Foundations of Education

Third Edition

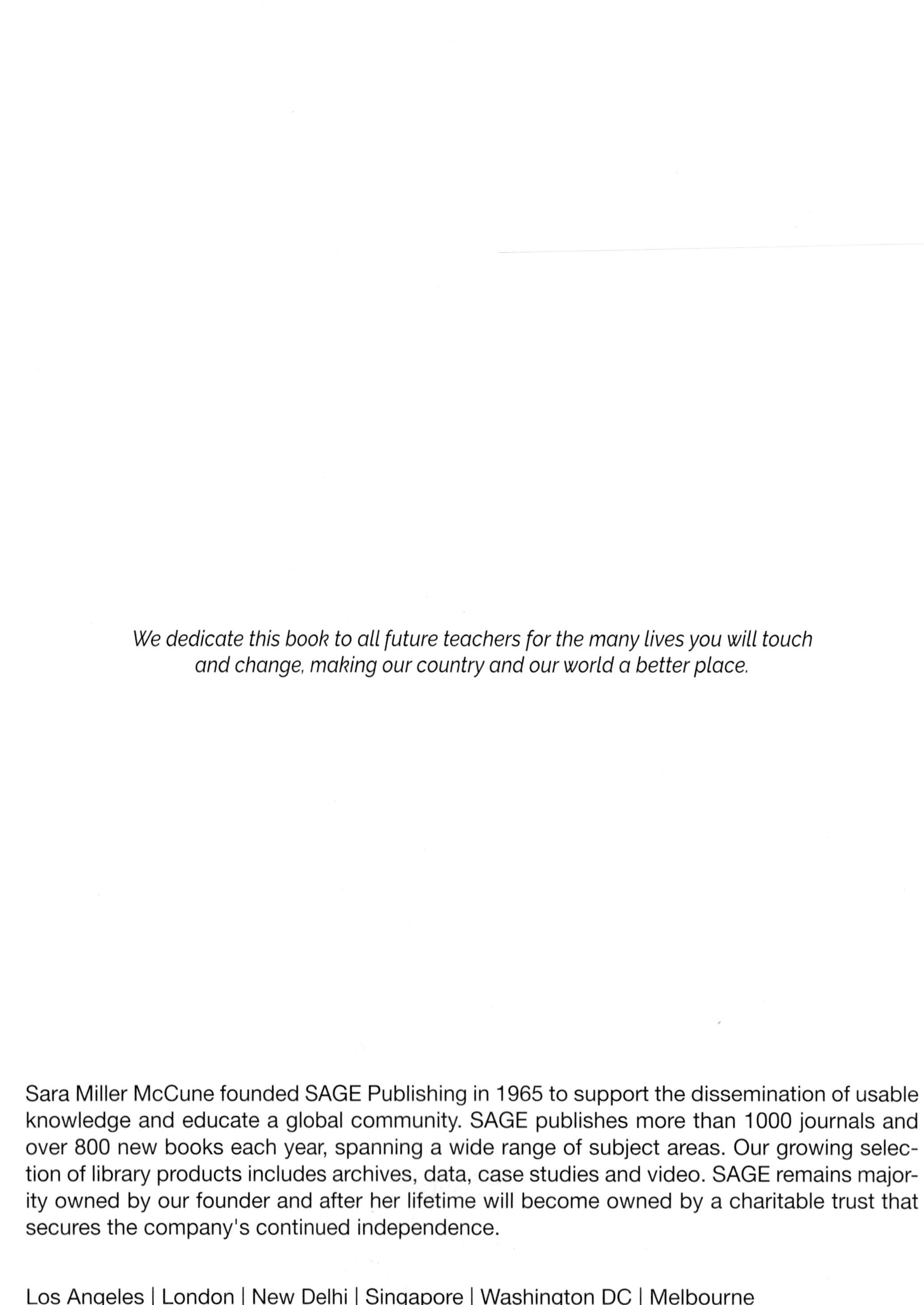

We dedicate this book to all future teachers for the many lives you will touch and change, making our country and our world a better place.

Sara Miller McCune founded SAGE Publishing in 1965 to support the dissemination of usable knowledge and educate a global community. SAGE publishes more than 1000 journals and over 800 new books each year, spanning a wide range of subject areas. Our growing selection of library products includes archives, data, case studies and video. SAGE remains majority owned by our founder and after her lifetime will become owned by a charitable trust that secures the company's continued independence.

Los Angeles | London | New Delhi | Singapore | Washington DC | Melbourne

Foundations of Education

Third Edition

Leslie S. Kaplan

Newport News Public Schools (Retired)

William A. Owings

Old Dominion University

Los Angeles | London | New Delhi
Singapore | Washington DC | Melbourne

FOR INFORMATION:

SAGE Publications, Inc.
2455 Teller Road
Thousand Oaks, California 91320
E-mail: order@sagepub.com

SAGE Publications Ltd.
1 Oliver's Yard
55 City Road
London, EC1Y 1SP
United Kingdom

SAGE Publications India Pvt. Ltd.
B 1/I 1 Mohan Cooperative Industrial Area
Mathura Road, New Delhi 110 044
India

SAGE Publications Asia-Pacific Pte. Ltd.
18 Cross Street #10-10/11/12
China Square Central
Singapore 048423

Printed in Canada

Library of Congress Cataloging-in-Publication Data

Names: Kaplan, Leslie S., author. | Owings, William A., 1952- author.
Title: Foundations of education / Leslie S. Kaplan, William A. Owings. Other titles: American education
Description: Third edition. | Los Angeles: SAGE, [2022] | Revised edition of: American education. 2009; and, Educational foundations. Second editon. 2015.
Identifiers: LCCN 2021026406 | ISBN 9781071803912 (paperback) | ISBN 9781071803967 (epub)
Subjects: LCSH: Education--United States--Textbooks.
Classification: LCC LA212 .K25 2022 | DDC 370.973--dc23 LC record available at https://lccn.loc.gov/2021026406

Acquisitions Editor: Leah Fargotstein

Content Development Editor: Chelsea Neve

Production Editor: Veronica Stapleton Hooper

Copy Editor: Amy Hanquist Harris

Typesetter: diacriTech

Proofreader: Dennis W. Webb

Cover Designer: Janet Kiesel

Marketing Manager: Victoria Velasquez

This book is printed on acid-free paper.

21 22 23 24 25 10 9 8 7 6 5 4 3 2 1

BRIEF CONTENTS

DETAILED CONTENTS

PREFACE

This third edition of *Educational Foundations* is written to help those considering a career in education make sense of today's schools and students. We do this by making traditional educational foundations topics relevant and personally meaningful to young and mature adult learners. At the same time, we offer the comprehensive scope, the scholarly depth, and the conceptual analyses and critiques of contemporary issues that demanding professors expect.

College students taking their first education course often do not see the links between foundations topics and their future careers. While reviewing "the competition" to prepare for this edition, the authors saw why. Many well-regarded foundations textbooks read like encyclopedias: 400-page compendia of "edu-facts." In contrast, less comprehensive but popular textbooks feature attention-grabbing photos but few in-depth discussions of foundations topics or provocative appraisals of current education issues. They read as if authors had checked off a list of "must-have" foundations subjects but did not develop them in any impactful way. No wonder students assigned to read these texts respond with a big, "So what?"

Given this reality, many professors choose to construct their own foundations curricula, collecting relevant articles for each key topic to generate critical thought and analyses. Although this practice generally keeps professors and students interested in the course, its curricular content tends to be highly idiosyncratic. It favors the professors' pet topics rather than presents the full scope of education foundations that prepares future educators for the institution in which they will be working.

So rather than over- or underwhelm readers, the authors decided to create an educational foundations textbook that meets both students' needs for relevance and meaning and professors' needs for respected foundations content, contemporary scholarly sources, and conceptual challenge. In short, we wrote *Educational Foundations, Third Edition* to be effectively taught and deeply learned.

In addition, we recognize that most teachers in American public schools *differ* racially, ethnically, and culturally from their students.[1] Yet regardless of family backgrounds, all students must succeed in school if they are to become self-sufficient, responsible citizens. Research affirms that working with highly effective teachers year after year can increase children's learning and, ultimately, expand their life options. This is especially critical for minority and low-income students who depend on public schools to give them the knowledge and skills needed to access bright futures.

Although students do not require teachers who look like them in order to learn, they do need teachers who respect and understand them enough to provide high expectations, academic rigor, and (academic and moral) supports needed to gain a high-quality education. Nonetheless, studies assert that "most teachers are not prepared to work in diverse classrooms and communities of color."[2] Teachers enable student learning by developing caring and respectful relationships with them. This connection is especially critical with children whose backgrounds differ from the teachers' own. So in addition to presenting the traditional educational foundations' topics, we include issues purposefully chosen to help future teachers develop empathy, understanding, and insight for *all* their students. Understanding the cultural influences and perceptions that minority and low-income children and their families

[1] Partelow, L., Spong, A., Brown, C., & Johnson, S. (2017, September 14). Americans need more teachers of color and a more selective teaching profession. *Center for American Progress*. https://www.americanprogress.org/issues/education-k-12/reports/2017/09/14/437667/america-needs-teachers-color-selective-teaching-profession/; Figlio, D. (2017, November 16). The importance of a diverse teaching force. *Brookings*. https://www.brookings.edu/research/the-importance-of-a-diverse-teaching-force/

[2] Marchitello, M., & Trinidad, J. (2019, March). Preparing teachers for diverse schools: Lessons from minority serving institutions. *Bellwether Education Partners*, p. 4. https://bellwethereducation.org/sites/default/files/Preparing%20Teachers%20for%20Diverse%20Schools_Bellwether.pdf

bring to school helps teachers more effectively bond with them, enabling educators to better assist and advance their students' learning. We also help future educators recognize the systemic school practices that can either advance—or limit—students' learning so if present, teachers may work to resist or change them. And, just as importantly, we show future teachers how they, their schools, and communities can help children avoid or overcome many obstacles in the path of their educational attainment.

The text's authors and instructors teaching an introductory course in education share many common goals for their students:

- To use a textbook that college and adult students will find readable, interesting, balanced, and significant
- To address what future educators need to know and understand so they may smoothly transition into the education profession
- To respect the traditional educational foundations content
- To give immediacy and relevance by continually linking foundation topics to "hot-button" contemporary education issues
- To provide scholarly support for important concepts with current research findings
- To *educate*, not *inculcate*,[3] by introducing students to varied perspectives on American public education and the larger social and political contexts so they can assess the information and draw their own conclusions
- To infuse teaching and learning's "best practices" by continuously engaging students and professors in reading meaningful sections of narrative, applying the content in real-world contexts, and reflecting on its meaning
- To generate socially mediated learning experiences where students can foster deeper understanding of ideas and issues by discussing them with peers and professors
- To develop culturally responsive teachers who respect and understand diverse students and recognize (and use) the cultural assets these students bring to school to increase their learning
- To cultivate reflective practitioners by providing ongoing occasions for students to think about what they are reading, interact with fellow students and their professors around the content to create fuller meaning, and develop their own philosophy of education
- To involve students in using an array of digital tools—conceptual, visual, and graphic—in learning activities as part of the instruction to advance their own learning.

Teacher educators affirm that "teaching and learning are intellectual and affective engagements."[4] Preparing future teachers should include examining their own personal and professional values as well as the larger educational and cultural ones. College education should offer students opportunities to practice reflective self-discernment as well as develop critical cultural understanding. It is through these actual changes in thought, comprehension, and—hopefully—in behavior that real learning occurs.

SPECIFIC MARKET FOR *EDUCATIONAL FOUNDATIONS, THIRD EDITION*

Educational Foundations, Third Edition is a core textbook appropriate for any introductory teacher preparation program. This course typically focuses on the describing the profession, its history in the United States, and its philosophical, structural, legal, financial, and curricular underpinnings. Almost

[3] Liston, D., Whitcomb, J., & Borko, H. (2009). The end of education in teacher education. Thoughts on reclaiming the role or social foundations in teacher education. *Journal of Teacher Education, 60*(2), 107–111. https://doi.org/10.1177/0022487108331004
[4] Liston et al., 2009, p. 109.

all teacher preparation programs require teacher education students to take an educational foundations course.

In 2018, about 23% of all bachelor's degrees awarded in the United States were in education;[5] 96% of undergraduate education BA degrees and certificates are in fields that prepare students for teaching.[6] Many of these programs offer an MA degree in teaching for candidates who, for a variety of reasons, did not pursue teaching as undergraduates.

Although community colleges have traditionally been a primary access point for minority and low-income students, the rising cost of college is swaying more middle-class families to view community college as the first 2 years of a bachelor's degree.[7] Many students stay longer. More than 120 public community colleges in 25 states now offer more than 400 baccalaureate degree programs,[8] almost half with programs in teacher preparation.[9] Studies have shown that more than 50% of teachers attended a community college for at least part of their education.[10]

Unfortunately, between 19% and 30% of teachers leave the profession before their fifth year.[11] It doesn't have to be this way. Research finds that teachers with strong teacher preparation backgrounds are more likely to increase student learning and achievement *and* continue in the profession.[12] In our view, a strong teacher preparation background begins with its first courses. We believe that our text provides the high-interest subject matter and engaging learning activities to enable future teachers to make a smooth transition into the profession, continually strengthen their skills and confidence, and stay.

Two- and four-year college education departments and courses, including Foundations of Education, Foundations of Teacher Education, and Introduction to Education, are primary markets for this book. A secondary market would be the course Introduction to Teaching.

MAJOR FEATURES OF *EDUCATIONAL FOUNDATIONS, THIRD EDITION*

This text offers special features and pedagogical aids to facilitate student learning.

- **Learning Objectives**: Correlated to each chapter's main sections, learning objectives engage students in analytical thinking about the chapter topics. To have students demonstrate high levels of cognitive reasoning, we ask them to "assess, defend, critique, compare and contrast, predict, support or argue" the section's main ideas. After completing the chapter, students should be able to show that they understand and can analyze, synthesize, evaluate, and apply their new knowledge and insights.

---

[5] One source reports that 82,621 BA degrees awarded in education, 2018. See: Bustamante, J. (2019, June 8). College graduation statistics. Educationdata.org. https://educationdata.org/number-of-college-graduates/

[6] King, J. E. (2018). *Colleges of education: A national portrait*. American Association of Colleges of Teacher Education. https://secure.aacte.org/apps/rl/res_get.php?fid=4178&ref=rl

[7] Spencer, K. (2018, April 4). Middle-class families increasingly look to community colleges. *The New York Times*. https://www.nytimes.com/2018/04/05/education/learning/community-colleges-middle-class-families.html?rref=collection%2Fsectioncollection%2Feducation-learning&action=click&contentCollection=learning®ion=rank&module=package&version=highlights&contentPlacement=2&pgtype=sectionfront

[8] Povich, E. S. (2018, April 26). More community colleges are offering bachelor's degrees—and four-year universities aren't happy about it. *PEW*. https://www.pewtrusts.org/en/research-and-analysis/blogs/stateline/2018/04/26/more-community-colleges-are-offering-bachelors-degrees

[9] The National Association of Community College Teacher Education Programs. (2013). *The crucial role of community colleges in teacher preparation and professional development*. http://nacctep.riosalado.edu/Drupal/PDF/CR_2013.pdf

[10] National Association of Community College Teacher Education Programs. (2019). About us. http://nacctep.riosalado.edu/new/About_Us.html

[11] Castro, A., Quinn, D. J., Fuller, E., & Barnes, M. (2018). *Policy brief 2-18-1: Addressing the importance and scale of the U.S. teacher shortage*. University Council for Educational Administration. http://www.ucea.org/wp-content/uploads/2018/01/Addressing-the-Importance-and-Scale-of-the-US-Teacher-Shortage.pdf

[12] See: American Association of Colleges for Teacher Education (AACTE). (2012, Spring). How teacher preparation affects student achievement. *What We Know*. https://secure.aacte.org/apps/rl/res_get.php?fid=485&ref=rl; Boyd, D. J., Grossman, P. L., Lankford, H., Loeb, S., & Wyckoff, J. (2009). Teacher preparation and student achievement. *Educational Evaluation and Policy Analysis, 31*(4), 416–440. http://citeseerx.ist.psu.edu/viewdoc/download?doi=10.1.1.866.5199&rep=rep1&type=pdf

- **Standards**: The text has been thoroughly revised to reflect current standards, including 2013 InTASC Standards. Each chapter begins with a list of the relevant InTASC Standards it addresses. A summary of where each InTASC standard appears below.
- **American Education Spotlight**: Each chapter contains personal and professional portraits of notable individuals in education from varied backgrounds or viewpoints who contribute in a major way to the topic under study. *Spotlight* profiles include Nel Noddings (Chapter 1); Linda Darling-Hammond (Chapter 2); Diane Ravitch (Chapter 3); Horace Mann (Chapter 4); Ruby Bridges (Chapter 5); Richard Rothstein (Chapter 6); Pedro Noguera (Chapter 7); Derald Wing Sue (Chapter 8); Amy June Rowley (Chapter 9); Rick Hess (Chapter 10); Michael Rebell (Chapter 11); Lisa Delpit (Chapter 12); Robert Marzano (Chapter 13); and Ronald Edmonds (Chapter 14).
- **FlipSides**: In every generation, education debates roil the profession. FlipSides presents readers with a range of philosophical and practical education dilemmas, garners arguments for each position, and invites readers to decide for themselves. Attention-grabbing FlipSides issues include Is Teaching an Art or a Science? (Chapter 1); Should Effective Teachers Receive Performance (Merit) Pay? (Chapter 2); Essentialist or Critical Theory? Which Philosophy of Education Should Guide Today's Schools? (Chapter 3); Traditional Teaching Versus Culturally Responsive Teaching: Which Approach Will Help Today's Diverse Students Learn to High Levels? (Chapter 8); The Case For and Against Standardized Testing (Chapter 13); and Which Matters Most in Student Achievement: Families or Schools? (Chapter 14). In short, FlipSides helps professors bring more relevance and conceptual challenge to the foundations classroom and, ideally, helps students learn to argue with data and facts (rather than opinion) and to disagree without being disagreeable.
- **Reflect & Engage Activities**: Successful teachers know that asking students to think about and actively use newly learned information in personally meaningful ways helps them better understand and retain the information. Located immediately following each chapter's major concepts, these "minds-on," "hands-on," small-group, and class activities include problem-solving, role-playing, and using digital tools for mind mapping and constructing "wordles" (word clouds) and graphic images. These learning activities help students clarify what they are learning, make it relevant and personally meaningful, increase retention and transfer, and enhance students' facility using digital tools to extend learning. Professors can adapt and revise these activities as they desire to accomplish their instructional goals.
- **Teacher Scenarios: It's Your Turn:** In this new feature at each chapter's end, we present a brief, real-world education situation with a dilemma. Readers must apply the chapter's ideas in innovative ways to address the scenario's problem effectively. Professors can use these scenarios as culminating in-class activities or as individual or small-group assignments. It is the type of highly appealing learning that most young (and older) adults enjoy.
- **Key Take-Aways**: Rather than an end-of-chapter summary, key take-aways (organized by the chapter's learning objectives) remind readers of each section's "big ideas" worth remembering. This helps to answer the readers' question, "So what?"
- **Diverse Voices** (in the online instructor's manual): Disability, race, sexual identity, poverty, academic capacity: How do these dynamics affect teaching and learning? Just as a picture can be worth a thousand words, getting a firsthand experience can make an abstraction real—and memorable. The instructor's manual contains personal essays and excerpts (with links to the original articles) from individuals who have lived the issues discussed and suggests ways teachers can help students like they were. For example, in "Scott's Journey," a young man with cerebral palsy tells his experiences moving from a totally segregated school setting for children with disabilities to a regular high school. As his peers, teachers, and administrators looked beyond what Scott could not do to what he *could* do, he became a participating member of his school community.

NEW TO THIS EDITION

The 7 years between the second and third editions of *Educational Foundations* witnessed substantial shifts in education research, thought, and practice. New data are available about how education reform, policy changes, societal influences, and student diversity are affecting teaching and learning. The heightened need to educate *every* student to high levels while recognizing (and trying to remedy or end) the factors that work against their academic success, the increasing political and legal sway toward education privatization, the growing need to teach using technology and internet platforms, and the evolving nature of the education profession toward greater teacher career options shaped how we approached this edition. In addition to updating our tables and figures, our chapters now explore these current topics and their impacts on teachers, students, and the profession.

- **Chapter 1**: Teachers Shape the Future begins with a new title to better recognize what our profession does and presents a new section on Technology and Education in a Global Environment.
- **Chapter 2**: Teaching as a Profession now describes how the teaching profession is evolving, looking at how millennials are changing expectations for careers in education, citing teacher career advancement initiatives, and critiquing the new national teacher preparation accreditation organizations (CAEP and AAQEP).
- **Chapter 3**: Philosophy of Education now has Reflect & Engage activities that ask students to identify the parts of the chapter's four educational philosophies with which they agree and begin to construct their own philosophy of education.
- **Chapter 4**: The History of American Public Education introduces Catherine Beecher, a prominent 19th century educator who advanced teaching as a career for women. The chapter also focuses new attention on private schools in the new American nation and asks whether education's purpose should be religious or secular.
- **Chapter 5**: Education Reform—1900 to Today has a Recent Trends section that now analyzes the growing influence of education privatization (i.e., the economic/political orientation, charter schools, school vouchers, and virtual education), social–emotional learning, and personalized learning, as well as their impact on student attainment (each with related research findings). The latest version of the Elementary and Secondary Education Act—the Every Student Succeeds Act—also appears.
- **Chapter 6**: Competing Goals of Public Education now explains "critical consciousness." It also highlights how the disparities in academic quality and learning climates between schools serving affluent as compared with low-socioeconomic-status students create an "opportunity gap" rather than simply an "achievement gap" stemming from the systemic obstacles to low-income children's school success.
- **Chapter 7**: Cultural, Social, and Educational Causes of the Achievement Gap and How to Fix Them debates the "melting pot" theory of cultural assimilation versus a nation of separate ethnic groups and "cultural pluralism" theory and suggests how integrate the two concepts. In considering how school factors may reduce the "achievement/opportunity gap," we now include evidence that a well-functioning preschool experience supports students later in school and life. We also address ways of reconciling cognitive dissonance so teachers can become fully aware of (and work to change) unfair school and teaching practices.
- **Chapter 8**: Diversity and Cultural Assets in Education expands our understanding of student diversity to include often marginalized gifted and LGBTQ+ students. We also analyze how students' perceptions of microaggressions influence their learning and appraise how white privilege theory and "white fragility" theory may shape the learning environment. Likewise, we introduce the intersectionality concept with which teachers can better understand and appreciate their students' natural complexities (and reduce stereotyping).

- **Chapter 9**: Teachers, Ethics, and the Law presents the Model Code of Ethics for Educators (2015) to guide preK–12 educators in their decision-making and to help teacher preparation programs nurture their teacher candidates' ethical problem-solving capacities. We also spend extra time on "cyberbullying of students and staff" to inform future teachers about what cyber behaviors are (or are not) legal.
- **Chapter 10**: School Governance and Structure expands diversity of thought with an American Education Spotlight featuring Rick Hess, a conservative public intellectual and education policy analyst.
- **Chapter 11**: School Finance places extra emphasis on how money—the total amount and how it is spent—matters in improving student outcomes. The chapter now gives students the opportunity to compare two schools' budgets in an eye-opening exercise in fiscal (in) equity, and it includes an analysis of recent trends of using taxpayer dollars to pay for private education.
- **Chapter 12**: Curriculum and Instruction combines two previously separate chapters to better focus on the key concepts in each area. We highlight types of curricular organization and new scientific understanding of how people learn and its influence on classroom instruction. We also consider how the COVID-19 pandemic changed how we use technology to plan and deliver instruction, maybe forever, and the equity issues it raises.
- **Chapter 13**: Standards, Assessment, and Accountability includes a new discussion of the "opting out" movement in response to the overuse (and misuse) of standardized testing.
- **Chapter 14**: Educating Everyone's Children begins with a more apt name and concludes with a discussion of "public schools as a public good" and "teaching as a public service."

Although Chapters 8 and 12 sustained lengthy revisions to better focus on new trends and "big picture" concerns, most chapters required important but unobtrusive updates in data and content. Similarly, to increase diversity of thought on education topics, we expanded the American Education Spotlight section to introduce a wider range of influencers and ideas in education policy and practice with the additions of Pedro Noguera, USC dean and education professor (Chapter 7); Derald Wing Sue, Teachers College Columbia professor and originator of the microaggression theory (Chapter 8); Rick Hess, resident scholar and director of education policy at the American Enterprise Institute (Chapter 10); and Robert Marzano, American education researcher and author (Chapter 13).

Lastly, in COVID-19's wake, we see preK–16 schooling's reshaping. Today, we are all learners. By trial and error, teachers are learning to design and conduct engaging lessons for internet platforms, deliver learning remotely, and flexibly pair hybrid and in-class instruction as necessary to meet societal conditions. Parents homeschooling their children (with their teachers' learning materials and encouragement, although at a distance) are developing a deeper and more tangible appreciation for teachers' essential roles in educating our children and schools' vital roles in structuring community life. Many of these technological and social innovations likely will continue. Trends currently remaking the teaching profession may even accelerate. What remains constant is our unshaken confidence that teachers shape the future and our desire to help prepare future educators to make successful transitions into tomorrow's classrooms.

A NOTE ON LANGUAGE IN THE THIRD EDITION

Culture and language evolve over time. This includes how we describe historically and socially marginalized persons. In earlier editions, the authors used the term "minority," a word without specificity that can conflate or erase important differences or identities. In this edition, however, the authors have actively tried to reduce this use of the term and be as specific as possible in each context, using more contemporary terms to describe these student demographics in common parlance today. When we do use the term "minority" without more nuance—such as in Chapter 8's The Racial and Cultural

Identity Development Model—it is a legacy term from the original model or written as used at the time of the source's original publication. Today, we strive to use more modulated, complex terms that groups use to define themselves.

ORGANIZATION OF THE THIRD EDITION

Chapter 1: Teachers Shape the Future includes discussion of teaching as an inspiring, satisfying, and important profession; the personal qualities of effective teachers; the moral purposes of education; technology and trends affecting education in a global environment; and what 21st century students need to learn. We discuss the 2013 InTASC (Interstate New Teacher Assessment and Support Consortium) 10 Model Core Standards for the knowledge, dispositions, and skills expected of effective teachers.

Chapter 2: Teaching as a Profession includes information about factors that make teaching a profession; how the teaching profession has evolved; research on teacher preparation, teacher quality, student achievement, and teacher longevity; and the impacts of schools' professional culture on teacher retention. The chapter also considers the teaching profession's changing career expectations and advancement initiatives (including alternative salary structures such as performance pay, knowledge- and skills-based pay, differentiated salary schedules, and career pathways).

Chapter 3: Philosophy of Education includes traditional, progressive, existential, and critical theories of education; considers valid and enduring insights from each of the philosophies; and shows how teachers may use each of them.

Chapter 4: The History of American Public Education discusses cultural influences on education in early colonial America; early education in the New England colonies; early education in the middle colonies; and early education in Virginia, southern colonies, and elsewhere. We also review early education of African Americans and Native Americans; public schooling during the early national period; and the movement toward universal schooling.

Chapter 5: Education Reform—1900 to Today talks about challenges to traditional concepts of schooling (i.e., education as human development); describes how national reports and scientific management theory influenced public schools' organization and curriculum; and explains how Booker T. Washington, W. E. B. DuBois, and legal and legislative actions advanced African Americans' education. We consider world wars, the Great Depression, vocational education, the *Coleman Report*, special education, and *A Nation at Risk* through the Every Student Succeeds Act, as well as virtual education, education privatization, social–emotional learning, and personalized learning.

Chapter 6: Competing Goals of Public Education considers the general and wide-ranging nature of American education goals; presents conservative, liberal, and critical theories and their competing educational aims; reflects on realizing education's purpose (investing in human capital); and asks, "Is education still the key to the American dream?"

Chapter 7: Cultural, Social, and Educational Causes of the Achievement Gap and How to Fix Them looks at education through the lens of society and schools. It introduces an analysis of our culture's evolving view of diversity (from the "melting pot" to cultural pluralism) and the public schools as socializing agents; the relationships among family resources and school success, outlooks, and opportunities; poverty and education; segregation and the achievement/opportunity gap; and school practices that either contribute to—or reduce—the unequal opportunities for diverse students.

Chapter 8: Diversity and Cultural Assets in Education looks at education through the individual student's lens. It discusses today's student diversity (including gifted students, English language learners, students with disabilities, LGBTQ+ students, and immigrants); race as a social (not scientific) construct; and how people develop cultural and racial/ethnic identities. The chapter also considers underrepresented students' perceptions (oppositional culture theory, stereotype theory, and microaggressions theory) and academic performance; discusses how white identity theory affects teachers and students; and suggests ways to foster student resilience and achievement.

Chapter 9: Teachers, Ethics, and the Law introduces the Model Educator Ethical Standards (2015); discusses why teachers have standards for professional behaviors, teacher certification/licensure, and contracts; what tenure is (and is not); and teachers' and students' constitutional freedoms (and their limits) in schools. Written largely in a question-and-answer format, the chapter attempts to make the problematic legal issues and their adjudication more immediately clear and relevant to future teachers.

Chapter 10: School Governance and Structure includes sections on the federal role (Department of Education, legislative, and judicial) in education; student assessment at the national level; the state players in education policy and practice; the local leaders and support staff who shape education policy (and student success); and structural issues that affect schools' effectiveness.

Chapter 11: School Finance highlights how money matters in education, focusing on how a country's investment in education builds its nation's human capital, increases individuals' employability and earning potential, and reduces public social costs. The chapter also discusses federal, state, and local sources of school revenues; identifies the budget categories in which school districts spend money; clarifies how equity and adequacy issues in school funding impact student learning and achievement; and discusses taxpayer resistance and using taxpayer dollars to pay for private schooling.

Chapter 12: Curriculum and Instruction describes the separate yet interdependent relationships among curriculum, instruction, and society's goals for students; traces the ways in which public school curricula respond to intellectual, societal, and political influences; discusses how a school's curricular balance impacts children's personal, social, and intellectual growth and development; explains how groundbreaking advances in our understanding of how people learn impacts classroom instruction; and talks of the potentially lasting impact of the COVID-19 pandemic on technology, teaching, learning, and equity.

Chapter 13: Standards, Assessment, and Accountability critiques how educational standards contribute to student achievement, school accountability, and teachers' professional growth; describes how teachers and schools use assessment to enhance teaching and learning; predicts how the principles of school assessments should influence teachers' ethical practices to advance student learning; and argues how accountability for educational outcomes means more than students' achievement test scores.

Chapter 14: Educating Everyone's Children examines the effective schools practices that enable public schools to provide high-quality education for every child, especially low-income and underrepresented students. These include strong instructional leadership, clear and focused mission, safe and orderly environment, a climate of high expectations, frequent monitoring of student progress, positive home–school relations, and the opportunity to learn. We also consider what they look like as practiced in schools today.

TEACHING RESOURCES

This text includes an array of instructor teaching materials designed to save you time and to help you keep students engaged. To learn more, visit www.sagepub.com or contact your SAGE representative at www.sagepub.com/findmyrep.

ACKNOWLEDGMENTS

Writing this book has been a genuinely interesting, enjoyable, and collaborative experience. Our sincere thanks and appreciation go to the following:

Leah Fargotstein, our SAGE acquisitions editor, and Chelsea Neve, our highly skilled and always conscientious SAGE content developer, gave us invaluable support. Both knowledgeably guided us through the redevelopment and revision processes with always excellent suggestions, new challenges, consistent encouragement, sunny good humor, and capable eyes for making text both reader-friendly and intellectually engaging.

We also thank Victoria Velazques, SAGE marketing manager, for her efforts to get this text into professors' hands, and Shelly Gupta, who helped both find engaging photos to illustrate each chapter and manage the entire permissions process.

Appreciation also goes to our production team: Veronica Stapleton Hooper, our SAGE senior project editor and Amy Hanquist Harris, our copy editor.

Lastly, we would be remiss if we did not also thank our editors on earlier *Educational Foundations* editions. Dan Alpert, now Corwin's publisher and program director: equity/diversity, professional learning, was our first development editor who guided us when we began transitioning from preK–12 practitioners to education writers. We collaborated with Dan on *American Public School Finance* (2006), *Educational Foundations* (2011), and our *Culture Re-Boot* (Corwin, 2013). Always generous with invaluable suggestions about creating a winning content with an authentic voice, Dan nurtured our confidence and maturity as writers. He remains a dear and trusted friend. Sincere thank-yous also go to Mark David Kerr and Kate Scheinman, who helped us develop several innovative features for our second edition that continue in this current edition.

Notably, our peer reviewers provided extremely valuable and useful feedback. They told us when we were on the right track, suggested what to add, identified when we needed to clarify or present linkages to other chapters, and advised ways to infuse more "teaching with technology" and digital learning activities into the text. These reviewers became welcome and virtual collaborators as we developed and refined this text, and we sincerely thank them:

Karen L. Anderson, *Stonehill College*
Denise Baldwin, *University of Arkansas at Monticello*
Brandi Burton, *University of West Alabama*
Rhonda Clements, *Manhattanville College*
Madeline Craig, *Molloy College*
Tracey Lahey, *Manhattan College*
Mark Malisa, *University of West Florida*
James Rigney, *University of Florida*
Beth Sanders-Rabinowitz, *Atlantic Cape Community College*
Brenda S. Tinkham, *Chowan University*
Joanne Tressel, *American International College*
Jennifer Zakrzewski, Charleston Southern University

INTASC STANDARDS CHAPTER GUIDE

Interstate Teacher Assessment and Support Consortium (InTASC) Standards for Beginning Teacher Licensing and development.

InTASC Standard	Description of Teacher Performance	Text Chapters
1 **Learner Development**	The teacher understands how learners grow and develop, recognizing that patterns of learning and development vary individually within and across cognitive, linguistic, social, emotional, and physical areas, and designs and implements developmentally appropriate and challenging learning experiences.	Chapter 1 Chapter 2 Chapter 3 Chapter 4 Chapter 5 Chapter 6 Chapter 7 Chapter 8 Chapter 9 Chapter 10 Chapter 11 Chapter 12 Chapter 13 Chapter 14
2 **Learning Differences**	The teacher uses understanding of individual differences and diverse cultures and communities to ensure inclusive learning environments that enable each learner to meet high standards.	Chapter 1 Chapter 2 Chapter 3 Chapter 5 Chapter 6 Chapter 7 Chapter 8 Chapter 9 Chapter 10 Chapter 11 Chapter 12 Chapter 13 Chapter 14

InTASC Standard	Description of Teacher Performance	Text Chapters
3 **Learning Environments**	The teacher works with others to create environments that support individual and collaborate learning, and that encourage positive social interaction, active engagement in learning, and self-motivation.	Chapter 1 Chapter 2 Chapter 3 Chapter 5 Chapter 6 Chapter 7 Chapter 8 Chapter 9 Chapter 10 Chapter 11 Chapter 12 Chapter 13 Chapter 14
4 **Content Knowledge**	The teacher understands the central concepts, tools of inquiry, and structures of the discipline(s) he or she teaches and creates learning experiences that make these aspects of the discipline accessible and meaningful for learners to assure mastery of the content.	Chapter 1 Chapter 2 Chapter 3 Chapter 5 Chapter 6 Chapter 7 Chapter 8 Chapter 10 Chapter 12 Chapter 13 Chapter 14
5 **Application of Knowledge**	The teacher understands how to connect concepts and use differing perspectives to engage learners in critical thinking, creativity, and collaborative problem solving related to authentic local and global issues.	Chapter 1 Chapter 3 Chapter 5 Chapter 6 Chapter 7 Chapter 8 Chapter 10 Chapter 12 Chapter 13 Chapter 14
6 **Assessment**	The teacher understands and uses multiple methods of assessment to engage learners in their own growth to monitor learner progress, and to guide the teacher's and learner's decision making.	Chapter 1 Chapter 2 Chapter 3 Chapter 5 Chapter 8 Chapter 10 Chapter 12 Chapter 13 Chapter 14

InTASC Standard	Description of Teacher Performance	Text Chapters
7 **Planning for Instruction**	The teacher plans instruction that supports every student in meeting rigorous learning goals by drawing upon knowledge of content areas curriculum, cross-disciplinary skills, and pedagogy, as well as knowledge of learners and the community context.	Chapter 1 Chapter 2 Chapter 3 Chapter 5 Chapter 6 Chapter 7 Chapter 8 Chapter 10 Chapter 12 Chapter 13 Chapter 14
8 **Instructional Strategies**	The teacher understands and uses a variety of instructional strategies to encourage learners to develop deep understanding of content areas and their connections, and to build skills to apply knowledge in meaningful ways.	Chapter 1 Chapter 2 Chapter 3 Chapter 5 Chapter 6 Chapter 7 Chapter 8 Chapter 10 Chapter 12 Chapter 13 Chapter 14
9 **Professional Learning and Ethical Practice**	The teacher engages in ongoing professional learning and uses evidence to continually evaluate his/her practice, particularly the effects of his/her choices and actions on others (learners, families, other professionals, and the community), and adapts practice to meet the needs of each learner.	Chapter 1 Chapter 2 Chapter 3 Chapter 5 Chapter 6 Chapter 7 Chapter 8 Chapter 9 Chapter 10 Chapter 11 Chapter 12 Chapter 13 Chapter 14

InTASC Standard	Description of Teacher Performance	Text Chapters
10 **Leadership and Collaboration**	The teacher seeks appropriate leadership roles and opportunities to take responsibility for student learning, to collaborate with learners, families, colleagues, other school professionals, and community member to ensure learner growth, and to advance the profession.	Chapter 1 Chapter 2 Chapter 3 Chapter 5 Chapter 6 Chapter 7 Chapter 8 Chapter 9 Chapter 10 Chapter 12 Chapter 13 Chapter 14

ABOUT THE AUTHORS

Leslie S. Kaplan, a retired school administrator in Newport News, Virginia, is a full-time education writer and former researcher with Old Dominion University's Research Foundation. She has provided middle school and high school instructional leadership as well as central office leadership as a director of program development. Before becoming a school administrator, she worked as a middle school and high school English teacher and as a school counselor with articles frequently published in *The School Counselor*. Kaplan's scholarly publications, coauthored with William A. Owings, appear in numerous professional journals. She also has coauthored several books and monographs with Owings, including *American Public School Finance* (3rd ed.); *Organizational Behavior for School Leadership: Leveraging Your School for Success; Introduction to the Principalship: Theory to Practice; Culture Re-Boot: Reinvigorating School Culture to Improve Student Outcomes; Leadership and Organizational Behavior in Education; Educational Foundations* (2nd ed.); *American Education: Building a Common Foundation; American Public School Finance* (2nd ed.); *Teacher Quality, Teaching Quality, and School Improvement; Best Practices, Best Thinking, and Emerging Issues in School Leadership*; and *Enhancing Teacher and Teaching Quality*. In addition, their chapter on privatizing American public schools appears in *The Oxford Encyclopedia of Educational Administration* (2021). Kaplan also serves on the NASSP *Bulletin* Editorial Board. As a person with experiences in a variety of education roles, she has the unique distinction of being honored as both Virginia's Counselor of the Year and Assistant Principal of the Year. She is a past president of the Virginia Counselors' Association and the Virginia Association for Supervision and Curriculum Development, and she served as board member and secretary for Voices for Virginia's Children. She is a 2014 National Education Finance Academy Distinguished Fellow of Research and Practice.

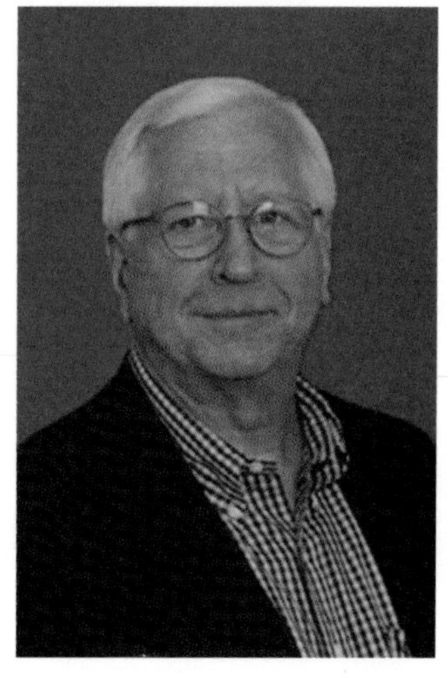

William A. Owings is a professor of educational leadership at Old Dominion University in Norfolk, Virginia. Owings has worked as a public school teacher, an elementary school and high school principal, assistant superintendent, and superintendent of schools. His scholarly publications, coauthored with Leslie S. Kaplan, include books on educational leadership, school finance, and educational foundations, as well as articles in *National Association of Secondary School Principals (NASSP) Bulletin, Journal of School Leadership, Journal of Education Finance, Journal of Effective Schools, Phi Delta Kappan, Journal of Academic Perspectives, Teachers College Record*, and the *Eurasian Journal of Business and Economics.* Owings has served on the state and international boards of the Association for Supervision and Curriculum Development (ASCD) and is a member of the *Journal of Education* Finance Editorial Advisory Board. He also reviews articles for the NASSP *Bulletin Educational Administration Quarterly, Eurasian Journal of Business and Economics, Asia Pacific Journal of Education*, and *International Journal of Education Research.* He is a frequent presenter at state and national conferences and a consultant on educational leadership, school finance, and instructional improvement. He is a 2014 National Education Finance Academy Distinguished Fellow of Research and Practice. Owings and Kaplan share the 2008 Virginia Educational Research Association Charles Edgar Clear Research Award for Consistent and Substantial Contributions to Educational Research and Scholarship.

iStock/kali9

1 TEACHERS SHAPE THE FUTURE

InTASC Standards Addressed: 1, 2, 3, 4, 5, 6, 7, 8, 9, 10

LEARNING OBJECTIVES

After you read this chapter, you should be able to

1.1 Support the view that teaching is an inspiring, satisfying, and important profession.

1.2 Identify the personal qualities of effective teachers.

1.3 Critique education's moral purposes and how teachers enact these through caring.

1.4 Assess technology's role in educating students in today's global environment.

1.5 Identify and explain the 21st century skills today's students need to learn.

1.6 Describe the InTASC Model Core Standards and key themes for teachers.

"Teachers are heroes. Doctors save lives, but teachers help to create and shape them. What work could be more valuable?"[1] In fact, the 2020 COVID-19 pandemic validated teachers as frontline workers essential to our children, our economy, and the American way of life.

Today's American educators are engaged in an endeavor without precedent: supporting high standards for every student and providing the needed academic and affective scaffolding to ensure that every student reaches them. Effective teachers are vital if every American child is to receive a first-class education and the life-enhancing opportunities that it brings. But to be effective, teachers need a strong academic and professional preparation—a solid grounding in content knowledge and pedagogy and, increasingly, teaching well on digital platforms—*plus* healthy doses of idealism and optimism if they are to respond successfully to their diverse students and meet daily classroom challenges. They need an *education*, not merely *training* to develop the essential knowledge, skills, and perspectives that inspire a sincere commitment to understand every learner's needs and obstacles, meeting the former and overcoming the latter. Future teachers also need an education that will enable them to become reflective decision-makers who work collegially and ethically with other educators, parents, and their communities in their students' best interests and who expect to improve their professional practice throughout their careers.

As an essential part of a high-quality teacher preparation program, this educational foundations text will help guide you to become this type of teacher.

1.1 TEACHING AS AN INSPIRING, SATISFYING, AND IMPORTANT PROFESSION

Being a teacher is important and demanding work. "It takes a great deal of dedication to walk into school every day with enthusiasm, energy, and love, often in spite of conditions that make doing so a constant struggle. Yet some teachers do it all the time, and many remain in the classroom for years with a commitment that is nothing short of inspirational."[2]

Noted education professor Sonia Nieto observes that teachers' values, beliefs, and dispositions energize them to stay in the profession. Their love for children, desire to engage with intellectual work, hope of changing students' lives, strong belief in public education's democratic potential, and anger at public education's shortcomings all lie at the heart of what makes for excellent and caring teachers.[3] Having a sense of mission, solidarity, and empathy for students, the desire to be lifelong learners, the courage to challenge conventional thinking, improvisational abilities, and a passion for social justice motivate and keep teachers in the profession.[4] Comfort with uncertainty, endless patience, and a sense of humor also help.

And students know the difference when they have teachers who care about them and want to help them learn. When asked how they make this determination, they answer: The teacher *teaches well* (makes the class interesting, stays on task, stops to explain), and the teacher *treats them well* (is respectful, kind, and fair).[5] In these ways, a "caring teacher" models how children can become both smart and good.

Teaching well is critical, taxing, and deeply satisfying work. Many educators enjoy sharing their professional journeys about haltingly yet successfully meeting classroom challenges. Several samples illustrate how notable teachers experience their role.

Josh Parker, the 2012 Maryland State Teacher of the Year, observes that teachers who love their work can have the power to change lives.

> [T]eaching is what love looks like in practice. Teaching children well is proof of the love that we have for children, for society, and for the future of the world. Expertise, maturity, and ethics may be the branches, but the root of even these disciplines is a deep and abiding love for the profession itself.
>
> "Mr. Parker, can I ask you a question?" a young man in class spoke up while everyone else was quietly completing their assignment. "You really love us, don't you?" I was a bit surprised but smiled in response. "Of course I do, what makes you say that?"
>
> "Well, you are here almost every day, you dress up like you're going to church, and you help us when we have problems," the young man said.
>
> I have taught disruptive students, unruly students, perfect students, hurting students, and every other type of student in between. What touches them is not the teachers' expertise, but the approach. Treat them. Talk to them. Listen. The love and empathy in your heart for who they are is the sanctifying quality of transformative instruction.[6]

Christie Watson, a National Board-Certified teacher, who teaches sixth-grade English language arts and social studies in North Carolina, writes,

> It is February, and as usual, I love my students. I no longer feel the polite, anxious, and determined love of August, but a more genuine affection that comes from really knowing them. By this point in the year, my students and I have figured each other out. I know their interests, work habits, and personality quirks. They know how to tease me and what questions will prompt me to tell a story. We have established a level of mutual respect, and now we laugh more heartily, grin more frequently, and feel a warmth in the classroom despite the gloomy weather outside.
>
> I'm in a similar season in my career. Somehow the weeks have turned into semesters, which have turned into years, and I find myself a veteran teacher. The love I have for my profession is deeply rooted in the person I've become, and I find a satisfaction in being an education veteran that I couldn't have predicted in those first turbulent years in the classroom. After all, love is a flame, a madness, a battlefield—pick your metaphor—and teaching can be too.
>
> Full of good intentions, I blazed through my first few years in the classroom, loving my students fiercely, putting in long hours, making countless mistakes, and shedding many tears. Fortunately, with persistence and a lot of support, I was able to survive those years. Now my relationship with teaching resembles all the best long-lasting loves—rich, fulfilling, still passionate, yet less likely to hurt.
>
> So how do we develop a love of teaching that lasts? [Veteran educators share] many of the same strategies:
>
> **Be a lifelong learner**. A key to long-term success in the classroom is a willingness to try new things. Public education is ever-changing, and while change can be intimidating, it is also incredibly rejuvenating. . . .
>
> **Be Invested**. Seeking opportunities for teacher leadership is both gratifying and invigorating. . . . It feels good to be heard, to know that we matter, and to aid in decision-making. Feeling invested in your school and community validates your hard work and makes it easy to stay. . . .

Find your support. I would not be the teacher I am today without many individuals investing time and effort into helping me be successful. My first principal believed in me, despite my disastrous classroom management, and my first teammates helped me navigate parent conferences. . . .

Choose to love it. [A] great piece of advice I received before marriage was that love is not just a feeling; it's a decision. This idea also applies to teaching. There are always bad days, difficult months, and sometimes even entire school years that feel more draining than others. In those challenging times, it's important to step back and *decide* to love teaching anyway. . . . Try to focus on the good . . . [and] choose to bring back the fun. . . . If you're not feeling the love, odds are your students aren't either.

Don't give up. People are not attracted to education for the money, respect, or recognition. We teach because we love helping students, we love learning, and we want to make a difference.[7]

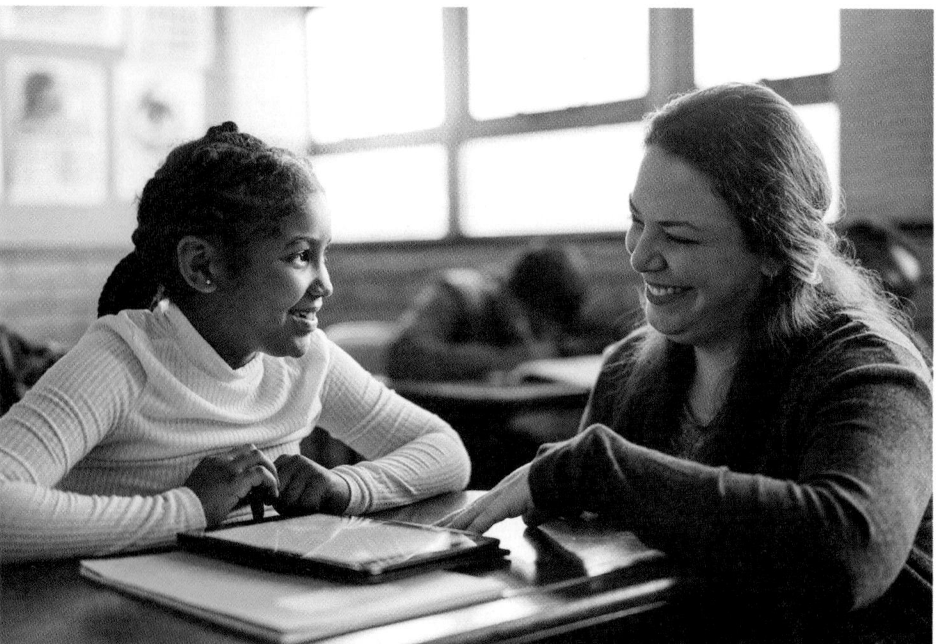

Teaching well is critical, taxing, and deeply satisfying work.
iStock/LumiNola

Veteran educator Laurie Barnoski, who retired after 32 years as an English teacher, offers this love letter to the profession:

It is true that teaching is a difficult job. It can be frustrating, exhausting, intimidating, and even frightening. Students know that if they choose a teaching career, they are going into a profession that does not pay well and is not highly respected by many people. Our current fixation on testing is a threat to teachers' job security and takes away some of their autonomy and creativity in the classroom. In addition, expectations of what teachers are supposed to accomplish can be overwhelming. Why would anyone choose to teach?

Take it from someone with experience: The positive aspects far outweigh the negatives. Here are [several] reasons why I think teaching matters.

- **Teaching is a worthy goal:** Teaching is a profession where you devote your life to helping young people develop into thoughtful, intelligent, positive human beings and citizens. You might not make a lot of money, but you will be given love, appreciation, and respect from your students. How many people get to say they have the same role in shaping the next generation and in shaping society?

- **Teaching is a skilled profession:** Though a large segment of the public thinks teaching is easy, those in the classroom know better. It tests your knowledge in many subject areas and your capacity to work with students of all abilities, backgrounds, and cultures. Your job is to develop each student's potential, and that takes skills and hard work.
- **Teaching is interesting:** Each day will be different. You will be working with many individual students and colleagues with distinct personalities and needs. Every year brings a new crop of young people to get to know. In addition, you can be creative as you plan your lessons and methods of instruction.
- **Teaching brings vitality:** Being around young people on a daily basis reminds you to not take life too seriously. They are inventive and funny. One night while I was sleeping, I heard a noise on the deck but thought it was a raccoon. The next day when I opened my front door, the front of the house was covered in paper hearts. "Mrs. Barnoski, " a note read, "you have been 'heart attacked'!"
- **Teaching provides autonomy:** Though you will have to follow mandates on state testing and other rules that you may not agree with, you can be autonomous on a daily basis. You are still the authority on how each student learns. When your classroom door closes, you're the one directing the interplay.
- **Teaching creates a legacy:** In my 30-plus years of teaching, I taught over 8,000 students. It feels great to bump into them unexpectedly and discover the impact I had on their lives. When my 103-year-old aunt, who was also an English teacher, passed away, several of her former students—some of whom were in their 70s—attended her funeral. Because of what your students have learned from you, small pieces of yourself will live on.
- **Teaching fosters meaningful relationships:** You will have the opportunity to develop lifelong relationships with many of your colleagues and students. Research has shown that to succeed in life, all children need at least one adult who cares about them. You can be that person. It is a privilege.

Teaching is an amazing profession, but it's not for everyone. It is only for those who can tackle challenges, work hard, and put in the time and effort it takes to help young people succeed.[8]

For one more look at how teaching inspires its best practitioners, Jennifer Wellborn, a middle school science teacher, writes about why she teaches:

> I may be naive, but I believe that what I do day in and day out *does* make a difference. Teachers *do* change lives forever. And I teach in public school because I still believe in public school. I believe the purpose of public school, whether it delivers or not, is to give quality education to all kids who come through the doors. I want to be part of that lofty mission. The future of our country depends on the ability of public schools to do that.[9]

Even as they celebrate the complex joys of being a teacher, these veteran educators concede that the profession has its discontents. Their grievances are legitimate. Many teachers are deeply frustrated and unhappy about the profession's present condition. A 2019 *Phi Delta Kappan* poll of the public attitudes toward public schools found that half of teachers say they've seriously considered leaving the profession in recent years; and 55% say they would not want their child to follow them into the profession.[10] Inadequate salaries and benefits, high job stress, and feeling disrespected or undervalued contribute to this broad dissatisfaction. In 2019, teachers from six states went on strike for higher pay, supplies, and better working conditions. The public was on their side.[11]

Acknowledging the present difficulties, however, does not discourage many future teachers from their commitment to public service. It does not dampen their desire to pursue a worthy goal and become part of a skilled and interesting profession that can shape young lives for the better. It does not diminish their wish to build meaningful relationships with students, colleagues, and parents, often in ways that change the trajectories of students' lives. Rather, the realities of teaching actually strengthen their choice to love teaching.

These teachers, and countless others, give clear voice to the belief that teaching is an inspiring, satisfying, highly demanding, and vitally important profession. Despite its challenges, they want to become effective teachers who show children how to become both smart and good. To learn more about what motivates and cautions you about entering the teaching profession, complete the activity in the **Reflect & Engage** box, Teaching as an Important, Demanding, Satisfying Profession.

REFLECT & ENGAGE: TEACHING AS AN IMPORTANT, DEMANDING, SATISFYING PROFESSION

Teaching matters. It is an interesting, complex, exacting, and highly satisfying profession that can make profound, positive differences in children's lives.

Each student takes a blank piece of notebook paper or newsprint and divides the paper top-to-bottom and side-to-side into four sections. Label each box *A, B, C,* or *D*. Then, respond to each question that follows by drawing freehand images or using clip art or a pictogram software as your answers. You may use colored markers or pencils. When finished, discuss your image answers in pairs and then as a class:

A. What satisfactions and cautions do these excellent teachers offer future educators?

B. What motivates you to consider a teaching career?

C. What discourages you from pursuing a teaching career?

D. Describe an experience you had as an elementary or secondary school student with an exceptional teacher who meaningfully influenced who you are as a person or who stirred you to become a teacher.

1.2 PERSONAL QUALITIES OF EFFECTIVE TEACHERS

Who the teacher is as a person influences students' learning experiences.

iStock/SDI Productions

Just as successful educators have vivid memories about their students, the reverse is also true. Although we may not always remember specific facts learned in a particular class, most of us can easily recall volumes about the teacher's personality. Arguably, the person who fills the role of teacher is the most important factor in teaching.

Before any individual becomes a professional, he or she is first a unique person of distinct appearance, personality, interests, abilities, talents, and ways of interacting with others. A teacher's personality is one of the first characteristics that students, parents, and administrators notice. Who the teacher is as a person has a tremendous influence on the classroom climate and students' learning experiences. Even more impressive, teachers' psychological influence on students has been linked to student achievement in various studies of educational effectiveness.[12] Although many aspects of effective teaching can be learned and developed, changing an individual's personality is difficult.

Here are some of the research-based findings about effective teachers' personal qualities.[13] See if you can identify some of your own favorite teachers here:

- *Effective teachers care about their students.* They show their caring in ways that students understand, see, and feel. They put in the extra time and energy to ensure that every student succeeds. These teachers bring out the best in students by affirming and encouraging them with patience, trust, honesty, courage, listening, understanding, and knowing their students as people and as learners.
- *Effective teachers show all students (and colleagues) fairness and respect.* They establish rapport and credibility by emphasizing, modeling, and practicing evenhandedness and showing esteem. For instance, they respond to student misbehavior on an individual level—rather than by punishing the entire class. They tell students what they need to do right—and get all the facts before speaking with students about what they did wrong. And they treat students equitably and do not show favoritism.
- *Effective teachers show interest in their students both inside and outside the classroom.* When students are having difficulties, these teachers work with them—rather than scold or ignore them. Attending football games, plays, and choral and band concerts in which their students participate also shows students that their teachers genuinely care about them. It also increases students' feelings of belonging in their classrooms. At the same time, teachers maintain the appropriate professional role with students. The ability to relate in these positive ways creates a learning environment that advances student achievement.
- *Effective teachers promote enthusiasm and motivation for learning.* Teacher excitement for teaching their subject matter has been shown to increase both positive relations with students and student achievement. Effective teachers know how to inspire all students—by understanding their individual interests and, whenever possible, making connections to students' familiar and valued prior knowledge. These teachers also give students choices about what and how they will study, thus intrinsically motivating student learning. Students want to work hard and learn for teachers they think like them and who believe in their ability to learn.
- *Effective teachers have a positive attitude toward their own learning and to the teaching profession.* They have a dual commitment to student learning and to personal learning. They believe that all students can learn the school's essential curriculum—and this is more than a slogan to them. Furthermore, effective teachers see themselves as responsible, capable, and willing to deliver for their students' success. They also work collaboratively with other teachers and staff, sharing ideas and assisting to resolve difficulties.
- *Effective teachers are reflective practitioners.* They continuously and thoughtfully review their teaching practice daily, class by class. Research consistently affirms the value of reflection in developing effective teaching.[14] Self-evaluation and self-critiquing are essential learning tools. Effective teachers seek greater understanding of teaching through experience, scholarly study, professional reading, and observing master teachers. Likewise, they desire feedback to

improve their performance. As they become better, their sense of **efficacy**—their belief in their own ability to make a difference—increases. They gain confidence both in their skills and in their results. Their students and colleagues see this transformation in action.

Clearly, teaching is more than what you know and can do in the classroom. Who you are as a person greatly affects how effective you are as a teacher. To learn more about the teacher characteristics that you find to be the most—and the least—helpful to you as a student, complete the activity in the **Reflect & Engage** box, Personal Qualities of Effective Teachers.

REFLECT & ENGAGE: PERSONAL QUALITIES OF EFFECTIVE TEACHERS

Who the teacher is as a person has a tremendous influence on the classroom climate and students' learning experiences.

A. Using the descriptors in this section, portray your favorite teacher—the one who you believe to be most influential in motivating you to become a teacher.

B. Using Table 1.1, respond in the box or on separate paper in a word, cartoon, or emoji to the descriptors about your favorite teacher. What did that teacher do or say that made him or her so influential for you? What behaviors and attitudes did the teacher regularly use in class?

C. Use the descriptors—or their reverse—to describe the "worst" teacher you had in school with a word, cartoon, or emoji and complete the table's second column.

D. As a class, identify and discuss characteristics of your favorite and least favorite teachers and describe how these behaviors affected you as a student in their class.

E. Using Table 1.2, assess the degree to which you currently have developed each of these positive teacher qualities and mark the appropriate boxes with a word, cartoon, or emoji.

TABLE 1.1 ■ Characteristics of My Most Influential Teacher

Teacher Characteristics	Favorite Teacher	"Worst" Teacher
Made difficult topics easy to understand		
Made me feel capable of learning, even when I made mistakes		
Taught with excitement for the subject and for teaching		
Made learning relevant and personally meaningful to me		
Taught in ways that made me want to learn		
Encouraged independent thought and accepted criticism		
Gave me some control and choice over my learning		
Connected new content to what I already knew		
Provided opportunities for interaction		
Gave helpful feedback in timely manner		
Taught me new ways to learn better		
Created a positive, safe emotional climate in class		
Was fair in grading and discipline		

Source: Leslie S. Kaplan and William A. Owings [Original by authors].

TABLE 1.2 ■ Personal Assessment of Positive Teacher Qualities

	Personal Assessment: The Degree to Which I Have the Quality		
Positive Teacher Qualities	Less Developed	Moderately Developed	Highly Developed
1. I have personal experiences working with young people as a tutor, teacher, counselor, or mentor.			
2. I am optimistic about life and my ability to help every student learn.			
3. I have the capacity to build positive relationships with students.			
4. I have consistently high expectations for every student.			
5. I communicate clearly.			
6. I admit my mistakes and quickly correct them.			
7. I think about and reflect on my behavior so I can improve.			
8. I have a sense of humor (and others agree that I do).			
9. I dress appropriately for the teaching profession.			
10. I am organized but also flexible and spontaneous.			
11. I like to collaborate with peers, families, and the community.			
12. I am enthusiastic about teaching students from varied backgrounds.			
13. I look for a win-win resolution in conflict situations.			
14. I respond to students respectfully, even in difficult situations.			
15. I consistently express high expectations and high confidence.			
16. I treat every student fairly.			
17. I have positive conversations with students outside the classroom.			
18. I maintain a professional manner in all public settings.			

Source: Leslie S. Kaplan and William A. Owings [Original by authors].

1.3 THE MORAL PURPOSE OF EDUCATION

Teaching affects the individual, the local community, and the larger society. Accordingly, Michael Fullan, professor emeritus at the University of Toronto and an international leader in teacher education, explains that schools have a moral purpose. Schools are charged with improving their students' lives, regardless of those individuals' backgrounds, and developing citizens who can live and work productively in increasingly dynamic and complex societies.[15] The individual teacher is the building block of this educational endeavor, linking caring and competence through professional practice. In this view, teachers' personal purpose has a social dimension: They are the agents of educational change and societal improvement.

Likewise, John Goodlad, a leader of educational renewal and a researcher on teacher education, maintains that schools have four moral imperatives: preparing students for responsible citizenship, providing essential knowledge and skills, building effective relationships, and practicing sound stewardship.[16] In this vein, he continues, "[E]ducation must be evaluated not just according to goal attainment [i.e., students' academic outcomes] but also according to the means employed."[17] The ends of education do not justify using inappropriate ways to reach them. Rather, education should prepare our children for "the kind of society we want [ourselves and them] . . . to live in."[18]

1.3a Preparing Students for Responsible Citizenship

First, a public school is the only national institution specifically assigned to prepare students to live responsibly in a democratic republic. Our federal government, state, and local communities have charged public schools as the agents of societal well-being. Children need to develop the information, skills, and habits of mind that make them informed citizens who can effectively participate in our representative government and can constructively fulfill their obligations as voters, law abiders, neighbors, and taxpayers. Through school, students acquire the knowledge and reasoning skills that allow them to become self-supporting and productive contributors to our society.

For those of us who live in the United States, democracy requires getting along with other people who hold viewpoints that may differ from our own. Students tend to live in neighborhoods with others like themselves. Schools, by contrast, gather several neighborhoods together into a larger and more diverse educational community. In schools, students develop the interpersonal skills they need to understand and appreciate the common ties they share with classmates from different families, genders, races, cultures, and economic backgrounds. Schools help both native-born individuals and immigrants, as well as people from different regions of the same state and the country, to identify and celebrate their unifying American traditions and beliefs and to build a common civic ethic. Students also get to know unfamiliar peers with different backgrounds as pleasant individuals much like themselves and learn how to show respect and appreciation for their individual traditions.

Classrooms create diverse communities.

iStock/fstop123

1.3b Providing Essential Knowledge and Skills

U.S. schools provide students access to knowledge. Schools help students develop communication skills through verbal, numerical, media, and digital fluency and learn about the Earth as a series of physical and biological systems. They help students learn the historical, political, social, economic, and cultural realities in which they live. In addition, schools provide students with instruction on how to gather, assess, evaluate, and judge information, use it to create new ways of knowing, and to express informed, well-reasoned opinions. They also ensure that no belief, attitude, or practice keeps students from getting the necessary knowledge.

1.3c Enacting Schools' Moral Purpose Through Caring Relationships

Although teaching is a professional activity, it is also an acutely personal one. Teaching entails much more than just the mechanics of delivering content. It involves caring about and interacting with individual students in a group setting and, when necessary, remotely. And when students spend more than 1,000 hours with their teacher in a typical school year, that's plenty of time to build a relationship that can either advance or limit learning.[19]

At their core, relationships are about caring. In fact, research suggests that a caring relationship with teachers can help students do better in school and act more kindly toward others.[20] A 2017 *Review of Educational Research* analysis of 46 studies found that strong teacher–student relationships were associated in both short- and long-term improvements in higher student academic engagement, attendance, grades, fewer disruptive behaviors and suspensions, and lower school dropout rates—even after controlling for individual, family, and school differences.[21] Teacher caring has been identified as essential for effective teaching and learning at all educational levels.[22] And the benefits are mutual. A study in the *European Journal of Psychology of Education* found a teacher's relationship with students to be the best predictor of how much the teacher experiences joy rather than anxiety in the classroom.[23]

Effective teachers are often described as those who develop relationships with students that are emotionally supportive, safe, and trusting; who show concern about students' emotional, intellectual, and physical well-being; and who regularly give children resources—modeled behavior, information and advice, specific experiences, and encouragement—to develop their social and academic skills.

Simply developing good relationships with students is not enough to promote student learning, however. Highly effective teachers leverage that foundation to promote students' deeper thinking and engagement. Caring teachers create and sustain a safe, considerate, and intellectually challenging environment. In this view, teachers are socializing agents who create interpersonal contexts that influence the quality and levels of student motivation and engagement with school's academic and social life. For instance, a caring teacher may notice that a certain child is struggling with peer relationships. This teacher would assess this child's needs, decide how to meet them, and then take the necessary action. What is more, students know when teachers respect and like them. They know when teachers hold high expectations for their achievement—and when they don't. And students respond accordingly—by engaging in the material or by withdrawing from it. Table 1.3 gives examples of how to build caring relationships with students.

TABLE 1.3 ■ How Teachers Show Their Care and Connectedness With Students[25]

Principle	Description of Caring and Connectedness in Action
Know your students as individuals.	Use the first days of class to survey or interview students about their interests, likes, dislikes, goals, and expectations. Teachers need to know their students and let their students get to know them.
Every student is unique.	Accept that students are individuals who have different backgrounds and ways of learning. To the extent possible, teach with varied approaches, activities, and assignments to connect every student with the lesson.
Research cultural differences.	Learn the differences between teachers and students to avoid cultural misunderstandings around norms, styles, and language.

(Continued)

TABLE 1.3 ■ How Teachers Show Their Care and Connectedness With Students (Continued)

Principle	Description of Caring and Connectedness in Action
Invite student input.	Listen to students and be aware and responsive to the classroom climate.
Provide a safe, supportive, and fair learning environment.	Encourage students to share their ideas and ask questions without fear of being punished or humiliated if wrong.
Give clear expectations.	Students need clarity about your expectations for classroom and school behavior and academic performance. Show how class activities will help build the necessary and required career skills later in life.
Give timely, specific, and constructive feedback.	Students need to know as early as possible how they are progressing on their class activities, assessments, and assignments and what they need to change so they may succeed in class.

Although important interpersonal and professional boundaries exist—a "relationship" with a student does not mean "friend"—good teachers combine teaching's generalizable principles and subject-specific instruction with a genuine sensitivity to their students' uniqueness and humanness as learners. Unlike their emotionally supportive relationship with parents, however, students report that their relationships with their teachers tend to be domain and classroom specific.[24]

AMERICAN EDUCATION SPOTLIGHT: NEL NODDINGS

A leader in the field of educational philosophy, Nel Noddings, the Jacks Professor Emeriti of Child Education at Stanford University, winner of numerous prizes for her teaching excellence and scholarly accomplishments (and a former public elementary and high school teacher and administrator) believes that caring relationships should be the foundation for teaching and learning.

In her view, American schools have traditionally promoted the belief that students develop character through academic skills and intellectual pursuits.[26] Knowledge of "the basics" (whether classical studies or basic reading and math) along with self-sacrifice, success, determination, ambition, and competition would enable students to build the attitudes and skills appropriate to live successfully in a capitalist society. Noddings objected to this approach. To her, schools should address human values and concerns, not merely cognitive ones.[27]

Noddings argues that contemporary teachers enact schools' moral purpose through *caring*,[28] involving physical proximity and a degree of nurturance; and our schools should produce

Courtesy of Nel Noddings

competent, considerate, loving, and lovable people.[29] As a teacher, caring involves listening to students, gaining their trust, and engaging in dialogue about their needs, working habits, interests, and talents. Teachers use this knowledge to build their lessons and plan for their individual progress.

Caring relationships also involve moral and ethical behaviors. Ethics and morals are theory and practice, respectively. This **ethical caring** is more highly abstract, less intense or intimate, than mother–child caring, also known as *natural caring*. With an ethic of caring, one acts out of affection or inclination rather than simply from duty and principle. For teachers and students, these caring relationships occur within the school and classroom settings during the teaching and learning process.

Teachers model caring for students in many ways. They consistently treat students with respect and consideration and expect them to treat other students in the same way. Teachers and students must trust and respect one another well enough to express differing viewpoints or decisions and carefully consider the reasons given that oppose their original position. Caring teachers show students how intellectual activity is useful, fun, and important. They limit lectures to the presentation of essential information and then use class time for students to interact and explore how the information addresses issues that are real and relevant to them. Teachers work with students to develop learning objectives that meet both the school's and the students' needs; they use discussion to elicit and respond thoughtfully to students' ideas; and they give students timely, specific written feedback on their work. Caring teachers assume that students are well intentioned and act from worthy motives: They try to understand and address the purposes that underlie students' sometimes annoying behaviors rather than responding quickly and punitively to the overt behavior itself. When teachers respond to students with respect for the quality person that student either is now or can become, the student feels confirmed, validated as worthy and competent.

Ideally, the students recognize and respond to teachers' caring by thoughtfully completing assigned work. The ethic of caring, therefore, is often characterized as responsibility and response. Students learn and develop this caring outlook and behaviors through their relationships with their teachers. But since caring is an unselfish act, teachers must demonstrate care for students even when it is not reciprocated, although it is more difficult.

As Nodding sees it, all children must learn to care for other human beings as well as for animals, plants, the physical and global environments, objects, instruments, and ideas—in addition to developing academic competencies. Caring teachers want to help their students grow into likable and ethical people: "persons who will support worthy institutions, live compassionately, work productively but not obsessively, care for older and younger generations, be admired, trusted, and respected."[30] For this type of maturation to happen, teachers need to know both their subjects and their students very well.

Noddings's critics include feminists (who see the one caring as naively carrying out the traditional female role in our culture while receiving little in return, perpetuating inequity, and reinforcing oppressive institutions) and those favoring more traditional (masculine) approaches to ethics (who believe the partiality given to those closest to us is inappropriate). Others view the problematic nature of building an ethical theory upon those in unequal relationships.[31]

Critics aside, Noddings believes that by furthering students' development in this way, schools produce people who can care competently for their own families and contribute effectively to their communities, both local and international. In her view, caring is the strong, resilient backbone of human life.

1.3d Practicing Good Stewardship

Goodlad affirms that schools and teachers must practice good **stewardship**.[32] A steward is a caretaker who looks out for and manages an estate's or organization's affairs. Stewardship is how we track and account for the resources we have been given, what we do with them according to our values and beliefs, and how we guarantee that they are ably used to those purposes. Stewardship requires consciously, purposefully, and intentionally aligning our goals and actions with our values.

Similarly, teaching involves more than working with students behind the classroom door or online. By virtue of their faculty membership and school district employment, teachers have ethical duties and obligations that go beyond the classroom. As good stewards, they attend to the school's mission and protect the school's reputation in the community. Similarly, teachers have an ethical obligation to protect the reputation of the teaching profession as a whole.

As stewards, teachers ensure that they and their school are committed to each student's advancement and to society's well-being. To do so, they assure the highest quality teaching and learning for all students in the school (not just those inside their own classrooms). This means that teachers must be constructive and helpful to colleagues who share the goal of making the school an increasingly effective and satisfying place and experience for everyone to learn and work. It means remaining professional in attitude and behaviors in the face of unwelcome disruptions. Stewardship also means keeping the community informed about the school's accomplishments and activities and enlisting local support to make school even better. It means practicing responsible citizenship, thinking critically, and acting deliberately in a pluralistic world—and educating students to do the same.

Contemporary education stewards also provide students with attitudes, knowledge, and skills for responsibility in a global environment. With 21st century communications, work environments, challenges, and outcomes extending across the global stage, interdependence across national borders has become necessary. Teachers preparing young people to negotiate such complexity and become "thoughtful stewards" in tomorrow's world need to ready them with more "literacies." For instance, what attitudes, knowledge, and skills will today's students need to work with international colleagues to successfully ensure that we all have clean air to breathe and water to drink? Young people need to develop scientific, cultural, and global understanding; skills and dispositions to comprehend multiple viewpoints; the capacities to work collaboratively with others to address shared concerns; and a greater commitment to act beyond narrow self-interest if they are to take on this essential role.[33]

Finally, fulfilling the demands of teacher stewardship means becoming a transformational learner. Changing the world begins with changing oneself. Teachers must be enthusiastically engaged with their own learning, continue to learn, and show students how to learn. Students are more likely to find learning a specific subject fascinating and motivating when they see that their teacher finds it fascinating as well. They may be more willing to persist in learning new knowledge and skills when they see their teachers patiently struggling to master new content and practices, too. Put simply, teachers encourage student learning by being enthusiastic learners themselves.

As stewards, teachers are committed to each student's advancement and society's well-being.

iStock/ferrantraite

Enacting these four moral imperatives—acculturating students, providing essential knowledge and skills, developing effective relationships with students, and providing stewardship—are more than a matter of teachers' personal preferences. Fullan and Goodlad believe teachers are morally obligated to take on these roles. Teaching is clearly more than a job or career. As teachers, we touch our entire community and nation through the students we educate. In a similar way, **Flip Sides** asks you to consider whether teaching is an art or a science.

For the relationship between teachers and students to develop, they need to spend time together. Creating opportunities to greet and interact with students every day through welcoming them into the classroom, talking about students' interests, and providing engaging lessons are positive starting points for forging such connections. Similarly, creating smaller schools, limiting class sizes, and keeping students and teachers working together over multiple years can provide the extra time needed to develop strong teacher–student relationships. Working to create more caring schools would help both teachers and students develop more ethical selves. To think more deeply about how teachers express their moral purpose in their classrooms and schools, complete the activity in the **Reflect & Engage** box, Education's Moral Purpose.

REFLECT & ENGAGE: EDUCATION'S MORAL PURPOSES

Education has a moral purpose that affects the individual, the local community, and the larger society. Let's see what this assertion looks like enacted in actual schools.

Divide the class into four groups and assign each group one of the following questions to answer in graphic form by drawing a picture or cartoon to express their ideas (using newsprint and markers or colored pencils if available) and then explain it orally to the class:

A. Illustrate how every teacher, regardless of subject taught, can prepare students for responsible citizenship.

B. Illustrate how every teacher, regardless of subject taught, can help students attain essential knowledge and skills.

C. Illustrate how every teacher, regardless of subject taught, can enact schools' moral purpose through caring relationships.

D. Illustrate how every teacher, regardless of subject taught, can practice good stewardship. Reconvene the class and have each group explains their graphic answers. Then, discuss as a class, with examples:

1. In what ways are teachers "agents of educational change and societal improvement"?
2. To what extent do you agree or disagree with Nel Noddings's view that teachers should address human values and concerns, not merely cognitive ones? Explain your reasons.
3. Explain how a teacher's "caring" can increase student learning.
4. Explain why building caring relationships with students is *a necessary but not sufficient condition* to generate high student learning.

FLIPSIDES

Is Teaching an Art or a Science?

Is teaching an art or a science? Over the years, many have debated whether good teachers rely on native instinct and in-the-moment spontaneous behaviors to engage students in powerful learning or whether good teachers rely on a systematic, predictable set of choices based in research and experience. Read the following debate and decide where you stand on this issue.

Effective teaching is an art.	Effective teaching is a science.
• Great teachers are born, not made.	• Teaching is an applied science derived from research in human learning and behavior that can be learned.

(Continued)

Effective teaching is an art.	Effective teaching is a science.
• Teaching involves complex judgments that unfold during the instructional process. Teachers must deal creatively with the unexpected in the moment, often relying on tacit knowledge from prior experiences.	• Teaching has an explicit knowledge base in the social sciences that provides a basic structure that can be learned, is open to new evidence, and can guide teachers' decisions and behaviors about practice.
• Teaching requires spontaneity and intuition activated on the spot to fuel new clarifying insights and creativity.	• Teaching is a sequential, predictable, rational, step-by-step process in an identifiable cause-and-effect relationship with learning.
• Effective teaching is affective, flexible, and expressive, responding to events in the moment and communicating in ways that actively engage learners in learning.	• Effective teaching is rational and logical, observing and analyzing the environment as a means to planning and making the appropriate instructional decisions to actively engage learners in learning.
• The best research can do is tell us which strategies have a good chance of working well with students, but individual classroom teachers must determine which strategies to use with the right student at the right time.	• Intuition is functional but inarticulate knowledge that cannot travel well; it cannot be transmitted to others, it must be invented anew in each situation, and it cannot be depended on to appear in all situations.
• Teaching skills cannot all be prelearned and rehearsed. They must respond to events in the moment.	• Effective teaching behaviors can be taught, learned, and improved with conscious practice, observation, and feedback and is generalizable to all content areas.
• Teaching is holistic, considering the complex interactions among the teacher, the situation, the content, and the learner that cannot be fully understood in making any decisions and behaviors about practice.	• An effective teaching model, and teacher practice and feedback using it, can guide successful teacher behavior regardless of the content, learners' age, socioeconomic status, or ethnicity.
• Much art involves science. Artists know the nature of their materials and their effects singly or combined; they know how to use media to convey emotion and experience; and they actively critique their work to generate feedback to improve performance.	• Much science involves art. Teachers learn and apply a set of research-based principles and rules but use art in situations when rules don't work and teachers must improvise. Effective teaching can be, but is not always, an art.

Effective teaching is both an art *and* a science. The science of teaching—the knowledge base—provide the key foundation from which teachers' creativity and artistry can emerge. In short, teaching is a science; what you do with it is an art. Effective teachers need them both.

Sources: Brandt, R. (1985, February). On teaching and supervising: A conversation with Madeline Hunter. *Educational Leadership, 42*(5), 61–68; Costa, A. L. (1984). A reaction to Hunter's knowing, teaching, and supervising. In P. L. Hosford (Ed.), *Using what we know about teaching: 1984 ASCD Yearbook* (pp. 196–203). ASCD; Hunter, M. (1984). Knowing, teaching, and supervising. In P. L. Hosford (Ed.), *Using what we know about teaching: 1984 ASCD Yearbook* (pp. 169–195). ASCD; Hunter, M. (1979, October). Teaching is decision making. *Educational Leadership, 37*(1), 62–67; Hunter, M. (1985, February). What's wrong with Madeline Hunter? *Educational Leadership, 42*(5), 57–60; Lambert, L. (1985, February). Who is right—Madeline Hunter or Art Costa? *Educational Leadership, 42*(5), 68–69.

1.4 TECHNOLOGY AND EDUCATION IN A GLOBAL ENVIRONMENT

Throughout most of human history, people lived and organized their lives around boundaries structured by local geography and topography, family and kinship, community social organizations, religions, and local worldviews. This is no longer true. Today's world is rapidly changing, and so is our understanding of what it means to be "educated." At present, youth grow up linked to economic realities, social media, technologies, and cultural movements that spill over local and national borders.

Just to get a sense of how the world has changed, consider these examples: The cost of an overseas telephone call in 1927 cost $75 for 3 minutes from New York to London.[34] In 2019, this call could cost from two to five cents a minute.[35] In the 1960s and 1970s, immigrants working in London relied on the postal system and personal letter carriers to communicate with family back home in India, Malaysia, or China. They waited 2 months to receive a reply to each letter. Calling by phone was not even possible. By the late 1990s, however, their grandchildren used mobile phones that linked them instantly with their cousins in Calcutta, Singapore, or Shanghai.[36]

As discussed in considering "stewardship," our world is complex. Unlike when your parents were in preK–12 schools, you will teach in a highly interconnected, globalized world. Accordingly, "education's challenge will be to shape the cognitive skills, interpersonal sensibilities, and cultural sophistication of children and youth whose lives will be both engaged in local contexts and response to larger transnational processes."[37] Technology as a teaching and learning tool is increasingly integral to this process.

1.4a Technology, the Workplace, and Globalization

Globalization—the trend of deterritorializing skills and competencies so that people working anywhere in the world can collaborate with those working elsewhere—and technology are reshaping the American workplace. These dynamics have major implications for American education and students' eventual careers and lifestyles. Now, teachers not only have to teach students how to receive knowledge, but they also have to teach them how to transfer and apply what they know to new situations or problems.[38] At the same time, teachers themselves are learning the skills to plan, deliver, and assess engaging lessons digitally.

The U.S. economy is shedding simpler, labor-intensive manufacturing processes and moving increasingly toward more mechanized, digitized, high-value efforts that require fewer workers and a more well-educated and prepared workforce. Anything that can be digitized can be outsourced to either the smartest or the cheapest producer—or the producer that fits both descriptions. Many manufacturing jobs that traditionally provided middle-class salaries for relatively low-skilled workers have already been automated (using fewer workers) or moved offshore. The results create prosperity for some as well as substantial societal disruptions. Income disparities between wealthy and poor have increased; educated workers see greater earning opportunities, whereas the less skilled and less educated have fewer. This economy affects what students worldwide need to know and be able to do.

1.4b Competing in a Global Environment

It is almost universally recognized that the effectiveness of a country's educational system is a key factor in establishing a competitive advantage in an increasingly global economy. Education is a fundamental part of a country's economic and social development as well as its citizens' personal development. Education is a primary means to reduce social and economic inequalities. Keeping U.S. education strong and viable in a globalized world is essential to maintain the U.S. citizens' standard of living and our national security. In this context, effective teachers and effective schools are essential facets of our national well-being.

When jobs in a globalized world go to those with the best skills for the lowest wage (wherever they are) and artificial intelligence (AI) technologies can perform much routine physical and cognitive work, any serious skill gaps place many future U.S. workers at a serious disadvantage. Widespread use of automation could lead to a future of widespread unemployment and more low-wage jobs unless U.S. schools can find a way to perform apace with top school systems around the world. More and more, this new reality includes teachers.

1.4c Teaching With Technology

From texting friends on smartphones to relying on GPS (global positioning system) in your car to find the best route to unfamiliar places, technological innovation and digital devices have reshaped our lives. But generally speaking, this has been less true for teaching. Until 2020, U.S. public schools provided about only one computer for every five students and spent $3 billion annually on digital content.[39] Then, in 2020, the coronavirus pandemic exploded, and the related school closures pushed some schools closer to providing one computer for every student, years ahead of schedule. Still, by May 2020 only 59% of teachers said their schools had at least one device for every student.[40] Perhaps this scarcity of 1:1 digital learning devices reflects the reality that until now, U.S. teachers reported that technology had not led to meaningful innovation in the way they teach.[41]

Studies affirm this unhurried adoption. A significant body of research makes clear that, even with new digital devices in their classrooms, most teachers have been slow to transform their instructional practices. Plus, limited evidence suggests that technology is improving students' learning outcomes.[42] The two factors are likely related because most teachers' lack of familiarity with how to use digital tools as a crucial part of their daily planning affects student learning.

Then, virtually overnight, teaching and learning went online. Although teachers did their best to adapt, most were not ready to teach remotely. Many schools did not have the necessary resources to switch on cue to virtual instruction—likewise for some teachers and many students. As a result, in many places learning during spring 2020 (and beyond) was hit or miss.

The COVID pandemic pushed technology-infused teaching and learning to the front burner. Suddenly, teachers discovered that digitally informed instruction was more than using Google Docs to replicate worksheets, delegating teaching algebra to Khan Academy videos day after day, or positioning the internet-linked computer as an "add-on" before the bell rings.[43] Once-reluctant classroom teachers are now hands-on, actively rethinking, redesigning, and delivering their lessons for digital platforms. No longer an accessory to instructional practice, technology-infused instruction has become central to teaching and learning. And it will be—either online or in a hybrid schedule with in-classroom teaching—for the foreseeable future.

Increasingly adept teachers will find that well-designed and enacted digitally infused instruction can strengthen and enrich learning. When used effectively, it supports **deep learning**—the conceptual skills that prepare students to "master core academic content, think critically and solve complex problems, work collaboratively, communicate effectively, and learning how to learn."[44] Technology-infused learning enables teachers to personalize and customize student education, making it possible for teachers to prompt them to explore topics of interest related to the curriculum more fully. With higher student interest and motivation to learn, teachers can guide them in how to direct and manage their own learning, gather information, think critically, differentiate reliable from unreliable sources, work alone and with others (including receiving ongoing feedback from teachers), and demonstrate coherently their content mastery as projects or other products. Similarly, teachers can infuse lessons with digital tools such as blogging platforms, portfolio tools, and video publishing resources to help students improve their writing and become digital storytellers. With internet access and regular practice, students become able to learn anywhere at any time, facilitating lifelong learning. These are skill sets that effectively prepare students to succeed in college and careers.

What is more, technology-infused instruction brings new opportunities. Subject matter is constantly changing, and digital textbooks embed links to relevant and timely materials. Online polling and other digital tools help engage all students (including those who normally resist raising their hand in class) and provides regular feedback on students' learning progress and needs, allowing teachers to adjust their coursework accordingly. Using technology-informed instruction can help build credibility with students (who are already digital natives). Additionally, technology can reduce tedious, time-consuming "housekeeping" tasks, such as recording and monitoring student attendance and performance. McKinsey & Company suggest that technology can help save teacher time—up to 2 hours a week—in administrative paperwork.[45]

To make digital learning work for all parties, today's classroom teachers need intensive and ongoing professional development on how to design, enact, and assess engaging instruction delivered digitally. Tomorrow's teachers need preservice training and/or intensive and ongoing professional development and support (ideally, with classroom coaching) once on the job to master these approaches. Both veteran and novice teachers will need many occasions to experiment with these tools and receive timely constructive feedback.

Likewise, all teachers need to learn how to build students' **digital citizenship**—the ability to participate safely, intelligently, productively, and responsibly in the computerized world. Digital citizenship includes keeping technical devices free from malware and protecting one's self from data loss, following ethical behaviors and legal standards in the digital sphere, identifying and avoiding harmful content, and using cultural rules for online interactions.[46] Digital citizenship must be taught, learned, and applied.

Digital learning comes with pros and cons. Some argue that technology in the learning space can be distracting and even enable cheating.[47] Critics observe that whether in the classroom or at home, students who use computers or tablets during lectures tend to find it difficult to concentrate and tend to earn worse grades.[48] Students may choose to check Instagram instead of watching and listening to the teacher. Technology can foster cheating in class and on assignments, allowing students to copy and paste from another's work. Then, too, not all students have equal access to technology resources; not everyone can afford tablets, smartphones, or broadband, worsening the "opportunity" gap (although library and community resources and other creative solutions may be available). These circumstances raise equity issues. Digital-infused instruction also makes lesson planning more labor intensive for teachers. And the rise of "big data" has led to new worries about how schools can protect and secure students' sensitive information. Most believe, however, that the benefits outweigh the negatives—especially when the teacher–student relationship remains pivotal to the learning process—and teachers can learn how to use these digital tools as a learning enhancer, not a teacher alternative.

Beyond the technology concerns are the students. Learning occurs best within trusting and caring relationship. In schools, teachers and students build these ties over time, verbally and nonverbally, from person-to-person interactions. No matter how digitally proficient the teacher, this cannot replace our children's profound need for meaningful, in-person connections with teachers, peers, and others. Especially in unusual times of social upheaval with dramatically altered daily routines, children can feel anxious, angry, and fearful. These emotions may interfere with learning regardless of teachers' digital expertise. With this in mind, teachers and administrators will want to find innovative ways to address students' social and emotional needs and nurture respectful, trusting relationships within the digital or hybrid environments.

Despite our new reliance on digital platforms to conduct schooling, it remains to be seen whether these changes will be medium-term stopgaps or a transformational way to conduct teaching and learning. Effective teachers will learn to how to use technology-enabled instruction as an essential, responsibly used learning modality as a regular part of their classrooms, online or in person. No longer can it remain "just casually layered on top of an outdated, industrial-era system."[49] Chapter 12 further considers how the COVID-19 pandemic made teaching with technology integral to student learning and the challenges this brings for instructional quality, student learning, and equity.

1.5 WHAT 21ST CENTURY STUDENTS NEED TO LEARN

We do not know what the world will be like in 5 years, let alone in 60 years when today's kindergartners retire. As part of globalization, our students are facing many emerging issues, including worldwide financial crises, global pandemics and related economic harm, retreats from government spending on public services and institutions (including public schools), climate change, poverty, health issues, a growing and educated global middle class, and other environmental and social issues. Our economy is generating fewer jobs in which workers engage in repetitive, assembly line–type tasks throughout their day and producing more information-rich jobs that confront employees with novel problems that require knowledge, analysis, and teamwork. These realities oblige students to learn how to skillfully function, communicate, and create change personally, socially, economically, and politically on local, national, and global levels.

To be successful in the 21st century, our students will need more than a factory-model education based on the needs of Industrial Age employers. Through the late 19th and early 20th centuries, good preparation for factory employment meant schoolchildren "sat and listened" while teachers "stood and delivered" textbook lessons; and students changed classrooms to ringing bells. Today, companies have altered how they organize and do business. Workers have more responsibility and contribute more to productivity and innovation. Advanced economies, groundbreaking industries and firms, and high-growth jobs require more educated workers with the ability to respond flexibly and knowledgeably to complex problems, communicate effectively, manage information, work in teams, and produce new knowledge. By 2030, workers are likely to spend more time using higher cognitive and technical skills, social and emotional skills, and less time on physical, manual, and basic cognitive skills.[50] To do this, employees are expected to be thoughtful consumers of digital content but also effective and collaborative creators of digital media. Many of these workers can reside in any country with internet connectivity.

Many agree that competencies critical for the 21st century include developing capacities in the cognitive, intrapersonal, and interpersonal domains. The *cognitive domain* includes thinking, reasoning, and related skills. The *intrapersonal domain* involves conscientiousness, self-management, and the ability to regulate one's actions and emotions to reach goals. The *interpersonal domain* concludes communicating information to others, interpreting others' messages, and responding appropriately. The available research supports the consistent, positive correlations between these factors and desirable adult outcomes, although more research is needed to determine whether the relationships are causal.[51] Table 1.4 identifies these 21st century competencies.

TABLE 1.4 ■ Skills Required to be an Effective 21st Century Employee

Cognitive skills	• Deep understanding of core subject matter—knowing the facts and how they fit together • Critical thinking, logical reasoning, and complex, open-ended problem-solving—tied to content; using evidence and assessing information • Cognitive flexibility and adaptability—to use information and skills in new ways and to adjust oneself to new realities new roles, lifelong learning • Information access and analysis—to find necessary resources, critique its accuracy and value, make reasoned decisions, and take purposeful action • Curiosity, imagination, and creativity—thinking "outside the box" to solve novel problems
Interpersonal skills	• Collaboration—with colleagues, teams, and experts across several networks • Leadership—have social influence with others • Express empathy—understand others' needs, resolve conflicts, develop trusting relationships
Intrapersonal skills	• Communicate oral and written communications effectively—to interpret information clearly and interact competently and respectfully with others across geographic and cultural boundaries • Regulate one's behaviors and emotions—in order to reach a goal • Use initiative, entrepreneurialism, and leadership—make well-reasoned decisions and take appropriate actions • Think and act ethically—self-regulation, perseverance, intellectual openness; thinking short and long term.

These cognitive, interpersonal, and intrapersonal skills are not "habits of mind" or competencies that students can learn by sitting passively at their desks listening to teacher lectures within their four classroom walls. Increasingly, 21st century students will be assessed on what they can do with what they have learned rather than on what they can memorize or accumulate by seat time. Teachers' expectations for every student's learning will be high. Teachers will ensure that the curriculum is connected to students' interests, goals, experiences, talents, and the real world, made relevant rather than meaningless to students. Lessons will include occasions for students to analyze, synthesize, evaluate, and create rather than merely recognize or comprehend information or practice context-free skills. Students will be actively involved in making their learning happen and making choices about study topics and projects rather than on receiving teachers' accumulated wisdom.

Likewise, 21st century students will work collaboratively with classmates—onsite and around the world—rather than learn at their solitary desks in their classrooms. The curriculum will be thematic and interdisciplinary, as it is in the real world, rather than artificially fragmented into separate departments. Literacy will expand from the 3Rs to multiple media that reflect the communication platforms of our globalized world. Frequently, students show their learning through performances and projects upon which they are assessed rather than relying primarily on standardized tests. In short, the concept and practice of 21st century education will need to be different from the one most college students experienced earlier in their education careers. And teachers' roles will change, from primary content deliverer to major learning facilitator. Teachers' unexpected immersion into digital teaching beginning in spring 2020 and its continuation into subsequent school years will likely advance this outcome, especially if they receive the professional support and resources they need.

Should America's teachers and best students worry? Maybe. This new reality poses a challenge to all industrialized nations. Although Americans and Western Europeans produced many 20th century innovations, we have no guarantee that we will permanently lead in technological development. After World War II, the United States had no serious economic or intellectual competition. In recognition of its dominance, the 20th century was often called the American Century. Some believe that this economic, military, and cultural preeminence "bred a sense of entitlement and cultural complacency" in the United States.[52] Achieving a prominent place in this century will not be as easy for Americans as it was in the late 20th century.

Even though education means much more than securing a well-paying job, "learning more to earning more" is still a realistic goal. Americans who want to compete successfully for decent-paying employment will need the right attitudes, knowledge, and skills to vie for the information-rich careers in new specialties that will likely become available in this country. By comparison, individuals with low-knowledge skills whose jobs can be moved elsewhere have reason to worry. As the accounting profession's "grunt work" (that is, bookkeeping, preparing payrolls) moves overseas, the job of designing and creating complex tax-sheltering strategies with quality-time discussions with clients remains anchored in the United States.

Thomas Friedman, the three-time Pulitzer Prize–winning author and *The New York Times* columnist, writes that when he was young, his parents used to tell him to finish his dinner because people in China and India would love to have his food. Now, his advice to his daughters is, "Finish your homework. People in China and India would love to have your jobs."[53]

Preparing students for citizenship, work, and lifestyle in a globalized world has clear implications for teaching and learning. Globalization is changing the nature of life from labor to knowledge, from retaining information to using it for analysis, synthesis, evaluation, and creativity. Young people will need the ability to understand, communicate, work with, and get along with people different from oneself and be ready for full participation in democratic self-government. And it is worth remembering that a high-quality education is lifelong and focuses on living an aware, productive, personally and socially responsible, happy life. To be sure, effective 21st century teachers are learning to teach very differently than they were taught.

1.6 INTASC MODEL CORE PERFORMANCE STANDARDS FOR TEACHERS

New teachers enter the profession motivated and enthused about their new role. They want to be prepared, confident, and able to meet their classroom demands and to continue to grow their expertise throughout their careers. The profession has built frameworks to support this effort.

The **Interstate Teacher Assessment and Support Consortium (InTASC)**, a program of the Council of Chief State School Officers, developed Model Core Teaching Standards for licensing teachers.[54] Updated in 2013 and aligned with other state and national standards,[55] InTASC standards define what teachers should know and be able to do to ensure that by high school graduation, every preK–12 student is ready to enter college or today's knowledge-based workforce. These professional practice standards contain a continuum of expectations for teachers, appropriate from their first days leading their own classrooms through accomplished practice (although the professional practice looks different at different stages of a teacher's career).

InTASC standards—essential knowledge, critical dispositions, and performances—are common to all teachers, regardless of academic discipline or specialty area. **Performance** refers to the teaching behaviors that can be observed and assessed in teaching practice. **Essential knowledge** notes the importance of declarative and procedural knowledge as the bedrock of effective practice. **Critical dispositions** indicate the habits of professional action and moral commitments that anchor teacher actions. Meeting these standards—including knowledge of student learning and development, curriculum and teaching, and contexts and purposes that create a set of professional understandings, abilities, and ethical commitments that all teachers share—ensures that all their students learn to high levels. They also describe the conditions needed to support their professional growth along the way.

The InTASC standards are performance-based and assessable. They permit states and schools to incorporate more innovation and diversity in their teacher education programs by looking at teacher *outcomes* rather than *inputs*, such as lists of courses taken. These standards are based on five key themes that will propel improved student learning:

1. ***Personalized learning for diverse learners***: Teachers will need to know how to customize learning for children with a range of individual differences and multiple approaches to learning for each student.
2. ***A stronger focus on applying knowledge and skills***: Since today's learners need both academic and global skills—including applying knowledge to problem-solving and attributes such as curiosity, creativity, innovation, communication, and interpersonal competence—to make their way in the world, teachers need cross-disciplinary skills to help students explore in multiple perspectives.
3. ***Improved assessment literacy***: Teachers are expected to use data—gathered through a range of ongoing and annual formative and summative assessments—to improve instruction, understand each learner's progress, and support each learner's success.
4. ***A collaborative professional culture***: Effective teaching involves collaboration—from opening classrooms to peer observation to embedded professional learning and collective inquiry—to improve practice and increase student learning.
5. ***New leadership roles for teachers and administrators***: Teacher are expected to lead by advocating for each student's needs; actively investigating and considering new ideas that would improve teaching and learning and advance the profession; participating in a collaborative culture; and engaging in efforts to build a shared vision and supportive culture within a school or classroom by working together with administrators, families, and community to meet common goals.

InTASC groups the standards into four general categories to help users organize their thinking about the 10 standards:[56] the learners and learning, content, instructional practice, and professional responsibility.

1.6a Learners and Learning

Teaching begins with the learner. Teachers must understand individual differences, have high expectations for every learner, and implement appropriate, challenging learning experiences to help every learner meet high standards and reach their full potential.

Standard #1: Learner Development

"The teacher understands how learners grow and develop, recognizing that patterns of learning and development vary individually within and across the cognitive, linguistic, social, emotional, and physical areas, and designs and implements developmentally appropriate and challenging learning experiences."

Standard #2: Learning Differences

"The teacher uses understanding of individual differences and diverse cultures and communities to ensure inclusive learning environments that enable each learner to meet high standards."

Standard #3: Learning Environments

"The teacher works with others to create environments that support individual and collaborative learning, and that encourage positive social interaction, active engagement in learning, and self motivation."

1.6b Content

Teachers must understand their content deeply and flexibly. They are able to draw upon it using multiple means of communication as they work with learners to access information, apply knowledge in real-world settings using cross-disciplinarity skills (e.g., critical thinking, problem-solving, creativity, communication), and address meaningful issues by connecting them to relevant local, state, national, and global issues to assure learner mastery of the content.

Standard #4: Content Knowledge

"The teacher understands the central concepts, tools of inquiry, and structures of the discipline(s) he or she teaches and creates learning experiences that make the discipline accessible and meaningful for learners to assure mastery of the content."

Standard #5: Application of Content

"The teacher understands how to connect concepts and use differing perspectives to engage learners in critical thinking, creativity, and collaborative problem-solving related to authentic local and global issues."

1.6c Instructional Practice

Effective instructional practice requires that teachers understand and integrate assessment, planning, and instructional strategies in coordinated and engaging ways.

Standard #6: Assessment

"The teacher understands and uses multiple methods of assessment to engage learners in their own growth, to monitor learner progress, and to guide the teacher's and learner's decision making."

Standard #7: Planning for Instruction

"The teacher plans instruction that supports every student in meeting rigorous learning goals by drawing upon knowledge of content areas, curriculum, cross-disciplinary skills, and pedagogy, as well as knowledge of learners and the community context."

Standard #8: Instructional Strategies

"The teacher understands and uses a variety of instructional strategies to encourage learners to develop deep understanding of content areas and their connections, and to build skills to apply knowledge in meaningful ways."

1.6d Professional Responsibility

Teachers' main responsibility is creating and supporting safe, productive learning environments that result in learners achieving at the highest levels. To do this well, teachers must engage in meaningful, intensive professional learning and self-renewal by a continuous cycle of examining their practice through ongoing study, self-reflection, and collaboration.

Standard #9: Professional Learning and Ethical Practice

"The teacher engages in ongoing professional learning and uses evidence to continually evaluate his/her practice, particularly the effects of his/her choices and actions on others (learners, families, other professionals, and the community), and adapts practice to meet the needs of each learner."

Standard #10: Leadership and Collaboration

"The teacher seeks appropriate leadership roles and opportunities to take responsibility for student learning, to collaborate with learners, families, colleagues, other school professionals, and community members to ensure learner growth, and to advance the profession."[57]

In deciding that these standards apply to every teacher, regardless of their career development stage, InTASC concluded that the differences between beginning and advanced practice rested more in the increasing degree of complexity and sophistication of teaching practice teachers use in applying their knowledge than in the kind of knowledge they need. Over their careers, teachers move from basic competence to more complex teaching practices. All teachers must be able to meet these 10 standards, but they will differ in the expertise with which they do.

For example, advanced practitioners have developed the ability to deal simultaneously with more of the complex facets of teaching, moving from limited instructional strategies to a broader, deeper repertoire, and adapting their performances to meet students' individual needs. To eventually become an expert practitioner, beginning teachers must have at least an awareness of the kinds of knowledge and understandings needed—as well as the resources available—to develop these skills, knowledge, dispositions, and behaviors that increase all students' learning. Having a core content of common knowledge gives teachers a professional base from which to learn, grow, and perform.[58]

The InTASC competencies accurately reflect the complex and high-stakes world of today's diverse classrooms. Many content areas have their own additional standards that teachers must meet. Learning to become an effective teacher takes time, learning experiences, quality feedback, and increasingly extended doses of practice and reflection. Becoming a teacher blends the individual's personality with the professional attitudes, knowledge, and skills shared by the profession as a whole. It is a moral and ethical commitment for a lifelong journey. To learn more about what the InTASC Standards mean and look like in practice—and consider your own experiences with them as students—complete the activity in the **Reflect & Engage** box, Understanding InTASC Expectations for Teachers.

REFLECT & ENGAGE: UNDERSTANDING INTASC EXPECTATIONS FOR TEACHERS

This is a group activity that involves role play. In an era of heightened teacher accountability for every student's learning to high levels, the InTASC Model Core Teaching Standards describe what effective teachers are expected to do—*what effective teaching and learning look like*—in professional practice that helps increase every student's learning. Let's look at some of them more closely and use role play to make them more vivid.

A. Each group of three students will consider one of the following sets of standards: Standards 1, 2, and 3 (The Learner and Learning); Standards 4 and 5 (Content); or Standards 6, 7, and 8 (Instructional Practice). Decide what these standards mean and what they *look like* in teacher and student behaviors. Identify when and how you experienced these as a student yourself. Select a vignette to present a role play of these "standards in action" that you will present to the class. In the role play, explain why they are important if every student is to have strong learning outcomes and identify how and when you expect to develop the knowledge and skills to be able to teach competently in this way.

B. After about 15 minutes, reassemble the class, and each group will present its role play of their InTASC standards. After each group performs, discuss answers as a whole group. Identify the key findings for each set of standards.

C. Discuss as a whole class: How do these expectations differ from those under which you were taught as a preK–12 student? In what ways do you find these standards to be both challenging and exciting? What do these standards tell you about the teaching profession today and your role as part of it?

KEY TAKE-AWAYS

Learning Objective 1.1 Support the view that teaching is an inspiring, satisfying, and important profession.

- Effective teachers are essential if every American child is to receive a first-class education and the life-enhancing opportunities that it brings.
- Having a sense of mission, solidarity, and empathy for students, the desire to be lifelong learners, the courage to challenge conventional thinking, comfort with uncertainty, improvisational abilities, endless patience, a sense of humor, and a passion for social justice motivate and keep teachers in the profession.

Learning Objective 1.2 Identify the personal qualities of effective teachers.

- Who the teacher is as a person has a tremendous influence on the classroom climate and students' learning experiences.
- Effective teachers are people who care about their students inside and outside the classroom, treat all students with kindness and respect, motivate student learning, have a positive attitude toward their own learning and the profession, are reflective practitioners, and continue to learn throughout their career.

Learning Objective 1.3 Critique education's moral purposes and how teachers enact these through caring.

- Schools and teaching have moral purposes—to support individual and societal well-being by helping students develop the cognitive and interpersonal skills and habits they need to thrive as people, workers, and citizens.
- Education must be evaluated not just according to goal attainment (i.e., students' academic outcomes) but also according to the means employed. Desirable ends do not justify inappropriate means to get there.
- Caring teachers maintain important interpersonal and professional boundaries with their students. Having a "relationship" with a student does not mean being a "friend."

Learning Objective 1.4 Assess technology's role in educating students in today's global environment.

- Globalization and technology are reshaping the American workplace, including schools.
- Globalization links today's youth to economic realities, social media, technology, and cultural movements that cross local and national boundaries; and teachers must help prepare students to live and work within this broader, more competitive arena.
- The 2020 COVID-19 pandemic dramatically reshaped how U.S. teachers conduct "school." Now, virtually all teachers are learning to prepare, deliver, and assess digitally infused instruction for online classes.

Learning Objective 1.5 Identify and explain the 21st century skills today's students need to learn.

- Teaching students 21st century knowledge and skills means preparing them with cognitive, interpersonal, and intrapersonal skills that enable them to respond knowledgeably and flexibly to complex real-world problems, to think creatively, to communicate effectively, to manage information, to manage themselves, to work well in teams, and to produce new knowledge.

Learning Objective 1.6 Describe the InTASC Model Core Standards and key themes for teachers.

- InTASC standards—essential knowledge, critical dispositions, and performances—are common to all teachers, regardless of academic discipline or specialty area.
- Five key themes supporting InTASC are personalized learning for diverse learners; a stronger focus on teachers applying cross-disciplinary knowledge and skills to help students deal with multiple perspectives; teachers' improved assessment literacy and using data to improve instruction and understand each learner's progress; a collaborative professional culture in which teachers work together to improve practice and increase student learning; and new leadership roles for teachers and administrators within a supportive school climate.

TEACHER SCENARIO: IT'S YOUR TURN

Charles was different than the rest of us in the Educational Foundations class. He had just finished his master's degree in English and wanted to be an English teacher. He said he really didn't need to know "all the stuff" from this class. His plan was to teach for only about 3 or 4 years until he got his PhD so he could teach at the college level. Teaching middle or high school English was only a "short gig" to pay tuition so he could teach people who really wanted to learn—not the "little brats who don't matter and don't care about literature."

1. After reading this chapter, what would you say to Charles?
2. How does Charles's attitude about teaching in public secondary schools violate InTASC standards?

NOTES

1. Jeffrey Young, a former superintendent of schools in Cambridge, MA, as cited in Giegerich, S., & Levine, J. (2019, Spring/Summer). A changed landscape: Class action. The case for empowering our teachers. *TC Today*, 14.
2. Nieto, S. (2009). From surviving to thriving. *Educational Leadership, 66*(5), 8–13.
3. Nieto, S. (2003). What keeps teachers going? *Educational Leadership, 60*(8), 14–18.
4. Nieto, S. (Ed.). (2009). *Why we teach.* Teacher College Press.
5. Davidson, M., Lickona, T., & Shmelkov, V. (2007, November 14). Smart schools and good schools: A paradigm shift for character education. *Education Week, 27*(12), 31, 40.
6. Parker, J. (2017, February 13). Love and teaching: A transformational connection. *Education Week.* https://blogs.edweek.org/teachers/teacher_leader_voices/2017/02/love_and_teaching_a_transforma.html?cmp=eml-eb-sub-love-021419&M=58746433&U=23232&UUID=2b4d84db033572aee9bfdaf6faa06317
7. Watson, C. (2017, February 14). Fostering a long-lasting love of teaching. *Education Week Teacher.* https://www.edweek.org/tm/articles/2017/02/14/fostering-a-long-lasting-love-of-teaching.html?cmp=eml-eb-sub-love-021419&M=58746433&U=23232&UUID=2b4d84db033572aee9bfdaf6faa06317
8. Barnoski, L. (2018, January 3). A veteran educator's love letter to teaching. *Education Week.* https://www.edweek.org/tm/articles/2018/01/03/a-veteran-educators-love-letter-to-teaching.html?cmp=eml-eb-sub-love-021419&M=58746433&U=23232&UUID=2b4d84db033572aee9bfdaf6faa06317
9. Wellborn, J. (2005). The accidental teacher. In S. Nieto (Ed.), *Why we teach* (pp. 15–22). Teachers College Press.
10. Heller, R. (2019, September). Broad discontent leads half of teachers to consider quitting their jobs. *Phi Delta Kappan, 101*(1), K3–K5. https://pdkpoll.org/assets/downloads/2019pdkpoll51.pdf

11. Teacher strikes in 2019 occurred in West Virginia, Oklahoma, Arizona, Colorado, California, and North Carolina.

12. We will discuss the teacher's influence (i.e., expectations for students, preparation to teach diverse students, teaching effectiveness, disciplinary practices, and school/classroom climate) on student achievement in Chapter 7, Cultural, Social, and Educational Causes of the Achievement Gap and How to Fix Them.

13. Stronge, J. H. (2002). *Qualities of effective teachers*. ASCD.

14. Korthagen, F. A. J., & Wubbels, T. (2001). Evaluative research on the realistic approach and on the promotion of reflection. In F. A. J. Korthagen (Ed.), *Linking practice and theory: The pedagogy of realistic teacher education* (pp. 88–107). Lawrence Erlbaum.

15. Fullan, M. (1993). *Change forces: Probing the depths of educational reform*. Falmer Press.

16. Goodlad, J. (1990). Studying the education of educators: From conception to findings. *Phi Delta Kappan, 71*(9), 698–701; Goodlad, J. I. (1983, March). A study of schooling: Some findings and hypotheses. *Phi Delta Kappan, 64*(7), 465–470.

17. Goodlad, J. I. (1979). *What schools are for*. Phi Delta Kappa Educational Foundation, p. 8. https://files.eric.ed.gov/fulltext/ED178400.pdf

18. Goodlad, 1970, p. 14.

19. Sparks, S. D. (2019, March 3). Why teacher–student relationships matter. *Education Week, 38*(25), 7–8. https://www.edweek.org/ew/articles/2019/03/13/why-teacher-student-relationships-matter.html

20. For a more complete discussion of this topic, see: Owusu, A., & Kyei-Blankson, L. (2016). Going back to the basics: Demonstrating care, connectedness, and a pedagogy of relationship in education. *World Journal of Education, 6*(3), 1–9. https://files.eric.ed.gov/fulltext/EJ1158355.pdf; Wentzel, K. R. (2016). Students' relationships with teachers as motivational contexts. In K. R. Wentzel & D. B. Miele (Eds.), *Handbook of motivation at school* (2nd ed.; pp. 211–230). Routledge.

21. Quin, D. (2017). Longitudinal and contextual associations between teacher–student relationships and student engagement: A systematic review. *Review of Educational Research, 87*(2), 345–387.

22. Forrester, G. (2005). All in a day's work: Primary teachers "performing" and "caring." *Gender & Education, 17*(3), 271–287.

23. Hagenauer, G., Hascher, T., & Volet, S. E. (2015). Teachers' emotions in the classroom: Associations with students' engagement, classroom discipline, and the interpersonal teacher–student relationship. *European Journal of Psychology of Education, 30*(4), 385–403.

24. Wentzel, 2016.

25. Hawk, T. F., & Lyons, P. R. (2008). Please don't give up on me: When faculty fail to care. *Journal of Management Education, 32*(3), 316–338; Meyer, D. (2009). Entering the emotional practices of teaching. In P. A. Schutz & M. Zembylas (Eds.), *Advances in teacher emotional research: The impact on teachers' lives* (pp. 73–91). Springer; Sparks, S. D. (2019, March 12). Why teacher–student relationships matter. *Education Week, 38*(25), 8; Owusu & Kyei-Blankson, 2016.

26. For a more complete discussion of the traditional education view of "mental discipline and the curriculum for developing students' character," see Chapter 5: Education Reform—1900 to Today.

27. Noddings, N. (1988, February). An ethic of caring and its implications for instructional arrangements. *American Journal of Education, 96*(2), 215–230.

28 Noddings, 1988.

29. Noddings, N. (1995, January). A morally defensible mission for schools in the 21st century. *Phi Delta Kappan, 76*(5), 365–368.

30. Noddings, N. (1999). Caring and competence. In G. Griffen (Ed.), *The education of teachers* (pp. 203–220). National Society for the Study of Education.

31. Diller, A. (1988). Review: The ethics of care and education: A new paradigm, its critics, and its educational significance. *Curriculum Inquiry, 18*(3), 325–342; Hoagland, S. L. (1990). Some concerns about Nel Noddings' *Caring. Hypatia. A Journal of Feminist Philosophy, 5*(1), 109–114.

32. For a fuller discussion of John Goodlad's view of educational stewardship, see: Fenstermacher, G. D. (n.d.). *Teaching on both sides of the classroom door*. University of Michigan. http://www-personal.umich.edu/~gfenster/jigms.pdf

33. Bennett, D. D., Cornwell, G. H., Al-Lail, H. J., & Schenck, C. (n.d.). An education of the twenty-first century: Stewardship of the global commons, *Liberal Education*. Association of American Colleges & Universities. https://www.aacu.org/publications-research/periodicals/education-twenty-first-century-stewardship-global-commons

34. *The New York Times*. (1982, May 19). Rates on overseas phone calls decline. Section C, p. 14. https://www.nytimes.com/1982/05/19/garden/rates-on-overseas-phone-calls-decline.html

35. McGreevy, L. (2019, February 1). International calling rates: How much do international calls cost? *FitSmall* Business.com. https://fitsmallbusiness.com/how-much-does-international-calling-cost/

36. Watson, J. L. (2004). Globalization in Asia: Anthological perspectives. In M. M. Suarez-Orozco & D. B. Qin-Hilliard (Eds.), *Globalization: Culture and education in the new millennium* (p. 147). University of California Press.

37. Suarez-Orozco, M. M., & Qin-Hilliard, D. B. (2004). *Globalization: Culture and medication in the new millennium* (p. 3). University of California Press.

38. Little evidence supports the view that individuals can develop general-purpose cognitive competencies that transfer to any new discipline, problem, or context, in or out of school. Research does show that students can learn to transfer knowledge and skills to new situations *within* a subject area or discipline when teachers use effective teaching methods. See: National Research Council. (2012). *Education for life and work. Guide for practitioners* (p. 5). The National Academies of Sciences, Engineering, Medicine. http://sites.nationalacademies.org/cs/groups/dbassesite/documents/webpage/dbasse_084153.pdf

39. Herold, B. (2016, February 5). Technology in education: An overview. *Education Week*. https://www.edweek.org/ew/issues/technology-in-education/index.html

40. Rauf, D. S. (2020, June 2). Coronavirus pushes schools closer to a computer for every student. *Education Week*. https://www.edweek.org/ew/articles/2020/06/03/coronavirus-pushes-schools-closer-to-a-computer.html

41. Bushweiler, K. (2019, April 23). What educators really think. *Education Week, 38*(30), 2. https://www.edweek.org/ew/articles/2019/04/24/what-educators-really-think.html

42. Bouygues, H. L. (2019, June). Does educational technology help students learn? An analysis of the connection between digital devices and learning. *Reboot*. https://reboot-foundation.org/wp-content/uploads/docs/ED_TECH_ANALYSIS.pdf; Herold, 2016.

43. Jones, S. (2019, October 3). A&A with an ed-tech expert: Don't focus on the tools. *Education Week Teacher*. https://www.edweek.org/tm/articles/2018/10/03/qa-with-an-ed-tech-expert-dont-focus.html

44. The Flora and William Hewlett Foundation. (2013, November). Deeper learning advocacy cluster evaluation: Key findings. The William and Flora Hewlett Foundation, p. 2. *ORS* Impact.com. https://hewlett.org/wp-content/uploads/2016/08/Hewlett%20Deeper%20Learning%20Key%20Learning%20Memo.PDF

45. Bryant, J., Heitz, C., Sanghvi, S., & Wagle, D. (2010, January). How artificial intelligence will impact K–12 teachers. *McKinsey & Company*. https://www.mckinsey.com/~/media/McKinsey/Industries/Social%20Sector/Our%20Insights/How%20artificial%20intelligence%20will%20impact%20K%2012%20teachers/How-artificial-intelligence-will-impact-K-12-teachers.ashx

46. Digital Citizenship Utah. (2017). Digital citizenship. *DigCitUtah*. http://digcitutah.com/resources-library/. For digital citizenship resources, see https://digcitutah.com/digital-citizenship/.

47. Himmelsbach, V. (2019, July 15). Technology in the classroom in 2019: 6 pros & cons. *TopHat*. https://tophat.com/blog/6-pros-cons-technology-classroom/

48. Himmelsbach, 2019.

49. VanderArk, T., & Schneider, C. (n.d.). How digital learning contributes to deeper learning. *Getting Smart*. p. 6. http://www.worldwideworkshop.com/pdfs/GettingSmart_DigitalLearningDeeperLearning.pdf; Bushweiler, K. (2019, April 23). What educators really think. Technology Counts 2019, National Survey. *Education Week, 38*(30), 2. https://www.edweek.org/ew/articles/2019/04/24/what-educators-really-think.html

50. Madgavkar, A., Manyika, J., Krishnan, M. Ellingrud, K, Yee, L., et al. (2019, June 11). *The future of women at work: Transitions in the age of automation*. Jumpforme.eu. http://jumpforme.eu/companies-gender/statistics-reports/2019/06/11/the-future-of-women-at-work-transitions-in-the-age-of-automation/

51. National Research Council. (2012). *Education for life and work. Guide for practitioners*. The National Academies of Sciences, Engineering, Medicine. http://sites.nationalacademies.org/cs/groups/dbassesite/documents/webpage/dbasse_084153.pdf

52. Friedman, T. (2007). *The world is flat: A brief history of the twenty-first century* (p. 339). Farrar, Straus, and Giroux.

53. Friedman, 2007, p. 279.

54. Council of Chief State School Officers (CCSSO). (2013, April). *InTASC Model core teaching standards and Learning progressions for teacher 1.0 A resource for ongoing teacher development.* https://ccsso.org/sites/default/files/2017-12/2013_INTASC_Learning_Progressions_for_Teachers.pdf

55. InTASC is aligned with Common Core State Standards for students in mathematics and English language arts, the National Board for Professional Teaching Standards (NBPTS), Council for Accreditation of Teacher Education Programs (CAEP); Learning Forward, and School Leader Licensure Consortium (ISLLC, 2008) educational leadership policy standards.

56. The standards offer much more detail about performances, essential knowledge, and critical dispositions and give more examples of how novice teachers can progress through each set of performances, knowledge, and dispositions throughout their career than we can repeat here. We encourage readers to take a closer look.

57. Council of Chief State School Officers, 2013.

58. InTASC has also translated the Model Core Teaching Standards into learning progressions, expressing teaching performances, knowledge, and dispositions in more specificity for teachers to use to advance and support their professional growth.The advanced model is called *Learning Progressions for Teachers 1.0: A Resource for Ongoing Teacher Development* (2013). For details, see pp. 10–47 at https://ccsso.org/sites/default/files/2017-12/2013_INTASC_Learning_Progressions_for_Teachers.pdf.

iStock/track5

2 TEACHING AS A PROFESSION

INTASC Standards Addressed: 1, 2, 3, 4, 6, 7, 8, 9, 10

LEARNING OBJECTIVES

After you read this chapter, you should be able to

2.1 Compare and contrast the factors that make—or weaken—the status of teaching as a profession.

2.2 Defend the view that the teaching occupation has become increasingly professionalized over the generations.

2.3 Critique the research findings relating teacher preparation, teaching quality, student achievement, and teacher longevity.

2.4 Describe teacher licensure's rationale, state licensure practices, and the relationship between teacher certification and student achievement.

2.5 Identify the organizations that support teaching professionals and explain how they help professionalize teaching.

2.6 Argue how a school's professional culture and well-designed induction and mentoring programs can help new teachers transition into effective professional educators.

American education's future has become the focus of national attention. In 2018 and 2019, teacher strikes and walkouts made bold headlines across the country as educators from Arizona to Oklahoma and West Virginia and in cities including Denver, Los Angeles, and Oakland, California, protested low salaries and school-funding cuts. In March 2020, the COVID-19 virus forced many governors to shutter their schools and try to educate children through a mix of teacher-made work packets and/or online instruction. Arguably, American parents suddenly trying to "homeschool" their children were never more appreciative of teachers' essential role in their daily lives.

Today's teaching profession faces huge challenges. Teacher preparation programs have seen a 23% decline in the number of people completing their coursework.[1] Expanded career opportunities for undergraduate women (who earn 80% of education degrees) account for part of this decline.[2] The increasing responsibilities, long working hours, high stress without commensurate compensation (salary and benefits), the high accountability demands, the constant evaluations, too much testing and paperwork, and the lack of support are among reasons. Local issues also factor in. It is no surprise that some schools are chronically short of teachers, unable to find educators able and willing to work at current wages and conditions. Given these realities, most American parents do not want their children to become public school teachers.[3]

At the same time, the teaching profession has never been more essential. Like medicine or law, most developed nations regard education as vital for individual citizens and the larger society. Teaching is complex and intellectually demanding work that requires high levels of cognitive and emotional intelligence. Never more so than today, teaching is recognized as an essential public service, a meaningful and rewarding profession that improves children's lives and prepares them for satisfying and responsible adulthood. And most notably, for a large proportion of our children, their social mobility and life options *depend* on working repeatedly with highly effective teachers. Studies confirm that consistently working with highly effective teachers can overcome the academic limitations placed on students by their family backgrounds.[4] Ironically, these challenges can also become incentives to enter the profession where teachers – individually and collegially – can make life-changing differences for children.

Similarly, teachers' expectations for their working lives are shifting. Millennial teachers bring fresh ways of envisioning their teaching careers. New roles and career paths are opening, and school districts are exploring innovative approaches to teacher compensation and leadership. Seeing teaching as a profession; considering how it has evolved over the generations; understanding the research on the relationships between teacher preparation, teaching effectiveness, and student outcomes; acknowledging the organizations that increase teacher development and the field's professionalization; and recognizing the school factors that help new teachers develop their classroom efficacy and expertise bring a heightened respect for the teaching occupation and its critical importance to local and national life.

2.1 FACTORS THAT MAKE TEACHING A PROFESSION

Teachers are professionals with expert knowledge about instruction and curriculum in their particular disciplines. They understand child development and the ways in which learners learn. As a group, teachers are well organized and increasingly participate in making decisions about educational practices and their work conditions.

2.1a Defining a Profession

Sociology professor Andrew Abbott defines a **profession** as an exclusive occupational group that applies abstract knowledge and specialized skills to particular cases and has expertise and influence to practice in a given domain or field.[5] Likewise, every profession claims competence by successfully showing they have met their profession's high standards of practice.[6] Establishing a profession means that individuals in a certain occupation claim an authority—power, confidence, and right—to practice that livelihood. Because they can demonstrate expertise, these individuals receive the opportunity to do the profession's work.

Broadly defined, **professionalism** means accepting responsibility for developing and growing one's expertise. For teachers, professionalism means incorporating specialized knowledge about student learning, curriculum, instruction, and assessment; particular attention to students' unique needs and well-being; self-regulation; ethical behavior; and infusing autonomous performance and responsibility into their practice. In addition, teacher professionalism implies a sense of stewardship, of caring and doing everything possible to improve teaching and learning—even beyond their own classroom and school. Accomplishing all this requires values such as honesty, fairness, and integrity in the practitioner.

A profession can keep its authority if the public accepts its claims of expertise and if the profession's internal structure of well-defined and agreed-upon knowledge and skills support it. For instance, people believe that physicians are professionals because they know anatomy, physiology, biochemistry, and pathology, and have specialized information and abilities gained through their study in an accredited medical school. The medical profession includes organizing groups that provide written and performance tests that enable doctors to become board certified and earn advanced credentials.

"Few would require cardiologists to deliver babies, real-estate lawyers to defend criminal cases, chemical engineers to design bridges, or sociology professors to teach English. The commonly held assumption is that such traditional professions require a great deal of skill and training; hence, specialization is assumed to be necessary."[7]

Characteristics of a profession include the following elements:[8]

- A clearly defined, highly developed, specialized, and theoretical knowledge base beyond that understood by laypersons
- An orientation toward social or public service and a lifetime commitment to career
- Agreed-upon standards of professional practice shaped by practitioners to ensure or certify minimal competence for group membership
- Autonomy for individuals and the occupational group in making decisions about selected aspects of work
- A code of ethics to help clarify ambiguous issues related to services rendered
- A lengthy period of specialized training
- Control of licensing and certification standards and entry requirements
- Control over training new entrants

- Self-governing and self-policing authority by members of the profession, especially about professional ethics (acceptance of responsibility for judgments made and acts performed related to services rendered)
- Professional associations and elite groups that provide recognition for individual achievements
- High prestige and economic standing

Let's look more closely at education as a profession in four key areas as they compare with law, engineering, and medicine: (1) a defined body of knowledge and skills beyond that which laypersons recognize as unique and special; (2) control over licensing standards and/or entry requirements; (3) autonomy in making decisions about certain work areas; and (4) high prestige and economic standing. We will consider professional associations, unions, and elite groups later in this chapter and discuss teachers and ethics in Chapter 9.

A Defined Body of Knowledge and Skills

All professions have a certain knowledge and skills specialty requiring complex reasoning and problem-solving with large amounts of information that separates their members from the general public. When members make this clearly defined expertise widely known, they protect the public from untrained amateurs by denying them professional membership.

Until relatively recently, however, "teaching" had no agreed-upon specialized body of knowledge.[9] Traditionally, teaching has not been guided by extensive procedural rules as found in law or by established methods such as those found in the physical sciences and health care. As a result, many people talk about education as if they—the laypersons—were also experts. To them, teaching holds no mystery because they have all had personal experiences as students. Because they cannot see teachers' store of professional knowledge and skills or examine the complex mental planning decisions or the moment-by-moment thinking choices made in a dynamic classroom, laypeople assume that teaching does not require any extraordinary talent apart from knowing their subject. In fact, Daniel C. Lortie, professor emeritus of education at the University of Chicago, has coined the phrase **"apprenticeship of observation"** to describe the phenomenon where laypersons who have spent thousands of hours as schoolchildren watching and judging teachers in practice develop many false ideas about teaching and mistakenly consider themselves to be "experts."[10]

Furthermore, until recently, teaching's less well-defined body of knowledge than law or the physical sciences has allowed teacher education course requirements to vary from state to state, and even among teacher training institutions within a given state. While teacher education usually includes three major components—general education, specialized subject education, and professional education—heated discussions often arise over which is more important and by how much. For instance, how many credit hours should a prospective teacher have in professional practice (pedagogy) compared to course hours in a specialized subject field? How much clinical experience in actual school settings should be required? Should students learn the subject discipline in a liberal arts college or within specialized teacher education schools? One might logically ask, if leaders in teacher education cannot clearly agree on the profession's body of knowledge, how can the general public expect to see teachers as true professionals?

Over the past few decades, heightened expectations for student learning have led to heightened expectations for teaching effectiveness. As a result, the body of knowledge for teaching has become clearer, more consensual, and tied to high performance standards. Increasingly, states have adopted a common set of high-quality teacher performance standards using national professional benchmarks.[11] Further, research finds that this increased professional knowledge about teaching effectiveness is making a measurable difference in student learning. Teachers using effective teaching behaviors have been empirically shown to increase student learning linked to increased student achievement.[12]

We now have the means to help teachers master these essential dispositions and practices. For example, educators now have research-validated observation tools to assess teachers' classroom and professional performance and guide professional growth. For example, Charlotte Danielson's research-based *Framework for Teaching* provides clear descriptions of good teaching in all its complexity at four different performance levels and offers a comprehensive approach to teacher professional learning across their careers, from preservice teacher preparation through teacher leadership.[13] The *Framework* has been repeatedly validated as a means for teachers to improve their teaching practice in ways that increase measured student achievement.[14] Likewise, Robert Marzano and colleagues' Focused Teacher Evaluation Model[15] offers a standards-based evaluation model that also identifies essential behaviors to measure teacher effectiveness. It focuses on student results and gives actionable feedback teachers can use to improve their instructional practices. Research on Marzano's model finds a correlation between the model, student learning gains, and increased student achievement on state math and reading scores.[16] Both instruments measure teacher growth and promote teacher development.

Additionally, since 1954, national teacher education accrediting organizations (discussed later in this chapter) have been setting high, clear standards for teacher preparation programs that specify the courses to be taken and the faculty qualifications for teaching them. Increasingly, teacher preparation programs have adjusted their programs to become accredited, recognizing that having a nationally recognized, respected, and defined body of knowledge strengthens their students' knowledge and skills as well as enhances teaching as a profession.

Controlling Requirements for Entrance and Licensing

Unlike other professions that have a standard path to licensure, teaching has historically lacked uniform requirements for professional entry. Prospective teachers who want to teach in U.S. public schools must receive certification in their desired subject areas and grade levels by the state in which they choose to practice. Certification requirements vary from state to state, differing in time, cost, and difficulty. Nearly every state requires teachers to pass a licensure exam before entering the classroom. Some states require a performance assessment and/or a pedagogical skills exam (to assess teachers' mastery of the professional competencies they gain during teacher preparation to help students learn their subject) plus a content subject assessment and/or a basic skills exam. Certain states offer 1- to 3-year "emergency credentials" that allow candidates to bypass the regular licensure requirements. For the most part, states make these decisions based on political influences and other local considerations.

This array of requirements prompts a variance in teacher preparation programs (i.e., How many hours are required in different course areas? Must teacher candidates pass the licensing exam before or after they complete the teacher preparation program?). Some states issue certificates valid for only 3 to 5 years. To renew them, teachers must meet additional requirements—usually proof of a set number of professional development or graduate education or subject course hours—and pay new fees. All these disparities make it difficult to assess how "classroom ready" entering teachers actually are.

The trend toward testing teachers to assess their basic knowledge and skills remains controversial. Many different teacher licensure exams exist, and states hold teachers to widely different standards of rigor. But because states control the "cut scores" that mark the difference between passing and failing, a teacher who receives a certain score may "pass" in one state but "fail" in another.

Reciprocity of teaching certificates among states is another concern. **Reciprocity** is an agreement between states to accept each other's teaching credentials. Each state often imposes its own state-specific requirements as part of the interstate reciprocity agreements. Because different states have different certification requirements, teachers often find it difficult to move between states and continue to be certified. Teachers must apply for a new license if they wish to teach in a state where they do not currently hold a teaching certificate. States review the request for reciprocity case by case.[17]

The subject of teaching certification requirements generates controversy. Those who want stricter entry requirements insist that these will help upgrade teacher quality and qualifications. Others argue that the entry gates be loosened to allow access to midcareer changers into teaching and allow alternative certification programs that permit college graduates without formal education training to teach immediately. Both sides see their approach as attracting and keeping talented candidates into teaching. But the outcomes of such initiatives could be to diminish teaching's professional status.

Autonomy in Deciding Work Responsibilities

Every profession considers all group members qualified to make expert judgments about their work; outsiders are deemed unqualified to make such decisions. Nonetheless, teachers traditionally have had little input about what they teach or the resources they use. School officials often hire outside "experts" with little teaching experience to help teachers select textbooks, write grant proposals, or resolve local community issues. Likewise, school reform ideas often come from government officials, business leaders, and civic groups—not from teachers. More and more, this situation is changing. Educators at all levels are having increased input, individually and collectively, into education policy decisions.

Research finds that teacher autonomy—such as selecting textbooks and other classroom materials; choosing content, topics, and skills to be taught; deciding on teaching techniques; and evaluating, grading, and disciplining students—is positively associated with teachers' job satisfaction and teacher retention.[18] A 2015 national report found that, from 2003 to 2012, teachers perceived significant declines in their autonomy, with many having less control over factors that affected their classrooms.[19] Many elements, from high-stakes testing to common core state standards and locally developed curriculum, may have contributed.

Limits to teacher autonomy may be necessary as school leaders and policy makers must consider local and national expectations for accountability, consistency, and equity. But as teachers expand their knowledge about effective teaching and learning practices, become increasingly skilled at generating student learning, and actively participate in site-based school leadership, they are expanding their autonomy in influencing their own work responsibilities.

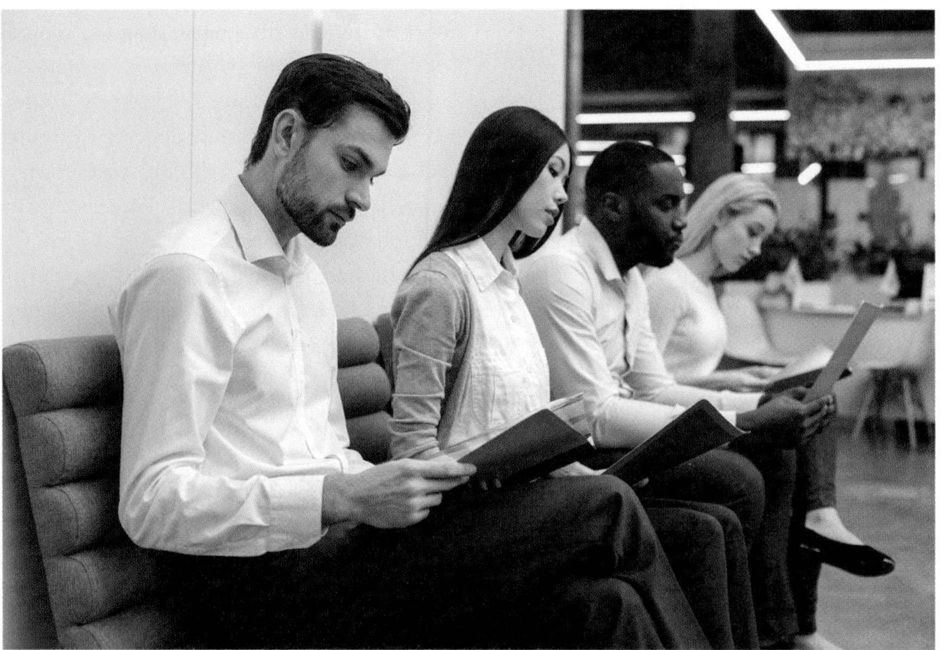

Today's teachers enter the profession from a variety of backgrounds, including prior careers.
iStock/dima_sidelnikov

Prestige and Economic Standing

Prestige is the level of social respect or standing, the good reputation, and high esteem accorded to an individual or a group because of their position's status. Occupations have high prestige if the public sees them as holding a relatively lofty position in the hierarchy of occupations and believes the people who are in that occupation make especially valuable contributions to society. In our culture, the most prestigious occupations require an advanced level of formal education or skill, practitioner autonomy, a recognized knowledge base, a self-governing professional body, a code of ethics, and little physical or manual labor. **Status** refers to the position or standing in society that confers certain benefits and privileges. Factors such as remuneration, knowledge, responsibility, social utility, and prestige contribute to social status. In addition to this "objective" definition, status also has a "personal" dimension. **Subjective status** refers to the self-perception of rank or prestige that emphasizes personal achievement.

Generalizing about teachers' occupational prestige is not clear cut. Some consider teaching as a semiprofession seeking full professional status,[20] whereas others assert that official statistics give teaching formal professional status.[21]

Many features may account for the teaching's midrange prestige and social status. For 50 years, sociologists have studied how the public evaluates occupations' relative prestige. The data show that teaching, like many other female-dominated occupations, rates in the middle, lower than physicians, military officers, engineers, or scientists and higher than business executives, entertainers, or member of Congress.[22] The large teacher workforce, the wide variations in teacher education program expectations and state licensure requirements, and the taxpayer-paid salaries tend to limit their compensation and undermine their socioeconomic status. Similarly, teachers' connections with childhood rather than adulthood, working with groups of children (*required* to attend school) rather than with individuals (usually adults who *voluntarily* go to physicians or lawyers), and the confusion about whether teaching has a specialized body of professional knowledge to justify higher salaries also figure in to determining occupational prestige and status.[23] And since virtually everyone has been a student at one time, teaching has less professional "mystique" than less familiar occupations.

In the 2014 Harris Poll asking respondents to say how much prestige each job had, teaching did not even make the top 10.[24] Thus, status of teaching as a prestigious occupation is debatable. Since prestige and status are relatively independent, a teacher may have the general public's high esteem for being competent, dedicated, and caring in his or her work, but the occupation itself may lack prestige because of teaching's relatively low compensation.[25] As a profession, teaching has most—but not all—of the requisite attributes.

Nonetheless, teaching as a career has experienced changes that have improved its status. First, teachers' average education level has increased significantly over the past century. Now, all teachers have bachelor's degrees; many have master's degrees and even doctorates. Second, teaching has become increasingly complex. Effective teachers use high-level thinking in selecting appropriate subject content, planning and targeting instruction to meet diagnosed student learning needs, facilitating student engagement and mastery, and assessing learning outcomes in ways that increase students' knowledge and skills and improve teaching. Likewise, effective teachers have high levels of language proficiencies in reading, writing, and speaking and expertise using a wide array of media to promote learning. Teachers also work successfully with a variety of people—students, colleagues, parents, and administrators. All these factors positively impact teachers' prestige and esteem in their communities.

Occupational prestige and status are not the last word in measuring teachers' value, however. Sociologists are careful to separate **professionalization** from **professionalism**. The former descriptor refers to the occupations' qualities (typically enhanced by increasing training or raising required qualifications), whereas the latter refers to the attitudes or psychological attributes of those who think they are (or aspire to be) professionals. The latter orientation sees a professional as someone, not an amateur, who is committed to a career and to public service.[26] Teachers can be highly professional in their attitudes, expertise, behaviors, and commitment in their work lives even though their occupation, overall, may not meet some of the stringent criteria more evident in high-prestige professions. This positive orientation raises teachers' esteem and subjective status. Subjective status also improves when teachers feel valued within the profession; feel their school leaders' trust when they receive challenges and the time and support to meet them; get funds to participate in further professional education; work with high-quality resources and facilities; and provide continuing professional development to other teachers. Voters, through their governmental representatives, can elevate the profession's prestige by raising both the salaries and the academic-level requirements for education and to receive professional licenses.

Studies find that several indices of professionalization—namely, teachers' autonomy, authority, and decision-making influence, as well as induction and support for new teachers—are associated with positive student outcomes.[27] Researchers observe that in all the most successful education systems, teachers' high quality and status are common features and assert that the professional status is one factor that attract new teachers to the profession.[28]

Teacher Salaries

As the old cliché goes, teachers are not in it for the money. Fifty-five percent of teachers said they are not satisfied with their teaching salary.[29] Nearly one in five public school teachers have second jobs during the school year.[30] In the view of many, American public school teachers are not being paid anything near what they are worth.

Salary plays a key role in determining an occupation's prestige. As discussed, teachers are not as highly paid as physicians, lawyers, engineers, business executives, and college professors because the public believes that these other professionals deal with more abstract and complex material than preK–12 teachers do, and they work with individuals (usually adults) who come to them voluntarily (as compared to teachers' "captive audience" of children). In addition, these fields require more demanding academic preparation and licensure than does public school teaching. Yet increasingly, the public favors raising teacher pay.[31]

In most preK–12 school districts, teachers' uniform salary schedules determine their compensation (salary, benefits, extra pay, and pensions), with adjustments made for educational credentials ("lanes") and teaching experience ("steps"). Developed in the early to mid-20th century, teacher salary schedules reflect an effort to reduce wage inequality stemming from favoritism, gender, race, and ethnicity in assigning compensation. In the 2011–2012 school year (the most current year available), an estimated 89% of public school districts paid teachers according to uniform salary schedules.[32] But this approach to compensation may not offer the best incentive to attract, develop, and keep effective teachers.

For more than 50 years, teachers' salary and overall compensation have been eroding. An analysis of U.S. census data from 1940 to 2000 shows that the annual salary teachers received fell sharply relative to the annual pay of other workers with college degrees.[33] According to the Economic Policy Institute, a nonpartisan think tank, public school teachers' average weekly wages, adjusted for inflation, have fallen, whereas the weekly wages of other college graduates have risen: Teachers are paid nearly $350 *less* each week in salary, or 23% *less* than their non-teaching college-educated peers. Teachers' 1960 "wage premium" (when women teachers were paid more than comparably educated and experienced women employees in other careers) has become a 21.4% "wage penalty" in 2018. Although teachers do receive better benefits than other college-educated workers, even after considering these in the analysis, the total teacher compensation penalty was 13.1% in 2018. These wage penalties vary across the states, ranging from 0.2% to 32.6%.[34]

Table 2.1 highlights the national 2018 mean average salaries for occupations requiring a college degree. The average secondary school teacher earns $11,280 less than a registered nurse and $14,590 less than an accountant each year (the next closest professions listed) than other college graduates, even though entry into each of these fields requires a 4-year college degree.

TABLE 2.1 ■ Annual Mean Wages for Occupations Requiring a College Degree, 2018

Occupation	Annual Mean Wage
Recent college graduate starting average salary	$ 50,944*
Engineers	$ 99,230
Elementary and secondary school administrators	$ 98,750
Computer programmers	$ 89,580
Social workers	$ 85,900
Accountants, auditors	$ 78,820
Registered nurses	$ 75,510
Secondary school teacher	$ 64,230
Elementary and middle school teachers	$ 51,290

Note: *Miller, S. (2019, August 22). Average starting salary for recent college grads hovers near $51,000. *SHRM*. https://www.shrm.org/resourcesandtools/hr-topics/compensation/pages/average-starting-salary-for-recent-college-grads.aspx

Source: Bureau of Labor Statistics. (2019). *May 2018 National occupational employment and wage estimates United States*. United States Department of Labor. https://www.bls.gov/oes/current/oes_nat.htm#00-0000

Of course, it is a mistake to assume that every college degree-requiring occupation should receive the same salary, and supply and demand for certain skills—not years of schooling—determine wages. Additionally, not all agree that teachers are underpaid.[35]

Then, too, teacher salary analyses typically look at teachers' average salary levels of particular types of schools, localities, and states. This can be misleading because each state determines its own education funding amounts,[36] and teacher salary levels are often standardized according to a uniform schedule based on education levels and years of experience. When considering average salaries, therefore, it is difficult to know whether the salary differences are due to the geographic location (and its cost of living), a more mature teacher workforce (who are paid higher for their extra years on the salary scale), or actual differences in compensation.

Teacher compensation consists of more than salary; it also includes benefits. States and localities often choose to contribute to teacher pension benefits—which promise future advantages—rather than provide present-day increases in teacher salaries.[37] Typically, both teachers and employers make annual contributions to a pension trust fund. Pension rights are typically considered part of a contract between the employer and the employee, often the result of collective bargaining agreements. Once approved, these plans have constitutional protections in certain states. As a rule, public school teachers and other government employees have a total compensation and benefits package that is lower (or at least not higher) than comparable private-sector workers receive.[38]

Most states use **defined benefit (DB) plans**—in which employers guarantee employees a special annual retirement benefit based on a formula, generally considering final average salaries and years of services. Notably, individual benefits are not tied to contributions. Because retirees are guaranteed a certain benefit amount—in addition to features often including cost of living adjustments, young age for normal retirement, and retiree health benefits—the government (taxpayers) must make up any shortfalls resulting from less-than-expected actual pension fund investment returns. Such features are rare in private-sector pensions. Depending on the state, other types of pension plans may also be available. Considering teachers' pension benefits as part of their compensation places salary in a different context.

Traditionally, teachers accepted a "trade-off," receiving relatively low salaries and low-to-no cost health care premiums while working in exchange for regular payments (pensions) and subsidized health care after retirement. But today, this compact is unraveling. Although most state and local governments promise this benefit to employees, few states or municipalities have reserved the monies to honor this commitment.[39] In 2018, teacher pensions made up about $500 billion in unfunded liability,[40] with most state pension funds in debt, falling short of their investment targets and without enough money set aside to fund the pension promise they made to public employees. As a result, many states are either reducing or ending this benefit.

Moreover, health care costs—including premiums, copayments, and deductibles—are spiraling, and teachers' salaries are not keeping up with inflation. On average over the past decade, teacher salaries have increased 1.4% a year as compared with increases of 4% for health insurance and 7.8% for retirement.[41] In fact, most teacher compensation increases go to pay for health insurance and unfunded pension liabilities rather than increased salaries.[42]

Teachers have other ways of supplementing their salaries. Most school districts offer teachers opportunities to earn stipends as club sponsors, department heads, coaches, and summer school instructors, with additional money for earning advanced degrees. Although teachers can make a comfortable living, depending on their subject specialty, their state and school district, and their initiative, recruiting and keeping capable, qualified, and committed teachers is critical. Given our market-driven economy, persons with high-demand skills can find attractive incentives in occupations other than education; the law of supply and demand does not stop at the schoolhouse door.

The issues of teacher salaries, teacher quality, and student achievement are connected. Effective teachers are the most important school-based determinant of student achievement, and the evidence linking teaching quality and student achievement is overwhelming.[43] Salary is a proven method of attracting a larger applicant pool, and selecting the highest-quality teachers from that pool is key (although it may also take meaningful adjustments in school culture and climate to keep them).[44] The growing wage and compensation differences make it more difficult to recruit and retain talented

Research findings show teaching requires knowledge of subject, pedagogy, and learners.
iStock/monkeybusinessimages

teachers. States with lower salaries and poorer working conditions have larger teacher shortages, especially for schools serving children of color, children with disabilities, and English learners.[45] Raising teachers' salaries is a critical part in any strategy to recruit and retain a better teacher workforce.

Lastly, teaching as a profession has always been about more than the money. Teachers have the essential task of ensuring children's intellectual growth and preparing each new generation to competently enter the economic, political, and social realms. It would be reasonable to expect that our society would reward such important work with high status and appropriate compensation. Yet as Table 2.1 shows, the average teacher earns less than colleagues in professions requiring similar educational preparation. But since states' legislators and governors are largely responsible for funding schools—and teachers' compensation packages—informed and motivated voters can influence the financial and community support that their state's education and teachers receive.

2.2 HOW THE TEACHER PROFESSION HAS EVOLVED

Today's teachers bear society's expectations of higher achievement for every student, regardless of background or life circumstances. The labor market welcomes highly intelligent, well-educated employees of every race, ethnicity, and gender. As a result, teaching and schooling have changed more dramatically in the past few decades than they did in the two centuries before. Teachers today are working by a whole new set of rules.

2.2a Changes Over the Decades

Although the first American teachers were male "schoolmasters," by 1870 women outnumbered men as teachers across the nation—an imbalance not reversed since it began.[46] As a result, teaching has been a profession largely shaped by a "gendered bureaucracy" in which men, viewed as professionals, supervised and trained women, who actually taught. For the most part, young women teachers did not remain in their classrooms for long. Many married and left to have families. Female teacher turnover was an expected part of the school culture. Because they were seen as a source of cheaper and less aggressive labor than men throughout the 19th century and into the 20th century, women teachers were paid less than their male counterparts.

In the early 20th century, the U.S. educational system organized teaching and learning in simple and mechanistic ways. Administrators—usually men—maintained their schools' continuity. They hired departing teachers' replacements and tried to get newcomers up to speed as efficiently as possible. To achieve this feat, schools typically took an unsophisticated view of teaching. The hiring protocol addressed basic questions:

- Did teachers know their subjects (at least better than their students)?
- Could teachers keep their classrooms orderly, quiet, and purposeful?
- Could teachers move all students out of the halls by the time the next class's bell rang?
- Could teachers' students score highly on tests (so administrators could infer what they learned)?

Thus, although teachers considered themselves to be professionals, the organizations in which they worked—schools—often did not always treat them as such.

In the two decades following World War II, teaching changed from an occupation requiring relatively little specialized training to a profession that demanded increasing levels of preparation and competence. Yet partially in response to the earlier political and life-choice realities, teaching remained an **"unstaged" career**, lacking a progression of steps through which one could advance. Teachers' responsibilities seldom changed over the years, from their first to their last workdays.

Lack of Career Stages

Analysts offer differing explanations for teaching's traditional lack of career stages. Because teaching was widely regarded as "woman's work," some concluded that it did not require the same kinds of promotions that signaled advancement in male-dominant careers. And because child rearing has traditionally shaped women's employment patterns, teaching has been a high-turnover field, not easily plotted out into stages. In 1956, a national survey of first-year teachers found that whereas 80% of the male respondents expected to remain continuously employed as teachers or administrators, only 25% of the female respondents had similar expectations. The vast majority of women who planned to leave education listed "raising a family" as their reason, even though many of those same women returned to teaching after their children were in school.[47] With women living in a society that expected mothers to stay home with their children, personal and family changes often dictated career changes.

Other analysts point to schools' customary **"egg crate" structure**, in which teachers work alone rather than as members of an integrated and tiered organization, for the lack of career stages. In this view, hiring teachers to fill vacant classrooms could supposedly occur with relatively little disruption to the rest of the organization. Some blame the lack of career steps on the influence of teaching's conservative milieu, which discourages efforts to distinguish individuals by competence. Finally, certain analysts conclude that teaching's unstaged nature results from teachers' tendency to define their success based on their work inside the classroom rather than their ability to move up to higher-status positions outside it. This may be circular reasoning because teachers may have looked for success markers from those items available to them. Such has traditionally been teaching's professional culture: rationalizing and minimizing the absence of teaching career stages, promotions, and tangible rewards.

2.2b Changing Career Expectations

Typically, careers are marked by upward movement in responsibly, status, and earnings. Teaching's flat, or narrow, career structure is not compatible with the modern workforce's expectations.[48] But those entering teaching today have different expectations for their careers than did the teachers who entered the profession two generations ago. As a result, the profession's structure is changing to meet modern workplace demands and accommodate the new teaching workforce.

Until the mid-1960s, teaching was the primary career option for large numbers of well-educated women and people of color to whom other professions were formally or informally closed. This is no longer true. Today, persons considering teaching have many more career options than did the retiring veterans of the current school system. Many of these alternative careers offer higher salaries, greater status and prestige, and better working conditions than does teaching. As a result, many of today's prospective teachers are drawn from a narrower population than the one that filled the teaching ranks decades earlier.

In addition, today's new and prospective teachers differ from retiring teachers in other important ways: They enter teaching at different career stages, they take multiple routes to the classroom, and they plan to spend fewer years there. Approximately 60% of new teachers enter the field through traditional undergraduate teacher preparation programs, while a growing trend sees mature adults enter teaching as a second career.[49] About 40% enter the profession through an alternative route. Many mid-career new teachers come to teaching believing that it offers more meaningful work than their previous employment.

Moreover, the concept of work and career has evolved over the past century. Traditionally, careers were thought to progress in linear career sequence within the context of one or two firms. Success was defined by the organization and measured in promotions and salary increases. In comparison, by 2000, most Americans changed jobs every 4.5 years.[50]

Consequently, whereas veteran teachers expected to remain in their classrooms from novice days until retirement, many new teachers approach teaching tentatively, conditionally, or as one of several careers they expect to have over their working lives. Few see themselves remaining in the classroom for the long term. Although first-career teachers expect to be excellent teachers, they do not plan to make classroom teaching their life's work.[51]

At the same time, the United States is facing a teacher shortage. Unique dynamics of the state and local teacher labor market—as well as school level, school location, and subject area—experience more serious shortages than others. Half of the almost 500,000 teachers who leave their school each year leave the teaching profession; and 90% of the nationwide annual demand for teachers comes from teachers leaving the profession.[52] This topic is more fully discussed elsewhere.[53]

In sum, new teachers have more career choices available to them and do not expect to make classroom teaching their sole occupation. Many have solid employment experiences in other career fields and arrive at teaching with a maturity born of greater chronological age and life-earned wisdom. But in many ways, teaching's current career structure is not attractive to many new or prospective educators. Given these factors, it is the teacher's preparation, potential structural changes in the profession, and the school's professional culture that often make the difference between teachers who enter, teachers who leave, and teachers who stay.

2.2c Teacher Career Advancement Initiatives

Many new teachers observe that while the nature of teaching has becoming increasingly demanding and their career expectations for teaching have changed, the structure of public school teaching careers and the teachers' workday have not. In their view, "we are asking teachers to deliver 21st century instruction in a job structure designed for the demands of the past century."[54] Although mostly true, educators and policy makers are asking questions about whether traditional practices are worthwhile and are exploring interesting new ideas that may redesign teaching's traditional career structure.

Paying for Masters' Degrees and Experience

A sizable body of research investigating the relationship between teachers' coursework and degrees beyond a bachelor's and their students' academic achievement finds attaining a master's degree correlates with higher student achievement *only* for certain subjects (i.e., mathematics and science).[55] It makes sense that a chemistry teacher with a master's in chemistry is more likely to get better student outcomes than an earth science teacher with a master's in educational leadership. But when measured across all teachers and all types of degrees, the average master's degree shows little correlation to student achievement.[56] Nonetheless, of the 56.4% of all U.S. preK–12 teachers who hold a master's degree or higher (up from 47.1% in 1987–1988),[57] about 10% hold credentials in math or science.[58] This extra stipend can amount to an extra $10,000 a year or more by the time the teacher reaches the top of the salary scale, regardless of whether the degree is in the same subject the teacher is teaching.

From the data, it is unclear how much of the "master's-and-above" supplement actually attracts or rewards effective teachers. A 2012 report observed that it cost an estimated $14.8 billion, annually, to pay teachers for earning advanced degrees.[59] Some encourage school districts to stop this practice and, instead, use the money more flexibly to attract and keep effective teachers.[60]

By comparison, teaching experience does appear to positively impact student achievement. Advances in research methods and data systems now allow investigators to conclude that teachers continue to "grow on the job," and these gains continue into their second and third decades of teaching.[61] This is especially true when they teach in a supportive and collegial working environment and when they amass experience in the same grade level, subject, or district.[62] Of course, variations in teacher effectiveness exist at every career stage. Not every experienced teacher is more effective and not every inexperienced teacher is less effective, on average. Additionally, teacher education and experience are an equity issue because the least experienced teachers tend to be disproportionately concentrated in low-income schools with large populations of underrepresented students and English language learners.[63]

Alternative Pay Structures to Advance Teaching as a Career

Education policy makers currently are looking at alternative approaches to teacher compensation to achieve key policy goals: attract and retain quality teachers and improve and enhance their teaching skills once hired. A broader, more flexible salary structure may be an idea whose time has come. Alternative compensation may take the forms of performance pay, knowledge- and skill-based pay, differentiated salary schedules, and career pathways. A closer look at each approach and related research can help inform compensation policy decisions.

Performance (Merit) Pay and Research **Performance pay**—sometimes called *merit pay* or *performance awards*—usually means a system of employee compensation that links salary to measures of work quality or goals such as increasing student achievement. Advocates assert that paying educators more can enhance their effectiveness as well as attract and retain high performers. Most often, districts' performance pay can be either an annual salary increase (where the performance-based compensation becomes a guaranteed part of the teacher's base salary in all future years) or an annual bonus (where a teacher receives the monetary award based on performance in a given year and must be re-earned annually). Forty percent (51) of the 124 largest school districts in the country offer some form of performance pay, usually tied to permanent salary increases.[64]

Research is inconclusive about whether teacher performance pay improves student outcomes.[65] While some studies have found positive (if modest) effects on student achievement,[66] most studies have not.[67] Findings greatly depend on how the program is structured and implemented in the school context.[68] Moreover, research indicates that performance pay is almost always force-fit upon existing compensation plans, and piecemeal, short-term approaches are not likely to strongly affect teacher motivation or student achievement.[69] Performance pay also assumes that teachers can perform better if they have the "right" incentives, a problematic notion. A more complete discussion of these studies' limitations is available elsewhere.[70]

Critics of performance pay note, among other things, that they lack teacher support; they discourage teacher collaboration and harm school culture; teacher performance is difficult to monitor in reliable, valid, and fair ways; and many unintended and harmful consequences result (such as encouraging teacher transfers from low-performing schools or behaving opportunistically by "teaching to the test" or cheating).[71] The National Education Association (NEA) and the American Federation of Teachers (AFT) offer qualified support for performance pay.[72]

Knowledge- and Skills-Based Pay and Research **Knowledge- and skills-based pay** incentive programs give teachers extra compensation for acquiring new knowledge and practices the school and district believe are critical to their goals, such as improved student outcomes. Qualifying for these rewards may include completing teaching portfolios, obtaining dual certification, or earning a graduate degree in their taught subject. Occasionally, these professional proficiencies are linked to external assessments that gauge teacher competency (such as Educational Testing Service's Praxis exams) or evaluate effective practices (such as earning National Board for Professional Teaching Standards [NBPTS] certification).

NBPTS-certified teachers often receive higher salaries and overall higher earnings than noncertified peers. As of July 2019, 25 states awarded stipends ranging from $1,000 to $10,000 annually (and up to 12% above base pay) to teachers holding NBPTS certification. Almost every state allows teachers to use their NBPTS certification as credits toward obtaining or renewing their professional educator credential.[73]

Differentiated Salary Schedules Paying effective teachers more than their colleagues with similar years of experience to teach hard-to-staff subjects or work in hard-to-staff schools—also known as using **differentiated salary schedules**—is becoming more commonplace. In a 50-state sample of the 100 biggest school districts in the country and the largest districts in each state, differentiated pay is currently available in 124 of 145 school districts.[74]

Districts are twice as likely to offer extra compensation for teaching hard-to-staff subjects (i.e., STEM, English as a second language, and special education) as they are for working in high-needs schools.[75] Most award annual salary supplements (stipends), start new hires in these subject areas at a higher level on the salary schedule, or pay an increased base salary on a separate salary schedule. One-time stipends may take the form of recruitment bonuses. Annual stipends can vary district to district, ranging from $100 to $20,000, annually. For example, the Hawaii Department of Education gives a one-time $10,000 recruitment bonus to special education teachers who agree to work in a special education classroom for 3 years (paid over the 3 years).[76] Additional financial incentives include paying the newly hired teacher's moving or housing expenses if they teach in critical subject areas; offering up to 10 extra days of paid professional development; providing loan forgiveness, mortgage assistance, or tuition reimbursement; or leave the differential pay to the superintendent's discretion.

Studies suggest that teacher vacancies in hard-to-staff subjects or schools could benefit from differentiating salaries along these dimensions.[77] Some argue that boosting salaries for a small subset of teachers would be more cost effective than paying supplements to teachers earning master's degrees.[78] Similarly, some conclude that since performance pay is not cost effective over time (because the teacher costs outpace the student achievement), providing differentiated pay for effective teachers to transfer to high-needs schools becomes more cost effective in the long term.[79]

Neither the AFT and the NEA oppose changes to the salary scales but insist it must be done at the local level with teachers' support and input.[80] To gain their support, teachers must believe that the differentiated pay is based on credible and believable grounds. In locales where teachers are union members, union involvement will ensure the plans conform with contracts. Likewise, state- and local-level policy makers' involvement will be needed to guarantee sufficient monies will be available over time to sustain the program.

Career Pathways As professionals, teachers need more than a "one-size-fits-all" career. **Career pathways** (sometimes called *career ladders or career lattice)* offer teachers multiple routes to new roles and responsibilities that best fit their career interests and goals. They earn additional pay as they increase their capacities and take on new roles that contribute to improved student outcomes.[81] Career pathways offer coherence to teachers' career development.

Locally designed and negotiated career pathways may include placing highly effective teachers in **hybrid roles**—providing "release time" or a part-time classroom schedule—that support teacher instructional leadership activities during (and after) the school day. For example, expert teachers with release time can model lessons, observe peers and give feedback on their instruction, mentor novice teachers, participate in peer assistance and review, or lead professional development. They may train to become their school's data experts, analyzing and using data to improve instruction. Interested teachers can also take on more teacher leadership roles, receive job-embedded professional development, have a voice in school leadership decisions, and receive increased compensation (ranging in amounts from minimal to substantial based on role, responsibilities, additional contract days, and annual funding). Career pathways establish clear criteria for eligibility to help interested teachers self-select (and be chosen for) these roles. Both the NEA and the AFT endorse the teacher career pathways concept.[82]

Studies on teachers' attitudes suggest that they want to grow as teachers and leaders and serve in different capacities as educators over their career.[83] The variety of opportunities for professional growth and increased responsibilities—especially when linked to differentiated pay—make a teaching career more attractive. Research indicates that successfully established career advancement initiatives that include these career pathways with features including increased compensation can positively impact teacher recruitment, retention, job satisfaction, and student achievement.[84] But unless local leaders adjust their existing career structures and systems to effectively implement career pathways and find sustainable funding, efforts to create, implement, and sustain career pathways will be disappointing.

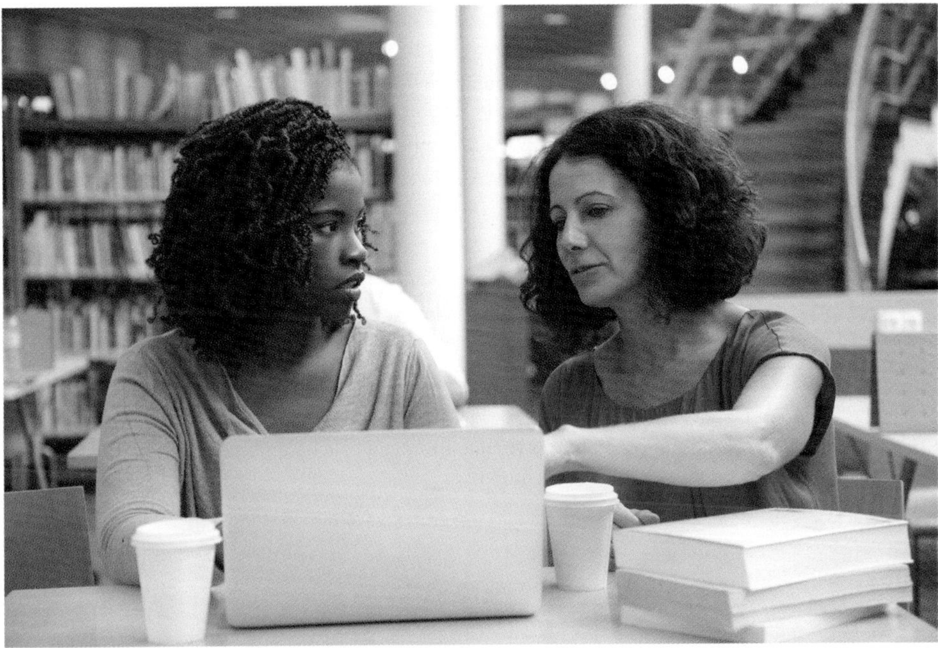

Induction programs provide caring, experienced colleagues who help ease the transition into successful teaching and the profession.

iStock/MangoStar_Studio

Millennials and Teaching

The idea of career pathways is of particular interest for millennials or Generation Y (Gen Y), those born between 1980 and 1996, who now comprise a majority of the teacher workforce.[85] Typically, millennials do not equate "jobs" with "careers." Because they arrived in a job environment of massive turnover rates, an unstable economy, and a more competitive business environment, they want to take on responsibility quickly and build their own professional equity and skills to use as future bargaining chips for their next job move. As a result, millennial teachers often want their careers to function as personalized paths that fit their individual interests and career development goals. Studies find that nearly all (98%) of millennial teachers plan to stay in the education profession for their careers, but only half wish to remain classroom teachers.[86]

Millennials seek more control over their work situation; desire career-long professional growth; expect rapid career advancement in experience, expertise, and compensation; and want new challenges and opportunities to prevent burnout.[87] They also value having a work–life balance (despite the fact that 91% aspire to reach leadership positions); believe their work evaluations should be based on outcomes produced (rather than on age or tenure); and seek ongoing feedback about their performance.[88] These beliefs may help propel changes to the teaching profession's structure.

To assess the factors that you deem most important in the early stages of your "ideal career pathway" as a teacher, complete the activity in the **Reflect & Engage** box, Teacher Career Advancement Initiatives.

REFLECT & ENGAGE: TEACHER CAREER ADVANCEMENT INITIATIVES

In many locations, school districts are exploring innovative ideas that may redesign teaching's traditional career structure and compensation. What do you think of these changes?

A. As individuals, create a graphic image using a digital tool such as Piktochart to design your own "ideal career pathway" to take you through your first 5 to 10 years as a teacher.

B. In groups of four, display and explain your graphic images; consider the following issues and discuss the varied factors that make each proposal either attractive or unattractive to you as a future teacher, and explain your thinking.

- Receiving an annual increase to your salary for teaching experience
- Receiving an annual increase for earning a master's degree in your subject area *only* if it is math or science
- Receiving performance (merit) pay based on your students' achievement
- Receiving an annual salary increase for acquiring additional professional knowledge and skills (such as earning NBPTS certification)
- Receiving extra pay through a differentiated salary schedule for teaching a hard-to-staff subject or work in a highly challenging school
- Having frequent opportunities to receive feedback on your teaching performance effectiveness
- Having opportunities to learn new skills and take on extra teacher and/or leadership responsibilities

C. Reassemble the class, and each group reports its preferences and disagreements about the discussed teacher career advancement initiatives.

D. As a class, design three possible "ideal" career pathways available to teachers.

FLIPSIDES

Should Effective Teachers Receive Performance (Merit) Pay?

Effective teachers are the most important school contributor to student learning, and every school would like more of them. Accordingly, policy makers are asking whether schools should use higher salaries, stipends, and bonuses to reward their best performers and to attract and keep teachers who demonstrate superior capacity to generate student learning. As a future teacher, do you think performance (merit) pay for teachers is a good idea whose time has come?

Pay Teachers More Based on Their Performance	Don't Pay Teachers More Based on Their Performance
• The idea of merit pay for teachers is a popular market-based way to improve teachers' compensation.	• Research on whether teacher pay for performance improves student outcomes is small and has mixed findings.
• Some argue that using merit pay for outstanding performance will attract more highly effective individuals into the teaching profession.	• Links found between teachers' merit pay and increased student learning may be correlational, not cause and effect.
• Many studies confirm that teacher and teaching quality (teacher attributes and effectiveness) are among the strongest school determinants of student achievement. Bonuses for high performance may attract and keep higher-quality teachers.	• Since varied factors that affect student achievement lie outside the teacher's influence (i.e., students' prior knowledge and experiences, students' health, attendance, family mobility), paying teachers' bonuses for their students' high achievement would unfairly advantage certain teachers while unfairly disadvantaging others.

Pay Teachers More Based on Their Performance	Don't Pay Teachers More Based on Their Performance
• Salary schedules (in which all teachers with the same years of teaching experience receive the same salary) do not reflect 21st century labor market realities (and do not effectively recruit or retain highly effective teachers).	• Money does not necessarily motivate teachers' best efforts in helping students learn. • Most teachers do not hold back their best instructional practices while waiting for merit pay to incentivize their use. They use the instructional skills they have.
• Labor market realities insist that more effective professionals should be able to earn more than the least effective professionals. • Performance (merit) pay for teachers would motivate teaching excellence throughout the school.	• Cultural differences between schools (which value collaboration) and businesses (which value competition and profits) make merit pay unworkable in schools. • Merit pay within a department may foster competition rather than collaboration, reducing teachers' willingness to share successful methods, experiences, and sources—to students' detriment.
• Salary should distinguish between high- and low-demand fields (such as math and science as compared with social studies). • Salaries should attract—not discourage—high-achieving college graduates into a profession.	• Serious limitations make performance pay for teachers invalid, unreliable, and unethical. • Studies find measurement errors in the data used to identify effective teachers.[89] Studies find cheating, narrowing the curriculum, and other opportunistic behaviors may result.
• Not recognizing and rewarding the organization's highest performers encourages mediocrity rather than excellence.	• Reducing teacher and teaching quality to a test score is inaccurate and unethical. • Monies to award merit pay to teachers with outstanding performance are not always available (making merit pay programs unsustainable).

Given the reasoning and data about giving teachers' performance pay, do you think schools should pay teachers more for outstanding performance? If no, why? If yes, how?

2.3 RESEARCH ON TEACHER PREPARATION AND TEACHER–STUDENT OUTCOMES

In *Doing What Matters Most: Investing in Quality Teaching*, education scholar Linda Darling-Hammond concludes that reviews of more than 200 studies contradict the myth that "anyone can teach" and that "teachers are born and not made." She writes,

Teachers who are fully prepared and certified in both their discipline and in education are more highly rated and are more successful with the students than are teachers without preparation, and those with greater training... are more effective than those with less.[90]

2.3a Teacher and Teaching Quality, Teacher Preparation, and Student Achievement

Teacher preparation refers to a "state-approved course of study, the completion of which signifies that an enrollee has met all the state's educational or training requirements for initial certification or licensure to teach in the state's elementary or secondary schools."[91] The search for highly effective teachers had led school districts to look for candidates who have met all the state's initial certification or licensure requirements to teach the states' elementary and secondary students.

Despite the plethora of research about teacher education, relatively few studies connect aspects of teacher preparation and certification to students' learning.[92] Nonetheless, of these studies, many find that effective teacher preparation and teaching behaviors learned in their preparation programs linked to increased student achievement.

In a national survey, Darling-Hammond found that factors such as student poverty, minority status, and language background appear less important in predicting individual achievement levels than "teacher quality" variables. Fully certified teachers who had a college major in the subject they were teaching had a greater positive impact on student achievement than could be predicted from students' poverty, minority status, or language. Similarly, teacher preparation had a stronger connection with student achievement than class size, overall spending, or teacher salaries, even after taking students' backgrounds into account.[93]

Similarly, preservice teacher preparation that includes coursework, class observation, practice, and feedback on their teaching can help novice teachers be more effective in improving their elementary students' measured achievement in English language arts and mathematics in their first 3 years in the classroom. This tends to be true even in high-poverty schools where students have the greatest need for effective instruction and where novice teachers often start their careers.[94] Investigators determined that informed practice to be the most impactful learning opportunity to affect new teachers' teaching effectiveness.[95]

Of course, not all teacher preparation programs are alike. Each has its own strengths and weaknesses, and many produce teachers who are no more or less effective than teachers graduating from other schools. Nonetheless, certain programs tend to produce more effective teachers.[96]

Darling-Hammond believes that effective teacher education requires students to integrate and relate knowledge of the learners' characteristics with knowledge of the subject taught and then to connect both of these factors to the relevant teaching practices. Only when these three dimensions—the learner, the subject, and the pedagogy—overlap and interact in professional practice can effective teaching and learning occur.[97]

2.3b Research on Alternative Versus Traditional Teacher Preparation Routes

The concern for high-quality teacher preparation has focused on both 4- or 5-year traditional programs and alternative programs. Although they may vary widely across states, **alternate teacher routes** typically allow candidates to begin teaching while working on program coursework and requirements at the same time to speed entry into the teaching occupation. Teach for America (TFA) and The New Teacher Project (TNTP) Teaching Fellows are two examples. According to the National Center for Education Statistics (2018), approximately 18% of public schools teachers in 2015–2016 had entered the profession through an alternative preparation pathway.[98] Given its relatively brief professional preparation, many question whether what schools gain in speed of teacher entry sacrifices teacher knowledge, skills, and student outcomes.

A review of recent research finds that traditional teacher preparation programs consistently produce teachers with better knowledge of instruction,[99] self-efficacy,[100] and teacher retention[101] as compared with alternative programs across all schooling levels except kindergarten.[102] When comparing traditional and alternative preparation programs, studies find mixed results in relation to student achievement, with less selective alternative preparation progress either substantially less effective[103] or slightly less effective[104] than traditional programs for generating student learning. One study found that almost half of teachers from alternative preparation programs did not complete practice teaching as compared to eight percent of traditional program graduates.[105] These differences are especially meaningful for teacher outcomes as teachers who complete more practice teaching and pedagogy coursework feel more prepared for teaching and report a higher likelihood of remaining the profession.[106]

At the same time, some investigations find that it may not be the type of professional certification but the increased classroom experience that leads to student achievement gains. With two or three years of successful teaching experience, studies find that alternatively certified teachers can match traditionally prepared teachers in student achievement gains.[107]

Some argue that choosing between alternative certification programs and traditional teacher preparation programs is a false choice since wide variations in quality and effectiveness exist within each category.[108] Likewise, others observe that traditional and alternative programs have morphed into one another, making broad comparisons between them useless.[109] So to the question, "Which type of preparation program produces the most effective teachers?" the answer is, "It depends."

2.3c Preparedness and Teacher Longevity

More than 42% of new teachers leave the profession within 5 years of entry,[110] a percentage that has steadily increased over the past 20 years.[111] In his seminal 2003 investigation (updated in 2018), Richard Ingersoll, a University of Pennsylvania professor, observed that 11.9% of beginning teachers left after 1 year, and another 11.1% left after the second year; thus, a cumulative total of 23% of all new teachers had abandoned teaching after only 2 years in the classroom. After 5 years, fully 44.6% of the original teaching pool had exited the profession (Figure 2.1).[112]

FIGURE 2.1 ■ Cumulative Percentage of Beginning Teacher Attrition by Years of Experience

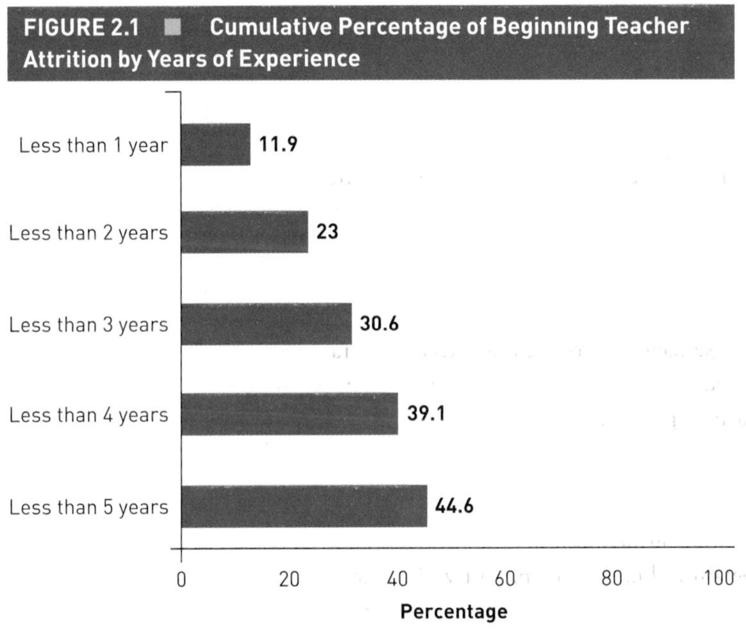

Source: Ingersoll, R., Merrill, E., Stuckey, D., and Collins, G. (2018). *Seven trends: The transformation of the teaching force, updated October 2018.* Research Report (#RR 2018-2). Consortium for Policy Research in Education, University of Pennsylvania. Figure 13, p. 19. https://repository.upenn.edu/cgi/viewcontent.cgi?article=1109&context=cpre_researchreports

Beginning teachers vary widely in the preservice education and preparation they receive, and the nature of their preparation to teach strongly impacts how long they stay in the classroom. Studies find that new teachers with more training in teaching methods and pedagogy—knowing *how* to teach (especially practice teaching, observation of other classroom teaching, and feedback on their own instructional practices)—were much less likely to leave teaching after their first year in their own classrooms. Novice teachers who had taken three or four pedagogy courses in in how to teach were 36% less likely to leave than those who took no such courses.[113] In fact, one study of new-teacher attrition rates 5 years after college graduation found that those with no pedagogical training were 3 times more likely to leave teaching during any given year as compared with peers with the pedagogical training.[114]

Specifically, the presence of four types of new teacher pedagogical preparation—how to select and adapt instructional materials; coursework in learning theory or child psychology; observation of others' classroom teaching; and formal feedback on their own teaching (through practice teaching)—was significantly related to whether new teachers left teaching or not.[115] First-year teachers who had at least 12 weeks of practice teaching before employment were more than 3 times less likely to leave the profession than those who had no practice teaching at all.[116] In short, lower levels of preparation in how to teach accounted for higher new-teacher attrition. Figure 2.2 illustrates how these teacher preparation factors reduce novice-teacher attrition.

FIGURE 2.2 ■ Teacher Preparation Reduces Attrition of First-Year Teachers

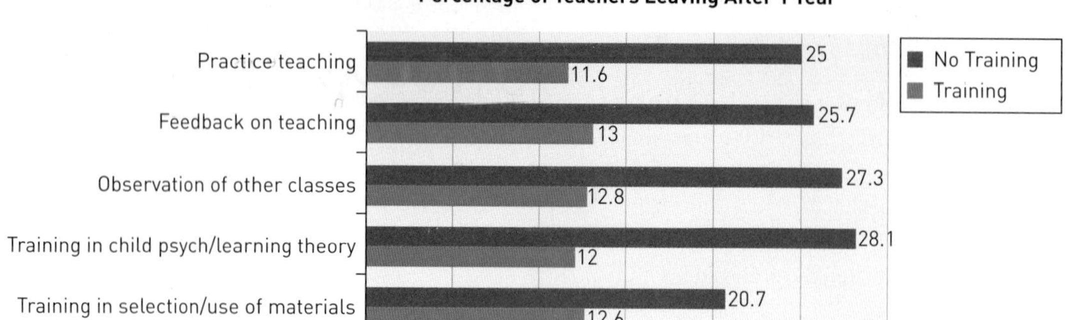

Source: Darling-Hammond, L., and Sykes, G. (2003). Wanted: A national teacher supply policy for education: The right way to meet the "highly qualified teacher" challenge. *Education Policy Analysis Archives, 11*(33), p. 24.

Additionally, during their first 3 to 5 years in the profession, teachers who are satisfied with their preparation and who receive supports as they transition into the profession are less likely to leave the teaching field early.[117] It makes sense that studies find the more effective teachers—regardless of preparation pathway—and who receive their colleagues' and administrators' encouragement tended to remain in teaching, whereas those who were less effective were more likely to leave.[118] Other studies confirm these findings.[119] Of course, it is possible that teacher selection effects enter the attrition picture: Those who are committed to teaching as a career may be more likely to enroll in teacher preparation programs that provide many opportunities to learn how to teach.

The research on teacher preparation, teaching effectiveness, and teacher longevity is clear and consistent. High-quality preservice teacher preparation provides beginning teachers with the knowledge and skills needed for effective teaching in today's diverse classrooms. Effective teachers know their subjects very well, and they know how to teach them so that students learn and increase their measured achievement. Teachers understand and apply knowledge of child and adolescent development to motivate and engage students. They are able to diagnose individual learning needs and use multiple methods to engage students in learning and assess their growth. They know how to work with others to make their classroom a safe and stimulating learning environment. In addition, when prospective teachers have sufficient opportunities to practice their learning in real classroom settings with effective supervision from experienced teachers and mentors who give them accurate, detailed, real-time feedback, both they and their students are more likely to be successful.

When it comes to answering, "Which type of preparation generally leads to higher teacher longevity in the profession," the answer is, "Those with traditional preparation." But the bottom line needs emphasizing: Although content knowledge is essential, by itself it cannot ensure that the teacher is able to teach or that his or her students will learn.

To learn more about how teacher preparation programs can make you—and future colleagues—ready for classroom effectiveness, complete the activity in the **Reflect & Engage** box, Teacher Preparation, Student Outcomes, and Teacher Longevity.

REFLECT & ENGAGE: TEACHER PREPARATION, STUDENT OUTCOMES, AND TEACHER LONGEVITY

Conventional wisdom asserts that "teachers are born and not made." One either has the inborn talent to teach or doesn't. Today, we know from ample research that this "wisdom" is untrue.

Working in pairs, discuss the following:

A. Identify what would you like to learn regarding the learner, the subject, and the pedagogy that would make you a more effective teacher.

B. As a teacher, would you rather have a colleague from a traditional or alternative teacher preparation program; explain your answer.

C. Consider the teacher preparation factors that contribute to novice teachers staying—or leaving—the profession after 1 to 5 years in the classroom. Identify the factors that your present teacher preparation program provides to you (you may have to check your college or university course catalog and/or ask your professor) that prepare you to become an effective teacher.

D. If you were a new teacher in a hiring interview with a principal, how might you explain how your teacher preparation readies you to be an effective teacher?

After the paired talks, discuss these issues as an entire class.

AMERICAN EDUCATION SPOTLIGHT: LINDA DARLING-HAMMOND

"I have always felt that the most exciting thing any person could do is to learn, and the most challenging and satisfying thing anyone could do is to teach."*

Courtesy of Linda Darling-Hammond

Sometimes called the "Michael Jordan of educational policy," ** Linda Darling-Hammond is an authority on teacher effectiveness, school reform, and educational equity. Currently the Charles E. Ducommun Professor of Education Emeritus at Stanford University, in 2015 she became the founding president and CEO of the Learning Policy Institute, a "think tank" that brings high-quality research evidence into education policy discussions. In 2016, Darling-Hammond was named the most influential education scholar in the country. In 2019, she became president of California's State Board of Education.

Darling-Hammond propelled the issue of teacher quality into the national education debate. As founding executive director of the National Commission on Teaching and America's Future, a blue-ribbon panel, she spearheaded its 1996 report, *What Matters Most: Teaching for America's Future*, providing research that supports teacher quality and which led to sweeping policy changes that affected teaching in the United States. She also led the development of licensing standards for beginning teachers—Interstate New Teacher Assessment and Support Consortium (InTASC)—that reflect current knowledge about what teachers need to know and be able to do to teach challenging content to diverse learners. And as an early member of the National Board for Professional Teaching Standards (NBPTS), Darling-Hammond helped design performance assessments that allow teachers to demonstrate their classroom teaching skills in authentic ways. As the author or editor of more than 500 publications, including award-winning books on issues of policy and practice, she is a prolific and adroit communicator.

Darling-Hammond started her own education career as a teacher's aide. She began teaching in "grossly underfunded" Camden, New Jersey, where she faced educational inequity firsthand, working in a "crumbling warehouse high school managed by dehumanizing and sometimes cruel procedures and staffed by underprepared and often downright unqualified teachers. It had a nearly empty book room and a curriculum so rigid and narrow that teachers could barely stay awake to teach it."*

Darling-Hammond acknowledges that because teaching has not yet acquired the features that mark a profession—namely, the commitment of everyone who enters the field to their clients' well-being; that everyone entering the field has demonstrated mastery of a common knowledge base they use to serve their clients; and a field in which members take responsibility for defining, transmitting, and enforcing some standards of practice to protect people who they serve—teaching is not yet a profession. Moreover, she observes that state certification does not ensure good teaching because not all states' certification requirements are up to date and are easily waived to allow unprepared persons to teach. By comparison, she argues, NBPTS certification can increase teaching quality and help professionalize teaching.

In her ongoing efforts to strengthen the teaching profession, Darling-Hammond has also done significant work to strengthen the quality of assessments, improve the quality of teacher preparation (even when it is delivered through alternative routes), and advance the quality of schools, including charter schools (including those that she founded or worked with as a board member).

Darling-Hammond received her BA from Yale University in 1973 and her doctorate in Urban Education from Temple University in 1978. She is married to husband Allen and has three children, Kia, Elena, and Sean. Like their mother, Kia and Elena have become well-prepared and deeply committed teachers.

Notes:

*Darling-Hammond, L. (1997). *The right to learn: A blueprint for creating schools that work* (pp. xii–xiii). Jossey-Bass.

**Berry, B., as cited in Arizona State University (2019). Reflections on Linda Darling-Hammond. *Inside the Academy.* https://education.asu.edu/inside-the-academy-of-education/reflections-family-friends/reflections-linda-darling-hammond

Sources: AERA. (2019). Meet Linda Darling-Hammond. #THANKASCIENTIST. http://www.aera.net/Newsroom/Thank-A-Scientist-Week/Meet-Linda-Darling-Hammond; Arizona State University. (2019). Reflections on Linda Darling-Hammond. *Inside the Academy.* https://education.asu.edu/inside-the-academy-of-education/reflections-family-friends/reflections-linda-darling-hammond; Barnum, M. (2016, February 23). Opinion: Where Linda Darling-Hammond's bold claims on testing, teachers, and New Orleans go wrong. *The 74.* https://www.the74million.org/article/opinion-where-a-top-scholars-bold-claims-on-testing-teachers-and-new-orleans-go-wrong/; Freedberg, L. (2019, March 15). Linda Darling-Hammond becomes president of California's State Board of Education. *EdSource.* https://edsource.org/2019/linda-darling-hammond-sworn-in-as-new-president-of-californias-state-board-of-education/609870; Hess, R. (2016, January 6). The 2016 RHSU Edu-Scholar public influence rankings. *Education Week.* http://blogs.edweek.org/edweek/rick_hess_straight_up/2016/01/the_2016_rhsu_edu-scholar_public_influence_rankings.html; PBS Online. (n.d.). Interview with Linda Darling-Hammond: Only a teacher. *Teachers Today.* https://www.pbs.org/onlyateacher/today2.html; Stanford Graduate School of Education. (2018, July 21). Teaching is the profession on which all other professions depend: Linda Darling Hammond on transforming education. *School's In.* https://ed.stanford.edu/news/teaching-profession-which-all-other-professions-depend-linda-darling-hammond-transforming

2.4 STATE LICENSURE

If students are to be held to high standards, their teachers must also be held to high standards. *Licensure* and *certification* indicate the state's formal approval of teaching candidates for professional practice. These two terms are often used interchangeably.

2.4a Why States License Teachers

Since education in the United States is mainly a state and local concern, each state can set its own requirements for aspiring teachers. Depending on the region, a teaching certificate may be called a *teaching credential* or a *teacher's license.* When someone earns this credential, it means they have earned at least a bachelor's degree from an accredited college or university, successfully completed a teacher preparation program, and passed the needed exams in the certification field. Candidates must meet a minimum score requirement, pass a background check, and complete the necessary forms to apply for licensure. States also accredit their teacher preparation programs, as we will discuss later in this chapter.

States have a compelling interest in setting meaningful teacher standards. We expect our schools—when successful—to provide benefits to society that go beyond the sum of those conferred upon individual students. Students and communities cannot afford to work with unqualified teachers. Without strong, meaningful, and well-enforced licensure and accreditation requirements, not only will districts lack important data about the teacher candidates, but parents will lack important information about the individuals to whom they entrust their children's learning and safety. Likewise, states will lack the policy tools needed to encourage improvements in teacher training and make quality teachers available to all schools and students.

2.4b State Variations in Licensing Teachers

Because public schools want to ensure that the educators it hires are qualified to teach, most states require prospective teachers to pass a standardized exam that attempts to measure the teacher's knowledge and skills. Individual states may require teachers who wish to hold certain certification levels to pass more than one formal test. Each state sets its own standards, making testing requirements vary state by state. Presently, most teacher licensing exams focus mainly or exclusively on new teachers' knowledge of the content they are expected to teach.[120] For example, California asks its teacher candidates to pass the California Basic Education Skills Test to earn certification, whereas New York expects teachers to pass a state-administered New York State Teacher Certification Examination. It is essential, therefore, for teaching candidates to learn about the specific licensing and testing requirements in the state where they plan to teach.[121]

Most states (45 of them) require future teachers to pass the Praxis series of exams to become teachers.[122] Praxis basic skills tests include reading/language arts, mathematics, science, and social studies, and each state has a designed a minimum score that candidates must meet in order to pass. Some states require passing this test before candidates can be admitted to the teacher preparation program. States also require subject tests to assess a candidate's knowledge in the subject or level in which they wish to become certified. Moreover, teacher preparation programs in 18 states require candidates to take the edTPA (Education Teacher Performance Assessment), a subject-specific portfolio-based test that demonstrates a candidate's readiness for a full-time classroom teaching assignment.[123] Again, each state sets its own minimum score.

Given the reliance on content knowledge without equal emphasis on know-how to teach (pedagogy), some argue that most teacher licensure tests today provide incomplete evidence of the essential competencies that comprise the core work of teaching.[124]

2.4c How New Teachers Become Licensed

"Are you licensed?" is one of the first questions school district employers will ask candidates applying for teaching positions. Becoming licensed or certified usually means the individual has completed the appropriate academic training and satisfied the requirements specified by state procedures and regulations. Each state has its own specific rules and regulations for teacher certification, but most require a combination of some or all of the following:

- *Formal academic training.* General elementary teachers need a major or minor in education and must have taken college-level courses in math, science, English, and social studies. To become a secondary teacher, one usually is required to major in the subject area to be taught.
- *Completion of an accredited teacher preparation program.* Traditional college and university teacher education programs are designed so that students can work toward the major or minor coursework while also taking teacher preparation courses. These programs include *practica*—a course of study designed especially to prepare teachers that involves the supervised hands-on application of previously studied theory (a required number of hours) and a student-teaching internship, usually a semester long. Many education programs lead to teacher certification upon graduation. One-year teacher preparation programs after a person has obtained a bachelor's degree are also available.
- *Statewide assessments and testing.* Each state requires teachers to pass a series of tests that evaluate their basic liberal arts knowledge as well as their teaching skills. Many states use Educational Testing Service's (ETS) Praxis series or the National Evaluation Services (NES) exams. Some states allow candidates to take the test within a year or two of being granted a provisional license.
- *Additional checks.* All states now require applicants to complete a background check and may require fingerprinting to ensure that only persons without a criminal record are working with children.

Because each state has different licensure or certification requirements, it is best to contact the education department or licensing office in the state where one plans to teach for more information about its teacher-related requirements.

2.4d Research on Teacher Certification and Student Achievement

Although states try to increase teacher and teaching quality by setting licensure and certification requirements, the literature on the relationship between teacher certification and student achievement has produced mixed results. On the one hand, Darling-Hammond and others have found that teacher preparation and certification are the strongest correlates of students' math and reading achievement.[125] On the other hand, some argue that teacher effectiveness may depend on general academic ability or strong subject matter knowledge as much as on any special preparation in how to teach.[126] Others assert that because little research on teacher testing or licensing prior to 2003 meets the standard for scientific evaluation, those studies that did meet this standard have yielded tentative and inconclusive results.[127]

Nevertheless, the emerging studies on teacher certification and student achievement are bringing a fuller understanding closer. Overall, the teacher certification evidence suggests that existing credentialing systems do not distinguish very well between effective and ineffective teachers. Wide variation in teacher effectiveness exists within each certification type with effective (and ineffective) teachers coming from both traditional and nontraditional certification routes.[128] Additionally, research finds that teacher experience, rather than type of certification, tends to make a difference in increasing student achievement, with improved student achievement with increases in teacher experience during the first 3 to 5 years in the classroom.[129] Therefore, teacher certification may be a necessary, but not a sufficient, condition for increasing student achievement.

2.5 ORGANIZATIONS THAT SUPPORT TEACHING PROFESSIONALS

Over the years, the rules governing teachers' behavior and working conditions have evolved. For example, a 1922 Wisconsin teacher's contract forbade a female teacher from dating, marrying, staying out past 8 p.m., smoking, drinking, loitering in ice cream parlors, dyeing her hair, and using lipstick or mascara.[130] More significantly, until the mid-20th century, married women teachers were not allowed to earn tenure.[131] Professional organizations for teachers, such as the National Education Association (NEA) and the American Federation of Teachers (AFT), have long worked to improve teachers' quality of work life and advance teaching as a profession. National teacher education program accrediting associations, the Interstate New Teacher Assessment and Support Consortium (InTASC), and the National Board for Professional Teaching Standards (NBPTS) have also increased teacher professionalization.

2.5a Teacher Unions

Teacher organizations—the National Education Association (NEA) and the American Federation of Teachers (AFT)—have become among the most influential special interest groups in national and state politics. Often referred to as unions, these teacher organizations are considered powerful because of their size, resources, and their statutory authority in certain states to negotiate the contents of collective bargaining agreements with district school boards about teachers' compensation, working conditions, and benefits. The influence of the teacher union depends on the state.[132]

Broadly defined, a **union** is a group of employees who come together voluntarily with the shared goal of improving their working conditions and having a voice at their place of employment. **Collective bargaining** is a formal process that gives union members a voice in decisions that affect its members' compensation and work lives. For teachers, collective bargaining spells out many facets of education policy and practice in the school and district workplace and the day-to-day interactions among teachers, students, and administrators. Union officials represent their teacher members in legal contract discussions to determine salary, benefits, work hours, and working conditions. These may include class schedules, health insurance, layoffs, pay for special duties, seniority, salary schedule, job security, duty-free lunch, hours of work, sick leave, transfers, pupil discipline, parental complaints, and grievance procedures. Collective bargaining negotiations also help protect teachers from receiving unfair treatment. Many agree that traditional labor unions made America's largest, wealthiest middle class possible by broadly sharing our nation's economic growth.[133] Since the state controls the legal right to collectively bargain, teacher unions may or may not be permitted to operate in any state.

Teacher association or union participation is down over time. About 70% of U.S. public school teachers participate in unions or employee association, down from 74% in 2011–2012 and 79% in 1999–2000.[134] Since the late 1970s, voters and the business community have sought to reduce taxes, limit government expenditures, or both. Yet despite the 2018 U.S. Supreme Court ruling in *Janus v. American Federation of State, County, and Municipal Employees Council 31* that concluded public employee unions could not garnish nonconsenting workers' paychecks to fund their collective bargaining for taxpayer-funded wages and benefits, teacher unions have not seen the predicted mass exodus of teachers. In fact, the AFT has added members since the *Janus* ruling.[135]

The National Education Association and the American Federation of Teachers

Started in 1857, the NEA is the largest professional organization and largest labor union in the United States, formed to promote the professional side of teaching and advocate for teachers. It also represents education support professionals, higher-education faculty, school administrators, retired educators, and education students who plan to become teachers. In 2019, the NEA had 3.2 million members,[136] and in 2017–2018, operated on a $366.7 million budget.[137] Most NEA funding comes from its members' dues.

Founded in 1916, the AFT, an affiliate of the AFL-CIO, formed to represent classroom teachers' interests in bargaining negotiations and other interactions with district and state administrators. Today, it represents more than 1.7 million preK–12 teachers and other educators, paraprofessionals, higher-education faculty, and professional staff; federal, state, and local government employees; and nurses and other health care professionals, as well as early childhood educators and nearly 250,000 retirees in more than 3,000 local affiliates nationwide.[138] In 2017, it operated on a $220.3 million budget.[139]

At various times during the late 20th century, the NEA and AFT considered merging their two teacher organizations, but irreconcilable differences at the national level prevented it. Mergers did occur in certain states. Meanwhile, the two unions established the AFT-NEA Joint Council to develop common positions on issues of mutual interest.

Teacher Unions and Education Reform

In recent years, the NEA and AFT have argued for a new collective bargaining model that recognizes that teachers and administrators hold common goals and share joint responsibility for improving school performance. These educators are not adversaries. In this context, both groups view collaboration as a useful approach in deciding governance, instructional, and personnel issues.

Both NEA and AFT believe that teachers should be held accountable for their students' academic performance, and they want an accountability system that does not limit or distort instruction. For example, an NEA 2011 policy statement proposed using student achievement test scores as part of teacher evaluation and accountability and to also include a mix of observations and a process for supporting teachers with below-par evaluations.[140] Controversy remains, however, about how to determine teacher accountability and what the outcomes from that assessment should be.[141]

Likewise, the AFT acknowledges that teachers and teaching must change, and instructional effectiveness depends on evidence of adequate student learning. Rather than protecting ineffective teachers from accountability, the AFT wants to substantially improve teacher evaluation practices to include rigorous reviews by trained experts, peer evaluators, and principals based on professional teaching standards, best practices, and student achievement. The AFT also asserts that student achievement—including student test scores based on valid and reliable assessment that show students' real growth while in the teacher's classroom—should be an essential component of teacher evaluation.[142] Despite the many complexities involved in making this intention into a reality, willingness to consider teacher accountability for student learning is an important ethical and professional advance in teacher unions' thinking.

Teacher Unions and Student Achievement

The relationship between teacher unionization and student achievement is complex, and findings are mixed. Studies differ on whether collective bargaining results in a higher quality of teacher applicants.[143] Many of the studies that examine the relationship between teacher unions and student achievement find modestly higher achievement on standardized tests (SAT and ACT scores) and on high school graduation rates in unionized schools, especially for middle-range students and students of color. Below-average and above-average students appear to fare worse.[144] Whether the overall student achievement gain is worth the higher costs in teacher compensation and improved working conditions is a matter of debate. Clearly, researchers have much to learn about how unions affect student outcomes. But union leadership and teacher membership that assume more responsibility for student outcomes is a good thing.

Teacher Union Critics

While advocates argue that unions are necessary to protect teachers from arbitrary and potentially unfair administrator decisions and to help teachers gain the compensation, benefits, and voice to impact their working conditions, opponents see it differently. Antiunion sentiment is growing among the public—largely because they perceive that teacher unions protect ineffective teachers and block school reform and accountability, putting teachers' interests ahead of students. Some point to NEA and AFT's opposition to labor market competition by fighting vouchers, tuition tax credits, and homeschooling and by rejecting privatization by "contracting out" school services and rebuffing a lower compulsory minimum age for leaving school. What is more, teachers' collective bargaining impacts district policies, teacher salaries and benefits, and working conditions—typically increasing school district spending by upward of 15%.[145] And unions' political arms advocate for teachers as a special-interest group in local, state, and national elections. As a result, teacher unions have become a flash point in contemporary policy debates.

In a similar vein, some critics wonder if the AFT and NEA's "good faith" plans for reform actually represent the unions' sincere effort to get in front and lead reform rather than have reform "done" to them. Likewise, certain detractors object to what they view as unions advancing certain "quality of life" objectives, such as allegedly promoting a gay rights agenda. The organizations' internal practices have also been subject to critical scrutiny.[146] Partly in response to these criticisms, states have begun to weaken teacher job security and change seniority provisions. As noted, the U.S. Supreme Court in *Janus* (2018) limited public sector unions' ability to collect agency fees from nonmembers.[147]

2.5b Should Teachers Strike?

Teachers face ethical dilemmas when they are expected to behave in ways about which they have conflicted feelings. Participating in a teacher strike is one example. Acting professionally in problematic situations involves thoughtfully addressing issues of personal, moral, and ethical significance.

Causes of Teacher Strikes

Between 1918 and 1960, more than 120 teacher **strikes**—that is, employee work stoppages in support of demands made on their employer, such as higher pay or improved conditions—occurred. In 2018, teacher strikes in six states advocated for increased school spending and teacher salaries.[148] Teachers also strike to express their strong objections to educational policy and practices over which they feel powerless to influence, seeking a voice in their schools' decision-making about educational programs and improved educational services for students.

The legality of strikes varies from state to state. Teachers who decide to strike in states where this practice is illegal can be fired from their jobs. Likewise, the public often reacts negatively to striking teachers, accusing them of acting illegally, victimizing children, violating their contracts, disregarding their districts' poor financial circumstances, and following small groups of "malcontents."

What Strikes Can Accomplish

Teachers walk out because it produces results. Having the legal right to strike affords teachers greater power to increase the dollar value of their work. Even where strikes are illegal, teachers who strike win better salaries and working conditions. A national 43-state analysis conducted in 1996 found evidence that when teachers go on strike, whether legally or illegally, or have a neutral party arbitrate their dispute, they win salary increases of 3.6% to 11.5% and reduce class hours between 37 and 70 minutes per day. In contrast, fact-finding missions and voluntary arbitration have no significant influences on outcomes.[149] More currently, teachers are striking not only to improve their paychecks, save their pensions, and acquire more classroom resources. They are also pushing back against education reform policies such as charter schools, performance (merit) pay, and fighting for social justice initiatives such as protections for undocumented students.

The Dilemma for Teachers

Considering whether to participate in a strike requires teachers to ponder several dilemmas involving their personal and professional code of ethics, their employment, their colleagues, their students, and their administrators. For professionals, the first ethical principle is "Do no harm." Teachers must consider all of the following as they decide:

- *Personal/professional ethics.* As individuals and as professionals, teachers develop a set of ethical guidelines that influence their thoughts and actions about what is "right and appropriate." Teachers' understanding of professional stewardship and their personal values play into how they define the correct behavior in this situation.
- *Employment.* If participating in a strike is not legal, teachers who strike may lose their jobs. An individual teacher must consider whether participating in an illegal walkout is worth the possibility of forfeiting one's employment (and perhaps future positions if the teacher cannot get a letter of recommendation from this employer).
- *Colleagues.* Some teachers interpret "collegiality" as having unquestioned loyalty, group solidarity, and the belief that teachers as professionals should not interfere in other teachers' business or criticize them or their practices, even at the expense of students' well-being. In the face of this "peer pressure," individual teachers may feel coerced into not "breaking ranks" with colleagues, even if they believe that such loyalty compromises students' needs and welfare.
- *Students.* Teachers transmit societal values by providing formal instruction and by acting as role models. They may feel torn between advocating for improved professional benefits and meeting their responsibilities toward their students. Teachers are aware that their respect (or lack of it) toward school rules and commitment to their students' well-being sends powerful messages about integrity and appropriate behavior.
- *Administrators.* Walking out in a strike may place teachers in an adversarial relationship with their administrators and school boards (their actual employers). Teachers must consider whether participating in a strike is worth jeopardizing the collaborative and trusting relationship they have built with each.

Applying abstract ethical standards to actual situations is very difficult. When teachers are unsure how to act, they must rely on their own sense of what is right and appropriate as well as on the expressed and shared professional norms about what constitutes ethical behavior. Prospective educators—in fact, all educators—can develop more mature ethical judgment when they reflect seriously on their own values, expectations, and professional norms as well as consider with colleagues how to act ethically and professionally in given situations.

To consider more fully how teacher organizations can benefit—or harm—the teaching profession, complete the activity in the **Reflect & Engage** box, Organizations That Support Professional Teaching.

REFLECT & ENGAGE: ORGANIZATIONS THAT SUPPORT PROFESSIONAL TEACHING

Teacher unions advocate for teacher professionalism and for improved salary and working conditions that strengthen teaching and learning.

A. In pairs, create a *wordle* (word cloud) using a digital tool such as Vizzlo to answer whether you think that teacher unions like the NEA and AFT are good or bad for the teaching profession and for you as a future teacher. Why? Show and explain your wordle to another pair of classmates.

B. In groups of four, consider whether the teacher unions' shift from their traditional adversarial position in relation to administrators to a collaborative one can benefit or harm teaching and learning.

C. Discuss the pros and cons of teachers going on strike. If you were in a school or district in which the teachers went on strike, what would you do? Explain how you might weigh the various factors in making your decision (including your state laws regarding teacher strikes).

After the groups have finished their discussions, reassemble the entire class to report out and consider their answers.

2.5c National Teacher Preparation Accreditation Organizations

Since teachers are the school's most important factor in increasing student learning, students in teacher education programs want to know that they are receiving the best-possible preparation to become successful, classroom-ready teachers. Completing an accredited teacher education program is one such route.

For almost a century, professional accreditation has played a key role in quality assurance in medicine, and more recently, law, psychology, physical therapy, and other established professions. Its success is due—in large part—to an uncompromising expectation for preparation programs to apply high-quality and rigorous external standards. Receiving a public or private accrediting body's endorsement is one way that teacher education programs show their worth and assure the public that it will receive adequately prepared teachers. Like most other academic fields, **accreditation** in teacher education programs is a means of self-policing and quality control. Although national accreditation of teacher programs is voluntary in most states, about 900 of the approximately 2,100 different providers participate; most of them are traditional schools and departments of education at college and universities.[150] States also have their own teacher preparation program review processes.

Briefly, in the past, two independent accrediting bodies served teacher education: the National Council for Accreditation of Teacher Education (NCATE) and the Teacher Education Accreditation Council (TEAC). Separately, each organization accredited undergraduate and graduate professional education programs at colleges and universities across the country, judging them on how well they prepared teachers. In October 2010, the two groups merged into the Council for the Accreditation of Educator Preparation (CAEP) in an effort to raise the profession's stature with a single set of high standards. CAEP has 798 programs participating in 43 states and has awarded accreditation to 238 programs.[151]

CAEP accreditation is rigorous, focusing on evidence and outcomes through external peer review that typically occurs every 7 to 10 years on a regular basis. For example, CAEP requires teacher-candidates' grade point averages and information on how the beginning teacher perform in the field. This is a challenging and costly process, especially for states that lack the infrastructure to collect these data. Also, while initially offering teacher education programs a choice of three pathways to accreditation, in 2016, CAEP narrowed these to one. Many teacher-preparation programs were not happy with the changes.

In 2017, the Association for Advancing Quality in Educator Preparation (AAQEP), a new teacher preparation accrediting group, arrived on the scene. AAQEP has certain "must haves," such as teachers' content knowledge and flexibility to programs to be innovative within their local contexts. The group also collaborates with education-preparation programs to self-identify areas of improvement and strengths. As of 2019, AAQEP had 14 states participating, had accredited nine programs, and 83 programs more were applying.[152] Meanwhile, CAEP is not sure the kind of flexibility—that some call "accreditation light"—is the answer to improving schools of education.[153] In return, AAQEP supporters call their approach "collegial" as compared with CAEP's "top-down compliant" or "one-size-fits all."

As it now stands, colleges can "shop around" for the accreditor they prefer, seeking the one they believe will give them the most favorable treatment. All this suggests that accreditors and universities are divided about how to ensure that teachers graduating from teacher education programs are ready to lead their own classrooms. The impact of two competing accreditation organizations (once again) with two different sets of standards on the public's perceptions of teaching's professionalization is unclear.

2.5d Interstate Teacher Assessment and Support Consortium (InTASC)

Created in 1987, the Interstate Teacher Assessment and Support Consortium (InTASC) is a group of state education agencies and national educational organizations dedicated to reforming teacher preparation, licensing, and ongoing professional development. *InTASC Model Core Teaching Standards and Learning Progressions for Teacher 1.0* (2013), based on the best understanding of current research on teaching practice, outlines what teachers should know and be able to do. This includes the performances, essential knowledge, and critical dispositions—to ensure that every K–12 student will be ready to enter today's college or workforce. One basic premise guides its work: An effective teacher must be able to customize learning for learners with a range of individual differences and integrate content knowledge with students' specific strengths and needs to ensure that *all* students learn and perform at high levels.[154]

InTASC aligns itself with the range of current standards for curriculum, professional development, and leadership from other education associations. By offering consistency among these documents, InTASC ensures that teachers have a coherent continuum of expectations from the first days in the classroom through accomplished practice and the conditions needed to support professional development along this continuum. In InTASC's view, only the degree of sophistication in performances, knowledge, and dispositions distinguishes the beginning from the accomplished teacher.[155]

InTASC's philosophy asserts that teachers need to recognize that all learners come to school with varying experiences, abilities, talents, and prior learning, as well as language, culture, and family and community values. These factors are assets that teachers can use to promote learning. To do this effectively, teachers must have a deeper understanding of their own frames of reference (e.g., culture, gender, language, abilities, ways of knowing) and their own potential biases that will likely impact their expectations for and relationships with learners and their families. Also, teachers need to provide each student with multiple approaches to learning.

In addition, InTASC promotes teacher collaboration and teacher leadership. Teachers must open their practice to colleagues' observation and scrutiny and engage in ongoing, embedded professional learning where teachers participate in collective inquiry to improve practice. Professional collaboration and leadership include actively participating as a school improvement team member in decision-making for a shared vision and supportive culture, identifying common goals, and monitoring progress towards these goals. All these roles focus on teachers' responsibility for student learning and their ongoing maturation as effective professionals.

2.5e National Board for Professional Teaching Standards (NBPTS)

The National Board for Professional Teaching Standards (NBPTS), established in 1987, operates a voluntary system to provide a national advanced teaching credentials for most preK–12 teachers by assessing and certifying high-quality teaching. NBPTS sets high standards for what highly effective teachers know and do. Its goal is to improve the teaching profession and positively influence student learning. It complements but does not replace a state's teacher license. Teachers who achieve National Board Certification (NBC) have met high standards through study, self-assessment, expert evaluation, and peer review. As of 2018, more than 122,000 teachers in 25 certificate areas spanning 16 disciplines across all 50 states—about 3% of all U.S. teachers—had earned NBPTS certification. Forty-seven percent of new certificate holders teach in high-need schools.[156]

The Certification Process

NBPTS candidates must hold at least a bachelor's degree, a valid state teaching license, and have 3 years of successful teaching experience in the same state-supported school district. The assessments are performance based. Teachers must also complete the assessment (of content knowledge) and submit portfolio entry components (typically using videotaped lessons showing the teacher differentiating instruction, demonstrating effective teaching practice and a positive learning environment), as well as provide essays describing themselves as an effective and reflective practitioner for their certificate area. Trained teachers in the candidate's certification area review the assessments. Candidates (sometimes with their school district's help) must also pay a fee.[157] The certification process can take from 1 to 3 years. Certified teachers must renew their certification every 10 years.

Research on NBPTS Teachers and Student Achievement

Nationwide studies tend to find that National Board Certified Teachers (NBCTs) are more effective than other teachers of similar experience in raising student achievement in elementary and secondary schools.[158] Students taught by NBCTs learn more—equal to approximately 1 to 2 months more of additional instruction—than students taught by their noncertified colleagues,[159] with an impact even stronger for minority and low-income students.[160] Additionally, students of NBCTs show evidence of deeper learning nearly 3 times more often than their peers in classrooms of non-NBCTs (74% versus 29%).[161] Moreover, NBCTs have also been found to impact the overall quality of teaching in schools where they work by mentoring their colleagues.[162] The improved student outcomes are matched by NBCTs achieving stronger results on key measures of teacher effectiveness, especially noteworthy when compared to the lack of consistent findings about the effectiveness of teachers with master's degrees.[163] Most (91%) NBCTs choose to remain in the classroom; the others often become school leaders.[164] Whether NBPTS produces better teachers or simply identifies accomplished teachers is unclear.[165]

Other Gains From NBPTS Certification

National board certification also has positive teacher outcomes. NBPTS certification provides a valid, reliable, and highly respected assessment and credentialing system to recognize accomplished teachers. It affords the teaching profession a way to create stages to an otherwise "unstaged" profession, while keeping excellent teachers teaching. Studies find that teachers with NBPTS certification showed a higher level of self-efficacy in instruction, management, engagement and participation in leadership roles,[166] and increased knowledge of teaching[167] than non-NBCTs.

Similarly, schools and school districts frequently use board-certified teachers for instructional leadership. They can model excellent classroom practices that increase students' learning, mentor novice teachers, provide professional development to their colleagues, serve as peer assessors, and work as curriculum coordinators. When used (and appropriately compensated) in these ways, board-certified teachers can help transform schools into high-achieving and professionally rewarding learning communities and create another stage in a teacher's career.

2.6 PROFESSIONAL CULTURE AND TEACHER RETENTION

Teaching is the only profession without a built-in apprenticeship period. Most schools expect new teachers to do the same job as 15-year veterans—a tall order. And new teacher initiation is often a trial by fire. If school districts want to keep and develop the teachers they hire, schools need to build a **professional culture**—the set of beliefs, values, assumptions, and relationships that educators and staff share about teaching and learning that influence every aspect of how a school functions—that includes and celebrates practices that support new teachers both as they begin working and throughout their tenure.

2.6a Induction and Mentoring

The terms "induction" and "mentoring" are often used interchangeably. In reality, the two terms mean slightly different things. **Induction** is a comprehensive, coherent, and sustained professional development process that the school district organizes to train, support, and retain new teachers. Good induction seamlessly moves new teachers into a lifelong learning program. Beginning before the first day of school and continuing through the first 2 or 3 years of teaching, induction includes new teacher orientation, support, and guidance programs. By comparison, **mentoring** is a specific type of induction program. It consists of a collegial, supportive relationship developed between a veteran and a new teacher to ease the transition into the realities of daily classroom teaching. Typically, mentoring includes giving moral support and practical suggestions.

In both induction and mentoring, teachers "who know the ropes" help novices understand and successfully handle events happening in their classrooms and schools. These programs acculturate the new teachers, who use the guidance and practical advice to learn how to prevent and solve problems on their own. With a variety of caring and knowledgeable colleagues to help the novice make sense of the transition to teaching, develop new skills, and gain essential insights, a new teacher can quickly build competence and a feeling of "I can do this!" No wonder that more than half of the deans, faculty, alumni, and principals believe that inadequate induction and mentoring are among the key reasons why so many new teachers leave the profession.[168]

Induction

Effective induction programs recognize that the art and craft of teaching develops over time. Typically, induction programs focus on learning the district's culture—its philosophy, mission, policies, procedures, and goals—and improving the novice's teaching effectiveness. Although no two induction programs are alike, high-quality induction programs include classroom observations of and by beginning teachers; formative assessment of or feedback on teaching from mentors; and participation in a professional learning community or beginning educator peer network. New teachers are not alone: Their schools ensure that they connect with colleagues and contribute to a group in which new and veteran teachers interact respectfully and value one another's contributions. Teachers tend to remain in teaching when they belong to professional learning communities based in high-quality interpersonal relationships founded on trust and respect.[169]

Mentoring

Although mentoring has become the most popular teacher induction practice during the past 25 years, the program formats vary widely. Mentoring may consist of only one hasty meeting during the first week of school, or it may involve weekly hour-long meetings apart from teachers' regular teaching schedules. Some school districts value mentoring enough to invest many hours of preparation to ready their mentors to be effective in their coaching and relationship roles with new teachers. Others simply make mentoring assignments without much forethought. Without strong administrative support to visibly endorse its value, mentoring rarely works.

Research on Induction and Mentoring

The quality and effectiveness of local schools' induction and mentoring programs vary. Their success with new teachers depends on the funding availability, the quality and number of mentors, and principals' and superintendents' commitment to make the programs work. The most effective induction programs include a package of supports, especially mentors from the same field, the chance to participate in group or collective planning, and collaborative learning activities.

Increasingly, research is showing that well-conceived and implemented high-quality teacher induction and mentoring programs successfully increase new teachers' job satisfaction, efficacy, and retention rates.[170] Effective induction programs increase teacher commitment and retention (except in large, urban, low-income schools), improve teacher classroom instructional practices, and have students earning higher academic achievement scores or learning gains than teachers without such induction programs.

Likewise, research shows that teachers learn more in collaborative teacher networks and study groups than with mentoring. They learn more in professional development programs that are longer, more sustained, and more intensive than they do in shorter ones. Additionally, they learn more when there is collective participation and when they see teacher learning and development as part of a coherent professional growth program in which all teachers—veterans and newbies alike—participate.[171] Demonstrating that quality teaching is a group responsibility—not just an individual concern—is another hallmark of successful induction programs.

Unfortunately, a 2016 50-state report finds only a few states provide a high-quality system of new teacher supports. Only 16 states provide some dedicated funding for teacher induction, and only 15 states require a research-based, multiyear course of support for all beginning teachers.[172]

According to Linda Darling-Hammond, "An occupation becomes a profession when it assumes responsibility for developing a shared knowledge base for all of its members and for transmitting that knowledge through professional education, licensing, and ongoing peer reviews."[173]

Today, the teaching profession is at an inflection point. We recognize teachers' critical role in making the American economy and democracy work. Teachers now have clearly articulated standards for what they should know and be able to do that are tied empirically to student learning. We know the types of teaching practices and educational access that enable every student to learn and grow into competent citizens. The alignment of teacher preparation accreditation standards, InTASC, and NBPTS are establishing powerful professional models to guide preservice and practicing teachers along a continuum of professional growth from novice to master teacher. We also recognize the types of career advancement initiatives and compensation options that can bring professional satisfaction to educators who wish to grow and advance throughout their careers. High-quality new teacher induction and mentoring have been shown to help beginning teachers succeed in their classrooms, their schools, and throughout their work lives. As a result, teaching, as a profession, has never been better positioned to make a difference to teachers, students, and their communities.

KEY TAKE-AWAYS

Learning Objective 2.1 Compare and contrast the factors that make—or weaken—the status of teaching as a profession.

- The teaching profession is critically important to local and national life, providing an essential public service that prepares children for responsible adulthood. Many of our children's social mobility and life options *depend* on working repeatedly with highly effective teachers.
- Teachers can be highly professional in their attitudes, expertise, behaviors, and commitment in their work lives even though their occupation, overall, may not meet some of the strict criteria more evident in high-prestige professions.
- The issues of teacher compensation and pension are problematic. Traditionally, teachers accepted a "trade-off"—relatively low salaries and low-to-no cost health care premiums—while working in exchange for regular payments (pensions) and subsidized health care after retirement. Today, this compact needs renewed attention and constructive action.

Learning Objective 2.2 Defend the view that the teaching occupation has become increasingly professionalized over the generations.

- The structure of teaching as a career is becoming more compatible with the modern workforce's expectations, providing an array of career advancement options to fulfill teachers' desire for professional growth, new roles and responsibilities, leadership opportunities, increased occupational prestige, and higher compensation during their education careers (inside and outside the classroom).

Learning Objective 2.3 Critique the research findings relating teacher preparation, teaching quality, student achievement, and teacher longevity.

- Research supports the view that teaching behaviors learned in effective preparation programs are linked to increased student achievement.
- Wide variations in quality can be found in both traditional and alternative teacher preparation pathways. Teaching effectiveness depends on the individual, the particular preparation program, and the actual school and classroom milieu. Several years of successful teaching experience may matter more than certification type or preparation pathway in increasing student achievement.
- Sufficient knowledge and skills in pedagogy—*knowing how to teach*—increases teacher effectiveness and longevity in the profession.

Learning Objective 2.4 Describe teacher licensure's rationale, state licensure practices, and the relationship between teacher certification and student achievement.

- States need strong, meaningful, and well-enforced licensure and accreditation requirements as a "quality control" for school districts and parents. Unfortunately, studies find that existing credentialing systems do not distinguish very well between effective and ineffective teachers. Therefore, teacher certification may be a *necessary, but not a sufficient,* condition for increasing student achievement.

Learning Objective 2.5 Identify the organizations that support teaching professionals and explain how they help professionalize teaching.

- The National Education Association (NEA) and the American Federation of Teachers (AFT), often called teacher unions, have long worked to improve teachers' quality of work life and advance teaching as a profession.
- The Council for the Accreditation of Educator Preparation (CAEP) and the Association for Advancing Quality in Educator Preparation (AAQEP) give teacher preparation programs a means of self-policing and quality control. But giving colleges the opportunity to "shop around" for the accreditor they believe will give them the most favorable treatment feeds the belief that accreditors and universities cannot agree on how to ensure that teacher education program graduates are classroom ready. The impact of this on the public's perceptions of teaching's professionalization is unclear.
- The Interstate New Teacher Assessment and Support Consortium (InTASC) and the National Board for Professional Teaching Standards (NBPTS), both aligned to the same high standards, have increased teacher professionalization, guiding teachers' professional growth and effectiveness throughout their careers.

Learning Objective 2.6 Argue how a school's professional culture and well-designed induction and mentoring programs can help new teachers transition into effective professional educators.

- If school districts want to keep and develop the teachers they hire, schools need to build a professional culture that includes varied supports—including strong induction and mentoring programs—for new teachers as they begin working and throughout their tenure.

TEACHER SCENARIO: IT'S YOUR TURN

You have gone home for the semester break and are ready to celebrate the holidays with the family. You and your grandmother have always been close. In fact, her background as a teacher is what inspired you to become a teacher. You are excited to share with her what you have learned in your teacher preparation classes. She retired from teaching 25 years ago, and you love hearing stories about her time in the classroom. After dinner, you asked her why she became a teacher, and she responded that way back then there were only four jobs available for women: being a teacher, a nurse, a secretary, or a housewife.

She knew she was going to college and wanted to earn her "MRS degree." But along the way, she liked the idea that she would take her one class in teaching methods and spend 6 weeks in a school doing her practice teaching.

A. Explain to your grandmother how teaching has changed professionally in terms of preparation, professionalization, and the research supporting pedagogy.

B. Describe to your grandmother how teaching is becoming less of an "unstaged" career.

C. Explain to your grandmother why, despite all the occupations now open to intelligent women, you chose a career in teaching.

NOTES

1. King, J. E. (2018). *Colleges of education: A national portrait.* American Association of Colleges for Teacher Education. https://secure.aacte.org/apps/rl/res_get.php?fid=4178&ref=rl
2. King, 2018.
3. PDK. (2019, September). Broad discontent leads half of teachers to consider quitting their jobs. 51st annual poll supplement. *Phi Delta Kappan, 101*(1), K3–K5.
4. Darling-Hammond, L. (2000, January 1). Teacher quality and student achievement: A review of state policy evidence. *Educational Policy Analysis Archives, 8*(1). https://epaa.asu.edu/ojs/article/view/392/515; Walsh, K. (2001). *Teacher certification reconsidered: Stumbling for quality.* Abell Foundation. https://www.abell.org/sites/default/files/publications/ed_cert_rejoinder_1101.pdf
5. Abbott, A. (1988). *The system of professions: An essay on the division of expert labor.* University of Chicago Press.
6. Abbott, 1988; Larson, M.S. (1977). *The rise of professionalism.* University of California Press.
7. Ingersoll, R. M. (2008, January). A researcher encounters the policy realm: A personal tale. *Phi Delta Kappan, 89*(5), 371.
8. See: Ingersoll, R., & Collins, G. J. (2018). *The status of teaching as a profession.* University of Pennsylvania Scholarly Commons. https://repository.upenn.edu/cgi/viewcontent.cgi?article=1226&context=gse_pubs; McPeck, J. E., & Sanders, J. T. (1974). Some reflections on education as a profession. *Journal of Educational Thought, 8*(2), 33–66.
9. Yinger, R. J., & Nolen, A. I. (2003, January). Surviving the legitimacy challenge. *Phi Delta Kappan, 84*(5), 386–390; Johnson, S. M. (2001, January). Can professional certification of teachers reshape teaching as a career? *Phi Delta Kappan, 82*(5), 393–399.
10. Lortie, D. (1975). *Schoolteacher: A sociological study.* University of Chicago Press.
11. Virginia Department of Education. (2011). *Uniform performance standards for teachers.* http://www.doe.virginia.gov/teaching/performance_evaluation/research_base_ups_teachers.pdf;Virginia Department of Education. (2012). Virginia standards for the professional practice of teachers. http://www.doe.virginia.gov/teaching/regulations/uniform_performance_stds_2011.pdf
12. Goldhaber, D., & Startz, R. (2017). On the distribution of worker productivity: The case of teacher effectiveness and student achievement. *Journal of Statistics and Public Policy, 4*(1), 1–12; Kane, T. J., McCaffrey, D. F., Miller, T., & Staiger, D. O. (2013, January). Have we identified effective teachers? Validating measures of effective teaching using random assignment. *MET Project.* Research Paper. The Bill & Melinda Gates Foundation. http://citeseerx.ist.psu.edu/viewdoc/download;jsessionid=5B4DD024EAC5AA92D4221FF7F0A6F3A7?doi=10.1.1.638.2716&rep=rep1&type=pdf; Marzano, R., Toth, M., & Schooling, P. (2012). *Examining the role of teacher evaluation in student achievement. Contemporary research base for the Marzano causal teacher evaluation model.* White Paper. Marzano Center; Sartain, L., Stoelinga, S. R., & Brown, E. R. (2011, November). *Rethinking teacher evaluation in Chicago. Lessons learned from classroom observations, principal-teacher conferences, and district implementation.* Consortium on Chicago school research. https://files.eric.ed.gov/fulltext/ED527619.pdf.
13. Danielson, C. (2007). *Enhancing professional practice: A framework for teaching* (2nd ed.). ASCD; Danielson, D. (2014). *The framework for teaching. Evaluation instrument. 2013 edition.* https://danielsongroup.org/downloads/2013-framework-teaching-evaluation-instrument; Danielson, C., & McGreal, T. L. (2000). *Teacher evaluation to enhance professional practice.* ASCD.

14. See: Archibald, S. (2006). Narrowing in on educational resources that do affect student achievement. *Peabody Journal of Education, 81*(4), 23–42; Borman, G. D., & Kimball, S. M. (2005). Teacher quality and educational equality: Do teachers with higher standards-based evaluation ratings close student achievement gaps? *University of Pennsylvania ScholarlyCommons.* University of Pennsylvania Graduate School of Education. https://repository.upenn.edu/cgi/viewcontent.cgi?article=1010&=&context=cpre_articles&=&sei-redir=1&referer=https%253A%252F%252Fscholar.google.com%252Fscholar%253Fhl%253Den%2526as_sdt%253D0%25252C47%2526q%253DBorman%252BKimball%252B2005%252Bteacher%252Bquality%252Band%252Beducational; Kane et al., 2013.

15. Marzano, R. J., & Toth, M. D. (2013). *Teacher evaluation that makes a difference: A new model for teacher growth and student achievement.* ASCD; Carbaugh, B., Marzano, E., & Toth, M. (2017 March). *The Marzano focused teacher evaluation model.* Learning Sciences International. https://www.learningsciences.com/wp/wp-content/uploads/2017/06/Focus-Eval-Model-Overview-2017.pdf

16. Learning Sciences Marzano Center. (2016, March). *The research base for the Marzano teacher evaluation model and correlations to state VAM.* https://www.learningsciences.com/wp/wp-content/uploads/2018/05/The-Research-Base-for-the-Marzano-Teacher-Evaluation-Model-Correlation-to-State-VAMs.pdf

17. For information about teacher certification reciprocity guidelines by states, see: *The teacher certification reciprocity guide.* (2019). https://www.teachercertificationdegrees.com/reciprocity/

18. Guarino, C. M., Santibañez, L., & Daley, G. A. (2006). Teacher recruitment and retention: A review of the recent empirical literature. *Review of Educational Research, 76,* 173–208; Ingersoll, R., & May, H. (2012). The magnitude, destinations, and determinants of mathematics and science teacher turnover. *Educational Evaluation and Policy Analysis, 34*(4), 435–464.

19. Sparks, D., Malkus, N., & Ralph, J. (2015, December). *Public school teacher autonomy in the classroom across schoolyears 2003–04, 2007–08, and 2011–12.* NCES 2015-089. *Stats in Brief.* U.S. Department of Education. https://nces.ed.gov/pubs2015/2015089.pdf

20. Etzioni, A. (Ed.). (1969). *The semi-professions and their organizations: Teachers, nurses, and social workers.* Free Press; Hoyle, E. (2001). Teaching: Prestige, status and esteem. *Educational Management Administration & Leadership, 29*(2), 139–152; Lortie, 1975.

21. Hoyle, 2001.

22. Pollack, H. (2014, September 10). Doctors, military officers, firefighters, and scientists seen as among America's most prestigious occupations. *Axios Harris Poll 100.* https://theharrispoll.com/when-shown-a-list-of-occupations-and-asked-how-much-prestige-each-job-possesses-doctors-top-the-harris-polls-list-with-88-of-u-s-adults-considering-it-to-have-either-a-great-deal-of-prestige-45-2/

23. Hoyle, E. (1995). Social status of teaching. In L. Anderson (Ed.), *International encyclopedia of teaching and teacher education* (2nd ed.). Pergamon; Hoyle, E. (2001). Teaching prestige, status, and esteem. *Educational Management and Administration, 29*(2), 139–152.

24. Sixty percent of survey respondents rated the teaching profession as having "more prestige." See: Pollack, 2014, September 10.

25. Hoyle, 2001.

26. Ingersoll, R., & Collins, G. J. (2018). The status of teaching as a profession. *University of Pennsylvania Scholarly Commons.* University of Pennsylvania Graduate School of Education. https://repository.upenn.edu/cgi/viewcontent.cgi?article=1226&context=gse_pubs

27. Ingersoll, R. (1997). *Teacher professionalization and teacher commitment: A multilevel analysis.* National Center for Education Statistics; Ingersoll, R. (2003). *Who controls teachers' work? Power and accountability in America's schools.* Harvard University Press; Ingersoll, R. (2012). Beginning teacher induction: What the data tell us. *Phi Delta Kappan, 93*(8), 47–51; Ingersoll, R., & Collins, M. (2018). Accountability, control, and teachers' work in American schools. In J. Ponticell & S. Zepeda (Eds.), *Handbook of educational supervision* (pp. 157–182). Wiley-Blackwell.

28. Barber, M., & Mourshed, M. (2007). *How the world's best performing systems come out on top.* McKinsey.

29. Will, M. (2018, May 30). Nearly half of public school teachers are satisfied with their salaries, data show. *Education Week.* http://blogs.edweek.org/edweek/teacherbeat/2018/05/teacher_salary_job_satisfaction.html

30. Will, M. (2019, June 19). To make ends meet, 1 in 5 teachers have second jobs. *Education Week.* https://www.edweek.org/ew/articles/2018/06/19/to-make-ends-meet-1-in-5.html

31. Will, M. (2018, August 21). Teachers are winning public support for pay raises, survey finds. *Education Week, 38*(1), 14.

32. Schools and Staffing Survey (SASS). (2017). Percentage of public school districts that had salary schedules for teachers, 2011–12. Table 2. National Center for Education Statistics, Institute of Education Sciences, U.S. Department of Education. https://nces.ed.gov/surveys/sass/tables/sass1112_2013311_d1n_002.asp

33. Hurley, E. (n.d.). *Teacher pay 1940—2000: Losing ground, losing status.* National Education Association. http://www.nea.org/home/14052.htm

34. Allegretto, S., & Mishel, L. (2019, April 24). *The teacher pay weekly wage penalty hit 21.4 percent in 2018, a record high.* Economic Policy Institute. https://www.epi.org/files/pdf/165729.pdf

35. Biggs, A. G., & Richwine, J. (2018, April 27). No, teachers are not underpaid. *American Enterprise Institute.* http://www.aei.org/publication/no-teachers-are-not-underpaid/; Dorfman, J. (2014, August 7). Low teacher pay and high teacher pay are both myths. *Forbes.* https://www.forbes.com/sites/jeffreydorfman/2014/08/07/low-teacher-pay-and-high-teacher-pay-are-both-myths/#7a0406d331af

36. For a look at how states' average salaries compare, see: Will, M. (2018, April 24). See how our state's average teacher salary compares. Average teacher salary by state. *Education Week.* http://blogs.edweek.org/edweek/teacherbeat/2018/04/teacher_pay_2017.html

37. For a more detailed discussion of how teachers' salaries. pensions, and benefits work in schools, see: Will, M., & Sawchuk, S. (2018, March 30; Updated 2019, January 25). Teacher pay: How salaries, pensions, and benefits work in schools. *Education Week.* https://www.edweek.org/ew/issues/teacher-pay/index.html

38. Allegretto, S., & Mishel, L. (2016, August 9). *The teacher pay gap is wider than ever.* Economic Policy Institute. https://www.epi.org/publication/the-teacher-pay-gap-is-wider-than-ever-teachers-pay-continues-to-fall-further-behind-pay-of-comparable-workers/

39. For a more complete discussion of retirees' health care benefits' fiscal impact, see: Lutz, B., & Sheiner, L. (2014). *The fiscal stress arising from state and local retiree health obligations.* NBER Working Paper 19779. National Bureau of Economic Research. http://www.nber.org/papers/w19779.pdf

40. EducationNext. (2018, March 1). *EdStat: States' teacher pension plans are now underfunded by $500 billion.* https://www.educationnext.org/edstat-states-teacher-pension-plans-now-underfunded-500-billion/

41. Aldeman, C. (2018, April 9). Aldeman: Teachers have the nation's highest retirement costs. But they'll never see the benefits. *The 74.* https://www.the74million.org/article/aldeman-teachers-have-the-nations-highest-retirement-costs-but-theyll-never-see-the-benefits/

42. Schmitz, K., & Aldeman, C. (2017, June). *Retirement reality check: Grading state teacher pension plans.* TeacherPensions.org. Bellwether Education Partners. https://www.teacherpensions.org/sites/default/files/Retirement%20Reality%20Check_Grading%20State%20Teacher%20Pension%20Plans.pdf

43. See: Darling-Hammond, L. (2000). Teacher quality and student achievement: A review of state policy evidence. *Education Policy Analysis Archives, 8*(1). https://epaa.asu.edu/ojs/article/view/392/515; Goe, L., & Stickler, L. M. (2008, March). Teacher quality and student achievement: Making the most of recent research. *TQ Research & Policy brief.* National Comprehensive Center for Teacher Quality. https://files.eric.ed.gov/fulltext/ED520769.pdf; Harris, D. N., & Sass, T. R. (2007, March). *Teacher training, teacher quality, and student achievement.* CALDER, National Center for Analysis of Longitudinal Data in Education Research, and Urban Institute. https://files.eric.ed.gov/fulltext/ED509656.pdf

44. Wong, A. (2016, February 18). What if America's teachers made more money? *The Atlantic.* https://www.theatlantic.com/education/archive/2016/02/what-if-americas-teachers-made-more-money/463275/. A 2015 work life survey found that slightly less than half the teachers surveyed (46%) said salary was a major source of stress in the workplace. Experienced teachers rated working conditions as more stressful than modest salary. See: American Federation of Teachers and Badass Teachers' Association. (2015). *Quality of worklife survey.* https://www.aft.org/sites/default/files/worklifesurveyresults2015.pdf

45. Darling-Hammond, L. (2017, September 20). *Where have all the teachers gone?* Learning Policy Institute. https://learningpolicyinstitute.org/blog/where-have-all-teachers-gone

46. Donohue, D. M. (2002, Spring). Rhode Island's last holdout: Tenure and married women teachers on the brink of the women's movement. *History of Education Quarterly, 42*(1), 50–74.

47. Simpson, R. L., & Simpson, I. H. (1969). Women and bureaucracy in the semi-professions. In A. Etzioni (Ed.), *The semi-professions and their organization* (p. 209). Free Press.

48. Coggshall, J. G., Behrstock-Sherratt, E., & Drill, K. (2011). *Workplaces that support high performing teaching and learning: Insights from Generation Y teachers.* American Federation of Teachers and American Institutes for Research. http://www.air.org/sites/default/files/AFT_AIR_GenY_Workplaces_April2011.pdf

49. Feistritzer, C. E. (2011). *Profile of teachers in the U.S. 2011.* National Center for Education Information. https://www.edweek.org/media/pot2011final-blog.pdf

50. Sullivan, S. E. (1999). The changing nature of careers: A review and research agenda. *Journal of Management, 25*(3), 457–484.

51. Johnson, S. M. (2001, January). Can professional certification for teachers reshape teaching as a career? *Phi Delta Kappan, 82*(5), 393–399.

52. Castro, A., Quinn, D. J., Filler, E., & Barns, M. (2018, January). Policy Brief 2018-1: Addressing the importance and scales of the U.S. teacher shortage. University Council for Educational Administration. http://www.ucea.org/wp-content/uploads/2018/01/Addressing-the-Importance-and-Scale-of-the-US-Teacher-Shortage.pdf

53. See: Castro et al., 2016; Flannery, M. E. (2016, March 15). Survey: Number of future teachers reaches all-time low. Education Policy. *NEA Today.* http://neatoday.org/2016/03/15/future-teachers-at-all-time-low/

54. Kelly, P. (2017, December 4). I've been teaching for 12 years and I love my job but we've got to change some things. *Educationpost.* https://educationpost.org/ive-been-teaching-for-12-years-and-i-love-my-job-but-weve-got-to-change-some-things/

55. National Council on Teacher Quality. (2010, December). Restructuring teacher pay to reward excellence. https://www.nctq.org/dmsView/Restructuring_Teacher_Pay_To_Reward_Excellence_NCTQ_Report

56. See, for example: Goldhaber, D. D., & Dominic, J. B. (1998). When should we reward degrees for teachers? *Phi Delta Kappan, 80*(2), 134–138; National Council on Teacher Quality. (2010, December). *Restructuring teacher pay to reward excellence.* https://www.nctq.org/dmsView/Restructuring_Teacher_Pay_To_Reward_Excellence_NCTQ_Report; Rice, J. K. (2003, August). Teacher quality: Understanding the effectiveness of teacher attributes. *Economic Policy Institute.* https://www.epi.org/files/page/-/old/books/teacher_quality_exec_summary.pdf

57. Snyder, T. D., de Brey, C., & Dillow, S. A. (2018, February). *Digest of education statistics, 2016* (52nd ed.). NCES 2017-094. Chapter 2, Table 209.10, p. 153. https://files.eric.ed.gov/fulltext/ED580954.pdf

58. National Center for Education Statistics, Schools and Staffing Survey, Public Teacher File, 2003-04 as cited in Roza, M., & Miller, R. (2009, July). *Separation of degrees: State-by-state analysis of teacher compensation for master's degrees.* Center for Reinventing public Education. https://www.crpe.org/sites/default/files/rr_crpe_masters_jul09_db_0.pdf

59. Miller, R., & Roza, M. (2012, July). *The sheepskin effect and student achievement.* Center for American Progress, https://cdn.americanprogress.org/wp-content/uploads/issues/2012/07/pdf/miller_masters.pdf

60. Sawchuk, S. (2009, August 12). Halt urged to paying teachers for earning master's degrees. *Education Week, 28*(37), 6.

61. Kini, T., & Podolsky, A. (2016, June). *Does teaching experience increase teacher effectiveness? A review of the research.* Learning Policy Institute. https://learningpolicyinstitute.org/sites/default/files/product-files/Teaching_Experience_Report_June_2016.pdf; Rockoff, J. E. (2004). The impact of individual teachers on student achievement: Evidence from panel data. *The American Economic Review, 94*(2), 247–252; Papay, J. P., & Kraft, M. A. (2015). Productivity returns to experience in the teacher labor market: Methodological challenges and new evidence on long-term career improvement. *Journal of Public Economics, 130*, 105–119.

62. Kini & Podolsky, 2016.

63. See: Goldhaber, D., Lavery, L., & Theobald, R. (2015). Uneven playing field? Assessing the teacher quality gap between advantaged and disadvantaged students. *Educational Researcher, 44*(5), 293–307; U.S. Department of Education. (2014, March). *Civil rights data collection. Data snapshot: Teacher equity.* Office of Civil Rights. https://www2.ed.gov/about/offices/list/ocr/docs/crdc-teacher-equity-snapshot.pdf

64. Nittler, K., & Duncan E. (2018, January). A new look at performance pay. *Teacher Quality Bulletin.* National Council on Teacher Quality. https://www.nctq.org/blog/A-new-look-at-performance-pay

65. Springer, M. D. (2012). *No evidence that incentive pay for teacher teams improves student outcomes. Results from a randomized trial.* RAND. https://www.rand.org/pubs/research_briefs/RB9649/index1.html

66. See: Balch, R., & Springer, M. (2015). Performance pay, test scores, and student learning objectives. *Economics of Education Review, 44*(1), 114–125; Dee, T., & Wyckoff, J. (2015). Incentives, selection, and teacher performance: Evidence from IMPACT. *Journal of Policy Analysis and Management, 34*(2), 267–297; Goldhaber, D., & Walch, J. (2012). Strategic pay reform: A student outcomes-based evaluation of Denver's ProComp teacher pay initiative. *Economics of Education Review, 31*(6), 1067–1083; Nittler & Duncan, 2018; Springer, M., & Taylor, L. (2016). Designing incentives for public school teachers: Evidence from a Texas incentive pay program. *Journal of Education Finance, 41*(3). 344–381.

67. Chiang, H., Speroni, C., Herrmann, M., Hallgren, K., Burkander, P., & Wellington, A. (2017, December). *Evaluation of the teacher incentive fund: Final report on implementation and impacts of pay-for-performance across four years.* (NCEE 2017-4004). Washington, DC: National Center for Education Evaluation and Regional assistance, Institute of Education Sciences, U.S. Department of Education. https://ies.ed.gov/ncee/pubs/20184004/pdf/20184004.pdf

68. Pham, L. D., Nguyen, T. D., & Springer, M. G. (2017, April 3). *Teacher merit pay and student test scores: A meta-analysis.* Vanderbilt University. https://aefpweb.org/sites/default/files/webform/42/Teacher%20Merit%20Pay%20and%20Student%20Achievement%20Test%20Scores%20LP_TN_MGS%20MASTER.pdf

69. Natale, C., Gaddis, L., Bassett, K., & McKnight, K. (2013). *Creating sustainable teacher career pathways: A 21st century imperative.* A joint publication of Pearson & National Network of State Teachers of the Year. https://www.nnstoy.org/download/career_pathways/Final%20updated%20Research%20Report.pdf

70. See: Chiang, H., Wellington, A., Hallgren, K., Speroni, C., Herrmann, M., Glazerman, S., & Constantine, J. (2015). *Evaluation of the teacher incentive fund: Implementation and impacts of pay-for-performance after two years.* U.S. Department of Education, Institute of Education Sciences, National Center for Education Evaluation and Regional Assistance. https://ies.ed.gov/ncee/pubs/20154020/pdf/20154020.pdf

71. Goldhaber, D., DeArmond, M., Player, D., & Choi, H.-J. (2008). Why do so few public school districts use merit pay? *Journal of Education Finance, 33*(3), 262–289; Podgursky, M. J., & Springer, M. G. (2007). Teacher performance pay: A review. *Journal of Policy Analysis and Management, 26*(4), 909–949.

72. National Education Association. (2017). *Fact sheet on NEA's views regarding mandated performance pay for educators.* http://www.nea.org/home/15069.htm; National Education Association. (2017). Myths and facts about educator pay. http://www.nea.org/home/12661.htm;DeLisio, E. R. (2017, July 17). Pay for performance: What are the issues? *The Educator's Network.* https://www.educationworld.com/a_issues/issues/issues374a.shtml

73. NBPTS. (2019, July). *State financial incentives for national board certification.* https://www.nbpts.org/wp-content/uploads/state_incentive_chart.pdf

74. Nittler, 2017; Gerber, N. (2018, May). How are districts and states using pay to staff high-need schools and subjects? *District Trendline.* https://www.nctq.org/blog/How-are-districts-and-states-using-pay-to-staff-high--need-schools-and-subjects

75. High-needs schools are those with the lowest student achievement, the highest student poverty rates, or in special schools in specific geographic area. Gerber, 2018.

76. Pereira, A. (2016, April 14). Hawaii wants teachers, is offering "financial incentives" to relocate. *SFGATE, San Francisco Chronicle.* https://www.sfgate.com/business/article/Hawaii-wants-teachers-offering-financial-7249036.php

77. Dee, T. S., & Goldhaber, D. (2017, April). *Understanding and addressing teacher shortages in the United States.* The Hamilton Project. https://www.brookings.edu/wp-content/uploads/2017/04/es_20170426_understanding_and_addressing_teacher_shortages_in_us_pp_dee_goldhaber.pdf

78. Iasevoil, B. (2017, September 25). Teacher salary schedules were meant to equalize pay. Do they have the opposite effect? *Teacher Beat blog. Education Week.* http://blogs.edweek.org/edweek/teacher-beat/2017/09/teacher_salary_schedules.html

79. Chaing et al., 2017.

80. Miner, B. (2018). The debate over differentiated pay: The devil is in the details. *Rethinking Schools.* http://rethinkingschools.aidcvt.com/special_reports/quality_teachers/24_01_pay.shtml

81. The concept and terms "career pathways" or "career lattice" often replace the term "career ladder" because "ladder" suggests a teacher is on a "higher rung" than colleagues, a concept that sometimes creates resentment.

82. American Federation of Teachers. (2012). *Raising the bar.* http://www.highered.nysed.gov/pdf/raisingthebar2012.pdf; American Federation of Teachers. (2013). *Reclaiming the promise. Career ladders.* https://www.aft.org/sites/default/files/rtp_careerladders.pdf; National Education Association. (2011). *Leading the profession: NEA's three-point plan for reform.* https://www.nea.org/assets/docs/NEA_3point_plan_for_reform.pdf

83. Coggshall, J. G., Behrstock-Sherratt, E., & Drill, K. (2011, April). *Workplaces that support high-performing teaching and learning: Insights from Generation Y teachers.* American Institutes for Research and the American Federation of Teachers. https://growththroughlearningillinois.org/Portals/0/Documents/Workplaces-that-support-high-performing-teaching-and-learning.pdf

84. Natale, C. F., Gaddis, L., Bassett, K., & McKnight, K. (2016, January). *Teacher career advancement initiatives: Lessons learned from eight case studies.* A report prepared for the National Network of State Teachers of the Year (NNSTOY) and Pearson. NNSTOY and Pearson. https://files.eric.ed.gov/fulltext/ED581291.pdf

85. Jenkins, S. (2013, December 2). Voices: Get with it: Millennials are the future of teaching. *Chalkbeat.* https://www.chalkbeat.org/posts/co/2013/12/02/voices-get-with-it-millennials-are-the-future-of-teaching/

86. Coggshall, J., Ott, A., Behrstock, E., & Lasagna, M. (2009). *Retaining teacher talent: The view from Generation Y.* Learning Point Associates and Public Agenda. https://files.eric.ed.gov/fulltext/ED508142.pdf

87. Coggshall et al., 2011.

88. Loewus, L. (2018, December). Millennial teachers: Things to consider in trying to recruit and retain them. *Teaching Now Blog, Education Week.* http://blogs.edweek.org/teachers/teaching_now/2018/12/millennial_teachers_things_to_consider_in_trying_to_recruit_and_retain_them.html

89. See: Jacob, B., & Lefgren, L. (2005). Principals as agents: Subjective performance measures in education. National Bureau of Economic Research Working Paper No. 11463. Cambridge, MA: NBER; Rebora, A. (2009, October). Teacher evaluations get poor grades. *Education Week, 30*(1), 7; Weisberg, D., Sexton, S., Mulhern J., & Keeling, D. (2009). *The widget effect. Our national failure to acknowledge and act on differences in teacher effectiveness.* The New Teacher Project; Popham, W. (2008). A misunderstood grail. *Educational Leadership, 66*(1), 82–83; Murnane & Cohen, 1986.

90. Darling-Hammond, L. (1997). *Doing what matters most: Investing in quality teaching.* National Commission on Teaching & America's Future. https://files.eric.ed.gov/fulltext/ED415183.pdf

91. U.S. Department of Education. (2016). Title II Higher Education Act. Washington, DC., p. 6. https://title2.ed.gov/public/TA/Glossary.pdf

92. Cochran-Smith, M., Villelgas, A. M., Abrams, L., Chavez-Moreno, L., Mills, T., & Stern, R. (2015). Critiquing teacher preparation research: An overview of the field, Part II. *Journal of Teacher Education, 66*(2), 109–121.

93. Darling-Hammond, L. (2000). Teacher quality and student achievement. *Education Policy Analysis Archives. 8* (1). ISSN 1068-2341. https://epaa.asu.edu/ojs/article/view/392/515

94. Bruno, P., Rabovsky, S., & Strunk, K. (2019). *Taking their first steps: The distribution of new teachers into school and classroom contexts and implications for teaching effectiveness and growth* (Working Paper No. 212-0119-1). National Center for Analysis of Longitudinal Data in Education Research. American Institutes for Research.

95. Goodson, G., Casell, L., Price, C., Litwok, D., Dynarski, M., Crowe, E., Meyer, R., & Rice, A. (2019, September). *Teacher preparation experiences and early teaching effectiveness.* U.S. Department of Education, Institute of Education Sciences. https://ies.ed.gov/ncee/pubs/20194007/pdf/20194007.pdf; Sparks, S. D. (2019, October 9). Preservice feedback and practice boost teacher effectiveness. *Education Week, 39*(8), 6. https://www.edweek.org/ew/articles/2019/10/09/preservice-feedback-and-practice-boost-teacher-effectiveness.html

96. Goldhaber, D., & Liddle, S. (2011). The gateway to the profession: Assessing teacher preparation programs based on student achievement. Center for Education Data & Research. http://www.nnstoy.org/download/CEDR%20WP%202011-2%20Teacher%20Training%20(9-26).pdf

97. Darling-Hammond, L. (1996). *What matters most. Teaching and America's future.* National Commission on Teaching and America's future. Columbia University Teachers College, p. 28; Darling-Hammond, L., & Bransford, J. (Eds.), *Preparing teachers for a changing world: What teachers should know and be able to do.* National Academy of Education. Jossey-Bass.

98. National Center for Education Statistics. (2018, May). Characteristics of public school teachers who completed alternative route to certification programs. *The condition of education.* Institute for Education Sciences. https://nces.ed.gov/programs/coe/indicator_tlc.asp

99. Darling-Hammond, L., Chung, R., & Frelow, F. (2002). Variation in teacher preparation how well do different pathways prepare teachers to teach? *Journal of Teacher Education, 53*(4), 286–302.

100. Zientek, L. R. (2007). Preparing high-quality teachers: Views from the classroom. *American Educational Research Journal, 44*(4), 959–1001.

101. Carver-Thomas, D., & Darling-Hammond, L. (2017, August 16). Teacher turnover: Why it matters and what we can do about it. Learning Policy Institute. https://learningpolicyinstitute.org/sites/default/files/product-files/Teacher_Turnover_REPORT.pdf; MacIver, M. A., & Vaughn, E. S., III. (2007). "But how long will they stay?" Alternative certification and new teacher retention in an urban district. *ERS Spectrum, 25*(2), 33–44.

102. Darling-Hammond, 2002; Jang, S. T., & Horn, A. S. (2017, March). The relative effectiveness of traditional and alternative teacher preparation programs. A review of recent research. *MHEC Research Brief.* Midwestern Higher Education Compact. https://www.mhec.org/sites/default/files/resources/teacherprep2_20170301_1.pdf

103. Clotfelter, C. T., Ladd, H. F., & Vigdor, J. L. (2010). Teacher credentials and student achievement in high school a cross-subject analysis with student fixed effects. *Journal of Human Resources, 45*(3), 655–681; Darling-Hammond, L., Holtzman, D. J., Gatlin, S. J., & Heilig, J. V. (2005). Does teacher preparation matter? Evidence about teacher certification, Teach for America, and teacher effectiveness. *Education Policy Analysis Archives, 13*(42), 2–50; Henry, G. T., Bastian, K. C., Fortner, C. K., Kershaw, D. C., Purtell, K. M., Thompson, C. L., & Zulli, R. A. (2014). Teacher preparation policies and their effects on student achievement. *Education Finance and Policy, 9*(3), 264–303.

104. Guarino, C. M., Hamilton, L. S., Lockwood, J. R., & Rathbun, A. H. (2006). *Teacher qualifications, instructional practices, and reading and mathematics gains of kindergartners.* Research and Development Report. NCES 2006-031. National Center for Education Statistics.

105. Ronfeldt, M., Schwartz, N., & Jacob, B. A. (2014). Does preservice preparation matter? Examining an old question in new ways. *Teachers College Record, 116*(10), 1–46.

106. Ronfeldt et al., 2014.

107. Bos, H., & Gerdeman, D. (2017, May 4). Alternative teacher certification: Does it work? *American Institutes for Research.* https://www.air.org/resource/alternative-teacher-certification-does-it-work;Boyd, D., Grossman, P., Lankford, H., Loeb, S., & Wyckoff, J. (2005). How changes in entry requirements alter teacher workforce and affect student achievement. *Education Finance and Policy, 1*(2), 176–216; Gordon, R., Kane, T. J., & Staiger, D. O. (2006). *Identifying effective teachers using performance on the job.* The Brookings Institution. www.brookings.edu/views/papers/200604Hamilton_1.pdf; Kane, T. J., Rockoff, J. E., & Staiger, D. O. (2006). *What does certification tell us about teacher effectiveness? Evidence from New York City.* Graduate School of Education. http://www.gse.harvard.edu/news/features/kane/nycfellowsmarch2006.pdf

108. Berry, B. (2005, October 19). Teacher quality and the question of preparation. *Education Week, 25*(8), 44, 34.

109. Johnson, S. M., & Birkeland, S. E. (2006, February 15). Fast-track certification. Can we prepare teachers both quickly and well? *Education Week, 25*(23), 48, 37; Johnson, S. M., Birkeland, S. E., & Peske, H. G. (2005). *A difficult balance: Incentives & quality control in alternative certification programs.* Harvard Graduate School of Education. http://www.nctq.org/nctq/research/1135274951204.pdf

110. Perda, D. (2013). *Transitions into and out of teaching: A longitudinal analysis of early career teacher turnover* (Unpublished doctoral dissertation). University of Pennsylvania.

111. Ingersoll, R. M., Merrill, E., & Stuckey, D. (2018, November 30). *Seven trends: The transformation of the teaching force—updated October 2018.* Consortium for Policy Research in Education (CPRE) Research Reports. https://repository.upenn.edu/cgi/viewcontent.cgi?article=1109&context=cpre_researchreports

112. Ingersoll et al., 2018.

113. Ingersoll, R., Merrill, L., & Jay, H. (2014, July). What are the effects of teacher education and preparation on beginning teacher attrition? *Research Report* (RR-82). Consortium for Policy Research in Education (CPRE), University of Pennsylvania. https://www.cpre.org/sites/default/files/researchreport/2018_prepeffects2014.pdf

114. Shen, J. (2003, April). *New teachers' certification status and attrition pattern: A survival analysis using the Baccalaureate and Beyond Longitudinal Study, 1993–97.* Paper presented at the annual meeting, Chicago.

115. Ingersoll et al., 2014.

116. Even one semester of practice teaching was less likely to exit than those with less than a semester of practice. See:. Ingersoll et al., 2014.

117. DeAngelis, K. J., Wall, A. F., & Che, J. (2013). The impact of preservice preparation and early career support on early- to mid-career teachers' career intentions and decisions. *Journal of Teacher Education, 64*(4), 338–355.

118. Boyd, D., Dunlop, E., Lankford, H., Loeb, S., Mahler, P., O'Brien, O. H., & Wyckoff, J. (2011) *Alternative certification in the long run: Achievement, teacher retention, and the distribution of teacher quality in New York City.* Center for Education Policy and Analysis, Stanford. https://cepa.stanford.edu/sites/default/files/Alternative%20Certification%20in%20the%20Long%20Run%20Preliminary%20Report%287Dec2010%29_0.pdf; Ingersoll et al., 2014.

119. Van Overschelde, J. P., Saunders, J. M. J., & Ash, G. E. (2017). "Teaching is a lot more than just showing up to class and grading assignments": Preparing middle-level teachers for longevity in the profession. *Middle School Journal, 48*(5), 28–38. https://www.tandfonline.com/doi/abs/10.1080/00940771.2017.1368319

120. Gitomer, D. H., & Zisk, R. C. (2015). Knowing what teachers know. *Review of Research in Education, 39*(1), 1–53.

121. For more information on state testing requirements, see: Teach.com. (2019). Become a teacher: Get your teaching credential. https://teach.com/careers/become-a-teacher/teaching-credential/state-requirements/

122. See: ETS. (2019). State requirements. Praxis. https://www.ets.org/praxis/states/

123. Will, M. (2020, March 25). Student-teachers caught in middle by shutdowns. *Education Week, 39*(27), 8.

124. Phelps, G. A., & Sykes, G. (2020, March). The practice of licensure, the licensure of practice. *Phi Delta Kappan, 101*(6), 19–23; edTPA. (2020). *About EDTPA. Overview.* https://edtpa.aacte.org/about-edtpa https://edtpa.aacte.org/about-edtpa

125. Clotfelter, C. T., Ladd, H. F., & Vigdor, J. L. (2007). *How and why do teacher credentials matter for student achievement. Working Paper 2.* CALDER. https://caldercenter.org/sites/default/files/1001058_Teacher_Credentials.pdf; Darling-Hammond, L., Holtzman, D. J., Gatlin, S. J., & Heilig, J. V. (2005, October 12). Does teacher preparation matter? Evidence about teacher certification, Teach for America, and Teacher effectiveness. *Education Policy Analysis Archives, 13*(42), https://www.redalyc.org/pdf/2750/275020513042.pdf

126. Ballou, D., & Podgursky, M. (2000). Reforming teacher preparation and licensing: What is the evidence? *Teachers College Record, 102*(1), 1–27; Finn, C. E. (1999). Foreword. In M. Kanstoroom & C. Finn, Jr. (Eds.), *Better teachers, better schools.* The Thomas B. Fordham Foundation; U.S. Department of Education. (2002). *The Secretary's report on teacher quality.* U.S. Department of Education.

127. Podgursky, M. (2003). *Improving academic performance in U.S. public schools: Why teacher licensing is (almost) irrelevant.* Paper presented at the Teacher Preparation and Quality: New Directions in Policy and Research Conference. Washington, DC: October 18–20, 2003. https://www.researchgate.net/profile/Michael_Podgursky/publication/237427643_Improving_Academic_Performance_in_US_Public_Schools_Why_Teacher_Licensing_is_Almost_Irrelevant/links/02e7e53c9325eaf3a0000000/Improving-Academic-Performance-in-US-Public-Schools-Why-Teacher-Licensing-is-Almost-Irrelevant.pdf

128. See: Boyd, D., Grossman, P., Lankford, H., Loeb, S., & Wyckoff, J. (2005). How changes in entry requirements alter teacher workforce and affect student achievement. *Educational Finance and Policy, 1*(2), 176–216; Kane, T. J., Rockoff, J. E., & Staiger, D. O. (2006). What does certification tell us about teacher effectiveness? Evidence from New York City. Harvard Graduate School of Education. https://www0.gsb.columbia.edu/faculty/jrockoff/certification-final.pdf; Nunnery, J. A., Kaplan, L. S., & Owings, W. A. (2009, December). The effects of troops to teachers on student achievement: A meta-analytic approach. *National Association of Secondary School Principals Bulletin, 93*(4), 249–272.

129. See: Boyd et al., 2005; Kane et al., 2006; Rivkin, S. G., Hanushek, E. A, & Kane, J. F. (2005). Teachers, schools, and academic achievement. *Econometrics, 73*(2), 417–458.

130. Clark County History Buffs. (n.d.). Wisconsin teacher's contract for 1922 ($75 a month). *Clark County Wisconsin History.org.* https://www.wiclarkcountyhistory.org/0data/11/11120.htm

131. Cooke, D. H. (1937). Local residents and married women as teachers. *Review of Educational Research, 7*(3), 267–272.

132. For a state-by-state comparison, see: Northern, A. M., Scull, J., & Zeehandelaar, S. (2012, October 29). *How strong are U.S. teacher unions? A state-by-state comparison.* Thomas B. Fordham Institute. https://fordhaminstitute.org/national/research/how-strong-are-us-teacher-unions-state-state-comparison

133. Greenhouse, S. (2019). *Beaten down, worked up*. Penguin Random House.

134. Loewus, L. (2017, October 12). Participation in teachers' unions is down, and likely to tumble further. *Education Week.* http://blogs.edweek.org/edweek/teacherbeat/2017/10/participation_teachers_unions_down_likely_to_tumble_further.html

135. Will, M. (2019, June 27). Teachers' unions expected big membership loses. Here's why those haven't panned out. *Education Week.* https://www.edweek.org/ew/articles/2019/06/27/teachers-unions-expected-big-membership-losses-heres.html;Until this ruling, public section unions assigned "fair share" fees to nonunion members who still profited in higher wages and benefits from union negotiated collective bargaining agreements. Unions asserted that none of these "fair share" dues went to politics or political candidates. In the Court's view (5–4 vote), the collective bargaining process was inherently political, and forcing employees to pay ""shop" or "agency" fees violated their First Amendment rights of property, expression, and choice, See: *Janus v. American Federation of State, County, and Municipal Employees, Council 31,* et al. No. 16-1466, 585. (2018). https://www.supremecourt.gov/opinions/17pdf/16-1466_2b3j.pdf

136. NEA. (2019). Our members. http://www.nea.org/home/1594 htm

137. NEA. (2018, June). *2018-2020 strategic plan and budget. Presented to the representative assembly July 2018* (p. 7). https://ra.nea.org/wp-content/uploads/2018/06/Strategic_Plan_and_Budget_2018.pdf

138. AFT. (2019). *About us.* https://www.aft.org/about

139. AFT. (2018, June 30). Consolidated financial statements. https://www.aft.org/sites/default/files/aft-consolidatedaudit063018.pdf

140. NEA. (2011). *Teacher evaluation: A resource guide for National Education Association leaders and staff.* http://www.nea.org/assets/docs/teacherevalguide2011.pdf

141. Wise, A. E., & Udan, M. D. (2013, March 12). The political future of the teaching profession. *Education Week, 32*(24), 26, 32.

142. AFT. (2009). The instructional demands of standards-based reform. https://www.aft.org/sites/default/files/instructionaldemands0609.pdf

143. Loeb, S., & Page, M. (2000). Examining the link between teacher wages and student outcomes: The importance of alternative labor market opportunities and non-pecuniary variation. *Review of Economics and Statistics, 82*(3), 393–408; Johnson, S. M., & Donaldson, M. (2006). The effects of collective bargaining on teacher quality. In J. Hannaway & A. Rotherham (Eds.), Collective *bargaining in education: Negotiating change in today' schools* (pp. 111–140).

144. Carini, R. M. (2002). School reform proposals: The research evidence. *Teacher unions and student achievement.* Arizona State University. https://nepc.colorado.edu/sites/default/files/Summary-10.Carini.pdf; Eberts, R. W. (2007, Spring). Teachers unions and student performance: Help or hindrance? *The Future of Children, 17*(1), 175–200. https://files.eric.ed.gov/fulltext/EJ795878.pdf

145. Eberts, R. W. (2007, Spring). Teachers unions and student performance: Help or hindrance? *The Future of Children, 17*(1), 175–200. https://files.eric.ed.gov/fulltext/EJ795878.pdf

146. For example, see: Lieberman, M. (2000). *Teacher unions: How they sabotage education reform and why?* Encounter Books.

147. National Council on Teacher Quality. (2014). District policy/State influence fact sheet. Retrieved February 4, 2014, from *Janus v. American Federation of State, County, and Municipal Employees, Council 31* et al. No. 16-1466, 585. (2018).

148. Van Dam, A. (2019, February 14). Teachers strikes made 2018 the biggest year for worker protest in a generation. Economic Policy. *The Washington Post.* https://www.washingtonpost.com/us-policy/2019/02/14/with-teachers-lead-more-workers-went-strike-than-any-year-since/

149. Zigarelli, M. A. (1996, Winter). Dispute resolution mechanisms and teacher bargaining outcomes. *Journal of Labor Research, 17*(1), 135–148.

150. Will, M. (2019, August 21). Teacher-prep accreditors competing once again. *Education Week, 39*(1), 32. https://www.edweek.org/ew/articles/2019/07/24/teacher-preparation-programs-again-have-a-choice-of.html

151. Will, M. (2019, July 24). Teacher-preparation programs again have a choice of accreditors. But should they? *Education Week*. https://www.edweek.org/ew/articles/2019/07/24/teacher-preparation-programs-again-have-a-choice-of.html

152. Will, 2019, July 24.

153. Loewus, L., & Sawchuk, S. (2017, October 12). Yet another group sets out to accredit teacher-prep programs. *Education Week, 37*(10), 8. https://www.edweek.org/ew/articles/2017/10/12/yet-another-group-sets-out-to-accredit.html; Will, 2019, August 21.

154. Chapter 1 describes these standards in more detail.

155. For more information on INTASC, see: Council of Chief State School Officers. (2013, April). *InTASC. Model core teaching standards and learning progressions for teachers* 1.0. https://ccsso.org/sites/default/files/2017-12/2013_INTASC_Learning_Progressions_for_Teachers.pdf

156. National Board for Professional Teaching Standards. (2018, December). 3,907 teachers achieve national board certifications, bringing national total to more than 122,000. https://www.nbpts.org/newsroom/new-nbcts-2018/

157. For more specifics on applying for NBPTS certification, see: NBPTS. (2018). *National board certification. Eligibility verification forms and instructions*. https://www.nbpts.org/wp-content/uploads/Eligibility_Forms_and_Instructions.pdf; NBPTS. (2018). *National board process overview*. https://www.nbpts.org/wp-content/uploads/National-Board-Process-Overview-1.pdf

158. See: Cowan, J., & Goldhaber, D. (2015). *National board certification and teacher effectiveness: Evidence from Washington*. The Center for Data & Research, University of Washington Bothell. http://ww.cedr.us/papers/working/CEDR%20WP%202015-3_NBPTS%20Cert.pdf; Chingos, M. M., & Peterson, P. E. (2011). It's easier to pick a good teacher than to train one: Familiar and new results on the correlates of teacher effectiveness. *Economics of Education Review, 30*(3), 449–465; National Board for Professional Teaching Standards. (2015, March). *Board certification: A proven tool for identifying quality teaching. Summary of Research*. https://www.nbpts.org/wp-content/uploads/policy_implications_of_new_research.pdf;Strategic Data Project. (2012). SDP human capital diagnostic: Los Angeles Unified School District. *Center for Education Policy Research, Harvard University*. https://sdp.cepr.harvard.edu/files/sdp/files/sdp-lausd-hc.pdf

159. Cowan, J., & Goldhaber, D. (2015). *National board certification and teacher effectiveness: Evidence from Washington*. The Center for Data & Research, University of Washington. http://www.cedr.us/papers/working/CEDR%20WP%202015-3_NBPTS%20Cert.pdf; NBPTS. (2018). Elevating teaching, empowering teachers. *Research*. https://www.nbpts.org/research/; Vandervoort, L.G., Amrein-Beardsley, A., & Berliner, D. C. (2004). National board certified teachers and their students' achievement. *Education Policy Analysis Archives, 12*(46), 1–117.

160. Goldhaber, D., & Anthony, E. (2007). Can teacher quality be effectively assessed? *The Review of Economics and Statistics, 89*(1), 134–150; Cavalluzzo, L. C. (2004). Is national board certification an effective signal of teacher quality? *The CNA Corporation*. https://pdfs.semanticscholar.org/2530/2da018db3d54983847972f8e241290bbcdf7.pdf

161. National Board for Professional Teaching Standards. (n.d.). *The proven impact of board-certified teachers on student achievement*. https://www.nbpts.org/wp-content/uploads/impact_brief_final.pdf; Smith, T., Baker, W., Hattie, J., & Bond, L. (2004). Chapter 12. A validity study of the certification system of the national board for professional teaching standards in assessing teachers for professional certification: The first decade of the national board for professional teaching standards. In R. E. Stake, S. Kushner, L. Ingvarson, & J. Hattie (Eds.), *Assessing teachers for professional certification: The first decade of the national board for professional teaching standards* (pp. 345–378). Emerald.

162. Frank. K., Sykes, G., Anagnostopoulos, D., Cannata, M., Chard, L., Krause, A., & McCrory, R. (2008). Does NBPTS certification affect the number of colleagues a teacher helps with instructional matters? *Educational Evaluation and Policy Analysis, 30*(1), 3–30; Sun, M., Penuel, W., Frank, K., Gallagher, H., & Youngs, P. (2013). Professional development to promote the diffusion of instructional expertise among teachers. *Educational Evaluation and Policy Analysis, 35*(3), 344–369.

163. Clotfelter, C., Ladd, H., & Vigdor, J. (2007). *How and why do teacher credentials matter for student achievement?* NBER Working Paper 12828. National Bureau of Economic Research; Betts, J. R., Zau, A. C., & Rice, L. A. (2003). *Determinants of student achievement: New evidence from San Diego*. Public Policy Institute of California; Goldhaber & Anthony, 2007.

164. Kennelly, A. (2001, April 12). *Teachers survey data report.* As cited in Sato, M., Hyler, M. E., & Monte-Sano, C. B. (2014, Fall). Learning to lead with purpose: National board certification and teacher leadership development. *International Journal of Teacher Leadership, 5*(1), 1–23. https://files.eric.ed.gov/fulltext/EJ1137495.pdf; Stokes, L., St. John, M., Helms, J., & Maxon, D. (2004). *Investing in a teacher leadership infrastructure for Washington education. A summative assessment of the Washington initiative for national board teacher certification.* http://www.inverness-research.org/reports/2004-06-Rpt-WashInitiativeAssessment-WI-NBTC.pdf

165. Lustick, D., & Sykes, G. (2006). National board certification as professional development: What are teachers learning? *Education Policy Analysis Archives, 14*(5).

166. Hines, L. A. (2013). *National board for professional teaching standards certification and teacher self-efficacy* (Unpublished doctoral dissertation). Western Kentucky University, KY.

167. Lustick, D., & Sykes, G. (2006). National board certification as professional development: What are teachers learning? *Education Policy Analysis Archives, 14*(5), 1–46. The study identified this finding for science teachers.

168. Levine, A (2006. September). *Educating school teachers.* The Education Schools Project. http://edschools.org/pdf/Educating_Teachers_Report.pdf

169. For details on what teacher induction programs in schools may include, see: Ingersoll, R., & Strong, M. (2011). The impact of induction and mentoring programs for beginning teachers: A critical review of the research. *Review of Educational Research, 81*(2), 201–233.

170. Ingersoll & Strong, 2011; Ingersoll, R., & Smith, T. M. (2004). Do teacher induction and mentoring matter? *NASSP Bulletin, 88*(638), 28–40.

171. Garet, M. S., Porter, A. C., Desimone, L., Birman, B. F., & Yoon, K. D. (2001). What makes professional development effective? Results from a national sample of teachers. *American Educational Research Journal, 38*(4), 915–945; Wong, H. K. (2004, March). Induction programs that keep new teachers teaching and improving. *NASSP Bulletin, 88*(638), 41–58.

172. Goldrick, L. (2016, March). *Support from the start. A 50-state review of policies on new educator induction and mentoring.* New Teacher Center. https://newteachercenter.org/wp-content/uploads/2016CompleteReportStatePolicies.pdf

173. Darling-Hammond, L. (1997). *The right to learn: A blueprint for creating schools that work.* Jossey-Bass, p. 30.

iStock/kirkikis

3 PHILOSOPHY OF EDUCATION

InTASC Standards Addressed: 1, 2, 3, 4, 5, 6, 7, 8, 9, 10

LEARNING OBJECTIVES

After you read this chapter, you should be able to

3.1 Compare and contrast an educational *philosophy* with an *opinion*.

3.2 Support how traditional education philosophy contributes to our understanding of school's purposes and practices.

3.3 Defend how progressive education philosophy contributes to our understanding of school's purposes and practices.

3.4 Assess how existential education philosophy contributes to our understanding of school's purposes and practices.

3.5 Critique how critical theory education philosophy contributes to our understanding of school's purposes and practices.

3.6 Argue the key characteristics of the four educational philosophies that influence today's public schools.

No decision is more important than determining what to teach and toward what ends. The "right thing to do," regardless of context or profession, always relies on values as well as facts. Communities' system of values and beliefs about education—that is, their philosophy of education—influences to what purposes, what, and how schools teach. Different philosophies lead schools in different directions.

Competing views exist about schools' purposes and practices:

- Traditionalist educators believe that schools' purpose is to foster students' intellectual development by teaching the Western European classics and thought to prepare students for further education and work.
- Progressive educators believe that schooling *is* life, not preparation for life, and should be child centered, not subject centered. According to this view, schools should prepare students for an informed life in a democratic society.
- Existentialist educators believe that education's most important goals are to awaken human consciousness to the human condition and to the freedom to choose and create the personal self-awareness that helps make each individual unique.
- Critical theorist educators believe that schools should create the conditions for teachers to act as public intellectuals to challenge the present power structure and create a more democratic society.

Our philosophy shapes us and determines how we approach the world. Our philosophy of education influences our views about what schools are for and how we should educate our children. Deciding what, why, and how to teach is a value-laden enterprise, influenced by plural beliefs available in a multicultural democracy. Understanding the merits and limits of each approach will help prospective teachers develop, articulate, and enact their own views about education's purpose and process.

3.1 WHAT IS AN EDUCATIONAL PHILOSOPHY?

Philosophy comes from two Greek words: *philos*, meaning "love," and *sophy*, meaning "wisdom." Literally, philosophy means love of wisdom. In everyday usage, this term refers to the general beliefs, concepts, and attitudes that an individual or group possesses. Most people have a set of ideas, values, and attitudes about life and education.

3.1a What Is Philosophy?

"Philosophy" is difficult to define. Put simply, philosophy is the investigation of causes and laws underlying reality. It is also "a basic theory or viewpoint" or "system of values by which one lives" as well as "the critique and analysis of fundamental beliefs as they come to be conceptualized and formulated."[1] Since philosophy means questioning the nature of things, it is grounded in logical reasoning rather than empirical methods. In short, analytic questioning and thinking about a reality's true nature creates a philosophy (a motivating viewpoint and value system), which then directs one's beliefs and actions concerning that reality.

Having a *philosophy* involves more than simply having an *opinion*. An opinion requires only a point of view; one does not have to support it with data or rational analysis. By contrast, a philosophy requires intellectual and rational inquiry, a systematic critical thinking without reference to experiments or religious faith. A philosopher pursues knowledge for its own sake to more fully understand the world and its ideas. Having a philosophy or discerningly analyzed point of view gives people a frame of reference by which to make sense of their experiences and to anticipate future ones.

3.1b What Is an Educational Philosophy?

Unlike philosophy as an academic discipline that stands on its own as a way of making abstract sense of the world, educational philosophy focuses on practice. **Educational philosophies** are viewpoints that help educators interpret, find meaning, and guide their work. Different educational philosophies exist because educators and policy makers hold different ideas and values about education's purposes and practices.

Educational philosophy asks (and answers) many questions, such as these:

- What is education?
- What are its goals?
- What is school?
- What is an educated person?
- Which knowledge, attitudes, and skills should schools teach?
- Who should decide what is taught?
- How should students be taught?
- What is the teacher's role?
- What is the student's role?

Educational philosophies reflect our society's pluralism. The philosophies considered in this chapter have well-established roots in educational thought and practice. Although science can provide guidance, it cannot yet verify that one educational philosophy is empirically and objectively superior to any other. Nor can science determine the world's "best" culture or the "truest" religious faith. All of these decisions are part of value-driven, affective belief systems. For most humans, our beliefs more powerfully determine our thoughts and actions than do any scientific conclusions—that is, unless scientific rationality as the basis for thought and actions is part of our belief system.

3.1c Influences on Educational Philosophies

As one might expect in a pluralistic society, Americans' sets of beliefs, concepts, and attitudes—their educational philosophies—about what should happen in schools vary greatly. Factors such as the historical era, the geographic location, the local and larger cultures, the ease of communication and travel between those cultures and others, and the specific persons involved all influence the prevailing educational philosophy. For example, an educational philosophy that grows and flourishes during an era of limited communication and transportation between and among different world cultures and limited education among its society's members may not be the same educational philosophy that develops in a more fluent, interconnected world that depends on a highly educated populace to survive economically and politically. Naturally, educational philosophies change over time as events and personalities emerge and affect thinking and living.

3.1d The Values Behind Education

Philosophy matters. Americans place great faith in education because it prepares individuals to live as responsible and productive citizens in a democratic republic, and it extends our country's cherished values into the future. At their best, public schools are the "great equalizer," bringing together students of diverse backgrounds and giving them a common American heritage and the knowledge and skills to negotiate the larger society. Indeed, schools have been the agency of Americanization for generations of immigrants. Likewise, a solid education can overcome limitations on students imposed by their background, creating opportunities for social and economic mobility. These beliefs and values underlie American schools.

Clearly, education is not a mechanical or neutral act. Rather, it is a value-laden process that influences the direction, knowledge, and nature of the students' learning experiences. Through a philosophy of education, or logical systematic point of view, a school, district, state, or nation selects which information and skills students will learn and how they will learn them. A philosophy of education provides answers about *why* one does things. Learning *why* to do something is an essential first step before teachers can learn *how* to do it. Educational philosophy offers the frame of reference that guides and makes sense of all other educational decisions. It provides a rationale and justification for making choices about curriculum, instruction, assessment, and student–teacher relationships.

3.1e Educational Foundations and Future Teachers

Educational foundations coursework has the potential to give prospective teachers the ability to make sense of pedagogy and policy decisions within the larger social context. It helps future teachers understand the ideologies and values that shape and inform their future school districts' actions as well as their own teaching choices. Effective foundations experiences encourage teacher education students to consider their personal values and determine how they want to relate to others and how the educational concepts they choose reflect these perspectives.

As such, educational philosophy offers an essential conceptual base for future teachers. A philosophy of education allows current and future practitioners to apply informed systematic approaches to making decisions in schools. It also highlights larger issues in the complex relationship between schools and society.

At the same time, understanding their own educational philosophy and being able to better express their beliefs and values can help future educators relate to those who view the world differently. Listening closely to others' views and speaking thoughtfully about the teacher's own educational philosophy can help defuse tensions among those who care about improving schools but who bring different perspectives and value sets to the discussion.

When looking at educational philosophies, it is tempting to oversimplify the arguments and define clear-cut "either–or" categories. The "traditional" educational philosophy versus the "progressive" educational philosophy, for instance, pits one set of ideas against a different set of ideas. To draw either–or comparisons between educational philosophies, however, would be imprecise and incorrect. In the real world, differences exist within each category as well as between the various categories. As so often happens with ideas in the real world, the process of drawing distinctions between philosophies is not always neat and orderly.

The following pages discuss four major perspectives on educational philosophy that have influenced—and continue to influence—the way people view and practice American education. The classical and contemporary educational philosophies affect the ways people today think about schools. Understanding these educational philosophies will make prospective teachers more knowledgeable educational consumers and reflective practitioners.

3.2 KEY IDEAS OF TRADITIONAL PHILOSOPHY OF EDUCATION

Conservative traditionalists adapt educational beliefs and practices extending back to ancient Greece and the Middle Ages. The **liberal arts** vision of education believes that mastering the academic disciplines—mathematics, logic, philosophy, sciences, history, literature, and the arts—characterizes the educated person. Students pursue liberal studies to develop both their intellectual and moral excellence.

Traditional educational philosophies reflect two educational approaches. **Perennialists** focus on teaching what they view as universal truths through the Western civilization's classics. **Essentialists** prefer to select those subjects from the Western tradition that would be most relevant to the current student generation. Both are considered to be teacher- or subject-centered philosophies. Table 3.1 compares the key ideas of these two traditional approaches that continue to influence contemporary U.S. education.

TABLE 3.1 ■ Traditional Philosophies' Conceptual Features: Perennialist and Essentialist

Key Ideas	Perennialist	Essentialist
Learning is teacher and subject centered. The teacher and the text are the classroom's central focuses.	X	X
Western European civilization provides the core curriculum. This store of knowledge carries the accumulated "universal and eternal truths" and virtues that all students need to develop their minds and live productive lives.	X	X
Schools' purposes are to preserve and transmit this common cultural knowledge and to develop students' minds. Teachers and curriculum socialize students into society's essential dimensions of truth, beauty, values, and wisdom taught in a systematic, disciplined manner to help students learn to think rationally and critically.	X	X
Educators select the knowledge and skills deemed most important ("essential") to help students function successfully in a particular time and society.		X
Educators work with the community to identify essential knowledge and skills.		X
The purpose of school is to prepare students for further education and work.		X

Source: Leslie S. Kaplan and William A. Owings [Original by authors].

3.2a The Essentialist Philosophy of Education

Both conservative in tradition, essentialists and perennialists view the Western classics and Western thought as the canon in which American children should be educated. The two approaches differ, however, in how they use the classics. As noted in Box 3.1, perennialists think students should learn the classics as timeless truths that are able to guide contemporary reasoning and life. Essentialists, in contrast, want to select from the Western classics those most suitable to adaptability and usefulness in contemporary life. Box 3.2 highlights essentialists' conceptual features. Because essentialists adapt the classic liberal arts curriculum to meet more contemporary societal demands, they are sometimes called pragmatic traditionalists. The essentialist curriculum largely underlies today's U.S. public schools' curriculum.

3.2b The Essentialist Curriculum

Over time, society has found that certain skills—such as reading, writing, mathematics, and, most recently, digital literacy—are essential for people to function effectively in their world. Core knowledge subjects include reading, writing, math, science, history, foreign language, and technology. Both perennialists and essentialists share a basic commitment to train the intellect through subject-centered knowledge. Their differences revolve around what they consider to be most worth knowing.

Essentialist thinking has its roots in the *mental discipline learning doctrine* of early American schooling, which suggested that studying certain rigorous academic subjects strengthens the student's mind and character. According to the essentialist perspective, schools' focus should be subject centered, academic, and cognitive. Curriculum is a logically organized sequence of separate and academic disciplines, consisting of increasingly difficult topics, such as one would see in a high school or college course handbook. Students experience highly structured study in language and grammar, mathematics, sciences, history, and foreign languages. This subject matter lays the intellectual foundation necessary for students to understand and function successfully within their society's shared culture.

Essentialists believe that every student needs this general education to succeed in life in our democratic society. To deny this course of study to any student, essentialists argue, would be inequitable, regardless of that student's ability, interest, or career direction. In their view, one curriculum fits all. The subject matter itself is the important variable, just as it would be for a perennialist.

At the height of essentialism's popularity, essentialist concerns were more nationalistic than democratic. During the Cold War (i.e., the latter half of the 20th century), essentialists saw their discipline-centered academic education as a shield protecting the United States against the Soviet Union's imperialistic intentions. The Soviets' 1957 launch of the *Sputnik* satellite humiliated the United States, which had fully expected to be first nation into space. Some blamed the Americans' public education system for not producing enough sufficiently talented scientists and engineers to propel the United States into outer space ahead of its adversary.

In addition, the controversial report *A Nation at Risk* (1983) concluded that U.S. children lagged behind other nations' achievement level in basic subjects. American students were not mastering the basics in reading, writing, math, science, and technology to the level that would enable the United States to compete successfully internationally. Public schools needed to improve their teaching and improve students' skills in these areas, the report's authors concluded. Wide support for the "back-to-basics" curriculum followed.

The essentialist curriculum emphasizes subject-centered learning to build reasoning skills, character, and shared culture.

iStock/fstop123

Educators responded by developing a more intellectually demanding curriculum. The math, sciences, and reasoning skills fostered in the essentialist curriculum, proponents claimed, would produce the scientists, engineers, and technology workers who would defend and protect the United States from outside threats. Students' intellectual training became a critical weapon of national defense. To this day, most American high schools continue to rely on an essentialist curriculum.

3.2c Essentialist Instruction

The national security panic about public schools' failings led in two directions. First, students would have to study the core subjects in greater depth and with more application to real situations. Second, essentialist schools would be strictly academic learning centers. Teachers and administrators expect students to leave their emotional or behavioral concerns behind. Nonacademic activities interfere with schools' primary purpose, so schools' aim does not include remedying these types of problems in students' lives.

Instructionally, this means an increase in inquiry teaching strategies to enhance thinking, reasoning, and problem-solving by schools' high achievers. Classroom practices tend to rely on lecture, recitation, discussion, demonstration, question and answer, and competency-based assessments to determine student mastery of subjects. Drill and practice are also commonly employed learning strategies.

Essentialist teachers use a variety of learning materials to make sure that students learn the content. Typically, students learn from listening to teacher lectures, talking in response to teachers' questions, watching demonstrations, and taking notes rather than from engaging in firsthand exploration of the content. They demonstrate their learning of content and skills on achievement tests, teacher made and standardized.

3.2d The Essentialist Teacher's Role

In the essentialist classroom, teachers transmit cultural and community-valued knowledge and expect students to learn it (see Table 3.2). To be successful, teachers must know their subjects very well. They organize the curriculum into a series of topics and teach in sequence, progressing from less complex to more complex ideas and skills through successive grade levels. The teacher's role is to engage students in mastering the content and manipulating it with high-level thinking, reasoning, questioning, evaluating, and problem-solving. In addition, teachers show students that clear standards and criteria exist for judging literature, music, poetry, and art; and they show students how to evaluate and assess these works.

As intellectually satisfying as the essentialist classroom might be for teachers of high-achieving students, helping more slowly achieving students learn rigorous content can be less exciting. Slower-learning students typically spend more classroom time recognizing and comprehending the basic material through lecture, drill, and practice, while their faster-learning peers devote more time to extending their understanding and competency of the material through discussion of concepts and supporting details, analysis, evaluation, synthesis, and creative problem-solving.

TABLE 3.2 ■ Essentialists' Conceptual Features Summary
Ideal of learner: Learners develop a rational mind capable of critical thinking by studying the core academic disciplines of Western thought.
Ideal of subject matter: Teachers present a strictly academic and discipline-centered curriculum selected for its relevance for today and its respect for yesterday that strengthens students' mental powers and celebrates the Enlightenment's traditional values.
Ideal of school: School is a rational, organized place that transmits important cultural knowledge and skills to students.
Ideal of society: Our American society is a democratic republic that depends on a common or shared core of academic knowledge to build societal cohesion.

Source: Leslie S. Kaplan and William A. Owings [Original by authors].

3.2e A Contemporary Essentialist Educator: E. D. Hirsch Jr.

Educators in the mid-1950s and 1960s focused on teaching students specific academic disciplines needed to ensure our national defense and to create responsible citizens for a democratic republic. But by the late 1980s, educators had returned to the idea of general, less rigorous essentialist education.

Spurred to action by what they saw as a lax approach to teaching and learning, essentialists identified two factors that had been neglected in youths' education in the previous decades. First, schools were not effectively training students' minds. Second, students were failing to gain the cultural background knowledge—that is, the shared vocabulary and information—they needed to develop a common national identity and participate fully in their culture. E. D. Hirsch Jr. proposed a remedy for this situation: bringing the academic disciplines back to the curriculum's center.

Eric Donald Hirsch, Jr.

Eric Donald Hirsch Jr. (born 1928) is an American educator and literary critic. He is the originator and chair of the Core Knowledge Foundation and professor emeritus of education and humanities at the University of Virginia. A former English professor and literary critic, Hirsch recalls being "shocked into education reform" while researching written composition. During these studies, he noticed that a student's ability to comprehend a passage was determined partly by its relative readability but even more by the student's background knowledge.[2] This insight led him to develop his concept of **cultural literacy**—the belief that reading comprehension depends on formal decoding skills, a wide vocabulary, and on far-ranging background knowledge that literate writers and speakers assume their audiences already share. It is cultural literacy that gives educated persons access to opportunities in the larger society.

Recently, Hirsch suggested that over the past 60 years, changes in the early elementary curriculum have contributed to the "decline of communal sentiment... [u]nder the banner of "Teach the child not the subject!" with a stress on skills rather than content.[3] Similarly, schools' neglect of factual knowledge, including American history and its civil underpinnings, with a general distaste for "rote learning," has led to a decline in Americans' common knowledge base. In Hirsch's view, this has weakened students' ability to read and communicate, diluted feelings of patriotism, and left many Americans with less sense that they are "all in the same boat" with Americans of other races, ethnicities, and political persuasions. The result: Many Americans feel a sense of loss, disunity, and belonging with the larger society that propels them into more narrow "tribes" of those just like themselves. This situation threatens to undermine our sense of community and national unity needed for psychological, public, and societal harmony.

Hirsch proposes a coherent, national common-core knowledge curriculum that begins in the early grades and includes the basic principles of constitutional government and civics; important events of world history; essential elements of math and oral and written expression; masterpieces of art and music; and stories and poems passed down through the generations. He asserts that general factual knowledge is a vital part of learning and suggests that schools should measure this learning with high-stakes standardized tests based on specific nationwide educational standards.

Further, Hirsch sees access to a very good school and a high-quality curriculum as an equity issue, a civil right that promotes social justice. High-quality curriculum is especially important for economically disadvantaged children whose families cannot provide the same extensive vocabulary and knowledge—the "cultural capital"—that more privileged children have available when they enter school. In fact, Hirsch asserts that starting in the early grades, teaching a high-quality curriculum—with its vocabulary and related background knowledge—to every student would raise verbal achievement and reduce both the achievement gap and the equity (fairness) gap.[4] To not teach all students the high-status curriculum hurts their chances of economic, social, and cultural advancement—limiting the social mobility that is the touchstone of American public education.

In Hirsch's view, if we are to increase our compatriots' sense of belonging and national solidarity, increasingly, schools' "responsibilities must [also] include teaching the national public culture to all and encouraging loyalty to the national community and to its best ideals."[5]

Criticism of Hirsch's Ideas

Hirsch's educational ideas have been controversial. Some critics note that Hirsch may be wrong in decrying that schools don't teach core knowledge. The reality may be that this content is routinely *taught* (but not well) but is *not learned*. Others criticize him as a conservative advocate for a "lily-white" curriculum, a promoter of "drill and kill" pedagogy, and a reactionary force. Some challenge his view of educational history as skewed. By emphasizing content, critics claim, Hirsch underestimates the importance of pedagogy—that is, good teaching practices. Some assert that Hirsch views schooling as simply **transmission of meaning**: Teachers hold knowledge in their heads, and their job is to transmit it in the most efficient way into students' heads. Frequently, critics add, Hirsch's approach leads to whole-class instruction, telling, and rote memorization as the most effective means for accomplishing this transmission.[6] The **Reflect & Engage** activity—Essentialist Education—offers a deeper exploration of Hirsch's ideas and their implications for teaching and learning.

REFLECT & ENGAGE: ESSENTIALIST EDUCATION

E. D. Hirsch believes that all school children should have rigorous, demanding academic learning in a core curriculum. He disagrees with Americans who think that children shouldn't be asked to do difficult things with their brains while they are young, rejecting the view, "Let them play now; they'll study at the university."

In groups of four, discuss the following questions:

A. Hirsch writes that American schools have operated on the assumption that challenging children academically is unnatural for them. Do you agree? What examples can you cite to support your opinion?

B. Hirsch believes that giving all students the "cultural capital" necessary to succeed in a highly competitive, information-based economy is a "civil right." Do you agree or disagree? If you agree, how can schools provide the "cultural capital" to students whose families cannot provide it? If you disagree, how can our society avoid ending opportunities for meritocracy and social mobility?

C. As a student, what would you have liked and disliked if your teachers had used Hirsch's educational approach and curriculum?

D. Discuss current examples that support Hirsch's view that schools no longer provide a shared knowledge base in American history and our civic underpinnings, contributing to a sense of loss, disunity, and belonging with the larger society and the implications for societal harmony.

Source: Hirsch, E. D., Jr. (1996). *The schools we need and why we don't have them.* Doubleday.

AMERICAN EDUCATION SPOTLIGHT: DIANE RAVITCH

"For years, people would say to me, 'Well, I don't agree with everything you write,' and I would think, 'Thanks a lot, that's some compliment.' But now I say, 'Well, I don't agree with everything I write, so why should you?'... I think the hardest thing is just to say you've made a mistake."*

Diane Ravitch (1938–), research professor of education at New York University and senior fellow at the Brookings Institution, has become a champion among public school teachers in what they see as a governmental and business assault on their profession.

An 83-year-old grandmother, education historian, and education policy activist, Ravitch is a native of Houston, the third of eight children, and a public schools graduate. She received a BA from Wellesley College in 1960. Married soon after college, Ravitch had two children and became a housewife. At 32, she returned to graduate school and earned a PhD in History of American Education from Columbia University. A highly respected voice in the profession, Ravitch has written education histories, champions the need for a strong and balanced curriculum, and promotes the idea of voluntary state and national curriculum standards. She is the author or editor of over 20 books—most recently, *Left Back: A Century of Failed School Reforms* (2020).**

Considered an essentialist in her advocacy for a rigorous, coherent national curriculum, Ravitch *had been* a visible and vocal promoter of standardized testing, accountability, charter schools, voucher programs, and evaluating teachers based on their students' test scores. Ravitch served as an education official for President George H. W. Bush, and President Bill Clinton appointed her to the National Assessment Governing Board, which oversees federal testing. She left government service in 1993.

Over time, Ravitch became disillusioned with the strategies that once seemed so promising. Since 2004, she has renounced her earlier positions and is now looking for solutions that she believes are compatible with schooling for democracy.

Briefly, her current education views include these:

- *Standardized testing*: Outcomes of high-stakes testing often compromise education by lowering standards, narrowing the curriculum, "gaming the system", teaching to tests, and cheating. Emphasizing accountability that relies on testing basic skills guarantees that students will have less time for science, history, the arts, or foreign language, those very subjects that encourage creativity, innovation, and imagination.
- *Curriculum*: Teachers should rely less on textbooks as curriculum. Texts have been so highly censored, sanitized, and homogenized by politicized pressure groups that they make students bored and cynical. Students need a curriculum that allows them to engage with controversy, see the bad and good in world events, and gain a broader, richer perspective.
- *Charter schools*: The overwhelming majority of high-quality research studies on charters show that some are excellent, some are awful, and most are no better than public schools. Charters should not be for profit; they should be answerable to students and parents, not stockholders, and public charters should help students with the highest needs.
- *Corporate-driven reforms*: Public schools are not a business. "Venture philanthropy" such as the Broad Foundation or the Bill and Melinda Gates Foundation—which begin with a strategy or reform idea and give schools the money to do it—are using their money to control public policy without accountability.
- *Poverty and education:* Poverty impacts academic achievement, and our society must both improve schools and reduce poverty. We must invest in parental education, prenatal care, and preschool to make sure that children arrive in school well nourished, healthy, and ready to learn.

Critics of Ravitch's ideas say that apart from her calls for better curriculum, child health care, and increased funding for early education, she does not offer clear alternative solutions for education policy makers; and she ignores the complexity of school accountability policy. Others attack her for changing her position.

Ravitch concludes that there is no single answer to educational improvement. She argues that our schools need experienced and well-respected teachers and principals. Students need to learn the subjects that prepare them for the duties of citizenship. After all, isn't the primary purpose of public education to sustain our democracy?

Notes:

*Schultz, K. (2010, May 17). Diane Ravitch on being wrong. *Slate*. https://slate.com/news-and-politics/2010/05/diane-ravitch-on-being-wrong.html; **Ravitch, D. (2020). *Left back: A century of failed schools reforms.* Simon & Schuster.

Sources: Ballotpedia. (2019). Diane Ravitch. https://ballotpedia.org/Diane_Ravitch; Phillip, A. (2011, August 1). Ravitch rallies teachers vs. "astroturf." *Politico*. http://www.politico.com/news/stories/0711/60279.html; Ravitch, D. (2011, July 1). Invitation to a dialogue: Fixing the schools. *The New York Times*. https://www.politico.com/story/2011/07/ravitch-rallies-teachers-vs-astroturf-060279; Ravitch, D. (2010, March 9). Why I changed my mind about school reform. *The Wall Street Journal*. https://www.wsj.com/articles/SB10001424052748704869304575109443305343962;

Ravitch, D. (2011, May 31). Waiting for a school miracle. The New York Times. https://www.nytimes.com/2011/06/01/opinion/01ravitch.html; Rizga, L. K. (2011, May 16). The education of Diane Ravitch. *Mother Jones*. http://motherjones.com/politics/2011/03/diane-ravitch?page=2; Rotherham, A. J. (2010, March 17). Is education on the wrong track? *The New Republic*. https://newrepublic.com/article/73944/education-the-wrong-track-5; Wattenberg, B. (2003, June 13). The language police/Textbook PC. PBS. *Think tank with Ben Wattenberg*. http://www.pbs.org/thinktank/transcript1116.html

3.3 THE PROGRESSIVE PHILOSOPHY OF EDUCATION

Just as the conservative traditionalists seek to preserve and transmit a core culture through schools, adherents to the progressive educational philosophy aim to change the society and culture. A relatively contemporary perspective, **progressive** is defined as moving forward, ongoing, advancing; a person who favors or strives for reform in politics, education, or other fields. Likewise, **progressive education** is an educational reform movement that focused on educating the "whole child"—intellectual, physical, and emotional—begun as a reaction to the alleged narrowness and formalism of traditional education.

The term "progressive" arose from a period (roughly 1890–1920) during which time many Americans took a critical look at the political and social effects of vast concentrations of corporate power and private wealth. From the inception of their movement, progressives argued that state systems of public schooling have primarily tried to achieve cultural uniformity, not diversity. The schools' goal, they proposed, should be to educate reasoning—not passive—citizens. Progressivism consistently rejected the traditional teacher-centered, curriculum-centered education in favor of a more student-centered approach. From the 1920s to the 1940s, progressive education had become the standard practice in the U.S. public school classrooms.

Briefly stated, the **progressive philosophy** of education views students—rather than content—as education's focus. In this perspective, education's purpose is to prepare students to be lifelong learners in an ever-changing democratic society.

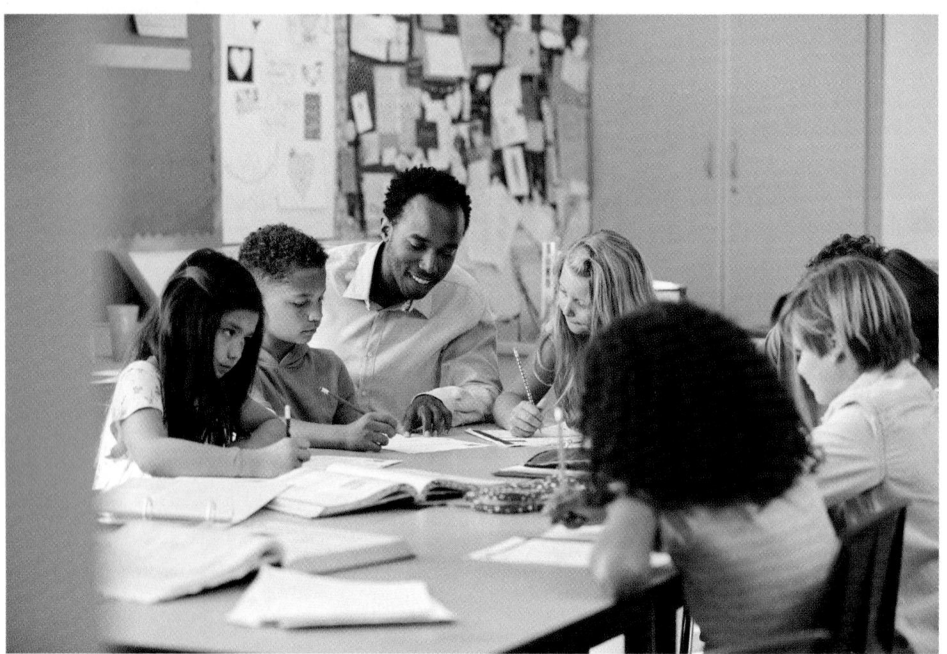

Progressive educators focus on both student and curriculum.

iStock/monkeybusinessimages

As a movement, progressive education incorporated a variety of viewpoints and practices. Educational progressives were pluralistic and often self-contradictory, yet always closely tied to broader currents of social and political progressivism. In this section, we first discuss the general progressive philosophy. Next, we review John Dewey's approach. Later, we will investigate the critical theory, a radical contemporary offshoot of progressive philosophy.

3.3a Key Ideas of Progressivism

During most of the 20th century, progressive educators shared the belief that representative democracy means active participation by all citizens in social, political, and economic decisions that will affect their lives. This progressive approach contrasted with the U.S. educational model that prevailed in the early 1900s, which used a traditional curriculum with classroom methods based in **social efficiency**—that is, an emphasis on classroom control, management, obedience to authority, and a structured curriculum that focused on memorization and rote skills. (Chapter 5 discusses American education in the early 20th century in fuller detail.)

3.3b The Progressive Curriculum

Progressives believe that because learning is a natural response to students' curiosity and their need to solve problems, students' interests and desire to seek solutions should guide the curriculum (see Table 3.3). Accordingly, the progressive curriculum focuses on adapting the program of study to students' needs—academic, social, and physical. The formal written curriculum is interdisciplinary, reflecting knowledge as it appears in the real world. The teacher, the student, and the curriculum need to work together to find the best fit to promote the most learning.

In addition, progressives believe that although the past produced great ideas and thoughts, knowledge and social environments constantly change. Given this dynamic nature, reliance on a classical Western—or any—tradition of thought would quickly lead to an outdated curriculum. The students' job is to learn how to learn so they can cope successfully with new life challenges and discover relevant truths in the present. Learning how to learn and making learning personally meaningful to students are more important than transmitting a set body of once-valued knowledge to students.

TABLE 3.3 ■ Progressive Educators' Key Ideas
Education should be child centered. Each individual should be free to develop naturally. Students' interests should guide teaching. Debate exists on the extent to which a school should encourage children to freely develop these potentialities.
Schools are a means of social reform and improvement. A child-centered school is the best guarantee that the larger society will be truly devoted to human worth and excellence.
Education's purpose is to create engaged citizens for a democratic republic. Schools create small communities in which students and teachers show respect for one another and work together in mutually beneficial ways.
Educators should respect diversity. They should recognize each individual for his or her own abilities, interests, ideas, needs, and cultural identity, as well as encourage students to be independent thinkers and creative beings.
Students are whole people. Developing the whole student—physically, mentally, socially, and morally—is essential for the student's intellectual and personal growth.
Teachers should motivate learning. In this role, they should serve as guides, not taskmasters.
Schools and homes should cooperate to meet students' needs. Parents are children's first educators and should work with schools to help children learn.

Source: Leslie S. Kaplan and William A. Owings [Original by authors].

3.3c Progressive Instruction

Progressives believe that education's aim is to prepare students for life. For this reason, they suggest, instruction should begin with concrete, real-world objects rather than abstract concepts. Teachers show young children how to observe, describe, classify, assess, and eventually generalize what they see and touch. Older children's education includes the traditional curriculum, but it is taught in an interdisciplinary fashion. Teachers help students learn appropriate moral behavior by connecting students' acts with natural consequences. Because bodily health is essential to cognitive health, teachers also encourage students in physical play and activity. In these ways, teachers provide the range of knowledge and skills that will enable people to adapt more readily to their circumstances.[7]

Progressive teachers engage students in inquiries or investigations that the students develop themselves. Students learn from one another in cooperative learning groups. This approach fosters both intellectual and social learning. In the progressive classroom, the teacher becomes a facilitator, a resource person, and a co-inquirer. Through students' own investigations, they continuously develop new and deeper understandings. Students learn in a hands-on, minds-on, interactive classroom.

3.3d The Progressive Teacher's Role

From the beginning, progressive approaches placed high demands on teachers' knowledge, time, and ability. Teachers must know their subjects inside and out to integrate them with related disciplines and, at the same time, connect them to students' social, physical, and cultural environments. Teachers must be lifelong learners so they can continually introduce students to new scientific, technological, literary, and artistic developments to illustrate that knowledge is constantly changing. Similarly, teachers need a repertoire of effective instructional skills and an extensive array of teaching materials to accommodate students' preferred ways of learning.

In addition, teachers should get to know their students very deeply as individuals and as learners, looking for opportunities to connect students to content through these learner-centered (personal and background knowledge) factors. Because students' needs have academic, social, and physical aspects, teachers must design learning activities to have children interact with one another around the content in cognitive, social, hands-on, and minds-on ways.

3.3e Progressive Education Critics

In the hands of first-rate instructors, progressive innovations were highly successful. In the hands of average teachers, however, they led to bedlam. Done poorly, progressive education could be worse for children's learning than the formalism it sought to replace.

Some progressive advocates greatly expanded this perspective's child-centered focus. In doing so, they unwittingly turned progressive education into a gross and anti-intellectual caricature, quickly and inaccurately popularized as "the child controlling the classroom." As a result, in too many classrooms, "license began to pass for liberty, planlessness for spontaneity, and chaos for education."[8] Many viewed the progressive approach in public schools as "dumbing down America's youth."[9] Phrases such as "whole child" and "creative self-expression" became clichés, too vague to serve as useful guides to constructive or rigorous educational practice.

Critics also claimed that progressive educators were trying to "re-engineer society along collectivist lines by eliminating competition and independent thought from schools."[10] Because progressive educators appeared to be "replacing systematic and sequential learning" with "activities,"[11] a few even attacked progressive educators as Communists.[12] By the mid-1950s, the progressive movement had lost its central influence on school practice, and it eventually disintegrated as an identifiable educational movement.

3.3f Enduring Progressive Contributions

Despite the controversy over certain educational practices enacted under the progressive umbrella, by the end of World War II much progressive philosophy had become conventional wisdom. Education policy discussions routinely included phrases such as "recognizing individual differences," personality development," "the whole child," "social and emotional growth," "the learners' needs," "intrinsic motivation," "discovery learning," "bridging the gap between home and school," and "teaching children, not subjects." Many aspects of progressive education simply had become accepted as good education.

In the late 20th and early 21st centuries, various educational groups rediscovered and revised progressive beliefs and practices to address the changing needs of schools, children, and society. Open classrooms, schools without walls, cooperative learning, multiage approaches, whole language, the social–emotional curriculum, experiential education, and numerous forms of alternative schools all have important philosophical roots in progressive education. The progressive philosophy offers hopeful alternatives to the one-size-fits-all curriculum and assessments and the mechanized school organization that characterize today's schools. Table 3.4 highlights progressive education philosophy's key features.

TABLE 3.4 ■ Progressivism's Conceptual Features Summary

Ideal of the learner: The student is a whole person with cognitive, emotional, social, and physical needs central to learning to use his or her mind well and interact effectively with others.

Ideal of the subject matter: Interdisciplinary, problem-focused, inquiry-based learning in a real-life context and using real-world resources enables students to learn to use their minds well and see education as relevant to their real world.

Ideal of the school: A small community teaches the cognitive and interpersonal skills necessary for all students to live an American democratic life.

Ideal of the society: A democratic society is made up of caring, responsible, interacting, intelligent citizens respecting each other and working for the common good.

Source: Leslie S. Kaplan and William A. Owings [Original by authors].

3.3g A Notable Progressive Educator: John Dewey

In the 1920s and 1930s, John Dewey (1859–1952), a philosopher and educator, became one of the key figures in the progressive education movement. Considered an American pragmatist (pragmatism was a very influential philosophy during his time), Dewey inspired but did not lead the progressive education movement. In fact, over time he became one of the movement's most vocal critics. Through his writings and laboratory work at the University of Chicago, Dewey tested and refined his ideas about how to best help students learn. Chapter 5 discusses Dewey's broad influence on 20th century education.

John Dewey's View of Education

To John Dewey, education's aim was ultimately to make human beings who would live life to the fullest, continually add to the meaning of their experiences, and increase their abilities to direct their lives. Educated students had both personal initiative and adaptability and were able to control (or at least influence) their surroundings, rather than simply adjust to them. Likewise, Dewey saw intelligence as the purposive reorganization, through action, of actual world-based experience.[13]

Dewey believed:

- *Each student is unique*, both genetically and experientially.[14] Children have their own cognitive, emotional, social, and physical differences and growth rates. Even when teachers present a standard curriculum using established pedagogical methods, each student will respond uniquely to the experience. Thus, teaching and curriculum must be designed in ways that allow for such individual differences if all students are to learn effectively.
- *Education must serve a broader social purpose.* Education must help people become more effective members of a democratic society. Democracy, for Dewey, is more than just a form of government; it incorporates all of the associated living and shared experiences. Students practice successful democratic citizenship through their classroom behaviors. Schools that place students in the center of active, meaningful, shared learning can become levers of social change.
- *Teaching practices must be democratic.* Dewey argued that authoritarian schools' one-way delivery style, from teachers to students, does not provide a good model for life in democratic society. Instead, students need educational experiences that will enable them to become valued, equal, self-directed, and responsible citizens.
- *Students' experiences affect their learning.* People do not experience one common reality. Instead, each person experiences his or her own reality, depending on his or her previous experiences; these experiences, in turn, influence the individual's perceptions and actions in the present situation.

- *Curriculum includes real-world experiences.* Each school is an embryonic community, alive with the various types of occupations that reflect the larger society. Through interaction, students learn the spirit of service and the capacity for self-direction. Increasing the number of student viewpoints, their number of shared interests, their freer interactions, and mutual adjustments will eventually create a more democratic society.
- *Schooling is life, not preparation for life.* Learning's outcome is behavior. Schooling is a means to improve students' thinking, skills, capacities, democratic interactions, and eventually to improve society.
- *Curriculum integrates culture and vocation.* Curriculum should be both egalitarian and democratic, always stressing use of the mind and applying learning to real-world situations.

Defining a Balance

Dewey rejected the idea that traditional liberal arts curriculum was the only education students needed. He also challenged the age-old separation between culture and vocation. For centuries, "culture" and higher social standing had meant possessing certain kinds of knowledge associated with wealth, leisure, and theory—as opposed to poverty, labor, and practice. In Dewey's view, the traditional curriculum was thoroughly useful to statesmen, professionals, and intellectuals, but it was largely irrelevant for most other persons. Dewey, therefore, rejected it as both exclusive and inequitable.

Dewey did not simply discard the traditional subject matter but rather sought to balance it with teaching that accounted for the principles of children's growth and development, children's needs and interests, and preferred ways of learning at different ages. Schools became "child centered" to the extent that teachers tailored the curriculum and instruction to facilitate the child's learning in concert with the individual student's development. This "child-centered" curriculum considered the child's physical, intellectual, and emotional growth as these forces interacted with the curriculum. In this context, the curriculum's role was seen as developing children's own capacities and intelligence and nurturing children's own thinking rather than simply transmitting knowledge and facts. Dewey's educational vision included was "both–and," not "either–or."

When following Dewey's approach, teachers designed learning experiences for students that would provide data for students' observations, reflections, meaning creation, and learning. The resulting curriculum was both hands-on and minds-on. The younger the students, the more concrete and hands-on the curriculum. As a result, the curriculum was largely interdisciplinary, problem focused, and inquiry based, and it connected students to the real world outside the classroom.

Dewey believed in three types of subject matter:

- The active pursuit of occupations, such as carpentry, sewing, or cooking
- Studies dealing with the background of social life, such as history and geography
- Studies that provided command of the forms and methods of intellectual communication and inquiry, such as reading, grammar, and arithmetic

Generally, this curriculum moved from the concrete, which was immediately knowable by physical experience, to the social, which focused on a more abstract interpersonal knowing, to intellectual abstraction and reasoning.

The Importance of Teaching and Learning

The child-centered approach contrasted in key ways with the traditional "teacher-centered" classroom. In teacher-centered classrooms, the teacher transmitted skills, facts, and values largely through lecturing and seatwork. Teachers talked. Students listened and took notes. Thus, knowledge was transferred from teacher to students; the direction went one way, with teachers determining the subjects, standards, and methods of teaching. Children's participation in deciding on learning processes and purposes was minimal; their task was to receive and retain the information and through practice (usually rote memorization) and to master the information and skills.

By comparison, in a "child-centered" classroom, the teacher considered both the individual children's needs and the prescribed curriculum. Therefore, the teacher's role changed from transmitter of the official curriculum to facilitator of student learning. Teachers now designed and enacted ways to connect students to content through activities that made sense and had meaning *to the learners*. In addition, they encouraged student collaboration in real-world problem-solving with learned content to build deeper understanding through analysis, synthesis, evaluation, and application of what they learned in practical and creative ways. At the same time, teachers helped students work collaboratively to increase their interpersonal skills. This knowledge and skill base, Dewey thought, would best prepare students to live responsibly in a democratic society.

Dewey believed that teachers needed thorough knowledge of two arenas: subjects and students. First, teachers needed a deep and wide knowledge of their academic disciplines. They needed to understand how to connect their subject content to the meaningful themes and related disciplines that students studied. Second, teachers needed a strong awareness of those common childhood experiences that they could use to lead children toward understandings that the knowledge represented. Making this connection successfully required teachers to know sufficient detailed information about children's physical, cognitive, psychological, and social growth and development.

Beyond the Paradigm War

Progressive education accommodated a substantial variety of curricula and teaching approaches. Although many people identify John Dewey with progressive education, throughout the 1920s he became less the progressive education movement's interpreter and synthesizer and more its prime critic.

Dewey saw traditional educational philosophy and progressive education philosophy as representing two extremes in the education paradigm. On one side, the traditional philosophy encouraged a relatively structured, disciplined, ordered, didactic, teacher-directed education; on the other side, the progressive philosophy advanced a relatively unstructured, highly flexible, student-directed education. Although each approach might have some merit, neither approach alone could be successful.

In Dewey's view, the traditional education brought a constructive structure and order to learning, although it lacked a holistic understanding of students. Further, the traditional approach led to design of a curriculum that was too focused on content and not enough on how teachers could help diverse students learn it. Dewey suggested that teachers must consider both the subject and the learners' needs it if they were to make a positive difference in their students' lives.

Similarly, Dewey argued that progressive education misapplied freedom. He disapproved of completely "student-driven" education. He recognized that students often did not know how to structure their own learning experiences for maximum benefit. Many progressive teachers did not sufficiently direct or constrain students. All too often, they provided freedom without really knowing how or why freedom could be most useful to promote student learning. They used the superficial trappings of progressive philosophy while missing its central core. Freedom, without structure and focus, was not the answer.

Dewey proposed that education move beyond this "paradigm war" and seek first to understand the nature of human experience. Learning needed structure *and* awareness of how children learned—both–and, not either–or. Learning should be based on a clear theory of experience, not simply teachers' or students' whims.

Discarding the traditional versus progressive paradigm, Dewey suggested that American education follow a middle ground. According to him, teachers need content knowledge along with strong attention to students' subjective experiences, present and past. Education needs a systematic organization of activities and subject matter for students to become knowing and thinking individuals. Furthermore, education becomes scientific, Dewey observed, only as teachers attempt to be more intelligent about their goals and practices used to achieve these ends.

In Dewey's view, schooling's goal was to develop an educated person, able to reason effectively, act creatively, behave responsibly within a democratic society, adapt when necessary, initiate and control when possible, and continue lifelong learning.

3.3h Reconciling Traditional and Progressive Viewpoints

For more than 100 years, the pendulum has continued to swing between traditional and progressive educational approaches. One approach takes hold, influences school programs, and inevitably has some glaring failings in its outlook and implementation. Then, its opponents reject the approach and substitute its opposite. A while later, the cycle repeats itself, exasperating educators, policy makers, and teachers while confusing students, parents, and the general public.

Good intentions are one of the teaching profession's strengths. Both traditionalists and progressives continue to offer educational theories based on sincere positive aims. Both viewpoints have cadres of dedicated and enthusiastic supporters. Yet no evidence exists that good intentions increase learning beyond a basic level.

Clearly frustrated by the tug of war over American educational philosophy, Stanley Pogrow, education professor at San Francisco State University, writes, "Pure traditionalists are brain dead. Pure progressives live in a fairy-tale land. And while good intentions are better than bad intentions, relying primarily on their power is not effective."[15] Likewise, as the late writer Michael Crichton, author of *State of Fear*, has observed, the combination of good intentions and bad information is "a prescription for disaster."[16]

In reality, both traditional and progressive approaches have strengths and weaknesses. Each philosophy supplies an important piece of the puzzle in our quest to create better schools. Although these two educational philosophies appear at loggerheads, they are, in fact, complementary. As David B. Ackerman, a former school superintendent and curriculum administrator observes, "They are intertwined taproots of our professional outlook, the warp and woof of the fabric of beliefs that guide us when we walk into a classroom."[17] In their extreme versions, however, neither approach works. In their reasonable versions, one approach will not work without the other.

The problem comes when influential groups seeking to establish their philosophical (and political) dominance take their ideas to illogical extremes. Educators and policy makers all too often use exaggerated rhetoric as a means to capture the most followers. As Dewey and others observed, both extremist traditional and progressive positions are mistaken on how teaching and learning occur for most students. The vast majority of students do not function or learn best in a purely structured or purely unstructured approach. Meanwhile, the current research cannot smooth out the pendulums' oscillations. The traditional and progressive educational philosophies' lasting insights appear in Table 3.5.[18]

TABLE 3.5 ■ Enduring and Valid Insights From Traditional and Progressive Philosophies
Traditionalists:
• **Teach students what is of deepest value.** Choose texts that will help young people understand and appreciate the best of the world's thoughts and words as they relate to truth, beauty, goodness, meaning, and pleasure. Choose content that will lift students beyond themselves, thereby creating a sensibility and vision of a thoughtful and well-lived life.
• **Teach with rigor.** Tactfully insist that students and teachers engage with challenging materials and express their thoughts clearly to open minds and better express ideas.
• **Uphold standards of excellence.** Hold students' work to high standards to promote real achievement.
• **Use instructional time in meaningful ways.** Lecture is not inherently "bad," and cooperative learning is not inherently "good." In the time available, identify and use the pedagogical pathways most likely to lead all students to the most learning.
• **Acknowledge that discipline-based knowledge is the firm foundation for any transdisciplinary learning.** Subject disciplines provide important essential information about the nature of human beings and the world, as well as powerful, indispensable perspectives and tools of inquiry. Content knowledge is a necessary (but not a sufficient) condition for learning.

Progressives:

- **Children are whole people.** Students have intellectual, psychological, and social characteristics that affect how well they learn.
- **One standard does not fit all.** Standards of excellence are absolute, but individual students' performance standards may not reach them at a particular time. We teach individual students, not categories of them.
- **A child's mind is not a receptacle.** Meaning is not inert. Students need to think actively about what they have seen, heard, or read and relate it to prior knowledge and experience so they may create sense and meaning from it, comprehend it, and learn it. They need to be minds-on.
- **Children bring their unique beliefs and attitudes into the classroom.** Teachers must consider these existing assets as part of students' learning experiences and use them to facilitate new learning.
- **Students find holistic knowledge more meaningful.** Teachers need to help students make disciplinary knowledge personally germane by connecting information fragments into a coherent, relevant, and harmonious set of lenses—tied to prior knowledge or experiences—for understanding the world.

Source: Leslie S. Kaplan and William A. Owings [Original by authors].

An educational philosophy that takes the best of both traditional and progressive approaches values both the teacher and the student having an engaged mind during the learning process. It provides a strong disciplinary focus as well as knowledge integration. It understands the values and limitations of both content "depth" and "coverage" and balances the necessary tradeoffs. It uses student ability grouping—and ungrouping—when appropriate to the learning tasks at hand. It evaluates students on their progress toward achieving personal excellence as they grow toward meeting standards of measurable excellence.

In this way, prospective teachers can find the positive aspects in varied educational philosophies. It is not necessary to take each approach as absolute and extreme. Rather, it is important to acknowledge that each can make a positive contribution in the classroom. Although existential and critical theory approaches do not routinely appear in American public schools, they offer perspectives that can give teachers more choices about ways to make learning more attainable and meaningful for our diverse students.

To more fully understand how John Dewey's ideas about teaching and learning influence yours, complete the activity in the **Reflect & Engage box,** John Dewey and Progressive Education.

REFLECT & ENGAGE: JOHN DEWEY AND PROGRESSIVE EDUCATION

John Dewey believed that education's ultimate goal was to make human beings who had initiative, adaptability, and good citizenship continually add to the meaning of their experience and increase their abilities to direct their own lives.

A. After reading Dewey's beliefs about what education should be, work in pairs to identify which aspects you would want to include in your own teaching practice and why.

B. Explain the value of having a "hands-on" and "minds-on" education. To what extent was your preK–12 education hands-on and minds-on? To what extent is your university education hands-on and minds-on? What percentage of each do you think would create your optimal education for a young learner, for a secondary student, and for a college student?

C. Regroup as a class and discuss how you see the traditional and progressive approaches to education—in their nonextreme versions—able to reinforce each other to strengthen teaching and learning. Which specific approaches would work best in your teacher education program?

3.4 EXISTENTIAL PHILOSOPHY OF EDUCATION

As a philosophy, existentialism represents both the desperation and the hope inherent in modern living. An **existential philosophy of education** is a viewpoint in which curriculum and instruction encourage deep personal reflection on one's identity, commitments, and choices. Its approach is cognitive, affective, and highly individual.

3.4a Key Ideas of Existential Philosophy of Education

Existentialism is a relatively modern philosophy that became prominent after World War II. Its roots, however, trace back to the Bible. As a philosophy relevant to today's education, one may date its modern influences to the 19th century European philosopher Søren Kierkegaard (1813–1855). More recently, philosophers advocating this approach include Martin Buber (1878–1965), Karl Jaspers (1883–1969), Jean Paul Sartre (1905–1986), and the more contemporary educator, Maxine Greene (1917–2014).

Existentialist philosophy reacts against two factors. First, it rejects the conservative education tradition that respects only the Western classics and shows little regard for the individual. Second, it recoils from the horrors of World War II and the Holocaust as vivid examples of a world gone mad. Instead of the world's chaos, **existentialism** focuses on the existence of the individual and individual responsibility. Existentialists believe that people must create themselves by shaping their own meaning and choices. The key ideas associated with this perspective appear in Table 3.6.

TABLE 3.6 ■ Existentialism's Key Ideas
The world is chaotic, producing anxiety and hurt. People free themselves from this disorder through heightened awareness and making choices.
People are responsible for defining themselves through their choices. Although people may not be able to control events, they can control their responses to these events. Accordingly, they create personal meaning and value through the decisions they make and the knowledge they wish to possess.
People's most significant realities are personal and nonscientific. Although people live in a world of physical realities and have developed scientific and useful knowledge about these realities, their subjective experiences are the ones most meaningful to them.
Education's most important goal is to awaken human consciousness to the human condition and to the freedom to choose and create the personal self-awareness that helps make each person authentic, genuine, and unique.
Education should focus on both cognitive and affective dimensions. Both aspects are necessary if an individual is to become a fulfilled whole person.

Source: Leslie S. Kaplan and William A. Owings [Original by authors].

Existentialism rejects any source of allegedly objective, authoritative truth about the world. Instead, existentialists emphasize that people are responsible for defining themselves. The only "truth" is the "truth" that the individual determines is true. Therefore, individuals create their own realities—and themselves—through the choices they make. To exist is to choose. According to existentialists, people have two options. They can either define themselves or have others define them. Humans always face the threat of people, institutions, and agencies imposing an artificial truth on them and restricting their individual freedom. Existentialists believe that individuals are in a constant state of becoming, creating chaos or order, creating good or evil. Each person has the potential for loving, producing, and being an inner-directed, authentic person. An authentic person recognizes this freedom and knows that every choice is an act of personal value creation.

Education, say existentialists, should focus on individuals' cognitive and affective needs, stressing students' individuality. It should include topics about the rational and irrational world and the anxiety that conflict generates. In this way, education can give individuals the cognitive and emotional tools they need to liberate themselves from the world's disorder and absurdity. By studying aspects of literature, history, science, and the arts and learning how to think and communicate about them effectively, young people gain the power to make choices and create meaning in their lives.

3.4b Existential Versus Traditional Views on Education

Existentialists and traditionalists view the world and education very differently. Existentialists reject the traditionalists' views about the primacy of Western classics as the source of universal virtue and wisdom. To existentialists, one curriculum does not fit all. Instead, existentialists see each student as a separate individual needing a highly personalized education. Whereas traditionalists see the world as stable and able to benefit from unchanging truths, existentialists see the world as unstable and indifferent to human wishes. Individuals, however, have the responsibility to impose a meaning and order on the world. Death is the only given.

3.4c The Existentialist Curriculum

Existentialists believe that the great thinkers of the past had their own ways of considering life and the natural world, and they developed their own conclusions. Likewise, today's students need to find their own ways of thinking about these issues and make up their own minds. To this end, the existential curriculum is heavily geared toward the humanities.

The humanities provide students with vicarious experiences that will help them better understand the world and respond to it with their own imagination and self-expression. For example, rather than emphasizing historical events, existentialists focus on historical figures' actions, which serve as possible models for students' own behaviors. In deference to the humanities, the existentialist curriculum may deemphasize math and the natural sciences, presumably because their subject matter would be considered "cold," "dry," "objective," and, therefore, less useful to increasing students' self-awareness.

Literature, especially biography, plays an important role in an existentialist classroom. Drama and movies also provide ample material to illuminate the human condition. Because these media re-create the author's experiences, thoughts, emotions, and images around profound life issues, they depict conditions in which individuals make choices. This learning increases readers' levels of awareness.

Art in essentialist classrooms helps students learn about self-expression, meaning, and options.

iStock/skynesher

What is more, art, drama, and music encourage personal interaction with the content. From an early age, children in existentialist classrooms receive exposure to life's problems and possibilities, humanity's horrors and accomplishments. In such contexts, students can better learn about their own personal preferences and values that anchor future choices. Similarly, existentialist educators regard vocational education as a method of teaching students about themselves, enabling them to recognize their own potential rather than as a means for earning a livelihood.

In the existential classroom, students create their own means of self-expression. They learn to freely employ language and artistic media to clarify and communicate their emotions, thoughts, and insights. Using educational technology and multimedia enhances students' range of self-expression, encouraging personal creativity and imagination rather than copying and imitating established models. In these classrooms, students write plays, create graphic images, produce films, and craft poems to identify and express their own voices.

In the existentialist classroom, subject matter takes second place to helping students understand and appreciate themselves as unique individuals who accept complete responsibility for their thoughts, feelings, and actions. The existentialist curriculum is a means to an end, not an end in itself, as traditionalist educators would have it. Instead, teachers and schools offer the topics they consider appropriate for students at each grade level to study. From these subjects, students make personal decisions and select what they need to study. Because every student is different, no single set of learning outcomes is appropriate for all students. Likewise, because feeling is not divorced from reason in decision-making, the existentialist expects the school to educate the whole person—mental, emotional, social, and physical.

Although many existentialist educators provide some curricular structure, existentialism—more than other educational philosophies—affords students an extensive variety of curricular options from which to pick. As a result, students are actively involved in a range of different topics and activities at the same time. For instance, in one classroom, several students may watch a video of Martin Luther King Jr.'s "I Have a Dream" speech, two or three may listen on headphones to Abraham Lincoln's Gettysburg Address, several students may dissect a frog, others may read books, and a few others may draw pictures of the human skeletal system. The teacher moves from group to group, working to help advance students' understandings, furthering their investigations, asking questions to prompt their thinking, challenge their conclusions, and refine their products.

3.4d The Existentialist Teacher's Role

Existentialists believe that both teachers and students should have opportunities to ask questions, suggest answers, and participate in dialogue about humanity's important issues—namely, life, love, and death. An existentialist teacher encourages students to philosophize, question, and discuss life's meaning, using whatever curriculum engages students in that dialogue. Since the answers to these questions are often personal and subjective, they are not measurable by standardized tests.

As a resourceful guide and facilitator, the teacher's role is to help students define their own essence by exposing them to various paths they may take in life. To do so, teachers create an environment in which students may freely choose their own preferred way. Teachers work with each student to help him or her find appropriate materials and the best study methods to address the student's interests. In this kind of classroom, the teacher is a resource—along with other students, books, classical masterpieces, contemporary works, the internet, television, newspapers, magazines, and other people.

Obviously, existentialist educators reject the standards movement, opposing the imposition of one common curriculum and the use of standardized testing as a way to measure academic success. Rather, they see this movement as a trend away from individuality, personal choice, and freedom, and toward conformity and loss of freedom.

Additionally, teachers in an existentialist classroom face demands on their own affective and cognitive dimensions. When teaching under the existentialist umbrella, teachers need to understand their own personal lives and the values and beliefs they have constructed from their personal experiences. Without this personal experience, introspection, and reflection, they cannot help their students make sense and reasonable choices in their own lives. Likewise, teachers need to be able to take intellectual and emotional risks to open their thinking and feelings to students, to let students know them as reasoning and experiencing individuals. Such intimate sharing helps students become awake to the possibilities within themselves in their own worlds. In this role, teaching is intensely personal and carries significant responsibility because the line between the teachers' personal and professional behaviors is notably more fluid than in a traditional classroom.

3.4e Existential Instruction

Existentialist classrooms are open learning environments. Instruction is largely self-directed and self-paced and includes a great deal of individual contact with the teacher. Existentialist methods focus on the individual. Because each student has a different set of background experiences, unique learning style, and different learning topic, the teacher's main job is to discover what works for each student and then provide the student with the necessary resources and unobtrusive guidance to let learning happen.

In this kind of environment, instruction is frequently informal and highly interpersonal. The teacher relates to each student openly and honestly. In an intense relationship with each one, the teacher helps every pupil understand the world by posing questions, generating activities, and working together. Martin Buber, an existential philosopher, wrote about an "I–thou" approach, in which a student and teacher learn cooperatively from each other in a nontraditional, nonthreatening "friendship."[19]

3.4f A Notable Existentialist Educator: Maxine Greene

Maxine Greene, whom *The New York Times* described as "one of the most important education philosophers of the past 50 years,"[20] a professor emeritus of philosophy and education at Teachers College, Columbia University, was an influential contemporary existentialist educator. In her view, "creative thinking and robust imagining" were the foundations to both a person's lifelong learning and to a democratic society's flourishing, a way for students to engage the world as it might be.[21] Her philosophy sees education as a process of awakening diverse persons, enabling them to develop their talents and work with one another. With her belief in the intersection of the arts with social action, Greene saw educated persons' common goal as bringing a better and more just social order and more meaningful way of being in the world into existence.

Greene saw education's goals as helping students to realize their deep responsibility for themselves and recognize their connections to other human beings who share this world. Learning's purpose, in her view, is to nurture students' intellectual talents so they can construct a more democratic, just, and caring society. Citizens must be well informed and have the educational abilities and sensitivities needed to critically examine our world.

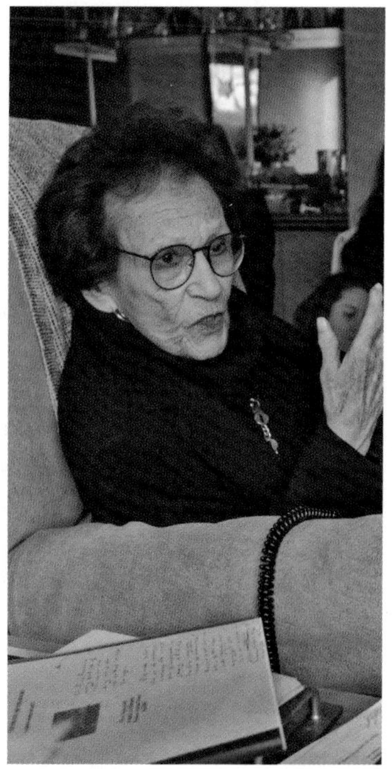
The late Maxine Greene, an advocate for existential education.

Associated Press

In today's hyperconnected, fast-paced environment, finding a calm, optimistic, personal space can be difficult. Technology makes everyone's pain and society's violence instantly visible to anyone with a TV, internet hookup, or smartphone. As a result, the current world is a challenging place to live and to teach children to have a positive outlook. For these reasons, Greene believes in an education that stresses self-defining, choosing, and acting responsibly.

Greene put her beliefs into action. The Maxine Greene Foundation for Social Imagination, the Arts, and Education awards as much as $10,000 to everyday educators who are capable of inventiveness and who go "beyond the standardized and ordinary."[22] The Foundation also supports artists whose works embody new social visions and individuals who radically challenge or alter the public's imagination around social policy issues.

Greene mourned that many schools have become "boot camps run by drill sergeants."[23] She wrote, "We should realize that we are in a very inhospitable environment.... Imagination is given a very small place in the way people talk about learning today, but it is a way to go beyond, to break through boundaries."[24] She saw teachers as intellectuals working with ideas, not merely testing students for memorized facts. Likewise, she sees the existential classroom as being rich in humanities and the arts and staffed by caring, aware teachers; in these refuges from unsafe external realities, teachers help students find occasions for constructive possibilities.

Greene expected teachers to create communities in their classrooms. Students and teachers listen carefully to one another as they try to make sense of others' and their own experiences, learning how to respect their individual differences. With their teachers' support, students integrate their responses to these experiences into their intellectual and emotional growth and their quests for decency and social justice.

Table 3.7 highlights the essential features of existential education philosophy.

TABLE 3.7 ■ Existentialism's Conceptual Features Summary

Ideal of learner: A learner is a unique individual who discovers his or her identity, makes choices, creates his or her own meaning, and brings order to the world's chaos.
Ideal of subject matter: The humanities bring opportunities for students to explore life's heights and depths and to develop personal insights to inform future choices.
Ideal of school: Schools create an environment for individuals to learn how to define self and create meaning for their life choices in a disorderly world.
 **Ideal of society:** The world is chaotic and absurd, and individuals must decide who they are and how they wish to respond to events in their lives. The ideal society would be composed of such unique, authentic, knowledgeable, and responsible individuals.

Source: Leslie S. Kaplan and William A. Owings [Original by authors].

3.4g Criticism of Existential Philosophy in Schools

Existentialism is a highly individualistic philosophy with educational implications. Although elements of existentialism occasionally appear in public schools, this perspective has found wider acceptance in private schools and in some alternative public schools founded in the late 1960s and early 1970s. To be effective as an educational approach, existential philosophy requires a smaller, more homogeneous school environment where students have family backgrounds rich in learning experiences before and during their school years so they do not need to spend much time mastering basic skills, developing the "appropriate" social behaviors, or building the "**cultural capital**"—the accumulation of knowledge, behaviors, and skills that demonstrate one's competence and status in society—needed to succeed in life. As Chester E. Finn Jr., an advocate of rigorous educational standards, asserts, "You can't structure a policy regimen for any kind of large education system around those artistic, romantic ideas."[25]

To consider how the existential philosophy of education shapes your own ideas about teaching and learning, complete the activity in the **Reflect & Engage** box, Existential Philosophy of Education.

REFLECT & ENGAGE: EXISTENTIAL PHILOSOPHY OF EDUCATION

The existential philosophy of education is highly individualized and rooted in the humanities. Its goal is for students as individuals to develop the thinking and affective skills for self-definition, self-expression, and the capacity to impose a meaning and order on their world. Discuss answers to the following questions with a partner:

A. After reading about the existential curriculum and teaching practices, what do you think you might have gained from being a student in a preK–12 existential educational experience? What do you think you might have missed?

B. What aspects of teaching in a school with an existential philosophy do you think you would most enjoy? Which aspects do you think you would find most frustrating?

C. Explain what Maxine Greene meant by saying that one educational goal is to help individuals find their calm, optimistic, personal space. Why would this be important to learning? Where do you find yours?

D. Reassemble as a class and debate the benefits and limitations of an existential philosophy of education in practice. Which students would likely benefit, and which would lose ground? Explain.

3.5 THE CRITICAL THEORY PHILOSOPHY OF EDUCATION

Critical theory is a social philosophy oriented toward using education to increase human freedom from domination by our society's social, economic, and political elites.

The progressive education movement led to the development of a more radical offshoot in the 1930s, known as **social reconstruction**. These progressive educators looked to schools for leadership in creating a new and more equitable society than the one that had given birth to the Great Depression. As a consequence, social reconstructionists advocated for serious societal reform. Critical theory developed from this progressive offshoot.[26]

Critical theory is well known within the education mainstream, and its development revitalized the debate about democratic schooling in this country.[27] The late 1970s saw a reaction to the conservative movement of the 1950s and 1960s, which sought to strengthen public schools' liberal arts and sciences curricula. Working independently, a group of American scholars began to critique public schooling. They saw public school as an arena for ideological struggle with a *hidden curriculum*—the unwritten, unofficial, and often unintended lessons, norms, values, and viewpoints that students learn in school—and socialization for capitalistic needs that neglects issues of class, race, and gender that create large societal inequities.

3.5a Key Ideas of Critical Theory

Critical theorists reject schools' transmission of traditional mainstream culture and values as indoctrination. They see schools' traditional purpose as a way for the wealthy and powerful in our culture to convince most people that their privileged interests are also society's interests. As a result, these influential persons shape our schools by making their curriculum our "official knowledge."[28]

Critical theorists believe that students from less privileged socioeconomic backgrounds begin school with unequal opportunities. These limitations, they argue, can be removed only by changing the society's political and economic systems (see Table 3.8). Critical theorists would change both schools and the society that makes and keeps people unequal.

Critical theory suggests that schools can sow the seeds of societal transformation. Peter McLaren, Michael W. Apple, and Henry Giroux, for example, see schools' potential for serving as a positive fulcrum for social justice.[29] As presently organized, public schools simply replicate and reinforce the status quo, including its inequities and undemocratic practices. Sounding the call for pedagogical empowerment, these critical theorists see teachers' role as helping students make sense of and engage the world around them. When necessary, teachers should help students change the world for the better. In this way, schools can become the agents that raise children to question and challenge their society's

TABLE 3.8 ■ Critical Theory's Key Ideas

Education is values based. Education, rather than pursuing child development or human achievement in a norms-free vacuum, revolves around the particular culture's values.
Education involves types of imposition and indoctrination. Because education has its roots in both culture and values, the real question is not whether imposition and indoctrination of students will take place, but rather from which source it will come.
Education represents a political activity. Education involves degrees and types of imposition and indoctrination that follow the ruling groups' and classes' wishes.
Teachers engage in political activity. Teachers' "political activity" usually occurs without conscious awareness of their work's political nature. They are not teaching an objective "truth," but rather the social elites' values. Teachers need to respond to the genuine interests of people other than the upper-middle class and upper class who use schools to keep their power by reproducing the status quo (and reinforcing their places in it).
 **Teachers should work for social justice.** Teachers can help students critique the status quo and unequal power relations and work for social justice in their society. Schools can transform society.

Source: Leslie S. Kaplan and William A. Owings [Original by authors].

constraints and failings. When students learn how to push against the status quo's "fit," they will be well prepared to improve their communities and the nation as a whole. Thus, adoption of the critical theory perspective raises educators' consciousness beyond the classroom and schoolyard to consider broader social and cultural concerns.

3.5b Critical Theory Curriculum

A curriculum based on critical theory is designed around contemporary social life rather than traditional academic disciplines. It includes whatever will help a culture to evolve, change, and solve real problems.

A critical theory curriculum has several organizing ideas. First, it views culture as a product of power relations. Next, it helps students investigate issues of inequality in their own environments and encourages them to take constructive action against those conditions. It conceptualizes culture and identity as complex and dynamic, and it considers all cultures to be integral parts of the curriculum.

In addition, a curriculum based on critical theory organizes studies that incorporate students' backgrounds, preferred ways of learning, and prior experiences. It purposely uses schools as laboratories to prepare students to participate actively in a democratic society and become change agents in their culture. Lastly, such a curriculum creates an environment that celebrates diversity, and it teaches students to build coalitions and develop cooperative learning strategies.[30]

To accomplish these goals, the critical theory curriculum integrates all traditional subjects into single-theme, interdisciplinary units. By interacting with this highly relevant, contemporary, and interdisciplinary academic content and its societal context, teachers can help their students understand current social problems' validity and urgency. With teachers' guidance, students decide which problems to study and which educational objectives they want to reach.

For example, a mathematics lesson on "sweatshop accounting" could help students look closely at profit distribution for shoes and clothes in different areas of the world. The class might receive sets of data to extract and analyze what the price of a brand-name shoe represents and determine the relative salaries going to the shoemaking workers, retail store owners, and marketing spokespersons.[31] Similarly, a social studies class could consider the world's distribution of wealth, where cookies represent wealth and students are assigned to different continents. Some continents would receive more cookies than others, and students can eat what they have been given. When one or two students receive many cookies apiece at the same time as other students must share only a few, the obvious unfairness becomes apparent.[32] Likewise, issues such as equal justice under law, terrorism, poverty, inequality, racism, and homelessness might all become relevant topics for class study.

Working together, the teacher and students explore the issues at hand, suggest alternative viewpoints for fuller understanding, analyze the topic, and form conclusions. Throughout this endeavor, the teacher models the democratic process, listening carefully and respecting diverse viewpoints.

Curriculum materials may come from a variety of sources inside and outside the school. Students can learn through internships, work–study programs, and other cooperative relationships with the community and outside resources.

3.5c Critical Theory Instruction

Critical theorists believe that students learn through a cultural context and participation in a democratic process. Key elements of this type of learning include use of a problem-based framework and cooperative investigation. As exemplified by the "sweatshop accounting" case, students learn that history is influenced by past and present cultural, social, and political environments; gather and analyze relevant data; and use their findings to inform their decision-making. Along the way, students acquire skills and knowledge as they continually interact among the curricular content, their school, and key persons in their community.

Similar to what happens in an existentialist classroom, students in a critical theory-based classroom engage in many different activities to study the agreed-upon topic. Teachers guide and facilitate them to learn the scientific method—observe, ask a question, research the topic, experiment or test, gather data, assess, draw conclusions, and report findings. This inquiry approach applies not just to physics, chemistry, or biology, but to the whole of life, including students' personal and social lives.

For example, one math lesson grew out of student-raised real-life concerns about how fast the middle school was growing. The school district's lack of space forced the school to occupy the top floor of an older building with a leaky roof. The student body doubled in size, from 100 to 200 students. After the terrorist attacks on September 11, 2001, the students worried about being trapped in a fire and stampeded in an emergency. Their teacher organized them into groups and challenged them to use math to make their case for more school space.

A critical theory curriculum helps students identify and solve real problems in their communities.
iStock/franckreporter

After taking measurements, comparing their school with one in a more affluent neighborhood, and collecting and analyzing data, the sixth graders compiled their findings and presented their report to the school advisory council, which reported directly to the school board.[33]

Critical theory recommends use of a variety of instructional methods, including simulations, demonstrations, group research, reports, analysis of current issues, reading, guest speakers, small-group discussion, field trips, interviews, internships, and essay writing. In addition, students can conduct internet research, read case histories, analyze multiple aspects of the topic, formulate predictions, propose and justify revisions and solutions, and act to implement these solutions.

3.5d The Critical Theory Teacher's Role

Critical theory sees teachers as change agents and the classroom as a site for political action. Critical theorists encourage teachers to empower themselves by conducting a challenging review of their school's purpose, its curriculum content and organization, and the teaching profession's role and mission. Critical theorists recommend that teachers take responsibility for shaping their own futures and for helping students shape their own lives and the world in which they will live.

To make this happen, critical theorists believe that teachers need greater self-awareness regarding their political role in maintaining the existing governmental and social power structure. Teachers must understand how a society constructs knowledge from various positions if they are to understand how to create equitable and culturally responsive teaching strategies. Remember, "history is written by the victors,"[34] not grounded in facts but in their interpretation by those with the societal and political power to declare it so.

In this regard, many U.S. teachers may be at a significant disadvantage. Critical theorists claim that because most prospective teachers are heterosexual white women from European American, middle-class backgrounds, they may not immediately recognize the unique ways in which their racially privileged, class-dominant, gender-oriented (either an advantage or disadvantage), and heterosexually-oriented positions influence their teaching. How they teach shapes how their students view and experience the world—specifically, it encourages students to adopt the teacher's own perspective.

The task of teacher preparation programs, critical theorists argue, is to awaken prospective teachers' awareness of the same oppression that they might potentially reinforce in their classrooms. This process can be very difficult, and even threatening, to undergraduates who are still forming their collegiate and young adult identities—and to their professors who espouse a different philosophical orientation. In fact, every individual's identity has multiple aspects that must be considered: A person can be a son or a daughter; male or female or gender non-conforming; brother or sister; white, Black, Latinx, Asian, or mixed race; thin or stout; marathon runner or homebody. Each individual has more than one persona; reality is complex. We discuss this concept of *intersectionality* more fully in Chapter 8. To emphasize only one of these aspects of self, instead of recognizing and accepting them all, critical theorists claim, leads to cognitive dissonance. Likewise, valuing teaching the common beliefs and heritage that all Americans share—and at the same time criticizing how different power groups in our society create persistent inequities among families and children—can lead to cognitive dissonance. Rather than pick one view over the other, a mature mind may be able to accept the reality that both views contain aspects that may be true.

3.5e A Notable Critical Theory Educator: Henry Giroux

Henry A. Giroux, an American and Canadian professor at McMaster University in Ontario, Canada, offers a clear definition of the public schools as a battleground of political ideas. With a thorough understanding of public school education from life experiences as a teacher and intellectual experiences as a scholar, Giroux developed a **critical pedagogy**, an instructional perspective whose purpose is to transform teachers, schools, and society into agents for social justice. Giroux clearly articulates his views about critical pedagogy (see Table 3.9).

Ultimately, Giroux says public schools need to rethink their purpose. Educators should abandon the long-held assumption that school credentials provide the best route to economic security and class mobility. In his view, the U.S. economy has experienced long-term stagnation with real incomes declining for low- and middle-income groups. Instead of training students for specific labor tasks, teachers should facilitate students in thinking differently about the meaning for work and prepare

Henry Giroux

Maya Sabados, Secretary. Reprinted with permission from Henry Giroux.

TABLE 3.9 ■ Henry Giroux's Critical Pedagogy's Central Ideas

Struggling for democracy is both a political and educational task. Education must be treated as a public good. More than a place to benefit individual students, schools are crucial sites where students gain a public voice and come to understand their own power as individual and societal agents. Giroux believes that incorporating different groups' experiences and voices into the curriculum and having students reflect on these perspectives help build a democratic community.[35]

Teaching is a political activity. Teaching is not objective and value neutral. Instead, teachers are cultural producers who are deeply implicated in public issues. If public schools' purpose is to indoctrinate students into preserving the society and political power structure as they are,[36] teachers must become transformative intellectuals, helping students identify where their society's power is located and how the power structure communicates its ideology and values. Educators should teach "students how to think in ways that cultivate the capacity for judgment essential for the exercise of power and responsibility by a democratic citizenry," expanding the possibilities of a democratic society and social transformation.[37]

Ethics is a central concern of critical pedagogy. Knowledge has ethical value. Education is more than just "economic capital" necessary to get a job. Education should be about self-definition, social responsibility, and individuals' capacities to expand the range of freedom, justice, and democratic practices. Without an ethical perspective, students cannot see a society's ideology as being deeply implicated in individuals' struggles for identity, culture, power, and history. Nor can knowledge without ethics help teachers and students push against the oppressive boundaries of gender, class, race, and age domination.

The curriculum should include diverse student voices. The curriculum should expand beyond the Western European tradition. In 1940, 70% of new U.S. immigrants came from Europe. In 1992, by comparison, only 15% came from Europe, while 44% came from Latin America, and 37% came from Asia.[38] The "melting pot" metaphor, in which schools "Americanize" all newcomers to accept traditional Western thought and values, no longer works for such a diverse population with multiple narratives, cultural myths and beliefs, and ready access to worldwide communications media and travel. Schools need to adopt a multicultural curriculum to accommodate their more diverse populations.

Critical pedagogy should be politically transformative. Knowledge is not just to *learn*; it is to *use* to make the world better and more democratic. Students need to understand how the curriculum presents different viewpoints, voices, and identities; how these relate to historical and social forces; and how they can be used as the basis for change. In addition, teachers and students need to analytically address issues related to life in a vastly more globalized, high-tech, and racially diverse world than has existed at any other time in history.[39]

An interdisciplinary curriculum permits students to consider important social issues. Although the traditional curriculum does contain some content useful for the critical theory classroom, the curriculum best suited to developing critical reflection among students and the community is interdisciplinary in scope and recognizes that knowledge is partisan and culturally determined. It should examine the hidden examples of power in everyday life.[40] Giroux believes that reading the liberal curriculum as popular culture rather than viewing it as an immutable canon or great narrative could be useful.

Source: Leslie S. Kaplan and William A. Owings [Original by authors].

them to demonstrate the skills and attitudes necessary to hold multiple jobs over the course of a career. Achieving this goal will require a curriculum characterized by new forms of literacy, vastly expanded understanding of how power works within a culture, and an appreciation for how the mass media play a decisive role in constructing multiple and diverse social identities.[41] Table 3.10 summarizes critical theory's philosophy of education.

TABLE 3.10 ■ Critical Theory's Conceptual Features Summary

Ideal of learner: A learner is a liberated individual seeking genuine meaning and identity in a diverse and complex world.

Ideal of subject matter: Knowledge is understood in relation to its connection to the society's dominant ideology and power structure.

Ideal of school: Public school is an agency of societal transformation to provide more economic and political equality in a democratic society.

Ideal of society: An ideal society is one in which individuals and groups find identity, understanding, and meaning in an unjust world and work to improve it.

Source: Leslie S. Kaplan and William A. Owings [Original by authors].

FLIPSIDES

Essentialist or Critical Theory:

Which Philosophy of Education Should Guide Today's Schools?

American public schools should keep essentialist tradition to guide curriculum and instruction.	American public schools should use a critical theory approach to guide curriculum and instruction.
• The essentialist philosophy underlies the current U.S. public school curriculum. Schools' purposes should continue to transmit and preserve the common Western (European) culture and knowledge.	• The critical theory philosophy is well-known within education mainstream. Incorporating different groups' experiences and voices into the curriculum and having students reflect on these perspectives help build a democratic community.
• Schools should provide students with the intellectual training required for thinking, reasoning, and problem-solving to prepare them for further education and work.	• Schools should provide students with the intellectual, reasoning, problem-solving, self-definition, and social responsibility skills to prepare them for further education, multiple jobs over a career, and to make their society more equitable and fairer.
• Learning is a subject-centered, intellectually demanding academic curriculum that builds knowledge and moral character necessary for life in a democratic society.	• Learning is a values-based, political activity that occurs within a specific culture; public schools should respond to the genuine interests regarding class, gender, and race—rather than only to upper-middle and upper-class interests.
• The teacher and the text should be the classroom's main focus.	• The teacher should use the curriculum beyond the text to work for social justice, helping students understand and critique the status quo and challenge unequal power relationships.
• Teachers' role is to engage students in high-level thinking, reasoning, questioning, evaluating, problem-solving, and meeting clear academic standards.	• In addition to the cognitive goals, teachers' role is to become change agents who guide students to work cooperatively and use their knowledge and skills to constructively improve their environments.
• Curriculum should strictly emphasize Western European civilization, which is most suitable to adaptability and usefulness to contemporary life.	• Curriculum should include all cultures and diverse students' voices, using highly relevant, contemporary, single-theme interdisciplinary units organized around contemporary social life rather than academic disciplines.
• Dominant instructional practices should include lecture, discussion, demonstration, question-and-answer recitation, drill and practice, students researching and writing reports, making oral presentations, and completing assessments.	• Dominant instructional practices should include identifying and solving problems, collaborative study, research, respecting alternative viewpoints, analyzing topics, making informed conclusions, and taking informed actions to solve problems and develop personal agency.
• Modes of student engagements should include listening, reading, talking, watching, practicing, report writing, making oral presentations, and test taking.	• Modes of student engagement should include cooperative investigations of contemporary problems and helping them take informed action against inequalities in their own environment.

American public schools should keep essentialist tradition to guide curriculum and instruction.	American public schools should use a critical theory approach to guide curriculum and instruction.
• Educators work with the community to identify essential knowledge and skills to teach students.	• Educators work with the community to provide students with actual problems to solve, feedback on student-proposed solutions, and internships and work-study programs using outside resources.
• Criticism of essentialist education concludes that it is too Eurocentric; it leaves slower-learning students behind in achievement; and its strictly academic approach excludes students' nonacademic needs.	• Criticism of critical theory education is that it undermines the status quo in school, community, nation; it has little empirical research supporting its benefits to student learning; and it has little connection of theory to practice.

Which philosophical approach to curriculum and instruction do you believe is best for 21st century American public school students? How might a teacher incorporate strengths from each approach into the classroom?

3.5f Criticism of Critical Theory in Schools

Like other educational viewpoints, critical theory has its opponents. First, according to many of these detractors, critical theory education writers use a language that is difficult to understand; this makes it challenging to clearly comprehend what they are saying and use it for changing public schools. Second, critical theories usually avoid using empirical research methods to study schools. As a consequence, they have much to say but little evidence to back it up. Finally, critical theories of education often fail to connect theory to practice in ways that practitioners can find meaningful or useful.

To explore how critical theory influences your own views about teaching and learning, complete the activity in the **Reflect & Engage** box, Critical Theory.

REFLECT & ENGAGE: CRITICAL THEORY

Critical theorists would change both schools and society that make and keep people unequal. Teachers' role is to help students to challenge, make sense of, and engage constructively with the world around them. Work with a partner to answer the following questions:

A. Describe any aspects of critical theory philosophy that you saw or experienced in your preK–12 education. If you did not see it, why do you think this is so?

B. Explain the reasons why a community or national groups might favor a critical theory philosophy of education. What reasons might a community or group reject them?

C. What aspects of critical theory do you think you might want to use as a teacher? Which aspects would you not want to use? Explain.

D. Reassemble as a class to debate the benefits and limitations of critical theory philosophy of education in practice. Which students might benefit? Which students might not?

3.6 REFLECTIONS ON THE FOUR EDUCATIONAL PHILOSOPHIES

Educational philosophies construct a lens through which a teacher filters ideas about education's purpose, teaching and learning in way that guides their professional practice.

Not all educational philosophies have equal respect and standing in today's public schools or policy circles. Yet any philosophy may have some merit. Where educational philosophy seeks to improve a classroom, it must offer insight into the learner, the subject matter, and the society. If taken to illogical extremes, however, no educational philosophy can support all students' learning. In addition, philosophies that seek to overturn the prevailing culture are not well received by those who stand to lose their influence and social, economic, or political power under the new schema. Given this context, four perspectives inform the educational philosophy that governs today's public schools: traditional, progressive, existential, and critical theory.

Traditional views are deeply subject centered, anchored in the psychology of mental discipline and the purpose of transmitting the Western European culture through knowledge of the time-honored academic subjects. Through an academically rigorous curriculum, essentialists attempt to build a common set of knowledge, understandings, and loyalty among diverse students to a shared American society.

Progressives—in many varieties—focus less on the strict academic disciplines and mental exercises and rely more on relating the subject content to the learners' prior knowledge (experiences) and needs. Though instructionally geared toward how children learn developmentally, ideally, the curriculum is academically rigorous. Teachers seek to teach the knowledge, skills, competencies, and attitudes children need to lead an intelligent, reasoning, and economically sustainable life in a pluralistic democratic society. Part of this approach entails applying the scientific method to social thinking.

Existentialists stress the importance of individuals' choices in creating their identity, values, and personal meaning from the world around them. Teachers and students develop close emotional and intellectual bonds that enable teachers to guide students' learning in directions the student wants to go. Because they facilitate self-awareness and self-expression, the humanities and arts form the basic curriculum. And because this approach is so highly individualized, it is not widely used in today's public schools.

Lastly, critical theorists see public schooling as a political activity. By using a relevant and varied curriculum and engaging in intellectual inquiry, teachers have the power to challenge the inequitable power bases inherent in schools' curriculum and society's structure. Teachers can use students' cognitive growth and problem-solving skills in social action to build their efficacy to radically improve our society as a whole. They can also give diverse students a voice in selecting what to learn.

To begin developing your own philosophy of education by considering aspects you value in essentialist, progressive, existential, and critical theories, complete the activity in the **Reflect & Engage** box, Your Emerging Philosophy of Education.

REFLECT & ENGAGE: YOUR EMERGING PHILOSOPHY OF EDUCATION

After reading about the four major philosophies of education, identity the components you would want to include in yours.

A. Think about your emerging philosophy of education for several minutes. Jot down words or phrases that you believe important to describe it. From which philosophies are you taking ideas? Which philosophies are you ignoring?

B. Individually, create a mind map using a digital tool such as Bubbl to illustrate your emerging philosophy of education and its intellectual "roots."

C. In groups of four, share your mind maps and discuss the components of your emerging philosophy of education and their intellectual "roots."

D. Reassemble as a class and discuss your findings. Which philosophies of education seem to be the most—and least—popular among members of this class? How did this chapter inform (or not) your ideas about philosophy of education? How does your educational philosophy provide a rationale and justification for making choices about curriculum, instruction, assessment, and student–teacher relationships?

KEY TAKE-AWAYS

Learning Objective 3.1 Compare and contrast an educational *philosophy* with an *opinion*.

- An opinion requires only a point of view; one does not have to support it with data or rational analysis. By contrast, a philosophy requires intellectual and rational inquiry, a systematic critical thinking without reference to experiments or religious faith.
- An educational philosophy is a theoretical map that guides viewpoints about schools' purpose and the nature of teaching and learning.
- Teaching is a value-laden enterprise influenced by the many beliefs available in a multicultural democracy. Many different viewpoints about education's purposes and practices exist.
- Prospective educators benefit from developing a philosophy of education because it provides a frame of reference to help them interpret and find meaning in data and events and make informed choices about why and how they want to teach. They also help educators relate to those who see the world differently than they do.

Learning Objective 3.2 Support how traditional education philosophy contributes to our understanding of school's purposes and practices.

- Traditional essentialist education philosophy contributes to the preservation and transmission of core Western cultural knowledge and skills believed to be essential to enable society's children function successfully within their environment.
- In the essentialist classroom, teachers transmit a subject-centered, cultural, and community-valued knowledge through a rigorous **subject-centered curriculum** and expect students to learn it.

Learning Objective 3.3 Defend how progressive education philosophy contributes to our understanding of school's purposes and practices.

- According to John Dewey, progressive education philosophy contributes student-centered practices that combine academic rigor with real-world relevance; develops children's intellectual, physical, social, and moral dimensions; prepares children for lifelong learning; creates engaged citizens for a democratic republic; and serves as a vehicle for societal reform and improvement.
- The formal written progressive curriculum is interdisciplinary, reflecting knowledge as it appears in the real world. Learning how to learn and making learning personally meaningful to students are more important than transmitting a set body of once-valued knowledge to students.
- Because students' needs have academic, social, and physical aspects, teachers must design learning activities to have children interact with one another around the content in cognitive, social, hands-on, and minds-on ways.

Learning Objective 3.4 Assess how existential education philosophy contributes to our understanding of school's purposes and practices.

- Existentialist education philosophy contributes a highly individualized, largely arts-and-literature curriculum and instruction that encourages deep reflection and self-expression to help students understand themselves and their choices in a chaotic world.
- Teachers work with each student to help him or her find appropriate materials and the best study methods to address the student's interests. Existentialist classrooms are open learning environments. Instruction is largely self-directed and self-paced and includes a great deal of individual contact with the teacher who prompts and deepens their thinking.
- An existentialist teacher encourages students to philosophize, question, and discuss life's meaning, using whatever curriculum engages students in that dialog. Since the answers to these questions

are personal and subjective, they are not measurable by standardized tests. Likewise, existentialist educators reject the standards movement, imposing a standard curriculum and standardized tests to measure student achievement.

Learning Objective 3.5 Critique how critical theory education philosophy contributes to our understanding of school's purposes and practices.

- Critical theory education philosophy contributes a belief that schools are places where teachers act as "public intellectuals" and use an interdisciplinary curriculum around contemporary issues in students' lives to help students think critically and act thoughtfully in order to create a more just society.
- Critical theory gives diverse students voice in selecting issues to learn, see themselves in the content studied, and occasions to express their views to receptive and respectful peers.

Learning Objective 3.6 Argue the key characteristics of the four educational philosophies that influence today's public schools.

- Each philosophy of education is anchored in a community's values and beliefs about education's purposes; the types of knowledge, skills, and attitudes students will need to competently enter their society; teachers' and curriculum's roles in facilitating learning; and the students' role in the learning process.
- The four major American education philosophies vary in the degrees to which they view
  - education's ends as social stability or as societal improvement;
  - curriculum as Western European or as interdisciplinary, affective, and multicultural;
  - curriculum as relying solely on traditional content or as infusing content with other perspectives, including students' real-life experiences;
  - teachers' role as information transmitters or as learning facilitators;
  - knowledge and skills as things to hold and assess or as assets to amass and use;
  - students' role in the learning process as active or passive;
  - students as developing into knowledgeable, self-aware individuals or as information possessors who find no relevance or personal meaning in what they are learning;
  - students as holders or users of information.
- Educators can successfully reconcile the traditional, progressive, existential, and critical theory viewpoints by selecting and using each approach's strengths and avoiding each's weaknesses.

TEACHER SCENARIO: IT'S YOUR TURN

You have just arrived for your first job interview as a teacher. Before the conversation starts, the human resources supervisor escorts you to a room with a laptop and a printer. The first part of the interview involves you preparing a written response to an education question. You have 30 minutes to complete the assignment. The question to which you are to respond is this:
From an educational philosophy perspective, using the best of traditionalist, progressive, existentialist, and critical theory,

- What are your goals for educating your students?
- What types of subject matter will you be teaching?
- What will your classroom look like, sound like, and feel like for you and your students?

NOTES

1. Philosophy. (1970). *The American heritage dictionary of the English language*. American Heritage and Houghton Mifflin, p. 985.
2. Core Knowledge Foundation. (2019). E.D. Hirsch, Jr. https://www.coreknowledge.org/about-us/e-d-hirsch-jr/

3. Hirsch, E. D., Jr. (2017). A sense of belonging. *Democracy: A Journal of Ideas, 44*(Spring). https://democracyjournal.org/magazine/44/a-sense-of-belonging/

4. Hirsch, E. D., Jr. (2007). Narrowing the two achievement gaps. A presentation at the 18th Educational Trust National Conference, Nov. 9, 2007, Washington, DC: Core Knowledge Foundation, Charlottesville, VA. https://www.coreknowledge.org/wp-content/uploads/2017/01/EDH-narrowing-the-two-achievement-gaps.pdf

5. Hirsch, 2017.

6. For a sample of Hirsch's critics' views, see: Kohn, A. (1999). *The schools our children deserve.* Houghton Mifflin; Macedo, D. (1994). *Literacies of power.* Westview Press; Provenzo, E. (2006). *Cultural literacy: A critique of Hirsch and an alternative theory.* Paradigm Press; Wiggins, G. (2013, October). It's time to retire E. D. Hirsch's tired refrains. Granted, and . . . thoughts on education by Grant Wiggins. https://grantwiggins.wordpress.com/2013/10/13/its-time-to-retire-e-d-hirschs-tired-refrains/

7. Cremin, L. A. (1961). *The transformation of the school: Progressivism in American education., 1876–1957* (pp. 93–94). Random House, Viking Books.

8. Cremin, 1961, p. 207.

9. Golub, A. B. (2004, August). *Into the blackboard jungle: Educational debate and cultural change in 1950s America.* Unpublished dissertation, University of Texas, Austin, TX, p. 63. https://repositories.lib.utexas.edu/bitstream/handle/2152/1211/goluba86500.pdf%3Bjsessionid%3D162A00E6F8CC141AC301C9F1CE96A8C4?sequence%3D2

10. Golub, 2004, p. 63.

11. Bagley, W. C. as cited in Evers, W. M. (1998, October 30). How progressive education gets it wrong. *Hoover Digest*, 4. https://www.hoover.org/research/how-progressive-education-gets-it-wrong

12. Jones, K., & Oliver, R. (1956). *Progressive education is REDucation.* Meador; Raywid, M. A. (1962). *The ax-grinders: Critics of our public schools.* Macmillan, pp. 35–49.

13. Cremin, 1961, p. 123.

14. Dewey called his educational approach "experientialist" rather than progressive.

15. Pogrow, S. (2006). The Bermuda Triangle of American education: Pure traditionalism, pure progressivism, and good intentions. *Phi Delta Kappan, 88*(2), 142.

16. Crighton, M. (2004). *State of fear.* Avon Books, p. 531.

17. Ackerman, D. B. (2003, January). Taproots for a new century: Tapping the best traditional and progressive education. *Phi Delta Kappan, 84*(5), 346.

18. Ackerman, 2003, pp. 344–349.

19. Buber, M. (1923/2004). *I and thou.* Paulist Press.

20. Weber, B. (2014, June 4). Maxine Greene, 96, dies; Education theorist saw arts as essential. *The New York Times.* https://www.nytimes.com/2014/06/05/nyregion/maxine-greene-teacher-and-educational-theorist-dies-at-96.html?_r=1

21. Weber, 2014.

22. For more information about the Maxine Greene Foundation, see: https://fconline.foundationcenter.org/fdo-grantmaker-profile/?key=GREE427

23. Arenson, K. W. (2001, October 3). One philosopher's alchemy: Teaching as romance. *The New York Times*, A, 19. https://www.nytimes.com/2001/10/03/nyregion/one-philosopher-s-alchemy-teaching-as-romance.html

24. Arenson, 2001.

25. Arenson, 2001.

26. Berube, M. R. (2004). Radical reformers: *The influence of the left in American education.* Information Age.

27. Counts, G. S. (1932). *Dare the school build a new social order?* John Day, pp. 11–26.

28. The term "official knowledge"—the formal curriculum that the society's dominant culture transmits in schools—was coined by Michael Apple: Apple, M. W. (1993). *Official knowledge: Democratic education in a conservative age.* Routledge.

29. See: McLaren, P. (1994). *Life in schools.* Longman; McLaren, P. (2000). *White terror and oppositional agency: Toward a critical multiculturalism.* State University of New York Press; Apple, 1990; Giroux, H. (1988). *Teachers as transformative intellectuals; Towards a critical pedagogy of learning.* Bergin & Garvey; Giroux, H. (1983). *Theory and resistance: Towards a pedagogy for the opposition.* Bergin & Garvey.

30. Gutstein, E., & Peterson, B. (2005). Rethinking mathematics: Teaching social justice by the numbers. Milwaukee, WI: *Rethinking schools*. Cited in Adair, J. K. (2008, November/December). Everywhere in life there are numbers: Questions for social justice educators in mathematics and everywhere else. *Journal of Teacher Education, 59*(5), 408–415.

31. Gutstein & Peterson, 2005.

32. Gutstein & Peterson, 2005.

33. Gutstein & Peterson, 2005.

34. A quotation attributed to various people including Winston Churchill, Hermann Goering, and Robespierre, but its actual origins are unknown. See: Phelan, M. (2019, November 26). The history of "History is written by the victors." *Slate*. https://slate.com/culture/2019/11/history-is-written-by-the-victors-quote-origin.html

35. Giroux, H. (2002, October). The corporate war against higher education. https://louisville.edu/journal/workplace/issue5p1/giroux.html

36. Giroux sees the traditional "Americanization" of diverse students into a common American democratic culture, which has been American public schools' guiding purpose since the 18th century, as indoctrination.

37. Giroux, H. (1994). Doing cultural studies: Youth and the challenge of pedagogy. *Harvard Educational Review, 64*(3), 278–309.

38. Giroux, H. A. (1994, Fall). Slacking off: Border youth and postmodern education. *Journal of Advanced Composition, 14*(2), 347–366.

39. Giroux, 1994.

40. Aronowitz, S., & Giroux, H. (1985). *Education under siege. Critical studies in education and culture*. Bergin & Garvey.

41. Giroux, 1994.

North Wind Picture Archives/Alamy Stock Photo

4 THE HISTORY OF AMERICAN PUBLIC EDUCATION

InTASC Standards Addressed: 1, 3, 4, 8, 9

LEARNING OBJECTIVES

After you read this chapter, you should be able to

4.1 Assess the major cultural influences on education in early colonial America.

4.2 Critique the characteristics of education in the early New England colonies.

4.3 Identify the characteristics of education in the Middle and Southern colonies.

4.4 Trace how public schooling changed during the early national period.

4.5 Defend how certain factors and persons influenced the U.S. movement toward teaching's increasing professionalization and universal public schooling.

4.6 Assess the status of schooling in the late 19th century.

This chapter looks at American education from early colonial days through the movement toward universal public schooling. We will consider how the earliest settlers brought European educational ideas and institutions to their new homeland, as well as how our American environment transformed these Old World beliefs and practices. We will see how the early interaction of three key factors—the economy, religion, and the view of governmental control—led to the types of schools that each community, and then state, developed. The extension of the right to vote, the rise of manufacturing, the increasing diversity of the American population, and the widespread entrance of women into teaching as a profession all encouraged public schools' expansion to higher grades and its spread across the nation. Many of the educational challenges we face and are overcoming today have their roots in these earlier schools.

4.1 CULTURAL INFLUENCES ON EDUCATION IN EARLY COLONIAL AMERICA

When the European settlers arrived, the North American continent was not empty. Native Americans had been here for centuries, developing their own civilizations. Culture contact, the initial reality of American education, also proved to be its ongoing challenge.

4.1a Settling North America

In December 1620, Pilgrims came as a community to America seeking to preserve their religious and cultural integrity. Although they were only a minority of the Plymouth, Massachusetts, population, their views dominated the colony's character. As in the earlier (but failed) Jamestown (1607) settlement in Virginia, family and church initially were responsible for educating the colony's children. A key reason: The settlers included few people with formal learning.[1]

Like the Pilgrims before them, the Puritans who settled Massachusetts in later years arrived as a community linked by family, friendship, and common loyalty. They were attempting to preserve their religious and cultural heritage by creating a Christian commonwealth. Within such a society, education would transmit their intellectual traditions and prepare young people to pursue the Puritans' cultural ideal. Family, church, school, university, and community all provided education dedicated to molding persons into religious and civil responsibility.

Other countries also settled America. The Spanish founded the first permanent European settlement north of the Gulf of Mexico at St. Augustine, Florida, as early as 1565. The French had permanent colonies in Nova Scotia and Quebec in 1605 and 1608. By 1664, New Amsterdam (later renamed New York) was a prosperous Dutch market town of about 1,500 inhabitants. Englishmen, Swedes, French, Portuguese, and Africans lived in its extensive colonial province. There were scattered settlements of French Huguenots, Spanish and Portuguese Jews, Scottish Presbyterians, and German sectarians. These early immigrants came as individuals, as independent families, and in groups of families looking to share a common life in a new land under unfamiliar but tolerant civil authorities.[2]

From its inception, diversity and cultural competition, accommodation and blending were fundamental facts of American life.[3] By 1689, English settlements stretched from Maine to the Carolinas and east to the West Indian Islands. Of the 200,000 Europeans on the North American continent, the English represented the largest group. Owing to their greater numbers than the French, Dutch, and Spanish settlers and their technological superiority to the Native Americans and the enslaved Africans, the English were uniquely positioned to influence colonial development.

English colonists spread their decisive cultural influence in North America through their educational system. By the 1620s, England saw its colonies as permanent, self-sustaining communities. These villages and towns embraced families, churches, missions, print shops, and schools, which would systematically advance English ideas, customs, language, law, and literature. Although settlers from other countries had families in North America during the 17th century and some had churches, missions, and schools, none of these groups managed to develop an educational system as extensive as the English version. As a result, England achieved intellectual as well as political influence that, although challenged, would not be overthrown.[4]

4.1b Renaissance Influences on Early Colonists' Intellectual Traditions

The Renaissance and its contradictions influenced those who came to America. Colonists were both overly believing and skeptical, idealistic yet pragmatic. Colonists accepted witchcraft and the new sciences. They believed in improving themselves while preserving valued customs. Their books included Christian classics and ancient texts. Renaissance scholarship looked backward toward the past exemplars and focused on contemporary religious works as well as manuals of law, medicine, politics, surveying, agriculture, and conduct. Poetry, drama, history, and fiction offered colonists opportunities to experience refined living once they ensured basic survival. Wanting to safeguard their civilization's continuity in the New World, the colonists used these books to express their shared aspirations and the forms of education they would support.

The early settlers' intellectual tradition included humanistic ideas about education developed by Desiderius Erasmus, Sir Thomas Elyot, and John Locke. Erasmus's *The Education of a Christian Prince* (1516) identified education as necessary to develop a competent ruler who uses his power to advance the people's welfare rather than his own—or his friends'—economic and social gains. To fulfill this essential educational responsibility, a tutor of fine character, high morals, pure life, and affable manner was widely sought and highly valued. The tutors' curriculum would include the Bible, Greek and Roman literature, and classical historians.[5]

Influenced by Erasmus, Sir Thomas Elyot's *The Boke Named the Governour* (1531)[6] extended a good education's value from hereditary monarchy to those who would govern. The key idea affirmed that common-born administrators and professionals needed a proper education if they were to join with traditional aristocracy in government service.

Widening educational access further, British philosopher John Locke believed in the principle that the people, not their kings, had civil and political rights.[7] As a result of his contractual theory of government, some would consider Locke to be the grandfather of the American Declaration of Independence.[8] Locke believed education had useful purposes—for the business of living (not simply for the university) and for the possibility of advancing progress. In *Some Thoughts Concerning Education* (1693), Locke advised parents on how to raise their children into moral, social persons with the virtue (have a good life based on Christian principles) and the wisdom (able management of one's business affairs) necessary for living in the world. In his view, education helped shape the child's psychological and motivational structure, enabling the child to take rational control over his or her own life.

The Renaissance's religious conflicts also influenced American education. The 16th century's Protestant Revolution challenged the Catholic Church's authority, and this revolt did not stop at the Atlantic Coast. Individual responsibility for salvation became more dominant than the church's collective influence. Accordingly, individual responsibility required all people to be educated. Education became viewed as a vital necessity, requiring a new type of school—elementary, for the masses, and in the native tongue. The American colonies would faithfully reflect this belief.[9]

In short, 16th century political and religious thought culminated in a significant humanistic shift in how the English viewed education. The same education that Erasmus, Elyot, and Locke realized would prepare the aristocracy to rule wisely could also prepare common persons to live moral, productive lives as citizens and workers. Convinced of education's value, "it is but a short step from an education that *confirms* status to an education that *confers* status."[10] Education, it was realized, could lift individuals up to a higher station in life. It did not just humanize those who ruled; rather, education could *qualify* persons to rule, whatever the circumstances of their birth and the conditions of their early life. Education would make meritocracy possible.

To look more deeply at how the Renaissance advanced a novel view of education as the basis for a meritocratic society, complete the activity in the **Reflect & Engage** box, A New View of Education.

REFLECT & ENGAGE: A NEW VIEW OF EDUCATION

The Renaissance advanced a humanistic view of education: It could prepare common persons to rule and live productive lives.

A. As a class, discuss the difference between "an education that *confirms* status to an education that *confers* status."

B. How does this idea of education's worth fit with the American belief in the values of meritocracy and social mobility?

C. Individually, create a wordle (word cloud) using a digital tool such as Vizzlo to describe what the belief in "education that confers status" mean for your own schooling and life opportunities if you were a student in colonial America. Discuss these with the class.

4.1c Schooling in the Early Colonies: Three Key Factors

Available schooling in the early colonies depended on three key factors that influenced people's thoughts and actions about educating their children: the local economy, local religious practices, and the locality's views on government involvement in their schools. Table 4.1 clarifies these relationships and identifies

TABLE 4.1 ■ Types of Early Colonies and Types of Schools

	Geographic Regions		
Factors Influencing the Type of School Desired	New England*	Middle Colonies (Pennsylvania, New Jersey, New York, Delaware, Maryland)	Virginia and Southern Colonies
Economy	Small farms; trades; lived in small villages, towns, and cities.	Small farms; trades; lived in small villages, towns, and cities.	Large plantations; highly stratified society of great wealth disparities.
Religion	Mostly Puritan. Wanted a church-based society.	Varied. Did not want one religion dominating the others.	Varied. Did not want one religion dominating the others.
Community's view of government involvement in its schools	State and local control favored to require, pay for, and maintain public schools.	No government involvement with schools wanted.	No government involvement with schools wanted.
Type of school	Church-run, later becoming public schools for all.	Home or private education for the wealthy; parochial or charity schools for the rest.	Home or private education for the wealthy; parochial and charity schools for the rest.

Note: *New England is generally considered to include Maine, Vermont, New Hampshire, Massachusetts, Connecticut, and Rhode Island.

Source: Original table by Leslie S. Kaplan and William A. Owings. ©SAGE.

the type of schooling each region developed.[11] Of course, diverse viewpoints existed in every region, but general trends can be described.

Early American public education arose from collaboration between churches and colonial governments. Most of the first colonists arrived from Western Europe and had a range of ideas about what education in the New World should be. Figure 4.1 shows their settlements along the Atlantic Coast.

Outside New England, settlers rejected the idea that church and state should join as partners in running the colonies, including their educational systems. They also rejected the notion of using public monies for public schools. Because these other colonies varied from one another in religious backgrounds, social classes, and economies, they did not want one sect's religious leaders controlling all students' learning. Furthermore, the Southern caste system—in which wealthy whites ruled over enslaved African Americans and white indentured servants—made the idea of publicly funded education of diverse social and economic classes and races totally unthinkable. Adding to the mix, every colony had private-venture schools whose owners, for a price, promised to teach their students whatever they wanted to learn. The push-and-pull between local and state control of public schooling that emerged during this period continues to this day.

FIGURE 4.1 ■ Immigrant Groups in the U.S. Colonies

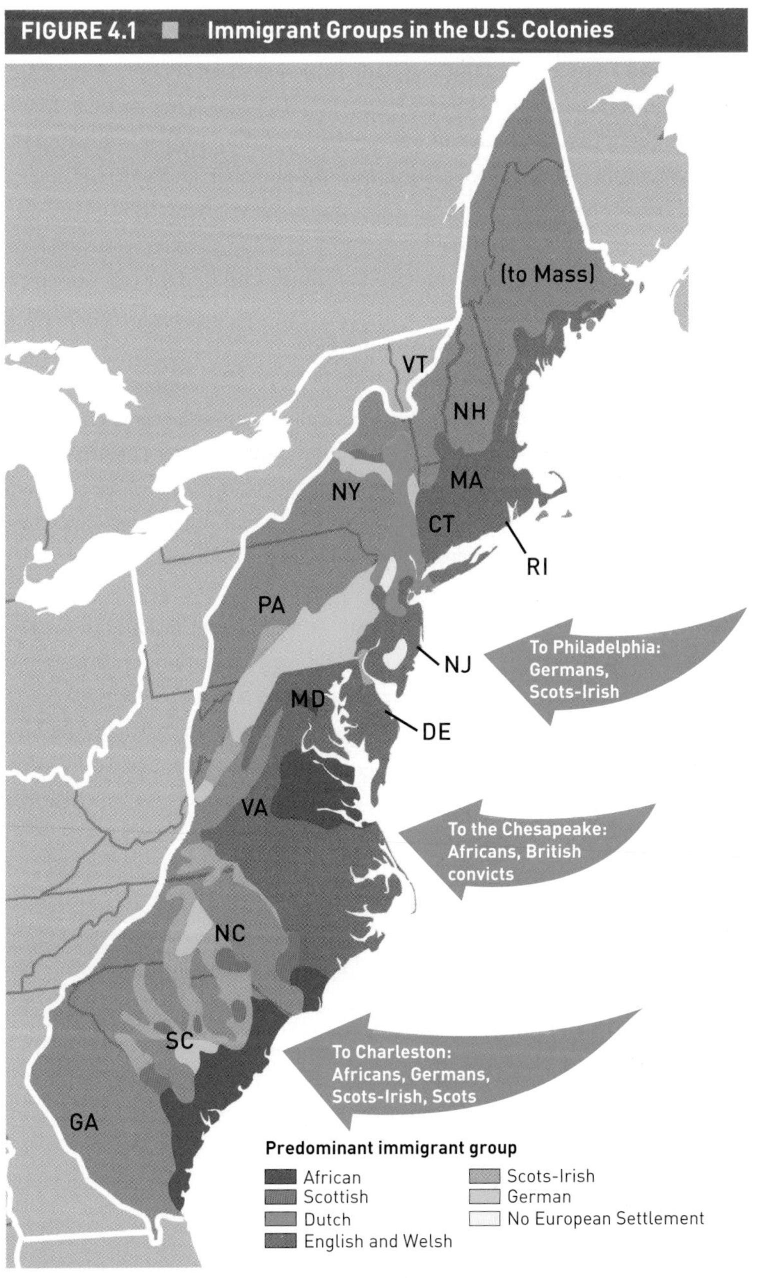

4.2 EARLY EDUCATION IN NEW ENGLAND COLONIES

The New England colonies shared a small farm and trades economy. Most people lived in little villages. Many shared a common religious faith and believed that government should have a role in establishing and maintaining public schools.

4.2a Puritans Shape Early New England Education

New England's Puritans viewed education as the essential backbone of their society and government. While still living in England, Puritans opposed close church–state connections. Instead, they wanted their churches and congregations to be free to practice their own style of Calvinist Protestantism. Many Puritans fled England for America to save their lives and gain religious liberty.

The Puritans settled along the Atlantic Coast in a small farm-based economy, living together in villages, sharing a similar religious background, and the philosophy that education, religion, and the state all served a common good. Because most of the colony's early residents were English Calvinist Puritans, they felt comfortable having the state or locality collect fees or taxes to pay for, build, maintain, and require attendance in local church-run schools.

The Family as an Educational Agency

In the early New England colonies, the family was the principal means of educating children. Through home instruction, colonists taught their children to read the Bible and participate in family and congregational worship. Families often used a **hornbook** (an early reading primer consisting of a single page protected by a transparent sheet of flattened cattle horn), the alphabet, and a *primer* (an elementary book of religious material) or *catechism* (a series of questions and answers giving the fundamentals of religious belief) to teach reading.[12] In this way, children learned to read using passages with which they were probably familiar. The early colonial family also undertook training children for labor or employment, with fathers teaching their sons the multiple arts required to manage the household, farm, and workshop, and mothers instructing their daughters in varied domestic skills.

When they wished to follow a vocation not pursued in their own homes, children would apprentice in another household, where a parent-surrogate systematically taught the new trade. Apprentices learned by direct example with immediate participation and appraisal by the parent or master. Young men who wanted to enter a more learned profession might substitute a period of formal schooling for the apprenticeship. The masters of the school stood in *loco parentis* (in place of the parents), and the curriculum of reading, writing, and principles of religion either incorporated or supplemented the trades portion of the education.

This educational arrangement did not hold for all New England families, however. The English settlers sharply disrupted the Native Americans' family life and education, and many indigenous people eventually withdrew from the tribal environment and attempted to live as Europeans did. An even sharper rupture of family life and education occurred among the Africans brought forcibly to America to be enslaved and placed as property within colonial households. We know practically nothing about the education provided in such families. These involuntary immigrants likely transmitted African stories to their children and adapted their tribal lore to their New World circumstances.[13]

New England Laws Regarding Town Schools

In New England, the Plymouth Colony originally left education to households and churches. Different towns experimented with providing grammar (elementary) schools. By the end of the settlement's first decade, seven of the 22 Massachusetts towns had taken some public action on behalf of schooling, although not all of these attempts survived.[14]

Because most colonial townships had not provided formal schooling for their residents, the state government felt compelled to act. In 1642, Massachusetts passed groundbreaking legislation that empowered each town's selectmen to periodically visit local homes where they expected parents or masters to explain how they were providing for their children's education. Parents presumed their children would learn how to read well enough to understand religious and secular laws.

With this law, education became compulsory for all youths in the Massachusetts Bay Colony—boys and girls alike.[15] To the Puritans, both genders' eternal souls were at stake. Most notably, the responsibility for encouraging and overseeing family education now moved from the clergy to secular officials.

Intended more for parental guidance than as a legal requirement, these laws were not usually enforced. From time to time, Massachusetts towns would crack down on parents and masters whose dependents remained ignorant and illiterate. After 5 years, the general court realized that the school law was not working as intended.

Early School Finance Laws

Acting more firmly, the court established the law of 1647—the famous "Ye Olde Deluder Satan" law. Because Puritans saw children as depraved—prone to idleness and foolishness—the law assumed that those who could read and understand the Bible could not be lured to follow Satan's temptations (and possibly offend God and neighbors).

The 1647 law required towns that had at least 50 households to appoint and pay for a teacher to instruct all children to read and write. Any town with 100 or more households was required to set up a grammar school and hire a teacher to prepare youth for university. Towns generated school funds by direct taxation of the entire town, by taxing all those with boys of school age (typically 6- to 12-year-olds), by charging tuition, by selling some town land, or by some combination of such measures.[16]

Selectmen were authorized to impose fines on those parents who were not educating their children. Violators might endure public humiliation in the stockades.[17] Despite the legal penalties, most towns responded with a variety of strategies, ranging from outright noncompliance to meeting the letter of the law but compromising on its spirit.[18]

Most importantly, civil authorities—not religious ones—retained functional control over schools. Town funds—not church funds—financed schools. Elected local officials now had the duties that had formerly belonged to ministers—hiring teachers, inspecting schools, supervising curriculum, and encouraging student attendance.

The Puritans had few objections to moving the school into civil government's hands. After all, they saw religious and civic government as one in the same, sharing a common purpose in educating children to prepare them for a righteous religious and civic life. Not until 1789, after the American Revolution, did Massachusetts require community (secular) sponsored schools.

Initially, Massachusetts's approach to state-controlled education had limited impact outside what are now the neighboring states. In Connecticut, the law of 1650 ordered that children and apprentices be taught to read. Like its neighboring colony to the north, Connecticut established Latin grammar schools to prepare male students for the state college, Yale College, where they would study for the ministry.

To the New England Puritans, education's primary goal was not to advance a child's personal interests, but rather to protect and enhance the community and the state. Public schools were not supposed to replace parents' role in teaching and socializing their children. An educated populace was as much a moral issue as a civic necessity. The state, however, was in a better position than parents to enforce this expectation for learning. State oversight and control of schools had begun.

4.2b Four Types of Schools

Most New England colonials saw the family unit as the source for all education—practical, moralistic, and religious. The family controlled its children's future social and economic mobility. Wealthy (and many middle-class) families could financially afford to educate their children rather than have them work as laborers or apprentices. They could pay for private tutors, enroll their children in private, tuition-based schools, or send them to Europe to receive a cosmopolitan education. If they wanted their sons to become lawyers, physicians, or ministers, they could send them to college.

Not all families believed that women needed an education to meet their household and social responsibilities.[19] Families with means who wanted to educate their daughters could send them to an entrepreneurial school, if one were available.[20] As for children from poor families, unless they lived in a town that required school attendance for a few years, they received no formal instruction at all. Their future economic survival depended on gaining an apprenticeship or undertaking hard, backbreaking manual or household labor.

New England colonists re-created the dual-track system they had seen in England. The dual track included a minimum education for most children (at the English elementary, town, or common school) and preparation for college for affluent young men (at the Latin grammar school). A third type of school, the dame school, became available to prepare young children with the skills to enter elementary (common) school. A fourth type, the academy, was a newer and less well-defined institution for older students not attending college.

4.2c English (Elementary) Town Schools

The New England town (elementary) schools were controlled locally and welcomed both boys and girls, ages 6 through 13 or 14. Attendance was irregular, depending on the weather and the need for children to work on their families' farms. The schools' curriculum included reading, writing, arithmetic, catechism, and religious hymns. Children learned the alphabet, syllables, words, and sentences by memorizing the hornbook. Older children read the *New England Primer*, which included the Ten Commandments, the Lord's Prayer, and the Apostles' Creed. Math went as far as counting, adding, and subtracting.

Town School Teachers

Initially, all teachers in New England town schools were men. Some were earning a living as a teacher while preparing to become ministers or enter another profession. Some became teachers to repay debts owed for their trips from Europe to North America. In the late 17th century when a few towns did hire women ("school dames") for teaching, they employed them only as adjuncts to the town schoolmaster, who remained the "revered and accepted instructor of children."[21]

Eventually, the schoolmasters' jobs went to itinerant teachers and college students in the winters and to women teachers in the summers. Girls were usually admitted to the summer school with the female instructors but not to the winter schools.[22] Girls, therefore, learned a small amount of reading, writing, religion, and *ciphering* (using arithmetic to solve problems). Only toward the end of the colonial period—and then only for girls "from the best families"—did girls receive education beyond domestic training for the home.[23]

Teaching salaries remained modest. Reading and writing masters in smaller rural communities could earn 10 pounds per year. Meanwhile, distinguished grammar schoolmasters could earn a more generous 25 to 50 or 60 pounds per year. Given colonial New England's labor shortages, salaries for competent teachers could sometimes approach 75 to 100 pounds per year.[24] What these amounts are worth in today's dollars is unknown and difficult to determine. Unfortunately, because parents did not always pay their school fees, teachers were often not paid on time. On the plus side, teachers occasionally received special grants and benefits, such as gifts of land, houses, and firewood; a share of tuition fees; and exemptions from taxes and military service.[25]

Teacher turnover was high during this era. In fact, most schoolmasters changed jobs yearly.[26] Only about 3% of the graduates remained in teaching permanently because ongoing labor shortages opened attractive alternatives to talented schoolmasters. The result was a chronic scarcity of schoolmasters and the presence of many transient, part-time teachers. The best teachers soon left the classroom for higher-paying careers in medicine, business, public service, and the ministry. Many teachers "doubled up," simultaneously serving as ministerial assistants, practicing law and medicine, acting as justices of the peace and captains of the militia, and working as brewers, tailors, innkeepers, and gravediggers.[27]

As a result, pupils were taught by anyone and everyone, including parents, tutors, clergymen, lay readers, physicians, lawyers, artisans, and shopkeepers. In large towns such as Boston, New York, and Philadelphia, "virtually anyone who could command a clientele could conduct classes." The content and sequence of learning remained fairly well defined, and each student progressed from textbook to textbook at his or her own pace.[28]

School Buildings

Formal schools started wherever space could be found: a meeting room, a barn, or a spare room in a large home. Without models for schools to copy, townsfolk built utilitarian and practical shelters—one room, with benches and a stove. Multiple grades of students attended the same school, taught by a single teacher.

More often than not, these schools were built cheaply and quickly and deteriorated almost as fast. In 1681, one Roxbury, Massachusetts, citizen complained that the local schoolhouse was "not fitting for to reside in; the glass broken and thereupon very raw and cold; the floor very much broken and torn up to kindle fires; the hearth spoiled; the seats, some burnt and others out of kilter, so that one had as well nigh as good keep school in a hogsty as in it."[29]

In most cases, school furnishings were threadbare, consisting of a rough floor and planks on barrels or stakes for desks, and benches running around the walls for seats. Paper greased with lard often substituted for windows.[30] In the winters, many schools went unheated. Those that were heated often relied on poorly vented fireplaces or stoves, sometimes making breathing difficult. Heating the school building used much wood, which sometimes led to a wood tax levy on families with children attending school.[31]

If the town did not build schoolhouses, and classes in winter needed warmth as well as space, schoolmasters rented a room with a fireplace—sometimes a kitchen. Summer school might be held in barns, watch houses, or meeting houses.

Teaching Resources

Teachers had an almost complete lack of teaching supplies, books, and effective teaching methods. Desks would not appear for many years, and blackboards did not appear until 1820s. Pencils and steel pens were not available until later still. Paper was expensive and of poor quality, so pupils used it as little as possible. Sometimes, students wrote their letters and numbers on birch bark or traced letters in sand. One of the schoolmaster's job requirements was the ability to make and repair goose quill pens. Meanwhile, the ink was homemade and often poor quality.[32]

Instructional Methods

Instructional methods in the colonial era were relatively unsophisticated. The vast majority of schools were ungraded, and most instruction was individual, with pupils approaching the master's desk or lectern and reciting orally or displaying their work for praise or correction.[33] Other students practiced their drills and waited their turns. Memorizing was the norm. The teaching-and-learning process was so inefficient and ineffective that students could attend school for years and gain only the most minimal reading and writing skills.

Teachers' time was spent on listening to individual students' recitations, assigning students new tasks to learn, preparing copies, making quill pens, dictating math addition problems, and keeping order.[34]

Classroom Management

Townsfolk considered teachers to be failures if they could not keep their students under tight control. As a consequence, school discipline was severe. Even college men occasionally received whippings. Being thrashed, standing in the corner, wearing a dunce cap, and other humiliating consequences were commonplace. Some classrooms even had their own whipping posts—or the post stood in the schoolyard or street.[35]

Milder punishments included forcing students to sit on air or "standing in the corner, face to the wall; stooping down to hold a nail or peg in the floor, the culprit often getting a stinging slap on his rear to keep him from bending his knees. Another punishment included being forced to sit among the girls, which in time came to be called '*capital* punishment.'"[36] In colonial schools, students frequently received blistered hands, swollen ears, and throbbing limbs along with their ABCs.

4.2d Dame (Primary) Schools

Town schools made no provisions for beginning learners. Students were supposed to learn how to read at home before they entered the town school at age 8.[37]

Providing something between day care and primary reading instruction, dame schools began to prepare certain students for the town school. These schools were fee-based lower-elementary or primary schools typically held in a widowed or unmarried townswoman's home. If young children could "stand up and keep their places," they could attend. For a few pennies a week from parents or the town treasury, the dame took neighbors' children into her home and helped them learn the beginnings of reading and spelling, basic writing, and counting. More often, dames taught what they knew best—and students learned rudimentary sewing and knitting. In time, schoolmasters' daughters were trained to keep a dame school to prepare boys for the town's grammar school.[38]

Dame schools, run by widows or unmarried women, were a cross between day care and primary reading instruction.
Bettmann/Getty Images

Unlike today's kindergartens and early primary grades, the dame schools were not pleasant, colorful, child-friendly places. The alphabet and the Bible formed the heart of the curriculum, and the atmosphere was stern and dogmatic.[39]

Knowing the ABCs and basic reading and writing soon became a prerequisite for admission to the town grammar school. Eventually, compulsory attendance legislation provided regular public funding for the dame school, and it evolved into the town primary school.

By 1750, most New England towns had elementary or common schools available to children, with primary schools available after 1820 to bring education to beginning learners. For most children, however, formal education ended at age 7. Girls left school to attend to their household duties. They were generally excluded from Latin grammar schools and higher education. Similarly, after attendance at a dame school, most boys went on to apprenticeships or farm work. For both girls and boys, the household and workplace continued to be the most frequent sources of education.

4.2e Latin Grammar Schools

At a time when the more fortunate poor and middle-class students completed their education in the town schools, upper-class sons ages 7 or 8 went to Latin grammar schools, which prepared them to begin college at age 15. America's 17th and 18th century Latin grammar schools were often modest, one-room structures. The "Latin School" at Boston was established in 1635 (and still exists today as the nation's oldest school) with others soon following in Massachusetts towns.

Latin Grammar School Teachers

The towns' best teachers worked in Latin grammar schools, and their pupils called them "Master." These instructors were frequently well-educated men who held college degrees and enjoyed a higher social position than did the elementary teachers. They were strictly religious and capable instructors. Because they served wealthy men's children, their salaries were relatively higher and more consistently paid than the salaries of their town school colleagues.[40]

Curriculum

Because Latin was considered the sacred language of religion and advanced learning, students studied works by ancient Roman writers Cicero, Caesar, Virgil, and Horace. More advanced students studied works by Greek authors such as Socrates and Homer. Any given grammar school could include an additional offering that ranged from introductory reading and writing in English to arithmetic, geometry, trigonometry, navigation, surveying, bookkeeping, geography, rhetoric, logic, algebra, and astronomy.[41] Vocational subjects and instruction in fine arts were not available.

After Latin grammar school, upper-class boys often applied for admission to Harvard or Yale College to prepare for the ministry. Middle-class boys and girls did not expect to attend college. Students had to demonstrate competency in Latin and Greek to be admitted to Harvard, where they received an education in grammar, logic, rhetoric, arithmetic, geometry, astronomy, ethics, metaphysics, and natural science, in addition to Hebrew, Greek, and ancient history (useful for Bible study).

The middle and Southern colonies did not share New England's fondness for classical studies, but a few Latin grammar schools were founded in several large towns in those regions. Instead of focusing on classical languages and curriculum, these schools leaned toward more commercial and practical courses and introduced merchants' accounts, navigation, surveying, and higher math as subjects of study. In time, these schools evolved to become English grammar schools.[42] By the mid-18th century, classical Latin grammar schools had declined in popularity, even in Massachusetts.[43]

4.2f The Academy

The **academy**, an institution providing "higher schooling," was the most flexible and loosely defined of provincial schools. Academies were a good educational "fit" with commercial and early industrial economies, which demanded a modest number of people to fill those professions—later called "white-collar" positions—that required higher schooling. The academy was incorporated to ensure financial support beyond that available through tuition alone. The families of small businessmen, merchants, professionals, and large landowners—that is, the "middling classes"—generated enough youths to provide the base population for an academy. In addition, by accommodating part-time and older students, academies fit the varied life cycles pursued by people of the time and maximized their enrollments.[44]

Most academies catered to common school students. At their highest level, academies overlapped with colleges. For the most part, early academies offered as their curriculum what the master was prepared to teach, what the students were prepared to learn, what the academy's sponsors were prepared to pay for, or some combination of the three.[45]

Governance

Although open to the public, academies were not free; they were reasonably affordable. Many academies were church-sponsored institutions. Other academies were supported by gifts or estates left by wealthy, civic-minded individuals in their wills for the purpose of educating children. Many others were organized by private subscriptions or as private stock companies. They usually retained private management.[46]

In time, towns, counties, or states began to charter and help maintain the academies, and they evolved into semipublic institutions. Many mingled private and public funds to support their activities. Almost all charged students a tuition or fee, and most had dormitories and boarding halls. A few even provided some form of manual labor—an early work–study program—to defer school expenses.

Additionally, with the creation of boards of trustees to oversee the development of curriculum and assessment, academies became more accountable to the community for the quality of their students' learning.

Curriculum and Instruction

Academies maintained a degree of curricular choice and flexibility distinct from both the earlier Latin grammar schools and the later public high schools. Unlike the Latin grammar schools, academies were not devoted solely to college preparation; they also sought to prepare students for business life and the rising professions. Teachers taught classes in English. Although students might still have learned Latin and Greek, the curriculum now included English grammar, English literature, oratory, arithmetic, algebra, geometry, geography, botany, chemistry, general history, American history, surveying, rhetoric, and natural and moral philosophy. Courses in navigation, needlework, vocal music, or dance might have been available as well.[47] The curriculum was both traditional and, for its day, contemporary.

Rote memorization and student recitation remained the usual practice in schools at all levels through much of the 19th century. The system of *emulation*—a form of competition in which prizes were generally awarded in public—was another popular instructional method. Teachers encouraged students to imitate and surpass their highest-achieving peers.[48]

Women's Education

Although girls attended dame schools, only a small percentage attended town schools or academies. Town schools did not allow girls to attend until the 19th century. When town schools at last accepted girls, they usually attended at different times of the day than the boys or on holidays or summer when the boys did not attend.[49] The growing economy and women's active participation in the family business and commerce increased their need for literacy.

The Latin grammar schools had been created exclusively for boys, but the academies rather freely admitted girls.[50] Supply and demand played a role in bringing young women into this "advanced education." In 1800, the United States had only 25 colleges but hundreds of academies. The increased number of academies meant there was more competition for students, which in turn required academies to appeal to a broader constituency. Thus, academy education was the only form of higher schooling available to women in the early republic.

The academies soon became teacher training schools, the chief supply source for the best-educated elementary teachers. Although they rarely offered instruction in how to teach, their advanced instruction in subjects related to the common schools' curriculum made their future common school teachers more knowledgeable about the subjects they would be teaching. Normal schools would eventually replace academies as sources of teacher preparation. Likewise, the public high school became the main provider of what became known as "secondary" education. Eventually, academies were converted into high schools, became private, tuition-based "prep" schools, or ceased to exist.[51]

Facilities

Academies' special contribution to the U.S. educational system included its good-quality facilities and resources for educating students. A larger school building replaced the resource-poor, one-room schoolhouse that had long served as the town school and Latin grammar school. Academies included a public hall for meetings and rhetorical exercises, and they provided maps, charts, globes, and libraries for students' use. The extra funds available to this kind of semipublic institution brought teachers and students a wider range of educational assets to improve their learning climate and their learning.

Academies took students who had completed the common schools' English education and gave them an advanced education in modern languages, the sciences, mathematics, history, and the more useful subjects of the time. In this way, they built upon the common school courses but marked a transition from the aristocratic and largely exclusive college-preparatory colonial Latin grammar schools to the more democratic public high schools we have today.

To consider more deeply the educational opportunities, climate for learning, teaching quality, and life options available to children from varied social classes in early New England schools, complete the activity in the **Reflect & Engage** box, Early New England Schools.

REFLECT & ENGAGE: EARLY NEW ENGLAND SCHOOLS

Although early New England colonists valued a basic education for most children, parents' wealth often determined how much and what type children would receive.

A. Separate into three groups of early colonial New England children: those from poor families, those from middle-class families, and those from well-to-do families. Each group of "children" will prepare and give a 3-minute role play discussing the following topics:

- Their educational experiences (which schools or training they received)
- What they were taught and what they learned
- Their teachers' main instructional methods and learning resources
- Their teachers and school facilities
- Discipline received for misbehavior or failing to learn one's lessons
- Their present life and/or career options
- Their parents' reasoning for making these educational decisions for them

B. After the role play presentations, as a class discuss how children's social strata and gender dramatically affected their educational, work, and life options in the early colonies.

C. As individuals, explain how this system would have personally affected you had you been living in New England at that time.

4.3 EARLY EDUCATION IN THE MIDDLE AND SOUTHERN COLONIES

Early education in other colonies took unique forms reflecting the people settling there, the geographic and economic conditions under which they lived and worked, and the locality's socioeconomic strata. Additionally, colonists' cultural and linguistic backgrounds as well as the religious, ethnic, and racial differences dividing one group from another shaped whether and how they chose to educate their own and other people's children.

4.3a Early Education in the Middle Colonies

In the heterogeneous middle-colony communities, people believed that responsibility for education belonged to the family, church, charitable organizations, or private efforts. Reflecting the immigrants' many different cultures and religious sects, this region's early colonists did not want the state controlling their children's education. They feared having one group or religion force its views on all students through a state-sponsored curriculum or teachers dedicated to a particular faith. Instead, the state's only responsibility was to maintain pauper schools to provide a minimal education for the students living in or near poverty. Colonies adhering to this view included Pennsylvania, New Jersey, New York, Delaware, and Maryland.

At the same time, middle colonies' settlers supported church (parochial) or private schools for those who could afford to attend. Each family paid tuition to send its children to the school run by its own religious denomination. Students often received lessons in the dominant community group's native language. Church schools also emphasized the sponsoring church's religious beliefs along with reading, writing, and math.[52] A few of the larger towns opened private, tuition-based schools to educate children from more affluent families.

Impoverished children, if their families allowed, could attend church or philanthropic charity-run schools (if available), where they received a nominal education. Many of the charity-run schools were geared toward sons and daughters of "middling income" who could not afford tuition but whose families were not in need of financial support.[53] These charity schools' curriculum was similar to dame schools, and they focused on teaching the ABCs, basic reading, and counting. Orphans and children in very poor families typically received their education through apprenticeships.

Teachers in the middle colonies' parochial schools were usually clergymen until a regular schoolmaster could be found and hired. The local churches employed schoolmasters if they were solid believers in their denomination's faith, had a respectable education of their own, and were willing to work hard. For a small extra fee, many parochial school teachers were part-time choir masters, church chorus members, bell ringers, sextons, and janitors.[54]

Different middle colonies developed some unique educational features. In New York City, which served as a commercial port, several private, for-profit schools charged students fees to study navigation, surveying, bookkeeping, Spanish, French, and geography. In the 17th century, these private entrepreneurial schools came to shoulder an increasing share of New York City's formal education burden. During the 18th century, they expanded to educate more pupils. These private schools were popular because teachers taught in English and because artisans, tradesmen, and shopkeepers presented a practical curriculum.[55]

Pennsylvania's Quaker settlers took a special interest in their local schools. Active since 1683, Quaker schools displayed a strong social-justice bent, educated girls and boys, white people, African Americans, and Native Americans, emphasizing reading, writing, arithmetic, and religion as subjects of study. Quakers also sponsored a network of charity-run schools throughout the colonies to educate African American and Native American children. Reflecting the Quakers' practical-minded view, their curriculum included vocational training, crafts, and agriculture. Pacifists and conscientious objectors by religious principle, Quaker teachers did not use corporal punishment to control their students.

Centrally located between different colonies, New Jersey developed an educational system that reflected influences coming into the colony from varied directions. Each settler group brought its own education traditions. After the English colonized New York in 1664, however, English methods and practices came to influence most of New Jersey. As a consequence, education in New Jersey became limited to families with money or was provided haphazardly through charitable schools for poor children.

Thus, the middle colonies depended on a mixture of church-run and private schools for their educational opportunities. Without state involvement, education was very rudimentary, of limited availability, and often nonexistent. Each parochial (church) school did what it wished. Poor and orphaned children, if lucky, attended charity schools or entered apprenticeships. Meanwhile, children from wealthy families still had private tutors or attended private-tuition schools.

4.3b Early Education in Virginia and Southern Colonies

Colonized by wealthy, successful European immigrants, Virginians and other Southern colony settlers came to America with—or seeking—their fortunes. Although religion was important to them, it was not the central guiding force in their lives.

Climate, crops, and social class influenced Virginians to develop large plantation-style settlements rather than the compact towns found in New England. The introduction of indentured servants and enslaved Africans—along with well-to-do planters, landholders, and independently wealthy gentlemen—led to a highly stratified class-based society instead of New England's popular democracy. What is more, these settlers believed that education was the family's—not the state's—business. Given these social realities, early Virginians had no motivation, from a public policy standpoint, to provide free and common public schools.

Virginians held traditionally English views about education. High-quality schooling was reserved for the elite. Wealthy students received private tutoring at home, attended small private or church-sponsored select schools, or received their education abroad. Young men learned basic academic skills, social graces and good manners, and plantation management skills. Daughters of wealthy families learned how to be successful hostesses. Children of self-taught, literate poor white farmers often learned from their parents. Students from meager backgrounds learned through apprenticeships, in charity-provided pauper schools (if available), or in church-run schools. At best, impoverished children received a scant education, lasting only a few years.

With parents under no legal requirement to educate them, most children of penniless Southerners ended up as field laborers without any training in reading, writing, or arithmetic. In 1642, the Virginia legislature passed a law providing compulsory apprenticeship education to children of indentured servants, orphans, and poor children, usually little more than simple vocational training.

Meanwhile, girls' education in Virginia and the South was generally more restricted than it was in the North. Virginians' expectations for women's education were modest. Girls were expected to learn the domestic skills such as cooking and sewing. As far as schooling, girls could learn the basics of reading, writing, and arithmetic. If their parents permitted, girls were able to attend charity schools, private schools, and—for the wealthiest—tutoring, boarding, or finishing schools. Most young women received informal instruction at home to do those things that would make them better wives, mothers, and housekeepers.

4.3c Early Education in Other States

Given their economies, religions, and views about government control, settlers in Rhode Island, North Carolina, Tennessee, Kentucky, Alabama, and Mississippi resisted the idea of the local or state government having a role in educating children. Among the New England states, only Rhode Island did not adopt the Massachusetts education laws. Desiring religious freedom, Rhode Island residents did not want one religious group dominating thought in schools. Instead, their first public schools did not emerge until the early 19th century.

Initially, these states were indifferent to providing a common education for their populace. As in other states, parents with money bought their children an education. If parents did not have the means, if parents did not want their children formally educated, or if no schools were available locally, children went without.

Farther west, Indiana and Illinois settlers held conflicting views about education, depending on their backgrounds before emigrating. Those coming from New England wanted a strong state hand in establishing and regulating schools. Those coming from the South believed the state had no legitimate role in educating children—and even if it did, mixing students from various social classes was unthinkable. In the end, settlers reached a stalemate, substantially limiting education's development in each state.

Although not all of the early states have been mentioned in these discussions, the economy, religion, and local views about government involvement in education contributed to the settlers' varying beliefs and practices regarding public schools.

4.3d Early Education of African Americans and Native Americans

> Both schooling for democratic citizenship and schooling for second-class citizenship have been basic traditions in American education.... Both were fundamental American conceptions of society and progress, occupied the same time and space, fostered by the same governments, and usually embraced by the same leaders.[56]

Attempts to provide formal schooling for Native Americans or African immigrants and their descendants throughout the early 1700s were limited in scope and local in influence. Some missionary societies continually taught small numbers of free and unfree African Americans and Native Americans, eventually baptizing many of them. The pupils' day-to-day realities, however, often undermined their formal education.

Not until after the Civil War was it legal in most Southern states to teach African Americans to read.

O'Sullivan, Timothy H., 1840–1882, photographer, Library of Congress

Educating Enslaved African Americans

The successful campaign to contain and repress literacy among enslaved people grew just as efforts to provide popular education for free people began to flourish. Between 1800 and 1835, most Southern states enacted laws making it a crime to teach enslaved children to read or write. Wanting to create and maintain a submissive and obedient labor force, slaveholders understood that education could undo their economic system by liberating the thoughts of enslaved Africans and African Americans (those born in the New World). Learning to read, write, add, and subtract would give enslaved people "dangerous" notions about their own abilities and destinies. In addition, many Southern slaveholders believed that enslaved Africans and African Americans were racially inferior to European Americans and did not have the intellect to learn. Some free Southern African Americans attended Quaker schools and missionary schools set up by abolitionists. In spite of the dangers and difficulties, thousands of enslaved people somehow managed to learn to read and write. By 1860, approximately 5% of enslaved people were literate.[57]

Some education occurred as slaveholders and their families taught African American children the lessons related to their status and work. Certain lessons taught the skills and manners required to properly complete their tasks, whether as field hands or as skilled and semiskilled craftsmen, house servants, coachmen, midwives, preachers, healers, and parent-surrogates. All lessons were expected to nurture submissive and obedient attitudes in enslaved people toward the slaveholder in particular and toward white people in general. For the most part, "it was the whip and the Bible that served as the two most important pedagogical instruments in instructing... [African Americans] in the [w]hite version of their place in the world."[58]

Although missionaries hoped that enslaved African Americans and Native Americans would welcome conversion to Christianity, slaveholders objected. They feared that conversion would imply setting enslaved people free or at least impose certain obligations on slaveholders, such as charity, humanity, and keeping enslaved families together. To quell this concern, missionary societies did their best to convince slaveholders that baptism did not imply earthly freedom.[59] On some plantations, enslaved people were allowed to attend church services to learn their duties and obligations in Christianity that supported white oppression. At the same time, African Americans learned covert lessons necessary to their survival as a people and as human beings rather than as property through teachings by their enslaved community, their families, and their clandestine religious congregations.

The pedagogy of the African American family helped their children learn gardening, hunting, fishing, quilting, sewing, cooking, and loyalty to kin that endured in spite of physical separation. Parents also taught their children lessons about personal dignity and pride, family and community solidarity, resistance to white oppression, and aspirations to freedom and salvation. Music and stories transmitted the African culture from one generation to the next, perpetuating itself, expressing and inspiring an essential educational message. The pedagogy of their secret congregations located in the woods or swamps adjacent to their living areas provided enslaved adults with emotional release, a sense of camaraderie and community support, and expression of the belief that they would transcend their daily miseries. Similarly, the family and the church were the chief institutions that free African Americans relied on for their own education, with churches often establishing and maintaining schools for these individuals.[60]

To hypothesize about your own educational and lifestyle futures as a child living in the early American colonies, complete the activity in the **Reflect & Engage** box, American Education in the Early Colonies.

REFLECT & ENGAGE: AMERICAN EDUCATION IN THE EARLY COLONIES

The early colonies took different approaches toward educating their young people. Much depended on how similar the settlers were—in terms of religion, ethnicity, and economic assets—to their town neighbors.

Given the realities of early colonial schooling, suppose that you were growing up as a person of your same racial or ethnic background, socioeconomic class, and gender. Answer the following questions:

A. In which colony would you have *most* preferred to have grown up? Which type of schooling opportunities would have been available to you? How would have your educational opportunities made a difference in your adult options and lifestyle?

B. In which colony would you have *least* preferred to have grown up? Which type of schooling opportunities would have been available to you? How would have your educational opportunities made a difference in your adult options and lifestyle?

C. Working in pairs, create a mind map using a digital tool such as Bubbl to depict your type of schooling and life opportunities available to someone of your family's means and of your race and gender in colonial America. Discuss these with the class.

4.3e Educating Native Americans

In New England, the Puritans remained ambivalent about the Native Americans' capacity to be educated or converted to Christianity. In the early years, the colony vigorously promoted Native American schooling. Evidence exists that as early as 1650, Native American children attended Massachusetts common schools alongside white classmates. Harvard's charter even mentions educating "English and Indian youth of this country." Nevertheless, efforts to provide Native American children with formal schooling had few permanent results because pupils' tribal folkways overwhelmed any white teachings.[61] Then, too, the immense gap between what missionaries said about the brotherhood of man and how white people actually treated enslaved Native Americans and Africans made skeptical students question any religious teachings. No other region did as well as New England in trying to educate America's original inhabitants, although missionaries tried to provide schooling for Native Americans in all the colonies.

The Native American educational experience was no more successful in the South, although native children had an early history of education there. In 1622, Virginia settlers established a school, called Henrico, to educate native children in reading and knowledge of Christian principles. The purpose was wholly evangelistic: to save these innocents' souls. This endeavor had limited success. Hostile relations frequently arose between the Native American population and the English settlers who wanted the young students to reject their tribal traditions in favor of the Western belief system and culture. In addition, Native American children were highly susceptible to European diseases; as a result, many who attended the settlers' schools got sick and died.

The large variety of Native American tribes and forms of social organization make generalizing about their education difficult, but for the most part, the family carried important teaching responsibilities in these groups. A clear division of labor occurred between the genders. Women assumed responsibility for planting, cultivating, harvesting, preparing foods, and making clothes. Men engaged in hunting or fishing and making war. Training the young occurred continuously through showing, explaining, and imitating, with young men undergoing instruction in age cohorts. Most tribes relied on praise, reward, and prophesy rather than physical punishment to stimulate knowledge and skill mastery. Competition provided an additional incentive. Likewise, tribes imposed meaning on the world through songs, stories, dances, and ceremonies. This family and community pedagogy were very powerful. Compared to it, any curriculum taught to Native American children by white "outsiders" in "school" appeared weak, disruptive, or meaningless.[62]

Although many Native Americans and African Americans became Christian, only some of them became literate. A few were permitted to pursue respectable careers as free tradesmen. A handful even influenced the thinking of their time, such as the Native American clergyman Samson Occom and the African American scientist, Benjamin Banneker. Nevertheless, tribal values continued to dominate Native American thought and action, and most African Americans were constrained by the slave system and the attitudes toward race that supported it.

4.4 PUBLIC SCHOOLING DURING THE EARLY NATIONAL PERIOD

Schooling had been firmly transplanted to America during the initial decades of this country's settlement, especially in New England, by a population that highly prized education. As the colonies grew economically, the demand for schooling kept pace. People widely perceived and used schooling as a vehicle for personal advancement, such as moving artisans' children into the professions. Schools also increased in number as competing Protestant sects used schools for missionary purposes. Finally, a growing interest in public affairs during the last half of the 18th century increased the incentive for schooling. One needed to know how to read to keep up with the newspapers, almanacs, pamphlets, and books dealing with current events, especially after the Stamp Act crisis of the 1760s lit the fuse to the American Revolution.

By the middle of the 18th century, secular schooling gained popularity. In New England, secular schools replaced earlier religious schools. In the middle colonies, many of the parochial schools had closed. In the Southern colonies, the highly stratified class-based society, the large distances between communities, and the ongoing presence of enslaved African Americans still made common schools socially and politically unrealistic.

4.4a The Secular Mandate

Colonial leaders, proud of what they had accomplished in their new homeland, worked to gain their political and economic independence from England. The American Revolution, 1776 to 1781, ultimately ended British rule in the 13 colonies.

The new republic's leaders agreed that a self-governing people needed universal education that would motivate all citizens to choose public over private interest.[63] Although the U.S. Constitution does not mention education, the nation's leaders agreed that public education was essential to maintaining a republican form of government. This meant consciously fashioning schooling based on American art, history, and law, independent thinking, and commitment to the promise of an American culture.[64] Education's task was to erect and maintain the new American nation.

The first U.S. president, George Washington, believed in widespread public education. A free people would inevitably have opinions about their government, and Washington preferred that these views be enlightened.[65] John Adams, the second U.S. president, observed that to act as a free person and participate in self-government, "I must judge for myself, but how can I judge, how can any man judge, unless his mind has been opened and enlarged by reading."[66] Continental Congress leaders and future presidents, Thomas Jefferson and James Madison; Continental Congress president and future first U.S. chief justice, John Jay; and revolutionary pamphleteer, Thomas Paine, all advocated for education as a necessary source of general knowledge for citizens in a democracy.

By the 1820s, the need of a self-governing people for universal education had become a familiar part of American politics. Although the country's founders advocated educating the nation's children for a few years at state expense, they disagreed about how to do it. Consensus would not arrive until the early 19th century. Education for self-government would have three central parts: popular schooling for literacy along with a certain common core of knowledge, morality, and patriotism; a free press to express multiple views on important public issues to inform public opinion; and a variety of voluntary associations to serve the public good. Schooled for literacy and armed with newspapers containing up-to-date information, a free American citizenry would learn how to become self-governing by doing it.

Separating Church and State

The new United States was a land of increasing religious and cultural diversity. The Constitution's authors supported the free exercise of religious faith for all by banning any state-sponsored religion. In this new nation, church and state could no longer be partners in public education. In turn, the public school began its transformation from an institution dominated by religious purpose and content into one charged with enlightening a diverse citizenry for civic participation. Its rationale became wholly civic, not religious. This essential idea laid the foundation for our system of free, common, public, tax-supported, nonsectarian schools that endures to this day.

4.4b Social, Political, and Economic Changes

After the Revolutionary War ended and the United States formed a national government, significant social, political, and economic movements continued to alter the fledgling nation's character and direction. Three of the most important influences were the rise of cities and manufacturing, extension of voting rights, and the growth of a new social class's demands for schools. All of these forces would change the U.S. system of public education.

Growth of City Populations and Manufacturing

When the U.S. national government was originally formed, almost every American lived on a farm or in a small village. As late as 1820, the country had only 13 cities of 8,000 people or more in 23 states, containing only 4.9% of the total national population.[67]

After 1825, an increasing number of villages evolved into the cities of the future. Some developed near waterfalls where cheap power made large-scale manufacturing possible. For instance, Lowell, Massachusetts, did not exist in 1820. Yet by 1840, more than 20,000 people lived there, largely to work in the mills powered by the Merrimack River. Cincinnati and Detroit grew because their locations made them good trade and commerce centers. Driven by the improving economy after the 1812 War with England, U.S. cities increased rapidly in both size and number.

The emergence of new cities and the rapid growth of older ones appreciably altered education by producing an entirely new set of economic, social, and educational conditions. Cities along the Atlantic

Coast—especially in Pennsylvania, New York, and New England—rapidly developed a manufacturing economy. Factory work meant the beginning of the end of the home-and-village industries. Eventually, the informal apprenticeship system foundered. Rural populations moved toward the cities and employment in large factories. More people lived and worked in close proximity with others different from themselves.

The factory system altered village and home life as well as education. Living in large, crowded cities of diverse people brought to the fore many social and moral problems that were not evident when people lived in a small, familiar community. The villages' church, private, and charity school systems broke down under the strain of trying to educate many more children than they had the resources to do successfully. As a result, people started demanding that state funds or grants partially support both church and philanthropic society schools. Likewise, several charity organizations arose in various cities to help address poverty, juvenile delinquency, and other urban problems.

Manufacturing growth moved many agricultural workers to cities, significantly changing education by producing new economic and social realties.

Niday Picture Library/Alamy Stock Photo

These economic and societal changes did not affect everyone. The South's economy and society—which continued to be based on plantation life, enslaved African Americans, indentured servants, and lack of manufacturing—remained largely unaffected by the changing economic and social conditions until well after the Civil War. Its educational practices changed very little over this period. Likewise, Native Americans were considered alien members of their respective tribes with whom the United States negotiated treaties, and they received few of the traditional benefits given foreign neighbors.

Extending Voting Rights

Women, men who were not citizens or were not wealthy enough to own property, and people of color could not vote in the nation's early days. During this time, women could only vote in states where the constitutions did not specifically deny them this right.

Change in voting rights came slowly. Western states, formed by people who lacked "old money" or large estates and judged persons more on their earned merits than on their inherited family backgrounds, championed the voting rights movement. By 1828, all white men could vote, giving rich and poor, Westerners and members of the Eastern manufacturing classes, employers, and laborers greater influence in their government and their own affairs.

Poor and Working-Class Demand for Schools

Gaining the right to vote made white men of all social classes recognize that general education for knowledge and civic virtue was a basic necessity for their own and society's well-being. Governors began to recommend that their legislatures establish tax-supported schools. The new labor unions formed after 1825 joined in the demands for schools and education because their members saw the free education of their own children as their natural economic and political right.

The 19th century's second quarter witnessed the movement for tax-supported, publicly controlled and directed, nonsectarian common schools. Bitter arguments, legislative fights, religious jealousies, and private interests characterized the process of establishing free public schools. By 1850, however, tax-supported, nonsectarian public schools had become a reality in almost every Northern state. In North Carolina, free taxpayer-supported schools were established, marking the first implementation of this trend in the South.

Two developments—the newly invented steam printing press and the first low-cost modern newspapers—also appeared at this time. These widely read publications strongly influenced popular opinion to support free common public schools. In time, the desirability of common, free, tax-supported, nonsectarian, state-controlled schools—open to all students—became clear to most American citizens as a means to perpetuate a democratic republic and to advance public well-being.

Developing a National Educational Consciousness

The post–Revolutionary War period signaled a turning point in American education. The schools' tradition of promoting religious doctrine could no longer hold, although it took time for this practice to fade. Now, people would have to share a collective national loyalty and political allegiance with others whom they did not know, who did not live in their towns or states, and who saw and acted upon the world in different ways than they did. Secular purposes would direct schools. A new generation of young people had to be socialized to adopt the attitudes and behaviors needed to responsibly participate in the young constitutional democracy.

Before 1820, outside New England and New York, people had not developed an educational consciousness for a variety of reasons. First, no economic demand for education existed. The era's simple agricultural life—the colonies' largest occupation—did not require formal schooling. A person who could read, write, and cipher was considered educated, and those who could not lost no respect.

Second, after the Revolutionary War, the United States was very poor. The country had few industries, a huge war debt, and weak foreign trade. Political leaders focused on immediate problems: strengthening the existing government and finding necessary resources to make essential infrastructure improvements. These critical responsibilities demanded their attention at the expense of providing universal education.

Until this time, travel and communication were difficult, and people did not often interact with others holding differing views and values. It was not necessary for everyone to speak the same language or speak a common language in the same way. They did not need formal schools to acculturate them to their shared society. Similarly, the early colonies had few cities that would bring diverse people together and require that they get along with each other if they were to survive and advance. Instead, the colonial villages' isolation and independence allowed them to remain indifferent to providing a universal, free education to their children unless, like the Puritans and Quakers, religious and humanity concerns motivated the residents to establish private sectarian schools.

In addition, no widespread voting eligibility, behaviors, or institutions existed in which citizens could publicly express their views or agitate for widespread education. The day's politics did not envision popular voting to settle important local or national questions. Political decisions, including those of war, taxes, the military draft, or writing a national Constitution, still remained in the hands of wealthy white men—and these influential individuals could always afford to educate their own children.

By the War of 1812 to 1814, when Americans finally pushed the defeated British out of the United States, they had built a democratic national consciousness. Confident that the Union would survive as a stable political entity, the citizens of the United States finally had the energy, the self-assurance, the money, and the interest in creating a democratic system of public schools, a communal language, and shared traditions. As a consequence, plans for education and national development began to receive serious consideration.

Private Schools in the New Nation

Private (nonpublic) schools are usually controlled by a private corporation, religious or nonaffiliated (not a government agency or board), and mainly supported by private funds and tuition. As early as the 16th century, Catholic missionaries opened private schools in Florida and Louisiana, even before formal education began in Massachusetts.[68]

In the American colonies, private schools operated alongside town schools. In some places, public schools operated under both civil and religious supervision. Tuition-based venture schools in every colony offered to teach their students whatever they wanted to learn. Many academies were privately owned and managed, although some received public tax and land subsidies and state and local tuition assistance. The first colonial colleges—Harvard, Yale, and Princeton—were all private colleges. As the 19th century began, the line between public and private schools remained unclear.[69]

After the American Revolution, the strong sense of national identity created a demand for public, secular schools. Rather than continue to rely on church-sponsored and private schools to create a literate citizenry, the new nation needed taxpayer-supported, nonsectarian, free, compulsory, and universal education as a state function. During this time, private schools—especially those with a religious affiliation—became viewed as divisive, perhaps even un-American.

Despite widespread poverty, Catholic churches ran parish elementary schools, using a dedicated corps of religious women teachers and supportive members. Other denominations also established private elementary schools. Presbyterians, for instance, established nearly 300 schools in the mid-19th century in response to their concern over the common schools' alleged secularism. Other religious groups, including Lutherans, Quakers, Mormons, and Mennonites, also supported their own private schools. By 1900, 7.6% of the total U.S. student enrollment was in private schools.[70]

To consider more intensively whether public schools should have a religious or secular-based orientation—and how this issue may have affected your own education—complete the activity in the **Reflect & Engage** box, Education in the Colonial and Early National Period.

REFLECT & ENGAGE: EDUCATION IN THE COLONIAL AND EARLY NATIONAL PERIOD

During the colonial and early national periods in American history, public schools had distinctive philosophical underpinnings. Controversy still rages, however, about whether our public schools were—or should be—religious or secular in purpose and practice.

A. The issue of schools teaching religion is often a family issue. Create a wordle (mind cloud) using a digital tool such as Vizzlo that depicts your family's views on you receiving a secular or a religion-based education. Consider the factors that went into their decision about your education. How do you think your family's decision on this issue influenced your education and current worldview?

B. Discuss your wordle with a partner.

C. As a class, discuss the extent to which early American colonists practiced religion in public schools. Where did it occur and for what reasons? Where did it not occur and for what reasons? How did this influence the schools available—and the children who could be educated—in your own state?

D. Why is it still important to keep American public schools secular in outlook and practice?

4.4c Schools in the Early National Era

The early national era saw the common school, the Latin grammar school, and the academy continue while three new types of schools began: the infant school, the public high school, and "supplementary" schools.

Infant (Primary) Schools

Infant schools were an educational innovation that prepared very young children to attend the common school. In 19th century England, children as young as 5 often worked up to 14 hours a day in factories. One philanthropic factory owner, Robert Owen, offered an education to children between the ages of 3 and 5, partly to let youngsters have some fun before they entered factory life and partly to provide them with moral and intellectual training. These schools were known as infant schools because their students were virtually babies!

In 1816, infant schools arrived in America as an English import to supplement the common school. Established initially in the eastern cities, they were designed for children between the ages of 4 and 7. Women were the teachers. Infant schools created a homelike learning environment for young children, resembling a large nursery with the purpose of engaging and amusing the pupils. The innovation flourished for a while but then fell out of favor. Later, in the 1850s, the infant school was revived as the kindergarten.

Infant schools tried to advance a new teaching theory propelled by a psychological view of children. For the first time, American schools considered the learner's needs and interests and the teaching methods needed to help them best learn.[71]

Over time, New England's infant schools evolved into kindergartens. Primary schools took over the dame school and infant school instruction as a public function and added the primary grades to the existing common schools. To this day, we still use the term "primary grades" to describe kindergarten through Grade 3 of elementary school.

Public High Schools

Empowered with new money and new political rights, the middle class and businesspeople clamored for the taxpayer-supported public high school as a cooperative effort to benefit their children.

The public high school originated in 1821 in Boston as an alternative to the Latin grammar school. Its practical aim was to prepare young men for a private and public life in a profession (not requiring college) at no fee. English was the only language taught, along with reading, writing, grammar, science, math, history, and logic. This type of school quickly developed into a public institution offering the option of an English or a classical curriculum.

Under public control, the high school largely reproduced the academy's upper-academic levels, making available to the day students at modest cost or for free the same education that had once been available only to boarding students at a substantial cost. Where high school extended education beyond primary, grammar, or intermediate school, it created an additional step on the American educational ladder, which was clearly evolving into a unitary school system for all the community's children.

Several factors provided the momentum for establishing public high schools. First, colleges required that students receive advanced education between elementary school and college, but no fully free, tax-supported schools yet bridged that gap. As city dwellers became more affluent and could afford to allow their children to attend school (rather than going to work), more students completed the elementary courses and wanted advanced training.

Second, the new manufacturing and commercial activities of the time required job applicants to have more—and different—knowledge and skills to be effective. Workers in these emerging jobs needed learning beyond elementary school but not as much as college.

Supplementary Schools

Supplementary schools were educational units that filled in the learning gaps for individuals whose school attendance had ended prematurely. Such schools emerged during the early national era under private, quasi-public, and public auspices for groups of students having unique educational needs that the community thought best met in separate facilities. These students included children with disabilities, youths alleged to be delinquent, and African American and Native American children judged to be unacceptable in regular classrooms.[72]

Localities in the early 1800s also established several private or semiprivate voluntary alternatives to tax-supported schools. These included the Sunday School Movement, the Public School Society, philanthropic societies for education, and monitorial schools. These innovations, however, remained local institutions rather than serving as national models.

4.4d Teaching and Learning in the Early National Era

Schooling's popularization brought a change in the teaching profession's character and composition. During the 19th century, teaching became an increasingly female-dominated profession, especially in the primary and intermediate grades.

The Learning Environment

During this time, the one-room district school with one teacher instructing between 40 and 60 boys and girls of varying ages remained the rule in most parts of the United States. Teachers informally grouped students for different subjects taught at different levels, trying to keep youngsters focused and working. Sometimes, the entire student group would learn through a sing-song drill together, spelling a group of words, reciting a multiplication table, or listing state capitals. At other times, groups of three or four students would recite together. Occasionally, individual students would take turns going through a question-and-answer drill with the teacher. Students occasionally helped one another. It was, however, a relatively inefficient process, especially for inexperienced teachers.[73]

Discipline problems often arose in these large classes. It was often the new teacher's job to test his or her charisma and classroom management skills against the "big boys" before the class could begin its serious work.[74] Harsh physical punishment of wayward students using whips, canes, paddles, and birch rods was common.

Successful efforts to limit physical punishment began in the 1820s and 1830s. Bureaucratic and affectionate discipline came to replace harsh physical punishment for student misbehavior or failure to learn their lessons. With **bureaucratic discipline**, an impersonal institutional authority other than the teacher, often advanced students acting as monitors, a status earned by merit, enforced the school's rules. **Affectionate discipline**, by comparison, depended on teachers and students forging deeply personal, warm, individualized relationships, like an ideal family. In theory, these positive emotional ties would trigger students' conscience, self-surveillance, and automatic obedience. Both approaches encouraged students to internalize the authority and created incentives to help students motivate and mange themselves. By the last quarter of the 19th century, some urban schools had banned corporal punishment altogether. Where it was not forbidden, it often fell into disrepute.[75]

Catharine Beecher helped professionalize teaching and advocated for women to make it a career.

The original uploader was AlexPlank at English Wikipedia/ public domain.

Normal Schools

In the early 1800s, American society did not require a highly educated workforce. Instead, it needed large numbers of people with basic skills to drive its economy. The public schools met this need. As the society became more complex and job entry requirements increased, states saw the need to train teachers to be more effective. New York governor DeWitt Clinton advocated for better teacher preparation, noting that "the mind and morals of the rising and perhaps the destinies of all future generations, be not entrusted to the guardianship of incompetence."[76]

In 1834, the New York legislature enacted the country's first law providing for elementary school teachers' professional education in a teacher training institute called a normal school. **Normal schools** were 1- or 2-year training institutions for prospective teachers. The first normal schools were actually secondary schools that prepared teachers for elementary schools; they were not college-level institutions. Most of their students had only an elementary education. Because a high proportion of normal school students needed remediation, the curriculum included an eclectic mix of basic subject matter and pedagogy. Normal schools operated locally and enrolled neighborhood students who would teach for community schools. By 1860, nine states had established state normal schools. By 1865, the United States had 22 state normal schools. After that time, public and private teacher training schools grew rapidly. By the end of the 19th century, most normal schools had become 4-year teacher education colleges.[77]

Prospective teachers could also receive training in academies. The academy teacher training program was entirely academic because no professional body of teaching knowledge existed at the time. In these institutions, lecturers taught principles of teaching and school management primarily by using personal anecdotes drawn almost entirely from their own school experiences. Future teachers reviewed elementary school subjects and advanced academic studies.

Catherine Beecher Advanced Teaching as a Career for Women

During the early national period, many believed that women were meant to move only within the private world of family. Nonetheless, societal shifts pushed women toward teaching. The growth of common schools increased the need for teachers. Social norms viewed women, as compared to men, as more temperamentally and morally suited to work with younger children. Notably, they were also willing to work for half (sometimes one-third) the salary of men, and schools' male supervisors found women more open to suggestions. By 1830, factory work was becoming more onerous, less well paid, and increasingly seen as work for immigrant women.[78] As a result of these forces, by 1860, women outnumbered men as teachers in most of the northeastern states.[79] During the same era, teaching became more professional, making it a sacred calling second only to the ministry in its importance to society. Catherine Beecher's advocacy helped move women and the teaching profession forward.

Catherine Esther Beecher (1800–1878), a 19th century educator, reformer, and author, popularized the idea of women's equal access to education, curricular reform, and advanced teaching as a profession for women.[80]

The eldest child of a famous preacher, Lyman Beecher, Catharine became a surrogate mother to her seven younger siblings at age 16 when her mother died of tuberculosis. In this role, she became intimately familiar with motherhood's responsibility and nobility. In 1821, she became a schoolteacher. When her fiancé suddenly died in 1822, Catharine, devastated, never married. With these formative experiences and as an unmarried woman in the 19th century, she advocated for women as teachers and mothers, citing their nurturing traits as well suited to children's moral and intellectual development. Bucking prevailing norms about "women's place," she argued that each woman, like each man, should be educated for a paying career.

In 1823, Beecher founded a girls' school that in 4 years became the innovative Hartford (Connecticut) Female Seminary. Her seminary offered young women a full range of subjects beyond the fine arts, languages, and etiquette typical of female education of the time. She challenged the prevailing belief in women's "fragility," introducing physical education and calisthenics courses to improve women's health.[81] She later opened the Western Female Institute in Cincinnati and worked on the McGuffey Readers, the first nationally adopted textbooks for elementary students.

During the 1840s, she founded the Central Committee for Promoting National Education, an organization that promoted teacher education and contributed to establishing education as a profession. In 1852, she helped found the American Woman's Educational Association to establish higher learning institutions for women in Illinois, Wisconsin, and Iowa and then to recruit and train teachers to staff schools on the burgeoning frontier.

Disgusted that teaching's important work was largely regarded as drudgery performed out of financial need by men with little preparation or interest for the work, Beecher proposed that teaching become a profession for women. By defining teaching as natural nurturance for women, Beecher (and later, Horace Mann) saw it as "*not really* work in the public sphere so much as expanding the private sphere to include teaching."[82] At this time, "private sphere" was wherever women and children were.[83] Female teachers could benefit children as well as elevate women by giving them a respectable way to earn a living. To Beecher, giving women the opportunity for a career in teaching was more important than women getting the right to vote.[84] Nonetheless, with her tireless efforts to advance teacher education for women and her desire to provide every child, regardless of social class, with a basic education, some consider her a "co-pioneer" (along with Horace Mann) of American public education.[85]

4.4e Varied Opportunities for Varied Students

Schooling was far less available for African Americans and Native Americans than for white children. Many Southern states made it illegal to teach enslaved people to read and write. Likewise, schooling was less accessible and less used by first-generation immigrants than by their children and native-born whites. Lastly, comparatively few women attended academies and colleges before the Civil War, and their choices among these institutions were limited.

Freed African Americans expressed their liberty through their struggle for education. After the Civil War, formerly enslaved people campaigned for universal schooling. The wealthy planters did not believe in state-enforced public education, however, and other classes of white Southerners with whom they shared economic, psychological, and social interests did not disagree. Nevertheless, with help from Republican politicians, formerly enslaved people gained influence in state governments and laid the foundation for public schooling.

Without free schools, now-free African Americans taught themselves to read and write. By 1866, they had created at least 500 "native schools" in which the newly educated would teach other pupils. Formerly enslaved people also initiated free, church-sponsored "Sabbath" schools that operated mainly in the evening and on the weekend, providing basic literacy instruction. Newly liberated African Americans accepted help from Northern missionary societies, the Freedmen's Bureau, and certain Southern whites, but their own actions were the primary force that brought schools to their children.[86]

At the heart of both African American and Native American education in the 19th century was the racist notion that neither group could be assimilated into the larger society. In general white people believed educating African Americans would raise their hopes for a lifestyle and privileges that they could never attain. Native Americans who learned Western knowledge and skills in an effort to become part of the larger society found that no amount of "civilizing" would make their white neighbors accept them as equals. The prevailing assumption on the part of white people was that while people could be educated to transcend ethnic and religious barriers to become full-fledged members of the American community, they could not be educated to overcome the barriers of race,[87] even though these barriers were rooted in the racism of the early national era and forcibly placed on African Americans and Native Americans by American society itself.

4.4f Increasing Access to Colleges

The earliest colleges—Harvard, William and Mary, Yale—were initially created with religious and state support to prepare men for ministry professions. Nationhood, however, brought a demand for more higher-education opportunities for more citizens beyond those training for a religious vocation.

After nationhood, the nine original colonial colleges[88] reorganized to bring themselves more in line with the new government's ideas. Columbia and Pennsylvania changed for a time into state universities. At Harvard and Yale, divinity as a focus of study declined in importance while history and modern languages became more popular.

The Western migration also influenced college availability. Immediately after the Revolutionary War, settlers began to move to the new western territories along the Ohio River. When "The Ohio Company" (a New England-based company) bought 1.5 million acres in south-central Ohio, the U.S. Congress granted it land for schools and a university. In 1788, upon the sale of 1 million acres near Cincinnati, Congress granted the township land for educational purposes. The former university became Ohio University at Athens, and the latter became Miami University at Oxford. The practice of granting townships land for schools and for state universities continued with the admission of each new western and southern state.

After 1820, with the growing national consciousness favoring free public education, interest in founding new colleges increased. The already widespread dissatisfaction with colleges' exclusivity and curricular narrowness grew. Until about 1870, providing higher education was largely a private effort. Most colleges required students to pay tuition. Because most colleges were founded by different religious denominations, people viewed them as representing and advancing their own parochial interests rather than the state's—or general public's—interests.

When some states discovered that they could not legally take over existing denominational colleges, they began to create their own universities. The University of Virginia, the University of North Carolina, and the University of Tennessee were just some of the resulting schools. The period of great state university expansion came after 1850. By 1860, the public educational stepladder spanning from first grade through college had become a reality.

Over time, colleges opened their doors to women. In 1800, no college admitted women. By 1860, 61 colleges admitted women. After the Civil War, during which time many women filled work positions formerly held by men—especially in teaching—regular colleges began welcoming women as students. Every state west of the Mississippi River made its state university coeducational from its first days of admitting students. Many eastern universities followed suit later in the 19th century.

The New Land-Grant Colleges

Before 1825, eight states had started building future state universities. The national government further encouraged the development of state-sponsored higher-educational institutions by granting to each new state, beginning with Ohio in 1802, two entire townships of land to help endow a "seminary of learning" in each. This practice eventually led to the founding of a state university in every new state.

In 1862, the federal government granted funds under the Morrill Act to establish colleges of agriculture and the mechanical arts, thereby encouraging the founding of new institutions and expanding older ones. The Morrill Act granted 30,000 acres for each U.S. senator and U.S. representative that the state had. The result: More than 11 million acres of public land was given to states to endow institutions for teaching these new college subjects, an area half as large as the state of Indiana. The educational return on the land-grant colleges has been very large. Today, all states still receive federal money to carry on this work.

4.5 MOVEMENT TOWARD UNIVERSAL PUBLIC SCHOOLING

As public schools expanded in number and variety to meet increased workplace and literacy demands, immigrants from around the world began arriving in the United States. By the 1850s, more than 500,000 immigrants entered the United States each year, representing an increasingly wider range of backgrounds and cultures. Between 1840 and 1870, the country's population doubled; it then doubled again between 1870 and 1900. By 1900, one out of every seven Americans was foreign born.[89] Public schools became the socializing institution to help newcomers adjust to their new homeland and serve as a means to promote a unifying national experience.

The 19th century's second and third quarters saw the rise of local school districts. But by the decade 1840 to 1850, serious organizational and practice defects had become obvious. State control of school systems would appear as a solution to better and more equitable education for America's increasingly diverse students.

4.5a Creating School Systems

The formal legal movement toward the creation of public school systems was uneven. State constitutions would adopt principles, which their legislatures would then interpret or ignore. For instance, Indiana's 1816 constitution made it the general assembly's duty to make a law for a general education system from township to state university "as soon as circumstances will permit." Circumstances did not "permit" for more than 30 years.[90]

Finding popular support for a state-governed education system was difficult. In the mid-1800s, political control remained firmly lodged at the district, town, or county level. The technology and concept of state control had not yet been fully developed. Local citizens squared off over highly divisive financial and symbol-laden issues, including levying taxes and allocating public monies, drawing school districts, selecting curriculum, and maintaining discipline.

These growing state systems drew in an increasing number of amateurs, semiprofessionals, and professionals advocating for public schooling. Before the Civil War, these "friends of education" appeared in every state, spearheading the public school movement, articulating and publicizing its goals. Horace Mann and Henry Barnard helped to make the public school movement one of the most enduringly successful of all pre–Civil War reforms.

4.5b Horace Mann

In 1837, Massachusetts created the first state board of education and named Horace Mann as its first appointed secretary of education. In the 19th century, no one did more to convince the American people that education should be universal, nonsectarian, and free, and its aim should be social efficiency, civic virtue, and character building. Under Mann's leadership, an unorganized and differing series of community school systems became a unified state school system, both in his state and throughout the northern states. In recognition of his accomplishments, Mann is sometimes called "The Father of American Education."

Neither the Massachusetts State Board of Education nor its secretary had any powers to enforce their ideas. Their job was to investigate conditions, report facts, expose defects, and make recommendations regarding actions to the legislature. Any influence that they had would entirely depend on the secretary's intellect, energy, and charisma.

Mann's Vision and Leadership

As an educational leader, Mann's central purpose was to put Adams and Jefferson's democratic educational vision into widespread practice. Aware of America's diversity in origins and traditions, he called for a publicly supported, publicly controlled "common school" that would be open to all students regardless of race, class, or gender with the goal of fostering a sense of community by sharing a "public philosophy."[91] Rather than a school for the common people, Mann's vision was a school common to all the people, rich and poor alike. In his view, public schools would become "the great equalizer," helping end poverty and social class distinctions.[92] By bringing children from such diverse backgrounds together, schools would enable them to develop friendships and mutual respect that would create societal harmony and reduce adult life conflicts. Mann concluded, "As the child is father to the man, so may the training of the schoolroom expand into the institutions and fortunes of the state."[93]

To Mann, education and freedom were inextricably linked. Education was necessary for all citizens to learn the self-discipline required to live responsibly in a democratic republic. If the ordinary people were wise, the problem of leadership would take care of itself. He observed, "A republican form of government, without intelligence in the people, must be, on a vast scale, what a mad-house, without superintendent or keepers, would be on a small one."[94]

Mann did not believe that the self-regulating district system, which was not accountable to local or state concerns, was an effective way to identify and spread successful teaching practices. Instead, Mann suggested, local schools needed a shared mission under an overseeing agency devoted to maintaining certain standards in all children's education. He advanced the idea of an education system, a functional organization of individual schools and colleges that put them into regular relationship with one another and with the state.

To this end, Mann articulated general principles on which intelligent educational choice could depend. His goal was to ensure educational equity and rationality (not uniformity) to all students in all locations. In his *Fourth Annual Report* in 1840, he asked small districts to consolidate into larger ones—and sought to bring them under state authority. The societal costs for not educating all students in effective schools, he reasoned, were greater than the cost of doing so.[95]

The fundamental issues underlying the American Revolution spoke to human rights. As an outgrowth of this movement, some advocated that women were the natural equals of men in terms of rights, liberties, and abilities, and pointed out that a proper education (and employment) would make them equals in actuality. Mann asserted that mothers needed an education even more than leaders because of their critical influence on the next generation of citizens. Many disagreed with this view, however, and flatly opposed female education on the grounds that it was harmful and wasteful.[96]

Mann successfully met this challenge, making a difference through his intelligence, presentation of relevant data, personal charisma, excellent writing and speaking skills, and persistence. He held forums at teachers' institutes and public meetings in every county, raising public consciousness about the issues at hand. Besides public speaking, Mann's other instrument of persuasion and influence was his *Annual Report* (of which he wrote 12) that set out his vision of what education should be in a free society.

Arousing Critics

Overturning the status quo incited critics of Mann's views, actions, and outcomes—asserting that he did not go far enough or that he went too far. In all his writings and commentary, Mann did not raise difficult questions that might have undermined the fragile coalitions he had cobbled together to support public schools. For example, he was unable to reconcile his desire to train students for responsible citizenship and his need to avoid controversial classroom topics.[97] Although Mann served in Congress after 1848 as an uncompromising abolitionist, he did not address providing education for African American children. Nor did he argue for public education exclusively.[98] He did not call for free higher education because his concern was with the greatest general proficiency of average students rather than the exceptional progress of a few.[99] Although he exhorted against parental indifference to schooling, he did not recommend compulsory attendance. Rather, Mann advocated regulations that would require children to attend either regularly or not at all. Eventually, organized labor and reform groups pressed for compulsory school attendance to end youthful idleness and prevent youth exploitation.[100]

From the other side, Mann's contemporary critics viewed his call for school systems, educational consistency, and equity as partisan and political rather than as common sense. Edward A. Newton and Matthew Hal Smith suggested that no idealistic equity could ever justify a rigid educational uniformity.[101] Likewise, Orestes A. Brownson, a Unitarian minister who later joined the Catholic Church, vigorously criticized Mann's advocacy for children's attendance of state-sponsored secular schools, seeing them as promoting a "civil religion" that was a plot to end Christianity.[102] For the first (but not the last) time in our history, public school opponents cried, "The public schools are Godless schools!"

AMERICAN EDUCATION SPOTLIGHT: HORACE MANN

Through force of personality, Horace Mann (1796–1859) convinced the American people that education should be universal, nonsectarian, and free; and he educated public opinion to support schools' value to the community.

Born in a small Massachusetts town in 1796, young Horace was educated in the local one-room schoolhouse. Reading extensively at the town library, he learned enough to be admitted to Brown University. As a lawyer elected to the Massachusetts State Senate, and then as the senate president, he helped pass the bill creating the Massachusetts State Board of Education. In 1837, Mann shocked family and friends by taking the job as the board's first secretary. He now worked for an agency with no money or control over local schools—and which paid him a meager $1,500 salary; no provision for rent, clerical help, or supplies; and a title without honor.

Horace Mann, the "father" of American education.
Hulton Archive/Stringer/Getty

Mann's was a time of tremendous social change: Immigrants were flooding into the northeastern states, farmers were leaving rural areas to work in factories, and cities were growing rapidly with rising crime and poverty. In response, Mann and other reformers promoted state-regulated public education as a way to bring order and discipline to the working class in this rapidly changing society. They believed that educating youths would reduce crime and moral vices such as violence and fraud. This perspective supplemented their ideals about preparing an educated public for a representative democracy.

Despite their potential for civic good, public schools of Mann's era were unpleasant and inefficient. Visiting almost 1,000 schools while Massachusetts Secretary of Education, he found poor facilities lacking adequate heating, lighting, and ventilation. Schools had no blackboards and no regular textbooks. Memorization and recitation were the primary pedagogy. Inequality of educational opportunity was everywhere. Wealthy children attended school for longer periods, and the poorest often did not attend because they could not afford the minimal tuition. At one point, Mann commented that Massachusetts took better care of its livestock than its children. He also vigorously opposed the punishment used by schoolmasters, noting that they "crowd from forty to sixty children into that ill-constructed shell of a building, there to sit in the most uncomfortable seats that could be contrived, expecting that with the occasional application of the birch [a tree branch used to hit uncooperative students] they will then come out educated for manhood or womanhood."*

When it came to teaching and learning, Mann was an innovator who recognized the student as a learner. He observed that children differed from one another in temperament, ability, and interest. Teachers would need to adapt their lessons to accommodate these differences. Rather than have students passively memorize and recite their lessons, Mann wanted classroom interactions that allowed students to ask questions and hold group discussions, arrive at answers for themselves, and receive more humane and caring treatment. Teachers should help children build their own powers of seeing, judging, and reasoning and encourage their initiative. Mann's regard for learners led him to develop a statewide teacher training system that would produce teachers who used instructional practices that helped students learn. Because his concern lay with the greatest general proficiency for average students—rather than the remarkable progress of the few—teaching for all students' learning was of critical importance.

During Mann's 12 years as secretary, public education appropriations more than doubled, teachers' salaries greatly increased, and the school term added a full month—increasing the school year's length to 6 months. He wrote and spoke persuasively to modify the conditions of existing schools and build new ones. Mann's efforts led to providing more free nonreligious public schools for boys and girls, better schoolbooks, improved teaching, higher pay for teachers, better student attendance, and a more educated population.

Mann's influence was significant and permanent. His vision and efforts helped realize the founders' dreams about education of all for a democratic society.

Note: *Sarah Mondale and Sarah B. Patton. (Eds.). (2001). *The story of American public education.* Beacon Press, pp. 27–28.

Sources: Cubberley, E. P. (1947). *Public education in the United States.* Riverside Press; PBS, n.d.; Mondale & Patton, 2001.

4.5c Henry Barnard

At the end of the colonial period, Connecticut schools had greatly deteriorated. An 1838 investigation showed that only one-half of 1% of the state's children attended school. The available public schools—poor, private-tuition-charging institutions—were increasing; citizens objected to taxation; and teachers lacked training or professional interest.[103] Henry Barnard's work restored this state's educational effectiveness and its pride in its public schools.

Henry Barnard, American education scholar.
Hulton Archive/Stringer/Getty

Henry Barnard accomplished important educational improvements in both Connecticut and Rhode Island. A Yale-educated lawyer, he became deeply interested in teaching. He subsequently spent much of his personal fortune to publish journals advocating educational reform. Influenced by European educators who respected children as learners, Barnard helped pass the Connecticut state law setting up the state board of education with a secretary, like the Massachusetts plan. Barnard was then elected the first secretary—at the grand salary of $3 per day plus expenses.[104]

As Connecticut's secretary of the board of commissioners of the common schools, Barnard visited many schools and issued a series of reports identifying and detailing the problems he hoped to solve. He invoked the state government's authority to force each district to meet certain standards for buildings, teachers, attendance, and textbooks. In 1839, he organized the first teachers' institute in America for educators to learn new instructional techniques, helping to professionalize teaching. Likewise, he worked to improve schools' physical conditions by writing extensively about schoolhouse construction. He studied school data and used the statistical returns about school activities and accomplishments to engage public interest in education.

Barnard's educational innovations met with active resistance. When the Connecticut legislature abolished both the board and his position in 1842, Barnard moved to Rhode Island to examine and report on the conditions in that state's schools. He served as Rhode Island's commissioner of public schools from 1845 to 1849. Like Mann, Barnard was a strong campaigner and fearless organizer, holding public meetings across the state to generate interest in the state's educational system. He organized a series of town libraries throughout the state and developed a traveling model school for his teachers' institutes, demonstrating lessons that showed current and prospective teachers how to teach.

In 1851, Barnard returned to Connecticut as head of the state normal school (teachers' college) and ex-officio secretary of the state board of education. In this role, he rewrote school laws, increased taxation for schools, checked the power of local school districts, and laid the foundation for Connecticut's state schools system. In 1855, Barnard also began editing his *American Journal of Education*, a large encyclopedia of educational information, which provided American educators with an understanding of their professional inheritance as well as recent teaching practices. By some opinions, Barnard became American's first great education scholar.

Mann and Barnard were two highly visible, extremely influential leaders during the formative period of American education. Their work to build and strengthen state departments of education, create statewide school systems, and professionalize teaching inspired educators throughout the northern states and encouraged friends of education elsewhere.

4.6 THE STATUS OF PUBLIC SCHOOLING IN THE LATE 19TH CENTURY

By the last half of the 19th century, public schools reflected regional differences. The northern and mid-Atlantic states saw substantial growth in their public school systems. Public schools in the Midwest expanded; public schools in the South grew only modestly.

Within the various regions, schools differed in the school term's length and education's availability beyond the primary level. Significant racial, ethnic, gender, and religious differences continued to affect access to schooling. In addition, the sizable differences in teacher qualifications and effectiveness made a year of schooling in one institution or locality significantly different from a year of schooling in another institution or locality.

During this era, school was intended to prepare youngsters for productive work outside the household, where literacy and punctuality, the ability to follow rules and procedures, and cooperation with others would be expected. After receiving an education, American citizens could read and appreciate newspapers. They knew social norms beyond the family. Whatever their limitations, by the late 19th century, public schools were preparing increasingly more students for adult life in a democracy. As Alexis de Tocqueville, the French political thinker and historian who toured the early 19th century United States and wrote *Democracy in America* (1835), observed that if the United States had few individuals who could be described as learned, it also had fewer illiterates than anywhere else in the world.[105]

At the same time, the white community's cultural assumptions affirmed that people could be educated to transcend ethnic and religious barriers to become fully functioning American citizens, but they could not be educated to transcend the barriers of race. African Americans, Native Americans, and other peoples of color largely remained outside this American cultural community and its public education system.

KEY TAKE-AWAYS

Learning Objective 4.1 Assess the major cultural influences on education in early colonial America.

- Because English settlers represented the largest immigrant group in North America, they spread their decisive cultural influence through their extensive educational system.
- The early English settlers' intellectual tradition included humanistic ideas that education could *qualify* men to rule and enable children to take rational control over their own lives. Since they believed that an education *conferred*—not only *confirmed*—status, they valued education as the essential backbone of their society and democratic republic government.

Learning Objective 4.2 Critique the characteristics of education in the early New England colonies.

- The early interaction of three key factors—the local economy, local religion, and the local view of governmental control—led to the types of schools that each community and state developed. The push-and-pull between local and state control of public schooling that emerged during this period continues to this day.
- From early colonial days, family wealth, a child's gender, and race/ethnicity typically determined how much and what type of education their children received.
- Massachusetts Puritans saw religious and civil authorities as one in the same so did not object to having local secular officials use town funds to run schools to educate children for a moral religious and civic life. Less homogeneous communities in other regions did not support the idea of government-run schools. After the American Revolution, with the nation's increasing religious and cultural diversity, public schools became wholly civic, not religious institutions.

Learning Objective 4.3 Identify the characteristics of education in the Middle and Southern colonies.

MIDDLE COLONIES

- Because its settlers represented many different cultures and religious sects, the middle colonies rejected state control of education and depended on a mixture of church-run and private schools for their educational opportunities.
- Without state involvement, education was very rudimentary, of limited availability, and often nonexistent. Each parochial (church) school did what it wished. Poor and orphaned children, if lucky, attended charity schools for a few years or entered apprenticeships. Meanwhile, children from wealthy families still had private tutors or attended private, tuition schools.

VIRGINIA AND THE OTHER SOUTHERN COLONIES

- Climate, crops, and social class influenced Virginians to develop large plantation-style settlements, and the introduction of indentured servants and enslaved Africans led to a highly stratified class-based society instead of New England's popular democracy.
- High-quality schooling was reserved for the elite, mostly young men. Virginians' expectations for women's education were modest. Children of self-taught, literate poor white farmers often learned from their parents. Students from meager backgrounds learned through apprenticeships, in charity-provided pauper schools (if available), or in church-run school. Impoverished children received a minimal education, at best, lasting only a few years.

OTHER STATES

- The economy, religion, and local views about government involvement in education contributed to the settlers' varying beliefs and practices regarding public schools.
- Initially, these states were indifferent to providing a common education for their populace. As elsewhere, parents with money bought their children an education. If parents did not have the

means, if parents did not want their children formally educated, or if no schools were available locally, children went without.

Educating African Americans and Native Americans

- Both schooling for democratic citizenship and schooling for second-class citizenship have been basic traditions in American education.
- Attempts to provide formal schooling for Native Americans or enslaved Africans and their descendants throughout the early 1700s were limited in scope and local in influence.
- Some education occurred as slaveholders of enslaved families taught African American children the lessons related to their status and work.
- African Americans learned covert lessons necessary to their survival as a people and as human beings rather than as property through teachings by their enslaved community, their families, and their clandestine religious congregations.

Learning Objective 4.4 Trace how public schooling changed during the early national period.

- The new republic's leaders—Washington, Adams, Jefferson, Madison, and others—agreed that a self-governing people needed universal education that would (ideally) motivate all citizens to choose public over private interest. Education's task was nothing less than to erect and maintain the new American nation.
- After the Revolutionary War, the need for all Americans to share a common national loyalty, language, traditions, and skills to participate in a constitutional democracy required tax-supported, secular schools open to all students. But the 19th century's movement for public schools faced bitter arguments and legislative fights over local control, funding, curriculum, religious jealousies, and private interests.
- Recognizing the new nation's increasing religious and cultural diversity, the U.S. Constitution supported the free exercise of religious faith for all by banning any state-sponsored religion. Church and state could no longer be partners in public education, and public schools changed from an institution dominated by religious purpose and content into one charged with enlightening a diverse citizenry for civic participation.

Learning Objective 4.5 Defend how certain factors and persons influenced the U.S. movement toward teaching's increasing professionalization and universal public schooling.

- Teachers in early colonial schools were initially men who earned a living while preparing for another profession or to repay a debt. In general, teaching was ineffective and inefficient and took place in poor facilities with no resources.
- Catherine Esther Beecher (1800-1878), a 19th century educator, reformer, and author, popularized the idea of women's equal access to education, curricular reform, and advanced teaching as a profession for women. By the mid-19th century, women became the majority of educators, especially in elementary and primary grades.
- Throughout the 18th and 19th centuries, white Americans largely assumed that people could be educated to transcend ethnic and religious barriers to become full-fledged members of the American community, but they could not be educated to overcome the barriers of race.
- By 1860, the public educational stepladder spanning from first grade through college had become a reality.
- By 1900, one out of every seven Americans was foreign born. The public schools became the socializing institution to build a unifying national experience, bring order and discipline to the working class, and help the newcomers adjust to their new homeland.
- Horace Mann and Henry Barnard helped professionalize teaching as a career and made the public school movement one of the most enduringly successful of all pre–Civil War reforms.

Learning Objective 4.6 Assess the status of schooling in the late 19th century.

- By the last half of the 19th century, public schools reflected regional differences in the school term's length, the availability of school beyond the primary level, which children had access to schooling, and differences in curriculum, teacher qualifications, and effectiveness. These variations made a year of schooling in one institution or locality significantly different from a year of schooling in another institution or locality.
- At the same time, the white community's cultural assumptions affirmed that people could be educated to transcend ethnic and religious barriers to become fully functioning American citizens, but they could not be educated to transcend the barriers of race. African Americans, Native Americans, and other peoples of color largely remained outside this American cultural community and its public education system.

TEACHER SCENARIO: IT'S YOUR TURN

You have been asked to deliver the opening speech for an education job fair where individuals are exploring the idea of pursuing a career in education. Since 77% of the American public school teachers are female, your talk will address how education came to be a female-dominated profession today whereas it started out in colonial days to be male-dominated. Additionally, trace how education has become increasingly professional in terms of the preparation, qualifications, and instructional skills needed for teachers now versus in colonial days. Your talk should last between 5 and 10 minutes. Write out your speech.

NOTES

1. Cremin, L. A. (1970). *American education: The colonial experience, 16071783.* Harper & Row.
2. Many contemporary historical scholars recognize the need for a more comprehensive approach to American history than the narrow focus on British New England settlements and seek to include Spanish, Dutch, French, West African, and other influences. See: MacDonald, V. M. (2001, Autumn). Hispanic, Latino, Chicano or "other": Deconstructing the relationship between historians and Hispanic-American educational history. *History of Education Quarterly, 41*(3), 365–413.
3. Cremin, 1970.
4. Cremin, L. A. (1977). *Traditions of American education.* Basic Books, pp. 1–10.
5. Erasmus, D. (1936). *The education of a Christian prince*, trans. by L. K. Born. Columbia University Press.
6. Elyot, T. (1883). *The Boke named the governour*, ed. by H. H. S. Croft. Kegan Paul Trench & Co. Cited in Cremin, 1970, pp. 61–63.
7. Barzun, J. (2000). *From dawn to decadence: 1500 to the present.* HarperColllins.
8. Darnton, R. (2003). *George Washington's false teeth: An unconventional guide to the eighteenth century.* Norton, p. 97.
9. Cubberley, E. P. (1947). *Public education in the United States.* Riverside Press, pp. 6–10.
10. Cremin, 1970, p. 67 (italics added).
11. Cubberley first defined four basic types of schooling practices that we cite here. See: Cubberley, 1947, pp. 97–105.
12. Cremin, 1970, p. 129.
13. Vaughan, A. T. (1963). *New England frontier: Puritans and Indians, 1620–1675.* Little Brown; Degler, C. N. (1959–1960). Slavery and the genesis of American race prejudice. *Comparative Studies in Society and History, 11*, 49–66.
14. Cremin, 1970, p. 180.
15. The law of 1642 made no distinction between educating boys or girls because both genders needed to be able to read the Bible to practice their religion appropriately. In practice, however, its application may have been more arbitrary.

16. Perlman, J., Siddali, S. R., & Whitescarver, K. (1997, Summer). Literacy, schooling, and teaching among New England women, 1730–1820. *History of Education Quarterly, 37*(2), 117–139.

17. Cubberley, 1920, p. 365.

18. Perlman et al., 1997.

19. Sklar, K. K. (1993, Winter). The schooling of girls and changing community values in Massachusetts towns, 1750–1820. *History of Education Quarterly, 33*(4), 511–542.

20. Preston, J. A. (2003, September). "He lives as a Master": Seventeenth century masculinity, gendered teaching, and careers of New England schoolmasters. *History of Education Quarterly, 43*(3), 360–371.

21. Preston, 2003, p. 371.

22. Sklar, 1993.

23. Cubberley, 1947, p. 52.

24. Cremin, 1970, p. 558.

25. Cremin, 1970, pp. 187–188.

26. Preston, 2003.

27. Cremin, 1970, pp. 188–189; Preston, 2003.

28. Cremin, 1970, p. 558.

29. Small, W. H. (1914). *Early New England schools.* Ginn, p. 258.

30. Cubberley, 1947, p. 56.

31. Small, 1969.

32. Cubberley, 1947, p. 56.

33. Cremin, 1970, p. 505.

34. Cubberley, 1947, pp. 57–58.

35. Cubberley, 1947, p. 57.

36. Small, W. H. (1914/1969). *Early New England schools.* Ginn, p. 391.

37. Cubberley, 1920, p. 664.

38. Cubberley, 1947, pp. 27–29.

39. Rippa, S. A. (1984). *Education in a free society: An American history.* McKay.

40. Cubberley, 1947, pp. 51–52.

41. Cremin, 1970, p. 503.

42. Cubberley, 1947, p. 31.

43. Reese, W. J. (1995). *The origins of the American high school.* Yale University Press.

44. Beadie, N. (2001, Summer). Academy students in the mid-nineteenth century: Social geography, demography, and the culture of academy attendance. *History of Education Quarterly, 41*(2), 251–262; Leslie, B. (2001, Summer). Where have all the academies gone? *History of Education Quarterly, 41*(2), 262–270.

45. Cremin, 1970, p. 505.

46. Leslie, B. (2001, Summer). Where have all the academies gone? *History of Education Quarterly, 41*(2), 262–270.

47. Cubberley, 1947, p. 113.

48. Nash, M. A. (2001, Summer). Cultivating the powers of human beings: Gendered perspectives on curriculum and pedagogy in academies of the new republic. *History of Education Quarterly, 41*(2), 239–250.

49. Riordan, C. (1990). *Girls and boys in school: Together or separate*? Teachers College Press.

50. Because the grammar schools intended to prepare young men for the ministry, a wholly male occupation at that time, girls could not attend.

51. Leslie, 2001.

52. Hayes, W. (2006). *Horace Mann's vision of the public schools: Is it still relevant?* Rowman and Littlefield Education. http://www.publiceducation.ord/newsblast/pdf/Chapter_One.pdf

53. Sundue, S. B. (2007, April). Confining the poor to ignorance? Eighteenth century experiments with charity education. *History of Education Quarterly, 47*(2), 123–148.

54. Cubberley, 1947, p. 53. This extra fee was often difficult to collect.

55. Cremin, 1970, p. 537.

56. Anderson, J. D. (1988). *The education of blacks in the South, 1860–1935*. University of North Carolina Press, p. 1.

57. Anderson, 1988, p. 16.

58. Cremin, 1980, pp. 221–222.

59. Cremin, 1970, pp. 348–349.

60. Cremin, L. A. (1980). *American education: The national experience, 1783–1876*. Harper & Row, pp. 224–229.

61. Cremin, 1970, pp. 194, 350.

62. Cremin, 1980, pp. 239–241.

63. *Education* meant the full array of institutions that helped shape human character, including families, churches, schools, colleges, newspapers, voluntary associations, and laws.

64. Cremin, 1980, pp. 2–3.

65. Cubberley, 1947, p. 89.

66. McCullough. D. (2001). *John Adams*. Simon & Schuster, p. 223.

67. Cubberley, 1922, p. 363.

68. Hunt, T. C., & Carper, J. C. (2019). *Private schooling*. https://education.stateuniversity.com/pages/2334/Private-Schooling.html

69. Hunt & Carper, 2019.

70. Hunt & Carper, 2019.

71. Cubberley, 1947, p. 139.

72. Cremin, 1980, p. 390.

73. Cremin, 1980, pp. 395–396.

74. Cremin, 1980.

75. Butchart, R. E. (1998). Punishments, penalties, prizes, and procedures: A history of discipline. In R. E. Butchart & B. McEvan (Eds.), *Classroom discipline in American schools* (pp. 19–49). State University of Albany Press.

76. Cubberley, E. P. (1947). *Public education in the United States*. Houghton Mifflin, p. 375.

77. For a more complete discussion of normal schools, see: Bohan, C. H., & Null, J. W. (2007, Summer/Fall). Gender and the evolution of normal school education: A historical analysis of teacher education institutions. *Educational Foundations*, 1–26. https://files.eric.ed.gov/fulltext/EJ831197.pdf

78. Dublin, T. (1979). *Women at work*. Columbia University Press as cited in Weller, K. (1989). Women's history and the history of women teachers. *The Journal of Education, 171*(3), 9–30.

79. Woody, T. (1929). A history of women's education in the United States. Science Press. As cited in Weller, K. (1989). Women's history and the history of women teachers. *The Journal of Education, 171*(3), 9–30.

80. Cedrone, S. (2017, February 289). Catharine Beecher educates the west. *Connecticut Explored*. https://www.ctexplored.org/catharine-beecher-educates-the-west/; Sturges, M. (2019, September 5). *Catharine Beecher, champion of women's education*. Connecticut History.org. https://connecticuthistory.org/catharine-beecher-champion-of-womens-education/; Weiler, K. (1989). Women's history and the history of women teachers. *Journal of Education, 171*(3), 9–30.

81. Michals, D. (2015). *Catharine Beecher*. National Women's History Museum. https://www.womenshistory.org/education-resources/biographies/catharine-esther-beecher

82. Weiler, K. (1989). Women's history and the history of women teachers. *Journal of Education, 171*(3), 17.

83. Baker, R. (1984). The domestication of politics: Women and American political society 1780–1920. *American Historical Review, 89*(3), 620–647.

84. Burstyn, J. N. (1974, September). Catharine Beecher and the Education of American women. *The New England Quarterly, 47*(3), 386–403.

85. Sturges, 2019.

86. Anderson, 1988, pp. 4–12.

87. Cremin, 1980, pp. 242–245.

88. The nine original colonial colleges were Harvard (founded in 1636), William and Mary (1693), Yale (1702), Princeton (1746), University of Pennsylvania (1753–1755), Kings (later Columbia University; 1754), Brown (1764), Rutgers (1766), and Dartmouth (1769).

89. Butts, R. F. (1955). *A cultural history of Western education: Its social and intellectual foundations*. McGraw Hill.

90. Cremin, 1980.

91. Barzun, 2000, p. 489.

92. Mann, H. (1848). *Report no. 12 of the Massachusetts board of education*. Dutton and Wentworth.

93. Mann, H. (1845). *Ninth annual report of the board of education, together with the ninth annual report of the secretary of the board*, p. 69. Cited in Cremin, 1980, p. 139.

94. PBS. (n.d.). Horace Mann (1796–1859): Only a teacher. Schoolhouse Pioneers. *PBS Online*. http://www.pbs.org/onlyateacher/horace.html

95. Cubberley, 1947, pp. 225–226.

96. Cremin, 1980, pp. 143–144.

97. Rothstein, R., Jacobsen, R., & Wilder, T. (2008). *Grading education: Getting accountability right*. Economic Policy Institute and Teachers College Press.

98. Barzun, 2000, p. 489.

99. Cremin, 1980, pp. 141–142.

100. Cremin, 1980, pp. 156–157.

101. Cremin, 1980, p. 155.

102. Brownson, O. A. (1966). *The works of Orestes A. Brownson, vol. XIX*, collected and arranged by H. F. Brownson. AMS Press, pp. 442–443.

103. Cubberley, 1947, p. 227.

104. Cubberley, 1947, p. 226.

105. De Toqueville, A. (1945). *Democracy in America* (vol. II), edited by P. Bradley. Alfred A. Knopf.

iStock/monkeybusinessimages

5 EDUCATION REFORM—1900 TO TODAY

InTASC Standards Addressed: 1, 2, 3, 4, 5, 6, 7, 8, 9, 10

LEARNING OBJECTIVES

After you read this chapter, you should be able to

5.1 Assess how G. Stanley Hall and John Dewey's views of education as human development challenged the traditional subject-centered views and practices.

5.2 Explain how national reports, Frederick Taylor's scientific management theory, and common schools influenced the organization, curriculum, and instruction in schools.

5.3 Compare and contrast how Booker T. Washington, W. E. B. DuBois, and legal and legislative actions advanced education for African American and other underserved students.

5.4 Summarize how World War I, the Great Depression, and vocational education influenced public education in the 20th century.

5.5 Argue how the 1966 *Coleman Report*, including later analyses of the report, ultimately shifted the focus of educational reform.

5.6 Describe how Public Law 94-142 and IDEA components provide free and appropriate education to students with disabilities.

5.7 Assess how *A Nation at Risk* and federal legislation increased public schools' accountability for educating every student.

5.8 Critique how popular trends and innovations—including education privatization, charter schools, virtual education, voucher programs, and social–emotional and personalized learning—are affecting American education.

As a society, we have adopted Horace Mann's vision that public schools are our society's great equalizers. Our early national leaders believed universal education was necessary to ensure the political and social well-being of the United States. They foresaw a country with a unified history, traditions, and common language—all rooted strongly on their own English traditions, religion, language, democratic principles, and school practices.

Ideals about education for all children outran the early national leaders' abilities to put these values into action, however. Societal ignorance and prejudice prevented African Americans, economically disadvantaged students, and students with disabilities from attending—let alone benefiting from—America's public schools. To a large extent, the second part of American public schools' history demonstrates our nation's attempts to extend and address these unmet needs.

In this chapter, we discuss the changing concepts of schooling emerging from the late 1800s through the first two decades of the 21st century. Along the way, we look at educational figures who shifted the focus and practice of public education. We consider the legal, legislative, and financial interventions used to increase access and success of all students, especially the underserved, and consider several contemporary education trends. Finally, we examine the ways American public schools have tried to meet these goals.

5.1 CHALLENGES TO TRADITIONAL CONCEPTS OF SCHOOLING

Colonial and early national educators believed that certain book knowledge, such as studying the Christian Bible and devotional texts and the *New England Primer*, would give students the training necessary for life and citizenship. They assumed that all children learned in the same ways. Memorization and recitation—getting the facts into students' heads through practice and then repeating them back to the teacher—were the most frequently used teaching and learning methods.

As the 20th century approached, the idea of **pedagogy** —that is, teaching as a profession with certain methods, techniques, and materials to promote student learning—took new scientific and philosophical directions. Fresh ideas challenged traditionalist thinking about curriculum and instruction. Heated debates would soon follow between those favoring a child-centered approach that considered how children actually learned and those who focused on a subject-centered approach for transmitting important cultural knowledge.

5.1a The Subject-Centered Education Approach

Between 1860 and 1890, **faculty psychology** became popular. This viewpoint held that intellect, will, and emotions all had their own "place" or compartments in the mind, and the mind could be trained by a uniform procedure of mental discipline and drill. According to **mental discipline theory**, building the "powers of the mind"—attention, will, memory, imagination, feelings, judgment, reasoning, observation, and sense discrimination through memorization, practice, and recitation—developed children's moral character while they learned important information.

If "mental discipline" was the pedagogy, then traditional Western European subjects formed the curriculum. Latin, Greek, French, German, mathematics, rhetoric, grammar, history, physics, chemistry, government, biology, and the Great Books were seen as the anchors of a strong education. The rationale was simple and circular: The more difficult the curriculum, the more the students had to exercise their minds. The more exercise, the more value attributed to the subject. Any academic subjects that could not find a mental discipline rationale remained outside the curriculum.

The mental discipline approach required a very detailed set of courses that precisely spelled out the work that all pupils in each grade in all town or city schools would master. Regardless of students' age, past experiences, future prospects, or physical or mental condition, one course of study was assumed to be appropriate for all. Proponents viewed this system as egalitarian because everyone received the "elite" curriculum. Teachers taught. Intensive drill, practice, and memorization were keys to learning. Students either learned or left school. Many aspects of this traditional approach remain to this day.

5.1b The Child-Centered Education Approach

In the late 1800s, a new academic discipline, psychology, made many educators rethink the teaching and learning processes. **Psychology** entailed the scientific study of human behavior in general and the mind in particular. Reversing the traditional subject-centered model, psychologists now placed students—not subjects—at teaching's center. The educational focus moved to the learner and the ways the learners learned.[1] In turn, the view that a school's purpose was to assist children to develop their inborn capacities began to gain favor.

Many of the early impulses toward placing students rather than subjects at the center of education efforts came from Europe, influenced by the work of Italian educator Maria Montessori.[2] Advocates of a "new education" insisted that young children should be educated in kindly and natural ways and that they learned best not through books but through sensory experience and contact with actual objects.[3] These concepts would profoundly influence American thinkers about the most effective ways of educating children.

5.1c G. Stanley Hall

In the 1880s and early 1890s, members of the **child study movement** investigated how children's minds and personalities developed. An American psychologist, G. Stanley Hall (1844–1924), pioneered the experimental study of child development. In 1878, he earned Harvard's first doctorate in psychology.[4] Soon thereafter, he began to study children's minds at the age when they entered school. Using questionnaires, Hall and his colleagues systematically observed, questioned, and measured children, tabulating a variety of traits, opinions, and facts. Hall's scientific approach to observing children brought credibility to the child study movement. As a result, by 1900 the child study movement had become a key part of educational psychology.

G. Stanley Hall, child study movement pioneer.

Frederick Gutekunst, public domain, via Wikimedia Commons

Hall believed that a child's psychological life and behaviors develop through a series of stages that correspond more or less to the stages through which the human race has traveled from savagery to civilization. Children's normal mental growth requires living through each of the stages, and each stage provides the building blocks for the next. According to this belief, the task of family and school is to adjust to and foster that development rather than to try to shape or control it. "To a nation about to celebrate 'the century of the child,' his doctrines had enormous appeal."[5]

First at Johns Hopkins University and later at Clark University, Hall and his colleagues concluded that teachers using child study findings could be more effective by adapting their instructional practices to meet students' learning needs. For teachers, this meant extending kindergarten's informality upward into the elementary grades and adjusting the curriculum to fit children's natural rhythms of interest and need. Hall introduced art, music, gardening, manual training, domestic science, and physical education into the school program and encouraged development of parks and playgrounds.[6]

Hall's work helped shift teaching's focus from the subject to the student through his assertion that no education could be worthy, much less efficient, if it ignored students' true nature, needs, and development. His work placed a new emphasis on the scientific study of students' feelings, dispositions, and attitudes as part of the learning process. Most importantly, Hall's approach "subtly shifted the burden of proof in the educational situation, and in so doing, the meaning of equal opportunity as well."[7] This view would later lead to substantial changes in both curriculum and instruction.

Hall's child-centered approach risked moving school too close to the student, creating schools dedicated to allowing students to set all the terms and conditions on the learning content and process. Reacting to education's traditional overemphasis on control, order, and disregard for the learners' interests and welfare, the child-centered movement pulled too far in the other direction. Neither approach was fully in the students' best interests. The middle ground between the subject-centered and child-centered extremes would be a more reasonable and effective place for teaching and learning.

5.1d John Dewey

John Dewey brought education reform back to the middle. An education philosopher (as discussed in Chapter 3), Dewey advanced a pedagogy that included both content and students within their social contexts. In turn, the struggle over school curriculum would become a broader struggle over how the schools would contribute to social progress. With Dewey, educational concerns affecting African Americans, women, the poor, and immigrants became public policy issues connected to social improvements.

John Dewey focused on subjects and students in their social contexts and worked to improve teaching and learning.

Underwood & Underwood, NY/Library of Congress, LC-USZ62-51525

John Dewey did not coin the term "**progressive**" (that credit goes to an educational movement begun in the late 19th century in which children were believed to learn best from real-life experiences with other people), but it ultimately became associated with him.[8] Educated as a psychologist, Dewey completed his doctoral studies at Johns Hopkins University. He eventually set up a laboratory school at the University of Chicago to test his ideas about teaching children. In 1905, he left Chicago for Columbia University, where he worked until his death in 1952.

Calls for educational improvement characterized Dewey's era. Businesses and labor unions wanted schools to provide students with apprenticeships to prepare them for work. Settlement workers and municipal reformers wanted schools to provide poor residents and immigrants with instruction in hygiene, domestic science, manual arts, and child care. Patriots wanted schools to teach children how to become better Americans. Agrarians wanted schools to train students to appreciate country life and stop moving to the cities. All of these demands reflected a common message: The family, neighborhood, and workshop were no longer fulfilling their time-honored educational functions. Schools had inherited the educational role from other social institutions that could no longer do what they had always done because the modern world was too complex and too large.[9]

In Dewey's view, schools had the mission to advance democratic principles and form common democratic communities. Rather than strictly focusing on child-centered self-expression and self-development or on the traditional curriculum that left students unconnected to their real world, Dewey believed that the larger society was a vitally important part of education. "Democracy has to be born anew every generation, and education is its midwife," Dewey observed. He emphasized the importance of students developing social insights and a sense of community consciousness. Schools, he thought, could become a miniature democracy where students learned about their differences and commonalities, where vocational studies coexisted with academic ones, and where tolerance and diversity partnered with critical mindedness. To this end, Dewey pressed insistently for the type of common schooling that would bring the children of all classes, creeds, and ethnic backgrounds into little "embryonic communities."[10]

At the same time, Dewey regarded the traditional curriculum as undemocratic: "A democracy cannot flourish where there is a narrowly utilitarian education for one class and broadly liberal education for another. It demands a universal education in the problems of living together, one broadly human in outlook."[11] He recognized that the classical subject-centered curriculum served as a means to preserve social and class status through exclusivity and inequity. Unless students were planning to become statesmen, professionals, or intellectuals, they did not need to learn Latin and Greek languages. Instead, students needed to learn English and other practical knowledge and skills. Dewey believed in a common culture based on individual growth and development linked with social integration.

To connect formal learning and the real world, Dewey's lab school built its curriculum around social occupations such as cooking, carpentry, and sewing. From these occupations, students learned arithmetic, reading, writing, and sciences as each developed from their experiences with their lives outside school. In this context, motivating student learning no longer depended on threats or punishments. Students were genuinely interested in the learning activities that they saw as worthwhile, relevant, and understandable.

Effective teaching interested Dewey. Based on his laboratory work, he determined that good teaching must address three factors. First, teachers need to understand the learners' interests, problems, and developmental level. Second, teachers must present knowledge in ways that are relevant and make sense to the learners. Third, classrooms should reflect society's highest democratic values: tolerance, cooperation, critical mindedness, and political awareness.[12]

Armed with this innovative perspective, Dewey merged ideas about science with those of democracy. He advocated using the scientific method in teaching and learning, believing that intelligent inquiry could transform problems into progress. He believed that school should teach students how to be problem solvers by helping them learn how to think rather than simply having them memorize large amounts of information. Students in a healthy democracy needed to know how to think by themselves and act with social responsibility. Good learning, he concluded, originates in genuine life experiences, framed intellectually as problems to be investigated, hypotheses generated and tested to bring new insights on the original problem.

For Dewey, education did not consist solely of transmitting information to passive learners. Instead, education was an act of reconstruction: adding to experiences' meaning in ways that made sense to students and increased their ability to direct later experiences and control their surroundings. Active learning, Dewey insisted, was essential to education. Intelligence was the purposive reorganization of experience.

Dewey's educational ideas tried to reconcile the seemingly unworkable dualism between the subject-centered and child-centered views. Over time, his work would change teaching and learning in American public schools.

FLIPSIDES

Child-Centered Versus Subject-Centered Education

For over 100 years, educators have been arguing the merits of child-centered teaching as compared with subject-centered teaching. As a future teacher, which approach do you think best supports and advances student learning?

Children—not subjects—should be at the center of learning.	Subjects—not children—should be at the center of learning.
• All children are different and learn in different ways.	• All children learn the same way.
• Teachers should consider children's actual nature, needs, and development in planning and delivering their lessons.	• Teachers should provide students with intensive drill and practice of new learning through memorization and recitation to help them remember what they are learning and build the students' moral character.

Children—not subjects—should be at the center of learning.	Subjects—not children—should be at the center of learning.
• Educators' job is to adapt their instructional practices in ways that foster children's development of their inborn capacities.	• Educators' job is to transmit our important cultural knowledge by stressing the subject content.
• Children learn best through sensory, real-life experiences with other people (rather than solely by books and lectures).	• Children learn best by mental practice, memorization, and recitation of what they have learned.
• Theory of learning developed through systematic observations, questioning, and measurement of how actual children learned.	• Theory of learning developed on belief that the human mind can be strengthened through exercise and mental discipline.
• All students should study academic subjects as well as art, music, physical education, and vocational subjects that naturally fit children's interests and needs. This makes education universal and democratic.	• All students should study the same "elite" curriculum, regardless of their past experiences and future goals. This makes education egalitarian.
• Schools' mission is to advance democratic principles and practices by having students learn the common culture that all Americans share.	• Students who do not learn the "elite" curriculum can either work harder or leave school.
• Students need to develop critical thinking skills and learn to be problem solvers.	• Students need to learn the big ideas of Western culture.
• Students need to develop social insights and a sense of community—learning how to get along with others who may be different than themselves—to prepare them to live in a democratic society.	• Students need to learn the subjects that reflect our cultural heritage.
• Teaching effectiveness matters: Understand students' needs; present knowledge in ways that are relevant and meaningful to students; maintain tolerant, cooperative, critical minded, and politically aware classrooms.	• Teaching effectiveness depends on giving students the "elite" curriculum with sufficient drill and practice to help them learn it.
• Teachers motivate students by making learning relevant and interesting to them.	• Teachers motivate students by threats and punishment.
• Main criticism of the other view: Subject-centered/traditional pedagogy tends to overemphasize control, order, and disregard for learners' interests or well-being.	• Main criticism of the other view: Child-centered pedagogy, when misapplied, lets children (rather than experts) set the terms and conditions and keeps them unconnected from the real world.

What do you see as the strengths and weakness of each approach for educating 21st century children? How might you as a teacher use aspects of each approach to generate student learning?

5.2 NATIONAL REPORTS AND SCIENTIFIC MANAGEMENT THEORY INFLUENCE PUBLIC SCHOOLS' ORGANIZATION AND CURRICULUM

In the late 1800s and early 1900s, as waves of varied and impoverished newcomers arrived to make their homes and futures in America, well-to-do citizens realized that their country's best interests lay in educating the "lower" classes. To tackle this problem, between 1842 and 1918 all states passed compulsory education attendance laws.

At the same time, differences among the nation's schools increased. In the North, African American children were attending separate, segregated schools resulting from neighborhood segregation or gerrymandered school districts. Southern law and custom largely closed public education to students of color. Vocational high schools were becoming common in the larger cities, sorting students along class and gender lines, as did the vocational tracks within comprehensive high schools. A fresh look at curriculum was imminent.

5.2a Liberal Arts and the High School Curriculum

In the 1890s, less than 5% of the U.S. student-age population attended high school.[13] Almost all of those individuals went on to graduate and enroll in college. Because each college had its own requirements, policy makers thought a common high-status high school curriculum could ensure that all prospective college students had the appropriate academic background.

Committee of Ten

In 1893, the National Education Association (NEA) appointed a Committee of Ten to establish a standard high school curriculum for students planning to attend college.[14] The committee's final report advanced a highly traditional set of liberal arts studies: Latin, English literature, modern languages (such as German or French), algebra, geometry, physics, chemistry, natural history, history, and geography. All students were to take these courses, regardless of their background, educational plans, or career directions.

The Committee of Ten never imagined that secondary school would become universal or that students preparing for the workforce would need such an academically oriented curriculum. Nevertheless, the subject-centered emphasis of its report and its active disregard for differing students' needs would find a strong reaction among future educators.

Committee of Fifteen

Next, the NEA formed the Committee of Fifteen to address elementary education. In 1895, the Committee of Fifteen endorsed the traditional subject-centered courses: grammar, literature, arithmetic, geography, and history. Unlike the high school report, however, the elementary curriculum report urged that academic topics be "correlated" with—not taught in isolation from—the arts (vocal music, drawing, physical exercise, and hygiene). For seventh- and eighth-grade boys, it recommended manual training, such as woodwork; for girls, it recommended sewing and cooking.[15]

The *Cardinal Principles Report* of 1918

During the early 1900s, high schools prepared increasing cohorts of middle-class students for work and college. From 1890 to 1930, public high school enrollments virtually doubled every decade, bringing in more students who were not preparing for college.[16] High schools began to include alternatives to traditional liberal arts, permitting different students to study different subjects within the same school.

Recognizing the trend toward a more diverse student body, the NEA sponsored a new report on high schools. The resulting *Cardinal Principles* report of 1918 became one of the 20th century's most influential education documents. It called for expanded and differentiated high school programs that would better serve the new, highly dissimilar secondary school student population.

The proponents of the *Cardinal Principles* believed that requiring all students to follow the same traditional academic course of study increased educational inequality. The 1918 report recommended that high schools adopt a more comprehensive approach, placing equal value on traditional liberal arts, vocational development, citizenship education, physical activity, and such personal needs as instruction in personal hygiene, the "worthy use of leisure," and wholesome boy–girl relationships.[17]

To do this, *Cardinal Principles* advocated a common core of knowledge and courses that would be far less academically substantial than the traditional college preparatory curriculum. Reflecting what was actually occurring in public high schools, *Cardinal Principles* established a blueprint for the modern comprehensive high school. Intending to develop the whole student for life and work, high schools dropped the preoccupation with academic and intellectual disciplines and replaced it with a broadened curricular scope and a sorting function related to students' perceived abilities and future vocations.

This new vision of schooling affected high schools in several ways. Schools' differentiated curriculum allowed students to follow their own academic or vocational interests and plans. All students took courses in general education, designed as unifying learning experiences to promote the common knowledge and shared values needed for responsible citizenship. To help students make curricular and career selections, guidance and counseling programs along with intelligence and achievement tests and other educational measurement instruments became integral parts of education.

Criticism of the Comprehensive High School

If the Committee of Ten's recommendations were weighted too heavily toward a classical academic curriculum, then the *Cardinal Principles* recommendations went too far in the opposite direction, diluting high schools' academic focus.[18] Designed to meet individual differences, the comprehensive high school developed a tracked curriculum and did not do enough to raise all students to high academic standards. The availability of advanced, average, and below-average courses ensured that all students moved through the program at varying levels of intellectual rigor. The common learning intended to provide a shared experience in American ideas and values became a required core curriculum that "tracked" students did not share. Advanced, average, and below-average students might enter the same school building in the morning and never meet in the classrooms. Nevertheless, this commitment to educating all high school students under the same roof with a range of curricular choices has remained a mainstay of the U.S. educational system.

5.2b Frederick Taylor and Scientific Management of Schools

Early 20th century business and industry leaders saw education as an important way to promote efficiency and profitability. Highly influenced by industrialization's mechanisms, factory productivity, and good organization, educators and business proposed applying **scientific management**, a process for increasing institutional competence, to ensure quality, standardized school outcomes. This organizational approach fit well with the *Cardinal Principles* report in arranging high schools for maximum cost-effectiveness.

Frederick Taylor (1865–1915), an engineer and the world's first efficiency expert, developed the concept of scientific management to provide businesses and factories with increased production and lower costs. To implement his ideas, Taylor contracted with companies to rearrange their production processes, simplifying each employee's tasks. According to Taylor, the "best practices" were those that gained the highest productivity with the least effort. Instead of doing many different things, workers in "Taylorized" factories executed the same simple tasks over and over. This increased production reduced an employer's need for skilled labor and lowered management's costs.

Educators adapted Taylor's views on organizational efficiency to American schooling. For schools, scientific management was not a natural fit, however. Laboring on an assembly line was not the same as educating dissimilar children. In making a factory model work in schools, teachers had to identify actual learning outcomes and take measurements to determine whether students had achieved those outcomes. The adaptation of Taylor's approach to the classroom, therefore, begat the science of school measurement: finding supposedly objective and numerical ways to demonstrate student achievement. Other efficiency reforms required teachers to document their teaching activities to prove that they were minimizing "waste." Because many of Taylor's education disciples were not educators themselves, they seldom tried to tell teachers what or how to teach.

How Scientific Management Worked in Schools

Scientific management in schools had curricular, instructional, and social implications. Schools developed tracking practices, placing students into unique programs of study, such as college-preparatory or vocational education, based on their demonstrated or assumed intelligence. In this way, high schools sorted and selected society's future leaders and workers.

Educators liked this system because it appeared to reward student merit. Students who learned well received rewards; students who did not learn as readily did not. Likewise, students saw themselves either as intelligent, superior, and worthy of a promising future or as not intelligent and unworthy. As a consequence, self-fulfilling prophesies were set in motion.

Between 1900 and 1930, school administrators began to see themselves as managers rather than as educators. They used scientific management ideas to help their schools accommodate the large numbers of immigrant children at low cost. Children entered school and moved through the grades with their age-peers, changing classes at predetermined intervals to ringing bells. Today, we know that children grow and develop at different and variable rates, so automatically moving students in tandem with those of their chronological age rewarded students who showed quicker development. Those who developed more slowly fell behind and dropped out. Many of these practices persist in schools today.

Criticism of Scientific Management in Schools

In the long run, the factory model proved ill-suited to both business and schools. Although mass production and its industrial ethos were brilliant innovations in their time, by the late 20th century, they had become liabilities for companies having to survive in competitive, rapidly evolving world markets. Daily work routines have a powerful impact in shaping an organization's culture. Instead of dividing work into smaller and less meaningful tasks in which quality was someone else's responsibility, organizations in the late 20th and 21st centuries had to educate, empower, and engage all of their employees in a process of continuously improving their product's quality—and their own knowledge and skills.

Scientific management had a similar effect in schools, which became increasingly bureaucratic, impersonal, departmentalized, and isolated from the larger society. School codes and procedures spelled out exactly how to address every detail of school life. Students moved through the fragmented curriculum, and standardized tests purported to measure the quality of their learning. Self-fulfilling prophesies meant lower aspirations, less learning, and worse life outcomes for lower-track students. And, as learning became less meaningful to students, misbehavior increased, absences and dropouts increased, and academic quality and student achievement declined.[19]

5.2c The Myth of the Common School

John Dewey, like Horace Mann before him, believed in the common school's power to integrate students of varied economic, ethnic, and cultural backgrounds and help them become educated people capable of living in and supporting a democratic republic. How well did this vision become a reality?

The common school was essentially a phenomenon in America's North and West, thriving best where a reasonable homogeneity of race, class, and religion already existed. Common schools were decidedly less common in the South and in America's large cities. Three trends undermined this ideal in those areas.

First, newly freed African Americans in the South were systematically barred from access to common schools. Public elementary schools became available to the majority of southern African American children only during the first third of the 20th century, long after common schools became available for other American children.[20] For many southern African American youth, high school education did not become available until later still.

Second, on religious grounds, some parents would not forgo their own sacred doctrine for that of another group or for schools' secular needs. Roman Catholics created Catholic schools for all their children. Several ethnic groups—Pennsylvania Amish, for instance—resisted common schooling on the belief that it would prevent their children from properly appreciating their Old World language and customs.

Third, members of the eastern upper classes often sent their children to private schools while residential segregation separated students by social class on a geographic basis. Living in neighborhoods reflecting their parents' level of wealth, children of different classes went to different neighborhood schools. One celebrated common school, however, was the single-social-class slum schools that brought together immigrant children of different ethnic and religious backgrounds.[21]

Certain parents did not want their children to mix with students from other social classes or ethnic/racial/religious groups. Others expressed genuine concern about the common schools' poor academic quality, preferring to educate their children in private schools rather than upgrade the public educational programs. These arguments remain with us, influencing some of our most difficult educational and political problems.

To consider in depth how late 19th and early 20th century education innovations affected public schools, some which continue today, complete the activity in the **Reflect & Engage** box, Late 19th and Early 20th Century American Education.

REFLECT & ENGAGE: LATE 19TH AND EARLY 20TH CENTURY AMERICAN EDUCATION

This is a group activity that involves a role play. The mid- to late 19th and early 20th centuries saw many innovations in thought and practice that would define modern American public schools at all levels (K–12).

A. Complete Table 5.1, using the text and a partner as debate resources.

TABLE 5.1 ■ Public School Innovations and Practices, Early 20th Century

Rationale/Philosophy	Description of Key Ideas and Practices		Major Proponent/s	Where This Aspect Is Seen in Public Schools Today
	Curriculum	Instructional Practices		
Mental discipline/subject-centered education				
Child-centered education				
Scientific management and *Cardinal Principles*, 1918				

B. Role Play: John Dewey and Frederick Taylor plan to debate "The Purpose and Practice of School" at your local college. In groups of four, prepare their arguments that express their views on the following five issues:

- The purpose of public education
- The structure of public education
- The impact of psychology on teaching and learning
- The role of teachers in educating children
- The types of curriculum and instruction that will best prepare students to live in a rapidly changing world

C. Divide the class into small groups, half preparing Dewey's talk and the other half preparing Taylor's talk.

D. Each group selects a member to represent Dewey or Taylor and deliver their argument to the rest of the class. "Deweys" can present together, and "Taylors" can present together.

E. After the debates, discuss these ideas as a class: Which approach is best for today's world, and why?

5.3 WASHINGTON, DUBOIS, LAWSUITS, AND LEGISLATION ADVANCE AFRICAN AMERICAN EDUCATION

African Americans emerged from being enslaved with a strong belief in the desirability of learning how to read and write, and they demanded universal schooling. Mostly impoverished, they had to find a new way of life—one that included education to make the other promises possible.

5.3a Seeking Educational Gains

From 1865 to 1872, the Bureau of Refugees, Freedmen, and Abandoned Lands (more simply called the Freedmen Bureau) helped resettle African Americans. It constructed and operated schools for African American children, collecting money from various private-aid agencies and philanthropic societies to purchase buildings, provide curriculum materials, and hire teachers. During its first few years, it had no congressional appropriations.

Without publicly supported Southern schools, many formerly enslaved African Americans established their own educational collectives and associations and staffed schools entirely with African American teachers. At least 500 of these "native schools" were found throughout the South.[22] By the 1870s, African American Southerners had constructed and maintained a semblance of a common school system using their own scant resources.[23]

In the late 19th century, many Southern whites opposed universal schooling. They feared political instability if educated African Americans competed for jobs with white laborers. In addition, they recognized that teaching African Americans to read and write would enable them to read and sign their name to voting ballots. In many Southern states, African Americans accounted for 40% to 60% of the total population, giving the principle of "one man, one vote" ominous implications. Therefore, during the Southern education movement of 1901 to 1915, the region resisted educational reforms that might benefit African Americans, opposed public school appropriations, and excluded these students from compulsory school laws.

Despite the Fourteenth Amendment's due process protections, African Americans were neither safe nor equal under the law. The South witnessed 49 racially based lynchings in 1882, and 155 of these murders 10 years later.[24] In the South, "separate but equal" became the dominant social doctrine, officially approved in the 1896 *Plessy v. Ferguson* Supreme Court ruling (this case is discussed in more detail later in this chapter). Hate groups like the Ku Klux Klan became popular. It would take compelling African American leaders, U.S. Supreme Court rulings, and federal legislation to make high-quality public education a possibility for African American students and other students of color.

5.3b Booker T. Washington

Booker T. Washington, educator and advocate, developed educational and economic opportunities for African Americans.

Frances Benjamin Johnston Collection, Library of Congress, LC-J694-255

Born in Virginia, the son of an African American mother and a white father, Booker Taliaferro Washington (1856–1915) grew up enslaved. In 1865, when freedom came, his family moved to a

West Virginia mining town, where his stepfather found work. As a young boy, Washington took a job in a salt mine that began at 4 a.m. so he could attend school later in the day. He learned to read and write at the local African American Baptist church. At age 10, he took a servant's job at a wealthy general's home and educated himself in the family's library. These experiences formed Washington's intelligence and attitudes, likely giving him an early orientation in accommodation and compromise.

At 16, with his parents' permission, Washington walked 200 miles to attend the Hampton Institute (now University) in Virginia, arriving with 50 cents in his pocket. He paid his tuition and board by working as the janitor. The head teacher was suspicious of Washington's country ways and ragged clothes, and she admitted him only after he had cleaned a room to her satisfaction.[25]

At Hampton Institute, Washington aspired to become a lawyer but received a vocational education. Hampton's mission was to provide an industrial education as a dignified pursuit and a reasonable first step in assisting African Americans to move out of poverty. Students learned vocational practices as well as attitudinal and moral ones: thrift, abstinence, order, and cleanliness. At Hampton, it was understood that once people of color had job skills, they could assimilate and become part of the larger culture.[26] Washington adopted this practical philosophy for himself.

Strongly believing that education would raise his people to equality in this country, Washington became a teacher. In 1881, he founded the Tuskegee Normal and Industrial Institute in Tuskegee, Alabama, with the goal of training teachers, farmers, and tradesmen. He encouraged graduates to return as educated individuals to their hometowns to raise African American education levels. As the head of Tuskegee Institute, he traveled the country to raise funds, and he became a well-known speaker.

A practical realist, Washington saw African Americans' social and economic improvement as a long struggle to be won one step at a time. Education for people of color meant developing practical wage-earning skills and diligent work habits that set the foundation for self-sustaining, segregated communities. Washington encouraged a peaceful apartheid between Blacks and whites and worked to develop educational and economic opportunities for his people. Only later could African American communities demand and expect increased political, educational, and economic opportunities.[27] As Washington saw it, by working within the system, African Americans would transcend it.

Washington's vision was pragmatic and sometimes controversial. A believer in self-reliance, he asserted that African Americans could secure their constitutional rights through their own economic and moral advancement rather than through legal and political changes. For instance, to prevent racial strife, Washington discouraged African Americans from voting, running for political office, and pursuing civil equality.[28]

To accomplish his ends, Washington advanced African American interests without offending white people who were in positions to stop African American progress. He wrote, "In all things that are truly social, we [Blacks and whites] are as separate as the fingers, yet one as the hand in all things essential to mutual progress."[29] This clear image suggesting racial separation made white people feel comfortable with African American advancement. Washington's vision for African American advancement did not include competing with white people for higher education, professional jobs, or social status—so his message did not threaten them. His agenda was peaceful adjustment.

Although Washington's conciliatory stance angered some African American intellectuals who feared it would encourage the equal rights foes, his major achievement was to win over varied groups of Southern whites without whose support the programs he envisioned and brought into being would have been impossible. Other African American leaders like W. E. B. DuBois wanted to move faster and farther.

5.3c W. E. B. DuBois

William Edward Burghardt DuBois was a scholar dedicated to attacking racial injustice and defending individual freedom. Endorsing a policy of "educate and agitate," he demanded full and immediate political and civil gains—including voting rights, access to liberal (not vocational) education, and equal economic opportunities—for African Americans.

W. E. B. DuBois, scholar and writer, agitated for African American educational, economic, and civic equality.

Cornelius M. Battey, 1918, Library of Congress, LC-DIG-ppmsca-38818

DuBois (1868–1963) was born in Great Barrington, Massachusetts. DuBois's great-grandfather had fought in the American Revolution, and the Burghardts had been an accepted part of the community for generations. Yet from his earliest years, DuBois was aware of differences that set him apart from his Yankee neighbors. In addition to the hymns sung in his village Congregational Church, he learned his grandmother's songs passed through the generations from Africa. As a youngster, DuBois believed himself part of an earlier tradition that stood in sharp contrast to the detailed chronicle of Western civilization learned at school.[30]

Intellectually gifted, Dubois received a scholarship to attend Fisk College (now University) in Nashville, Tennessee. In his first trip south, he saw the discrimination, poverty, inferior land, ignorance, and prejudice directed toward African Americans and witnessed African Americans' desire for knowledge. He completed his bachelor's and PhD degrees at Harvard—the first African American to earn a Harvard doctorate.

While on a University of Pennsylvania fellowship, DuBois conducted intensive social research on African Americans as a social system, the first time anyone had undertaken such a scientific approach to studying social phenomena.[31] As a sociology professor at Atlanta University, DuBois studied African American morality, urbanization, African Americans in business, college-bred African Americans, the African American church, and African American crime. He repudiated the widely held view of Africa as a vast cultural unknown by presenting a historical version of Africa's complex, civilizing development.

As a result of these rich and varied experiences, DuBois developed a broader and more radical perspective on American social reform than did Booker T. Washington. Essentially, they represented two sides of an ideological divide. DuBois rejected Washington's accommodation policy, calling instead for "ceaseless agitation and insistent demand for equality" and the "use of force of every sort: moral suasion, propaganda, and where possible even physical resistance."[32] DuBois asserted that Washington's emphasis on industrial education, conciliation, and silence about African American civil and political rights led to bad policy, which limited African Americans' advancement.

DuBois stressed that African Americans needed a traditional liberal arts education so that they could move forward intellectually, politically, and economically. At a minimum, he believed, 10% of the African American population—the "Talented Tenth"—should receive a classical education at the leading American universities, much like his own. In his view, this Talented Tenth would use their liberal arts education and knowledge of modern culture to guide the African Americans to a higher civilization.

Continually pushing for African Americans' full civil and political rights, in 1910 DuBois and his advocacy colleagues joined with white intellectuals and activists—including John Dewey—and formed the National Association for the Advancement of Colored People (NAACP). DuBois became its director of publications and research.[33] After World War I, DuBois's angry editorials in the NAACP magazine, *Crisis*, about the injustices done to African American veterans influenced Congress to pass legislation that established a federal work plan for returning veterans, opened officer training schools for African Americans, and prompted law enforcement to bring legal action against lynchers.

Over the years, DuBois concluded that only struggle and protest could bring social change in the racist culture of the United States. Although he supported integration and equal rights for everyone regardless of race, his thinking often exhibited black separatist–nationalist tendencies.[34]

Both Washington and DuBois saw school and educational opportunities as the foundation for improving African Americans' lives. Both advocated for improved African American schooling. It would take many years to accomplish even part of their goal, and decisions in groundbreaking court cases—rather than public opinion—would lead the way.

5.3d Gaining Access to Universal Education

In 1900, only 36% of African American children aged 5 to 14 attended school. Only 22% of those aged 5 to 9 years and slightly more than half of children aged 10 to 14 years attended school. Those fortunate enough to go received less than 6 months of instruction per year.[35]

From 1880 to the 1930s, almost all southern rural communities with significantly large African American populations and more than half of the major southern cities failed to provide any public high schools for African American youths.[36] By contrast, by the early 1930s, state-sponsored and state-funded building campaigns had made public secondary schools available to all classes of white children.[37] For African American youths in the South, the struggle to attain public high school enrollment would continue until after World War II. This lack of educational opportunity fundamentally hindered their social and economic adjustment.

Meanwhile, courts were challenging discriminatory practices that affected African American students' access for free public schooling. The *Roberts* case, *Plessy v. Ferguson*, and *Cummings v. Board of Education* would pave the way for the 1954 U.S. Supreme Court's *Brown* ruling that desegregated America's public schools. Table 5.2 identifies and briefly describes these early cases.

TABLE 5.2 ■ Court Challenges to Open Public Schools to African American Children

Court Case Importance	Description and Outcome
***Roberts v. City of Boston*, 1849** Initiated the legal and educational concept of "separate but equal" that would remain entrenched for more than 100 years.	Five-year-old Sarah Roberts had to walk past five nearby Boston elementary schools for white children (that refused to enroll her) to reach the dilapidated Smith Grammar School, established in 1820 for African Americans. Finally, her father contacted lawyer Charles Sumner to challenge the unequal treatment. Massachusetts Chief Justice Lemuel Shaw ruled that all citizens should have "equality before the law," but this did not mean that there could not be separate schools for African American children.
***Plessy v. Ferguson*, 1896** U.S. Supreme Court established racial discrimination—"separate but equal"—as a national standard for society and schools.	In 1892, 30-year-old Homer Plessy, a "colored" shoemaker (one-eighth African American) was arrested and jailed for sitting in the "white" car of the East Louisiana Railroad. Plessy agreed to work with a small group of African American New Orleans professionals to challenge this law's arbitrariness. The U.S. Supreme Court decided that a Louisiana law requiring "separate but equal" accommodations for Blacks and whites on intrastate railroads was constitutional.
***Cummings v. Richmond County Board of Education, Georgia*, 1899** U.S. Supreme Court decision confirmed that both the Fourteenth Amendment's equal protection clause and *Plessy's* "separate but equal" rule were virtually meaningless.[38]	The Richmond County school board closed the African American high school, turned the building into an African American elementary school (rather than improve the original elementary school's facilities), and it recommended the displaced African American students try to enroll in church-affiliated schools. When this decision was legally challenged, the U.S. Supreme Court replied that education was a state concern. Public school boards did not have to offer secondary education for African American youths, and a state could constitutionally maintain separate education systems for African Americans and white students in public and private institutions.

The *Roberts* case established the legal and educational concept of "separate but equal." *Plessy* made racial discrimination a legal national standard for society and schools. The *Cummings* precedent required African American children to attend schools in substandard facilities and receive poor instruction, frequently with school in session only a few months of the year. Additionally, funding for African American and white schools, although separate, was far from equal. In 1931, southern states spent an average of $45.63 for each white child's education and only $14.95 for each African American student. Of the total school expenditures in the South, only 10.7% went to support African American students.[39]

5.3e *Brown v. Board of Education*, 1954

In *Brown v. Board of Education*, African American children of elementary school age living in Topeka, Kansas, had a suit filed on their behalf to be allowed to enroll in the public schools serving white children. They said that segregated public schools were not equal and could not be made equal, thereby depriving the children of the equal protection of the laws.

Children involved with *Brown v. Board of Education*. The U. S. Supreme Court decided that public school segregation is unconstitutional.

Carl Iwasaki / Contributor / Getty Images

In a unanimous 1954 ruling, the U.S. Supreme Court agreed. They wrote that "separate but equal" was "inherently unequal." According to this decision, the practice of segregating public school children solely on the basis of race deprived children of color of equivalent educational opportunities, even though the physical facilities and other "tangible" (material) factors might be identical. The ruling in the *Brown* case became a watershed moment for American education and for larger society as well.

The Court concluded that education was the most important state and local government function: to prepare children to live as good citizens in a democratic society, make them aware of our cultural values, and ready them for later professional training. Segregated educational facilities provided unequal educational opportunities. To separate children from others of similar age and qualifications solely because of their race generated feelings of inferiority about their status in the community in ways that could not be repaired. These feelings, in turn, affected children's motivation to learn. Segregated schools, the Court determined, tended to limit African American students' educational and mental development. Giving African American children access to racially mixed classrooms would help to equalize their educational resources and improve their academic and life outcomes.

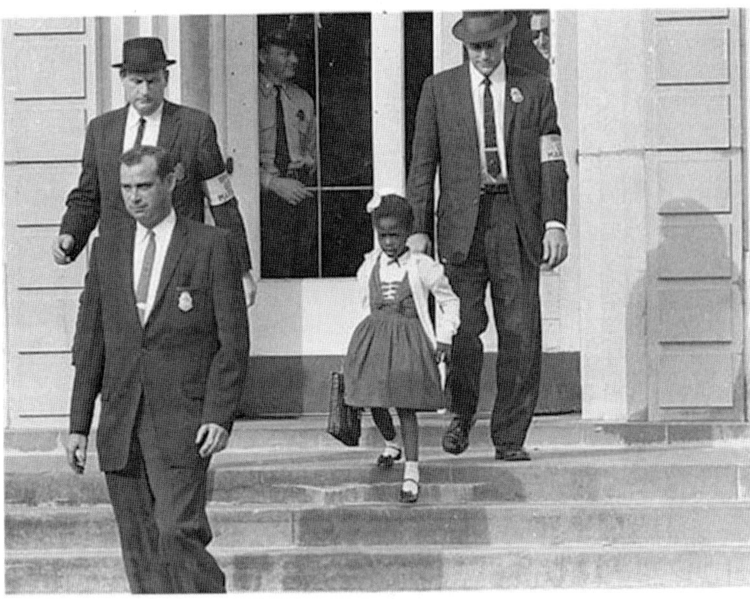

U.S. Marshals escort 6-year-old Ruby Bridges from her elementary school, November 1960.

Uncredited DOJ photographer, public domain, via Wikimedia Commons

Education After *Brown*

Despite the Supreme Court ruling, **massive resistance**—closing public schools to keep African American students from enrolling with white students—characterized several southern states' efforts to block racially desegregated education. Yet even with popular defiance toward the *Brown* decision, by 1970, southern schools were less segregated than schools in any other region of the country.[40] Desegregation in the North, West, and Midwest faced different challenges. After World War II, many middle-class white people had moved out of cities and into the surrounding suburbs. As a consequence, meaningful school desegregation could not happen without crossing city–suburb lines. Because this kind of racial separation resulted from a seemingly[41] "natural" outgrowth of individuals choosing where to live, courts considered it legally permissible.

In a reversal of *Brown*'s intent, courts in the 1990s began releasing districts from desegregation orders issued in the 1970s. Both federal and state courts are now declaring that formerly segregated districts have made "good faith"—if unsuccessful—efforts to desegregate. Called "unified," these school districts are relieved of any more duty to integrate their schools. These same courts are declaring "race-based admissions policies" unconstitutional. These later rulings allowed the return to neighborhood schools, even if that meant that some schools resegregated. As a result, in fall of 2015, 58% of African American students attended schools that enrolled 75% or more students of color (as compared with 51% in 2000).[42] And as of the past 15 years, a larger share of Latinx students than African American students attend "intensively segregated" schools.[43]

The *Brown* Legacy

Despite the limited legal retreat since the 1954 ruling, *Brown*'s move to desegregate schools was appropriate, both morally and educationally. Current research shows that African American children achieve more—and reduce the achievement gap between their test scores and those of white and Asian American students—in racially integrated schools.[44] Today, neither the government nor schools can use "a binary concept of race" to discriminate among individual students. Schools cannot put a collective social goal (racial balance) ahead of an individual's rights. Such racially based measures would now be considered "extreme."

To more fully explore the personal meaning of *Brown v. Board of Education* and "separate but equal," complete the activity in the **Reflect & Engage** box, "Separate but Equal" in American Education.

AMERICAN EDUCATION SPOTLIGHT: RUBY BRIDGES

Although school desegregation was a societal issue, it was also a personal one affecting real children. In the black-and-white photo above, first-grader Ruby Bridges walks from her elementary school escorted by federal marshals ordered by President Dwight D. Eisenhower. Ruby was the first African American child enrolled in the William Frantz Elementary School, and she needed an armed escort to keep her safe.

Ruby Bridges was born in Mississippi in 1954, the oldest child of Abon and Lucille Bridges. She loved living on the farm that her paternal grandparents sharecropped. It was a hard life, so her parents moved to New Orleans to seek greater opportunities for themselves and their children. As she got older, while her father worked as a service station attendant and her mother worked nights to help support their growing family, Ruby's job was to keep an eye on her two younger brothers and sister. Home, church, and her all-black school kindergarten were the boundaries of her life—until a federal court order forced New Orleans schools to desegregate. During the summer of 1960, Ruby was chosen to attend the all-white William Frantz Elementary School for first grade.

The first day Ruby enrolled, crowds of angry white parents gathered around the school to scream horrible things and shake their fists at her. Four federal marshals had to escort Ruby to and from the school to protect her. Every day after that, Ruby would hurry past the angry crowds without saying a word. Her mother had told her not to be scared, but if she were afraid, she should pray. Prayer would protect her.

Once inside, Ruby sat at her desk among a room full of other desks—all vacant. None of the white parents would send their children to the school. Her teacher, Mrs. Henry, was impressed by Ruby's unfailing politeness and hopeful spirit. It was a very lonely experience for Ruby, but with Mrs. Henry's help and companionship, she learned to read and write.

One morning, Mrs. Henry noticed Ruby walking toward the school as usual but then she stopped, turned toward the angry, howling crowd and seemed to even be trying to speak to them. The crowd seemed ready to jump on her while the marshals tried to keep Ruby moving. Finally, she stopped talking and walked into the school.

Mrs. Henry immediately asked Ruby why she tried to talk to such an angry, hostile crowd. Ruby responded that she didn't stop to talk with them.

"Ruby, I saw you talking," Mrs. Henry pressed. "I saw your lips moving."

"I wasn't talking," replied Ruby. "I was praying.... I was praying for them."

Evidently, Ruby had stopped every morning a few blocks away from the school to pray for the people who hated her. But on this morning, she had forgotten until she was already in the middle of the malevolent mob.

Later that year, two white boys joined Ruby at the school. Other children soon followed. The next school year, the mobs gave up their struggle. Ruby finished Frantz Elementary, graduated from high school, then studied travel and tourism at a Kansas City business school and worked for American Express as a world travel agent. In 1984, she married Malcolm Hall and later became a full-time parent to their four sons.

Texas A&M University-Commerce Marketing Communications Photography, CC BY 2.0, via Wikimedia Commons

On January 8, 2001, President Bill Clinton awarded Ruby the Presidential Citizens Medal. Today, Ruby Bridges Hall, chair of the Ruby Bridges Foundation, speaks to groups around the country about her experiences with education. Sometimes when she visits schools, Mrs. Henry, her first-grade teacher (now retired) goes with her. They tell others that school is a place to bring people together—from all races and backgrounds.

Sources: Michals, E. (2015). *Ruby Bridges*. National Women's History Museum. https://www.womenshistory.org/education-resources/biographies/ruby-bridges?gclid=EAIaIQobChMIpKjVrvic5gIVEz0MCh1-oA8xEAAYASAAEgJg1_D_BwE;

Hall, R. G. (n.d.). The education of Ruby Nell. The Ruby Bridges Foundation. http://toolboxforteachers.s3.amazonaws.com/PBL/Hampton1/Stereotyping/Math/Stereotyping_Ruby-Nell.pdf; Elliot, L. (2000, May 25). Rare Ruby. *The Toronto Star*. Reprinted by The Ruby Bridges Foundation.

REFLECT & ENGAGE: "SEPARATE BUT EQUAL" IN AMERICAN EDUCATION

"Separate but equal" was a social doctrine used to keep Blacks and whites physically apart in public (and private) spheres. The *Brown* decision ended this practice in public schools.

A. Individually, using colored markers or pens on notebook paper, create a wordle (mind cloud) using a digital tool such as Vizzlo that illustrates the meaning of *Brown v. Board of Education.*

B. Have the class members identify the words or phrases they chose to center their wordle and those they considered as most important issues to educating all children well.

C. Discuss the extent to which you think each issue *Brown* sought to improve is present in your home community and in the larger society. Cite evidence to support your view.

D. What do you think students—African American and white—felt and thought during the first few days and weeks after their schools became integrated? How do you think integration affected teachers' roles as instructors and classroom managers?

5.4 WORLD WAR I, THE GREAT DEPRESSION, VOCATIONAL EDUCATION, AND PUBLIC EDUCATION

World War I and the Great Depression, increased high school enrollments, and vocational education would all affect American public schools. These 20th century forces initiated important changes whose effects are still apparent today.

5.4a World War I and Standardized Tests

Modern standardized tests were a by-product of World War I. They emerged when military services needed to rapidly classify millions of recruits based on their general intellectual level. In 1917, Army psychologists developed group tests to meet this urgent practical need.

In spite of their limitations, these early 20th century intelligence exams have remained the basis for standardized achievement tests ever since. Able to be efficiently administered to large groups and after many revisions, the Army Alpha and Army Beta intelligence tests became the models for most group intelligence tests. Soon, group intelligence tests were being devised for all ages, from preschool children to graduate students. Designed for testing large numbers of individuals at the same time by using simplified instructions and administrative procedures, the tests were both efficient and cost-effective.

5.4b The Great Depression and Education

During the Great Depression in the 1930s, President Franklin D. Roosevelt and his advisors initially saw employment—rather than education—as the answer to the "youth problem." For this reason, they devoted their greatest attention to providing federal relief and creating jobs. Nonetheless, these jobs sometimes provided educational benefits to those most in need.[45]

For example, the Works Progress Administration (WPA) gave money to schools to hire more teachers, buy supplies, and provide free hot lunches for students. The WPA and Public Works Administration

(PWA) built larger schools to replace the one-room schools that had prevailed in some parts of the country. Primarily to keep youths off the labor market, the National Youth Administration (NYA) provided work–study programs at the high school and collegiate levels. The Civilian Conservation Corps (CCC) put unemployed young men to work on conservation projects, while its voluntary education programs taught 35,000 illiterate youths how to read and write and granted more than 1,000 high school diplomas and 39 college degrees. Under these programs, thousands more studied everything from industrial trades to philosophy, economics, and social problems.

5.4c Increasing High School Enrollments

After World War I ended, states began to enforce child labor and compulsory attendance laws. Secondary school enrollments in the United States rose from approximately 1.1 million in 1910 to 2.5 million in 1920 to 4.8 million in 1930.[46] Later, the Great Depression's economic collapse prompted another boost in high school enrollments, as large number of jobless adolescents returned to school. By 1940, 7.1 million students between the ages of 14 and 17 were enrolled in high school, representing more than 73% of that age group in this country. Amid this unprecedented enrollment surge, education leaders argued that the new high school entrants' intellectual abilities were weaker than those of previous student groups; they needed access to less demanding courses.[47]

The economic crisis and resulting high school enrollment boom combined to produce a profound shift in high schools' nature and function. Increasingly, the schools' task became custodial in nature—to keep students out of the labor market instead of immediately preparing them for it. As a result, educators channeled increasing numbers of pupils into undemanding, nonacademic courses while lowering standards in the academic courses required for graduation.

Proponents of these actions argued that these curriculum changes increased equal educational opportunities. In reality, they had a generally unequal impact on the low-income white and African American students who entered high schools in the 1930s and 1940s. These students were disproportionately assigned to nonacademic tracks and less demanding academic courses.[48] Although high schools met their short-term goals of removing these students from the adult labor market, they failed to meet these students' long-term needs for appropriately rigorous and marketable knowledge and skills.

5.4d The Growth of Vocational Education

After the Civil War, rapid industrialization prompted many Americans to leave farming for factories. Public schools struggled to meet the demands for a work force that was moving from an agrarian society to an industrial economy.[49] To deal with this paradigm shift, the idea of vocational education took hold.

In 1906, the National Society for the Promotion of Industrial Education advanced vocational schools as the ideal way to prepare young people for work. Business and industry liked having already-prepared high school graduates because it helped reduce businesses' training costs and increase profits. Politicians and economists encouraged these programs as a way to increase their local and national competitive advantages. In addition, vocational education appeared to effectively train and integrate into the public school system low-income and new immigrants' children who were seeking skilled trades or manual labor occupations.[50]

Since the passage of the Smith-Hughes Act of 1917, federal legislation has continued to provide funds to support vocational education in public schools.[51] Over the years, the Smith-Hughes Act and its successors expanded these vocational education programs to keep more students in secondary education and provide trained workers for a growing number of semiskilled positions.

Today's vocational education in comprehensive high schools focuses its curricula on having students develop both vocational and academic skills to prepare them for college and careers. For example, High Schools That Work (HSTW) is a national program that blends traditional college preparatory academic studies with quality vocational and technical studies to improve learning and achievement for all career-bound students. Its research shows that vocational students in schools that participated in HSTW for at least 2 years exceeded the national average scores of vocational students in reading, math, and science achievement.[52]

Similarly, high school **career academies** are designed to equip each student for both college and career. These "schools within schools" combine core academic subjects with a career-technical class related to an occupational theme such as health and bioscience, business and finance, arts and communications, education and child development, or engineering and information technology. Longitudinal studies of matched comparison groups have found that academy students have better attendance, earn more course credits, receive higher grades, and are less likely to leave high school before graduation. In addition, 4 years after leaving high school, career academy graduates tend to be working and earning substantially more than their nonacademy counterparts.[53]

5.5 THE *COLEMAN REPORT*: FAMILY, SCHOOL, AND EDUCATING THE DISADVANTAGED

In the years after the *Brown* decision, many people wanted to know if school desegregation had actually improved learning opportunities for all American students. In 1964, the U.S. Office of Education commissioned James S. Coleman, a Johns Hopkins University sociology professor, to assess whether children of different races, income groups, and national origins had equal educational opportunities.[54] Published in 1966, the *Coleman Report* concluded that family background—not schools—was the most important determiner of children's academic success.[55]

5.5a *Coleman Report* Findings

Documenting an African American–white achievement gap, the *Coleman Report* found that African American children started out academically behind their white peers and stayed behind, regardless of whether equal resources were available in their schools. Achievement disparities were large. In sixth grade, the average African American student was 1.9 years behind his or her white peers. By 12th grade, the average achievement gap had widened to nearly 4 years. Desegregating schools did not appear to increase African American school achievement.

Additionally, the *Coleman Report* showed that African American children typically attended more poorly equipped schools—they had less access to physics, chemistry, and language; fewer laboratories available; and fewer books per pupil. But the differences were smaller than expected for African American and white schools in the same geographic regions. Few school inputs seemed to make a difference, except for teachers' verbal abilities. The report also found that 10 years after *Brown*, most students still attended segregated schools, and school segregation in the North was just as pervasive as it was in the South.

Not all of the Coleman findings were discouraging. Its second-most important finding was that after family characteristics, a student's sense of control of his or her own destiny was the most important determinant of academic achievement. The students with whom youngsters attended school were almost as important as family background in predicting academic success. African American students did better in schools that were predominantly middle class than they did in schools dominated by low-income students, even though the improvements were not large enough to make up for achievement differences due to family background. Desegregation advocates viewed this finding as a point in favor of their movement.

5.5b The *Coleman Report*: A Second Look

Several attempts have been made to reanalyze the Coleman data to ensure that the original interpretations were correct. It is true that although the Coleman methodology would not meet today's standards for scientific research, it was considered to be in the "vanguard" in 1966.[56]

One study found that teacher bias noted on Coleman's questionnaire might have possibly contributed to lower scores for African American students.[57] Achievement gaps in the same school between African American and white students were higher where most of the teachers had expressed preference for teaching college-oriented children of white-collar professionals. Thus, teacher expectations may have played an important role in influencing their students' outcomes.[58]

At the end of the day, what most people took away from the *Coleman Report* was that "schools don't matter": Smart families—not schools—make students smart. Substantial research supports the link between family systems and children's school success.[59] Even so, considerable evidence suggests that these conclusions greatly oversimplify and distort the findings. Both school and family factors influence student learning.

Importantly, the *Coleman Report*'s conclusions shifted the policy and research focus toward student achievement—as opposed to school facilities—as a measure of the public schools' quality. Stimulated by Coleman's findings, the "effective schools" research since the 1970s (discussed more fully in Chapter 14) has shown how schools can make a difference—and even overcome—many students' background characteristics.[60]

5.6 SPECIAL EDUCATION: PROVIDING FREE AND APPROPRIATE EDUCATION TO STUDENTS WITH DISABILITIES

Public prejudice and ignorance kept most students with disabilities from having access to a full and appropriate education until the late 20th century. Right up to the mid-century, only students with the least serious disabilities received public schooling.

5.6a Advances in Special Education in the Mid-20th Century

Inspired by *Brown's* precedent, parents of students with disabilities began to form organizations, such as the National Association for Retarded Citizens (the Arc), to advocate for publicly educating their children. Responding to their persistence, Congress authorized the 1958 Public Law 85-926 to support the training and preparation of special education teachers. Special education leaders began arguing for the rights of students with disabilities to be educated alongside their nondisabled peers in more normal school settings.

5.6b Public Law 94-142: IDEA

The 1970s saw courts and Congress deciding in favor of students with disabilities attending public schools based on equality of opportunity. Congress noted that of the more than 8 million children with disabilities in the United States in 1975, more than half did not receive appropriate educational services that would allow them to have full equality of opportunity. One million children with disabilities were excluded entirely from the public school system.[61]

Children with disabilities are entitled to a free and appropriate public education.

iStock/FatCamera

Early in the decade, court decisions in Pennsylvania (1971) and in the District of Columbia (1972) established the right of all children labeled as "intellectually disabled" to a free and appropriate education. These rulings made it more difficult for public schools to exclude students with disabilities. Further, in 1973 the Rehabilitation Act, Section 504, and later amendments guaranteed the rights of disabled individuals in employment settings and in schools that receive federal monies. Finally, parental pressure, court decisions, and legislative actions persuaded Congress to pass the Education for All Handicapped Children Act (Public Law 94-142) in 1975. Amended several times, in 1990 it became the Individuals With Disabilities Education Act (IDEA).

PL 94-142 and Beyond

PL 94-142 defined **children with disabilities** as those who are intellectually challenged, hard of hearing, deaf, speech and language impaired, visually impaired (including blindness), seriously emotionally disturbed, orthopedically impaired, or otherwise health impaired, as well as children with specific learning disabilities. To ensure their basic educational rights, this law specified that they must have the following requirements met and services available to them:

- A free and appropriate public education (FAPE)
- An individualized education program
- Special education services
- Related services
- Due process procedures
- The least restrictive learning environment (LRE) in which to learn

At last, all children with disabilities from ages 3 to 21, inclusive, were eligible to receive these educational services in public schools.

Over the years, additional amendments extended and clarified these rights. By 1976, all states had laws subsidizing public school programs for students with disabilities. IDEA amendments of 1997 (PL 105-171) addressed the need for high educational performance standards for all students and teachers, including those in special education. By the early 1980s, students considered to have mild or moderate disabilities were usually integrated into general education classrooms on at least a part-time basis. In addition, many students who were not served in the past—including those with severe disabilities—started receiving educational services in their local neighborhood schools, including participation in regular cafeteria, playground, library, hall, bus, and restroom activities.

Later court cases have tried to clarify the true intent of the IDEA statute. Cases have addressed issues such as FAPE, procedural safeguards, individualized education program, LRE, separate school placement, related services, discipline, attorneys' fees, and tuition reimbursement. Chapter 9 discusses the Supreme Court decisions around meaningful educational progress that states must provide to students with disabilities. Table 5.3 identifies a few of the key rulings.

TABLE 5.3 ■ Special Education Issues

Issue	Legal Clarification
Free and appropriate public education (FAPE)	Schools must prepare an educational program of specialized instruction and related services purposely designed to meet the child with disabilities' unique needs. When initially adjudicated in 1982, "free and appropriate" meant a "basic floor of opportunity" that schools must deliver.[62] In 2017, the U.S. Supreme Court decided on a higher standard, unanimously ruling that FAPE meant giving these students the chance to make meaningful, "appropriately ambitious" progress in keeping with the child's circumstances. Without clarifying what "appropriate" progress looks like, the Court deferred to school authorities' "expertise" and "judgment."[63]

(Continued)

TABLE 5.3 ■ Special Education Issues (*Continued*)

Issue	Legal Clarification
Procedural safeguards	Schools must use fair and proper steps in a highly regulated process to ensure that children with disabilities receive appropriate educational services. The most important procedures give parents prior notice and opportunity to participate in developing their child's individual educational plan and be informed about methods and procedures they can use to appeal and resolve any conflicts or grievances with school officials if they disagree about how to best educate their child.
Individualized educational program (IEP)	Schools must prepare a written educational plan, updated annually by a multidisciplinary team including the parents, that identifies the child's educational needs, the annual instructional goals and objectives, the specific educational programs and services to be provided, and the evaluation procedures that will measure the child's progress. Teachers are expected to implement the plan as written until the multidisciplinary team and parents change it.
Least restrictive environment (LRE) **(sometimes called inclusion)**	Schools must ensure that children with disabilities are educated in the general education classroom with normally developing children whenever possible, while providing them with the supports necessary for them to succeed.[64] This placement gives the child with disabilities more opportunities to socialize and interact with other typically developing children, reduces the stigma of being "different," and offers students with disabilities the opportunity to learn the rigorous regular curriculum at the same pace and depth as other children. From 1995 to fall of 2015, the percentage of students with disabilities who spend 80% or more of their school day in regular classrooms increased from 45% to 62.5%, respectively.[65]
Response to intervention (RTI)	In 2004 IDEA legislation, RTI encourages earlier, structured, increasingly intense, and highly individualized interventions for students experiencing difficulty learning to read or understand math. Teachers monitor students' progress to see if their responses to this intervention bring adequate academic growth. If not, a multidisciplinary team may decide that the student is eligible for special education services. Research suggests that implementing RTI components with fidelity is an effective strategy to increase student learning in reading and mathematics.[66] Critics note RTI's limitations.[67]

5.7 FEDERAL INFLUENCE OVER EDUCATION, ACCOUNTABILITY INCREASES

In the last half of the 20th century, American public schools saw increased federal attention. The report *A Nation at Risk* criticized the public schools for their low expectations and weak student performance, leading to a renewed focus on rigorous academic standards and measurable student outcomes. In addition, U.S. congressional legislation continued investing more money for state and local schools in attempts to increase schools' accountability for every child's achievement.

5.7a *A Nation at Risk* Impacts Public Schools

In 1983, *A Nation at Risk*, a report of the National Commission on Excellence in Education, sharply criticized public schools. It claimed that world competitors were challenging the United States' former preeminence in commerce, industry, science, and technological innovation. American students were scoring poorly on international tests, not taking enough science and math courses, and showing weak critical thinking skills. American schools, once a source of justifiable pride, were "presently being eroded by a rising tide of mediocrity that threatens our very future as a Nation and as a people."[68] These realities placed the nation at risk.

Complaining that U.S. public schools had moved from standards-centered to student-centered, the authors of *A Nation at Risk* wanted the direction reversed. The report advocated high expectations for every student by having all complete a reasonably demanding academic curriculum and meet high standards before they received a high school diploma. Textbooks and standardized tests would drive the improvement.

As a report, *A Nation at Risk* was highly controversial. Some questioned the assumed cause-and-effect relationship between public schooling and market dominance or industrial productivity. Others raised broader issues, asking whether schools could either cause or cure America's social, economic, and political dilemmas.[69] Writers criticized the fallacy of comparing the highly dissimilar United States with European and Asian education systems.[70] Some observed that the report included a very narrow definition of "excellence" and noted that the report's recommendations placed an ever-growing group of educationally and economically disadvantaged students at even greater risk of failure.[71]

Many saw *A Nation at Risk* as propaganda meant to advance a political agenda[72] using a "golden treasury" of selective, distorted, and spun statistics. It hyped bad news about schools, they said, while deliberately suppressing or ignoring the good news.[73] In addition, public school defenders asserted, the United States was not failing in the global marketplace.[74]

Despite these criticisms, *A Nation at Risk* delivered some key educational benefits. It spurred policy makers to increase public schools' accountability and educational rigor as evidenced through standardized tests. By 1983, 34 states required minimum-competency testing for grade-to-grade promotion or high school graduation.[75]

5.7b Federal Support and Increased Accountability for Educating All Students

The 2015 **Every Student Succeeds Act (ESSA)** signals the latest effort to ensure public school accountability, linking federal dollars to rigorous evidence that schools are raising traditionally underserved students' academic achievement. It reflects the latest reauthorization of earlier legislation aimed at providing federal aid to public schools.

1965 Elementary and Secondary Education Act

In 1965, President Lyndon Johnson led Congress to pass the Elementary and Secondary Education Act (ESEA), the forerunner of ESSA. Part of Johnson's 1964 Civil Rights Act and the "War on Poverty" legislation, ESEA was possibly the most important congressional action to fund education programs until that time.

Head Start and Title I

ESEA introduced the federal **Head Start** programs, which were preschool education classes intended to give children ages 3 to 5 from economically disadvantaged homes the cognitive and social development or readiness for school success. The **Title I** legislation was intended to supplement academic resources for low-income children who needed extra reading and math help in the early grades. Although states received extra money to support low-income schools, the law did little to hold state governments responsible for academic outcomes at those schools.

Title I has not been as successful as hoped. Two large-scale Title I evaluations conclude that it has not substantially narrowed achievement gaps between disadvantaged and middle-class students as policy makers intended,[76] in part due to low per-pupil spending (averaging about $500 to $600 a year) or accountability for how funds are used.[77] More positively, reanalyses of the data and related studies conclude that Title I may have kept the achievement gap from widening.[78]

By comparison, the effects of Head Start on children's short- and long-term outcomes are very positive. They improve educational outcomes, increasing the likelihood that participants graduate from high school, attend college, and receive a postsecondary degree, license, or certification. Especially among African American children, Head Start also promotes social, emotional, and behavioral development that shows itself in adult measures of self-control, self-esteem, and positive parenting practices.[79]

No Child Left Behind Act

In 2002, President George W. Bush signed the reauthorization of ESEA funds, called the **No Child Left Behind Act (NCLB)**. Seeking equity and excellence, NCLB represented the federal government's first serious attempt to hold states, districts, and schools accountable for remedying the unequal achievement among different student populations, especially low-income students, students of color, English language learners, and students with disabilities. The ESSA is its current replacement.

NCLB required schools to **disaggregate**—or separate—their data annually and show academic progress at all tested grades, in all tested subjects, by all tested student subgroups. By requiring the achievement data to be separated in this way, policy makers sought to prevent schools from "hiding" or glossing over underserved students' low achievement by averaging their scores with the higher scores earned by more economically advantaged and better-achieving students. If any one group failed to make the adequate yearly progress goal, the whole school received a failing grade. "Failing" schools were liable for a range of penalties, including school closing.[80]

Although it is not possible to compare NCLB student achievement across states—because each state defined "proficiency" its own way and used varying assessments—the **National Assessment of Educational Progress (NAEP)**, a common metric for all states, can be used to assess this progress. Research has found that the states that experienced the greatest gains on NAEP, post-NCLB, were those with the most rigorous academic standards.[81] Results indicate the gaps separating African American and Latinx students from white students during this period were the smallest in our nation's history.[82]

Critique of NCLB

Although NCLB can claim some elementary and middle school achievement gains, the accountability program appeared to have "unforeseen problems, unintended consequences, and unworkable features" that limited its effectiveness.[83] Its practice of comparing one student group's performance against a different group, the narrowing of the curriculum by placing an excessive focus on reading and math, statistical issues that interfere with drawing accurate conclusions, cheating, and a misleading definition of "teacher quality" all created difficulties in improving student learning and achievement.

Every Student Succeeds Act

The ESSA is the U.S. Congress's efforts to improve upon NCLB's strengths while ending its weaknesses. A reauthorization of ESEA, the law reduces much of the federal government's imprint in education policy and gives states new leeway to determine and implement education reform.[84]

Briefly, ESSA[85] allows states to pick their own interim and long-term accountability goals in four areas: proficiency on state tests, English language proficiency, graduation rates, and one additional "nonacademic" indicator such as student engagement, school climate/safety, or whatever the state thinks makes sense. Each assessment's results must be broken out by student subgroup. States are required to adopt "challenging" academic standards, and state goals must set the expectation that all student groups that are furthest behind close gaps in achievement and graduation rates. States also decide how much the individual indicators will count.[86]

States must also identify and intervene in the bottom 5% of performance and in high schools where the graduation rate is 67% or less. ESSA also requires schools to annually issue updated "easily accessible and user-friendly" report cards, including new school-by-school spending data[87] (that will help show whether schools that are spending similar amounts of money are getting similar academic results), teacher-pay averages, and academic and discipline disparities between student groups.

Critique of ESSA

Although ESSA promised to open states to educational innovation, a review of state accountability plans finds that although states are using new strategies and law-driven initiatives, innovation is lacking.[88] The concern about "teaching to the test" remains. Additionally, many district administrators fear that showing school spending amounts—the financial transparency requirement—will have school board members and parent groups (among others) facing off about budgeting priorities.[89] Although ESSA pushes for more equitable funding between high-poverty schools and other campuses, determining the per-pupil expenditure is highly challenging.[90] Moreover, ESSA ended NCLB's mandate that teachers must be "highly "qualified"—have a bachelor's degree in the subject they were teaching plus state certification—and allows states to define for themselves what is an "effective teacher."[91] When it comes to an ESSA progress report, the *Phi Delta Kappan* in 2019 found that states are "all over the map."[92]

The Common Core Standards

The 2010 **Common Core State Standards** Initiative is a state-led effort coordinated by the bipartisan National Governors Association Center for Best Practices (NGA Center) and the Council of Chief State School Officers (CCSSO) to provide K–12 schools and parents with a clear and consistent framework about what students are expected to learn and be able to do in English language arts and mathematics to prepare them for college and the workforce regardless of where they live. Since many students move from one school district and state to another during their K–12 years, having a shared set of national standards in every locale delivering a rigorous curriculum benefits them academically. Motivated to prevent American schoolchildren from falling behind academically, administrators, state education officials, policy-making groups, teachers, and experts collaborated to develop the standards that

- include rigorous academic content using higher-order thinking skills,
- are evidence based, and
- are informed by other top-performing countries.

Forty-one states and the District of Columbia currently use the Common Core State Standards[93] These include reading more nonfiction to develop students' facility for comprehending argument-driven essays and understanding key math concepts rather than simply "plugging" a number into an algorithm to solve an equation. Overall, these yardsticks are more intellectually demanding than those many states had been using. States and localities used the standards to develop or purchase their own aligned curriculum, and the federal government paid to have companion examinations available to measure student progress toward meeting these performance expectations.

Political and logistical obstacles made the Common Core State Standards controversial. Some saw it as government overreach into state and local education turf. Implementation issues compromised its arrival in classrooms; not all administrators and teachers received adequate professional development on how to use the standards to improve student learning. Educators and parents vehemently objected to assessing students on more difficult material and receiving lower test scores than earned on earlier, less rigorous tests. Often, the pressure to have students perform well on Common Core assessments led to a narrowed curriculum, omitting science and social studies lessons. Moreover, teachers did not want their professional evaluations to include student achievement metrics from this unfamiliar and untested curriculum. Parents complained that they could no longer help children with their homework.

By the mid-2010s, Common Core's public relations problem led to more than 20 states repealing, revising, renaming, or rolling back parts of the program. Nonetheless, currently the Common Core has deeply penetrated many American classrooms, and many see growth in student reading comprehension as an outcome.[94]

Teacher Evaluation and Student Achievement

Because research confirms that teacher effectiveness is the most important school factor in improving student achievement, finding, developing, and keeping effective teachers is an important school goal. Since student learning is teaching's most important outcome, it makes sense to base their evaluations, in part, on student achievement, as long as it is done fairly and efficiently. Nonetheless, evaluating teachers and finding ways to assess their impact on student learning remain subjects of intense debate.

For decades, teacher evaluation has suffered from several weaknesses. They have been infrequent, seldom consider students' academic progress, are unable to give teachers worthwhile feedback, and rarely used to make important decisions about professional development, salary, promotion, or tenure. Additionally, evaluation protocols typically allow principals only to rate teachers as "Satisfactory" or "Unsatisfactory," making it impossible to separate great teachers from satisfactory teachers or marginal teachers from poor teachers. Nearly 99% of teachers receive "Satisfactory" ratings.[95]

As a result, ineffective tenured teachers rarely lose their jobs over their poor performance, top-performing teachers go unrecognized, and moderately effective, diligent teachers lack opportunities to grow. In addition, the public is misled into thinking that all teachers perform the same.

In 2009, only 15 states required teacher evaluations to include some measure of students' academic growth. By 2015, 43 states were doing so.[96] But many states are backing away from NCLB-era policies that offered fiscal grants in exchange for using student-growth measures and standardized test scores in assessing teaching quality. Instead, localities are using ESSA's flexibility to decide what elements of student learning to include in teacher evaluations. In 2019, only 34 states required student growth metrics in teacher evaluations.[97]

Studies have found that well-designed teacher evaluation programs can have a direct, beneficial, and lasting effect on individual teacher performance. Teachers are found to be more effective at raising student achievement during the school year when they are being evaluated than they were previously. Several years after the evaluation, they are found to be even more effective.[98]

According to the New Teacher Project[99] and others,[100] improving teacher evaluation should be comprehensive, meaningful, and fair. Table 5.4 illustrates their suggested criteria.

TABLE 5.4 ■ Proposed Teacher Evaluation Criteria

Standard	Description
An annual process	All teachers should be evaluated at least once a year.
Comprehensive	A wide-ranging performance evaluation system should fairly, accurately, and credibly observe and measure teachers' ability to help students learn and succeed.
Clear, rigorous expectations	Evaluations should be anchored in clear, precisely worded, and observable standards of instructional excellence that highlight student learning.
Multiple valid measures	Evaluations should include an array of data points that focus on teachers' impact on students' academic growth, each with its own weight, and present a complete picture of teacher performance. Such data may include **value-added**[101] models, classroom observations (using a research-affirmed metric of effective teaching), samples of student work connected to learning standards, examples of typical assignments or other evidence of student mastery from classroom assessments, and other quantitative and qualitative information.
Multiple ratings options	Expectations should use four to five rating levels to describe differences in teacher effectiveness, such as *highly effective, effective, needs improvement*, and *ineffective* or *exemplary, strong, effective, developing*, and *needs improvement*.
Increased teacher involvement	Teachers and administrators should participate in designing, implementing, and assessing the effectiveness of any teacher evaluation program in their schools.
Regular feedback	Evaluations should encourage regular, frequent observations and constructive critical feedback to teachers about student progress, professional goals, and developmental needs and the support school leaders will provide to support those needs.
Professional development	Evaluations should be tightly linked to teachers' evaluation on performance standards and professional growth activities targeted to teachers' needs.
Significant	Evaluation outcomes should be a major factor in human resources policies and practices regarding hiring, assignment, professional development, pay increases, promotions, retention, and dismissal.
Regular assessment of the assessment	Educators and others should routinely "assess the assessment" by looking for evidence of inconsistent findings, bias, "gaming the system," and/or lack of transparency and redesigning their instruments and procedures to remedy these.

Although teachers' evaluations should not be based only on a single measure, such as standardized test scores, teachers should be accountable for helping students make measurable progress toward rigorous learning standards. These fair and accurate evaluation approaches go a long way in making teaching a rewarding career that attracts talented, growth-oriented individuals.

5.8 RECENT TRENDS: EDUCATION PRIVATIZATION, VIRTUAL EDUCATION, NEW CURRICULA

An array of current education policies is upending assumptions about who educates our children and who pays for it. The education privatization movement—sometimes called **school choice**—wants to give parents more options about how and where to educate their children, using taxpayer dollars. As more families are participating in these alternative schools, research is providing answers to whether these innovations are enhancing student achievement. Social–emotional learning and personalized learning are curriculum innovations to enhance student learning and well-being. Research findings also clarify their effectiveness.

5.8a Education Privatization

Education privatization reflects a confluence of trends—social, political, demographic, and technological. The increasing importance of education for social and economic success; civil rights struggles to secure high-quality education for every marginalized child; free market economists and policy makers who believe the private sector is more fiscally efficient than the public sector; conservative parents' focus on educating their children with "traditional American" values; technology's capacity to offer education outside a formal schoolhouse; and 50 years of persistent criticism of "failing public schools" have reframed and reshaped the policy debate.[102] Privatizing public schools by creating charter schools, using vouchers, and engaging in public–private partnerships where schools contract out education services—such as hiring private custodial crews to clean schools or food service companies to manage school cafeterias—are key tenets. A more complete accounting of American education privatization is discussed elsewhere.[103]

In 2019, 7,000 charter schools across 44 states and the District of Columbia served 3.2 million children.[104] Approximately 29 states and the District of Columbia currently use taxpayer-funded school vouchers or similar fiscal programs,[105] costing about $2.3 billion in 2017 to 2018.[106] Clearly, education privatization is big business.

Charter Schools

Briefly, charter schools are public or private schools that claim to offer students more innovation and higher performance than available in traditional public schools (TPS) in exchange for taxpayer dollars, greater flexibility, and less oversight.

Charter laws vary by state. Studies find that the most successful charter laws specify high regulation, require high-quality operators to ensure academic and fiscal accountability, and close low-performing schools.[107] Nonprofit, public schools open to all and accountable to public authorities tend to be the best.[108]

Nationally, research finds mixed results about how well charter schools are educating their students with wide state-by-state (and city-by-city) differences in student achievement. Although certain charters show high academic performance,[109] many charter students are not achieving as well (and some worse) as their peers in TPS; and privately run charters have a high risk of fiscal mismanagement.[110] Additionally, research also finds that charter schools increase racial and socioeconomic segregation[111] and often siphon money away from public schools.[112]

Voucher Programs

School vouchers are certificates for a fixed amount of public funding that parents can use to enroll their child in any school the parent chooses that accepts vouchers, including private, religious, and home schools. Voucher regulations vary, depending on the state's legislation. Education savings accounts, tax credit scholarships, and newly expanded 529 accounts are all voucher-type programs that use taxpayer dollars (actual or potential) to support tuition and supplies at private or home schools.[113] Disagreement exists about whether vouchers save taxpayer dollars, as proponents claim.[114]

Over the past 30 years, extensive research on educational vouchers in the United States shows little evidence that vouchers improve educational outcomes. Benefits to student achievement and school district performance are mixed or limited.[115] Studies do show some evidence of small improvements in high school graduation and college enrollment rates; but this has been a decade-plus national trend. Scholars have criticized voucher advocates for misrepresenting empirical results.[116] Research on student outcomes from tax credit scholarships, education savings accounts, or expanded 529 accounts is limited, in part, because these initiatives do not require participating schools to formally assess student performance.

Computers can personalize and expand learning opportunities.
iStock/monkeybusinessimages

Virtual Schools

Virtual (online) charter schools are scholastic programs that attempt to educate full-time students primarily through the computer, via the internet, with synchronous or asynchronous lessons. Online schools are intended to serve an atypical student population, including those far behind academically who want credit recovery to earn their diplomas on time; those with severe health problems; sports or music prodigies; students in unstable households; and rural students who want to take AP or foreign language courses not available in their schools. Ideally, all these youngsters could benefit from the highly flexible and student-centered schedule that permits other needs or interests.

In 2017 to 2018, 501 full-time virtual schools enrolled 297,712 students.[117] Most virtual schools are charter schools.[118] About 163 virtual charter schools educate over 30,000 seniors nationally (as determined by the adjusted cohort graduation rate, according to federal numbers).[119]

Although virtual charter schools vary in effectiveness, most are not performing well. Academic achievement is poor, and dropout rates are high. Nationally, in the 2016–2017 school year, half of all virtual charter high schools had graduation rates below 50%.[120] Virtual schools run by school districts show the highest student performance, whereas for-profit operators have the lowest performance.[121] Academic growth in reading and math for students in poverty, students with disabilities, and English language learners is especially weak.[122]

Nonetheless, virtual charters collectively receive more than $1 billion in taxpayer dollars annually.[123] Given their performance, several states are calling for stricter oversight, regulations, and closer monitoring of virtual schools' student attendance and engagement.[124]

5.8b New Curricula

Over the past 2 decades, brain research and investigations in cognitive, social, and developmental psychology have generated findings that educators are now using to inform classroom practice. Social–emotional learning and personalized learning make it clear that the transfer from laboratory to classroom can be tricky.

Social–Emotional Learning

Social–emotional learning (SEL), a form of emotional intelligence,[125] is the process by which children and adults gain and effectively apply the knowledge, attitudes, and skills needed to manage their emotions, set and realize worthwhile goals, feel and show empathy for others, keep positive relationships, and make responsible decisions.[126] These competencies are believed to improve students' academic performance, generate prosocial behaviors, improve relationships during their school years, and prepare them for successful college and adulthood. ESSA has given states permission to use SEL measures as one nonacademic metric to assess their school's success.

Briefly, SEL is a set of learning activities that teachers infuse into in all classrooms, at all times of the day, and encourage their use when children are home in their communities. The learners' cognitive ability and overall maturation—and their positive relationships with their teacher and other students—influence how teachers instruct SEL competencies. Schools can either prepare their own SEL curriculum or purchase high-quality SEL materials.

A 2018 Pew Research Center survey found that 70% of students ages 13 to 17 say that they are under stress and think anxiety and depression are major problems for their peers.[127] Educators realize that young people dealing with stress or trauma may not be able to fully engage as classmates or learners. Thus, teaching SEL is believed to help students realize the skills and competencies that allow them to successfully learn and get along well with others.

Research from the United States and Europe of several hundred thousand K–12 students strongly supports the view that well-designed and implemented SEL programs have significant benefits—social, emotional, interpersonal, behavioral, and academic—for participating individuals.[128]

Critics of social–emotional learning call it "fuzzy" and ask whether it encourages educators to "pathologize childhood" and invites schools to intrude deeper into children's lives.[129] These detractors remind us that normal childhood ups-and-downs are not "trauma." Meanwhile, educators also point to the lack of time and training to prepare teachers to address issues of students' relationships, well-being, and motivation in addition to academics.

Personalized Learning

In contrast to the "one-size-fits-all" approach to teaching, **personalized learning (or personalization)** is a student-centered approach to tailoring education to meet different students' needs.[130] In truth, however, "personalized learning still means whatever people want it to mean."[131] The term is ambiguous and can mean any number of educational arrangements. It may mean reconfiguring an entire school to provide students with theme-based academies. It can mean placing students in front of a computer screen with assignments selected specifically to remedy, teach, or advance that student's knowledge and skills in a particular subject. Or it can mean allowing a student to use a computer in a regular school classroom to find information for a science project. Accordingly, some call personalized learning a "mindset" rather than a program.[132] Therefore, it is important that educators carefully define what they mean when they ask what it is, how it works, and how effective it is in generating student achievement.

Research on technology-driven personalized learning is weak and generally not supportive,[133] in part because the term means so many different things. A 2019 National Education Policy Center report on personalized learning recommends that schools and policy makers "pause in their efforts to promote and implement personalized learning" until "rigorous review, oversight, and enforcement mechanisms" can be established.[134]

5.8c Successfully Educating *Every* Student: Where We Stand Today

Ultimately at stake is whether all children in our pluralist society will have access to high-quality schooling and achieve the knowledge and skills essential for 21st century competence, social mobility, and a reasonably satisfying adult quality of life. Today's achievement disparities will ultimately lead to socioeconomic differences among tomorrow's families. Such large discrepancies among families have serious moral and political implications for our society's future. Educational change comes slowly. Because education is fundamentally and primarily about a society's values, educational consensus and adjustments are realized even more gradually in a diverse society. Nonetheless, change does occur.

The COVID-19 pandemic has exposed more clearly the inequities in American families and their capacities to actively support their children's education. Families with ample resources provided their children with the needed digital tools—tablets, smartphones, computers, Wi-Fi capacity, and parents working from home who could supervise and assist their learning—while their schools were closed to in-person classes. Despite the unusual circumstances, their learning moved forward. By comparison, families with many fewer resources lacked sufficient digital tools for every school-aged child, lacked the broadband access, and did not have the professional flexibility to work from home. For many children, learning during spring 2020 and the 2020–2021 school year was sporadic and stalled. After-action reports in school districts considered new policies, new funding, and new teacher professional development to ensure continued learning for every child in future years.

Over America's history, this country's educational system has moved from a religious orientation to a largely secular one. In the 20th and 21st centuries, court decisions, legislation, and case law have brought traditionally underserved students into our public schools. Educational trends and innovations are promising to make students more successful learners. Some are succeeding; others—despite their popularity—are not. Nonetheless, today, we expect all students to master the high-status curriculum, and we are closer to making this goal a reality.

To consider more fully the changes in American public schools since World War II, complete the activity in the **Reflect & Engage** box, Education in the Past 70+ Years.

REFLECT & ENGAGE: EDUCATION IN THE PAST 70+ YEARS

American education since World War II has experienced many changes: (1) National reports prompted thinking about public schools' weakness; (2) the federal government invested more funding for public schooling and student equity; (3) rigorous curriculum standards became available; (4) teacher evaluation was reimagined; (5) education privatization gained momentum; and (6) new curricula arrived to address unmet student needs.

A. Working in small groups, each group considering a different issue (see 1–6), create a mind map using a digital tool such as Bubbl to depict the issues' key features, benefits to children, drawbacks, public reception, any possible personal experience with the topic, along with what your group sees as its lasting impact on American education.

B. After completing the mind maps, present your findings visually and orally to the rest of the class.

C. As a class, consider the benefits, limitations, and lasting influence of each American education issue in numbers 1 through 6.

KEY TAKE-AWAYS

Learning Objective 5.1 Assess how G. Stanley Hall and John Dewey's views of education as human development challenged the traditional subject-centered views and practices.

- Our founders saw public education as a way to ensure our nation's well-being. But our ideals about education for all children outran the early national leaders' abilities to put these values into practice.

- By the early 20th century, schools had inherited the educational role from other social institutions that could no longer do what they had always done because the modern world was too large and complex.
- Stanley Hall and colleagues' scientific approach to observing children and adapting teaching practices to meet students' learning needs brought credibility to the child study movement. As a result, by 1900 the child study movement had become a key part of educational psychology.
- John Dewey saw education not as an act of transmitting information to passive learners but rather an act of reconstruction: adding to experiences' meaning in ways that made sense to students and increased their ability to direct later experiences. Intelligence was the purposive reorganization of experience.
- Neither education's traditional subject-centered approach (and its overemphasis on control, order, and disregard for the learners' interests and welfare) nor the child-centered movement (placing students, not subjects, at teaching's center) best served students' interests.

Learning Objective 5.2 Explain how national reports, Frederick Taylor's scientific management theory, and common schools influenced the organization, curriculum, and instruction in schools.

- From 1900 to 1930, school administrators used Frederick Taylor's scientific management ideas to help their schools efficiently accommodate the large numbers of children and organize learning time. Scientific management practices shaped the schools' culture, students' aspirations, and outcomes (and to a large degree, still do so today).
- The Committee of Fifteen (1895) designed a model elementary school curriculum, urging academic topics be "correlated" with the arts and physical education.
- *Cardinal Principles* (1918) established a blueprint for the modern comprehensive high school. To prepare students for life and work, it broadened the curriculum, sorted students using testing and academic "tracking" according to their perceived abilities and assumed future vocations, and set self-fulfilling prophesies in motion.
- If the Committee of Ten's (1893) recommendations were weighted too heavily toward a classical academic curriculum, then the *Cardinal Principles* recommendations went too far in the opposite direction, diluting high schools' academic focus.
- Horace Mann and John Dewey believed in the common school's power to integrate and educate diverse students capable of living in a democratic republic. Many factors caused this goal to be more aspirational than reality.

Learning Objective 5.3 Compare and contrast how Booker T. Washington, W. E. B. DuBois, and legal and legislative actions advanced education for African American and other underserved students.

- Without publicly supported Southern schools, many formerly enslaved African Americans established their own educational collectives and associations, staffing schools entirely with African American teachers.
- Both Booker T. Washington and W. E. B. DuBois saw school and educational opportunities as the foundation for improving African Americans' lives, but their approaches to accomplish this—"accommodate and educate" versus "educate and agitate," respectively—differed dramatically.

Learning Objective 5.4 Summarize how World War I, the Great Depression, and vocational education influenced public education in the 20th century.

- Booming enrollment after World War I and during the Great Depression produced a profound shift in high schools' nature and function. They could meet many students' short-term goals (staying out of the adult labor market) but failed to meet their long-term needs (for appropriately rigorous and marketable knowledge and skills).

- Today's vocational education in comprehensive high schools focuses its curricula on having students develop both rigorous vocational and academic skills to prepare them for college and careers.
- In *Brown v. Board of Education* (1954), the U.S. Supreme Court unanimously decided that segregated schools provided unequal educational opportunities. Although school desegregation became law, in many locations, it did not become common practice.

Learning Objective 5.5 Argue how the 1966 *Coleman Report*, including later analyses of the report, ultimately shifted the focus of educational reform.

- The 1966 *Coleman Report*'s conclusions—that after family characteristics, a student's sense of control of his or her own destiny was the most important determinant of academic achievement—shifted the policy and research focus toward student outcomes (as opposed to school inputs) as a measure of the public schools' quality.

Learning Objective 5.6 Describe how Public Law 94-142 and IDEA components provide free and appropriate education to students with disabilities.

- The 1970s saw courts and Congress deciding in favor of students with disabilities attending public schools based on equality of opportunity.
- To ensure the basic educational rights of students with disabilities, this law specified that they must have the following requirements met and services available to them: a free and appropriate public education; an individualized education program; special education services; related services; due process procedures; and the least restrictive learning environment in which to learn

Learning Objective 5.7 Assess how *A Nation at Risk* and federal legislation increased public schools' accountability for educating every student.

- *A Nation at Risk* (1983)—claiming that U.S. public schools were "presently being eroded by a rising tide of mediocrity that threatens our very future"—spurred policy makers to increase public schools' accountability and educational rigor, as evidenced through state academic content standards and standardized achievement tests.
- The Elementary and Secondary Education Act of 1965 introduced Head Start preschool and Title I early grades programs to address educational equity for economically disadvantaged children. Head Start research outcomes include increased likelihood of participants graduating from high school, attending college, and receiving a postsecondary degree, license, or certification. Title I research outcomes appear less successful in making achievement gains but may have prevented further academic losses.
- The No Child Left Behind Act (NCLB) represented the federal government's first serious attempt to hold states, districts, and schools accountable for remedying the unequal achievement among different underserved student populations. Unintended outcomes included teaching to the test and a narrowed curriculum, creating difficulties in improving student learning and achievement.
- The Every Student Succeeds Act is the latest legislation linking federal dollars to states' public accountability for raising traditionally underserved students' academic achievement. ESSA ended NCLB's mandate that teachers must be "highly qualified," and critiques of state ESSA accountability plans find that innovation is lacking and the concern about "teaching to the test" remains.
- Political, logistical, and implementation hurdles made the rigorous academic Common Core State Standards in language arts and mathematics—informed by other top-performing countries—controversial.
- Well-designed and implemented teacher evaluation, based in part on student achievement, has been shown to improve teaching and learning.

Learning Objective 5.8 Critique how popular trends and innovations—including education privatization, charter schools, virtual education, voucher programs, and social-emotional and personalized learning—are affecting American education.

- An array of current education policies—education privatization (school choice), charter schools, and voucher programs—are upending assumptions about who educates our children and who pays for it. Wide state-by-state differences in charter and voucher regulations, academic quality, accountability expectations, and oversight lead to very mixed student and fiscal outcomes.
- Research finds that well-designed and implemented social and emotional learning programs have significant benefits for participating individuals. By comparison, personalized learning's many definitions make it difficult to research effectively, but studies on technology-driven personalized learning is weak and generally not supportive.
- Today's achievement disparities will ultimately lead to socioeconomic differences among tomorrow's families. Such large discrepancies among families have serious moral and political implications for our society's future.
- Today, we expect all students to master the high-status curriculum, and we are closer to making this goal a reality.

TEACHER SCENARIO: IT'S YOUR TURN

By a trick of imagination, you are a 125-year-old veteran teacher. The National Education Association (NEA) has invited you to give a keynote address at its annual conference about how certain events and influences over the past 100 years have shaped today's public schools.

Write a 5-minute presentation that discusses events from the past 100 years that have affected public schools in the following ways:

1. Shaped schools' organizational structure for teaching and learning
2. Affected curriculum and instruction
3. Reflected U.S. Supreme Court decisions
4. Increased diverse children's access to public schools
5. Reflected federal legislation
6. Influenced national reports

NOTES

1. Cremin, L. A. (1988). *American education: The metropolitan experience 1876–1980*. Harper and Row, p. 226.
2. Rathunde, L. (2001, Winter). Montessori education and optimal experience: A framework for new research. *NAMTA Journal, 26*(1), 11–43. http://citeseerx.ist.psu.edu/viewdoc/download?doi=10.1.1.186.6082&rep=rep1&type=pdf
3. Reese, W. J. (2001, Spring). The origins of progressive education. *History of Education Quarterly, 41*(1), 1–24.
4. Cremin, L. (1961). *The transformation of the school: Progressivism in American education 1876–1957.* Vintage, p. 101.
5. Cremin, 1961, p. 102.
6. Cremin, 1988, pp. 280–306.
7. Cremin, 1961, p. 104.

8. For a full discussion of the progressive education movement and its origins, see Reese, 2001.
9. Cremin, 1961, p. 117.
10. Cremin, L. A. (1965). *The genius of American education*. Vintage, p. 61.
11. Cremin, 1961, p. 125.
12. Cremin, 1961, p. 118.
13. Mirel, J. (2006, Winter). The traditional high school: Historical debates over its nature and function. *Education Next, 6*(1). Stanford University, Hoover Institution. http://educationnext.org/the-traditional-high-school/
14. Only one committee member actually worked in a public school. See: Rippa, S. A. (1984). *Education in a free society: An American history*. McKay.
15. Committee of Fifteen. (1895). *Report of the Committee of fifteen on elementary education: National Education Association of the United States*. American Book Company.
16. Cremin, 1988, p. 546.
17. Commission on the Reorganization of Secondary Education. (1918). *Cardinal principles of secondary education*. Department of the Interior, Bureau of Education, Bulletin No. 35. U.S. Government Printing Office.
18. Rothstein, R., Jacobsen, R., & Wilder, T. (2008). *Grading education: Getting accountability right*. Economic Policy Institute and Teachers College Press.
19. Wilms, W. W. (2003, April). Altering the structure and culture of American public schools. *Phi Delta Kappan, 84*(8), 606–615.
20. Anderson, J. D. (1988). *The education of blacks in the south, 1860–1935*. University of North Carolina Press, pp. 148–149.
21. Cremin, 1965.
22. Anderson, 1988, pp. 4–7.
23. Anderson, 1988, pp. 148–150.
24. Curti, M. (1968). *The social ideas of American educators*. Littlefield, Adams, p. 294.
25. Washington, B. T. (1901/2000). *Up from slavery: An autobiography*. Doubleday/Bartleby.com. https://www.bartleby.com/1004/
26. Hampton Institute's founder, General Samuel Armstrong, had commanded African American troops in the Civil War and was committed to providing an industrial education for African Americans and Native Americans. For a fuller discussion, see: Hlebowitch, P. S. (2001). *Foundations of American education* (2nd ed). Wadsworth/Thomson Learning, p. 302.
27. Anderson, J. D. (1990, Summer). Black rural communities and the struggle for education during the age of Booker T. Washington, 1877–1915. *Peabody Journal of Education, 67*(4), 46–62; Harlan, L. R. (1988). *Booker T. Washington in perspective*. University of Mississippi Press.
28. Anderson, 1988, pp. 102–103.
29. Washington, B. T. (1895/1969). The Atlanta compromise. In D. Calhoun (Ed.), *Educating for Americans: A documentary history (p. 350)*. Houghton Mifflin.
30. Buckley, K. W. (n.d.). *W. E. B. DuBois: A concise biography*. University of Massachusetts, Amherst. https://hollingsworthpeonies.com/i/u/10078242/f/W.E.B._du_Bois_Short_Bio_Photo.pdf
31. As a consequence, DuBois is acknowledged as the "Father of Social Science."
32. DuBois, W. E. B. (2012/1940). *Dusk of dawn. An essay toward an autobiography of a race concept*. Transaction, Rutgers University, p. 193.
33. DuBois thought that African Americans should lead the NAACP and that if white people were to be included at all they should serve in supportive roles.
34. In 1961, completely disillusioned with the United States, DuBois moved to Ghana and joined the Communist Party. A year later, he renounced his American citizenship. He died in 1963 at the age of 95.
35. Anderson, 1988, pp. 148–152.
36. For a thorough discussion with photos of African American education in the South between 1890 and 1940 and the unrealistic expectations placed on African American teachers, see: Fultz, M. (1995, March). African American teachers in the South, 1890–1940: Powerlessness and the ironies of expectations and protests. *History of Education Quarterly, 35*(4), 401–422.

37. Anderson, 1988, pp. 186–87, 235.

38. Anderson, 1988, p. 192.

39. Curti, 1968, pp. 306–307.

40. Ferguson, R. F., with Mehta, J. (2004, May). An unfinished journey: The legacy of *Brown* and the narrowing of the achievement gap. *Phi Delta Kappan, 85*(9), 656–669.

41. Starting in the 1930s, U.S. government policy and local practices often kept suburbs white by denying mortgage loans to African Americans. See: Rothstein, R. (2017). *The color of money.* Liveright.

42. DeBrey, C., Musu, L., McFarland, J., Wilkinson-Flicker S., Diliberti, M., Zhang, A., Branstetter, C., & Wang, X. (2019, February). *Status and trends in the education of racial and ethnic groups, 2018,* NCES 2019-038. U.S. Department of Education, National Center for Education Statistics, Institute of Education Sciences, p. iv. https://nces.ed.gov/pubs2019/2019038.pdf

43. Frankenberg, E., Ee, J., Ayscue, J. B., & Orfield, G. (2019, May 10). *Harming our common future: America's segregated schools 65 years after* Brown. The Civil Rights Project. https://www.civilrightsproject.ucla.edu/research/k-12-education/integration-and-diversity/harming-our-common-future-americas-segregated-schools-65-years-after-brown?smid=nytcore-ios-share

44. Bohrnstedt G., Kitmitto, S., Ogut, B., Sherman, D., & Chan, D. (2015, June). *School composition and the black-white achievement gap.* NCES 2015-018. U.S. Department of Education. https://files.eric.ed.gov/fulltext/ED560723.pdf; The Century Foundation. (2019, April 29). The benefits of socioeconomically and racially integrated schools and classrooms. https://tcf.org/content/facts/the-benefits-of-socioeconomically-and-racially-integrated-schools-and-classrooms/?session=1;Reardon, S. F. (2016). School segregation and racial academic achievement gaps. *The Russell Sage Foundation Journal of the Social Sciences, 2*(5), 34–57. https://www.rsfjournal.org/content/rsfjss/2/5/34.full.pdf

45. Kantor, H., & Lowe, R. (1995, April). Class, race, and the emergence of federal education policy: From the New Deal to the Great Society. *Educational Researcher, 24*(3), 4–11, 21.

46. Cremin, 1988, p. 311.

47. Mirel, 2006.

48. Mirel, 2006.

49. Gordon, H. R. D. (1999). *History and growth of vocational education in the United States.* Allyn & Bacon.

50. Benavot, A. (1983, April). The rise and decline of vocational education. *Sociology of Education, 56*(2), 63–76.

51. The Smith-Hughes Act called for specific entry-level skill training for youths in separate vocational schools, teacher training, and separate state boards for vocational education.

52. Bottoms, G., & Presson, A. (2000). *Finishing the job: Improving the achievement of vocational students.* Southern Regional Education Board, High Schools That Work, pp. 3, 6–7; Hoachlander, G., Alt, M., & Beltranena, R. (2001, March). *Leading school improvement: What research says—A review of the literature.* Southern Region Education Board, High Schools That Work; Kaufman, P., Bradby, D., & Teitlebaum, P. (2000, February). *High schools that work and whole school reform: Raising academic achievement of vocational completers through reform of school practices.* National Center for Research in Vocational Education.

53. Association for Career and Technical Education. (2009, March). The role of career academies in education improvement. *Issue Brief.* http://www.ncacinc.com/sites/default/files/media/research/ACTE%20Issue%20Brief%20Career_academies.pdf; Hoye, J. D., & Stern, D. (2008, September 10). The career academy story: A case study of how research can move policy and practice. *Education Week, 28*(3), 24–26.

54. Coleman, J. S. (1966). *Equality of educational opportunity.* U.S. Department of Health, Education, and Welfare, Office of Education/National Center for Education Statistics.

55. The Coleman study was the first time that testing data were used to measure educational disparities by looking at what students actually learned. The data collected through Coleman's questionnaire addressed characteristics of schools, teachers, and students; educational resources; physical facilities; socioeconomic backgrounds and racial composition, as well as attitudes toward race, integration, busing, and achievement.

56. Viadero, D. (2006b, June 21). Race report's influence felt 40 years later: Legacy of Coleman study was new view of equity. *Education Week, 25*(41), 1, 21–22.

57. When Geoffrey Borman of the University of Wisconsin–Madison and his colleague N. Maritza Dowling reanalyzed the original Coleman data with more sophisticated statistical models than were available in 1966, they found they could attribute as much as 40% of the variation in achievement differences

between students to in-school factors rather than to family background. For more details, see: Viadero, D. (2006a, June 21). Fresh look at Coleman data yields different conclusions. *Education Week, 25*(41), 21; Borman, G. D., & Maritza Dowling, N. (2006, April). *Schools and inequality: A multilevel analysis of Coleman's equality of educational opportunity data.* Paper presented at the Annual Meeting of the American Educational Research Association, San Francisco, CA.

58. Viadero, 2006a.

59. Epstein, J. L. (1991). Effects on student achievement of teachers' practices of parent involvement. In S. Silvern (Ed.), *Advances in reading/language research, vol. 5: Literacy through family, community and school interaction* (pp. 261–76). JAI Press; Epstein, J. L. (1989). Family structures and student motivation: A developmental perspective. In C. Ames & R. Ames (Eds.), *Research on motivation in education: vol. 3: Goals and cognitions* (pp. 259–295). Academic Press; Hoover-Dempsey, K. V., & Sandler, H. M. (1997). Why do parents become involved in their children's education? *Review of Educational Research, 67,* 3–42; Ketsetzis, M., Ryan, B. A., & Adams, G. R. (1998). Family processes, parent–child interactions, and child characteristics influencing school-based social adjustment. *Journal of Marriage and the Family, 60,* 374–387.

60. Brookover, W. B., Beady, C., Flook, P., Schweitzer, J., & Wisenbaker, J. (1979). *School social systems and student achievement: Schools can make a difference.* Praeger; Clark, D. L., Lotto, L. S., & McCarthy, M. M. (1980). Factors associated with success in urban elementary schools. *Phi Delta Kappan, 61,* 469–470; Edmonds, R. (1979). Effective schools for the urban poor. *Educational Leadership, 37*(1), 15–24; Purkey, S. C., & Smith, M. S. (1983). Effective schools: A review. *Elementary School Journal, 83,* 427–454; Rutter, M., Maugham, B., Outson, J., & Smith, A. (1979). *Fifteen-thousand hours: Secondary schools and their effects on children.* Harvard University Press.

61. McCarthy, M. M. (1991). Severely disabled children: Who pays? *Phi Delta Kappan, 73*(1), 66–71.

62. For more details on the initial interpretation of "free and appropriate education," see the U.S. Supreme Court decision, *Board of Education of Hendrick Hudson Central School District v. Rowley*, 1982, 458 U.S. 176, 102 S. Ct. 3034. Cited in Alexander & Alexander, 2005, pp. 499–502.

63. Dunn, J. (2017, Summer). Special education standards. *EducationNext, 17*(3). https://www.education-next.org/special-education-standards-supreme-court-raises-level-benefit-endrew-f-v-douglas-county/; *Endrew F v. Douglas County School District*, 580 US__2017. https://www.supremecourt.gov/opinions/16pdf/15-827_0pm1.pdf; Kamenetz, A., & Turner, C. (2017, March 22). The supreme court rules in favor of a special education student. *NPR ED.* https://www.npr.org/sections/ed/2017/03/22/521094752/the-supreme-court-rules-in-favor-of-a-special-education-student

64. Necessary supports to meet the inclusion mandate may include sending teachers, assistants, assistive technology, and adapted texts and curriculum into the general education classroom along with the student with disabilities.

65. EducationNext. (2018, July 24). *EdStat: 60 percent of all students with disabilities spend 80 percent or more of their school day in regular classrooms.* https://www.educationnext.org/edstat-60-percent-students-disabilities-spend-80-percent-school-day-regular-classrooms/; National Center for Education Statistics. (2019). Students with disabilities, inclusion of. *Fast Facts.* U.S. Department of Education. http://nces.ed.gov/fastfacts/display.asp?id=59; The Condition of Education. (2007, June*). Inclusion of students with disabilities in general classrooms.* NCES 2007-064. U.S. Department of Education, Indicator 31, p. 68. https://nces.ed.gov/pubs2007/2007064.pdf

66. Fuchs, L., & Vaughn, S. (2012). Responsiveness-to-intervention: A decade later. *Journal of Learning Disabilities, 45*(3), 195–203; Herman, R., Dawson, P., Dee, T., Greene, J., Maynard, R., Redding, S., et al. (2008). *Turning around chronically low-performing schools: A practice guide* (NCEE #2008-4020. U.S. Department of Education. https://ies.ed.gov/ncee/wwc/Docs/PracticeGuide/Turnaround_pg_04181.pdf; Gersten, R., Compton, D., Connor, C. M., Dimino, J., Santoro, L., Linan- Thompson, S., et al. (2008). *Assisting students struggling with reading: Response to intervention and multi-tier intervention for reading in the primary grades. A practice guide* (NCEE 2009-4045). U.S. Department of Education. http://ies.ed.gov/ncee/wwc/pdf/practice_guides/rti_reading_ pg_021809.pdf; Gersten, R., Beckmann, S., Clarke, B., Foegen, A., Marsh, L., Star, J. R., et al. (2009). *Assisting students struggling with mathematics: Response to intervention (RTI) for elementary and middle schools* (NCEE 2009-4060). U.S. Department of Education. http://ies.ed.gov/ncee/wwc/pdf/practice_ guides/rti_math_pg_042109.pdf

67. Samuels, C. (2008, January 23). "Response to intervention" sparks interest, questions. *Education Week, 27*(20), 1, 13.

68. National Commission on Excellence in Education. (1983, April). *A nation at risk: The imperative for educational reform: An open letter to the American people.* http://www.ed.gov/pubs/NatAtRisk/risk.html

69. Yeakey, C. C., & Johnston, G. S. (1985, February). High school reform: A critique and a broader construct of social reality. *Education and Urban Society, 17*(2), 157–170.

70. Husen, T. (1983, March). School standards in America and other countries. *Phi Delta Kappan, 64,* 455–461.

71. Yeakey & Johnston, 1985.

72. Writer Gerald Bracey concluded that *A Nation at Risk* was not intended to objectively examine the condition of American education, but rather to document the terrible things that Terrell Bell, President Ronald Reagan's Secretary of Education, had heard about schools.

73. For example, in 1990, politics delayed the Sandia Report's publication for several years because its positive findings about public schools might undercut the critical perspective taken by *A Nation at Risk*.

74. Bracey, G. W. (2003, April). April foolishness: The 20th anniversary of *A Nation at Risk. Phi Delta Kappan, 84*(8), 616–621.

75. Linn, R. L. (n.d.). *Test-based accountability.* The Gordon Commission on the Future of Assessment in Education. https://www.ets.org/Media/Research/pdf/linn_test_based_accountability.pdf

76. See Puma, M. J., Karweit, N., Price, C., Ricciuti, A., Thompson, W., & Vaden-Kiernan, M. (1997, April). *Prospects: Final report on student outcomes.* U.S. Department of Education; Carter, L. F. (1983). *A study of compensatory and elementary education: The sustaining effects study.* U.S. Department of Education.

77. Dynarski, M., & Kainz, K. (2015, November 10). Why federal spending on disadvantaged students (Title I) doesn't work. *Evidence Speaks Reports, 1*(7). Economic Studies at Brookings. https://www.brookings.edu/wp-content/uploads/2016/07/Download-the-paper-2.pdf

78. Borman, G. D., et al. (2001). Coordinating categorical and regular programs: Effects on Title I students' educational opportunities and outcomes. In G. D. Borman, S. C. Stringfield, & R. E. Slavin (Eds.), *Title I: Compensatory education at the crossroads* (pp. 79–116). Lawrence Erlbaum; Borman, G. D., & D'Agostino, J. V. (2001). Title I and student achievement: A quantitative synthesis. In G. D. Borman, S. C. Stringfield, & R. E. Slavin (Eds.), *Title I: Compensatory education at the crossroads* (pp. 25–58). Lawrence Erlbaum.

79. Schanzenbach, D. W., & Bauer, L. (2016, August 19). Report. The long-term impact of the Head Start program *Brookings.* https://www.brookings.edu/research/the-long-term-impact-of-the-head-start-program/

80. Klein, A. (2015, April 10). No child left behind: An overview. *Education Week.* https://www.edweek.org/ew/section/multimedia/no-child-left-behind-overview-definition-summary.html

81. Viadero, D. (2010, March 26). Study suggests NCLB impact on NAEP scores. *Education Week.* http://blogs.edweek.org/edweek/inside-school-research/2010/03/if_you_think_the_last.html

82. National Assessment of Educational Performance. (2012). *NAEP—mathematics 2011: Summary of major findings.* http://nationsreportcard.gov/math_2011/summary.asp; National Assessment of Educational Progress. (2011). *Top stories in NAEP reading 2011.* http://nationsreportcard.gov/reading_2011/

83. Hess, F., & Finn, C. Jr. (2004, September). Inflating the life rafts of NCLB: Making public school choice and supplementary services for students in troubled schools. *Phi Delta Kappan, 86*(1), 34–58.

84. Every student succeeds Act (ESSA). (2015). https://www.ed.gov/essa?src=rn

85. For an ESSA overview, see: Klein, A. (2016, March 31). The every student succeeds act: An ESSA overview. *Education Week.* https://www.edweek.org/ew/issues/every-student-succeeds-act/index.html; for a more thorough discussion of ESSA and how states are faring with its requirements, see *Phi Delta Kappan*, October 2019 issue.

86. Although academic indicators will count "much" more.

87. This includes schools reporting their exact per-pupil costs by program.

88. Klein, A. (2019, April 2). States, districts tackle the tough work of making ESSA a reality. *Education Week, 38*(27), 4–6. https://www.edweek.org/ew/articles/2019/04/03/states-districts-tackle-the-tough-work-of.html

89. Burnette II, D. (2019, April 2). A heavy lift to make school data transparent—and easy to use. *Education Week, 38*(27), 10–12. https://www.edweek.org/ew/articles/2019/04/03/a-heavy-lift-to-make-school-data.html

90. Klein, A. (2019, April 2). Answering your ESSA question. *Education Week, 38*(27), 20–21. https://www.edweek.org/ew/articles/2019/04/03/answering-your-essa-questions.html

91. Klein, 2019.

92. Heller, R. (2019, October). From what it's not to what it is: The editor's note. *Phi Delta Kappan, 101*(2), 4.

93. Common Core State Standards Initiative. (2019.) *Standards in your state*. Council of Chief State School Officers. http://www.corestandards.org/standards-in-your-state/

94. Goldstein, D. (2019, December 7). Common core after 10 years: Pass? Or Fail? *The New York Times*, A, 1. https://www.nytimes.com/2019/12/06/us/common-core.html?smid=nytcore-ios-share

95. Weisberg, D., Sexton, S., Mulhern, J., & Keeling, D. et al. (2009) *The widget effect: Our national failure to acknowledge and act on differences in teacher effectiveness* (2nd ed.). The New Teacher Project. https://tntp.org/assets/documents/TheWidgetEffect_execsummary_2nd_ed.pdf

96. National Council on Teacher Quality. (2019). State of the states 2019: Teacher & principal education evaluation policy. https://www.nctq.org/pages/State-of-the-States-2019:-Teacher-and-Principal-Evaluation-Policy. This url shows teacher evaluation requirements by state, 2015–2019.

97. National Council on Teacher Quality, 2019.

98. Taylor, E.S., & Tyler, J. H. (2012, Fall). Can teacher evaluation improve teaching? *EducationNext, 12*(4). https://www.educationnext.org/can-teacher-evaluation-improve-teaching/

99. National Council on Teacher Quality. (2012). *State of the states, 2012: Teacher effectiveness policies*. https://www.nctq.org/dmsView/State_of_the_States_2012_Teacher_Effectiveness_Policies_NCTQ_Report

100. Close, K., & Amrein-Beardsley, A. (2018, August 24). Learning from what doesn't work in teacher evaluation. *Phi Delta Kappan, 100*(1), 15–19; Skedsmo, G., & Huber, S. G. (2018, February). Teacher evaluation: The need for valid measures and increased teacher involvement. *Educational Assessment, Evaluation, and Accountability, 30*(1), 1–5.

101. Value-added methodology is a statistical technique that determines the amount of teacher influence on students' academic progress that controls students' prior characteristics (such as prior achievement, parental income, or socioeconomic status). Although it can be used correctly for large-scale studies, the research finds that it has questionable use at the secondary level, and the consensus exists that this technique should not be used to make high-stakes decisions about individual teachers.

102. Boyd, W. L. (2007). The politics of privatization in American education. *Educational Policy, 21*(1), 7–14.

103. Abrams, S. E. (2016). *Education and the commercial mindset*. Harvard University Press; Burch, P. (2009). *Hidden markets. The new education privatization*. Routledge; Debray-Pelot, E. H., & McGuinn, P. (2009). The new politics of education: Analyzing the federal education policy landscape in the post-NCLB Era. *Educational Policy, 23*(1), 15–42.

104. Hinton, M. (2019, January 23). Charter debates could be coming to state legislatures. *Education Week, 38*(19), 14, 16; Jones, S. (2019, February 27). What form can charter schools take? A brief field guide. *Education Week, 38*(23), 7.

105. EDChoice. (2019, August 23). School choice. School choice in America dashboard. https://www.edchoice.org/school-choice/school-choice-in-america/

106. Catt, D. (2019, December 2). *The states ranked by spending on school choice programs, 2018 edition*. Engage. https://www.edchoice.org/engage/the-states-ranked-by-spending-on-school-choice-programs-2018-edition/

107. National Association of Charter School Authorizers. (2017). *Principles & standards*. http://www.qualitycharters.org/for- authorizers/principles-and-standards/

108. Carey, K. (2017, February 23). Dismal voucher results surprise researchers as DeVos era begins. The Upshot. *The New York Times*. https://www.nytimes.com/2017/02/23/upshot/dismal-results-from-vouchers-surprise-researchers-as-devos-era-begins.html

109. Abdulkadiroğlu, A., Angrist, J. D., Dynarski, S. M., Kane, T. J., & Pathak, P. A. (2011). Accountability and flexibility in public schools: Evidence from Boston's charters and pilots. *The Quarterly Journal of Economics, 126*(2), 699–748; Tuttle, C. C., Gill, B., Gleason, P., Knechtel, V., Nichols-Barrer, I., & Resch, A. (2013). *KIPP middle schools: Impacts on achievement and other outcomes*. Mathematica Policy Research. http://files.eric.ed.gov/fulltext/ED540912.pdf

110. Center for Research on Education Outcomes [CREDO]. (2009). *Multiple choice: Charter school performance in 16 states*. https://credo.stanford.edu/reports/MULTIPLE_CHOICE_CREDO.pdf; CREDO. (2013. January 11). *Charter school performance in Michigan*. Stanford University. https://credo.stanford.edu/pdfs/MI_report_2012_FINAL_1_11_2013_no_watermark.pdf; Cremata, E., Davis, D., Dickey, K., Lawyer, K., Negassi, Y, Raymond, M. E., & Woolworth, J. L. (2013). *National charter school study 2013*. CREDO. http://credo.stanford.edu/documents/NCSS%202013%20Final%20Draft.pdf

111. Frankenberg, E., Siegel Hawley, G., Ee, J., & Orfield, G. (2017, May 23). *Southern schools: More than a half-century after the civil rights revolution.* The Civil Rights Project at UCLA. https://www.civilrightsproject.ucla.edu/research/k-12-education/integration-and-diversity/southern-schools-brown-83-report/Brown63_South_052317-RELEASE-VERSION.pdf;CREDO. (2015b). *Urban charter school study report on 41 regions 2015.* https://urbancharters.stanford.edu/download/Urban%20Charter%20School%20Study%20Report%20on%2041%20Regions.pdf

112. Kaplan, L. S., & Owings, W. A. (2018). Funding school choice: Implications for American education. *Journal of Education Finance, 44*(2), 199–217.

113. For a more complete discussion of these voucher programs, see: Kaplan, L. S., & Owings, W. A. (2018). Betsy DeVos's education reform agenda: What principals—and their publics—need to know. *NASSP Bulletin, 102*(1), 58–84; Kaplan, L. S., & Owings, W. A. (2018, Fall). Funding school choice: Implications for American education, *Journal of Education Finance, 44*(2), 199–217.

114. Costrell, R. M. (2009, Winter). Who gains, who loses? The fiscal impact of the Milwaukee parental choice program. *Education Next, 9*(1). http://educationnext.org/who-gains-who-loses/; EdChoice. (2017). *Does school choice drain public schools' funding and resources?* https://www.edchoice.org/school_choice_faqs/does-school-choice-drain-public-schools-funding-and-resources/

115. Carey, K. (2017, February 23). Dismal voucher results surprise researchers as DeVos era begins. The Upshot. *The New York Times.* https://www.nytimes.com/2017/02/23/upshot/dismal-results-from-vouchers-surprise-researchers-as-devos-era-begins.html; Carnoy, M. (2017, February 28). School vouchers are not a proven strategy for improving student achievement. *Economic Policy Institute.* http://www.epi.org/publication/school-vouchers-are-not-a-proven-strategy-for-improving-student-achievement/; Epple, D., Romano, R., & Zimmer, R. (2015, June). Charter schools: A survey of research on their characteristics and effectiveness. (NBER Working Paper No. 21256). The National Bureau of Economic Research. http://202.119.108.161:93/modules/ShowPDF.aspx?GUID=e74e5fbcefdb4e05846c6c35f86c7a49;Dynarski, M. (2016). On negative effects of vouchers. *Evidence Speaks Series.* https://www.brookings.edu/research/on-negative-effects-of-vouchers/

116. Critics assert that empirical results show little consensus or consistency across the reported findings; and the positive effects do not translate to different contexts, populations, programs, grade levels, or subjects. See: Lubienski, C., & Brewer, T. J. (2016). An analysis of voucher advocacy: Taking a closer look at the uses and limitations of "gold standard" research. *Peabody Journal of Education, 91*(4), 455–472.

117. Molnar, A., Miron, G., Elgeberi, N., Barbour, M. K., Huerta, L., Shafer, S. R., & Rice, J. K. (2019). *Virtual schools in the U.S. 2019.* National Education Policy Center. http://nepc.colorado.edu/publication/virtual-schools-annual-2019

118. Prothero, A. (2016, November 3). Outsized influence: Online charters bring lobbying "A" game to states. *Education Week, 36*, 11.

119. Prothero, A., & Harwin, A. (2019, April 18). Many online charter schools fail to graduate even half of their students on time. *Education Week, 38*(31), 8. https://www.edweek.org/ew/articles/2019/04/18/many-online-charter-schools-fail-to-graduate.html

120. Prothero & Harwin, 2019.

121. Molnar et al., 2019.

122. CREDO, 2015a.

123. Fang, L. (2014, September 25). Venture capitalists are poised to "disrupt" everything about the education market. *The Nation.* http://www.thenation.com/article/181762/venture-capitalists-are-posed-disrupt-everything-about-education-market;Prothero, 2016.

124. Barnum, M. (2017 February 27). Online charter schools have poor track record, but they can reach places other schools can't. *The74 Million.* https://www.the74million.org/article/online-charter-schools-have-poor-track-record-but-they-can-reach-places-other-schools-cant/

125. *Emotional intelligence* is the capacity to be aware of, manage, and express one's emotions, and to handle the emotions of others. High emotional intelligence improves one's capacities in leadership and relationships.

126. Weissberg, R. P., & Cascario, J. (2013). Academic learning + social-emotional learning = national priority. *Phi Delta Kappan, 95*(2), 8–13.

127. Horowitz, J. M., & Graf, N. (2019, February 20). *Most U.S. teens see anxiety and depression as major problems among their peers.* Pew Research Center. https://www.pewsocialtrends.org/2019/02/20/most-u-s-teens-see-anxiety-and-depression-as-a-major-problem-among-their-peers/

128. Durlak, J. A., Weissberg, R. P., Dymnicki, A., Taylor, R. D., & Schellinger, K. B. (2011). The impact of enhancing students' social and emotional learning: A meta-analysis of school-based universal interventions. *Child Development, 82*(1), 405–432; Sklad, M., Diekstra, R., De Ritter, M., Ben, J., & Gravesteijn, C. (2012). Effectiveness of school-based universal social emotional and behavioral programs. Do they enhance students' development in the area of skill, behavior, and adjustment? *Psychology and Schools, 49*(9), 892–909; Wiglesworth, M., Lendrum, A., Oldfield, J., Sott, A., ten Bokkkel, I., Tate, K., & Emery, C. (2016). The impact of trial stage, developer involvement and international transferability on universal social and emotional learning program outcomes: A meta-analysis. *Cambridge Journal of Education, 46*(3), 347–437.

129. Hess, R. (2019, April 18). Is social and emotional learning encouraging educators to pathologize childhood? *Education Week*. http://blogs.edweek.org/edweek/rick_hess_straight_up/2019/04/is_social_and_emotional_learning_encouraging_educators_to_pathologize_childhood.html

130. The Glossary of Education Reform. (2015, May 14). *Personalized learning*. https://www.edglossary.org/personalized-learning/

131. Herold, B. (2018, November 7). Personalized learning still means whatever people want it to mean. *Education Week, 38*(12), 5.

132. Herold, 2018, 5.

133. Boninger, F., Molnar, A., & Saldaña, C. M. (2019, April 30). *Personalized learning and the digital privatization of curriculum and teaching*. National Education Policy Center. https://nepc.colorado.edu/sites/default/files/publications/RB%20Personalized%20Learning%20revised_0.pdf; Bulger, M. (2016, July 22). Personalized learning: The conversations we're not having (pp. 11, 14–15). *Data & Society*. https://datasociety.net/pubs/ecl/PersonalizedLearning_primer_2016.pdf; Enyedy, N. (2014). *Personalized instruction: New interest, old rhetoric, limited results, and the need for a new direction for computer-mediated learning*. National Education Policy Center. https://nepc.colorado.edu/publication/personalized-instruction; Pane, J. F. (2018). *Strategies for implementing personalized learning while evidence and resources are underdeveloped*. RAND. https://www. rand.org/pubs/perspectives/PE314.html

134. Boninger et al., 2019.

iStock/skynesher

6 COMPETING GOALS OF PUBLIC EDUCATION

InTASC Standards Addressed: 1, 2, 3, 4, 5, 7, 8, 9, 10

LEARNING OBJECTIVES

After you read this chapter, you should be able to

6.1 Assess the general goals of American education and explain their importance.

6.2 Critique the wide-ranging nature of American education goals and the challenges these bring.

6.3 Compare and contrast how conservative, liberal, and critical theory education critics offer differing views of schools' role in society and how schools can improve.

6.4 Support how education is an investment in human capital.

6.5 Defend the ways that education is still the key to achieving the American Dream.

For more than 300 years, Americans have expected much from our schools. Starting with narrowly academic and religious goals in the 17th century, we added civic, vocational, and social goals in the 18th and 19th centuries. Fully including underrepresented children and children with disabilities in public education and addressing personal or self-realization goals entered in the 20th century. The 21st century extends these trends. In reviewing these expectations, John Goodlad, an American education scholar, concluded, "These goals now encompass such a wide range of knowledge, skills, and values along with a kaleidoscopic array of scientific, humanistic, and aesthetic sources of human enlightenment."[1] It seems as if public education is trying to do it all.

With so many purposes, it is understandable that we would occasionally disagree about which are more important and how well our schools are accomplishing them. Relentless attacks on public schools since at least *Sputnik*'s launch in 1957—along with disillusionment with public organizations in general—have made people question all public institutions. Today, political hyperbole often cynically depicts our public schools in dystopian terms: "failing," "crumbling," a "dead end." Movies like *Waiting for Superman* (2010)[2] have advanced this narrative.

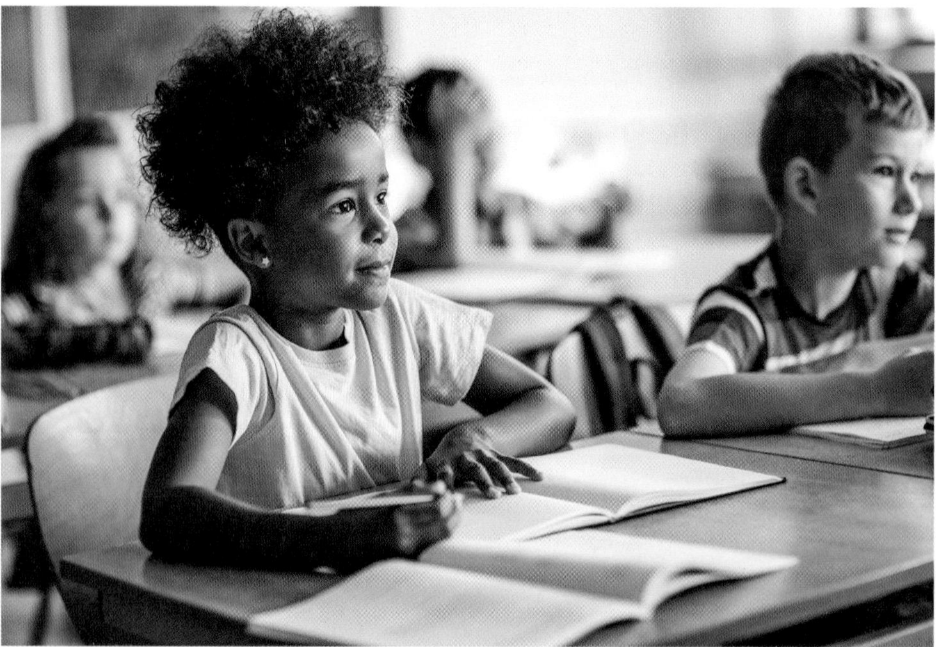

Education socializes each generation in the knowledge and skills required for mature citizenship and economic participation.

iStock/skynesher

Imploring us to keep our perspective on public schools' goals, Mike Rose, professor of education at the University of California at Los Angeles, observes, "In the midst of the culture wars that swirl around schools; the fractious, intractable school politics; the conservative assault on public institutions; and the testing, testing, testing—in the midst of all this, it is easy to lose sight of the broader purpose and grand vision of the common public school."[3] It is also easy to lose sight of the value of respectful dialogue.

As citizens in a democratic republic, it is our responsibility to continually assess how well our public institutions are performing. We need to repeatedly review their purposes and gauge the extent to which they are fulfilling their promises. At times, we as a society need to revise schools' goals in response to our changing world. To do this is natural—and does not imply failure. Rhetorical overkill makes thoughtful analysis and reflection more difficult. Only when we can listen thoughtfully and respectfully to those with whom we disagree can we avoid the false choices and find improved, more meaningful solutions for our national community.

If we are to equip all our children with the intellectual, cultural, civic, and interpersonal knowledge and skills that will enable them to become self-directed, employable, and contributing citizens, we will need to find ways to identify and successfully reconcile our competing goals for their education. Only then will our children be able to turn our goals into their personal realities.

Schools prepare children to become informed, active citizens and responsible neighbors.

iStock/fstop123

6.1 THE GENERAL GOALS OF PUBLIC EDUCATION

Education exists to serve society by socializing each generation in the knowledge and skills required for mature citizenship and economic participation. In a diverse society, finding a common set of values and goals for schools to address presents many challenges.

6.1a Defining a Set of Common Values

American public schools have many responsibilities. Their historical mandate requires them to provide learning experiences that contribute to students' intellectual, academic, civic, vocational, personal, and social growth. In fact, society has charged schools with remedying virtually every societal ill while simultaneously providing students with the intellectual, civic, and creative capacities they need to lead and defend our nation.

The idea of education to serve the social order is a respected tradition. In Plato's time, the idea of a good society implied a set of educational policies and practices that would support the public's highest ideals. In those days, societies could only exist through the conscious, deliberate socialization process, established on a community-by-community basis.

In the early United States, the idea of common public school became popular. American intellectuals like John Adams and Thomas Jefferson advanced the widespread availability of public schooling as essential to an enlightened citizenry. Democracy could not exist, they avowed, unless future generations had the knowledge, skills, ethical beliefs, and the will to stay informed. Self-governance depended on it. In this way, mass public schooling became seen as a way to continue our republic, nationhood, and culture.

This notion extended into the 19th century when Horace Mann, as Massachusetts superintendent of schools, used his position to require public school attendance through the elementary grades. Mann envisioned public schools as teaching shared political values with the ultimate aim to maintain public order. Other thinkers agreed with him, framing education's goals even more broadly.

In recent times, defining a shared set of political values has become more difficult. Since the 19th century, vigorous community debates over what schools should teach have shaken the schoolhouse. During the late 20th century, liberal organizations and labor unions pressed the schools to teach their type of political ideology, whereas conservative political groups pressured public schools not to teach what they considered to be "left-wing ideas." The range of educational alternatives now available—including private schools, homeschooling, virtual schools, charter and parochial schools—means that a community's children do not all attend a common school. Economically, ethnically, and racially segregated neighborhoods also keep children from sharing universal educational experiences. Chapter 7 discusses how residential and school segregation and school integration impact students' academic achievement and life outcomes.

Nevertheless, if the United States can survive as a democratic republic, we all must live together in an economically viable, law-abiding, patriotic, fair, and civil society. Public schools' purpose, then, is to attempt to create a more democratic, integrated, and socially mobile society in what is arguably a less-than-perfect world.

6.1b Defining Schools' Goals

Societies always make ongoing distinctions between what schooling's purposes are and what they ought to be. For example, many believe that schooling should educate citizens to fit into the existing society. Others believe that schools should educate citizens to improve—not reproduce—the society. Different educational visions mean different ideas of what makes a "good society," and varying social visions influence what makes a "good education."

Schools' **intellectual goals** are to teach essential cognitive skills such as reading for comprehension, writing for clarity of expression, mathematics for numerical reasoning in life and sciences, and digital literacy to know how to access, evaluate, and communicate information over the internet. Schools are charged with transmitting the culture's knowledge and values through reading and discussing the society's language, literature, history, sciences, and arts. Schools also address intellectual goals when they teach students to use higher-order thinking and reasoning through analysis, synthesis, and evaluation to manipulate and use information creatively to solve problems.

Similarly, schools' **political goals** aim to instill allegiance to the country and to its existing political order. Schools are supposed to encourage patriotism and responsible public behaviors. They are tasked with preparing children to become citizens who will participate in our civil processes by obeying the laws, paying taxes, and voting for persons to represent them in the state and national government. In schools, our young citizens learn about current local, national, and world events and how to appropriately and effectively gather accurate information and express and debate their views about important issues of the day. Likewise, schools help assimilate members of different cultural groups into a shared political society with unifying traditions and values.

Many believe that schools' **social goals** include helping prevent or solve societal problems. Schools work as one of many institutions—along with the family and religious organizations, among others—to socialize children into society's various roles, behaviors, and values. By bringing the community's children together in a common facility to pursue a common endeavor, schools teach students how to respect and work effectively with people from other backgrounds or traditions. This **socialization process**—developing in its members shared culture, behaviors, values, and loyalty—is essential to any society's stability.

Finally, schools' **economic goals** intend to prepare students for their later occupational roles and to select, train, and distribute individuals into the society's division of labor. The extent to which schools directly prepare students for their work varies from society to society, but most schools have at least some indirect role in this process.

Ironically, these purposes sometimes produce contradictory impulses. If schools are to increase students' intellectual ability by teaching and encouraging critical thinking, reasoning, and evaluating, they can also create students who thoughtfully challenge—rather than accept—their society's norms and rules. As Lawrence A. Cremin, an education historian, noted,[4]

> Schooling, like education in general, never liberates without at the same time limiting. It never empowers without at the same time constraining. It never frees without at the same time socializing. The question is not whether one or the other is occurring in isolation but what the balance is, and to what end, and in light of what alternatives.

The natural tension between schooling's role in maintaining the status quo and its potential to bring about change lies at the heart of differing views of education and schooling—and it often creates competing goals. Those who support society tend to stress schools' role in preserving it. Those who believe that society needs improvement stress schools' role in either improving or transforming it. In this chapter, you will read about how different political perspectives on education view its goals and how each contributes a fuller dimension to the others.

6.2 THE WIDE-RANGING NATURE OF AMERICAN EDUCATION GOALS

Today, American schools' basic governance is decentralized, with most power wielded at the state level. As a result, we actually have 51 school systems, one for each state (and one for the District of Columbia). All regulate themselves in slightly different ways. Given this context and America's broad pluralism, any effort to advance a single set of educational goals for American schools is likely to promote disagreement and debate.

6.2a National Goals in a Decentralized Education System

Over the years, improved communications and travel have allowed some nationalizing influences to affect schools in similar ways. In addition, federal legislation and targeted funding have encouraged certain school reforms in schools across the country. The national popularity of certain exams and textbooks in the school curriculum has also contributed to a degree of consistency among schools.

In our decentralized school governance system, the challenge is to provide a set of national educational goals for schools that gives guidance and direction without giving requirements or prescriptions. The national goals have to be general enough to mean different things to different people. To gain widespread acceptance, these goals must leave room for interpretation and adaptation according to the state and local circumstances. At the same time, they must be clear enough to give a shared sense of national purpose and identity. And, increasingly, the goals must be attuned to the international educational benchmarks that reflect the knowledge and skills our children will need to compete for jobs with well-educated peers around the world.

When we talk about educational purposes, we refer to goals and objectives. All three terms—purposes, goals, and objectives—describe a direction, or what we are seeking to accomplish. Many educators use the terms "goals" or "purposes" to refer to broad directions, whereas **objectives** are more specific. Many educators refer to these as the "ends" of education.

6.2b Goals for U.S. Education

All education endpoints reflect two major influences: current social forces and prevailing educational philosophies or theories. Social forces and philosophies interact to shape the goals that are adapted at the national or state levels. These goals, in turn, affect the more specific school and classroom goals and objectives. As time passes, changes in society, knowledge, and beliefs about the nature of the world and the nature of learning may produce related changes in educational theories and purposes.

Benchmarks for U.S. Academic Performance

The U.S. Department of Education continues to monitor the nation's progress on a set of national education goals originally developed in 1990. Published in a report, *America 2000: An American Educational Strategy*,[5] these ambitious educational targets continue to define expectations for our national, state, and local school performance because they have yet to be fully met.

These educational goals are as follows:

1. All children will start school ready to learn, with their preparation being ensured by participating in preschool programs.
2. The national high school graduation rate will increase to at least 90%.
3. All students will leave Grades 4, 8, and 12 having demonstrated competency in English, mathematics, science, foreign languages, civics and government, economics, art, history, and geography.
4. Teachers will have opportunities to acquire the knowledge and skills needed for preparing students for the 21st century.
5. U.S. students will be first in the world in mathematics and science achievement.
6. Every American adult will be literate and will possess the knowledge and skills necessary to compete in a global economy.
7. Every school will be free of drugs, violence, and the unauthorized presence of firearms and alcohol.
8. Every school will promote partnerships to increase parental involvement in their children's social, emotional, and academic growth.

To assess how well U.S. schools are meeting these aspirational goals, the National Center for Education Statistics (NCES) developed a set of performance benchmarks. This organization collects data on an ongoing basis to allow states and policy makers to determine how well schools are meeting these goals.

Comprehensive Education Goals

Whereas *America 2000* goals are mostly academic, more comprehensive educational goals also exist. While studying school goals in 1979, John Goodlad (1920–2014), a noted education professor, researcher, and writer, reviewed lists of desired outcomes published by local school boards across the country. From these, Goodlad identified a cluster of 12 major American schools' goals that reflect a complete, humanistic perspective about what communities wanted their schools to accomplish and gave each a rationale.[6] These American public schools' purposes remain valid today:

1. **Mastery of basic skills or fundamental processes.** In our technological civilization, an individual's ability to participate in society's activities depends on mastering the following: verbal and mathematical literacy, the ability to communicate clearly and effectively with varied media, and knowledge of subjects that affect one's ability to live with awareness and make informed decisions as citizens in a democratic republic.

2. **Career or vocational education.** An individual's satisfaction in life will be significantly related to satisfaction with her or his job. Intelligent career decisions will require knowledge of personal aptitudes, interests, and ambitions in relation to career possibilities.
3. **Intellectual development.** As civilization has become more complex, people have had to rely more heavily on their cognitive abilities. Full intellectual development of each member of society is necessary.
4. **Enculturation.** Studies that illuminate our relationship with the past yield insights into our society and its values; moreover, these strengthen an individual's sense of belonging, identity, and direction for his or her own life.
5. **Interpersonal relations.** Schools should help every child understand, appreciate, and value persons belonging to social, cultural, and ethnic groups different from his or her own.
6. **Autonomy.** Schools must produce self-directed citizens, or else they have failed both society and the individual. Schools help prepare children for a rapidly changing world by helping them develop the capacity to adapt to new situations and assume responsibility for their own needs.
7. **Citizenship.** To counteract the present human ability to destroy humanity and the environment requires citizen involvement in this country's political and social life. A democracy can survive only through its members' participation.
8. **Creativity and aesthetic perception.** The abilities to create new and meaningful things and appreciate other people's creations are essential both for personal self-realization and for society's benefit.
9. **Self-concept.** An individual's self-concept serves as a reference point and feedback mechanism for personal goals and aspirations. The school environment can help facilitate development of a healthy self-concept.
10. **Emotional and physical well-being.** Emotional stability and physical fitness are necessary conditions for attaining other goals, and they are also worthy ends in themselves.
11. **Moral and ethical character.** Individuals need to develop the judgment that allows them to evaluate behavior as right or wrong. Schools can foster the growth of such judgment as well as a commitment to truth, moral integrity, and moral conduct.
12. **Self-realization.** Efforts are necessary to develop a better self and contribute to the development of a better society.

Americans still want their schools to meet comprehensive education goals. Responding to the test-driven accountability ethos, which they saw narrowing educational goals to English and math proficiency, Richard Rothstein, an education policy scholar, and his colleague, Rebecca Jacobsen, attempted to synthesize Americans' goals for public education developed over our 250-year history. They defined eight broad goal areas that appeared prominent in different eras and presented these goals to representative samples of all American adults, including school board members, state legislators, and school superintendents. Respondents assigned a relative importance to each of the goal areas. Their average responses were very similar and appear in Table 6.1. Rothstein and Jacobsen conclude that the yawning gap between the surveyed respondents' broad preferences and the narrow educational standards established through political processes "reflected a widespread policy incoherence." What Americans wanted and what education policy makers wanted did not match. Although today's policy makers appear to emphasize the limited goals of reading and mathematical proficiency as measured by standardized tests, contemporary community leaders still desire our schools to accomplish a broad array of goals—including many not easily reduced to a single test score.

To maintain school accountability for successfully teaching to these ends, Rothstein and Jacobsen suggest a balanced, valid, but less standardized exam-based accountability system to measure all

TABLE 6.1 ■ Selected Americans' Views on Relative Importance of Public School Goals

Goal Area	Relative Importance of the Goal Area (%)
Basic academic skills in core subjects Reading, writing, math, knowledge of science and history	22
Critical thinking and problem-solving Ability to analyze and interpret information, use [the internet] to develop knowledge, apply ideas to new situations	18
Social skills and work ethic Good communication skills, personal responsibility, ability to get along well with others, and work with others from different backgrounds	12
Citizenship and community responsibility Knowledge of how government works and of how to participate in civic activities like voting, volunteering, and becoming active in communities	11
Preparation for skilled work Vocational, career, and technical education that will qualify youths for skilled employment that does not require a college degree	10
Physical health A foundation for lifelong physical health, including good habits of exercise and nutrition	9
Emotional health Tools to develop self-confidence, respect for others, and the ability to resist peer pressure to engage in irresponsible personal behavior	9
The arts and literature Capacity to participate in and appreciate the musical, visual, and performing arts; develop a love of literature	9

Source: Adapted from Rothstein, R., and Jacobsen, R. (2006, December). The goals of education. *Phi Delta Kappan, 88*(4), 264–272 (Table 1, p. 271).

these areas. In this way, American schools could be faithful to its tradition as well as to contemporary expectations.

Ideally, during the process of developing a school district's or individual school's goals, school leaders invite local citizens, parents, and students to give meaningful input. Working as partners with professional educators who understand child development and the learning process, the community members can provide valuable perspectives on what the local schools should teach.

Whether school goals are formulated at the national, state, school district, or school level, the goals are written generally. That is, they are not directly connected to any particular content or subject matter; instead, they are intended to be long-lasting guides, providing direction for what the school is supposed to accomplish. Such goals are too vague for teachers and students to directly apply in the classroom. For their part, teachers must translate these broad goals into more specific objectives—and consider the best way for students to learn them.

To explore how schools' competing goals have personally affected your education, complete the activity in the **Reflect & Engag**e box, Schools' Competing Goals.

AMERICAN EDUCATION SPOTLIGHT: RICHARD ROTHSTEIN

Richard Rothstein sees a myriad of factors—inside and outside school—that affect student achievement.

Courtesy of Economic Policy Institute

"Making teacher quality the only centerpiece of a reform campaign distracts our attention from other equally and perhaps more important school areas needing improvement.... Blaming teachers is easy. These other areas are more difficult to improve."*

Richard Rothstein is a Distinguished Fellow of the Economic Policy Institute, a Senior Fellow, emeritus, at the Thurgood Marshall Institute of the NAACP Legal Defense Fund, senior fellow of the Chief Justice Earl Warren Institute on Law and Social Policy at the University of California (Berkeley) School of Law, author, and popular speaker on education policy issues. Formerly the National Education Columnist of *The New York Times* and a visiting professor at the Teachers College, Columbia University, Rothstein is the author of several books, including *The Color of Law: A Forgotten History of How Our Government Segregated America* (2017), *Grading Education: Getting Accountability Right* (2008), and *Class and Schools: Using Social, Economic and Educational Reform to Close the Black-White Achievement Gap* (2004). His analysis helps us consider the myriad factors—inside and outside school—that contribute to the Black-white achievement gap and suggests ways to reduce them.

Rothstein contends that although the single biggest *in-school* factor in students' success is their teacher's "quality" or effectiveness, good teachers alone cannot fully compensate for the disadvantages many children bring to school. Decades of social science research demonstrate that differences in the quality of schools can explain about one third of the variation in student achievement. In addition to teacher quality, in-school factors include inspiring principal leadership, a well-designed curriculum, and teacher collaboration to raise student achievement. But the other two-thirds affecting student achievement is attributable to *nonschool* factors. Poor nutrition, inferior housing, and unstable families also add to a child's failure to learn at high levels. When combined with low-income students' concentration in segregated schools, their cumulative effect helps explain much of the educational achievement gap. In fact, Rothstein argues with evidence that segregation was—and is—a public policy choice. Rothstein asserts the following points:

U.S. government policies have created racial segregation. In the 20th century, federal, state, and local housing policies and laws have created, encouraged, and enforced racial segregation in housing. These policies have worsened economic inequalities and produced large academic gaps between white and African American schoolchildren. Even if these policies are no longer in force, their effects live on. We cannot solve our educational problems in segregated schools. And to believe that *de facto* segregation in housing—and in schools—arose randomly from income differences, demographic trends, and white and African Americans families' choices reflects "colossal historical amnesia."**

Poverty negatively affects learning. Closing or substantially narrowing achievement gaps requires combining school improvement with reforms that narrow the vast socioeconomic status (SES) inequalities in the United States. Outside influences such as social class differences in parenting and available resources, health, nutrition, and attendance contribute to a school's effectiveness.

Balanced accountability is in the best interest of both schools and students. Most Americans want schools to have both an academic focus and social and political outcomes. Although emphasis among the eight major goals (identified in Table 6.1) has shifted over the generations, the goals still remain important. A balanced accountability system—beyond test scores alone—would use measures that may be more difficult to standardize but are equally valid and true to American traditions.

Some critics call Rothstein an apologist for public schools. Others contend that he ignores the fact that hundreds of schools are successfully educating low-income students with clear and replicable practices. Although they may disagree with his conclusions, few dispute that his positions are thoughtfully reasoned and well-supported with data.

Rothstein reflects, "Of course, every teacher should attempt to inspire every [student] with encouragement that greater effort could lead to college and a professional career. But no sane teacher believes that this encouragement will be effective with every single child. When an institution promises such universal success, it undermines its own legitimacy."***

Notes:

Rothstein, R. (2010, October 14). How to fix our schools. Economic Policy Institute. http://www.epi.org/publications/entry/ib286/, p. 3.

***Rothstein, R. (2013, December). Misteaching history on racial segregation. School Administrator, 70(11), 38–40.*

****Rothstein, R. (2010, March 27). A blueprint that needs more work. Economic Policy Institute. http://www.epi.org/page/-/pdf/pm162.pdf?nocdn=1, p. 5.*

Sources: Tianga, K. A. (2018, May 22). The not-so hidden truths about the segregation of America's housing, *Shelterforce*. https://shelterforce.org/2018/05/22/the-not-so-hidden-truths-about-the-segregation-of-americas-housing/; Mishel, L., & Rothstein, R. (2007, October). Schools as scapegoats. *The American Prospect*, 44–47. http://epi.3cdn.net/2210a55cb9b1c98ee5_tpm6b5yvr.pdf; Rothstein, 2010; Rothstein, R. (1993, Spring). The myth of public school failure. *The American Prospect*, 20–34; Rothstein, R. (2008, April). Whose problem is poverty? *Educational Leadership, 65*(7), 8–13. http://www.epi.org/publications/entry/ascd_whose_problem_is_poverty/; Rothstein, R., & Jacobsen, R. (2006, December). The goals of education. *Phi Delta Kappan, 88*(4), 264–272.

REFLECT & ENGAGE: SCHOOLS' COMPETING GOALS

Schools' goal is to contribute to students' growth in five areas—intellectual, social, political, personal, and economic.

A. Working in groups of four students, create a mind map with a digital tool such as Bubbl using Rothstein and Jacobsen's eight categories as central themes and Goodlad's "12 major goals of American schools" as related associations that radiate from them. How well (or not) do these two sets of school goals fit together?

B. Have each student in the group give specifics of how his or her personal K–12 educational experiences did or did not contribute to meeting each of these eight goal categories. Where did your prior school succeed or fall short in meeting these goals? What might you do now and while in college to increase your growth in domains that you identify as less well developed?

C. Each group presents its mind map to the class, identifying similarities and differences.

D. As a class, discuss how these numerous goals can lead to heated public debates about what schools should be teaching.

E. Discuss how school boards can use these goals to identify key purposes for their own schools.

6.2c Personal Goals of Education

Just as Goodlad and Rothstein and Jacobsen provide comprehensive looks at American public schools' goals, Elliot W. Eisner (1933–2014), Stanford University professor of education and art, brings the goals to the individual student level. Although he believes that "schools are part of the furniture of our communities... [that we] take as much for granted as the streets upon which we walk,"[7] Eisner sees schools' purpose as uncommon: helping students to live personally satisfying and socially productive lives by fully developing their minds.

"Mind is a form of cultural achievement," says Eisner.[8] Humans are *born* with brains, but their minds are *made*. In other words, the cultures into which they are born shape how they think. For children, school is the primary culture for their cognitive development. Therefore, school decisions about its priorities are fundamental decisions about the kinds of minds our children will have the opportunities to develop.

Likewise, schools are cultures for growing minds. Through both cultural transmission and self-actualization,[9] schools provide opportunities that influence the direction this growth takes. Both the curriculum schools teach and the time allotted for different subjects tell children what adults believe are important for them to learn. These factors also influence the kinds of mental skills children have the opportunity to acquire.[10] Reading and math are certainly essential skills, but they are not all an educated person needs to know. Eisner argues that education's aim is not merely to enable our children to do well in school; it is also to enable our children to do well in life.[11] In this view, students' test scores are merely proxies for learning; the scores themselves are not learning.

Developing the mind is related to the modes of thought that teachers enable and encourage students to use. A valuable education uses a curriculum that encompasses various ways of thinking and knowing the world, including exploration of both the arts and the sciences. These thought processes incorporate the rational and the affective, the planned and the serendipitous. In the last analysis, the most important curriculum is the one that will help students navigate successfully in the lives they lead outside school so students can ably and continually adapt to complex and changing circumstances.

To foster this mental development, insightful teachers understand that not all problems have a single right answer, purposeful flexibility is an important learning tool, and students need opportunities for varied types of self-expression.

First, not all problems have one correct answer. Solutions to problems take many forms. Whereas spelling, arithmetic, writing, and reading are taught with deliberately constricting conventions and rules, the arts celebrate imagination, multiple perspectives, and the importance of personal interpretation. Both ways of knowing are important. Students need opportunities to see and explore the world in a variety of formats so they can learn how to think in varied ways.

Next, in a technologically oriented world, people tend to believe that objective rationality is the shortest distance between two points. The scientific method illustrates this view: define, hypothesize, experiment, and evaluate. Although this is a reasonable approach to solving certain problems, it is not the only way to understand experiences. Wise teachers realize that rationality is broader. In the arts (as in scientific research), for instance, goals need to be flexible and surprise can be valuable. For example, in 1928 Alexander Fleming accidentally discovered penicillin when he found that a mold growing in his petri dish secreted a "juice" that inhibited bacterial growth. Educated individuals are open to unanticipated opportunities that inevitably emerge and that increase insight. The work of art is an act of creation, an unfolding journey. Ending a learning experience too soon—by stopping explorations at the first "right" answer—short-circuits the potential of deeper and more personal understanding.

"While we say that the function of schooling is to prepare students for life, the problems of life tend not to have fixed, single correct answers" like the problems students find in school, Eisner remarks. The problems students find in life are much more like the problems they find in the arts[12]; they are often subtle and occasionally ambiguous. "Life outside school is hardly ever like a multiple-choice test."[13]

Effective teachers create learning experiences for students that increase their opportunities to experience the world fully and meaningfully. They make schools *intellectual* rather than merely *academic* places. They understand that students' minds can be developed, knowledge is greater than what literal language might convey, and intelligence deepens and expresses itself in many forms. For students, education means learning how to use their minds well. This is the best preparation for life. Eisner concludes, "What's at stake is not only the quality of life our children might enjoy but also the quality of the culture that they will inhabit."[14]

To understand more deeply how learning to use your mind well can make your own life more personally satisfying and socially productive, complete the activity in the **Reflect & Engage** box, Exploring Personal Goals of Education.

REFLECT & ENGAGE: EXPLORING PERSONAL GOALS OF EDUCATION

Education leads students to more personally satisfying and socially productive lives. Elliot Eisner observes that education's goal should be for young people to do well outside school by developing and expanding their minds in a nourishing school culture.

A. Working individually, create a graphic image using a digital tool such as Piktochart to illustrate the types of "learning how to use your mind well (beyond the math and reading skills) that will enable you to do well in life." Also include the deep awareness and appreciation of life experiences that you had in school that will enhance your capacity to live a personally satisfying and socially productive life.

B. After 15 minutes, discuss your graphic images in pairs.

C. Divide into three groups to consider your high school and college curriculum and how it impacted (or not) your thinking and creative skills. The first group will consider the traditional English and math curriculum (subjects typically covered by high-stakes achievement testing). The second group will consider the fine arts (poetry, music, visual arts, and theater). The third group will consider examples that integrate a wider range of subjects (including English, math, sciences, social studies, foreign languages, and physical education) with fine arts. Thinking back on their experiences in high school and college, identify the types of personal goals—including thinking, problem-solving, leadership, teamwork, and life appreciation experiences—most developed by the disciplines each group represents. To what extent did your teachers encourage this kind of personal and academic growth?

D. All groups report their findings back to the class.

E. Discuss as a class how you can use this awareness to increase your future students' meaningful mind-developing and person-developing learning experiences in your classes.

6.2d Social Goals of Education

Schools have long had social goals. In 1900, Edward Alsworth Ross, an American sociologist, referred to education as "an economical system of police."[15] He divided social control into internal and external forms. Traditionally, he asserted, internal forms of social control centered on the family, the church or synagogue, and the community. The family and religious institution inculcated moral values and social responsibility into the child. This process ensured social stability and cohesion. In modern society, however, school has largely replaced the family and church as the community's most important institution for instilling internal values. In this sense, the school exerts external social control. "The ebb of religion is only half a fact," Ross observed. "The other half is the high tide of education. While the priest is leaving the civil service, the schoolmaster is coming in."[16]

Whether the family and religious institutions are collapsing is debatable. Yet our society often views education as assuming the responsibility for teaching moral values, thereby enacting a social role.

Historically, public schools have delivered moral and social instruction in a variety of ways. Horace Mann, for example, believed that schools were the key to reforming society; he assumed that properly trained youths would not want to commit criminal acts. As a consequence, compulsory school attendance evolved as a means to reduce juvenile delinquency. Similarly, the need to keep young people off the streets became a justification for starting summer schools in the late 19th and early 20th centuries. More recently, schools have assumed the responsibility for reducing traffic accidents by providing drivers' training programs, improving family life through courses in home economics, ending drug abuse, preventing sexually transmitted diseases, and reducing teen pregnancy through health education.[17]

Frequently, schools are asked to solve social problems by finding solutions that do not challenge economic and political interests. For instance, alcoholism might result from family stresses or other adverse conditions. For schools to solve the problem of alcoholism through health classes assumes that the problem is one of individual training, unrelated to other causes. It is easier for a community to provide and require students to take a health course than to change work conditions, improve urban environments, or send a family into counseling. Schools are less threatening than direct interventions that target businesses, unions, city government, or family privacy.

Schools are often the safest and least controversial way of planning for social improvement. "Let the schools do it" allows community leaders to "check the box" without actually solving the problem. Assigning these responsibilities to schools allows legislators, policy makers, and local government officials to appear to do the right thing without offending any important interests. Yet regardless of schools' good intentions, their social influence has only gone so far toward remedying society's ills.

For instance, our society has used schools to help end poverty. The relationships between schools and poverty are many and complex. Inadequate education is linked to low-income jobs, low-quality housing, poor diet, poor medical care, and high rates of school and work absenteeism. The community finds it difficult and expensive to intervene to break these interactions, even though programs such as Medicare and Medicaid, food stamps, and public housing subsidies try to make a difference. Meanwhile, schools offer Head Start, Title I, and other compensatory education programs for low-income children who begin school at an economic disadvantage in comparison to children from middle- and high-income families. These programs' success has been either limited or mixed.

In addition, not all societal groups agree on which social values schools should teach. Horace Mann argued that all religious groups could agree on certain moral values, and these shared values would become the backbone of schools' moral teachings. Religious groups disagreed with his supposition, however. The Catholic Church voiced the strongest opposition to this notion and established its own school system. More recently, the 1990s witnessed heated value conflicts about AIDS education between those who believed in a family and church-taught strong moral code to control sexual behavior in opposition to those who believed that prevention through education was a legitimate public health interest. Viewing American education as a cure-all for America's social ills raises questions about whose social and moral values and goals our schools should reflect. It also raises the question of whether using schools for social control is actually a way to avoid more direct and controversial approaches to solving societal problems. These questions remain unanswered.

6.2e Economic Goals of Education

Public schools also have economic goals. Economists note that schools can advance economic growth in two ways. First, they can socialize future workers for the workplace. Through their academic curriculum, attendance requirements, tardiness rules, practice in following directions and completing assigned tasks, and emphasis on obedience to authority, schools provide the preparation and training future workers need. Second, schools can increase national wealth by sorting, selecting, and training students for the labor force, determining the best type of education and future employment appropriate for each student.

Both of these goals have historical support. In the 19th and early 20th centuries, schools emphasized marching, drills, and orderliness as preparation for factory work. In the 20th and early 21st centuries, public schools served as a "**sorting and selecting machine**" that separates "human capital" (students) by their observed or presumed abilities and interests into certain curricular programs matched to appropriate future jobs. Standardized tests identify students' abilities, aptitudes, and interests, and counselors or other school officials then match these factors to the suitable school programs. When schools sort and select students in this way, proponents suggest the economy will prosper and workers will be happy.

In the 21st century, although the "sort and select" process appears much the same as in the previous century, the economic environment into which U.S. students graduate has clearly changed. Chapter 1 discusses how American workers are now competing in a global labor market. Globalization exposes the average U.S. worker to much more competition and job insecurity. As the world becomes more interconnected and high-level skills more widespread, jobs become more mobile. U.S. companies seek cheaper labor in foreign countries, even for white-collar professional jobs, and many American workers are forced to take reduced wages and benefits to compete with foreign workers (or, increasingly, be replaced by robots).

To make U.S. workers more competitive in world labor markets, policy makers and schools have called for world-class standards, teaching skills needed for 21st century success, and raising the educational level of U.S. workers to those achieved in other industrialized countries (usually identified as Canada, Finland, or Singapore). Having U.S. students take international achievement tests and comparing their scores with those of other industrialized nations is believed to be one way to monitor our students' performance vis-à-vis their international competitors.

In addition, a learning society and lifelong learning are considered essential parts of global education systems. Both concepts assume a world of constant technological change that will require workers to continually update their skills. This means that schools will be required to teach students how to learn so that they can keep gaining knowledge and expanding their skills throughout their working lives.

Likewise, American society is much different today than it was 50 years ago, when a one-income household could support the American working- and middle-class family. The proportion of American adults who are middle class nationally is shrinking.[18] In 2016, about half of American adults lived in middle-income households.[19] According to Pew Research Center, in 1960, only 25% of families with children under age 18 had both spouses working.[20] By comparison, the Bureau of Labor Statistics (2020) finds that dual-income households with children under 18 make up 66% of the total households with children.[21]

These new economic and global realities on education reprise unsettling questions about treating students as human capital. Should schools emphasize a broad liberal education, or should they prepare students for specific careers? In a labor market based on educational attainment and marketable skills, will inequality of educational opportunity cause increased stratification between the educational haves and have-nots? Will producing many well-educated graduates lead to **educational inflation**, in which the supply of well-educated individuals increases yet employee wages and advanced degrees' value decline because so many qualified and available persons exist to fill the positions? Should economic opportunities be based on the outcomes on high-stakes tests? These are important questions on which a national consensus and debate are missing.

Certainly, students need to learn the intellectual tools and knowledge for making decisions about their lives. What is more, given the wide variations in school quality in the United States[22] (in terms of students' cognitive readiness for academic learning, teacher effectiveness, class size, instructional standards and resources, and career and college readiness preparation, for instance), if the ability to compete in the labor market depends on the quality of education they receive, then some graduates will be more advantaged than others. Those persons who arrive at school ready to learn and with access to better schools have increased opportunities to better jobs and higher wages. These important issues should influence our ongoing discussions about schools' economic purpose.

In the future, schools will continue to serve comprehensive intellectual, political, social, economic, and personal purposes. It remains essential that prospective and present educators, policy makers, and our society as a whole consider these goals, some of which are contradictory, when deciding how to move forward.

If you want to more thoughtfully explore how American education's various goals have personally impacted you, complete the activity in the **Reflect & Engage** box, Education's Many Goals.

REFLECT & ENGAGE: EDUCATION'S MANY GOALS

Society has assigned schools many goals. Consider them and decide what you think.

A. Form five groups that each represent one of the following categories: intellectual, social, political, personal, and economic education goals. In these small groups, brainstorm all K–12 school goals or objectives that fit into your group's category. Create a wordle (word cloud) using a digital tool such as Vizzlo to display the goals and their relative importance to you. As you do, consider these questions:

Which goals had the most impact on you as a K–12 and college student, and how?

Which ones helped you realize and reach your personal aims?

Which goals do you see as possibly contradictory or pulling in different directions?

Which goals do you think are realistic and achievable? Which do you think are beyond the school's means to achieve? Why do you think this?

Which goals reinforce the "status quo"?

Which goals are likely to reduce the "achievement/opportunity gap"?

Which goals have the potential to change the society?

Which goals have the most community support in your hometown? Which goals have the least support in your hometown?

B. Each group describes its wordle to the entire class and discusses its responses to the previous questions. What does this discussion tell you about what a meaningful education should include? What does it tell you about the difficulty of determining educational goals?

FLIPSIDES

Should American Schools Stress Reading and Math Proficiency or More Comprehensive Educational Goals?

Educators and policy makers often disagree about what measures to use for public school accountability. Should accountability for a 21st century American education focus on reading and math skills, which can be accurately measured, or should it focus on a more comprehensive set of goals, which, although important, cannot be accurately measured with a paper and pencil test?

To be accountable, American education should focus on reading and math skills, using rigorous content.	To be accountable, American education should focus on developing reading and math skills, using rigorous content plus a more comprehensive set of goals.
• Reading and math skills are basic academic skills that are essential for success in all other academic subjects.	• Reading and math skills are essential academic skills, but these are not all that an educated person in the 21st century needs to know and be able to do.
• Schools are not equipped to teach our students everything our society has asked schools to teach them.	• Schools' important cognitive, social, political, economic, and personal goals are necessary to make our communities and nation stronger, safer, and fairer.
• Public school accountability depends on assessing reading and math skills by using easy-to-administer, efficient, valid, reliable, and relatively cost-effective standardized tests.	• Valid measures exist for assessing the performances and products that result from students meeting other important educational goals, but some may not be standardized; may take more time, effort, and cost to assess; or may appear in later behavior (such as voting).

To be accountable, American education should focus on reading and math skills, using rigorous content.	To be accountable, American education should focus on developing reading and math skills, using rigorous content plus a more comprehensive set of goals.
• Students' test scores are evidence of effective education and accountability.	• Test scores are not learning itself; they are proxies (stand-ins) for learning. In the real world, not all problems have fixed, single, correct answers.
• Students should learn how to solve problems and provide the right answers.	• Students should learn various ways of thinking so they solve problems and can live well outside school.
• As academic places, schools should teach students to think objectively and rationally with the subject matter they study and in response to events occurring in their lives outside school.	• As intellectual places. schools should teach students to use their mind flexibly (cognitively and affectively), value and adapt to surprises, and deal with ambiguity to prepare for life in a complex, changing world.

After reading the arguments in favor and against accountability based on a rigorous reading- and math-focused curriculum, which approach do you believe would be best for 21st century American students and public school accountability?

6.3 CONSERVATIVE, LIBERAL, AND CRITICAL THEORY EDUCATION CRITICS: DIFFERING VIEWS AND GOALS ABOUT SCHOOLS' ROLE IN SOCIETY

Although public schools intend to transmit our best traditions and values, our culture is not static. Rather, schools reflect changes in their host society—from putting computers into every classroom (or digital devices into every student's home) to having security guards patrol the halls. What is more, the "official knowledge" included in the school curriculum evolves, faces challenges, and changes. Struggles over curriculum, teaching, and policy are actually battles for power over children's thoughts and for the direction of society's future.

For all, knowledge is power. Whoever controls the knowledge—and the policies, textbooks, and lessons that contain it—holds the power. In fact, vigorous community debates over textbook adoptions illustrate cultural politics in action. They are skirmishes in the national conflict for cultural authority. And the winners' views will prevail.

Debates about educational issues often focus on different ideas about what schools' goals—and what our society—should be. From our early days as a young republic through today, many different visions of U.S. education and schools' role in society have been advanced. In Chapter 3, we consider these varying belief systems in detail. Although the views are complex, it helps to simplify and frame them by using a political typology—specifically conservative, liberal, and critical theory perspectives. The remainder of this section presents broad and general descriptions of how each viewpoint sees education and its goals.

6.3a The Conservative Perspective

The origins of the conservative perspective lie in the 19th century Darwinist view that individuals and groups must compete in their societal environment to survive. According to this stance, human progress depends on individual initiative and effort. Conservatives also believe the capitalist free market as the economic system most respectful of human needs. They see individuals as rational actors who can make decisions on a cost–benefit scale.[23] Lastly, conservatives believe that individuals are responsible for their own well-being; people create society's problems by making uninformed or selfish choices.

Conservatives believe that schools should provide the educational training necessary to ensure that the most talented and hard-working individuals receive the tools they need to become the most socially and economically productive. Under this approach, schools socialize children into the adult roles needed to maintain society as it is. Students learn cultural traditions through the curriculum and school norms. Schools are essential to both economic growth and social stability. Nevertheless, individuals or groups of students rise or fall based on their own intelligence, effort, and initiative. Achievement requires hard work and sacrifice. Schools give students the opportunity to succeed, but it is the individual's responsibility to do the work to make accomplishment happen. To this end, market-based education reforms—such as charter schools and voucher programs—give parents more choices about how and where to educate their children.[24] And since educated children benefit the larger society, taxpayer funding for these private options is appropriate.

Generally, conservative critics believe that today's educational problems have occurred for the following reasons:

- Schools have watered down the curriculum and lowered academic standards in response to 1960s and 1970s cries for greater societal equality and catering to students' calls for more choices about what they studied.
- Multicultural education that responds to the needs of all groups has weakened the traditional curriculum, reducing the school's ability to pass on American and Western civilization's heritage and the rigorous cognitive skills that go with them.
- Liberal demands for cultural relativism (the belief that every culture's values and beliefs are equally valid) have forced schools to lose their traditional role of teaching absolute ("correct") values and moral standards.
- Schools' acceptance of individuality and freedom has meant the loss of traditional discipline and decline of authority in the classroom and in the school.
- Schools are state-controlled public institutions, immune from laws of a competitive free market and choked by bureaucracy and inefficiency.

Many of today's religious and social conservatives express strong views about public schools, bringing their beliefs about faith and ethical behavior into the political arena. They criticize public schools for undermining what they see as time-honored values. Further, they believe that society would be better if schools contained more religion (typically Protestantism)—or at least did not advance secular ideas, values, or practices that undermine it. They believe that schools should return to more traditional religious values and practices as once applied in early American common schools, restoring the connection between church and state.[25]

Indeed, some conservatives no longer want to send their children to American public schools. The publication of *A Nation at Risk*[26] almost 40 years ago confirmed conservatives' worst fears about public schools' harmful effects on their children. The report, compiled by a panel appointed by President Ronald Reagan, sharply criticized American education—and gave many a scapegoat on which to pin society's problems. Similarly, the report blamed schools' "rising tide of mediocrity" for skyrocketing divorce rates, teenage pregnancy, and sexually transmitted diseases.

Finally, conservative educational reformers want to make the following changes to modern-day public schools:

- *Return to the basics*—reading, writing, math, and other traditional subjects.
- *Return to the traditional academic curriculum*, which focuses heavily on Western civilization's history, thought, and literature.
- *Make students and schools accountable* for minimum performance standards at specific grade levels (i.e., fourth, eighth, and 11th grades to assess teachers' cumulative impact on student learning), enforced through standardized testing and public accountability.

- *Introduce free-market mechanisms* into the education marketplace. This includes tuition tax credits, vouchers, "opportunity scholarships," charter schools, and public school choice programs (allowing parents to send their children to the public school of their choice, regardless of where they live).
- *Create more exacting teacher evaluation* practices that rely heavily on their students' achievement results.

Conservatives are currently reaching some of their objectives with practices that support increased school accountability and give parents more taxpayer-funded options about where to educate their children. Since education is a state's responsibility, laws in many states help them achieve these goals.

6.3b The Liberal Perspective

In the 20th century, liberal perspectives on education arose from U.S. philosopher and educator John Dewey's ideas and President Franklin Delano Roosevelt's New Deal policies. Although supporting the conservative view of a market capitalist economy, liberals believe that an unregulated free market is open to abuses and that certain government functions should not be shared with for-profit enterprises. Since unregulated capitalism is particularly hurtful to economically and politically disadvantaged groups, society needs government involvement in economic, political, and social arenas to ensure fair treatment of all citizens and to guarantee a healthy economy. Liberals, therefore, balance capitalism's economic productivity with individuals' social and economic needs. Good governance is not as simple as choosing "individual liberty" over "government control." Rather, liberals seek the best equilibrium of individual freedom with the essential legal protections for individuals, their contracts, and their businesses, which only a government of laws can provide.

Like conservatives, liberals believe that individual effort is very important. But since people do not all begin life's journey with the same resources, personal exertion may not be enough. By placing a strong emphasis on equity and equality of opportunity, liberals try to minimize the differences in life outcomes between the country's richest and poorest citizens. When individual effort falls short, government must sometimes intervene on behalf of those in need. Liberals also believe that societal conditions affect groups as well as individuals. Accordingly, solutions to societal problems must address group—not only individual—well-being.

Liberals value schools for their ability to educate and socialize students into the society, as do conservatives. Liberals, however, stress schools' role in creating a more equal playing field for every student to succeed. They argue that individual students or groups of students begin school with different life advantages, different types of prior knowledge, and different levels of "academic readiness." Schools must be equitable to all of these children through policies and programs that give disadvantaged students a better chance to make the most of their educational opportunities. Further, they recognize America's pluralism and emphasize schools' role in helping all young people learn how to thrive in a diverse nation. According to this perspective, education entails balancing individual and societal needs in ways consistent with democracy and meritocracy. School is a means for every student to receive a fair and equal opportunity for upward mobility—economically, politically, socially, and personally.

Liberals believe that today's educational problems exist for the following reasons:

- Schools need to level the playing field experienced by economically disadvantaged or culturally different students because their backgrounds have limited these students' chances for a good life, allowing them to underachieve.
- Schools place too much emphasis on discipline and authority, not allowing students to develop fully as individuals.
- Academic quality and climate disparities between schools serving affluent as compared with low-socioeconomic-status students create unequal opportunities for achievement and advancement. This disparity more accurately reflects an "opportunity gap" than an

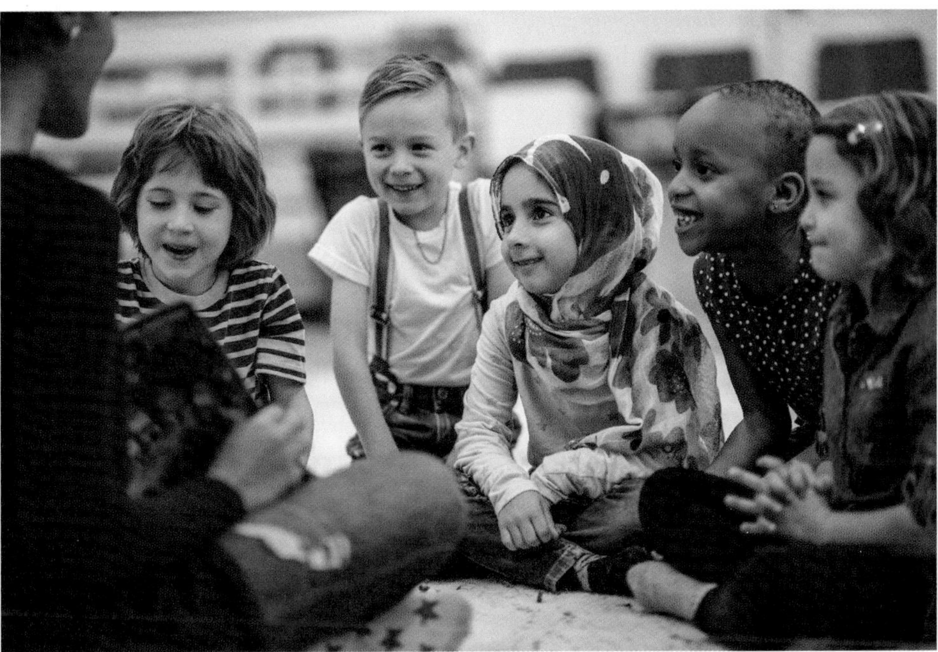

The liberal perspective supports education policies that connect equity and excellence.
iStock/fstop123

"achievement gap" stemming from the systemic obstacles to low-income children's school success.[27]

- The traditional curriculum leaves out the diverse voices and cultures of groups that make up our pluralistic society. Students need to see and feel that they have value before they can learn.

The **achievement gap**—sometimes called the **opportunity gap**, or the unequal achievement shown by different student populations—greatly concerns liberals. At present, liberal critics strongly influence educational policy and practice. In particular, they have employed federal approaches to support disadvantaged students. For example, liberal critics voted for categorical funds, such as Title I, aimed at improving education for schools with a high percentage of students living in poverty. Likewise, liberals worked closely with conservatives to write and pass the 2002 federal No Child Left Behind Act (NCLB) and its successor, the 2015 Every Student Succeeds Act (ESSA). These education laws are intended to make sure that all students, including traditionally underserved students (ethnic or racial minority, economically disadvantaged, special education, and English language learners) receive the high-quality education that every student needs. During this process, conservatives focus on the high accountability requirements and sanctions for public schools not successfully meeting them, whereas liberals approve giving schools added resources to help them be more accountable for ensuring the high achievement of the traditionally underserved and underperforming student groups.

Liberal critics want education reforms that include the following measures:

- *Connecting equity with excellence*, making high-quality education a reality for every student. Treating different students the same is inherently unequal, they say.
- *Providing full-day preschool* for low-income children to help them become "school ready." Studies show that preschool participation can have significant short- and long-term benefits.[28]
- *Improving failing schools*, especially urban schools. Programs should include site-based management (decentralized school control), teacher empowerment (teachers have a say in the way schools run), effective schools programs (based on research about what works),[29] and public school choice programs that support public education.

- *Adequately compensating high-quality, highly effective teachers who work in high-challenge urban schools* to attract and keep the most talented teachers and to create a stable school culture of academic achievement.
- *Creating more equal opportunity for disadvantaged students*, such as Head Start, Advancement via Individual Determination (AVID), affirmative action, and compensatory higher-education programs.[30]
- *Balancing the curriculum* of Western thought and values along with readings and history of other groups in a culturally diverse setting.
- *Linking high standards with high supports.* Do both: Set acceptable and high performance standards and ensure that every student can meet these standards (by providing students with additional academic and social supports rather than lowering expectations).
- *Making teacher evaluation practices more rigorous* and including student achievement data as part of a fair and comprehensive look at a teacher's effectiveness.

Liberals are currently reaching some of their objectives with the practices that support diverse students learning to high levels. These goals, however, are only in the process of being achieved.

6.3c The Critical Theory Perspective

As discussed in Chapter 3, **critical theory** is an educational philosophy that concerns itself with issues of struggle, power, culture, and domination within a society.[31] Developed in the United States as an offshoot of the progressive education movement,[32] critical theorists recognize that humans are the architects of their own destinies. They urge individuals to develop a critical consciousness that can create new truths both for themselves and for society. Historically, schools transmitted a society's culture—the one usually belonging to society's dominant group, extending its norms, values, and practices into the future. As a result, the culturally influential and powerful shape our schools and determine our "official knowledge."[33]

Critical theorists believe that our public schools practice a **cultural hegemony** (control by one dominant worldview) by imposing the colonial Western European settlers' traditions on today's ethnically and culturally diverse students. What is more, according to critical theorists, the dominant class deliberately controls, shapes, and manipulates the subordinate groups' beliefs to ensure that the dominant group's views become familiar, common sense, accepted, and taken for granted. In these ways, critical theorists argue, schools perpetuate the socioeconomic conditions that keep poor people poor, ignorant, and powerless.

Critical theorists reject this in-group dominance. Similar to liberals, they believe that students from lower-socioeconomic backgrounds begin school with unequal resources and opportunities. Unlike liberals, critical theorists believe that these limitations can be removed only by changing the society's political–economic system. Liberals would adapt school practices to increase disadvantaged students' achievement, but critical theorists would go even further: They would change both schools and the society that make and keep people unequal by diverting more resources to the disadvantaged.

Critical theorists believe that school and society have problems for the following reasons:

- The educational system has failed the poor, racial and ethnic minorities, people with disabilities, and women through continuation of classist, racist, ableist, and sexist policies and practices.
- Schools have stifled analysis, deep understanding, and criticism of American society's problems by implementing a curriculum and teaching practices that promote conformity and docility to the established powers.
- The traditional curriculum ignores cultures, genders, and races that are present in the classroom and that have contributed to society. It disrespects diverse students when it leaves out underrepresented voices.
- The educational system promotes inequality of both opportunity and results.

As part of their perspective, critical theorists hold dual views of schools. Schools have the means to reinforce the societal status quo as well as the potential to transform the larger society. First, critical theorists believe that schools are a means to reproduce traditional (that critical theorists call "oppressive") social patterns. Education favors the dominant culture's **cultural capital**—its language, values, and meanings. As such, schooling confirms, legitimizes, and reproduces the status quo. This influence does not happen through force or coercion, but rather occurs through a process of gaining the students' passive, legitimate consent. In short, through schooling's socialization, all social and economic classes learn to accept the elite social group's beliefs, values, and practices as right and natural.

For example, critical theorists see school practices such as **tracking** (placing certain students into a low-status, low-interest, low-ability, dead-end curriculum) and assigning "special education" labels to students who cannot keep up with the traditional curriculum as grave injustices, designed to keep certain groups down while holding up others. This differential access to knowledge and occasions to learn, differential opportunities to think and use language effectively, and differential access to high-quality curriculum and teaching are all part of this educational process, say critical theorists, deliberately designed to keep "less desirables" out of the cultural mainstream.

Similarly, critical theorists contend that a U.S. history course that reflects only the white Euro-American experience does not show respect for the contributions of other races and cultures in creating today's America. Such a course delivers an implicit message to students: This is a Caucasian society; if you are not white, you are marginal in tradition and importance, and Western thought and culture are superior to any other traditions and cultures.

Second, critical theorists believe that schools contain the seeds of societal transformation. Henry Giroux and Peter McLaren, for example, see schools as able to exert positive power for social justice.[34] Sounding the call for pedagogical empowerment, they see teachers' role as helping students make sense of and engage the world around them and—when necessary—change the world for the better. Through this type of effort, schools can become the agents that raise children to question and challenge their society's limitations and failings. When students learn how to push against the status quo's beliefs and practices, they can improve both their community and the nation. In this way, critical theory raises our consciousness beyond the classroom and schoolyard to broader social and cultural concerns. In other words, people are capable of creating and transforming their own culture because people are both the products and the creators of their social world.[35]

"Schools must be moral, just, and inclusive of those who most need access to the educational process that is imperative to sustaining a democratic community," says educator Louise Anderson Allen.[36] Schools can be a vehicle for social change.

Critical theorists believe that schools can improve by focusing on the following goals:

- *Changing society.* For the most part, critical theorists do not believe that school reform alone can solve educational problems because many problems begin with the larger community. Many critical theorists seek significant social change.
- *Implementing programs that lead to more democratic schools*—with teachers, students, and parents having more input into decision-making.
- *Developing curriculum and teaching that involve "critical pedagogy"*—allowing teachers and students to understand the current social and educational problems and propose potential (perhaps radical) solutions to these ongoing issues.
- *Developing curriculum and teaching that are multicultural, antiracist, antisexist, and anticlassist*—offering a positive curricular treatment of the varied groups that make up U.S. society and U.S. classrooms.
- *Making teacher evaluation more rigorous* and including both student achievement data and documentation of "social transition" projects in which the students engaged to improve their school or community with evidence of its success.

Critical theory can provide current and future educators with a lens through which to view, test, and challenge their assumptions about diversity and find better answers to inform school practices that can help every student learn to high levels. As critical theorists observe, although schools' curriculum conveys the dominant cultural values through its choice of subjects and topics for study, it also teaches the cognitive and intellectual means to challenge those assumptions and improve our society.

The critical theory perspective believes that teachers and students can improve society.

iStock/SDI Productions

6.3d Learning From the Critics

All critics—conservative, liberal, and critical theorists—offer perspectives on the society they want and how to improve schools (see the summary in Table 6.2). Each offers a somewhat competing set of goals.

TABLE 6.2 ■ Comparing Education Critics' Perspectives

	Conservative	Liberal	Critical Theory
Role of individual and government	Individuals must compete in social environments to survive. Individuals are responsible for their own choices.	Individual effort may not be enough. Government and school must ensure fair treatment of citizens in economic, political, and social arenas.	A need exists to change schools and society that make and keep students—and people—unequal.
Role of school	Schools provide opportunities for education to let young people become economically and socially productive. Socialize children into adult roles. Provide opportunities to let individual initiative and effort lead to success (or not).	Schools provide education and socialization. Schools must create equal and equitable opportunities for all students to succeed in a diverse society by leveling the playing field for economically and culturally disadvantaged students.	Public schools advance the dominant class's interests through injustices. Schools and teachers need to instill in students a critical awareness to help them understand, challenge, and transform their society.

	Conservative	Liberal	Critical Theory
Curriculum	Curriculum should meet high standards and follow the traditional Western European/American curriculum.	Curriculum should meet high standards while including diverse voices along with traditional Western European and American history, thought, and values.	Move beyond white European/American experiences to include diverse cultures, genders, and voices in a high-quality curriculum.
Accountability	Make schools, teachers, and students accountable for meeting high standards of academic performance.	Government and schools have major roles in reducing "achievement/ opportunity gaps" by assisting traditionally underperforming students. Ensure that every student can and does meet high standards.	Teachers should help students develop a critical awareness of society's power and inequalities so they can learn the knowledge and skills to challenge and transform their society for the better.

Source: Leslie S. Kaplan and William A. Owings [Original by authors].

Conservatives remind us that our democratic republic and Western tradition have brought important values to this country, and they deserve a prominent place in the curriculum. The United States is a nation of immigrants and a nation of laws. Coming from different countries, cultures, and family backgrounds, persons living here need to develop a common commitment—to become one people, one nation, indivisible, with liberty and justice for all. We deeply value our freedoms to think, speak, assemble peacefully, and worship as we choose. We also appreciate the opportunities to advance ourselves through knowledge and hard work. Likewise, conservatives remind us that respect for individual differences includes accepting students' religious beliefs that can be accommodated within the school. Students, in turn, must recognize that others may also have their own views. In the end, schools must maintain a respectful, appropriate, and safe learning environment. Finding the appropriate balance is not easy, but it is essential.

Liberals remind us to have high expectations for every student's achievement. They recognize that not all students start from the same point, through no fault of their own. Schools can provide academic and social **scaffolding**—the extra time and academic and moral supports necessary to help economically and culturally diverse students and students with disabilities overcome their education gaps and learn to the highest levels. Liberal critics see equity and excellence as compatible and doable. Closing the achievement/opportunity gap means schools must do things differently—teaching, staffing, curriculum, assessing. The results will change both the lives of individual students and our society as a whole.

Critical theorists' core ideas have merit when we look at how U.S. schools have traditionally educated low-income, underrepresented, and disabled students. Our success in fully educating disadvantaged and disenfranchised students has important implications for our own democracy's well-being. We are living in a globalized world. Global systems of production, exchange, and technology bring people together economically. Divisive belief systems and social practices—such as nationalism, racism, sexism, and contempt for those with disabilities—keep people in poverty and outside the mainstream, leaving them without opportunities to advance and improve their lives or their society. Democracy loses—unless people have access to the means and supports to improve their own lives and the lives of their children.

When a society has too many individuals without the means or opportunities to improve their lives, social revolution becomes a possibility. Those who see themselves as disadvantaged become increasingly resentful and angry about their situation. They blame those with the political power and economic means for keeping them down. With little to lose, disenfranchised citizens may engage in violence against the society. The 20th century Communist revolutions in Russia and

China as well as 21st century "Arab Spring" revolts in Tunisia, Libya, Egypt, and Syria are cases in point. The bottom line: A democratic republic cannot long thrive—or even exist—without a well-educated, vibrant, widespread middle class, whose members have access to means of improving their own well-being. By taking this view, critical theorists sound much like the U.S. Founding Fathers.

Clearly, education can improve the quality of life for individuals, communities, and nations alike. Literacy—deep cognitive understanding of how to extract information accurately from the printed page, spoken language, or internet—can empower people to take constructive action to improve their lives. Teachers need to understand their students as individuals and design appropriate and challenging learning experiences within safe and inclusive environments. Likewise, the curriculum needs to be critically understood and challenged for its application to real life, used for collaborative problem-solving, and assessed in multiple ways to guide and monitor student progress. In addition, when teachers respect and understand their students' unique lives and diverse cultures—and give the time and supports needed to learn—they can better connect students' experiences to the curriculum and help them learn the attitudes, knowledge, and skills to mature into economic self-sufficiency and responsible democratic participation.

Taking the best from these three perspectives, for U.S. schools to achieve their purposes and promises, educators should do the following:

- *Provide high-quality opportunities* for every student to learn a rigorous curriculum.
- *Develop student literacy and critical thinking* to apply to curriculum, life experiences, and the larger society.
- *Create inclusive classrooms* characterized by respect between teacher and students—and among students themselves.
- *Offer challenging and relevant learning activities* (that make sense and have meaning to students) and foster interpersonal skills.
- *"De-track" students* from low-interest, low-challenge classes and provide them with opportunities (and supports) to learn the important, high-status curriculum from effective teachers.
- *Increase educational scaffolding* for those students who start from further back or learn differently or more slowly so they can learn to high levels.
- *Teach for learning,* using the insights about how students actually learn and providing the activities and quality feedback to help all students master and use what they are learning.
- *Teach for "minds on"*—help students learn how to engage in critical thinking, collaborative problem-solving, applying knowledge to real-world events, analyzing, synthesizing, evaluating, and creating in meaningful ways with what they learn.
- *Ask questions about current events* and to what extent they represent—or deny—the democratic ideals on which our country is founded. Help students propose solutions when societal practices fall short of its ideals.
- *Educate all our students* to have the knowledge and skills they need to lead more productive, creative, and satisfying lives, not just display compliance inside the classroom or work setting.
- *Continue professional learning* and use evidence to regularly evaluate and refine teaching practice to meet each learner's needs.
- *Seek appropriate leadership roles and opportunities* to advance student learning, collaborate with colleagues, learners' families, and community members to ensure learner growth and advance the profession.

No society can sustain a large gap between the poor and the rich. If we ignore the fact that our economically disadvantaged, underrepresented students and students with disabilities are not graduating from high school at high rates and are not performing well on national and international assessments, we put our entire society and way of life at risk. Here is where education can be the agent for positive social change.

Educational policy makers and critics ask, "What type of society do we want?" and "What is education's role in developing a democratic citizenry, an economically and socially mobile society, and an economically vibrant country?" We can answer these questions more thoughtfully when we consider our critics' ideas.

Conflict—that is, courteous discussion of different viewpoints to reach consensus for the common good—is essential to living in a democratic society. We should neither fear nor blindly defend against our critics. We want to teach our students to think searchingly, listen carefully and respectfully, and act responsibly. Our society is not perfect, and we can help students develop the cognitive tools, constructive attitudes, and interpersonal behaviors to make both their lives and our communities better. As educators and citizens, we can do no less. Public schools gain strong community support when they present their "official" curriculum within the larger context of "democratic education for a more democratic society" rather than as a means to advance the agenda of certain special-interest groups.

If you want to more deeply explore how cultural conservative, liberal, and critical theory ideas influence your own thinking and values, complete the activity in the **Reflect & Engage** box, Analyzing the Three Perspectives.

REFLECT & ENGAGE: ANALYZING THE THREE PERSPECTIVES

Generally speaking, cultural conservatives criticize public schools because they believe educational benefits should rest on individual merit, family, free enterprise, patriotism, and Christianity. They believe that public schools sometimes undermine traditional values based on religious morality and individual merit.

Liberal critics believe that public schools must level the playing field between affluent and economically disadvantaged students through policies and programs that give disadvantaged students a better chance to make the most of their educational opportunities. They see education as balancing the individual and social needs in ways consistent with democracy and meritocracy.

Critical theorists would change both schools and the society that made and keep people unequal. They believe that the traditional curriculum aims to make students conforming and docile. Instead, they suggest, schools should be moral, just, and inclusive of those who most need access to the educational process. Schools can be a vehicle for social change when they implement curriculum and teaching that are multicultural, antiracist, antisexist, and respect the diversity of today's students.

Working first in pairs and then discussing as a whole class, consider the information in this text, and answer the following questions:

A. On which issues do you agree with each of the three different perspectives?

B. On which issues do you disagree with each of them?

C. Using the "best" ideas from each perspective, what might this look like if practiced in your school?

D. In what ways do you think public schools would change if schools accepted each approach's ideas regarding curriculum, library resources, need for extra academic support for underserved and disadvantaged students, school rules, prayer in schools, achievement testing, and availability of school support personnel (counselors, nurses)?

6.4 REALIZING EDUCATION'S GOALS: INVESTMENT IN HUMAN CAPITAL

From varying perspectives, U.S. education has many worthy goals. Implicit in conservative, liberal, and critical theory views is the belief that education is an investment in human capital, making our lives more satisfying, our communities better places to live, and our national well-being stronger.

6.4a Investing in Human Capital

Education as an investment in **human capital**—the idea that educating everyone benefits the community—is a relatively new concept. In earlier times, governments provided extended formal schooling to educate the social and financial elites. Laborers, members of the working classes, and the poor remained largely undereducated. We will discuss the concept of education as an investment in human capital more fully in Chapter 11.

Adam Smith's *The Wealth of Nations* (1776) formally introduced the notion of human capital.[37] In this seminal work, Smith discussed society members' learned abilities (education) as part of a society's resources. He viewed investment in human capital as providing workers with vocational training related to production. His original concept, which was quite revolutionary at the time, provided an early first step toward the larger view of educated workers contributing to the economy and to society at large.

People feel rich when they can give their children an education that promises them a successful future.
iStock/andresr

Two hundred years later (in the 1960s), Theodore W. Schultz's work on investment in human capital expressed the idea that laborers' primarily intellectual attributes have value.[38] Schultz, an agricultural economist, often visited farms and spoke with farmers. After World War II, while interviewing an old, apparently poverty-stricken farm couple, he noticed their contentment. When he asked them why they were so satisfied with their lives—even though they were poor—they answered that they were not poor. They felt rich because they had used their farm to send four children to college and believed that education would make these children productive, successful, and happy. This perspective quickly led Schultz to the concept of human capital as capital produced by investing in knowledge.

To meet its goals, education requires a significant financial and cultural investment. Schultz suggested that investing in people's minds was economically valuable for the larger community. His theory of investing in human capital won the 1979 Nobel Prize for Economic Science. Schultz's work became the basis for considering education as an excellent investment—a significant contributor to a society's economic development.

An educated citizenry makes many tangible, positive, and measurable impacts on society. More than any other social investment, education is a community's investment in its own best interests. It raises the standard of living by increasing employability and spendable income while reducing a

FIGURE 6.1 ■ Percentage of Labor Force by Race and Educational Attainment, 2016

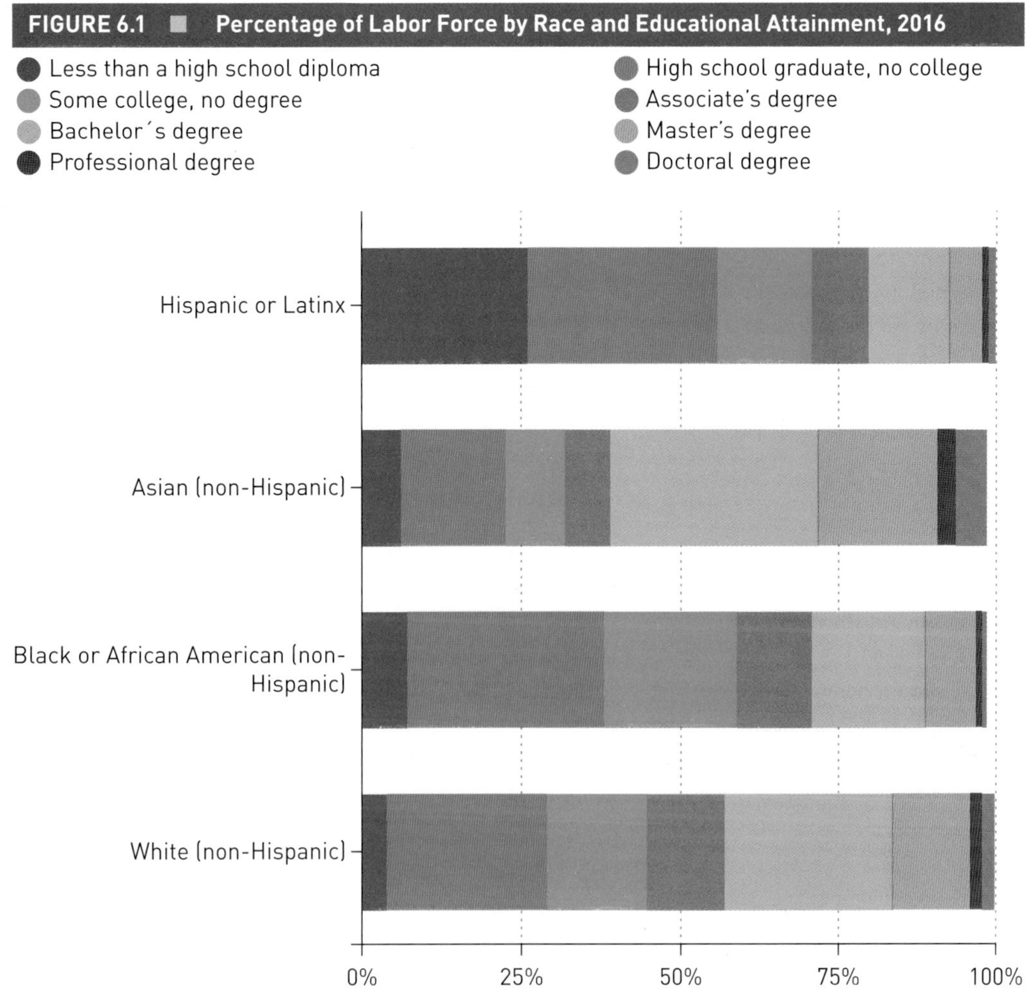

Source: U.S. Bureau of Labor Statistics. (2019). Percentage of labor force by race and educational attainment, 25 years and over, 2016 annual averages, p. 4. *Spotlight on Statistics.* https://www.bls.gov/spotlight/2017/educational-attainment-of-the-labor-force/home.htm.

community's social services costs. In addition, a good public education system is a major drawing card for local business development and expansion. Managers realize that well-educated workers make good employees. In a dynamic synergy, education enhances the quality of life not just for the educated individuals themselves, but for the entire community as well. More immediately, education directly affects the personal living standard by influencing how much people earn.

Every ethnic group gains economically from increased education. Figure 6.1 shows that although different ethnic and racial groups in the United States may earn different amounts for the same level of education,[39] each group is making gains, and all members of each ethnic group earn more than their ethnic peers who have attained lower education levels.

Undoubtedly, education is a major contributor to the U.S. economy's financial health. As a rule, citizens with higher levels of educational attainment earn more money, return more tax dollars to support government services, add more to the general consumer economy to enhance their lifestyles, and draw fewer resources from society than do those with less education.[40]

6.5 IS EDUCATION STILL THE KEY TO THE AMERICAN DREAM?

One of our nation's most enduring myths sees the United States as the land of endless opportunity. For hundreds of years and to this day, immigrants have come here from around the world to build better lives for themselves and for their families. To these newcomers, the streets of the United States are figuratively "paved with gold." Within one or two generations, immigrants' children typically become part of the American mainstream. This is the American Dream: the freedom to live your life as you choose and, through hard work, become successful. But today, does the myth of the American Dream match its reality?

In the American Dream, a person's economic or social standing does not depend on his or her parents' wealth or social status, but rather on the individual's own efforts. In other words, America is a meritocracy. With an expanding economy and political freedom, those individuals (and their children) with desirable talents and a strong work ethic have the opportunity to join the middle class. But such social mobility has slowed over the past few decades. Two thirds of individuals born in the 1940s were able to attain better jobs than their parents—were upwardly mobile—as compared with slightly over half of those born in the 1980s.[41] A growing body of research questions whether this ideal of social mobility and economic opportunity is still a possibility for many of our most economically disadvantaged students.

6.5a Slowing Social and Economic Mobility

Today, the upward mobility that many take for granted—that children will do better economically than their parents—may now be at risk. **Social mobility** refers to the upward or downward movement, socioeconomically, for children from less advantaged families. It also refers to the downward movement, or its lack, for children from more advantaged backgrounds. The truth is that research finds that social and economic mobility in the United States is less than it is in other industrialized countries[42] and has been falling since 1940.[43]

Stanford economist Raj Chetty observes, "Your chances of achieving the 'American Dream' are almost two times higher if you're growing up in Canada relative to the U.S." [44] In his study, U.S. children have a 7.5% chance of achieving economic mobility,[45] Canadian children have a 13.5% probability, and children in the United Kingdom and Denmark have a 9% and 11.7% probability, respectively. Prime culprits for this lack of upward mobility include an area's degree of segregation (with mixed-income communities producing improved outcomes for disadvantaged children); income inequality (less income inequality means higher rates of upward mobility); family structure (with stable two-parent families having higher rates of upward mobility); and public schools (better public schools tend to have much higher rates of upward mobility). [46]

Further, studies in the United States and the United Kingdom find a "glass floor": Children from advantaged families are protected from downward mobility. At the same time, on average, less-able children from more affluent families do better in income and earnings than more-able children from poorer families. And the most important protective factor: a college degree. [47]

Intergenerational wealth can be measured by examining the place on the economic ladder where a child is raised and then determining the step (quintile) that the child reaches as an adult. Figure 6.2, reflecting data through 2009, depicts mobility experiences of Americans at different points on the economic landscape.[48] The wealth ladder's ends appear to have a "stickiness": 66% of those raised in the bottom remain on the bottom two rungs as adults, and 66% of those raised in the top of the wealth ladder remain on the top two rungs as adults. Rising from "rags to riches" is virtually impossible: Only 4% of adults raised in the bottom 20% rise to the top. Meanwhile, 63% of Americans raised at the top of the income ladder remain above the middle quintile as adults. Notably, a 4-year college degree promotes upward mobility from the bottom and prevents downward mobility from the middle and top. As a result, over generations people move up and down the social–economic ladder, and completing a college education affects mobility in positive ways regardless of where one begins.

In *Pursuing the American Dream: Economic Mobility Across Generations* (2012), the Pew Charitable Trusts finds that 84% of Americans exceed their parents' family income. Earning a 4-year college degree makes someone 3 times more likely to rise from the income ladder's bottom to its top and less likely to fall down the income ladder. In comparison, more than one third of children raised in the middle of the family income ladder who do not complete a 4-year college degree tend to fall to lower income levels.[49] In an information- and intelligence-based economy, in a globalized world, social and economic mobility require a strong education to make advancement more likely and loss of social mobility less likely.

FIGURE 6.2 ■ Intergenerational Wealth: Chances of Moving Up or Down the Family Income Ladder, by Parents' Quintile

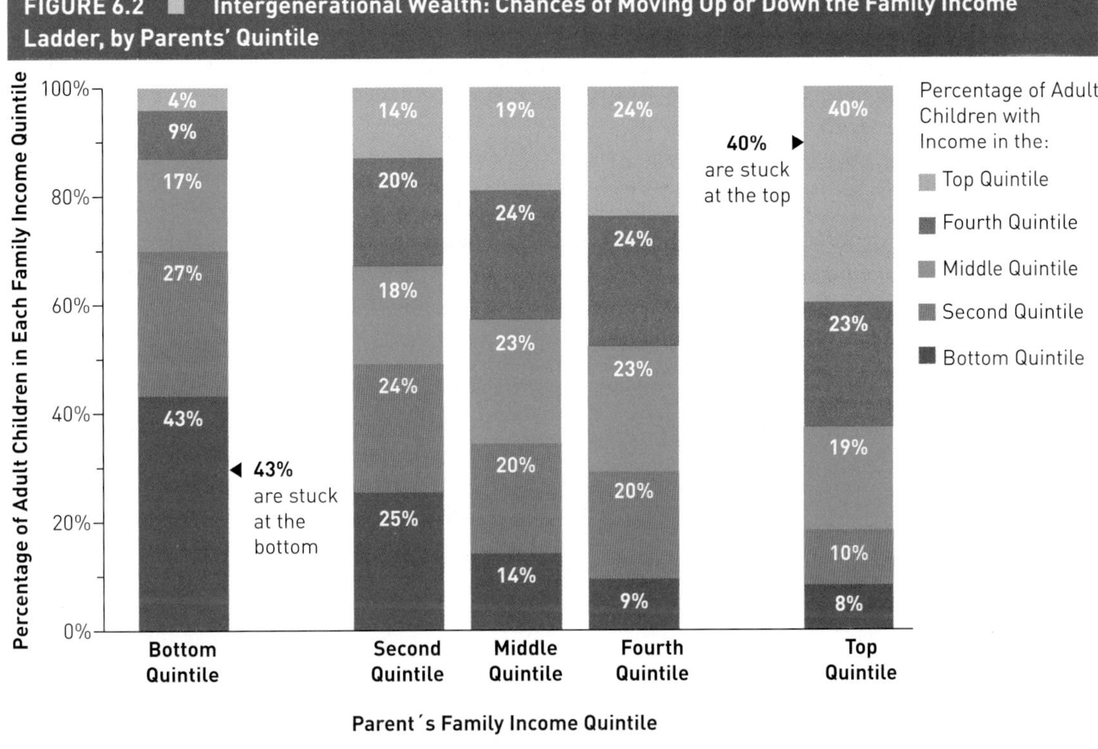

Source: Urahn, K., Currier, E., Elliott, D., Wechsler, L., Wilson, D., & Colbert, D. (2012, July). *Pursuing the American dream: Economic mobility across generations.* The PEW Charitable Trusts, Figure 3, p. 6. https://www.pewtrusts.org/~/media/legacy/uploadedfiles/wwwpewtrustsorg/reports/economic_mobility/pursuingamericandreampdf.pdf

Importantly, the overall college enrollment rate for young adults increased from 35% in 2000 to 40% in 2017, and students from varied demographics were among these. In 2017, as compared with 2000, the college enrollment rates were higher for students who were white (41% vs. 39%), Black (36% vs. 31%), Hispanic (36% vs. 22%), and Asian (65% vs. 56%).[50]

Education's potential to increase social mobility is an important topic because statistics show that the income gap between America's poorest and richest has widened since the 1970s. Beginning in the 1970s, economic growth slowed, and the income gap widened. For households in the middle and lower parts of the income distribution, income growth slowed sharply, whereas incomes at the top continue its strong growth. Wealth—the value of a household's property and financial assets (less the value of its debts)—is even more highly concentrated. The share of wealth held by the top 1% rose from just under 30% in 1989 to nearly 39% in 2016, while the share held by the bottom 90% fell from just over 33% to less than 23% over the same period.[51]

Greater inequality means it takes longer for income differences to disappear in later generations, a situation that jeopardizes the health of our entire society. "The United States could be in danger of creating a poverty trap at the bottom and an enclave of wealth at the top," observes Isabel Sawhill, a senior fellow at the Brookings Institution.[52] Education is essential for children from less advantaged families to move up the economic ladder. The overwhelming majority of research finds that students who earn postsecondary credentials—from 2- and 4-year college degrees to industry-recognized postsecondary credentials—have an improved path into the workforce and an enhanced chance of rising into the middle class.[53]

But preparation for postsecondary education begins well before senior year in high school. Performance gaps by social class among children begin in their earliest years. By kindergarten, these gaps are visible and do not narrow in the following years without interventions. Greater investments in preK programs to develop strong cognitive and noncognitive skills essential for success in school and beyond can narrow the gap between low-SES children's capacities and what they need to start school.

Schools can also provide ongoing comprehensive academic, health, nutrition, and emotional support for children throughout their school years. Added access and supports for rigorous academic, as well as high-quality career and technical education (with an earned industry-recognized credential), are also routes into the well-paying workforce and the middle class.[54]

From an economic viewpoint, the question is not only whether people will find jobs but also whether they will be able to find jobs with long-term opportunities that will allow them to productively use their knowledge and skills and increase their economic and social mobility. Without significant increases in students' knowledge and skill levels when they enter the job market and without the appropriate jobs to enter, they will not be able to improve their lifestyles. Although 4-year college degrees may not be the right path for each student in the 21st century, each student will need mastery of complex knowledge and skills, critical thinking, and the abilities to communicate well and work effectively in teams. A rigorous high school education and most likely a few years of formal schooling beyond that will be critical, depending on the career path chosen. In short, a quality education for each student remains a must-have if social and economic mobility are to continue.

6.5b Optimism About Achieving the American Dream

Despite some discouraging indicators, most Americans remain optimistic about achieving the American Dream. A 2018 study finds that most Americans believe they have achieved the American Dream because they have "freedom to choose how to live" (85%) and have "a good family life" (83%). Only 16% believe that becoming wealthy is essential, and only 18% reported that the American Dream was out of their reach.[55] This optimism was true for varied ethnic and racial groups.[56] The same was true for those earning under $35,000 a year (72%) and those earning over $100,000 a year (90%). Differences were generational, however. Eighty-three percent of baby boomers, 80% of GenXers, and 81% of millennials were optimistic about achieving the American Dream as compared with 73% of Gen Z (Americans born in 1997 or later).[57] These differing responses may reflect an acceptance of the slowed social and economic mobility available today. Instead, most Americans identify their success beyond money, home ownership, and social prestige—to individual freedom, family, and community. More than ever, a strong education—a rigorous and relevant curriculum taught by highly effective teachers—remains essential.

Questions of larger social and political movements cannot be divorced from educational philosophy, nor should educational philosophy and reflection on practice simply be reduced to acting according to the day's prevailing political winds. As thoughtful citizens, we need to examine these issues carefully. The competing goals in contemporary U.S. schools actually stem from competing social visions. In a diverse society, this debate is both expected and beneficial.

KEY TAKE-AWAYS

Learning Objective 6.1 Assess the general goals of American education and explain their importance.

- Since our nation's founding, our leaders believed that a democratic republic could not exist without a well-educated, widespread middle class whose members have access to means of improving their own well-being and enacting responsible citizenship. Public education would be the key to making this a reality. It continues to be.
- Defining a common set of shared political values and goals for schools to address as it socializes each generation in the knowledge and skills required for mature citizenship and economic participation in a dynamic and diverse society presents many challenges.
- Schools work as one of many institutions—along with the family and religious organizations, among others—to socialize children into society's various roles, behaviors, and values.
- Different educational visions mean different ideas of what makes a "good society," and varying social visions influence what makes a "good education." Struggles over curriculum, teaching,

and policy are actually battles for power over children's thoughts and for the society's future direction.

- The natural tension between schooling's role in maintaining the status quo and its potential to bring about change lies at the heart of differing views of education and schooling—and it often creates competing goals. Similarly, as time passes, changes in society, knowledge, and beliefs about the nature of the world and the nature of learning may produce related changes in educational theories and schools' purposes.
- Although today's policy makers appear to emphasize the limited goals of reading and mathematical proficiency as measured by standardized tests, contemporary community leaders want our schools to accomplish a broad array of goals—including many not easily reduced to a single test score.

Learning Objective 6.2 Critique the wide-ranging nature of American education goals and the challenges these bring.

- In our decentralized school governance system, the challenge is to provide a set of national educational goals for schools that gives guidance and direction without giving requirements or prescriptions. The national goals have to be general enough to mean different things to different people and aligned with international education benchmarks.
- What Americans want from their education system and what education policy makers want do not always match.
- School decisions about its priorities are fundamental decisions about the kinds of minds our children will have the opportunities to develop. Education's aim is not merely to enable our children to do well in school; it is also to enable our children to do well in life.
- Schools will continue to serve comprehensive intellectual, political, social, economic, and personal purposes. It remains essential that prospective and present educators, policy makers, and our society as a whole consider these wider goals, some of which are contradictory, when deciding how to move forward.

Learning Objective 6.3 Compare and contrast how conservative, liberal, and critical theory education critics offer differing views of schools' role in society and how schools can improve.

- Conservative educational theorists remind us that our democratic republic and Western tradition have brought important values to this country, and they deserve a prominent place in the curriculum. As a nation of immigrants, we need to develop both individual responsibility and a common commitment to become one people, loyal to this nation, able to improve our lives by gaining knowledge and working hard.
- Liberal educational theorists remind us that every student deserves opportunities to learn at the highest levels. Schools should provide a high academic challenge for every student plus give the academic and social assistance needed to help economically and culturally diverse students overcome their opportunity gaps. Education balances individual and social needs in ways consistent with democracy and meritocracy, making equity and excellence compatible and doable.
- Critical theorists would change both schools and the society that made and keep people unequal. They remind us that our success in fully educating disadvantaged and disenfranchised students has important implications for our own democracy's well-being. As such, the curriculum needs to be analytically understood, challenged for its application to real life, used for collaborative problem-solving, and assessed in multiple ways to guide and monitor student progress.

Learning Objective 6.4 Support how education is an investment in human capital.

- Education is a community's investment in its people (its "human capital"), enabling individuals to address their intellectual, political, social, economic, and personal needs and then contribute to the larger society. Every ethnic group gains economically from increased educational attainment.

Learning Objective 6.5 Defend the ways that education is still the key to achieving the American Dream.

- Education increases social and economic mobility. Although social and economic mobility has slowed in past decades, the American Dream—defined as the freedom to live your life as you choose and have a good family life—continues to generate optimism.
- Over generations, people move up and down the social–economic ladder, but without successfully completing a rigorous and relevant high school curriculum and a postsecondary education, most do not have improved paths into the workforce or chances of entering the middle class.

TEACHER SCENARIO: IT'S YOUR TURN

The politics in your state have become increasingly polarized. Far Right and Far Left voices in the legislature are making education policy decisions difficult. As someone who has studied conservative, liberal, and critical education theories and education as an investment in human capital, the State Secretary of Education has asked you to prepare a briefing paper explaining which aspects of each education theory could have the greatest impact on improving the human capital and economic mobility of high school graduates in your state. How could these theories' ideas and practices be implemented at the preK–12 levels? The secretary hopes that combining the best educational perspectives and practices of each theory will improve student outcomes and decrease the political partisanship. Write out your recommendations and your rationale for the secretary.

NOTES

1. Goodlad, J. I. (1979, January). Can our schools get better? *Phi Delta Kappan, 60*(5), 342.
2. *Waiting for Superman* (2010) is an American documentary that uses what some consider "incomplete or misleading statistics and unsupported claims" to criticize the American public education system, especially teachers and unions, by following several students as they tried to gain acceptance into competitive charter schools. See: Harvard Educational Review. (n.d.). Waiting for "Superman." https://www.hepg.org/HER-Home/Issues/Harvard-Educational-Review-Volume-80-Number-4/HerBookNote/Waiting-for-Superman"_360
3. Rose, M. (2006, October 11). Grand visions and possible lives: Finding the public good through the details of classroom life. *Education Week, 26*(7), 32–33. http://www.edweek.org/ew/articles/2006/10/11/07rose.h26.html
4. Cremin, L. A. (1977). *Traditions of American education.* Basic Books, p. 37.
5. U.S. Department of Education. (1990). *America 2000.* The Clinton Administration Education Program. https://www3.nd.edu/~rbarger/www7/goals200.html. These goals refer to national goals that public schools were to have reached by the year 2000.
6. Adapted from Goodlad, J. I. (1979). *What schools are for.* Phi Delta Kappa Educational Foundation, pp. 44–52. Reissued in 2006 by Phi Delta Kappan International.
7. Eisner, E. W. (2003, May). Questionable assumptions about schooling. *Phi Delta Kappan, 84*(9), 648–657.
8. Eisner, E. W. (1992, April). The misunderstood role of the arts in human development. *Phi Delta Kappan, 73*(8), 592.
9. Eisner, 1992.
10. Eisner, E. W. (2001, January). What does it mean to say a school is doing well? *Phi Delta Kappan, 82*(3), 367–372.
11. Eisner, E. W. (1999, May). The use and limits of performance assessment. *Phi Delta Kappan, 80*(9), 658–660.
12. Eisner, 1992, p. 595.
13. Eisner, 1992, p. 595.

14. Eisner, 1999, p. 660.
15. Ross, E. A. (1900, January). Social control XIV: Education. *American Journal of Sociology, 5*(4), 483.
16. Spring, J. (2002). *American education*. McGraw-Hill, pp. 10–15.
17. Spring, J. (2002). *American education*. McGraw-Hill, pp. 10–15.
18. Pew Research Center. (2015, December 9). *The American middle class is losing ground*. https://www.pewsocialtrends.org/2015/12/09/the-american-middle-class-is-losing-ground/
19. Similarly, 29% of American adults lived in lower-income households, and 19% lived in upper-income households. See: Fry, R., & Kochhar, R. (2018, September 6). *Are you in the American middle class? Find out with our income calculator*. Pew Research Center. https://www.pewresearch.org/fact-tank/2018/09/06/are-you-in-the-american-middle-class/
20. Pew Research Center. (2015, June 18). *The rise or dual income households*. https://www.pewresearch.org/ft_dual-income-households-1960-2012-2/
21. This percentage is higher than for the overall population because retired couples (in which both are not working) are more prevalent in the overall population than among households with children. See: Bureau of Labor Statistics. (2020, September). Comparing characteristics and selected expenditures of dual- and single-income households with children. *Monthly Labor Review*. https://www.bls.gov/opub/mlr/2020/article/comparing-characteristics-and-selected-expenditures-of-dual-and-single-income-households-with-children.htm
22. Owings, W., Kaplan, L. S., Myran, S., & Doyle, P. (2017). How variations in state policies and practices impact student outcomes: What principals and professors need to know. *NASSP Bulletin, 101*(4), 299–314. https://doi.org/10.1177%2F0192636517745582
23. "Cost–benefit scale" is an economics term meaning that a person makes decisions by taking into account the relative advantages as compared to the expenses (financial, emotional, physical, social) of making a particular decision.
24. "Neoliberal" is another term to describe those who use political processes to privatize or direct state institutions in ways that favor their interests, such as by establishing charter schools with public funds (to improve learning opportunities for children of color) or hiring private vendors to enact roles currently run by public institutions (such as providing food or transportation to school children). Some scholars consider neoliberals to be conservatives. See: Bailey, C. (2015). Neoliberal standardization and its discontents: An interview with Diane Ravitch. *Alternative Routes: A Journal of Critical Social Research*, *26*, 327–331. http://alternateroutes.ca/index.php/ar/article/view/22324; Wubbena, Z. D. (2015, April 15). Breathing secondhand smoke: Gatekeeping for "good" education, passive democracy, and the mass media. An interview with Noam Chomsky. *Critical Education, 6*(8). http://ices.library.ubc.ca/index.php/criticaled/article/view/185227
25. The phrase "a wall of separation between church and state" does not appear in the U.S. Constitution. The phrase comes from a letter written by Thomas Jefferson on January 1, 1802, to the Danbury Baptist Association. For that reason, we refer to that concept as a *doctrine*.
26. National Commission on Excellence in Education. (1983). *A nation at risk*. U.S. Government Printing Office.
27. Some argue that "opportunity gap" is a more appropriate term than "achievement gap" when referring to students from low-income communities. The arbitrary circumstances into which people are born (such as their race, ethnicity, zip code, and socioeconomic status) determine their life opportunities rather than every person having the chance to achieve to the best of his or her potential. It places responsibility on the inequitable system that does not provide chances for every child to thrive and succeed. This provides educators and policy makers with a more solutions-oriented language to promote systemic reforms. See: Mooney, T. (2018, May 11). Why we say "opportunity gap" instead of "achievement gap." *Teach for America*. https://www.teachforamerica.org/stories/why-we-say-opportunity-gap-instead-of-achievement-gap; Schott Foundation for Public Education. (n.d.). Opportunity gap—talking points. http://schottfoundation.org/issues/opportunity-gap/talking-points
28. See: Barnett, W. S., & Boocock, S. S. (Eds.). (1998). *Early care and education for children in poverty*. State University of New York Press; Claessens, A., Engel, M., & Curran, F. (2014). Academic content, student learning and the persistence of preschool effects. *American Educational Research Journal, 51*(2), 403–434; Conner, C., Morrison, F., & Slominski, L. (2006). Preschool instructional and children's emergent literacy growth. *Journal of Educational Psychology, 98*(4), 665–689; Karoly, L. A., Kilburn, M. R., Bigelow, J. H., Caulkins, J. P., & Cannon J. S. (2001). *Assessing costs and benefits of early childhood intervention programs: Overview and applications to the starting early starting smart program*. RAND; Reynolds, A. (2019). The power of P-3 school reform. *Phi Delta Kappan, 100*(6), 27–33.
29. See: Chapter 14, Educating Everyone's Children.

30. Compensatory higher-education programs for disadvantaged students, such as Upward Bound, prepare middle school- and high school-aged, underserved students for college.

31. *Critical consciousness* can be defined as "the ability to recognize and analyze systems of inequality and the commitment to take action against these systems" as a means for marginalized students to achieve well academically. See: El-Amin, A., Seider, S., Gravs, D., Tamerat, J., Clark, S., Soutter, M., Johannsen. J., & Malhotra, S. (2017, June 4). Critical consciousness: A key to student achievement. *Phi Delta Kappan, 98*(5), 18–23.

32. Giroux, H. (1994, Fall). *Slack off: Border youth and postmodern education.* http://www.gseis.ucla.edu/courses/ed253a/Giroux/Giroux5.html; Giroux, H. (n.d.). *Doing cultural studies: Youth and the challenge of pedagogy.* http://www.gseis.ucla.edu/courses/ed253a/Giroux/Giroux1.html; McLaren, P. (1994). *Life in schools.* Longman; McLaren, P. (2000). White terror and oppositional agency: Toward a critical multiculturalism. In E. Duarte & S. Smith (Eds.), *Foundational perspectives in multicultural education.* SAGE.

33. The term "official knowledge"—the formal curriculum that the society's dominant culture transmits in schools—comes from Apple, M. W. (1993). *Official knowledge: Democratic education in a conservative age.* Routledge.

34. Giroux, 1994; Giroux, H. (n.d.). *Doing cultural studies: Youth and the challenge of pedagogy.* http://www.gseis.ucla.edu/courses/ed253a/Giroux/Giroux1.html; McLaren, 1994; McLaren, 2000.

35. See: Kozol, J. (1967). *Death at an early age: The destruction of the hearts and minds of Negro children in the Boston Public Schools.* Bantam Books; Kozol, J. (1991). *Savage inequalities: Children in American schools.* Crown; Freire, P. (1970). *Pedagogy of the oppressed.* Continuum; Freire, P. (1973). *Education for critical consciousness.* Herder and Herder; Freire, P. (1985). *The politics of education.* Bergin & Garvey; Freire, P. (1998). *Pedagogy of freedom.* Rowman & Littlefield.

36. Allen, L. A. (2006). The moral life of schools revisited: Preparing educational leaders to "build a new social order" for social justice and democratic community. *International Journal of Urban Education Leadership, 1,* 1–13.

37. Smith, A. (1937). *The wealth of nations* (Rev. ed). Modern Library.

38. Schultz, T. W. (1961, March). Investment in human capital. *American Economic Review, 51,* 1–17.

39. Unequal earning levels for different ethnic groups with the same education can have a variety of causes, such as inability to find high-paying employment in urban neighborhoods where many live or differential job descriptions (and salaries) for similar work. Here may be an example of a promise yet to keep.

40. Owings, W. A., & Kaplan, L. S. (2019). *American education finance* (3rd ed.). Routledge.

41. Hout, M. (2018, July 18). *Americans' occupational status reflects that status of both of their parents.* PNAS [Proceedings of the National Academy of Sciences of the United States of America]. https://www.pnas.org/content/pnas/115/38/9527.full.pdf

42. Ball, F. (2019, April). Middle class at risk as social mobility slows. *Economia.* https://economia.icaew.com/news/april-2019/middle-class-at-risk-as-social-mobility-slows;Wilkinson, R., & Pickett, K. (2009) *The spirit level: Why more equal societies almost always do better.* Penguin.

43. Chetty, R., Grusky, D., Hell, M., Hendren, N., Manduca, R., & Narang, J. (2017, April). The fading American dream: Trends in absolute income mobility since 1940. *Science, 356*(6336), 398–406.

44. Chetty, R. (2016). Improving opportunities for economic mobility: New evidence and policy lessons. In R. Chetty (Ed.), *Economic mobility: Research & ideas on strengthening families, communities, & the economy* (p. 37). Federal Reserve Bank of St. Louis. https://www.stlouisfed.org/~/media/files/pdfs/community%20development/econmobilitypapers/section1/econmobility_1-1chetty_508.pdf?d=l&s=tw

45. The probability of achieving economic mobility in the U.S. varies with the geographic area of the country.

46. Chetty, 2016.

47. McKnight, A., & Reeves, R. V. (2017, July 26). Glass floors and slow growth: A recipe for deepening inequality and hampering social mobility. *Social Mobility Memos.* Brookings. https://www.brookings.edu/blog/social-mobility-memos/2017/07/26/glass-floors-and-slow-growth-a-recipe-for-deepening-inequality-and-hampering-social-mobility/

48. *Absolute mobility* measures whether a person has more or less income, earnings, or wealth than his or her parents did at the same age. *Relative mobility* measures a person's rank on the income, earnings, or wealth ladder as compared with his or her parents' rank at the same age. See: Urahn et al., 2012, p. 1.

49. Uhran et al., 2012.

50. National Center for Education Statistics. (2019). *College enrollment rates: The condition of education 2019.* https://nces.ed.gov/programs/coe/pdf/coe_cpb.pdf

51. Stone, C., Trisi, D., Sherman, A., & Taylor, R. (2019, August 21). *A guide to statistics on historical trends in income inequality*. Center on Budget and Policy Priorities. https://www.cbpp.org/research/poverty-and-inequality/a-guide-to-statistics-on-historical-trends-in-income-inequality

52. Sawhill, I. V. (2006). *Opportunity in America: The role of education*. Brookings Institution. https://www.brookings.edu/research/opportunity-in-america-the-role-of-education/

53. Petrilli, M. (2017, October 13). Education is still a sturdy path to upward mobility. *Flypaper*. Thomas B. Fordham Institute. https://fordhaminstitute.org/national/commentary/education-still-sturdy-path-upward-mobility;Petrilli, M. J. (2016, March 15). *Education for upward mobility*. Thomas Fordham Institute. https://fordhaminstitute.org/national/research/education-upward-mobility-0

54. Petrilli, 2017.

55. Abrams, S. J. (2019, February 6). The American dream is alive and well. *American Enterprise Institute*. https://www.aei.org/articles/the-american-dream-is-alive-and-well/

56. Non-Hispanic whites (81%); Blacks, Hispanics, and mixed race (80%); and Asian heritage (85%) said they had achieved or were on their way to achieving the American Dream.

57. Abrams, 2019.

iStock/Wavebreakmedia

7 CULTURAL, SOCIAL, AND EDUCATIONAL CAUSES OF THE ACHIEVEMENT GAP AND HOW TO FIX THEM

InTASC Standards Addressed: 1, 2, 3, 4, 5, 7, 8, 9, 10

LEARNING OBJECTIVES

After you read this chapter, you should be able to

7.1 Argue how America's view of immigrants and assimilation shifted from the "melting pot" metaphor to "cultural pluralism" and its implications for American education.

7.2 Critique how the American public schools became a major socializing agent for generations of children.

7.3 Support the view that family socioeconomic status influences U.S. students' skills, social capital, outlooks, and opportunities.

7.4 Assess the contradictory roles of American public schools, how these appear in practice, and their implications for the social mobility and the achievement/opportunity gap.

7.5 Describe the poverty factors that can adversely affect a child's school success.

7.6 Assess how residential and school segregation and school integration impact students' academic achievement and life outcomes.

7.7 Identify and discuss the school factors and practices that contribute to the achievement/opportunity gap.

7.8 Identify and describe the school factors and practices that can reduce the achievement/opportunity gap.

Americans established public schools, in part, to become the great social equalizers, placing every student on the path to social mobility and economic survival. If we look closely, however, we find that schools typically reinforce—rather than overcome—our communities' social, economic, racial, and ethnic divides.

Although school doors open to all children, schools have never served all children or their families fairly or well. Both social class (as defined by parents' income, education, occupation, resources, and expectations) and school practices (such as teacher expectations, academic tracking, and school/instructional climate) influence student learning and contribute to the achievement/opportunity gap.

In addition, we structure our schools to accomplish goals we set for them: to educate, acculturate, and prepare young people for viability in the larger society. Nonetheless, unfair school practices, societal barriers, and cultural values that schools use to realize these ends make it possible for schools to limit certain students' access to the high-quality education they need and deserve. Frequently, educators do not see the schools' inequities because these practices are so familiar and well rationalized that they seem neutral, normal, and appropriate rather than unfair.

This chapter looks at the various ways in which both society and schools may present obstacles to underserved and low-income students receiving the education they need and that contribute to the *achievement gap*—the disparity in academic performance between groups of students. The more we understand how schools typically function, however, the achievement gap can look like an *opportunity gap*—the lack of access to resources needed for low-income children to learn apace with more affluent peers. In this vein, the chapter also examines the practices (i.e., opportunities) educators and communities can adopt to better support every student's learning and higher achievement.

7.1 FROM MELTING POT TO CULTURAL PLURALISM

The United States is proud of its tradition of successfully incorporating people from around the world into our society. From the young nation's earliest day, its founders recognized that their new government's survival depended on its ability to create a new nation from a heterogeneous population. "Ethnic diversity was the norm"[1] and "*E Pluribus Unum*" (out of many, one) was its de facto motto. The bald eagle on the Great Seal of the United States—embodying long life, courage, strength, and freedom—affirmed this unity. The "paradox and ambiguity" in the concept of an American nation—melting pot or cultural pluralism—continues to this day.[2]

The Great Seal of the United States affirms our national unity.

U.S. Government, public domain, via Wikimedia Commons

Until the 1960s, the United States considered itself a nation of assimilated immigrants, a "melting pot"[3] in which all its citizens' individual ethnic, religious, and cultural differences dissolved into a unifying civic American culture. The Declaration of Independence declared that "all men are created equal," and the Constitution and its amendments gave individuals freedom of speech, religion, and the right of peaceful assembly. Anyone who came to this country and believed and lived by these (and other) American ideals could become an American.

Membership in the American political community rested on an overt allegiance to the U.S. and its constitutional principles. After the Revolutionary War, this commitment also included sharing homegrown cultural norms: an American identity separate from Europe, a commitment to broad economic opportunity, social mobility, and a rejection of rigid social class and political distinctions.

Sometime in the 1960s and 1970s, this image of assimilation lost favor. The civil rights movement upended the traditional idea that the path to American success lay in obscuring racial and ethnic differences. At the same time, the societal divisions created by the Vietnam War exploded the 1950s consensus view of American society. To many, the "melting pot" analogy idealized the original settlers' Western European culture, disrespected the ethnic communities' cultural assets, and ignored African Americans' continued struggle for first-class citizenship. Newly empowered ethnic groups—many already acculturated, accepted, and successful—pressed to affirm their previously "undervalued self-identities" (as in bumper stickers reading, "Kiss Me, I'm Polish").[4] Instead of celebrating their complete assimilation from ethnic national to all-American, images of "stews," "salads," "patchwork quilts," and "mosaics" became fashionable, a mixing of the intact unique pieces as part of the whole American banquet/fabric.[5] These new images tried to portray becoming American as finding a proper balance between fully assimilating—totally embracing American identity and citizenship—and retaining the best parts of one's previous culture.

Cultural pluralism—the concept that individual ethnic groups can keep their cultural heritages, their ancestral pride, within the larger society even as they become full-hearted and patriotic Americans—became part of our lexicon.[6] Ethnic identity was applauded, and "*Ozzie and Harriet* gave way to *Kojak* and *Colombo* [1950s, 1970s, and 1960s television shows, respectively], heritage travel," and other symbols of pride in one's ethnic identity.[7]

The genius of the "American Experiment" is that we are a heterogeneous nation committed to sharing an American civic ethic and norms. Cultural pluralism has enabled Americans to realize that diversity can bring richness of experiences and perspectives, and social cohesion does not require a forced conformity. In the United States, although "melting pot" and "cultural pluralism" viewpoints on assimilation may conflict in theory, they overlap in practice. In their most extreme forms, neither benefits the larger society. What's important is that we recognize that our differences are less important than our shared values and loyalty to our common American nation. As David Brooks, *The New York Times* columnist, observes, "America is a diverse country joined more by a common future than by common pasts."[8]

7.1a Increasing U.S. Diversity and Our Future Quality of Life

The U.S. census confirms our increasing diversity. As our white, slow-growing, and aging population declines in its percentage of the population, racial minorities increasingly will become the main demographic engine of the nation's workforce. By 2045, the U.S. Census Bureau projects that more than half of all Americans will belong to a minority group,[9] and by 2060, nearly one in five is projected to be foreign born.[10] Figure 7.1 illustrates the projected racial profile of the U.S. population in 2045 (white, 49.7%, Hispanic, 24.6%, Black, 13.1%, Asian, 7.9%, Multiracial, 3.8%).

FIGURE 7.1 ■ Racial Profile of U.S. Population, 2045

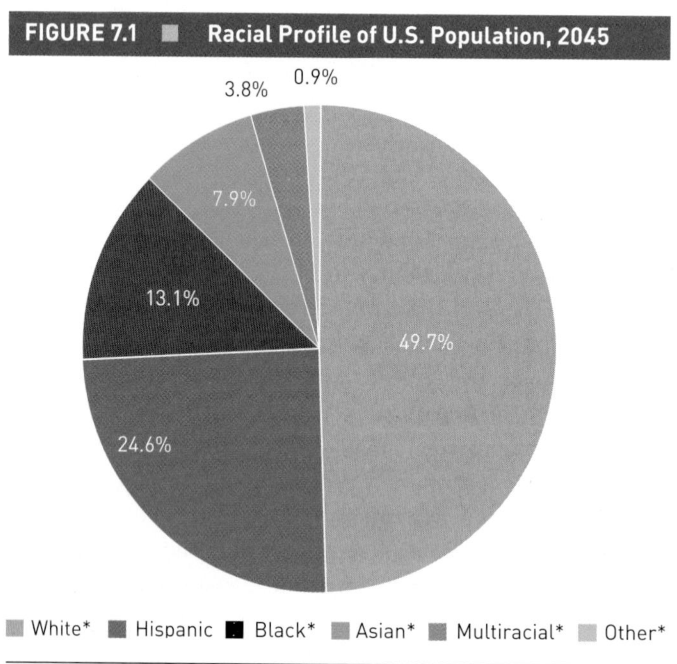

Source: Frey, W. H. (2018, September 10). The US will become "minority white" in 2045, census projects. *The Avenue*. Brookings. https://www.brookings.edu/blog/the-avenue/2018/03/14/the-us-will-become-minority-white-in-2045-census-projects/

Increasingly, racial minorities will become the source of growth in our nation's youth, our working age population, our voters, and much of our consumers and tax base. In a related demographic, by 2030 the U.S. Census Bureau predicts that all baby boomers will be older than age 65; one in every five U.S. residents will be retirement age.[11] As a result, the more rapidly growing, largely white older adults demographic will increasingly rely on racial minority individuals' contributions to the economy and to government programs such as Social Security and Medicare. Unless this upcoming workforce has the high-quality education and skills to provide national, statewide, and local leadership and to earn strong and consistent wages, our body politic may suffer and our social networks may not be able to meet their obligations.

The need to educate fully every one of these young people to high levels has significant implications for the nation's future well-being. When one looks at high school graduation rates by demographic in 2017—African Americans, 77.8%; Latinx, 80%; low-income students, 78.3%; Native American/ Alaska Natives, 72.4%; Asian Americans, 91.2%; whites, 88.6%; and English learners, 66.4%[12]—the challenge for educators is clear.

7.1b A Complex Reality

According to Richard Rothstein, Economic Policy Institute research associate (profiled in Chapter 6), "Policy makers almost universally conclude that these existing and persistent achievement gaps must be the result of wrongly designed school policies—expectations that are too low, teachers who are insufficiently qualified, curricula that are badly designed, classes that are too large, school climates that are too undisciplined, leadership that is too unfocused, or a combination of these factors."[13] In short, many Americans have decided that the achievement gap is the result of "failing schools."

The reality, however, is much more complex. Although certain school perspectives and practices do tend to limit educational opportunities for poor students and students of color in the United States, the larger social class-stratified society, a history of inequality, and even today's courts perpetuate inequities. Nonetheless, each student's personal future, as well as our nation's governance, economy, and security, will increasingly depend on these same underrepresented children we are *not* effectively educating now.

7.2 PUBLIC SCHOOLS AS SOCIALIZING AGENTS

About 400 years ago, when Europeans arrived in the New World with their own language, culture, myths, and ideologies, the land was not empty. Native Americans speaking 300–350 different languages in North America greeted them.[14] Before the Pilgrims stepped off the *Mayflower* onto Plymouth Rock, the Spanish had already settled the Southwest; the French had populated the Mississippi Valley from St. Paul, Minnesota, to New Orleans, Louisiana; and enslaved Africans had arrived in Jamestown, Virginia.

In spite of the cultural diversity already in place, our early political leaders envisioned a country with one unified history, shared mores, and a common language. Indeed, the first colonists' Anglo-Saxon orientation set the stage for the symbolic politics of language and ethnic identity in the United States. A European American tradition was born, and it became the public schools' dominant culture.

From the 1600s to the 1800s, the U.S. frontier's physical and psychological openness allowed varied people to establish their own communities and preserve their Old World customs. Holding on to their ancestral practices and languages gave newcomers a strong and valued sense of who they were, even when living in an unfamiliar country. If those emigrating to their community did not like these customs, they could move on to settle elsewhere.

Throughout U.S. history, schools have served as a powerful agency to socialize ethnic and racial communities to the founders' white Anglo-Saxon, Protestant norms. Developing a common heritage and loyalty to this country, unifying a varied population, preparing students for citizenship in a democratic society, and teaching students to be economically self-sufficient were essential elements in ensuring this country's economic, social, and political survival. Portraying their own Western intellectual, political, historical, and cultural roots positively, public schools' curriculum was seen as a means to make this national unity and prosperity happen.

Although many ethnic group members who immigrated to the United States by choice appreciated the schools helping their children to become Americans, not all ethnic communities welcomed this approach. Many groups did not want to be forced, taught, or encouraged to let go of their own cultural language, beliefs, and traditions. This was especially true for indigenous Native American communities, African Americans brought here against their will, conquered Mexican Americans in 1848, and Puerto Rican communities after the 1898 Spanish American War.[15]

It is easy to see, therefore, how educators and students (along with their families and communities) could make different judgments about the same school practices. Educators acted in ways that they sincerely believed were best for the students and for society as a whole. Meanwhile, those students who were told to leave their cherished family heritages at the schoolhouse door might have experienced their school-led Americanization differently.

To more fully explore the idea of public schools as socializing agents for making all immigrant children into "Americans" with a common civil culture, complete the activity in the **Reflect & Engage** box, Public Schools and Student Diversity.

REFLECT & ENGAGE: PUBLIC SCHOOLS AND STUDENT DIVERSITY

From its earliest days, the United States was a heterogeneous nation. Public schools became socializing agents to assimilate newcomers into a common civic culture.

Separate the class into several small groups (4–6 students) and assign each group one of the following topics (A–C) for them to discuss for about 10 minutes.

A. Explain what "*E Pluribus Unum*" means from an educational and civic perspective.

B. Discuss how the concepts of "the melting pot" and "cultural pluralism" reflect two differing approaches to assimilating immigrants into the American society. Which reflects your own family's experiences? Which do you think is more realistic? Which do you think is better for the country?

C. Describe how the projected racial profile of the United States in 2045 and related demographics will affect public education and the larger society.

D. As a small group, create a mind map that depicts how the melting pot and cultural pluralism ideas relate and differ.

E. Reconvene the entire class and have each group summarize their findings. Discuss these topics as a class.

7.3 SOCIAL CLASS AND CHILDREN'S SKILLS, OUTLOOKS, AND OPPORTUNITIES

Since the 19th century, American schools have increased in number, seeking to impart knowledge and skills to all children regardless of family background, race, class, gender, or national origin. This democratic ideology of providing equal opportunity to each citizen through a free public education has always been a highly motivating and worthy ideal. The question remains, however: To what extent is it actually happening?

7.3a The Relationship Between Social Class and Educational Outcomes

Extensive research concludes that children's social class is one of the most significant predictors of their educational success. Performance gaps by social class begin in children's earliest years, and children who start behind tend to stay behind.[16]

Social class and **socioeconomic status (SES)** are two terms used to distinguish a person's position relative to others within that society. Parental occupation, educational level, income, housing value, and political influence are the basis for determining a student's social class or SES. Socioeconomic level also includes parents' attitudes toward education, their aspirations for their children, and their families' intellectual activities, such as taking cognitively stimulating trips to museums, historical sites, and national parks. Social class position creates a selective perception and set of experiences that shape a person's perspective, behaviors, and life options.

Additionally, social class distinctions tend to determine the quality of schooling students receive, their worldviews, and their relationships to others in society. Although a student's SES is highly associated with academic achievement, factors other than family background also impact student achievement.[17]

Typically, the **upper class** is usually defined as wealthy persons with considerable money, property, and investments. At the level below the upper class, the **middle class** includes professionals, managers, and small-business owners (upper-middle class) as well as technical workers, technicians, sales personnel, and clerical workers (lower-middle class). Generally, the **working class**[18] includes skilled craftsworkers (upper-working class) and unskilled manual and service workers (lower-working class). Skilled workers may either be middle or working class, depending on their education, income, and home neighborhood. **Underclass** refers to a group within the working or lower class. Many of its members are the third or fourth generation living in poverty. They depend on public assistance to maintain a relatively spare existence and tend to live clustered in inner-city slums or in rundown rural areas. After several generations without visible social or economic progress, members of the underclass usually lose hope of improving their economic and social situation.[19]

Social class also influences the degrees of social capital (sometimes called cultural capital) available to students to help them succeed in school. **Social capital** can be understood as the individual's capacity to access scarce resources because of their membership in networks or broader social structures.[20] Studies conclude that parental social capital can facilitate their children's academic achievement.[21] Socioeconomically advantaged upper- and middle-class students may have social or professional ties with community and school leaders that allow them to request—and receive—treatment favorable to their children. Working-class and low-income parents tend not to have these connections.[22] Moreover, relatively affluent adults also bestow human capital on their children: advising on course selection, assisting on homework or science projects, joining the PTA, or calling the principal to request placement in the "best teacher's" classroom. With their conversations and actions, parents with social capital can teach these skills to their children, implicitly or explicitly, who then use it to achieve academic, social, and career success.

On a daily basis, social class differences may be difficult to recognize. Because observers see individuals only in limited situations, the patterns of class differences may not be clearly visible to outsiders. In addition, it is a mistake to generalize based on social class because many variations in attitudes, values, and beliefs exist within each category.

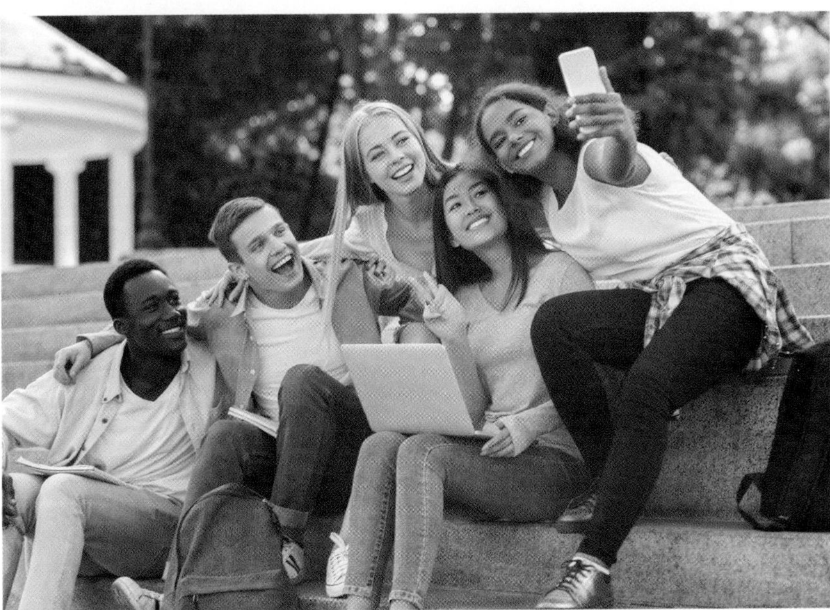

Many students dress to obscure their social class differences.

iStock/Prostock-Studio

7.3b Family Resources and School Success

Family income strongly influences students' educational success and future income in spite of schools' attempts to provide equal opportunity. In general, higher social class status correlates with high levels of education attainment and achievement. A low-income child is roughly twice as likely to be a low academic achiever as a child who is not from a low-income family.[23] From the time they enter kindergarten, students in the bottom quintile of family SES score more than a standard deviation below those in the top quintile on a standardized test of reading and math; and these gaps don't seem to narrow as children progress through the grades.[24] Nobel laureate economist James Heckman observes that the achievement gaps between the advantaged and the disadvantaged appear by age 5, and schooling plays a minor role in creating or perpetuating the gaps. The middle classes fall somewhere in between.[25] In fact, children's **school readiness**—their physical, cognitive, social, and emotional development that enables them to benefit from early formal schooling—to succeed academically typically reflects their parents' SES.

American sociologist Sean Reardon observes that while the relationship between parental education and children's achievement has remained relatively stable over the past half century, the relationship between income and achievement has grown sharply. Because families with plentiful resources can invest relatively more time and financial/social assets in their children's cognitive development than do lower-income families, family income is almost as strong a predictor in children's school achievement as parental education. Families with ample resources can also afford to live near—or pay tuition for their children to attend—well-resourced, high-achieving schools.[26]

It is important to remember that parenting approaches change over time as cultures and eras shift. The real issue is how parenting strategies match up with expectations of schools, the labor market, and other societal demands.

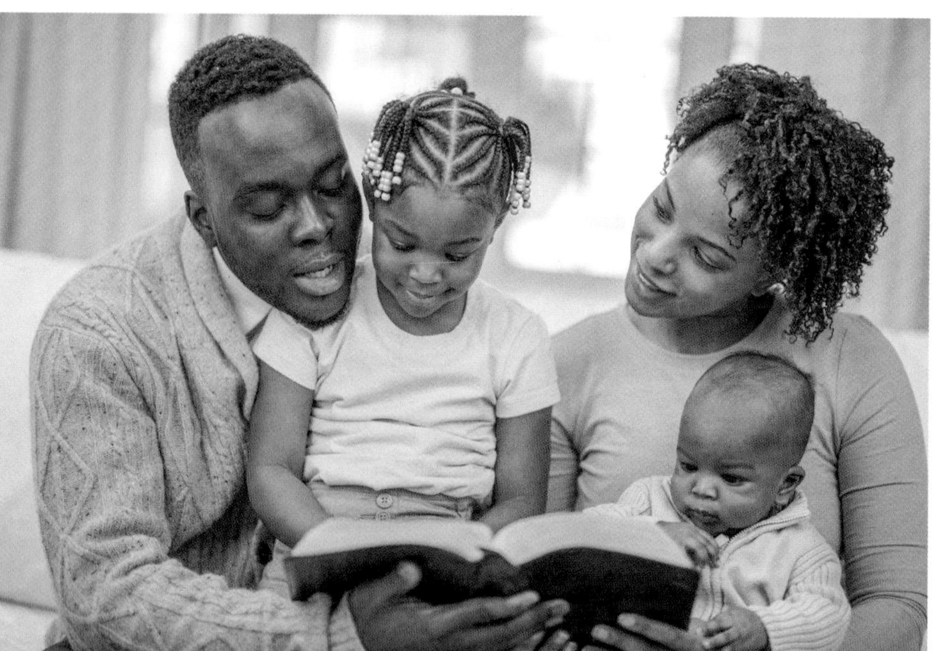

Reading to children prepares them for learning.
iStock/FatCamera

7.3c Equal Opportunity in Schools

Do schools help students achieve equality of opportunity? Or do our schools reproduce and reinforce social class differences—maintaining the achievement gap? To some degree, the answer to each question is yes.

Equality of opportunity means that all members of a society have the same chances to enter any occupation or social class and to compete for any place in society. It does not mean that everyone will have the same income and status. Nor does it mean than everyone will achieve the same outcome. But children receive very different educational opportunities depending on their readiness to attend school and the quality of their schools and teachers.

Unequal Starting Lines

Providing actual equal opportunity requires all persons to start at the same place, as if all were running a race. In this perfect world, all runners would be physically fit and in excellent health. All would arrive wearing first-rate equipment, walk up to the starting line, take their positions, and push off at the starting gun at the same time. During this race, some people would lead, and others would follow. In this equality model, schools would guarantee that either everyone begins on equal terms at the starting line or schools can control the race to ensure that competition remains fair. In the first case, everyone must have an equal education and readiness before they reach the starting block. In the second, everyone must identify and develop their abilities during the race.

Of course, not all American children begin at the same place. The American goal of equal opportunity has been an attempt to balance the equality ideal with the inherently unequal societal reality. Schools contribute to society's stability by promising to be the "great equalizer." Our society believes that getting a good education creates opportunities for students' economic and social advancement and political participation. Over many years and for many students, this is true. For many others, it is not.

In America, some say, "It is better to be born rich than smart."[27] Despite unequal realities, believing that schools give everyone the chance to achieve wealth and power allows people to rationalize that those who fail to reach those goals simply "did not work hard enough" or "did not take advantage" of these opportunities. This reasoning keeps our social system steady by shifting responsibility for the inequality from the institution and society to those without the money, power, or status.

7.4 CONTRADICTORY ROLES OF AMERICAN SCHOOLS

American public schools have roles that often contradict each other. Our public schools are intended to be "the great equalizer," bringing together students from different backgrounds to learn society's shared norms and values that make them educated, loyal, and responsible members of our democratic republic. At the same time, our public schools have traditionally had the responsibility for "sorting and selecting" students into educational paths leading to varying occupations and social status. What initially was intended as a unifying experience for diverse students has become one that increasingly separates them.

7.4a Sorting and Selecting

In colonial times, family economics did the sorting and selecting before students ever reached the common (elementary) school. A family's income and survival needs affected which students entered school and how long they remained. Many children left school to help support their families before finishing their studies. Other children were not allowed to attend. As a result, those who remained in school were already among life's select.

Beginning in the late 19th century, all U.S. children were required to attend school. Using what it considered "scientific," impartial, and professional opinions from teachers (and later from guidance/school counselors and standardized tests), schools classified—sorted and selected—students according to their presumed individual talents or abilities. Educators then placed them into program "tracks" intended to lead to appropriate education for their future occupations and societal roles.

Students determined to have the highest cognitive abilities (approximately 10% of those enrolled) received a rigorous academic education to prepare them for college and the few professional careers that required a respectable fund of knowledge, high-level reasoning, and effective communication skills.

The other 90% of students received a less rigorous academic education appropriate to work at home, farm, and factories. Educators did not need to consider that not all students arrived at the schoolhouse door physically fit, healthy, well fed, properly shoed, fully trained, cognitively nourished, well coached, and ready for the same race.

Because the educational system is inherently tilted to favor middle- and upper-class children (traditionally the only children with the family resources to permit continuous school attendance), their parents believe that schools are doing right by their offspring. By comparison, circumstances of poverty, racial/ethnic minority status, disability, or other factors keep some children from consistently accessing these opportunities for equal outcomes. Consequently, they tend to be consistently underserved in public schools.

7.4b School Quality and Social Mobility

Despite the formidable influence of social class on school success, a high-quality education still can help young people overcome the disadvantages their family background may place on them and propel their upward mobility.[28] The PEW Charitable Trusts and the Economic Mobility Project (2012) found that a 4-year college degree promotes upward mobility from the bottom and prevents downward mobility from the middle and top of the family wealth income and wealth ladders. Having a college degree makes a person more than 3 times more likely to rise from the bottom of the family income ladder to the top. In reverse, PEW found that 39% raised in the middle of the family income ladder who do not earn a college degree fall from the middle, compared with 22% of those with a degree.[29]

Of course, getting into and through college depends on receiving a high-quality preK–12 education. Studies find a strong link between school quality and opportunities available later in life. Poor school quality can lead to a variety of economic and social ills: The lower the school quality, the higher the dropout rate and increase in teen pregnancies (which limit upward mobility).[30] Studies also find that factors linked with upward mobility include geographic regions with higher-quality K–12 schools,[31] along with less residential segregation, less income inequality, greater social capital, and greater family stability (fewer single-parent families).[32] The study was correlational, not causal.

Of course, high-quality schools by themselves cannot propel students' social and economic mobility. Additional out-of-school factors—such as parental income and education, their social capital, family stability, health care, and the local labor market, along with other influences—also play major roles. Given these realities, a high-quality education may be a *necessary* but not *sufficient* condition to advance low-income students' social and economic mobility.

To more fully explore the relationships among public schools, children's family cultures, and social mobility, complete the activity in the **Reflect & Engage** box, Children's SES and Educational Outcomes.

REFLECT & ENGAGE: CHILDREN'S SES AND EDUCATIONAL OUTCOMES

Although America's public schools aspire to be the "great equalizers" that give children from varied backgrounds the opportunity for social mobility, children's social class has always played a major role in shaping their educational outcomes. Individually and as a class, complete the following:

A. Individually, create a mind map of the relationship between social class and students' educational outcomes. Draw a circle around every item that reflects a child's social capital. Share in small groups.

B. As a class, explain how parents' social capital affects their children's educational outcomes. Describe how your parents' social capital influenced you.

C. As a small group, draw a cartoon or graphic image using a digital tool such as Piktochart that explains why "equality of opportunity" in public schools is difficult to accomplish.

D. Describe the relationship between school quality and social mobility.

E. Have the class break into three groups to debate the question: "Yes, no, or sometimes: Are public schools the great equalizers? And, if so, when?"

7.5 POVERTY AND EDUCATION

Despite its flaws, public education is the engine of social mobility. Yet in reality, the achievement gap begins well before kindergarten. Profound risk factors in many children's early life may greatly compromise their future school attainment. As the risk factor that intensifies all other risk factors,[33] poverty places children at a tremendous educational disadvantage.

The federal government considers a family of four "poor" when their annual income falls below $26,200.[34] The Children's Defense Fund finds the U.S. child poverty rate in 2018 was 16%, representing nearly 11.9 million children living in poverty; [35] the average U.S. student poverty rate was 52.1%.[36] More than half the students in U.S. classrooms are considered to be poor. And even though poverty is a worldwide phenomenon, the United States has one of the highest child poverty rates in the industrialized world. According to the World Economic Forum, only five prosperous nations had higher child poverty rates than the United States.[37]

Poverty limits children's opportunities to learn.

Poverty published August 12, 2011, by Bill Day, politicalcartoons.com. Reproduced with permission.

7.5a Poverty, Cognitive Development, and School Success

As discussed, a family's socioeconomic status, its accompanying lifestyle, and available resources for early learning—not race or ethnicity—are strongly related to children's cognitive skills. Generally, the more years a child lives in poverty, the lower his or her academic achievement relative to other age peers, with deficits in verbal, mathematical, and reading skills that may be 2 to 3 times larger than that of higher-SES children.[38] This cognitive deficit has many causes, including lower birthweight, early childhood learning differences, language differences, and housing instability. Let's look at each.

Low Birth Weight

About one in every 12 babies in the United States (8%) is born with **low birth weight** (that is, less than 5 lbs. 8 oz.). Low birth weight babies tend to come from mothers in poor health or from lower-SES women (who may have poor pregnancy nutrition, inadequate prenatal care, and pregnancy complications).[39] Premature and low birth weight infants may experience disruptions in their normal brain development, resulting in impaired cognitive growth.[40] Experiences during a child's first 3 years—including 9 months in the womb and the next 12 months as a baby—are when specialized brain cells are forming connections with each other, creating the neural networks that make thinking, learning, and feeling possible.

Fewer Early Childhood Learning Experiences

As discussed, lower-SES children tend to have fewer childhood academic learning experiences before enrolling in kindergarten than children from higher-SES families.[41] Studies find that children in lower-SES quintiles often had younger mothers, less frequent parent reading, fewer books at home, less computer use, lower preschool attendance, and lower parental expectations that children would earn a college degree.[42]

Early Language Differences

Language differences (fluency, elaboration, verbal exchanges with children) from interacting between higher- and lower-SES mothers also impact children's cognitive development, and these differences appear by 18 months of age.[43] By age 5, on some measures, low-SES children score more than 2 years behind on standardized language development tests by the time they enter school.[44] The results can be weaker language, memory, and self-regulation skills than their more affluent peers.

7.5b Poverty and Chronic Health Concerns

The relationship between SES and health is strong and well documented.[45] Children growing up in poverty tend to have more health concerns than children growing up in affluence. This relationship is reciprocal: Poverty makes it more difficult to stay healthy, while poor health detracts from the educational and employment paths to economic and social mobility.[46] In addition, studies affirm that children who do not live in safe, quality housing—whether due to health hazards (such as lead in paint or toxins in drinking water), housing instability (including homelessness), lack of enough nutritious food,[47] or for other reasons—experience high rates of physical, mental, and emotional problems.[48]

Toxic stress—the term for hormonal changes that happen in response to severely or repeated frightening or threatening events or conditions (e.g., growing up in unsafe and unstable environments)—can also disrupt children's behavior, cognitive capacity, and emotional and physical health.[49] Living in communities where rampant gun violence and death may occur at any time of day or night can undermine anyone's sense of safety and ability to focus on learning. Cognitive and neuroscience studies show traumatic stress interferes with memory and attention, good health, and emotional stability, interfering with students' ability to perform well academically, cognitively, and behaviorally.[50]

Ill and ailing children often miss school. In fact, at any grade, children experiencing any risk factor were more often **chronic absentees**—missing 10% or more of the school year—than children without these family risk factors.[51] Absenteeism becomes problematic as early as preschool and kindergarten.[52] Chronic absenteeism occurs at rates 3 to 4 times higher in high-poverty areas.[53] Outcomes from this poor school attendance include lower achievement in reading and math, grade retention, academic failure, more behavioral issues, lower high school graduation rates, increased achievement gaps, and involvement with the juvenile justice system.[54] Because students raised in poverty benefit the most from being in school, their high level of absences seriously undermines their academic progress and future economic well-being.

Any—or all—of these may interfere with school attendance, consistent learning, and school success. Of course, many children in poverty grow up to show resilience, high levels of social and behavioral health, and strong academic performance. This is especially true when caring, reliable adults safeguard them from chronic stressors. Chapter 8 discusses children's resilience in more detail.

7.5c Poverty and Housing Instability

Child Trends reports that children in poor families (with incomes below the federal poverty line [FPL]) were more than 4 times as likely to have experienced five or more moves as were children in families with incomes twice or more than the FPL (5.5% and 1.2%, respectively).[55] With rising housing costs (rents and utilities), stagnant or declining wages among the poor, and a shortage of federal housing assistance, most poor renting families spend over half (52%) their income to housing costs, up from 42% in 1991. As a result, eviction among low-income communities has become a common reality.[56]

Children's housing instability, especially with multiple moves, is associated with a lower school engagement, higher rates of absenteeism, lower grades in reading and math, a higher risk of dropping out of high school,[57] and lower standardized test performance.[58] Every time children change schools, they generally lose about 3 months growth in reading and math.[59] Mobility is especially difficult for children in the early grades whose physiological, cognitive, and affective domains are developing rapidly. Additionally, older children and teens who frequently change schools have difficulties bonding with teachers and must adjust to new classmates and curriculum, disadvantaging them socially and academically. And the negative effects increase with each additional move.[60] The lack of consistent attendance means they miss opportunities to learn the foundational skills essential for school and life success.

Although the ways that poverty may undermine children's success in schools do not end here, poverty is not destiny. Rather, it is a complex economic and social condition. Therefore, it is not accurate to assume that all low-SES children will perform poorly in school. Nonetheless, children from low-SES backgrounds may need additional academic and time supports, along with ongoing educator and family encouragement and high expectations, to move through the grades successfully.

7.6 SEGREGATION, EDUCATION, AND THE ACHIEVEMENT/OPPORTUNITY GAP

Although the landmark 1954 *Brown v. Board of Education* decision ruled against the "separate but equal" education of poor students and students of color, courts in the 1990s began releasing school districts from 1970s desegregation orders. Today, school segregation (and re-segregation) on the basis of socioeconomic status, race, and ethnicity is widespread and increasing. Court-ordered desegregation may soon be a memory. This is a concern because current figures show that 51% of public school students attend schools where a majority of their classmates qualify as poor or low-income under federal guidelines; and nationally, about 75% of both African American and Latinx students attend majority low-income schools (as compared with about 33% of white students attending such economically disadvantaged schools).[61] And since the 1980s, high-quality studies clearly and consistently find that schools' racial and SES composition influences student outcomes, both short and long term.[62]

7.6a Residential Segregation by Race, Class, and Income

People tend to live in neighborhoods with others like themselves, residentially segregated by several common dimensions, including age, SES, race, and ethnicity. Scholars have extensively documented housing discrimination practices against African Americans, and, to a lesser extent, Hispanics, largely shaping where people live.[63] Whatever the causes, income segregation creates very high-income and very low-income school districts, and on average, white families can better afford to live in affluent districts than can Black families.[64] These housing patterns make it more difficult to provide racially integrated schools.

Because neighborhood conditions appear to impact children's cognitive development and long-term educational outcome,[65] residential segregation may lead to achievement gaps if it means that children of different races systematically live in higher- or lower-wealth neighborhoods. Neighborhood and school segregation may each contribute independently to academic achievement gaps.[66]

Apart from housing, school districts sometimes find ingenious ways to promote policies and practices that create segregated schools. They manipulate school attendance zones, establish school sites in predominantly underserved or white neighborhoods, and develop neighborhood school policies. More recently, affluent and mostly white communities are splitting off from larger school districts to form their own, smaller, less economically diverse school districts.[67] All of these practices serve to create racially and ethnically segregated schools, a discriminatory practice that courts have found unlawful.[68]

7.6b Segregated Schools and Student Outcomes

Across the country, white, Black, and Latinx students are highly segregated between schools and school districts. On average, white students attend a school in which 69% of the students are white, Latinx students attend a school in which 55% of the students are Latinx, and Black students attend schools that average 47% Black or a combined Black and Latinx enrollment, averaging 67%.[69]

The research consensus is clear: A school's racial and SES composition is strongly related to student outcomes.[70] Although these findings are correlational rather than causal in nature, they suggest that any effects of racial segregation on student achievement patterns are at least partly the result of factors associated with the students' SES—for instance, instructional focus and quality, parental social/economic capital, social norms, material resources, and peer effects—rather than their racial composition, as such.[71] In fact, studies find the disparity in average school poverty rates between white and Black students' schools is consistently the single-most powerful correlate of achievement gaps: Poverty, not race, drives the achievement gap.[72] Achievement gaps are more highly linked with school segregation than residential segregation.[73] This finding suggests that students' exposure to poverty—as a proxy for general school quality of curriculum, instruction, and opportunities to learn—contributes most to the achievement gap. By comparison, research is mixed on whether segregated schools and neighborhoods have a minimal[74]—or beneficial—impact[75] on affluent students' academic achievement.

Research also finds that school segregation has additional negative individual and social outcomes, including increased student exposure to the criminal justice system,[76] worsened educational and professional outcomes,[77] a lowered ability to live and work in diverse environments,[78] and more racially prejudiced views later in life.[79] Racial isolation from attending segregated schools also tends to deprive children of color from developing "networks of opportunity," the social capital connections many people rely on to get a job or get into college.

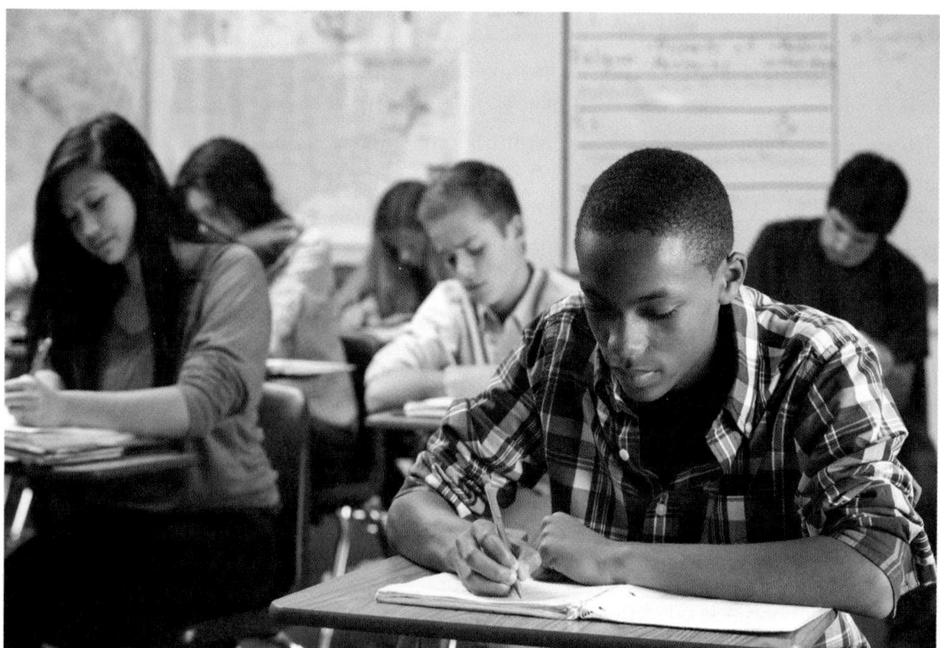

Students tend to struggle academically in high-poverty schools.

iStock/monkeybusinessimages

7.6c Integrated Schools and Student Outcomes

A growing body of social science research agrees that students attending socioeconomically and racially integrated schools tend to benefit academically, economically, and socially. Students in integrated schools have higher average achievement,[80] are more likely to graduate from high school,[81] and are more likely to enter and graduate from college.[82] Integrated schools also help reduce racial achievement gaps[83] as teachers encourage deeper learning, critical thinking, problem-solving, and creativity.[84] And integrated schools are likely to give students more equal access to essential resources, such as better school facilities, highly qualified and effective teachers, rigorous courses, private and public funding, and social and cultural capital.[85]

The positive outcomes of attending integrated schools extend well beyond high school. Students who attend integrated schools have higher occupational and income attainment,[86] as well as reduced individual levels of racial and ethnic prejudice[87] and better adult health and wellness.[88] Since integrated schools encourage friendships across group lines, students who attend them are more likely to seek out integrated settings later in life.[89] Studies have identified additional civic, social–emotional, and economic benefits.[90] What is more, these benefits are intergenerational, extending from grandparents who attended desegregated schools to their own children and grandchildren.[91] Although middle-class white youths experience benefits from student diversity in their classrooms, low-income and disadvantaged students appear to gain the most.[92]

Many reasons explain why all learners—middle- and upper-class children included—are likely to benefit from attending integrated rather than racially and SES segregated schools. These tend to include more experienced and highly qualified teachers and school leaders,[93] who are less likely to transfer to other (more challenging) schools;[94] more stable student populations;[95] school climates more supportive of learning and studying;[96] more parent involvement; [97] and more high-quality, consistent teacher resources.[98] In addition, researchers have affirmed that students' exposure to other students who differ from themselves and the new ideas and complexities that these interactions bring lead to improved cognitive skills, including critical thinking, creativity, and problem-solving, plus an increased understanding and respect for others.[99] Research strongly suggests that integrated schools can foster a greater belief in democratic values, build a community's civic capacity, and serve as building blocks for greater social cohesion in a multiethnic, fair, democratic society.

To more fully explore how poverty can undermine children's school success—and what good schools can do to help struggling students achieve well—complete the activity in the **Reflect & Engage** box, Poverty, Segregation, and Educational Outcomes.

REFLECT & ENGAGE: POVERTY, SEGREGATION, AND EDUCATIONAL OUTCOMES

The activity involves a role play. When it comes to education, poverty is the risk factor that exacerbates all other risk factors, and school integration has beneficial short- and long-term student outcomes. Separate the class into groups of four, each group representing three future teachers of varied subjects and one parent. Divide the groups into Groups A and Groups B and provide them with the following scenario:

> Your principal knows you are caring, effective, and highly regarded teachers and informal leaders in your high-poverty school. For a variety of reasons, many of your students are having serious academic difficulties. Your school has an activity bus to take children home 1 hour after the regular afternoon dismissal 3 days a week, but it is rarely full. Your district also has many schools that tend to be poorly integrated.

A. Groups A and B: Using the information in this section, develop a rationale for why your school should provide extra time for academic and social support to failing and struggling students. What forms would this extra help take? Include suggestions about how to identify eligible students, how to make it an attractive activity that they would be pleased to join, how to staff it, and how to involve parents. What incentives (apart from a stipend) might attract teachers to participate?

B. Reassemble as a class and have each group present a 5-minute rationale for additional support for students having academic difficulty, with practical suggestions for how to make it work.

C. As a class, identify and discuss what you see as the five top issues involved with educating high-poverty students and how schools and communities might successfully address their learning needs.

7.7 SCHOOL PRACTICES THAT CONTRIBUTE TO THE ACHIEVEMENT/OPPORTUNITY GAP

Although societal factors such as social class, family income, and residential and school segregation affect students' preparation for learning and their eventual academic achievement, school practices also influence whether all students' learning opportunities are truly equal. Teacher expectations and their instructional effectiveness, tracking, curriculum rigor, grade retention, disciplinary practices, and school/instructional climate all have tremendous impacts on students and their future educational, employment, social, and lifestyle opportunities.

7.7a Teacher Expectations

Teachers' beliefs about which students are likely or unlikely to succeed in school significantly influence how they teach diverse children. The following studies support this theory.

Hawthorne Studies

The classic Hawthorne studies illustrate how expectation affects performance. From 1927 to 1932, researchers at Western Electric's Hawthorne Plant in Cicero, Illinois, examined the workplace's physical and environmental influences (such as brightness of lights and humidity) and its psychological aspects (such as work breaks, group pressure, working hours, and managerial leadership). No matter which experimental manipulation the investigators used, the workers' production improved. Researchers determined that the workers enjoyed receiving the researchers' attention, also known as the "novelty effect."[100]

Their conclusions have implications for educators. The classroom is a powerful social network, and students' feelings about both their teachers and their classmates have important implications for how hard and how much they are willing to work and succeed at learning.

"Pygmalion in the Classroom"

In Greek mythology, Pygmalion was a king and sculptor who created a statue of a woman, fell in love with it, and through his love, brought the statue to life. In their 1965 article, "Pygmalion in the Classroom," Robert Rosenthal and Lenore Jacobson, a Harvard University professor and an elementary principal, respectively, describe how they told elementary school teachers that based on their students' standardized test scores, certain children were "late bloomers" and could be expected to be "growth spurters." In truth, the test did not exist, and children designated as "spurters" were chosen randomly. Rosenthal and Jacobson hoped this experiment would determine the degree (if any) to which changes in teacher expectations can produce changes in student achievement. In the end, the researchers found that when teachers expect students to do well, students tend to do well; when teachers expect students to fail, they tend to fail.[101]

Coleman Study

Teacher expectations for students' achievement may have played a large role in the landmark Coleman Study (1966). Coleman's teacher survey data suggested that achievement gaps between African American and white students in the same school were higher where most of the teachers had expressed preference for teaching college-oriented children of white-collar professionals.[102] They expected less achievement from their underrepresented and low-income students, and—in a self-fulfilling prophecy—they got it.

Oakes Study on Teachers' Expectations for Students' Futures

Jeannie Oakes, a University of California at Los Angeles education professor, found evidence suggesting that teachers (consciously or unconsciously) treat bright students as future peers and less bright students as future subordinates.[103] When asked to list the five most important lessons to be learned by high school students, teachers' list for the bright students differed markedly from their list for the rest of the student population. Teachers hoped the brightest would learn to think logically and critically (important skills for future leaders). Meanwhile, they hoped that the less bright would learn good work habits, respect for authority, and practical or work-related skills (all important attributes for future subordinates).

Growth Mindset

Growth mindset is the belief that intelligence is not fixed and one's brain is capable of change—with dedicated effort, trying new strategies, asking for help when needed, and persistence—when faced with challenges. A relevant metaphor conveys its meaning: The brain is like a muscle that grows stronger and smarter when it exercises with rigorous learning experience.

A 2019 national study of nearly 12,000 ninth graders in urban, suburban, and rural public high schools found that giving students an opportunity—even briefly—to understand and reflect on their mindsets for learning can make them more likely to take on more difficult academic tasks and improve.[104] Notably, participating low-performing students developed the mindset that skills are developed over time and through effort rather than being innate and "fixed." By the end of the year, putting in their best efforts, the students had earned higher grade point averages in core academic classes, especially in math and science, and were more likely to enroll in advanced or honors math courses in 10th grade than peers in the control group. Similarly, high-achieving students with the growth mindset, already earning top grades, were more willing to enroll in more demanding courses. This is meaningful because the difficulty of math courses taken in high school strongly predicts later educational attainment,[105] which itself is a leading predictor of longevity and health.[106]

7.7b Preparation to Teach Diverse Students

American public schools have had a difficult time providing highly effective teachers for students of color. Part of this reflects the high teacher turnover in high-poverty schools.[107] But most teachers say they feel prepared to teach diverse students. A recent RAND study of nationally representative educators found that 68% of teachers "somewhat" or "strongly" agree that their preparation programs left them feeling prepared to work with Black, Latinx, and low-income students.[108] That means that more than 30% of teachers say they felt *unprepared* to teach diverse students.

Schools of education and teacher preparation programs have the challenge of introducing teacher candidates to varied perspectives and experiences. Coursework must confront teacher candidates' "naïve optimism," "unexamined stereotypes," and unconscious biases.[109] For instance, many teachers mistakenly believe that the poorer the community, the more "dysfunctional" its culture and that its values conflict with those taught in schools. These mistaken views can become problematic because the "cultural mismatch" between the largely white (80%) public school teachers and the 51% of public school enrollment who are students of color can shape the effectiveness of the instruction that they receive. These factors further reinforce preK–12 schools' inequities.[110]

To meet this challenge, successful teacher preparation programs continually update their curricula to include varied voices and perspectives, teach effective methods of instruction and classroom management, and build strong ties to underserved communities so they may provide authentic preservice practicum field experiences in settings where their graduates eventually will work. It is essential that all teachers develop their awareness, knowledge, and skills in working with others who differ from themselves and learn cultural competence—and value diversity as an asset that deepens everyone's learning. Chapter 8 will discuss "culturally competent" pedagogy and related issues.

7.7c Tracking and Restricted Curricula

Since the 1920s, most schools enrolling adolescents have offered a *"tracked" curriculum*—a sequence of academic classes that range from slow-paced remedial courses to intellectually demanding academic ones—along with an array of electives, exploratory, vocational, and physical education classes. Tracking can be defined as rigidly sorting students into homogeneous groups according to their perceived abilities, past academic achievements, presumed educational needs, and expected vocational directions and keeping students in these placements throughout their schooling. Tracks can be identified by ability (high, average, or low) or by the kind of educational preparation they provide (academic, general, vocational). Tracking and students' SES are related. Research suggests that factors including students' academic preparedness and ability,[111] their access to resources (i.e., family assets, access to test prep, and social capital),[112] and teachers' unconscious biases[113] all play roles in identifying students for different academic tracks.

Curriculum Tracking

Curriculum tracking offers different learning opportunities to different student groups. Typically, higher-track classes offer a more cognitively challenging and extended academic curriculum linked with higher-quality instructional practices than do low-track classes.[114] This practice has been shown to have negative consequences for the future educational opportunities and schooling outcomes of children placed in the lower tracks, especially for low-income, African American, and Latinx children.[115] Since curriculum tracking provides the basis for organizing schools, integrated schools may become segregated once students enter their classrooms.

Tracking Versus Ability Grouping

Tracking differs from ability grouping in important ways. Whereas almost all tracking is a form of ability grouping, not all ability grouping results in tracking. Generally speaking, tracking is rigidly determined. Once placed into a "track," the student tends to stay in it. In contrast, **ability grouping**, which also separates students into homogeneous groups according to perceived abilities, past academic achievements, and presumed educational needs, tends to be more flexible and related to the purpose of study. Students can change ability groups for different subjects or learning purposes by the day, week, or project. The FlipSides feature asks readers to consider this issue in more detail.

Opportunities, Effort, and Ability

Some argue that differences in student achievement can be explained by three factors: learning opportunities, effort, and ability.[116] Tracking removes many learning opportunities.[117] Research strongly suggests that students in higher tracks and ability groups tend to learn more content at more rigorous cognitive levels than do comparable students in lower tracks and ability groups.[118] Not surprisingly, studies find that students in higher tracks expend substantially more **effort**—the amount of time and energy that students spend in meeting teachers' or schools' formal academic requirements (such as completing homework, attending school, coming to class prepared)—than do students in lower tracks.[119] If **ability** is having the means or skill to do something, it stands to reason that lack of learning opportunity and lack of effort will lead to lack of ability (although this has been argued in reverse as a rationale to keep "low-achieving" [presumed low-ability] students out of high-challenge courses). Students' beliefs in their own chances of academic success—and their perceptions of what their teachers expect of them—likely contribute to their effort in school.[120] A self-fulfilling prophesy may begin, reinforced with each successive course.

FLIPSIDES

Should Ability Grouping or Open Access Be the Way to Place Students Into High-Status Courses?

Teachers have long argued about how best to group students for instruction. Should students' ability and achievement or their interest and willingness to work hard be the criteria for their enrollment in rigorous courses? Which approach do you think is best for student learning and meeting long-term goals?

Group students for instruction according to their abilities, prior achievement, and career goals.	Group students for instruction according to their interests, goals, and willingness to work hard to learn.
• Placing students into courses based on their prior school achievement, achievement test results, and discipline records is an objective and reliable way to organize students for learning.	• Placing students into courses based on prior school achievement, achievement test results, and discipline records is unfair and ineffective. Report card grades are highly subjective, achievement tests may be culturally biased, and weak students are capable of maturing and improving.
• Grouping students by ability and goals reinforces a meritocracy in which all students with ability and drive can get a world-class education.	• Grouping students by ability and goals disproportionately excludes African Americans, Latinx, and students with disabilities from opportunities to learn in high-track, college preparatory classes. Tracking is neither equitable nor effective.
• Grouping students for instruction by ability or test results allows teachers to make the content and learning activities challenging and relevant for each student.	• Grouping students for instruction based on ability or test results is unfair to those who lack extensive opportunities outside school to learn; limits access to experienced, effective teachers; harms achievement; and prevents enrollment in courses needed for college and careers.
• Grouping students by ability and career goals gives them the curriculum that will prepare them for their future vocations.	• Grouping students by ability and career goals is unrealistic and unfair because students' vocational goals change with experiences, maturity, and successes.
• Grouping students for instruction by ability gives teachers a manageable range of student abilities in the classroom. "Teaching to the middle" hinders learning for the highest and lowest achievers.	• Teachers can and should learn how to teach a high-status content effectively to a wide range of student abilities through differentiated instructional practices and additional support when needed. Access to high-status courses "with a future" is a student's civil right.
• Students who plan to go to work immediately after high school do not need to learn the same 21st century knowledge and skills as those going to college.	• Every student today needs to have the same 21st century high-level knowledge and skills as those going to college because most well-paying noncollege jobs also require these skills.
• To allow weak students to enroll in college preparatory courses would be setting the students up for failure.	• Many nontraditional students can succeed in college preparatory classes if they are motivated to work hard, if they have parents'/guardians' support, and if the teacher provides extra learning time and help.
• Students will be uncomfortable in classrooms with students who are unlike themselves and who have different cultural backgrounds and life goals.	• Students become comfortable when they get to know unfamiliar students as competent, likable, motivated individuals who are both different and like themselves. Tracking segregates and negatively polarizes peer group attitudes about others unlike themselves.

7.7d Lower Teacher Quality

Research consistently affirms the relationship between teacher quality factors and student achievement.[121] Briefly, these "quality" factors include teachers' academic skills and knowledge (especially their vocabulary), their mastery of the content they teach, their experience on the job throughout their careers (steepest improvements occur between their second and fifth years), their teaching effectiveness (pedagogy), and the interaction among these factors.[122]

Decades of research have documented that teacher quality is inequitably distributed. Large and persistent gaps in teacher quality exist between advantaged and disadvantaged students.[123]Typically, lower-quality teachers—as evidenced by fewer years of teaching experience, degree level, certification, and college attendance—are more likely to teach in schools with low-performing students.[124] One study from California and New York found that districts serving the highest proportions of underrepresented and low-income students tended to have twice as many uncredentialled and inexperienced teachers as do their more affluent peers.[125] Similarly, an analysis from the 2015 NAEP assessment finds that teachers whose students scored low in NAEP reading, math, and science reported being less likely to ask their classes to engage in higher-order thinking or offer them advanced academic work than teachers whose students scored high.[126] Teacher quality appears in their expectations, curriculum, and related instructional practices for different students' learning and achievement.

Since studies confirm that consistently working with highly effective teachers can overcome the academic limitations placed on students by their family backgrounds,[127] when teacher quality varies across schools and districts in ways that systematically disadvantage poor, low-achieving, and racially isolated schools, it becomes an equity issue.[128]

7.7e Grade Retention

For decades, educators and policy makers have debated whether struggling students would benefit more from repeating a grade or by moving ahead with their same-aged peers. Retention proponents argue that students who had not met grade-level criteria would fall further behind if they moved ahead via so-called "**social promotion**"—when struggling students are advanced to the next grade with their same-age peers despite not having mastered the grade-level expectations. In their view, allowing children more time to develop adequate academic skills would make them more successful in later grades.

But by 1954, research evidence concurred that students retained in grade did not made educational gains, and investigators since then agree.[129] As compared with retained students, promoted struggling students had higher-achievement growth, fewer referrals to special education, were less likely to drop out of school, and had better personal and social adjustment[130] than their retained peers. Nonetheless, the grade retention practice continues.

Because retention rates vary across locales, no systematic, reliable, and well-validated means currently exists to quantify exact grade level retention rates; but several investigators are trying to improve this methodology. A 2014 report found about 4.2% of all students were retained; grade retention was highest in first (6.2%) and ninth (2.9%) grades; higher among boys than girls (especially in later grades); highest among African American and Latinx children; and higher among children of less educated parents and among children born outside of the United States.[131] Likewise, in 2018 Child Trends, a nonprofit, nonpartisan research group that focuses exclusively on improving children's lives, found that children living in homes with incomes at or below the federal poverty level were more likely to repeat a grade (8%) than classmates in households with higher incomes (3%).[132] Between 2000 and 2016, the percentage of students retained in grade decreased from 3.1% to 1.9%, a pattern observed among white, Black, and Hispanic students, although a higher percentage of Black than white students were retained. The percentage of white (1.7%) and Latinx (1.9%) students were not measurably different.[133]

7.7f Disciplinary Practices

Typically, schools' disciplinary policies and practices offer a prescribed response to disturbing student behaviors—such as verbal disrespect, physical fighting, or other disruptive conduct—that make teaching and learning difficult. But even as educators view schools' prevailing disciplinary practices as fair, objective, unbiased, and race neutral, research is increasingly finding that disciplinary practices are culturally loaded.[134] Most school district discipline codes leave ample room for "professional judgment," allowing teachers' conscious or unconscious beliefs about their students to influence their discipline decisions.

A large amount of national and state data show that punitive, exclusionary discipline practices have a disproportionate and growing impact on African American students who are differentially selected for discipline referrals.[135] In 2015–2016, African American males made up 25% of all students suspended out of school at least once, and African American females accounted for another 14%, even though they each only represented 8% of all students.[136] Black students make up nearly one third of all students arrested at school or referred to law enforcement.[137] Student with disabilities also continue to be disciplined at higher rates than their abled peers.[138]

School discipline policies may inadvertently encourage discrimination. The schools' tendency to interpret all conflict as a threat to the institution's stability encourages educators to oversimplify conflict. Thus, teachers and administrators believe that any classroom disruption should be swiftly and efficiently ended. Vaguely worded rules against "defiance" leave much to teacher discretion. Educators tend to view behaviors that clash with the operating norms as aberrant and deserving punishment. In this way, they fail to notice problems and inequities that their organizations are creating, such as the disproportionately high suspension rates of racially and ethnically minority students, their overrepresentation in low-track classes, or the relationship between these facts. In disciplining students, educators often punish the symptom rather than address the cause.

This disproportionate discipline of children who are underserved or who have disabilities—the cycle of misbehavior, disciplinary action, and removal from the classrooms—may contribute to the achievement gap. In fact, one large study of student records determined that school suspensions account for approximately one fifth of the Black–white gap in school performance.[139] A suspended student may miss from one period to 10 or more school days, depending on the violation and school policies. This results in lost opportunities to learn. According to 2014 research from Johns Hopkins University, being suspended even once in ninth grade appears to double the possibility of dropping out, from 16% for students not suspended to 32% for those suspended even once. What is more, disciplinary incidents are related to other indicators of student detachment from school: course failures and absenteeism.[140] Because student suspensions appear related to their academic engagement and success, addressing the disparity in disciplinary practices is an essential part of closing the achievement/opportunity gap.

Although it is true that all students must be held accountable for their behaviors, it is equally true that teachers should be held accountable for their classroom management skills and the learning climate and supports they provide that enable every student to succeed. Both teachers and student can learn to do better. Studies find that when teachers adopt an empathic (rather than punitive) mindset, learn to value students' perspectives, and sustain positive relationships with their students while encouraging better behavior, their suspensions rates dropped by half, especially for at-risk underserved students with prior suspensions.[141] As one investigator observed, "Changing the mindset of one teacher can change the social experience of that child's entire world."[142]

7.7g School and Instructional/Classroom Climate

Both academic and disciplinary practices affect school climate. **School climate** refers to the physical, intellectual, psychological, and social environment in which teachers' and students' behaviors occur within schools. School climate is the school's "feel" at the building and classroom levels. Some schools "feel" positive, encouraging, high achieving, and respectful of all its members; others do not. **Instructional or classroom climate** refers to the teaching, behavioral, and personal aspects of the classroom experience that can propel or hinder student learning.

School and instructional/classroom climate are multidimensional constructs. Teaching practices, student and faculty diversity, and the relationships among administrators, teachers, parents, and students all contribute to their formation. The number and quality of teacher–student interactions, students' and teachers' perceptions of the school's personality, environmental factors (such as the facility's or classroom's attractiveness, cleanliness, and state of repair), the academic performance expected and received from all students, the school's size and feeling of safety, and the feelings of mutual trust and respect among students and teachers all come into play. In total or viewed separately, these factors can have a positive influence on the learning environment—or they can create significant barriers to learning.

For example, tracking, retention, and disproportionate discipline affect school and instructional climates. They can adversely influence the relationships among different groups within the schools, isolating students along cognitive, cultural, racial, and economic lines.[143] When the lower-track seats are overwhelmingly occupied by low-income and students of color at the same time as white, Asian American, and middle-class or affluent students predominantly fill the upper-track classrooms, the different student groups do not have opportunities to move beyond stereotypes and get to know one another as persons. Separated daily by high- and low-status courses, teachers' behaviors toward them, and their relative expectations for success and "appropriate" behavior, students in the disparate groups tend to make uninformed judgments about one another. As a consequence, distrust and disrespect grow.[144]

A safe and supportive school environment fosters student learning.

iStock/monkeybusinessimages

Ineffective school practices, antisocial behaviors, and academic failure reinforce one another. The school's psychosocial climate—in the halls, classroom, cafeteria, gym, and anywhere on campus—becomes negative. A pattern of academic failure provides few opportunities for the student to receive positive affirmation. Students perceived as being at risk of antisocial conduct, particularly males and students of color, are more likely to be punished and excluded from school. From the failing student's perspective, school becomes a bad, unfair place. No students want to anxiously sense that they are in danger, whether physically or psychologically. In such conditions, students cannot learn. Further, when they perceive a threat, students react quickly, often disruptively. The cycle of bad grades and low expectations (perceived as disrespect toward the student) leads to disorderly student behaviors, suspensions from school, lost learning opportunities, further failure, and eventual dropping out. By comparison, the greater the school's academic quality and more positive its emotional climate, the lower the level of school crime and violence. And the more the students learn. Ample research supports these observations.[145]

7.8 SCHOOL FACTORS THAT MAY REDUCE THE ACHIEVEMENT/OPPORTUNITY GAP

We have discussed an array of factors that create a negative school climate, which in turn hurt students' learning opportunities, attitudes, behaviors, and achievement. Now, we will consider several factors that enhance school and classroom climate, increase students' opportunities to learn, and reduce the achievement gap.

7.8a Early Childhood Education and Student Achievement

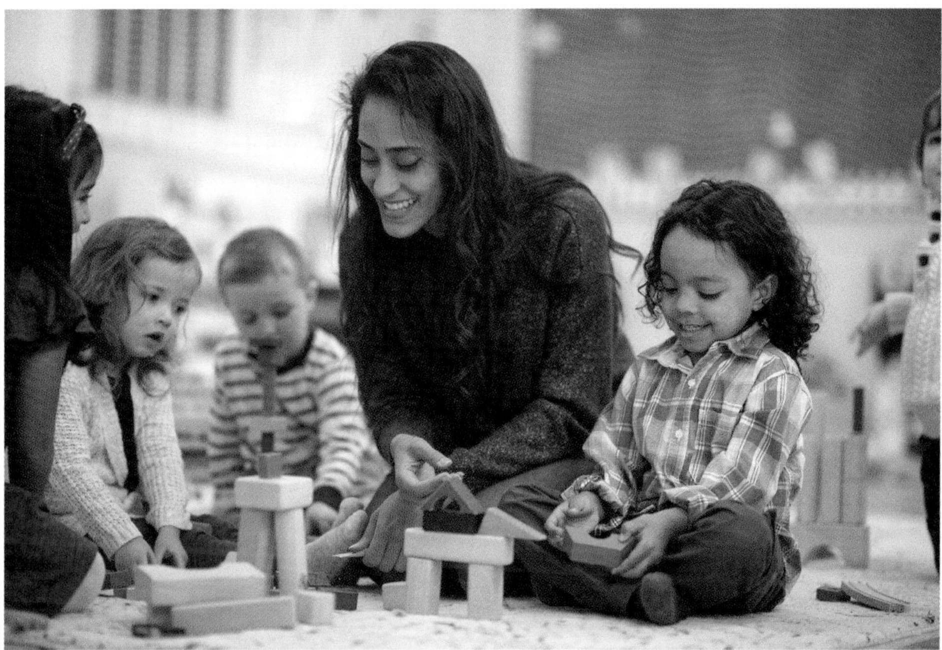

Preschool is a time when children develop key physical, emotional, and cognitive skills.
iStock/FatCamera

Early childhood—from birth to age 8—is widely accepted as a distinct phase of human development in which children acquire key physical, emotional, and cognitive skills. Early gaps in school readiness increase over time and add to differences in achievement proficiency and school completion. In the face of a large and increasing 32-point achievement gap between affluent (52%) and low-income fourth graders (20%) scoring proficient on the 2015 NAEP reading test,[146] **early childhood education (ECE)**—**preschool** (birth to age 3) and **prekindergarten**, age 4—is becoming an important national priority. Today, about 55% of 3- and 4-year-olds attend full-day preschool programs, with more than 80% of kindergartners attending full-day programs.[147] Both percentages represent large increases from earlier decades. But as compared with other industrialized wealthy nations that enroll 82% of their 3- and 4-year-olds,[148] participation in U.S. early childhood education is lagging.

Studies of three early landmark preK programs—Abecedarian Project,[149] the High/Scope Perry Preschool,[150] and the Child-Parent Centers (CPC)[151]—offer evidence that high-quality early education increases short- and long-term educational and economic success relative to program costs.[152] Substantial evidence based on several large-scale, multiyear studies find that preK–3 educational alignment as a coherent instructional unit helps close the achievement gap.[153] A strong body of empirical research also suggests children who participate in high-quality prekindergarten programs have advanced cognitive growth, improved school readinesss skills in kindergarten, greater word recogniton skills, a larger oral vocbulary, and prereading skills as compared to age-appropriate peers without ECE exposure.[154] Studies also find that ECE participants had fewer special education referrals, fewer rententions in grade, and were more likely to graduate from high school as compared to those with no ECE experience. [155]

Long-term student outcomes also show the difference. Studies find that children with high-quality ECE experience also have higher levels of academic achievement, graduate from high school on time, are more likely to seek further education, attain and keep stable employment, earn a higher salary, and are less liable to commit juvenile or adult crimes.[156] Remarkably, studies even find that the advantages to the Perry Preschool participants persist: Their siblings and own children obtain the same benefits (likely because participation improved the home environments).[157] In the face of these data, investigators conclude that investments in high-quality prekindergarten programs—providing early, organized social and academic learning opportunities aligned with the district's K–3 curriculum—outweigh the total economic debt burden of remedial reading services and criminal justice expenses (predominantly juvenile and adult incarceration) and rehabilitation costs.[158]

Despite the positive outcomes, ECE's impacts across all cultural and social contexts vary greatly in size, consistency, and duration. Too much variation in program quality and lack of alignment with later education are major factors.[159] For instance, states vary widely in their ECE investments. Three states enroll over 70% of their state's prekindergarten students, 10 states serve at least 50% of their 4-year-olds, and 14 states serve fewer than 10%, while seven states have no formal early childhood programs, services, policy, or funding.[160] Citing budgetary concerns for shortchanging ECE programs is shortsighted: two early high-quality ECE programs found that for every $1 spent, the state saved an estimated $2.50 to $10.83 in educational savings for remediation, special education, grade retention, increased earnings and tax revenues, averted criminal justice, and child welfare systems.[161] Put another way, existing research suggests that expanding early learning initiatives could benefit society by approximately $8.60 for every $1 spent, about half of which comes from children's increased earnings as adults.[162]

States need to assess their ECE programs and provide additional resources where needed to increase available seats and length of participation for eligible children, strengthen and align curriculum, and enhance teacher quality. As an investment in individual and community well-being, many credibly argue that preK participation is the most effective strategy to address achievement and learning opportunity gaps among different social and economic groups.

7.8b Multicultural Education

Multicultural education—the form of education or teaching that incorporates the histories, texts, values, beliefs, and perspectives of people from varied cultural backgrounds—is a response to the U.S. cultural pluralism and the relative absence of underrepresented viewpoints in the public school curriculum and society. It explicitly promotes the Western values of democracy, freedom, human dignity, equality, and respect for diversity by using multiple, nonstereotyped perspectives and underrepresented voices in primary sources in an expanded and deepened high-quality, standards-based curriculum. At the same time, teachers continue to provide students with instruction on basic and complex academic skills, to think critically and incorporate complexity, to recognize multiple ways of understanding information while holding pupils to high performance expectations. Its goal is to help all students understand and appreciate human differences and commonalities, to respect individual differences, recognize social inequities, and to learn about and celebrate cultural diversity among Americans.

Research affirms that multicultural education can increase students' basic and advanced academic skills and improve intergroup relations. Using ethnically informed materials, experiences, and examples infused into academic subject matter makes the instruction more interesting to many students, increases its personal meaning, heightens the practical relevance of the skills to be learned, and improves students' time on task.[163] Together, this combination of motivating conditions leads to greater student efforts, task persistence, skill mastery, and academic achievement. It also can help students learn to interact successfully with those of different races, ethnicities, and experiences.

When teachers understand and welcome their diverse students' assets, hold high expectations for their learning, and use a curriculum and instruction that invites all students to participate in the American experience, occasions for miscommunications decrease. In these ways, teachers practice **culturally responsive teaching**.[164] We will discuss this more fully in Chapter 8.

7.8c Factors Beyond the School

Even with 50 years of research studying the achievement gap, no consensus exists as to which strategies work best to reduce or end it. The amount of literature on the topic is, frankly, overwhelming, making it hard to draw simple actionable conclusions.

From birth to age 18, children spend only a small portion of their lives in school. As we discussed, many factors—family background; parental beliefs and expectations about education; family SES and the resources available to nurture and encourage children's learning; stability and safety in a child's life; cognitive, social, and emotional readiness for school; physical and mental health that permits regular school attendance and focus on learning—all impact the achievement/opportunity gap. Similarly, the strength of school and community links (including youth-oriented organizations such as the YMCA, 4-H, Scouts, Boys and Girls Clubs, and Little Leagues) and their interactions also affects students' academic achievement. Nonetheless, despite the family's enormous influence on student achievement, it does not determine it. Students from backgrounds that would seem to undermine their school success often find ways to overcome their limitations and achieve at high academic levels. Similarly, children from affluent backgrounds may not achieve well in school.

The total picture of a child's environment—in school and beyond—includes conditions that either support learning or present challenges to overcome. Scholars, educators, community leaders, and policy makers need to think more comprehensively if every student is to succeed in school.

AMERICAN EDUCATION SPOTLIGHT: PEDRO NOGUERA

Pedro A. Noguera, a prominent sociologist, education researcher, and former public school teacher, is the dean of the University of Southern California's Rossier School of Education and expert of educational equity. An author, teacher, and recipient of many prestigious awards, his research focuses on the ways in which social, economic, and demographic factors influence schools and the conditions that promote student achievement.

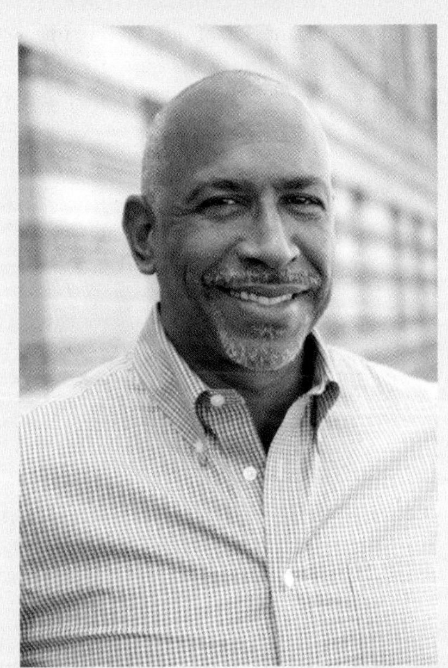

Courtesy of Pedro A. Noguera

Noguera believes that *equity* (recognizing that not all students are the same and giving them what they need, academically and socially, to be successful) and *excellence* (learning and performing to high standards) are compatible goals. In his view, schools often ignore this truism and fail to ensure that every child has the opportunity to learn.

Children come to school with individual differences as well as disparities in family economic well-being, health, housing stability, and parental employment, all variables that affect academic performance. The achievement gap mirrors these other disparities in students' lives. Yet schools often make these differences worse by using traditions and routines that reward privilege and punish the disadvantaged. These include how highly effective and ineffective/inexperienced teachers are assigned to low- and high-poverty schools, respectively; rigid academic tracking that limits students' preparation and denies access to high-challenge courses; teachers using ineffective instructional strategies with unchallenging curriculum; applying punitive rather than preventive school discipline practices; exercising top-down accountability rather than mutual accountability; and not partnering with parents to advance their children's learning.

Noguera sees that many educators have low performance expectations for low-income students of color, accepting their low-achievement pattern as "normal." They rationalize the poor academic performance by blaming students, their parents, or their communities. Similarly, many educators believe that intelligence is fixed, inherent, and unchangeable rather than recognizing children's cognitive ability as malleable and capable of growth and development in the right environment. Noguera wants all students—including those who are economically disadvantaged, English language learners, students with disabilities, and those who are overage and undercredited—to have access to teachers who help them learn to think critically; solve problems; conduct independent research, evaluation, and comparative analysis; and provide occasions to acquire the knowledge and skills needed for college and career readiness. When teachers give low-income, underrepresented, and other high-needs children the opportunity to learn in school and provide the necessary academic supports that affluent children typically have outside school, educators "begin to rebuild the possibility that education can serve as a path to mobility."*

Likewise, rather than continually stressing high-stakes testing (and more testing) to determine school accountability, Noguera prefers that policies and strategies to help underperforming schools build the capacity to create conditions that promote higher levels of student achievement. Educators need preservice and inservice learning to develop the attitudes, skills, and techniques they need to boost underserved students' achievement. Moreover, all stakeholders—teachers, principals, students, parents, legislatures, and governors—need to accept their share of the mutual accountability for student learning. Plus, educators need to treat parents as trusted, respected partners in the educational process, so they are more likely to reinforce learning at home.

Noguera also believes that the disproportionate rate of school discipline sanctions—from office referrals to corporal punishment, suspensions, and expulsion of Black, Latinx, and Native American students—contributes to their academic achievement gap. Although low-income and low-achieving students who live in high-crime/high-poverty neighborhoods with histories of low achievement may be at greater risk for engaging in behaviors that lead to office disciplinary referrals and school suspensions,[165] differential selection for disciplinary consequences for what the teacher perceives as "defiance" or "noncompliance," fewer resources, higher teacher turnover, and lower percentage of highly qualified teachers all need to be considered as possible contributors to the "overselection and oversanction" of these students of color.**

Finally, Noguera concludes that educators will know they are succeeding in closing the gap when their students' backgrounds—particularly race and social class—stop being predictors of academic achievement. "In the long term," he observes, America's future "will be determined not only by what happens in Washington but by what happens to our children in our nation's schools."***

Notes:

*Ferlazzo, L. (2016, August 4). "Excellence through equity": An interview with Pedro Noguera & Alan Blankstein. *Education Week.* https://blogs.edweek.org/teachers/classroom_qa_with_larry_ferlazzo/2016/08/excellence_through_equity_an_interview_with_pedro_noguera.html

**Gregory, A., Skiba, R. J., & Noguera, P. A. (2010). The achievement gap and the discipline gap: Two sides of the same coin? *Educational Researcher, 39*(1), 59–68. https://pdfs.semanticscholar.org/5e29/3a4598fece049e2e33b1254dd46d73106780.pdf

***Noguera, P. (2019, April 29). It's time to develop a progressive education agenda. *The Nation.* https://www.thenation.com/article/progressive-education-agenda/

Sources: Noguera, P. A. (2016). *Excellence through equity.* https://www.vassonline.org/images/vass/resources-2016-spring-conference/Pedro%20Noguera%20-%20Excellence%20Through%20Equity.pdf; Noguera, P. A. (2017, September). *Taking deeper learning to scale.* Learning Policy Institute. https://learningpolicyinstitute.org/sites/default/files/product-files/Taking_Deeper_Learning_Scale_REPORT.pdf

7.8d Building Awareness of Unfair School Practices

Parents know that not all schools are created equal. Homebuyers routinely ask realtors to show them houses in school attendance zones with high test scores. With few exceptions, most students end up replicating their parents' place in the social hierarchy. Educators, in contrast, tend to believe that schools are fair systems of opportunity. Although well intentioned, teachers do not always see that the educational system is tilted in their favor.

Teachers did not create the institutions in which they work; they simply fit themselves into their schools' existing patterns and norms. Most educators genuinely believe that schools are a meritocracy that provide a level playing field to all students. According to this perspective, it is the students' job to work hard, learn, and move ahead. If they don't, their failure is on them.

Likewise, educators are not often aware of how their sometimes-inaccurate assumptions affect their interactions with others. Educators generally believe that they are wholly objective professionals fully capable of interpreting situations and treating individuals in totally neutral and evenhanded ways. Likewise, future educators often come to teaching with little cross-cultural experience and knowledge and tend to have limited visions of what teaching students unlike themselves entails. This lack of awareness creates one of the greatest obstacles to establishing more trusting and equitable relationships with the schools' multiple communities.

Thinking of this type reflects a strong acceptance of "difference blindness."[166] Teachers want to be fair and try to see and treat every student the same way—seemingly "blind" to racial, ethnic, and gender differences. Because teachers were socialized as Americans and as transmitters of our cultural heritage, they simply may not see, understand, or value that other ways of knowing and understanding the world exist. Yet when teachers are not aware that others see the world differently than they do, communication and trust become more difficult.

7.8e Reconciling Cognitive Dissonance

"Difference blindness" is a form of cognitive dissonance. Cognitive dissonance is a theoretical construct used to explain how people respond to information that does not coincide with their current understandings or beliefs.[167] According to **cognitive dissonance theory**, an individual can experience an unpleasant psychological tension or dissonance when new knowledge or information does not fit with what he or she already knows or believes, and this anxiety motivates the individuals to reduce it.

Here is an example of cognitive dissonance: A future teacher tries to make sense of two contradictory beliefs—an established belief and a newer belief that challenges the first one,

The established belief: "Schools are fair and advance *every* student's best interests."

The newer belief: "Schools can be unfair when their practices systematically disfavor lower-income children and students of color."

To reduce the psychological discomfort, the future teacher may react in any of three ways:

- *Change the new cognition* to make it consistent with the preexisting cognition (i.e., deny or devalue the research or anecdotal evidence that school practices may be unfair to lower-income students and children of color). For example, "The investigators are biased, and their conclusions are, too."
- *Add new cognitions to bridge the gap* between the conflicting cognitions (i.e., find additional information that supports the idea that many teacher assumptions and school practices systematically disadvantage lower-income and racial/ethnic minority children). For example, "Although I had not viewed academic tracking as unfair, credible and ample evidence suggests that it might be true."
- *Change his or her behavior* (i.e., challenge your own assumptions, stop uncritically supporting institutional practices such as rigid academic tracking, and instead, support moves to end rigid tracking and use students' cultural assets to help them learn the academic content).[168] For example, "I am going to recommend my best students who work hard and want to go to college for the honors' classes next semester. I will speak to them and their parents to help them understand the course expectations, and if they agree to put in the time and effort to learn the interesting but challenging material, I'll enroll them."

Helping future teachers become fully aware of cognitive dissonance's internal discomfort *before* they experience it helps reduce their resistance to the unfamiliar ideas. It also prevents them from automatically rejecting the unsettling information, encourages their critical thinking, and promotes a classroom environment conducive to learning.[169] Accepting one's own cognitive dissonance as an internal signal that one may be about to learn something new is a form of emotional intelligence. Improved relationships with colleagues, students, parents, and others may result, along with improved teaching and learning.

7.8f Closing the Achievement/Opportunity Gap

Schools too often fail to take seriously their responsibility to educate all children. As Colleen Larson and Carlos J. Ovando, multicultural scholars, assert, "Although we have expanded our geographical borders in many of our school systems, we have failed to expand our psychic circles of community."[170]

Becoming conscious of student differences can be a way of valuing, supporting, and genuinely relating to children rather than a way of diminishing them. Developing this awareness of difference is not easy. All people have an unconscious tendency to confirm what they believe and to explain away what they do not. They unconsciously magnify those features that fit with their expectations and overlook the rest. Difference, however, does not necessarily mean "less than."

Our cognitive maps and feelings about student differences affect the ways we interact with others. When we can critically examine how our own assumptions, behaviors, systems, and practices may contribute to underserved students' problems in school, we can truly become professional educators for a pluralist society. Chapter 8 discusses these issues in more detail. Recognizing and accepting student differences also helps educators become advocates for making schools better places for all students.

Although schools are only one of the societal forces that influence students' learning, educators must do what they can to remove obstacles to students' opportunities and provide necessary supports to help underserved students become fully educated for 21st century economic viability and democratic citizenship.

To explore more deeply how teachers and schools can contribute to—or reduce—the achievement gap, complete the activity in the **Reflect & Engage** box, School Practices and the Achievement/Opportunity Gap.

REFLECT & ENGAGE: SCHOOL PRACTICES AND THE ACHIEVEMENT/OPPORTUNITY GAP

This activity involves a role play. School practices can either contribute to—or reduce—the achievement/opportunity gap. For this activity, separate the class into groups of four. Half the groups will address teachers' and schools' current practices that may *limit* student achievement. The other groups will address things that teachers, the school district, and the locality can do to *support and improve* student opportunity and achievement.

A. You are a team of four (teachers, principals, parents, and community members) who want to improve achievement for your schools' low-income and underserved students as well as students with disabilities.

B. Your group will prepare a 5-minute presentation to your local school board and city council on your selected/assigned topic.

C. Present your recommendations to your entire class and receive feedback.

D. For a field experience, interview a local principal, assistant principal, or central office administrator about what their school/s are currently doing to better support student achievement, what more they would like to do, and whether any of the limiting practices described in this chapter are still part of the school organization.

KEY TAKE-AWAYS

Learning Objective 7.1 Argue how America's view of immigrants and assimilation shifted from the "melting pot" metaphor to "cultural pluralism" and its implications for American education.

- We rely on our public schools to provide Americans of differing backgrounds with a shared set of values and loyalties to the United States. Without this common ground, societal and political tensions will likely increase.
- Our nation's founders recognized that their new government's survival depended on its ability to create a new unified nation from a heterogenous population. Anyone who came to this country and believed and lived by these (and other) American ideals could become an American.
- In the 1960s and 1970s, the "melting pot" vision of assimilation was replaced by cultural pluralism, a celebration of individuals' ethnic and cultural differences within their American identity. Yet we recognize that our differences are less important than our shared values and loyalty to our common American nation.

Learning Objective 7.2 Critique how the American public schools became a major socializing agent for generations of children.

- The first American colonists' Western European orientation set the stage for the nation's symbolic politics of language and ethnic identity.

- Throughout U.S. history, schools have served as a powerful agency to socialize ethnic and racial communities to the founders' norms. Although most immigrants valued this chance to become "true Americans," not all immigrant groups viewed this favorably.

Learning Objective 7.3 Support the view that family socioeconomic status influences U.S. students' skills, social capital, outlooks, and opportunities.

- Social class differences—including parents' education, family wealth, and income—tend to determine the quality of schooling students receive, their worldviews, and their relationships to others in society.
- A student's SES is highly associated with academic achievement, although factors other than family background impact student achievement. Social class also influences the degree of social capital (sometimes called cultural capital) that is available to students to help them succeed in school. Performance gaps by social class begin in children's earliest years, and children who start behind tend to stay behind.
- Parenting approaches change over time as cultures and eras shift. The real issue is how parenting strategies match up with expectations of schools, the labor market, and other societal demands.

Learning Objective 7.4 Assess the contradictory roles of American public schools, how these appear in practice, and their implications for the social mobility and the achievement/opportunity gap.

- Our public schools are intended to be "the great equalizer," bringing together students from different backgrounds to learn society's shared norms and values that make them educated, loyal, and responsible members of our democratic republic. At the same time, our public schools have traditionally held the responsibility for "sorting and selecting" students into educational paths leading to varying occupations and social status. What initially was intended as a unifying experience for diverse students has become one that increasingly separates them.
- A high-quality education, especially a 4-year college degree, can help young people overcome the disadvantages their family background may place them in and propel their upward mobility. Studies find a strong link between school quality and opportunities available later in life.

Learning Objective 7.5 Describe the poverty factors that can adversely affect a child's school success.

- Poverty is the risk factor that intensifies all other risk factors. The achievement/opportunity gap begins well before kindergarten. Profound risk factors in many children's early life may greatly compromise their future school attainment.
- Low-income children's cognitive deficit from living many years in poverty has many causes, including lower birth weight, early childhood learning differences, language differences, housing instability, chronic health concerns, and segregated schools,

Learning Objective 7.6 Assess how residential and school segregation and school integration impact students' academic achievement and life outcomes.

- Although the landmark 1954 *Brown v. Board of Education* decision ruled against the "separate but equal" education of poor and underrepresented students, courts in the 1990s began releasing school districts from 1970s desegregation orders. Today, school segregation (and re-segregation) on the basis of socioeconomic status, race, and ethnicity is widespread and increasing.
- Since the 1980s, high-quality studies clearly and consistently find that the school's racial and SES composition influences student outcomes, short and long term. Achievement/opportunity gaps are more highly linked with school segregation than residential segregation.
- A growing body of social science research agrees that students attending socioeconomically and racially integrated schools tend to benefit academically, economically, and socially. Integrated schools tend to include more experienced and highly qualified teachers and school leaders; more

stable student populations; school climates more supportive of learning and studying; more parent involvement; and more high-quality, consistent teacher resources.

- Research strongly suggests that integrated schools can foster a greater belief in democratic values, build a community's civic capacity, and serve as building blocks for greater social cohesion in a multiethnic, fair, democratic society.

Learning Objective 7.7 Identify and discuss the school factors and practices that contribute to the achievement/opportunity gap.

- Teacher expectations and their instructional effectiveness, teachers' and students' growth mindsets, tracking, curriculum rigor, grade retention, disciplinary practices, and school/instructional climate all strongly impact students and their future educational, employment, social, and lifestyle opportunities.
- Some argue that differences in student achievement can be explained by three factors: learning opportunities, effort, and ability. Academic tracking removes many learning opportunities, reducing the need for effort and limiting growth of ability.
- American public schools have had a difficult time providing highly effective teachers for students of color. Education preparation programs' curricula and coursework do not always challenge teacher candidates' "naïve optimism," "unexamined stereotypes," and unconscious biases.
- Decades of research have documented that teacher quality (effectiveness) is inequitably distributed. Large and persistent gaps in teacher quality exist between advantaged and disadvantaged students. When this uneven distribution of effective teachers systematically disadvantages poor, low-achieving, and racially isolated schools, it becomes an equity issue.

Learning Objective 7.8 Identify and describe the school factors and practices that can reduce the achievement/opportunity gap.

- Since research finds that early gaps in school readiness increase over time and add to differences in achievement proficiency and school completion, early childhood education (ECE)—preschool (birth to age 3) and prekindergarten, age 4—is becoming an important national priority. Several studies provide evidence that high-quality early education and its social and academic learning opportunities increase short- and long-term educational and economic success relative to program cost.
- Research affirms that multicultural education can increase students' basic and advanced academic skills and improve intergroup relations. Similarly, culturally responsive teaching—teachers understanding and welcoming diverse students' assets, holding high expectations for their learning, and using a curriculum and instruction that invites all students to participate in the American experience—improves student outcomes.
- Despite the family's enormous influence on student achievement, it does not determine it.
- Awareness of their own assumptions and schools' inequitable norms and practices helps educators recognize and overcome schools' institutional biases and make cultural pluralism and higher achievement for all students a reality.

TEACHER SCENARIO: IT'S YOUR TURN

You have just been given your first student teaching placement in a "low-achieving" urban school system where 90% of the students in your school qualify for free or reduced-price lunch, and the student body demographics are 72% Black, 14% white, and 14% Hispanic. The principal meets with each of the new student teachers. Before she meets with you, she asks you to respond in writing to four questions:

1. How will your life's background help you to be a good teacher at this school or hinder you from being a good teacher in this school?

2. What do you need to know about your students to better help them learn, and how will you obtain that information?

3. Describe and explain your initial comfort level with working in a "low-achieving" urban school.

4. What help might you ask for as a new student teacher and why?

NOTES

1. Archdeacon, T. J. (1990). Melting pot or cultural pluralism? Changing views on American ethnicity. *Revue Européenne de Migrations Internationales, 6*(1), 11–28. https://www.persee.fr/doc/remi_0765-0752_1990_num_6_1_1224
2. Archdeacon, 1990, p. 11.
3. The metaphor of U.S. assimilation as a "melting pot" was coined by Israel Zangwill, a Jewish playwright born in London in 1864 to Eastern European immigrants. His play *The Melting Pot* opened in Washington, DC, in October 1908. He wrote, "America is God's crucible, the melting pot where all the races of Europe are melting and reforming!" For a fuller discussion, see: Chametzky, J. (1989). Beyond melting pots, cultural pluralism, ethnicity—or *DejaVu* all over again. *MELUS, 16*(4), 3–17; Gleason, P. (1964). The melting pot: Symbol of fusion or confusion?" *American Quarterly, 16*(1), 20-46; Kraus, J. (1999). How the melting pot stirred America: The reception of Zangwill's play and theater's role in the American assimilation experience. *MELUS, 24*(3), 3–19.
4. Chametzky, 1989.
5. These terms did not become part of our long-term assimilation vocabulary because they are essentially static, not involved in a transformation process as assimilation is. See: Gleason, 1964.
6. Horace M. Kallen coined the term "cultural pluralism" but did not use it as we do today See: Kallen, H. (1915). *Democracy versus the melting pot: Horace Kallen, 1915*. The Pluralism Project, Harvard University. http://pluralism.org/document/democracy-versus-the-melting-pot-horace-kallen-1915/
7. DeParle, J. (2019, August 11). What makes an American? News analysis. *The New York Times*. Section SR. https://www.nytimes.com/2019/08/09/sunday-review/immigration-assimilation-texas.html?smid=nytcore-ios-share
8. Brooks, D. (2020, May 29). If we had a real leader. *The New York Times*, A, 27. https://www.nytimes.com/2020/05/28/opinion/coronavirus-trump.html?referringSource=articleShare
9. Frey, W. H. (2018, September 10). The US will become 'minority white' in 2045, Census projects. Brookings. https://www.brookings.edu/blog/the-avenue/2018/03/14/the-us-will-become-minority-white-in-2045-census-projects/
10. Colby, S. L., & Ortman, J. M. (2015, March). Projections of the size and composition of the U. S. population: 2014 to 2060. *Current Population Report*. P25-1143. https://www.census.gov/content/dam/Census/library/publications/2015/demo/p25-1143.pdf
11. United States Census. (2018, March 13). Older people projected to outnumber children for the first time in U.S. history. *Newsroom*. https://www.census.gov/newsroom/press-releases/2018/cb18-41-population-projections.html
12. Gerwertz, C. (2019, January 24). U.S. high school grad rate reaches another all-time high. But what does it mean? *Education Week*. https://blogs.edweek.org/edweek/high_school_and_beyond/2019/01/2017_high_school_graduation_rate.html
13. Rothstein, R. (2004, October). A wider lens on the black-white achievement gap. *Phi Delta Kappan, 86*(2), 106.
14. Larson, C. L., & Ovando, C. J. (2001). *The color of bureaucracy: The politics of equity in multicultural school communities*. Cengage Learning, p. 8.
15. Larson & Ovando, 2001, pp. 8–9.
16. Garcia, E., & Weiss, E. (2017, September 27). *Education inequalities at the school starting gate*. Economic Policy Institute. https://www.epi.org/files/pdf/132500.pdf
17. Coleman, J. S., Campbell, E., Hobson, C., McPartland, J., Mood, A., Weinfield, F., & York, R. (1966). *Equality of educational opportunity*. U.S. Government Printing Office; Caldas, S. J., & Bankston, C. (1997. May/June). Effect of school population socioeconomic status on individual academic achievement. *Journal of Educational Research, 90*(5), 269–277; Sirin, S. R. (2005, Fall). Socioeconomic status and academic achievement: A meta-analytic review of research. *Review of Educational Research, 75*(3), 417–453.

18. Although more respectful than the term "lower class," the term "working class" is a misnomer because most people of every social class "work." The authors of this book sometimes use the term "low income" to refer to lower or "working class" social status, reflecting the group's economic situation.

19. Jencks, C., & Peterson, P. E. (Eds.). (1991). *The urban underclass*. Brookings; Wooster, M. M. (1998, May–June). Inside the underclass. *American Enterprise, 9*(3), 83–84.

20. Portes, A. (1998). Social capital: Its origin and applications in modern sociology. *Annual Review of Sociology, 24*(1), 1–24.

21. Jaeger, M. M. (2009, June). Equal access but unequal outcomes: Cultural capital and educational choice in a meritocratic society. *Social Forces, 87*(4), 1943–1971; Parcel, T. L., & Dufur, M. J. (2001). Capital at home and at school: Effects on student achievement. *Social Forces, 79*(3), 881–912.

22. Ream, R. K., & Palardy, G. J. (2008, June). Reexamining social class differences in the availability and the educational utility of parental social capital. *American Educational Research Journal, 45*(2), 238–273.

23. Wolf, A. (1978). The state of urban schools. *Urban Education, 13*(2), 179–194.

24. Duncan, G., & Magnuson, K. (2011). The nature and impact of early achievement skills, attention skills, and behavior problems. In G. J. Duncan & R. J. Murnane (Eds.), *Whither opportunity? Rising inequality, schools, and children's life chances* (pp. 47–70). Russell Sage Foundation. http://inequality.stanford.edu/sites/default/files/The%20Widening%20Income%20Acheivement%20Gap%20Between%20the%20Rich%20and%20The%20Poor.pdf

25. Heckman, J. (2008, June). *Schools, skills, and synapses* (NBER Working Paper No. 14064). National Bureau of Economics Research, pp. 4, 12.

26. Reardon, S. F. (2011, July). The widening academic achievement gap between the rich and the poor: New evidence and possible explanations. In G. J. Duncan & R. J. Murnane (Eds.), *Whither opportunity? Rising inequality, schools, and children's life chances* (pp. 91–116). Russell Sage Foundation. http://inequality.stanford.edu/sites/default/files/The%20Widening%20Income%20achievement%20Gap%20Between%20the%20Rich%20and%20The%20Poor.pdf

27. Carnevale, A. P. (2019, June 12). It's better to be born rich than smart. *Education Week, 38*(35), 24. https://www.edweek.org/ew/articles/2019/06/05/better-to-be-born-rich-than-smart.html

28. The PEW Charitable Trusts. (2012, July). *Pursuing the American dream: Economic mobility across generations*. https://www.pewtrusts.org/~/media/legacy/uploadedfiles/wwwpewtrustsorg/reports/economic_mobility/pursuingamericandreampdf.pdf

29. The PEW Charitable Trusts, 2012.

30. Minghao, L., Goetz, S. J., & Weber, B. (2018). Human capital and intergenerational mobility in U.S. counties. *Economic Development Quarterly, 32*(1), 18–28.

31. In this study, proxies for higher-quality schools include mean public school expenditure per student (higher), mean class size (smaller), test scores (higher), and dropout rate (lower).

32. Chetty, R., Hendren, N., Kline, P., & Saez, E. (2014). Where is the land of opportunity? The geography of intergenerational mobility in the United States. *The Quarterly Journal of Economics, 129*(4), 1553–1623; Rothstein, J. (2017, August 15). Inequality of educational opportunity? Schools as mediators of the intergenerational transmission of Income. *Washington Center for Equitable Growth*. https://equitablegrowth.org/working-papers/inequality-of-educational-opportunity-schools-as-mediators-of-the-intergenerational-transmission-of-income/

33. Owings, W. A., & Kaplan, L. S. (2020). *American public school finance* (3rd ed.). Routledge, p. 209.

34. U.S. Department of Health and Human Services. (2020, January 21). *2020 poverty guidelines*. https://aspe.hhs.gov/2020-poverty-guidelines

35. Children's Defense Fund. (2020). *The state of America's children 2020*. https://www.childrensdefense.org/policy/resources/soac-2020-child-poverty/

36. The child poverty rate ranged from 76.4% in District of Columbia to a low of 28.3% in New Hampshire. See: Snyder, T. D., de Brey, C., & Dillow, S. A. (2019). *Digest of education statistics 2017* (NCES 2018-070). U.S. Department of Education. Table 204.10, p. 10. https://nces.ed.gov/programs/digest/d16/tables/dt16_204.10.asp

37. Nations with higher child poverty rates than the United States are Lithuania, Bulgaria, Romania, Turkey, and Mexico. See: Edmond, C. (2017, June 28). *These rich countries have high levels of child poverty*. World Economic Forum. https://www.weforum.org/agenda/2017/06/these-rich-countries-have-high-levels-of-child-poverty/

38. Huffman, L. C., Mehlinger, S. L., & Kerivan, A. S. (2000). Risk factors for academic and behavioral problems at the beginning of school. Paper commissioned by The Child Mental Health Foundations and Agency Network (FAN). National Institutes of Mental Health. https://files.eric.ed.gov/fulltext/ED476378.pdf; McLoyd, V. (1998). Socioeconomic disadvantage and child development. *American Psychologist, 53*(2), 185–204.

39. Children's Hospital of Philadelphia. (2018). *Low birthweight.* http://www.chop.edu/conditions-diseases/low-birthweight; Currie, J., & Moretti, E. (2007). Biology as destiny? Shorthand long-run determinants of intergenerational transmission of birth weight. *Journal of Labor Economics, 25*(2), 231–263.

40. Cepeda, I. L., Grunau, R. E., Weinberg, H., Herdman, A. T., Cheung, T., Liotti, M., Amir, A., Synnes, A., & Whitfield, M. A. (2007). Magnetoencephalography study of brain dynamics in young children born extremely preterm. *International Congress Series 1300*, 99–102; Morse, S. B., Zheng, H., Tang, Y., & Roth, J. (2009). Early school-age outcomes of late preterm infants. *Pediatrics, 123*(4), e622–e629; Raznahan, A., Greenstein, D., Lee, N. R., Clasen, L. S., & Giedd, J. N. (2012). Prenatal growth in humans and post-natal brain maturation into late adolescence. *Proceedings of the National Academy of Sciences of the United States of America, 109*(28), 11366–11371.

41. Duncan, G. J., Yeung, W. J., Brooks-Gunn, J., & Smith, J. R. (1998). How much does childhood poverty affect the life chances of children? *American Psychological Review, 63*, 406–423; Moore, K. A., & Zedd, Z. (2002). Children in poverty: Trends, consequences, and policy options. *Child Trends Research Brief.* Child Trends.

42. Larson, K., Russ, S. A., Nelson, B. B., Olson, L. M., & Halfon, N. (2015, February) *Pediatrics, 135*(2), e440–e448. https://pediatrics.aappublications.org/content/pediatrics/135/2/e440.full.pdf

43. Hart, B., & Risley, T. R. (1995). Meaningful differences in the everyday experience of young American children. Paul H. Brookes; Hart, B., & Risley, T. R. (2003). The early catastrophe: The 30 million word gap by age 3. *American Educator, 27*(1), 4–9. https://www.aft.org/sites/default/files/periodicals/TheEarlyCatastrophe.pdf; Huttenlocher, J. (1998). Language input and language growth. *Preventive Medicine, 27*(2), 195–199; Huttenlocher, J., Haight, W., Bryk, A., Seltzer, M., & Lyons, T. (1991). Early vocabulary growth: Relation to language input and gender. *Developmental Psychology, 27*(2), 236–248.

44. Carey, B. (2013, September 25). Language gap between rich and poor children begins in infancy, Stanford psychologist find. *Stanford News.* https://news.stanford.edu/news/2013/september/toddler-language-gap-091213.html

45. Brooks-Gunn & Duncan, 1997; Currie, J., & Stabile, M. (2003). Socioeconomic status and child health: Why is the relationship stronger for older children? *The American Economics Review, 93*(5), 1813–1823.

46. Case, A., Lubotsky, D., & Paxson, C. (2002). Economic status and health in childhood: The origins of the gradient. *The American Economics Review, 92*(5), 1308–1334; Currie, J. (2005). Health disparities and gaps in school readiness. *The Future of Children, 15*(1), 117–138; Palloni, A. (2009). Luck, wallets, and the enduring effects of childhood health. *Demography, 4 3*(4), 587–615.

47. Sastry, N., & Pebley, A. R. (2003). *Neighborhood and family effects on children's health in Los Angeles.* RAND; Wertheimer, R. (2003). Poor families in 2001: Parents working less and children continue to lag behind. *Child Trends.* https://www.childtrends.org/wp-content/uploads/2003/05/Child_Trends-2003_05_01_RB_PoorFamilies.pdf

48. Park, J. M., Fertig, A. R., & Allison. P. (2011). Physical and mental health, cognitive development, and health care use by housing status of low-income young children in 20 American cities: A prospective cohort study. *American Journal of Public Health, 101*(Supplement), S1, S255; Coley, R. L., Leventhal, T., Lynch, A.D., & Kull, M. (2013). Relations between housing characteristics and the well-being of low-income children and adolescents. *Developmental Psychology, 49*(9), 1785–1787; Stipek, D. J., & Ryan, R. H. (1997). Economically disadvantaged preschoolers: Ready to learn but further to go. *Developmental Psychology, 33*(4), 711–723.

49. Morsy, L., & Rothstein, R. (2019, May 1). Toxic stress and children's outcomes. *Economic Policy Institute and Opportunity Institute.* https://www.epi.org/files/pdf/164823.pdf; Shonkoff, J. P., Garner, A. S., Siegel, B. S., Dobbins, M. I., Earls, M. F., McGuinn, L., Pascoe, J., & Wood, D. L. (2012, January). The life-long effects of early childhood adversity and toxic stress. *Pediatrics, 129*(1), 232–246.

50. Yeager, D. S., Hanselman, P., Walton, G. M., Murray, J. S., Crosnoe, R., Muller, C., Tipton, E., Schneider, B., Hulleman, C. S., Hinojosa, C. P., Paunesku, D., Romero, C., Flint, K., Roberts, A., Trott, J., Iachan, R., Buontempo, J., Yang, S. M., Carvalho, C. M., . . . Dweck, C. S. (2019, August). A national experiment reveals where a growth mindset improves achievement. *Nature.* https://www.nature.com/articles/s41586-019-1466-y

51. Romero, M., & Lee, Y.-S., (2008, January). *The influence of material and family risk on chronic absenteeism in early schooling.* National Center for Children in Poverty. https://files.eric.ed.gov/fulltext/ED522733.pdf

52. Chang, H., & Balfanz, R. (2017). *Preventing missed opportunity: Taking collective action to confront chronic absence.* Attendance Works and Johns Hopkins University. http://attendanceworks.org/wp-content/uploads/2017/09/PreventingMissedOpportunityFull_FINAL9.8.16_2-1.pdf

53. Balfanz, R., & Byrnes,V. (2012, May). The importance of being in school: A report on absenteeism in the nation's public schools. Johns Hopkins University School of Education. https://coseboc.org/sites/coseboc.org/files/assets/ChronicAbsenteeismReport.pdf

54. Chang & Balfanz, 2017.

55. Jellyman, T., & Spencer, N. (2008). Residential mobility in childhood and health outcomes: A systematic review. *Journal of Epidemiology and Community Health, 62*(7), 584–592; Scanlon, E., & Devine, K. (2001). Residential mobility and youth well-being: Research, policy, and practice issues. *Journal of Sociology and Social Welfare, 28*(1), 119–138.

56. Desmond, M. (2015, March). Unaffordable America: Poverty, housing, and eviction. *Fast Focus No. 22-2015.* Institute for Research on Poverty, University of Wisconsin–Madison. https://www.irp.wisc.edu/publications/fastfocus/pdfs/FF22-2015.pdf

57. Rumberger, R. W., & Larson, K. A. (1998). Student mobility and the increased risk of high school drop-out. *American Journal of Education, 107*(1), 1–35.

58. Mehana, M., & Reynolds, A. J. (2004). School mobility and achievement: A meta-analysis. *Children & Youth Services Review, 26*(1), 93–119; Selya, A. S., Engel-Rebitzer, E., Dierker, L., Stephen, E., Rose, J., Coffman, D. L., & Otis, M. (2016). The causal effect of student mobility on standardized test performance: A case study with possible implications for accountability mandates within the elementary and secondary education act. *Frontiers in Psychology.*https://www.frontiersin.org/articles/10.3389/fpsyg.2016.01096/full; Voight, A., Shinn, M., & Nation, M. (2012). The longitudinal effects of residential mobility on the academic achievement of urban elementary and middle school students. *Educational Research, 41*(9), 385–392.

59. Sparks, S. D. (2016, August 11). Student mobility: How it affects learning. *Education Week.* https://www.edweek.org/ew/issues/student-mobility/index.html

60. Lee, V. E., & Burkham, D. T. (2002). *Inequality at the starting gate. Social background and differences in achievement as children begin school.* Economic Policy Institute. http://www.epi.org/publication/books_starting_gate/

61. Brownstein R., & the National Journal. (2015, November 12). Why poverty and segregation merge at public schools. *The Atlantic.* https://www.theatlantic.com/politics/archive/2015/11/why-poverty-and-segregation-merge-at-public-schools/433380/

62. See: Linn, R., & Welner, K. G. (2007). *Race conscious policies for assigning students to schools: Social science research and Supreme Court cases.* National Academy of Education; Mickelson, R. A. (2008). Twenty-first century social science research on school diversity and educational outcomes. *Ohio State Law Journal, 69,* 1173–1228; Mickelson, R., & Nkomo, M. (2012). Integrated schooling, life course outcomes, and social cohesion in multiethnic democratic societies. *Review of Research in Education, 36*(1), 197–238.

63. Practices such as real estate agents steering racial groups to certain neighborhoods, unequal access to mortgage credit, exclusionary zoning, and resistant neighbors all play roles. Even with identical incomes, Black families may live in lower-income areas than white families due to racialized housing search processes and discrimination. Massey, D. S., & Denton, N. A. (1993). *American apartheid: Segregation and the making of the underclass.* Harvard University Press; Ross, S. L., & Turner, M. A. (2005). Housing discrimination in metropolitan America: Explaining changes between 1989 and 2000. *Social Problems, 52,*152–180; Reardon, S. F., Fox, L., & Townsend, J. (2015). Neighborhood income composition by household race and income, 1990–2009. *Annals of the American Academy of Political and Social Science, 660*(1),78–97.

64. Owens, A. (2018). Income segregation between school districts and inequality in students' achievement. *Sociology of Education, 91*(1), 1–27. https://www.asanet.org/sites/default/files/attach/journals/jan18soefeature.pdf

65. See: Burdick-Will, J., Ludwig, J., Raudenbush, S. W., Sampson, R. J., Sanbonmatsu, L., & Sharkey, P. (2011). Converging evidence for neighborhood effects on children's test scores: An experimental, quasi-experimental, and observational comparison. In G. J. Duncan & R. J. Murnane (Eds.), *Whither opportunity? Rising inequality and the uncertain life chances of low-income children* (pp. 255–276). Russell Sage Foundation; Chetty, R., Hendren, N., & Katz, L. F. (2015). *The effects of exposure to better neighborhoods on children: New evidence from the moving to opportunity experiment.* Harvard University.

66. Reardon, S. F. (2015, October). *School segregation and racial academic achievement gaps*. CEPA Working Paper No. 15-12. Stanford University: Center for Education Policy Analysis. https://cepa.stanford.edu/sites/default/files/wp15-12v201510.pdf

67. Samuels, C. A. (2019, September 11). Secession exacerbates segregation, study finds. *Education Week, 39*(4), 6.

68. Cohen, R. M. (2019, January 3). New Jersey is getting sued over school segregation. *CityLab*. https://www.citylab.com/equity/2019/01/new-jersey-school-segregation-lawsuit-brown-v-board-housing/579373/

69. Orfield, G., Frankenberg, E., Ee, J., & Ayscue, J. B. (2019, May 10). *Harming our common future: America's segregated schools 65 years after Brown*. The Civil Rights Project. https://www.civilrightsproject.ucla.edu/research/k-12-education/integration-and-diversity/harming-our-common-future-americas-segregated-schools-65-years-after-brown?smid=nytcore-ios-share

70. See: Coleman, J. S., Campbell, E. Q., Hobson, C. J., McPartland, J., Mood, A. M., Weinfeld, F. D., & York, R. L. (1966). *Equality of educational opportunity*. U.S. Department of Health, Education, and Welfare, Office of Education; Borman, G. D., & Dowling, M. (2010). Schools and inequality: A multilevel analysis of Coleman's equality of educational opportunity data. *Teachers College Record, 112*(5), 1201–1246.

71. Reardon, 2015.

72. Samuels, C. A. (2019, October 2). Poverty, not race, fuels the achievement gap. *Education Week, 39*(7), 5.

73. Reardon, 2015.

74. Quillian, L. (2014). Does segregation create winners and losers? Residential segregation and inequality in educational attainment. *Social Problems, 61*(3), 402–426; Vigdor, J. L., & Ludwig. J. O. (2008). Segregation and the test score gap. In K. Magnuson & J. Waldfogel (Eds.), *Steady gains and stalled progress: Inequality and the Black–white test score gap* (pp. 181–211). Russell Sage Foundation.

75. Owens, 2018.

76. Tegeler, P., Mickelson, R. A., & Bottia, M. (2010, October). *What we know about school integration, college attendance, and the reduction of poverty*. The National Coalition on School Diversity. https://www.school-diversity.org/pdf/DiversityResearchBriefNo4.pdf

77. Mickelson, R. A. (2016, October). *School integration and K–12 outcomes: An updated quick synthesis of the social science evidence*. The National Coalition on School Diversity. https://school-diversity.org/pdf/DiversityResearchBriefNo5Oct2016Big.pdf

78. Eaton, S., & Chirichigno, G. (2010, October). *The impact of racially diverse schools in a democratic society*. The National Coalition on School Diversity. https://www.school-diversity.org/pdf/DiversityResearchBriefNo3.pdf

79. Siegel-Hawley, G. (2012, October). *How non-minority students also benefit from racially diverse schools*. The National Coalition on School Diversity. https://www.school-diversity.org/pdf/DiversityResearchBriefNo8.pdf

80. Goldsmith, P. A. (2004). Schools' racial mix, students' optimism, and the Black–white and Latino–white achievement gaps. *Sociology of Education, 77*(2), 121–147; Palardy, G. (2008). Differential school effects among low, middle, and high social class composition schools. *School Effectiveness and School Improvement, 19*(1), 21–49.

81. Billings, S., Deming, D., & Rockoff, J. (2014). School segregation, educational attainment, and crime: Evidence from the end of busing in Charlotte-Mecklenburg. *Quarterly Journal of Economics, 129*(1), 213–256; Saatcioglu, A. (2010). The hidden value of school desegregation: Disentangling school- and student-level effects of desegregation and resegregation on the dropout problem in urban high schools: Evidence from the Cleveland Municipal School District, 1977–1998. *Teachers College Record, 112*(5), 1391–1442.

82. Choi, K., Raley, K., Muller, C., & Riegle-Crumb, C. (2008). Class composition: Socioeconomic characteristics of coursemates and college enrollment. *Social Science Quarterly, 89*(4), 846–866; Fletcher, J., & Tienda, M. (2010). Race and ethnic differences in college achievement: Does high school attended matter? *The Annals of the American Academy of Political and Social Science, 627*(1), 144–166.

83. Card, D., & Rothstein, J. (2006). *Racial segregation and the Black–white test score gap*. Working Paper 12078. The National Bureau of Economic Research. https://www.nber.org/papers/w12078.pdf; Reardon, S., Kalogrides, D., & Shores, K. (2018. May). *The geography of racial/ethnic test score gaps*. CEPA Working Paper No.16-10. Stanford Center for Education Policy Analysis. https://cepa.stanford.edu/sites/default/files/wp16-10-v201712.pdf

84. Page, S. E. (2008). *The difference: How the power of diversity creates better groups, firms, schools, and societies.* Princeton University Press; Chang, M. (2006, May/June). The educational benefits of sustaining cross-racial interaction among undergraduates. *Journal of Higher Education, 77*(3),430–455.

85. Chiu, M. M., & Khoo, L. (2005). Effects of resources, inequality, and privilege bias on achievement: Country, school, and student level analyses. *American Educational Research Journal, 42*(4), 575–603; Schneider, M. (2002). Do school facilities affect academic outcomes? *National Clearinghouse for Educational Facilities.* http://www.ncef.org/pubs/outcomes.pdf

86. Ashenfelter, O., Collins, W., & Yoon, A. (2006). Evaluating the role of *Brown v. Board of Education* in school equalization, desegregation, and the income of African Americans. *American Law and Economics Review, 8*(2), 213–248; Johnson, R. C. (2011 January; Rev. August 2015). *Long-run impacts of school desegregation & school quality on adult attainments.* National Bureau of Economic Research. Working Paper 16664. https://gsppi.berkeley.edu/~ruckerj/johnson_schooldesegregation_NBERw16664.pdf

87. Braddock, J. H. III, & Gonzales, A. D. C. (2010). Social isolation and social cohesion: The effects of K–12 neighborhood and school segregation on intergroup orientations. *Teachers College Record, 112*(6), 1631–1653; Davies, K., Tropp, L. R., Aron, A., Pettigrew, T. F., & Wright, S. C. (2011). Cross-group friendships and intergroup attitudes: A meta-analytic review. *Personality and Social Psychology Review, 15*(4), 332–351.

88. Johnson, 2011.

89. Phillips, K. J. R., Rodosky, R. J., Muñoz, M. A., & Larsen, E. S. (2009). Integrated schools, integrated futures? A case study of school desegregation in Jefferson County, Kentucky. In C. E. Smrekar & E. B. Goldring (Eds.), *From the courtroom to the classroom: The shifting landscape of school desegregation (pp. 239–270).* Harvard Education Press.

90. For a more complete discussion of this topic with citations for further study, see: The Century Foundation. (2019, April 29). *The benefits of socioeconomically and racially integrated schools and classrooms.* https://tcf.org/content/facts/the-benefits-of-socioeconomically-and-racially-integrated-schools-and-classrooms/?session=1

91. Johnson, 2011.

92. See: Benner, A. D., & Crosnoe, R. (2011). The racial/ethnic composition of elementary schools and young children's academic and socioemotional functioning. *American Educational Research Journal, 48*(3), 621–646; Clayton, J. (2011). Changing diversity in schools: The impact on elementary student performance and achievement. *Education and Urban Society, 43*(6), 671–695; Siegel-Hawley, G. (2013). *How nonminority students also benefit from racially diverse schools.* The National Coalition on School Diversity. https://files.eric.ed.gov/fulltext/ED571621.pdf

93. Jackson, K. (2009). Student demographics, teacher sorting, and teacher quality: Evidence from the end of desegregation. *Journal of Labor Economics, 27*(2), 213–225.

94. Jackson, 2009; Lankford, H., Loeb, S., & Wyckoff, J. (2002) Teacher sorting and the plight of urban schools. *Education Evaluation and Policy Analysis, 24*(1), 37–62.

95. Jackson, 2009; Lankford et al., 2002.

96. Jackson, 2009; Lankford et al., 2002.

97. Epstein, J. L. (2011). *School, family, and community partnerships: Preparing educators and improving schools* (2nd ed.). Westview Press.

98. Condron, D., & Roscigno, V. J. (2003) Disparities within: Unequal spending and achievement in an urban school district. *Sociology of Education, 76*(1), 18–36; Klugman, J. (2012) How resource inequality among high schools reproduces class advantages in college destinations, *Research in Higher Education, 53*(8), 803–830.

99. Wells, A. S., Fox, L., & Cordova-Cobo, D. (2016, February 9). How racially diverse schools and classrooms can benefit all students. *The Century Foundation.* https://tcf.org/content/report/how-racially-diverse-schools-and-classrooms-can-benefit-all-students/

100. This phenomenon of improved performance without obvious intervention is now known as the "Hawthorne effect" in honor of the initial Hawthorne studies.

101. Rosenthal, R., & Jacobson, L. (1968). *Pygmalion in the classroom: Teachers' expectations and pupils; intellectual development.* Rineholt and Winston.

102. Viadero, D. (2006, June 21). Fresh look at Coleman data yields different conclusions. *Education Week, 25*(41), 21.

103. Oakes, J. (1985). *Keeping track: How schools structures inequality.* Yale University Press.

104. The study found that two sessions of 25 minutes online at the start of ninth grade could increase students' grades and willingness to take advanced classes. See Yeager et al., 2019; Sparks, S. D. (2019, August 21). National study finds that lessons on "growth mindset" boost grades. *Education Week, 39*(1), 14–15. https://www.edweek.org/ew/articles/2019/08/07/national-study-shows-how-a-simple-growth.html?cmp=soc-edit-tw

105. Schiller, K. S., Schmidt, W. H., Muller, C., & Houang, R. (2010). Hidden disparities: How courses and curricula shape opportunities in mathematics during high school. *Equity and Excellence in. Education, 43*, 414–433.

106. Carroll, J. M., Muller, C., Grodsky, E., & Warren, J. R. (2017). Tracking health inequalities from high school to midlife. *Social Forces, 96*(2), 591–628.

107. Simon, N. S., & Johnson, S. M. (2015). Teacher turnover in high-poverty schools: What we know and can do. *Teachers College Record, 117*(3), 1–36.

108. Johnston, W. R., & Young, C. J. (2019). *Principal and teacher preparation to support the needs of diverse students.* RAND, pp. 8, 12. https://www.rand.org/pubs/research_reports/RR2990.html

109. Marchitello, M., & Trinidad, J. (2019a, March). *Preparing teachers for diverse schools. Lessons from minority serving institutions.* Bellwether Education Partners. https://bellwethereducation.org/sites/default/files/Preparing%20Teachers%20for%20Diverse%20Schools_Bellwether.pdf; Sleeter, C. (2008). Preparing white teachers for diverse students. In M. Cochran-Smith, S. Feiman-Nemser, & D. J. McIntyre (Eds.), *Handbook of research on teacher education* (3rd ed.; pp. 551–582). Routledge; Yuan, H. (2018). Preparing teachers for diversity: A literature review and implications from community-based teacher education. *Higher Education Studies, 8*(1), 9–17.

110. Marchitello, M., & Trinidad, J. (2019b). *Authors' analysis of public school enrollment data from the National Center for Education Statistics.* https://nces.ed.gov/ccd/elsi/tableGenerator.aspx

111. Hamilton, R., McCoach, D. B., & Tutwiler, M.S. (2017). Disentangling the roles of institutional and individual poverty in the identification of gifted students. *Gifted Child Quarterly, 62*(1), 6–24.

112. Oakes, J. (1995). Matchmaking: The dynamics of high school tracking decisions. *American Educational Research Journal, 32*(1), 3–33.

113. Grissom, J. A., & Redding, C. (2016,). Discretion and disproportionality: Explaining the underrepresentation of high-achieving students of color in gifted programs. *AERA Open, 2*(1), 1–25.

114. Lankford et al., 2002; Kalogrides, D., & Loeb, S. (2013). Different teachers, different peers: The magnitude of student sorting within schools. *Educational Researcher, 42*(6), 304–316.

115. Groeger, L.V., Waldman, A., & Eads, D. (2018). Miseducation: Is there racial inequality at your school? *ProPublica.* https://projects.propublica.org/miseducation/; Oakes, J. (1995). Matchmaking: The dynamics of high school tracking decisions. *American Educational Research Journal, 32*(1),3–33.

116. Sorensen, A., & Hallinan, M. (1977). A reconceptualization of school effects. *Sociology of Education, 50*(4), 273–289.

117. Brewer, D. J., Rees, D. L., & Argyrs, L. M. (1995, November). Detracking America's schools: The reform without cost. *Phi Delta Kappan, 77*(3), 210–215; Gamoran, A. (1990). *The effects of track-related instructional differences for student achievement.* Paper presented at the Annual Meeting of the American Educational Research Association, Boston, MA.

118. Gamoran, A. (1986). Institutional and instructional effects of ability grouping. *Sociology of Education, 59*(4), 85–98; Gamoran, A. (1987). The stratification of high school learning opportunities. *Sociology of Education, 60*(3), 135–155; Hoffer, T. (1992). Middle school ability grouping and student achievement in science and mathematics. *Education Evaluation and Policy Analysis, 14*(3), 205–227.

119. Carbonaro, W. (2005, January). Tracking, students' efforts and academic achievement. *Sociology of Education, 78*(1), 27–49. https://pdfs.semanticscholar.org/8628/ecc9283e53b6dc9d8f077373eab0ab843a22.pdf?_ga=2.209773779.734898398.1567366078-1101960874.1567366078

120. For a more complete discussion of student effort in school and achievement, see Carbonaro, 2005.

121. Darling-Hammond, L. (2000, January 1). Teacher quality and student achievement: A review of state policy evidence. *Education Policy Analysis Archives, 8*(1), 1–44; Goe, L., & Stickler, L. M. (2008, March). *Teacher quality and student achievement: Making the most of recent research.* https://files.eric.ed.gov/fulltext/ED520769.pdf

122. For a fuller description of teacher effectiveness qualities, see: Darling-Hammond, 2000; Kini, T., & Podolsky, A. (2016, June 3). *Does teaching experience increase teacher effectiveness? A review of the research*. Learning Policy Institute, pp. 15–27. https://learningpolicyinstitute.org/sites/default/files/product-files/Teaching_Experience_Report_June_2016.pdf; Whitehurst, G. J. (2002, March 5). *Scientifically based research on teacher quality: Research on teacher preparation and professional development*. http://citeseerx.ist.psu.edu/viewdoc/download?doi=10.1.1.468.8079&rep=rep1&type=pdf

123. Bailey, M. J., & Dynarsky, S. M. (2011). *Gains and gaps: Changing inequality in U.S. college entry and completion*. Working Paper No. 17633. National Bureau of Economic Research; Reardon, 2011.

124. Kalogridis & Loeb, 2013.

125. Adamson, F., & Darling-Hammond, L. (2012). Funding disparities and the inequitable distribution of teachers: Evaluating sources and solutions. *Education Policy Analysis Archives, 20*(37), 1–46.

126. The Nation's Report Card. (2019). *2015 student questionnaires results: Classroom instruction for mathematics, reading, and science*. https://www.nationsreportcard.gov/sq_classroom/#mathematics

127. Darling-Hammond, 2000.

128. See: Boyd, D. J., Lankford, H., Loeb, S., Rockoff, J., & Wyckoff, J. (2008). The narrowing gap in New York City teacher qualifications and its implications for student achievement in high-poverty schools. *Journal of Policy Analysis and Management, 27*(4), 793–818; Goldhaber, D., Theobald, R., & Fumia, D. (2018., January). *Teacher quality gaps and student outcomes: Assessing the association between teacher assignments and student math test scores and high school course taking*. Working Paper 185. National Center for Analysis of Longitudinal Data in Education Research (CALDER). https://caldercenter.org/sites/default/files/WP%20185.pdf; Isenberg, E., Max, J., Gleason, P., Johnson, M., Deutsch, J., & Hansen, M. (2016, October). *Do low-income students have equal access to effective teachers? Evidence from 26 districts. NCEE 2017-4007*. U.S. Department of Education. https://ies.ed.gov/ncee/pubs/20174008/pdf/20174007.pdf

129. Goodlad, J. (1954). Some effects of promotion and on-promotion upon the social and personal adjustment of children. *Journal of Experimental Education, 22*(4), 301–328; Owings, W., & Magliaro, S. (1998, September). Grade retention: A history of failure. *Educational Leadership, 56*(1), 86–88.

130. David, J. L. (2008, March). What research says about . . . grade retention. *Educational Leadership, 65*(6), 83–84.

131. Warren, J. R., Hoffman, E., & Andrew, M. (2014). Patterns and trends in grade retention rates in the United States, 1995–2010. *Educational Researcher, 43*(9), 433–443.

132. Child Trends. (2018, December 28). *Children who repeated a grade*. https://www.childtrends.org/indicators/children-who-repeated-a-grade-2

133. National Center for Education Statistics. (2019, February). *Status and trends in the education of racial and ethnic groups. Indicator 154: Retention, suspension, and expulsion*. Institute of Education Sciences. https://nces.ed.gov/programs/raceindicators/indicator_RDA.asp

134. Applied Research Center. (2000). *Facing the consequences: An examination of racial discrimination in U.S. public schools*; Noguera, P. (1997). Reconsidering the crisis confronting California black male youth: Providing support without further marginalization. *Journal of Negro Education, 65*(2), 219–236.

135. Skiba, R. J., Michael, R. S., Nardo, A. C., & Peterson, R. L. (2002). The color of discipline: Sources of racial and gender disproportionality in school punishment. *Urban Review, 34*, 317–342.

136. Blad, E., & Mitchell, C. (2018, May 1). Black students bear uneven brunt of discipline, data show. *Education Week, 37*(29), 10.

137. Blad & Mitchell, 2018.

138. Blad & Mitchell, 2018; Barbee, B., & Blackburn, C. (2019, June 11). SPLC report: Corporal punishment in school disproportionately affects black students, students with disabilities. *Southern Poverty Law Center*. https://www.splcenter.org/news/20190611/splc-report-corporal-punishment-in-school

139. Morris, E. W., & Perry, B. L. (2016, February). The punishment gap: School suspension and racial disparities in achievement. *Social Problems, 63*(1), 68–86.

140. Balfanz, R., Byrnes, V., & Fox, J. (2014). Sent home and put off-track: The antecedents, disproportionalities, and consequences of being suspended in ninth grade. *Journal of Applied Research on Children: Informing Policy for Children at Risk, 5*(2), 1–19.

141. Okonofua, J. A., Paunesku, D., & Walton, G. M. (2016). *Brief intervention to encourage empathic discipline cuts suspension rates in half among adolescents*. https://www.pnas.org/content/113/19/5221.abstract; Sparks, S. D. (2016, July 10). One key to reducing school suspension: A little respect. *Education Week, 35*(36), 1, 10.

142. Jason A. Okonofua, Stanford University social psychologist who led experiments on helping teachers and students empathize and develop respect for each other to reduce school suspensions, said this. See: Sparks, 2016.

143. Hallinam, M., & Williams, R. (1989). Interracial friendship choices in secondary school. *American Sociological Review, 54*(1), 67–78; Oakes, J., Gamoran, A., & Page, R. N. (1992). Curriculum differentiation: Opportunities, outcomes, and meanings. In R. W Jackson (Ed.), *Handbook of research on curriculum* (pp. 570–608). Macmillan.

144. Darling-Hammond, L. (1998). Unequal opportunity: Race and education. *Brookings.* https://www.brookings.edu/articles/unequal-opportunity-race-and-education/; Hallinam & Williams, 1989; Oakes et al., 1992; Miller, V. J. (2018). Access defined: Tracking as a modern roadblock to equal educational opportunity. *New York University Law Review.* https://www.nyulawreview.org/wp-content/uploads/2018/10/NYULawReview-93-4-Miller.pdf; Hamilton, R., McCoach, D. B., & Tutwiler, M. S. (2017). Disentangling the roles of institutional and individual poverty in the identification of gifted students. *Gifted Child Quarterly, 62*(1), 6–24; Oakes, 1985.

145. See: Cohen, J., McCabe, E. M., Mitchell, N. M., & Pickeral, T. (2009, January). School climate: Research, policy, teacher education, and practice. *Teachers College Record, 111*(1), 180–213; MacNeil, A. J., Prater, D. L., & Busch, S. (2009). The effects of school culture and climate on student achievement. *International Journal of Leadership in Education. Theory and Practice, 12*(1), 73–84; Uline, C., & Tschannen-Moran, M. K. (2007). The walls speak: The interplay of quality facilities, school, climate, and student achievement. *Journal of Educational Administration, 46*(1), 55–73.

146. National Center for Education Statistics. (2016). *The nation's report card: 2015.* U.S. Department of Education; Braveman, P., & Gottlieb, L. (2014). The social determinants of health: It's time to consider the causes of the causes. *Public Health Reports, 129* (Suppl. 2), 19–31; Piketty, T. (2014). *Capital in the twenty-first century.* Harvard University Press.

147. National Center for Education Statistics. (2020). Preprimary education enrollment. *Fast Facts.* https://nces.ed.gov/fastfacts/display.asp?id=516

148. National Center for Education Statistics. (2019, May). Preschool enrollment rates by country. *The Condition of Education.* https://nces.ed.gov/programs/coe/indicator_cgh.asp

149. Campbell, F., Ramey C., Pungello E., Sparling, J., & Miller-Johnson, S., (2002). Early childhood education: Young adult outcomes from the Abecedarian Project. *Applied Developmental Science, 6*(1),42–57.

150. Schweinhart, L., Montie, J., Zongping, X., Barnett, W., Belfield, C., & Nores. M. (2005). *Lifetime effects: The high/scope perry preschool study through age 40.* High/Scope Press; Sparks, S. D. (2019, May 14). Like father, like son: Preschool benefits cross generations, says landmark study. *Education Week.* http://blogs.edweek.org/edweek/inside-school-research/2019/05/perry_preschool_early_childhood_intergenerational_benefits.html

151. Reynolds, A., Temple, J., White, B., Ou, S.-R., & Robertson, D. (2011). Age 26 cost–benefit analysis of the child parent center early education program. *Child Development, 82*(1), 379–404.

152. Karoly, L. (2001). Investing in the future: Reducing poverty through human capital investments. In S. Danziger & R. Haveman (Eds.), *Understanding poverty* (pp. 314–346). Harvard University Press; Knudsen, E., Heckman, J., Cameron, J., & Shonkoff, J. (2006). Economic, neurobiological, and behavioral perspectives on building America's future workforce. *Proceedings of the National Academy of Sciences, 103*(27), 10155–10162; Bartik, T. (2011). *Investing in kids: Early childhood programs and local economic development.* W. E. Upjohn Institute for Employment Research.

153. Reynolds, A. (2019). The power of P-3 school reform. *Phi Delta Kappan, 100*(6), 27–33.

154. Claessens, A., Engel, M., & Curran, F. (2014). Academic content, student learning and the persistence of preschool effects. *American Educational Research Journal, 51*(2), 403–434; Conner, C., Morrison, F., & Slominski, L. (2006). Preschool instructional and children's emergent literacy growth. *Journal of Educational Psychology, 98*(4), 665–689; Duncan, G., & Magnuson, K. (2013). Investing in preschool programs. *Journal of Economic Perspectives, 27*(2), 109–132; Karoly, L., Kilburn, M., & Cannon, J. (2005). *Proven benefits of early childhood interventions.* RAND. https://www.rand.org/content/dam/rand/pubs/monographs/2005/RAND_MG341.pdf; Phillips, D., Lipskey, M., Dodge, K., Haskins, R., Bassok, D., Burchinal, M., Duncan G., Dynarski, M., Magnuson, K., & Weiland, C. (2017). *Puzzling it out: The current state of scientific knowledge of pre-kindergarten effects.* https://www.brookings.edu/wp-content/uploads/2017/04/consensus-statement_final.pdf

155. Barnett, W. S., & Boocock, S. S. (Eds.). (1998). Early care and education for children in poverty. State University of New York Press; Karoly, L. A., Kilburn M. R., Bigelow, J. H., Caulkins, J. P., & Cannon J. S. (2001). *Assessing costs and benefits of early childhood intervention programs: Overview and applications to the starting early starting smart program.* RAND; Samuels, C. (2018). Quality is crucial to sustaining benefits of pre-k, studies stress. *Education Week, 37*(29), 7.

156. See: Claessens et al., 2014; Conner et al., 2006; Duncan & Magnuson, 2013.

157. Heckman, J. K. J., & Karapakula, G. (2019, May). *Intergenerational and intragenerational externalities of the perry preschool project.* NBER Working Paper No. 25889. The National Bureau of Economic Research. https://www.nber.org/papers/w25889.pdf

158. Campbell, F. A., & Ramey, C. T. (1994). Effects of early intervention on intellectual and academic achievement: A follow-up study of children from low-income families. *Child Development. 65*(2), 684–698; Garcia, J., Heckman, J., Leaf, D., & Prados, M. (2017). Quantifying the life-cycle benefits of a prototypical early childhood program. IZA DP No. 10811. http://ftp.iza.org/dp10811.pdf; Gayl, C. (2008). Pre-kindergarten: The research on pre-k. *Center For Public Education.* http://www.centerforpubliceducation.org/Main-Menu/Pre-kindergarten/Pre-Kindergarten; Yoshikawa, H., Weiland, C., Brooks-Gunn, J., Burchinal, M., Espinosa, L., Gormley, W., . . ., & Zaslow, M. (2013). *Investing in our future: The evidence base on preschool education.* Society for Research in Child Development. https://www.fcd-us.org/assets/2016/04/Evidence-Base-on-Preschool-Education-FINAL.pdf

159. Camilli, G., Vargas, S., Ryan, S., & Barnett, W.S. (2010). Meta-analysis of the effects of early education interventions on cognitive and social development. *Teachers College Record, 112*(3), 579–620.

160. Friedman-Krauss, A. H., Barnett, W. S., Weisenfeld, G. G., Kasmin, R., DiCrecchio, N., & Horowitz, N. (2018). *The state of preschool 2017: State preschool yearbook.* National Institute for Early Education Research. http://nieer.org/wp-content/uploads/2018/07/State-of-Preschool-2017

161. The Abecedarian and the Child-Parent Center Early Education Program, respectively, netted these cost-benefits. See: Campbell, F. A., & Ramey, C. T. (1994). Effects of early intervention on intellectual and academic achievement: A follow-up study of children from low-income families. *Child Development. 65*(2), 684–698; The Carolina Abecedarian Project. (n.d.). *Groundbreaking follow-up studies.* University of North Carolina. https://abc.fpg.unc.edu/groundbreaking-follow-studies; Reynolds, A. J., Temple, J. A., White, B. A., Ou, S.-R., & Robertson, D. L. (2011). Age-26 cost-benefit analysis of the child-parent center early education program. *Child Development, 82*(1), 379–404.

162. Executive Office of the President of the United States. (2014, December). *The economics of early childhood investments.* https://obamawhitehouse.archives.gov/sites/default/files/docs/the_economics_of_early_childhood_investments.pdf

163. Zirkel, S. (2008, June). The influence of multicultural education practices on student outcomes and intergroup relations. *Teachers College Record, 110*(6), 1147–1181.

164. Banks, J. A. (1992). Multicultural education: For freedom's sake. *Educational Leadership, 49*(4), 34.

165. For example, exposure to violence can lead children to suffer from anxiety, irritability, stress, and hypervigilance that can express itself in negative classroom behaviors, such as presenting a "tough front" to prevent becoming victims; underperforming students grow frustrated and disaffected with continued poor academic achievement and are more likely to act disruptively. See: Miles, S. B., & Stipek, D. (2006). Contemporaneous and longitudinal associations between social behavior and literacy achievement in a sample of low-income elementary school children. *Child Development, 77,* 103–117.

166. Larson & Ovando, 2001.

167. Festinger, L. A. (1957). *A theory of cognitive dissonance.* Row, Peterson.

168. McFalls, E. L., & Cobb-Roberts, D. (2001). Reducing resistance to diversity through cognitive dissonance instruction: Implications for teacher education. *Journal of Teacher Education, 52*(2), 164–172. Authors conclude that the ultimate decision to accept or reject information is the learner's responsibility.

169. McFalls & Cobb-Roberts, 2001.

170. Larson & Ovando, 2001, p. 82.

iStock/Ridofranz

8 DIVERSITY AND CULTURAL ASSETS IN EDUCATION

InTASC Standards Addressed: 1, 2, 3, 4, 5, 6, 7, 8, 9, 10

LEARNING OBJECTIVES

After you read this chapter, you should be able to

8.1 Assess the demographic mismatch between today's students and today's teacher workforce, misconceptions about race, and the implications for teachers' "cultural competence."

8.2 Critique how people develop cultural and racial identities that impact their learning; how the theories of white privilege and white fragility challenge white people's awareness of themselves in the world; and the influence of intersectionality on understanding diversity.

8.3 Clarify the relationship between underrepresented students' perceptions—including oppositional culture theory, stereotype threat theory, and microaggression theory—and their academic performance.

8.4 Support how teachers using students' assets (rather than deficits) can improve their teaching effectiveness with all students, especially underrepresented students.

8.5 Argue how teachers can use diverse students' personal, family, and cultural assets and culturally responsive pedagogy to foster student resilience and success in school.

"Teaching and learning are cultural processes that take place in a social context,"[1] observes Geneva Gay, multicultural scholar. She elaborates: "To make teaching and learning more accessible and equitable for a wide variety of students, students' cultures need to be more clearly understood. Such an understanding can be achieved by analyzing education from multiple cultural perspectives and thereby removing the blindness imposed on education by the dominant cultural experience."[2]

Students' personal, familial, and cultural factors all influence how well they achieve in school. The achievement/opportunity gap persists for students who are Black, low income, Latinx, Native American, English language learners, children without permanent homes, children of migrant workers, and children with special disabilities. Although racial differences are not biological, they do have social and cultural implications. In addition, schools are increasingly educating students who identify as having a variety of sexual and gender orientations who bring unique concerns into the learning environment. Apparently, members of any student group that largely differs from the white middle-class heterosexual model around which many public schools are organized face challenges to their school success.

When dealing with people who are different than we are, it is important to check ourselves for **unconscious, implicit bias**—stereotypes or beliefs—that affects our actions in a prejudiced way. Since a person's **explicit or conscious bias** (i.e., discrimination against people of certain races, ethnicities, religions, or abilities) exists within conscious awareness, the individual acts intentionally to express these prejudices, such as with verbal harassment or by not calling on a student with a disability to participate in class. By comparison, *implicit* or *unconscious bias* operates outside a person's mindful awareness, appearing in the person's attitudes, understandings, and behaviors and directly contradicting what a person says he or she values. Implicit bias, such as negative stereotypes, can interfere with relationship building and decision-making, tainting the learning climate and harming both teacher and student. When teachers can recognize their own cultural beliefs, biases, and assumptions and acknowledge others' ethnic, cultural, personal, and other differences in a nonjudgmental manner, they can better provide the caring, culturally supportive classrooms and high academic expectations to help every student succeed.

8.1 TODAY'S DIVERSE LEARNERS

Diverse learners are children who differ in visible and invisible ways from the stereotypical "white Anglo-Saxon" student of America's colonial past. They include students from racially, ethnically, culturally, and linguistically different families, communities, and socioeconomic statuses (SES).[3] Diverse learners also include students who do not differ demographically from the mainstream white student but who come to school with their own educational, social, or physical needs that must be acknowledged so they may succeed academically.

8.1a Meet Our Students

Many ethnically and racially diverse learners are already very familiar; they may be yourself, your siblings, relatives, friends, neighbors, and classmates. Other diverse learners may be less familiar, so we will briefly introduce them to you.

Students with disabilities may be identified with one of 13 different disability conditions that adversely affect their educational performance. In 2017–2018, about 7 million students, ages 3 through 21 received special education services.[4] These categories may overlap, and many variations appear within and between each category.[5] These students' educational and physical needs vary widely, from needing instructional supports and accommodations in regular or self-contained classrooms to using mechanical transportation to propel themselves through the halls to advanced academic classes. To the maximum extent possible, students with disabilities learn in classrooms with their abled peers.

Culturally diverse learners may differ from their peers and teachers by ethnicity, race, socioeconomic status, language, gender, learning preferences, and/or cognitive and social development. American citizens or immigrants, they may practice different communication styles—such as using nonverbal gestures or a more reserved response to teachers' questions—than students from the dominant culture. Over 1,000 different cultures are represented in today's schools.[6]

English language learners come from a range of home languages, cultural backgrounds, and levels of English proficiency. They may be U.S. born or refugees. They may have extensive or no prior school experiences. As of May 2019, the United States enrolled 4.9 million students (9.6% of public school students) across all 50 states.[7]

Gifted students have been formally or informally identified as having superior abilities in areas of academic achievement, cognitive abilities, creative thinking, and or visual/performing arts. On the other hand, gifted children from marginalized groups may be underidentified. Roughly 3.2 million children are currently enrolled in gifted and talented programs in U.S. public schools (about 6% of public school students).[8]

LGBTQ+ is an acronym for people who are lesbian, gay, bisexual, transgender, and queer or questioning their sexual orientation or gender identity.[9] In 2017, LGBTQ+ persons, or sexual minority youth, represented about 4.5% of the U.S. population,[10] comprising about 1.3 million students (around 8%) of all high school students.[11] Yet despite the umbrella label, this group is not homogeneous; members have different interests and priorities. A Center for Disease Control (CDC) health survey found that they were twice as likely to be bullied, both online and at school, and more than twice as likely to stay home from school to avoid violence they might face going to school or once there.[12] By self-defining as LGBTQ+, these individuals become part of a subculture who share these characteristics.[13] This complex topic is discussed more fully elsewhere.[14]

While each learner can benefit from the school environment, those who arrive with backgrounds unlike the "typical" student may need additional academic and social supports to take the best advantage of school's academic and cocurricular programs. Teachers need to know each student as an individual to determine what each needs to succeed at school.

8.1b Student Diversity and Teacher Demographics

American public school students are more diverse than their teachers. The 2015–2016 school year was the first in which the majority of American public school children were students of color.[15] The elementary and secondary educator workforce remains overwhelmingly white (80%) and female (77%).[16] Of the teachers of color (20%), 34% work in high-poverty districts; and about 80% of students live where Black or Latinx teachers comprise less than 5% of the faculty.[17] Black men are teaching's most underrepresented demographic.[18]

Table 8.1 indicates the percentage of students and teachers by race in 2015 to 2016.[19] The demographic mismatch between students and their teachers is striking.

TABLE 8.1 ■ American Public School Student and Teacher Demographics, 2015–2016

Students	Teachers
White 48.2 %	White 80.1 %
Latinx 26.4 %	Latinx 8.8 %
Black 15.3 %	Black 6.7 %
Asian 5.1 %	Asian 2.3 %
Native American/Alaska Native 1.0 %	Native American/Alaska Native 0.4 %
Native Hawaiian/Pacific Islander 0.4 %	Native Hawaiian/Pacific Islander 0.2 %
Two or more races 3.6 %	Two or more races 1.4%

Source: Adapted from Riser-Kositsky, M. (2019, February 5). Education statistics: Facts About American Schools. *Education Week*. https://www.edweek.org/ew/issues/education-statistics/index.html

A growing body of research suggests that children often benefit from having a teacher of the same race or ethnicity. Studies find that Black students have better attendance, more positive attitudes, and higher graduation and college attendance rates when their teachers share their race and/or ethnicity. They perform better in reading and math and are less likely to be suspended from school for infractions that involve teacher discretion (such as arguing in class, insubordination, and disrupting instruction) when they have Black teachers.[20] Likewise, Black teachers of Black students tend to have significantly higher expectations for their educational attainment than do white teachers;[21] confront issues of racism; serve as advocates and cultural brokers; and develop more trusting relationships with students, especially those who share their cultural background.[22] At the same time, teachers of color also provide a positive role model for white students, breaking down negative stereotypes and preparing students to live and work in a multiracial society.[23]

Despite these benefits to student learning, people of color are less likely to enter the teaching profession and less likely to remain. That's partly because African American and Latinx teachers are more likely to work in urban schools where students have higher needs and where burnout is high for everyone, experts say.[24] Education requirements, low pay, stressful workplaces, and lack of respect all can contribute to the shortage of teachers of color, as well as their high turnover rates. This situation creates high stress and turnover for many teachers.

While the teaching workforce has become slightly more diverse recently, no signs suggest that these teacher demographics will change.[25] Nonetheless, all teachers can improve school climate and increase their effectiveness in raising every student's achievement when they develop a keener self-awareness of their racial, cultural, and subcultural assumptions and biases and adjust their behaviors accordingly. Building a better understanding of their diverse students as individuals and as members of their particular cultures can aid this process of professional growth. The rest of this chapter provides insights and practices to do this.

8.2 DEVELOPING CULTURAL AND RACIAL IDENTITIES

Our cultural heritages and backgrounds affect our lives in many ways. **Culture** is "the systems of values, beliefs, and ways of knowing that guide communities of people in their daily lives."[26] Culture shapes one's thinking and actions, identifying for members what is and is not acceptable behavior. Culture always intersects with individuals' race, ethnicity, social class, gender, age, ability, status, family traditions, and personal identity. These beliefs, common traditions, language, values, and agreement about norms for living help people organize their world through language and other symbol systems. Culture also influences how various groups approach learning and problem-solving, how they construct knowledge, and how they pass information through the generations.[27]

8.2a Culture and Learning

Research suggests that two broad cultural value systems—individualism and collectivism—shape people's thoughts and actions in almost all aspects of life.[28] Cultures that value individualism encourage their children to "live their own lives." Generally, the traditional American mainstream culture is individualistic, emphasizing self-reliance, rugged individualism, self-expression, and personal achievement. "Every man for himself" might describe the individualistic culture. In contrast, cultures that favor a collectivist orientation make family and kinship ties lifetime priorities. Cultures including African American, Latinx, Native American, Asian American, and many immigrant groups can be collectivistic, stressing interdependence, cooperation, family unity, family and group success, respect, and social development.[29] The expressions "Many hands make light work" and "It takes a village" reflect the collectivist perspective. Table 8.2 compares individualistic and collectivist perspectives about schooling.

TABLE 8.2 ■ Cultural Perspectives on Schooling

Individualistic Perspective	Collectivist Perspective
Children socialized to see learning as achieving personal goals and celebrating individual achievement.	Children socialized to see learning as working toward group goals. Group success is more important than individual achievement.
As independent individuals, students are responsible for their own learning and focus on their own needs. If students need help, they must ask the teacher for help.	Learning is interdependent and embedded in a social context. Students are encouraged to work collaboratively to help others with their tasks before considering their own assignments.
The primary learning relationship is between teacher and student.	The student and teacher relationship is central but not the only important relationship in the classroom.
The academic work is the highest priority; relationships come second.	Relationships are the highest priority; academic tasks come second.
Education's goal is for students to perform well academically and show ability through good grades and on-time promotions.	Education's goal is to produce decent and knowledgeable persons who respect others and do not place themselves above others in value.
Social and ethical development are separate.	Social and ethical development are integrated.

Source: Based on Trumbull, E., Rothstein-Fisch, C., and Greenfield, P. M. (2000). Bridging cultures in our schools: New approaches that work. *WestEd.* https://www.wested.org/online_pubs/lcd-99-01.pdf

As noted in Table 8.2, the basic difference between these two viewpoints is the relative emphasis placed on individual versus group well-being. Every culture has both individualistic and collectivist values. Wide variations appear within each culture, and both approaches have advantages and disadvantages. In addition, factors such as SES, rural or urban setting, and parents' formal educational level affect tendencies toward individualism versus collectivism. In our Western culture, higher SES, urban settings, and increased parental education are associated with greater individualism.

8.2b Race as a Social, Not Scientific Construct

From American colonization to the present day, racial categorization is a fact of public and private life. **Race** is a social construction, a cultural invention based on physical appearance (such as facial features and skin or hair color and texture), ancestry, nationality, and culture. People invented the idea of race to make sense of their experiences in a world filled with people who lived elsewhere and looked and acted unlike themselves. Anthropologists say that from a biological standpoint, races do not exist; it is not a scientifically validated biological category. So-called racial traits are not reliably measurable, and DNA evidence shows that contemporary humans are one variable species.[30]

Nonetheless, race does carry tremendous social importance. The concept of race is used to identify individuals and place them into demographic groups for various purposes, including classification, public policy, and population demographics. People so identified accept that externally imposed designation and make it part of their psychosocial identity, influencing their sense of self in society.

Children's racial and ethnic attitudes tend to crystallize around age 10.
iStock/fstop123

Europeans brought the concept of race with them to the new world, along with the view of racial hierarchy. To European settlers in America, whiteness stood for European nobility and became the category to protect them from the threat of racial dilution by mixing with African Americans—free, enslaved, or emancipated and their descendants—or Native Americans. In the United States, race is a highly salient organizing social category.

The 17th and 18th century slave trade fortified the use of race as a social and physical factor. As the colonial and early U.S. census counted the American population, a state's enslaved population counted as three fifths of its free population. The U.S. Constitution only recognized enslaved people as three fifths of a person. Enslaved descendants from Africa and Native Americans were denied U.S. citizenships, freedom, and human rights. Similarly, language and physical differences marked Asian American immigrants as nonwhite, and Latinx people were noted for their language and occasionally for their physical appearance as being nonwhite.[31] By 1900, European and American scientists viewed races as natural, long-standing divisions of the human species evolving at different biological and cultural rates. In this way, they rationalized, accepted, and legitimized racial inequality.

Understanding race as a social—not biological—construct can help teachers understand the historical, economic, social, and political conditions that encouraged and sustained this country's social inequality. It also enables teachers to respect each student's individuality and create the learning environment that allows each student to grow and learn to high standards.

8.2c A Racial/Cultural Identity Development Model

People develop cultural and racial identities through their interactions and responses to persons, events, media, and institutions that highlight the degree to which they are alike or different than others in their environment. Society and culture assign relative values to these similarities and differences. In turn, the sense and meaning that individuals derive from these experiences and the value judgments they make about them help define their self- and group identities. Other historically and socially marginalized groups, such as women, individuals with disabilities, and LGBTQ+ youth, experience similar processes.[32]

Racial, Ethnic, and Cultural Identities

Identity is who you are, the way you think about yourself, and the way the world views you. **Racial, ethnic, and cultural identities** are defined as a sense of collective self, based on a person's perception that he or she shares a common heritage with a particular racial, ethnic, or cultural group. These identities are critical parts of how persons see themselves both as individuals and as part of a larger group. Although the development of this collective identity does not necessarily happen in an inflexible chronological sequence, scholars believe that most underrepresented group members go through relatively similar stages. White persons also experience development of their racial identity (to be discussed later).

For underrepresented adolescents, race, ethnicity, and culture play important roles in their identity development. Racial and ethnic attitudes among children appear to crystallize by about age 10.[33] Their home, community, and school experiences all contribute to how children come to view and value themselves as individuals and as minority group members.

Observers have noted that underrepresented groups share similar patterns of adjustment to living in a culture that does not value them.[34] In past decades, African Americans, Asian Americans, Latinx, and Native Americans have experienced changes in the ways they view themselves within American society. With an increasing sense of self-worth, they celebrate their own traditions and challenge the larger society to respect their value. Their sense of cultural oppression is the mutually unifying force. As a result, researchers have integrated various cultural identity models to identify common features that cut across minority populations.

Table 8.3 illustrates a conceptual framework to help educators understand their culturally and racially/ethnically diverse students' attitudes and behaviors. This theoretical model defines five stages of development that those growing up outside the mainstream experience as they struggle to understand themselves in terms of their own culture, the dominant culture, and what they view as the unfair relationship between the two: conformity, dissonance, resistance and immersion, introspection, and integrative awareness. At each identity level, attitudes and beliefs reflect the individual's experiences at that stage.[35] Critics take issue with some of these characterizations, as we will discuss more fully in a later section.

TABLE 8.3 ■ The Racial and Cultural Identity Development Model

Phases of Minority Development Model	Attitude Toward Self	Attitude Toward Dominant Group
Stage 1: Conformity	Self-depreciating or neutral	Group appreciating
Stage 2: Dissonance	Conflict between self-depreciating and group appreciating	Conflict between group appreciating and group depreciating
Stage 3: Resistance and Immersion	Self-appreciating	Group depreciating
Stage 4: Introspection	Concern with the basis of self-appreciation	Concern with the basis of group depreciation
Stage 5: Integrative Awareness	Self-appreciating	Selective appreciation

Source: Adapted from Sue, D. W., and Sue, D. (2016). *Counseling the culturally diverse: Theory and practice* (7th ed.). John Wiley & Sons, p. 367, Table 11.1. [They cite as their source: Atkinson, D. R., Morten, G., and Sue, D. W. (1998). *Counseling American minorities: A cross cultural perspective* (5th ed.). McGraw.]

Conformity Phase

Racial and ethnic minority individuals strongly prefer the dominant cultural values over those of their own culture. They strongly identify with white Americans' lifestyles, value systems, and cultural and physical characteristics as "superior." At the same time, they accept the "inferiority" of all other lifestyles and related characteristics, and they may act negatively toward their own racial and cultural heritage.

For instance, Malcolm X (1925–1965), the African American leader, went to great lengths to straighten and dye his hair so that he would appear more like white males.[36]

Dissonance Phase

Racial and ethnic minority individuals receive information or have experiences that contradict the dominant culture's beliefs, attitudes, and values. The individual begins to question and challenge the conformity stage's attitudes and beliefs—and his or her current self-concept. The person becomes aware that racism exists, that not all aspects of the minority or majority culture are either good or bad, and one cannot escape one's cultural heritage. Feeling pride in one's racial or ethnic minority culture changes the way the person sees himself or herself—and the way the person sees others.

For example, an Asian American who believes that all Asians are inhibited, passive, and academically oriented math whizzes may meet someone who breaks all these stereotypes, such as encountering a dynamic, gregarious Asian American teacher. Likewise, a Black youngster may view playing professional sports as the fast track to adult wealth and fame but sees top Black athletes who are very well educated.

Resistance and Immersion Phase

The culturally different individual tends to completely endorse racial or ethnic minority-held views and rejects the dominant society's values and culture. The person actively seeks information and artifacts of his or her own group's history that enhance the individual's sense of identity and worth. The person may feel embarrassed and angry that he or she once devalued his or her own racial or cultural group and now feels intense pride and honor about that group's cultural and racial characteristics. Individuals may feel strong anger toward the dominant society's oppression and racism, as well as a solid, unquestioning identification with—and commitment to—one's own group. As a result, individuals tend to withdraw from the dominant culture and immerse themselves in their own.

For example, the 1960s "Black Is Beautiful" movement encouraged African Americans to stop "relaxing" their hair in the European American fashion and to celebrate their African heritage by embracing their hair's texture and wearing it in natural styles as a way to raise self-esteem and pride in one's ancestral traditions.

Introspection Phase

The underrepresented individual becomes uncomfortable with the rigid views of the resistance and immersion stage. The "all or nothing" approach is too simplistic (and often both exhausting and inaccurate) for the complex world they are coming to know. Rather than wanting to react negatively to the dominant culture, the person wants to develop a positive sense of self within the larger society. Similarly, the person no longer wants to hold back his or her own expanding views and choices in an effort to please the group. The racial or ethnic minority individual must choose between responsibility and loyalty to his or her own personal independence or go along with group conformity.

For example, a Latinx teen who develops a close friendship with a white classmate may feel considerable pressure from his or her culturally similar peers to end the relationship with the "gringo." Or a low-income Black youth who takes schoolwork seriously, aspires to attend college, and considers white classmates as friends may feel shunned by racial peers.

When underrepresented students have experiences that contradict the dominant culture's beliefs, attitudes, and values, they begin to question how they see themselves.

iStock/Courtney Hale

Integrative Awareness Phase

Persons of color have developed an inner sense of security, a positive self-image, autonomy, and confidence, and they can appreciate the unique aspects of their own culture as well as those of the dominant U.S. culture. They realize that underrepresented and white cultures are not always in conflict: All cultures have both acceptable and unacceptable aspects. With the prior phases' conflicts resolved, their empathy for others increases, and they seek to understand others' cultural values and beliefs. They become bicultural or multicultural—an individual who is a member of his or her own race/group, a member of the larger society, and a member of the human race.

To illustrate, a Latinx person can be good friends with other Latinx people, white people, Black people, and any other persons, gay or straight, who have the qualities that make for strong, mutually respectful relationships.

Cultural identity development influences individuals' own identity development. Different persons experience these stages at different times and at varying rates, depending on their experiences and personalities. For this reason, teachers cannot expect all of their students from historically or socially marginalized groups to be at the same stage at the same time. Students may grow and change in their cultural or racial identity development throughout the year. When teachers understand that this process occurs, they can better understand and accept their diverse students as maturing individuals.

8.2d White Identity Model

Just as race is a social construct, so is whiteness. In our culture, "whiteness" is more than skin color. Rather, **"white" and "whiteness"** are a set of social processes and practices, a way white people see themselves and others, and a set of cultural behaviors usually "unmarked and unnamed."[37]

White persons also have a racial/cultural identity. But being white is so interwoven into everyday living that, at times, they cannot step outside and see their beliefs, values, and behaviors as creating a distinct cultural group.

White educators benefit when they can understand their own racial/cultural identity within a pluralistic society. Like persons of color, white people go through racial identity changes.[38] In any multicultural encounter, the status of white racial identity development affects the process and outcome of interracial relationships. By going through the same stages as discussed previously in the racial/cultural minority identity development model (plus one earlier phase and one later phase), white persons experience their own racial/cultural self-awareness.[39]

Naiveté Phase

During life's first 3 years, the child experiences immature, neutral, open, and spontaneous curiosity about racial differences. Between ages 3 and 5, the young white child begins to associate positive meaning with his or her own ethnic group and negative meaning with other groups, gradually developing a sense of superiority about the concept of whiteness from the media and significant others in the child's life.

For instance, a white 4-year-old meets a Black 4-year-old on the local playground, and they begin to play together. Their parents exchange quick glances, and after a few minutes, the white parent declares, "It's time to go now" and takes the child away.

Conformity Phase

The white person consciously or unconsciously comes to believe that the white Euro-American culture is the most highly developed and that all other cultures are primitive or inferior. The person has minimal awareness of the self as a racial being and strong belief that his or her values and norms governing behavior are universal. With limited accurate knowledge of other cultural or racial groups, the white person tends to rely on stereotypes as the main source of information. Many white people deny that they belong to a race, profess to "color blindness," and deny that people are different or that discrimination exists. This stance allows them to deny responsibility for perpetuating a racist system. Instead, they see the "problem" as resting with the marginalized groups.

For instance, a white person insists that he or she does not notice another's skin color, asserting, "People are people!" But when confronted with a historically and socially marginalized group or subgroup member's achievement gap, he or she responds, "These students would not have problems if they worked harder, assimilated, spoke better English, and used the restroom that matches their birth gender."

Dissonance Phase

The white person is forced to deal with the inconsistencies that he or she has compartmentalized when confronted with information or experiences at odds with his or her denial of racial differences or with the inaccurate stereotypes he or she holds about others. Most often, individuals must acknowledge "whiteness" (at some level), must examine their own cultural values, and decide which are correct—their stereotypes or their actual experiences with others unlike themselves.

For example, a white person who consciously believes that "all human are created equal" and does not knowingly discriminate suddenly has qualms about having a Black family move next door or have their teenager date a person of color. Similarly, a "straight" white person gets to know someone from the LGBTQ+ community and finds that this individual does not fit the stereotype.

Resistance and Immersion Phase

The white person begins to question and challenge his or her own racism. The individual sees stereotypes portrayed and perpetuated in advertising, television, social media, interpersonal interactions, and U.S. culture and institutions. The person has increased awareness of how racism operates and its pervasiveness in American culture and institutions. In addition, the person recognizes how being white has provided him or her with certain advantages that are denied to various underrepresented groups. The white person feels angry at the larger society and guilty about having been part of an oppressive system.

A white "liberal" may want to protect historically and socially marginalized group members from unfair treatment or may overidentify with a particular underrepresented group. In an extreme but true example, in 2015, Rachel Dolezal, a Pacific Northwest civil rights activist—the local NAACP president whose friends thought she was an African American—made international news when her parents "outed" her as a white woman. In 2016, she changed her name to Nkechi Amare Diallo.[40]

Introspective Phase

The white person reflects on what it means to be white, accepts their whiteness, and recognizes the benefits from white privilege and the reality that they may never fully understand the racial or ethnic minority experience. At the same time, they also feel disconnected from the Euro-American group. The person speaks with and observes the white group and also actively initiates experiences and interactions with various underrepresented group members.

A white person with racial or ethnic minority friends feels somewhat confused making the transition from one perspective to another. Although the person is white and no longer holds racist stereotypes, the individual cannot fully experience what it means to be an underrepresented group member in this culture.

Integrative Awareness Phase

The white person understands self as a racial/cultural being, recognizes the social and political forces that influence racism, appreciates racial/cultural diversity, and shows increased commitment to ending racial/cultural mistreatment. The person develops a nonracist white Euro-American identity, values multiculturalism, and feels comfortable and strongly connected with members of culturally diverse groups.

A white person develops a white, Euro-American nonracist identity and the inner security and strength needed to navigate smoothly in a pluralistic, multicultural society that only marginally accepts such an integratively aware white person.

Commitment to Antiracist Action Phase

The white person enacts an increased commitment to end oppression—sees "wrong" and actively works to make it "right."

In this phase, a white person openly objects to racist jokes, tries to educate family and colleagues about racial issues, and takes direct action to end racism in schools and the workplace. A future teacher decides to consciously develop and refine his or her own culturally competent pedagogy during professional teacher preparation and extend it further in the classroom.

8.2e White Privilege and White Fragility Theories

Generally speaking, white people tend to think that "race" is a trait that belongs to "other people" and are surprised to learn that the way they see themselves in the world is not the same as how people of color see them. "White privilege" and "white fragility" are theories that help explain how white people may be perceived as enacting their racial position in our society.

White Privilege Theory

White privilege theory[41] refers to the unseen, unconscious, built-in advantage that white people gain—having more access to power and resources than people of color in the same situation—from being white in our Western culture.[42] According to whiteness theory scholars, in the United States (as well as in Canada and Western Europe) white persons hold social, political, economic, cultural, and institutional power—*privilege*—over people of color. The distribution of benefits and resources is unequal and advantages white people and disadvantages people of color.[43] This is a historic, traditional, normalized, and deeply fixed feature in American society,[44] and socialization into this culture shapes white persons' thinking. Research suggests that children develop a concept of race and a sense of white superiority as early as preschool.[45]

For example, white people don't generally have to worry about "stop and frisk" laws (i.e., "because they look suspicions") or be assumed guilty if accused of a crime. They tend to receive the benefit of the doubt. This "privilege" is a phenomenon that until recently most white people did not see whereas most people of color in our society do.

White privilege theory does not assume that everything that each white person has is unearned or undeserved. Most white people who have achieved a high level of success have worked very hard to get there. Many white people don't feel powerful. Instead, white privilege is more psychological, a subconscious bias that white people maintain by their lack of awareness that they hold this power. At the same time, because legislatures, corporate leaders, and educators—largely white persons—often make deliberate choices in laws, hiring practices, and discipline procedures that keep the advantage intact, white privilege may be "unconsciously enjoyed and consciously perpetuated... both on the surface and deeply embedded into American life."[46]

Despite white privilege theory's influence in encouraging white persons to recognize their complicity in racial injustice,[47] it has its critics. Some say the theory's language ("privilege") and message unfairly suggests that all white persons in all situations and in all settings benefit from unearned advantage, confusing a structural inequality of a group with the circumstances of every individual within that group,[48] intensifying "identity politics" and "tribalism" that increase distrust and harm civil discourse.[49] Some decry the lack of discussion about white privilege's historic, social, economic, and political forces and the structural practices that contribute to the legacy of racial discrimination and oppression.[50] Others claim that white privilege theory ignores or downplays the role of ethnicity and social class, assuming that all persons of color are a homogeneous group who have experienced the same injustices (such as minimizing the differing historical experiences between American and Caribbean Black people).[51]

White Fragility Theory

According to this theory, white people's relatively infrequent interactions with people of color lead them to expect racial comfort in diverse group settings. Anticipating psychological ease lowers their capacity to tolerate racial stress in situations where race is discussed.

White fragility theory can be understood as a state of reduced psychological stamina in which even a minimal amount of racial stress for white persons becomes seemingly unbearable, "triggering" a range of defensive behaviors.

According to Robin DiAngelo, a professor at the University of Washington who studies how whiteness appears in everyday exchanges (and coined the term "white fragility"[52]), "[W]hite people in North America live in a social environment that protects and insulates them from race-based stress."[53] Socialized to American culture as white persons, many experience a sense of entitlement that gives them unwarranted advantages–what some call *privilege*. Many white persons are not consciously aware of this bias and its benefits. As a result, when faced with a challenge to their "identities as good, moral people," they experience "racial stress."

Examples of "white fragility" include blaming others with less social power for a white person's discomfort or portraying themselves as "victims". When attending programs on multicultural awareness, they may claim that they "already had a class on this." These behaviors are samples of resistance that racial insulation encourages.[54] The continual retreat from the discomfort of authentic racial engagement in a culture infused with racial disparities limits individuals' capacity to form genuine links across racial lines and perpetuates the cycle that anchors racism in place.

Despite widespread praise for DiAngelo's contribution to interracial understanding,[55] critics argue that the white fragility construct is flawed by measurement weaknesses and has little empirical support from social science research.[56] Others call it an "inherently racist concept" that demeans white persons on the basis of their skin color and group identity, dismisses disagreement as "guilt-fueled argumentation," and puts those who object to its concept into a "double bind"—that is, if you reject the idea and enactment of white fragility, you are exhibiting white fragility,[57] making it more difficult to facilitate a larger meaningful conversation about racism.[58] Another critic contends that "white fragility" is "surreal" in presenting its contemporary slights (i.e., bad manners) as compared to the many historic injustices this country has inflicted on persons of color (i.e., lynchings).[59] Other critics find minor weaknesses in the book's omissions[60] or claim it is of interest mainly to those in particular academic circles.[61]

Nonetheless, DiAngelo reminds us that each of us is responsible for either perpetuating or transforming our society that keeps racism in place.[62] One cannot change what one refuses to see. Understanding white privilege and white fragility may help future white educators become more conscious of how their actions may appear to others in a pluralist society and gain the insight and humility that may help them become more effective teachers.

8.2f Limitations of the Racial/Cultural Identity Models

Cultural identity development is a dynamic process. Some persons show behaviors and attitudes characteristic of several stages at the same time. For example, they may exhibit conformity characteristics in certain situations, yet show resistance and immersion behaviors in other circumstances. Some individuals move through the stages in a straight line at differing rates, whereas others may move back and forth between stages. These theoretical models are a conceptual framework intended to help understand student development; they are not a set of fixed, rigid rules.

In addition, the cultural identity development model does not fit all historically and socially marginalized students' situations. For instance, recent Asian American immigrants to the United States tend to hold very positive and favorable views of their own culture and already possess an intact racial/cultural identity.[63]

Another criticism notes that racial/cultural identity models imply a value judgment, assuming that some cultural resolutions are healthier than others. For example, the racial/cultural identity model suggests that the integrative awareness stage represents a higher form of healthy functioning. Likewise, the models also lack an adequate consideration of gender, class, sexual orientation, and other group identities. Nor is racial/cultural identity a simple, global concept. Additionally, evidence is mounting that although identity may move sequentially through identifiable stages, affective, attitudinal, cognitive, and behavioral components may not develop in a uniform manner.[64]

Finally, sociocultural forces affect identity development. Many of the early African American identity development models arose as a result of perceived and real experiences of oppression in our society. The increasingly visible racial/cultural movements of Native Americans, Latinx, and African Americans happened at a time of heightened racial and cultural awareness and pride. Similarly, the LGBTQ+ movement gained significant momentum over the past few decades as popular media—starting with television's Ellen DeGeneres's sitcom, *Ellen* (1994–1998), and the popular show and reboot *Will and Grace* (1998–2006, 2017–2020), as well as Tom Hanks's portrayal of a lawyer dying from AIDS in the movie *Philadelphia* (1993)—brought gay and lesbian characters into our lives who were considered mainstream except for their sexual orientation.[65] In June 2015, the U.S. Supreme Court ruled that states could not ban same-sex marriage and legalized it in all 50 states.[66] Clearly, the times themselves, in conjunction with the cultural forces in play, can greatly affect—either advance or impede—cultural identity development.

8.2g Intersectionality and Identity

People have multiple social identities and ways of experiencing the world. Social, cultural, and political histories of certain groups in a society play defining roles in shaping these social identities and the benefits or disadvantages that these roles bring.

Intersectionality, a relatively recent theory, stresses that individuals develop their social identities in a holistic, integrated manner and considers their meaning and consequences for the person or group in the larger society. Legal scholar and civil rights activist Kimberlé Crenshaw coined the term in 1989 as a way to explain the overlapping discriminations against African American women.[67] Today the term is applied more widely. A person's identity development reflects the complexity of lived experience. A person's racial, ethnic, class, gender, nationality, faith tradition, gender identity, and other identities can be understood as complex and holistic, influenced by specific historical and social contexts and the systemic power and privilege that lie beneath the hierarchical relations among social groups of that specific time and place.[68]

These social identities operate in the world all at the same time to open or limit opportunities for a particular person or groups in a given society. For example, a Black person can also be a middle- or upper-middle-class professional woman, with both the drawbacks and privileges that these four overlapping categories can bring in the United States today. With this focus, the intersectionality concept is often used in feminist (especially women of color) and critical race theory scholarship as a lens to study the hierarchies of privilege and power and in international discourses of human rights.

Despite its useful insights about power, subjectivity, and inclusivity, intersectionality is a contested concept. Critics decry its subjectivity of interpretation, its openness to misuse and misrepresentation, the difficulty of using the complex concept in research (or even in daily life, as in, "Am I being discriminated against because of my gender or my accent?"), and other discipline-specific "politics" and "word play" among feminist and critical theory scholars.[69]

In short, those who share the same race, gender, or class identity may or may not have a basis for shared experiences because their identities consist of more than one thing. For teachers, intersectionality means using caution when generalizing about individual students based on their superficial characteristics or on only one aspect of their total personality. It is important to know each student as an individual. This is how one builds mutually respectful and trusting relationships and to find the way each student learns best.

8.2h Research on Racial and Cultural Identities in School

The link between a healthy racial–ethnic identity and high academic achievement is complex. Historically, close ties of young African Americans with the African American community have been linked to highly valuing learning and education.[70]

Students' racial and cultural identities are strongly related to their feelings about themselves, their racial identity, and their place in the world. Specifically, many studies find that students with positive racial and cultural identities are more likely to be successful in middle school,[71] high school,[72] and college.[73] Positive racial and cultural identity is associated with more active coping, fewer beliefs supporting aggression, and less hostile or combative behaviors.[74] Advanced levels of racial and cultural identity development are a significant predictor of positive social adaptation and emotional adjustment for Black and white adolescents.[75]

Additionally, scholars have found that cultural minority adolescents who interacted more with peers of the same cultural background had more developed levels of cultural identity.[76]

Although research suggests that simply being a member of a racial or cultural minority group does not predict higher or lower levels of self-esteem, the studies find that the *sense of belonging* that students feel toward their racial or cultural group does predict their self-confidence and self-esteem.[77] Conversely, those persons who have not examined or developed a clear sense of racial or cultural identity tend to have low self-regard and feelings of inadequacy. This relationship holds true for all racial and cultural groups.

Lastly, studies have found that social support from family and friends can help youths develop cultural identity and a higher level of self-esteem.[78] When young people have positive family, community, and cultural reinforcement for their racial and cultural identity, the more ably they can resist and accommodate any negative social and media messages. Students who feel good about themselves and have a positive sense of their own value are more likely to work hard and achieve highly in school.

To more fully explore how people—including you—develop their racial identities, complete the activity in the **Reflect & Engage** box, Developing a Racial Identity.

REFLECT & ENGAGE: DEVELOPING A RACIAL IDENTITY

People develop a racial/cultural identity through various cognitive and emotional stages.

A. Using Table 8.1 and the discussion of underrepresented and white racial/cultural identities, create a wordle (mind cloud) that describes how you personally experienced your own racial/cultural identity development. After you finish, share your wordle with a partner.

Which commonalities do you and your partner find in your racial/cultural identity development experiences? What differences?

As a class, discuss how your racial/cultural identity development experiences compare with those noted in this chapter and compared with one another.

How would white privilege theory be a useful concept to you as a future teacher? Why or why not?

How would white fragility theory be a useful concept to you as a future teacher? Why or why not?

How would intersectionality theory be a useful concept to you as a future teacher? Why or why not?

In what ways is discussing racial and cultural identity development an uncomfortable topic for you? What can you or others do to make you more at ease discussing it with friends and classmates?

8.3 UNDERREPRESENTED STUDENTS' PERCEPTIONS AND ACADEMIC PERFORMANCE

Students' perceptions and performances seem to have a chicken-and-egg complexity. Generally speaking, do underrepresented students perceive and behave as they do because of how they are treated and taught in schools? Or are they treated and taught in schools because of the ways they perceive and behave? The answer seems to be yes to both.[79] Many preservice teachers also have unquestioned and inaccurate assumptions about which students can—and cannot—perform to high levels in school. Both teachers and students benefit when they challenge their preconceived ideas about underrepresented students' ability to succeed in school.

In addition to the research-documented connection between socioeconomic status and school success, group cultural patterns or the relationships between these groups and the larger society may also frustrate underrepresented students' relationship with school. John Ogbu's ideas about "oppositional" culture, Claude Steele's stereotype threat theory, and Derald Wing Sue's theory of microaggressions describe how many underrepresented students' views and emotions may affect their academic achievement. Although some of these theories have more research support than others, they all offer meaningful perspectives on racial or ethnic minority student achievement.

8.3a Oppositional Culture Theory

Low-income and underserved students' underachievement is a very complex phenomenon with a variety of causes. John Ogbu, the late University of California–Berkeley professor, believed that although structural barriers and school factors affect racial and ethnic minority students' school performance, these young people are also autonomous human beings who actively interpret and respond to their situation in ways that can either help or hurt themselves.[80]

To Achieve Is to "Be White"

"**Acting white**" is a cultural meme[81] describing a set of social interactions in which racial and ethnic minority adolescents who get good grades in school enjoy less social popularity than white students who do well academically.[82] For example, when asked to identify "acting-white" behavior, Black students name actions ranging from speaking standard English, enrolling in an Advanced Placement or Honors classes, and sporting shorts in winter.[83]

In the 1980s, anthropologists Signithia Fordham and John Ogbu helped bring this phenomenon to public attention. They suggested an **oppositional culture theory** (sometimes called academic disengagement theory) that seeks to explain why racial and ethnic minority students often do poorly in school. According to this theory, some racial and ethnic groups underachieve academically because they view schooling and the education system as extensions of the dominant culture that threatens their group's cultural identity and reproduces societal inequities. These underrepresented students respond to institutionalized racism by believing that high achievement in school would cause them to lose their racial or ethnic identity or betray their demographic peers by "acting white."[84] Ogbu saw these behaviors as a functional adaption to the reality of a racially stratified "job ceiling" and fewer returns on their educational investment that discourages students of color from working hard to excel in school.[85]

Ogbu later observed that "oppositional identities" appear in Black students from all SES backgrounds. In this way, middle- and upper-income Black youths may succumb to peer pressure and may devalue academic pursuits and adopt self-defeating behaviors that jeopardize their academic success.[86]

These behaviors may also be true for other students of color from varied SES backgrounds.

These oppositional beliefs can create dilemmas for racial and ethnic minority students. They feel forced to choose between (1) conforming to the school's demands and rewards and achieving well but risking their demographic community's rejection, or (2) accepting their community's disapproval of (or at the least ambivalence toward) those mainstream ("white") attitudes and behavior by not performing well in school. As a result, many lower their aspirations to adapt to what they see as a hostile social environment.

Despite its once widespread popularity, oppositional culture theory and "acting white" has been somewhat discredited.[87] Critics challenge the concept's validity,[88,89] claiming that it lacks research explicit support. Some observe that this theory does not account for the African American community's long history of pursuing schooling and academic excellence, even when threatened with violence or death.[90] Others argue that resistance to academic success is not racialized: high-achieving white students and students of color both are exposed to negative peer sanctioning.[91] Moreover, students' markers of personal style, such as speech codes, clothing, or music preferences may reflect cultural, not academic reasons (often to raise their social status among same-race peers).[92] Recent studies in sociology suggest some Black students' low performance is more related to underdeveloped prior educational skills in literacy and numeracy than in an intentional resistance to education.

Nonetheless, many continue to find Ogbu's work about academic disengagement useful in pointing to underrepresented students' attempts to resist inequitable schooling.[93] But the reasons for this underachievement are complex and many. Teachers cannot accurately assume that a poorly achieving student of color is "oppositional" and rejects school or academic achievement.

8.3b Stereotype Threat Theory

It may seem logical—but is inaccurate—to assume that the Black, Latinx, or other students of color's educational disadvantages affect only low-income students. In reality, even middle- and upper-class Black students can have perceptions that limit their education.[94] Claude M. Steele, a Stanford University social psychology professor, has suggested that stereotype threat is a coping strategy that hurts high-striving, middle-income Black students' achievement. The theory also applies to other underrepresented groups. Put simply, **stereotype threat theory** is the idea that people tend to underperform when confronted with situations that might confirm negative stereotypes about their social group.

Stereotype threat occurs when an individual who really cares about doing well is placed in a circumstance in which a negative group stereotype could apply. For example, a Black student does not want to accidentally do something (such as perform poorly on an important exam) that might inadvertently confirm a stereotype (of unintelligent Black students) to observers. This fear of confirming the stereotype may be distracting enough to the individual that the person actually makes careless mistakes.

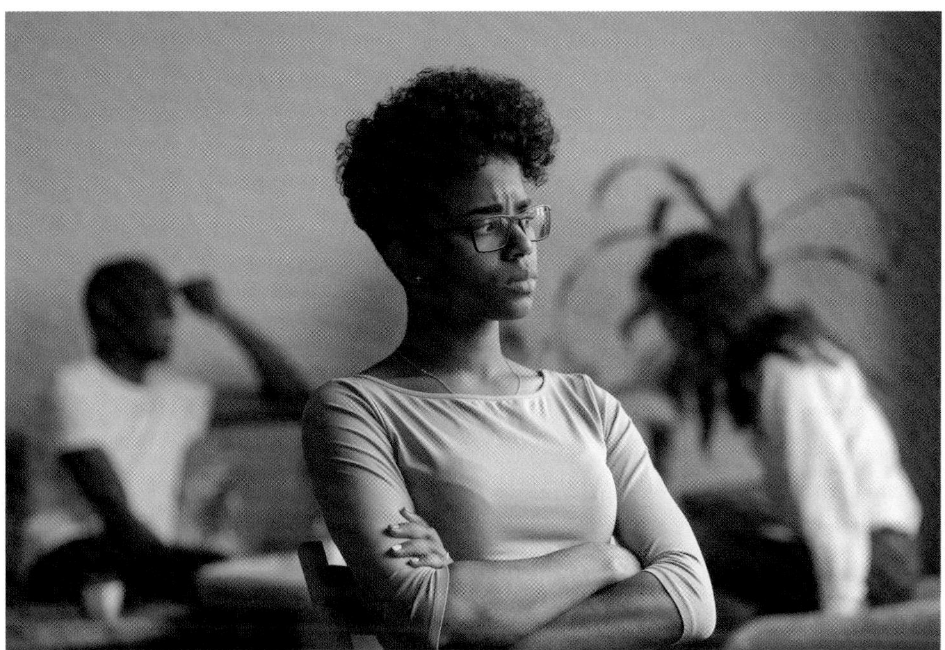

Stereotype threat undermines capable students' capacity to succeed.
iStock/fizkes

In a series of ingenious experiments, Steele found that when students were told that the test they were about to take tended to produce achievement differences such that women and students of color scored at a lower level, that outcome was exactly what happened. In the control groups, where students took the same test but were not told about any expected performance differences among different student groups, no performance differences appeared.[95] These effects have been documented in more than 300 studies involving a variety of situations.[96]

In Steele's studies, highly capable students seemed to be trying too hard. They reread the questions and multiple choices and rechecked their answers more often than when they did not face stereotype threat. When this finding is applied to schools, it implies that when any capable underrepresented students take a difficult test, their anxiety about not wanting to perform poorly may cause them to make mistakes. Their perceptions of the threat become self-fulfilling prophecies. Other studies have suggested that under stereotype threat, physiological stress, heightened performance monitoring, anxiety, mind wandering, and negative thoughts and efforts to suppress them undermine a person's working memory resources[97] and consume executive mental resources needed to perform well on cognitive and social tasks.[98]

Stereotype threat appears to affect different social groups in different ways. Sometimes, students respond to stereotype threat by pretending that school is not important. Steele posits that some students use **disidentification**—or withdrawal of psychic investment—to remove themselves from this perceived threat. To save face, they rationalize their poor performance as a lack of interest in the subject rather than as an inability to master it. Appearing not to care about school success may even become a group norm.[99] In avoiding potentially threatening situations, these students may set up a negative spiral. In contrast, while these students respond to stereotype threat by underperforming, others work even harder to achieve.[100]

Interestingly, stereotype threat is not limited to racial or ethnic minority students. Scholars have found evidence of stereotype threat occurring among elementary schoolgirls as young as 7 or 8 years old taking mathematics tests,[101] older adults given a memory test, and white men being assessed on athletic ability.[102] When researchers told white males that the same exams were being used to compare their abilities with those of Asian Americans, white male performance worsened. Even something as subtle as asking students to indicate their race or gender on a test form can trigger the phenomenon.

Teachers can create learning environments that reduce stereotype threat's negative outcomes. Studies have found that students are more motivated and able to achieve when they believe that intelligence is malleable rather than a trait fixed at birth, that hard work and a positive outlook can improve their grades and close achievement gaps, and when classroom activities "affirm" their values and boost their confidence.[103]

Critics challenge stereotype theory, correctly asserting that students' vulnerability to stereotype threat and disidentification are universal characteristics—that is, they do not belong solely to Black or other underrepresented students.[104] Some contest the methodology of stereotype threat research,[105] noting that stereotype threat is simply another term for test anxiety,[106] and assert that eliminating stereotype threat would not remove the Black–white achievement gap, as some suggest.[107]

8.3c Microaggression Theory

Racial discrimination does not have to mean receiving racial epithets or taunts. Once Black children reach school, they find themselves subject to more subtle forms of prejudice, such as when teachers overreact to their "disruptive" conduct, do not recommend them for advanced courses, or decide to omit racially representative content from the curriculum. For more than two decades, Derald Wing Sue, Teachers College of Columbia University professor, has studied these behaviors, and his extensive writings on the subject helped to broaden our understanding of **microaggression theory** and the historically and socially marginalized groups' experience.[108]

Briefly, **microaggressions** are short, everyday, indirect, subtle, intentional or unintentional statements, actions, put-downs, insults, or environmental slights that communicate hostile, derogatory, or negative messages to target persons based solely on their marginalized group membership. The microaggression construct is an intellectual framework for understanding some of the behaviors that make underrepresented group members feel disrespected, even though the white speaker or doer may have not intended insult. Religious minorities, women, people with disabilities, and LGBTQ+ individuals are also subject to microaggressions.[109] Microaggressions' power lies in their seeming invisibility to the perpetrator and often to the recipient.

Well-intentioned people who sincerely believe they are unbiased individuals are often blind to how others perceive their behaviors as insulting, as well as to the cumulative effects of those behaviors. Although microaggressions may be explained away by valid and nonbiased reasons, recipients always wonder whether disrespect really happened. For instance, a third-generation Pakistani-American frequently is asked, "What country are you from?" While each interaction itself is only a tiny annoyance, easily ignored, the cumulative effect of these inactions adds up over time to be burdensome: The implicit assertion is that persons with West Asian features are somehow "less American" than their white peers.

Microaggressions frequently occur in schools.[110] Examples include teachers raising their eyebrows when a student of color sits down in their Advanced Placement physics classroom; a teacher not learning how to pronounce (or continuing to mispronounce) the students' names after being corrected; teachers scheduling tests and project due dates on religious or cultural holidays or setting low expectations for students from particular groups or neighborhoods; and teachers using inappropriate humor in class that demeans students from different groups.[111] This topic is more fully discussed elsewhere.[112]

Table 8.4 offers examples of racial microaggressions. It includes the main idea, the microaggression behavior, and the message the receiver takes from the exchange.

The microaggression construct has its detractors. Scientists critique the concept for its lack of scientific basis, overreliance on subjective evidence, weak methodology, and promotion of psychic fragility.[113] Some claim it is not useful and lends itself toward a culture of "victimhood,"[114] lessening one's ability to manage small interpersonal matters on one's own, and creating a society in which people compete for victim status or as victim defenders.[115] Others suggest that the objectionable behavior may be unfortunate, but it is not "aggressive." Calling it such confuses the people involved and ratchets up the tension between them. Likewise, efforts to publicly shame or punish "microaggressors" does not improve the organization's climate or culture, making it more difficult to address and remedy the offending behaviors. Lastly, the self-policing of individual thoughts or actions to prevent committing

TABLE 8.4 ■ Examples of Racial Microaggressions

Microaggression's Main Idea	Microaggression Behavior	Message Received by Recipient
Alien in own land (When Latinx and Asian Americans are assumed to be foreign born)	"Where are you from?" "You speak good English."	You are not American. You are a foreigner.
Crediting with intelligence (Assigning intelligence to a person of color based on their race/ ethnicity)	"You are a credit to your race." "You are so articulate." Asking an Asian American person to help solve a math or science problem.	People of color are not usually as intelligent as white people. All Asians are good at math and science.
Color blindness (Statements indicate that a white person does not want to acknowledge race)	"When I look at you, I don't see color." "There is only one race—the human race."	Assimilate to the dominant culture (white). Deny the individual as a racial/ ethnic/cultural being.
Denial of individual racism (Statements when white people deny their racial biases)	"I have several Jewish friends." "I have friends of color." "As a woman, I know what you go through as a racial minority."	I cannot be a bigot because I have friends of other religions or races/ ethnicities. Your racial oppression is no different than my gender oppression. I am like you, so I cannot be a racist.
Myth of meritocracy (Statements that assert that race does not play a role in life success)	"I think the most qualified person should get the job." Everyone can succeed in this society with an education and hard work.	People of color are given unfair benefits because of their race. People of color are lazy and/or incompetent and need to work harder.
Pathologizing cultural values and communication styles (Statements that the dominant white culture's values and communication styles are the best)	Asking a Black person: "Why do you have to be so loud/animated? Just calm down." Asking an Asian American woman: "Why are you so quiet? Speak up more." Dismissing an individual who raises the subject of race/culture in work/school setting	Assimilate to the dominant culture. Leave your "cultural baggage" outside. "Your culture is wrong to prevent you from speaking up." "Things are fine as they are. Don't stir things up."
Environmental microaggressions (Large-scale microaggressions more obvious on systemic and environmental levels)	A college or university names all its buildings after white, heterosexual, upper-class males Overcrowding public schools in communities of color	You don't belong here. You won't succeed here. You can only go so far. People of color don't/shouldn't value education.

Source: Adapted from Sue, D. W., Cadodilupo, C. M., Torino, G. C., Bucceri, J. M., Holder, A. M., Nadal, K. L., and Esquilin, M. (2007). Racial microaggressions in everyday life. Implications for clinical practice. *American Psychologist, 62*(4), 271–286.

microaggressions is poor preparation for professional life, which requires intellectual engagement with people and ideas that differ from one's own.[116]

Nonetheless, racial stress is real. Researchers have found that such stressors tend to have a significant and negative physical and psychological effect on these children and their families' well-being.[117] For Black youth, the negative physical, psychological, and academic effects of racism include traumatic symptoms (including hypervigilance about potential racist actions), depression, impaired academic self-concepts, and lowered school engagement that may result in lower school performance [118] and may contribute to academic achievement gaps.[119] There is no reason to think that these effects are no less harmful to other microaggression targets.

For a more in-depth look at how preservice teachers—including you—become more effective teachers when they identify and challenge their preconceived ideas about underrepresented students' ability to succeed in school, complete the activity in the **Reflect & Engage** box, Theories of Oppositional Culture, Stereotype Threat, and Microaggressions.

AMERICAN EDUCATION SPOTLIGHT: DERALD WING SUE

An African proverb says that "the true tale of the lion hunt will never be told as long as the hunter tells the story." History is written by the winners. Adding to this quote, Professor Derald Wing Sue observes that both empirical reality (i.e., objectivity, testing, data, facts, and evidence) and experiential reality (i.e., subjective experiences, emotions, values, and beliefs) have validity (truth) in understanding the human condition.* And they must be tempered with balance.**

Considered to be "the most influential multicultural scholar in the United States"*** Dr. Derald Wing Sue, an Oregon-born son of immigrant Chinese parents, grew up in a mostly white neighborhood after his parents moved their family from Portland's Chinatown to a nearby suburb. He recalls his elementary school classmates repeatedly ridiculing him and his younger brother because of their Asian heritage. This unsettling and puzzling experience led to Dr. Sue's deep interest in human behavior. With his PhD in counseling psychology from the University of Oregon and influenced by the civil rights movement that brought heightened attention to racial and ethnic identity, he developed a keen interest in multicultural studies. Currently, Dr. Sue is a professor of psychology and education at Teachers College, Columbia University.

Because of his life-changing experience with racism directed toward his family, Dr. Sue's research direction has increasingly turned to the psychology of racism and antiracism. In addressing President Bill Clinton's Race Advisory Board (1997) and his book, *Overcoming Our Racism: The Journey to Liberation* (2003), Dr. Sue realized that the invisibility of "whiteness" and ethnocentric monoculturalism—many white people not seeing themselves as racial or cultural beings—harmed not only people of color but white people also. In his view, generally speaking, white people avoid an honest dialogue about race and racism, deny that race is an important factor in people's lives, prefer to believe that "people are people," insist they are "color blind" ("I don't notice a color, so I can't be racist"), and swear that "differences" are not important—all to avoid facing their own unconscious and unintentional participation in racism. They keep silent because they fear anything they say will mark them in others' eyes as "racist." Or they stay mute because they may uncover unconscious racial biases and prejudices and realize that they are indeed racist or see how they may have benefited from historical and current societal practices. And if white people benefit from white privilege, the American value of meritocracy may be a "myth" since all groups do not operate on a level playing field.

The intense and difficult dialogue resulting from this discussion prompted Dr. Sue and his research team to undertake a 6-year study on the causes, expressions, and impact of *racial microaggressions*, the brief, daily slights and indignities, intentional or not, that communicate hostility or disrespect to a target person or group. His microaggression research is now expanding to include religion, gender, disability, sexual orientation, and other marginalized groups.

Dr. Sue offers suggestions to help educators deal with race. Because talking about race, a "hot button" topic, often generates intense and powerful emotions and creates a threatening environment for participants, he recommends that educators at all levels develop racial sensitivities and skills to facilitate such discussions. Teachers need the classroom competencies to enable true listening and exchanging ideas (rather than angry, defensive monologues, avoidance, or quick shutdown). To do this, they first must recognize their inherited biases, cultural conditioning, fears, and anxieties about race and work to understand themselves as racial and cultural beings. Next, they need education and special training to develop these skills. In addition, they need occasions for true interracial interactions that go beyond intellectual book learning and lectures—with people who differ in race, culture, and ethnicity and in real-life settings and situations—even though it may make participants feel uncomfortable. Dr. Sue cautions that undergoing such personal and interpersonal experiences requires courage, honesty, openness, and truthfulness.

An internationally recognized author or coauthor of over 15 books, 150 publications, and many media productions, Dr. Sue has led cultural diversity training for many Fortune 500 companies, institutions of higher education, business, industry, government, and other organizations. For his outstanding contributions to cross-cultural understanding and distinguished service, he has received numerous awards from professional organizations, educational institutions, and

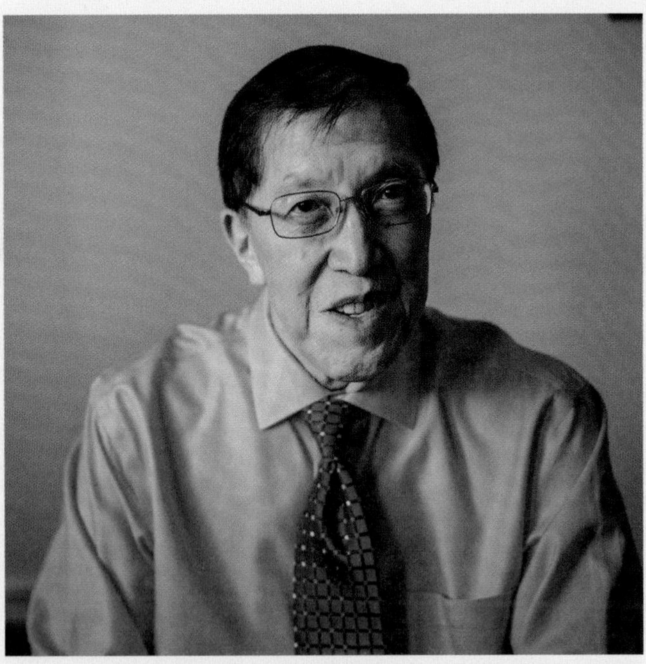

Bill Cardoni/reprinted by permission of Derald Wing Sue

community groups. He reminds us that we are each a product of our society, and each of us has the responsibility to make the "invisible" visible by stopping the denial of our unconscious biases, trying to understand other perspectives and experiences, and taking real steps to end racism.

Notes:

*Sue, D. W. (2017). Microaggressions and "evidence": Empirical or experiential reality? *Perspectives on Psychological Science, 12*(1), 170–172.

**Schneider, K. J. (1998). Toward a science of the heart: Romanticism and the revival of psychology. *American Psychologist, 53*, 277–289.

***Psychology Today. (2020). Derald Wing Sue, PhD. https://www.psychologytoday.com/us/experts/derald-wing-sue-phd

Sources: Levine, J. (2019, Fall/Winter). Weighing your words. Derald Wing Sue is challenging America to think about microaggressions. *TC Today, 44*(1), 10–23; Munsey, C. (2006, February). A family for Asian psychologists. *American Psychologist, 37*(2). https://www.apa.org/monitor/feb06/family; Sue, D. W. (2011). The challenge of white dialectics: Making the "invisible" visible. *The Counseling Psychologist, 39*(3), 415–422; Sue, D. W. (2013, November). Race talk: The psychology of racial dialogues. *American Psychologist, 68*(8), 663–672; Sue, D. W., Lin, A. I., Torino, G. C., Capodilupo, C. M., and Rivera, D. P. (2009). Racial microaggressions and difficult dialogues on race in the classroom. *Cultural Diversity and Ethnic Minority Psychology, 15*(2), 183–190.

REFLECT & ENGAGE: THEORIES OF OPPOSITIONAL CULTURE, STEREOTYPE THREAT, AND MICROAGGRESSIONS

The following activity involves creating graphic images and role play. Many preservice teachers have unquestioned and inaccurate assumptions about which students can—and cannot—perform to high levels in school. If teachers are to effectively educate every student, educators must identify and challenge these preconceived ideas about underrepresented students' ability to succeed in school.

A. Individually, draw a graphic image using a digital tool such as Piktochart about a time that you saw or heard the phrase "acting white." Where were you, and what did it mean to you?

B. Working in groups of four, share your graphic images and your explanations of their meaning. Discuss.

C. As a small group, create a brief role play (that you will later enact for the class) of the following theories. As you do, consider where you were and to whom the behavior was addressed. What did it mean to you? What appeared to be the effect on the receiver and other observers? How did the receiver of the microaggression or the observers respond?

- An incident of oppositional culture theory
- An incident of stereotype threat theory
- An incident of microaggression theory

D. As a class, discuss key findings from your small groups and suggest how knowing about these theories can be helpful—or harmful—to teachers wanting to educate every student.

8.4 USING STUDENT ASSETS TO INCREASE LEARNING

Over the years, research has clearly affirmed that when teachers lack the necessary skills to teach all students effectively—regardless of race, class, or culture—students are less likely to achieve, and classrooms are more likely to be disruptive and disorderly.[120] The reason? Good relationships with teachers motivate students to learn. In contrast, when educators have difficulty establishing mutually respectful, caring, and helpful relationships with the students they teach, it becomes difficult to create a classroom climate in which children want to put in the effort to learn.

Although race, class, language, and cultural differences between students and teachers do not cause the achievement gap, they do perpetuate it and may complicate efforts to reduce or end it. For public schools to become the equalizers of opportunity, educators need to develop the "cultural competence" to work successfully with children who differ from themselves. Part of becoming culturally competent means learning to identify the range of student assets—those personal, family, and cultural strengths children bring with them to school—and use these to provide the classroom conditions that facilitate learning.

8.4a Student Assets: Interpersonal Relationships and Compatible Learning Goals

According to Professors A. Wade Boykin, Howard University, and Pedro Noguera, University of Southern California, students have many assets that encourage learning.[121] The first of these is the students' capacity to enter into a mutually respectful, caring, and helpful relationship with their teachers. Additional student assets include existing or emerging interests and preferences; motivations, passions, and commitments; attitudes, beliefs, opinions, and self-perceptions; personal or collective identities; and prior experiences, knowledge, understandings, skills, and competencies. For our purposes, we will look at three distinct but interrelated types of student assets that teachers can harness for school success: interpersonal relationships with teachers, compatibility of learning goals between student and teacher, and cultural/family influences.

Interpersonal relationships involve the quality of the teacher–student relationship and teacher expectations. **Compatible learning goals** address the extent that teachers' and students' interests, values, perceptions, and learning objectives are "on the same page" and work together toward the same ends in mutually satisfying ways. **Cultural/family influences** take in traditional values that reflect the student's culture as they play out in the family and community. We will look at the first two student assets in this section. Cultural/family influences will appear in the next section.

Research on Teacher–Student Relationship Quality

Much evidence supports the importance of the teacher–student relationship quality (TSRQ)[122] in closing the achievement/opportunity gap. Classroom behaviors that reflect this interpersonal dimension include the degree to which teachers show empathy, support, encouragement, and optimism about students' capacity to master the material and the extent to which students perceive teachers as fair, genuine, and respectful in their praise and feedback. Qualities that studies find in the teacher–student relationship that increase student achievement, especially with underrepresented students, include these:

- The TSRQ predicts academic achievement[123] and helps close the achievement gap.[124]
- Teachers display proactive communication with students, anticipating problems and addressing them before they happen, as well as building a positive rapport and positive classroom climate.[125]
- Academically successful African American students say their teachers are accessible and approachable, validate their capabilities, and hold high expectations for their achievement.[126]
- The TSRQ affects student engagement in the present and predicts student engagement and achievement in later years.[127]
- The TSRQ is positively related to African American and Latinx students' language skills and reading scores It increases student engagement and motivates these students to learn not simply *from*, but *for* their teachers.[128]

Clearly, the teacher–student relationship—and the degree that traditionally underserved students recognize that their teachers care about them as people and as academic learners—has a positive and measurable effect on their classroom engagement and achievement. Payoffs occur not only in the current classroom but also in later years. In particular, "warm, demanding pedagogy"—described as sternness short of scolding students who don't live up to expectations in a compassionate, supportive, and nurturing way—may be especially effective with low-income, African American, and Latinx students.[129]

Research on Compatible Learning Goals

Classroom learning goals deal with how teachers and students decide on and approach their purposes for teaching and learning. For instance, **mastery goals** focus on gaining skills, comprehension, or competence based on student effort and personal improvement, whereas **performance goals** stress being best as compared with others. Mastery goals tend to rely on students' effort (over which students believe they have control), whereas performance goals tend to rely on students' ability (which students tend to believe is inherited and beyond their control).

Likewise, the degrees to which teachers use students' values, interests, and learning priorities with the curriculum to make learning personally meaningful and relevant to students impacts how well any students, especially students of color and low-income students, achieve. At the same time, a positive learning climate encourages students to invest their efforts in their learning; a negative learning climate discourages these learning behaviors.

Evidence suggests that the way teachers structure students' learning goals—as well as the way students identify their own and their teachers' learning goals—can significantly affect their academic functioning. Studies show that goal compatibility is especially critical for African American and Latinx students (but these approaches most likely succeed with most students):

- The ways students understand and respond to achievement experiences are associated with distinctly different patterns of cognition, affect, and behavior. Mastery goals lead to more favorable student ratings of their classroom's emotional tone and peer relationships, higher levels of student engagement, higher academic outcomes, greater self-efficacy, more personal interest in math, less text anxiety, more adaptive help seeking, and more success on unit exams among ethnically diverse students than for diverse students with a high level of performance goal orientation; and the more students of color perceive that the teacher stresses performance goals, the more they show disruptive behaviors and less self-efficacy.[130]

- With a mastery approach to learning, students facing challenge or failure are likely to attribute the result to lack of enough effort on their part, rather than to a lack of ability where others are smarter or more capable.[131]
- Students more readily link mastery goals to changeable beliefs about one's competence and smartness (effort is within their control), whereas performance goals are linked to ideas of fixed ability (beyond their control).[132]
- Teachers who center the learning process on children of color's actual experiences, relating what students learn to matters of personal interest and relevant events in their lives, and drawing connections across topics have better achievement outcomes for students.[133]
- A learning climate that fosters a properly structured collaboration for learning, such as peer tutoring or peer-assisted learning, can boost academic performance—particularly for students of color from low-income backgrounds.[134]

Teachers who treat their low-income, African American, Latinx, and other underserved students with genuine caring and meaningful support plus high expectations for learning and achievement tend to generate favorable achievement outcomes. The effects are reciprocal: Increased TSRQ leads to higher student achievement, which, in turn, leads to a greater TSRQ. Providing personally relevant learning for low-income and underrepresented students—indeed, *for all students*—makes schoolwork more meaningful to them and easier to learn. Similarly, focusing the classroom climate on mastery rather than performance and using well-designed collaborative learning activities also result in higher achievement for underrepresented and low-income students.

Family loyalty and respect contribute to the identity and well-being of families of color.
iStock/monkeybusinessimages

8.4b Student Assets: Cultural and Family Resources

Culture matters in student learning. *Culture*, a society's set of concepts, values, assumptions, sensibilities, or ways of thinking, creates a perceptual lens through which people interpret life events. Their culture helps them define what makes sense, what is appropriate. Beginning with the 17th century Massachusetts town schools, American public schools promoted an Anglo-Protestant culture that largely has shaped public schools nationally. But a pluralistic society is home to additional cultures. Low-income students, student of color, and students with disabilities—in fact, every student—bring cultural factors with them to school that teachers can use to help them learn. American public schools—with their purposes, rules, regulations, and procedures—are also a cultural context. As discussed previously, when teachers can align students' experiences and values with the curriculum and make the content personally relevant and meaningful to students, engagement and learning increase.

Considering a child's culture brings certain cautions, however. "Cultural differences" are not the underlying cause of every difficulty a child of color experiences in school. It is wise not to make general cultural assumptions about individual students. The same behaviors may occur for a variety of reasons, or different behaviors may occur for the same reason. In fact, the behaviors in question may or may not be related to culture. Simply because a student is Latinx does not mean he or she must automatically act, think, or feel certain ways. Generalizing about culture is especially problematic when factors are attributed to historically marginalized groups and mistakenly used to explain why group members perform poorly or are unable to function as well as other members of cultural groups. Actually, more variation exists within cultural groups than between cultural groups. In short, the complexity of culture urges restraint in what we infer from our observations or from what we are told.

Given this caution, scholars increasingly are advocating for culturally relevant pedagogy: getting to know each student as an individual, drawing on the student's fund of knowledge found in their family and community experiences, and linking these to instructional practices and curriculum content. This creates greater understanding among teachers, students, and their families and identifies student assets that teachers can use to increase classroom engagement.

8.5 FOSTERING STUDENT RESILIENCE AND ACHIEVEMENT

Helen Keller (1880–1968), a woman who earned a Radcliffe College (Harvard) degree and was deaf and blind (and whose life was later dramatized in a play and several movies called *The Miracle Worker*), campaigned relentlessly for social justice. In her work, she emphasized that it was others' attitudes about people with disabilities, rather than the disability itself, that caused problems. She wrote, "We have been accustomed to regard the employed deaf and blind as the victims of their infirmities. Facts show that it is not physical blindness but social blindness which cheats our hands of the right to toil."[135]

The same "social blindness" often afflicts teachers when they are working with culturally, racially, and ability diverse students. This "blindness" is most evident when educators look at what these students *cannot do* rather than at what they *can and might do* with support from high expectations, respect for the personal and cultural assets they bring with them, and a variety of means to help them learn and achieve.

8.5a Deficit Thinking

Deficit thinking—looking at students' weaknesses rather than their strengths—is socially defined. It is based on the "normal" development of middle-class, usually white students whose homes and communities have prepared them for schooling long before they enter the classroom. Children who come to school without that preparation and without the continuing support of family members who can reinforce schooling's goals often face teachers' expectations that they cannot easily meet. Instead of seeing human variation, teachers and schools have been encultured to see "pathology." All too often, when students do not learn new material at the same pace—or behave in the same ways—as their classmates, frustrated teachers quickly refer them for special education evaluation for suspected "disability."

Viewing "disability" or cultural/racial difference as the opposite of "normal" falsely limits our expectations for diverse students' achievement. The traditional or medical model of disability centers on individuals' functional limitations or impairments as the cause of their disadvantages. For instance, a person has a "disability" because he or she has cerebral palsy, cannot walk, and moves around in a motorized chair. A student is "disadvantaged" because he or she represents an underrepresented culture or has a low-income background. In this view, the person owns both the problem and the associated limits. Similarly, teachers who assume that their urban students of color "don't work hard enough to improve their life circumstances" are operating from a deficit-thinking framework. In fact, some even consider using the term "at-risk" as deficit thinking because it focuses on what certain students don't have and can't do as compared with what assets they do have and can do.[136]

In contrast, the asset model shifts the focus. Instead of looking at the individual's "lack of ability" or "otherness" as the problem, **asset thinking** identifies and uses the student's personal strengths and interests and identifies and remedies the limiting social, environmental, and attitudinal barriers that hinder the person's learning. Teachers with asset thinking find occasions where the student is competent and capable in settings important to the learners, encourage their decision-making and initiative, and view them as resources for educating others about their communities and cultures. In the same way, we modify public buildings to create wider doorways to rooms, build wider private restroom stalls, and construct ramps to ease accessibility from the street. These are all means of creating access and opportunity.

Likewise, we provide inclusive classrooms and multiple instructional interventions for struggling learners. We expand our curriculum to include authentic voices from culturally diverse groups who make up the American society. We look for and use our students' cultural and personal strengths—such as high family and extended family support and encouragement, religious orientation, strong parental work ethic with high aspirations to achieve, and students' skills and interests in nonacademic areas—in our efforts to educate them to 21st century competence.

In short, the asset model rejects the "deficit" model's language and belief system. It sees student difficulties and differences not as "pathology" or sickness, but rather as normal human variations. Educators would do well to end deficit thinking in how they approach teaching and learning for all children.

To more deeply consider how deficit thinking and asset thinking influence teachers' expectations for diverse students' achievement—and what this might look like in schools—complete the activity in the **Reflect & Engage** box, Using Cultural/Family Assets (and Discarding Deficit Thinking).

High expectations and respect for personal assets help students with disabilities succeed.

iStock/simonkr

REFLECT & ENGAGE: USING CULTURAL/FAMILY ASSETS (AND DISCARDING DEFICIT THINKING)

Viewing "disability" or cultural/racial difference as the opposite of "normal" falsely limits our expectations for diverse students' achievement. Discuss these questions in pairs and then as a whole class:

A. In groups of four, create a graphic image using a digital tool such as Piktochart of "deficit thinking" and "asset thinking" as they might appear in schools. Display and explain these graphic images to the class as a whole.

B. As a whole class, do the following:

- Discuss why aligning students' experiences and values with the curriculum can increase their engagement and learning.
- Explain the benefits and limitations of considering students' cultural influences when designing meaningful learning activities.
- Give examples of how "deficit thinking" of student "normality" affects teachers' expectations and limits access to high-quality educational opportunities for diverse students in schools.
- Explain how a poor-quality classroom and school climate can contribute to students' learning difficulties.
- Describe what you think teachers can change in their instructional practices to help diverse students learn more effectively without needing to make a special education referral.
- Identify what you as a future teacher are likely to do or not do in teaching diverse students as a result of reading this chapter.

8.5b Fostering Students' Resilience

Children can overcome difficult conditions and happily succeed in the mainstream culture. **Resilience** can be defined as the process or capacity to have successful outcomes despite challenging or threatening circumstances. Resilience cannot be measured directly but is inferred from the presence of major stress or adversity that has the potential to threaten healthy development linked with the observation of positive outcomes. It may be influenced by the interplay between an individual's characteristics, as well as social and environmental factors.

For examples, studies find that resilient children demonstrate four personal characteristics: social competence, problem-solving skills, autonomy, and a sense of purpose.[137] Likewise, research finds that children who experience chronic adversity fare better or recover more successfully when they have a positive relationship with a competent adult, are good learners and resourceful problem solvers, are likable, are assertive, have a strong work ethic and are persistent, and are perceived as effective in a variety of situations by self and others.[138] Notably, relationships developed in the school setting with peers and teachers, high academic quality, and challenging cocurricular and extracurricular activities can influence children's ability to thrive in adverse situations.[139]

Drawing Upon Students' Resources

Each child has an array of personal, family, and cultural resources from which teachers can draw to help the student succeed. Emotional, mental, spiritual, physical, and relationship resources and knowledge of school's "unspoken rules" can help individuals become resilient.

Emotional resources such as stamina, persistence, and good decision-making give children the ability to control their emotional responses, particularly to negative situations, without engaging in self-destructive behaviors. Mental resources include those abilities and skills such as reading, writing, computing, and reasoning needed for daily life. Spiritual resources give children some belief in a divine or higher purpose and guidance upon which they can rely for direction and support. Physical resources include good physical health and mobility or the capacity to use what abilities they have to influence and control their environment. Support systems include family, friends, and additional people who are available in times of need. Relationships and role models nurture the child and engage in self-affirming behaviors. Finally, learning the verbal and nonverbal knowledge, assumptions, and behaviors—the "unspoken rules"—that in-group members continuously use can help resilient children move easily through the system as they find ways to meet their needs. This may mean deliberately teaching these rules to students.

School success requires a number of assets that schools do not necessarily provide. Teachers can informally assess each child in their classrooms through conversations, observations, student records, and other interactions to identify and employ these assets in the service of a high-quality education. The more resources each student has at hand and the greater the extent to which the teacher can access and use these for teaching and learning, the more resilient the student is likely to become and the more that learning is likely to occur.

8.5c Making Connections

Caring about young people and finding ways to help them achieve will build connections between teachers and students. Educators have daily opportunities to develop relationships that can foster educational aspiration and performance. It begins by knowing each student as an individual, as a learner, and as a member of a particular family and community.

Lisa Delpit, an educational leadership expert who focuses on education and race (featured in *Education Spotlight* in Chapter 12), writes that cultural differences between teachers and students can undermine them creating strong connections in at least two ways:

When a significant difference exists between the students' culture and the schools' culture, teachers can easily misread students' aptitudes, intent, or abilities as a result of the difference in styles of language use and interactional patterns. Secondly, when such cultural differences exist, teachers may utilize styles of instruction and/or discipline that are at odds with community norms.[140]

Such miscommunications limit students' access to learning. When teachers do not understand their students' potential, they will "underteach them no matter what the methodology."[141]

Likewise, Sonia Nieto, Geneva Gay, and Gloria Ladson-Billings write about **culturally responsive pedagogy**—the idea that students' backgrounds are assets that students can and should use in the service of their learning and that teachers of all backgrounds should develop the skills to teach all students effectively.[142] Their views come from linking their firsthand experiences teaching in public school classrooms to scholarly research to gain a wider understanding of how students of color learn. For example, after over a decade teaching, Ladson-Billings could not understand why Black students were not successful in schools. She puzzled, "I knew too many smart Black people, and their school outcomes just didn't make sense." During her PhD studies at Stanford University, she decided to flip upside down the popular perspective on Black children as "deficient." Instead of asking what is "wrong" with Black children, she began to ask what is "right." That meant taking an unblinking look at how children were taught and what teachers could do to help their students succeed.[143] Effective educators still look for "what is right" about each child and use these insights to propel their learning.

Evidence is growing that all teachers—regardless of race, ethnicity, or gender—who care about, mentor, and guide their students can have a dramatic positive impact on those children's futures, even when these students face seemingly insurmountable obstacles related to poverty, racism, and other social ills.[144] Developing the personal and professional awareness, knowledge, and skills to use culturally responsive pedagogy is a paramount responsibility for all educators who want all of our children to succeed.

Culturally responsive pedagogy, typified by those strategies noted in Table 8.5, can help underrepresented students succeed in school.[145] Table 8.5 describes what culturally responsive teaching looks like.

TABLE 8.5. ■ Culturally Responsive Teaching

Teacher Quality	Behaviors
As a teacher, be willing to learn.	Low-income, underrepresented populations, and students with disabilities may differ in attitudes, work habits, learning styles, and behaviors from middle-class white students. Be prepared to learn about them—and every student—as individuals, as learners, and as members of specific families and cultures to gain insights and tools to help these children succeed in school.
Be welcoming.	When teachers warmly and genuinely welcome low-income students, students of color, students with disabilities—and every student—into their classrooms and provide the social and academic supports to help them succeed, the positive learning climate will help them focus and learn.

TABLE 8.5. ■ Culturally Responsive Teaching (*Continued*)

Teacher Quality	Behaviors
Be culturally sensitive and respectful.	Understand the ways your students' cultural values, language, behaviors, social, and economic background may influence their attitudes and actions. See your students' cultural values and strengths as motivators and resources in the learning environment. Remember that communication styles vary with the culture and don't misinterpret students' actions as disrespect, misbehavior, or inability to learn. Students may be choosing "not to learn" until the teacher can make the classroom discussion more welcoming, personally and culturally meaningful, and respectful.
Build relationships based on respect and caring.	Holding high expectations, insisting on high-quality work, and offering academic and moral supports to reach these goals demonstrate respect and caring. Calling each student by the correct name, answering students' questions and talking to each of them respectfully, saying "Hello!" outside the classroom, and helping students when they need it let students know whether the teacher really respects and cares about them—or not. Teachers can also attend sports or extracurricular activities to show support outside the classroom.
Assess each student's resources.	Identify each student's assets, including financial, emotional, mental, spiritual, and physical resources; support systems; relationships; and role models. Use these resources to help support student learning. If certain students are not familiar with the school's "hidden rules," find a respectful way to clearly teach them how to behave appropriately and successfully in the school environment as bicultural individuals.
Use culturally responsive pedagogy.	Instructionally, one size does not fit all. Teachers who know and understand their students' cultural backgrounds, values, and learning and interacting styles look for and use their strengths, not their deficits. Noted educator Jaime Escalante, celebrated in the movie *Stand and Deliver*, prepared low-income Latinx students to pass the calculus Advanced Placement tests by referring to their ancestors, "You *have* to learn math. The Mayans discovered zero. Math is in your blood!"[146]
Reduce the "cognitive load."	Learning is always more effective when it is tied to the students' existing knowledge and background[147] and starts where the students are. Each child has his or her own educational and life history, and the more the teacher can have them use what they already know, the more they can extend and deepen their learning.
Reduce the "cultural load."	Build personal relationships with your students and their families and make an effort to include aspects of each child's culture in the classroom regularly. Pronounce each student's name correctly, find out where each student is from, and gather a little personal history about each.
Reduce the language load.	Keep the concepts and rigor high but explain the language in simpler academic terms. Break up complex sentences into smaller ones, point out new and difficult words, define them, and explain how they are used. Give information both visually (in writing, pictures, and gestures) and verbally.
Don't underestimate students' ability to achieve well in your class.	Just because diverse students' school behaviors may not be the same as those of white, middle-class students does not mean that they lack the intelligence and motivation to learn at high levels when given a high-quality academic curriculum and any needed supports (encouragement, material, tutoring, and extra time). Offer high expectations with high supports.
Identify past leadership experiences.	Review with students any past formal or informal leadership experiences and connect these to their ability to make good decisions for themselves—including those regarding schoolwork and their lives.
Help students know themselves as students and learners.	Give students useful and respectful feedback about what they are doing well and how they can improve. Let them know that they control the effort needed to build their abilities to successfully master their schoolwork and meet other life challenges. Students who can recognize and accept their own academic weaknesses and who work to correct them are more likely to perform well in school.

(*Continued*)

TABLE 8.5. ■ Culturally Responsive Teaching (*Continued*)

Teacher Quality	Behaviors
Work with parents or extended family.	Research indicates that students are more likely to exhibit significant academic achievement when parents or family members are involved with their education,[148] especially for diverse students whose cultures place a high value on parents and extended family. Include flexibility in your schedule so that you can meet with parents or guardians who work during the day, greet them with a smile, find interpreters if needed to make understanding and communication easier, speak without education jargon, and provide bilingual information about school practices and ways that parents can help their children learn at home. Let parents know that you care about their children.
Work with parents as a team.	Encourage parents to speak with their children in their language at home and use family and community stories to complete school assignments, support students' adjustment to their new culture, know what is happening in their children's lives, and encourage student involvement in community events that help promote ethnic languages and cultures. Teachers can also invite parents to visit the classroom to talk about their cultures and display items from their countries.
Establish partnerships with community organizations and school liaisons.	Finding and developing parent liaisons who are fluent in the languages spoken by students' families can facilitate relationships between schools, students, and families. These intermediaries can teach parents about schools' "chain of command," assist counselors in interpreting immigrant students' home-country transcripts, help reduce miscommunications among staff and parents of color, and explain students' culture and values to staff.

8.5d Resetting Our Perspectives, Priorities, and Expectations

The process of learning involves more than intellectual ability and mastery of cognitive content. It also includes teachers' and students' psychological and emotional dispositions, their relationships with each other, and the teaching and learning climates in which they occur.

Unequal educational opportunities still exist in American's schools. Increased understanding of students' social class, race, culture, and special learning needs can help educators better relate to all of their students and find resourceful ways to increase each child's learning opportunities and outcomes.

As Delpit concludes, "If we are to successfully educate all of our children, we must work to remove the blinders built of stereotypes, monoculture instructional methodologies, ignorance, [and] social distance."[149] In the words of a Native Alaskan educator, "In order to teach you, I must know you."[150]

FLIPSIDES

Traditional Teaching Versus Culturally Responsive Teaching: Which Approach Will Help Today's Diverse Students Learn to High Levels?

What are the most effective ways to teach a challenging and rigorous curriculum to low-income and underrepresented students? For the sake of argument, we call one teaching approach "traditional" and the other "culturally responsive." Each position reflects a different era and guiding assumptions, expectations, and practices. Which viewpoint do you support?

I support the traditional view.	I support the culturally responsive view.
• Teachers should be color blind (or indifferent) to students' race, ethnicity, or culture in order to treat all students the same.	• Teachers should think of each child as a unique individual. Students' personality, race, ethnicity, and culture contain assets that can facilitate their learning.

I support the traditional view.	I support the culturally responsive view.
• Because low-income and children of color are economically or otherwise "disadvantaged," it is not fair to make them compete with middle-class "advantaged" students. Keep expectations "realistic" and don't set up these students for failure.	• High expectations are for every child. Low-income and underrepresented children have personal and cultural assets that teachers can use to help facilitate their learning. Teachers can also provide the academic, time, and social supports to help these students reach high goals.
• Public schools are a meritocracy in which students who work hard can achieve high standards.	• For meritocracy to function, certain children may need to work hard and receive added teacher supports so they can catch and keep up with better-resourced peers.
• American schools are the social agency that "Americanizes" and socializes immigrants and other outsiders into the American culture and democratic participation. The curriculum should focus solely on American history, norms, and values.	• Learning to live effectively in a pluralistic American democracy means widening the curriculum to include both our unifying history, traditions, and values as well as diverse voices that contribute to the whole. Curriculum should include these diverse stories as American stories.
• The economy has room for low-skill workers, so if students cannot keep up academically, it is OK for them to leave before high school graduation and get a job.	• The 21st century economy has few places for low-skill workers to earn a living wage. Even students not planning on college need to develop high-level knowledge and skills in order to find meaningful paid employment.
• Students should be placed into classrooms with curriculum appropriate for their ability, achievement, and future career goals.	• Making assumptions about students' ability or achievement is often based on data that are subjective, shortsighted, incomplete, or wrong and do not consider student motivation or effort.
• Parents are essential partners in children's education. If they cannot make the time to attend teacher conferences or school events, they must not care about their children's education.	• Many parents care deeply about their children's education and have high expectations for their achievement but for a variety of reasons may not be able to attend school conferences or events.
• Teachers' jobs are to teach and assess students—not "coddle" them.	• Positive interpersonal relationships between teachers and students can motivate students to learn from and for their teachers.

The traditional view was popular from the 19th to the late 20th centuries, while the culturally responsive view is becoming more widespread now. Which viewpoint makes sense if one is to become an effective teacher today?

KEY TAKE-AWAYS

Learning Objective 8.1 Assess the demographic mismatch between today's students and today's teacher workforce, misconceptions about race, and the implications for teachers' "cultural competence."

- The process of learning involves more than intellectual ability and mastery of cognitive content. It also includes teachers' and students' psychological and emotional dispositions, their relationships with each other, and the teaching and learning climates in which they occur.
- Educators can improve school and classroom climate and increase their teaching effectiveness when they develop a keener self-awareness of their implicit or unconscious racial, cultural, and subgroup assumptions and biases and adjust their attitudes and behaviors accordingly.

Learning Objective 8.2 Critique how people develop cultural and racial identities that impact their learning; how the theories of white privilege and white fragility challenge white people's awareness of themselves in the world; and the influence of intersectionality on understanding diversity.

- *Race* is a social construction, a cultural invention based on physical appearance, ancestry, nationality, and culture. Although race is not a scientifically validated biological category, it carries tremendous social importance in this country.
- Cultural identity development is a complex, dynamic process affected by sociocultural forces. Many studies find that students with positive racial and cultural identities are more likely to be successful in school.
- White persons have a racial/cultural identity. Because being white is the U.S. cultural norm, white persons have consciously or unconsciously learned racial biases, prejudices, misinformation, and negative stereotypes through cultural conditioning. White educators benefit when they can understand their own racial/cultural identity within a pluralistic society.
- A person's identity development reflects the holistic complexity of their lived experience. Those who share the same race, gender, class identity, disability, or sexual/gender orientation may or may not have a basis for shared experiences because their identities consist of more than one thing. Thus, it is wise not to make general cultural assumptions about individual students.

Learning Objective 8.3 Clarify the relationship between underrepresented students' perceptions—including oppositional culture theory, stereotype threat theory, and microaggression theory—and their academic performance.

- John Ogbu's ideas about "oppositional" culture, Claude Steele's stereotype threat theory, and Derald Wing Sue's theory of microaggressions describe how many underrepresented students' perspectives affect their academic achievement. Although some of these theories have more research support than others, they all offer meaningful perspectives on underrepresented student achievement. Critics challenge aspects of these theories.
- White privilege and white fragility are theories that help explain how white people may be perceived as enacting their racial position in our society and encourage white people in our culture to recognize their complicity in racial injustice. Both theories have critics.
- Teachers and students benefit when they challenge their preconceived ideas about underrepresented students' ability to succeed in school. Viewing cultural/racial difference or "disability" as the opposite of "normal" falsely limits teachers' expectations for diverse students' achievement.

Learning Objective 8.4 Support how teachers using students' assets (rather than deficits) can improve their teaching effectiveness with all students, especially underrepresented students.

- Good relationships and learning goal compatibility with teachers motivate students to learn and achieve. With a mastery approach to learning, students facing challenge or failure are likely to attribute the result to lack of enough effort (that they can control) rather than to a lack of ability (that they cannot control).
- For public schools to become the equalizers of opportunity, educators need to develop the "cultural competence" to work successfully with children and families who differ from themselves. When teachers can align students' experiences and values with the curriculum and make the content personally relevant and meaningful to students, engagement and learning increase.

Learning Objective 8.5 Argue how teachers can use diverse students' personal, family, and cultural assets and culturally responsive pedagogy to foster student resilience and success in school.

- Each child has an array of personal, family, and cultural resources from which teachers can draw to help the student succeed. The more resources each student has and the greater the extent to which the teacher can access and use these for teaching and learning, the more resilient the student is likely to become and the more that learning is likely to occur.
- Evidence is growing that all teachers who care about, mentor, and guide their students and use culturally responsive pedagogy can have a dramatic positive impact on those children's futures, even when these students face seemingly insurmountable obstacles related to poverty, racism, and other social ills.

TEACHER SCENARIO: IT'S YOUR TURN

You are an experienced teacher in diverse middle school. The school's student demographics are 38% white, 41% Black, 15% Latinx, and 6% Asian American; 15% are eligible for special education services; 91% are eligible for free or reduced-price lunch. Overall school achievement is low. It is now August before school begins.

Seeking to improve student achievement, your principal asks you to work with the new faculty during the coming year about how to develop a positive classroom environment and use instructional practices in which every student can succeed. You will present a monthly series of 2-hour professional development to facilitate their awareness and understanding of the following:

1. Their common assumptions and biases about racial and cultural populations and students with disabilities
2. How everyone develops a racial and cultural identity and its role in student achievement
3. The importance of knowing each student's needs and backgrounds
4. Factors that may interfere with their learning
5. The benefits to students by using culturally responsive pedagogy

On the Friday before school begins for students, you will have 15 minutes to introduce this program. Develop a monthly outline for the series' content, the rationale for each topic, and a description of what teachers will explore during each session.

NOTES

1. Gay, G. (1994). *A synthesis of scholarship in multicultural education.* North Central Regional Laboratory. https://files.eric.ed.gov/fulltext/ED378287.pdf
2. Gay, 1994.
3. In this chapter, we will respectfully use the self-referent terms that these groups prefer that others call them: children of poverty and low income, Latinx, African American and Black, Native American, students with disabilities, and LGBTQ+.
4. National Center for Education Statistics. (2019a, May). *Children and youth with disabilities: The condition of education.* U.S. Department of Education. https://nces.ed.gov/programs/coe/indicator_cgg.asp
5. The 13 current disability categories are autism, blindness, deafness, emotional disturbance, hearing impairment, intellectual disability, multiple disabilities, orthopedic impairment, other health impaired, specific learning disability, speech or language impairment, traumatic brain injury, and visual impairment.
6. IRIS Center. (2020). *Cultural diversity* (p. 3). Vanderbilt University. https://iris.peabody.vanderbilt.edu/module/div/cresource/q2/p03/

7. National Center for Education Statistics. (2019b, May). *English language learners in public schools: The condition of education.* U.S. Department of Education. https://nces.ed.gov/programs/coe/indicator_cgf.asp

8. Office of Civil Rights. (2012). 2011–12 state and national estimations: Gifted and talented enrollment estimations. *Civil Rights Data Collection.* U.S. Department of Education. https://ocrdata.ed.gov/StateNationalEstimations/Estimations_2011_12

9. *Lesbian* is a woman whose enduring physical, romantic, and/or emotional attraction is to other women; some lesbians prefer to identify as gay. *Gay* is used to describe people whose enduring physical, romantic, and/or emotional attractions are to people of the same sex. *Bisexual* is a person who has the capacity to form enduring physical, romantic, and/or emotional attraction to those of the same gender or to those of another gender. *Transgender* is an umbrella term for those whose gender identity and/or gender expression differs from what is typically associated with the sex they were assigned at birth. *Queer* is an adjective that some use to describe a person whose sexual orientation is not exclusively heterosexual and believe that the terms "lesbian," "gay," and "bisexual" are thought of as too limiting and/or tied to cultural connotations that they feel do not apply to them. *Questioning* is another alternative for defining the *Q* at the end of *LGBTQ* and describes someone who is questioning their sexual orientation or gender identity. The "+" (plus) signifies that the LGBTQ community also includes other variations on sexual orientation or gender identity, such as pansexual, intersex, asexual, ally, and others.

10. Newport, F. (2018, May 22). In U.S., estimate of LGBT population rises to 4.5%. *Gallup News.* https://news.gallup.com/poll/234863/estimate-lgbt-population-rises.asp;. LGBT Demographic Data Interactive. (2019). *LGBT proportion of population: United States.* The Williams Institute, UCLA School of Law. https://williamsinstitute.law.ucla.edu/visualization/lgbt-stats/?topic=LGBT#density

11. Schlanger, Z. (2017, June 25). A teen health survey crucial to US public policy is finally asking kids about their sexual orientation. *Quartz.* https://qz.com/1014142/a-teen-health-survey-crucial-to-us-public-policy-is-finally-asking-kids-about-their-sexual-orientation/

12. Schlanger, 2017.

13. UCLA Center. (n.d.). *About sexual minority (LGBT) youth subculture.* http://smhp.psych.ucla.edu/pdfdocs/youth/lgbt.pdf

14. See: Blackburn, M. V., & Pennell, S. M. (2018, September 24). Teaching students to question assumptions about gender and sexuality. *Phi Delta Kappan, 100*(2), 27–31; Human Rights Campaign. (2018). *2018 LGBTQ youth report.* https://www.hrc.org/resources/2018-lgbtq-youth-report; Prescott, S. (2019, October). Supporting LGBTQ-inclusive teaching. NewAmerica.org. https://d1y8sb8igg2f8e.cloudfront.net/documents/Supporting_LGBTQ-Inclusive_Teaching_2019-10-23_002327_KHHvQn6.pdf

15. Geiger, A. W. (2018, August 27). America's public school teachers are far less racially and ethnically diverse than their students. *FactTank.* Pew Research Center. https://www.pewresearch.org/fact-tank/2018/08/27/americas-public-school-teachers-are-far-less-racially-and-ethnically-diverse-than-their-students/

16. U.S. Department of Education. (2016, July). *The state of racial diversity in the educator workforce.* Office of Panning, Evaluation, and Policy Development; Loewus, L. (2017, August 15). White women still dominate the teaching force. *Education Week, 37*(1), 11. https://www2.ed.gov/rschstat/eval/highered/racial-diversity/state-racial-diversity-workforce.pdf

17. Meckler, L., & Rabinowitz, K. (2019, December 27). America's schools are more diverse than ever. But the teachers are still mostly white. *The Washington Post.* https://www.washingtonpost.com/graphics/2019/local/education/teacher-diversity/

18. Mitchell, C. (2016, February 16). Black male teachers a dwindling demographic. *Education Week, 35*(21), 1, 9–10.

19. Riser-Kositsky, M. (2019, February 5). Education statistics: Facts about American schools. *Education Week.* https://www.edweek.org/leadership/education-statistics-facts-about-american-schools/2019/01

20. See: Bates, L. A., & Glick, J. E. (2013). Does it matter if teachers and schools match the student? Racial and ethnic disparities in problem behaviors. *Social Science Research, 42*(5), 1180–1190; Lindsay, D. A., & Cassandra, M. D. (2017). Exposure to same-race teachers and student disciplinary outcomes for Black students in North Carolina. *Educational Evaluation and Policy Analysis, 39*(3), 485–510; Egalite, A. J., Kisidan, B., & Winters, M. A. (2015). Representation in the classroom: The effect of own-race teachers on student achievement. *Economics of Education Review, 45*(1), 44–52.

21. Downer, J. T., Goble, P., Myers, S. S., & Pianta, R. C. (2016). Teacher-child racial/ethnic match within pre-kindergarten classrooms and children's early school adjustment. *Early Childhood Research Quarterly, 37* (Supplement C), 26–38; Gershenson, S., Holt, S. B., & Papageorge, N. W. (2016). Who believes in me? The effect of student-teacher demographic match on teacher expectations. *Economics of Education Review, 52*(C), 209–224.

22. Villegas, A. M., & Irvine. J. J. (2010). Diversifying the teaching force: An examination of major arguments. *The Urban Review, 42*(3), 175–192.

23. Klopfenstein, K. (2005). Beyond test scores: The impact of black teacher role models on rigorous math taking. *Contemporary Economic Policy, 23*, 416–428.

24. Meckler & Rabinowitz, 2019.

25. Hussar, W., & Bailey, T. (2013). *Projections of education statistics to 2022* (NCES 2014-051). U.S. Department of Education.

26. Trumbull, E. (2005). Language, culture, and society. In E. Trumbull & B. Farr (Eds.), *Language and learning: What teachers need to know* (pp. 33–72). Christopher-Gordon, p. 35.

27. Rothstein-Fisch, C., & Trumbull, E. (2008). *Managing diverse classrooms: How to build on students' cultural strengths*. Association for Supervision and Curriculum Development, pp. 2–3.

28. Greenfield, P. M. (1994). Independence and interdependence as developmental scripts: Implications for theory, research, and practice. In P. M. Greenfield & R. R. Cocking (Eds.), *Cross-cultural roots of minority child development*. Lawrence Erlbaum, pp. 1–37; Hofstede, G. (2001). *Culture's consequences: Comparing values, behaviors, institutions, and organizations across nations* (2nd ed.). SAGE; Markus, H., & Kitayama, S. (1991). Culture and the self: Implications for cognition, emotion, and motivation. *Psychological Review, 98*, 224–253.

29. Greenfield, 1994; Nelson-Barber, S., Trumbull, E., & Wenn, R. (2000). *The coconut wireless project: Sharing culturally responsive pedagogy through the World Wide Web*. Pacific Resources for Education and Learning.

30. Mukhopadhyay, C., & Henze, R. D. (2003, May). How real is race? Using anthropology to make sense of human diversity. *Phi Delta Kappan, 84*(9), 669–678; Renn, K. A. (2012). Creating and re-creating race: The emergence of racial identity as a critical element in psychological, sociological, and ecological perspectives on human development (pp. 11–32). In C. L. Wijeyesinghe & B. W. Jackson III (Eds.), *New perspectives on racial identity development* (2nd ed.). New York University Press.

31. Renn, 2012.

32. Cass, V. C (1979). Homosexual identity formation: A theoretical model. *Journal of Homosexuality, 4*(3), 219–235; Downing, N. E., & Roush, K. L. (1985). From passive acceptance to active commitment: A model of feminist identity development for women. *Counseling Psychologist, 13*(4), 695–709; Olkin, R. (1999). *What psychotherapists should know about disability*. Guilford Press; Kin, J. (2012). American Asian identity development theory. In C. Wijeyesinghe & B. W Jackson (Eds.), *New perspectives on racial identity: A theoretical and practical anthology* (pp. 138–160). New York University Press; Sue, S., & Sue, D. W. (1971). Chinese American personality and mental health. *Amerasian Journal, 1*(1), 36–49.

33. Rotheram, M. J., & Phinney, J. S. (1988). Introduction: Definitions and perspectives in the study of children's ethnic socialization. In J. S. Phinney & J. Rotheram (Eds.), *Children's ethnic socialization: Pluralism and development* (pp. 10–28). SAGE.

34. Berry, G. (1965). *Ethnic and race relations*. Houghton Mifflin; Sue, D. W., & Sue, D. (1999). *Counseling the culturally different: Theory and practice* (3rd ed.). John Wiley & Sons; Sue, D. W., & Sue, D. (2016). *Counseling the culturally diverse: Theory and practice* (7th ed.). John Wiley & Sons.

35. The following discussion reflects the work of Derald Wing Sue and David Sue. See: Sue & Sue, 2016, pp. 366–377.

36. Haley, A. (1966). *The autobiography of Malcolm X*. Grove Press.

37. Frankenberg, R. (1993). *The social construction of Whiteness: White women, race matters*. University of Minnesota Press.

38. The following discussion reflects the work of Derald Wing Sue and David Sue. See: Sue & Sue, 2016, pp. 406–412.

39. Sue & Sue, 2016, pp. 406–412.

40. Haag, M. (2018, May 25). Rachel Dolezal, who pretended to be black, is charged with welfare fraud. *The New York Times*. https://www.nytimes.com/2018/05/25/us/rachel-dolezal-welfare-fraud.html

41. The term "white privilege" is attributed to Peggy McIntosh's 1988 paper, *White Privilege and Male Privilege: A Personal Account of Coming to See Correspondences Through Work in Women's Studies*. See: Rothman, J. (2014, May 12). The origins of "privilege." *The New Yorker*. https://www.newyorker.com/books/page-turner/the-origins-of-privilege

42. Kendall, F. E. (2013). *Understanding white privilege* (2nd ed.). Routledge; McIntosh, P. (1998). *White privilege: Unpacking the invisible knapsack*. https://www.racialequitytools.org/resourcefiles/mcintosh.pdf;. Collins, K. (2018, Fall). What is white privilege, really? *Teaching Tolerance*. https://www.tolerance.org/magazine/fall-2018/what-is-white-privilege-really

43. Hilliard, A. (1992). *Racism: Its origins and how it works*. Paper presented at the meeting of the Mid-West Association for the Education of Young Children, Madison, WI.

44. McIntosh, P. (1988). White privilege and male privilege: A personal account of coming to see correspondence through work in women's studies. In M. Anderson & P. Hill Collins (Eds.), *Race, class, and gender: An anthology* (pp. 94–105). Wadsworth; Mills, C. (1999). *The racial contract*. Cornell University Press; Feagin, J. R. (2006). *Systematic racism: A theory of oppression*. Routledge.

45. Clark, K. B. (1963). *Prejudice and your child*. Beacon Press; Derman-Sparks, L., Ramsey, P., & Olsen Edwards, J. (2006). *What if all the kids are white: Anti-bias multicultural education with young children and families*. Teachers College Press.

46. Collins, 2018.

47. Blum, L. (2008). "White privilege": A mild critique. *Theory and Research in Education, 6*(3), 309–321.

48. Gordon, L. (2004). Critical reflections on three popular tropes in the study of whiteness. In G. Yancy (Ed.), *What white looks like: African American philosophers on the whiteness question*. Routledge; Jilaji, Z. (2019, May 23). What does teaching "white privilege" actually accomplish? Not what you might think (or hope). *Quillette*. https://quillette.com/2019/05/23/what-does-teaching-white-privilege-actually-accomplish-not-what-you-might-think-or-hope/

49. Hanson, V. D. (2018, October 23). The white-privilege tedium. *National Review*. https://www.nationalreview.com/2018/10/white-privilege-debate-elizabeth-warren/

50. Andersen, M. (2003). Whitewashing race: A critical perspective on whiteness. In W. Doane & E. Bonilla-Silva (Eds.), *White out*. Routledge.

51. Blum, 2008; Corlett, J. A. (2003). *Race, racism, and reparations*. Cornell University Press; Feinberg, W. (1998). *Common schools/uncommon identities: National unity and cultural difference*. Yale University Press; Hanson, 2018.

52. DiAngelo, 2011; DiAngelo, R. (2018). *White fragility. Why it's so hard for white people to talk about racism*. Beacon Press.

53. DeAngelo, 2011, p. 54. DiAngelo notes that white racial insulation is somewhat mediated by social class. Poor and working-class urban white people are generally less racially insulated than suburban or rural white people. Nonetheless, the larger social environment insulates and protects white persons as a group through institutions, media, school textbooks, movies, advertising, among other factors.

54. Whitehead, K. A., & Wittig, M. A. (2005). Discursive management of resistance to a multicultural education programme. *Qualitative Research in Psychology, 1*(3), 267–284; Horton, J., & Scott, D. (2004). White students' voices in multicultural teacher education preparation. *Multicultural Education, 11*(4), 12–16.

55. Frey, W. R. (2019). White fragility: Why it's so hard for white people to talk about racism. Robin DiAngelo. *Journal of Social Work, 20*(1), 123–125.

56. Frey, 2019; Church, J. (2018, August 24). The problem with "white fragility" theory. *Quillette*.https://quillette.com/2018/08/24/the-problem-with-white-fragility-theory/

57. Church, 2018; Lile, J. (2019, June 18). "White fragility" is an inherently racist idea that should be retired immediately. *The*Federalist.com.https://thefederalist.com/2019/06/18/white-fragility-inherently-racist-idea-retired-immediately/

58. Lile, 2019.

59. Sanneh, K. (2019, August 12). The fight to redefine racism. *The New Yorker*. https://www.newyorker.com/magazine/2019/08/19/the-fight-to-redefine-racism

60. Frey, 2019.

61. Corrigan, L. M. (2016) On rhetorical criticism, performativity, and white fragility. *Review of Communication, 16*(1), 86–88.

62. For more DiAngelo readings on white fragility, see: DiAngelo, R. (2006). My class didn't trump my race: Using oppression to face privilege. *Multicultural Perspectives, 8*(1), 51–56; DiAngelo, R. (2012, February). Nothing to add: A challenge to white silence in racial discussions. *Understanding and Dismantling Privilege, 2*(1), 1–17.https://www.marypendergreene.com/bookshelf/docs/Nothing-to-Add-Published.pdf;DiAngelo, R. (2015, April 9). *White fragility: Why it's so hard to talk to white people about racism.* http://www.kooriweb.org/foley/resources/whiteness/white%20fragility.pdf;. DiAngelo, R. (2006). The production of whiteness in education: Asian international students in a college classroom. *Teachers College Record, 108*(10), 1983–2000.

63. Sue & Sue, 2008, p. 257.

64. Sue & Sue, 2008, p. 258.

65. A 2015–2016 study found that most LGBTQ+ characters were male and white but becoming increasingly diverse. See: Townsend, M. (2015, October 37). GLAAD's "where we are on tv" report calls for more diverse, substantive LGBT characters. *GLAAD.* https://www.glaad.org/blog/glaads-where-we-are-tv-report-calls-more-diverse-substantive-lgbt-characters

66. *Obergefell v. Hodges*, 576 U.S. 644. (2015).

67 Crenshaw, K. (1989). Demarginalizing the intersection of race and sex: A Black feminist critique of antidiscrimination doctrine, feminist theory, and antiracist politics. *University of Chicago Legal Forum, 1*(8), 139167. https://chicagounbound.uchicago.edu/cgi/viewcontent.cgi?article=1052&context=uclf; Crenshaw, K. (1991). Mapping the margins: Intersectionality, identity politics, and violence against women of color. *Stanford Law Review, 43*(6), 1241–1299. https://doi.org/10.2307/1229039; Perlman, M. (2018, October 23). The origin of the term 'intersectionality'. *Columbia Journalism Review.* https://www.cjr.org/language_corner/intersectionality.php

68. For a more complete discussion of *intersectionality*, see: Cole, E. R. (2009, April). Intersectionality and research in psychology. *American Psychologist, 64*(3), 170–180; Renn, K. A. (2012). Creating and re-creating race: The emergence of racial identity as a critical element in psychological, sociological, and ecological perspectives on human development). In C. L. Wijeyesinghe & B. W. Jackson III (Eds.), *New perspectives on racial identity development* (2nd ed.; pp. 11–32). New York University Press.

69. Carathathis, A. (2014). The concept of intersectionality in feminist theory. *Philosophy Compass, 9*(5), 304–314; Cho, S., Crenshaw, K. W., & McCall, K. L. (2013, Summer). Toward a field of intersectionality studies: Theory, application, and praxis. *Signs, 38*(4), 785–810; May, V. M. (2014, Winter). "Speaking into the void "? Intersectionality critiques and epistemic backlash. *Hypatia, 29*(1), 94–112.

70. Perry, T., Steele, C., & Hilliard, A. (2003). *Young, gifted, and Black. Promoting high achievement among African-American students.* Beacon.

71. Carlson, C., Uppal, S., & Prosser, E. C. (2000). Ethnic differences in processes contributing to the self-esteem of early adolescent girls. *Journal of Early Adolescence, 20*, 44–67.

72. Phinney, J. S. (1989). Stages of ethnic identity in minority group adolescents. *Journal of Early Adolescence, 9*, 34–49.

73. Phinney, J. S., & Alipuria, L. (1990). Ethnic identity in college students from four ethnic groups. *Journal of Adolescence, 13*, 171–184.

74. Phinney, J. S., Horenczyk, G., Liebkind, K., & Vedder, P. (2001). Ethnic identity, immigration, and well-being: An interactional perspective. *Journal of Social Issues, 57*, 493–510; Wright, 2009.

75. Yasui, M., Dorham, C. L., & Dishion, T. J. (2004). Ethnic identity and psychological adjustment: A validity analysis for European American and African American adolescents. *Journal of Adolescence, 19*, 807–825.

76. Phinney, J. S., Romero, I., Nava, M., & Huang, D. (2001). The role of language, parents, and peers in ethnic identity among adolescents in immigrant families. *Journal of Youth and Adolescence, 30*, 135–153; Wright, B.L. (2009, Spring). Racial-ethnic identity, academic achievement, and African American males: a review of Literature. *Journal of Negro Education, 78*(2), 123-134.

77. Helms, J. E. (1993). *Black and white racial identity: Theory, research, and practice.* Praeger; McMahon, S. D., & Watts, R. J. (2002). Ethnic identity in urban African American youth: Exploring links with self-worth, aggression, and other psychosocial variables. *Journal of Community Psychology, 30*, 411–431; Martinez, R. O., & Dukes, R. L. (1997). The effects of ethnic identity, ethnicity, and gender on adolescent well-being. *Journal of Youth and Adolescence, 26*, 503–516; Phinney, J. S. (1992). The multigroup ethnic identity measure: A new scale for use with diverse groups. *Journal of Adolescent Research, 7*, 156–176; Phinney, J. S., & Kohatsu, E. L. (1997). Ethnic and racial identity development and mental health. In J. Schulenberg, J. L. Maggs, & K. Hurrelmann (Eds.), *Health risks and developmental transitions during adolescence.* Cambridge University Press, pp. 420–443; Bracey, J. R., Bamaca, M. Y., & Umana-Taylor, A. J. (2004). Examining ethnic identity and self-esteem among biracial and monoracial adolescents. *Journal of Youth & Adolescence, 33*, 123–132.

78. Blash, R. R., & Unger, D. G. (1995). Self-concept of African American male youth: Self-esteem and ethnic identity. *Journal of Child & Family Studies, 4*, 359–373; Carlson, C., Uppal, S., & Prosser, E. C. (2000). Ethnic differences in processes contributing to the self-esteem of early adolescent girls. *Journal of Early Adolescence, 20*, 44–67.

79. Evans, R. (2005, April). Reframing the achievement gap. *Phi Delta Kappan, 86*(8), 582–589.

80. Ogbu, J. U., & Simons, H. D. (1998). Cultural-ecological theory of student performance with some implications for education. *Anthropology and Education Quarterly, 29*(2), 155–188.

81. "Acting white" is a term that originated with the first school integration practices over 50 years ago and the idea that Black students were educated well only if a white student were sitting next to them. Since then, attitudes on race have changed, but the cultural meme of viewing school as "white"—the psychological association between school achievement and whiteness—became self-perpetuating. See: McWhorter, J. (2019, July 20). The origins of the "acting white" charge. *The Atlantic*. https://www.theatlantic.com/ideas/archive/2019/07/acting-white-charge-origins/594130/

82. Fordham, S. (1996). *Blacked out: Dilemmas of race, identity, and success at Capital High*. Chicago: University of Chicago Press; Noguera, P. A. (2003). How racial identity affects school performance. *Harvard Education Letter 19*, 1–3; Fryer, R. G. (2006, Winter). "Acting white": The social price paid by the best and brightest minority students. *Education Next, 6*(1). Stanford University. https//educationnext.org/actingwhite/

83. Neal-Barnett, A. (2001). Being black: A new conceptualization of acting white. In A. M. Neal-Barnett, J. Contreras, & K. Kerns (Eds.), *Forging links: African American children clinical development perspectives* (pp. 75–88). Greenwood.

84. Fordham, S., & Ogbu, J. (1986). Black students' school successes: Coping with the burden of "acting white." *Urban Review, 18*, 176–206; Lundy, G. F. (2003, March). The myths of oppositional culture. *Journal of Black Studies, 33*(4), 450-467.

85. For a more detailed discussion of oppositional culture and "acting white" theory and criticism of this theory, see: Wildhagen, T. (2011, Fall). Testing the "acting white" hypothesis: A popular explanation runs out of empirical steam. *The Journal of Negro Education, 80*(4), 445-463.

86. Ogbu, J. U. (1991). Low performance as an adaptation: The case of Blacks in Stockton, California (pp. 249–285). In M. A. Gibson & J. U. Ogbu (Eds.), *Minority status and schooling*. Grand.

87. Ogbu, J. U., with Davis, A. (2003) *Black American students in an affluent suburb: A study of academic disengagement*. Lawrence Erlbaum.

88. Ogbu, J. U. (1991). Low performance as an adaptation: The case of Blacks in Stockton, California (pp. 249-285). In M. A. Gibson & J. U. Ogbu (Eds.), *Minority status and schooling*. New York: Grand Publishing.

89. Downey, D. B., & Ainsworth-Darnell, J. W. (2002). The search for oppositional culture among Black students. *American Sociological Review, 67*, 156–164; Farkas, G., Lleras, C., & Maczuga, S. (2002). Does oppositional culture exist in minority and poverty peer groups? *American Sociological Review, 67*, 148–155; Ferguson, R. F. (2001). A diagnostic analysis of Black–white GPA disparities in Shaker Heights, Ohio. *Brookings Papers on Education Policy, 2001*, 347–414; Harper, S. R. (2006). Peer support for African American male college achievement: Beyond internalized racism and the burden of "acting white." *Journal of Men's Studies, 14*(3), 337–358.

90. Anderson, J. D. (1988). *The education of Blacks in the south, 1860–1935*. University of North Carolina Press; Perry, T., Steele, C., & Hilliard, A. (2003). *Young, gifted, and Black: Promoting high academic achievement among African-American students*. Beacon.

91. Tyson, K., Darity, W. Jr., & Castellino, D. (2006). It's not a "Black thing": Understanding the burden of acting white and other dilemmas of high achievement. *American Sociological Review, 70*(4), 582–605.

92. Carter, P. L. (2005). Keepin' it real: School success beyond Black and white. Oxford University Press.

93. Brown, K. D., & Brown, A. L. (2012, Winter-Spring). Useful and dangerous discourse: Deconstructing racialized knowledge about African-American students. *Educational Foundations, 26*(1–2), 11–26; Foley, 2004.

94. Steele, C. M. (1999, August). Thin ice: "Stereotype threat" and black college students. *Atlantic Monthly, 284*(2), 44–47, 50–54; Steele, C. M. (1997, June). A threat in the air: How stereotypes shape intellectual identity and performance. *American Psychologist, 52*(6), 613–629.

95. Steele, 1997.

96. Rutgers School of Arts and Sciences. (2020). *Stereotype threat*. Department of Philosophy. https://philosophy.rutgers.edu/climate-v2/climate-issues-in-academic-philosophy/stereotype-threat

97. Pennington, E. R., Helm, D., Levy, A. R., & Larkin, D. T. (2016, January). Twenty years of stereotype threat research: A review of psychological mediators. *Public Library of Science, 11*(1), e0146487. PubMed.gov. https://www.ncbi.nlm.nih.gov/pubmed/26752551

98. Schmader, T., Johns, M., & Forbes, C. (2008, April). An integrated process model of stereotype threat on performance. *Psychology Review, 155*(2), 336–356.

99. Steele, J., James, J. B., & Barnett, R. (2002). Learning in a man's world: Examining the perceptions of undergraduate women in male-dominated academic areas. *Psychology of Women Quarterly, 26*, 46–50.

100. Viadero, D. (2007, October 24). Experiments aim to east effects of "stereotype threat." *Education Week, 27*(9), 10.

101. Neuville, E., & Croizet, J. (2007). Can salience of gender identity impair math performance among 7-8 years old girls? The moderating role of task difficulty. *European Journal of Psychology of Education, 22*(3), 307–316; Ambady, N., Shih, M., Kim, A., & Pittinsky, T. L. (2001). Stereotype susceptibility in children: Effects of identity activation on quantitative performance. *Psychological Science, 12*(5), 385–390.

102. Viadero, 2007.

103. Good, C., Aronson, J., & Inzlicht, M. (2003). Improving adolescents' standardized test performance: An intervention to reduce the effects of stereotype threat. *Journal of Applied Developmental Psychology, 24*(6), 645–662; Sherman, D. K., Hartson, K. A., Binning, K. R., Purdie-Vaughns, V., Garcia, J., Taborsky-Barba, S., Tomassetti, S., Nussbaum, A. D., & Cohen, G. L. (2013, April). Deflecting the trajectory and changing the narrative: How self-affirmation affects academic performance and motivation under identity threat. *Journal of Personality and Social Psychology, 104*(4), 591–618; Walton, G., & Cohen, G. L. (2007). A question of belonging: Racial, social fit, and achievement. *Journal of Personality and Social Psychology, 92*(1), 82–96.

104. Evans, 2005.

105. Stoet, G., & Geary, D. C. (2012). Can stereotype threat explain the gender gap in mathematics performance and achievement? *Review of General Psychology, 16*(1), 93–102; Spencer, S. J., Logel, C., & Davies, P.G. (2016). Stereotype threat. *Annual Review of Psychology, 67*, 415–437; Wei, T. E. (2014, October). *Stereotype threat, gender, and math performance: Evidence from the National Assessment of Educational Progress*. Harvard University. https://www.researchgate.net/profile/Thomas_Wei2/publication/228776168_Stereotype_Threat_Gender_and_Math_Performance_Evidence_from_the_National_Assessment_of_Educational_Progress/links/56e6b35808aedb4cc8af75a5/Stereotype-Threat-Gender-and-Math-Performance-Evidence-from-the-National-Assessment-of-Educational-Progress.pdf

106. Jensen, A. R. (1998). Population differences in g: Causal hypothesis. In A. R. Jensen (Ed.), *The g factor: The science of mental ability* (pp. 513–515). Praeger.

107. Sackett, P. R., Hardison, C. M., & Cullen, M. J. (2004). On interpreting stereotype threat as accounting for African American–white differences on cognitive tests. *The American Psychologist, 59*(1), 7–13.

108. See, for example, Sue, D. W., Cadodilupo, C. M., Torino, G. C., Bucceri, J. M., Holder, A. M., Nadal, K. L., & Esquilin, M. (2007). Racial microaggressions in everyday life: Implications for clinical practice. *American Psychologist, 62*(4), 271–286; Sue, D. W. (2010). *Microaggressions in everyday life: Race, gender, and sexual orientation*. Wiley.

109. Sue, 2010; Sue et al., 2007.

110. Jernigan, M. M., & Daniel, J. H, (2011). Racial trauma in the lives of Black children and adolescents: Challenges and clinical implications. *Journal of Child and Adolescent Trauma, 4*(2), 123–141.

111. For more examples of microaggressions in the classroom, see: Portman, J., Bui, T. T., Ogaz, J., & Trevino, J. (2013). *Microaggressions in the classroom*. University of Denver. http://otl.du.edu/wp-content/uploads/2013/03/MicroAggressionsInClassroom-DUCME.pdf

112. Cadodilupo, C. M. (2016). Microaggressions in counseling and psychotherapy. In D. W. Sue & D. Sue (Eds.), *Counseling the culturally diverse: Theory and practice* (7th ed.; pp. 180–208). John Wiley & Sons.

113. Lilienfeld, S. O. (2017). Microaggressions: Strong claims, inadequate evidence. *Perspectives on Psychological Science, 12*(1), 138–169.

114. Friedersdorf, C. (2015, September 14). Why critics of the "microaggressions" framework are skeptical. Politics. *The Atlantic*. https://www.theatlantic.com/politics/archive/2015/09/why-critics-of-the-microaggressions-framework-are-skeptical/405106/; Campbell, B., & Manning, J. (2014). Microaggression and moral cultures. *Comparative Sociology, 13*(6), 692–726.

115. Haidt, J. (2012). Where microaggressions really come from: A sociological account. *The Righteous Mind.* https://righteousmind.com/where-microaggressions-really-come-from/

116. Lukianoff, G., & Haidt, J. (2015, September). The coddling of the American mind. *The Atlantic.* https://www.theatlantic.com/magazine/archive/2015/09/the-coddling-of-the-american-mind/399356/

117. English, D., Lambert, S. F., Tynes, B. M., Bowleg, L., Zea, M. C., & Howard, L. C. (2020). Daily multidimensional racial discrimination among Black American adolescents. *Journal of Applied Developmental Psychology, 66* (Jan.–Feb.), 1–12; Krieger, N. (1990). Racial and gender discrimination: Risk factors for high blood pressure? *Social Science and Medicine, 30*(12), 1273–1281; Murry, V. M., Butler Barnes, S. T., Mayo Gamble, T. L., & Inniss Thompson, M. N. (2018). Excavating new constructs for family stress theories in the context of everyday life experiences of Black American families. *Journal of Family Theory & Review, 10*(2), 384–405; Saleem, F. T., & Lambert, S. (2016). Differential effects of racial socialization messages for African American adolescents: Personal versus institutional racial discrimination. *Journal of Child and Family Studies, 25*(5), 1385–1396; Murray et al., 2018.

118. Chavious, T. M., Rivas-Drake, D., Smalls, C., Griffin, T., & Cogburn, C. D. (2008). Gender matters too: The influence of school racial discrimination and racial identity on academic engagement outcomes among African American adolescents. *Developmental Psychology, 44*(3), 637–654; English et al., 2020; Jernigan & Daniel, 2011; Wang, M. T., & Huguley, J. P. (2012). Parental, racial socialization as a moderator of the effects of racial discrimination on educational success among African American adolescents. *Child Development, 83*(5), 1716–1731.

119. Saleem, F. T., Anderson, R. E., & Williams, M. (2019). Addressing the "myth" of racial trauma: Developmental and ecological considerations for youth of color. *Clinical Child and Family Psychology Review,* 1–14. doi:10.1007/s10567-019-00304-1

120. Irvine, J. J. (2003). *Educating teachers for diversity: Seeing with a cultural eye.* Teachers College Press; Lipman, P. (1995). Bring out the best in them: The contribution of culturally relevant teachers to education. *Theory Into Practice, 34*(3), 203–208; Sleeter, C. E. (2000). Creating an empowering cultural curriculum. *Race, Gender, & Class in Education, 7*(3), 178–196.

121. Boykin, A. W., & Noguera, P. (2011). *Creating the opportunity to learn: Moving from research to practice to close the achievement gap.* ASCD.

122. Boykin and Noguera, 2011..

123. See: Hamre, B. K., & Pianta, R. C. (2001). Early teacher–child relationships and the trajectory of children's school outcomes through eighth grade. *Child Development, 72*(2), 625–638; Reyes, M. R., Brackett M. A., Rivers, S. E., White, M., & Salovey, P. (2012, March). Classroom emotional climate, student engagement, and academic achievement. *Journal of Educational Psychology, 104*(3), 700–712; Roorda, D. L., Koomen, H. M. Y., Spilt, J. L., & Oort, F. J. (2011). The influence of affective teacher–student relationships on students' school engagement and achievement: A meta-analytic approach. *Review of Educational Research, 81*(4), 493–529.

124. See: Hamre & Pianta, 2005; Griffith, J. (2002). A multi-level analysis of the relation of school learning and social environments to the minority achievement in public elementary schools. *Elementary School Journal, 102*(5), 353–366; Balfanz, R., & Byrnes, V. (2006). Closing the mathematics achievement gap in high-poverty middle schools: Enablers and constraints. *Journal of Education for Students At-Risk, 11*(2), 143–159; Liew, J., Chen, Q., & Hughes, J. (2010). Child effortful control, teacher–student relationships, and achievement in academically at-risk children: Additive and interactive effects. *Early Childhood Research Quarterly, 25*(1), 51–64.

125. See: Baker, J. A. (1999). Teacher-student interaction in urban at-risk classrooms: Differential behavior, relationship, quality, and student satisfaction with school. *Elementary School Journal, 100*(1), 57–70; Byrnes, J. P., & Miller, D. C. (2007). The relative importance of predictors of math and science achievement: An opportunity-propensity analysis. *Contemporary Educational Psychology, 32*(4), 599–629; Hamre, B. K., & Pianta, R. C. (2005). Can instructional and emotional support in the first-grade classroom make a difference for children at risk of school failure? *Child Development, 76*(5), 949–967; Urdan, T., & Schoenfelder, E. (2006). Classroom effects on student motivation: Goal structures, social relationships, and competence beliefs. *Journal of School Psychology, 44*(5), 331–349.

126. See: Brand, B. R., Glasson, G. E., & Green, A. M. (2006). Sociocultural factors influencing students' learning in science and mathematics: An analysis of the perspectives of African American students. *School Science and Mathematics, 106*(5), 228–236; Stewart, E. (2006). Family- and individual-level predictors of academic success for African American students: A longitudinal path analysis utilizing national data. *Journal of Black Studies, 36*(4), 597–621.

127. See: Ladd, G. W., Burch, S. H., & Burs, B. S. (1999). Children's social and scholastic lives in kindergarten: Related spheres of influence? *Child Development, 70*(6), 1373–1400; Hughes & Kwok, 2007; Sutherland, K. S., & Oswald, D. P. (2005). The relationship between teacher and student behavior in classrooms for students with emotional and behavioral disorders: Transactional processes. *Journal of Child and Family Studies, 14*(1), 1–14; Hughes, J. N., Luo, W., Kwok, O., & Loyd, L. (2008). Teacher-student support, effortful engagement, and achievement: A 3-year longitudinal study. *Journal of Educational Psychology, 100*(1), 1–14.

128. See: Burchinal, M. R., Peisner-Feinberg, E., Pianta, R., & Howes, C. (2002). Development of academic skills from preschool through second grade: Family and classroom predictors of developmental trajectories. *Journal of School Psychology, 40*(5), 415–436; Ferguson, R. (2003). Teachers' perceptions and expectations and the black-white test score gap. *Urban Education, 38*(4), 460–507; Tucker, C., Zayco, R., Herman, K., Reinke, W., Truijillo, M., Carrawa, K., Wallack, C., & Ivery, P. (2002). Teacher and child variables as predictors of academic engagement among low-income African American children. *Psychology in the Schools, 39*(4), 477–488; Ware, F. (2006). Warm demander pedagogy: Culturally responsive teaching that supports a culture of achievement for African American students. *Urban Education, 41*(4), 427–456; Wooley, M., Kol, K., & Bowen, G. I. (2009). The social context of school success for Latino middle school students: Direct and indirect influences of teachers, family, and friends. *Journal of Early Adolescence, 29*(1), 43–70.

129. See: Dweck, C. S., & Leggett, E. L. (1988). A social-cognitive approach to motivation and personality. *Psychological Review, 95*(2), 256–273; Gutman, L. M. (2006). How student and parent goal orientations and classroom goal structures influence the math achievement of African Americans during the high school transition. *Contemporary Educational Psychology, 31*(1), 44–63; Friedel, J. M., Cortina, K. S., Turner, J. C., & Midgeley, C. (2010). Changes in efficacy beliefs in mathematics across the transition to middle school: Examining the effects of perceived teacher and parent goal emphases. *Journal of Educational Psychology, 102*(1), 102–114; Kaplan, A., & Maehr, M. L. (1999). Achievement goals and student well-being. *Contemporary Educational Psychology, 24*(4), 330–358; Walker, C., & Greene, B. A. (2009). The relations between student motivation beliefs and cognitive engagement in high school. *Journal of Educational Research, 102*(6), 463–472.

130. Kaplan, A., & Maehr, M. L. (1999). Achievement goals and student well-being. *Contemporary Educational Psychology, 24*(4), 330–358; Schiefele, U., & Schaffner, E. (2015). Teacher interests, mastery goals, and self-efficacy as predictors of instructional practices and student motivation. *Contemporary Educational Psychology, 42* (July), 159–171.

131. Graham, S., & Golan, S. (1991). Motivational influences on cognition: Task involvement, ego involvement, and depth of information processing. *Journal of Educational Psychology, 83*(2), 187–194.

132. Mueller, C. M., & Dweck, C. S. (1998). Praise for intelligence can undermine children's motivation and performance. *Journal of Personality and Social Psychology, 75*(1), 33–52.

133. See: Cohen, G. L., Garcia, J., Apfel, N., & Master, A. (2006). Reducing the racial achievement gap: A social-psychological intervention. *Science, 313*(5791), 1307–1310; D'Ailly, H. H., Simpson, J., & MacKinnon, G. E. (1997). Where should "you" go in a math compare problem? *Journal of Educational Psychology, 89*(3), 562–567; Davis-Dorsey, J., Ross, J., & Morrison, G. R. (1991). The role of rewording and context personalization in the solving of mathematical word problems. *Journal of Educational Psychology, 83*(1), 61–68.

134. See: Ginsburg-Block, M., Rohrbeck, C., Lavigne, N., & Fantusso, J. W. (2008). Peer-assisted learning: An academic strategy for enhancing motivation among diverse students. In C. Hudley & A. E. Gottfried (Eds.), *Academic motivation and the culture of school in childhood and adolescence* (pp. 247–273). Oxford University Press; Maheady, L., Mitchielli-Pendl, J., Harper, G., & Mallette, B. (2006). The effects of numbered heads together with and without an incentive package on the science test performance of a diverse group of sixth graders. *Journal of Behavioral Education, 15*(1), 25–39; Rohrbeck, C. A., Ginsburg-Block, M. D., Fantusso, J. W., & Miller, R. R. (2003). Peer-assisted learning interventions with elementary school students: A meta analytic review. *Journal of Educational Psychology, 95*(2), 240–257; Slavin, R., Lake, C., & Groff, C. (2009). Effective programs in middle and high school mathematics: A best-evidence synthesis. *Review of Educational Research, 79*(2), 839–911.

135. Disability History.org. (n.d.). EDGE curriculum culture: Charity images. *Education for Disability and Gender Equity.* http://www.disabilityhistory.org/dwa/edge/curriculum/cult_contenta5.htm

136. In January 2020, California lawmakers changed the term "at-risk" to "at-promise" in the state's educational and penal codes, a term that lawmakers view as less stigmatizing. California's change in terminology does not change the definition of students who would fall under this description. See: Samuels, C. A. (2020, January 15). "At-promise": Can a new term change a student's trajectory? *Education Week, 39*(18), 6.

137. Bernard, B. (1993). Fostering resiliency in kids. *Educational Leadership, 51*, 44-48.

138. Bondy, E., Ross, D. D., Gallingane, C., & Hamnbacher, E. (2007). Creating environments of success and resilience. Culturally responsive classroom management and more. *Urban Education, 42*(4), 326–348; Masten, A. S., Best, K. M., & Garmezy, N. (1990). Resilience and development: Contributions from the study of children who overcome adversity. *Development and Psychopathology, 2*(4), 425–444; Noltenmeyer, A. L., & Bush, K. R. (2013). Adversity and resilience: A synthesis of international research. *School Psychology International, 34*(5), 474-487.

139. Noltenmeyer & Bush, 2013.

140. Delpit, L. (1995). *Other people's children: Cultural conflict in the classroom.* New Press, p. 167.

141. Delpit, 1995, p. 175.

142. Gay, G. (2000). *Culturally responsive teaching: Theory, research, and practice.* Teachers College Press; Gay, G. (2013). Teaching to and through cultural diversity. *Curriculum Inquiry, 43*(1), 48–70; Ladson-Billings, G. (1994). *The dream-keepers: Successful teachers of African American children.* Jossey-Bass; Nieto, S. M. (2002/2003, December/January). Profoundly multicultural questions. *Educational Leadership, 60*(4), 6–10.

143. Knutson, K. (2019, April 16). Gloria Ladson-Billings: Daring to dream in public. *University of Wisconsin-Madison News.* https://news.wisc.edu/gloria-ladson-billings-daring-to-dream-in-public/

144. Flores-Gonzales, N. (2002). *School kids, street kids: Identity and high school completion among Latinos.* Teachers College Press; Noddings, N. (1992). *The challenge to care in schools: An alternative approach to education.* Teachers College Press; Stanton-Salazar, R. D. (1997). A social capital framework for understanding the socialization of racial minority children and youth. *Harvard Educational Review, 67*(1), 1–40.

145. For information about helping Native Americans, Latinx students, and English language learners succeed in school, respectively, see: Fore, C. L., & Chaney, J. N. (1998). Factors influencing the pursuit of educational opportunities in American Indian students. In S. M. Manson (Ed.), American Indian and Alaska Native mental health research. *Journal of the National Center, 8*(2), 54–59. National Center for American Indian and Alaska Native Mental Health Research. http://www.ucdenver.edu/academics/colleges/PublicHealth/research/centers/CAIANH/journal/Documents/Volume%208/8(2).pdf; Wainer, A. (2004). *The new Latino south and the challenge to public education: Strategies for educators and policymakers in emerging immigrant communities.* Tomas Rivera Policy Institute. https://files.eric.ed.gov/fulltext/ED502060.pdf; Miller, P. C., & Endo, H. (2004, June). Understanding and meeting the needs of ESL students. *Phi Delta Kappan, 85*(10), 786–791.

146. As cited in Delpit, 1995, p. 164.

147. Elmore, R., Peterson, P., & McCarthey, S. (1996). *Restructuring in the classroom.* Jossey-Bass; McLaughlin, M. W., & Talbert, J. W. (1993). Introduction: New visions of teaching. In D. Cohen & J. E. Talbert (Eds.), *Teaching for understanding: Challenges for policy and practice* (pp. 1–10). Jossey-Bass; National Research Council. (2000). *How people learn: Brain, mind, experience, and school.* National Academy Press; Wiggins, G., & McTighe, J. (1998). *Understanding by design.* Association for Supervision and Curriculum Development; Wiske, M. S. (1997). *Teaching for understanding: Linking research with practice.* Jossey-Bass; Richardson, V. (2003, December). Constructive pedagogy. *Teachers College Record, 105*(9), 1623–1640.

148. Henderson, A. T., & Berla, N. (Eds.). (1994). *A new generation of evidence: The family is critical in student achievement.* National Committee for Citizens in Education; Epstein, J. L. (1991). Effects of students' achievement of teacher practices of parent involvement. In S. B. Silvern (Ed.), *Advances in teaching/language research. Vol. 5: Literacy through family, community, and school interaction* (pp. 261–276). JAI Press; Henderson, A. T., & Mapp, K. L. (2002). *A new wave of evidence: The impact of school, family and community connections on student achievement, annual synthesis 2002* (Eric Document No. ED 474521). Center of Family and Community Connections with Schools, Southwest Educational Development Laboratory.

149. Delpit, 1995, p. 182.

150. Cited in Delpit, 1995, p. 183.

iStock/Slavica

9 TEACHERS, ETHICS, AND THE LAW

InTASC Standards Addressed: 1, 2, 3, 9, 10

LEARNING OBJECTIVES

After you read this chapter, you should be able to

9.1 Defend the importance of having an Educators' Code of Ethics.

9.2 Assess how case law, teacher licensure, and a contract to teach affect the teaching profession.

9.3 Describe how teachers' constitutional freedoms, such as freedom of speech, freedom of religion, and protection from unreasonable search and seizure, operate in schools.

9.4 Examine how students' privacy rights in school regarding discipline, property, and student records affect students and teachers.

9.5 Critique how schools protect and limit student rights.

Sooner than you think, you will sign a contract to become a teacher. A teaching contract creates a legal agreement between a new teacher and a school district. By signing this document, you accept certain legal rights, professional responsibilities, and ethical obligations that will guide your behavior.[1]

Schools accept a profound responsibility for educating students, and teachers play a unique role in their students' lives. While students are in school or on school-sponsored trips, teachers are responsible for their students' physical and emotional safety as well as for helping them learn. Additionally, teachers demonstrate leadership by being role models for ethical behavior whose actions children notice and copy. The state must balance individual teachers' and students' constitutional rights against the necessity of maintaining a controlled and safe learning environment. Courts have allowed schools to behave in reasonable ways to keep students safe, healthy, and able to learn. For teachers to carry out their professional actions ethically and legally, they must first know how their ethical code and the law protect and limit teachers' and students' conduct.

This chapter reviews teaching's ethical and legal considerations. Relevant issues include codes of ethics, the teaching license or certificate, the teaching contract, how teachers' constitutional freedoms operate in schools, students' rights at school and how they affect themselves and teachers, and ways in which schools may limit freedom of speech and privacy. Rights of students with disabilities and students' freedom from harassment (cyberbullying and sexual) in schools are discussed as well. Although this chapter does not cover every legal aspect future educators need to know, it will help beginning teachers make informed decisions.

9.1 WHY HAVE STANDARDS FOR PROFESSIONAL ETHICS?

Hippocrates, the ancient Greek physician and author of what is arguably the first code of ethics—the Hippocratic oath—wrote, "First, do no harm." This is a concept that serves members of all professions well.

Professions unite their members through common training, shared values, and collective purposes. Professional expertise confers a degree of authority and power on its holders. But professional autonomy is never without societal limits. Because every profession affects the well-being of others who depend on those professionals' skills and services, professional behaviors have both technical and moral dimensions. Society holds practitioners accountable for both aspects through a professional code of ethics.

A 2019 *American Educational Research Journal* study finds that about 80% of teachers surveyed in an urban Midwest district report that they had witnessed other staff doing things that were "morally wrong," and 45% said that they themselves had acted on the job in ways that betrayed their values.[2] Teachers elsewhere likely have similar concerns. Raising future educators' awareness of the complex situations and ethical choices that lie ahead may help them enact their educator roles more professionally.

9.1a What Is a Code of Ethics?

Ethics can be described as the rules or widely accepted standards of practice—the voluntary norms, values, beliefs, habits, and attitudes—that govern members' professional conduct. Along with certification or minimum requirements needed to complete a teacher education program and licensing or professional development as part of a teaching career, ethical codes of conduct are part of professional standards. As Pulitzer Prize–winning author Thomas Friedman observes, "Laws regulate behavior from the outside in. Ethics regulate behavior from the inside out."[3]

The word "ethics" is derived from the Greek word meaning "moral philosophy." To behave "ethically" means being able to *choose* the "right" behavior, whereas being "moral" means being willing to *practice* that right behavior. The difference is between thinking and doing.

The tension between a profession's desire to control its own practice and the public's demand for accountability has led to many professions developing codes of ethics. **Professional codes of ethics** can be described as the rules that guide professional decisions and actions. Professional codes of ethics perform three essential purposes: to ensure high standards of practice, to protect the public, and to guide practitioners in their decision-making.[4] These codes serve as both a foundation and a guide to professional behavior in morally ambiguous situations.

Society grants a profession power and privilege only when its members are willing and able to contribute to the general well-being and to conduct their affairs in a manner consistent with broad social values. In this sense, the profession serves as a norm reference group for its practitioners. Its code of ethics visibly clarifies for practitioners and the general public the rules and customs that guide its members' actions. Because the ethical code is open to public scrutiny, it inspires public confidence in the profession and its practitioners. Medicine, law, accounting, pharmacy, teaching, and other professions have all developed their own codes of ethics to improve professional practice and maintain the public's confidence in their practitioners.

9.1b Teachers' Code of Ethics

When teachers enter the classroom, they represent the education profession to the local community and to the nation. From that standpoint, a teacher's professional and ethical behaviors are important on many levels.

InTASC Standard #9, Professional Learning and Ethical Practice, states that "the teacher engages in on-going professional learning and uses evidence to continually evaluate his/her practice, particularly the effects of his/her choices and actions on others (learners, families, other professionals, and the community), and adapts practice to meet the needs of each learner."[5] In 2015, the National Association of State Directors of Teacher Education and Certification (NASDTEC) released a Model Code of Ethics for Educators (MCEE) to guide preK–12 educators in their decision-making and to help teacher preparation programs nurture their teacher candidates' ethical decision-making capacities.[6] The ethical code for educators focuses on five principles and identifies appropriate teacher responsibilities and behaviors for each. Table 9.1 identifies and explains these principles. Tables 9.2 and 9.3 define Principle I (Responsibility to the Profession) and Principle III (Responsibility to Students), respectively.

These model ethical standards frequently refer to respecting "appropriate" and "professional" boundaries. **Professional boundaries** are the legal, ethical, and organizational frameworks of care, expectations, and limits within which the worker–client relationship occurs. **Teachers' professional boundaries** are "the verbal, physical, emotional, and social distances that an educator must maintain in order to ensure structure, security, and predictability in an educational environment."[7] Defining clear limits to what teacher behaviors are (and are not) suitable in a school or community setting protects the student from potential harm, intentional or unintentional; ensures that teachers maintain ethical standards; protects teachers from unreasonable or increasing student or parental demands or expectations; enables teachers to set clear limits and deal properly with student behavior; and reduces teacher "burnout." It also helps teachers keep their private life private.

For example, not keeping accurate records of student performance; giving a student a higher (or lower) grade because the teacher likes (or dislikes) the student; having inappropriate physical contact with (or making a sexually provocative statement to) a student; or extending your relationship with student or family beyond the professional teaching role violate professional boundaries. Conflicts of

TABLE 9.1 ■ Model Code of Ethics for Educators

Principle	Description
Responsibility to the profession	The professional educator is aware that trust in the profession depends upon a level of professional conduct and responsibility that may be higher than required by law. This entails holding oneself and other educators to the same ethical standards.
Responsibility for professional competence	The professional educator is committed to the highest levels of professional and ethical practice, including demonstration of the knowledge, skills, and dispositions required for professional competence.
Responsibility to students	The professional educator has a primary obligation to treat students with dignity and respect. The professional educator promotes the health, safety, and well-being of students by establishing and maintaining appropriate verbal, physical, emotional, and social boundaries.
Responsibility to the school community	The professional educator promotes positive relationships and effective interactions with members of the school community while maintaining professional boundaries.
Responsible and ethical use of technology	The professional educator considers the impact of consuming, creating, distributing, and communicating information through all technologies. The ethical educator is vigilant to ensure appropriate boundaries of time, place, and role are maintained when using electronic communication.

Source: NASDTEC. (2015). *Model Code of Ethics for Educators* (CEE). https://edprepmatters.net/2015/06/nasdtec-releases-model-code-of-ethics-for-educators/

TABLE 9.2 ■ Principle I: Responsibility to the Profession

A. **The professional educator demonstrates responsibility to oneself as an ethical professional by**

- Being aware of, knowing, or understanding the Code of Ethics. Not being aware is not, in itself, a defense to a charge of unethical conduct.
- Holding oneself responsible for ethical conduct, regardless of one's views about the procedures, policies, laws, and regulations.
- Monitoring and keeping sound mental, physical, and emotional health needed to perform professional duties and services; and taking appropriate steps when personal or health-related issues may interfere with work-related duties.
- Taking responsibility and credit only for work you actually performed or produced and acknowledging others' contributions.

B. **The professional educator fulfils the obligation to address and attempt to resolve ethical issues by**

- Confronting and taking reasonable steps to resolve conflict between the Code and a person or the organization's implicit and explicit demands.
- Taking proactive steps when having reason to believe that another educator may be approaching or involved in an ethically compromising situation.
- Cooperating fully during ethics investigations and proceedings.

C. **The professional educator promotes and advances the profession within and beyond the school community by**

- Influencing and supporting decisions and actions that positively impact teaching and learning, educational leadership, and student services.
- Engaging in respectful communications regarding issues that impact the profession.
- Staying current with ethical principles and decisions from relevant sources including professional organizations and associations.

Source: Adapted from NASDTEC. (2015). *Model Code of Ethics for Educators* (MCEE). https://edprepmatters.net/2015/06/nasdtec-releases-model-code-of-ethics-for-educators/

TABLE 9.3 ■ Principle III: Responsibility to Students

The professional educator respects the rights and dignity of students by

- Respecting students by considering their age, gender, culture, setting, and socioeconomic context.
- Interacting with students with transparency and in appropriate settings.
- Considering how appearance and dress can affect one's interactions and relationships with students.
- Acknowledging that no circumstances allow educators to engage in romantic or sexual relationships with students.

The professional educator demonstrates an ethic of care through

- Seeking to understand students' educational, academic, personal, and social needs as well as students' values, beliefs, and cultural background.
- Respecting the dignity, worth, and uniqueness of each student including, but not limited to, actual and perceived gender, gender expression, gender identity, civil status, family status, sexual orientation, religion, age, disability, race, ethnicity, socioeconomic status, and culture.
- Establishing and maintaining an environment that promotes the emotional, intellectual, physical, and sexual safety of all students.

The professional educator maintains student trust and confidentiality when interacting with students in a developmentally appropriate manner and within appropriate limits by

- Respecting student privacy and keeping confidential certain types of student communication, documents, or information and releasing personal data in accordance with prescribed state and federal laws and local policies.
- Upholding parents'/guardians' legal rights and legal requirements to reveal information related to legitimate concerns for the student's well-being.

Source: Adapted from NASDTEC. (2015). *Model Code of Ethics for Educators* (MCEE). https://edprepmatters.net/2015/06/nasdtec-releases-model-code-of-ethics-for-educators/

interest and financial improprieties between teachers and students or their families also breach professional boundaries. Although many school districts define and illustrate "professional boundaries" in their teachers' handbook code of conduct, ultimately the teacher is responsible for managing these boundary issues.

Professional codes of ethics are not without shortcomings. Many professions have a poor record of reporting their own violators.[8] Some contend that any ethical code represents a professional consensus, yet to reach this agreement likely means using general statements that everyone can interpret to their own liking, making the code relatively useless for providing moral guidance.[9] Skeptics suggest that ethical codes exist mainly to make the professionals *look* moral, not to advance morality in the profession.[10] It is true, however, that to be effective, ethical codes must be integral parts of the organization's culture and applied equally to all organizational levels. Distributing teacher handbooks is not enough to promote ethical values or behaviors. For the most part, professional codes of ethics are only as "ethical" and "moral" as the individuals following them.

To more fully explore teachers' ethical responsibilities to the teaching profession and to students, complete the activity in the **Reflect & Engage** box, Teachers' Code of Ethics.

REFLECT & ENGAGE: TEACHERS' CODE OF ETHICS

This activity includes a role play to explore some ethical limits that teachers face. Although professional expertise confers a degree of authority and power on its holders, professional autonomy is never without societal limits.

A. Divide the class into two sets of small groups. One set of groups will address Principle I, Responsibility to the Profession. The other set of groups will address Principle III, Responsibility to Students.

B. *Principle I Group*: Design a role play in which Colleague A observes another teacher, Colleague B, violating professional ethics by taking credit for creating an award-winning curricular unit that Colleague A actually wrote. Very upset, Colleague A reports the situation to an assistant principal known for his or her personal integrity and highly developed sense of professional ethics. Using Table 9.1, Responsibility to the Profession, create a brief role play in which Colleagues A and B meet with each other and with the assistant principal (separately, sequentially, and/or together) to discuss and successfully resolve this situation. Use as many of the bulleted points in Table 9.1 as you can to make your point.

C. *Principle III Group*: Design a role play in which Colleague X is considering accepting an invitation from a student's parents to attend the student's birthday party at a local restaurant. Colleague X plans to attend, but other teachers (Colleagues Y and Z) say it is not a smart thing to do. Colleague X seeks advice from an assistant principal known for sound ethical judgment. Colleagues Y and Z may or may not attend. Use as many of Principle III's bullet points as you can to make your point.

D. Each group presents their role play to the whole class. After the role play, the class members identify the ethical guidelines used.

E. The whole class discusses the dilemmas of ethical decision-making and how to address them.

9.1c Teachers, Ethics, and Social Networking Websites

Both current and prospective teachers may confront ethical issues when they put personal information online. In general, workers expect their supervisors to monitor them closely while they are on the job. After work hours, however, employees expect that as long as they break no laws, what they do is not the employer's concern. Unfortunately, the internet, by its very nature, makes some off-the-job activities more visible to more people than was previously possible. Posting personal information on the internet makes it public. This reality creates ethical concerns—and occasionally employment consequences—for educators.

In today's world, the line between their personal and professional lives is not clear-cut.[11] Teachers have lost their jobs and forfeited their opportunities to enter the profession because of material they posted on social networking pages. Even if teachers avoid losing their jobs and break no laws, the ethical concerns and potential abuses raised by communicating "inappropriately" with students through online social networking sites make the situation hazardous to teachers' reputations, effectiveness, and credibility.

Social Networking and Privacy

Social networking sites such as Facebook, Instagram, and Snapchat are interactive websites designed to build online communities for individuals who have something in common—an interest in a hobby, a topic, or an organization—and who share a simple desire to communicate across physical boundaries with other interested people. Most social networking sites include the ability to chat in real time, send email, blog, participate in discussion groups, and share files. Users can also post links to photos, music, and video files, all of which have the potential to create a virtual identity. An estimated 72% of Americans use social networking websites.[12]

Many teachers use social networking sites as an avenue to enhance their instruction by reminding students of upcoming homework, tests, and deadlines. Other teacher social networking uses are coming under fire for what school districts consider "inappropriate activity," including posting candid photos, racy or suggestive song lyrics, and references to sex, alcohol, or drug use.[13] Venting online about personal frustrations at work has also caused problems for teachers.[14]

Risks of Communicating Outside the "Controlled Environment"

Teachers who communicate with their students outside the controlled classroom environment must make decisions about what and how much personal information to reveal. Although teachers may have control over the content they disclose on their university-housed web pages, friends, strangers, or other students can post discrediting or defamatory messages on users' Facebook websites.

Apart from banning teachers outright from using these sites to communicate with their students, some school districts have used a range of disciplinary actions—including dismissal—against what they consider to be teachers' questionable uses of social networking sites. In 2018, a school district suspended a sixth-grade teacher (who moonlighted as a pole-dancing fitness instructor) for posting a video of herself pole dancing in her home; they said it was in violation of the county's social media policy and the state department of education's ethics policy for educators.[15] Additional examples of teachers having employment problems with their social media use are easily found.[16]

Online social networking can even cause problems before someone enters the profession.[17] Becoming a professional educator means recognizing that what may be acceptable in their lives as undergraduate students may not be when they are looking for their first teaching job or heading their own classroom.

Ethical Behavior: A Higher Standard

Like it or not, teachers are held to a higher standard of moral behavior than is the population in general. This expectation is reflected in the clauses of various state certification procedures, which mandate that teachers shall not "engage in conduct that would discredit the teaching profession." Under these state clauses, teachers have been denied entry into or dismissed from their profession based on their behavior outside the classroom. The legal issues concerning the impact of using social media on employment is discussed elsewhere in this chapter.[18] Many states also have professional codes of ethics for teachers, with guidelines for teachers' participation in social networking sites.[19]

Even when the law is clear, the higher standard to which teachers are held means they must rely on their good judgment and professional ethics to govern their public and professional behaviors. Ethics regulates behavior from the inside out. Teachers need to always ask themselves how any conduct—whether inside the classroom or over the internet—will protect students' well-being, motivate other teachers, and inspire public trust and confidence in the education profession.

It is wise to be judicious before posting details about one's personal life online or participating in relationships with students outside clearly defined professional boundaries.

To consider teachers' ethical behaviors on social media—including your own—complete the activity in the **Reflect & Engage** box, Teaching and Social Media.

REFLECT & ENGAGE: TEACHING AND SOCIAL MEDIA

Posting personal material on social networking sites makes it public. Although this behavior may now be part of our culture, it also raises serious ethical and employment issues when viewed in a professional context.

A. Working alone, create a graphic image using a digital tool such as Piktochart that depicts the ethical concerns of teachers when using social media. Share and discuss your images and your ideas with a partner.

B. Review your own social networking sites from the perspectives of a future employer, a parent of a future student, and a future principal. Identify all "questionable" writings and images that may appear attractive to peers but that might appear "inappropriate" to an employer or parent.

C. Pair with a classmate to review each other's social networking sites through the eyes of a potential employer or a student's parent. What otherwise harmless words or images might these other parties consider "inappropriate"?

D. Report back to the class on your findings.

E. If you find items that might be "inappropriate," what will you do, and when?

9.2 TEACHERS AND CASE LAW, LICENSURE, AND CONTRACTS

School law is a fast-growing field of study. Courts keep making decisions that affect how states and localities conduct education and how schools balance teachers' constitutional freedoms with the responsibility to provide a safe, orderly, and efficient learning environment. **Case law**, the legal precedents that judges create in their written opinions when they decide legal cases, influences virtually every aspect of education.[20] In case law, judges can either interpret statutory law or interpret prior judicial decisions. As your teacher preparation and teaching experiences grow, these issues will become more familiar to you, and you can make more-informed decisions.

9.2a A Legal Context

The U.S. Constitution, federal statutes, state constitutions, state statutes, case law, and regulations all influence educational practice. Although states have substantial power to manage schools, their control is not absolute. Federal and state constitutions limit the state's authority to enact statutes controlling education's operations. In other words, if the state legislature enacted a law calling for a practice that conflicted with the federal or state constitution, a court would strike down that law.

Case law frequently references amendments to the Constitution. Many court cases that involve education's general or guiding practices come from the U.S. Supreme Court and focus on either the First or the Fourteenth Amendment. The First Amendment, ratified in 1791, deals with freedom of religion, speech, press, and assembly. It reads as such:

> Congress shall make no law respecting an establishment of religion, or prohibiting the free exercise thereof; or abridging the freedom of speech, or of the press; or the right of the people peaceably to assemble, and to petition the Government for a redress of grievances.

This amendment is important to schools because it affects church–state relations, school prayer, religious exercises in schools, and individuals' right to practice their religion in schools. It also affects student assemblies, drama programs, and newspapers (freedom of speech and freedom of the press) and becomes an issue when someone seeks a way to appeal an unfairness that is government imposed.

The Fourteenth Amendment, ratified in 1868 and designed to promote the rights of newly freed enslaved people, addresses due process and equal protection. It reads in part as such:

> All persons born or naturalized in the United States and subject to the jurisdiction thereof, are citizens of the United States and of the State wherein they reside. No State shall make or enforce any law which shall abridge the privileges or immunities of citizens of the United States; nor shall any State deprive any person of life, liberty, or property, without the due process of law; nor deny to any person within its jurisdiction the equal protection of the laws.

This amendment guarantees that states cannot take away citizens' constitutional rights. It affects teachers' freedom of speech and freedom of religion, for example. The term "due process of law" has implications for teacher contract issues, student suspensions, and a host of other legal areas. Significantly, the last clause, known as *equal protection*, states that equal protection—that is, equal application—of the law shall not be denied to any *person* (not just a citizen) by a state.

9.2b Teaching License or Certificate

Each state has the authority to establish the criteria for teacher eligibility and certification.[21] For the most part, each state has developed its own specific certification requirements, though many states have reciprocal licensure agreements with other states. This **reciprocity** means if a person qualifies for licensure in a state that has a reciprocal agreement with another state, the individual qualifies for licensure in both states. For instance, if someone qualifies for a teaching license in Virginia, and Virginia has a reciprocal agreement with California, the individual also qualifies for a California teaching license. The general rule is that if a person satisfies all the requirements established for receiving a state teaching license, the licensing agency cannot arbitrarily refuse to issue a license to that individual but may require additional coursework.

Having a teaching license or certificate, however, does not guarantee its holder a teaching position. A teaching certificate is not a contract. Rather, **certification** is simply a state's way of saying that the certificate or license holder has met the minimum requirements to hold a teaching job. Once the individual has the license, it is that person's responsibility to persuade school district officials through a written or online job application and during an interview that he or she is the best-qualified candidate for the position.

Generally, states issue teaching licenses and keep them active for a specific period of time, usually 5 years. Over that period, teachers must prepare to renew the license by taking classes, participating in professional development activities, and updating and expanding their professional knowledge and skills. Because most states require a valid teaching license to obtain a teaching contract, a teacher's job may be in jeopardy if his or her teaching license expires.

Can my teaching license be revoked once it is issued to me?

Yes. Most states have criteria for revoking a teaching license and have established a process to do so. Needless to say, an educator who loses his or her professional license will not be able to earn a living as a teacher in that state. Revoking a license is a severe penalty, similar to a lawyer being disbarred or a physician losing his or her license to practice medicine.

States require a "just cause" to revoke a teaching license. These reasons may include conviction of a felony, moral turpitude,[22] or falsifying teaching credentials. Virginia, for example, allows the Virginia Board of Education to revoke a teaching license it issued for three causes: obtaining or attempting to obtain a license by fraudulent means or through misrepresenting material facts; falsification of school records, documents, statistics, or reports; or conviction of any felony. [23] Because community standards vary, the state may base these decisions on how the community reacts to certain situations. Whether or not a certain conduct will result in losing a teaching license depends on the exact details of the situation and the state and locale in which the behavior occurs.

9.2c A Teaching Contract

When teachers sign a contract, state statutes and state department of education regulations govern the employment conditions. Generally, the contract is between the teacher and the local school board. The contract will specify the nature of the job to be performed and the compensation to be paid. Some contracts are very specific and say, for example, "fifth-grade teacher at Oak Hill Elementary School." Other contracts are less specific and may simply state, "teacher." Most often, the teacher cannot be assigned to teach a content area outside of his or her certification without the teacher agreeing to do so. Finally, once a contract is offered it must be accepted within a reasonable time frame or the contract becomes null and void. The contract will usually stipulate this time frame.

Most teaching contracts have a provision for teachers to serve a **probationary period**—usually 3 years working under an annual contract (sometimes called *untenured*). Some states have shorter probationary periods; others have longer ones. Generally, the range is from 1 to 5 years. Once a teacher satisfactorily serves the probationary period, states have a provision for *tenure*, sometimes called **continuing contract status.**

Tenure—the policy that restricts a school's ability to fire teachers without "just cause"—provides a degree of job security and a right of continued employment for teachers. Tenure laws tend to have three main components: tenure requirements, reasons for dismissal, and a process for appeals. Once tenured, a teacher cannot be dismissed without due process. Tenure *does not* guarantee lifelong employment.

Due process includes a formal hearing and presentation of proof of sufficient cause to meet the statutory requirements for removal from the position.[24] The teacher has an opportunity to have a lawyer present and challenge the evidence. Generally, the tenured teacher must be notified of the detailed charges in a timely manner and given sufficient opportunity to prepare a defense. The hearing must be held before an impartial body (which may be the school board unless bias can be proved). The teacher's attorney may cross-examine witnesses and challenge any evidence brought in the case. In addition, the teacher can appeal an unfavorable decision in court.

An untenured teacher, by contrast, may be dismissed at any time for any reason so long as the decision is neither arbitrary nor capricious nor discriminatory. An untenured teacher may simply be notified that his or her annual contract will not be renewed. The employing school district may give no reason for the termination. However, if the employing school district gives an illegal reason, the teacher may decide to sue the school district.

Teachers also face a range of legal issues once they are employed and teaching. Teachers' rights sometimes come with complex responsibilities. Legal factors regarding academic freedom, free speech, teacher privacy, and freedom of religion may all affect how teachers do their jobs.

9.3 TEACHERS' CONSTITUTIONAL RIGHTS IN SCHOOLS

Teachers keep their constitutional rights in their professional roles. But in the interest of student safety and organizational well-being, their rights to free speech, privacy, and religious expression may be curtailed.

9.3a Freedom of Speech

As citizens, teachers have a right to disagree publicly with a school principal's decision. However, if a teacher in a school makes public comments about "what a stupid decision the principal made," the teacher may get into legal trouble if those comments disrupt the school's operation. Teachers' freedom of speech is subject to certain limits.

Do teachers have academic freedom in the classroom?

It depends. The concept of academic freedom encompasses two separate aspects—the freedom to learn and the freedom to teach. In the United States, academic freedom is bound up in the First Amendment ideal of free speech. **Academic freedom** means that teachers have some choices in the teaching methods they use as long as the teaching methods meet professional standards. Teachers have the professional freedom to monitor and adjust their teaching strategies if their students are not mastering the content.

Academic freedom does *not* mean that teachers can say whatever they would like—or teach whatever they want—in the classroom. In public schools, school boards set the curriculum. They have legal rights to decide what materials and speech are appropriate for the classroom. For example, suppose a third-grade teacher wants to teach a unit about skin, muscles, and bones, but that content belongs in the fourth-grade curriculum. The teacher has no right to teach the subject out of the school system's established curriculum sequence.

Reviewing several court cases helps clarify teachers' academic freedom. In *Cockrel v. Shelby County School District et al.* (2001),[25] Donna Cockrel, a fifth-grade teacher, was teaching a unit on "saving the trees" and discussing industrial hemp (hemp is derived from the same plant as marijuana). At the same time, popular actor Woody Harrelson was speaking with the Kentucky Hemp Growers Association. With the principal's permission, Harrelson spoke to the class. As a visual aid, he passed (illegal) hemp seeds around the class. The extensive media reporting on Harrelson's activities alerted local parents about the hemp seeds, and they complained about the lesson's appropriateness. After the school superintendent asked the Professional Standards Board to investigate and report back on the incident, the board found insufficient cause to take any action against the teacher. At that point, the school district put a "controversial topics" policy into place in its schools. Complying with the new policy, Cockrel received permission for Harrelson to return for another class discussion, and the school board then fired her. The court ruled that the teacher's speech was constitutionally protected as a matter of public concern and that she could not be fired. The school board had violated its own policy; the teacher had not.

In another case, *Keefe v. Geanakos* (1969), a high school teacher gave his class copies of an article published in *Atlantic Monthly* that used a rather vulgar and literal term to describe an incestuous son.[26] The teacher explained the word's etymology to the class and clarified why the author had used that specific word in the story. Any students finding the article offensive were allowed to select an alternative reading. The school board dismissed the teacher, and he sued to recover his teaching position. The court agreed with the teacher in finding the article to be thoughtful; deleting the offending word would have made understanding the article impossible. The teacher was reinstated.

Teachers may go beyond legal bounds when they select classroom material that is "offensive and unnecessary to the accomplishment of educational objectives... [where]... such questions are matters of degree involving judgment on such factors as the age and sophistication of the students, relevance of the educational purpose, and context and manner of presentations."[27] In other words, a teacher does not have total freedom to select materials for classroom use that are not age or educationally appropriate.

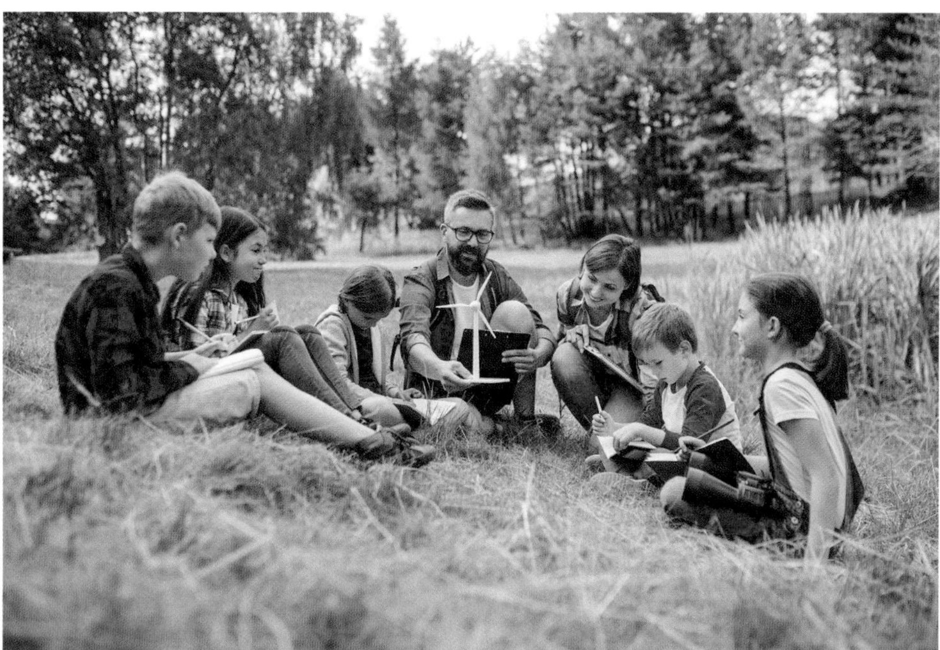

Teachers have choices in teaching methods as long as they meet professional and local standards.

iStock/Halfpoint

How can "speaking out on a matter of public concern" affect my job?

Free speech means that government must tolerate and cannot restrain the people's right to express information, ideas, and opinions in open public debate, regardless of whether that speech is offensive, tumultuous, or discordant (subject to reasonable limitations).[28] Yet over the years, the U.S. Supreme Court has concluded that practical reality requires that government, at certain times and under certain conditions, be able to restrict employees' speech to fulfill its responsibilities to operate effectively and efficiently.

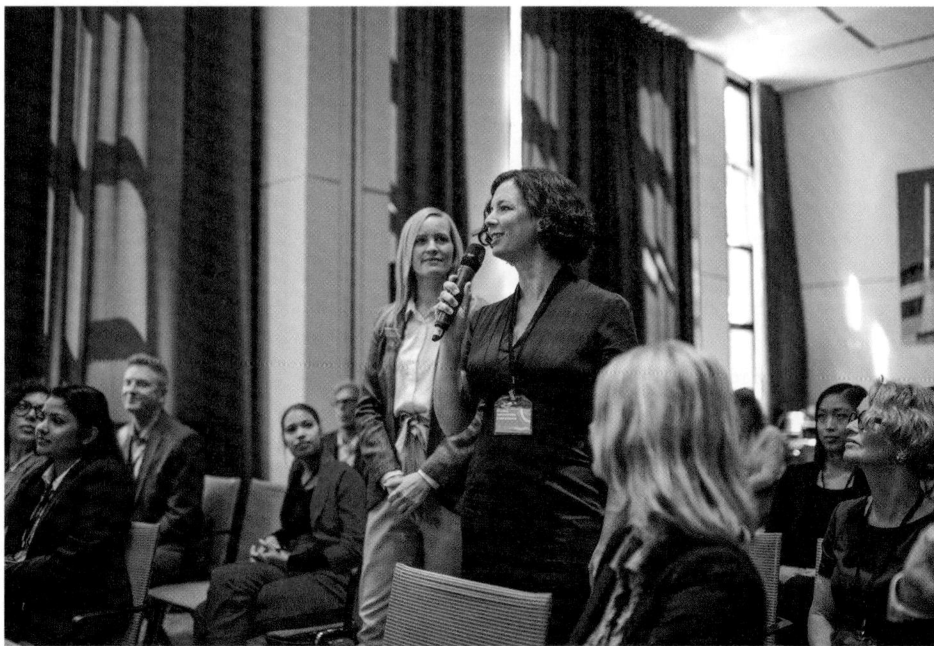

Public school teachers may have limits on their rights to free speech.

Luis Alvarez/Getty Images

Defining what a *public concern* is can be tricky. Today, speaking out publicly as a teacher about tax increases or a proposed policy where public comment is encouraged is clearly a matter of public concern. The Supreme Court has decided, however, that a public school teacher or other school employee may be restrained in the exercise of speech depending on whether it involves a matter of public concern or private concern.

Early in American history, public employment was viewed as a privilege, not as a right. As such, many courts held that contracts between teachers and school boards curtailed certain teacher rights and freedoms. If a teacher spoke out on an issue that violated the contract's terms, the teacher could be dismissed, and the courts would uphold the dismissal. Until 1968, schoolteachers were hesitant to become too involved in politics for fear that they would be penalized or even fired for such activities. But in its 1968 ruling in *Pickering v. Board of Education*, the U.S. Supreme Court decided that teachers have a right to speak out freely on matters of public concern.[29]

Marvin Pickering was a teacher at Township High School in Illinois. The locality was considering a tax increase to raise school revenue, and Pickering wrote a letter to the editor of the local newspaper. Pickering criticized the earlier bond issue (that did not allocate funds to his liking) and alleged that the superintendent of schools tried to prevent teachers from opposing the proposed bond issue. Pickering's letter contained several factual errors. After a school board hearing to determine if Pickering's letter had "been detrimental to the efficient operation of the schools of the district," which, if true, under state statute required the teacher's dismissal, the board fired him.

In accordance with state law, the board held a hearing on Pickering's dismissal and found many of the board's allegations about harmed reputations to be false, but it upheld the dismissal, as did the Illinois Supreme Court. The U.S. Supreme Court disagreed, noting that "without proof of false statements knowingly or recklessly made by him, a teacher's exercise of his right to speak on issues of public importance may not furnish the basis for his dismissal from public employment." In their view, Pickering's statements did not harm the school district's operations and did not affect the teacher's performance. Pickering won the case.

To guide lower federal courts in future cases of this nature, the Supreme Court stated what has come to be called the *Pickering* balance test. Writing in the Court's opinion, Justice Thurgood Marshall explained:

> The problem in any case is to arrive at a balance between the interests of the teacher, as a citizen, in commenting upon matters of public concern and the interest of the State, as an employer, in promoting the efficiency of the public services it performs through its employees.[30]

In other words, a balance must be found between a person's rights to speak out on matters of public concern and an organization's interest in doing its job efficiently.

Fifteen years later in *Connick v. Myers* (1983), the U.S. Supreme Court clarified the limitations on public employees' free speech.[31] Although a public employee's speech is protected when he or she is speaking out on a matter of *public* concern, balancing the employee's and state's interests, the First Amendment does not protect a public employee's speech or expression concerning a *private* or *personal* interest in matters of public concern. Even though this case did not involve educators, it is relevant because Myers was a public employee, and the precedent established in this case has been cited in legal actions involving educators.

Assistant District Attorney Sheila Myers, opposed to her reassignment to another area of criminal law, circulated a questionnaire to other assistant district attorneys about staff morale and related issues. Told that the questionnaire amounted to insubordination, she was fired. The Supreme Court upheld her dismissal, stating that the matter was basically a private issue and not a public one. It became a personal issue because the questionnaire went out after the transfer was announced. The Court believed that Myers's First Amendment interest was outweighed by the disruptive nature of the questions she was circulating to colleagues, which "substantially interfered with the operation of the office."

Placing additional limits on teachers' speech, the ruling in *Stroman v. Colleton County School District* (1993) specified that teachers' First Amendment (free speech) rights do not extend to encouraging dishonest conduct and conduct that violates policy.[32] In this case, because teacher John Stroman was upset about a change in the Colleton County School District's summer pay policy (from lump sum to bimonthly), he wrote and circulated a letter to fellow teachers, criticizing the central office for fiscal mismanagement and being administratively "top heavy" and encouraging teachers to participate in a "sick out" during final exams week. Meeting with the superintendent and his principal the next day, Stroman admitted writing and circulating the letter, claiming that the pay schedule treated him unfairly. The superintendent handed Stroman a dismissal letter dated that day, citing unfitness for teaching by proposing to and encouraging others to abandon their duties. Stroman sued to be reinstated as a teacher, claiming that his free speech rights were denied.

The Fourth Circuit Court of Appeals[33] affirmed the teacher's First Amendment free speech rights but stated that the First Amendment did not cover a grievance (in this case, the change in summer pay policy). The court ruled that speaking out in self-interest about the summer pay changes made the matter one of self-concern and not public concern, eliminating the free speech rights claim. It upheld Stroman's dismissal.

This decision has had a major legal impact on teachers' rights to speak out on issues that are part of their official duties. At present, the courts appear to be moving more toward protecting employers than protecting employees in what might be considered free speech issues and employment.

9.3b Teacher Privacy

The word "privacy" is not found in either the Bill of Rights or the Constitution. Nonetheless, it is considered to be a basic and fundamental right, a logical offshoot of the constitutional protection against unreasonable search and seizure. Therefore, a compelling state interest must be demonstrated to warrant violating a person's privacy. The Fourth Amendment of the U.S. Constitution reads like this:

> The right of the people to be secure in their persons, houses, papers, and effects, against unreasonable searches and seizures, shall not be violated, and no Warrants shall issue, but upon probable cause, supported by Oath or affirmation, and particularly describing the place to be searched, and the persons or things to be seized.

Although teachers keep their right to privacy in schools, this right has certain limits.

Can my classroom, desk, closet, and file cabinets be searched?

Yes. A teacher's right to privacy in the classroom comes under the concept of a workplace. In *O'Connor v. Ortega* (1987), the Supreme Court defined the **workplace** as "those areas and items that are related to work and are generally within the employer's control."[34] This would include offices, hallways, cafeterias, desks, file cabinets, lockers, and other areas. In these locations, an employee does not have an expectation of privacy, and the school may search them. By comparison, a teacher's personal effects, such as purses, briefcases, and closed luggage, are not considered as belonging to the workplace. These items may not be searched without a warrant.

The Supreme Court did not establish any ground rules on when or how an employer's "interest in supervision, control, and the efficient operation of the workplace" would outweigh an employee's "legitimate expectations of privacy." It left to the lower courts the job of applying the simple "balance" formula on a case-by-case basis.

Can I be forced to take a drug test?

Yes. The Fourth Amendment safeguards individuals against arbitrary and unwarranted intrusions into their privacy. It does not limit *all* searches and seizures, however—only those that are unreasonable. What is "reasonable" depends on the circumstances and the nature of the search and seizure itself. What is "reasonable" remains an open question.

To search citizens, the police must have **probable cause**—a reasonable belief that a person has committed a crime. Due to schools' unique nature in which they serve **in loco parentis (in the place of the parent)**, the standard for school searches is lower than that required for the police to search an ordinary citizen. In schools, the government has a special interest that allows warrantless searches based on **reasonable suspicion**—credible information from a reliable source—a less demanding standard than probable cause. This standard of reasonable suspicion justifies searches of students on school property.

In addition, the increased prevalence of illegal drug use has prompted courts to define privacy rights in a new context that does not neatly fit with probable cause or reasonable suspicion. As a result, courts have formulated a new category of reasonable searches called **suspicionless searches,** which permit testing for drugs and alcohol without showing individualized suspicion.

In *Hearn v. Board of Education* (1999), the school district had a zero-tolerance policy for drugs and alcohol on school property.[35] During a routine "drug dog" search of the parking lot, the dog sniffed drugs in a teacher's car. The teacher claimed the search was illegal. The school district policy required that anyone suspected of having or having used drugs submit to a urine test within 2 hours; refusal to comply with the policy could result in the employee being fired. The teacher refused to take the urine test and was later fired. The teacher sued, and the court held that the search was legal based on the probable cause of the dog sniff identification of the vehicle.

Additionally, the U.S. Supreme Court has held that under certain conditions, suspicionless searches of people employed in safety-sensitive positions may take place.[36] A federal court has ruled that teachers fall under the safety-sensitive positions and may be compelled to submit to drug searches in the form of urine testing.[37]

Can school authorities test teachers for illegal drug use without having a reasonable suspicion of drug use?

Yes. In *Knox County Education Association v. Knox County Board of Education* (1998), the U.S. Court of Appeals ruled that school authorities could conduct suspicionless drug testing of teachers.[38]

In this case, the court ruled that suspicionless testing was justified based on the unique role that teachers play in schoolchildren's lives. In the school setting, where teachers act *in loco parentis*, the public interest in drug testing outweighs teachers' privacy interests in not being tested. The court further pointed out that the teaching profession is by nature and of necessity heavily regulated, and teachers have a diminished expectation of privacy. The drug testing regimen employed in this school system was limited, narrowly tailored, and relatively unobtrusive in its monitoring and disclosure.

9.3c Teachers' Freedom of Religion

As U.S. citizens, teachers have rights defined by the U.S. Constitution that accompany them into the classroom. Freedom of religion is one of these protected rights. As with freedom of speech, however, this right is not unlimited. The First Amendment to the U.S. Constitution dealing with freedom of religion states,

> Congress shall make no law respecting an establishment of religion, or prohibiting the free exercise thereof...

And the 1972 amendment to Title VII of the Civil Rights Act further expands this religious freedom:

> It shall be an unlawful employment practice for an employment agency to fail or refuse for employment, or otherwise to discriminate against, any individual because of his race, color, religion, sex, or national origin, or to classify or refer for employment any individual on the basis of his race, color, religion, sex, or national origin.

May I be required to teach something that goes against my religious beliefs?

Yes. Although these laws guarantee Americans freedom of religion, this religious freedom is not unlimited. In *Palmer v. Board of Education of the City of Chicago* (1980), a teacher refused to teach part of the city-designated curriculum, stating that to do so would violate her religious beliefs.[39] Although the court acknowledged the teacher's right to freedom of belief, it also pointed out the school district's interest in providing a proper education to all students. The ruling in this case further stated that teachers "cannot be left to teach the way they please." When a teacher has a religious belief that interferes with teaching the required class content, the content takes priority over the religious beliefs.

However, if a teacher's religious tenets prohibit the teacher from pledging to the flag, the teacher cannot be forced to recite the Pledge of Allegiance with the class as part of his or her professional duties. If school rules require the Pledge to be recited, the teacher may be required to be in the classroom with the students as they recite the Pledge of Allegiance.[40] The courts have continued to uphold teachers' freedom of religion as long as it does not encroach on students' rights and does not harm the school's good conduct.

What should teachers know about the courts' position on intelligent design?

The U.S. Supreme Court[41] and a federal court in Pennsylvania[42] ruled that teaching creationism or intelligent design is unconstitutional teaching of religion in public schools.

Are teachers legally responsible for teaching intelligent design alongside evolution?

No. In *Edwards v. Aguillard* (1987),[43] the U.S. Supreme Court ruled that requiring a "balanced" treatment of creation science and evolution science was unconstitutional because it violated the bar against teaching religion in public schools. Likewise, in *Kitzmiller v. Dover Area School District* (2005),[44] a federal court, in a strongly worded opinion, struck down as unconstitutional a local school board's attempt to insert teaching of intelligent design into the classroom as an attempt to "discredit evolution," which has the scientific community's support.

As a teacher, am I permitted to celebrate my religious holidays?

Usually. As an employment practice, school boards must reasonably accommodate aspects of teachers' religious observances and practice unless it can be shown that such accommodations produce undue hardships on the employer's business. The teacher has the initial burden of proof to show that a school board's decision was religiously motivated or involved the denial of a religious freedom. If the teacher does so, the burden then moves to the school board, whose members must show they made a good-faith effort to accommodate the teacher's religious beliefs.

In *Wangsness v. Watertown School District No. 14-4* (1982), the court ruled in favor of a teacher who requested to be absent from school without pay for 7 days to attend a religious festival.[45] The teacher's request was denied, but the teacher attended the festival anyway. Before leaving for the event, the teacher prepared lesson plans and met with the substitute teacher to review the lessons. The school district dismissed the teacher, and the teacher sued. The court found that the classes had run well in the teacher's absence, and the school district had not suffered a hardship due to the teacher attending the religious festival. The court determined that the dismissal was not warranted and had violated the teacher's rights under Title VII.

In another case, *Pinsker v. Joint District No. 28J* (1983), a Jewish teacher requested more than the 2 days allowed to celebrate the religious holidays.[46] He showed that teachers of the Christian faith had more days to celebrate their holidays and that the school calendar was built around Christian holidays. The school board denied the teacher's request, and the teacher went to court. Eventually, the court found in favor of the teacher, stating that his Title VII rights were violated because the employer had punished an employee by placing the employee in a position in which a tenet of faith must be ignored to retain employment.

What could happen if I share my religious beliefs in class with my students?

It depends. Teachers are employees of the school board. As government employees, teachers accept limits about sharing their personal religious beliefs with students. According to U.S. Supreme Court interpretations of the First Amendment, the state cannot endorse religion or promote one religion over another. When teachers speak as a teacher on school property, they are speaking to children who see them as authority figures. By sharing his or her religious faith with others, a teacher is implicitly endorsing a religion. This places impressionable students under pressure to accept the teacher's religion.

In two relatively recent cases, in 2000 and 2007, two different U.S. Courts of Appeals ruled that teachers could not post "overly religious" materials on their classroom or school bulletin boards because that content violated the First Amendment's Establishment Clause and was not directly related to the curriculum.[47] If school administrators learn that a teacher is sharing his or her religion with students, the administrators can tell the teacher to stop this practice for the reasons mentioned earlier. If the teacher continues to speak with students about his or her religious beliefs, the teacher can be fired for insubordination.

What are my rights and obligations as a teacher regarding Bible reading, prayers, and moments of silence in my classroom?

It depends. The U.S. Supreme Court has made decisions related to a variety of religious activities when they occur on school grounds. In *School District of Abington Township v. Schempp* and *Murray v. Curlett* (1963),[48] the Court found that state-enforced Bible reading and prayer in public schools were religious exercises and, therefore, unconstitutional. Likewise, in *Wallace v. Jaffree* (1985),[49] the Court ruled that a state-authorized period of silence for meditation or voluntary prayer is unconstitutional. In *Brown v. Gilmore* (2000),[50] however, the Fourth Circuit Court of Appeals in Virginia found that a "minute of silence" was constitutional because its purpose was secular.

9.3d Other Legal Issues Affecting Teachers

Teachers also face legal issues arising from actions that occur while they are teaching.

Is there such a thing as "educational malpractice," and can I be sued if students do not learn in my class?

No. The good news here is that there has never been a successful suit for educational malpractice. Educational malpractice is a professional issue, not a legal one.

Can I be sued if my actions as a teacher cause harm to a student?

Yes. Not only may teachers be sued personally for causing student injury, but they may also lose their jobs. Harming another person is the subject of the legal arena called *torts*. A **tort** is a civil wrong or some type of harm that one person causes another person, outside of a contract, for which the courts may award damages. Courts have not been hesitant to rule on torts. It is important to note that torts involve a civil—and not a criminal—wrong.

Most people are aware of the terms *assault* and *battery*, but many do not understand the difference between the two. **Assault** is a mental violation or the threat that someone will receive a physical injury. **Battery** is what happens when the assault becomes physical. Almost every school district has regulations that protect students and teachers against assault and battery, and offending parties face severe consequences. Students who threaten to harm another person or who give an unlawful or unwanted touch with the intention of harming or offending another person could be suspended or even expelled from school. In addition, the victim may file criminal and civil charges against the student who threatened or hit that individual. Similarly, teachers who threaten to harm or who give an unwanted or unlawful touch with the intent to harm or offend a student could be fired from their jobs and may lose their teaching licenses. What is more, a teacher could be criminally or civilly charged as a result from the incident.

In *Spears v. Jefferson Parish School Board* (1994), the Louisiana Court of Appeals held the school district liable for a teacher's intentional act that resulted in emotional harm to a child.[51] In 1989, kindergartner Justin Spears and two friends became disruptive while their physical education class watched a movie. When one of the coaches, Mr. Brooks, asked the boys to sit by him, they began to play with the teacher's hair and ears. He told the boys if they did not stop, he would "kill them." Brooks took two of the boys into an adjacent office while Justin remained behind with another teacher. Brooks and the boys agreed to play a trick on Justin by having them pretend to be dead. When Justin entered the office, he saw one boy on the floor with a rope tied around his neck. When Justin began to cry, Brooks tried to calm him down by telling him the boys were not really dead.

After this incident, Justin began to behave strangely at home, using infantile behaviors and becoming more attached to his mother. He refused to go to the bathroom alone, fearing Brooks would jump out of the mirror and harm him. A psychologist diagnosed Justin as having post-traumatic stress

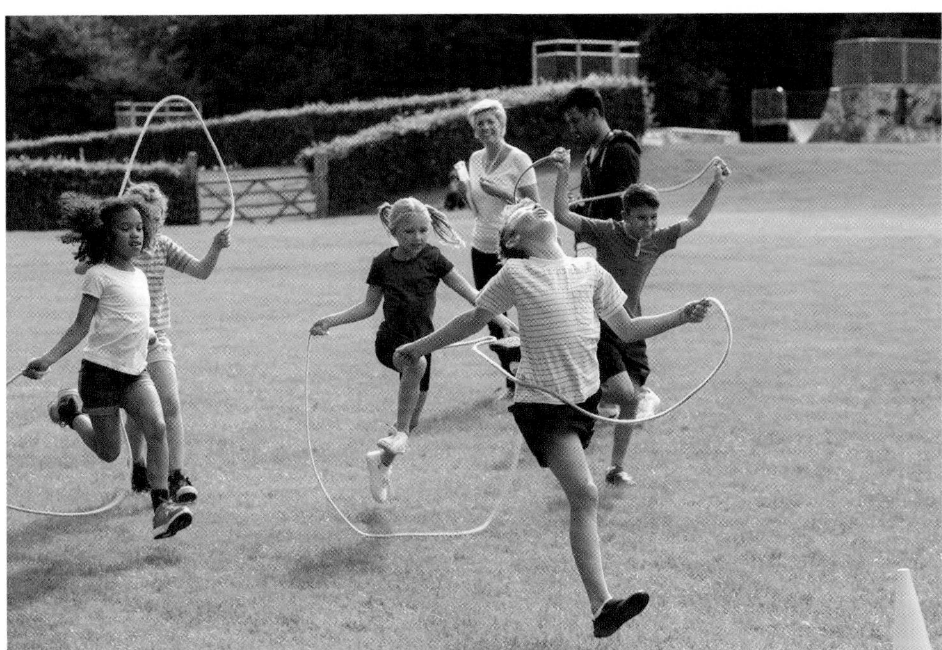

Being professional means proactively minimizing the potential for harm.

iStock/SolStock

syndrome. The parents then sued both the school district as an entity and Brooks as an individual for this injury to their son. The trial court found in favor of the parents, awarding the family general damages of $100,000 for the additional therapy Justin would need, as well as money damages to the parents for losses they received from the incident.

Is it considered "negligence" on my part if something happens in my classroom and someone gets hurt?

Maybe. As long as there are children, there will be accidents. Nonetheless, a student injury that results from an unintended mishap does not mean that the supervising adult is legally blameless. **Negligence** is generally defined as conduct that is blameworthy because it falls short of what a reasonable person would do to protect another individual from a foreseeable risk of harm. In short, being a professional means minimizing the potential for injuries to occur by acting proactively in an informed manner to avoid potentially unsafe situations.

A teacher is negligent when, without intending any wrong, he or she either acts or fails to take a precaution that under the circumstances an ordinary prudent and reasonably intelligent teacher ought to foresee would expose another person to unnecessary risk of harm. In certain school functions where children face greater risks, a teacher has an increased level of obligation or duty to the children.

For example, whenever pupils perform a dangerous lab experiment, the teacher has a greater responsibility to ensure the students' safety than when the teacher is supervising a study hall. Likewise, a woodshop teacher has a higher standard of care than a librarian because the risk of harm is greater when students are working with power tools than when they are reading books. Students face more dangers when they are running around the schoolyard than they do when they are sitting quietly studying in the classroom. Clearly, teachers' standards of care vary with the students' ages and with the situations and circumstances.

No definite rules exist about what constitutes negligence. What is negligent in one situation may not be negligent under a different set of circumstances. For teachers and other educators, the generally accepted standard of care would be that of a reasonably prudent *teacher*, not that of a reasonably prudent *layperson*.[52] As professionals, courts expect teachers to have more informed awareness and judgment about potential risks than ordinary people and to take necessary preventive actions.

Of course, sometimes pure accidents occur in which someone is injured, and no one is actually at fault. For instance, when a child closed a music room door, cutting off the tip of another student's finger, the court found no negligence had occurred; the event was merely an accident.[53]

9.4 STUDENT RIGHTS AT SCHOOL: DISCIPLINE AND PRIVACY

Given that students enjoy many of the same constitutional rights as adults, courts have been very careful in ensuring that they are protected. School officials have broad authority to establish rules and regulations governing student conduct in the school setting. These powers are not absolute, however; they are subject to the standard of *reasonableness*. Generally, rules are considered reasonable if they are needed to maintain an orderly and peaceful school environment and advance the educational process.

In determining the enforceability of school policies, rules, and regulations, courts require school authorities to provide evidence to sufficiently justify their need to enforce these directives. Fair and reasonable exercise of administrative authority will stand up to a judge's scrutiny. Of course, determining exactly what is fair and reasonable depends on the situation.

9.4a Student Discipline and Due Process Rights

Courts have ruled that for schools to operate properly, teachers and principals must be given certain authority to maintain an orderly environment. Practically and legally, parents give schools some level of control when they enroll their children. Nevertheless, students do not lose all of their constitutional privileges when they enter the school building. Schools must balance the individual students' rights with those of the public good.

Just as parents must discipline their children from time to time, so teachers have the authority to guide, correct, and occasionally rebuke their students under the *in loco parentis* concept, unless state law or school board policy does not authorize such a role. Teachers are taught how to maintain an orderly classroom environment. When students disrupt the learning process, teachers must redirect or discipline them. However, neither parents nor teachers have unlimited control over students: Child abuse is illegal whether it is committed by parents or by teachers.

For the most part, teachers' classroom management is preventive in nature; that is, it focuses on identifying and stopping small problems before they become bigger. When a student overtly and maliciously does not comply with classroom rules, the teacher usually refers the student to an administrator, who handles the misbehavior privately with the student. When punishment is required, parents are called and detention, in-school suspension, or out-of-school suspension typically result. When the answer to what rules are "reasonable" is unclear, the courts must decide.

Suspending a student from school disrupts his or her right to an education. According to the Fourteenth Amendment, due process is required if a citizen's right is being taken away.[54] In *Goss v. Lopez* (1975), the U.S. Supreme Court ruled that a temporary suspension of fewer than 10 days from school requires **procedural due process**. Students must be given oral or written notice of the charges, an explanation of the evidence against them, and an opportunity to present their side of the story. Due process is required whenever a student is separated from school.

The due process procedures become even more formal when the school recommends a student for **expulsion**, which involves long-term or permanent separation from the school program. Similarly, the court's ruling in *Honig v. Doe* (1988) gave students with disabilities additional protections in situations involving disciplinary action, thereby limiting schools' ability to make unilateral decisions about removing a disruptive student with disabilities from school.[55]

Giving students their due process rights takes time. An administrator must speak with students and other teachers who may have witnessed the event, determine what actually happened, and decide a reasonable consequence. The administrator must then present the gathered evidence to the offending student and his or her parent or guardian to explain, justify, and document any disciplinary action taken. This process ensures that schools treat all students fairly and legally.

Is it OK for teachers to use corporal punishment on a student?

Even if it is legal in your state, it is prudent not to use it. Although the U.S. Supreme Court determined in *Ingraham v. Wright* (1977)[56] that **corporal punishment in schools**—any punishment in which physical force is used and intended to cause a degree of pain or discomfort, however mild—was acceptable, the public's acceptance of hitting (i.e., pinching, smacking, slapping, or spanking) in schools has declined substantially in recent decades. In fact, today a teacher or a principal may be charged with assault and battery for paddling a child in school. If convicted of criminal charges, the educator may be subject to a fine or imprisonment. If convicted on civil charges, the educator may have to pay monetary damages. Currently, 31 states and the District of Columbia ban corporal punishment.[57]

When are disciplinary actions considered to be child abuse?

It depends. For many educators and parents, it is not clear precisely which actions make up "child abuse." Corporal punishment as a common-law school privilege often conflicts with most child abuse statutes. In *Arkansas Department of Human Services v. Caldwell* (1992), the court ruled that reasonable force in paddling a student does not constitute child abuse.

In this case, an assistant principal in Mountain Home, Arkansas, paddled three fifth-grade students who had been caught smoking on the playground. The following afternoon, one child's mother noticed bruises on her daughter's buttocks and reported these actions as suspected child abuse to the appropriate state agency. Because the bruises had resulted from the paddling, the caseworker ruled the child abuse charges were substantiated and placed the administrator's name on the State Central Registry of Child Abuse. The administrator appealed to have her name removed. The court ruled that the paddling was not abusive and noted that reasonable paddling may be legal, although excessive punishment may be abusive.

Where allowed, the corporal punishment administered must be moderate, delivered with a proper instrument, and take into account the child's age, gender, size, and overall physical strength. Within these broad limits, a teacher must balance the seriousness of the offense with the extent of punishment assigned. Because teachers are usually present when student misbehavior occurs and teachers normally know the manner, look, tone, gestures, language, setting, and general circumstances of the offense, courts will allow teachers considerable latitude in judgment. At the same time, courts will not tolerate punishment that is cruel and excessive. Any sign that teachers acted out of malice will override the teacher's *in loco parentis* privilege.

9.4b Student Privacy: Search and Seizure of Student Property

Educators must occasionally decide whether to search a student's locker, desk, book bag, or pockets. At the heart of the issue is the right of privacy guaranteed by the Fourth Amendment, which states, "The right of people to be secure in their person, houses, papers, and effects, against unreasonable searches and seizures shall not be violated, and no warrants shall issue, but upon probable cause...."

Just as parents do not need to prove to a judge that they deserve a warrant so they can check their children's book bags or bedrooms, educators operating *in loco parentis* are held to the less rigorous legal standard of reasonable suspicion. Suspicion, by definition, implies a belief; it does not equal proof. The courts have ruled that students' right to privacy and freedom from unreasonable search and seizure must be balanced against schools' need to maintain order and provide a safe and secure environment for all students.

The reasonable suspicion standard is not unlimited, however. Public school officials have restraints on their rights to search students' persons, book bags, desks, or lockers.[58] Some facts must provide reasonable grounds for performing the search, the search must be conducted to further a legitimate school purpose such as maintaining school safety, and the search may not be overly intrusive.

Can school officials search students' personal possessions?

Yes, under certain conditions, school administrators can search students' personal possessions. A landmark 1985 U.S. Supreme Court case, *New Jersey v. T. L. O.*, provides guidance for school administrators in the area of student searches and seizure of property.[59] In this case, a teacher found a 14-year-old freshman student, T. L. O. (her initials), smoking in the bathroom with another student. The assistant principal asked to see the girl's purse and found cigarettes, rolling papers, marijuana, a pipe, plastic bags, a substantial amount of money, a list of students who apparently owed the girl money, and two letters implicating her in selling marijuana at school. The parents sued, claiming the search unreasonable. On appeal, the U.S. Supreme Court ruled that a student search is permissible if it is "justified at its inception," reasonable, and "not excessively intrusive." What is reasonable, therefore, varies flexibly with the context.

Can school administrators search student lockers?

Yes. *New Jersey v. T. L. O.* found that teachers and administrators' need to maintain order outweighs students' privacy interests. But that does not mean that school officials can search anybody at any time. According to the U.S. Supreme Court, school searches are only justified "when there are reasonable grounds for suspecting that the search will turn up evidence that the student has violated or is violating either the law or the rules of school." Random searches and searches of student lockers based on hunches or rumors are not justified. And when a locker search is justified, it must be not "unreasonable" or "overly intrusive."

Can students expect privacy in their school lockers?

No. In *Isiah B. v. State of Wisconsin* (1993),[60] the Supreme Court of Wisconsin found that a student does not have reasonable expectation of privacy when storing personal items in a school locker. In this case, a school security guard found a gun in a student's coat during a random locker search. The student, Isiah B., also admitted to having cocaine in his coat.

Since the ruling in the *T. L. O.* case, most courts have concluded that students have no expectation for privacy from search in school lockers. Schools make lockers available to students for the limited purpose of storing legitimate educational materials. Students' constitutional protections must be balanced against the necessity of maintaining a controlled and disciplined environment in which all children can accomplish their education.

Can schools randomly test student athletes for illegal drug use?

Yes. Across the United States, illegal drugs affect students' health and safety. Controlling students' drug and alcohol use challenges school authorities, leading many school districts to seriously consider implementing drug testing programs.

In 1989, the U.S. Supreme Court made key rulings in two drug-related cases, concluding that a drug test—regardless of the method used to conduct the test—constitutes a search. Even so, such a search is legal because of the government's compelling interest in promoting public safety by minimizing accidents and protecting the public.[61] The Supreme Court did not hear a case involving drug testing in public schools until 1995.

Does random drug testing of student athletes violate their privacy?

No. In *Vernonia School District 47J v. Acton* (1995), the U.S. Supreme Court ruled that schools could conduct random drug tests on student athletes.[62] According to the court's decision, student athletes voluntarily choose to participate in interscholastic athletics and, therefore, have no legitimate privacy expectations. In a later case, the Supreme Court extended the drug testing rule to include students beyond athletes.

Can all students who participate in competitive extracurricular activities be required to take random drug tests?

Yes. In *Board of Education of Independent School District No. 92 of Pottawatomie County v. Earls* (2002), the U.S. Supreme Court ruled that a policy requiring all students who participated in competitive extracurricular activities to submit to a drug test was reasonable and did not violate the Fourth Amendment.[63] According to the Court, the policy reasonably served the school district's important interest in detecting and preventing students' drug use, and it was constitutional.

Students who participate in competitive extracurricular activities can be required to take random drug tests.
iStock/monkeybusinessimages

9.4c Student Records and Privacy Rights

Schools collect and keep student records for purposes that include educational planning, counseling, program development, individualized instruction, grade placement, and college admissions, among other uses. Students' files typically include family background information, health records, progress reports, achievement test results, psychological data, disciplinary records, previous report cards, and other confidential material.

Do teachers and other educators have unlimited rights to use student records?

No. Common law, specific state and federal statutes, and case law all limit the ways educators can access and use student records to protect students' privacy and rights.

The federal Family Educational Rights and Privacy Act (FERPA) of 1974 guarantees parents and students a degree of confidentiality and fundamental fairness in maintaining and using student records. FERPA was adopted to ensure that certain types of students' personally identifiable and sensitive information would not be released without parental consent. The act establishes standards for schools to follow in handling student records. In 2011, the Department of Education proposed amendments to FERPA to permit use of student data in statewide longitudinal data systems to help evaluate and improve educational programs and end those that don't work. Student information would continue to be protected, with students' personally identifiable information disclosed only for authorized purposes and under the circumstances permitted by law.

Parents have the right to inspect all records that schools maintain on their children, must have an opportunity to challenge these records' accuracy, and must consent before the school can release a student's records to agencies outside designated educational categories. Once a student reaches age 18 or enters postsecondary school, the student may give consent in lieu of the parent to release his or her own records. Schools that do not follow the required procedures risk losing federal education funds.

9.5 STUDENTS' RIGHTS AT SCHOOL: FREEDOM OF SPEECH, HARASSMENT, AND DISABILITY

Although free speech is a highly valued right, it is not absolute. Courts recognize that students keep their constitutional rights in school, although schools can regulate and balance them with the school's obligation to provide students with a safe and orderly learning environment.

9.5a Schools Can Regulate Student Speech and Expression

If the exercise of free speech creates a "clear and present danger" to the state, then schools can repress the speech without violating the individual's freedom. The ongoing tension between these two interests complicates the issue of free speech in schools, however.[64]

Can students express their political views silently and nondisruptively in school?

Yes. In *Tinker v. Des Moines Independent School District* (1969), student speech became protected unless the public schools could justify a reasonable forecast of "material and substantial disruption."[65] In December 1965, Mary Beth Tinker, John Tinker, and three other students were suspended because they wore black armbands to school to protest the Vietnam War, which was in violation of a hastily made school policy banning the wearing of black armbands. The U.S. Supreme Court ruled in the students' favor, holding that armbands were a symbolic act of free speech protected by the First Amendment that did not disrupt the school environment.

Mary Beth and John Tinker's black armbands were protected symbolic speech.

Bettmann/Contributor/Getty Images

In its ruling, the Court concluded, "It is hardly argued that either students or teachers shed their constitutional rights to freedom of speech or expression at the schoolhouse gate.... Students in school as well as out of school are 'persons' under our Constitution. They are possessed of fundamental rights which the State must respect just as they themselves must respect their obligations to the State.... To prohibit... expression of one particular opinion without evidence that it is necessary to avoid 'material and substantial interference' with schoolwork or discipline is not constitutionally permissible."[66]

The *Tinker* ruling changed the relationship between administrators and students. It affirmed that school officials must respect students' constitutional rights in school. School officials cannot justify a ban on student activity unless the officials can reasonably and legitimately forecast substantial disruption to the school's orderly and safe learning environment.

Are all student speech and expressions protected while in school?

No. Although the *Tinker* case affirmed students' rights to free political speech in school, not all student speech is permissible. In *Bethel School District No. 403 v. Fraser* (1986), the U.S. Supreme Court ruled that the First Amendment does not protect students' lewd and indecent speech.[67] Likewise, in *Morse v. Frederick* (2007), the Court ruled that the First Amendment does not protect students' speech encouraging illegal drug use at a school function.[68]

On April 26, 1983, Matthew Fraser, a student at Bethel High School in Bethel, Washington, delivered a nominating speech for a student elective office at a school assembly. Although two teachers had reviewed the speech beforehand and advised him that it was "inappropriate" and he should not deliver it and risk "severe consequences," Fraser gave it anyway. Throughout the entire speech, Fraser referred to his candidate in terms of an elaborate, graphic, and explicit sexual metaphor.

A Bethel High School disciplinary rule prohibited the use of obscene or profane language or gestures in school. The next day, Fraser admitted and explained his conduct to the assistant principal. With the teacher witnesses' written statements and Fraser's admission, the administrator suspended Fraser from school. Fraser appealed the suspension and then brought suit, claiming protected speech as decided in *Tinker*.

The U.S. Supreme Court ruled that, in this situation, *Tinker* did not apply. Students' silent political speech that did not disrupt the learning environment was not the same as a student's indecent speech and lewd behavior during a school assembly. Sexually provocative speech in school was offensive, had no political message, and was not constitutionally protected.

In *Morse v. Frederick* (2007), Joseph Frederick, a high school junior, brought and displayed a sign reading "Bong Hits 4 Jesus" to a school-sponsored event. The school's Drug Free Schools and Communities policy required schools to promote drug-free messages. The principal confiscated the banner and suspended Frederick. The Supreme Court ruled that the First Amendment regarding free speech does not require schools to tolerate at school events any student expression that contributes to the dangers of illegal drug use.

Can schools regulate the content of student newspapers?

Yes. Although a free press is essential to a democratic government's proper functioning, it has certain limitations. Published information is supposed to be true, without malice or harmful motives, and published for appropriate ends, no matter how difficult it may be for our society to ensure adherence to these goals. Similarly, courts tend to reject calls for prior restraint, in which a publication is censored before it can reach its readers.[69]

Freedom of the press in public schools, however, is governed by different constitutional precedents. In *Hazelwood School District v. Kuhlmeier* (1988), the U.S. Supreme Court ruled that schools may regulate the content of school-sponsored newspapers.[70] Hazelwood East High School's journalism class published the school newspaper, *Spectrum*, every 3 weeks during the 1982–1983 school year. Typically, the school principal reviewed page proofs before publication. For the May 13 edition, the principal objected to two of the scheduled articles—one story about three students' pregnancies, the other about a divorce's impact on students at the school. The principal was concerned that the pregnant girls' identities would become known, that the sexual references and birth control were inappropriate content for some younger students, and that the divorcing family did not have the chance to respond and consent to the story before its publication. The principal did not allow the stories to be published, and the student authors filed suit.

The U.S. Supreme Court noted that although students have First Amendment rights to free speech, these must be applied in light of the school environment's special characteristics. The Court ruled that educators could exercise editorial control over school-sponsored student expression activities as long as there is a reasonably related pedagogical concern. Because the student newspaper was intended as a supervised learning experience for journalism students, school officials were entitled to reasonably regulate its content.

In the wake of the *Hazelwood* ruling, schools have been permitted to impose reasonable restrictions on students' (and teachers') speech in school newspapers, theater productions, and other expressive activities that are part of the school curriculum, whether or not they occur in a classroom setting. When supervised by faculty members, such activities are designed to impart particular knowledge and skills to student participants and audiences. Students' freedom of speech and expression in a school newspaper, therefore, are not solely determined by the requirements of *Tinker*'s "material and substantial disruption" language. The Supreme Court ruled in *Hazelwood* that the principal was correct in deciding that the student authors and editors in question had not sufficiently mastered the ethical, moral, and legal restrictions that the journalism class taught about treating controversial and personal privacy issues. The principal had legitimate educational concerns.

Can students be disciplined for their speech on the internet/websites?

Yes, if the school can show the off-campus internet-distributed speech would substantially disrupt the school's operations.

In *Doninger v. Niehoff* (2008), a U.S. Court of Appeals for the Second Circuit in New York ruled that a school can apply disciplinary consequences to students when their off-campus internet-distributed comments create a "foreseeable risk of substantial disruption" at the school.[71] In spring 2007, planning setbacks threatened to postpone or cancel a Connecticut high school's yearly music festival. When Avery Doninger—a junior and incoming senior-class secretary—was unable to meet with the school's principal, Karissa Niehoff, to discuss the problems, Doninger and three other students sent a mass email asking community members to speak to administrators about rescheduling the event. After a later conversation in the school hallway, the principal informed Doninger that the event had been canceled.

That night, Doninger wrote a LiveJournal blog post criticizing the school officials' handling of the issue, calling the school officials "douchebags" and asking that readers complain to the school superintendent so as "to piss [her] off more" than the mass email had. In response to her derogatory comments about school officials, the school barred Doninger from serving as senior class secretary and from speaking at her graduation. The Doningers sued.

In May 2008, the court ruled in favor of the school officials. It determined that regardless of the fact that Doninger wrote the blog while off campus, the blog could be considered on-campus speech. Because the blog related to school issues, it was reasonably foreseeable that other students and school administrators would become aware of it. The court then noted that school administrators have the right, in certain situations, to restrict off-campus speech to promote school-related goals.[72]

Can students be disciplined for cyberbullying other students or staff?

Yes. **Cyberbullying** is the "willful and repeated harm inflicted through the use of computers, cell phones, and other electronic devices."[73] Frequently used by school-aged children against other school-aged children, this is a deliberate pattern of malicious behavior in which teens intend to hurt or embarrass another person using electronic equipment. Examples of cyberbullying might include spitefully posting online an intimate or humiliating photo or video of another person; spreading false rumors about someone; or threatening violence (i.e., "I'm going to get you at school tomorrow!!!"). The fact that friends, family, and acquaintances can view cyberbullying online makes it even more traumatizing for its victims.

According to the Cyberbullying Research left (2020), 15% of teens ages 9 to 12 years old[74] and 36.5% of teens ages 12 to 17 years old[75] report having been cyberbullied. Cyberbullying can result in physical and/or emotional harm. Its victims were 1.9 times more likely and offenders were 1.5 times more likely to have attempted suicide than those not involved in cyberbullying; and cyberbully victims and perpetrators were more likely to have suicidal thoughts, behaviors, and completed suicides than school bullying victims.[76] The trend appears to be growing.[77] And the seriousness of these incidents to the young people involved significantly impacts their ability to learn at school.[78]

By their nature, bullying and cyberbullying cases involve an array of legal issues. Some speech is protected by the First Amendment; other types of speech are not. Where the speaker (or message sender) seriously intends to inflict physical violence on a particular individual or group, it may become a "true threat"—not a joke, idle talk, or political argument—the speech is subject to regulation and penalty. Even when it is "only words," cyberbullying may be considered assault, and criminal punishment and award of monetary damages may result.

In response, more than half the states have enacted anticyberbullying laws[79] to prevent this behavior, to protect children, and to penalize offenders. Additionally, most state legislatures give school districts the responsibility for avoiding and resolving these behaviors, largely by instituting formal policies and procedures to address them.[80] Typically, school administrators must thoroughly investigate cases where students are being intimidated, threatened, or harassed online, even if the cyberbullying does not happen during school hours. Penalties range from school interventions (i.e., suspensions and/or expulsions) to jail time for felonies and even some misdemeanors. As with any form of harassment, teachers and administrators are responsible for identifying and ending it.

Few states have laws protecting teachers from students' cyberbullying, and what is considered "a threat" can vary from court to court.[81] Becoming familiar with your state's antibullying laws and your employing school district's policies on cyberbullying is essential for knowing your rights, responsibilities, and protections in this area.

Can schools regulate student dress and appearance?

Yes. Courts tend to support school boards' authority to regulate student dress and personal appearance if the attire becomes so extreme as to interfere with a school's favorable learning environment. For instance, school districts have the right to require pupils to participate in physical education and to wear clothing appropriate for these occasions. Students may not, however, be required to wear "immodest" attire.[82]

At present, whether schools can regulate students' hairstyles, headscarves, or headwraps is legally unclear. For example in 2018, a referee in New Jersey forced a 16-year-old mixed-race wrestler to cut his dreadlocks or forfeit his match.[83] In 2019, a suburban Atlanta public elementary school displayed several photos of African American children, including girls with braids, to display "inappropriate" haircuts and hairstyles.[84] Courts in different regions have decided divergent opinions.[85] Some see students' hair displays as protected speech, symbols of ethnic and cultural pride, whereas others see it as "distracting," "unprofessional," or promoting gangs. Nonetheless, cities and states across the nation have adopted legislation making it illegal to discriminate on the basis of a person's hairstyle.

Can public schools require students to follow dress codes?

Yes. Today, most states have laws that allow school boards to make dress code rules for their students. School officials face two irreconcilable issues when they consider student attire: maintaining a safe and effective educational environment and respecting students' constitutional rights. In these situations, courts usually support the school. For instance, dress codes that prohibit clothing with vulgar or obscene expressions or images or clothing worn in a manner that disrupts school activity—such as "gang-related" clothing, suggestively-themed T-shirts, and clothing that exposes underwear or body parts in a way that is indecent—are generally permitted. Dress codes that censor student expression because educators do not like the message are generally not permitted.

In the *Canady v. Bossier Parish School Board* decision (2001), the court ruled that a school's mandatory uniform policy does not violate students' First Amendment rights.[86] The court acknowledged that students have a constitutional right to free expression under the First and Fourteenth Amendments and noted that a person's choice of clothing can be a constitutionally protected form of expression. However, the right to free speech is not absolute. In many cases, courts have concluded that school boards' regulation of student behavior outweighs individual students' right to free speech. Adjusting the school's dress code by adopting a uniform policy is a constitutional means for school officials to improve the educational process, so long as that policy is not directed toward censoring the expressive content of student clothing. Educators have an essential duty to regulate school affairs and establish appropriate standards of conduct, and this responsibility takes priority over students' choice of clothing to wear in school.

9.5b Sexual Discrimination and Harassment of Students

Sexual harassment of students by educators is a disturbing problem. By the time they graduate from high school, an estimated 10% of K–12 students will experience sexual misconduct by a school employee.[87] After a 7-month investigation, the Associated Press (AP) found 2,570 educators who were sanctioned or whose teaching credentials were revoked, denied, or surrendered from 2001 through 2005 following allegations of sexual misconduct. More than 80% of the victims were students. At least half of the educators punished by their states were also convicted of crimes related to their harassing misconduct.[88]

The Education Amendments of 1972 contained Title IX, a law that specifically forbade discrimination based on gender.[89] Since the passage of the original legislation, the courts have expanded Title IX to address employee-to-employee, employee-to-student, and student-to-student harassment. Over time, court cases have determined that a school district is obligated to take reasonable steps to prevent and stop sexual harassment by school employees or students.

If a teacher sexually harasses a student, can the student sue both the school district and the teacher as an individual for monetary damages?

Yes. Two rulings established the case law regarding sexual harassment of students by adults in schools. In 1992, in *Franklin v. Gwinnett County Public Schools*, the U.S. Supreme Court ruled that students could recover compensatory and punitive monetary damages for sexual harassment under Title IX.[90] Further refining the scope of liability, in *Gebser v. Lago Vista Independent School District* (1998), the Supreme Court ruled that students could sue for monetary damages from the school district and the people involved if the school knew about the alleged sexual harassment and failed to respond adequately.[91]

Starting in the fall of her 10th-grade year (1986), Christine Franklin was subjected to continual sexual harassment from Andrew Hill, a sports coach and teacher employed by the district. Among other allegations, Franklin claimed that Hill engaged her in sexually-oriented conversations, asking about her sexual experiences with her boyfriend and inquiring whether she would consider having sexual intercourse with an older man. Hill forcibly kissed her on the mouth in the school parking lot and telephoned her at home, asking her to meet him socially. Three times during her junior year, Hill took her out of class and to a private office where he subjected her to coercive intercourse.

School officials were aware of the sexual harassment, but they took no action. Indeed, they discouraged Franklin from pressing charges against Hill. Franklin filed an action against the school board for monetary damages. Although the lower courts found for the school, the U.S. Supreme Court found for the student.

The Supreme Court unanimously held that damages were available under Title IX for intentional violations of the law. Where a student had been subject to sexual harassment, financial damages could be levied against the district and its supervisors as well as against the accused teacher.

In *Gebser v. Lago Vista Independent School District* (1998), the court ruled that school officials must take timely and positive actions in response to information that such inappropriate sexually harassing behaviors are occurring. A teacher's misconduct in sexually harassing a student does not make the school district liable under Title IX unless a school official had knowledge of the situation and responded with "deliberate indifference." If the school knows about the sexual harassment but does nothing to end it, the school and the individuals involved may be sued and the accuser may collect damages.

In spring 1991, eighth-grader Alida Star Gebser joined a high school book discussion group led by Frank Waldrop, a high school teacher in the Lago Vista Independent School District. During the discussion sessions, Waldrop often made sexually suggestive comments to the students. These inappropriate comments continued in ninth grade when Gebser was assigned to Waldrop's class, where he addressed many of these remarks to her. In the spring, the teacher initiated sexual contact with Gebser. They had sexual intercourse several times during the rest of the school year and the next year, often during class time, although never on school property. Gebser never reported the relationship to school officials, although she testified that she realized Waldrop's conduct was improper.

In October 1992, when parents of two classmates complained to the high school principal about Waldrop's inappropriate classroom comments, the principal met with the parents, and the teacher apologized. The principal advised Waldrop to be careful about his classroom comments but did not report the parents' complaint to the superintendent (who was also the district's Title IX coordinator). A few months later, a policeman discovered Waldrop and Gebser having sexual intercourse and arrested Waldrop. The school district fired him, and the state education department revoked his teaching license. During this time, the district did not have a sexual harassment complaints policy or a formal antiharassment policy, as federal regulations required. Gebser and others filed suit against the district, claiming damages under the Title IX statute.

The Supreme Court ruled that Title IX allowed damages only if a school official with authority to take corrective action had actual information about the harassment and showed "deliberate indifference" toward correcting the situation. Because school officials did not know about the sexual harassment and did not act with deliberate indifference, the Court found for the school district and against the student. If sexual harassment occurred but the school officials did not know about it at the time, school districts and individuals cannot be held liable for financial penalties.[92]

Can school boards be held liable for student-to-student sexual harassment?

Yes, but only when the school officials know about the harassment but do nothing to stop it. In *Davis v. Monroe County Board of Education* (1999), the U.S. Supreme Court ruled that a school board may be sued for damages in situations of peer-to-peer sexual harassment, but only when the educators acted with "deliberate indifference."[93]

Georgia fifth-grader LaShonda Davis was subject to frequent sexual harassment from a male classmate who tried to touch her breasts and genital area and made vulgar comments, such as "I want to get in bed with you." LaShonda reported each of these incidents to her mother and to her classroom teacher. When contacted by the parent, the teacher assured Mrs. Davis that the school principal had been informed of the incidents. Nonetheless, no disciplinary action was taken against the offending student, and the offensive conduct continued. After another harassing incident and Mrs. Davis meeting with the principal, the offending student still received no discipline, nor did the school separate LaShonda and the offender until after 3 months of reported harassment. The incidents finally ended when the student was charged with, and pleaded guilty to, sexual battery.

Mrs. Davis alleged that school officials failed to prevent LaShonda's suffering of sexual harassment by another student. The school's complacency created an abusive environment that deprived her daughter of educational benefits promised her under Title IX of the Education Amendments of 1972. Furthermore, the school district had not instructed its personnel on how to respond to peer sexual harassment and had not established a policy on the issue.

The U.S. Supreme Court concluded that a person could collect punitive damages against the school board in cases of student-on-student harassment, but only where the school district acted with deliberate indifference to known acts of harassment in its programs or activities. Because school officials had knowledge of the sexual harassment and did not act assertively to prevent future harassment, the Court found for the student. Further, the damages are warranted "only for harassment that is so severe, pervasive, and objectively offensive that it effectively bars the victim's access to an educational opportunity or benefit."

Can students be sued for harassing another student?

Yes. In *Nabozny v. Podlesny* (1996), a U.S. Court of Appeals ruled that schools had a responsibility to protect students from antigay verbal and physical abuse.[94]

For 4 years, Jamie Nabozny was subjected to relentless antigay verbal and physical harassment and abuse by fellow students at his public middle school and high school in Ashland, Wisconsin.[95] Students urinated on him and pretended to rape him during class. When classmates found him alone, they kicked him so many times in the stomach that he required surgery. Although they knew of the abuse, school officials once said that Nabozny should expect it if he were gay. Nabozny attempted suicide several times, dropped out of school, and ultimately ran away. To make sure that other students did not go through the same kind of nightmare, he sued his former school.

The federal appeals court found that a public school could be held accountable for not stopping antigay abuse. In this case, the school had violated the student's Fourteenth Amendment rights to equal protection based on gender or sexual orientation. The case went back to trial, and a jury found the school officials liable for the harm they caused to Nabozny. The case was ultimately settled for close to $1 million in damages.

To explore more fully the constitutional limits on teachers and students in schools, complete the activity in the **Reflect & Engage** box, Limits on Teachers' and Students' Constitutional Rights in Schools.

REFLECT & ENGAGE: LIMITS ON TEACHERS' AND STUDENTS' CONSTITUTIONAL RIGHTS IN SCHOOLS

Although teachers and students keep their constitutional rights to free speech, religion, and privacy while in school, these rights come with certain limits. Teachers' and students' constitutional protections must be balanced against the necessity of maintaining a controlled and disciplined environment in which all children can achieve their education.

This activity involves role play. Your college dean has asked you, as school law students, to present a 5-minute workshop to the local school district's incoming novice teachers during their new-teacher orientation about the "Five Most Important Legal Considerations for New Teachers."

A. Working in groups of four, identity what you think are the five most important legal issues that new teachers should know.

B. Develop a graphic image that displays these laws and a school or community situation in which they might be relevant.

C. Create a 5-minute talk to explain why you think it is extremely important that new teachers should know these laws or expectations that affect their teaching or their students in schools.

D. Role-play your talk with graphic aids to the "incoming new teachers" (your class).

E. As a class, discuss which legal issues discussed in this chapter have the most meaning for future teachers—and how this might influence how you conduct yourself and relate to students and other colleagues.

9.5c Students With Disabilities

Today, students with disabilities have additional legal protections to ensure their right to a public school education. Although Congress passed legislation stating that students with disabilities were entitled to a "free appropriate public education" (FAPE), it did not specifically define what an "appropriate education" meant. It deliberately left the definition broad and flexible, thereby allowing public schools to make this determination in accordance with the well-structured procedural process.

How much benefit should special education provide to students with disabilities?

Enough to provide students with disabilities a "reasonably ambitious" education calculated to enable them to "make progress appropriate in light of the child's circumstances."

Two special education cases reaching the U.S. Supreme Court 35 years apart reshaped the academic and functional standards for special education students. In *Board of Education of Hendrick Hudson Central School District v. Rowley* (1982), the U.S. Supreme Court ruled that "free and appropriate public education" as specified in PL 94-142 and the Individuals With Disabilities Education Act (IDEA) does not require a state to maximize the potential of each child with disabilities.[96] This was the first case in which the Supreme Court had an opportunity to interpret any of IDEA's provisions. In *Endrew F. v. Douglas County School District* (2017), the Court ruled that under IDEA, "a school must offer an IEP [individualized educational program] reasonably calculated to enable a child to make progress appropriate in light of the child's circumstances."[97]

Amy June Rowley, a deaf student in Peekskill, New York, had minimal residual hearing and was an excellent lip reader. Before she started kindergarten, Amy's parents and school administrators agreed to place Amy in a regular kindergarten class to see which supplemental services she would need. At the end of the trial period, all agreed that Amy should remain in the kindergarten class but with an FM[98] hearing aid to help her participate in certain classroom activities. Amy successfully completed her kindergarten year.

Amy's first-grade IEP kept her in a regular classroom with the FM hearing aid and assigned her additional tutoring and speech services. Agreeing with the plan, Amy's parents also requested that Amy receive a qualified sign language interpreter in all her academic classes instead of the other proposed services. After receiving an interpreter's services in kindergarten as part of a 2-week experiment, the interpreter reported that Amy did not need his services at that time. After consulting with the school district's Committee on the Handicapped, which had heard evidence from both sides, the school administrators concluded that Amy did not need the interpreter in first grade.

At a hearing that the Rowleys requested, the independent examiner who heard the evidence agreed with the school administrators. The interpreter was not necessary because "Amy was achieving educationally, academically, and socially" without such assistance. In an appeal, the New York Commissioner of Education also supported the school administrators' decision. The Rowleys then filed suit, claiming the denial of the sign language interpreter constituted a denial of the "free and appropriate public education" guaranteed by law.

The U.S. Supreme Court found that the state does not have to maximize the child's potential, but rather provide a program that benefits the child. The Court observed that the special education act did not define "appropriate education" or offer a substantive prescription about the level of education to be given to children with disabilities. According to the Court, IDEA "generates no additional requirement that the services so provided be sufficient to maximize each child's potential 'commensurate with the opportunity provided other children.'" Although this outcome might be desirable, ensuring that this goal is met was not the legislation's intent. In the *Rowley* decision, the Court "declined to establish any one test for determining the adequacy of educational benefits conferred upon all children covered by [IDEA] and confined its analysis to the facts of the case before it." The next case would challenge this view.

In the second case, Endrew F. ("Drew"), a child with autism spectrum and attention deficit/hyperactivity disorder, received annual IEPs in his Douglas County School District from preschool through fourth grade. During this time, his severe behavior problems increased. By fourth grade, Endrew's parents believed that his academic and functional progress had stalled. When the school district proposed a fifth-grade IEP that resembled those from past years, Endrew's parents removed him from public school and enrolled him in a specialized private school, where he made significant progress. When the school district later presented Endrew's parents with a new fifth-grade IEP, they thought it no more adequate than the original plan. They then sought reimbursement ($70,000 a year) for Endrew's private school tuition by filing a complaint under the IDEA with the Colorado Department of Education, which denied their claim. A federal District Court and the Tenth Circuit also affirmed that decision and denied the claim. Interpreting *Rowley*, the Courts declared that Endrew's IEP was "reasonably calculated to enable [him] to make some progress."

But in a unanimous decision, the U.S. Supreme Court raised the educational benefit for students with disabilities from "some educational benefit" to "reasonably ambitious" ones. It ruled that "an IEP must aim to enable the child to make progress... for pursuing academic and functional advancement. And the degree of progress... must be [appropriately ambitious] in light of the child's circumstances" and unique needs. Although "educational benefit" had to be tailored to each child's unique needs and circumstances, it always had to be more than trivial progress, a higher standard than *Rowley* or lower courts had determined. Not wanting to substitute their judgment for that of experts (that would encourage more lawsuits), the Court sent the *Endrew* case back to a lower court, and the judge that had decided in favor of the Colorado district reversed himself in February 2018, saying that the school system did not meet the new educational standard.[99]

IDEA and the courts give the primary responsibility for formulating students' education and choosing the educational methods to the state and local education agencies. They are expected to work in cooperation with the child's parent or guardian to ensure they are creating reasonably high expectations for their children with disabilities.

AMERICAN EDUCATION SPOTLIGHT: AMY JUNE ROWLEY

At age 10, Amy June Rowley became the center of a landmark U.S. Supreme Court case that helped shape education laws for students with disabilities. At its heart, *Hendrick Hudson Board of Education v. Rowley* is a very human story about a family fighting to make sure their child had an opportunity to learn.

Currently, Rowley, who is deaf, is an associate professor and coordinator of the American Sign Language Program in the Modern Languages and Literatures Department at California State University–East Bay in Hayward, California. In 2014, she completed her doctoral degree. Married, she and her husband have three children, two of whom are deaf and attend a California school for the deaf.

Amy's parents—Nancy and Clifford—were both born hearing but became deaf as a result of childhood illnesses. Amy's mother became a teacher of the deaf. She saw how much potential deaf students had, and she pushed them to achieve their best.

The Rowley's first child, John, was born hearing, and Amy's mother spoke to him as she would with any hearing child. When Amy was born, her mother assumed she could hear and spoke with her as if she were a hearing child. At 15 months old, however, Amy was not speaking as her brother did. She had started signing on her own by watching her parents signing, so her mother actively began teaching her bright daughter to sign, making certain that Amy understood everything happening around her. Although doctors confirmed Amy's deafness a few months later, Amy always had access to language, to knowledge of her world, and to high expectations for what she could learn and accomplish. The 1975 Education for All Handicapped Children Act (PL 94-142) gave Amy's parents the opportunity for her to receive better academic opportunities at a nearby public school in classes with hearing students than at a distant school for the deaf.

Nancy Rowley worked with her daughter after school at home to help Amy keep up with her studies. Amy recalls, "My mother would not allow me to fail."

As an adult, Amy has published articles both about special education litigation and relationships. She reflects on her personal experiences at the left of a legal, educational, and media storm:

"[Third grade was] the first time I really enjoyed school. I was able to follow along perfectly in classroom discussions, and my [sign language] interpreter made sure to interpret everything including my classmate's discussions.... I looked forward to recess where the interpreter would follow me out and interpret for me and other children to figure out what we wanted to do. Before, I had always followed other kids outside and usually kids wanted to play kickball, but I was often not included. So I would go to the playground and play alone or with a few other kids. But now... I felt I had a voice.... I wanted to play kickball, and they would make sure I was involved.... The added bonus of having an interpreter in the classroom meant that when I got home from school I only had to do my homework and not relearn everything I was supposed to have learned in class that day. So I really had a lot more time to play and 'just be a kid'" (Rowley, 2008, p. 322).

"Without an interpreter, I was a 'C' student. With an interpreter, I was an 'A' student," Amy asserts.

"Children should be allowed to be children. Too often, children are robbed of their right to grow up without the weight of the world on their shoulders. I know the weight of my world was squashing me in elementary school as my family and I pursued the educational experience I needed and deserved. With the case going all the way to the Supreme Court, I got a lot of national attention from the media. I didn't ask for that. Would I do this again? I was faced with that decision with my own children who are deaf. The school district I first worked with informed me that they wanted my oldest daughter to be able to function without an interpreter by the time she entered school.... They wanted to deprive me and her of communication. I had to explain to the school that American Sign Language is not a detriment to my daughter's education but actually an advantage that helps her thrive in school. Twenty-five years ago my parents asked for an interpreter for the exact same reasons. Twenty-five years later I know there has been progress, but it is not always evident. So would I do it again? Not at the expense of my children" (Rowley, 2008, p. 328).

Sources: Quirk, K. (2007, March 30). Deaf UWM professor helped shape education laws for students with disabilities. *Deaf News Network.* http://deafnn.wordpress.com/2007/03/30/uw-milwaukee-featured-stories-detail/; Rowley, A. (2008, July). *Rowley* revisited: A personal narrative. *Journal of Law and Education, 37*(3), 311–328; Rowley, A. J. (2019, March). Address by Amy June Rowley, PhD, Professor, California State University, East Bay. *New York Law Schools Law Review, 63,* 21. https://digitalcommons.nyls.edu/cgi/viewcontent.cgi?article=1001&context=nyls_law_review

Do school districts have to pay tuition for students with disabilities to attend private educational facilities?

Yes, sometimes. In 2016, 1.4% of all children with disabilities, the national average (about 85,000), received their education in private schools, and their local school districts paid for it with a "proportionate share" of their federal special education funding.[100] In 2007, New York City paid for private schools for more than 7,000 children with severe disabilities because it agreed that it could not properly instruct them, costing the city more than $57 million per school year.101

In 2009, the U.S. Supreme Court ruled in *Forest Grove School District v. T. A.* that parents of students with disabilities had the right to seek reimbursement through due process from their local school district for private school tuition for their child, even if the child had not been served in public schools.

Schools must balance the individual rights of teachers and students with the necessity of maintaining a safe and productive learning environment. Teachers who understand and follow their ethical and legal responsibilities will be more effective educators.

KEY TAKE-AWAYS

Learning Objective 9.1 Defend the importance of having an Educators' Code of Ethics.

- Because every profession affects the well-being of others who depend on those professionals' skills and services, professional behaviors have both technical and moral dimensions. Society holds practitioners accountable for both aspects through a professional code of ethics.
- Teachers' professional boundaries protect students and teachers from potential harm.
- Becoming a professional educator means recognizing that what may be acceptable in one's life as an undergraduate student may not be acceptable when looking for your first teaching job or heading your own classroom.

Learning Objective 9.2 Assess how case law, teacher licensure, and a contract to teach affect the teaching profession.

- States issue teaching licenses for a specific period of time. The license holder must maintain it with continued employment and professional learning, and the state can revoke it for "just cause."
- Most teaching contracts provide for teachers to serve a **probationary period** working under an annual contract. Tenure, or continuing contract status, provides a degree of job security because the teacher cannot be dismissed without the legal protection of due process (a formal hearing, presentation of evidence, and opportunity to have a lawyer and defend oneself). Tenure does not guarantee lifetime employment.

Learning Objective 9.3 Describe how teachers' constitutional freedoms, such as freedom of speech, freedom of religion, and protection from unreasonable search and seizure, operate in schools.

- **Academic freedom** means that teachers have some choices in the teaching methods they use as long as the teaching methods meet professional standards. Academic freedom does *not* mean that teachers can say whatever they would like—or teach whatever they want—in the classroom.
- A public school teacher or other school employee may be restrained in the exercise of speech depending on whether it involves a matter of *public* concern or *private* concern. A balance must

be found between a person's right to speak out on matters of public concern and an organization's interest in doing its job efficiently.

- Although teachers retain their constitutional rights while employed as educators, these rights are limited. Areas within their employers' workplace can be searched; teachers can be required to take drug tests; teachers must teach the required curriculum regardless of their religious beliefs; and they may not share their religious beliefs with students. The state must balance individual teachers' and students' constitutional rights against the necessity of maintaining a controlled and safe learning environment.
- While students are in school or on school-sponsored trips, teachers are responsible for their students' physical and emotional safety as well as for helping them learn. Teachers may be sued if their actions (or inactions) lead to student harm. For teachers and other educators, the generally accepted standard of care would be that of a reasonably prudent *teacher*, not that of a reasonably prudent *layperson*.

Learning Objective 9.4 Examine how students' privacy rights in school regarding discipline, property, and student records affect students and teachers.

- Courts recognize that students keep their constitutional rights in school, although schools can regulate and balance them with the school's obligation to provide students with a safe and orderly learning environment. Students can also be disciplined for their off-campus or internet-distributed speech if the school can show that it would substantially disrupt the school's operation.
- Common law, specific state and federal statutes, and case law all limit the ways educators can access and use student records to protect students' privacy and rights.

Learning Objective 9.5 Critique how schools protect and limit students' rights.

- Students who are sexually harassed at school by a teacher or another student can sue the school district and the teacher as an individual for monetary damages if the school knew about the alleged sexual harassment and showed "deliberate indifference" toward correcting the situation.
- Schools must provide students with disabilities a reasonably ambitious education calculated to enable them to make progress appropriate in light of the child's circumstances.

TEACHER SCENARIO: IT'S YOUR TURN

Sam, one of your teacher preparation classmates, is a gifted science student, but he is less adept in social skills with those in authority. You both are presently student teaching in a local high school, fulfilling your last requirement before graduation. His cooperating teacher, Mr. Jones, has given Sam constructive criticism regarding his classroom management and teaching practices. Annoyed, Sam has found "Facebook sympathy" with some of his students about his differences with Mr. Jones and has "friended" these students in spite of the high school and university prohibitions against such social media practice. As the semester continues, the tension grows between Sam and Mr. Jones. Six weeks before graduation, a group of the student teachers, all 22 years old or older, meet at a bar for the "6-week countdown." Sam has a bit too much to drink and asks you to video him while he finishes the "six-shots-in-6-seconds" ritual. He wants to place the video on his Facebook page with the caption, "Here's what I think of Mr. Jones!" What do you say to him in light of legal, ethical, and career consequences?

NOTES

1. We wish to thank our friends David and Kern Alexander for their help with this chapter. Much of the school law content is derived from their text, *American Public School Law* (9th ed., 2019) published by Cengage Learning. Text citations are from the ninth edition unless otherwise stated.
2. Schwartz, S. (2019, May 23). Teachers often experience "moral injury" on the job, study finds. *Education Week*. http://blogs.edweek.org/teachers/teaching_now/2019/05/moral_injury_teachers.html

3. Friedman, T. L. (2008). *Hot, flat, and crowded. Why we need a green revolution—and how it can renew America*. Ferrar, Straus, and Giroux, p. 192.

4. Barrett, D., Casey, J., E., Visser, R. D., & Headley, K. (2012). How do teachers make judgments about ethical and unethical behaviors? Toward the development of a code of ethics for teachers. *Teaching and Teacher Education, 28*, 890–898.

5. Council of Chief State School Officers. (2013, April). *InTASC. Model core teaching standards and learning progressions for teachers* 1.0. CCSSO's Interstate Teacher Assessment and Support Consortium (InTASC), p. 41. https://ccsso.org/sites/default/files/2017-12/2013_INTASC_Learning_Progressions_for_Teachers.pdf

6. NASDTE. (2015). *Model code of ethics for educators* (CEE). https://edprepmatters.net/2015/06/nasdtec-releases-model-code-of-ethics-for-educators/

7. NASTDE, 2015.

8. Frankel, M. S. (1989, February–March). Professional codes: Why, whom, and with what impact? *Journal of Business Ethics, 8*(2–3), 109–115.

9. Beyerstein, D. (1993). The functions and limitations of professional codes of ethics. In E. R. Winkler & J. R. Coombs (Eds.), *Applied ethics: A reader* (pp. 416–425). Blackwell.

10. Beyerstein, 1993.

11. Carter, H. H., Foulger, T. S., & Ewbank, A. D. (2008). Have you Googled your teacher lately? Teachers use of social networking sites. *Phi Delta Kappan, 89*(9), 681–685. See this article for a more complete discussion of social networking and teachers.

12. Pew Research left (2019, June 12). *Social media fact sheet*. Washington, DC: Retrieved from https://www.pewresearch.org/internet/fact-sheet/social-media/

13. Shannon, J. (2019, April 3). New York teacher, fired for a years-old topless selfie, claims sex discrimination in $3M lawsuit. Nation. *USA Today*. Retrieved from https://www.usatoday.com/story/news/nation/2019/04/02/lauren-miranda-selfie-new-york-teacher-topless-photo-firing/3348089002/; Waller, D. (2017, May 18). Ohio teacher in trouble over Snapchat post about "These damn kids and parents". Green Bay, MI: NBC26.com. Retrieved from https://www.nbc26.com/news/national/bedford-teacher-on-paid-leave-after-snapchat-complaint-made-public

14. The First Amendment does not protect a public employee who is airing personal grievances online. See: *Connick v Myers*, 461 U.S. 138, 103 S.Ct.1694 (1983).

15. Schwartz, S. (2018, August 24). A teacher was suspended for posting a video of herself pole dancing. But what are her rights? *Education Week*. http://blogs.edweek.org/teachers/teaching_now/2018/08/pole_dancing_teacher_social_media.html

16. See: Shannon, 2019; McCormack, S. (2017, December 6). Olivia Sprauer, former teacher, forced to resign after bikini modeling photo surfaces. *Huff Post*. https://www.huffpost.com/entry/olivia-sprauer-teacher_n_3230211; Sutter, L. (2019, May 2). Fifth-grade teacher on leave after vulgar social media post about students, officials say. *NBC5Chicago*. https://www.nbcchicago.com/news/local/5th-grade-teacher-on-leave-after-vulgar-social-media-post-about-students-officials-say/158522/

17. Rosen, J. (2010, July 25). The web means the end of forgetting. *The New York Times Sunday Magazine*, MM30.

18. O'Connor, K. W., & Schmidt, G. B. (2015, January-March). "Facebook fired": Legal standards for social media-based termination of K–12 public school teachers. *Journal of Workplace Rights*, SAGE. https://journals.sagepub.com/doi/pdf/10.1177/2158244015575636

19. Check with your own state's and school's professional teaching association or social media policies for specific guidance.

20. Case law is judge-made law. In contrast, statutes are laws passed by legislative bodies.

21. We use the terms "certification" and "licensure" interchangeably here, even while acknowledging that there are subtle, yet distinct differences between the two.

22. *Moral turpitude* can be defined as conduct that is considered to be so base, vile, or depraved that it is contrary to community standards of justice, honesty, or good morals.

23. Staples, S. R. (2017, November 3). Record review of cases involving a basis for license revocation. *Superintendent's Memo #312-17*. Department of Education. http://www.doe.virginia.gov/administrators/superintendents_memos/2017/312-17.shtml

24. Alexander, K., & Alexander, M. D. (2019). Tenure. In *American public school law* (9th ed.; p. 948). West Academic.

25. 270 F.3d 1036 (6th Cir. 2001), 53.

26. 418 F.2d 359 (1st Cir. 1969), 53.
27. *Brubaker v. Board of Education, School District 149, Cook County, Illinois* (7th Cir. 1974).
28. Alexander & Alexander, 2019, p. 992.
29. 391 U.S. 563, 88 S. Ct. 1731 (1968).
30. 391 U.S. at 568.
31. 461 U.S. 138, 103 S. Ct. 1684 (1983).
32. 981 F.2d 152 (4th Cir. 1993).
33. There are 13 Circuit Courts of Appeal in the United States, representing various geographic regions of the country. The Fourth Circuit Court of Appeals represents the mid-Atlantic states.
34. 480 U.S. 709, 107 S. Ct. 1492 (1987).
35. 191 F.3d 1329 (11th Cir. 1999).
36. *Skinner v. Railway Executives Association* (S. Ct. 1989) and *National Treasury Employees Union v. Von Raab* (S. Ct. 1989).
37. *Knox County Education Association v. Knox County Board of Education* (6th Cir. 1998) 158 F.3d 361.
38. Sixth Circuit, 1998, 158 F.3d 361.
39. 603 F2.d 1271, 1274 (7th Cir. 1979), cert denied. 444 U.S. 1026, 100 S. Ct. 689 (1980).
40. *Russo v. Central School District No. 1*, 469 F.2d 623 (2d Cir. 1972), cert denied, 411 U.S. 932. 93 S. Ct. 1899 (1973).
41. *Edwards v. Aguillard*, 482 U.S. 578 (1987).
42. *Kitzmiller v. Dover Area School District*, 400 F.Supp.2d 707 (M.D.Pa.2005).
43. 482 U.S. 578, 107 S. Ct. 2573.
44. 400 F. Supp.2d 707.
45. 541 F. Supp. 332 (D.S.D. 1982).
46. 544 F. Supp. 1049 (D. Colo. 1983).
47. *Lee v. York County School Division*, 484 F. 3d 687 (4th Cir. 2007), cert denied. 128 S. Ct. 387 (2007); and *Downs v. Los Angeles Unified School District*, 228 F. 3d 1003 (9th Cir. 2000).
48. 374 U.S. 203, 83 S. Ct. 1560.
49. 472 U.S. 38, 105 S. Ct. 2479.
50. 258 F. 3d 265 (4th Cir).
51. *Spears v. Jefferson Parish School Board*, 646 So. 2d 1104 (1994).
52. Alexander & Alexander, 2019, p. 767.
53. *Lewis v. St. Bernard Parish School*, 350 So. 2d 1256 (La. Ct. App. 1977).
54. There are two types of due process, procedural and substantive. We will deal only with procedural due process in this chapter.
55. 419 U.S. 565, 95 S. Ct. 729 (1975).
56. 430 U.S. 651, 97 S. Ct. 1401.
57. Caron, C. (2018, December 13). In 19 states, it's still legal to spank children in public schools. *The New York Times.* https://www.nytimes.com/2018/12/13/us/corporal-punishment-school-tennessee.html
58. In June 2009, the U.S. Supreme Court ruled that school officials could not strip-search a student while looking for ibuprofen because it violated the Fourth Amendment's prohibition against unreasonable search and seizure. See: Bravin, J. (2009, June 26). Court faults strip-search of student. *The Wall Street Journal/Law.* http://online.wsj.com/article/SB124593034315253301.html
59. 469 U.S. 325, 105 S. Ct. 733 (1985).
60. 176 Wis. 2d 639, 500 N.W2d 637.
61. Essex, N. L. (2005). *School law and the public schools: A practical guide for educational leaders.* Pearson, pp. 101–102.
62. 515 U.S. 646, 115 S. Ct. 2386.

63. 536 U.S. 822, 122 S. Ct. 2559 (2002).

64. Schools should base their rules and regulations on the school's legitimate interests. If the rule or regulation's purpose is unclear or nonexistent, courts say, then the rule should not exist.

65. 393 U.S. 503, 89 S. Ct. 733 (1969).

66. 393 U.S. 503, 89 S. Ct. 733 (1969).

67. 478 U.S. 675, 106 S. Ct. 3159 (1986).

68. 551 U.S. 127 S. Ct. 2618 (2007).

69. Okamoto, J. C. (1987, April 1). Prior restraint and the public high school student press: The validity of administrative censorship of student newspapers under the federal and California constitutions. *Loyola of Los Angeles Law Review.* Loyola Marymount University and Loyola Law School. https://digitalcommons.lmu.edu/cgi/viewcontent.cgi?article=1511&context=llr

70. 484 U.S. 260, 108 S. Ct. 562 (1988).

71. *Doninger v. Niehoff*, 514 F. Supp.2d 199 (D.Comm.2007).

72. Walsh, M. (2008, June 11). Student loses discipline case for blog remarks. *Education Week, 27*(41), 7.

73. Hinduja, S., & Patchin, J. W. (2015). *Bullying: Beyond the Schoolyard—Preventing and responding to cyberbullying* (2nd ed.). Corwin, p. 11.

74. Patchin, J. W., & Hinduja, S. (2020). *Tween cyberbullying 2020.* Cyberbullying Research left. https://cyberbullying.org/tween-statistics

75. Patchin, J. W. (2020). *2019 Cyberbullying data.* Cyberbullying Research left. https://cyberbullying.org/2019-cyberbullying-data

76. Hinduja, S., & Patchin, J. W. (2010). Bullying, cyberbullying, and suicide. *Archives of Suicide Research, 14*(3), 206–221; Stanglin, D., & Welch, W. M. (2013, October 16). Two girls arrested on bullying charges after suicide. *USA Today.* https://www.usatoday.com/story/news/nation/2013/10/15/florida-bullying-arrest-lakeland-suicide/2986079/; Engle, P. (2014, January 7). Teen in notorious Maryville rape case attempts suicide. *Business Insider.* https://www.businessinsider.com/daisy-coleman-suicide-attempt-2014-1

77. Patchin, J. W. (2020). School bullying rates increase by 35% from 2016 to 2019. Cyberbullying Research left. https://cyberbullying.org/school-bullying-rates-increase-by-35-from-2016-to-2019

78. Hinduja, S., & Patchin, J. W. (2019). Connecting adolescent suicide to the severity of bullying and cyberbullying. *Journal of School Violence, 18*(3), 333–346.

79. Hinduja, S., & Patchin, J. W. (2018, November). State bullying laws. *Cyberbullying Research left.* https://cyberbullying.org/Bullying-and-Cyberbullying-Laws.pdf

80. Cyberbullying Research left. (n.d.). *Bullying laws across America.* https://cyberbullying.org/bullying-laws

81. Morrison, S. (2017, May 15). How the law protects students who cyberbully their teachers. *Vocative.* https://www.vocativ.com/419694/teachers-victims-cyberbullying-social-media/index.html

82. Alexander & Alexander, 2019, p. 514.

83. Washington, J. (2019, September 18). The untold story of wrestler Andrew Johnson's dreadlocks. *The Undefeated.* https://theundefeated.com/features/the-untold-story-of-wrestler-andrew-johnsons-dreadlocks/

84. Vigdor, N. (2019, August 3). Georgia elementary schools is accused of racial insensitivity over hairstyle guidelines display. *The New York Times.* https://www.nytimes.com/2019/08/03/us/hairstyles-black-students-appropriate-inappropriate.html

85. Teaching Tolerance. (n.d.). *Can your school dictate your hair?* https://www.tolerance.org/sites/default/files/general/tt_can_school_dictate_hair_0.pdf

86. United States Court of Appeals, Fifth Circuit, 2001. 240 F.3d 437.

87. Shakeshaft, C. (2004). *Educator sexual misconduct: A synthesis of existing literature.* U.S. Department of Education. https://www2.ed.gov/rschstat/research/pubs/misconductreview/report.pdf

88. Irvine, M., & Tanner, R. (2007, October 24). Sex abuse: A shadow over U.S. schools. *Education Week, 27*(9), 1, 16–19.

89. Title IX prohibits discrimination not only within athletics and other extracurricular activities but also in regard to financial aid, testing, curricular offerings, pregnancy, and marital status.

90. 503 U.S. 60, 112 S. Ct. 1028 (1992).
91. 524 U.S. 274, 118 S. Ct. 1989 (1998).
92. Alexander & Alexander, 2019, p. 641.
93. 526 U.S.629, 119 S. Ct. 1662 (1999).
94. *Nabozny v. Podlesny*. 92 F. 3d 446 (1996).
95. Approximately 34% of LGBTQ+ students report being bullied while on school grounds; 27% report being physically harassed at school because of their sexual orientation; 13% have been physically harassed because of their gender identity. See: Dowd, R. (2018, March 22). *LGBT youth experiences discrimination, harassment, and bullying in school.* The Williams Institute, UCLA School of Law. https://williamsinstitute.law.ucla.edu/press/lgbt-youth-bullying-press-release/
96. 458 U.S. 176, 102 S. Ct. 3034.
97. 137 S.Ct. 988 (2017).
98. An FM hearing aid is one that uses frequency modulation to transmit sound over airwaves, allowing a user to hear more speech and less background noise as compared with AM hearing aids, which use amplitude modification.
99. Samuels, C. A. (2018, April 27). A year out, *Endrew F.* ruling leaves imprint. *Education Week, 37*(29), 14.
100. Samuels, C.A. (2018, August 2). How private schools and districts partner up on special education. *Education Week School Choice & Charters Blog.* https://www.edweek.org/policy-politics/how-private-schools-and-districts-partner-up-on-special-education/2018/08
101. Stout, D., & Medina, J. (2007, October 11). With justices split, city must pay disabled student's tuition. *The New York Times, Education*, B1. Retrieved from http://www.nytimes.com/2007/10/11/education/11school.html07.

RosalreneBetancourt 14/Alamy Stock Photo

10 SCHOOL GOVERNANCE AND STRUCTURE

InTASC Standards Addressed: 1, 2, 3, 4, 5, 6, 7, 8, 9, 10

LEARNING OBJECTIVES

After you read this chapter, you should be able to

10.1 Identify and explain the three areas of federal government's involvement in public education.

10.2 List the state leaders and legal entities who play key roles in shaping education policy and practice and describe their responsibilities.

10.3 Assess which local leaders, entities, and support staff play key roles in shaping education policy, practice, and student success.

10.4 Evaluate how the structural issues of school district size, school size, and grade-level configuration affect public schools' costs and effectiveness.

As a people, Americans are hardworking, pragmatic, and efficient—yet we prefer a little ambiguity when it comes to governing our public institutions. Purposefully, we have distributed accountability. "Anyone who has tried to change vehicle registration from Virginia to Maryland knows the true meaning of government by fragmentation," notes Michael J. Fuerer, dean of the George Washington University Graduate School of Education and Human Development.[1] The same can be said for education.

The United States does not have one national education system like France, Germany, England, or Japan. Instead, American education is largely controlled at the state level. Currently, the United States has one federal Department of Education, 50 state education agencies and one for the District of Columbia, and almost 13,600 school districts.[2] Most states allow localities within the state to manage education. In short, education is a federal interest, a state responsibility, and a locally administered concern. Local school districts are the primary operating units of the American public school system.[3]

In this chapter, we review the U.S. schools' governance and structure from the federal government to the classroom. We discuss how state boards of education and local school boards function. We look at how state and local school superintendents, school board office personnel, school building administrators, teachers, and school support professionals influence teachers' classroom practice and student achievement. Lastly, this chapter considers several structural issues that influence schools' costs and effectiveness.

10.1 THE FEDERAL ROLE IN EDUCATION

The U.S. Constitution defines the federal role in education. The Tenth Amendment to the U.S. Constitution reads,

> The powers not delegated to the United States by the Constitution, nor prohibited by it to the states, are reserved to the states respectively, or to the people.

Because education is not specifically assigned as a federal government responsibility, it becomes a state responsibility administered at the local level. As a result, the United States has 50 different education systems, with each state plus the District of Columbia directing its own.[4]

10.1a Brief History of the U.S. Department of Education

The U.S. Department of Education in Washington, DC, is the primary federal agency responsible for overseeing state spending of federal education dollars. Following the Civil War, President Andrew Johnson established the U.S. Department of Education in 1867 to help strengthen growing federal support for education. A Commissioner of Education received an annual salary of $4,000 to head the department and employed three clerks to assist at annual salaries ranging from $1,600 to $2,000.[5]

Poor management forced the first education commissioner to resign, however. Two years later, the Office of Education was transferred to the U.S. Department of the Interior and became the Bureau of Education. The Bureau focused on collecting information on schools and teaching to help states establish effective education systems.

In 1953, the U.S. Bureau of Education merged with other offices to become the Department of Health, Education, and Welfare (HEW). In 1979, President Jimmy Carter established the cabinet-level Department of Education, elevating its importance and influence.

In fiscal year 2019, the Department of Education Budget was $71.5 billion[6] and employed approximately 4,000 full-time workers[7] in addition to several thousand contractors. Although this is a large operation, the federal share accounts for only 8.3% of the nation's total education budget and represents less than 3% of the total federal budget.[8] The state and local levels contribute the remaining 92% of education dollars—47.0% and 44.8%, respectively.[9]

The federal government has traditionally had little jurisdiction over state and local education policies or practices. The U.S. Constitution and federal legislation limit the federal role in education to three areas:

- Providing funding approved by Congress and monitoring states' compliance in using those funds
- Ensuring state and local compliance with federal laws
- Assessing student achievement at the national level

10.1b The Legislative Branch

Through its legislative branch, the U.S. Congress, the federal government provides congressionally approved funding and monitors its use. Using categorical and competitive grants, the U.S. Congress sends states and schools federal dollars to help them accomplish their educational mission. Serving as incentives and resources, these federal monies tend to direct state and local educational efforts toward outcomes that the U.S. Congress, states, and localities deem as serving their best interests.

Using a complex system of funding mechanisms, policy directives, and the soft power of the President's and Education Secretary's "bully pulpit," the federal role in shaping public education is limited yet significant, pointing state and local leaders in certain directions. It can identify problems that need nationwide attention. For instance, when the Soviet Union in 1957 launched its *Sputnik* satellite into earth orbit, Americans were shocked and concerned that our Cold War enemies had beaten us in the "space race." In response, the U.S. Congress authorized a massive infusion of federal dollars into public education through the National Defense Education Act (NDEA) of 1958.[10] Congress believed that math and science education were essential to our national security. NDEA also increased spending for foreign language learning, technology, and other "critical" subjects. These new monies came with strings attached, however: To receive the funds, states and localities had to agree to spend the dollars in compliance with the grants' terms. Federal spending audits in local school districts soon became commonplace.

Federal legislation can also propose solutions to continuing challenges. Congress passed the original 1965 Elementary and Secondary Education Act (ESEA) to provide federal funding to support equal access, high standards, and accountability for public schools. Usually reauthorized every 5 years, its 2001 version, No Child Left Behind (NCLB), required each state to develop its own achievement standards and tests for language arts, mathematics, and science. Its 2015 reauthorization, the Every Student Succeeds Act (ESSA), continues its state-based achievement testing requirement.

ESEA and its later reauthorizations also offers states funding for education programs—such as Title I for low-income students, Title VI for students with disabilities, and Title VII for bilingual education—conditioned on the states agreeing to meet the requirements specified. In a "incentives-with caveats" approach, states receive these monies but may lose them if they do not live up to the agreed terms.[11] The federal influence over student testing across the country clearly shows how states are willing to comply with extensive federal rules for student achievement testing to secure more federal education dollars.

Federal oversight of preK–12 public education varies with the political climate. With No Child Left Behind's (2001) rigorous testing requirements, the federal oversight became intrusive. With Every Student Succeeds Act (2015), the federal control was reduced. In either case, the federal role has always tried to influence state and local decision-making about how to educate its children. By comparison, the federal government does not get involved in the basic functions of teaching and learning, and funds are not generally tied to specific mandates concerning school and classroom practices.[12] Exceptions to this "hands-off" approach come when addressing specific protected classes and disadvantaged populations.

Clearly, the federal government's role in preK–12 education continues to evolve, along with changes in society and education's growing importance in it. In these ways, federal dollars reach local classrooms.

AMERICAN EDUCATION SPOTLIGHT: FREDERICK "RICK" HESS

Frederick "Rick" Hess, a highly respected education reformer, believes that American schools can and should do better. The resident scholar and director of education policies studies at the American Enterprise Institute (AEI), a conservative public policy think tank, Hess's books and articles on K–12 and higher-education issues challenge conventional thought. Considered an "honest broker," people across the political spectrum pay attention.

Hess believes that meaningful educational change must occur at the local level and involve a range of key stakeholders. As he sees it, our schools and school systems are not built for what we are asking them to do today. But reimagining our schools requires big policy changes. And while policy can be the "blunt tool" to make people do things, it cannot make them do them well. As Hess sees it, we need to care about *how* things are done, not simply *whether* or not they are done. In reality, the work that makes the most positive differences for teaching and learning are always what educators, parents, and entrepreneurs are doing locally.

In Hess's view, education reform as practiced in the United States has "an insularity, a tendency to talk only to those who agree with us, a surety that we have the 'right' answers to big educational questions... and a conviction that things that go wrong are 'mere implementation problems.'"* He asserts that education reformers need to speak with people on both sides of the "Left–Right" political divides. He continues, "Expressing mainstream conservative concerns about federal overreach or the problem with race-based policy can be enough to get you called a clueless reactionary."* Progressive views (that design policies on structural issues such as race, class, and gender) and conservative views (that focus policies on individual responsibility) on education are not mutually exclusive. Both perspectives are important parts of the solution. Education can create the opportunities that give all children a more equitable start to equip them for successful lives and responsible citizenship. Political disagreements occur over how to do this.

And while impassioned reformers want to improve education, passion can make people "true believers" with little room for uncertainty, prompting them to "redouble rather than rethink" their efforts. He asserts that education reformers make a huge mistake when they mock and dismiss criticisms rather than answer them. In every field, "reformers need to pursue their passion with the professional discipline to match. [A] marine sergeant shouldn't be so gung-ho that he needlessly exposes his unit to danger." That holds for school reformers as well.

Although Hess endorses school and educator accountability for educating every child, he sees parent responsibility as an essential component of children's school success. "Education is always a handshake between families and teachers, between students and schools.... Part of a teacher's job is finding a way to open a student's heart and mind, and the job of parents and guardians is to raise children who are responsible, respectful, and ready to learn.... Everyone needs to step up."*

Starting his career as a high school social studies teacher in Baton Rouge, Louisiana, gaining firsthand classroom experience that was alternately "thrilling and unbearably frustrating," he quit.** Reflecting on that time, he observes, "From a personal level, the thing that struck me was how fundamental the act of learning and teaching is, and how natural it should be for learning to be an exciting, engaging activity.... [But] we've made it really hard for teachers and kids to have that kind of joyous, wondrous, liberating experience in a lot of schools and classrooms. And that pisses me off."** Today, Hess teaches (or has taught) at the University of Virginia, the University of Pennsylvania, Georgetown University, and Harvard University and has authored 13 books exploring various aspects of education reform.

Notes: *Shaughnessy, M. F. (2017, May 2). Interview—Rick Hess: Letters to a young education reformer. *Enterprise Instituted.* http://www.aei.org/publication/interview-rick-hess-letters-to-a-young-education-reformer/
**Unger, M. (2015). Hess, straight up. *Ed. Harvard Ed. Magazine.* https://www.gse.harvard.edu/news/ed/15/05/hess-straight

Source: Hess, F. M. (2019). Bio. *American Enterprise Institute.* https://www.aei.org/scholar/frederick-m-hess/

10.1c The Judicial Branch

A second area of federal education involvement, the judicial branch of the U.S. government, ensures that states comply with all federal laws and regulations. Sometimes, this requires the U.S. Supreme Court to clarify the law. *Griffin v. County School Board of Prince Edward County* and *Plyler v. Doe* offer two cases in point.

Griffin v. County School Board of Prince Edward County

In *Griffin v. County School Board of Prince Edward County* (1964), the Supreme Court ruled as unconstitutional a state's practice of closing some of its public schools and contributing instead to the support of private, segregated schools.[13]

On April 23, 1951, 16-year-old Barbara Johns, a student in Prince Edward County, Virginia, led the 450 students at all–African American Robert R. Moton High School out of their classes in a 2-week protest against the school's deplorable building conditions. Constructed in 1939 and designed to house 180 students, their school was massively overcrowded. Rather than build a new African American high school, the Prince Edward County school board erected three large plywood buildings covered with tar-paper to accommodate the overcrowding. Some classes were also held on an old school bus. Protesting these grossly unequal facilities and demanding a new high school, Jones contacted the National Association for the Advancement of Colored People (NAACP) for legal assistance. The students filed suit, alleging that they had been denied enrollment into public schools attended by white children and charged that Virginia's segregation laws denied equal protection of the Fourteenth Amendment.[14] In 1954, the Prince Edward group was one of the plaintiffs in the landmark U.S. Supreme Court's *Brown v. Board of Education* decision, which ruled that the state's segregation laws were unconstitutional because they denied African American students equal protection.

But through a series of political and legal maneuvers, Virginia and Prince Edward County did not desegregate their public schools. The Virginia General Assembly enacted legislation to close and cut off state funds to any public schools where "white and colored children" were enrolled together. When the Fourth Circuit Court of Appeals invalidated these laws in 1959, the Virginia General Assembly turned to a "freedom of choice" program, repealed compulsory attendance laws, and made school attendance a matter of local option. The vast majority of the county's 1,700 African American students and some white students received no formal education for 5 years, from 1959 to 1964.[15] In 1964, the U.S. Supreme Court ruled in *Griffin v. Prince Edward* that local authorities had to fund public education and reopen the schools to all students. The Court required that Prince Edward County enforce the nation's laws.

Plyler v. Doe[16]

Other education cases have gone to the U.S. Supreme Court to determine if states were correctly complying with federal laws. *Plyler v. Doe* involved the allocation of millions of dollars by the Texas state legislature to educate children of undocumented immigrants. At the time of the court case, Texas was educating an estimated 50,000 school-aged children of undocumented immigrants at an annual cost of approximately $100 million.[17]

The Texas legislature argued that because these children were in the country illegally, taxpayers should not have to finance illegal activity—that is, schooling the children. Subsequently, in 1975 the Texas legislature revised its laws to withhold state education funds from school districts that enrolled children who were not legally admitted into the United States. The law also allowed local school districts to deny enrollment to these children. Although the local school districts could accept these students if they wished, they would not receive state funding to educate them. When opponents of this policy brought suit, the Texas Supreme Court agreed with the legislature's position.

Ultimately, the U.S. Supreme Court decided the case, as in *Brown v. Board of Education*, based on the Fourteenth Amendment: "No State shall... deprive any person of life, liberty, or property without due process of law; *nor deny to any person within its jurisdiction* the equal protection of the laws." According to the Supreme Court justices, any "person" did not mean any "citizen." Although undocumented immigrants are not citizens, they are persons who cannot be deprived of equal protection under the law requiring compulsory school attendance.

Rowley and *Endrew* Special Education Cases

Although Congress can set education policy, judicial rulings can redefine what qualifies as policy implementation. As discussed in Chapter 9, the U.S. Supreme Court's ruling in *Endrew F. v. Douglas County School District RE-1* (2017)[18] interpreted the Individual With Disabilities Act (IDEA) as requiring school districts to provide an educational program "appropriately ambitious in light of [the child's] circumstances" for students with disabilities. This 2017 ruling raised the educational standard from the minimum educational benefit of a "basic floor of opportunity" as ruled in *Board of Education of the Hendrick Hudson Central School District v. Rowley* (1982).[19]

10.1d Student Assessment at the National Level

National assessment of students' academic progress represents the third area of federal involvement in education.[20] Until the 1960s, states generally educated their children as they saw fit—without regard to what other states were doing. Even if educators were curious about how well their students were achieving as compared to students in neighboring states, contrasting K–12 student achievement on a state-by-state basis was impractical, untraditional, and largely irrelevant. Because prior to the 1960s, students tended to leave school and find local employment, these individuals would have competed for jobs only with locally educated students. Competing with better-educated students from another state was not a realistic concern, so no nationwide assessment was needed.

National Assessment of Educational Progress (NAEP)

In the 1960s, this situation changed when the Kennedy administration focused government accountability on student assessment. As expected, states and various educational agencies were actively suspicious of the federal government's plan to hold states responsible for their students' educational attainment. To reduce states' misgivings about the potential for federal interference in state and local education, the Education Commission of the States (ECS) received the authority to design and conduct a national assessment.[21] Federal monies and the Carnegie Corporation would fund the project. In 1969, ECS received U.S. Office of Education assurances that it would give funds but not interfere with state policy or analysis. That compromise was sufficient for most states to allow federal involvement in collecting and monitoring their student achievement data.

Today, the federal Department of Education oversees the NAEP, also known as "the nation's report card." The NAEP data show regional, state, and national student achievement trends in the arts, civics, economics, foreign language, geography, math, reading, science, U.S. history, world history, and writing. Each state chooses a sample of students at identified grade levels in selected schools to take the NAEP tests.

10.2 THE STATE PLAYERS IN EDUCATION POLICY AND PRACTICE

Constitutionally, U.S. education is controlled at the state level. Table 10.1 shows how most states organize to administer the education function, noting the number of districts and average number of students per district in each state.

Every state has a legislative system similar to the federal government's three branches—executive, legislative, and judicial. Each state has a governor, a two-chambered legislature (except for Nebraska, which has a single chamber), a supreme court, and agencies that are funded by and report to the legislature. When we elect people to represent us in the legislative process, they pass many laws each year that directly affect education. For example, many years ago, Hawaiian legislators decided that they should have only one school district run by the state. As a result, Hawaii has no local school districts.

California's Proposition 13 provides another example of how voters can give the state a significant role in shaping schools. In what some call a "primal scream from angry voters,"[22] California taxpayers in 1978 chose to limit their local property tax rates. "Prop 13" resulted in hundreds of billions of dollars in lost revenues and chronic underfunding of schools, which, on average, lost half their local funding. Overall, school revenues decreased by as much as 15% in wealthy districts and by 9% in lower-income districts.[23] In short, Prop 13 shifted the fiscal control of California's public schools from local communities to the state with a decidedly negative impact on the state's education system.

We elect governors to become the state's CEO and choose representatives to the state legislature. Some want to lower taxes. Others want to increase public services. In recent years, state legislators have acted on many educational issues, including deciding the means by which the state will fund its schools, whether or not to permit charter schools and taxpayer-funded vouchers to attend private schools, teacher licensure laws, school curricula, testing issues, consolidation of school districts, school accreditation, and teacher retirement contributions and benefits.

10.2a The Public

The public influences education at the state level through the election process. In the United States, our form of government is called a democratic republic. With this system, we elect people to represent us and to make laws and enact policies that govern us. The Tenth Amendment to the U.S. Constitution makes education a state function. Therefore, each of the 50 states has its own constitution that details how the state will govern its education. By voting for governors and representatives to the state legislature who hold certain beliefs about education, the public elects officials to enact their preferences about the type of education their state will have.

For example, consider this scenario. During a governor's race, one charismatic candidate tells voters that, if elected, she promises not to cut education's general revenue or to raise taxes. Impressing a majority of voters with this pledge, the candidate wins the election. After she takes office, however, the governor's first 2-year state budget cuts more than $3 billion for education from preK–20, more than half of that ($1.8 billion) from kindergarten through 12th grade. In fact, the proposed budget would decrease per-student spending by 10%! To help offset the funding cuts, the governor asks teachers to put 5% of their salaries into their pensions, giving them less take-home pay. At the same time, the governor proposes cutting $1.5 billion from property taxes, meaning less money to support public schools. Needless to say, voters were shocked and dismayed when the governor not only trashed her election promises but did just the opposite. The lesson of this story: Voters in every state need to thoroughly "vet" their candidates for public office about their plans for public education, electing those with an unblemished record and reputation for integrity and who vow to fund and enact policies in accord with what voters view as the long-term public interest, Regardless of who is elected, once the public has voted, much of the funding and legislation for education come from the state legislature.

FIGURE 10.1 ■ Organizational Governance Flow Chart at the State Level

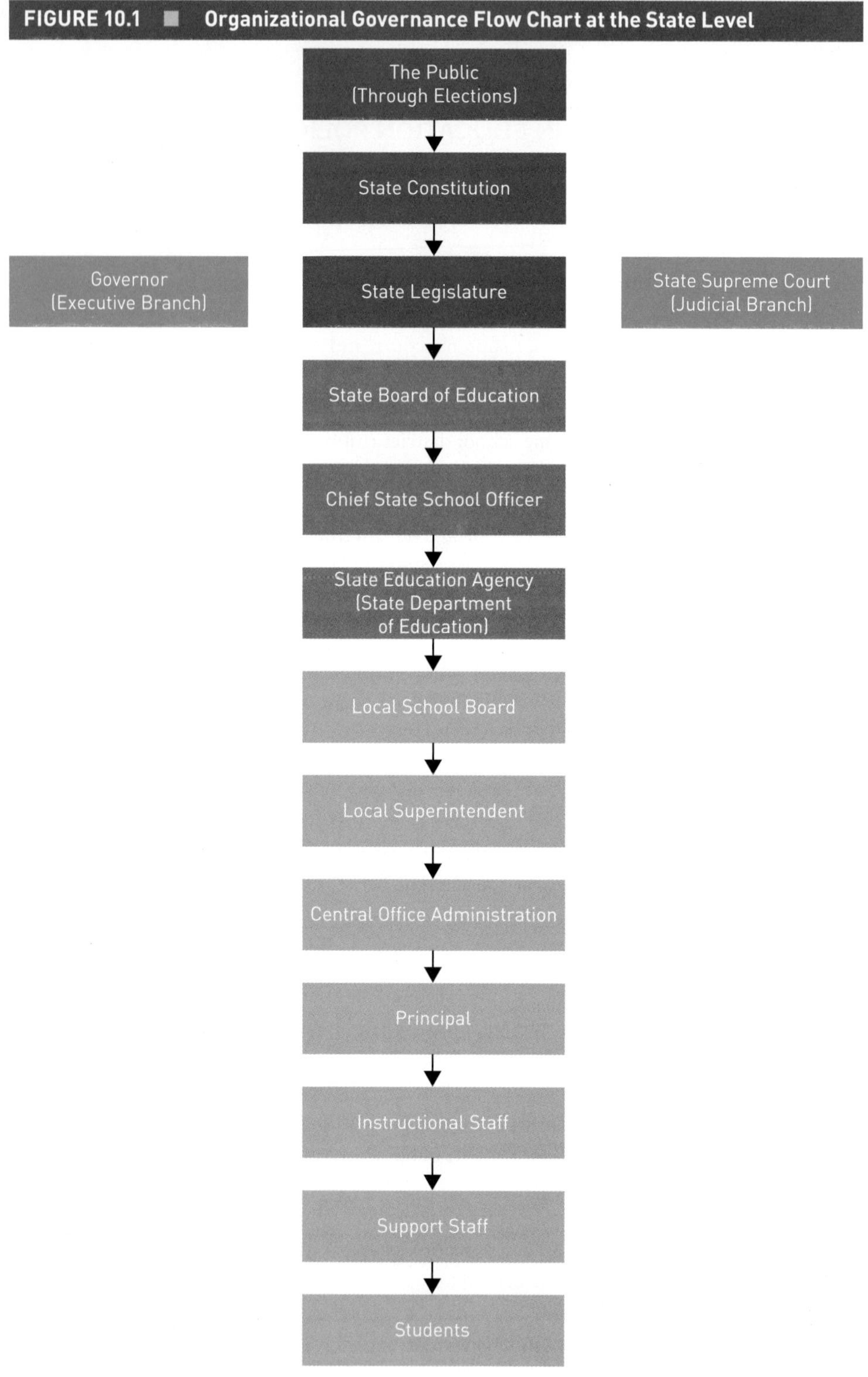

Source: Leslie S. Kaplan and William A. Owings [Original by authors].

10.2b The State Legislature

The legislature's education role varies from state to state, depending on the state constitution's wording. Basically, all state legislatures provide the laws and framework for how the state education system will function. State laws control how the state organizes and operates its department of education. State laws frame the procedures that localities must use to elect or appoint their school board members. State laws control how districts structure their superintendents' contracts, define their role in overseeing the school district, decide the length of the school day and the school year, and set curriculum parameters, testing programs, licensure regulations, and other matters.

Most frequently, the state legislature decides how the state will fund its schools. The legislature is responsible for establishing, maintaining, regulating, and determining the school funding formula. Virtually every state (and commonwealth) requires a formula to equalize state funding between affluent and poor communities. To do this, the state legislature establishes a basic floor level of education services that each locality must offer. Wealthier communities can afford to spend more on education than can poorer ones. Through its funding formula, the state finances more of the education costs for poorer areas and gives less state financial assistance to the wealthier ones. This more or less equalizes school funding throughout the states.[24]

Table 10.1 shows how the sizes of school districts and the number of pupils per district vary across the states. The state legislature makes these decisions. For example, Florida has, on average, more than 42,000 students per district; by comparison, North Dakota has, on average, slightly more than 600 students per district. Obviously, population density has a role in deciding size as legislators make the final decisions.

TABLE 10.1 ■ Number of School Districts in Each State, 2016–2017

State	Number of Students Fall 2016	Number of Districts Fall 2016	Average Number of Pupils per District
U.S. Total	50,615,189	13,598	3,722
Alabama	744,930	134	5,559
Alaska	132,737	53	2,504
Arizona	1,123,137	226	4,969
Arkansas	493,447	234	2,108
California	6,309,138	1,057	5,968
Colorado	905,019	178	5,084
Connecticut	535,118	169	3,166
Delaware	136,264	19	71,71
District of Columbia	85,850	1	85,850
Florida	2,816,791	67	42,041
Georgia	1,764,346	180	9,801
Hawaii	181,550	1	181,550
Idaho	297.200	115	2,584
Illinois	2,026,718	854	2,373
Indiana	1,049,547	294	3,569
Iowa	509.831	333	1,531
Kansas	494.347	307	1,610
Kentucky	684,017	173	3,953
Louisiana	716,293	69	10,381
Maine	180,512	249	724
Maryland	886,221	24	36,925
Massachusetts	964,514	326	2,958

(Continued)

TABLE 10.1 ■ Number of School Districts in Each State, 2016–2017 (*Continued*)

State	Number of Students Fall 2016	Number of Districts Fall 2016	Average Number of Pupils per District
Michigan	1,528,666	540	2,830
Minnesota	875,021	332	2,635
Mississippi	483,150	144	3,355
Missouri	915,040	518	1,766
Montana	146,375	401	365
Nebraska	319,194	245	1,302
Nevada	473,744	18	26,319
New Hampshire	180,888	180	1,004
New Jersey	1,410,421	565	2,496
New Mexico	336,263	89	3,778
New York	2,729,776	689	3,961
North Carolina	1,550,062	115	13,478
North Dakota	109,706	178	616
Ohio	1,710,143	620	2,758
Oklahoma	693,903	513	1,352
Oregon	606,277	179	3,387
Pennsylvania	1,727,497	500	3,454
Rhode Island	142,150	32	4,442
South Carolina	771,250	84	9,181
South Dakota	136,302	150	908
Tennessee	1,001,562	146	6,860
Texas	5,360,849	1,025	5,230
Utah	659,801	41	16,092
Vermont	88,428	278	318
Virginia	1,287,026	130	9,900
Washington	1,101,711	299	3,684
West Virginia	273,855	55	4,979
Wisconsin	864,432	421	2,053
Wyoming	94,170	48	1,961

Source: Snyder, T. D., de Brey, C., and Dillow, S. A. (2019). Number of public elementary and secondary education agencies, by type of agency and state or jurisdiction, 2015–2016 and 2016–2017. Tables 213.50, p. 117; 214.30, p. 120. *Digest of Education Statistics 2018* (NCES 2020-009). https://nces.ed.gov/pubs2020/2020009.pdf

10.2c The Governor

Governors generally serve a 4-year term.[25] At the state level, they fulfill much the same function as a company's CEO. The governor's role is usually defined in the state's statutes or constitution. In general, governors' roles appear to be increasing in power as they assume greater responsibilities.

The governor's authority affects many areas of policy making. The governor can propose and veto legislation, veto appropriations, and set general policies and regulations that apply to all aspects of state government. The governor can make budget recommendations to the legislature. In addition, the governor influences educational policies through his or her appointment authority—that is, the ability to name individuals to head state agencies, boards, and commissions to oversee the state's operations. These appointments affect education at all levels—preschool through college. The governor also exerts influence through the governor's office staffing for the liaison with education and through the governor's implementing federal laws and aid.

Perhaps the governor's most important education appointments (unless the position is elected) are the chief state school officer and the state board of education members. By enacting their agendas in personnel and policy choices, governors exercise powerful sway on directions given to the public schools.

10.2d The State Supreme Court

The state court system plays an important part in determining how public schools operate. Most state judicial systems consist of three levels similar to the federal system: a court of original jurisdiction, an intermediate appellate court, and a court of last resort. Although these courts have different names in different states, the state's highest court is usually called the state supreme court.

The state supreme court is rarely involved in education issues, but when these judges are, their decisions are usually vital to the schools. Generally, the state supreme court rules on whether the legislature's laws are consistent with the state's constitution. As the *Plyler v. Doe* case in Texas demonstrates, a state supreme court's decision can have major educational and financial consequences for the state.

10.2e The State Board of Education

The state board of education is the policy-setting agency that oversees and directs the state department of education. Depending on the state, the board's name may vary. It is similar to the local school board's oversight of the local school division, but with far broader impact.

All states have a state board of education.[26] In most states, governors appoint members to this board. In some states, the state legislature appoints members; in other states, the general public elects state board members. Still other states use a hybrid model combining election and appointment to the state board of education. Each state's constitution and laws define how the board operates. Some state boards hire and fire the chief state school officer; in other states, the governor appoints the chief state school officer; and in a few states, the public elects the chief state school officer. In many states, state board of education regulations have the effect of law.

State boards of education create policies in a variety of ways and for an array of reasons. Most often, these policies are intended to respond to state educational issues, needs, or perceived educational crises. These issues come to the board's attention through study sessions on topics that affect schools and students, from items brought forward by state and national trends and events, and from federal and state legislation.

State boards of education and state legislatures frequently share responsibility for making educational policy. Students' interests are best served when these bodies work together collaboratively to improve teaching and learning in schools. In recent years, however, increased executive and legislative interest in education policy has blurred the lines of responsibility. Establishing a strong relationship between key members of the state board, the governor's office, and the state legislature is essential to enhance communications and share responsibilities.

Although legislators introduce education policy initiatives with the best intentions, these initiatives often arrive at the state board without a comprehensive examination of existing policies addressing the issue or assessing those policies' effectiveness. State legislatures sometimes pass legislation in concept form while leaving the specific details of how that concept should be implemented for the state board to define. Because membership changes in legislatures and the governor's office, and state boards of education affect institutional memory and policy records, multiple and occasionally conflicting practices designed to address the same concern may result. Consequently, maintaining records to ensure continuity and accountability is a major board concern.[27]

10.2f The Chief State School Officer

Each state has a chief state school officer. This position goes by different names, depending on the state: superintendent of public instruction, commissioner of education, or state superintendent. It is also filled in a variety of ways. In some states, the governor appoints this person to carry out the governor's educational agenda. In others, the public elects this person directly. In still others, the state board of education appoints the individual. Alternatively, the governor may appoint the state board of education, which in turn appoints the state superintendent. The precise selection process employed often influences the way the chief officer enacts the role.

Although the chief state school officer's duties vary from state to state depending on the state's constitution, this person typically serves as the state department of education's chief administrator. As such, the chief state school officer recommends improvements to the state department of education, works with the governor in the state budgeting process, advises the state legislature on education issues, and ensures public schools' compliance with state regulations and statutes. He or she reports on the "state of education" within the state to the governor, the state legislature, and the public. Additionally, this official works with the department of education's licensure office to make recommendations regarding changes in licensure for educators.

10.2g The State Department of Education

Teachers generally do not have many dealings with the governor, the state legislature, the state supreme court, the state board of education, or the chief state school officer. Teachers do, however, deal with the state department of education, also known as the state education agency (SEA), mainly when they apply for or renew their professional teaching licenses. The chief state school officer heads this agency, which is usually located in the state capital. The state department of education makes policy and program recommendations to the state board of education. It also constructs the guidelines (more general) and regulations (quite specific) that translate education-related laws passed by the legislature into workable practices for the public schools.

Additionally, the state department of education ensures that the state is complying with the federal Department of Education's rules on federally funded programs. In the past, SEAs had provided curriculum and instruction assistance to schools. Since the early 1990s, however, budget cutbacks have reduced the number of SEA educators offering technical assistance to local schools. Nonetheless, SEAs continue to make certain that the local school districts are following exactly—that they are in compliance with—state and federal regulations regarding state testing, licensure regulations, and federal grants.

To explore more deeply how the federal and state laws, the Supreme Court, and other governance factors can influence public education, complete the activity in the **Reflect & Engage** box, Federal and State Education—Governance of Education.

REFLECT & ENGAGE: FEDERAL AND STATE EDUCATION—GOVERNANCE OF EDUCATION

This activity will involve creating graphic images using a digital tool such as Vizzlo and a debate. The federal, state, and local governments all impact education at your neighborhood school, directly or indirectly. How much influence should each government body have?

A. Working in groups of four, create a graphic image that depicts how each government level influences education. Consider factors such as Supreme Court cases; federal and state laws; accountability for student achievement; national assessments; school funding for facilities, teacher salaries and benefits, school resources; competitive federal grants; state and local government officials; state and local boards of education; and elections. Use images and words, sizes and colors to depict their relative importance.

B. Each small group selects one of two positions: (1) the federal government should be *more* involved in public education (and in what ways) or (2) the federal government should *not* be more involved in public education (and in what areas). Each group will prepare key arguments to debate their side of the issue. You may use graphic images as visual aids.

C. Each group presents their arguments and tries to persuade the other side of their case's merits. This can be informal, with one group making opening statements and the others adding points as needed and as recognized by the chair.

D. As a class, discuss how federal and state involvement with local education can be a benefit or a liability when it comes to educating all students to high levels and respecting teachers (in tangible ways) for the professionals they are.

10.3 THE LOCAL LEADERS WHO SHAPE EDUCATION POLICY AND PRACTICE

Education is a state function that draws federal interest and is administered locally. Most states allow localities to administer the community's schools in accordance with state law, to elect or appoint a local school board to set education policy, to hire and retain high-quality educators as superintendents, principals, teachers, and support staff, and to ensure that all students achieve to state standards.

This section discusses the role of the local school board, the local superintendent, the central office, the principal, teacher, and various educational support personnel—the positions and individuals with whom teachers are most closely involved.

10.3a The Local School Board

Local school boards play a critical part in preparing our children to be productive citizens and strengthen our communities. They aim to mirror the diverse communities they represent. All school boards derive their power and authority from the state. At the same time, all school boards generate their own "laws" by establishing the policies that govern their local schools. School boards everywhere are their communities' primary and—if state law permits—supreme educational authority.

Within every state except Hawaii, the local school board, as the local administrative unit, is responsible for implementing the state's policies and regulations.[28] The state's power over the local school board depends on the state's constitution. In some states, it is possible for the state to "take over" local school operations. In such instances, the state would assume direct management responsibility for running the schools—from hiring and firing personnel to designing the curriculum. In other states, this type of "takeover" of local schools is not constitutionally possible.

School district superintendents inform and advise their school boards.

iStock/fizkes

School district residents typically elect their local boards of education, but mayors or other executives of jurisdictions (such as cities or counties that encompass the school district) may appoint them. Through the election process, the community has the ability to change their representatives on the board and find people whose views more closely match their own. Whether school districts have elected or appointed boards often has more to do with local history than with any particular philosophical stand. When the current form of the school board was introduced in the early 1900s, municipalities that were incorporated as cities had appointed boards and all others had elected ones.

The local school district's power varies from state to state—again depending on the state constitution's wording. In some states, the local school board has the power to relieve the superintendent of his or her position and, if necessary, to change school policies.[29]

Likewise, the local school board's authority to request funding varies from state to state. Some local school boards have taxing authority to fund the school's operation. Others recommend funding levels, which the public must then formally approve. Still others make budget recommendations to the governing authority (a city council or board of supervisors, for example), which may or may not approve them.

Perhaps the local school boards' major responsibility is to hire the best superintendent of schools they can find. Additional responsibilities include approving the local school budget and establishing school district policies. According to the National School Boards Association, a school board should be responsible for eight key areas described in Table 10.2.[30]

As school board members make policy decisions, they try to pay attention to how these eight areas interact. When board members work together collaboratively and effectively, these eight components can optimize a local school board's ability to make positive and lasting school district improvements.

Most school board members are laypeople who volunteer their time or receive a modest stipend to meet once or twice a month to work for their local school system. Because board members often lack expertise in many education-related areas, many school boards tend to base their decisions on experts' (usually the superintendent's) recommendations and advice. Unfortunately, sometimes school board members overstep their responsibilities and try to micromanage the school system. For instance, a school board member cannot request a school bus route be changed to accommodate one of the ladies in her book group. This type of involvement can lead to problems in role definition with the superintendent and may distract the school board from its primary purposes. But as a result of the federal government's increased involvement in school affairs, relevant court decisions, and special-interest

TABLE 10.2 ■ Eight Characteristics of Effective School Boards

	Effective School Boards...
1	Set a vision of high expectations for student achievement and quality instruction for the district.
2	Have strong shared beliefs and values about what is possible for students and their ability to learn and of the system and its ability to teach all children at high levels.
3	Practice accountability; spend less time on operational issues and more time on policies to improve student achievement.
4	Establish strong, collaborative relationships with staff and the community; create strong communications structures to inform and engage internal and external stakeholder in setting and achieving district goals.
5	Use data-savvy members to embrace and monitor data, using negative information to drive continuous improvement.
6	Align and sustain resources, such as professional development, to meet district goals.
7	Lead as a united team with the superintendent, each from their respective roles, with strong collaboration and mutual trust.
8	Participate in team development and training, sometimes with their superintendents, to build shared knowledge, values, and commitments for their improvement.

Source: Adapted from Dervarics and O'Brien, 2011.

groups' actions, the local school board's once-considerable authority in curriculum policy has slowly diminished.

Pressure is on school boards to close achievement/opportunity gaps, increase high school graduation rates, and prepare more students for college and careers. In years past, unprecedented amounts of federal dollars have flowed to schools to achieve these goals. Some argue, however, that if mayors and political leaders are being held accountable for schools' academic, fiscal, or management failures, they may need deeper involvement with education issues. Accordingly, recent years have seen a mayoral takeover of some chronically low-performing, high-profile urban schools when school boards could not provide the leadership to overcome educational challenges. **FlipSides** presents the arguments on both sides for you to consider.

FLIPSIDES

Do School Boards Matter?

School governance needs to be effective, efficient, and accountable. But do local school boards have the capacity to provide a 21st century educational leadership? Or are they outmoded obstacles to education reform that should be replaced by local government control? What do you think?

Local school boards matter. Local citizens elected or appointed to school boards should run public schools.	Local school boards do not matter. Local government—the mayor, county manager, or state legislature—should run the public schools.
• For generations, the public has believed that local residents who are not education experts are qualified to set policy, to govern the schools, and to represent the local community values in public education.	• Local school boards don't have the know-how to deal with today's complex fiscal, legal, and academic achievement issues. They may micromanage or interfere with the superintendent's role or act a rubber stamp.
• The local school board has the sole responsibility and accountability for providing a high-quality education to the community's children. In contrast, mayors and states have many other responsibilities and priorities that compete with schools for attention and resources.	• Local school board members focus narrowly on education and may not be aware of the larger community's issues and needs. In contrast, mayoral or state governance of schools would have a larger, more comprehensive view of issues and needs.
• Local school board members are accessible to the parents and the community to discuss a problem in their neighborhood. They live in the communities they serve.	• Although mayors and state agents may not live or work in every neighborhood they serve, they can be contacted easily by social media, email, text, or phone and are highly responsive to voters' concerns.
• Voting for school board members is democracy in action. Often, elected board members represent different neighborhoods, bringing the entire community together to decide policies and practices for their schools.	• Only 10% to 15% of the electorate, on average, vote in school board elections. More voters cast ballots for mayors than for school board members.
• Local school board members can energize their community to action by articulating the community's needs to the schools and the schools' needs to the community.	• Mayors and state agents have a larger forum by which to communicate a community's and school's needs to the public and gain support.
• Local school boards have transparency, hold open meetings, have citizen input, debate issues, and have their records audited—unlike mayors and other politicians who often work behind closed doors or make decisions via executive fiat.	• Mayors and other political figures have staff persons who can gather necessary information about schools and communities necessary to make informed decisions—much of which can be made available publicly.

Local school boards matter. Local citizens elected or appointed to school boards should run public schools.	Local school boards do not matter. Local government—the mayor, county manager, or state legislature—should run the public schools.
• Data show mixed results for the effectiveness of state or mayoral school district governance and management. • When school governance is not local, education becomes less visible and loses public support. • State officials and mayors may grant contracts for education-related services in return for campaign contributions.	• Ideally, mayoral or state control of education would increase interagency collaboration between schools and health and social service organizations, business and civic groups, and wide coalitions of interest.
• Meaningful and sustainable education reform must occur from the inside, and it must have active local involvement from knowledgeable board members with influence over both educators and the local community.	• When change is imposed from the outside, those who assume control of a school or school system generally have greater flexibility and power in governance—for instance, in contract negotiations with teacher unions—than those previously in charge.
• School boards are sometimes the only entities that provide continuous institutional leadership through times of change.	• State or mayoral control brings regular personnel changes along with new ideas and solutions to address public school issues.
• Making school boards more effective—by clarifying and limiting their roles and responsibilities; by selecting good members; by educating members in the expectations, knowledge, and skills required of their role; and by improving communications with their communities—would be better for local schools than ending local school boards altogether.	• Many school boards lack the training or capacity to develop productive, positive, and long-term relationships with superintendents, leading to high turnover of urban superintendents. Many members may also lack the skills that would allow them to work together effectively in difficult situations.

After reading both sides of this issue, do you favor strengthening or ending local school boards? What reasons support your conclusion?

Sources: Land, D. (2002, January). Local school boards under review. Their role and effectiveness in relation to students' achievement. *Review of Educational Research, 72*(2), 229–278; Resnick, M., & Bryant, A. L. (2010, March). School boards. Why American education needs them. *Phi Delta Kappan, 91*(6), 11–14; Shober, A. F., & Hartney, M. T. (2014, March 25). *Does school board leadership matter?* Thomas B. Fordham Institute; Usdan, M. D. (2010, March). School boards. A neglected institution in an era of school reform. *Phi Delta Kappan, 91*(6), 8–10.

10.3b The School District Superintendent

The local school board's most important responsibility is to hire an excellent superintendent of schools. The superintendent is the school system's CEO and reports to the school board. He or she is a crucial part of the governance team for the school system and an essential link in the chain connecting the school board to the school system's people, programs, and activities.

Local school superintendents may be either appointed or elected. The Education Commission of the States reports that only Alabama and Mississippi have both elected and appointed local school superintendents. Cities tend to appoint their school superintendents, whereas county school systems tend to use a combination of elected and appointed school chiefs. Hawaii and Vermont have no local superintendents. The remaining 37 states tend to appoint their local superintendents.[31]

By and large, the superintendent oversees the school system's daily operations and advises the school board about policies and actions that need to be taken. The superintendent's specific responsibilities vary according to the school district's size; its location in a rural, suburban, or urban setting; and the superintendent's traditional duties within the organization.

In small, rural areas, the superintendent may be a "jack of all trades": He or she may evaluate all principals and central office staff and conduct professional development programs. In medium-sized suburban districts, two or more assistant superintendents may be available to assist with the work. Large urban and suburban districts may have area superintendents and assistant superintendents who report to the district superintendent, shouldering many of the duties associated with this position.

Superintendent Responsibilities

The school superintendent's work is threefold:

- **Organizing the school system for teaching and learning**. The superintendent must make certain that all students learn and achieve to high academic levels. He or she is responsible for developing and evaluating instructional programs and curriculum. The superintendent also influences curriculum policy by gathering and presenting data and responding to matters before the board of education, initiating programs for staff development, making district personnel aware of changes occurring in the schools, and moderating outside demands for change.
- **Operating the school system efficiently and effectively**. School systems are complex organizations that require not only good leaders but also good managers. For example, the superintendent must develop and oversee the school district's budget and consider federal and state requirements when developing the courses that the school system offers. Similarly, the superintendent is answerable for ensuring the efficacy of the school district's organization.
- **Maintaining good communication and relations with the school board**. The superintendent is the school board's primary advisor. Because the board members are laypeople, they rely on the superintendent and other specialists to give them the details and perspectives necessary to make informed decisions. Frequently, the superintendent serves as the school board's spokesperson in the community. Nonetheless, even when the board delegates many of its own powers to the superintendent and staff, especially in larger districts, the superintendent's policies remain subject to school board approval. In reality, the superintendent works for the school board and is always subject to the board's approval for continued employment in that district.

Some believe that the superintendent has lost much of his or her decision-making authority over curriculum policy in recent years because of the increased federal and state involvement in public education. Powers previously granted to the superintendent have been taken away through the courts and various legislative acts.[32] The role remains extremely important and highly challenging, however.

10.3c The District Central Office

The central office or school board office refers to the educators and support staffs who help the superintendent administer the school system. A typical central office organizational chart may look like Figure 10.2. It takes many people "behind the scenes" to support classroom teachers. Although students appear at the base, the entire pyramid could be turned upside down with the students placed at the top because they are the focus of the entire educational enterprise.

Most teacher candidates rarely think about how the central office personnel work to make their classroom efforts more successful. Teachers need to be recruited, hired, inducted, and developed into increasingly adept professionals. Instructional resources must be purchased, paid for, and inventoried. The achievement testing programs need to be coordinated, administered, interpreted, and analyzed to report on student achievement and schools' accountability and to modify curriculum and instruction. Paychecks need to be processed correctly and delivered on time. Bus transportation routes need to be established and drivers hired, trained, and evaluated. Food needs to be ordered and delivered to the school cafeterias. Food service workers need to be hired, trained, and supervised. Buildings need routine (or extensive) maintenance. The schoolyard grass needs to be cut. Leaking roofs and sputtering heating systems need to be fixed. The school district's budget needs to

FIGURE 10.2 ■ Typical School District Organizational Chart

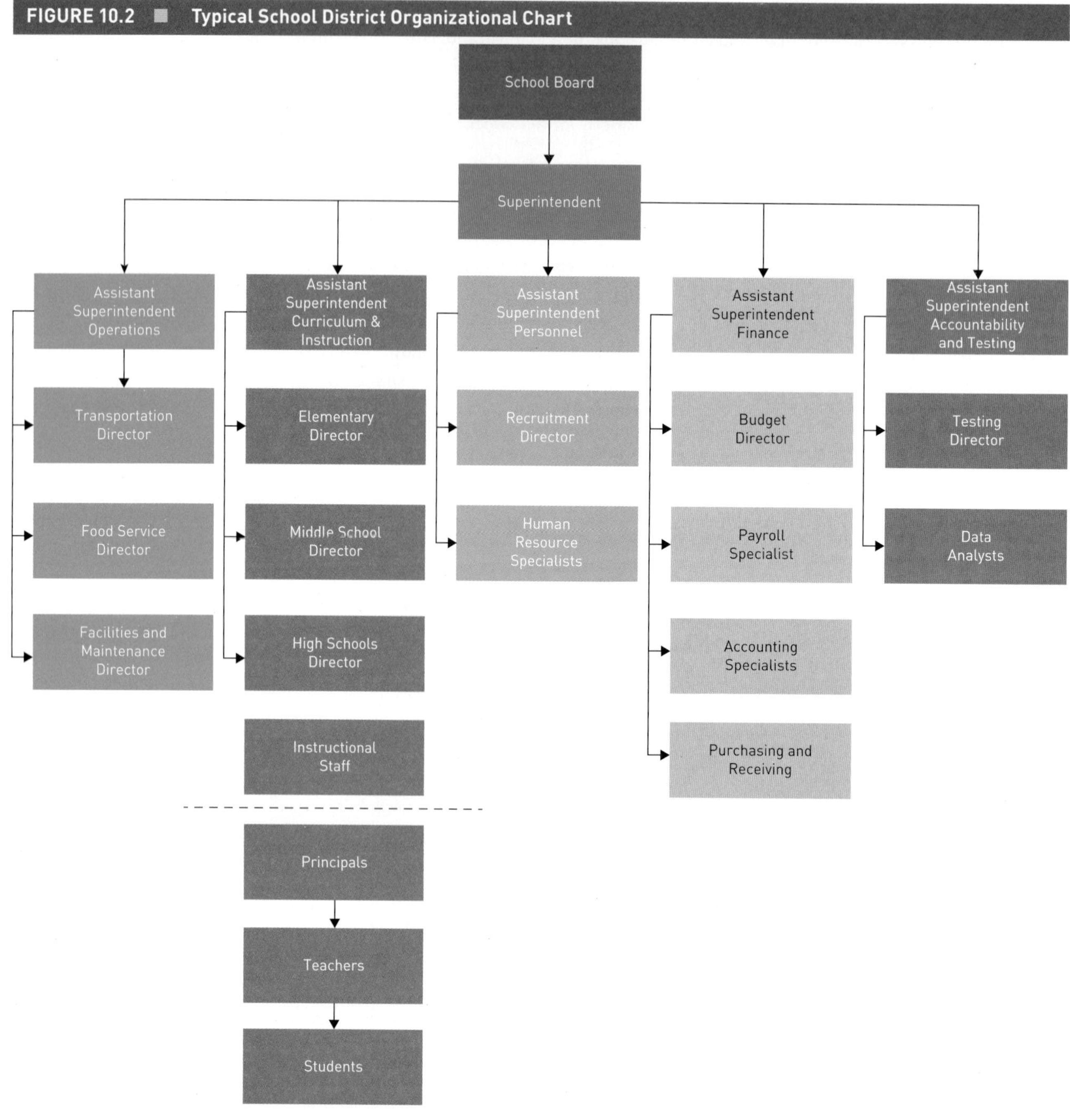

Source: Leslie S. Kaplan and William A. Owings [Original by authors].

be developed and monitored so the school system does not overspend its limits. These functions and many others are coordinated at the central office level, long before most teachers even think about teaching their lessons to students.

Work Responsibilities

Most importantly for teachers, a school district's central office assumes a variety of tasks that foster districtwide improvements in teaching and leadership. Many of these responsibilities focus on helping new teachers successfully adjust to their new role and work setting:[33]

- **Clarifying the district's instructional priorities** and how the school district's employees will meet them

- **Communicating the school district's information** to classroom teachers, parents, and the community
- **Fostering teacher leadership** by giving them opportunities to serve the school district in curriculum development, working on school district committees, and making presentations to illustrate their best programs and techniques at professional conferences
- **Providing service and expertise** to help teachers improve their professional practice, including the following: providing professional development programs to familiarize teachers with best practices for curriculum, instruction, and assessment; conducting the textbook or e-book adoption process; developing programs of studies; coordinating the special education and Title I programs; conducting formal teacher observations; assisting teachers who are having difficulties; and organizing districtwide activities such as science fairs, applying for grant-funded projects, and completing required state and federal reports
- **Ensuring consistency of practice** among district schools by developing common goals, curricula, instructional texts, instructional practices, assessments, teacher training, programs for special populations, resource staff, and much more, so all students have equal and equitable opportunities to learn
- **Orienting new teachers** to the district's culture, expectations, and practices, including helping new teachers learn to hold high expectations and provide high supports for each student's learning; showing them how to recognize and value student diversity; helping them to understand the school district's curriculum; and encouraging them to give (and receive) moral support to other new teachers

When one considers the many functions that schools require to operate smoothly, it becomes clear that the central office operations enable teachers to do their jobs well.

10.3d The Principal

Everyone knows the old spelling adage, "The principal is your pal." Many Americans agree. A 2019 report form the Pew Research left identified K–12 public school principals as the most trusted leaders in our country's most important institutions.[34]

Principals' job descriptions vary from state to state, depending on the laws and regulations. Virginia, for example, has defined the principal's position as the instructional leader of the school. Given the importance of achievement testing conducted since NCLB (2001) and ESSA (2015), most states now consider the principal's primary charges to be establishing a positive educational climate and culture for learning, managing the school's operations, and ensuring that all students learn to state achievement standards.

Teachers and their principals interact frequently. Larger schools have at least one assistant principal to help with these responsibilities, and teachers work repeatedly with these school leaders. Many of these principal–teacher exchanges occur in informal discussions about students, in teacher–parent conferences and faculty meetings, in the halls during class changes, and during the formal teacher observation and evaluation process. Most states require principals or assistant principals to observe and evaluate teachers as they are teaching at least twice a year—and perhaps more often before teachers are officially offered continuing contract status. In addition, many principals informally visit classrooms throughout the year to get a sense of the classroom climate, to speak briefly with students about what they are learning, and to monitor and support the teaching and learning process.

Principals Affect Student Achievement

Over three decades of school effectiveness inquiry concludes that successful schools have dynamic, knowledgeable, and focused principals. Research affirms that principals have an empirical link with improved student achievement.[35] Studies find that school leadership is second only to classroom instruction among all school-related factors as an influence on student learning.[36] Principals create the school conditions under which effective teaching and student learning can occur.

In a 2013 report, the Wallace Foundation identified five interacting key functions of principal leadership:[37]

- **Shaping a vision of academic success for all students**, one based on high standards
- **Creating a climate hospitable to education** in order that safety, a cooperative spirit, and other foundations for fruitful interaction prevail
- **Cultivating leadership in others** so teachers and other adults can participate in realizing the school's vision
- **Improving instruction** to enable teachers to teach at their best and students to learn to their utmost
- **Managing people, data, and processes to foster school improvement**

Effective principals ensure that each of these five tasks interact with the others for any part to succeed. It is difficult to carry out a vision of student success if the school climate is one of student disengagement and frequent classroom interruptions; if the principal doesn't attract, select, and keep outstanding teachers (and find fair, effective ways to improve or remove low-performing teachers); if teachers don't assume leadership for working together to see that every student learns to high standards; if teachers don't continually learn and refine instructional approaches that work best for their students; or if test data are not analysed and used formatively to inform instruction.

An outstanding principal has a measurable but indirect effect on student achievement.

iStock/kali9

Further, a meta-analysis of 30 years of research on the effects of principal practices on student achievement finds a significant, positive correlation between effective school leadership and student achievement. For the average school, having an effective principal can mean the difference between scoring at the 50th or 60th percentile on a given achievement test.[38] Similarly, a 2012 study estimated that highly effective principals raise a typical student's achievement in their school by between 2 and 7 months of learning in a single academic year, whereas ineffective principals lower their students' achievement by that same amount.[39]

In addition to instructional leadership, principals have considerable operations management responsibilities for security, public relations, finances, personnel, transportation, and technology.

Principals' behaviors make a tremendous impact on teachers' work life. In fact, research indicates that a teacher's decision to stay at a school largely depends on the principal's leadership.[40] Conversely, teachers cite a lack of administrators' support and weak or ineffective leadership as contributing factors in the negative working environment that add to teacher dissatisfaction and their decision to leave the profession.[41]

10.3e The Teacher

As discussed in Chapter 1, effective teachers who implement the InTASC standards understand the central concepts, tools of inquiry, and structures of the disciplines that they teach, and they create learning experiences that students can engage in fully and find meaningful. To better facilitate each student's learning, teachers build relationships with pupils so they can better understand the young person as a person and as a learner. Likewise, teachers understand how to link concepts and use varying viewpoints to involve learners in critical thinking, creativity, and collaborative problem-solving related to relevant local and world issues. Teachers also use multiple means of assessment to monitor learner progress, guide instruction, and involve learners in their own growth.

Then, too, teachers are school leaders inside and outside the classroom. They seek appropriate occasions to take responsibility for student learning and to work collaboratively with colleagues, students, families, and community members to foster student growth and advance the profession.

Although the classroom teacher may be the "teacher of record," increasingly she or he has colleagues in the building who will assist in the teaching-for-learning process. We will identify and discuss several critical support professionals next.

10.3f Support Staff

Teachers are not the only educators responsible for student learning. An array of skilled and specialized professionals and paraprofessionals may work with teachers to help make them and their students successful. Not every school has every support role on-site, but most have specialized resource professionals available through the school district.

The support professionals and paraprofessionals with whom teachers are most likely to work include school counselors, special education teachers, school nurses, school psychologists, reading specialists, instructional coaches, teachers' aides, and library media specialists. Each of these roles contributes a unique expertise that can help teachers do their jobs effectively.

10.3g School Counselors

As licensed professionals with a master's degree or higher in school counseling, school counselors are a major part of a school's education team. Focusing on students' academic development, career and college development, and social and emotional development, they are specifically educated to help maximize student achievement in schools. Professional school counselors develop strong rapport and largely confidential relationships with students to help them plan their educational program and resolve or cope with problems and developmental concerns that may interfere with their learning and future education and career planning.

School counselors support teachers' success by helping their students learn the essential behaviors that help them do well in school and life by helping students develop three skill sets that are the most powerful predictors of long-term school success (and seem to separate high achievers from low achievers):[42]

- **Cognitive and metacognitive skills** such as reflection, goal setting, progress monitoring, and memory skills
- **Social abilities** such as interpersonal skills, social problem-solving, listening, and teamwork
- **Self-management skills** such as controlling attention, motivation, and anger

Table 10.3 identifies and describes the programs that school counselors provide to students, parents, school staff, and the community.

TABLE 10.3 ■ School Counselors' Programs

Service	Description
School guidance curriculum	This curriculum consists of structured lessons designed to help all students achieve the knowledge, skills, and competencies appropriate for their cognitive, social, and emotional developmental level. Working collaboratively with K–12 teachers in their classrooms, professional school counselors develop and conduct interactive, comprehensive wellness programs within schools. Occasionally, counselors enact the curriculum with students individually and in small-group activities.
Individual student planning	School counselors coordinate and lead activities designed to help every student establish personal goals and develop future plans, including identifying upcoming courses, further education, work experiences, and eventual careers. Typically, counselors work with the same group of students during their entire time in a particular school so they can build caring, knowledgeable, strong, and trustful relationships with students and their families.
Responsive services	School counselors provide preventive and/or intervention activities to meet students' immediate or future needs—usually consisting of individual or group counseling—that are prompted by events and conditions in students' lives. Counselors may consult with parents, teachers, and other educators and make referrals to school support services or community resources. Additionally, school counselors can use student peer helping and information sharing as tools to prevent or resolve problems that interfere with learning.
System support	School counselors work with everyone in the school on behalf of students and teachers. Before the school year starts, counselors strategize with the school administrators to identify the school's needs and detail how the school counseling program will address them. They frequently partner with teachers to conduct parent conferences.

Developmental guidance and counseling program effectiveness is related directly to the school's counselor-to-student ratio. The number of counselors needed to staff the program depends on the students' and community's needs and on the local program's goals and design. The American School Counselor Association recommends a maximum ratio of 1:250 counselor to students (although the actual national average for 2017–2018 was 1:442).[43] Each state decides the school counselor-to-student ratio for each grade level that it will fund. For instance, Virginia accreditation standards require high

School counselors help students learn the skills they need to succeed in school and in life.

iStock/fstop123

schools to employ one full-time school counselor for every 350 students, one counselor for every 400 students at middle school, and one counselor for every 500 students at elementary school.[44] Depending on the state's requirements, counselors typically spend 60% to 80% of their time in direct service with students.

Research on School Counselors and Student Success

As it is for teachers and principals, accountability, program evaluation, and obtaining data about student outcomes are also counselors' concerns.[45] Research substantiates school counselors' ability to positively influence students through individual and group counseling and classroom guidance, changing their behaviors and increasing their achievement on classroom and standardized tests.[46] Studies find that greater access to school counselors (that is, a reasonable student-to-counselor ratio) is associated with higher graduation rates,[47] fewer disciplinary incidents,[48] and other improved measures of academic, emotional, and social performance.[49] Studies show school counselors can also improve students' college and career readiness.[50] In addition, schools with well-developed guidance and counseling programs have more positive climates.[51] When school counselor interventions target specific skills associated with school success and when they use research-based techniques to teach these critical skills, student outcomes show positive changes in classroom performance.[52]

Professional school counselors engage in continual personal and professional development and are proactively involved in professional organizations promoting school counseling at the local, state, and national levels. School counselors are evaluated regularly. Their principals and central office supervisor usually collaborate in assessing their performance, using basic standards of practice expected of professional school counselors who are implementing a school counseling and guidance program.

10.3h The Special Education Teacher

Today's public school students exhibit a range of disabilities, including specific learning disabilities, speech or language impairments, intellectual disabilities, emotional disturbance, hearing impairments, orthopedic impairments, visual impairments, autism spectrum disorders, combined deafness and blindness, traumatic brain injury, multiple disabilities, and other health impairments. After referrals, classroom interventions, rigorous screenings, and varied evaluations are complete, students may be classified under one of the various special education categories. Figure 10.3 depicts the percentage of students with disabilities in each category.

Because children with disabilities have more complex learning needs than their nondisabled peers, states have developed licensing standards for teachers who work with these students. Special education teachers are highly trained professionals who provide specially designed instruction to children with disabilities. Licensing requires the completion of a teacher training program and at least a bachelor's degree, although many states require a master's degree to qualify for this position.

A small number of special education teachers work with students with intellectual disabilities or autism, primarily teaching them life skills and basic literacy. The majority of special education teachers work with children with mild to moderate disabilities, using or modifying the general education curriculum to meet the child's individual needs.

In 2017–2018, the number of students ages 3–21 who received special education services under IDEA was 7 million, or 14% of all public school students.[53] As Figure 10.3 shows, about 34% of those students have specific learning disabilities, 19% have speech or language impairment, 14% have other health impairments, 10% have autism, 6% have intellectual disabilities, and 5% have emotional disturbance.

The law does not define special education as a place, but rather as the configuration of services and supports as the student's IEP (individualized education program) defines them.[54] Within the school, special educators deliver their services in a continuum of teaching settings. Increasingly, special education teachers work in general education classrooms using an **inclusion model**. In this paradigm, students with disabilities receive most, if not all, of their instruction in a general education classroom. In 2016, nearly 95% of students with disabilities spent at least part of their day in a regular education classroom; over half (63%) were in regular classes at least 80% of the time.[55]

FIGURE 10.3 ■ Percentage of Students Served Under IDEA by Disability Type, 2017–2018

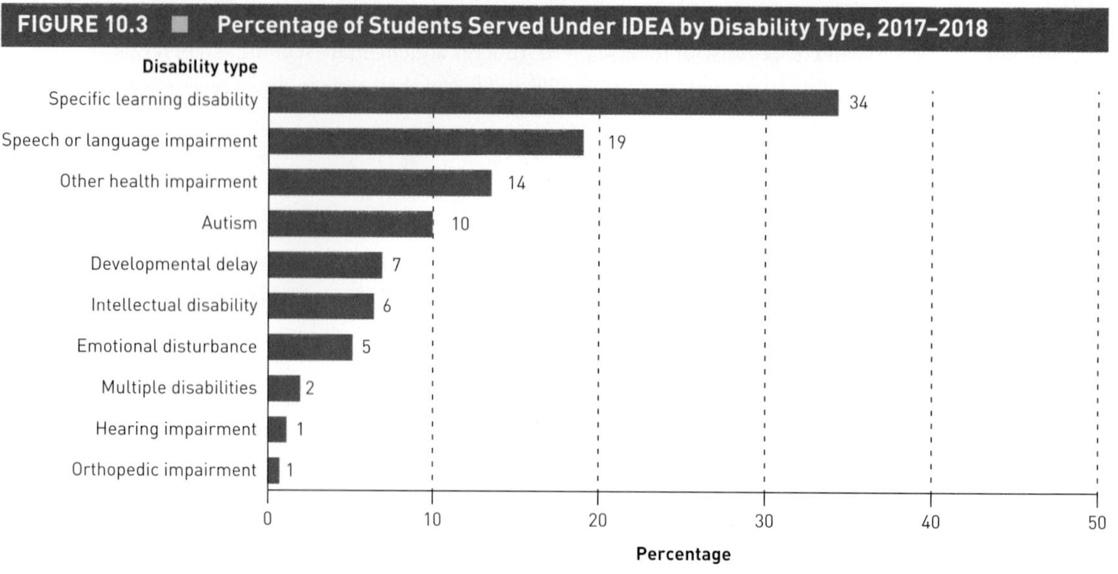

Source: McFarland, J., Hussar, B., Zhang, J., Wang, X., Wang, K., Hein, S., Diliberti, M., and others (2019, May). Children and youth with disabilities. Figure 1. Percentage distribution of students ages 3–21 served under the Individuals With Disabilities Education Act (IDEA), by disability type: School year 2017–18. *The Condition of Education* (NCES 2019-144). National left for Education Statistics. https://nces.ed.gov/pubs2019/2019144.pdf

Note: Total does not equal 100% due to rounding.

Other special educators teach students with disabilities in **self-contained classrooms**. Only 13.6% of students spend the majority of their school day (60%) in a classroom specifically set aside for children with disabilities.[56] The majority of special education teachers work in **resource rooms**, where they provide specialized instruction to students with disabilities who come in for part of the school day, either individually or in small groups.

Special education teachers design and teach appropriate curricula, assign work geared toward each student's needs and abilities, and grade papers and homework assignments. They are involved in the students' behavioral, social, and academic development. They help special education students feel comfortable in social situations and learn socially acceptable behaviors. Preparing these students for daily life after graduation is another important aspect of the job. In some instances, special education teachers assess students for possible careers or help them learn routine life management skills, such as balancing a checkbook.

A large part of a special education teacher's job involves collaborating with others: parents, social workers, school psychologists, occupational and physical therapists, school administrators, and regular education teachers. They coordinate the work of teachers, teacher assistants, and related personnel, such as therapists and social workers, to meet the students' individualized needs within inclusive special education programs.

Special education teachers represent a valuable resource for general education teachers. Because of their training, special education teachers are creative problem solvers who bring expertise in curriculum, teaching strategies, and learning styles into the classroom. They will help regular education teachers work with students with disabilities in their classroom or in the special educators' own classrooms. Either way, special educators bring resources or skills to help students with disabilities achieve academically and socially—and increase regular education teachers' effectiveness with diverse students.

10.3i The School Nurse

A growing body of evidence finds a connection between students' health and their learning, placing school nurses in the position of fostering student wellness and school success.[57] More than simply addressing the timeworn assumptions about "ice, lice, and band-aids,"[58] the school nurse supports student success by providing on-site emergency health care, health care assessments, interventions, and follow-up care for all children within the school setting. They work with actual and potential health problems that occur in schools; provide case management services for students with chronic and short-term illnesses; and actively collaborate with teachers, parents, students, and others to manage family health issues that affect learning.

Not all American children come to school healthy and ready to learn. Nearly 20% of students enter school with a chronic health condition such as asthma, life-threatening allergies, diabetes, and seizure disorders[59] that affect students' ability to be in school and ready to learn. The school nurse provides direct care (i.e., monitoring blood glucose several times a day, giving insulin injections) to students with these needs; helps students learn to manage their own chronic conditions; and works with students' health care providers, school staff, and the community to coordinate students' needs. The school nurse must be familiar with every student's treatment regimen, including any devices or medical procedures required as part of the treatment. Throughout the school day, school nurses have opportunities to detect illnesses early, prevent their spread, and identify students at risk while also advocating for the well-being of the entire school community.

By addressing students' health needs, professional school nurses support student success in the learning process. Table 10.4 briefly describes the school nurse's responsibilities.

TABLE 10.4 ■ The School Nurse's Responsibilities

Responsibility	Description
Providing direct health care to students and staff	The school nurse provides care to medically fragile, injured, or acutely ill students and staff, including administering emergency first aid, communicating with parents, and making referrals to other providers. The school nurse is responsible for administering student medications and performing health care procedures ordered by an appropriately licensed health caregiver. The school nurse also assists faculty and staff in monitoring students' chronic health conditions.
Providing leadership for administering health services	As the health care expert within the school, the school nurse assesses the overall system of care and develops a plan for ensuring that health needs are met. The school nurse also helps develop systemwide health policies and programs, including crisis/disaster management, disease management, mental health support and intervention, and school wellness policies.
Providing screening and referral for health conditions	The school nurse often conducts screening activities to address students' health problems that might potentially become barriers to learning or treats symptoms of underlying medical disorders. Screenings may include vision, hearing, dental, postural, weight (body mass index), or other conditions.
Promoting a healthy school environment	The school nurse monitors student compliance with state immunization laws, ensures appropriate exclusion from and reentry into school, and reports communicable diseases as required by law. The school nurse leads the school in implementing precautions for faculty and staff regarding blood-borne pathogens and other infectious diseases. This health care professional may also assess the school's physical environment and act to improve health and safety in areas such as the playground, perform indoor air quality evaluations, or review illness or injury patterns to determine a source of concern.
Promoting health with students, school, family, and community	The school nurse provides age-appropriate health information and self-management skills directly to individual students, groups of students, or classes, as well as to school staff, families, and the community. Health promotion activities may include helping develop school safety plans to address bullying and school violence; serving as liaison between school personnel, family, health care professionals, and the community; coordinating health fairs for students, families, or staff; consulting with food service personnel or physical education teachers regarding healthy lifestyles; and administering staff wellness programs.

Source: Based on American Academy of Pediatrics. (2008, May). Role of the school nurse in providing school health services. *Pediatrics, 121*(5). https://pediatrics.aappublications.org/content/121/5/1052

As the school's health expert, the school nurse participates as a part of students' individualized education program (IEP) and 504 team[60] and as part of a student and family assistance team. In the role as case manager, the nurse communicates with the family through telephone calls, emails, letters, and home visits as needed. The school nurse also speaks with local health providers and health care agencies while ensuring appropriate confidentiality, develops community partnerships, and serves on area coalitions to promote public health.

State law usually regulates the school's required nurse-to-student ratio; no national standard exists. The National Association of School Nurses recommends the following nurse-to-student ratios: 1:750 in general populations, 1:225 in student populations that may require daily professional school nursing services or interventions, and 1:125 in student populations with complex health care needs.[61] Yet only 33.7% of school districts report that they have a policy requiring schools to have a full-time school nurse, and only 18.1% of school districts are required to have at least a part-time nurse.[62] These figures vary by state.[63]

The National Association of School Nurses recommends each school have a full-time nurse with a minimum of a baccalaureate degree in nursing from an accredited college or university[64] and who has achieved school nurse certification. The school nurse needs expertise in pediatric, public health, and mental health nursing and must possess strong health promotion, assessment, and referral skills. School nurses also need to have knowledge of laws in education and health care that may affect children in the school setting. Each state sets its own eligibility and hiring requirements for this important school support person.

To consider more fully the professional and family influences on student learning in school, complete the activity in the **Reflect & Engage** box, Centering Students in the Education Process.

REFLECT & ENGAGE: CENTERING STUDENTS IN THE EDUCATION PROCESS

Figure 10.1 depicts the typical state education organizational chart. In this diagram, the public (through elections) sits at the top, and the students sit at the bottom. School district organization, starting with the local school board. The individual school level, starting with the principal, begins near the bottom. Ideally, all positions on the chart work to benefit the students.

A. Working in pairs, recreate this flowchart as a mind map using a digital tool such as Bubbl, starting with *students* in the left; identify all those professional and family roles, near and far, that impact students' learning and well-being.

B. Discuss where principals, teachers, school staff, and students are on your mind map. Explain the nature and strength of their influence on student learning and well-being.

C. Who holds the most and least power and influence inside the school system as it impacts students' learning and well-being? Which factors contribute to this status?

D. How can teachers use and enhance their power and influence to benefit students, their school, and the school district?

10.4 STRUCTURAL ISSUES THAT INFLUENCE SCHOOLS' EFFICIENCY AND EFFECTIVENESS

School district size, school, size, and grade configurations can vary substantially. The trend toward consolidating small school districts into larger ones and debates about the optimal school size and which grade configurations best help students learn are all structural issues that impact both schooling costs and student achievement. Local school boards have authority over most of these factors. And each has an impact on student learning.

Most school boards take their role as stewards of their neighbors' tax dollars very seriously. Where local boards feel cautious about spending tax revenues, they choose efficiency as an operational value. They are likely to build larger schools, assuming that two or three big schools are more cost-effective to operate than four or five smaller schools. Conversely, school boards may decide that effectiveness as an operational value is more important than efficiency. Reflecting this perspective, they may decide to build smaller schools, citing research that smaller schools may be better for student attendance and achievement gains than larger schools. Members' beliefs and values as well as research findings contribute to board decisions about school structure.

10.4a Consolidating School Districts

The questions about school size mirror the questions about the best size for school districts. Larger school districts, their supporters contend, offer a broader tax base and reduce the educational cost per student. As a result, these districts can better afford high-quality personnel, a wide range of educational programs and special services, and good transportation. Over the past half century, most studies of this issue have placed the most effective school district size at between 10,000 and 50,000 students.[65]

The 20th century witnessed a trend toward consolidating smaller school districts in an effort to increase efficiency. In 1939 to 1940 (the earliest year for which data are available), slightly more than 117,000 public school districts existed in the United States. By 2018, that number had dropped to just under 14,000, representing a loss of more than 100,000 school districts—a decrease of almost 90%.[66] Table 10.5 shows the main reasons driving school district consolidation.

TABLE 10.5 ■ Reasons for Consolidating School Districts

Factor	Explanation
Size	Larger schools, especially high schools, can accommodate broader curriculum offerings and specialized teachers.
Services	Larger schools can justify hiring school counselors, deans of students, assistant principals, lead teachers, and specialists not typically available in smaller schools.
Economics	Consolidating school districts lowers operating costs. Purchasing decisions can lead to significant savings when items are ordered in bulk; that is, the costs for books, paper, lab equipment, and art supplies may go down when schools can negotiate to buy them in larger quantities. Consolidation may allow schools to close older buildings and reduce the number of higher-paid central office administrators, both money savers. For example, instead of having three curriculum supervisors (one for each of the formerly separate school districts), a consolidated school district needs only one.

Figure 10.4 illustrates that larger schools are able to make more high-level, high-status courses available to students. These include dual-credit courses (simultaneous enrollment in a high school and college course), and Advanced Placement (AP) and/or International Baccalaureate (IB) courses. Only 78% of schools with enrollment less than 500 offer dual-credit courses to their students, and only 43% of high schools smaller than 500 students offer AP or IB courses to their students.[67] By comparison, schools with 500 to 1,199 and schools with more 1,200 students provide more advanced-level offerings to their students.

When school districts merge, the resulting district serves more students. Table 10.6 compares the number of pupils per school district in 1940 and 2017. The average school district in 1940 had approximately 239 students, and school districts in 2017 served more than 4,100 students on average.

During this 77-year period, the average number of students in school districts increased more than more than 17 times, from 239 to 4,155 (Table 10.6). The number of public schools and school districts decreased, even as their size and efficiency increased. Neighborhood schools and school districts gave way to larger ones covering multiple neighborhoods. Consolidation increased most districts' ethnic, geographic, and wealth diversity. Similarly, student population growth and school district consolidation has dramatically reduced the number of public schools over time. In 1939 to 1940, almost 250,000 public schools were in operation in the United States.[68] Today, that number stands at approximately 98,000.[69] The number of one-teacher schools has declined dramatically.

The empirical literature on the effects of district size on student outcomes is small and mixed.[70] Some studies have found that school districts with student enrollments between 2,000 and 4,000 students tend to be cost-effective, whereas districts enrolling more than 15,000 students achieve less cost savings.[71]

FIGURE 10.4 ■ Percentage of Public High Schools Offering Advanced-Level Courses, by Enrollment Size

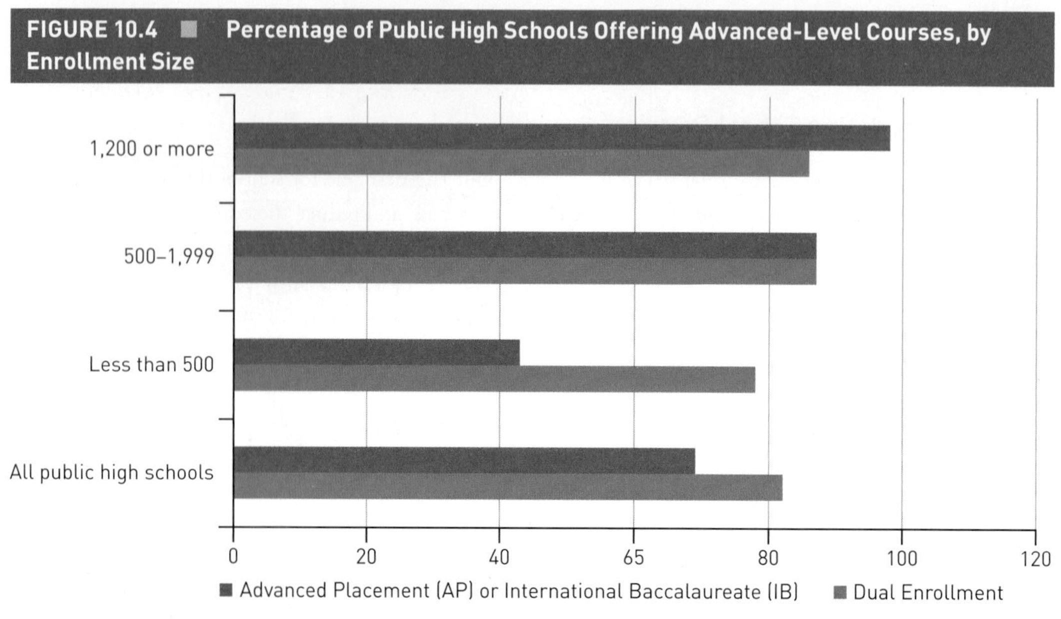

Source: U.S. Department of Education. (2013, February). *Dual-credit and exam-based courses in U.S. public high schools, 2010–2011: First look.* Table 1. https://nces.ed.gov/pubs2013/2013001.pdf

TABLE 10.6 ■ Number of Students Per School District, 1940 and 2017

	1940	2017
Total number of students	28,045,000	56,500,000
Total number of school districts	117,108	13,598
Pupils per school district	239	4,155

Source: Snyder, T. D., deBrey, C., and Dillow, S. A. (2019, December). *Digest of Education Statistics, 2018.* U.S. Department of Education. Tables 105.20, p. 43; 105.30, p. 44; 214.10, p. 118.

This changing structure posed crucial challenges for the localities affected. Feelings of community pride and ownership of local schools and school districts diminish as the schools and their leadership—and their children—move farther away: Local control is no longer local. At the same time, administrators and teachers work with more diverse students who need to learn more higher-level skills in order to survive in a globally competitive environment. School climate and student achievement, once taken for granted in small local schools with relatively homogeneous student populations, suddenly become urgent issues. Many educators need intensive professional development to gain the skills and attitudes needed to work effectively with students and parents who differ from themselves. In fact, distancing school districts from their communities has led some to call for replacing school boards with school councils, thereby returning public schools governance back to the "grassroots" level.[72]

Trying to improve student achievement by closing schools is even more tenuous. Studies of closures in Chicago and Pittsburgh suggest that academic performance is likely to decrease, at least in the short term, when students are transferred from closing schools. Indeed, students fare better academically only when they are transferred to higher-performing schools. Yet the supply of seats in high-performing schools is often limited, and even when they are available, increases in academic performance are modest.[73]

10.4b Reducing School Size

What is the best-sized school to support student success? Since 1990, a growing body of evidence questions whether larger schools provide better academic and school climate outcomes and whether they are more cost-effective. The existing literature offers conflicting conclusions.[74]

Studies suggest that students in smaller schools have more qualitative than quantitative benefits. These include enhanced school climate and student engagement: higher attendance, greater feeling of safety, fewer behavior problems, and higher participation in extracurricular activities;[75] lower high school dropout rates;[76] and better interpersonal relations.[77] Research on small schools also finds that these do not necessarily result in higher measured academic achievement.[78] These studies and others advanced the view that smaller schools lead to many—but not all—improved student outcomes.

Accordingly, the issue of school size and student achievement remains unclear and unresolved. Perhaps this is because several elements may influence the relationship between school size and student outcomes.[79] These include poverty, the student population served, and an "ideal" school size. Cost-effectiveness brings an additional consideration to the school size dilemma.

Importantly, the small school research points to the connection between student achievement and their socioeconomic status (SES).[80] Studies agree that students' SES—rather than school size—was the strongest predictor of student achievement results.[81] Smaller schools can help narrow the achievement gap between white, middle-class, affluent students and ethnic, underrepresented, and low-income students, likely a result of the individual attention that teachers in smaller schools can provide students in their classrooms as well as their help outside the classroom navigating the schools' complex social and administrative environments. But since studies point to the persistent effect of SES on achievement regardless of school size, researchers question whether school size has a *direct* effect on achievement.

Of course, the specifics of school size—what student enrollment is "small" or "large" and what the "ideal" school size—is debatable. In 1987, after reviewing several studies, two researchers determined that high schools should have no more than 250 students per school. Larger enrollments focused too much administrators' attention on control and order, harming the school climate. At the same time, the larger school population increased members' feelings of anonymity, making it more difficult to build a sense of community among students, teachers, and parents.[82] In contrast, other studies suggest that small and moderate-sized high schools (between 600 and 900 students) foster more positive social and academic environments compared to large high schools (those enrolling 2,100 students or more), especially for economically disadvantaged students.[83] These varied studies imply that students in very small high schools (fewer than 300 students) learn less than students in moderate-sized high schools but more than students in very large high schools (over 2,100 pupils).[84]

Cost-effectiveness is another consideration. It is true that while smaller schools are more expensive to operate on a *per-pupil* basis, researchers now assert that small schools can be more efficient when measured on a *cost-per-graduate* basis because they graduate more of their students[85] (as well as reduce social costs of lower earnings and higher rates of unemployment, incarceration, and welfare dependence).[86] Similarly, one study determined that moderately sized elementary schools (300–500 students) and high schools (600–900 students) may best balance costs and benefits in student performance and school services (relative to increased numbers of teachers, administrators, and support staff).[87]

Sometimes, larger schools create smaller schools by implementing the "school-within-a-school" concept. This approach may be a way to achieve the benefits associated with smaller school size without having to actually build expensive new school facilities. In this way, schools that personalize the learning environment for students can increase their engagement and academic achievement.

When considering the best school size to produce student achievement, school boards must consider the nature of their community and their student body, cost efficiency, and related factors and decide whether they, as stand-ins for the larger community, prefer to pay now or pay later.

10.4c Organizing Schools by Grade Levels

When Americans think of how schools are organized by grade levels, we tend to think of elementary, middle, and high schools. The reality, however, is much more varied. Figure 10.5 shows the breakdown of schools by elementary, secondary (middle and high school), and combined (the totals do not add up because of overlap in reporting).[88] Small schools are defined as schools with enrollments of fewer than 300 students, and large schools are those with 1,000 or more students.

FIGURE 10.5 ■ Percentage of Public School Enrollment, by Level, Fall 2000–Fall 2028

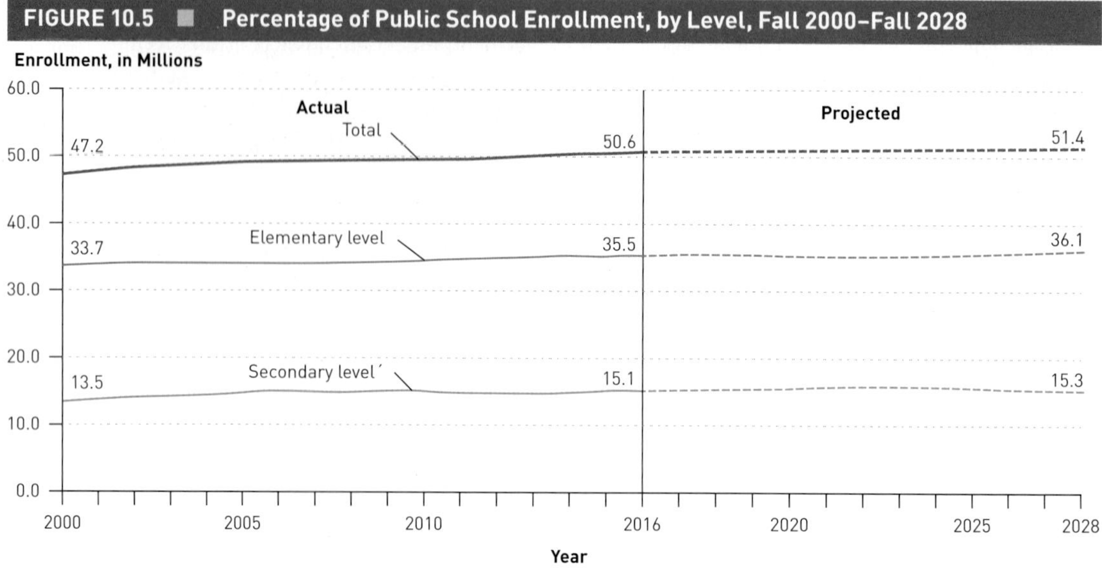

Source: U.S. Department of Education (2019, May). Public school enrollment. *The Condition of Education*. National Center for Education Statistics, Institute of Education Sciences, Figure 1. https://nces.ed.gov/programs/coe/indicator_cga.asp

Research on School Grade Configuration

Does a school's grade configuration affect student achievement? Do students achieve better in K–8 schools or in separate middle schools (Grades 6–8)? The research here is complicated and has yielded unclear results.[89] Although some research indicates that student outcomes vary among schools with different grade configurations—specifically, that K–8 schools can improve student achievement—the research as a whole suggests that the impact of grade configuration is less than the impact of instructional practices and school culture.[90] Although research finds that the transition to middle school has been associated with negative academic and social outcomes,[91] other studies have found adverse effects only in the Grade 6 transition year.[92]

Research does not conclusively suggest that any particular grade level configuration has a positive or negative effect on student achievement. When it comes to determining the "best" grade configuration to enhance K–8 student achievement, it may be, as one research review concludes, that "no sequence of grades is perfect or, in itself, guarantees student academic achievement and healthy social and emotional development."[93] Agreeing, another review notes that "what is most important for the education of young adolescent learners is what takes place inside each middle-grades school, not grade configuration per se."[94]

School governance is not the education issue that most new teachers think about. In all likelihood, principals and central office supervisors are probably the only "governance officials" with whom teachers interact on a daily basis. But many other individuals have a big say in the policies and practices that influence how teachers do their work.

To better understand how school district size, school, size, and grade configurations affect student outcomes, complete the activity in the **Reflect & Engage** box, Structural Issues That Influence School Effectiveness.

REFLECT & ENGAGE: STRUCTURAL ISSUES THAT INFLUENCE SCHOOL EFFECTIVENESS

This activity involves role play. School district size, school size, and grade configurations can vary substantially. Each of these factors has related costs, and each may impact teachers' work environment and student achievement. You and your class are expert education consultants who are very knowledgeable on school structure issues.

A local school board is pondering whether or not they should merge with a larger school district, combine smaller schools into larger ones to save money, and/or readjust their current grade configurations K–8 to create better learning environments for their students and teachers and more opportunities for parent participation in school activities. They need a basic conceptual framework of information to help guide their preliminary thinking. And they have asked your consulting firm to help them think through the initial considerations.

A. Separate the class into three teams that represent (1) school district size, (2) school size, and (3) grade configuration. Large teams can be organized into smaller work groups.

B. As teams, decide the questions would you want the school board to answer that you need to know in order to tailor your recommendations.

C. As teams, prepare separate 5-minute presentation on the factors that might help the board with their decision about district size, school size, or grade configuration.

D. Give your presentations, including the questions you want answered (and why you need to know), the research findings on these topics, and your recommendations about what to do about each.

E. As a class, discuss how these structural factors affected your own K–12 education experiences. As future classroom teachers, what do you find to be the most meaningful aspects of school structure?

KEY TAKE-AWAYS

Learning Objective 10.1 Identify and explain the three areas of federal government's involvement in public education.

- The United States does not have one national education system. Education is a federal interest, a state responsibility, and a locally administered concern. Local school districts are the primary operating units of the American public school system.
- The federal share accounts for only 8.3% of the nation's total education budget and represents less than 3% of the total federal budget.
- The federal government—through the Congress, the judiciary, and student assessment (at the national level)—has traditionally had little jurisdiction over state and local education policies or practices, except when addressing specific protected classes and disadvantaged populations. Although its role is limited, the federal government has a significant influence in pointing state and local leaders in certain directions.
- Education can create the opportunities that give all children a more equitable start to equip them for successful lives and responsible citizenship. Political disagreements occur over how to do this. Education reformers do well when they listen to and answer their critics.

Learning Objective 10.2 List the state leaders and legal entities who play key roles in shaping education policy and practice and describe their responsibilities.

- The public influences education at the state level through the election process.
- State laws control how districts structure their superintendents' contracts, define their role in overseeing the school district, decide the length of the school day and the school year, and set curriculum parameters, testing programs, licensure regulations, and other matters.
- In recent years, state legislators have acted on many educational issues, including deciding the means by which the state will fund its schools, whether or not to permit charter schools and vouchers to attend private schools, teacher licensure laws, school curricula, testing issues, consolidation of school districts, school accreditation, and teacher retirement contributions and benefits.

- By enacting their agendas in personnel and policy choices, such as for the chief state school officer and the state board of education, governors exercise powerful sway on directions given to the public schools.

Learning Objective 10.3 Assess which local leaders, entities, and support staff play key roles in shaping education policy, practice, and student success.

- The local school district's power (invested in the local school board) varies from state to state, depending on the state constitution's wording. Most school board members are laypeople who volunteer their time or receive a modest stipend to work for their local school system. But their authority has slowly diminished as the result of federal government's increased involvement in school affairs, relevant court decisions, and special-interest groups' actions.
- The superintendent is the school system's CEO and reports to the school board. The district superintendent organizes the school system for teaching and learning; ensures that the school system operates efficiently and effectively; and maintains good communication and relations with the school board.
- A school district's central office assumes a variety of tasks that foster districtwide improvements in teaching and leadership, and it manages operational tasks such as personnel, building and grounds maintenance, and finances.
- Most states now consider the principal's primary charges to be establishing a positive educational climate and culture for learning, managing the school's operations, and ensuring that all students learn to state achievement standards. Research affirms that principals' effectiveness has an empirical link with improved student achievement, an influence second only to classroom instruction among all school-related factors.
- An array of skilled and specialized professionals and paraprofessionals—including school counselors, special education teachers, and school nurses—often work with teachers to help make them and their students successful. Research affirms their positive impact on student learning and well-being.

Learning Objective 10.4 Evaluate how the structural issues of school district size, school size, and grade-level configuration affect public schools' costs and effectiveness.

- School board members' beliefs and values (about teaching, learning, and stewardship of their neighbors' tax dollars) as well as research findings contribute to board decisions about school size, district size, and grade configurations.
- Studies suggest that students in smaller schools have more qualitative than quantitative benefits. But since studies point to the persistent effect of SES on achievement regardless of school size, researchers question whether school size has a *direct* effect on achievement.
- While smaller schools are more expensive to operate on a *per-pupil* basis, researchers now assert that small schools can be more efficient when measured on a *cost-per-graduate* basis because they graduate more of their students as well as reduce social costs.
- Research does not conclusively suggest that any particular grade-level configuration has a positive or negative effect on student achievement. What takes place inside each middle grades school, not grade configuration per se, is the most important educational factor.

TEACHER SCENARIO: IT'S YOUR TURN

You are a retired teacher who has become a successful realtor and vice president of communications with a national realty chain. You have been tasked to add a section to the corporate website to inform potential clients about what factors to look for in school systems to ensure children achieve a high-quality education when buying a new home.

Using information from this chapter as well as previous ones, describe the following in a three-page document:

1. How school districts are generally organized and what to look for in terms of education policy from the governor, the state school board, the local school board, and the school leadership
2. What factors to consider in terms of school board and city/county council relations, school size, and grade-level configuration
3. The importance of principal and teacher quality to student achievement and what school characteristics reflect principal and teacher quality (e.g., key functions of principal leadership, InTASC teacher standards, years of experience in the school district, student achievement, and the like)
4. School consolidation issues.

NOTES

1. Fuerer, M. J. (2006, June 14). Moderation: A radical approach to education policy. Commentary. *Education Week 25* (10), 36.
2. Snyder, T.D., de Brey, C., & Dillow, S.A. (2019). Number of public school districts and public and private elementary and secondary schools: Selected years, 1898-70 through 2016-17. Table 214.10, p. 118. *Digest of Education Statistics 2018* (NCES 2020-009). National left for Education Statistics, Institute of Education Sciences, U.S. Department of Education. Washington, DC. Retrieved from https://nces.ed.gov/pubs2020/2020009.pdf
3. In some localities, these entities are called school districts. In others, they are called school divisions or local education agencies (LEAs).
4. The United States has 51 different education systems. The District of Columbia has its own education system, counting as the 51st.
5. Grant, W. V. (1993, January). Statistics in the U.S. Department of Education: Highlights from the past 120 years. In T. D. Snyder (Ed.), *120 years of American education: A statistical portrait* (pp. 1–4). National left for Education Statistics. http://nces.ed.gov/pubs93/93442.pdf
6. Ujifusa, A. (2018, October 1). See the new federal education budget signed into law by Donald Trump. *Education Week*. http://blogs.edweek.org/edweek/campaign-k-12/2018/10/donald-trump-education-spending-increase-second-straight-year.html
7. U.S. Department of Education. (2019). *Salaries and expenses overview: Fiscal year 2019 budget request.* https://www2.ed.gov/about/overview/budget/budget19/justifications/w-seoverview.pdf
8. New America Foundation. (2019). *Federal funding: Education policy.* https://www.newamerica.org/education-policy/topics/school-funding-and-resources/school-funding/federal-funding/
9. Snyder et al., 2019, Table 235.10, p. 187. Sums do not add up to 100% due to rounding error.
10. Public Law 85-864.
11. Pelsue, B. (2017, Fall). When it comes to education, the federal government in charge of . . . um, what? *Harvard Graduate School of Education*. https://www.gse.harvard.edu/news/ed/17/08/when-it-comes-education-federal-government-charge-um-what
12. Harris, D. N., Ladd, H. F., Smith, M. S., & West, M. R. (2016, December). A principled federal role in pre-K–12 education. *Brookings*. https://www.brookings.edu/wp-content/uploads/2016/12/gs_20161206_principled_federal_role_brownleft1.pdf
13. 377 U.S. 218, 84 S. Ct. 1226.
14. Friesen, K. J. (2013). Massive resistance in a small town. *Humanities, 34*(5). https://www.neh.gov/humanities/2013/septemberoctober/feature/massive-resistance-in-small-town
15. Friesen, 2013.
16. *Plyler v. Doe*, 457 U.S. 202 102 S. Ct. 2382 (1982).
17. Owings, W., & Kaplan, L. (2013). *American public school finance* (2nd ed.). Cengage, p. 222.
18. *Endrew F. v. Douglas County School District* Re-1, 580 U.S. (2017).
19. *Hendrick Hudson Central School District v. Rowley*, 458 U.S. 176, 102 S. Ct. 3034.

20. We will discuss student achievement and accountability in greater detail in Chapter 13. For the purposes of this section, we briefly address the topic as one of the federal roles in education.

21. Since 1983, Educational Testing Services (ETS) has held the NAEP contract.

22. Myers, J. (2019, August 15). Proposition 13 treats all California property taxes the same. Voters could change that in 2020. *Los Angeles Times*. https://www.latimes.com/california/story/2019-08-14/california-proposition-13-business-taxes-split-roll

23. *First to worst: Special challenge of* proposition 13. (n.d.). *The Merrow report*. Public Broadcast System, Learning Matters. http://learningmatters.tv/images/blog/First.pdf

24. We will go into more detail about this issue in Chapter 11.

25. Except in Vermont and New Hampshire, where the governors serve 2-year terms. In all states except Virginia, governors may succeed themselves.

26. Except in Wisconsin, which does not have a state board of education.

27. Kysilko, D. (2000, March). Building partnerships with the legislature. In *Boardsmanship review*. National Association of State Boards of Education.

28. Unique among the 50 states, Hawaii is a single state-run school district.

29. Alsbury, T. L. (2003, December). Superintendent and school board member turnover: Political versus apolitical turnover as a critical variable in the application of dissatisfaction theory. *Education Administration Quarterly, 39*(5), 667–678.

30. Dervarics, C., & O'Brien, E. (2011). *Eight characteristics of effective school boards: Full report*. left for Public Education. https://www.nyssba.org/clientuploads/nyssba_pdf/Events/nsbma-buffalo-07152016/Eight-characteristics-of-effective-school-boards_-full-report.pdf

31. Burnette, D., II. (2018, October 9). State school chiefs: Who's elected, who's not, and races to watch this year. *Education Week, 38*(8), 1, 15. States with elected school superintendents: Arizona, California, Georgia, Idaho, Indiana, Minnesota, North Carolina, North Dakota, Oklahoma, South Carolina, Washington, Wisconsin, Wyoming.

32. Andero, A. (2000, Winter). The changing role of school superintendent with regard to curriculum policy and decision making. *Education, 121*(2), 276–286.

33. Grove, K. F. (2002, May). The invisible role of the central office. *Educational Leadership, 59*(8), 45–47.

34. Pew Research left. (2019). *Why Americans don't fully trust many who hold positions of power and responsibility; Education Week*. (2019, October 2). Principals, when you're down, take heart, Americans trust you, p. 3.

35. Wahlstrom, K., Louis, K. S., Leithwood, K., & Anderson, S. E. (2010). *Investigating the links to improved student learning: Executive summary of research findings*. https://www.wallacefoundation.org/knowledge-left/Documents/Investigating-the-Links-to-Improved-Student-Learning-Executive-Summary.pdf; Wallace Foundation. (2013). *The school principal as leader: Guiding schools to better teaching and learning*. https://www.wallacefoundation.org/knowledge-left/Documents/The-School-Principal-as-Leader-Guiding-Schools-to-Better-Teaching-and-Learning-2nd-Ed.pdf; Waters, J. T., Marzano, R. J., & McNulty, B. A. (2003). *Balanced leadership: What 30 years of research tells us about the effect of leadership on student achievement*. Mid-Continent Research for Education and Learning.

36. Wahlstrom et al., 2010. In a 2019 revisit to this claim, Leithwood, Harris, & Hopkins now contend that the school factors that influence student achievement are too numerous to entitle the principal to claim the "second highest school factor" in generating student achievement (but imply that if there were a second most important factor, principals would hold it). See: Leithwood, K., Harris, A., & Hopkins, D. (2019, April). Seven strong claims about successful school leadership revisited. *School Leadership & Management, 40*(1), 5–22.

37. Wallace Foundation, 2013.

38. Marzano, R. J., Waters, T., & McNulty, B. A. (2005). *School leadership that works: From research to results*. Association for Supervision and Curriculum Development.

39. Branch, G., Hanushek, E. A., & Rivkin, S. G. (2013. Winter). School leaders matter. *Education Next, 13*(1), http://hanushek.stanford.edu/sites/default/files/publications/Branch%2BHanushek%2BRivkin%20 2013%20EdNext%2013%281%29_0.pdf

40. Johnson, S. M. (2006). *The workplace matters: Teacher quality, retention, and effectiveness*. National Education Association. www.nea.org/assets/docs/HE/mf_wcreport.pdf; Ladd, H. (2009, December). *Teachers' perceptions of their working conditions: How predictive of policy-relevant outcomes?* Paper presented at National left for Analysis of Longitudinal Data in Education Research (CALDER) conference, Washington, DC.; Scholastic and Bill & Melinda Gates Foundation. (2010). *Primary sources: America's*

teachers on America's schools. http://www.scholastic.com/primarysources/pdfs/Scholastic_Gates_0310.pdf

41. Garcia, E., & Weiss, E. (2019, May 30). Challenging working environments ("school climates"), especially in high-poverty schools, play a role in the teacher shortage. Economic Policy Institute. https://www.epi.org/publication/school-climate-challenges-affect-teachers-morale-more-so-in-high-poverty-schools-the-fourth-report-in-the-perfect-storm-in-the-teacher-labor-market-series/; Ingersoll, R. M. (2002, June). The teacher shortage: A case of wrong diagnosis and wrong prescription. *NASSP Bulletin, 86*(631),16–30.

42. Brigman, G., & Campbell, C. (2003, December). Helping students improve academic achievement and school success behaviors. *Professional School Counseling, 7*(2), 91–98.

43. For the student-to-counselor ratio 2017–2018 in each state, see: American School Counselor Association. (2019). *Student-to school-counselor ratio, 2017–2018.* https://www.schoolcounselor.org/asca/media/asca/home/Ratios17-18.pdf

44. Hankerson, M. (2019, May 9). How does the budget change Virginia's school counselor ratio? *Virginia Mercury.* https://www.virginiamercury.com/2019/05/09/how-does-the-budget-change-virginias-school-counselor-ratio/

45. Gysbers, N. C. (2004, October). Comprehensive guidance and counseling programs: The evolution of accountability. *Professional School Counseling, 8*(1), 1–14.

46. American School Counselors Association. (n.d.). Empirical research studies supporting the value of school counseling. https://www.schoolcounselor.org/asca/media/asca/Careers-Roles/Effectiveness.pdf

47. Carey, J., & Dimmitt, C. (2012). School counseling and student outcomes: Summary of six statewide studies. *Professional School Counseling, 16*(2), 146–153.

48. Lapan, R. T., Gysbers, N. C., Stanley, B., & Pierce, M. E. (2012). Missouri professional school counselors: Ratios matter, especially in high-poverty schools. *Professional School Counseling, 16*(2), 108–116; Lapan, R. T., Whitcomb, S. A., & Aleman, N. M. (2012). Connecticut professional school counselors: College and career counseling services and smaller ratios benefit students. *Professional School Counseling,* 16(2), 117–124.

49. Goodman-Scott, E., Sink, C., Cholewa, B., & Burgess, M. (2018). An ecological view of school counselor ratios and student academic outcomes: A national investigation. *Journal of Counseling and Development, 96*(10), 388–398; Reback, R. (2010). Noninstructional spending improves noncognitive outcomes: Discontinuity evidence from a unique school counselor financing system. *Education Finance and Policy, 5*(2), 105–137; Reback, R. (2010). Schools' mental health services and young children's emotions, behavior, and learning. *Journal of Policy Analysis and Management, 29*(4), 698–725; Webb, L. D., Brigman, G. A., & Campbell, C. (2005, June). Linking school counselors and student success: A replication of the student success skills approach targeting the academic and social competence of students. *Professional School Counseling, 8*(5), 407–413.

50. Lapan, R., Poynton, T., Balkin, R., & Jones, L. (2019). ASCA national model implementation and appropriate school counselor ratios promote more informed college decision-making. *ASCA Research Report.* https://www.schoolcounselor.org/asca/media/asca/Publications/Research-Release-Lapan.pdf; Jones, S., Ricks, J., Warren, J., & Mauk, G. (2019). Exploring the career and college readiness of high school students serviced by RAMP and non-RAMP school counseling programs in North Carolina. *ASCA Research Report.* https://www.schoolcounselor.org/asca/media/asca/Careers-Roles/Effectiveness-CCR-ResearchReport.pdf

51. Hernandez, T. J., & Seem, S. R. (2004, April). A safe school climate: A systemic approach and the school counselor. *Professional School Counseling,* 7(4), 256–262.

52. Brigman, G., & Campbell, C. (2003, December). Helping students improve academic achievement and school success behaviors. *Professional School Counseling, 7*(2), 91–98.

53. McFarland, J., Hussar, B., Zhang, J., Wang, X., Wang, K., Hein, S., Diliberti, M., et al. (2019, May). Children and youth with disabilities. (NCES 2019-144). *The condition of education,* National left for Education Statistics. https://nces.ed.gov/programs/coe/indicator_cgg.asp

54. For a more complete discussion of the laws, policy, and legislature concerning the placement of students with disabilities into school learning environments, see: National Council on Disability. (2018, February 7). *The segregation of students with disabilities.* https://ncd.gov/sites/default/files/NCD_Segregation-SWD_508.pdf

55. U.S. Department of Education. (2018, December) *40th annual report to Congress on the implementation of the Individuals With Disabilities Education Act, 2018.* Office of Special Education and Rehabilitative Services, p. xxvii. https://www2.ed.gov/about/reports/annual/osep/2018/parts-b-c/40th-arc-for-idea.pdf

56. National left for Education Statistics. (2018). Students with disabilities, inclusion of. *Fast Facts. The digest of education statistics, 2017* (NCES 2018-070). Table 204.60. https://nces.ed.gov/fastfacts/display.asp?id=59

57. Maughan, E. D., Bobo, N., & Butler, S. (2016). Framework for 21st century school nursing practice. *NASN School Nurse, 31*(1), 45–53.

58. Maugham, D. E. (2018, April). School nurses: An investment in student achievement. *Phi Delta Kappan, 99*(7), 8–13.

59. U.S. Health Resources and Services Administration. (2016). *Children with special health care needs.* https://www.hrsa.gov/about/news/press-releases/hrsa-releases-national-survey-child-health-data

60. The 504 team plans for reasonable accommodations for students' disabilities that impact their educational programs.

61. National Association of School Nurses. (2015, January). *School nurse workload: Staffing for safe care.* https://www.nasn.org/advocacy/professional-practice-documents/position-statements/ps-workload

62. lefts for Disease Control and Prevention. (2017). Results from the school health policies and practices study 2016. https://www.cdc.gov/healthyyouth/data/shpps/pdf/shpps-results_2016.pdf

63. Willgerodt, M. A., Brock, D., & Maugham, E. (2018). Public school nursing practice in the United States. The national school nurse workforce study. *Journal of School Nursing, 34*(3), 232–244.

64. National Association of School Nurses. (2016). *Education, licensure, and certification of school nurse.* https://www.nasn.org/advocacy/professional-practice-documents/position-statements/ps-role

65. Wahlberg, H. J. (1994, June–July). Losing local control. *Educational Researcher, 23*(5),19–26; Howley, C., & Bickel, R. (2002, March). The influence of scale. *American School Board Journal, 183*(3), 28–30; Andrews, M., Duncomb, W., & Yinger, J. (2002). Revisiting economics of size in American education: Are we any closer to consensus? *Economics of Education Review, 21*, 245–262; Pellicer, L. (1999, November). When is a school district too large? Too small? Just right? Lessons from Goldilocks and the three bears. *School Business Affairs, 65*(11), 4–6, 8–10, 26–29.

66. National Center for Education Statistics. (2018). Table 214.10. Number of public school districts and public and private elementary and secondary schools: Selected years, 1869–70 through 2016–17. *Digest of Education Statistics.* https://nces.ed.gov/programs/digest/d18/tables/dt18_214.10.asp

67. U.S. Department of Education (2013, February). *Dual credit and exam-based courses in U.S. public high schools: 2010-2011 First look.* Table 1. Percentage of public schools with students enrolled in dual credit courses, Advanced Placement (AP) or International Baccalaureate courses (IB), and AP course eligible for dual credit without the AP exam, by school characteristics:" School year 2010-11, p. 6. [latest available] Retrieved from https://nces.ed.gov/pubs2013/2013001.pdf

68. Berry, C. (2005). School district consolidation and student outcomes: Does size matter? In W. G. Howell (Ed.), *Besieged: School board and the future of education politics* (pp. 56–80). Brookings Institution Press.

69. U.S. Department of Education. (2019). Educational institutions. *Digest of Education Statistics, 2017* (NCES 2018-070), Table 105.50. https://nces.ed.gov/fastfacts/display.asp?id=84

70. Whitehurst, G. J., Chingos, M. M., & Gallaher, M. R. (2013, March). *Do school districts matter?* Brown left on Education Policy at Brookings. https://www.brookings.edu/wp-content/uploads/2016/06/Districts_Report_03252013_web.pdf; Driscoll, D., Halcoussis, D., & Svorny, S. (2003, April). School district size and student performance. *Economics of Education Review, 22*(2), 193–201.

71. Andrews et al., 2002.

72. Cunningham, W. G. (2003, June). Grassroots democracy: Putting the public back into public education. *Phi Delta Kappan, 84*(10), 776–779.

73. Shaw, K., & Schott, A. (2013, April 17). Proceed with caution. Districts must address school closures comprehensively. *Education Week, 32*(28), 32.

74. For thorough literature reviews, see: Andrews et al., 2002; Leithwood, K., & Jantzi, D. (2009). A review of empirical evidence about school size effects: A policy perspective. *Review of Educational Research, 79*(1), 464–490.

75. Fowler, W. J. (1995). School size and student outcomes. In H. J. Walberg (Series Ed.) & B. Levin, W. J. Fowler, Jr., & H. J. Walberg (Vol. Eds.), *Advances in educational productivity: Vol. 5. Organizational influences on educational productivity* (pp. 3–25). JAI Press; Lee, V. E., & Smith, J. B. (1993). *Effects of high school restructuring and size on gains in achievement and engagement for early secondary school students.* Wisconsin left for Education Research.

76. Fetler, M. (1989). School dropout rates, academic performance, size, and poverty: Correlates of educational reform. *Educational Evaluation and Policy Analysis, 11*(2), 109–116; Pittman, R. B., & Haughwout, P. (1987). Influence of high school size on dropout rate. *Educational Evaluation and Policy Analysis, 9*(4), 337–343.

77. Rutter, R. A. (1988). *Effects of school as a community.* National left on Effective Secondary Schools. (Eric Document Reproduction Service No. ED 313470).

78. See: Barrow, L., Claessens, A., & Schanzenbach, D. W. (2013, March). The impact of Chicago's small high school initiative. NBER Working Paper 18889. Cambridge, MA: National Bureau of Economic Research. http://www.nber.org/papers/w18889.pdf; Gerwitz, 2006; Hoff, D. J. (2008, May 21). Study of small high schools yields little on achievement. *Education Week, 27*(38), 10; Evan, A., Huberman, M., Means, B., Mitchell, K., Shear, L., et al. (2006, August). Evaluation of the Bill & Melinda Gates Foundation's high school grants initiative, 2001–2005: Final report. The American Institutes for Research and SRI International. http://www.gatesfoundation.org/learning/Documents/Year4EvaluationAIRSRI.pdf; Shear, L., Means, B., Mitchell, K., et al. (2008, September). Contrasting paths to small-school reform: Results of a 5-year evaluation of the Bill & Melinda Gates Foundation's national high school initiative. *Teachers College Record, 110*(9), 1986–2039.

79. Stevenson, K. R. (2006, April). *School size and its relationship to student outcomes and school climate. A review and analysis of eight South Carolina state-wide studies.* National Clearinghouse for Educational Facilities. https://pdfs.semanticscholar.org/32ce/d44fcbd0c9bacbdf57179a57dc422d4d6c9f.pdf

80. Fowler, W. J., Jr., & Walberg, H. J. (1991). School size, characteristics, and outcomes. *Educational Evaluation and Policy Analysis, 13*(2), 189–202.

81. See: Gerwitz, C. (2006, August 9). Chicago's small schools see gains, but not on tests. *Education Week, 25*(44), 5, 18; Howley, C. (2001). Research on smaller schools: What education leaders need to know to make better decisions. *ERS Informed Educator.* Educational Research Service; Jimerson, L. (2006, September). *The Hobbit effect: Why small schools work.* The Rural School and Community Trust; Johnson, J. D., Howley, C. B., & Howley, A. A. (2002*). Size, excellence, and equity: A report on Arkansas schools and districts.* Ohio University College of Education; Lamdin, D. J. (1995). Testing for effect of school size on student achievement within a school district. *Education Economics, 3*(1), 33–42; Lee, V. E., & Smith, J. B. (1997, Autumn). High school size: Which works best and for whom? *Educational Evaluation and Policy Analysis, 19*(3), 205–227.

82. Gregory, T. B., & Smith, G. R. (1987, January). High schools as communities: The small school reconsidered. *Phi Delta Kappan*; Sousa, R., & Skandera, H. (2003, June 30). Smaller Is better: *Hoover Digest, 1.* Stanford University.

83. Gerwitz, C. (2006, August 9). Chicago's small schools see gains, but not on tests. *Education Week, 25*(44), 5, 18.

84. Lee, V. E., & Smith, J. B. (1997, Autumn). High school size: Which works best and for whom? *Educational Evaluation and Policy Analysis, 19*(3), 205–227.

85. Stiefel, L., Berne, R., Iatarola, P., & Fruchter, N. (2000, Spring). High schools size: Effects on budgets and performance in New York City. *Education Evaluation and Policy Analysis, 22*(1), 27–39, at 36–37.

86. Lawrence, B. K., Bingler, S., Diamond, B. M., Hill, B., Hoffman, J. L., Howley, C. B., Mitchell, S., Rudolph, D., & Washor, E. (2002). *Dollars & sense: The cost-effectiveness of small schools.* Knowledge Works Foundation. http://www.ruraledu.org/user_up loads/file/Dollars_and_Sense.pdf

87. Andrews et al., 2002.

88. U.S. Department of Education. (2019, May). Public school enrollment. *The Condition of Education.* National left for Education Statistics, Institute or Education Sciences, Figure 1. https://nces.ed.gov/programs/coe/indicator_cga.asp

89. Hanover Research. (2015, January). *Reviewing grade level configurations.* https://www.napls.us/site/handlers/filedownload.ashx?moduleinstanceid=4047&dataid=8327&FileName=Hanover-Review-of-Grade-Level-Configurations-Morgan-Hill-Unified-School-District.pdf; Hong, K., Zimmer, R., & Engberg, J. (2018, May). How does grade configuration impact student achievement in elementary and middle school grades? *Journal of Urban Economics, 105*(1), 1–19.

90. Education Northwest. (2011, August 18). *What the research says (or doesn't say) about K–8 versus middle school grade configurations.* https://www.dps61.org/cms/lib07/IL01000592/Centricity/Domain/1/Elemiddle_Config_Research_Full.pdf

91. Juvonen, J., Le, V., Kaganoff, T., Augustine, C., & Constant, L. (2004). *Focus on the wonder years: Challenges facing the American middle schools.* RAND. https://www.rand.org/content/dam/rand/pubs/monographs/2004/RAND_MG139.pdf; Rockoff, J. E., & Lockwood, B. B. (2010). Stuck in the middle:

Impacts of grade configuration in public schools. *Journal of Public Economics, 94*(11–12), 1051–1061; Schwerdt, G., & West, M. R. (2013). The impact of alternative grade configurations on student outcomes through middle and high school. *Journal of Public Economics, 97*(C), 308–326.

92. Hong et al., 2018.

93. Anfara, V. A., Jr., & Buehler, A. (2005). Grade configuration and the education of young adolescents. *Middle School Journal, 37*(1), 57.

94. The National Forum to Accelerate Middle-Grades Reform. (2008, July). Policy statement on grade configuration. *Middle Grades Forum, 5*(5). https://files.eric.ed.gov/fulltext/ED528788.pdf

iStock/andresr

11 SCHOOL FINANCE

InTASC Standards Addressed: 1, 2, 3, 9

LEARNING OBJECTIVES

After you read this chapter, you should be able to

11.1 Explain how money matters in improving student learning and achievement.

11.2 Describe the ways that education is an investment in human capital.

11.3 Identify the federal, state, and local contributions to school funding.

11.4 Justify the reasons for increased education spending since 1960.

11.5 Identify the categories and purposes for which school districts budget and spend money.

11.6 Summarize the major equity issues in school funding.

11.7 Discuss two current trends in education finance and their implications for public schools.

The promise of equal opportunity, especially in education, is central to the American dream. To make this dream a reality, states and communities are responsible for ensuring that all schools have the essential resources to provide positive and intellectually engaging learning environments.

But this does not always happen. In fact, our schools are among the most unequally funded in the industrialized world.[1] The Organization for Economic Cooperation and Development (OECD) reports that among the 34 OECD nations, the United States is one of the few advanced nations where schools serving children from more affluent families usually have more educational resources than those serving poor students.[2]

Providing all American children with a preK–12 education is very expensive. The U.S. Census Bureau showed that the average per-pupil spending in fiscal year 2017 was $12,201.[3] This ranged from $23,091 per pupil in New York to $7,179 per pupil in Utah.[4] The public elementary and secondary revenue from all sources adds up to over $694 billion a year.[5] Yet some states can afford to spend more than double what others spend per pupil, and some districts within each state can afford to spend double or triple what others can allocate.[6]

Despite its considerable costs, excellent education for all of America's children is a good investment. When it comes to quality education, as a society we can pay now or pay later. Education is one of the largest determinants of an individual's life choices and chances. It affects students' future employment, income, health, housing, and many other aspects of life. PreK–12 schooling is a critical investment in a community's—and our nation's—cognitive, physical, social, and economic infrastructure.

11.1 MONEY MATTERS IN EDUCATION

Beyond receiving their salaries and benefits and ensuring that they have the instructional materials and resources to engage students effectively in the curriculum, teachers tend not to be overly focused on school funding. Much of what school funding provides—school buildings with HVAC[7] and electricity to allow classes to meet comfortably in well-lighted rooms in all seasons; sufficient curriculum materials; salaries and benefits for oneself, teaching colleagues, and support staff; specialists, including school counselors and school nurses, to help you do your job better; and food and transportation for students—tend to be "givens." These are expected and necessary factors that support public education. What future teachers do not realize, however, is that not all schools have these attributes. School funding is not always sufficient or fairly distributed. In short, financial factors directly impact your ability to do your job well and help your students learn to state standards.

Until recently, educators and policy makers disagreed about whether money mattered to student learning. The *Coleman Report* (1966) seemed to conclude that families, not schools, made the differences in student achievement.[8] In the years that followed, economists claimed that taxpayers were wastefully "throwing money at schools" because they found no direct relationship between school expenditures and student achievement.[9] Some politicians picked up and continued this theme.[10] Although family and their socioeconomic status do have a major influence on children's learning, effective schools can too. Chapter 14 will explore these "effective schools" more fully.

In fact, the research consensus is clear: Money—its *total amount* and *how it is spent*—can lead to increased student achievement.[11] Evidence affirms that increased spending directed to deliver high-quality instruction to students produces the greatest achievement return for the dollars spent. Specifically, increased spending on teacher quality (effectiveness),[12] teacher professional development,[13] increased teacher salaries,[14] and improved school faculties[15] can generate improved student outcomes. Moreover, this relationship is strong and consistent over time.[16]

Moreover, studies also find that increased spending to increase education quality and quantity yields large improvements in students' eventual educational attainment (as evidenced in rising standardized test scores and higher high school graduation rates) and improved labor market outcomes when they become adults. This is especially true for low-income children.[17]

In sum, educational and economic investigators conclude that money, by itself, may not guarantee improved student outcomes, but providing *adequate* funding may be a *necessary* condition. Simply giving schools more money—without directing and administering them differently—is not likely to generate systematic improvements in student results. Recognizing the critical importance of sufficient and well-targeted funds for public schooling and student learning, future teachers will be more able to understand the key influence of school finance as they prepare to enter the profession.

11.2 EDUCATION AS AN INVESTMENT IN HUMAN CAPITAL

Our country's democracy and economic well-being depend on an educated population, or as economists say, its human capital. **Human capital** includes the skills, knowledge, talents, social and personal attributes, and experiences that an individual or a population possesses that creates value to their organization or country. It can be possessed individually or collectively, and its cumulative total represents a form of wealth that organizations and nations can use to accomplish their goals. Education is foundational to its development.

Education provides individuals with the ability to enact responsible citizenship and to earn a living in career fields such as business, medicine, law, engineering, high-tech manufacturing, and services. In fact, education is the profession that enables all other professions. It fuels the American body politic and its economy's infrastructure like nothing else in our society. We can see the effects of education dollars in our own lives and communities because they amplify the value of the American economy and our quality of life by increasing residents'

- Earning potential and
- Employability.

At the same time, education decreases the following public social costs that we underwrite with our tax dollars:

- Crime rates
- Incarceration rates

Understanding education as an investment in human capital enables future teachers to see why adequate and well-directed school funding is essential if every school and every student (regardless of socioeconomic background) will be prepared to succeed in today's—and tomorrow's—economy. To this end, we will briefly discuss how education has an undeniably positive impact on each of these factors.

11.2a Earning Potential

The 2018 U.S. Census Bureau figures show that people with higher educational levels earn more money than people with lower educational levels. Figure 11.1 shows the median annual earnings of full-time young adult workers by their educational attainment. Of course, as income rises, so do the taxes one pays to the government.

FIGURE 11.1 ■ Median Annual Earnings of Full-Time Workers, Ages 25–34, by Educational Attainment, 2000–2017

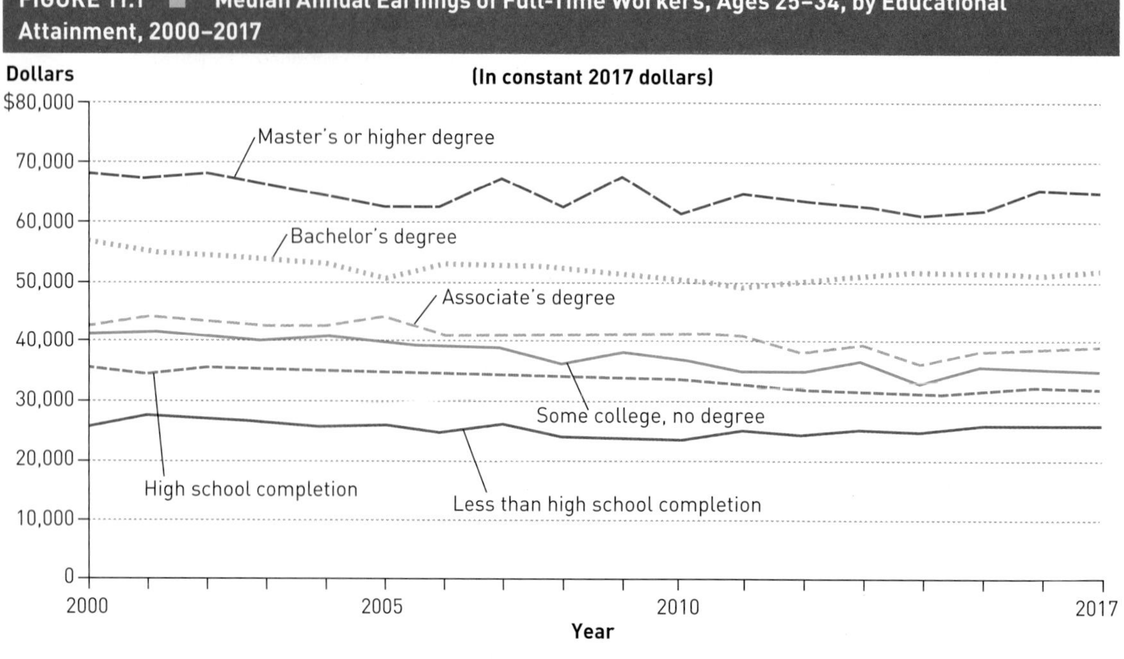

Source: U.S. Census Bureau. (2018). *Annual social and economic supplement, 2001–2018.* U.S. Department of Commerce, Figure 3. https://nces.ed.gov/programs/coe/indicator_cba.asp

Figure 11.1 shows the median annual earnings of full-time young adult workers, ages 25 to 34, by educational attainment in the years 2000 to 2017 (in 2017 constant dollars). The difference in earnings by educational level is clear: The higher the educational degree earned, the higher the median earnings over the nearly two decades.

For example, in 2018, the median earnings of young adults with a master's degree or higher were $65,000, about 19% higher than those of young adults with a bachelor's degree ($54,700). In the same year, the median earnings of young adults with a bachelor's degree were 57% higher than those of young adult high school completers ($34,900), and the median earnings of young adult high school completers were 25% higher than those of young adults who did not complete high school ($27,900). This earnings pattern holds true for both male and female young adults and for white, Black, Hispanic, and Asian young adults.[18]

Additionally, the more money earned, the more money paid in taxes to improve infrastructure (including schools), support social services, fund the military, and meet other expenses. If we assume a 40-year work life for an individual who is a high school dropout ($27,900 a year)[19] in constant 2018 dollars, the person will accumulate lifetime earnings of $1,116,000. Assuming that person paid a tax rate of 10%, over a working life he or she would have contributed $111,600 to the government coffers.

Similarly, a 2018, a person with a bachelor's degree would earn a median annual income of $54,700—about twice what a high school dropout would earn. Assuming a 40-year career in constant 2018 dollars, that person would have a lifetime earnings of $2,188,000. Assuming this person has a good accountant and pays the same 10% tax rate, the college graduate will have paid $218,800 in government taxes, almost 2 times more than the high school dropout would have paid. The higher the education, the more taxes paid over a lifetime. From the government's standpoint, an education is a very good investment, indeed.

Of course, this does not mean than every young person should attend a 4-year college. Many capable students are not interested in desk-bound academic learning. They prefer developing their technical expertise and problem-solving approaches in high-quality trade and technical programs in high schools, community colleges, or postsecondary technical schools. With this education, they can earn the skill and knowledge-based certificates and degrees that make them eligible for well-paid employment and the lifestyle that comes with it. They also support their communities and nation by paying taxes. The point is to help each student gain the type of advanced knowledge and skills needed to become competent in a competitive economy.

As we can see from these data, education acts as an economic stimulus. By providing good income to support a favorable quality of life—for the individuals themselves as well as for their families, communities, and nation through money given back in the form of taxes—education fulfills its promises for most individuals who engage it to the fullest advantage.

11.2b Employability

Before one can earn a salary, one must first get and hold a job. Education increases employability and decreases unemployment rates. Individuals with lower educational attainment are more likely to be unemployed or underemployed than those with higher educational attainment.

Figure 11.2 shows the labor force participation rates by education level for people ages 25 and over who were employed full-time, by educational attainment, in 2016. Only 58.1% of men and 33.3% of women high school dropouts are participating in the workforce.[20] The remaining percentages (41.9% men and 66.7% women) have not only dropped out of high school, but they have also dropped out of the workforce. They are no longer seeking employment, earning an income, or contributing income taxes. Many may be receiving government services, such as Temporary Assistance for Needy Families (TANF), Medicaid, or Supplemental Nutrition Assistance Programs (SNAP or "food stamps").

FIGURE 11.2 ■ Labor Force Participation Rates by Education, Ages 25+, 2016

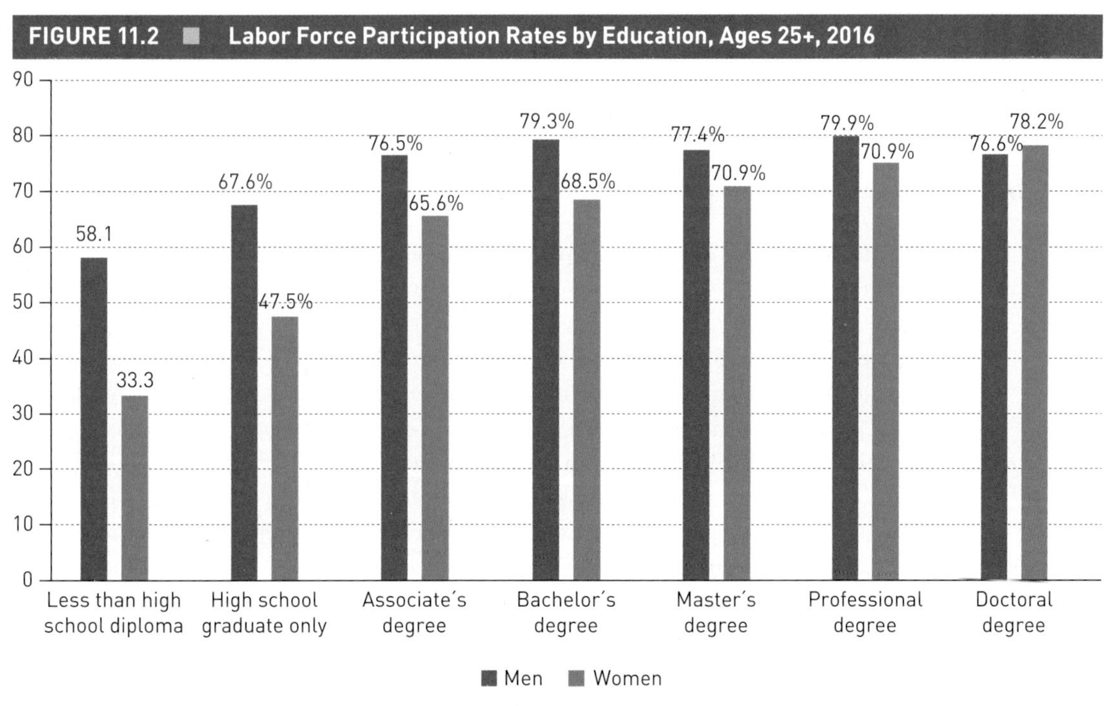

Source: Brundage, V., Jr. (2017, August). Profile of the labor force by educational attainment. Labor force participation rates by educational attainment and gender, 25 years and over, 2016 averages. *Spotlight on Statistics*. Bureau of Labor Statistics. https://www.bls.gov/spotlight/2017/educational-attainment-of-the-labor-force/home.htm

By comparison, almost 80% of men and 69% of women with a college degree are participating in the workforce and gainfully contributing to the economy and to the tax base. The remaining 20% and 31% of male and female college graduates, respectively, have left the workforce for variety of reasons, including unemployment and underemployment (accepting jobs lower than their academic or experience level) due to a mismatch between graduates' aspirations and available employment opportunities;[21] parents who took time off from work to raise their children; others who attend graduate school; or some combination of these.

The unemployment rate represents the other side of labor force participation. Figure 11.3 shows unemployment rates (by percentage) by education level and median usual weekly earnings (in dollars). The unemployment rate for high school dropouts is 2.5 times higher than that for college graduates.

FIGURE 11.3 ■ Unemployment Rates and Earnings by Educational Attainment, 2018

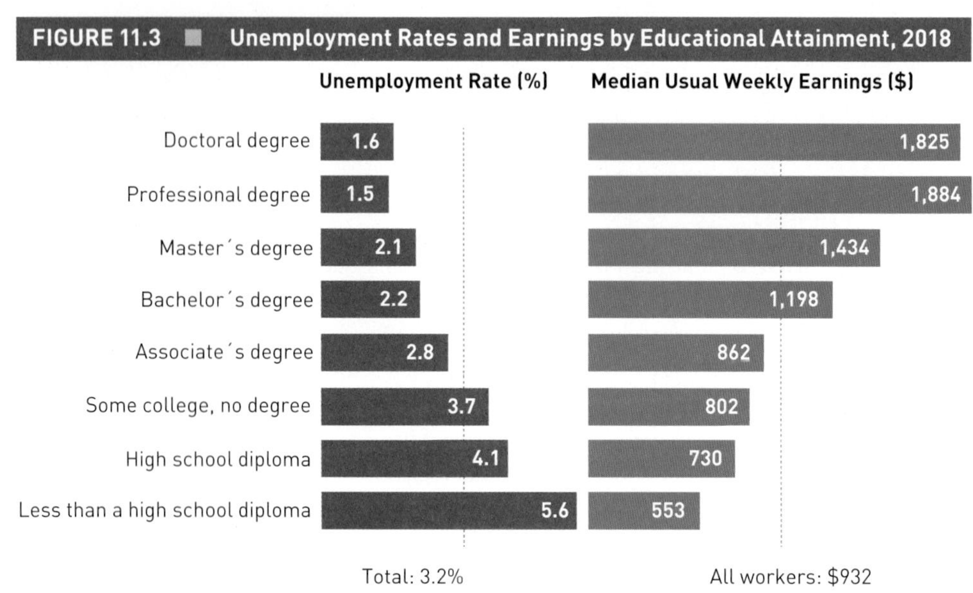

Note: Data are for persons age 25 and over. Earnings are for full-time wage and salary workers.

Source: U.S. Bureau of Labor Statistics. (2019, September 4). Unemployment rate and earnings by educational attainment. https://www.bls.gov/emp/chart-unemployment-earnings-education.htm

11.2c Public Social Costs

Although education increases revenue to individuals in income and to the government in tax dollars, it also tends to reduce public social expenses of unemployment costs, incarceration rates, and crime expenditures.

For instance, the Alliance for Excellent Education estimates that if the 1.2 million students who drop out each year earned high school diplomas instead, states could save $17 billion in health care costs over the graduates' lifetimes.[22] Likewise, studies affirm that high-quality preschool programs can provide children who live in poverty with foundational academic skills and social abilities for getting along with others with a positive attitude toward learning, hard work, and school that last well into adulthood.[23] In fact, the nonpartisan Committee for Economic Development determined that investing $4,800 per child in preschool can reduce teenage arrests by 40%. Meanwhile, the national nonprofit Coalition for Juvenile Justice reports that high school dropouts are 3 times more likely to be arrested than their peers who stay in school.[24]

In what is possibly the seminal study of the relationship between education and incarceration, Lochner and Moretti have determined that for each 1-year increase in educational level, arrest rates and crime levels decrease by 11%. Specifically, murder and assault decrease by 30%, motor vehicle theft by 20%, arson by 13%, and burglary by 6%. In addition, according to these authors, a 1% increase in the national graduation rate would save the nation nearly $2 billion each year in crime costs.[25] More recently, Lochner finds that improvements in education can lower crime, improve health, and increase voting and democratic participation.[26] Given these data, one can conclude that increased education brings sizable social benefits.

A person's educational attainment is one of the most important influences on his or her life chances regarding employment, income, health, housing, and other lifestyle factors. Although education is costly, inadequate education for large numbers of our young people may have public and social consequences that are even more costly.

11.3 FEDERAL, STATE, AND LOCAL SOURCES OF SCHOOL REVENUE

In 2017, public education revenues from all sources in the United States amounted to $705.3 billion.[27] Where does all the money come from to pay for these services? How is the money spent? How much of it goes to teachers' paychecks?

Money for schools comes from three major government sources: federal, state, and local. Increasingly, more school districts are supplementing these sources with grants from various foundations. Although education is a state function, the state is not always the largest source of school revenues. Figure 11.4 shows the percentages of school funds that have come from federal, state, and local sources over the past 40 years.

FIGURE 11.4 ■ Percentage of Revenue for Public Elementary and Secondary Education Schools by Source of Funds

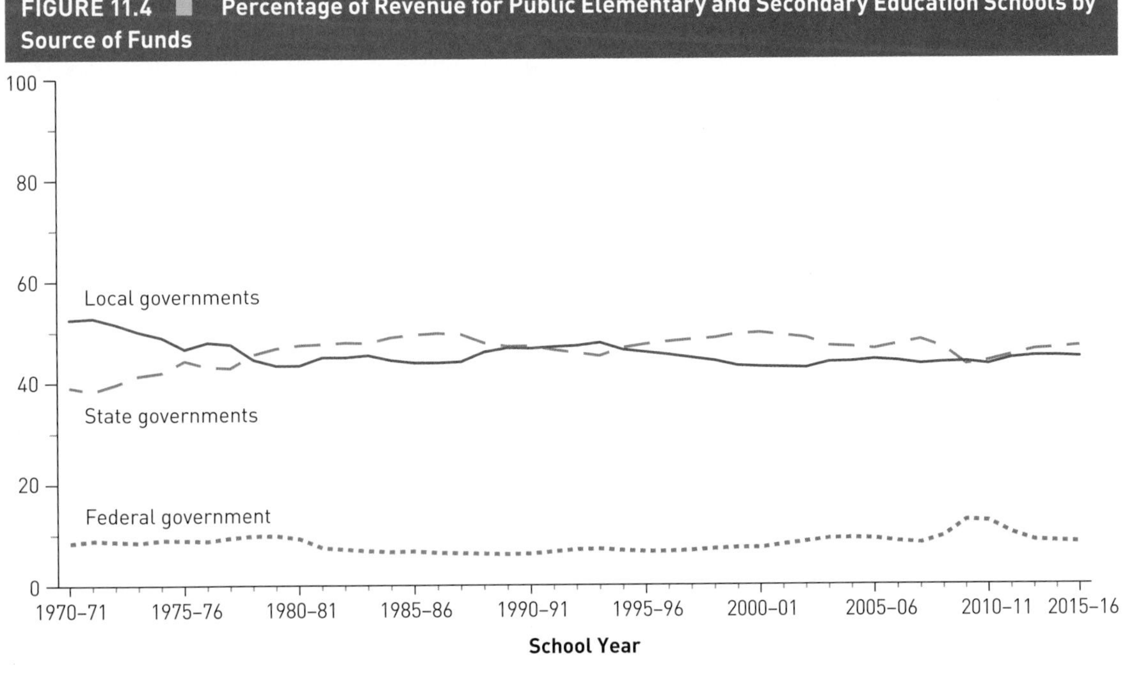

Source: Snyder, T. D., deBrey, C., and Dillow, S. A. (2019, December). *Digest of Education Statistics, 2018.* (NCES 2020-009). U.S. Department of Education. https://nces.ed.gov/pubs2020/2020009.pdf

In the 1970–1971 school year, the local governments, on average, contributed slightly more than 50% of schools' total operating revenue. State governments accounted for approximately 40% of these revenues, and the federal government paid for slightly less than 10%. Over the next 10 years, the state governments contributed more than the local government. Around the same time, the federal government's share began to drop. Since then, the federal share has remained relatively flat (around 8%), and the local and state governments have switched places several times in terms of which entity contributed more.

For the most part, American schools are a state function with a national interest that is operated locally. With the federal, state, and local governments all contributing to education, how does money come to school districts from each of the three government levels?

At the federal level, monies come back to the states once Congress has appropriated funds in an education budget. Those funds come from the federal taxes we pay.

At the state level, funding for the localities to help pay for schools is a bit more complex. A simple answer would be that states use their income and/or sales taxes to provide these funds—but not all states have income taxes, and some states have no sales taxes. Whatever ways a state raises revenues for its services, some mixture of those state funds goes to support education.

At the local level, the property tax is the predominant method for paying for schools. This tax dates back to the Massachusetts Law of 1647 that required landowners to pay a tax to support the local schools or face forfeiture of their acreage. At that time, the government taxed property because a person's real estate was the basis for his or her income.

In the days when "land was money," property was a realistic proxy for wealth. Today, for most of us this is no longer the case. Very few now derive income from our land. Instead, we earn our income from our place of employment, where that income is already taxed. Depending on the real estate market, most of us today will not realize any financial gain from our property until we sell it. That logic explains why some people object to using property taxes as the main revenue source for public schools. We will discuss taxpayers' resistance to property taxes and this movement's effects on school funding later in this chapter.

To explore the concept of why education is a smart community investment, complete the activity in the **Reflect & Engage** box, Education as an Investment in Human Capital.

REFLECT & ENGAGE: EDUCATION AS AN INVESTMENT IN HUMAN CAPITAL

Money—its *total amount* and *how it is spent*—can lead to increased student achievement. Despite its considerable costs, excellent education for all of America's children is a good investment. When it comes to quality education, as a society we can pay now or pay later.

This activity involves an individual role play.

A. You are a member of your community's school board. For at least a decade, and despite rising costs, state and local school funding has been flat. The local and state economies are fairly robust, recovered from the Great Recession. Nonetheless, teachers have not received cost-of-living raises in at least 12 years, and they complain that they lack the needed instructional supplies to keep their students engaged and learning. Resigning, retiring, and transferring teachers are not always replaced, and many classes (especially those for struggling students) now have over 35 students apiece. Achievement for the "high-flying" students is lagging, and achievement for the least able learners is falling.

B. Working in groups of four, prepare a 5-minute presentation to your school funding agency (township, county, or city governance officials) about your concerns regarding the condition of local teaching and learning.

C. In your presentation, using data and information from this chapter, explain why more adequately funding your public schools is a wise investment in human capital, and identify the areas of investment that research evidence suggests bring the greatest gains to student learning and achievement.

D. Present your arguments to your locality's governing board (the rest of the class). Be ready to answer questions that the governing board might have about your request and suggestions.

E. As a class, discuss the school finance facts that you find most surprising and important to you as a future teacher and voting citizen.

11.4 INCREASES IN EDUCATION SPENDING SINCE 1960

Education costs have been growing since we have been keeping figures on the subject. Figure 11.5 shows the change in the number of teachers and the student–teacher ratio since 1960 and the increase in total dollars spent on education during that same period. In examining this figure, it is easy to see that school expenditures have risen as the number of teachers has increased. That relationship makes sense: It costs money to hire additional teachers. It is interesting to note that the student–teacher ratios have been declining since at least 1960.

FIGURE 11.5 ■ Number of Teachers and Student–Teacher Ratio and Total Pupil Expenditures

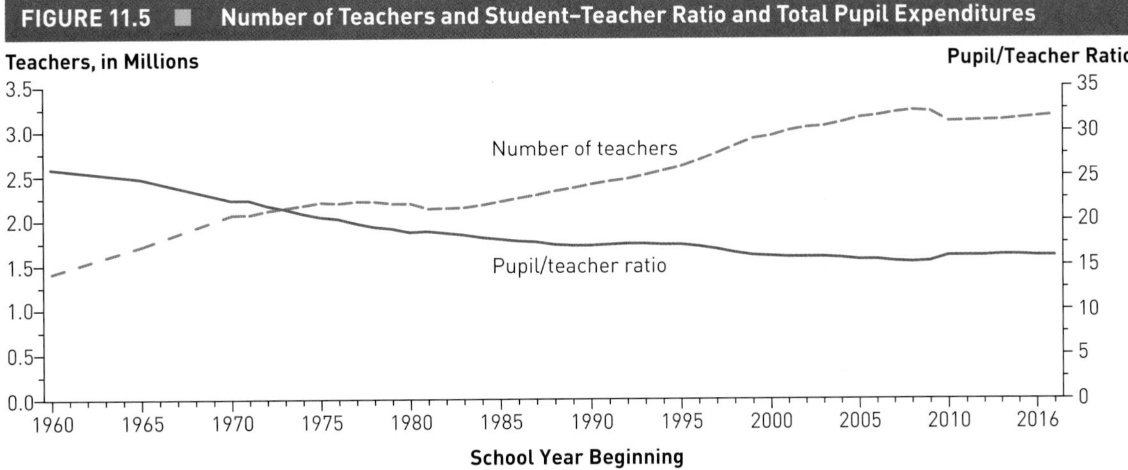

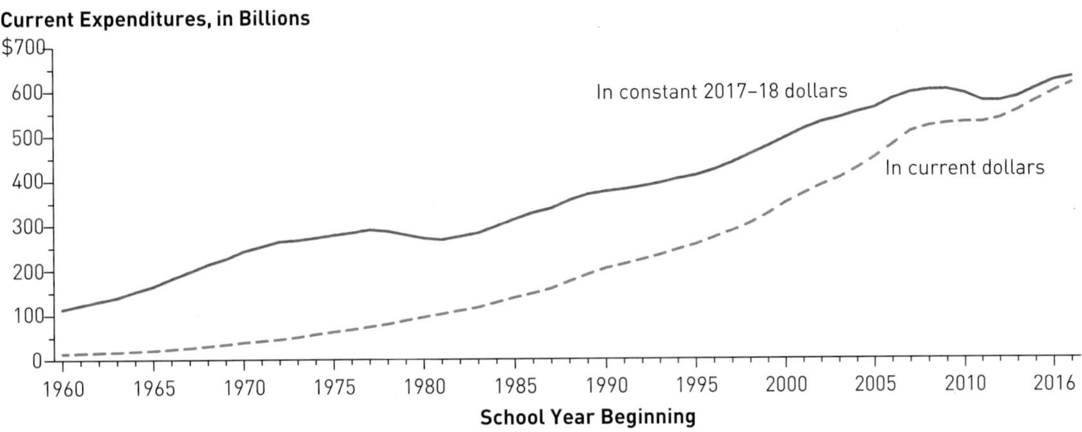

Source: Snyder et al., 2019. https://nces.ed.gov/pubs2020/2020009.pdf

11.4a Reasons for Increased Education Spending

Several reasons account for the increases in the number of public school teachers hired since 1960. In addition to the large baby boomer cohort entering high school, schools began serving more and increasingly diverse students as a result of court-mandated desegregation. This student population growth as well as court-ordered school desegregation required hiring more teachers and providing more equitable teacher salaries.[28]

Additionally, during this time more schools began to work with students with disabilities, whose education requires a teacher to work closely with fewer students. Although students with disabilities as a percentage of the total student population increased from 9.7% in 1978 to 11.6% in 1990 and although the number of special education teachers rose by more than 50% during these same years, this increase was responsible for only 18% of the growth in school spending over this period.[29]

Also during these years, educators concluded that having more than 30 to 40 students in every class was not an effective environment for teaching and learning. As a consequence, the pupil-to-teacher ratio declined: from 35:1 in 1890, to 28.1 in 1940, to 24.9:1 in 1960, to 20.5 in 1970, to 15.4 in 1990.[30] The two most important factors in the increased school expenditures since 1960 have been (1) the rising costs of instructional staff and (2) the declining pupil-to-teacher ratios as schools have attempted to raise school quality by reducing the pupil-to-staff ratios.[31]

In addition to the decrease in student–teacher ratios, increased student enrollments have affected U.S. school expenditures. Figure 11.6 shows the total student enrollment in U.S. public schools since 1960. From 1960 to 2016, total enrollments increased from 35 million to slightly over 50 million students. Along with greater expenditures devoted to decreasing class size and teaching more diverse

FIGURE 11.6 ■ Total Enrollment in U.S. Public Schools, 1960–2016

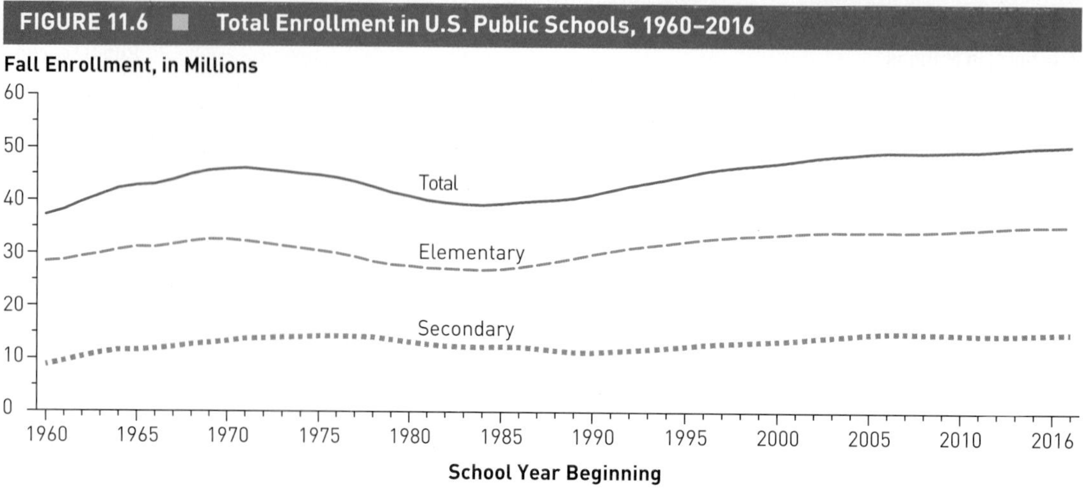

Source: Snyder et al., 2019. https://nces.ed.gov/pubs2020/2020009.pdf

students and those with disabilities, schools hired more teachers to meet the demand produced by increased student enrollments.

Knowing the full story behind the increasing cost figures helps to explain events with data. These data are especially important if you are considering a career in public education. Thinking of you as an "inside expert," friends and family may ask you, "Why are education costs increasing so much?" and "Why are we spending more money and not getting better results?" The information in this chapter will help you answer these challenging questions successfully and convincingly.

The pupil–teacher ratios have been reduced from 35:1 in 1900 to 16:1 in 2020.

thislife pictures/Alamy Stock Photo

11.4b National, Regional, and Local Education Expenses

How much does it cost to educate a child in the United States? The answer to this question varies widely according to the region, the state, and the locality. It also varies by the state and local wealth available to fund education: Affluent states and localities can fund education to higher levels.

Table 11.1 shows the average per-pupil expenditure for each state, the District of Columbia, and selected U.S. territories. Quite a variance appears in average state spending levels for each student.

TABLE 11.1 ■ Per-Pupil Spending by State, 2019

State	Per-Pupil Spending	State	Per-Pupil Spending
U.S. Average	**$12,756**		
Alabama	$10,386	Nebraska	$14,385
Alaska	$17,872	Nevada	$9,185
Arizona	$8,335	New Hampshire	$16,347
Arkansas	$11,951	New Jersey	$16,543
California	$10,281	New Mexico	$10,764
Colorado	$10,053	New York	$19,697
Connecticut	$17,798	North Carolina	$9,367
Delaware	$15,009	North Dakota	$14,381
District of Columbia*	$12,201	Ohio	$13,051
Florida	$9,764	Oklahoma	$9,250
Georgia	$10,114	Oregon	$11,905
Hawaii	$14,254	Pennsylvania	$16,122
Idaho	$8,677	Rhode Island	$15,320
Indiana	$11,626	South Carolina	$9,367
Illinois	$13,829	South Dakota	$11,430
Indiana	$11,626	Tennessee	$9,694
Iowa	$13,241	Texas	$8,619
Kansas	$11,753	Utah	$7,635
Kentucky	$11,210	Vermont	$20,540
Louisiana	$12,362	Virginia	$10,530
Maine	$16,006	Washington	$11,125
Maryland	$13,146	West Virginia	$12,915
Massachusetts	$14,529	Wisconsin	$12,558
Michigan	$13,016	Wyoming	$18,090
Minnesota	$13,068		
Mississippi	$10,240		
Missouri	$11,756	U.S. Virgin Islands**	$13,449
Montana	$14,229	Puerto Rico**	$7,591

Notes:

*U.S. Census Bureau. (2019, May 21). U.S. school spending per pupil increased for fifth consecutive year. https://www.census.gov/newsroom/press-releases/2019/school-spending.html

**For fiscal year, 2016. Cornman, S. Q., Zhou, L., Howell, M. R., & Young, J. (2018, December). *Revenues and expenditures for public elementary and secondary school education: School year 2015–16 (Fiscal Year 2016)—First look.* (NCES 2019-301). National Center for Education Statistics. https://nces.ed.gov/pubs2019/2019301.pdf

Source: Education Week. (2019, June 4). *Map–How much money each state spends per student: Quality counts 2019: Grading the states.* https://www.edweek.org/ew/collections/quality-counts-2019-state-finance/map-per-pupil-spending-state-by-state.html

The national average is $12,756 per pupil. Among the states, Vermont (on average) has the highest per-pupil expenditure ($20,540), and Utah has the lowest ($7,635). When the territories are examined, the average per-pupil expenditure drops even lower. Note that these figures are averages within each of the states; inside each state, large differences also occur between districts.

Just as differences exist among states in per-pupil spending, school districts also vary in the amount of funding they allot to each school within the same district. Fiscal policies assume that increased financial resources will be sent to schools and students most in need of academic assistance to educate every student to high academic standards. Too often, the reverse is happening. Schools with a high concentration of affluent students (so-called "alpha" schools) are receiving more funds per student than are schools serving concentrations of low-income and underrepresented students (so-called "omega" schools), even within the same school district.[32] Many reasons help explain this situation: increased costs for more experienced and academically credentialed teachers at the alpha schools;[33] within-district funding formulas that allocate positions rather than dollars to schools; teacher-sorting patterns that allow higher-paid teachers to systematically choose lower-needs schools;[34] and lack of transparency about intradistrict-funding decisions.[35] One study describes how for every dollar spent at one urban community's high-status high school, the district spends only 39.7 cents at the district's low-status high school.[36]

To more deeply explore the inequities and the role of "parent voice" in school funding decisions within the same school district, complete the activity in the **Reflect & Engage** box, Comparing Happy Valley and Dismal Swamp High School Budgets.

REFLECT & ENGAGE: COMPARING HAPPY VALLEY AND DISMAL SWAMP HIGH SCHOOL BUDGETS

This activity involves data analysis and role play. School districts often allocate more per-pupil funding to some of its schools than to all of its schools.

A. You are groups of concerned parents from Dismal Swamp High School. Working together in groups of three or four, analyze the data in Table 11.2 and make a persuasive case for why Dismal Swamp High School needs higher per-pupil funding than they are currently receiving.

B. Each group will present its case for more equitable funding to your local school board (the rest of the class).

C. Discuss the role of "parent voice" in school funding allocations. How might you enlist Happy Valley High School parents to join Dismal Swamp parents to support your argument for higher per-pupil funding at Dismal Swamp High School? How might you address the Happy Valley parents' concerns about losing money from their high school?

TABLE 11.2 ■ Comparing Happy Valley and Dismal Swamp High School Budgets

	Happy Valley High School	Dismal Swamp High School
Students	2,500	1,600
Administrators	Principal: $100,000	Principal: $85,000
	Assistant Principals (6): $540,000	Assistant Principals (4): $340,000
Professional staff	Deans (4): $300,000	Deans (1): $58,000
	Counselors (9): $585,000	Counselors (5): $275,000
	Instructors (190): $10,450,000	Instructors (100): $3,800,000
Classified	Secretaries (15): $480,000	Secretaries (8): $280,000
	Custodians (11): $440,000	Custodians (6): $240,000
Operations and maintenance	$850,000	$300,000

	Happy Valley High School	Dismal Swamp High School
Professional development	$60,000	$18,000
Field trip transportation	$50,000	$20,000
Instructional supplies	$400,000	$100,000
Total spending	$14,255,000	$5,264,000
Total per-pupil spending	$5,702	$3,290
Cents spent per dollar	$1 per pupil	57.7 cents per pupil
Notes	International Baccalaureate	No air conditioning
	12:2 pupil-to-teacher ratio	16:5 pupil-to-teacher ratio
	12 department chairs on 12-month contracts	4 department chairs on 11-month contracts
	Most teachers at top end of salary scale	Most teachers at lower end of salary scale

Source: Adapted from Owings, W. A., and Kaplan, L. S. (2010). The alpha and omega syndrome: Is intra-district funding the next ripeness factor? *Journal of Education Finance, 36*(2), 162–185.

11.5 EXPENDITURES: HOW SCHOOL DISTRICTS SPEND MONEY

Operating a school system is a complex undertaking, whose costs go far beyond teacher salaries and supplies. The growth in school spending outside teacher salaries has increased from one third of total expenditures in 1940 to more than one half of school costs in 1990.[37] These funds go toward items such as administrative support and utilities to keep the lights, heat, and air conditioning running. They cover the expense of operating and maintaining school buses or buildings, ordering all the cafeteria food and supplies, and accounting for meal prices and student lunch payments. With virtually every school system having a different budgeting process, comparing how states and school districts spend money is informative.

11.5a Spending Categories

The *Digest of Education Statistics, 2018* separates education expenditures into 10 defined categories. The *Digest* also provides dollar amounts and budget percentages for each category, as seen in Table 11.3.

Instruction includes teachers, teaching assistants, school-based curriculum support personnel, and anyone directly related to teaching children. These costs include salaries, benefits, supplies, tuition reimbursement, and the like for all persons included in this category. More than half of school expenditures (61%) are spent on classroom instruction.[38] Classroom instruction can mean literally inside a classroom or in other learning situations. As Table 11.3 shows, instruction is by far the largest budget category.

Student support includes school counselors, health care providers (school nurses), attendance personnel (the people who maintain attendance rolls and call students home if they are absent to make certain they are really sick), school psychologists, and speech pathologists.

Instructional staff services include curriculum development, staff professional development, libraries, media, and technology centers. Again, this category takes into account all salaries, benefits, supplies, equipment, and costs associated with these functions.

General administration involves the personnel who administer leadership responsibilities at the central office level whose responsibilities are not delineated in other named categories. The school administration category includes building-level principals and assistant principals and their associated costs.

TABLE 11.3 ■ National Average PreK–12 Education Budgets and Related Expenditures, 2015–2016

Budget Category	Expenditure (%)
Instruction	61
Student support	5.7
Instructional staff services	5.2
General administration	2.2
School administration	5.5
Operations and maintenance	9.2
Student transportation	4.1
Other support services	3.6
Food services	4.0
Enterprise operations	Less than 0.5
Total	100.5*

**Notes:* Error due to rounding. Does not include current expenditures for other programs, capital outlay, or interest on school debt.

Source: Avery et al., 2019. https://nces.ed.gov/pubs2020/2020009.pdf. Calculations by authors. The expenditure percentages totals to 100.5% due to rounding.

The operations and maintenance category includes the cost of using and keeping up the buildings. Operations include electricity, heat, and insurance on the buildings and their contents. Maintenance includes custodial workers, building and grounds upkeep, and supplies and equipment needed to keep the building clean and in good order.

Student transportation involves all costs of operating the familiar yellow school buses. It includes the price of buses themselves as well as the drivers, mechanics, fuel, tires, and equipment required to transport students.

The other support services category includes business support for paying, transporting, or exchanging goods and services for the school district. It includes central office support for planning; research; evaluation; and information, staff, and data processing as well as other central support services. In some smaller school districts, a small number of employees may assume responsibility for several functions, so this category is relatively small. In larger systems, more administrators, supervisors, and coordinators work on these tasks. For instance, a large school district may have assistant superintendents for instruction, school leadership, business, human resources, and evaluation, each with an entire professional and clerical staff to support this area.

Food services involves all the people, equipment, and supplies needed to feed students while they are at school. Someone must order the bulk food, plan menus, staff cafeterias, coordinate the federal free and reduced-price lunch information, and make certain that the operation does not lose money. Frequently, the school district's food service department operates the largest chain of "restaurants" in the locality.

Obviously, the operation of a school system and all of its finances are intricate and complex. They involve people, supplies, and processes that many teachers have never considered to be a part of education. Arguably, money should go where research informs us that money makes a difference to student learning. Later in this chapter, we will review research-based findings of how school spending can improve student achievement.

11.5b Teacher Salaries

In education, salaries and benefits generally account for approximately 60% to 70% of the total budget. The exact percentage depends on what the school district considers as instruction. For example, some states include instructional support staff and/or school principals under the instruction category. Because teachers are the largest group in education, most monies go to teacher salaries.

Table 11.4 shows the average teacher salary for each state from the National Education Association's *State Rankings 2018*. The U.S. average public school teacher salary for 2017 to 2018 was $60,477, with state average teacher salaries ranging from those in New York ($84, 384), California ($80,680), and Massachusetts ($80,357) at the high end to Mississippi ($44,926), West Virginia ($45,642), and Oklahoma ($46,300) at the low end. These salaries are not distributed equally across schools. Experienced and more highly paid teachers tend to teach in more affluent schools. And although the exact figures may vary year to year, states' relative position on teachers' salaries tends to remain constant. Table 11.4 averages the salaries to the state level to provide a comparison.

TABLE 11.4 ■ Rank and Average Public School Teacher Salaries, 2017–2018

Rank/State	Average Salary	Rank/State	Average Salary
1. New York	$84,384	27. Texas	$53,334
2. California	$80,680	28. Kentucky	$52,952
3. Massachusetts	$80,357	29. North Dakota	$52,850
4. District of Columbia	$76,486	30. Montana	$52,776
5. Connecticut	$74,517	31. Colorado	$52,701
6. New Jersey	$69,917	32. Virginia	$51,994
7. Alaska	$69,682	33. Wisconsin	$51,469
8. Maryland	$ 69,627	34. North Carolina	$51,231
9. Pennsylvania	$ 67,535	35. Tennessee	$50,900
10. Rhode Island	$66,758	36. Indiana	$50,614
11. Illinois	$65,721	37. Alabama	$50,568
12. Oregon	$63,061	38. Arkansas	$50,544
13. Michigan	$61,911	39. Louisiana	$50,359
14. Delaware	$61,795	40. South Carolina	$50,182
15. Vermont	$60,556	41. Kansas	$49,754
16. Wyoming	$58,352	42. Utah	$49,655
17. Ohio	$58,000	43. Missouri	$49,304
18. Hawaii	$57,866	44. Idaho	$49,225
19. New Hampshire	$57,833	45. Arizona	$48,723
20. Minnesota	$57,782	46. Florida	$48,168
21. Iowa	$57,018	47. South Dakota	$47,631
22. Georgia	$56,329	48. New Mexico	$47,152
23. Washington	$55,693	49. Oklahoma	$46,300
24. Nevada	$54,280	50. West Virginia	$45,642
25. Nebraska	$54,213	51. Mississippi	$44,926
26. Maine	$53,815	**United States**	**$60,477**

Source: National Education Association (NEA) Research. (2019, April). *Rankings of the states (2018) and estimates of school statistics (2019)*. http://www.nea.org/assets/docs/2019%20Rankings%20and%20Estimates%20Report.pdf

The range between the highest and lowest salaries is more than $39,000. Over a 30-year career in education, the difference between being paid at the highest and lowest salary ends could translate into a $1,170, 000—more than $1 million difference—in lifetime earnings.[39]

How do teacher salaries compare with salaries in other jobs that require comparable skill and education? As discussed in Chapter 2, according to a report by the Economic Policy Institute, weekly pay for teachers is 23% *less* than their nonteaching college-educated peers for jobs with comparable skill and education requirements.[40] No doubt, this salary disparity discourages many well-educated and talented individuals from seeking careers as teachers.

11.6 EQUITY ISSUES IN SCHOOL FUNDING

Considering how schools' funds should be allocated and spent are critical concerns. Most of us believe in equal treatment for individuals, yet students come to school with different learning needs. Should all students receive *equal* funding? What is an *adequate* amount of funding to bring all students to high levels of learning and achievement?

11.6a Spending per Pupil

Earlier, we saw the 50 states' differences in per-pupil spending. These differences raise this question: Should every state spend the same amount per pupil? Similarly, **Reflect & Engage**, Comparing Happy Valley and Dismal Swamp High School Budgets, asked you to think about whether needier schools within a district should receive more funding than less needy schools. Here lies the difference between equity and equality. Although the two concepts sound alike, they are very different. In its essence, **equity** is providing the services students actually need, whereas **equality** is providing the same services for all students regardless of the students' or locality's needs. Equity can be defined as a fairness issue for both students and taxpayers. The difference between equity and equality explains why equity, much more than equality, is a basic tenet of our school finance system.[41]

Adequacy—providing sufficient resources to accomplish the job of educating our children—is another money-related issue affecting fairness in school funding. A workable definition would be providing enough funds "to teach the average student to state standards, and then to identify how much each district/school requires to teach underserved students—those with learning disabilities, those from poverty backgrounds, and those lacking English proficiency—to the same high and rigorous achievement standards."[42] How much funding is adequate? As a fiscal concept, adequacy is value driven, with people defining it subjectively according to their own priorities and opinions. Although attempts have been made to quantify how much a state or school district needs to spend for its students, the actual figure remains unclear.

School funding adequacy has been a focus of active litigation. Since 1995, a number of school funding court cases have produced major changes in state education policy around the country. School finance litigation has forced states to not only change the way they fund schools but also to improve and update their state assessment and accountability systems. As of 2020, 45 states have been involved in some form of K–12 school finance litigation,[43] and 12 states are currently involved in active litigation.[44] These suits address the state's role in ensuring equitable spending among districts, providing suitable school facilities, and delivering adequate funding of programs designed for special education and at-risk students. Since 1989, plaintiffs have won almost 60% of adequacy cases.[45] When used wisely, the money awarded in these cases repeatedly translates into more resources for poorer districts and improved results for schools and students.

Consider the following scenario from Table 11.5. Two relatively similar school systems have roughly the same amount of money coming to them from the federal, state, and local governments: $10,600 per student. The two systems have roughly the same capacity to fund education, as seen from the average family income, and both have the same number of students to educate.

Both school systems draw from upper-middle-class neighborhoods where parents expect their children to go to college. In School System A, 3% of the students have been identified as eligible for special education services—far below the national average. In School System B, 18%—6 times as many—of

TABLE 11.5 ■ Equality Versus Equity Example

School System	Average Family Income	Federal Revenue	State Revenue	Local Revenue	Percentage of Students Eligible for Special Education
A	$65,000	$1,050	$3,550	$6,000	3
B	$65,100	$1,100	$3,450	$6,050	18

Source: Leslie S. Kaplan and William A. Owings [Original by authors].

the students have been identified as eligible to receive special education services, a rate higher than the national average.

If we look solely at the issue of equality, both school systems have the funds they need: $10,600 per pupil. If we look at the equity issue, however, the students' needs in School System B are greater than those in School System A. School System B must spend more money to meet the identified learning needs than does School System A. Equal funding for these systems may seem fair at first—until we consider the students' needs. Because of the varying student needs and the associated costs, treating these two systems equally on a financial basis would be neither fair nor equitable.

Consider this analogy. Imagine going to a physician who treats all patients equally. Each patient gets the same regimen at the same cost. It sounds ridiculous because we expect to be treated on the basis of our differing health needs. We expect to care for a common cold differently than we care for cancer, and we realize that managing cancer costs more than managing the sniffles. We want and expect to receive the medical care we require. The same is true in education. Although all students should have an equal opportunity for a good education, students may require a different level of services, depending on their unique situations.

Education is expensive, but providing poor and inadequate education for large numbers of students may be even more costly. Inadequately educated students bring steep public and social consequences. As discussed previously, money matters when it comes to student achievement. The more money spent wisely on student learning, the more students learn.

11.6b Funding Inequalities

Most parents and students in affluent school districts expect their children's schools to be clean, resource rich, and staffed with the best teachers that competitive (and regularly paid) salaries and excellent working conditions can provide. They make sure their schools have the funds to deliver on these expectations. As a result, schools serving different student populations often show large "funding gaps." School districts do not receive equal or equitable funding. Large differences exist between the monies available to educate low-income children as compared to affluent children. These disparities contribute strongly to the differences in their learning opportunities and outcomes.

Approximately 50% of schools' local financial support comes from local taxes, mostly from property taxes. As a result, the wealthiest districts are able to spend as much as 3 times the per-pupil amount spent by the most economically disadvantaged districts.[46] In other words, children attending schools in districts with a lot of taxable wealth may have more money spent on their education than children (often with higher educational needs) attending schools with little taxable wealth.

The differences between districts with high property values and poorer districts in the region are profound and show up vividly in per-pupil spending. States in which school funding relies mainly on local property taxes place property-poor districts at a severe fiscal disadvantage. Although state and federal subsidies help high-poverty districts, they usually don't close the funding gap. In 2018, Education Trust, a nonprofit, nonpartisan organization that advocates for high-quality education for low-income children, found that our nation's highest-poverty districts receive about $1,000 less per student than the lowest-poverty districts. And the differences between districts serving the most students of color and those serving the fewest is almost twice as large, about $1,800 per student.[47] Some districts spend 2 to 6 times more on students than other districts, even within the same state.[48]

Notably, the "spending gaps" also happen within school districts that draw from the same wealth base. Frequently, uneven amounts of per-pupil dollars appear to go to the schools with more white students. For example, a 2010 article described the "Alpha and Omega Syndrome"—an eye-opening actual funding difference between two high schools in the same community. The alpha high school (with 600 more students than the omega high school) spent $8,222 per pupil each year, whereas the omega high school across town spent $3,265 per pupil per year. Likewise, the alpha high school had twice as many teachers, 4 times as many deans, 50% more counselors, smaller class sizes, almost 4 times the monies allotted for field trips, twice the number of secretaries and custodians, and air conditioning, as compared with the omega school. Although real, this example is anecdotal and cannot be generalized to all schools—but it points to important fairness issues.[49]

School funding "gaps" affect student learning and achievement.

iStock/tacojim

Whether between or within school districts, this "spending gap" is a national equity concern. Research finds that schools in certain states receive up to 3 times more money per pupil than in other states.[50] Student demographics, costs of living, teacher pay and benefits, class sizes and tax structures—and legislative decisions in the state capital—all influence education spending. Regardless of the reasons, this disparity in resources translates into educational quality differences in such areas as teacher effectiveness, class size, facilities' upkeep, available technology, and other factors that can affect student learning opportunities, outcomes, and, ultimately, students' life chances. By contrast, adequate resources—such as well-prepared teachers and school leaders, smaller class sizes (especially in the early grades), and extended learning time—tend to result in improved student outcomes.[51]

Without a doubt, reliance on local property taxes is especially unfair to the African American, Latinx, and Native American students who are disproportionately concentrated in the lowest-funded, lowest-spending schools. Their families, on average, own less wealth and have lower per-capita and family incomes than white Americans.[52]

As the "Alpha and Omega Syndrome" illustrates, school districts create fiscal inequities between high- and low-poverty schools worse by the ways they choose to spend the funds they do have. In a study of spending patterns in dozens of school districts in 20 states, two major patterns emerged. First, school districts spent less money on salaries in high-poverty schools than in low-poverty schools within the same district (mainly because these teachers tend to have fewer years of teaching experience so receive salaries lower on the district's salary scale). Second, districts assigned a larger share of unrestricted funds to low-poverty schools (generally, where more affluent parents tend to have sway in educational decisions). Apparently, resource-rich schools keep getting more; resource-poor schools get less.[53]

11.6c The Cost of Educating Low-Income Students

To educate children growing up in poverty to common meaningful standards costs more than it does to bring more affluent students up to these standards. The Education Trust calculates that educating children from low-income families costs 40% more than educating their middle-class peers.[54] Children from low-income families typically have more educational and academic ground to cover in order to reach appropriate grade-level expectations than their more affluent peers (who usually have many educational and academic experiences—the cultural capital—as part of their lifestyles outside school). Low-income students need more instructional time, and they especially need well-prepared, effective teachers.

For instance, in 2016, suburban Chicago school districts spent more than $10,000 per pupil than schools in urban Chicago.[55]At the same time, states that invest in the resources that make a difference in student learning and achievement—low pupil-to-teacher ratios, especially for high-poverty districts, and competitive wages—tend to have higher academic outcomes among children from low-income families and show smaller income-based achievement gaps.[56] Many view this insufficient funding as shortsighted. A National Bureau of Economic Research report finds that a 20% increase in per-pupil spending a year for low-income children can lead to an extra year of completed education, 25% higher earnings as an adult, and a 20% reduction in the incidence of poverty in adulthood.[57] Similarly, a study finds that school funding reforms that intended to provide sufficient resources (adequacy) to accomplish the job of educating our children between 1990 and 2011 improved educational opportunity by raising student achievement in low-income districts. In fact, states with school finance reform saw decreasing achievement gaps between white students and students of color over the period studied, whereas states without school finance reform saw their achievement gaps increase.[58] Despite the compelling evidence, most states still have not enacted school funding reforms to meet the additional learning needs of all students, especially those from poverty, with disabilities, or who lack English fluency.[59]

School finance reforms that work include funding underserved students at higher levels, investing in growing educator capacity through professional development, ensuring assets' equitable distribution across schools, and guaranteeing access to quality preschool. Likewise, outcomes to society of providing sufficient educational resources to schools in low-income neighborhoods include increased graduation rates, hundreds of thousands of dollars added to the economy as graduates earn better wages and pay higher taxes, and reduced costs for health care, unemployment, crime, and incarceration.

AMERICAN EDUCATION SPOTLIGHT: MICHAEL REBELL

America invented the idea of public education and the ideal of educational equality. Yet the persistent gap between the American idea and the reality of blatantly inadequate schooling for low-income and underrepresented children threatens to undermine our nation's political and economic vitality. Money—where it comes from, how much is "enough," and how it's spent—is a critical factor affecting this disparity.

David Shankbone/CC BY-SA (http://creativecommons.org/licenses/by-sa/3.0/)

As an experienced lawyer and scholar, Michael A. Rebell litigates and studies school funding adequacy cases to advance the cause of high-quality education for every student. As executive director of the Campaign for Educational Equity, cofounder of The Campaign for Fiscal Equity, Inc., and Professor of Law and Educational Practice at Teachers College, Columbia University, Rebell is the foremost authority on children's educational rights and the education adequacy movement in the United States. He has pioneered the legal theory and strategy of educational adequacy. In recent decades, this legal strategy has proven successful in almost 60% of the cases challenging a state's failure to provide students with a sound, basic education.[60] As a result, states have directed more funds to schools serving primarily low-income and underrepresented students—those schools that need resources the most. As Rebell sees it, virtually all children need to meet rigorous academic standards if the United States is to remain a democracy and keep its competitive position in the global economy.

A prolific author, Rebell has written several books and dozens of articles on educational equity, education finance, testing, rights of students with disabilities, and dropout prevention. Rebell is a graduate of Harvard College and Yale Law School.

As a child of the 1960s and later as a law student, Rebell became fascinated by the courts' role in promoting social reform. He marveled at how principled judges could reshape failing social institutions while keeping their constitutional values. Wanting to become part of the process, he soon realized that reshaping complex institutions was itself a highly complex endeavor. He returned to graduate school and built a career that combined part-time teaching and scholarly writing with a substantial litigation practice focused on education reform. His professional life is characterized by reflection and practice mutually informing each other to determine what had been accomplished and what could be done next.

Rebell viewed the Great Recession's severe education budget cutting, which pink-slipped or "furloughed" teachers, raised class sizes to over 40 students, canceled classes, and shortened the school week, as both unconscionable and unconstitutional. He insists that the right to a quality education is not conditional and that the persistence of such conditions may permanently damage the life chances of entire generations of children. Children's right to education is not negotiable, he argues.

Critics brand adequacy lawsuit outcomes as "judicial activism" and question whether courts should be establishing policies for state spending or compelling governors and legislatures to make major policy decisions. Also, determining what a "sound, basic" education includes may require equal parts professional judgment and guesswork.

Rebell agrees that courts should not write education policy. He insists, however, that many of the critics' concerns are overstated. Additionally, he believes that only by involving those persons who must put school reforms into practice, including teachers, administrators, and students, will court rulings make positive impacts in classrooms.

Sources: Rebell, M. A. (2009). *Courts and kids: Pursuing equity through the state courts.* University of Chicago Press, pp. vi–viii; Rebell, M. (2010, February 8). Educational budget cuts unconscionable—and unconstitutional. *The Huffington Post.* http://www.huffingtonpost.com/michael-rebell/educational-budget-cuts-u_b_453636.html; Rebell, M. A. (1998). Fiscal equity litigation and the democratic imperative. *Journal of Education Finance, 24*(1), 23–50; Rebel, M. A., & Hughes, R. L. (1996). Schools, communities, and the courts: A dialogic approach to education reform. *Yale Law and Policy Review, 14*(1), 99–168; Rebell, M. A., & Wolff, J. (2008). *Moving every child ahead: From NCLB hype to meaningful educational opportunity.* Teachers College Press; Rebell, M. (2011). Faculty profile. Teachers College, Columbia University. https://www.tc.columbia.edu/faculty/mar224/; Richardson, L. (2003, July 3). Public lives: A child of the 60s and a keeper of the faith. *The New York Times.* http://www.nytimes.com/2003/07/03/nyregion/public-lives-a-child-of-the-60-s-and-a-keeper-of-the-faith.html

11.6d Salary Inequalities

We know from the extensive research at the state, district, school, and individual levels that teacher qualifications—their academic background, preparation for teaching, verbal fluency, certification status, and experience—significantly affect how much their students learn.[61] Students who live in poverty, who speak a language other than English, or have special education needs particularly benefit academically when taught by well-prepared, experienced teachers.

Typically, teachers in a school district receive salaries from a salary scale or schedule, with increased monies paid for increased years of teaching experience and more academic credentials. Teachers with little or no experience and fewer advanced degrees receive lower salaries. As a result, schools with higher-average teacher salaries tend to have the more experienced and well-educated teachers. Schools with lower-average teacher salaries tend to have the newcomers with the fewest years of professional experiences.

Teacher effectiveness factors are important to student learning outcomes.

iStock_M_a_y_a

These salary discrepancies affect classroom learning and school climate in varied ways. Some studies find that the most highly experienced and credentialed teachers are not randomly distributed within a school district. Instead, they are concentrated in high socioeconomic status (SES) schools, which tend to have both higher per-pupil expenditures and higher teacher salaries.[62] Such schools may be more attractive to teachers because of real or perceived differences in tangible resources, such as more books, more computers, wider availability of teachers' aides, and more achievement-oriented students. Conversely, the least qualified, least experienced, lowest-paid teachers tend to work in schools with the highest number of low-income and underrepresented students. Often, new teachers start their careers at such high-poverty schools. High teacher and student turnover and a greater percentage of novice teachers working in the lowest-achieving, high-poverty schools contribute to both inconsistent instruction and the neediest learners working year after year with the least experienced teachers. With constant teacher turnover, principals have difficulty establishing a culture for learning or providing a skilled, experienced, and caring teacher corps to positively impact student achievement.[63]

For instance, in California the average school district has relatively few inexperienced and uncredentialed teachers, but in several districts, they make up a large share—as much as 50% or more—of the teaching force.[64] Low-salary districts typically serve much larger proportions of student of color and English language learners than districts that offer the most competitive (highest) salaries.

Figure 11.7 shows the characteristics of low- and high-salary districts and their relationship to student demographics and classroom variables. Here, the lowest-salary districts with higher percentages of racial-ethnic minority students and English learners have class sizes that are about 20% larger than the highest-salary districts, a sign that these districts have fewer available resources overall. As a result, those districts serving the highest proportions of students of color have about twice as many uncredentialed and inexperienced teachers as do those serving the fewest students of color.[65] Differences in costs of living in certain regions accounts for some of this salary differential, but they persist after considering the cost-of-living and pupil needs.[66] In this way, the "salary gap" may be another "opportunity gap."

FIGURE 11.7 ■ Characteristics of Low- and High-Salary Districts

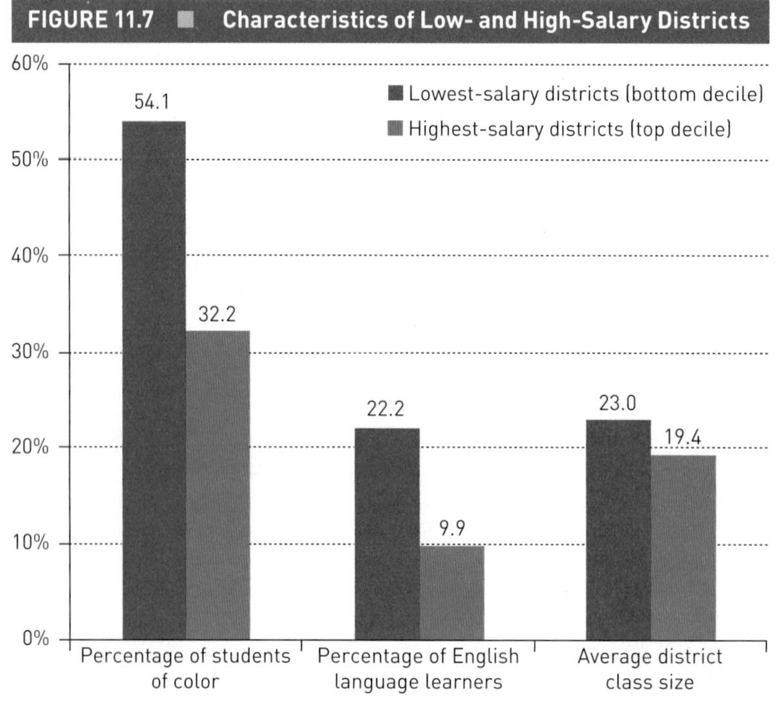

Source: Adamson, F., and Darling-Hammond, L. (2011, May). *Speaking of salaries: What it will take to get qualified, effective teachers in all communities.* Center for American Progress. www.americanprogress.org

As teachers gain experience and move up the pay scale, they often transfer to more affluent schools. District teacher transfer policies, sometimes written into teacher union contracts, aid this migration. Although teacher experience does not guarantee teacher quality, researchers agree that teacher effectiveness increases during the first 3 years in the classroom.[67] As a consequence, teachers' migration to affluent schools means that low-income and underrepresented students have less chance of working with an experienced, effective teacher than do students in a more affluent school with few low-income and underrepresented students.

11.6e Facility Inequalities and Student Achievement

School facilities contain the educational process and create the learning conditions, but the average public school building is over 50 years old, built around 1968. In 2017, the American Society of Civil Engineers rated U.S. public schools' infrastructure a quality grade of "D+": 53% of public schools needed to spend money on repairs, renovations, and modernization to put their building in good condition; 24% of schools were in "fair" or "poor" condition.[68]

This national underinvestment in public schools' facilities and their infrastructure—indoor and outdoor lighting, plumbing, heating/air conditioning, ventilation, electrical, security, fire suppression, telecommunications, furnishings, playgrounds, parking, and aesthetics—profoundly undermines teaching and learning. But despite the need, many schools lack the funds to renovate or modernize their outdated and crumbling structures. The *State of Our Schools, 2016* report documents a $38 billion per year shortfall on capital investments for public school construction and another $8 billion gap in spending on maintenance and operations.[69]

"Sick building syndrome" (SBS) is the name given to the relationship between unhealthy school facilities and teacher/student productivity. Its symptoms—the irritated eyes, nose, and throat; upper-respiratory infections; nausea; dizziness; difficulty concentrating; headaches; forgetting; irritability; and fatigue—can result from the schoolhouse's poor indoor air quality (IAQ).[70] Causes of SBS may include poor ventilation, high levels of dust, rooms with poor lighting, mold or fungus, chemicals in the air from cleaning products, heat or low humidity, insect or animal droppings, or noisy work environments. Although building components overall may not affect student performance, certain aspects such as noise can make it difficult for students to think, concentrate, and learn; they hinder students' cognitive skill development. In times of pandemics, poor classroom ventilation can increase the rate of disease transmission. Building conditions are especially influential at the elementary school level.

Strong evidence exists that school buildings' conditions impact students' health, student achievement, and teacher effectiveness. Earthman's 2002 seminal study found a 5- to 17-percentile point difference in standardized test scores for students in good facilities (well-maintained buildings with comfortable room and hall temperatures, satisfactory lighting, appropriate noise levels, good roofs, sufficient space) as compared with those in inadequate facilities (poorly maintained with too cold or hot rooms, inadequate lighting, high noise levels, leaky roofs, overcrowding), controlling for the students' SES. Older buildings typically lack the conditions necessary for proper learning environments, adversely affecting student achievement.[71] Researchers have found that exposures to mold, poor ventilation, inadequate lighting, overcrowding, and excessive noise all have potential to harm student and teacher health, contribute to absenteeism, and reduce cognitive abilities—all of which impact academic achievement.[72] Many studies confirm,[73] although some dispute,[74] these findings.

Most recently, a 2020 study found that Los Angeles schools that installed air filters in every classroom and common area following a nearby gas leak saw significant gains to reading and mathematics achievement compared to students' performance in schools that did not receive the air filters, with gains about equal to the learning benefits from reducing class size or providing intensive tutoring. On a cost-benefit basis, the improved indoor air quality outperformed other education reforms.[75]

Inadequate school facilities disproportionately affect low-income children. Because local school districts carry most of their capital facilities costs, poor and low-wealth districts are often unable to adequately maintain—or modernize—their buildings and grounds. As a result, districts and zip codes with higher enrollments of students from low-income families are more likely to have buildings in poor condition.[76]

In addition, perception often influences (and perhaps creates) a person's reality. Quality facilities are significantly related to school climate, and school climate plays a mediating role in the relationship between facility quality and student achievement.[77] Teachers working in buildings in poor condition state that the facility's design and appearance have a negative impact on the learning climate, whereas teachers in buildings in good condition report that the building has a positive influence on the learning climate.[78] Working in substandard buildings or in newer buildings that are poorly maintained undercuts teachers' morale and increases their work frustration; these attitudes likely transfer negatively into their classroom expectations and practices, possibly reducing student achievement. Similarly, inadequate school facilities likely impact a student's motivation, energy, attention level, listening capacity, and visual retention.[79] By comparison, a 2017 study found that improved ventilation and indoor air quality at schools improved teachers' self-reported job satisfaction.[80] Good working conditions appear to improve teaching experience and reduce teacher turnover, while poor school conditions make it more difficult to teach effectively.

Fixing school facilities is expensive. School construction projects are costly—and becoming more so. Between adding space to existing buildings ($3.2 billion), retrofitting and modernizing existing structures ($3.14 billion), and erecting new facilities ($7.8 billion), U.S. school districts spent more than $14 billion on completing construction projects during the 2014 calendar year. And construction costs keep rising. In March 2018, the producer price index for goods needed for construction—steel, concrete, lumber and plywood, diesel fuel, and other building materials—rose 5.8% over the prior 12 months.[81]

Providing satisfactory (or better) school building and infrastructure is both a learning and an equity issue. Too often, low-income students learn in facilities that need the most repair.[82] With research clearly affirming that school funding carefully targeted on enhancing teaching quality and providing safe, healthy, and comfortable facilities makes a measurable difference in student achievement, communities and school leaders benefit when they educate the public about the lost "opportunity costs" of attending school in inadequate facilities and then actively acquire the needed resources to improve them.

11.7 CURRENT TRENDS IN EDUCATION FINANCE

How and how much to fiscally support public education has become the focus of much national, community, and legal debate. We will briefly discuss two of the most contentious current education finance issues: taxpayer resistance to increased taxes for education and whether taxpayers should pay for families to send their children to private and religious schools.

Affluent communities usually find innovative ways to fund extra school resources.

Glen Martin/Contributor/Getty Images

11.7a Taxpayer Resistance to Increased Taxes for Education

Throughout history, virtually every political system has experienced its people's resistance to paying taxes. In the United States, the Massachusetts colonists in 1773 led a tax revolt as they dumped British tea into Boston Harbor. Two hundred years later, beginning in the 1970s, taxpayer resistance to funding public schools became a popular issue. And this resistance continues.

A well-developed body of research suggests that public sentiment about taxation reflects a number of factors. These include rational and economic self-interest, SES, and the symbolic politics of ideology and partisanship.[83]

People view public schools as providing young people with the knowledge and skills needed for their economic self-sufficiency and responsible citizenship. Taxpayers know that educated communities are safer and more prosperous. But homeowners resent having their property taxes increase year after year, especially when their property taxes grow faster than their personal income—and homeowners tend to vote. At the time of the Proposition 13 (1986) "taxpayer revolt," California taxpayers' residential property assessed values were rising 10% to 20% annually and as much as 40% in some areas[84]—and their property taxes were rising with them.[85]

Taxpayers also resent paying higher taxes to support public schools when they think that the money is not noticeably improving student learning and achievement. When headlines broadly assert that "public schools are failing"[86] (and in truth, some are, for many of the reasons mentioned in this chapter), the average taxpayer cannot help but wonder if public schools are performing well.[87] Many believe that it is unfair to increase property taxes on retirees with fixed incomes, possibly forcing them out of their homes through higher property taxes. Voters may lose confidence in the government's ability to spend tax dollars wisely on public goods and services. It is also possible that rejecting taxation may be rooted not so much in its financial pinch on taxpayers, but rather in the voter's ideological or political views about paying higher (or any) taxes.[88] All these variables play a role in taxpayers' views about funding schools through property taxes.

Taxpayer revolts tend to hurt low-wealth schools more than high-wealth schools. Affluent communities usually find innovative ways to provide additional resources to neighborhood schools. The California taxpayer revolt offers a case study.

After a brief lull following Proposition 13's passage, California schools began to make up for the lost property tax revenues, largely through rapidly growing nontax fees and charges. These alternative resources were both less constrained and less visible to voters than taxes. Fees, rental income, grants from outside agencies directly to classroom teachers, and monetary donations by parents to teachers to buy supplies circumvented the state's budgetary limitations on school funding.[89] Although little quantitative evidence is available, considerable anecdotal evidence indicates that schools' use of volunteer time increased, foundations were established to provide financial support for athletics and other extracurricular activities, and a variety of other methods (such as bake sales) were devised to get around the fiscal limitations.[90]

Taken together, these examples support the conclusion that individual actions to neutralize the schools' fiscal constraints play a major role in enabling high-wealth districts to keep their relative position of spending more resources per student and supporting higher student achievement. In contrast, less affluent communities can only rely on the state's fiscal support. The end result is that taxpayer revolts make school funding more inequitable.

11.7b Using Taxpayer Dollars for Private and Religious Schools

The education privatization movement—sometimes called *school choice*—wants to give parents more options about how and where to educate their children, using taxpayer dollars to create charter schools and provide voucher programs to pay private school tuition. Nearly 30 states have private school choice programs that directly (or indirectly through generous tax credits to incentivize businesses and individuals) pay students' tuition at private schools, some of which are religiously affiliated schools.[91] Current surveys disagree about the extent of Americans' support for the government giving public dollars to families to pay for tuition at private schools.[92]

The types of private school choice programs and their funding streams vary by states, with each legislature deciding whether to permit these programs and if they do, how many, the funding allowable, the fiscal caps that limit the amount of taxpayer dollars (or would-be taxpayer dollars) to be spent annually, student and family eligibility to receive taxpayer funds, and accountability provisions. In 2019, 29 states provided state support through direct voucher payments or tax credits for students to attend private schools.[93] EdChoice, a school choice organization, reports that the United States spends about $2.3 billion a year on school choice programs.[94]

School vouchers are fiscal programs in which parents receive a fixed amount of public funding allocated for their child's education to use toward tuition at their choice of a private school, including religiously affiliated schools, that accepts the vouchers. In 2019, the United States had 62 voucher programs operating across 29 states.[95] Wisconsin, for example, the state that pioneered school choice programs, spent $350 million on private school vouchers during the 2019–2020 school year. To fund these voucher programs, the state deducts or withholds the money from the school districts, leaving gaping holes in local school district budgets.[96]

Tax-credit scholarships (TCS) are state-offered tax credits to encourage businesses or individuals to donate to a scholarship-granting organization, which then gives the money to eligible students to use toward tuition expenses at a private school. Depending on how state legislators write the law, donors may deduct the value of their contribution—in some cases, the full amount—from their taxable incomes. Twenty states have established TCS programs, diverting a total of over $1 billion per year away from state treasuries and toward private schools.[97]

Education savings accounts (ESA) are taxpayer dollars set aside usually based on per-pupil funding formulas in individual savings accounts for participating students. Typically, these funds are reallocated from the state's public school budget. Parents can withdraw these dollars to spend on approved educational expenses, including private and parochial school tuition, home schooling, curriculum materials, standardized test fees, or transportation. Parents can rollover unused ESA funds for future K–12 and higher education costs. At present, six states have enacted ESA programs.[98] Each ESA created for a student means a loss of funds for the public school district in which the student resides. Private school choice programs in Arizona, Florida, Indiana, Ohio, and Wisconsin serve tens of thousands of students in their respective states who receive thousands of taxpayer dollars in scholarships, on average. [99]

529 Plans, formerly tax-advantaged college investment (savings) accounts, allows parents and grandparents to contribute to their child's college savings and deduct their annual contributions for "qualifying expenses" (including tuition, books, fees, supplies, and some room and board) from their income taxes. Since December 2017, the Tax Cuts and Jobs Act expands 529 accounts to include private and religious K–12 schooling.[100] The new law enables parents to deduct up to $10,000 a year for each child from personal state and local taxes for K–12 tuition and other school expenses. More than 30 states allow some kind of tax deduction or credit contributions into 529 accounts.[101]

The number of private school choice programs, including traditional vouchers, tax-credit scholarships, education savings accounts, 529 accounts, and the families using them have expanded markedly over the past decade. Influential advocacy groups and interested parents are fueling the increase. But these programs are not without critics.

Although school choice programs accept taxpayers' dollars, many lack transparency about how they use these funds. A 2020 *Education Week* Research Center report finds that despite the increasing influx of taxpayer monies, 29 states that have at least one of the three types of private school choice programs do not make public their teachers' qualifications to teach, their student results on state and national achievement tests, their willingness to admit students with disabilities, or their cooperation with audits or other measures to ensure sound fiscal management. Some states do not even require that they publicly list all the private schools participating in voucher programs.[102] Whereas public schools are publicly accountable for their spending decisions and student outcomes, private schools that accept public dollars are not (unless their state laws require it).

School choice funding often finds itself challenged by public school advocates who contend that it siphons public school monies away from public schools, reducing the educational resources available to public school students.[103] The U.S. Supreme Court does not always agree. In a sample of its decisions on school choice cases, the U.S. Supreme Court ruled in 1983 that state tax deductions (tuition tax credits) allowed to the parents of parochial school children for expenses incurred in education did not violate the First Amendment's Establishment clause;[104] in 2002 that vouchers could be used to pay for tuition at private religious schools as long as it is the parents' choice to do so;[105] and in 2017 that Missouri could not deny a religious school the opportunity to receive a state grant (public funds) to resurface its pea gravel playground with recycled rubber tires, a generally available, nonreligious public safety service—like police or fire protection—solely because of its status as a church.[106] Most recently, the

U.S. Supreme Court (2020) ruled that Montana's state government could not exclude religious school options for parents who want to participation in a generally available tax credit scholarship program, effectively ending constitutional provisions in as many as 38 states that bar taxpayer aid to parochial schools.[107] This ruling lowers further the traditional wall separating church and state.

FLIPSIDES

Should Taxpayers Support Public Funds for Private Education?

A fast-growing number of the nation's K–12 students attend private and religiously affiliated schools using public financing mechanisms, including vouchers, tax credit scholarships, education savings accounts, or 529 accounts. This practice either uses taxpayer dollars allocated for public schools or diverts monies that could be used for public services and schools away from state treasuries. Should public dollars support common or individual benefits? Should taxpayers pay to support students' tuition at private schools, including religiously affiliated ones?

Taxpayers should NOT support private education.	Taxpayers SHOULD support private education.
Public education funded by taxpayer dollars is a "common good" (benefitting the wider community) by teaching children how to understand, appreciate, and defend shared liberties and civic values while learning among diverse others.	Public and private education funded by taxpayer dollars is an "individual good" and (eventually) a "common good." The private schools' curriculum *may or may not* teach children about our shared liberties and civic values while learning among a diverse student body.
When families use public funds to pay for private school costs, the public schools lose dollars they could use to strengthen student learning.	School choice families are also taxpayers. They are using "their" tax dollars in ways they see appropriate for their children's education.
Public education dollars support public schools—a great equalizer that gives every child the chance for social and economic mobility.	Public education dollars to pay tuition at private schools offer a way to advance parents' own children's social and economic interests.
Public education brings together children from differing backgrounds to learn to understand and respect each other and work together as citizens in a diverse nation.	Public education dollars enable parents to enroll their children in a school that shares their family's values and lets their children learn among people like themselves.
Public education with heterogeneous student bodies prepares students for shared governance and the shared interests of a pluralistic community.	Private schools with homogeneous student bodies create fewer opportunities to work together across differences in ideology, religion, or ethnicity.
Public education, taxpayer dollars, and education policy are mainly state and locally generated and locally controlled.	Wealthy businesses, organizations, and individuals with no connections to local schools are lobbying legislatures nationally to advance a school choice/voucher agenda in your community.
Using public funds to pay for religious schools comes too close to allowing government funding to advance a particular religion, dismantling the wall between church and state.	Using public funds to pay for religious schools is essential because our county and its citizens now suffer from a lack of proper moral values.
Building a community of shared knowledge and civic values out of diverse citizenry is part of American schools' tradition.	Religious instruction in schools is part of our nation's schooling tradition, and it supports family values.
Public schools are designed to build the nation's human capital as well as for individuals to gain personal status through better educational qualifications and better jobs. Well-educated students benefit the nation.	Private schools are (also) a means for individual students to gain personal status through more rigorous courses, gain better educational qualifications, and obtain better jobs. Well-educated students benefit the nation.

Taxpayers should NOT support private education.	Taxpayers SHOULD support private education.
As more dollars leave the public schools, educational quality is lowered, and more parents want to leave the system, resulting in a downward academic and fiscal spiral.	If public schools want to keep their students, they need to improve education they deliver. Satisfied and dissatisfied parents "vote with their feet" when they enroll their child in a certain school.
Various surveys show that around one third to one half of Americans favors publicly funded school vouchers.	The popularity of publicly funded school vouchers is growing.
Education's effects are long lasting and affect the course of a person's entire life.	Education's effects are long lasting and affect the course of a person's entire life.

All parents want to give their children the education that they believe is best for them. What is the "common good"? What is our responsibility as taxpayers and as educators for ensuring the "common good"? To which schools, public or private, should taxpayer dollars go?

Sources: Abowitz, K. K., & Stitzlein, S. M. (2018, November). Public schools, public goods, and public work. *Phi Delta Kappan, 100*(3), 33–37; Cheuk, T., & Quinn, R. (2018, November). Dismantling the wall between church and state: The case of public education. *Phi Delta Kappan, 100*(3), 24–28; Ferguson, M. (2018, November). Money, power, and choices. Washington View. *Phil Delta Kappan, 100*(3), 64–65; Henderson, M. B., Huston, D., Peterson, P. E., & West, M. R. (2020, Winter). Public support grows for higher teacher pay and expanded school choice. *EducationNext, 20*(1). https://www.educationnext.org/school-choice-trump-era-results-2019-education-next-poll/; Larabee, D. F. (2018, November). Public schools for private gain: The declining American commitment to serving the public good. *Phi Delta Kappan, 100*(3), 8–13; Phi Delta Kappan. (2017, September). The 49th annual *PDK* poll of the public's attitude toward the public schools. *Phi Delta Kappan, 99*(1), K1–K32. Supplement. https://pdkpoll.org/timeline/2017

As the adage goes, "Money makes the world go 'round." Ample research affirms that sufficient and well-targeted money can increase student learning and achievement, with positive outcomes lasting into adulthood. But our society does not spend money equally or equitably to support all students' learning. Just as underrepresented, low-income, and affluent students show "achievement gaps," the schools in which they receive their educations reflect serious "spending gaps." In reality, spending gaps may also sometimes be "opportunity gaps."

Future teachers want to work in well-maintained schools with sufficient, up-to-date instructional supplies to actively support effective teaching and learning. When these resources are not available, the negative consequences for teachers and their students may last a lifetime.

KEY TAKE-AWAYS

Learning Objective 11.1 Explain how money matters in improving student learning and achievement.

- States and communities are responsible for ensuring that all schools have the essential resources to provide positive learning environments. But this does not always happen.
- The United States is one of the few advanced nations where schools serving children from more affluent families usually have more educational resources than those serving poor students.
- The research consensus is clear: Money—its *total amount* and *how it is spent*—can lead to increased student achievement. Specifically, increased spending on teacher quality (effectiveness), teacher professional development, increased teacher salaries, and improved school faculties can generate improved student (and later, adult) outcomes.

Learning Objective 11.2 Describe the ways that education is an investment in human capital.

- Education is foundational to the development of a nation's human capital. Data affirm that education increases individuals' earning potential and employability as it reduces public social costs.

- Adequate and well-directed school funding is essential if every school and every student (regardless of socioeconomic background) will be prepared to succeed in today's—and tomorrow's—economy.
- The more money earned, the more money paid in taxes to improve infrastructure (including schools), support social services, fund the military, and meet other expenses.

Learning Objective 11.3 Identify the federal, state, and local contributions to school funding.

- Money for schools comes from three government sources: federal, state, and local. The federal government pays about 8%, while state and local sources share the remaining costs. At the local level, the property tax is the predominant method for paying for schools.
- Changes in student demographics, costs of living, teacher pay and benefits, class sizes, tax structures, and legislative decisions in the state capital all influence education funding and spending.
- Typically, teachers in a school district receive salaries from a salary scale, with increased monies paid for increased years of teaching experience and more academic credentials.

Learning Objective 11.4 Justify the reasons for increased education spending since 1960.

- Reasons for the increased education costs since 1960 include increased student enrollments (from baby boomers entering high school, school desegregation, and students with disabilities), the hiring of more teachers to meet increased enrollments, more equitable teacher salaries, and reduced student-to-teacher classroom ratios.

Learning Objective 11.5 Identify the categories and purposes for which school districts budget and spend money.

- The *Digest of Education Statistics, 2018* separates education expenditures into 10 defined categories.
- More than half of school expenditures (61%) are spent on classroom instruction.
- Teacher salaries vary across the country.

Learning Objective 11.6 Summarize the major equity issues in school funding.

- Wide differences exist in levels of state and district per-pupil funding. Schools with a high concentration of affluent students tend to receive more funds per student than schools serving concentrations of low-income and underrepresented students, even within the same school district.
- Disparities in school resources translate into educational quality differences in teacher effectiveness, class size, facilities' upkeep, available technology, and other factors that can affect student outcomes and, ultimately, students' life chances.
- Studies find that the most highly experienced and credentialed teachers are concentrated in high socioeconomic status (SES) schools, which tend to have both higher per-pupil expenditures and higher teacher salaries, whereas the least qualified, least experienced, lowest-paid teachers tend to work in schools with the highest number of low-income and underrepresented students. With constant teacher turnover, principals have difficulty establishing a culture for learning or providing a skilled, experienced, and caring teacher corps to positively impact student achievement.
- Funding *equity* and *adequacy* are fairness issues for students and taxpayers. Different students require different levels of services, depending on their unique situations. To educate children growing up in poverty to common meaningful standards costs about 40% more than it does to bring more affluent students up to these standards.
- Since 1995, many school funding court cases have produced major changes in state education policy around the country, allocating more resources for poorer districts and generating improved results for schools and students.

- School finance reforms that work include funding underserved students at higher levels, investing in growing educator capacity through professional development, ensuring their equitable distribution across schools, and guaranteeing access to quality preschool.

Learning Objective 11.7 Discuss two current trends in education finance and their implications for public schools.

- A well-developed body of research suggests that public sentiment about taxation reflects rational and economic self-interest, socioeconomic status (SES), and the symbolic politics of ideology and partisanship.
- Taxpayers' resistance to paying higher taxes tends to hurt low-wealth schools more than high-wealth schools, making funding more inequitable.
- Nearly 30 states have private school choice programs—using taxpayer dollars to pay eligible students' tuition at private and religiously affiliated schools either directly (through vouchers or education savings accounts) or indirectly (through generous tax credits to incentivize businesses and individuals). Whereas public schools are publicly accountable for their spending decisions and student outcomes, private schools that accept public dollars are not (unless their state laws require it).
- Despite its considerable costs, excellent education for all of America's children is a good investment. When it comes to quality education, as a society we can pay now or pay later.

TEACHER SCENARIO: IT'S YOUR TURN

In your sociology class, you have been discussing the "cycle of poverty" and its impact on generations of people. Your final-exam assignment is to provide a solution to this problem. Knowing what you know now from this chapter, explain how education as currently funded contributes to this cycle and how increasing funding and targeting much of it to support instruction and facilities' maintenance to high-poverty schools might help reduce the problem. In your answer, include the research findings of how money matters in education, education as an investment in human capital, likely sources of school funding revenue, examples of funding inequities between high- and low-poverty schools, and how the placement of high- and low-experience teachers and their turnover rates make it difficult for schools to establish a culture of learning.

NOTES

1. Porter, E. (2013, November 5). In public education, edge still goes to rich. Economic Scene. *The New York Times*. https://www.nytimes.com/2013/11/06/business/a-rich-childs-edge-in-public-education.html
2. OECD. (2013). *Education at a glance, 2013: OECD indicators*. OECD. http://www.oecd.org/education/eag2013%20(eng)--FINAL%2020%20June%202013.pdf
3. U.S. Census Bureau. (2019, May 21). U.S. school spending per pupil increased for fifth consecutive year, U.S. Census Bureau reports. https://www.census.gov/newsroom/press-releases/2019/school-spending.html
4. Brewer, K. G. (2019, May 23). School spending on the rise, census shows. *U.S. News & World Report*. https://www.usnews.com/news/best-states/articles/2019-05-23/school-spending-on-the-rise-census-shows
5. U.S. Census Bureau, 2019.
6. Adamson, F., & Darling-Hammond, L. (2011, December). *Addressing the inequitable distribution of teachers: What it will take to get qualified, effective teachers in all communities*. Stanford Center for Opportunity Policy in Education. https://edpolicy.stanford.edu/sites/default/files/publications/addressing-inequitable-distribution-teachers-what-it-will-take-get-qualified-effective-teachers-all-_1.pdf

7. Forty-two percent of U.S. classrooms lack any or adequate air conditioning, according to the research led by Joshua Goodman. See: Sparks, S. D. (2018, May 31). As the temperature climbs, test scores drop in schools without air conditioning. *Education Week.* http://blogs.edweek.org/edweek/inside-school-research/2018/05/temperature_climbs_test_scores_drop.html

8. Alexander, K. (2016, September). Is it family or school? Getting the question right. *The Russell Sage Foundation Journal of the Social Science, 2*(5). https://muse.jhu.edu/article/633735

9. Hanushek, E. A. (1981). Throwing money at schools. *Journal of Policy Analysis and Management, 1*(1), 19–41.

10. Green, E. L. (2017, March 29). Betsy DeVos calls for more school choice, saying money isn't the answer. *The New York Times.* https://www.nytimes.com/2017/03/29/us/politics/betsy-devos-education-school-choice-voucher.html

11. Baker, B. D. (2018, July 17). *How money matters for schools.* Learning Policy Institute. https://learningpolicyinstitute.org/product/how-money-matters-brief?gclid=EAIaIQobChMI2qqxwaGB6AIViq_ICh38yg5SEAMYASAAEgIMB_D_BwE

12. Darling-Hammond, L. (2000, January 1). Teacher quality and student achievement: A review of state policy evidence. *Education Policy Analysis Archives, 8*(1). https://epaa.asu.edu/ojs/article/view/392/515;. Marzano, R., Toth, M., & Schooling, P. (2012). *Examining the role of teacher evaluation in student achievement: Contemporary research base for the Marzano causal teacher evaluation model.* White Paper. Marzano Center, Learning. http://www.marzanocenter.com/files/MC_White_Paper_20120424.pdf;. Whitehurst, G. J. (2002, March 5). *Scientifically based research on teacher quality. Research on teacher preparation and professional development.* http://citeseerx.ist.psu.edu/viewdoc/download?doi=10.1.1.468.8079&rep=rep1&type=pdf

13. See: Ball, D. L., & Cohen, D. K. (1999). Developing practices, developing practitioners: Toward a practice-based theory of professional development. In G. Sykes & L. Darling-Hammonds (Eds.), *Teaching as the learning profession: Handbook of policy and practice* (pp. 30–32). Jossey-Bass; Bill & Melinda Gates Foundation. (2012, January). *Gathering feedback for teaching. Combining high-quality observations with student surveys and achievement gains.* MET Project. http://k12education.gatesfoundation.org/download/?Num=2680&filename=MET_Gathering_Feedback_Research_Paper1.pdf;Yoon, K. S., Duncan, T., Lee, S. W.-Y., Scarloss, B., & Shapley, K. L. (2007, October). *Reviewing the evidence on how teacher professional development affects student achievement.* (Issues and Answers Report. REL 2007-No. 033). U.S. Department of Education. https://files.eric.ed.gov/fulltext/ED498548.pdf

14. Clodfelter, C., Glennie, E., Ladd, H., & Vigdor, J. (2008). Would higher salaries keep teachers in high-poverty schools? Evidence from a policy intervention in North Carolina. *Journal of Public Economics, 92*(5–6), 1352–1370; Steele, J. L., Murnane, R. J., & Willett, J. B. (2010). Do financial incentives help low-performing schools tract and keep academically talented teachers? Evidence from California. *Journal of Policy Analysis and Management, 29*(3), 451–478.

15. Earthman, G. (2002). Selected facility conditions and student academic achievement. *Williams Watch Series: Investigating the Claims of Williams v. State of California.* UCLA Institute for Democracy, Education and Access. https://nctaf.org/wp-content/uploads/ucla_2002_article.pdf; See: Baker, L., & Bernstein, H. (2012, February 27). *The impact of school buildings on student health and performance.* The McGraw-Hill Research Foundation and The Center for Green Schools. http://www.ncef.org/pubs/010715.McGrawHill_ImpactOnHealth.pdf;Lawrence Berkeley National Laboratories. (2018). Human performance: Indoor air quality. *Scientific Findings Resource Bank.* https://iaqscience.lbl.gov/performance-summary

16. Vcrstegan, D. A., & King, R. A. (1998). The relationship between school: A review and analysis of 35 years of production function research. *Journal of Education Finance, 24*(2), 243–262.

17. Jackson, C. K., Johnson, R. C., & Persico, C. (2016). The effects of school spending on educational and economic outcomes: Evidence from school finance reforms. *The Quarterly Journal of Economics, 131*(1), 157–218; Lafortune, J., Rothstein, J., & Schanzenbach, D. W. (2016, July). *School finance reform and the distribution of student achievement.* IRLE Working Paper #100-16. University of California, Berkeley. http://irle.berkeley.edu/files/2016/School-Finance-Reform-and-the-Distribution-of-Student-Achievement.pdf

18. National Center for Education Statistics (2020, May 20). Annual Earnings. Figure 2. Median annual earnings of full-time, year-round workers ages 25-34, by educational attainment: 2018. *The Condition of Education.* U.S. Department of Education. https://nces.ed.gov/programs/coe/indicator_cba.asp

19. National Center for Education Statistics (2020, May 20), Figure 2.

20. Brundage, V., Jr. (2017, August). Profile of the labor force by educational attainment. Labor force participation rates by educational attainment and gender, 25 years and over, 2016 averages, *Spotlight on Statistics*. Bureau of Labor Statistics. https://www.bls.gov/spotlight/2017/educational-attainment-of-the-labor-force/home.htm

21. Federal Reserve Bank of New York. (2020). *The labor market for recent college graduates*. https://www.newyorkfed.org/research/college-labor-market/index.html;. Kelly, J. (2019, November 14). Recent college graduates have the highest unemployment in decades—Here's why universities are to blame. *Forbes*. https://www.forbes.com/sites/jackkelly/2019/11/14/recent-college-graduates-have-the-highest-unemployment-rate-in-decadesheres-why-universities-are-to-blame/#17afd7b8320b

22. Amos, J. (2008, August). *Dropouts, diplomas, and dollars: U.S. high schools and the nation's economy*. Alliance for Excellent Education. https://all4ed.org/wp-content/uploads/2008/08/Econ2008.pdf

23. Barnett, W. S. (2011). Effectiveness of early educational intervention. *Science, 333*(6045), 975–978; Barnett, W. S., & Masse, L. N. (2007). Early childhood program design and economic returns: Comparative benefit-cost analysis of the Abecedarian program and policy implications. *Economics of Education Review, 26*(1), 113–125; Lamy, C. (2012). Poverty is a knot and preschool is an untangler. In R. C. Pianta, W. S. Barnett, L. M. Justice, & S. M. Sheridan (Eds.), *Handbook of early childhood education* (pp. 158–174). Guilford.

24. Carroll, T. (2008, March 26). Education beats incarceration. *Education Week, 27*(29), 32.

25. Lochner, L., & Moretti, E. (2004). The effect of education on crime: Evidence from prison inmates, arrests, and self-reports. *American Economic Review, 94*(1), 155–189. Social savings costs are reported in this source in 2006 dollars.

26. Lochner, L. (2011, January). *Non-production benefits of education: Crime, heath, and good citizenship*. Working Paper 16722. National Bureau of Economic Research. https://www.nber.org/papers/w16722.pdf

27. National Center for Education Statistics (2020, February). Revenues and expenditures for public elementary and secondary education: FY17. *Finance Tables*. NCES-2020-31. Institute of Education Sciences, U.S. Department of Education. https://nces.ed.gov/pubs2020/2020301.pdf

28. With desegregation, schools had to hire more teachers to reduce class sizes to more acceptable teacher–student ratios and increase African American teachers' salaries to levels comparable to what white teachers were earning.

29. Hanushek, E. A., & Rivkin, S. G. (1997). Understanding the twentieth century's growth in U.S. school spending. *Journal of Human Resources, 32*(1), 35–68.

30. Hanushek & Rivkin, 1997, p. 41.

31. Hanushek & Rivkin, 1997, p. 45.

32. Owings, W. A., & Kaplan, L. S. (2010). The alpha and omega syndrome: Is intra-district funding the next ripeness factor? *Journal of Education Finance, 36*(2), 162–185.

33. Roza, M., & Hill, P. T. (2004). How within district spending inequities help some schools to fail. *Brookings Papers on Education Policy, 7*, 201–227; Rubenstein, R., Schwartz, A. E., Stiefel, L., & Amor, H. B. G. (2007). District to schools: The distribution of resources across schools in big city school districts. *Economics of Education, 26*(5), 532–545.

34. Rubenstein, R., Schwartz, A. E., & Stiefel, L. (2006, April). *Rethinking the intradistrict distribution of school inputs to disadvantaged students*. Paper presented for the conference, Rethinking Rodriguez: Education as a fundamental right. University of California, Berkeley; Rubenstein et al., 2007.

35. Rubenstein et al., 2006.

36. Owings & Kaplan, 2010.

37. Hanushek & Rivkin, 1997.

38. U.S. Census Bureau. (2017, June 14). *More than half of school expenditures spent on classroom instruction*. U.S. Department of Commerce. https://www.census.gov/newsroom/press-releases/2017/cb17-97-public-education-finance.html

39. $39,301 (difference between highest and lowest teacher salary) times 30 years = $1,170,000.

40. Allegretto, S., & Mishel, L. (2019, April 24). *The teacher pay weekly wage penalty hit 21.4 percent in 2018, a record high*. Economic Policy Institute. https://www.epi.org/files/pdf/165729.pdf

41. Owings, W. A., & Kaplan, L. S. (2020). *American public school finance* (3rd ed.). Routledge, pp. 162–163.

42. Odden, A., & Picus, L. (2004). *School finance: A policy perspective* (3rd ed.). McGraw-Hill, p. 25.

43. SchoolFundingInfo. (2020). *School funding court decisions*. Center for Educational Equity at Teachers College. http://schoolfunding.info/school-funding-court-decisions/

44. Hunter, M. (2018, March 26). *School funding litigation from coast to coast*. Education Law Center. https://edlawcenter.org/news/archives/school-funding-national/school-funding-litigation-from-coast-to-coast.html

45. SchoolFundingInfo, 2020.

46. Condron, D. J., & Roscigno, V. J. (2003, January). Disparities within: Unequal spending and achievement in an urban school district. *Sociology of Education, 76*(1), 18–36.

47. Morgan, I., & Amerikaner, A. (2018, February). Funding gaps: An analysis of school funding equity across the U.S. and within each state. 2018 P-12 resource equity. *Education Trust*. https://edtrust.org/wp-content/uploads/2014/09/FundingGapReport_2018_FINAL.pdf

48. Maciag, M. (2018, August). Why school spending is so unequal. *Governing*. https://www.governing.com/topics/education/gov-education-spending-states.html

49. Owings & Kaplan, 2010.

50. Maciag, M. (2019, June 4). Stats that spend the most (and the least) on education. *Governing*. https://www.governing.com/topics/education/gov-state-education-spending-revenue-data.html

51. Baker, B. D. (2017). *How money matters for schools*. Learning Policy Institute. https://learningpolicyinstitute.org/sites/default/files/product-files/How_Money_Matters_REPORT.pdf

52. Noel, R. A. (2018, May). *Race, economics, and social status*. Bureau of Labor Statistics. https://www.bls.gov/spotlight/2018/race-economics-and-social-status/pdf/race-economics-and-social-status.pdf

53. Roza, M. (2006). How districts shortchange low-income and minority students: Funding gap 2006. *The Education Trust*, pp. 9–10. https://edunomicslab.org/wp-content/uploads/2013/12/EdTrustFundingGaps2006.pdf

54. Wiener, R., & Pristoop, E. (2006). How states shortchange the districts that need the most help: Funding gap 2006. *The Education Trust*, p. 6. https://files.eric.ed.gov/fulltext/ED496559.pdf

55. Raikes, J., & Darling-Hammond, L. (2019, February 18). Why our education funding systems are derailing the American Dream. *Learning Policy Institute*. https://learningpolicyinstitute.org/blog/why-our-education-funding-systems-are-derailing-american-dream

56. Baker, B. D., Farrie, D., & Sciarra. D. (2016). *Mind the gap: 20 years of progress and retrenchment in school funding and achievement gaps*. Research Report No. RR-16-15. Educational Testing Service. https://files.eric.ed.gov/fulltext/EJ1124843.pdf

57. Kirabo Jackson, C., Johnson, R. C., & Persico, C. (2016). The effects of school spending on educational and economic outcomes: Evidence from school finance reforms. *The Quarterly Journal of Economics, 131*(1), 157–218.

58. Lafortune, J., Rothstein, J., & Schanzenbach, D. W. (2016, July). *School finance reform and the distribution of student achievement*. IRLE Working Paper #100-16. IRLE Institute for Research on Labor and Employment. University of California, Berkeley. https://irle.berkeley.edu/files/2016/School-Finance-Reform-and-the-Distribution-of-Student-Achievement.pdf

59. Baker, B. D., Farrie, D., & Sciarra, D. (2018, February). *Is school funding fair? A national report card* (7th ed.). Rutgers University Graduate School of Education. https://drive.google.com/file/d/1BTAjZuqOs8pEGWW6oUBotb6omVw1hUJI/view

60. The win rate had been 75%, but the number went down after the 2008 Great Recession. Personal communication, March 29, 2020.

61. See Boyd, D., Grossman, P., Lankford, H., Loeb, S., & Wyckoff, J. (2006). How changes in entry requirements alter the teacher workforce and affect student achievement. *Education Finance and Policy, 1*(2), 176–216; Darling-Hammond, L. (2000). Teacher quality and student achievement: A review of state policy evidence, *Educational Policy Analysis Archives, 8*(1). https://epaa.asu.edu/ojs/article/view/392; Darling-Hammond, L., Holtzman, D. J., Gatlin, S. J., & Heilig, J. V. (2005). Does teacher preparation matter? Evidence about teacher certification, teach for America, and teacher effectiveness. *Education Policy Analysis Archives, 13*(42). https://epaa.asu.edu/ojs/article/view/147

62. Adamson, F., & Darling-Hammond, L. (2011, May). *Speaking of salaries. What it will take to get qualified, effective teachers in all communities*. Center for American Progress. https://files.eric.ed.gov/fulltext/ED536080.pdf

63. Kaplan, L. S., Owings, W. A., & Nunnery, J. (2005, June). Principal quality: A Virginia study connecting Interstate School Leaders Licensure Consortium (ISLLC) standards with student achievement. *National Association of Secondary School Principals Bulletin*.

64. Adamson & Darling-Hammond, 2011.

65. Adamson & Darling-Hammond, 2011.

66. Hall, D., & Ushomirsky, N. (2010). Close the hidden funding gaps in our schools. *The Education Trust.* https://files.eric.ed.gov/fulltext/ED511871.pdf

67. Kane, T. J., Rockoff, J. E., & Staiger, D. O. (2007, Winter). Teachers' certification doesn't guarantee a winner. *Education Next, 7*(1), 61–67; Ingersoll, R. (2003). *Is there really a teacher shortage?* Center for the Study of Teaching and Policy.

68. American Society of Civil Engineers. (2017). *Infrastructure report card.* https://www.infrastructurereportcard.org/wp-content/uploads/2017/01/Schools-Final.pdf

69. Filardo, M. (2016). *State of our schools: America's K–12 facilities, 2016.* 21st Century School Fund and Center for Green Schools.

70. Cherney, K. (2017, September 8). Sick building syndrome. *Healthline.* https://www.healthline.com/health/sick-building-syndrome

71. Earthman, G. (2002). Selected facility conditions and student academic achievement. *Williams watch series: Investigating the claims of* Williams v. State of California. UCLA Institute for Democracy, Education and Access. https://nctaf.org/wp-content/uploads/ucla_2002_article.pdf

72. Fisk, W. J., Paulson, J. A., Kolbe, L. J., & Barnett, C. L. (2016). Significance of the school physical environment: A commentary. *Journal of School Health, 86*(7), 483–487.

73. See: Baker, L., & Bernstein, H. (2012, February 27). *The impact of school buildings on student health and performance: A call for research.* The McGraw-Hill Research Foundation and The Center for Green Schools. https://www.usgbc.org/Docs/Archive/General/Docs18534.pdf;Lawrence Berkeley National Laboratories. (2018). Human performance: Indoor air quality. *Scientific Findings Resource Bank.* https://iaqscience.lbl.gov/performance-summary;. Gunter, T., & Shao, J. (2016). Synthesizing the effect of building condition quality on academic performance. *Education Finance and Policy, 11*(1), 97–123.

74. See: Cervantes, R. (1999). *The condition of school facilities as related to student academic achievement and behavior.* PhD Dissertation, University of Alabama at Birmingham; Picus, L. O., Calvo, N., Glenn, W. J., & Marion, S. (2005). Understanding the relationship between student achievement and the quality of educational facilities: Evidence from Wyoming. *Peabody Journal of Education, 80*(3), 71–95; Uline, C., & Tschannen-Moran, M. (2008). The walls speak: The interplay of quality facilities, school climate, and student achievement. *Journal of Educational Administration, 46*(1), 55–73; U.S. Department of Education, Office for Civil Rights. (2014). *Dear colleague letter: Resource comparability.* https://www2.ed.gov/about/offices/list/ocr/letters/colleague-resourcecomp-201410.pdf

75. Sparks, S. D. (2020, February 12). Air filters: A possible new tool to boost learning. *Education Week, 39*(21), 5, 7.

76. Alexander, D., & Lewis, L. (2014). *Condition of America's public school facilities: 2012–13* (NCES 2014-022). U.S. Department of Education; Filardo, M. W., Vincent, J. M., Sung, P., & Stein, T. (2006). *Growth and disparity: A decade of U.S. public school construction.* Building Educational Success Together.

77. Uline & Tschannen-Moran, 2008.

78. Leigh, R. M. (2012). *School facility conditions and the relationship between teacher attitudes.* Unpublished doctoral dissertation, Virginia Polytechnic Institute and State University, Blacksburg, Virginia. https://vtechworks.lib.vt.edu/bitstream/handle/10919/49572/Leigh_RM_T_2012_support_1.pdf?sequence=2;. Buckley, J., Schneider, M., & Shang, Y. (2004). *The effects of school facility quality on teacher retention in urban school districts.* National Clearinghouse for Educational Facilities.

79. Schneider, M. (2002). Do school facilities affect academic outcomes? National Clearinghouse for Educational Facilities, pp. 1–9. http://www.ncef.org/pubs/outcomes.pdf

80. Batterman, S., Su, F. C., Waid, A., Watkins, F., Goodwin, C., & Thun, G. (2017). Ventilation rates in recently constructed U.S. school classrooms. *Indoor Air, 27*(5), 880–890.

81. Concrete Construction. (2018, April 11). Construction costs increased in March. *Hanley Wood Media.* http://www.concreteconstruction.net/business/construction-costs-increased-in-march_o

82. Boser, U. (2015, June 3). If you build it, they'll learn better. *U.S. New & World Report.* https://www.usnews.com/opinion/knowledge-bank/2015/06/03/better-school-infrastructure-can-boost-student-learning

83. Cataldo, E. H., & Holm, J. D. (1983). Voting on school finances: A test of competing theories. *Western Political Quarterly 36*(4), 619–31; Reed, D. S. (2001, March). Not in my backyard: Localism and public opposition to funding schools equally. *Social Science Quarterly 82* (1), 34–50.

84. RealEstateabc.com. (2015). *California real estate median prices of existing homes since 1968.* https://www.realestateabc.com/graphs/calmedian.html

85. Prop 13 tied property taxes to 1% of the purchase price and capped annual increases at 2% a year.

86. Chen, G. (2018, January 23). Why 82% of public schools are failing. *Public School Review.* https://www.publicschoolreview.com/blog/why-82-of-public-schools-are-failing

87. Sixty percent of parents and 40% of nonparents give their local schools an A or B grade, whereas only 19% would give the nation's schools an A or B grade. See: *Phi Delta Kappan.* (2019). *How would you grade the public schools? PDK Poll of the public's attitudes toward the public schools.* https://pdkpoll.org/results/how-would-you-grade-the-schools. and https://pdkpoll.org/assets/downloads/2019pdkpoll51.pdf

88. RealEstateabc.com, 2015; Reed, 2001.

89. Downes, G. (1992, December). Evaluating the impact of school finance reform on the provision of public education: The case of California. *National Tax Journal, 45*(4), 405–419.

90. Henke, J. T. (1986, Fall). Financing public schools in California: The aftermath of the *Serrano v. Priest* decision. *University of San Francisco Law Review, 21*, 1–39.

91. Prothero, A., & Harwin, A. (2020, March 11). Transparency lacking on private school choice. *Education Week, 39*(25), 1, 14–15.

92. Henderson, M. B., Huston, D., Peterson, P. E., & West, M. R. (2020, Winter). Public support grows for higher teacher pay and expanded school choice. *EducationNext, 20*(1). https://www.educationnext.org/school-choice-trump-era-results-2019-education-next-poll/;. Phi Delta Kappan. (2017, September). The 49th annual PDK poll of the public's attitude toward the public schools. *Phi Delta Kappan, 99*(1), K1–K32. Supplement. https://pdkpoll.org/timeline/2017

93. Fiddiman, B., & Yin, J. (2019, May 13). *The danger private school voucher programs pose to civil rights.* Center for American Progress. https://www.americanprogress.org/issues/education-k-12/reports/2019/05/13/469610/danger-private-school-voucher-programs-pose-civil-rights/

94. EdChoice. (2019, November 4). How does school choice affect public schools' funding and resources? *Engage.* https://www.edchoice.org/engage/faqs/how-does-school-choice-affect-public-schools-funding-and-resources/

95. Fiddlman, B., & Yin, J. (2019, May 13). *The danger private school voucher programs pose to civil rights.* Center for American Progress. https://cdn.americanprogress.org/content/uploads/2019/05/10124230/Vouchers-and-Civil-Rights2.pdf

96. To fill the budget holes, localities can cut their budget by the lost amount, raise property taxes, or fill the hole with money from a fund balance. See: Conniff, R. (2019, October 18). Private school vouchers cost $350 million. State to spend $248M on school vouchers next school year. *Wisconsin State Journal.* https://urbanmilwaukee.com/2019/10/18/private-school-vouchers-cost-350-million/

97. Davis, C. (2017, May). *State tax subsidies for private K–12 education.* Institute on Taxation & Economic Policy. https://itep.org/wp-content/uploads/k12taxsubsidies-1.pdf

98. States with ESA programs: Arizona, Florida, Mississippi, Tennessee, Nevada, and North Carolina.

99. Prothero & Harwin, 2020.

100. Tax Cuts and Jobs Act of 2017. H.R. 1, 115th Congress of the United States, Part IV—Education, Sec. 110312. 529 Account Funding for Elementary and Secondary Education, (a)(1)(2017). https://www.congress.gov/115/bills/hr1/BILLS-115hr1enr.pdf

101. Flynn, K. (2017, December 22). New tax law brings big changes to 529 plans. Savingforcollege.com. http://www.savingforcollege.com/articles/coming-soon-big-changes-to-529-plans

102. Prothero & Harwin, 2020.

103. Arsen, D., DeLuca, T. A., Ni, Y., & Bates, M. (2015, November). *Which districts get into financial trouble and why: Michigan's story* (Working Paper #51). Michigan State University, The Education Policy Center. https://www.fundmischools.org/wp-content/uploads/2017/03/WP51-Which-Districts-Get-Into-Financial-Trouble-Arsen.pdf;. Epple, D., Jha, A., & Sieg, H. (2017, April 18). The superintendent's dilemma: Managing school district capacity as parents vote with their feet. University of Pennsylvania and NBER. http://www.sas.upenn.edu/~holgers/papers/ejs_qe_f.pdf;Epple, D., Romano, R., & Zimmer, R. (2015, June). *Charter schools: A survey of research on their characteristics and effectiveness.* (NBER Working Paper No. 21256). The National Bureau of Economic Research. http://202.119.108.161:93/modules/ShowPDF.aspx?GUID=e74e5fbcefdb4e05846c6c35f86c7a49

104. *Mueller v. Allen*, 463 U.S. 103 S. Ct. 3062 (1983).

105. *Zelman v. Simmons-Harris*, 536 US 639 (2002).

106. *Trinity Lutheran Church of Columbus v. Comer*, No. 15-577, S. Ct (2017).

107. *Espinoza v. Montana Department of Revenue*. See: Totenberg, N., & Naylor, B. (2020, June 30). Supreme court: Montana can't exclude religious schools form scholarship program. *NPR*. https://www.npr.org/2020/06/30/883074890/supreme-court-montana-cant-exclude-religious-schools-from-scholarship-program

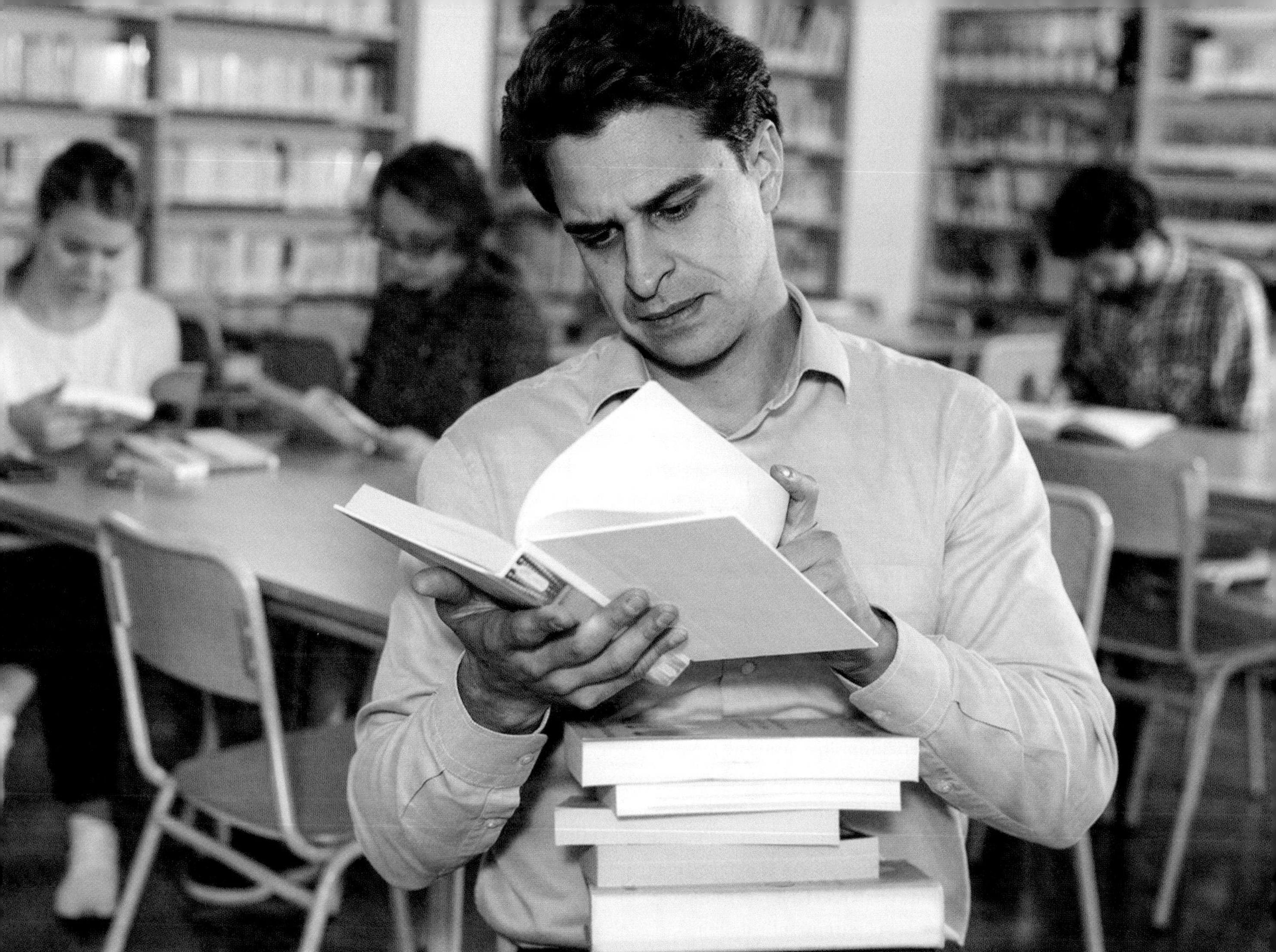

iStock/Ulza

12 CURRICULUM AND INSTRUCTION

InTASC Standards Addressed: 1, 2, 3, 4, 5, 6, 7, 8, 9, 10

LEARNING OBJECTIVES

After you read this chapter, you should be able to

12.1 Describe the separate but interdependent relationships among curriculum, instruction, and society's goals for students.

12.2 Defend the view that public school curricula respond to intellectual, societal, and political influences.

12.3 Assess how a school's curricular balance impacts children's personal, social, and intellectual growth and development.

12.4 Critique how conventional wisdom about the primary influencers of student learning expanded in the past few decades.

12.5 Support the view that educators must rethink effective teaching and learning technologies and consider both instructional and equity concerns.

Curriculum (the academic content we teach in school, a plan for learning) and instruction (the purposeful direction of the learning process) are foundational to schooling. *Curriculum* defines what schooling should accomplish. *Instruction* is the means by which teachers bring curriculum to life in the classroom. Once an education system has defined its curriculum, the teacher uses subject-matter (the content to be learned) and pedagogy (the theory and practice of education) to accomplish the curriculum's goals and facilitate student learning. Curriculum and instruction are separate yet interdependent concepts purposefully designed to generate student learning of those things their society deems most important.

Curriculum debates are nothing new. Since colonial days, educators and policy makers have argued about whether public schools should prepare the "select" children (they whose parents could afford to have them attend regularly) for the learned professions or prepare minimally literate citizens to be able to obey community norms and be informed voters. Later, industrialization brought the need for public schools to prepare children to enter vocational occupations while the most academically talented prepared for college.

We still wrestle with these issues today. In the 21st century, all students need a rigorous curriculum to develop the intellectual tools and self-discipline that will enable them to direct important life and career options. Additionally, all students need the knowledge, attitudes, and skills that will enable them to become engaged citizens who can responsibly influence public policy with their votes and interact constructively with others like—and unlike—themselves. And to facilitate learning this curriculum, school must provide every student with regular and ongoing access to highly effective teachers who understand how learning happens, know their students and their learning needs, create positive classroom learning environments, and have the deep content knowledge and pedagogical skills to help every student master it.

Joel Westheimer, professor of democracy and education at the University of Ottawa in Ontario, Canada, observes, "What we teach in schools is a proxy for the kind of society we hope to create."[1] But who decides what students should learn and if it's worth learning? Should we keep our society as it is, or should we change it? How should we teach it? How do we prepare enough highly effective future teachers to meet every student's needs? The debate continues because *what* teachers teach—and *how* they teach it—may either affirm or challenge our deeply held beliefs and commitments about who we are and how we want to live.

12.1 CURRICULUM HELPS TEACHERS AND STUDENTS MEET EDUCATIONAL GOALS

Curricula don't just happen. Society develops and uses curricula to prepare its young people for adult responsibilities. Accordingly, states and localities decide what students should learn based on their beliefs about what students need to survive in a complex environment and what it means to be an educated person in that culture. The governing body selects people, serving as the larger society's agents, to write curriculum reflecting these values and beliefs. These persons may include educators, professionals, politicians, and other community members.

In this way, curriculum planning occurs in a social context and involves translating views about human nature and the world into educational aims. Knowledge about how students learn and the educational program must be considered during this process.

12.1a What Is Curriculum?

The most common definition comes from the Latin root *currere*, which means "to run (around a racetrack)." For many students, curriculum is a race to be run, a series of obstacles (or courses) to be passed. Historically, curriculum referred to the subjects taught during the classical period of Greek civilization. In the mid-19th century, it came to mean a course of study at a school or university. The 20th century broadened the concept to include subjects other than the European classics.

In his book *What Works in Schools: Translating Research Into Action* (2003), educational researcher Robert Marzano argues that having a "guaranteed and viable curriculum" is the number-one factor that impacts student achievement.[2] Students need to learn and be able to act on the knowledge, skills, and perspectives that their community believes essential for mature, responsible adulthood in their society. So what is this essential building block for learning?

Defining *curriculum* is difficult because so many educational specialties call curriculum their professional home. Since the 1900s, the curriculum family has included people interested in subject content, teaching methods, teacher education, human development, social progressivism and conservatism, educational technologies, evaluation, and educational objectives. With so many related but competing professional interests, agreeing on one common definition is challenging.

Nonetheless, all agree that **curriculum** is the plan that guides the work of schools; and **teaching (instruction)** is the work that carries out the plan. Curriculum is the program; teaching/instruction is the method. The two are separate but interdependent concepts. In practical terms, curriculum is a document that designs, guides, and monitors the work that happens in schools.

12.1b How Curriculum Addresses Education's Goals

Our society believes that education should accomplish many, sometimes competing, goals. Once curriculum writers know a community's and schools' intents, they can select or develop the curriculum to help students achieve these ends.

Our contemporary schools' purposes include (but are not limited to) these goals:

- *National goals*—to preserve traditional American values and encourage good citizenship, economic growth, and social stability by transmitting our cultural heritage and traditions
- *Economic goals*—to socialize future workers for the workplace with appropriate attitudes, knowledge, skills, and behaviors
- *Social goals*—to help create a better culture, in part, by helping students learn to thrive in a diverse, pluralistic society
- *Personal goals*—to help students to live personally fulfilling and socially constructive lives by fully developing their minds and capacities[3]

Understanding education's purposes—along with a rich grasp of child development—helps curriculum writers make important decisions about how to elaborate their subjects. It also helps teachers plan how to teach and assess it.

12.1c Types of Curricular Organization

Schools can organize their curricula in various ways. These include subject-centered, student-centered, or problem-centered curricula; integrated curriculum; and a college and career-centered curriculum. Schools accompany these with a cocurricular program as well as an informal, hidden curriculum.

Subject-centered Curricula

In a **subject-centered curriculum**, schools organize learning around academic fields such as biology, mathematics, or literature as a way for students to acquire knowledge. For the most part, each teacher keeps instructional content to his or her own separate discipline. This approach is very familiar to most students who attended American public high schools and colleges with different subject departments.

Advocates of a subject-centered curriculum assert that it fosters students' intellectual development and presents a convenient, logical framework for organizing and interpreting information. This enables future teachers who major in specific content areas to learn the instructional techniques that best present these concepts and practices to students. Critics of the subject-centered curricula argue that this approach leads to fragmented learning as students are taught concepts and facts apart from relevant real-world contexts and, thus, with slight meaning for them. Also, it puts teachers "in charge" as the "authority" and leaves students as passive learners with little space for input or participation.[4] As a result, less motivated students may lose interest and fall behind.

Learner-centered Curricula

A **learner-centered curriculum** focuses on including student needs, interests, and goals in what is taught rather than strictly transmitting a prescribed set of facts and skills. This approach empowers learners to have input into their own education though their choices. Learning is viewed as the process of achieving full personal development. Teachers prepare differentiated instructional plans, allowing students to select assignments, learning experiences, or activities.

Advocates of this approach assert that this orientation intrinsically motivates students to learn, prompts critical thinking and active construction of knowledge, helps them become self-directed learners, and adapts to varied learning needs and styles. Critics contend that this curriculum design places substantial pressure on teachers to decide how much structure and independence to give students. Many students who are not mature enough to direct their own learning may fall behind academically. Teachers must also locate and secure the necessary resources specific to each student's interests and needs within a limited time. If they cannot, students receive insufficient instruction.

Problem-Based Curricula

A **problem-based curriculum** is an active, integrated, and constructive process that uses real-life issues to teach students how to identify a problem, search for solutions by gathering and evaluating relevant information from varied disciplines and sources, and devise a solution. Assigned problems are often complex, ill-structured, open-ended, and captivating enough to lead students toward investigation. Students must communicate, collaborate, and cooperate with classmates to solve the problems.

For instance, students might be assigned to redesign their high school's parking lot in ways that allow safe entries and exits from the street; give maximum parking availability for cars, SUVs, and trucks; and has sufficient open spaces for cars to move safely through the lot. To permit accurate planning, students would secure data from varied sources (interviews and written) about the designated area, and they would read and apply state and/or local regulations defining permissible locations for entry and exit points, adequate spaces for different types of vehicles, and width of driving lanes through the filled lot. Then, they would apply these rules to their designated lot. In problem-based curricula, teachers incorporate explicit instruction and scaffolding at key points, connecting the content students learn to the process they use to complete the activity.

Proponents note that this approach is learner-centered, engages students' intrinsic interest to motivate their learning, encourages creativity and collaboration, develops higher-order thinking skills, and transfers these skills to life outside the classroom. Some assert that a problem-solving curriculum ends the artificial separation between knowing and doing.[5] Critics note that constructing truly authentic problems is difficult, as is monitoring and assessing each student's work processes and outputs within their groups. Unless teachers are well-grounded in this curricular approach, they are likely to misunderstand and misapply its practices and fail to achieve the expected learning outcomes. Plus, schools need to provide sufficient investment in designing, preparing, and renewing learning resources and providing extra support for students with learning needs.[6]

Integrated Curricula

An **integrated curriculum** cuts across different areas of study by stressing the concepts that unify them, making connections for students, and engaging them in relevant, meaningful activities that can be linked to real life. For instance, an elementary teacher might have students study the concept of "patterns" by involving them in activities that explore "patterns" from math, science, language, social studies, music, and art perspectives.

Advocates of integrated curricula stress that it presents students with concepts and facts as they appear in the "real world" and increases student interest, involvement, and retention of information and skills, leading to improved student outcomes. Critics note that integrated curricula place a greater burden on teachers to know related content from varied disciplines and create challenging, enjoyable, and meaningful learning activities to help student understand and link the information.

College and Career Readiness Curricula

College and career readiness curricula are anchored in the belief that all students should graduate from high school ready for college, careers, and life, prepared to choose and enact their own futures. These curricula include mastery of rigorous knowledge and skills in core academic discipline of language, math, and sciences; the ability to communicate effectively orally and in writing; to think critically and develop informed arguments; to solve problems; to analyze information and data; and collaborate with others.

Cocurricular activities extend and reinforce classroom learning and have a positive effect on students' personal development and growth.

iStock/monkeybusinessimages

Proponents affirm that having successfully completed a college and career readiness program in high school helps students more successfully transition from secondary to undergraduate education and eventually to the well-paying professional workforce. Critics claim that this curricula for college readiness suffers from incoherence, with educators uncertain of how this approach should inform instruction, concern over the trillion-dollar student loan debt, and the doubt that, in an age of a rapidly changing workforce and the elimination of millions of high-skilled jobs over the last decade, educational attainment can still guarantee gainful employment.[7]

Cocurricula

Cocurricula[8] refers to the activities, programs, and learning experiences that complement what students are learning in their academic classrooms. These activities—such as student newspapers and yearbooks, musical performances, art exhibits, debate competitions, and engineering teams—may occur outside the classroom or after regular school hours. Outside organizations may run them.

Advocates note that research finds that participation in cocurricular activities extends and reinforces classroom learning; has a positive impact on students' personal development and growth; links to greater school attachment and sense of belonging, better academic achievement, and higher academic aspirations; and lowers risky social behaviors or the chance of dropping out of school.[9] Participation in cocurricular activities also helps students develop and refine particular skills in both academic and nonacademic areas, as well as acquire stronger time management, organization, and leadership abilities. Some critics say that these activities may detract time and effort from academics, with students so engaged in their off-time activities that they neglect to study or prepare for classes.

The Hidden Curricula

The **hidden curricula** refer to the unwritten, unofficial, and often unintended lessons, values, and viewpoints that students learn in school. As part of the school's culture and climate, it consists of the unspoken or implicit intellectual, social, and environmental messages—the social norms and expectations—that the school communicates to students. This curriculum is considered "hidden" because it is usually not acknowledged or examined by educators, students, or the community. Its lessons may either complement or contradict schools' formal curriculum.

Examples of the hidden curricula include the implicit messages that students receive when they see which students have the best teachers with the most rigorous coursework; how the school values student initiative and questioning authority; how the school recognizes, integrates, or honors diversity; how the school responds to biased or prejudicial statements and behaviors; or how teachers and students should view and interact with students of different abilities, social classes, or ethnicities. Do the books in school libraries and classrooms feature students of color and their experiences as well as those of white students? Do the books tell stories depicting a varied array of human experiences or a narrow one that reinforces stereotypes? Societal changes and social media are leading to a greater awareness of schools' hidden curricula as school communities, educators, and students reflect on their assumptions and actions.

Some say the hidden curricula should be acknowledged, examined (unhidden), and explicitly taught to ensure that every student can access mainstream beliefs, attitudes, and behaviors. Others say that the hidden curriculum reinforces existing social inequalities by educating students according to their social class and social status.

12.1d Selecting Curricula Emphases

Curriculum is more than core topics—reading, writing, language arts, mathematics, social studies, and science. Referencing their knowledge of how children of different ages learn, expectations from their academic disciplines, and state and local dictates, curriculum writers and teachers also have additional curricular considerations. Should the curriculum be mainly concerned with students' cognitive mastery or their affective responses to it? Should the subject be taught for depth or breadth? Should events discussed in social studies focus on state and local (here)—or international (there)—occurrences? Should the focus be on academic content or related skills? (Are these alternatives false choices or continua?) These five essential factors reflect some of the choices that educators make about how to translate a curriculum into student learning. Let's briefly consider each factor more closely.

Cognitive or Affective?

Teachers do not simply transmit information. They instruct actual children who have their own personalities, interests, life experiences, and cultures that impact learning preferences or needs. Research since the 1980s finds that cognitive and affective factors interact to influence student learning and achievement.[10] In fact, some educators believe that "all learning is social and emotional."[11]

Cognition is the act of acquiring knowledge. According to Bloom (revised), cognition includes remembering, understanding, applying, analyzing, evaluating, and creating.[12] **Affect** is the response to events that includes expression of emotion or feelings, values, and beliefs. In its narrowest sense, learning is the cognitive change that results from formal teaching: the capacity to hold more information mentally, to memorize and reproduce it. More broadly, learning is any development that occurs to learners, including cognitive, affective, and personal growth. **Learning** happens when the learner actively constructs knowledge—produces new understanding by reconciling prior knowledge with new information—that results in meaningful changes in the way they know, think, and act.[13]

Current neuroscience research suggests that learning occurs through a person's affective development.[14] Any behavior that has an emotional aspect is within the affective domain. Students' motivation to learn reflects an interaction between the context and what the student brings to that context. For example, in a largely cognitive-focused health lesson on "Bacteria and You," a teacher might list common bacteria on the board, define them, show pictures of how they look under a microscope, identify diseases they cause, and ask students to memorize the list. Class assessment would include matching bacteria names with their related illnesses. In this classroom, most of the students passively receive the information. By comparison, a teacher using a cognitive and affective instructional approach might begin by asking students to discuss these questions:

- Who has even had a cut that bled, even a little?
- What part of your body was injured?
- How did it happen?
- How did it feel?
- Did you ever have a cut become infected?
- What did it look like?
- How did you and your parents treat it?

Almost every student can relate to this topic and participate in the class discussion. By generating relevance and personal meaning around the "bacteria" topic, students become more encouraged to learn about microorganisms and how the human body fights infections. Teachers' assessment of student learning includes having them explain what bacteria are, describe how bacteria can cause infection, explain how the body reacts to them, and discuss how you can treat it to gain full recovery.

By integrating the cognitive and affective (motivational) factors in the lessons and classrooms, teachers stimulate cognitive and affective changes in students' knowledge and attitudes about bacteria and health. Affective change occurs when teachers adapt what they teach in ways that make sense and have personal meaning to students, heighten their interests, and enable them to willingly engage in the learning tasks and generate more learning.[15] This cognitive and affective learning tends to be remembered, recalled, and used later.

Teachers also motivate students by providing a safe learning environment. Like an athlete, a learner's affective state is a critical factor during performance. A student's motivation to learn can vary, depending on his or her own present condition and the situation in the classroom or school. A student who is anxious, worried, uncomfortable, frustrated, embarrassed, or afraid is less open to learning than one who is comfortable, interested, hopeful, curious, and confident. How teachers approach their curriculum and attend to both cognitive and affective dimensions directly impact student learning.[16]

Depth or Breadth?

How does one decide what to include in a curriculum? Given the amount of time allotted in the school year and school day, should the curriculum be wide and thin, covering many topics superficially so students have an "awareness" of many facts? Or should the curriculum include fewer topics but study each deeply and thoroughly so students truly understand and develop conceptual grasp and mastery of those subjects?

Those curriculum writers favoring *breadth* reflect the old saying, "Throw enough mud at the wall, and some of it is bound to stick." This view recognizes that not everything that is taught is learned. It suggests, nonetheless, that bombarding students with information is still a worthwhile effort because they will remember at least some of it.[17] For this theory's adherents, the traditional essentialist curriculum of separate subjects, each with many important topics studied apart from each other, is the right curriculum.

Those favoring *depth* follow the maxim, "Less is more." In the early 20th century, mathematician, teacher, and philosopher Alfred North Whitehead asserted that dumping vast amounts of information on students was counterproductive. He argued that humans were not mentally equipped to handle a great deal of random, "inert knowledge." The young, he advised, need to study in great depth a relatively few really powerful ideas that encompass and explain major aspects of human experience.[18]

For instance, according to this view, students should learn broad concepts that cut across all fields of knowledge and find their inherent connections. Concepts such as patterns, structures, relationships, and systems are central to all disciplines, including those not yet developed. By focusing on large-scale and meaningful mental organizers—the "big ideas" around which students can wrap (and remember) a variety of related ideas and details—students can explore new intellectual territories. Unless persons can integrate what they learn with an often-used larger meaning and prior knowledge, details are soon forgotten.

Some believe that young people should learn broad concepts—the "big ideas," such as teamwork—that cut across all fields of knowledge and find their inherent connections.

iStock/fizkes

Here or There?

Educators who think that individuals learn by connecting new information to personally meaningful experiences believe in starting each student's learning "here." *Here* reflects where the student is, cognitively, emotionally, socially, physically, and experientially. These curriculum writers would argue, for example, that second graders studying "society and family" would learn more by starting at home, looking at their own family members' relationships and behaviors. They could study society in the field by asking their parents or guardians focusing questions and then visiting with relatives or friends to look for additional answers.

By comparison, the "there" adherents might formally teach second graders in the U.S. about society and family in China, India, and ancient Greece—places far from some children's own experiences or present knowledge. Curriculum writers who stress *there* are thinking about the subject, not the learners.

To answer this question, wise curriculum writers must consider how students actually learn. Although it may be worthwhile for second graders to be able to locate China, India, and Greece on an atlas, real learning will come only by first developing authentic personal experiences with the concept of "society and family" and then extending it outward to the unfamiliar. By middle or high school, however, studying "there" with ongoing comparisons and contrasts with "here" might be more meaningful to students who are already very knowledgeable about their own families and society.

Conceptually dealing with the complex, the abstract, and the remote is very difficult, especially for young and teen learners. Immediate reality is a more practical place to begin to build the descriptive and analytical mental models—those "big ideas" that will cognitively scaffold the students' knowledge and enable them to integrate meaning from wider experiences. This lack of relevance and personal meaning often frustrates and bores students, undermining their desire or effort to learn.

Content or Skills?

Arguing whether to teach subject matter content or application skills is like asking, "Which came first, the chicken or the egg?" **Content** is the subject matter or topic, and **skills** are the abilities to use one's knowledge (the content) competently in performance. They are not an either/or dichotomy. Surely, certain skills are essential for being able to access content. Children must learn to recognize letters, singly and in combinations, and develop the phonic awareness to pronounce them in order to read. Simply put, young learners need to be taught *how* before they can be taught *what*.[19] More mature students need to master different skills before they can read and analyze varied texts, connect their learning across content areas, and correctly assess which information they find on Google or Facebook is credible, valid, and reliable (and which is not). But try to teach creative thinking without content! Try writing an essay on any topic without subject matter. One can't mentally manipulate nothing and come out with something.

Students need both content and related skills. Since the "how" and the "what" complement each other, the most effective instructors teach them together. The question then becomes how to sequence, integrate, and assess them. As teachers plan their lesson, they ask, "*What* do I want students to learn today, and *how* will I design the lesson to have students *use* and *practice* the new content in ways that they find interesting, engaging, and relevant? What will I have the students *do* to facilitate their learning?" By putting course content to use, students learn it more easily and are more likely to remember it and transfer it to new situations outside the classroom.

For a deeper look at the factors that shape a school's curriculum—and how the curricular emphasis affects you as a student—complete the activity in the **Reflect & Engage** box, Selecting Curricular Emphasis.

REFLECT & ENGAGE: SELECTING CURRICULAR EMPHASIS

This activity includes making a wordle (word cloud). Curriculum writers and teachers have considerations beyond meeting their discipline's state and local expectations for what students will learn. These additional factors shape how teachers impart the content to students. How might these factors look in actual lessons?

A. Separate the class into groups.

B. Have each group spend a minute to think about their most favorite—and least favorite—K–12 (or college) teachers.

C. Discuss the types of learning experiences in K–12 (or college) education that their favorite teacher provided the class. What type of learning experiences did their least favorite teacher assign the class?

D. Using words from this section and their individual recollections, each group collaborates to create a wordle to illustrate how their favorite teacher engaged them in learning. What did the teacher have you *do* with the new content/skill to facilitate your learning?

E. After completing their discussions and wordles, each group shows and reports their findings to the rest of the class.

F. Discuss: Which factors tended to create your most meaningful learning experiences?

Which factors tended to produce your most boring (and ineffective) learning experiences? How should the learner's age and academic maturity impact how the teacher uses each of the discussed factors?

FLIPSIDES

Should Students Be Schooled or Educated?

Mark Twain, the 19th century American writer and humorist, wrote, *"I try not to let my schooling interfere with my education." Schooling* is not the same as *educating*. Each offers a different view of what learners need to become responsible adults—and different views about what teachers and curricula need to provide learners so they might reach the desired outcomes. As a learner and a future educator, would you prefer a curriculum that provides *schooling* or *educating*?

As a student, myself, and as a future educator, I prefer to receive/provide practices for schooling.	As a student, myself, and as a future educator, I prefer to receive/provide practices for educating.
• As defined by state law, *schooling* is the program of formal instruction that occurs within a certain place (a classroom) and at a certain time (during the school day) for a specified number of days each year.	• Not defined by state law, *educating* includes more than what the state says children should know, is largely self-generating, and occurs across the lifespan, even outside of school.
• Schooling identifies what we want our students to know and be able to do to pass end-of-course tests.	• Educating identifies what we want our students to know, understand, do, and be as competent human beings.
• Schooling uses curricula that respect the traditions and content of separate academic disciplines so students can learn the habits of mind that each subject brings.	• Educating uses curricula that respect traditional content and integrate learning across "big ideas" and academic disciplines in ways that students find relevant, meaningful, and more likely to be remembered and used.
• Schooling provides individuals with the knowledge and skills approved by the larger community to preserve the status quo.	• Educating provides individuals with the knowledge and skills approved by the larger community in addition to those that assess, judge, and challenge conventional thinking.

As a student, myself, and as a future educator, I prefer to receive/provide practices for schooling.	As a student, myself, and as a future educator, I prefer to receive/provide practices for educating.
• Schooling relies on recognition, recall, application, and recitation of the curriculum to ensure that students are learning.	• Educating relies on recall, application, analysis, synthesis, evaluation, and creativity with the curriculum to ensure that students are learning and using their learning to solve problems.
• Schooling is mostly cognitive, focusing on transmitting culturally approved information to students.	• Educating is cognitive and affective, making the content relevant and meaningful to students.
• Schooling relies on curricula that are wide and thin so teachers can make students passingly familiar with many important topics.	• Educating relies on curricula that include essential concepts and themes that students can study deeply, understand, and master.

12.2 PUBLIC SCHOOL CURRICULUM RESPONDS TO INTELLECTUAL, SOCIETAL, AND POLITICAL INFLUENCES

Curriculum is not neutral. It is "always part of a **selective tradition**, someone's selection, and someone's vision of the knowledge that needs to be taught to everyone," says Michael Apple, professor at the University of Wisconsin–Madison.[20] Fundamentally, curriculum is about values. The decision to define a certain group's knowledge as the most important says much about who holds the power in a particular society and which values they seek to transmit through schooling.

12.2a Pendulum Swings

U.S. curriculum reflects an inherent tension between its focus on social control by transmitting our cultural history and its focus on developing the individual. On the one hand, we recognize that schools should acclimate students to the social order and allow them to learn the society's traditional values and culture. This is an important social and political responsibility that helps unite us as one nation with a common perspective and loyalty. On the other hand, we talk about individual dignity, self-actualization, individual potential, and the reality that education frees individuals to become their fullest, most satisfied, and most productive selves.

The contradictions in these two approaches are clear. As a result, our communities and curriculum writers have tried to find the appropriate curricular balance among society, subject, and child. This dynamic tension guides educational policy decisions at all levels and has influenced curriculum decisions for more than 100 years.

12.2b National Curriculum Standards

For over 30 years, education reform has focused on standards. Policy makers saw the need for all schools to be held accountable for delivering a core set of curricula anchored in high academic standards regardless of student populations, geographic locations, teaching styles, and curricular emphasis.

Goals 2000

Written by the U.S. state governors in 1989, *Goals 2000* introduced national curriculum standards as a way to ensure that public schools met the nation's academic achievement goals. States could voluntarily comply and adopt these proposed standards. In response to this push, professional educational organizations developed academic subject area standards in almost all curricular areas.

Common Core States Standards

In 2010, the National Governors Association (NGA), the Council for Chief State School Officers (CCSSO), and other influential stakeholders offered *K–12 Common Core State Standards*, a contemporary approach to improving public schools' curricula by focusing on rigorous academic content and the application of knowledge using higher-order thinking skills. Informed by curricula in top-performing countries, the standards incorporate the knowledge and skills that high school graduates need to master in order to succeed in college and careers in a global environment. Available for English language arts and mathematics, the standards clearly communicate what students at each grade level are expected to know and be able to do.

12.2c Debates Over Standards

In a nation that celebrates state and local control of education, national standards for content areas—even if local writers develop the actual curriculum—often meet with wide-ranging criticism. Many oppose federal intrusion into local schools. Others worry that the standards will be politicized, advocating only a certain interest group's viewpoint over others. Some critics observe that the standards might narrow the school experience, with too much emphasis on generating high test performance in certain subject areas while neglecting essential learning in nontested content areas. In this case, detractors worry, standards might result in *schooling* rather than in *educating*.[21] Additionally, critics complain that learning by standards would likely be subject-centered rather than child-centered, focusing too much on the text itself and ignoring the readers' affective experiences with it. Others assert that certain standards (such as the Common Core Standards) are too demanding, overestimating children's intellectual, physiological, and emotional capacities to engage in such rigorous study. Finally, some conclude that standards by themselves make no difference to student learning. Only robust curricula, highly effective teaching, valid and reliable assessment and accountability systems, among other things, must be in place if standards' promises are to be fulfilled. Successful implementation, not merely written standards, some argue, make the difference.

Ultimately, all curricula changes reflect intellectual, social, and political dynamics. Decisions about what the curriculum is, does, and includes are highly selective decisions made by those with social and political influence. The dramatic swings from subject-centered curriculum to student-centered curriculum and back again are clearly evident in the history of U.S. education. Unless the curriculum both connects with students in meaningful ways and enforces accountability for students mastering high-level and important knowledge and skills, the pendulum will continue to swing between subject-centered and child-centered approaches.

AMERICAN EDUCATION SPOTLIGHT: LISA DELPIT

"So often in the belief that we are 'being nice,' we fail to realize the brilliance of our students and teach down to them, demanding little.... [Research finds that] under the pressures of teaching and with all intentions of being kind, teachers had essentially stopped attempting to teach Black children.... If children come to us knowing less, and we put them on a track of slower paced, remedial learning, then where will they end up?"*

Lisa Delpit, education professor and Executive Director/Eminent Scholar, Center for Urban Education & Innovation at Florida International University, earned her MA and EdD from Harvard Graduate School of Education and a BA from Antioch College. She expresses concern about schools that place curricula and texts before students and relationships with those students and schools that consider some children as "our children" and many others as "other people's children."

Delpit's career goal was to teach African American children and teach them well. After completing a teacher preparation program in college, she student-taught kindergarten in an inner-city Philadelphia school enrolling 60% low-income African American and 40% high-income white students. Delpit used an "open classroom" concept to organize student learning. The results discouraged her.

"My white students zoomed ahead. They worked hard at the learning stations. They did amazing things with books and writing. My black students played the games; they learned how to weave; and they threw the books around the learning station. They practiced karate moves on the new carpets. Some of them learned how to read, but none of them as quickly as my white students. I was doing the same thing for all my kids—what was the problem?"**

Not until Delpit changed her classroom into a more "traditional," teacher-directed learning environment did her African American students begin to improve, although they still lagged behind. Delpit felt like a failure; she was teaching Black children, but she was not teaching them well.

Insights about how to best teach students in her own society who were living outside the mainstream culture came from Delpit's experiences living as an outsider in other cultures. During her graduate work, Delpit lived for extended periods in Papua New Guinea, and in Alaska, working with Native villagers. She observed that members of any culture transmit information implicitly to other members. Because Delpit did not grow up in these milieus, she found her work much easier and more effective when someone directly explained to her about how to dress appropriately, how to speak and listen to others in that community, and how to avoid taboo words or behaviors that might offend locals.

Delpit came to realize that children who do not receive the mainstream society's cultural learning at home—as middle-class children implicitly do—should explicitly be taught the content, perspectives, and tools, including critical thinking about what they are learning and the world at large, that they need to know at school. Only in this way would they be able to make sense and meaning of the core curriculum. She also advocates that teachers clearly teach underrepresented students the codes and rules needed to fully participate in mainstream American life, including how to speak standard English; how to present oneself; and how to write, dress, and interact in a mainstream-approved manner. These skills grant students access to other educational and career opportunities.

Delpit believes that effectively teaching low-income and underrepresented children requires teachers to establish relationships between themselves and their students, accept their students' culture and language, and help them to build on these. This requires teachers to have the humility to listen and learn from the students and their parents the issues that affect their lives.

In Delpit's view, the strongest relationship in the classroom is between student and teacher. Curricular content is only one aspect of their relationship. This model generates very different interactions than the academic, middle-class culture, which sees the relationship between speaker and listener as *less* important than that between speaker and content.

Research and instructional practice support Delpit's model. How much children of color like their teacher determines the amount of effort and time they will invest in classroom tasks. Effective teaching requires both aspects: strong rapport with students and deep knowledge of their curriculum content.

Next, Delpit advocates that teachers directly connect students to the curriculum by using "real-life" contexts and building on students' prior experiences. Delpit highlights a mathematics teacher who brought part of a bicycle wheel to her geometry class, saying that it came from her grandson's broken toy. Could they figure out how to fix it? After the students tried to solve the problem and reconstruct the wheel from its tiniest part, the teacher introduced a theorem related to constructing a circle given at any two points on an arc, and the students quickly learned the geometry content. Additionally, giving students access to the prescribed curriculum through relationships, relevance, and personal meaning is more likely to produce young people able to think critically and creatively in real problem-solving situations than by completing decontextualized problems.

Delpit stresses, "When teachers do not understand the potential of the students they teach, they will underteach them no matter what the methodology."***

**Delpit, L. (2006, May/June). Lessons from teachers. Journal of Teacher Education, 57(3), 221–231 (p. 221).*

***Delpit, L. D. (1986). Skills and other dilemmas of a progressive black educator. Harvard Educational Review, 56(4), 379–386 (p. 381).*

****Delpit, L. D. (1995). Other people's children. Cultural conflict in the classroom. W. W. Norton, p. 175.*

Sources: Delpit, 2006; Delpit, 1995; Delpit, 1986; Delpit, L. D. (1988). The silenced dialogue: Power and pedagogy. *Harvard Educational Review, 58*(1), 280–298; Delpit, L. D. (1988). The silenced dialogue: Power and pedagogy in education other people's children. *Harvard Educational Review, 58*(3), 280–298; Schwartz, S. (2019, September 18). Talking politics in school "when the world is on fire." Conversation with Lisa Delpit. *Education Week, 39*(5), 6.

12.3 EDUCATING THE WHOLE CHILD

Schools are "cultures for growing minds," and the opportunities that schools provide influence the direction this growth takes.[22] Educators' decisions about the amount of time allotted to a field of study influences the kinds of knowledge and mental skills children will have the chance to develop. As we have seen, the history of curriculum in the United States can be seen as a debate over which of three competing factors is most important—the individual child, the society, or the subject matter. The need to find the appropriate balance among these three essentials creates ongoing curriculum challenges.[23]

A disciplinary orientation to curriculum—the way most public schools are organized—is especially attractive to professors and researchers who work within separate subjects' structure. However, it may not reflect reality or provide excitement or connect to students' own experiences or provide personal meaning and relevance that would motivate and sustain learning.

Educators must teach students contemporary civilization's survival skills and balance the theoretical with the practical. Education needs to acknowledge the world's complexity, contradictions, and diversity. No subject stands alone in the real world—so why should it stand alone in the curriculum?

12.3a The Search for Curricular Balance

Every culture debates its education's aims. None, however, can produce final once-and-forever answers because education's intentions are inevitably tied to a particular society's goals and ideals at a particular time. In our pursuit of efficiency, some believe, we have remade ourselves into a collection of separate needs and attributes.[24] The same is true for our schools. Surely, we should educate our students for more than reading and math proficiency.

As discussed in Chapter 6, Richard Rothstein and Rebecca Jacobsen synthesized nearly 300 years of American education policy making into eight broad categories.[25] The eight categories include these:

- *Basic academic skills*—reading, writing, math, science, history, civics, geography, and foreign language
- *Critical thinking and problem-solving*—analyzing information, applying ideas to new situations, and developing knowledge using computers
- *Social skills and work ethic*—communication skills, personal responsibility, and getting along with others from varied backgrounds
- *Citizenship*—public ethics, knowing how government works, and participating by voting, volunteering, and becoming active in community life
- *Physical health*—good habits of exercise and nutrition
- *Emotional health*—self-confidence, respect for others, and the ability to resist peer pressure to engage in irresponsible personal behavior
- *The arts and literature*—participation in and appreciation of musical, visual, and performing arts, as well as a love of literature
- *Preparation for skilled employment*—qualification for skilled employment for students not pursuing a college education

If these goals reflect what yesterday's and today's civic and legislative leaders consider worth learning in school, our present school curricula are not faithful to American education's goals. In our "test mania," we now tend to focus almost exclusively on basic academic skills (reading, math) and critical thinking. If we were faithful to what our communities say they want, we would be addressing the other six categories as well.

Contemporary research results support the view that educating the whole child requires teaching a well-rounded curriculum. This includes more than those subjects tested for school accountability.

A well-rounded curriculum might also include, for example, civics, physical education, the arts, and social–emotional learning. Let's see why.

Civics

At a time when our nation is facing difficult choices, the lack of a high-quality civic education in American schools leaves millions of citizens without the facts and perspectives to make sense of—and trust in—our system of government or know their rights and responsibilities in it. Research indicates that students who receive high-quality civic learning are more likely than their peers to understand public issues, view political engagement as a way to meet common challenges, participate in civic activities, and practice civic equality.[26] Yet in 2018, it is estimated that only one in three Americans would pass the U.S. citizenship test.[27] Only half of eligible adults between the ages of 18 and 29 voted in the 2016 presidential election; just 20% of this group voted in the 2014 midterms, the lowest ever recorded.[28] Twenty-four states do not even require a semester of civics in high school.[29] Only a few states have civics requirements for middle schoolers.[30]

In an attempt to remedy this situation, a 2018 federal lawsuit argues that the failure of public schools to prioritize civics is depriving students of the knowledge they need to responsibly and effectively employ essential rights, such as voting, exercising free speech, peacefully petitioning the government, and actively participating in civic life.[31] In a democratic republic where the final authority rests with the people, "ultimately, schools are the guardians of democracy."[32]

Physical Education, the Arts, and Social–Emotional Learning

Other disciplines also bring educational benefits to the whole child. Studies find that exercise in physical education classes boosts brain function and academic achievement in children and adolescents.[33] Exercise puts students' brains in an optimal position to learn by increasing the amount of oxygen it receives, increasing their ability to focus and concentrate, and boosting their energy levels.[34] Likewise, studies in the arts (i.e., visual arts, music, drama, and dance)—disciplines that teach the value of learning through our senses, our intellects, and qualitative reasoning—find positive impacts on student learning and achievement as well as increasing students' capacities as whole persons.[35]

Research on social–emotional learning (SEL) programs in schools[36] finds developing children's social–emotional skills has multiple positive outcomes, both short and long term, for participating students, including enhanced positive social behavior, improved academic performance,[37] and significantly lower levels of conduct problems and emotional distress than nonparticipating students.[38] SEL has been found to be critical to their long-term success in and out of school[39] and can improve outcomes in adulthood.[40]

Engaging in SEL activities also has positive outcomes for teacher preparatory students: Taking time to teach future teachers to manage their emotions and to practice empathy, caring, and cooperation not only increased these behaviors but also increased students' academic achievement, as compared with a comparison group of students who were not exposed to these social–emotional programs.[41] Since studies find that teacher factors can affect the SEL program implementation in ways that may impact the program's quality and success,[42] some argue that this should be an area of increasing attention for teacher preparation programs.[43]

12.3b Rethinking Curriculum

Children respond to educational situations in intellectual, emotional, and social ways. To neglect their social and emotional development in the exclusive pursuit of measured academic performance is to ignore these young people's need to live satisfying lives. Ironically, it also limits their capacity to learn the prescribed content. If we fail to generate a relevant affective link—personal meaning—for the information, students will soon forget it.

Schools need to approach curriculum in a way that is sensitive to each learner's unique needs and developmental life stage. Curriculum needs to reach beyond literacy, math, and science to include civics, the arts, physical education, social–emotional skills building, and imaginative and ethical development. Future educators who fully understand the concept of curriculum and the need to educate the whole child can learn ways to meet local, state, national, and international standards and to teach their subject in ways that students find worth learning.

Additionally, in the human organism, all parts are interconnected. We need to recognize these connections when we teach. "Attention to such complex matters will not simplify our tasks as teachers but it will bring education closer to the heart of what really matter,"[44] insists Elliott Eisner, the late Stanford Graduate School of Education professor of art and education. Likewise, *curriculum* is no longer about running a racetrack. As Jacqueline Grennon Brooks of Hofstra University so eloquently observes, "Learning is not a race from point to point. It is a journey that changes pace, changes course, and, ultimately, changes us."[45]

To delve more deeply into your views about the importance of the individual child, the society, and the subject matter in selecting curriculum, complete the activity in the **Reflect & Engage** box, Educating the Whole Child.

REFLECT & ENGAGE: EDUCATING THE WHOLE CHILD

If the history of curriculum can be seen as a debate over which of three competing factors is most important—the individual child, the society, or the subject matter—how would you prioritize them?

A. Reassemble the class into groups of four.

B. In small groups, take 10 minutes to discuss the following questions and provide examples to explain your views:

- Considering Rothstein and Jacobsen's list, which five curriculum categories best describe your own K–12 education? Which curriculum categories would you have wished were included (but were not) in your K–12 education?
- Create 3 mind maps: one for your K–12 education, one for your college experiences, and one for this course. Prioritizes your group's rank order of the three main influencers of curriculum: the individual child, the society, or the subject matter. Make your top priority the largest theme. Add the "associated" courses—curricular and cocurricular courses and experiences that relate to these.

C. Reassemble as a class and discuss with examples at each education level how your own education experiences did (or did not) address the three main curriculum influencers (the society, the subject, or the child). To what extent did your education aim at educating the whole child? How might this awareness influence you as a teacher?

12.4 HOW PEOPLE LEARN

We have all had classes in which the teacher knew the subject very well but lacked the instructional skills to help you learn it. The relationship between curriculum (the content of education) and pedagogy (the process of teaching) is interdependent. Each factor is necessary but, by itself, is not enough to make an effective teacher. Each teacher's comprehension of how learning occurs influences how he or she ultimately understands and enacts teaching practices.

In a broad sense, **learning** happens when experience produces a stable change in someone's knowledge or behavior. It is a complex cognitive and affective process. We now know that learning is not merely a linear collection of memories, knowledge, and skills built up incrementally and stored in the brain like so many antiques in a cluttered attic. Rather, learning involves multiple processes that interact over time to influence the way people make sense of the world and their place in it. Moreover, learning is active; it is something people do, not something that is done to them. By engaging with the world, people have social, emotional, cognitive, and physical experiences. And they adapt as these experiences and environments affect their brain in ways that shape their knowledge, abilities, and desires to move ahead, as well as influence and organize a person's thoughts and actions into the future.

Effective teachers make learning happen through their choices about their curriculum, their knowledge of their students, and their selection of appropriate instructional strategies to connect students to curriculum. Doing this requires teachers to have a full and accurate understanding of the learning process and how to engage themselves and their students within it.

12.4a Instruction Makes Learning Happen

Although many excellent teachers have unique and vivid personalities, effective teaching also requires effective pedagogy and the decision-making that informs teaching as a profession.

Pedagogy is the art, science, or profession of teaching. Effective pedagogy involves three related areas: the teacher's instructional strategies, management techniques, and curriculum.[46] These are the tools to facilitate learning. **Instruction** is the means by which teachers bring curriculum to life in the classroom. Whatever the school district's curriculum, the teacher has tremendous influence over how to present it.

"The 'art' of teaching is rapidly becoming the 'science' of teaching."[47] Until recently, teaching had not been systematically studied in a methodical manner. Before then, a widespread belief held that school really made little difference in students' achievement. In the 1970s, however, researchers began to look at the effects of instruction on student learning.

Since then, research has shown that an individual teacher can have a powerful effect on his or her students *even if the school does not.* After reviewing hundreds of studies conducted in the 1970s, researchers Jere Brophy and Thomas Good confidently claimed, "The myth that teachers do not make a difference in student learning has been refuted."[48]

Groundbreaking advances from varied disciplines, including cognitive science and neuroscience, learning theory, educational psychology, developmental psychology, workforce development, social psychology, anthropology, and education offer insights about how people actually learn that teachers, parents, and policy makers can find relevant.[49] Appreciating these findings about how the context and culture influence learning, the learning process, knowledge and reasoning, motivation to learn, and the implications for teaching can help teachers make their instruction more effective. Briefly, learning occurs through the following contexts and processes.

12.4b Context and Culture Influence Learning

Learners do not learn in a vacuum. Learning is a social process, transferring culturally infused knowledge, attitudes, and practices across generations, shaping how individuals within that society mature and participate. In its broadest sense, *culture* is the learned behavior of a group of people that generally reflects their traditions, assigns group membership, and conveys a way of living in a particular community. Likewise, cultural values, historical perspectives, means of communication, and the importance attached to different kinds of knowledge and skills also impact *what* information and abilities are useful, *how* they learn them, and how to *use* them.

Of course, much diversity exists within each cultural community as people take on various roles, use different tools, and enact an array of practices.

While humans share basic brain structures, processes, and experiences such as relationships with families, learning does not happen the same way for everyone because cultural influences impact us from our life's start. As a result, each learner develops a unique set of knowledge and cognitive resources during his or her life, fashioned by the interplay of the learner's cultural, social, cognitive, and biological environments. Learning and brain development interact reciprocally. Brain development influences behavior and learning, and learning influences brain development and brain health; and all are affected by the learner's context and culture. And even as the individual constantly integrates many types of learning, both consciously and unconsciously, in response to the situation, the learner's social and physical environment also affect the present and future learning.

Culture also influences children's cognitive development, the rate at which they reach developmental milestones on problem-solving tasks, and the highest level of cognitive maturity attained. Routine cultural practices construct and mold how children think, remember, solve problems, and approach learning.[50] For example, our own advanced cultural tools such as computers and the internet have changed expectations about what and how people learn just as the absence of the printing press and low-cost reading materials amid pervasive poverty restricted widespread learning until the 15th century. In fact, researchers have identified cultural differences in what were once considered "basic" universal cognitive processes.[51]

Likewise, culture influences how children process emotional and social stimuli and experiences, affecting the development of brain networks. Emotions play a role in developing the neutral pathways for learning by helping people attend to, assess, and react to stimuli and situations in their immediate environment. Research affirms that the brain networks supporting emotion, learning, and memory are complexly and deeply intertwined,[52] with emotions as essential underpinning of cognition, steering behavior, thought, and learning.[53]—what grabs your emotions, gets your attention. Similarly, physical influences—such as nutrition, sleep, exercise, and exposure to environmental toxins—that impact learning can vary substantially across contexts and can be shaped by cultural practices.

Since race and ethnicity are social constructions (without scientifically meaningful genetic differences) that reflect complex, culture, history, socioeconomics, political status, and links to ancestors' geographic origins that vary over time,[54] a person's race or ethnicity tends to reflect these specific cultural features of their families, groups, or societies that influence learning and behavior. Students' cultural features, not their racial or ethnic ones, impact their learning.

Schools, too, are fashioned by their culture, imbued with the larger society's goals and values. They provide the knowledge and experiences young people need to adapt to their society's intellectual, economic, political, and social demands. Since a child's culture helps set the expectations for schooling and provides the content and context of what one learns in the school setting, the match between family expectations and practices and the schools' expectations and practices may help or hamper learning. For instance, given the child's culture and family influences, does the child learn best by observing or by teacher-directed verbal instruction? Should instructional practices be more individual or collaborative? And what knowledge and skills does a child need to demonstrate to be considered "intelligent"? Recognizing these cultural differences is central to teachers' understanding of how children learn and can make the difference between a child's successful and unsuccessful academic and social progress.

12.4c The Learning Process

Learning continues from before birth and throughout life as learners adapt to their experiences and environments, biologically and socially. As the brain matures, it becomes able to integrate a large assortment of complex cognitive functions. Research finds that infants are born ready and able to learn. Early childhood experiences and relationships are vital to development, and individual biology and social experiences are equally important in determining developmental outcomes—for good or ill.[55] A child growing up in a loving, safe, and stimulating environment will likely have different cognitive and social development and school outcomes that another child growing up in an environment marked by disorder, high stress, and adversity.

Memory, an essential foundation for most learning, plays a key role in how learners begin to integrate new information as knowledge. Memory is not a single construct that occurs in a certain part of the brain. Rather, it is made of up several distinct types of complex and interactive processes associated with different memory functions and learning processes. Learning involves building cognitive and affective skills for reconstructing memories based on past experiences and present environmental cues. Even short tasks, such has remembering five items on a grocery list, must be reconstructed through memory processes.

Sometimes, this cognitive reconstruction is so implicit and automatic that it feels effortless rather than mentally rebuilt. For instance, a person practicing the piano will see black ink symbols on a music sheet, feel the sensory-motor activity of their fingers on the keys, and hear the auditory sounds as they produce meaningful notes, understanding them as part of a musical pattern. Inputs from these different sense modalities register in different areas of the brain and come together in association areas, contributing to the coherent experience of "playing music." At the same time, the brain connects the current music making to prior experiences of music making and related occurrences and expectations, enriching the event.

Each person processes memories subjectively by what it means to that individual as colored by that person's prior knowledge, experiences, perceptual capacities, and brain processes. As a result, one's own

In the learning process, learners respond to triggering cues in their environment through which they reconstruct prior experiences and forge new connections to store in long-term memory.

iStock/FatCamera

memories and those of another may differ regarding the same information or event. That is why one person may see a glass of water as half empty while another sees it as half full, or why someone sees a lemon whereas another sees future lemonade!

In the learning process, learners respond to triggering cues in their environment through which they reconstruct prior experiences and forge new connections for them. Learning may come gradually with repetitions that become conditioned habits or may come through observing and modeling others' behaviors, attitudes, or emotional expressions. For example, learning not to litter relies on children observing the behaviors of their ecofriendly (or not) parents and neighbors. Infants learn their parents' language by noticing regular patterns in a particular environment over an extended time. Perceptual and motor learning enable individuals to learn primarily through sensory experiences. These support the development of seeing differences between colors, learning to ride a bike or drive a car, and gaining academic knowledge by seeing and discriminating letters for reading. Similarly, learning to differentiate the distinct features among different types and vintages of wine relies on increasingly sophisticated perceptual—sight, smell, taste, touch, and sound—learning.

Successful learning requires coordinating multiple cognitive processes that involve different networks in the brain. To coordinate these processes, an individual must be able to monitor and regulate his or her own learning, a capacity that matures and evolves throughout life and can be improved through appropriate interventions. Retrieving specific knowledge and skills varies with the cues that trigger the reconstruction and depend, in part, on the learner's emotional, social, and cognitive states at that moment. This is similar to hearing a song from years before that was playing during a very special event—the memory of that time and its emotions often come flooding back. A supportive learning environment can limit stress that hinders recall and reconstruction of prior knowledge and give appropriate cues to help a learner connect new instruction to what they already know.

Fact learning is another learning dimension. Research on memory concurs that repeated occasions to retrieve facts strengthens memory, especially if the occasions are spread over time, location, and learning contexts.[56] Moreover, facts placed into a structure that is meaningful to the learner makes them easier to remember. For example, it is easier to remember the color teal when already familiar with blue and green and to recall the colors of the rainbow with the acronym ROY G. BIV (red, orange, yellow, green, blue, indigo, and violet).

Research indicates that relevant learning means effective learning: Meaningful activities that both engage students emotionally and connect with what they already know cognitively help build neural connections and storage in long-term memory. If they are to remember—*learn*—it, students need a personal connection to any new knowledge. Since the brain stores information in the form of neural pathways, or networks, the student must be able to relate new information to something already in his or her brain if the new information is to "stick" to a neural network. Without the link, the new information goes, literally, "in one ear and out the other" because it has no mental scaffolding to hold it.[57]

Again, the relationship between brain development and learning is reciprocal. It involves the continuous shaping and reshaping of neural connections in response to stimuli and demands. As a result, the learner continually integrates many types of learning, some happening deliberately while some occurs unconsciously in response to environmental events and situations.

12.4d Knowledge and Reasoning

A person's **cognitive capacity**—the ability to identify and create relationships among pieces of information and develop increasingly complex structures for categorizing and using what they have learned—is an essential foundation for building knowledge and developing reasoning ability. Knowledge is a natural outcome of forming and consolidating episodic memories as learners associate representations of their experiences (sights, sounds, sensations, and ideas) with older memories and integrate them into new, more complex memories. For instance, a toddler's accumulation of sensory experiences with his or her grandparents—what they look like, how they sound, and what they do together, plus the emotions engendered by these interactions—creates a gradually enlarging and multifaceted memory of "grandparents." Individuals construct and mature their cognitive assets throughout their lives.

Expertise, possessing a high level of knowledge or skill in an area, comes with repeated involvement with a particular content or situation. Over time, learners construct mental representations that connect seemingly dissimilar facts and actions into more effective mental structures to use as a template for acting on the world. When college freshmen first arrive on campus, they may learn specific routes for walking to class, another way to reach the dining hall, and a different path to the library. Over time, they naturally develop a mental map of the campus that connects these separate routes together, and they can figure out the most effective way to travel between their dining hall and the library, even if they have never walked that way.

Experts have developed mental frameworks of information and understanding through their lengthy experiences in a certain domain. Acquiring knowledge and its increasingly differentiated mental representations that individuals can manipulate virtually has many well-documented benefits. These include the increased speed and accuracy of completing recurring tasks, the ability to solve increasingly complex problems, an increased capacity to identify relevant information (and ignore irrelevant information) in the environment, the enhanced ability to use the environment as a resource (knowing where to look for information), and making it easier to learn new and related information. Research literature supports the idea that what students already know about the content is one of the strongest indicators of how well they will learn the new information.[58] Prior or background knowledge can facilitate learning by reducing the demands on attention that introduction to new material requires and enabling students to see links between what they already know and what the teacher is presenting.

Certain prior experience can lead to adaptive behavior and save lives. Smelling gas odor from an unlit fireplace unit can alert the person to an unwanted gas flow and shut off the gas valve. On the other hand, prior knowledge also has disadvantages, including biases that may hinder learning. Despite the near universal agreement that global climate change is occurring and that human behavior strongly contributes to it, many adults do not accept these interpretations of the evidence. Rather, they look for information to reinforce their earlier beliefs.

In addition to acquiring, tagging, and integrating information, learners must also develop reasoning skills if they are to deepen and extend their knowledge. They need to make logical connections between bits of information. This enables them to organize knowledge for understanding and draw conclusions through the rational thought needed to generalize, categorize, and comprehend. Effective problem-solving usually requires the learner to adapt and transform retrieved knowledge in flexible ways to fit new situations.

Developing reasoning skills requires the brain's physical maturation along with opportunities to learn new approaches to gain, retrieve, and use prior knowledge in ways relevant to the circumstances. Over the lifespan, knowledge learners accumulate new information from direct (cognitive and/or sensory) experience and generate new information based on reasoning and imagining.[59] Reasoning ability is a major determinant of lifelong learning, allowing people to pursue their interest and continue gaining knowledge and forming perspective on what it means.[60] Much individual variability exists in persons' ability to reason with increased age, however, reflecting individual health, education, experiences, and social engagement.

12.4e Motivation to Learn

Clearly, learning depends on making conscious, sustained effort. People must want to learn and see the worth of what they are being asked to learn. **Motivation**—the condition that activates and sustains behavior toward a goal—develops and changes over time with adjustments in the individual's interests and goals, developmental skills, environment, and sociocultural influences. Motivation can be **intrinsic** (the experience of wanting to engage in an activity because it is interesting, enjoyable, or helps achieve one's chosen goals) or extrinsic (behavior prompted by rewards arising outside the person, such as grades, praise, or money).

Contemporary research on motivation finds that learners are active participants in their learning. Learners tend to persist in learning when they face manageable challenge (neither too easy nor too frustrating) and when they see the value and usefulness of what they are learning.[61] Likewise, learners who focus on learning rather than on performance (i.e., earning a high grade) or who have intrinsic motivation to learn tend to set themselves goals and value increasing their competence as an end.[62] A teacher who uses incentives to gain attention and stimulate interest in a topic (rather than force compliance), who encourages (rather than scolds) the student, or whom the student perceives as guiding (rather than monitoring) their progress can nurture the students' feelings of autonomy, competence, and academic achievement.[63] Praising students for their continued effort rather than for their ability is more likely to facilitate more learning.[64]

Mindset—the set of assumptions, values, and beliefs about one's self and one's world—includes how a person perceives, interprets, and acts upon his or her environment. Mindsets, developed over time as a function of learning experiences and cultural influences, play a critical role in motivation. For instance, if a student thinks intelligence is fixed (one is born with a certain amount of intelligence that doesn't change), he or she is less likely to put time and effort into learning. By contrast, a student who believes that intelligence is malleable and incremental (intelligence can be gained through experience and hard work) is more likely to invest personal attention, time, and effort into learning.[65]

Likewise, learners' expectations about their ability to accomplish a task—**self-efficacy**—and their values about the task greatly influence their willingness to persist in learning long enough to reach their goals. Students with a self-efficacy mindset work hard to learn and master new material or skills, rise to challenges, have higher levels of performance, put in more effort in response to failure, and pursue new opportunities to learn more. Research with varied-aged learners supports this idea; as learners experience success at a task or in a learning area (such as reading or math), their value for that activity can increase over time.[66] Some evidence suggests that it is possible to change students' mindsets in ways that improve their academic performance.[67]

Students' interests and social and cultural factors also influence students' motivation to learn. Students' interest in learning can be *personal*, a stable attribute that the person holds over time, or *situational*, a psychological state that arises spontaneously in response to specific features of the task or learning environment. Since situational interest is malleable, teachers can use practices that engage students and thus influence their attitudes, possibly increasing their personal interest and intrinsic motivation for learning over time.[68]

12.4f Lifelong Learning

Beyond formal education, people keep growing and learning throughout their lives. What and how much they learn and can transfer to new situations depend largely on their own choices and opportunities, as well as their capacities (cognitive and affective), interests, and resources.

Nonetheless, individuals' abilities to quickly generate, transform, and manipulate factual information starts declining in early adulthood even as their knowledge levels stay the same or increase. Yet as one's brain adapts throughout life, it gathers and organizes resources to make up for declines and adapt to circumstances. Good lifestyle—including involvement with meaningful work (especially complex work that involves both intellectual and social demands), social interaction, physical exercise, and sufficient sleep—are all associated with lifelong learning and healthy aging.

12.4g What This Means for Teaching

Teaching well is a complex task. Effective instruction depends on the complex interplay among the teachers, the curriculum, the students, and the learning environment. This includes the learners' cultural and social influences, prior knowledge, experiences, motivations, interests, language, and cognitive skills. It also includes the educators' own experiences and cultural influences.

Recent research on learning suggests that teachers' effective instruction include the following:

- **Know your students**. Learn each student's interests, cultural background, and family assets. Use your interactions with students to build mutual respect, trust, and understanding and use the information you gain of their prior knowledge to help motivate their interest and facilitate their learning.

Teachers' interactions with students to build mutual respect, trust, and understanding can be used to motivate their interest and facilitate their learning.

iStock/SDI Productions

- **Race and ethnicity are social (not biological) constructions**. Mankind invented the concept of race to fit particular societal needs. Students' race or ethnicity reflects complex culture, historic, socioeconomic, and political status, as well as ancestors' geographic origins. These cultural factors, not the race or ethnicity in itself, affect student learning.
- **Schools are cultural institutions.** A society's goals and values shape its schools and its curricula. Accordingly, the "goodness of fit" between schools' expectations and practices and family expectations and practices may help or hinder student learning. As teachers get to know

their students' family and cultural expectations for what and how children learn, the more teachers can adapt instruction in ways that facilitate children's education.

- **Learning is cognitive and affective.** People learn more when the new information is presented with meaningful (to them) cognitive and affective components. In turn, retrieving specific knowledge and skills depends, in part, on the learner's emotional, social, and cognitive state at that moment. Effective teachers create and maintain a positive classroom climate—calm, trusting, interesting, emotionally and physically safe—if children are to learn. Likewise, teachers are sensitive to students having a "bad day" or being "off," knowing that unhappy, frightened, hungry, or worried children will have a difficult time learning.
- **Make learning relevant and meaningful *to the student*.** Teachers who place facts into a structure that makes cognitive sense and has affective meaning for the learner and link it to what the learner already knows make facts easier to remember. Teachers who know students' backgrounds and prior knowledge can actively structure their learning and provide missing gaps in background knowledge until the students attain the skills and information to increasingly do more themselves.
- **Memory is made of several complex interactive processes.** Different learning processes develop and store different aspects of memory in different parts of the brain. Teachers who use a variety of learning activities—such as involving relevance to the learner and varied sense modalities (listening, writing, drawing, moving, and speaking)—will help students better remember and be able to reconstruct what they learn to use in familiar and new ways. Table 12.1 highlights the relative effectiveness of the instructional methods teachers use to promote student learning and retention.

TABLE 12.1 ■ Instructional Methods Impact Student Learning

Instructional Method	Students' Retention of Knowledge (%)
Lecture	5
Reading along with lecture	10
Audiovisual presentations	30
Discussion groups	50
Learning by doing	75
Learning by teaching others	90

Source: Adapted from NTL Institute for Applied Learning. Cited in Danielson, C. (2002). *Enhancing student achievement: A framework for school improvement.* Association for Supervision and Curriculum Development, p. 24.

- **Opportunities to learn make a difference.** If a student does not know what the teacher expects him or her to know, he or she might not have had the opportunity to learn it yet. The effective teacher can provide the opportunities for students to build the needed background knowledge to support their classroom learning.
- **Teachers can motivate student learning.** Teachers can motivate learning by making the lesson interesting (relevant and personally meaningful *to students*) and manageable; helping students set appropriately challenging learning and performance goals; attending to their engagement, persistence, and demonstrations of what they know and can do with the new information; using age-appropriate incentives (such as a degree of autonomy, and choice of teacher-designated alternate learning activities); encouraging their capacity to successfully handle the challenge or task and earn respect at achieving the desired outcome; praising their

effort (rather than their ability); and creating an emotionally supportive and nonthreatening learning environment.

- **Intelligence is malleable.** Help students accept that their intelligence is not fixed. Rather, it grows through experience, persistence, hard work, and thought. School is a place where one can become smart.

  - **Teachers' own backgrounds matter.** Teachers' own prior experiences and cultural influences affect their beliefs about their students, their instructional practices, and the classroom's learning environment. Effective teachers continually monitor (and sometimes challenge) their beliefs, assumptions, and practices to ensure that no personal bias or misinformation interferes with their professional roles.

Today, we know that effective instruction depends on understanding the complex interactions among learners' prior knowledge, experiences, motivations, interests, and language and cognitive skills; the educators' own experiences and cultural influences; and the classroom environment's cultural, social, cognitive, and affective qualities. Students' deep understanding occurs when fresh information prompts them to develop or refine the cognitive structures that enable them to rethink and expand their prior ideas. Effective instruction does not look for what students can unthinkingly repeat, but rather for what students comprehend and can do with the information to demonstrate their understanding. Research affirms that these instructional strategies can lead to strong academic achievement.[69]

Traditionally, American schools viewed learning as the process of students receiving and repeating (aloud or on written tests) newly presented information as evidence of learning. Today, we know more about how students actually learn, and this knowledge has instructional implications. Nonetheless, some traditional methods still belong in a teacher's instructional repertoire. Direct instruction and lecture are legitimate teaching methodologies. They can be stimulating and highly effective techniques, depending on the teacher's goals, the curriculum to be learned, the teacher's particular talents, and the students' characteristics.[70] Similarly, rote learning is not always bad. It has the advantage of automatizing aspects of problem-solving, thereby freeing the mind for more abstract thought. A student who has memorized the meaning of certain vocabulary words can more competently read and understand an essay that uses those words than a student who must constantly stop and look through a dictionary. Then, too, student interest and classroom involvement are necessary—rather than sufficient—conditions for worthwhile learning. Students' mastery of the content and ability to use it effectively in a variety of contexts is the ultimate goal, and the official curriculum remains the driver.

Urban teachers may incorrectly assume that because many of their students are so lacking in basic skills, they should be teaching for memorization and transmission of basic facts and abilities rather than teaching for personal meaning, concepts, generalizations, connections, and deep understanding—all of which will actually motivate student learning and skill development. Seeking equity and maintaining high expectations for every student's learning requires teachers to use meaning-making instructional approaches with *all* students.

One instructional approach does not fit all content with all students in all situations. Teachers become effective when they can develop a repertoire of instructional approaches, consider a wide array of impinging factors, and learn when and how best to use them to maximize each student's learning. Becoming a highly effective teacher takes time, varied experiences, timely and high-quality feedback, and lots of effort and reflection. And the results in student learning are the payoff.

12.5 TEACHING EFFECTIVENESS AND STUDENT ACHIEVEMENT

Conventional wisdom has long held that family backgrounds and economic status were the primary determiners of students' learning and school success. But in the last decade of the 20th century, researchers found that, aside from a well-articulated curriculum and a safe and orderly environment, the individual teacher is the most influential school-related factor in determining which students learn and how well they learn.[71]

The evidence linking teaching effectiveness with student learning and achievement is well established.[72] Linda Darling-Hammond, professor emeritus of education at Stanford University, asserts that only when these three dimensions—the *learner* (i.e., interests, prior knowledge, learning goals), the *subject* (i.e., the content), and the *pedagogy* (i.e., the effective instructional practices that motivate and engage the student with the new knowledge)—overlap and interact in professional practice can effective teaching and learning occur.[73] Chapter 2 discussed the research linking teacher and teaching quality, teacher preparation, and student achievement.

Research further indicates that qualitative variations among teachers can make large positive differences in their capacity to generate student learning year after year.[74] Studies confirm that consistently working with highly effective teachers can overcome the academic limitations placed on students by their family backgrounds.[75] Although teachers' content knowledge and verbal skills have been linked to higher student achievement,[76] teachers' subject knowledge may be a necessary but not a sufficient condition for high-quality teaching and learning.[77] Effective teachers also need competence in designing, enacting, and assessing instruction in both traditional and internet-based learning platforms. Continuing to develop pedagogical expertise is especially critical as technologies for teaching rapidly expand.

12.5a Rethinking Teaching With Technology

Milton Friedman, the Nobel Prize–winning economist, observed, "Only a crisis—actual or perceived—produces real change."[78] The COVID-19 pandemic that reached the United States in 2020 might "become the largest peacetime disruption to education in recent human history."[79]

From March through June 2020 and well into the next school year, over 50 million American public school students and 5.8 million private schools students found their school buildings closed.[80] Without warning or time to plan, they continued their classes from home. Despite educators' sometimes heroic efforts to keep students learning, a 2020 nationally representative survey of teachers found that many students' education suffered. Almost 80% of surveyed teachers reported that students' engagement with their schoolwork during the coronavirus school closures to be "much lower" or "somewhat lower" than their engagement levels before the closures. About 21% of students were essentially "truant" (i.e., not logging in or making contact with the teacher).[81] According to another survey, 45% of parents reported that their children were learning less than they normally would when attending school.[82] And by a two-to-one margin, the survey found that when students do return to the physical school classrooms, most parents do not want to go back to the status quo. They want schools to rethink how they educate students.[83]

Although experts have long predicted that technology would upend traditional education, until March 2020, most schools still taught in much the same way as their 19th century predecessors. Today's school calendar reflects a long-passed agrarian harvest season that needed children out of school for months of farm work during the summer. Some blame institutional inertia that resists change. Some blame this slow adoption of technology in teaching on equipment and software that simply weren't good enough. Clearly, the COVID-19 crisis disrupted K–16 education as we have known it, and it may never be the same.

Today, technology in the classroom is no longer simply a supplemental tool with which K–12 teachers can stream YouTube, SchoolTube, or Netflix videos to advance classroom learning,[84] personalize content for students wanting to extend and deepen their subject knowledge, or reinforce their lagging abilities in reading or math. Rather, in the COVID-19 era (with perhaps more pandemics to come), with most schools shuttered for in-person instruction, teaching with digital technology over the internet became the main event, an essential learning platform requiring a nonnegotiable skill set that teachers must have if they are to keep educating their students.

As a result, every teacher will have to become proficient in using instructional technology to deliver standards-based curricula remotely to students in instructionally effective ways. For many educators, teaching online is a new experience. It means rejiggering (or discarding) time-tested lectures and learning innovative ways suitable for a digital platform to organize and translate content into engaging lessons that facilitate student learning. Likewise, teachers and administrators will have to find ways to keep their learning expectations—and learning supports—high for each student so as not to stall their academic progress.

But moving to successful technology-infused instruction requires more than adjusted lesson plans. Lauren Scher, senior researcher at Mathematica, a nonpartisan research organization, asserts that effective digital learning requires resources and coordination.[85] A smooth transition to digital learning depends on meeting several conditions: all students have access to technology and the internet; teachers have the training, support, and expertise to use remote teaching to facilitate instruction aligned with their planned curriculum; and parents and caregivers are equipped to support and oversee students' involvement in digital learning activities. Hopefully, this guidance will inform state education budgets and educators' actions going forward.

But during spring 2020, these essential conditions were not in place for every teacher and student. School districts vary widely in their capacity to provide effective virtual learning to students and in teachers' comfort with instructional technology.[86] Although many teachers provided face-to-face synchronous class instruction through platforms such as Zoom and gave students self-paced digital learning activities, most schools conducted remote learning by distributing teacher-prepared paper "instructional learning packets."[87] Many teachers also held individual phone conferences with students and parents to aid families' at-home learning. Some provided asynchronous online learning tools (such as reading materials via Google classrooms and selected educational videos). Often, teachers became "case managers," tracking down students who did not log-on and asking how they could help. Many teachers joined online groups of teachers to share ideas about how to engage students and help them learn at their own pace. This large variance in teachers' digital competence and school districts' capacity to furnish digital learning present a serious learning and equity issue for students.

As schools move forward, remote learning likely will become a regular feature of K–12 education, either as a "hybrid" approach to teaching inside and outside the classroom or as full-time virtual teaching for weeks or months as circumstances require. For this to succeed, schools will need to collect information about families' technology needs. Teachers will need intensive and ongoing professional development and support to adapt their lessons aligned with the curriculum and state standards into cognitively engaging learning activities that can be delivered, monitored, and assessed effectively on a digital platform. Teachers must also learn how to operate the technology in ways that advance learning. And school leaders and teachers will need to understand how to integrate technology to support learning while ensuring student personal and data privacy. What had been an optional tool for academic enrichment or remediation has become an essential instructional medium integral to teaching and learning.

12.5b Equity and Internet-Based Learning

For all our societal advances in recent decades, the basics of connected life—web-enabled smartphones, reliable internet service—remain out of reach for many students and their families. Online conveniences have become daily necessities, especially in education. Yet a 2019 Microsoft study found that at least half of Americans did not have high-speed internet at home.[88] Another 2019 national study found approximately 12% of teachers, mostly from urban and rural Title I schools, reported that most of their students (61%–100%) did not have home access to the internet or a computer. Approximately one third of teachers (34%) said this lack of connectivity would limit their students' learning "a great deal" or "quite a bit" (as compared with teachers in schools with mixed-race students [26%] or mainly white students [27%]).[89] Similarly, some teachers (about 4%)[90] do not have reliable internet broadband at home, especially in rural areas where service is spotty, costly, or absent. To connect with their students during the pandemic, some teachers worked in school parking lots and empty buildings to use available Wi-Fi while following social distance protocols.[91] Part of digital equity means ensuring that students—and their teachers—can access devices or software that enable them to learn, communicate, and participate outside the traditional classroom.

Given this lack of digital access, low-income students, students with disabilities, and English learners are most in danger of losing ground academically. Many parents cannot afford to buy multiple smart devices for themselves and their children. It is also difficult to learn, especially remotely, if you lack adequate shelter, regular meals, parents with time to supervise learning, access to technology, and familiarity with the English language, as well as have concerns about family finances and health. These realities make it doubly difficult for these students to receive instruction or to successfully complete assignments that require internet access and digital devices, especially at higher grade levels.

For students with disabilities, online learning presents a special challenge. Schools are responsible for meeting their learning needs, even during times of disruption and school closures. But remote learning cannot usually provide these students with the full-time day programs, the part- or full-time aides, the specialists, or the assistive technology (AT) to help them perform certain important learning activities. Some of these services are not possible to implement effectively online; others (such as reading instruction or speech language therapy) are. Distance learning requires teachers to work with parents to make alternate arrangements for these services, to the extent possible, and restoring these services (with safety modifications) once schools reopen.

Many U.S. students—approximately 5 million children nationally[92]—are still learning to speak and read English. These English learners (ELs) have an especially challenging time learning virtually. In normal times, English learners participate in a structured curriculum with face-to-face interaction with teachers and peers. The classroom proximity enables EL students and their teachers to respond quickly to nonverbal cues, often subtle, that identify obstacles to learning. These cues may not be readily visible on a Zoom platform. Given the language difficulties of trying to learn in a virtual environment plus the lack of connectivity for many low-income English learners whose families cannot afford digital devices or internet access at home, the risk of their education stalling is high. The consequences of not mastering necessary knowledge and skills and of not graduating from high school or advancing to postsecondary education can jeopardize their chances for upward mobility and a secure lifestyle.[93]

The COVID-19 crisis forced states and school districts to recognize digital technology as a basic modality for educating students. Distance learning and related innovations are likely to become central, routine parts of their instructional programs. To do this, much planning and work lie ahead. Federal, state, local, and philanthropic resources must remedy the digital divide and improve the connectivity that make it possible for low-income and rural students to make academic progress. Current teachers need "upskilling" to expand and refine their capacities to prepare and deliver rigorous content via effective digital instruction. This includes becoming adept at actively engaging students in their learning and motivating them to "log on" and learn well in various delivery formats. Future teachers will want to develop many of these technology-related instructional skills preservice and continue to refine and expand them once in their own classrooms. And we can all rethink ways of achieving traditional and contemporary educational purposes with technology that serves every student.

Closing the "digital divide" is more than an educational or equity issue; it is also a funding issue. As the old saying goes, "Those who fail to plan, plan to fail."[94]

To more fully consider how what you are learning about learning will shape your own instructional practices as a teacher, complete the activity in the **Reflect & Engage** box, How What We Know About Learning Influences Instruction.

REFLECT & ENGAGE: HOW WHAT WE KNOW ABOUT LEARNING INFLUENCES INSTRUCTION

Effective instruction engages students emotionally and intellectually in learning. Research on how students learn can help teachers increase student achievement.

A. Working with a partner, identify the top-three instructional implications you and your partner most want to remember from this chapter and learn how to do well as a teacher—and why you believe these to be so important. Create a graphic illustration using a digital tool such as Piktochart to depict what you have learned.

B. In reviewing the implications for effective teaching, which strategies work best for you as a student? Which ones do your favorite or least favorite professors use? What differences—if any—do you see in the two lists? What might you do if you do notice important differences? Include these favorite teaching strategies as words on your graphic.

C. As a pair, present your graphic, observations, and conclusions about what we now know about student learning and their implications for effective teaching to the class. Discuss the commonalities and biggest surprises or "aha!-moments" you had reading this chapter.

KEY TAKE-AWAYS

Learning Objective 12.1 Describe the separate but interdependent relationships among curriculum, instruction, and society's goals for students.

- Curriculum (the learning program) and instruction (the method of enacting it) are separate, interdependent concepts purposefully designed to generate student learning of those things their society (national, state, and local) deems most important to live successfully in that culture.
- The relationship between curriculum (the content of education) and pedagogy (the process of teaching) is interdependent. Each factor is necessary but, by itself, is not enough to make an effective teacher.

Learning Objective 12.2 Defend the view that public school curricula respond to intellectual, societal, and political influences.

- Public school curriculum is not neutral. It is always part of a selective tradition that responds to intellectual, societal, and political influences. The debate over curriculum continues because *what* teachers teach—and *how* they teach it—may either affirm or challenge our deeply held beliefs and commitments about who we are and how we want to live.
- The U.S. curriculum reflects a dynamic tension between its focus on social control by transmitting our cultural history, traditions, and values and developing the individual. As a result, curriculum writers seek the appropriate balance among the society, the subject, and the child.
- Academic standards can be the center of intense controversy because they represent one group's strongly held beliefs and values about society and desired learning outcomes with which other groups strongly disagree.
- Educators can organize and present curriculum in varied ways, formally and informally, according to their community and school district's goals for learning, deep knowledge of child development, and needed resources.

Learning Objective 12.3 Assess how a school's curricular balance impacts children's personal, social, and intellectual growth and development.

- Contemporary research results support the view that educating the whole child requires teaching a well-rounded curriculum, including civics, physical education, the arts, and social–emotional learning. Each of these areas can have positive effects on student learning and achievement as well as their capacities as people.
- An appropriate curriculum includes more than those subjects tested for school accountability.
- The need to find the appropriate balance among the individual child, the society, and the subject matter creates ongoing curriculum challenges.

Learning Objective 12.4 Critique how conventional wisdom about the primary influencers of student learning expanded in the past few decades.

- Groundbreaking advances from varied disciplines, including cognitive science and neuroscience, learning theory, educational psychology, developmental psychology, workforce development, social psychology, anthropology, and education, offer insights about how people actually learn.

- **Learning** consists of multiple complex cognitive and affective processes that interact over time to influence the way people make sense of the world and their place in it.
- Learning happens when experience produces a stable change in someone's knowledge or behavior.
- While humans share basic brain structures, processes, and experiences such as relationships with families, learning does not happen the same way for everyone. Each learner develops a unique set of knowledge and cognitive resources during their lives, fashioned by the interplay of the learner's cultural, social, cognitive, and biological environments.
- Since learning involves both students' cognition and affect, teachers' instruction must be relevant, make sense, and have meaning *to students*, and their classroom learning environment must be physically and emotionally safe for everyone.
- *Schooling* is not the same as *educating*. *Educating* includes more than what the state says children should know, is relevant and meaningful to students, is largely self-generating, and occurs across the lifespan, even outside school.

Learning Objective 12.5 Support the view that educators must rethink effective teaching and learning technologies and consider both instructional and equity concerns.

- Before the 1970s, a widespread belief held that school really made little difference in students' achievement. Since then, research has shown that an individual teacher can have a powerful effect on his or her students *even if the school does not.*
- Teaching is both an art and a science.
- Today, technology in the classroom is no longer simply a supplemental tool. In the COVID-19 pandemic era, the internet has become an essential learning platform. As a result, every teacher will have to become proficient in using instructional technology to deliver standards-based curricula digitally to students in instructionally effective ways.
- As schools move forward, digital learning likely will become a regular feature of K–12 education, either as a "hybrid" approach to teaching inside and outside the classroom or as full-time virtual teaching for weeks or months as circumstances require.
- The COVID-19 pandemic brought new attention to digital inequities that hinder learning for low-income and rural students as well as students with disabilities and English learners.

TEACHER SCENARIO: IT'S YOUR TURN

Imagine this scenario: A 17th century American colonial schoolmaster appears in your college classroom. He wants to tell you about how he practices his profession. In turn, he wants you to explain 21st century teaching to him. In his day, he begins, he worked with two groups of students. One group consisted of township children whose parents had the financial resources to send them regularly, with the long-term goal of college preparation. The other group attended for a few years, appearing sporadically (depending on their work responsibilities at home) to learn enough reading, writing, and math to be able to read the Bible, obey the township's laws, and participate responsibly in civic activities. Instruction relied totally on memorization, practice, and rote recall of facts. Now it is your turn to describe 21st century teaching.

1. Describe the present-day curriculum, its influences and purposes, special considerations, and the major content areas (what is typically included and what should also be included).
2. Describe what we now know about student learning and how that influences instructional practices and the classroom's learning climate.
3. Describe the changes in the societal view of teachers' role in generating student learning.

NOTES

1. Westheimer, J. (2017, November). What kind of citizens do we need? *Educational Leadership, 75*(3), 15.
2. Marzano, R. J. (2003). *What works in schools: Translating research into action*. ASCD, p. 19.
3. Eisner, E. W. (1992, April). The misunderstood role of the arts in human development. *Phi Delta Kappan, 73*(8), 592.
4. Vasuthavan, E. S. (2017, November). *Problem centered curriculum (PCC) for a knowledge society.* Conference Paper. The 5th Malaysian International Conference on Academic Strategies in English Langue Teaching. https://www.researchgate.net/publication/322242964_PROBLEM_CENTERED_CURRICULUM_PCC_FOR_A_KNOWLEDGE_SOCIETY
5. Hiebert, J., Carpenter, T. P., Fennema, E., Fuson, K., Human, P., Murray, H., Olivier, A., & Wearne, D. (1996). Problem-solving as a basic for reform in curriculum and instruction: The case of mathematics. *Educational Researcher, 25*(May) 12–21.
6. Vasuthavan, 2017.
7. Duncheon, J. C. (2015). *The problem of college readiness.* State University of New York Press. https://www.sunypress.edu/pdf/63219.pdf
8. *Cocurricular* activities are extensions of the school's formal learning experiences, whereas *extracurricular* activities may be offered or coordinated by a school but may not be directly linked to academic learning. Sine the distinction is blurred in practice, the terms are often used interchangeably.
9. Darling, N., Caldwell, L. L., & Smith, R. 2005. Participation in school-based extracurricular activities and adolescent adjustment. *Journal of Leisure Research, 37*(1), 51–76.
10. For a more detailed discussion of student motivation, learning, and achievement, see: Linnenbrink, E. A., & Pintrich, P. R. (2002). Motivation as an enabler for academic success. *School Psychology Review, 31*(3), 313–327. http://citeseerx.ist.psu.edu/viewdoc/download?doi=10.1.1.520.1534&rep=rep1&type=pdf
11. Ferlazzo, L. (2019, February 6). Author interview: "All learning is social and emotional." Classroom Q & A Blog. *Education Week Teacher.* http://blogs.edweek.org/teachers/classroom_qa_with_larry_ferlazzo/2019/02/author_interview_all_learning_is_social_and_emotional.html
12. Anderson, L. W. (Ed.), Krathwohl, D. R. (Ed.), Airasian, P. W., Cruikshank, K. A., Mayer, R. E., Pintrich, P. R., Raths, J., & Wittrock, M. C. (2001). *A taxonomy for learning, teaching, and assessing: A revision of Bloom's Taxonomy of Educational Objectives.* Longman.
13. Siraj-Blatchford, I. (1999). Early childhood pedagogy: Practice, principles and research. In P. Mortimore (Ed.), *Understanding pedagogy and its impact on learning.* Paul.
14. Mahn, H., & John-Steiner, V. (2002). The gift of confidence: A Vygotskian view of emotions. In G. Wells & G. Claxton (Eds.), *Learning for life in the 21st century: Sociocultural perspectives on the future of education* (pp. 46–58).
15. For a more complete discussion of this topic, see: Shawer, S. F., Gilmore, D., & Banks-Joseph, S. (2008). Student cognitive and affective development in the context of classroom-level curriculum development. *Journal of the Scholarship of Teaching and Learning, 8*(1), 1–28. https://scholarworks.iu.edu/journals/index.php/josotl/article/download/1690/1688
16. Eisner, E. (1990). A development agenda: Creative curriculum development and practice. *Journal of Curriculum and Supervision, 6*(1) 62–73; King, M. B. (2002). Professional development to promote school-wide inquiry. *Teaching and Teacher Education, 18*(3), 243–257; Shawer, S. (2006). Communicative-based curriculum innovations between theory and practice: Implications for EFL curriculum development and student learning and motivation. *Faculty of Education Journal, 30*(4), 30–72.
17. Brady, M. (2000, May). The standards juggernaut. *Phi Delta Kappan, 81*(9), 649–651.
18. Brady, 2000, p. 650.
19. Sackstein, S. (2019, March 29). Content or skills? It's the chick or the egg conversation in education. *Education Week Teacher.* http://blogs.edweek.org/teachers/work_in_progress/2019/03/content_or_skills_its_the_chic.html
20. Apple, M. W. (1995). Facing reality. In J. A. Beane (Ed.), *Toward a coherent curriculum* (pp. 130–138). ASCD, p. 130.
21. For a fuller exploration of the differences and similarities between schooling and educating, see **FlipSides** in this chapter.

22. Eisner, E. W. (1992, April). The misunderstood role of the arts in human development. *Phi Delta Kappan, 73*(8), 591–595.

23. Schubert, W. H. (1995). Toward lives worth living and sharing: Historical perspectives on curriculum coherence. In J. A. Beane (Ed.), *Toward a coherent curriculum: The 1995 ASCD yearbook* (pp. 146–157). ASCD.

24. Noddings, N. (2005, September). What does it mean to educate the whole child? *Educational Leadership, 63*(1), 8–13.

25. Rothstein, R., & Jacobsen, R. (2006, December). The goals of education. *Phi Delta Kappan, 88*(4), 264–272. Table p. 271.

26. Campaign for the Civic Mission of Schools and the Lenore Annenberg Institute. (2011). *Guardian of democracy: The civic mission of schools*. University of Pennsylvania. https://cdn.annenbergpublicpolicyleft.org/wp-content/uploads/2011/09/GuardianofDemocracy_report_final-13.pdf

27. Riccards, P. (2018, October 3). *National survey finds just 1 in 3 Americans would pass citizenship test*. The Woodrow Wilson National Fellowship Foundation. https://woodrow.org/news/national-survey-finds-just-1-in-3-americans-would-pass-citizenship-test/

28. Wong, A. (2018, October 5). Civics education helps create young voters and activists. *The Atlantic*. https://www.theatlantic.com/education/archive/2018/10/civics-education-helps-form-young-voters-and-activists/572299/

29. Sawchuk, S. (2019, August 5). Americans say civics is a must and religion a maybe in schools. *Education Week*. http://blogs.edweek.org/teachers/teaching_now/2019/08/schools_should_require_civics_classes--and_offer_religion_courses_americans_say_in_new_poll.html; for a fuller discussion of teaching civics in U.S. public schools see: *Education Week*. (2019, September 23). Citizen Z: An *Education Week* project. https://www.edweek.org/ew/collections/civics-education/index.html

30. Campaign for the Civic Mission of Schools and the Lenore Annenberg Institute, 2011.

31. The case is *A. C. v. Raimondo*; see: Sawchuck, S. (2018, November 29). Education is fundamental to citizenship . . . and a constitutional right, new lawsuit alleges. *Education Week*. http://blogs.edweek.org/edweek/curriculum/2018/11/civics_education_is_a_constitutional_right.html

32. Campaign for the Civic Mission of Schools and the Lenore Annenberg Institute, 2011.

33. Viadero, D. (2008, February). Exercise seen as priming pump for students' academic strides. *Education Week, 27*(23), 14–15; Toporek, B. (2012, January 11). Physical activity linked to school success. *Education Week, 31*(15), 3.

34. Castelli, D. M., Hillman, C. H., Buck, S. M., & Erwin, H. (2007). Physical fitness and academic achievement in 3rd and 5th grade students. *Journal of Sport and Exercise Psychology, 29*(2), 239–252.

35. See: Bowen, D. H., & Kisida, B. (2019, February). *Research report for the Houston Independent School District*, 7(4). https://kinder.rice.edu/sites/g/files/bxs1676/f/documents/Investigating%20Causal%20Effects%20of%20Arts%20Education%20Experiences%20Final_0.pdf; Boyd, S. (2014, April 28). Extracurriculars are central to learning. *U.S. News & World Report*. https://www.usnews.com/opinion/articles/2014/04/28/music-art-and-language-programs-in-schools-have-long-lasting-benefits; Gerwertz, C. (2019, June 27). How arts teachers are strengthening students' social-emotional muscles. *Education Week*. https://www.edweek.org/ew/articles/2019/06/26/how-arts-teachers-are-strengthening-students-social-emotional.html; Hardiman, M. M., Bull, R. M. J., Carran, D. T., & Shelton, A. (2019, March). The effects of arts-integrated instruction on memory for science content. *Trends in Neuroscience and Education, 14*(1), 25–32.

36. SEL is broadly understood as the process through which children and adults gain and effectively apply the knowledge, attitudes, and skills needed to manage their emotions (self-control), set and achieve positive goals, feel and show empathy for others (develop social awareness), establish and maintain positive relationships, and make responsible decisions. See: Weissberg, R. P., & Cascarino, J. (2013). Academic learning + social-emotional learning = national priority. *Phi Delta Kappan, 95*(2), 8–13. Teachers need time and professional development to implement SEL programs successfully. See: Blad, E. (2017, November 7). Principals like social-emotional learning. Here's why schools struggle with it. *Education Week*;Social Emotional Learning. (2018). *Education Week Spotlight*, 6–7. https://www.edweek.org/media/spotlight-social-emotional-learning-2018.pdf

37. Claro, S., & Loeb, S. (2019, October). Self-management skills and student achievement gains: Evidence from California's CORE districts. *Search Ed Working Papers*. Annenberg, Brown University. http://www.edworkingpapers.com/ai19-138; Corcoran, R. P., Cheung, A. D. K., Kim, E., & Xie, C. (2018, November). Effective universal school-based social and emotional learning programs for improving academic achievement: A systematic review and meta-analysis of 50 years of research. *Educational Research Review, 25*(1), 56–72; Viadero, D. (2007, December 19). Social-skills programs found to yield gains in academic subjects. *Education Week, 27*(16), 1, 15.

38. Mahoney, J. L., Durlak, J. A., & Weissberg, R. P. (2018, November 26). An update on social and emotional learning outcome research. *Phi Delta Kappan, 100*(4), 18–23.

39. Bridgeland, J., Bruce, M., & Hariharan, A. (2013). *The missing piece: A national teacher survey on how social and emotional learning can empower children and transform schools.* Civic Enterprises and Hart Research Associates for CASEL.

40. Deming, D. J. (2017, June). *The growing importance of social skills in the labor market.* NBER Working Paper Series, Working Paper 21473. National Bureau of Economic Research. https://www.nber.org/papers/w21473.pdf; Nagaoka, J., Farrington, C. A., Ehrlich, S. B., Heath, R. D., Johnson, D. W., Dickson, S., Turner, A. C., Mayo, A., & Hayes, K. (2015). *Foundations for young adult success: A developmental framework.* University of Chicago Consortium on School Research; Schanzenbach, D. W., Nunn, R., Bauer, L., Mumford, M., & Breitwieser, A. (2016). *Seven facts on noncognitive skills from education to the labor market.* The Hamilton Project. https://www.hamiltonproject.org/assets/files/seven_facts_noncognitive_skills_education_labor_market.pdf

41. Melnick, H., & Martinez, L. (2019, May). *Preparing teachers to support social and emotional learning. A case study of San Jose State University and Lakewood Elementary School.* Learning Policy Institute. https://learningpolicyinstitute.org/sites/default/files/product-files/SEL_CaseStudies_SJSU_Lakewood_REPORT.pdf

42. Durlak, J. A., &. DuPre, E. P. (2008). Implementation matters: A review of research on the influence of implementation on program outcomes and the factors affecting implementation. *American Journal of Community Psychology, 41*(3–4), 327–350; Wanless, S. B., & Domitrovich, C. E. (2015). Readiness to implement school-based social-emotional learning interventions: Using research on factors related to implementation to maximize quality. *Prevention Science, 16*(8), 1037–1043.

43. Schonert-Reich, K. A. (2017, Spring). Social and emotional learning and teachers. *The Future of Children, 27*(1), 137–155. https://files.eric.ed.gov/fulltext/EJ1145076.pdf

44. Eisner, E. W. (2005, September). Back to the whole. *Educational Leadership, 63*(1), 14–18. (p. 18).

45. Brooks, J. G., Libresco, A. S., & Plonczak, I. (2007, June). Spaces of liberty: Battling the new soft bigotry of NCLB. *Phi Delta Kappan, 88*(10), 750.

46. Marzano, R. J., Pickering, D. J., & Pollock, J. E. (2001). *Classroom instruction that works: Research-based strategies for increasing student achievement*. ASCD.

47. Marzano et al., 2001, p. 1.

48. Brophy, J., & Murphy, T. (1986). Teacher behavior and student achievement. In M. Wittrock (Ed.), *Handbook of research on teaching* (p. 370). MacMillan.

49. The discussion here, 12.4a–12.4e, highlights material largely from: The National Academies Press. (2018). *How people learn II. Learners, contexts, and cultures.* https://www.nap.edu/catalog/24783/how-people-learn-ii-learners-contexts-and-cultures

50. See: Gauvain, M., Munroe, R. L., & Beebe, H. (2013). Children's questions in cross-cultural perspective: A four-culture study. *Journal of Cross-Cultural Psychology, 44*(7), 1–18; Greenfield, P. M. (2012). Cultural change, human activity, and cognitive development. *Human Development, 55*(4), 229–232.

51. Broesch, T. L., Callaghan, T., Henrich, J., Murphy, C., & Rochat, P. (2010). Cultural variations in children's mirror self-recognition. *Journal of Cross-Cultural Psychology, 42*(6), 1019–1031; Ojalehto, B. L., & Medin, D. L. (2015). Perspectives on culture and concepts. *Annual Review of Psychology, 66*(1), 249–275.

52. Panksepp, J., & Biven, L. (2012). *The archaeology of mind.* W. W. Norton.

53. Bechara, A., Damasio, H., & Demasiko, A. R. (2000, March). Emotion, decision making and the orbitofrontal cortex. *Cerebral Cortex, 10*(3), 295–307; Immordino-Yang, M. H., & Damasio, A. (2007). We feel, therefore we learn: The relevance of affect and neuroscience to education. *Mind, Brain, and Education, 1*(1), 3–10.

54. Figueroa, P. M. E. (1991). Education and the social construction of "race." Routledge; Kemmelmeier, M., & Chavez, H. L. (2014). Biases in the perception of Barack Obama's skin tone. *Analyses of Social Issues and Policies, 14*(1), 137–161; Smedley, A., & Smedley, B. D, (2005, January). Race as biology is fiction, racism as a social problem is real. *American Psychologist, 60*(1), 16–26.

55. Leisman, G., Mualem, R., & Mughrabi, S. K. (2015). The neurological development of the child with the educational enrichment in mind. *Psicologia Educativa, 21*(2), 79–96.

56. Benjamin, A. D., & Tullis, J. (2010). What makes distributed practice effective? *Cognitive Psychology, 61*(3), 228–247.

57. See: Bernard, S. (2010). Science shows making lessons relevant really matters. *Edutopia*. https://www.edutopia.org/neuroscience-brain-based-learning-relevance-improves-engagement; Immordino-Yang, M. H. (2015). *Emotions, learning, and the brain: Exploring the educational implications of affective neuroscience*. W. W. Norton; Willis, J. (2010). Current impact of neuroscience on teaching and learning. In D. A. Sousa (Ed.), *Mind, brain, education: Neuroscience implications for the classroom* (pp. 45–68). Solution Tree; Pekrun, R., & Linnenbrink-Garcia, L. (2012). Academic emotions and student engagement. In S. L. Christenson et al. (Eds.), *Handbook of research on student engagement* (Chap. 12, pp. 259–282). Springer Science + Business Media, LLC.

58. Marzano, R. (2004). *Building background knowledge for academic achievement: Research on what works in schools*. ASCD.

59. Salthouse, T. A. (2010). Influence of age on practice effects in longitudinal neurocognitive change. *Neuropsychology, 24*(5), 563–572.

60. Ackerman, P. L. (1996). A theory of adult intellectual development: Process, personality, interests, and knowledge. *Intelligence, 22*(2), 227–257.

61. See: Dweck, C. S., & Leggett, E. L. (1988). A social-cognitive approach to motivation and personality. *Psychological Review, 95,* 256–273; McClelland, D. (1960). The human side of enterprise. McGraw-Hill; Pintrich, P. R. (2003). A motivational science perspective on the role of student motivation and learning and teaching contexts. *Journal of Educational Psychology, 95*(4), 667–686.

62. Locke, E. A., & Latham, G. P. (1990a). *A theory of goal setting & task performance*. Prentice Hall; Locke, E. A., & Latham, G. P. (1990b). Work motivation and satisfaction: Light at the end of the tunnel. *Psychological Science, 1*(4), 240–246; Maslow, A. (1962). *Toward a psychology of being*. VanNostrand.

63. Vansteenkiste, M., Sierens, E., Soenens, B., Luyckx, K., & Lens, W. (2009). Motivational profiles from a self-determination perspective: The quality of motivation matters. *Journal of Educational Psychology, 101*(3), 671–688.

64. Experts and practitioners have debated whether external rewards encourage or discourage learning. They conclude that, in certain circumstances, external rewards such as praise or prizes can help encourage engagement and persistence *if* they do not undermine the person's sense of autonomy and control over behavior. See: Goswami, I., & Urminsky, O. (2017). How "effort balancing" explains dynamic effects of incentives on motivation. *Advances in Consumer Research, 45*(1), 129–134; Deci, E. L., Koestner, R., & Ryan, R. M. (2001). Extrinsic rewards and intrinsic motivation in education: Reconsidered once again. *Review of Educational Research, 71*(1), 1–27; Mueller, C. M., & Dweck, C. S. (1998). Praise for intelligence can undermine children's motivation and performance. *Journal of Personality and Social Psychology, 75*(1), 33–52.

65. Lin-Siegler, X., Dweck, C. S., & Cohen, G. L. (2016). Instructional interventions that motivate classroom learning. *Journal of Educational Psychology, 108*(3), 295–299; Sparks, S. D. (2019, April 3). Brain science backs up role of "mindset" in motivating students for math. *Education Week*. http://blogs.edweek.org/edweek/inside-school-research/2019/04/brain_study_mindset_math_motivation.html

66. Eccles, J. S., & Wigfield, A. (2002). Motivational beliefs, values, and goals. *Annual Review of Psychology, 53*, 109–132.

67. Rattan, A., Savani, K., Chugh, D., & Dweck, C. S. (2015). Leveraging mindsets to promote academic achievement: Policy recommendations. *Perspectives on Psychological Science, 10*(6), 721–726.

68. Hunsu, N. J., Adesope, O., & Van Wie, B. J. (2017). Engendering situational intertest through innovative instruction in an engineering classroom: What really mattered? *Instructional Science, 45*(6), 789–804; Guthrie, J. T., Wigfield, A., Humenick, N. M., Perencevich, K. D., Taboada, A., & Barbose, P. (2006). Influences of stimulating tasks on reading motivation and comprehension. *Journal of Educational Research, 99*(4), 232–245.

69. Abbott, M. L., & Fouts, J. T. (2003). *Constructivist teaching and student achievement: The results of a school-level classroom observation study in Washington*. Seattle Pacific University. https://files.eric.ed.gov/fulltext/ED481694.pdf; Schmoker, M. (2002). The real causes of higher achievement. *SEDL Letter, XIV*(2). SEDL Archive. http://www.sedl.org/pubs/sedletter/v14n02/

70. Baines, L. A., & Stanley, G. (2001). We *still* want to see the teacher. *Phi Delta Kappan, 82*(9), 686–696.

71. Hightower, A. M., Delgado, R. C., Lloyd, S. C., Wittenstein, R., Sellers, K., & Swanson, C. B. (2011, December). *Improving student learning by supporting quality teaching: Key issues, effective strategies*. Educational Projects in Education. https://www.rand.org/pubs/research_reports/RR4312.html; Opper, I. M. (2019). *Teachers matter: Understanding teachers' impact on student achievement*. RAND. https://www.rand.org/education-and-labor/projects/measuring-teacher-effectiveness/teachers-matter.html

72. Darling-Hammond, L. (2000). Teacher quality and student achievement: A review of state policy evidence. *Education Policy Analysis Archives, 8*(1). https://epaa.asu.edu/ojs/article/view/392/515; Darling-Hammond, L. (2006). Constructing 21st century teacher education. *Journal of Teacher Education,* 57(3), 300–314. https://doi.org/10.1177%2F0022487105285962; Goldhaber, D., & Startz, R. (2017). On the distribution of worker productivity: The case of teacher effectiveness and student achievement. *Journal of Statistics and Public Policy, 4*(1), 1–12. https://doi.org/10.1080/2330443X.2016.1271733; Kane, T. J., McCaffrey, D. F., Miller, T., & Staiger, D. O. (2013). *Have we identified effective teachers? Validating measures of effective teaching using random assignment.* Bill & Melinda Gates Foundation. https://files.eric.ed.gov/fulltext/ED540959.pdf

73. Darling-Hammond, 2006.

74. See: Kane, T. J., Rockoff, J. E., & Staiger, D. O. (2008). What does certification tell us about teacher effectiveness? Evidence from New York City. *Economics of Education Review, 27,* 615–631; Nye, B., Konstantopoulos, S., & Hedges, L. V. (2004). How large are teacher effects? *Educational Evaluation and Policy Analysis,* 26(3), 237–257; Rivkin, S. G., Hanushek, E. A., & Kain, J. F. (2005). Teachers, schools, and academic achievement. *Econometrica, 73*(2), 417–458.

75. Darling-Hammond, 2000; Walsh, K. (2001). *Teacher certification reconsidered: Stumbling for quality.* Abell Foundation.

76. Darling-Hammond, 2002; Whitehurst, G. J. (2002, March 5). *Scientifically based research on teacher quality. Research on teacher preparation and professional development.* http://citeseerx.ist.psu.edu/viewdoc/download?doi=10.1.1.468.8079&rep=rep1&type=pdf

77. Kaplan, L. S., & Owings, W. A. (2003, May). The politics of teacher quality. *NASSP Bulletin, 84*(9), 687–692.

78. Friedman, M. (1982). *Capitalism and freedom. Preface* (p. ix). University of Chicago Press.

79. Crabtree, J. (2020, March 12). Teaching technology stands to be rare winner from coronavirus. *Nikkei Asian Review.* https://asia.nikkei.com/Opinion/Teaching-technology-stands-to-be-rare-winner-from-coronavirus

80. *Education Week.* (2020, May 6). Map: Coronavirus and school closures. https://www.edweek.org/ew/section/multimedia/map-coronavirus-and-school-closures.html

81. *Education Week* Research Center. (2020, May 11). Survey tracker: Monitoring how K–12 educators are responding to coronavirus. https://www.edweek.org/ew/articles/2020/04/27/survey-tracker-k-12-coronavirus-response.html

82. The National Parents Union, an educational advocacy network, commissioned the poll. Lowe, B. (2020, May 11). New poll: Two-thirds of parents support keeping schools closed "until they are certain there is no health risk." *The 74.* https://www.the74million.org/new-poll-two-thirds-of-parents-support-keeping-schools-closed-until-they-are-certain-there-is-no-health-risk/

83. Lowe, 2020.

84. A 2019 report on a nationally representative sample of over 1,200 teaches found that approximately 60% of teachers used video-streaming services as an instructional digital tool. See: Vega, V., & Robb, M. B. (2019). *The Common Sense census: Inside the 21st century classroom.* Common Sense Media. https://www.commonsensemedia.org/sites/default/files/uploads/research/2019-educator-census-inside-the-21st-century-classroom_1.pdf

85. Scher, L. (2020, March 25). Learning in the midst of a pandemic: Four key education takeaways. *Mathematica.* https://www.mathematica.org/commentary/learning-in-the-midst-of-a-pandemic-four-key-education-takeaways

86. Richards, E. (2020, April 13). "Historic academic regression": Why homeschooling is so hard amid school closures. *USA Today.* https://www.usatoday.com/story/news/education/2020/04/13/coronavirus-online-school-homeschool-betsy-devos/5122539002/

87. Scher, 2019.

88. Kahan, J. (2019, April 8). It's time for a new approach for mapping broadband data to better serve Americans. *Microsoft on the Issues.* https://blogs.microsoft.com/on-the-issues/2019/04/08/its-time-for-a-new-approach-for-mapping-broadband-data-to-better-serve-americans/

89. Vega & Robb, 2019.

90. Will, M. (2020, April 29). Teachers without internet work in parking lots, empty school buildings during COVID-19. *Education Week, 39*(32), 17.

91. Will, 2020.

92. National left for Education Statistics. (2019, May). English language learners in public schools. *The Condition of Education.* https://nces.ed.gov/programs/coe/indicator_cgf.asp

93. Richards, E. (2020, May 14). Coronavirus online school is hard enough. What if you're still learning to speak English. *USA Today.* https://www.usatoday.com/in-depth/news/education/2020/05/14/coronavirus-online-classes-school-closures-esl-students-learn-english/5178145002/?build=native-web_i_t

94. Bailey, J. (2020, May 11). Analysis—A blueprint for reopening America' schools this fall: 21 former education chiefs identify 6 top priorities for districts & statehouses in returning amid coronavirus. *The 74.* https://www.the74million.org/article/analysis-a-blueprint-for-reopening-americas-schools-this-fall-21-former-education-chiefs-identify-6-top-priorities-for-districts-statehouses-in-returning-amid-coronavirus/

Siriporn Wongmanee/EyeEm/Getty Images

13 STANDARDS, ASSESSMENT, AND ACCOUNTABILITY

InTASC Standards Addressed: 1, 2, 3, 4, 5, 6, 7, 8, 9, 10

LEARNING OBJECTIVES

After you read this chapter, you should be able to

13.1 Compare and contrast the factors that contribute to an incomplete versus a comprehensive educational assessment of teaching and learning.

13.2 Critique how educational standards contribute to student achievement, school accountability, and teachers' professional growth.

13.3 Determine how the six principles of high-quality assessments should influence teachers' ethical practices to advance student learning.

13.4 Argue how accountability for educational outcomes means more than students' achievement test scores.

Educational testing in the United States began in the 20th century as an objective, relatively inexpensive tool to provide information for decision-making about large numbers of people. Over time, its cost has grown exponentially. Standardized testing costs states over $1.7 billion a year, overall, accounting for one quarter of 1% of the total U.S. K–12 spending.[1] This investment attests to the public's continued confidence in test scores—as a proxy for student learning—as one measure of accountability and as a means to make important educational decisions.

Standards, achievement, and accountability are highly visible topics. National leaders continue to hold states and school districts accountable for improving student outcomes. The Every Student Succeeds Act's (ESSA) use of multiple measures for statewide school accountability and improvement, determining student proficiency and achievement gains, and reaffirming schools' responsibility for student learning continues to be a prime concern for teachers, school leaders, and communities. Clear, relevant, and rigorous academic standards, an array of appropriate student performance assessments, and valid, reliable public accountability systems to understand where schools are struggling and how to improve them can be potent tools to accomplish this end.

Despite its often high-stakes nature, educational accountability does not have to intimidate future teachers. Accountability is a shared responsibility. Assessment is an ongoing and integral part of the teaching and learning process, not a once-a-year hurdle to be jumped. In fact, well-designed and effectively used assessments can motivate students' interest and boost their achievement. Larger than "tests and measurement," accountability involves helping students meet a variety of clear, high standards in fair ways. Becoming knowledgeable about standards, assessment, and educational accountability can help prospective teachers understand their benefits and limitations and learn how to use them to advance student equity and achievement as they increase their own teaching effectiveness.

13.1 HOW TEACHERS AND SCHOOLS USE ASSESSMENT TO ENHANCE TEACHING AND LEARNING

Parents, policy makers, and teachers want meaningful answers to all of the following questions:

- How is my student doing?
- Are the schools succeeding or failing?
- What works best to help students learn?
- Do test scores prove the effectiveness of educational programs?

Answering these reasonable questions requires teachers to have a variety of student assessment data accessible. An accountability system that contains test scores alone is incomplete without additional information about the curriculum and teaching practices. A teacher or school system that answers these questions (or bases its accountability) on test scores alone is like a physician evaluating your health based on body temperature or blood pressure but ignoring weight, height, blood tests, diet, exercise routines, or other medical or personal indicators that are essential to a competent (and accurate) diagnosis.

Teachers can know if they or their schools are succeeding or failing only if they have access to multiple sources of data gathered over an extended period. They need information about the measurable elements of the educational process—the curriculum standards, the learning assignments, types of available student support, and samples of students' completed work. They also need information about the results—students' project and performance grades and standardized test scores over many years. In addition, educators need to learn how to provide insights based on observations, descriptions, and qualitative understandings that explain what has happened beyond the test scores. In the end, teachers must gather enough meaningful information and use professional judgments to make sense out of what is happening in the classroom for each student.

13.1a The Educational Assessment Learning Cycle

People tend to use the words "measurement," "assessment," and accountability" interchangeably. All of these terms relate to data and the process of evaluating progress in a concrete way, but they mean somewhat different things.

Measurement involves assigning numbers to observations according to rules that fit the circumstances. Measurement must be as objective as possible, but it can never be completely objective. For example, in a spelling bee, the judge counts the number of words that the student spelled correctly and assigns that number as the student's score. This part of the process is objective: The spelling is either correct or not. Deciding on the words to be included in the spelling bee and whether the student's spelling score of 16 is "poor" or "excellent," however, requires the teacher to use his or her judgment and is subjective.

Assessment is broader than measurement. The word "assessment" comes from the Latin root *assidre*, meaning "to assist in the office of a judge." Assessment requires using professional judgment to determine what the measurement means. It is a comprehensive term that includes measurement, evaluation, and grading. **Educational assessment**, therefore, is a comprehensive process of describing, judging, and communicating the quality of students' learning and performances. As you see in Figure 13.1, assessment is the core of a continual learning cycle that includes measurement, feedback, reflection, and change. Assessment is not simply measuring learning. Rather, it is the first step in a continual learning cycle whose purpose is to foster improvement.

FIGURE 13.1 ■ The Assessment Learning Cycle

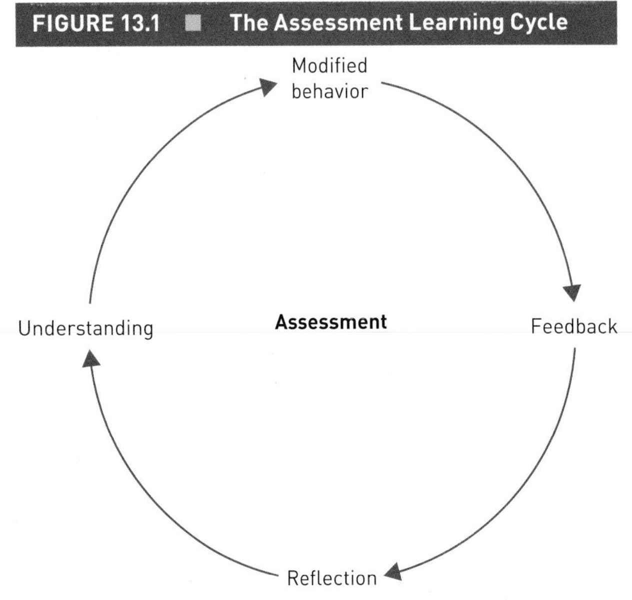

Source: Adapted from Frye, R. (1999, February 1). Assessment, accountability, and student learning outcomes. *Dialogue, 2,* 1–11. Figure 4, p. 7. Western Washington University, Office of Survey Research, 430. https://pdfs.semanticscholar.org/695c/5a5158acf743999e0909175717318715a2f5.pdf

A well-designed assessment gives both teacher and student high-quality feedback about how well the student is mastering the assigned curriculum. Upon receiving the feedback, teacher and student reflect and try to understand what the results mean. Has the student learned successfully? On which aspects does the student need additional instruction, practice, and feedback? What do the student and teacher do next with this feedback to change their behaviors? Does the teacher need to work with the individual or with large numbers of students in the class who did not show mastery on this or other important aspects of the assigned learning?

Answering these questions requires teachers to gather more evidence, reflect, and analyze deeply before acting. It allows them to use achievement data to guide their daily instructional plans and classroom actions. Thoughtful teaching needs to be driven by daily evidence, not solely by end-of-unit or course test scores.

Accountability systems include much more than students' achievement test scores. **Holistic accountability** considers the factors that support educational excellence, including teaching practices, curriculum practices, leadership practices, student behaviors, parent involvement, faculty communication and collaboration, and professional development. Thus, accountability addresses all aspects of the teaching and learning process. We will discuss holistic accountability in more detail later in this chapter.

13.1b Purposes of Assessment

The rationale for undertaking assessment is not merely to gather information. Rather, the intention is to combine data with professional judgment and relevant actions to create improvement. In schools, assessment has several purposes, including making placement decisions, determining how well students attain curricular and instructional goals, and diagnosing student learning needs.

Placement Decisions

Placement decisions occur before instruction begins. The goal is to gather information for making informed decisions on where to start and how to best teach students. Teacher awareness of what each student knows before trying to teach something new increases the likelihood that the teacher will be able to provide suitable instruction for each child. Knowing a child's background knowledge and skill levels enables teachers to make the new information personally meaningful and relevant to individual students by linking it to what they already know, understand, and can do. Data for placement assessment come from past records, observations of students' strengths and weaknesses, pretests, and student self-reports.

Likewise, assessments for placement are sometimes used as gatekeepers to determine who moves to the next grade, who is eligible to enroll the higher level courses, or who receives admission to a college or profession. Many states require high school students to pass one or more tests before they can receive a diploma. College admissions offices have long used the results of the American College Testing (ACT) program and the Scholastic Aptitude Test (SAT) as important data in making admissions decisions. Professions such as law, medicine, nursing, physical therapy, certified public accounting, and architecture require candidates to pass a specialized, standardized test before they are admitted to the profession. In the teaching profession, most state departments of education require new teachers to pass a licensure exam (i.e., typically a standardized test on content the teacher is expected to teach) to become eligible to receive a teaching license.

Determining Student Attainment

Teachers use information from students' homework, classwork, projects, and a variety of measures to help determine how much students learned. Formative and summative assessments help establish whether students have mastered the curriculum.

Formative assessments are assessment *for* learning. *Formative* does not refer to the content, but rather to the manner in which the assessments are used. As learners try to understand and apply their new knowledge and skills, teachers' formative assessments provide daily, continuous, and specific classroom feedback about students' areas of mastery and weakness as they relate to state standards. Formative assessments let everyone know where they stand in the learning process. Teachers can use this information to adjust instruction and to create appropriate work for groups of learners or individual students. Assessing *for* learning advances—not simply monitors—student learning in a variety of ways.

The formative approach makes a measurable difference in student achievement. Research studies have determined that:

- Feedback improves learning when teachers give students ongoing responses and guidance about how to improve their class work and tests.[2]
- Students benefit more from feedback than from grades.[3]
- Consistent, formative practices are linked to significant achievement gains and a reduced achievement gap, especially for the lowest achievers.[4]
- Formative assessments motivate students in positive ways that reinforce successful learning.[5]

Assessments are often used to make college placement decisions.

iStock/Prostock-Studio

Summative assessments involve the assessment *of* learning. Summative assessments are the final task at a unit's end used to make a concluding judgment about whether the student has met a certain required level of accomplishment. In addition to traditional examinations, teachers gather summative data through student demonstrations or performances, evaluating assigned projects and products, and systematically collecting portfolios that illustrate students' progress and achievements. Capstone assessments, such as science fairs, recitals, or art shows, celebrate a milestone accomplishment and demonstrate how well a person has mastered a knowledge or skill.

Because summative assessments help teachers and students determine the extent to which students have achieved the instructional goals, they support assigning grades to report cards or to conferring certificates of mastery. To a limited degree, teachers can also use these data to help them judge their teaching effectiveness.

Standardized tests will always be an important part of teachers' assessment repertoire as a means to find out if they are teaching the standard course of study in ways that generate students' learning. But they will not be the only data upon which teachers rely to inform their judgment about student performance.

Diagnostic assessments are a highly specialized intervention into student learning. They involve detailed and professionally prepared tests administered by a special education teacher, school psychologist, speech/language pathologist, occupational therapist, or regular teacher trained for this task. When a student experiences persistent learning difficulty despite the teacher's use of alternative instructional methods, diagnostic assessment is employed to determine the cause or causes of that student's ongoing learning problems. The findings enable teachers to develop plans for appropriate remedial attention to individual students and help them determine whether a student is eligible for special education or gifted services or accommodations.

Stephanie L. Bravmann, senior research consultant at the Center on Reinventing Education at the University of Washington, observes,

> Unlike formative assessment, which is intended to deal with the kinds of learning issues that respond to the classroom equivalent of bandages, hot-water soaks, or massage, diagnostic assessment helps find the underlying causes for learning problems that don't respond to purely palliative measures.[6]

Effective teachers learn how to balance assessment *for* and *of* learning. Teachers committed to educating each child appropriately collect and use ongoing student performance data. This helps them understand each student as a learner on a daily basis and make the necessary adaptations to support learning every day. Additionally, teachers partner summative assessments with the other available student learning data to fairly and equitably support—not merely evaluate—student learning. Using only summative assessments to gauge student learning is an incomplete measure of teaching and learning.

13.1c Types of School Assessments

Assessments come in a variety of styles and purposes. **Traditional assessments** commonly include paper-and-pencil or online formats with multiple-choice questions designed to compare students across the school district, state, or nation. Their scores on these tests identify whether students have developed the core knowledge and skills the standards expect. These are the assessment instruments that the U.S. education system traditionally uses. Although efficient, relatively inexpensive to administer and score, and a provider of useful information about student progress and educational programs, standardized tests cannot measure many of learning's important aspects. Typically, they do not often assess higher-level thinking, and they are not sensitive to students' ability to apply skills and knowledge to real-world problems.[7] Likewise, the assessments provided through standardized tests do not support many useful teaching strategies.[8]

Performance or authentic assessment refers to a type of appraisal that requires students to enact, demonstrate, construct, or develop a product or solution under defined conditions or standards. Performance assessments—such as presentations, portfolios, dramatic enactments or concerts, projects, exhibits and fairs, and debates—capture aspects of students' learning that standardized tests cannot. These assessments allow students to show what they know in a number of ways that meet standards in real-world settings. Although performance tasks provide meaningful intellectual challenge because they promote using learning beyond the classroom and can be tailored to fit individual student interests, performance assessments, too, have their benefits and limitations.

13.2 EDUCATIONAL STANDARDS CONTRIBUTE TO ACHIEVEMENT AND ACCOUNTABILITY

Accountability is tied to educational standards. **Educational standards** clearly identify what students should know and be able to do at a particular grade level. Accordingly, educational standards have become the foundation of curriculum and assessment in all 50 states, each of which has its own set of standards. Standards have come to be synonymous with rigor and setting high-achievement expectations for all students.

13.2a Educational Standards, Achievement, and Accountability

The emphasis on well-defined educational goals stems from the school effectiveness research conducted in the 1970s, which revealed that what students are taught in a specific subject and at a specific grade level varied greatly among schools and even among classrooms within a school.[9] For example, one report found that one elementary school teacher who was observed for more than 90 days did not teach fractions, despite the state mandate to teach the topic at that grade level. When asked about omitting the topic, the teacher replied, "I don't like fractions."[10] In a similar vein, another report showed a range of more than 4,000 minutes in the time spent on reading instruction in four fourth-grade classes.[11] Again, teacher preference accounted for such wide differences.[12] Across the country and within schools, students were learning according to teacher preferences and not based on high and clear educational benchmarks.

Notably, the focus of standards has shifted attention from *inputs* to *outcomes*. Before 1987, most standards focused on the curriculum, telling teachers what they should teach (inputs). In contrast, today's standards identify what students should know and be able to do (outcomes) when they finish a course, a grade, or a program. "Standards," "benchmarks," "indicators," and "objectives"—all refer to what students should know and be able to do. The standards-based education movement assumes that the only way to ensure that all students acquire specific knowledge and skills is to identify and teach them to expected performance levels.

Setting standards, teaching to the standards, and assessing the extent to which students meet the standards provide the basis for public school achievement and accountability. This systematic approach connects curriculum, instruction, assessments, and professional development to a set of performance indicators that the teachers, administrators, parents, and students endorse. Student learning is at the center, and standardized tests are frequently the means to measure students' performance.

What is more, today's standards apply to every student. The current U.S. educational reform movement finds it unacceptable that only a small percentage of students achieve at high levels. In response, schools have raised their expectations for every student's learning. This is not just the practical thing to do. It is the ethical thing to do if we want to provide more opportunities for talented and hard-working students from every racial, ethnic, and socioeconomic background to climb as high as their capabilities, energies, and opportunities will take them.

13.2b Why We Use Educational Standards

Many reasons exist for using educational standards. For example, such standards provide more accurate achievement measures than a comparison of students' scores to national norms. Meeting educational standards does not "sort and select" students into haves and have-nots. Instead, ideally, meeting educational standards provides the necessary intellectual challenge to above-average students at the same time that this assessment process is fair to all students.[13] In this section, we discuss more fully each reason for using these standards.

Standards and National Norms

First, standards are more accurate than norms as measures of student achievement. Garrison Keillor, the television and radio personality famous for *A Prairie Home Companion*, greeted his weekly audience with the words, "Welcome to Lake Wobegon, where all the women are strong, all the men are good-looking, and all the children are above average."[14] This boast is a proud tribute to Lake Wobegon's all-American families, but it tweaks the popular notion of "norm." Bragging that all children are "above average" pokes fun at the idea of the **bell curve**, a statistical concept in which random scores spread out around a range from high to low with half the scores above and half below the mean.

Figure 13.2 illustrates the bell curve and the **statistical norm** at the mean (average). The norm is the 34% below and 34% above (68% total) around the center line (50th percentile). The farther from the central line, the more outside the "norm." Because the Lake Wobegon population is not random (its fictional population has moved there by choice), the concept of statistical norm does not apply. There's the joke! Statistically, in a truly "normal" population, every child cannot be "above average." By definition, half must be below average. The concept of *norm* is less funny, however, when it is applied to student achievement.

Two ways exist to evaluate student performance. Either we can compare a student's performance to that of another student or to the average of a group of students. Or we can compare the student's performance to an objective standard. When educators use the norm approach, they accept the logic of the **normal distribution** or bell curve.[15]

Normed tests are specifically designed to distribute students' achievement scores along a continuum from high to low, while educational standards expect every student—given enough time and academic and social supports—to reach them. Normed tests are designed to produce few winners; standards are designed so that everyone can reach the designated proficiency. Comparing results and determining one winner and many losers may make sense when only one baseball team can win the World Series or when only one country can win the Olympic gold medal in figure skating. It does not make sense, however, when the educational goal is for every student to be a winner—that is, to learn the necessary knowledge and skills that mark excellent learning and that contribute to excellent

FIGURE 13.2 ■ The Bell Curve: Finding the Norm

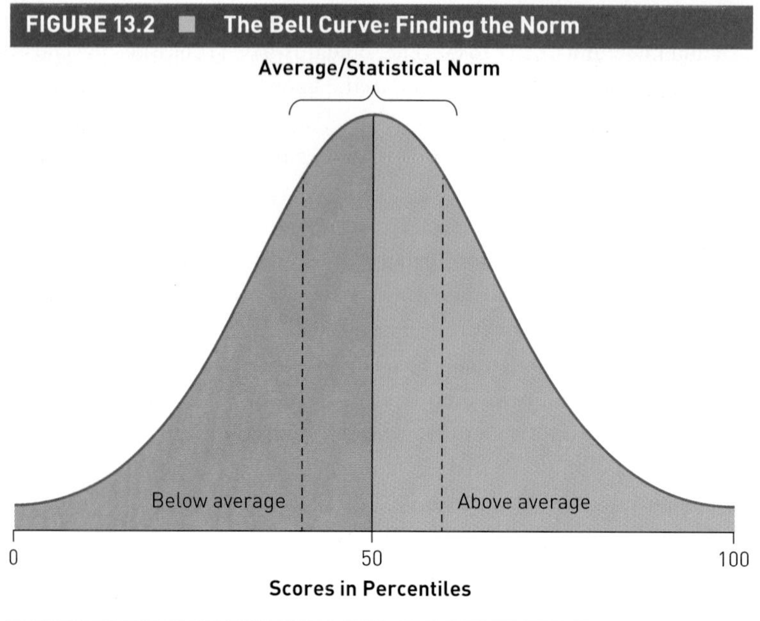

Source: Leslie S. Kaplan and William A. Owings [Original by authors].

performance. No teacher, parent, or employer wants his or her students to be in the "lower half" (below average).

Testing's central technical issue is accurately measuring students' performance and progress. This is accountability's most basic principle. Each student's challenge is to meet an objective standard. No one would want to be a passenger in an airplane flown by a pilot who merely scored "above average" on the Federal Aviation Administration (FAA) exam. Rather, we all would prefer to fly with an outstanding pilot such as "Sully" Sullenberger, who was able to save all on board his passenger flight in January 2009 by safely landing in the Hudson River after a "bird strike" disabled both plane engines.[16] Viewed in this way, academic standards provide accuracy and an acceptable performance level that comparisons to the average or norm cannot offer. Meeting academic standards can determine a student's proficiency, and every student can meet this goal.

Standards and Equity

Standards do not "sort and select" students. If the standards define what every student should know and be able to do, then every proficient student has the opportunity to earn the top grade—and demonstrate capable knowledge and skills.

As discussed in Chapter 7, U.S. public schools have traditionally sorted and selected students to prepare them for future societal roles. Curriculum tracking is one example of how schools accomplish this task. Traditional sorting and selecting practice denies certain students the educational opportunities to learn necessary knowledge and skills. As a result, curriculum tracking does not produce equitable results for underrepresented and low-socioeconomic status (SES) students, who need schools to help them create opportunities for social and economic mobility. Some call the inequity of curriculum tracking an ethical issue.[17]

What is more, using norms or standards becomes an ethical issue when teachers focus on how the results will be used and on their own responsibility for helping students learn. With norms, teachers expect students to perform at higher or lower levels. The mindset that the lower scores are "normal" and "expected" means that teachers need spend no extra effort to bring lower-scoring students up to the proficiency level. As a result, lower-performing students remain perpetually behind. Using standards, by contrast, brings the mindset that all students can and must reach proficiency—that is, they must all achieve the given standard. By adopting this perspective, teachers must invest extra time and use varied instructional and support practices with the lower achievers so that they, too, reach the standard.

Norm-referenced, high-stakes tests "are the equivalent of 'educational highways' with the smallest possible margin for error—an inch on either side—because *their* purpose is not to see that students 'arrive safely' but to nab them for violations," notes John Merrow, an education writer.[18] If the goal of U.S. public schools is to ensure that each student arrives safely at the proficiency level, using assessments tied to educational standards rather than norm-referenced assessments is more likely to get them there.

Standards and "Above-Average" Students

Although they may score highly on norm-referenced tests, many students classified as "above average" may not be able to write a coherent and persuasive essay, apply an algebraic concept to solve a real-world problem, or understand a complex literary passage's meaning. Although "above-average" scores make students and their parents feel good about their schools and their education, their expectations for proficiency are not high enough. They become inappropriately complacent when, in truth, their achievement as measured against rigorous academic standards (rather than norms) may be inadequate.

Comparison to the average does not only hurt disadvantaged students; it also hurts higher-achieving students who score well on tests but who still have much more to learn. They mistakenly believe that because they can "outscore" other students, they are successful and do not have to work harder to achieve a higher, more demanding level of mastery. They may not realize that their real competitors are not their peers across the room but those across the globe. Standards keep the challenges high and learning continuing for nearly all students.

Standards and Fairness

Standards communicate what students are expected to know and be able to do. **Benchmarks** identify specific content and performance expectations for certain grade levels or groups of grade levels. Scoring guides, sometimes called **rubrics**, provide the most specific expectations for students by identifying what they are supposed to accomplish on individual assignments and assessments. Students can reliably meet these expectations when the standards are clear and consistent, when students know and understand what they are, and when the teaching is effective.

This system is fair because unless the standards change, which occurs infrequently, the rules do not change in the middle of the game. What students learn, study, and practice is what is assessed. What is also fair, ideally, is that every student—regardless of gender, race, ethnicity, social class, or parental education level—has the chance to meet the same standards and show proficiency.

In the real world, however, academic standards' integrity depends on the connection among standards, teaching, and assessments. The state-approved tests must assess the same knowledge and skills that the teacher taught. Likewise, every student must have an opportunity to learn the state-approved curriculum and the standards set for that grade level. Although different students and teachers may approach mastering the standards in varying ways and with varying levels of help, every student should have access to what the community determines to be a demanding and excellent education to prepare each one for college and the workplace. In contrast, if the state standards, the teacher-taught curriculum, and the assessments do not match, the system is fair to no one.

13.2c Types of Educational Standards

Standards make statements about the expected level of attainment or performance, but they may mean very different things to different people. World-class standards, real-world standards, content standards, performance standards, and opportunity-to-learn standards all define different expectations for student achievement. Teachers have (professional) standards to meet. Education standards also have their critics.

World-Class Standards

Educators and policy makers may think of standards as world-class goals based on the performances of exceptional individuals such as Fields Medal–winning mathematicians, Nobel Prize–winning scientists, Pulitzer Prize–winning authors, and Olympic gold medal–winning athletes. Elementary and secondary students are not expected to meet these extremely high standards, of course. Instead, schools set world-class standards as aspirational goals and models of excellence meant to inspire ambition and greater effort.

Schools that adopt world-class standards take the long view. Educators see the curriculum as a developmental process. During each school year, students move toward the high standard. Teachers expect students to show improvement in many ways over time as they advance toward increasingly greater mastery.

Real-World Standards

Others believe that standards should be real-world goals that every student can actually achieve in school. Rigorous real-world standards for high school students reflect the knowledge and skills that will prepare them to enter and succeed in credit-bearing college courses or to gain entry-level positions in careers that pay a living wage and offer advancement opportunities. For example, 44 states and the District of Columbia have adopted the Common Core State Standards, which are modeled on those of high-achieving countries.[19] In an increasingly competitive global environment, policy makers and educators believe that American students should be held to the same mastery level as students in other nations with whom we compete politically and economically. Previously, states took a more local view, aligning their high school standards with the real-world expectations of local or regional employers. At the same time, postsecondary faculty offer guidance by spelling out what students need to know and be able to do to succeed in formal education after high school.

Content- or Discipline-Based Standards

Content- or discipline-based standards describe what teachers and students should know and be able to do in subject areas. Professional education organizations—representing mathematics, history/social studies, English/language arts, arts, behavior studies, career education, civics, economics, educational technology, foreign language, geography, health, history, life skills, mathematics, science, physical education, and early childhood professional preparation—have all developed standards based on national consensus.[20]

Usually, these content standards emphasize the subjects' core components or "big ideas" that students of a certain age or grade level should know. They are often accompanied by standards stating what teachers should know about the content or subject so they can teach at the preschool, elementary, or secondary levels.

As with the real-world standards, most states are using the Common Core standards in place of the older discipline standards in English language arts, math, and literacy in history, social studies, science, and technical subjects. For example, the Common Core reading standards note that all students must be able to comprehend texts of steadily increasing complexity in all their academic subjects as they move through the grade levels. By the time students are ready to graduate from high school, they must be able to read and comprehend independently and proficiently the challenging texts in each academic discipline typically encountered in college, workplace training programs, and careers. These reading standards attempt to correct an existing weakness: Although the reading demands of college, workplace, citizenship, and life have either stayed the same or increased over the past 50 years, K–12 texts have actually reduced their reading complexity. The result is a large gap between what most high school graduates can comprehend by reading on their own and what they are expected to be able to read independently—without teacher prompts, class discussion, or text summaries and clues—after they graduate.[21]

Table 13.1 provides a more complete idea about what increasing reading complexity in K–12 Common Core standards in literature and academic content means. It includes these areas of learning:

- Levels of meaning
- Structure
- Language
- Knowledge demands

TABLE 13.1 ■ Making Reading Texts in School More Complex

From Less Complex Text	→	To More Complex Text
Levels of Meaning (Literary Texts) or Purpose (Informational Text)		
• Single level of meaning	→	Multiple levels of meaning
• Explicitly stated purpose	→	Implicit purpose; may be hidden or obscure
Structure		
• Simple	→	Complex
• Explicit	→	Implicit
• Conventional	→	Unconventional (usually in literary texts)
• Events told in chronological order	→	Events told out of chronological order
• Traits of a common genre or subgenre	→	Traits specific to a particular discipline
• Simple graphics	→	Sophisticated graphics
• Graphics unnecessary to understanding	→	Graphics essential to understanding (may provide information not in the text)
Language Conventionality and Clarity		
• Literal	→	Figurative or ironic
• Clear	→	Ambiguous or purposefully misleading
• Contemporary, familiar	→	Archaic or otherwise unfamiliar
• Conversational	→	General academic and domain-specific
Knowledge Demands: Life Experiences (Literary)		
• Simple themes	→	Complex or sophisticated themes
• Single themes	→	Multiple themes
• Common, everyday experiences or clearly invented situations	→	Experiences distinctly different from one's own
• Single viewpoint	→	Multiple viewpoints
• Viewpoint(s) like one's own	→	Viewpoint(s) unlike or opposed to one's own
Knowledge Demands: Cultural/Literary Knowledge (Mainly Literary Texts)		
• Everyday knowledge and familiarity with genre conventions required	→	Cultural and literary knowledge useful
• Few, if any, references or allusions to other texts	→	Many references or allusions to other texts
Knowledge Demands: Content/Discipline Knowledge (Mainly Informational Texts)		
• Everyday knowledge and familiarity with genre conventions required	→	Extensive, maybe specialized discipline-specific content knowledge required
• Few, if any, references to/citations from other texts	→	Many references to/citations from other texts

Source: Adapted from Figure 2. Qualitative Dimensions of Text Complexity. National Governors Association and the Council of Chief State School Officers. (2020). *Common core state standards for English language arts & literacy in history/social studies, science, and technology* (p. 6). http://www.corestandards.org/assets/Appendix_A.pdf

Levels of meaning or purpose, for literary and informational texts, respectively, move from an easier text having one obvious meaning to one having multiple levels of meaning—such as satire or metaphor in literary works and hidden or obscure purpose in informational works. As used in Table 13.1, **structure** refers to the continuum between simple, well-marked, traditional organization to more complicated, implicit, and unconventional language construction. **Language conventionality and clarity** refers to the range of English from easily understood, clear, typical, conversational language to more challenging word-use that is figurative, ironic, ambiguous, or purposefully misleading. Finally, **knowledge demands** speak to the continuum between easier-reading texts that make few assumptions about the readers' life experiences and depth of their cultural and content knowledge and more demanding writings that make many assumptions about one or more of these areas. Clearly, such an increase in reading comprehension demands will create challenges for both teachers and students.

National Standards

The U.S. Constitution assigns the responsibility of education to the states. Each state has its own process of developing, adopting, and implementing educational standards. This means that what students can be expected to learn and be able to do vary widely from state to state. States prize their autonomy in the education domain, and they vigorously strive to keep it.

Prior to the Common Core standards, many educators expressed concerned that the curricula in use were unfocused, a superficial "mile wide and inch deep." In fact, researchers at Mid-continent Research for Education and Learning (McREL) identified some 200 standards and 3,093 benchmarks in national- and state-level documents for 14 different subject areas.[22] This material would take 15,465 hours to teach,[23] but U.S. public schools (K–12) had only 9,042 hours available to teach these standards and benchmarks.[24]

The Common Core State Standards reflect the shared desire among educators, experts, parents, and policy makers across the nation to voluntarily adopt the highest academic criteria benchmarked to those in the highest-achieving countries. But this would not be a national curriculum. Using the Common Core as a framework, each state sets its own content standards and uses these to write curricula. Local teachers, principals, superintendents, and school boards decide how they will meet the standards, and local teachers continue to create lesson plans and design instruction to the individual needs of the students in their classrooms.

As befitting a state-held responsibility, the federal government was not involved in developing the standards. But it has influenced their adoption. The U.S. Department of Education's Race to the Top grant program, which offered significant dollars tied to state education reform, provided an incentive to adopt by awarding states extra points for agreeing to use these voluntary standards. For moral, practical, and legal reasons, therefore, many believe that common national education standards are desirable.[25] And 7 years after their adoption, research finds positive changes in both teachers' instructional practices[26] and student learning.[27]

Criticism of Content Standards

Although high-quality content standards bring positive benefits to teaching, learning, and assessment, critics raise both legitimate and political concerns about their use. Because new academic standards brought new textbooks, new teaching methods, and new assessments, some parents complained that they could no longer help children with their math homework. Numbers of English teachers objected to the new emphasis on reading nonfiction text. In addition, critics complained about the frustrations of implementing a new curriculum—typically in areas of funding, identifying and/or evaluating curriculum materials, professional development, and developing educator evaluation systems—that significantly differed in complexity and rigor than the one teachers had been using.[28] Others opposed what they saw as federal government and private philanthropies' "political overreach" into state territory by offering states financial incentives to adopt the standards.[29]

Performance Standards

Performance standards are also statements about what a student or a teacher should be able to do in presentations that encompass combinations of knowledge and skills. Once teachers have identified the content standard, they design performance standards so each student can show what he or she understands and can do with what they learned. Assessments for the Common Core standards are expected to include performance tasks.

Because performance tasks require students to actively demonstrate what they know, performance assessments may sometimes be a more valid indicator of students' knowledge and abilities than a multiple-choice test. Answering a multiple-choice question correctly may require no more than recognizing or remembering a fact, relatively low levels of thinking. Making an oral presentation, in contrast, typically requires the student to invest time; conduct research; analyze, synthesize, evaluate, write, and practice; create graphic illustrations to accompany the talk; and have sufficient subject knowledge to correctly answer listeners' questions.

Setting and enforcing clear, high, and achievable performance standards is a challenging undertaking. Performance standards often differ from district to district and from classroom to classroom. Different educators prefer different levels of achievement specified in the rubrics. Some want rubrics with minimum national standards, whereas others prefer rubrics defining high levels of outstanding performance. State and school district expectations as well as personal preference and professional judgments all factor into the choice of rubrics teachers use and the performance levels students meet. And in the end, students must understand and know how to meet them.

Opportunity-to-Learn Standards

None of the Common Core standards will lift student learning and achievement unless students have sufficient high-quality occasions to study them.

Opportunity-to-learn standards define a set of conditions that schools, districts, and states must meet to ensure that every student has had enough occasions to learn what is needed to meet expectations for his or her performance. Student achievement depends not only on students' abilities but also on whether the student actually attended the class and whether the teacher has taught the subject in class with enough explanation, time, practice, feedback, and support in an appropriate learning environment necessary for students to comprehend and master it.

Opportunity-to-learn standards include the following factors:[30]

- *Content coverage.* The more the assessment matches the information the students actually learned, the more mastery students will show.
- *Content exposure.* The more time spent in learning experiences and the more complete and meaningful the information, the more students will learn.
- *Content emphasis.* The more the focus of teachers closely matches the standards and the assessments, and the more teachers help students develop higher-order thinking skills while using the content, the more students will learn.
- *Quality of instructional delivery.* The more teachers show cognitive understanding of the subject, structure presentations appropriately to students, relate new information to what students already know, monitor students' performance and provide corrective feedback during the lesson, and relate different parts of the lesson to each other, the more students will learn.

For instance, a student with disabilities who is not included in all regular core academic classrooms with appropriate supports may not have chances to learn a rigorous, high-challenge curriculum and the critical reading and thinking skills as a student who has all these classes. Likewise, a student who is frequently absent from school or whose teacher does not follow the school district's curriculum or pacing guide, or whose classroom is constantly disrupted by student outbursts does not have the same opportunities to learn as a classmate with perfect attendance, a teacher who closely follows the district's curriculum guide, and a calm, caring, focused, and orderly classroom environment. Even if the two students had identical academic abilities, the one in the latter class is more likely to master the expected standards. Differences in students' learning experiences can make tremendous differences in whether—and how much—they achieve.

Advocates of opportunity-to-learn standards often include family support, the school environment, and student behavior within their scope. Educators monitor and measure the opportunity-to-learn standards by using teacher logs, observations, and surveys; students' attendance records; and more structured interval testing and small-task assessment.

Regardless of how logical and important opportunity-to-learn standards appear, putting them into practice costs money. They have been the subject of state legislation and court cases dealing with school finance, assessment, and unequal opportunity.[31] Implicitly, all school funding adequacy court cases involve students' opportunity to learn. Ethically, teachers should stay vigilant to ensure that all their students receive ample opportunity to learn if their grades and test scores are to be fair and accurate reflections of their learning and achievement.

Professional Educator Standards

Professional education associations have also developed standards for teachers and other professional school personnel. These professional standards outline what educators should know and be able to do to teach or work as a school library media specialist, school counselor, principal, or other school professional. Prospective educators typically have to demonstrate the knowledge, skills, and dispositions of one or more sets of these standards before they can obtain a license to work in that field.

InTASC standards expect new teachers to appreciate and value human diversity.

iStock/skynesher

Standards may also include statements about the habits of mind or dispositions that teachers should demonstrate in their classrooms. Table 13.2 presents the Interstate New Teacher Assessment and Support Consortium (InTASC) standards for state licensure. These standards expect new teachers to demonstrate the following four dispositions related to Standard #2: Learning Differences: "The teacher uses understanding of individual differences and diverse cultures and communities to ensure inclusive learning environments that enable each learner to meet high standards."[32]

TABLE 13.2 ■ InTASC Standard #2: Teacher Dispositions for Student Learning Differences

InTASC Standard #2: Teacher Dispositions for Student Learning Differences	The teacher believes that all children can learn at high levels and persists in helping each learner reach his/her potential.
	The teacher respects learners as individuals with differing personal and family backgrounds and various skills, abilities, perspectives, talents, and interests.
	The teacher makes learners feel valued and helps them learn to value each other.
	The teacher values diverse languages and dialects and seeks to integrate them into his/her instructional practice to engage students in learning.

Source: Council of Chief State School Officers. (2013, April). *InTASC: Model core teaching standards and learning progressions for teachers 1.0*, p. 17. https://ccsso.org/sites/default/files/2017-12/2013_INTASC_Learning_Progressions_for_Teachers.pdf

Similarly, Table 13.3 presents the six types of InTASC performances to go along with these dispositions:[33]

TABLE 13.3 ■ InTASC Standard #2: Teacher Performances for Student Learning Differences

InTASC Standard #2: Teacher Performances for Student Learning Differences	The teacher designs, adapts, and delivers instruction to address each student's diverse learning strengths and needs and creates opportunities for students to demonstrate their learning in different ways.
	The teacher makes appropriate and timely provisions (e.g., pacing for individual rates of growth task demands, communication, assessment, and response modes) for individual students with particular learning differences or needs.
	The teacher designs instruction to build on learners' prior knowledge and experiences, allowing learners to accelerate as they demonstrate their understandings.
	The teacher brings multiple perspectives to the discussion of content including attention to learners' person, family, and community experiences and cultural norms.
	The teacher incorporates tools of language development into planning and instruction, including strategies for making content accessible to English language learners and for evaluating and supporting their development of English proficiency.
	The teacher accesses resources, supports, and specialized assistance and services to meet particular learning differences or needs.

Source: Council of Chief State School Officers. (2013, April). *InTASC. Model core teaching standards and learning progressions for teachers 1.0*, p. 17. https://ccsso.org/sites/default/files/2017-12/2013_INTASC_Learning_Progressions_for_Teachers.pdf

13.2d Determining Whether Students Have Met the Standards

Performance standards vary. Some specify a minimum level of performance or a range of performances, ranging from "unsatisfactory" to "outstanding." Other standards are expressed as a list of qualities, such as the organization and expression characteristics one would expect from a well-developed essay. Still other standards are stated as numbers, such as saying that a student must read a certain passage within 15 minutes and answer the related questions with 80% accuracy.

Sometimes, educators use "cut scores" to identify the lowest acceptable score that still meets the standard. The **cut score** is a point on the continuum from the lowest possible score to the highest. Those students who fall below the cut score have not been able to demonstrate that they meet the standard.

In short, the cut score separates those who reach the standard from those who do not. Classifying students as meeting the standard is relatively easy when the performance is either extremely high or extremely poor, but identifying passing somewhere in the continuum's middle is more complicated.

Although a cut score may appear to be objective and definitive, it is neither. Deciding where to place the cut score is both an objective (psychometric) problem and a subjective (professional judgment and values) problem. The cut score's location needs to consistently allow educators to distinguish between those students who meet the standard and those who do not. Cut scores may carry a heavy weight for students—determining who graduates or who enters a profession, for example. Those who fall short of the mark do not receive the desired rewards. Furthermore, the procedures used to determine the cut score must withstand painstaking scrutiny because they will be challenged if they appear arbitrary or misplaced.

Other standards are not either–or propositions. Sometimes, there are greater and lesser degrees of competency rather than all-or-nothing performance. A student writer may have creative ideas, authentic "voice," and coherent organization but may show inconsistent spelling and grammar. Even here, however, a point exists that separates those with some proficiency from those who lack it. Determining that precise spot between "just enough" and "not quite enough" is an objective and subjective decision.

As a result, a cut score or a passing score is often an arbitrary and unreliable benchmark. Professional and personal preferences or political philosophies can influence where these points lie on the continuum. Although no agreement exists on the best method for setting defensible standards on competency tests, consensus holds that this activity is technically and politically difficult.

To increase your skills in understanding and using a rubric to assess the quality of student work (in this example, teamwork), complete the activity in the **Reflect & Engage** box, Using Rubrics to Assess Performance.

REFLECT & ENGAGE: USING RUBRICS TO ASSESS PERFORMANCE

This activity involves role play. Performance standards often use rubrics to give students clear information by which to develop and assess their performance tasks. What follows is a rubric for conducting successful group work. Successful teamwork is a 21st century skill.

A. Working in groups of four, review the criteria and points assigned, describe what each behavior might look and sound like (and *not* look or sound like) at the 4-point (*Advanced*) and 1-point (*Beginning*) levels in a group of college undergraduates (possibly future teachers) working collaboratively on an assigned project.

B. Role-play these 4-point and 1-point behaviors in a brief scenario for the entire class.

C. After, as a whole class, discuss the questions that follow.

D. Discuss answers to these questions as a whole group:

TABLE 13.4 ■ Rubric for Cooperative Group Work and Ratings

Skills	4 (4 points) Advanced: Exceeds expectations	3 (3 points) Competent: Meets expectations	2 (2 points) Progressing: Does not fully meet expectations	1 (1 point) Beginning: Does not meet expectations
Contributions, attitudes	Consistently and actively works toward group goals, contributing knowledge, opinions, and skills.	Cooperative. Usually offers useful ideas. Has a positive attitude.	Works toward group goals with occasional prompting. Some useful ideas. Generally positive attitude.	Works toward group goals only when prompted. Rarely offers useful ideas. Is disruptive.

Skills	4 (4 points) Advanced: Exceeds expectations	3 (3 points) Competent: Meets expectations	2 (2 points) Progressing: Does not fully meet expectations	1 (1 point) Beginning: Does not meet expectations
Cooperation with others	Highly productive. Is sensitive to all group members' feelings and learning needs. Helps group identify necessary changes and encourages group action for change.	Cooperative. Accepts and fulfills individual role within the group. Shows sensitivity to others' feelings. Rarely argues.	Could do more of the work. Has difficulty. Requires structure, directions, and leadership. Shows sensitivity to others' feelings. Argues at times.	Contributes to group only when prompted. Does not work well with others. Needs occasional reminders to be sensitive to the feelings of others. Usually argues.
Team role fulfillment	Participates in all group meetings. Assumes leadership role as needed. Does assigned work. Values all group members' knowledge, opinion, and skills and encourages their contribution.	Participates in most group meetings. Contributes knowledge, opinions, and skills without prompting. Provides leadership when asked. Participates in needed changes.	Participates in some group meetings. Provides some leadership. Works toward group goals with occasional prompting. Participates in needed changes with occasional prompting.	Participates in few or no group meetings. Contributes to the group only when prompted. Provides no leadership.
Ability to communicate	Always listens to, shares with, and supports others' efforts. Provides effective feedback. Relays much relevant information.	Usually listens to, shares with, and supports others' efforts. Provides some effective feedback.	Often listens to, shares with, and supports others' efforts. Rarely listens; mostly talks. Provides little feedback. Relays little relevant information to teammates.	Rarely listens, shares with, or supports others' efforts. Always talks; never listens. Provides no feedback. Relays no information to teammates.

Source: Based on Center for Teaching Innovation. (2020). *Example of group work rubric*. Cornell University. https://teaching.cornell.edu/resource/example-group-work-rubric

- Describe the role you usually take in a cooperative group. Which point value would you typically receive?
- How can this rubric help you build your own skills and attitudes toward working cooperatively in small groups?
- Describe the role of teacher leadership and initiative in conducting a successful cooperative group.
- Discuss how a teacher might decide between "just enough" (3 points) and "not quite enough" (2 points) on student performance on this (or any) rubric.
- Discuss what you think are the difficulties in teachers developing and using a clearly expressed rubric to increase quality teaching and learning.

13.2e Why Standards Differ

Educators and policy makers of goodwill may disagree about standards' purposes. Different standards lead to different outcomes. Business leaders want high school graduates with polished reading, writing, math, and interpersonal skills who are ready for work on Day One. Policy makers, for their part, think about the long-term societal and economic needs. They want more demanding academic standards that will ensure a vibrant national economy in which U.S. workers have the complex knowledge and skills to earn high wages and keep the United States meeting world-class benchmarks. Each state's board of education has its own set of academic performance standards for schools to meet.

Parents typically choose standards based on their personal goals, family traditions, and expectations. Some parents expect their children to attend prestigious universities and aim for professional careers in architecture, medicine, law, engineering, or international banking. Others want their children to have employable skills by the time they graduate from high school or learn a respected and well-paying trade after a few years of apprenticeship, community college, technical school, and supervised internships.

School districts must reconcile these differing expectations when they adopt a set of learning standards. Although the process of setting standards is complex, both cognitively and socially, developing clear standards allows the schools' communities to clarify their needs and aspirations. In fact, the standard-setting process can become a community forum for discussing and negotiating what schools should do. Standards provide the criteria by which the locality holds schools, teachers, and students accountable, and they establish tacit performance expectations for teachers' professional growth. Given the transnational mobility of today's workers, a persuasive case can be made for implementing national standards tied to international benchmarks.

AMERICAN EDUCATION SPOTLIGHT: ROBERT J. MARZANO

Formerly a K–12 classroom teacher and then a professor of education, Robert J. Marzano, PhD, has spent over 40 years conducting action research and translating research and theory of teaching and learning into practical classroom strategies that teachers and administrators widely employ to improve teaching and raise student achievement. He asserts that "standards hold the greatest hope for significantly improving student achievement"* by making student learning and performance public education's central focus.

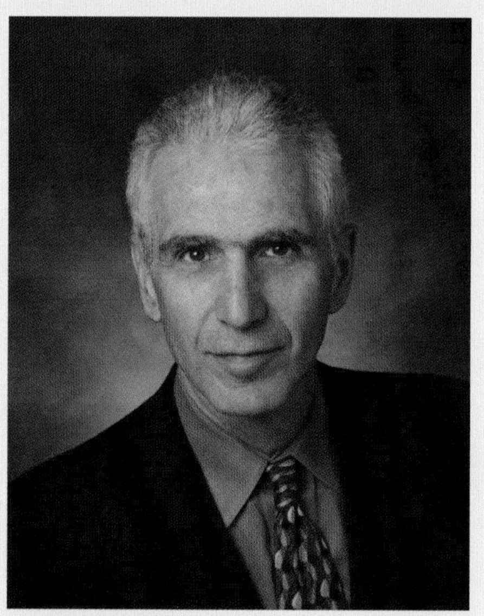

Courtesy of Robert Marzano

Presenting a context for the standards movement, Marzano recounts how *A Nation at Risk's* (1983) implicit and controversial assertion that America education had no academic standards prompted a presidential educational summit and spurred national subject matter organizations, such as the National Council of Teachers of Mathematics, to establish standards in their respective areas. In fact, from 14 "official" standards documents from educational groups, Marzano and his associate John Kendall calculated that if American educators were to teach all the knowledge identified, it would take 22 years (literally). In addition, then-available standards mixed too many dimensions of knowledge or skill in the same standard, making it difficult for teachers to teach or assess. Moreover, then-current standards were aligned neither with the textbooks nor the curriculum. In short, addressing all these standards would mean "curricular chaos."*** In Marzano's view, educators needed a more "judicious" approach to selecting standards to guide their teaching.

Marzano reminds us, "In the case of standards, quantity is not quality."** Successful organizations have a shared sense among its members about what they are trying to accomplish. Agreed-upon goals and ways to reach them strengthen the organization's capacity for rational planning and action. Schools and teachers need these common goals to direct their work. But when it comes to setting education standards, both practicality and understanding the nature of learning suggests that less—if taught well—is more. For instance, in 1999 Marzano and his colleague Mike Schmoker observed that although U.S. mathematics textbooks try to address 175% more topics than do German textbooks and 350% more topics than do Japanese textbooks, both German and Japanese students significantly outperform their U.S. peers in mathematics on international assessments. The same holds true for science textbooks and U.S. students' science performance on international assessments.*** Not only would U.S. students benefit from a more focused content, Marzano observes, but teacher morale and self-efficacy would also improve when they had a more manageable number of essential topics to teach and assess in greater depth.

Marzano supports having shared national education expectations for what children should learn and be able to do at each grade level. He explains that before the Common Core State Standards, each state had its own unique set of standards. What one state expected of students in a specific grade might be higher or lower than what another state expected of its students in the same grade. The fact that every state defined what it considered "proficient" performance complicates student mobility and making national comparisons. Students who moved from state to state could either miss a topic already taught (and not have a chance to learn that content at all) or have to sit through a repetition of something already learned and mastered, unable to move ahead. And "proficient" in one state might actually be considered "basic" in the state next door. Marzano believes that creating a common set of U.S. national standards—that are fewer, clearer, and higher than earlier standards; based on research about what students need to be ready for college and careers after high school; and internationally benchmarked to standards in high-performing countries—could fix many of these issues. Given the public's demand for accountability, Marzano reflects, "standards are here to stay."*

Of course, critics remind us that although standards may be necessary, they are not enough to ensure high student performance. Public schools need to make essential changes if high standards are to become a reality that ensures successful educational practice and improved student outcomes.[34]

An award-winning author of over 50 books (including *Classroom Instruction That Works* with over 1 million copies sold) and 200 articles and book chapters, as well as a developer of curriculum materials, Marzano's ideas are used internationally to improve student achievement and school outcomes.

Notes:

*Scherer, M. (2001, September). How and why standards can improve student achievement: A conversation with Robert J. Marzano. *Educational Leadership, 59*(1), 14–18.

**Marzano, R. J., & Kendall, J. S. (1998). *Awash in a sea of standards*. McREL. https://www.researchgate.net/profile/Robert_Marzano/publication/254675732_AWASH_IN_A_SEA_OF_STANDARDS/links/56f26c0708aee9c94d004303.pdf

***Schmoker, M., & Marzano, R. J. (1999). Realizing the promise of standards-based education. *Educational Leadership, 56*(6), 12–16.

Sources: Nyland, L. (2017). *Robert J. Marzano, Ph.D. Brock Prize Nomination*. https://brockprize.org/wp-content/uploads/2017/08/Marzano1.pdf; Marzano Research. (2019). *Robert J. Marzano*. https://www.marzanoresources.com/robert-j-marzano; Marzano, R. J. (1994). Lessons from the field about outcome-based performance assessments. *Educational Leadership, 51*(6), 44–50; Marzano, R. J., & Kendall, J. S. (1998). *Awash in a sea of standards*. McREL. https://www.researchgate.net/profile/Robert_Marzano/publication/254675732_AWASH_IN_A_SEA_OF_STANDARDS/links/56f26c0708aee9c94d004303.pdf; Marzano, R. J., & Kendall, J. S. (1998). *Implementing stands-based education*. National Education Association. https://files.eric.ed.gov/fulltext/ED430028.pdf; Marzano, R. J., Yanoski, D. C., Hoegh, J. K., Simms, J. A., et al. (2013). *Using common core standards*. Marzano Research Laboratory; Scherer, M. (2001, September). How and why standards can improve student achievement: A conversation with Robert J. Marzano. *Educational Leadership, 59*(1), 14–18; Schmoker, M., & Marzano, R. J. (1999). Realizing the promise of standards-based education. *Educational Leadership, 56*(6), 12–16.

13.3 PRINCIPLES OF SCHOOL ASSESSMENTS AND TEACHERS' PRACTICES

If standards are to have a real effect on schools and student achievement, other school elements must support them. These include an articulated curriculum that spells out what students should learn and be able to do and what teachers should teach. It includes professional development that connects teachers' instructional practices to this curriculum so they can better facilitate student learning.

Lastly, schools need a well-developed assessment process and materials that match the standards and the curriculum so teachers can fairly and accurately monitor and measure how well students are learning the knowledge and skills the standards require (and intervene instructionally when necessary to ensure that slower-learning students meet academic expectations).

13.3a Characteristics of High-Quality Assessments

Both traditional and performance assessments require certain essential technical and ethical components if they are to actually measure what they say they measure and if students and teachers are to think them reasonable. Test developers, educators, parents, and policy makers expect the tests their students take to meet high-quality professional standards for fairness, reliability, validity, controlled environmental conditions, ensured opportunity to learn, and ethical use.

Fairness

Children have an innate sense of fairness. No one wants to play in a game where the rules keep changing and are widely viewed as unreasonable. If the game score does not reflect their efforts or if they receive penalties for events over which they have no control, children wonder if the game is worth the effort. The same holds true for assessments.

Fairness means that everyone understands the rules of the game, the rules are applied consistently to each person, and everyone has the opportunity to play by the same rules. Standardized and performance tests, however, can sometimes be unfair.

A test is not fair when its items are biased. A test that shows provable and systematic differences in people's results based on group membership shows **test bias**. Test bias incorporates both psychometric and sociocultural factors, and both perspectives are necessary to draw a complete picture of test bias.

Psychometrically,[35] a test demonstrates bias when it consistently under- or overpredicts how well someone or some groups will perform. Because it has better predictive validity for some groups than for others, such a test is not valid for certain populations. Typically, this type of test bias places students from low-income families, underrepresented groups, students with disabilities, and English language learners at a serious disadvantage. Standardized tests often ignore the students' life experiences that may result in one group having a psychometric advantage over the others. For example, a student who recently immigrated to the United States from tropical Central America may not be able to write an essay question about a snow day.

Testing is not fair when all students taking it have not had the school learning, family and cultural experiences, or biological equipment needed to help them perform well on this assessment. Any number of factors may work against students having a common experience that would place them on equal footing when taking a standardized test. For instance, an affluent student may have the prior knowledge to identify correctly the analogy between "marathon" and "regatta"[36] on a college entry test as compared with a low-income urban student. Fairness in testing is, indeed, a complex and contentious problem.

Until the 1970s, most standardized tests writers were not so much culture biased as "culture blind."[37] In other words, test developers did not recognize that ways of knowing the world—other than their way—existed. Since then, test publishers have made special efforts to remove these biased depictions and content to avoid offensive, culturally restricted, or stereotyped materials. In fact, documented cases of test bias exist; the legal and financial implications are so important in high-stakes testing that today's test developers carefully screen their tests in a concerted effort to reduce bias and increase validity.[38]

Teachers and administrators must interpret traditional or performance test results within a context that includes the students' culture and the cultural assumptions under which the test was developed. How similar are our students to those in the norm group? Are underrepresented students' scores low because of low test-taking motivation, poor reading ability, frequent absences, or inadequate subject knowledge? Depending on the testing's purpose, the appropriate norms to measure the scores against may be the general norms, subgroup norms based on persons with comparable experiential backgrounds, or the individual student's own previous scores. The more differences between the individual student and the norm group—or the more the group depends on teacher instruction rather than home resources to provide the needed information and skills—the more caution teachers and administrators must use when interpreting the results.

Table 13.5 shows the percentage of test items linked to SES for different school subjects. Language arts, science, and social studies have the highest connection to students' outside school environments and experiences. The higher the percentage of SES items, the more chance for bias because scoring high depends more on what children learn outside school.

TABLE 13.5 ■ Academic Subjects and Socioeconomic Status

Subject	Percentage of SES Items (%)
Reading	15
Language arts	65
Mathematics	5
Science	45
Social studies	45

Source: Popham, W. J. (2001). *The truth about testing: An educator's call to action*. Association for Supervision and Curriculum Development, p. 65.

Validity

The most important question teachers must ask about any assessment is this: Does it really measure what it says it measures? **Validity** is the extent to which a test measures what it is supposed to measure. For instance, a measure of problem-solving ability should reflect how well learners can solve problems, not how accurately or rapidly they can read the question or guess the correct answers. Three important types of validity are face validity, content validity, and concurrent validity.

Face validity is the appearance of validity. This is not a technical aspect but rather a marketing one. For students to take tests seriously, tests need to look like "tests." For instance, a math test does not have face validity unless it includes obvious numbers and math problems.

Content validity focuses on whether the assessment provides an adequate sample or representation of the information that is supposed to be assessed. Although a test can never duplicate every detail of the subject matter, tests usually sample all the important dimensions of the content reasonably well. For instance, if a teacher inadvertently omits a topic, or if the teacher gives a topic either too much or too little emphasis, the assessment may not have enough content validity for that class.

Concurrent validity indicates the consistency or correlation between two independent measures of the same characteristic taken near the same time. Teachers can show an assessment has concurrent validity when the results of a teacher-made vocabulary test agree with the data from a standardized vocabulary test administered within a few days of the first test.

Reliability

To be valid, a test must be reliable; however, reliability does not guarantee validity. A test may produce consistent and repeatable results, yet the results may be meaningless and invalid. Reliability is an important technical aspect of high-quality assessments.

Test reliability is the extent to which a test is repeatable and yields consistent scores obtained by the same persons when retested with the identical test or with an equivalent form. Any single observation of a person gives only a rough estimate of the person's typical ability. If a child is shown to have an IQ of 110 when tested on Monday and an IQ of 80 when retested on Thursday, little confidence can be placed on either score. Likewise, if a student identifies 40 of 50 words correctly in one set of words but identifies only 20 words correctly on an equivalent set, neither score can be taken as a dependable index of the student's verbal comprehension; after all, both scores cannot be right. Conversely, high scoring reliability occurs when multiple scorings yield the same or very similar results.

Controlling Environmental Conditions

A test score is subject to many unwanted, irrelevant influences. Test scores may vary from one measurement to another for a variety of reasons—the student's attention or effort changes, the student is hungry or cold, the room is quiet or noisy. Likewise, test items may be more or less difficult for the student. For this reason, teachers need to ensure that every testing situation in their classrooms maintains the appropriate conditions that allow all students to do their best.

Every test imposes certain **environmental limitations**, the specific conditions under which the test must be administered. Instructors' manuals for standardized tests give clear directions to test administrators about these conditions. These constraints include how much time students have to complete the test or product, whether they work independently, and whether they can use calculators, smartphones, iPads, dictionaries, or math formula sheets. Can students stand up and stretch when they get tired? Can they walk around the room? Can they eat or drink while testing? Accordingly, regardless of the test location, all students are taking it under identical conditions if their scores are to be meaningful. These are the same conditions under which the test's norm group took the test, making a comparison to a norm group possible. Teachers and students need to know the limitations under which pupils will be assessed, and they must know this information ahead of time because it will affect their planning and test-taking behaviors.

The testing conditions affect students' results. A noisy, distracting classroom that is too hot or too cold can negatively influence students' thinking and final scores. Although some environmental conditions cannot be controlled, teachers can usually neutralize or reduce such factors as room temperature, noise, and visual stimuli (e.g., exciting posters or wall-mounted study guides) that might interfere—positively or negatively—with learners' performance.

Test length is an important assessment limitation. Brief assessments cannot provide a complete picture of student performance, but the amount of time available for testing is always finite. This is especially true for testing younger students. A tension always exists between the number of test items needed for greater assessment precision, the students' maturity, and the information that educators want to know. Additionally, imposing shorter time limits can reduce the test's reliability. Brief tests may be measuring how fast students produce the correct answers rather than how well the students understand the concepts supporting the questions that they might be able to answer correctly when they have enough testing time. In classroom testing, teachers want students to be able to show what they know without unduly worrying about "pencils down." Unless the test is deliberately looking to measure speed of response, student knowledge and capacity, not quickness, should be the focus.

Opportunity to Learn

As discussed with standards, high-quality assessments can be fair, valid, and reliable only when all students taking them have had the opportunities to learn the content being tested. Opportunity to learn is the single most powerful predictor of student achievement.[39] One cannot expect students to know what they have not been taught. This factor is not so much a technical aspect of the assessment instrument but rather a reflection of the students' school, classroom, and home experiences. As a principle of high-quality assessments, it bears repeating.

Students have not had an adequate opportunity to learn if they have not received the allotted time for instruction needed for them to master the subject matter at the level of depth necessary, if they have not received the appropriate content emphasis, or if they have not been given occasions to use higher-level thinking skills with the content. Further, unless teachers' instructional practices help students relate the new information to their prior knowledge, receive ongoing corrective feedback during the lessons, and have the lessons' parts related to other parts, the students will not have the opportunities to correctly answer the assessment questions or produce a meaningful, high-quality product or performance that meets the standard. Also, unless the school consistently provided an orderly and academically focused learning environment, students will have been denied the opportunity to learn.

Teachers must seriously consider all of these factors when they interpret their students' test scores. Issues of fairness, validity, reliability, environmental factors, and opportunities to learn all play key roles in determining students' learning and their performance on assessments. No matter how well regarded the assessment instrument, other variables can confound and weaken the meaning of students' test results. Until these issues can be successfully resolved, teachers need to exercise caution in using these data to make key and ethical decisions about individual students.

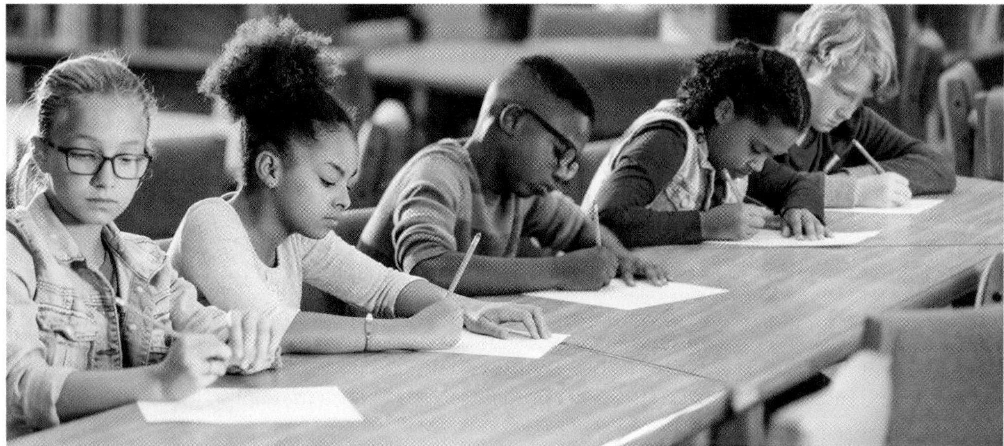

Technically and ethically appropriate assessments must be fair, valid, and reliable.
iStock/kali9

Using Tests Ethically

More than 40 years ago, Donald T. Campbell, a noted social psychologist, warned about the perils of measuring effectiveness with a single, highly important indicator. "The more any quantitative social indicator is used for social decision-making," he noted, "the more subject it will be to corruption pressures and the more apt it will be to distort and corrupt the social processes it is intended to monitor."[40] Simply put, when a measure becomes a target, it stops being a good metric. It means we must put a lot of thought into how we use these assessment measures.

Important judgments about students, teachers, and school effectiveness should not be based on a single test score. Overvaluing test scores for making important decisions promotes tests' misuse and often compromises the test scores' validity. Dozens of assessment experts have argued that high-stakes tests are psychometrically inadequate for the critical decisions that must be made about individual students, teachers, and schools. Although standardized and classroom assessments offer many advantages in gauging students' academic progress, educators must employ informed caution and judgment in using these test scores.

To determine the quality of the assessments you take at your college or university, complete the activity in the **Reflect & Engage** box, Assessing Your Assessments.

REFLECT & ENGAGE: ASSESSING YOUR ASSESSMENTS

This activity involves creating wordles (word clouds) and mind maps. High-quality assessments are fair, valid, and reliable; administered under appropriate environmental conditions; ensure that all students have had the necessary opportunity to learn; and are used ethically. How would you as a college student determine if the assessments you take in your classes have these six important qualities?

A. Working in pairs, create a wordle using a digital tool such as Vizzlo that describes a time when you had to take an important test that you did not think was fair, valid, or reliable; not administered under proper conditions; whose content you did not have an adequate opportunity to learn; or whose results were used unethically. Also consider the subject or skill that was supposed to be tested and how you felt while taking the test. How did the situation affect your scores? How were the test results used?

B. Class members will share their wordles.

C. As a class, discuss how you might determine whether an important test you had to take had fairness (lack of bias), validity, and reliability; was administered under appropriate conditions; had content or skills that you had the opportunity to learn, and was ethically used. What would you do if you believed—and could document—that these essential factors were *not* present?

D. Working in pairs, create a mind map using a digital tool such as Bubbl for five teacher behaviors that enhance and five teacher behaviors that jeopardize the fairness, validity, reliability, environmental conditions, opportunity to learn, or ethical use of classroom assessments.

E. Discuss your mind maps as a class and discuss the impact that teachers can have on the accuracy and meaningfulness of their classroom or standardized assessments.

13.3b The Cases for and Against Standardized Testing

A staple of school accountability, standardized, norm-referenced tests are an efficient and cost-effective way to assess large numbers of people from different backgrounds and learning experiences. All teachers are likely to use standardized tests as part of their schools' efforts to monitor and assess students' progress. Yet critics openly challenge these tests for a variety of reasons. Arguments both for and against standardized testing, as presented in the **FlipSides** table, deserve closer looks.

FLIPSIDES

The Cases for and Against Standardized Testing

Despite their efficiency and popularity, many argue against using standardized tests for accountability and high-stakes decisions. Some argue that the way educators use these tests actually harms student learning. Consider these differing views and then see where you stand.

Standardized tests should anchor student assessment and school accountability.	Standardized tests should not anchor student assessment and school accountability.
Efficiency	**Efficiency**
• Standardized tests are convenient, take less time to administer and score, are less expensive than other types of assessments for large numbers of students, and results are quickly available for informed decision-making.	• Efficiency is important but does not outweigh an assessment's capacity to produce accurate and meaningful results that show students' specific areas of mastery, high levels of reasoning and problem-solving, and use of the knowledge and skills in complex, well-designed performances.
Norm groups	**Norm groups**
• Comparing students against a norm group permits teachers and parents to judge how well their students are performing relative to students in other localities, states, and internationally. • Every student responds to the same questions without regard for opportunity to learn.	• Many underrepresented and low-income children are not similar to the tests' norming group in gender, ethnicity, social, or economic characteristics. When test bias exists, results are less valid for these students. • Children from affluent and middle-class families are more likely to answer certain test items correctly than children from low-income families.[41]
Generate a range of scores	**Generate a range of scores**
• Norm-referenced tests determine a student's relative standing as compared with other test takers. Teachers assume that some students will perform well, and others will not.	• Criterion-referenced tests and other performance measures assume that every child can learn to grade-level standards. Teachers expect to teach (and ensure) that every child can meet the criteria.

Standardized tests should anchor student assessment and school accountability.	Standardized tests should not anchor student assessment and school accountability.
Validity and reliability	**Validity and reliability**
• Educators can select those tests with sufficiently high levels of validity and reliability to justify their use for certain purposes.	• All assessments contain some bias and measurement error and may not be appropriate for making high-stakes decisions about individuals.
Curriculum scope	**Curriculum scope**
• Standardized tests measure broad characteristics such as verbal or math achievement and critical thinking that are not unduly sensitive to minor curriculum and experience differences.	• Curriculum narrowing occurs when teachers overly focus on raising their students' standardized test scores in certain subjects and they neglect to teach the nontested subjects.
Real-world applicability	**Real-world applicability**
• Many standardized tests focus on relatively low-level cognition skills of recognition, recall, and application and have one right answer.	• Standardized tests lack occasions for real intellectual work to produce novel solutions to actual problems, show disciplined inquiry, or have value beyond the classroom.
Data for high-stakes decisions	**Data for high-stakes decisions**
• Standardized tests are a central component of high-stakes decisions about students and, increasingly, about teachers and principals.	• No standardized test is accurate, valid, or reliable enough to be the basis for making high-stakes decisions about students' futures or for teacher or principal evaluation and compensation.

Although standardized assessments bring many advantages, educators must use their results cautiously. Given both sides of the argument, what is your opinion about the central role of standardized tests in individual and school assessment and accountability?

Ironically, overuse and misuse of standardized tests can actually undermine real education. "Teaching to the test," curriculum narrowing, and spending time in "test prep" practice not only affect what academic content teachers present but also influence the intellectual level of what they teach. To create space for "test prep," they limit the amount of time invested in having learning make sense and have personal meaning for students, and they shortchange the opportunities for students to have real-world application of what they are learning. In addition, the "test-prep" focus reduces the positive teacher–student interactions around regular classroom content that build strong and caring relationships.

The result is a seriously diminished education. This is especially true for high-performing students in low-performing schools who may lose ground academically, even as they earn top grades and score highly on standardized tests. As teachers emphasize helping the large number of low achievers or students in the middle meet the standard, the high achievers receive less attention. In turn, they continue to fall further behind their high-achieving peers in affluent public and private high schools where the primary goal remains on challenging bright students to higher achievement.[42]

Superior and Inferior Schools

It is natural—but incorrect and unfair—for people to assume that schools whose students have high test scores are superior to schools whose students have low test scores. A "failing" school's staff may actually be doing an outstanding instructional job, but their efforts may not be reflected by their students' scores on a high-stakes achievement test. Students' scores may increase, but not enough to meet the cutoff mark or standard. If the school's students came from traditionally underserved families, they may have started out far behind the norm group and actually make notable achievement gains during the year. Simply because their test results did not compare favorably with their more affluent peers does not mean the school, teachers, or students are "failing."

Likewise, identifying schools and teachers as successful simply because their students score well on standardized achievement tests is equally unfair and inaccurate. Much of what high-stakes tests measure is directly attributable not to what students learn in school, but to what they bring to school: their families' resources, their varied experiences and opportunities to learn outside school, or their inherited and home-nurtured academic aptitudes. Their high test scores do not prove that their school was effective. Until accountability systems include metrics that accurately reflect the contributions of those being judged, such as measuring how much progress a school's students make during the school year, and until assessments use statistical methods that account for the disadvantages (or advantages) that students may bring to school because of the quality of their prior instruction or their family learning opportunities, judgments about "superior" or "inferior" schools can be neither fair nor accurate.[43]

"Today's high-stakes tests often mask the actual quality of instruction in schools serving both low-income and high-income families,"[44] says educational assessment expert W. James Popham. This misidentification of schools leads to questionable recommendations for professional development. Skillful teachers in "failing" schools are told to change their instructional practices—even though their instruction may be highly effective. By comparison, weak teachers in high-scoring schools may allow themselves to be carried along with the elevated esteem of working in a "good school" when, in fact, they should be significantly improving how they teach.

13.4 ACCOUNTABILITY FOR EDUCATIONAL OUTCOMES

Traditional accountability systems use test scores as the primary indicator of educational quality. Educators and parents view these end-of-year test scores as the "results" or evidence of their students' learning. Not only is this perspective shortsighted and misleading, but recently, it has become controversial.

Some argue that the overuse (and misuse) of standardized testing is harming public education.[45] The "opting out" movement encourages parents, students, and teachers to refuse to allow their children to take standardized tests in order to protest the "educational malpractice" of a narrowed curriculum, wasted instructional time on "test prep," and the false narrative of "failing" schools in low-income communities. For instance, although in 2016 roughly 21% of eligible students in New York state Grades 3 through 8 "opted out" of taking federally mandated standardized tests,[46] most states have laws that ban this practice, considering it an act of civil disobedience, with a range of penalties for students who do.

Others contend that standardized tests help identify (and remediate) educational achievement gaps between affluent children and their peers in other neighborhoods, cities, or states. If our society believes that everyone is entitled to a meaningful education, then schools should work to ensure every child's academic success, even those living in low-income zip codes. According to this view, beyond demonstrating students' proficiency, testing is about equity—identifying the students who are not receiving the help they need and then getting them the resources they need to reach these educational outcomes. Viewing assessments as a way to ensure educational equity will benefit all families in ways that "will close the broader achievement gaps."[47]

Given these divergent views on the merits of standardized testing, what do we mean by "educational accountability," and what role do test scores play in it?

13.4a Accountability and Test Scores

Accountable means "to hold answerable for, to act in a creditable manner; and capable of being explained."[48] When a person is accountable, he or she is responsible for his or her actions and is obliged to explain and justify them. But does achievement testing as presently viewed and organized in public schools truly demonstrate accountability to parents, community members, and other stakeholders?

Educational accountability is "the process[es] by which school districts and states attempt to ensure that schools systems meet their goals."[49] Greater accountability is assumed to generate better alignment between public goals and the schools' intended purposes and improved student outcomes, typically defined by traditional achievement criteria.[50] Most Americans believe that schools and teachers must be held "accountable" for both taxpayer dollars and students' results. Tests—as a proxy for student learning—are an important way to determine this.

Although accountability includes academic assessment, accountability is much broader in scope. Education has numerous goals, many of which are not easily measured. Of course, our publics care about students' proficiency and graduation rates. But for our students to flourish as adults who make good judgments about key life decisions, who as citizens are active and informed voters, who as neighbors and coworkers treat others with respect, and who can compete successfully in the job market, our young people need to develop capacities that go well beyond what standardized tests can measure.

Considering test scores as education's "bottom line" is akin to the business model in which stock prices and reported earnings masquerade as quality indicators. In this view, critical factors such as accounting irregularities, deteriorating facilities, and restated earnings are "minor inconveniences." For instance, when Lehman Brothers, a Wall Street financial services firm and the fourth-largest investment bank in the world, collapsed and filed for Chapter 11 bankruptcy protection in 2008 as a result of its exposure to the subprime mortgage crisis, it threatened to take down the global financial system. Its failure eroded the trust needed among banks to fuel lending. It caused 26,000 employees to lose their jobs, caused millions of investors to lose all or almost all of their money, and began a chain reaction that produced the worst American financial crisis and economic downturn since the Great Depression. The proverbial "bottom line" had been an illusion. Lehmann executives had manipulated the balance sheets and falsified financial reports. The focus on corporate short-term windfalls had diverted attention from clear warning signs of larger, systemic problems.

In the same way, exclusive emphasis on test scores in educational accountability does not give a full and accurate picture of how well students are achieving or how well schools are performing. What is more, they offer no guidance about how to improve the performance of all players in the system.

Clearly, effective educational accountability systems extend well beyond test scores. Teachers' jobs are more complex than what a single test can measure. **Effective accountability systems** are comprehensive, containing multiple measures of student achievement. Students' poor or excellent school achievement never has only one single cause.

13.4b "Holistic" or Student-Centered Accountability

As compared with traditional educational accountability, **"holistic"** or **"student-centered" accountability** balances both quantitative and qualitative indicators: It presents the story behind the numbers. It considers individual students' progress by placing traditional test scores into a context that makes the data meaningful. Low or high scores tell us little if we do not know, for example, the type of curriculum the student studied; the teacher's expertise in the subject taught, the classroom experience, and instructional practices; the school's discipline climate; and the student's attendance in school during the year.[51]

Holistic accountability includes a variety of background factors that contribute to educational excellence[52] and make school accountability a shared responsibility:

- *Teaching practices,* including assessment, feedback, and collaboration
- *Curriculum practices,* including equity of opportunity for enrolling in advanced classes and academic supports to help students succeed once enrolled
- *Leadership practices,* including the use of resources to sustain the most important educational priorities (considering what teachers, administrators, school board members, and what other policy makers do)
- *Parent involvement,* including monitoring students' study at home and participating in relevant volunteer school and community activities
- *Faculty communication,* including intergrade and interdepartmental collaboration

- *Professional development,* including study of research, pedagogy, assessment, and content areas and adopting best practices in each for classroom and school use
- *Funding adequacy,* including schools receiving the needed and adequate resources to help each student achieve high levels of proficiency in his or her educational program

Holistic accountability is more motivating for teachers than other types of accountability. Teachers see holistic accountability as fair and significant because it includes indicators that they can directly manage or influence. They have a sense of control over the day-to-day learning they design for their students. When teachers know their success as educators will be judged based on a range of a student's learning activities and performances rather than on a single high-stakes test score, they feel less anxiety, stress, and resentment than if their entire year's worth of success depended on how well each student scored on one 3-hour test.

Likewise, holistic accountability motivates students because it gives them more ways to succeed. They have more occasions and formats in which to show what they have learned and can do. They can receive constructive feedback throughout the learning process and make continuous improvements. In addition, students often have occasions to choose their own topics, work partners, or performance methods to show what they have learned. Throughout the school year, they know where they stand relative to the standard, and they know exactly what they must do to successfully reach it. Because they exert more control over their own learning and academic fate, students are more committed to learning.

Holistic accountability is comprehensive, showing the importance not only of teacher effectiveness but also curriculum, principal leadership, parent involvement, student mobility, and other factors that traditional accountability practices ignore or obscure. All of these factors work together to build positive student outcomes.

Finally, holistic accountability extends the value of traditional accountability. It targets improving teaching and learning rather than merely providing an educational evaluation and a public report card. It recognizes that the purpose of student assessment is to improve student—and teacher—performance. We assess so we will know how to teach better and how to learn better. Poor performance on an appraisal inspires an improvement process rather than blame and humiliation. In this way, the assessment results spur the search to find the underlying causes of poor achievement and develop specific improvement strategies.

Every teacher should strive to help each student succeed. Student success motivates students and teachers alike—after all, everyone wants to feel competent and empowered with new skills, information, and insights. When teachers and students can engage in continuous improvement, the accountability system is oriented toward achieving constructive ends rather than making judgments about failure.

Holistic accountability includes a variety of background factors that contribute to excellent education.

Enigma/Alamy Stock Photo

13.4c Goals of Education and Accountability

Educational goals are broader than just generating high reading and math scores. Although these subjects are critical disciplines that underpin most learning and work in our complex world, shrinking the curriculum to these two areas actually increases the educational inequities that the accountability system is designed to remove.

Most school board members and state legislators think bigger. They say they want American students to learn critical thinking, social skills, citizenship and responsibility, physical and emotional health, preparation for skilled work, and appreciation for the arts and literature.[53] To them, these are the essentials of a high-quality education necessary for continued learning, good citizenship, interpersonal skills, esthetic appreciation, and economic self-sufficiency in a highly complex, information-rich world.

When schools receive sanctions based solely on their students' reading, math, or other single-subject scores, the accountability system inadvertently creates incentives to limit—or in some cases, to entirely end—time spent on other desirable parts of the curriculum. Skewing the curriculum toward reading, math, and "test prep" activities disproportionately affects low-income and underrepresented children, who need the most time and help becoming "proficient" in these test-directed areas. Instead of helping low-achieving students score well on the assessment, basing decisions about their academic growth solely on their standardized test scores may actually encourage practices that widen the achievement and opportunity gaps in areas that matter in life outside school but for which schools are not now being held accountable.

In fact, American schools should be held accountable for their results. Our students, our economy, and our national security depend on all students learning to high and measurable levels the knowledge, skills, and habits of mind necessary for 21st century viability. Nevertheless, when reviewing these broader goals, it is clear that basing school accountability only on student proficiency in reading and math is neither holistic nor in the best interests of the students and society.

An effective assessment program supports teaching and learning. True accountability weighs both quantitative and qualitative indicators, thereby delivering a fuller view of student learning. And our assessments must reflect what we value. If we value having every student learning to high standards, we must harness assessments for learning along with assessments of learning. These data can help us improve teaching and learning only when we learn how to use them—and the sources from which they come—wisely.

For a more complete understanding of the differences between "traditional" and "holistic" assessments for accountability, complete the activity in the **Reflect & Engage** box, Educational Accountability.

REFLECT & ENGAGE: EDUCATIONAL ACCOUNTABILITY

This activity involves creating a graphic image using a digital tool such as Piktochart or newsprint, pictures, words, shapes, and colors. Viewing end-of year test scores as evidence of school accountability for student learning is shortsighted and misleading. By comparison, "holistic" or student-centered accountability balances both quantitative and qualitative indicators: It presents the story behind the numbers.

A. Working in pairs, review the factors that comprise holistic accountability and identify what these elements might *look like*—discuss what teachers, principals, students, and parents would be doing and saying in schools.

B. Each pair will create a graphic image that compares and contrasts "traditional educational accountability" with "holistic accountability."

C. After each pair has completed its graphic image, each pair will present and explain its product to the rest of the class.

D. The class will discuss how holistic accountability would be more motivating to teachers and students than traditional school assessment.

E. The class will discuss the challenges that schools would have to overcome to make holistic accountability a reality.

KEY TAKE-AWAYS

Learning Objective 13.1 Compare and contrast the factors that contribute to an incomplete versus a comprehensive educational assessment of teaching and learning.

- Accountability is a shared responsibility.
- An accountability system that contains test scores alone is incomplete. Teachers can know if they or their schools are succeeding or failing only if they have access to multiple sources of data—quantitative and qualitative—gathered over an extended period and then apply professional judgment to determine what it means.
- Assessment is the first step in a continual learning cycle whose purpose is to combine data with professional judgment and relevant actions to foster improvement. A well-designed assessment gives both teacher and student quality feedback about how well the student is mastering the assigned curriculum.
- Assessment in schools has several purposes, including making placement decisions, determining how well students attain curricular and instructional goals, and diagnosing student learning needs.
- Effective teachers learn how to balance assessment *for* and *of* learning. Formative assessments help them understand each student as a learner on a daily basis and make the necessary adaptations to support learning every day. And they partner summative assessments with the other available student learning data to fairly and equitably support—not merely evaluate—student learning.

Learning Objective 13.2 Critique how educational standards contribute to student achievement, school accountability, and teachers' professional growth.

- Setting academic standards, teaching to the standards, and assessing the extent to which each student meets the standards provides the basis for public school achievement and accountability. These three elements must align if the system is to be fair.
- Academic standards define what *every* student should know and be able to do by the course's end. Because no student is expected to perform "below average," teachers' responsibilities include investing extra time and using varied instructional and support practices with the lower achievers so that they, too, reach the standard.
- World-class standards, real-world standards, content standards, performance standards, and opportunity-to-learn standards all define different expectations for achievement.
- Professional education associations have also developed standards for teachers and other professional school personnel. Interstate New Teacher Assessment and Support Consortium (InTASC) standards for state licensure include statements about the essential knowledge, habits of mind or critical dispositions, and performances for teachers.
- The Common Core State Standards reflect the shared desire among educators, experts, parents, and policy makers across the nation to voluntarily adopt the highest academic criteria benchmarked to those in the highest-achieving countries. Each state sets its own content standards and uses these to write curricula. Seven years after their adoption, research finds positive changes in both teachers' instructional practices and student learning.

Learning Objective 13.3 Determine how the six principles of high-quality assessments should influence teachers' ethical practices to advance student learning.

- Both traditional and performance assessments require certain essential technical and ethical components if they are to actually, accurately, consistently, and meaningfully measure what they say they measure: fairness, reliability, validity, controlled environmental limitations, ensured opportunity to learn, and ethical use.

- Teachers and administrators must interpret traditional or performance test results within a context that includes the students' culture and the cultural assumptions under which the test was developed.
- Important judgments about students, teachers, and school effectiveness should not be based on a single test score. Dozens of assessment experts have argued that high-stakes tests are psychometrically inadequate for the critical decisions that must be made about individual students, teachers, and schools.
- Standardized tests have both advantages and disadvantages in advancing and assessing student learning.
- Much of what high-stakes tests measure is directly attributable *not* to what students learn in school, but to what they bring to school: their families' resources, their varied experiences and opportunities to learn outside school, or their inherited and home-nurtured academic aptitudes. Until accountability systems include metrics that accurately reflect the contributions of those being judged, conclusions about "superior" or "inferior" schools can be neither fair nor accurate.

Learning Objective 13.4 Argue how accountability for educational outcomes means more than students' achievement test scores.

- Most American believe that schools and teachers must be held "accountable" for both taxpayer dollars and student outcomes, and tests are an important way to determine this. But education has numerous goals, many of which are not easily measured.
- Exclusive emphasis on test scores in educational accountability does not give a full and accurate picture of how well students are achieving or how well schools are performing. Nor do they offer guidance about how to improve the performance of all players in the system.
- Effective accountability systems are comprehensive, containing multiple measures of student achievement. Students' poor or excellent school achievement never has only one single cause.
- Holistic accountability is comprehensive. It includes academic achievement scores and specific information on curriculum, teaching and leadership practices, and funding adequacy. It weighs both quantitative and qualitative indicators, thereby delivering a fuller view of student learning. Our challenge is to find a workable balance between objectively and subjectively measured assessments for more comprehensive and valued educational ends.
- An effective assessment program supports teaching and learning. Such comprehensive assessment results spur the search to find the underlying causes of poor achievement and develop specific improvement strategies for a cycle of continuous improvement.

TEACHER SCENARIO: IT'S YOUR TURN

Sally Smith was the new eighth-grade science teacher at De Sade Middle School. Every Friday, she gave a rigorous five-question quiz to her students and recorded the letter grade from the percentage correct on the quiz. She said the quizzes gave her formative feedback on how the students were progressing. The weekly quiz counted for 50% of the marking period. She gave a unit test each month that counted 25% for the marking period. The remainder of the marking period grade comprised participation and a project.

At the end of the first marking period, more than half of Sally's students had a grade of D or F, while students in the other eighth-grade science classes had much higher grades. In fact, none of the other students had a grade of F, and 85% of the other students had a grade of C or higher. The school phones lit up with parent complaints.

1. Explain how Sally was using formative assessment incorrectly.
2. Explain how Sally's five-question quiz format lowered students' grades.
3. What do you think the principal should do? Why?

NOTES

1. Chingos, M. M. (2012, November 29). Strength in numbers: States spending on K–12 assessment systems. *Brookings*. https://www.brookings.edu/research/strength-in-numbers-state-spending-on-k-12-assessment-systems/; Ujifusa, A. (2012, November 29). Standardized testing cost states $1.7 billion a year, study says. *Education Week, 32*(13). https://www.edweek.org/ew/articles/2012/11/29/13testcosts.h32.html?tkn=VLMFJUQpeyvKkTzwuCHPd%2FuQG%2BPWLRrD1lNp&cmp=clp-edweek
2. Halverson, R. (2010). School formative feedback systems. Section 1: Mapping the terrain of interim assessments. *Peabody Journal of Education, 85*(2), 130–146; Black, P., & Wiliam, D. (1998a, October). Inside the black box: Raising standards through classroom assessment. *Phi Delta Kappan, 80*(2), 141–151.
3. Black & Wiliam, 1998a; Lipnevich, A. A., & Smith, J. K. (2009). "I really need feedback to learn:" Students' perspectives on the effectiveness of the differential feedback messages. *Education Assessment, Evaluation, and Accountability, 21*(4), 347–367.
4. Bloom, B. S. (1984, May). The search for methods of group instruction as effective as one-to-one tutoring. *Educational Leadership, 41*(4), 4–17; Black, P., & Wiliam, D. (1998b, March). Assessment and classroom learning. *Educational Assessment: Principles, Policy, and Practice, 5*(1), 7–74; Meisels, S., Atkins-Burnett, S., Xue, Y., Bickel, D. D., & Son, S.-H. (2003). Creating a system of accountability: The impact of instructional assessment on elementary children's achievement scores. *Educational Policy Analysis Archives, 11*(9). https://epaa.asu.edu/ojs/article/viewFile/237/363
5. Danielson, C. (2007). *Enhancing professional practice: A framework for teaching* (2nd ed.). Association for Supervision and Curriculum Development; Danielson, C. (2002). *Enhancing student achievement: A framework for school improvement.* Association for Supervision and Curriculum Development; Pitt, E., Berman, M., & Esterhazy, R. (2020). *Assessment & Evaluation in Higher Education, 45*(2), 239–250.
6. Bravmann, S. L. (2004, March 17). Assessment's "fab four": They work together, not solo. *Education Week, 23*(27), 56.
7. Kohn, A. 2000. *The case against standardized testing: Raising the scores, ruining the schools.* Heinemann; Schmoker, M. 2000. The results we want. *Educational Leadership, 57*(5), 62–65.
8. Madeus, G. F. (1991, November). The effects of important tests on students: Implications for a national examination system. *Phi Delta Kappan, 73*(3), 226–231; Shepard, L. A. (1991, November). Will national tests improve student learning? *Phi Delta Kappan, 73*(3), 233–238; Shepard, L. A. (2000, October). The role of assessment in a learning culture. *Educational Researcher, 29*(7), 4–14.
9. Marzano, R. J., Pickering, D., & McTighe, J. (1993). *Assessing student outcomes: Performance assessment using the Dimensions of Learning model.* Association for Supervision and Curriculum Development.
10. Fisher, C. W., Filby, N., Marliave, R. S., Cahen, L. S., Dishaw, M. M., Moore, J. E., & Berliner, D. C. (1978). *Teaching behaviors, academic learning time and student achievement.* Far West Laboratory of Educational Research and Development.
11. The actual range was from 5,749 to 9,965 minutes.
12. Berliner, D. C. (1979). Tempus educare. In P. L. Peterson & H. J. Walberg (Eds.), *Research on teaching* (pp. 120–135). McCutchan.
13. Reeves, D. B. (2004). *Accountability for learning: How teachers and school leaders can take charge.* Association for Supervision and Curriculum Development, pp. 106–113; Reeves, D. B. (2000). *Accountability in action: A blueprint for learning organizations.* Center for Performance Assessment, pp. 179–183.
14. Keillor, G. (2000, December). *National Geographic*: In search of Lake Wobegon. Originally published in *National Geographic* (2000, December). http://www.garrisonkeillor.com/national-geographic-in-search-of-lake-wobegon/
15. The *J* curve offers another way of looking at students' score distributions. In education, the classic bell curve represents the distribution of grades that occurs when small proportions of students get very low and very high marks and most students get average marks. A *J*-curve distribution implies that most students can occupy the rising part of the "J," which means most students can successfully learn and earn above-average marks. See Stewart, D. T. (2006). *The J curve: A new way of understanding why nations rise and fall.* Simon and Schuster.
16. St. John, A. (2019, January 15). What went right: Revisiting Captain "Sully" Sullenberger and the miracle on the Hudson. *Popular Mechanics.* https://www.popularmechanics.com/flight/a4137/sully-sullenberger-us-air-flight-1549-miracle-hudson/

17. Shaw, R. (2014, April 14). The tracking controversy: Practical ethics catalog—Practicing educators reflect on professional concerns. *Newfoundations.com*. https://www.newfoundations.com/PracEthics/Shaw.html

18. Merrow, J. (2001, May). Undermining standards. *Phi Delta Kappan, 82*(9), 659.

19. ASCD. (2020). *Common core standards adoption by state*. http://www.ascd.org/common-core-state-standards/common-core-state-standards-adoption-map.aspx

20. For an in-depth look at content standards, topics, and benchmarks, see Mid-continent Research for Education and Learning (McREL). (2020). *Content knowledge standards*. http://www.corestandards.org.

21. National Governors Association and the Council of Chief State School Officers. (2020). *Common core state standards for English language arts & literacy in history/social studies, science, and technology* (p. 6). http://www.corestandards.org/assets/Appendix_A.pdf

22. Kendall, J. S., & Marzano, R. J. (2000). *Content knowledge: A compendium of standards and benchmarks for K–12 education* (3rd ed.). Association for Supervision and Curriculum Development.

23. Marzano, R. J., Kendall, J. A., & Gaddy, B. B. (1999). *Essential knowledge: The debate over what American students should know*. Mid-continent Regional Educational Laboratory.

24. Marzano, R. J. (2003). *What works in schools: Translating research into action*. Association for Supervision and Curriculum Development, pp. 24–25.

25. Gordon, R. (2006, March 15). The federalism debate: Why the idea of national education standards is crossing party lines. *Education Week, 25*(27), 35, 48.

26. Kane, T. J., Owens, A. M., Marinell, W. H., Thal, D. R. C., & Staiger, D. O. (2016). *Teaching higher: Educators' perspectives on common core implementation*. https://pdfs.semanticscholar.org/fb6f/e6b4e4c64b2fdd4d0e1d925cea34a35f793a.pdf; Bay-Williams, J., Duffett, A., & Griffith, D. (2016). *Common core math in the K–8 classroom: Results from a national teacher survey*. Thomas B. Fordham Institute. https://files.eric.ed.gov/fulltext/ED570138.pdf

27. Scholastic & the Bill & Melinda Gates Foundation. (2014). *Teachers' views on the common core state standards one year later*. http://www.scholastic.com/primarysources/PrimarySources-2014update.pdf; Bay-Williams et al., 2016.

28. Barnum, M. (2019, April 29). Nearly a decade later, did the common core work? New research offers clues. *Chalkbeat*. https://chalkbeat.org/posts/us/2019/04/29/common-core-work-research/; Pondiscio, R., & Mahnken, K. (2014, November 12). *Responding to critics of common core math in the elementary grades*. Thomas Fordham Institute. https://fordhaminstitute.org/national/commentary/responding-critics-common-core-math-elementary-grades

29. McCardle, E. (2014, Fall). What happened to the common core? *Ed. Harvard Ed. Magazine*. Harvard Graduate School of Education. https://www.gse.harvard.edu/news/ed/14/09/what-happened-common-core

30. Stevens, F. I. (1996). Closing the achievement gap: Opportunity to learn, standards, and assessment. In B. Williams (Ed.), *Closing the achievement gap: A vision for changing beliefs and practices* (pp. 77–95). Association for Supervision and Curriculum Development.

31. Stanford Equality of Opportunity and Education. (2020). *Landmark US cases related to equality of opportunity in K–12 education. Section 4: Lawsuits*. https://edeq.stanford.edu/sections/landmark-us-cases-related-equality-opportunity-education

32. Council of Chief State School Officers. (2013, April). *InTASC. Model core teaching standards and learning progressions for teachers 1.0*, p. 17. https://ccsso.org/sites/default/files/2017-12/2013_INTASC_Learning_Progressions_for_Teachers.pdf

33. Council of Chief State School Officers, 2013.

34. Reeves, D. B. (2000). Standards are not enough: Essential transformations for school success. *NASSP Bulletin, 84*(620), 5–19.

35. *Psychometrics* is a field of study concerned with the theory and technique of mental measurement. In education, psychometrics deal with objective measurements of skills and knowledge, abilities, attitudes, personality traits, and educational achievement.

36. The SAT removed this question from their *Analogies* section in 2005.

37. Anastasi, A. (1976). *Psychological testing* (4th ed.). MacMillan, pp. 58–59.

38. Tanner, D. E. (2001). *Assessing academic achievement*. Allyn & Bacon, p. 269.

39. Berliner, D. C., & Biddle, B. J. (1997). *The manufactured crisis: Myths, fraud, and the attack on America's public schools*. Longman, p. 55.

40. Donald T. Campbell, cited in Hess, F. (2018, June 11). Education reforms should obey Campbell's law. *Education Week.* http://blogs.edweek.org/edweek/rick_hess_straight_up/2018/06/education_reforms_should_obey_campbells_law.html

41. Popham, W. J. (2001). *The truth about testing: An educator's call to action.* Association for Supervision and Curriculum Development, pp. 55–65.

42. Carnevale, A. P. (2007, September 26). No child gets ahead. *Education Week, 27*(5), 3; Viadero, D. (2007, August 1). Study: Low, high fliers gain less under NCLB. *Education Week, 26*(44), 7.

43. Toch, T., & Harris, D. N. (2008, October 1). Salvaging accountability: What the next president (and Congress) could do to save education reform. *Education Week, 28*(6), 30–31, 36.

44. Popham, 2001, pp. 17–19.

45. FairTest. (2018, April). *Just say no to standardized tests: Why and how to opt out.* https://www.fairtest.org/get-involved/opting-out

46. Samsel, H. (2017, October 26). 2 years after "opt out," are students taking fewer tests? *NPR Ed.* https://www.npr.org/sections/ed/2017/10/26/556840091/2-years-after-opt-out-are-students-taking-fewer-tests

47. Brighouse, H., Ladd, H., Loeb, S., & Swift, A. (2018 December/2019 January). Good education policy making: Data-informed but values-driven. *Phi Delta Kappan, 100*(4), 36–39; Snyder, S. (2018, April 23). Dad talk: Why parents shouldn't opt their kids out of standardized tests (Hint: It's not about your kid!). *T74.* https://www.the74million.org/article/dad-talk-why-parents-shouldnt-opt-their-kids-out-of-standardized-tests-hint-its-not-about-your-kid/

48. *The American Heritage Dictionary of the English language.* (1970). American Heritage, p. 9.

49. Rothman, R. (1995). *Measuring up: Standards, assessment, and school reform.* Jossey-Bass.

50. Leithwood, K., & Earl, L. (2000). Educational accountability effects: An international perspective. *Peabody Journal of Education, 75*(4), 1–18.

51. Reeves, 2004.

52. Reeves, 2004.

53. Rothstein, R., & Jacobsen, R. (2006, December). The goals of education. *Phi Delta Kappan, 88*(4), 264–272.

iStock/kali9

14 EDUCATING EVERYONE'S CHILDREN

InTASC Standards Addressed: 1, 2, 3, 4, 5, 6, 7, 8, 9, 10

LEARNING OBJECTIVES

After you read this chapter, you should be able to

14.1 Examine the Effective Schools Movement's beginnings and its findings about schools' capacity to provide high-quality education for low-income and underserved students.

14.2 Assess how each of the seven effective schools correlates contributes to student achievement and influences teachers' roles, as well as what each correlate looks like in schools.

14.3 Critique the rationale that the effective schools correlates by themselves cannot be completely successful in raising every student's achievement.

14.4 Defend the views of public schools as a public good and teaching as a public service.

American public schools provide everyone's children with opportunities to learn what they need to live adult lives as informed and responsible citizens and economic contributors. Nonetheless, sociological, economic, and cultural variables have often placed severe obstacles in the paths of underserved and low-income students as they struggle toward learning. Too often, a variety of poverty-related factors put low-income and racial-ethnic minority students cognitively and academically behind their middle- and upper-class peers even before they arrive at school. Likewise, schools' traditional sorting and selecting practices and institutional norms have kept many traditionally underserved students from entering the educational mainstream.

But this does not have to be the case. Research affirms that when teachers, administrators, and the community hold high expectations for students, effectively deliver a strong and appropriate curriculum, and provide high levels of support, learning typically improves. As Ron Edmonds, leader of the Effective Schools Movement, concludes, "We can, whenever and wherever we choose, successfully teach all children whose schooling is of interest to us. We already know more than we need to do that."[1]

In the mid-1970s, educators began investigating whether schools might be able to increase low-income and underserved students' achievement. They identified public schools that successfully educated all students regardless of their socioeconomic status (SES) or family background. These schools were located in varying regions and in communities both large and small.

Investigators noted that these high-achieving public schools had certain philosophies, policies, and practices in common: strong instructional leadership, a clear sense of mission, high expectations for all students, robust instructional behaviors, frequent monitoring of student achievement, a safe and orderly school environment, opportunities for students to learn, and positive home–school relations. Eventually, these attributes became known as the Correlates of Effective Schools. For approximately 50 years, research has continued to support these key practices.[2]

This chapter looks at the Effective Schools Movement and the research-based best practices that each school can employ to increase *every* student's academic learning. It provides an optimistic and realistic note on which to conclude a textbook for future educators.

14.1 A BRIEF HISTORY OF THE EFFECTIVE SCHOOLS MOVEMENT

Ronald R. Edmonds, the education professor and researcher (profiled later in this chapter) who first articulated the effective schools correlates, explains the rationale for the movement in this way:

> The very great proportion of the American people believes that family background and home environment are principal causes of the quality of pupil performance. In fact, no notion about

schooling is more widely held than the belief that the family is somehow the principal determinant of whether or not a child will do well in school.... Such a belief has the effect of absolving educators of their professional responsibility to be instructionally effective.[3]

In other words, when teachers expect little achievement from certain students, they usually get it.

In the 1950s and early 1960s, the efforts against poverty, racial prejudice, and unequal educational opportunity intensified. After 1960, Congressional legislation attempted to address these problems. The ensuing efforts to document and remedy the unequal educational opportunity, especially for low-income and underserved children, provided a major push for school effectiveness studies.

14.1a The Early Equal Opportunity Studies

The 1964 Civil Rights Act required the Commissioner of Education to conduct a nationwide survey of the availability of educational opportunity. The resulting 1966 report, *Equality of Educational Opportunity* (commonly referred to as the *Coleman Report* and discussed in Chapter 5) seemed to conclude that family background—not the school—was the major determinant of student achievement and life outcomes.[4] The *Coleman Report* suggested that schools were unable to overcome or equalize the disparity in students' academic achievement due to environmental factors. In 1972, Christopher Jencks, a Harvard University professor, and his colleagues corroborated Coleman's findings.[5]

Although these reports made for attention-grabbing headlines, their conclusions were wrong. What the Coleman and Jencks studies actually confirmed was the correlation linking higher family SES with their children's higher school achievement.[6]

As a result, the belief that, for academic achievement, "families matter, and schools don't" became part of our popular culture. In fact, Donald C. Orlich, a professor emeritus at Washington State University and an education assessment critic, believes that "many public school educators have uncritically accepted the hypothesis of familial effects, along with its corollary: that teachers cannot be held accountable for students' failure to learn when the students come from poor home environments."[7]

The Coleman and Jencks reports and the related literature prompted the federal government to create compensatory education programs. They also stimulated work by researchers and educators who believed the opposite—that effective schools *could* make a difference in student learning *regardless* of students' family backgrounds or socioeconomic status. These later investigators developed a body of research affirming that schools control the factors needed to ensure student mastery of the core curriculum, and the family plays a crucial role in promoting student learning.

14.1b Early Effective Schools Studies

For about 50 years, researchers have gathered ample evidence that shows schools can and do make a powerful difference in students' academic achievement. Their findings characterize today's "best practices."

Effective Schools Study Begins

In the late 1970s, independent researchers in the United States launched investigations to demonstrate that public schools could generate high academic achievement among low-income students and students of color. They began to identify public schools whose graduates scored higher than the national average on standardized tests. Academic growth—not decline—characterized these schools. Soon, hundreds of studies and research-based analytic papers tried to identify these schools' characteristics or "correlates" that were unusually successful with students regardless of their parents' education or income levels.

So began the Effective Schools Movement, a relatively small network of loosely coupled studies by like-minded persons looking to identify those in-school factors that affect students' academic achievement. Each study built on the previous investigations' findings.

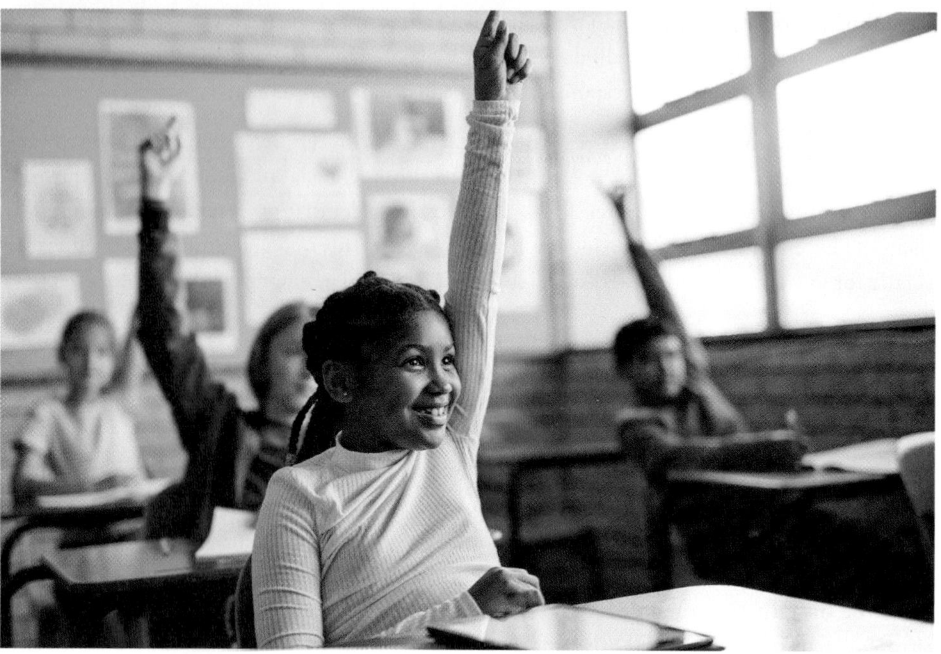

Effective schools successfully educate all students regardless of socioeconomic status or family background.
iStock/LumiNola

Types of Effective Schools Research

Much of the effective schools research might informally be considered as **outlier studies**.[8] In statistical terminology, an *outlier* is something that is relatively unusual and lies at the far end of the distribution. In other words, an outlier school might be one where all students were eligible for free or reduced-price lunch, yet the student achievement test scores were extremely high.

Other school effectiveness research focused on **case studies,** analyzing a small set of schools in depth. Typically, researchers organized the schools by outcome measures—that is, high-achieving schools versus low-achieving schools. The school characteristics in each group were then studied by demographic and survey techniques.

Despite their methodological limitations, these outlier and case studies clearly show that effective schools are characterized by good discipline, high teacher expectations for student achievement, and effective administrator leadership.[9]

14.1c Ronald Edmonds and the "Effective Schools" Concept

Until his death in 1983, Ronald Edmonds, an education professor at Michigan State University, was one of the key figures in the Effective Schools Movement. Thomas L. Good and Jere E. Brophy—themselves noted educational psychology researchers—noted that "Edmonds, more than anyone, had been responsible for the communication of the belief that schools can and do make a difference."[10]

Although Edmonds acknowledged that students' family background was a strong influence on student achievement, he refused to accept the *Coleman Report*'s conclusions. In 1979, as director of Harvard's Center for Urban Studies, Edmonds set out to find schools where students from low-income families were highly successful.

Effective Schools Correlates

In perhaps his most notable contribution to the education field, Edmonds verbalized five school-level variables that are strongly correlated with student achievement, more simply known as the original five effective schools "correlates"[11]:

- Strong administrative leadership with attention to instructional quality
- High expectations for all students' achievement

- A safe and orderly climate conducive to teaching and learning
- An emphasis on basic skill acquisition
- Frequent monitoring and measuring of pupil progress so teachers and principals are constantly aware of pupil growth in relationship to the instructional objectives

Edmonds's five correlates gleaned from schools that raised all children's academic achievement became the framework for thinking about school effectiveness.

Next, Edmonds defined an **effective school** as one in which low-income and racial and ethnic minority students' basic skills are at least as well developed as the middle-class children's skills. An effective school has closed the achievement gap between low- and high-SES students. In his view, "To be effective, a school need not bring all students to equal mastery levels, but it must bring an equal percentage of its highest and lowest social classes to minimum mastery."[12] As Edmonds saw it, in an "effective" school, one could not guess a student's SES by looking at reading test scores.

In addition, Edmonds found that schools that were instructionally effective for poor and underserved children were "indistinguishable" from instructionally less effective schools on SES factors (i.e., father's and mother's education, category of occupation, percentage of white students, mean family size, percentage of intact families). The large student performance differences, therefore, came not from differences in pupils' social class and family backgrounds[13] but from the schools' practices. By narrowing the students' "opportunity gaps," effective schools also narrowed the "achievement gaps." These findings directly contrasted with Coleman's and Jencks's conclusions that variations in student performance levels from school to school were only minimally related to the schools' characteristics.

Along with Wilbur Brookover, Lawrence Lezotte, and others, Edmonds looked for effective schools. They studied achievement data from schools in several major cities with student populations drawn mainly from poverty backgrounds. In one study, Edmonds and colleagues compared successful schools with similar schools in like neighborhoods where children were not learning or were learning at a low level, reaching the following conclusions:[14]

- Public schools can and do make a difference, even when the school population consists largely of students from poverty backgrounds.
- Children from poverty backgrounds can learn at high levels as a result of instruction and related practices delivered by public schools.
- Schools where all children are learning regardless of family background have common characteristics and processes.

Although Edmonds's studies had methodological limitations,[15] their findings provided valuable lessons about how schools could make a difference in low-income and underserved students' achievement. Edmonds's review of the effective schools literature and his own investigations led him to conclude that no one model explained school effectiveness for the poor or any other social class of students. Also, the relationship between the effective schools correlates and increased student achievement was correlational in nature, not a cause-and-effect relationship. In these studies, both the correlates and higher student achievement appeared together; no evidence proved that one factor caused the other.

More recently, researchers using sophisticated statistical models have determined that teachers can have more impact on student achievement than other school factors.[16] At the same time, methodological improvements in research studies have transformed Edmonds's initial narrow and managerial view of effective schooling into a more comprehensive notion of effective education that encompasses classroom instruction as well as staff and community relations.

Edmonds's contributions were primarily thought-provoking and conceptual.[17] His work and that of his colleagues in the United States and abroad motivated several decades of educators to improve their schools' capacities to help everyone's children succeed. And his influence continues today.

AMERICAN EDUCATION SPOTLIGHT: RONALD R. EDMONDS

Perhaps more than anyone, Ron Edmonds is responsible for communicating the belief that American public schools can and do make a difference.

Ronald R. Edmonds (1935–1983) initiated and led the Effective Schools Movement. In his view, the fact that many poor and racial and ethnic minority children do not master the school curriculum reflects *schools'*—rather than the children's—deficiencies. Edmonds introduced the concept of effective schools, and he tested and implemented successful programs of school reform based on it.

Lawrence W. Lezotte, Edmonds's colleague and close personal friend in the Effective Schools Movement, remembers the "biographical factors [that] seemed to propel [Edmonds] toward his work on issues of equity and social justice.

"Ron was a mixed race child with an upbringing that was in many ways parallel to that of President Obama with one important difference. Ron had a fraternal twin brother.

"Ron was an extremely accomplished student and his twin brother was not. Ron could never understand why Ron was treated so differently than his brother at school but no differently than his brother at home and in the community. This nagging issue may be the source of the belief that schools should be able to successfully educate all children.

"Ron Edmonds became a high school social science teacher in Ann Arbor, Michigan Public Schools. He used to tell the story that one year he was asked to teach two different sections of United

Courtesy of Michigan State Archives. Reprinted with permission from XOS Digital.

States History. One section was designated for the advanced placement students and the other for the lower performing students. He would tell that about the third week of school he came to the conclusion that he didn't need to have two different lesson plans for the different groups. He found that high expectations and engaging lessons worked for all the students. Again, this insight has a lasting impact on the effective schools research that was to follow years later."

As a high school teacher, Edmonds began doing project work with the University of Michigan. While in Michigan, he served as faculty at the University of Michigan, human relations director for the Ann Arbor, Michigan, public schools, and assistant superintendent in the Michigan Department of Public Instruction. For most of the 1970s, he directed the Harvard graduate education program's Center for Urban Studies and received a certificate of advanced study. Much of his work on the effective schools research and related policy discussions occurred while serving in that role. From 1978 to 1980, he served as a senior assistant for instruction with the New York City public schools. In 1981, Edmonds returned to Michigan as professor of education at Michigan State University (MSU), where he continued his research and advocacy until his untimely death in 1983.

Although critics don't challenge Edmonds's corelates, some decry how some educators have twisted his belief that schools can improve children's learning (by adopting effective policies and practices) into the popular phrase, "all children can learn" (without the qualification of adequate resources, extra support, and child-friendly policies). This simplistic phrase can confuse and mislead the public into assuming that all children can learn *the same curriculum* at *the same level* and in the *same amount of time*, that *every* student can meet state academic standards, and that the principal is the *sole* instructional leader. This misunderstanding also has unintended consequences, such as downplaying the need for early intervention of children who live in poverty. In fact, "the equal treatment of unequals is the greatest injustice of all."*

With his insights and research, Edmonds worked to dispel the hopelessness with which teachers of low-income and underserved children typically viewed their students. By 1990, the Effective Schools Movement had become a coalition of practitioners, citizens, and researchers working in over 700 school districts across the country and communicating their findings. And the effective schools process continues to improve.

Lezotte concludes, "Though much too brief, Ron's impact on the education of the children of the poor in the United States still reverberates throughout the efforts to reform public education today.... Without question, Ron Edmonds made a difference."

***Note**: Quote attributed to Edmond Burke (1729–1797), an Irish statesman and philosopher.

Sources: Lezotte, L. W. (2011, October 10). Personal communication with Bill Owings and Leslie Kaplan; Edmonds, R. (1996). *History of the effective schools movement*. Donnelley and Lee Library Archives, Chicago's National Liberal Arts College. https://www.lakeforest.edu/library/archives/effective-schools/HistoryofEffectiveSchools.php; *Hare, I. (1988, January). School social work and effective schools. Urban Education, 22(4), 413–428; Neisser, U. (1986). Introduction. In U. Neisser (Ed.), The school achievement of minority children. New perspectives. Lawrence Erlbaum; Raptis, H., & Fleming, T. (2003, October 1). Reframing education:* How to create effective schools. *C. D. Howe Institute, 188*(1), 1–24; Thomas, M. D., & Bainbridge, W. L. (2001, May). "All children can learn": Facts and fallacies. *Phi Delta Kappan, 82*(9), 660–662.

14.1d Additional Effective Schools Findings

Over time, the list of effective schools "correlates" expanded. In 1979, the Michigan Department of Education asked Wilbur Brookover and Lawrence W. Lezotte to investigate a set of eight Michigan schools enrolling large numbers of low-income and underserved children and characterized by consistent pupil performance improvement or decline. Trained interviewers visited schools and tried to identify the differences between improving and declining schools. The researchers found the following consistent differences between schools where students achieved well and where they didn't:[18]

- *Clear instructional focus.* Improving schools clearly accepted and emphasized the importance of the reading and math objectives, whereas declining schools gave less emphasis to such goals and did not specify them as fundamental.
- *High teacher expectations.* The staffs of improving schools tended to believe that *all* of their students could master the basic objectives. Teachers perceived that their principals shared this belief. Likewise, teachers at improving schools expected that their students would complete

high school or college, whereas teachers at declining schools had much lower expectations for their students' achievement and educational and employment futures.

- *Commitment to and responsibility for student achievement.* In improving schools, teachers and principals were more likely to assume responsibility for and were committed to teaching the basic reading and math skills. Staffs at declining schools felt that teachers could not do much to influence their students' achievement and displaced the responsibility for skill learning to parents or students.
- *High time on task.* Teachers in improving schools spent more time on achieving reading and math objectives, whereas teachers in declining schools spent less time in direct reading instruction.
- *Principal as instructional leader.* In improving schools, principals were more assertive in their institutional leadership role, held higher expectations for students' behavior, and were more regular in evaluating achievement of basic objectives. By comparison, principals in declining schools were more permissive, emphasized informal and collegial relationships with teachers, and emphasized general public relations rather than evaluating school effectiveness in providing a basic education for all students.
- *Accountability.* The improving schools showed greater acceptance of accountability and used measured student learning as one sign of their effectiveness.
- *Dissatisfaction with current achievement.* Generally, teachers in improving schools were less satisfied than staffs in declining schools. Staffs in declining schools were complacent and content with current achievement levels.
- *Unclear role of parent involvement.* Differences in parent involvement levels were not clear. Improving schools had higher levels of *parent-initiated* involvement but less overall parent involvement.
- *Compensatory education.* Classroom teachers in improving schools focused on teaching reading. By comparison, classroom teachers in declining schools spent more time identifying students to be placed in compensatory reading activities and placed greater emphasis on programmed instruction. Teaching children the academic basics appears to be "someone else's" job.

The 1979 Brookover and Lezotte findings present a relatively clear profile of achieving schools that are congruent with other urban school studies. They showed that teacher and principal expectations and behaviors created the school conditions that allowed low-income and underrepresented students to make achievement gains. They did not blame their students' low achievement on inherited, social, or family factors. At the same time, Brookover and Lezotte concluded that no single combination of variables will produce an effective school. Most importantly, they found that pupil family background neither causes nor prevents elementary school instructional effectiveness. Instructional effectiveness is the responsibility of principals and teachers.

Limitations of the Early Effective Schools Research

Effective schools research finds common characteristics but also shares serious limitations. The studies looked at too few schools with too-narrow student demographics to justify firm and generalizable conclusions. The findings were correlational, rather than indicating a cause-and-effect relationship. Furthermore, researchers looking at middle-class students and secondary schools did not find the same results as those studying elementary schools.[19] Despite these limitations, the studies' consistent findings of the school effectiveness "correlates"—strong principal or staff leadership, high expectations for student achievement, a clear set of instructional goals, an effective schoolwide staff professional development program to improve teacher pedagogy, an emphasis on order and discipline, and a system for monitoring students' progress—give substantial credibility to the varied studies' findings.[20]

In light of the previous two decades of effective schools research findings and the methodological critiques, in 1990 Levine concluded this:[21]

> The effective school correlates should be viewed more as prerequisites for attaining high and equitable student achievement levels. Their presence does not guarantee schools' success. All correlates must be present to make a difference. Additionally, "the correlates represented issues and challenges" for their schools. They were not "prescriptions" or "recipes" for attaining a high achieving status. Enacting each correlate takes many steps, and no specific action or steps is right for every school.
>
> Much of the positive results at unusually effective schools involve teachers and administrators identifying and addressing obstacles to student learning. Since schools are composed of interacting systems, changes in one place usually create ripples elsewhere. Ensuring that modifications in one sphere do not create negative repercussions elsewhere takes constant monitoring and adjusting that cannot easily be written in a "to-do" list. Schools cannot tackle all reforms at once, or they would go into overload.

14.1e Effective Schools Research, 1990 to Today

During the 1990s, educators made substantial conceptual and empirical advances in understanding and explaining effective schools.[22] In fact, school effectiveness is now understood as sets of interacting variables. The new models are more specific about the school factors and their interactions. In addition, the definition of effective schools expands to include public and private elementary, middle, and high schools from communities with all social classes in all types of communities. This second generation of effective schools models and research not only focuses on schools serving all types of students in all types of settings, but it also emphasizes growth in achievement and school improvement across all contexts.

In the 1990s, Jaap Scheerens and Roel Bosker, two education professors at the University of Twente, The Netherlands, reviewed a number of school effectiveness models. They conducted one of the most quantitatively sophisticated reviews of the research literature on the myriad factors influencing student achievement.[23] Using a complex statistical model to organize their research, they produced a meta-analysis of an international literature base. Their findings identify a pattern of support for academic pressure to achieve, parental involvement, orderly climate, and opportunity to learn.

Likewise, University of Hawaii education professor Ronald Heck's 2000 and 2005 studies find that schools with higher-quality educational environments (principal leadership, high expectations, frequent monitoring of student progress and climate) produced higher-than-expected achievement gains after controlling for the students' characteristics.[24]

Looking at influences beyond the school, investigators conclude that the school's community and socioeconomic context influence student achievement. Many observe that differences in student performance can be attributed to school and community characteristics even though these factors are beyond their schools' control. To help students learn, it is important for educators to understand and accommodate these outside factors.[25]

Researchers also conclude that implementing certain correlates without the others does not necessarily produce the desired results. Unless teachers have higher expectations for student learning or other effective schools correlates, teacher collaboration by itself will not significantly modify student achievement.[26] Similarly, principals' strong instructional leadership is important, but its impact on school effectiveness is indirect.[27] Evidence continues to emerge that principal leadership is second only to teaching among the school-related factors in its impact on student learning.[28] Research on these issues is ongoing.[29]

Despite positive findings, effective school research has been subject to much criticism of its principle, its theory, its methodology, its objectivity, and its practice.[30] Most of these fine-grained critiques are best left to education scholars. More practically, some critics assert that focusing on the essential corelates advances the wrongheaded idea that a few key "simple-sounding" factors

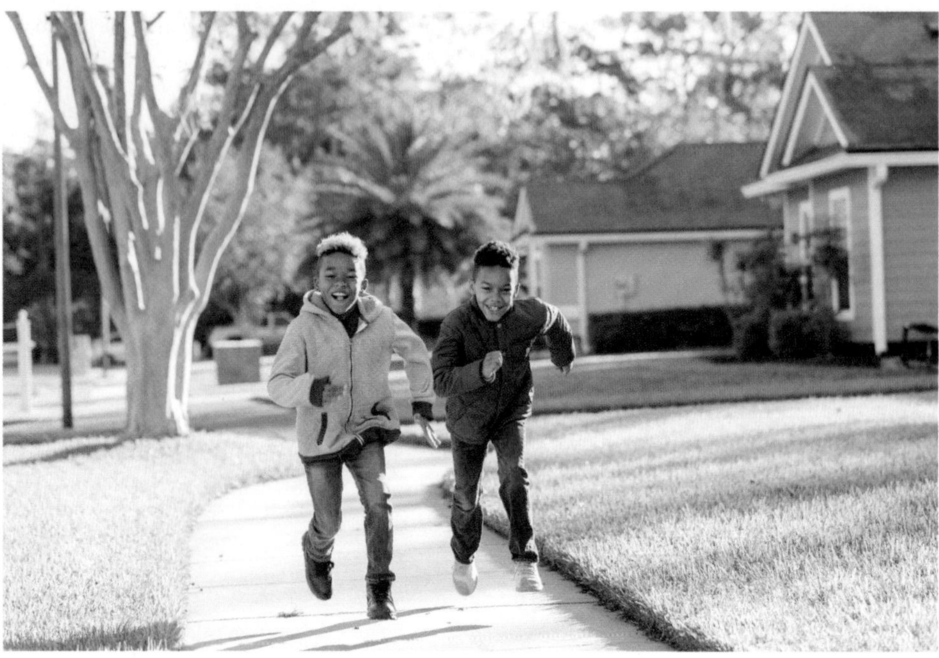

Many observe that differences in student performance can be attributed to their schools' and community's characteristics.

iStock/Imageegami

could solve complex problems in educating low-income children and ignores the varied outside factors that shape student learning and educational attainment.[31] Additionally, some of the criticisms are political in nature, meant to influence government policy makers wishing to advance their own ideological agenda.[32]

Perhaps the appraisal most relevant to future teachers is the reminder that *correlation does not equal causality*. Simply because the correlates appear to be operating together in successful schools does not justify the conclusion that one factor causes the other.

In answering its critics, much school effectiveness research recognizes the actual complexity of education that goes well beyond test scores.[33] In fact, the effective schools concept of schooling is the study of relationships among *school inputs* (such as the school's financial resources and teachers' professional experience), *school context* (the school's culture, climate, neighborhood, and prevailing societal philosophies), the direct and indirect *schooling process* (such as the nature of school leadership, teacher cooperation, and instructional quality at both school and classroom levels), and *school performance* (usually expressed as average student achievement) give insights into the schooling practices[34] and the factors that determine student achievement.[35] Perhaps they suggest avenues of positive change. At the same time, since schools function within a social, political, and cultural system, it is very difficult if not impossible to separate schools' functioning from the limits the larger society places on it. Accordingly, school effectiveness advocates acknowledge that efforts to improve school performance should carefully consider the "power of site or place."[36]

14.1f Effective Schools Practices Have Become Best Practices

Effective schools research and practice continue today but not always under the "brand-name" of Effective Schools.[37] In the 1980s under Ronald Reagan, U.S. Secretaries of Education Andrew Lamar Alexander and William Bennett talked about "good schools" and "effective schools" interchangeably, producing a popular book, *What Works: Research About Teaching and Learning*, that drew directly from the effective schools research.[38] By the late 1990s, the U.S. government began using the effective schools nomenclature and common features in the Comprehensive School Reform Act.[39] Policy advisors in Democratic administrations continued the use the effective schools research as a basis for advancing educational improvement and "systemic reform."[40]

In 2011, the National Center on Time & Learning reported on its study of 30 high-poverty schools nationwide that improved students' achievement by using extended time in their day to continuously strengthen instruction. These schools maximized time on task; prioritized time use according to focused learning goals; tailored instructional time to individual students' needs; built a culture of high expectations and mutual accountability; and relentlessly assessed, analyzed, and responded to student data.[41]

Additional schools studied include the "No Excuses Schools" (such as KIPP Academies),[42] "High Impact" schools,[43] and Village Academies.[44] Although the school-related factors contributing to their success are largely identical to those in the effective schools literature, the present practitioners do not publicly place themselves within the Effective Schools Movement. They represent elementary, middle, and high schools in various locations that are successfully raising low-income and racial and ethnic minority students' academic achievement by using the effective schools correlates. In short, effective schools correlates—with and without their provenance noted—are now widely accepted as best practice.

Over time, the effective schools correlates have evolved. Once reserved for schools working mainly with low-income children and children of color, and still highly effective with this group, effective schools correlates are now considered appropriate for schools with any student population regardless of students' SES. They follow, listed briefly:

- Strong instructional leadership
- Clear and focused mission
- Safe and orderly environment
- Climate of high expectations
- Frequent monitoring of student progress
- Positive home–school relations
- Opportunity to learn/student time on task

As schools continue to address contemporary issues, the correlates' meanings continue to mature, incorporating the available research findings. Today, their dimensions represent a higher developmental stage than when they first appeared.[45] Let's look more closely at each, see what the research literature has to say about their impact on student achievement, and describe what they look like when enacted in schools.

To gain a deeper understanding of how the effective schools correlates can improve every student's school performance—independent of family background—complete the activity in the **Reflect & Engage** box, Effective Schools Correlates Can Improve Student Outcomes.

REFLECT & ENGAGE: EFFECTIVE SCHOOLS CORRELATES CAN IMPROVE STUDENT OUTCOMES

This activity involves a role play. In 1979, Ronald Edmonds wrote, "The very great proportion of the American people believes that family background and home environment are principal causes of the quality of pupil performance.... Such a belief has the effect of absolving educators of their professional responsibility to be instructionally effective." After reading the first section of this chapter, are you ready to advocate to your school to take a deeper look at whether the effective schools model can improve student outcomes and teacher efficacy in your school and district?

A. You are four-person teams of teachers working in a high-poverty school. Together with your principal, you have been reading about the Effective Schools Movement and its correlates. Excited by your readings, you ask to meet with your superintendent to convince her to allow your faculty and parent organization to study and pilot an effective schools approach with your own students and community over the next few years. If successful, your school might even provide a model for other schools in the division.

B. Working in groups of four, prepare and present a persuasive 5-minute talk (with visual aids) about why you think the effective schools approach to educating children, its correlates, and its research findings encourage you to want to try it out in your school.

C. Present your talk to the whole class.

D. Discuss as a class the K–12 school experiences you had where the effective schools correlates (identify them) were—or were *not*—in place and how that affected you as a student.

E. Consider how the belief that "family background and home environment are the main influences on student performance" may affect a teacher's motivation to help every student learn to high standards. How does the effective schools orientation shape your own views of what's possible in educating low-income students?

14.2 CORRELATES OF EFFECTIVE SCHOOLS

Research and practice have shown that effective schools have seven correlates: strong instructional leadership, a clear and focused mission, a safe and orderly environment, a climate of high expectations, frequent monitoring of student progress, positive home–school relations, and the opportunity to learn/student time on task. We are going to consider each one separately—what it means, the research on its role in boosting student learning and achievement, and what it looks like when operating successfully in schools.

14.2a Correlate: Strong Instructional Leadership

Strong instructional leadership is an essential component of effective schools. Educational leadership scholars Phillip Hallinger (Mahidol University) and Joseph Murphy (Vanderbilt University) describe **instructional leadership** as the school's role that defines the school's mission, manages the instructional program, and promotes a positive learning climate.[46] More simply, instructional leadership is leadership for learning.[47] Kenneth Leithwood, an educational researcher and professor at the Ontario Institute for Studies in Education in Toronto, Canada, and his colleagues observe, "Indeed, there are virtually no documented instances of troubled schools being turned around without interventions by a dynamic leader. Many other factors may contribute to such turnarounds, but leadership is the catalyst."[48]

As the school's "official" leader, the principal sets the climate, creates the expectations, clarifies the school's direction, and delivers the resources needed to make teaching and learning satisfying and successful endeavors. Effective school leaders build their organizational cultures through participatory decision-making and collaborative planning. Working closely with teacher leaders, principals define and express a clear and focused school vision and mission, set goals, solve problems, and socialize their faculty to continue improving their pedagogy. In this way, teachers become leaders within their classroom and among colleagues, taking on broader responsibilities—such as expecting every student to master the state curriculum (perhaps with extra support); ensuring a safe, calm, and organized environment in their classroom and throughout the school; and monitoring student progress frequently—that enable students to learn to high levels.

In today's schools, however, the principal cannot be the only leader. As a "leader of leaders" rather than a "leader of followers," principals develop their skills as coach, partner, and cheerleader as well as organizational leader and manager. By consistently communicating and reinforcing the school's purpose in words and deeds and by sharing leadership with teachers, the principal creates a professional environment in which teachers can thrive and contribute to the overall school goals and environment.

Research and Discussion

A large body of high-quality evidence demonstrates the modest but consistently significant contributions that school leadership makes indirectly to student learning as well as the catalytic effects of this leadership on other essential aspects of the school and its community.[49] A meta-analysis of 30 years of research on the effects of principals' practices on student achievement finds that, for an average school, having an effective leader can mean achieving an achievement test score 10 percentile points higher than a peer in a school with a less effective principal.[50] And a 2012 study estimates that highly effective principals can raise a typical student's achievement in their school by between 2 and 7 months of learning in a single academic year, whereas ineffective principals lower their students' achievement by that same amount.[51]

Over the decades, educational leadership research has matured, using more sophisticated longitudinal designs, stronger statistical methods, more quantitative analyses, and more large-scale studies.[52] The results have deepened our understanding of school leadership's complexities. We now know that beyond classroom teaching, certain school factors (such as "academic optimism,"[53] academic culture,[54] and collective teacher efficiency[55]) and certain home factors (such as socioeconomic dynamics, home features, and home–school relationships) also substantially impact student achievement.

After years of study and reflecting on the principal leadership data, Kenneth Leithwood and colleagues in 2020 conclude that of all the school-related factors, "school leadership has a significant [indirect] effect on features of the school organization which positively influences the quality of teaching and learning. While moderate in size, this leadership effect is vital to the success of school improvement efforts."[56]

When administrators create school cultures that welcome shared leadership, spirited and inventive teachers will work willingly as part of the team to improve their schools. And when teachers participate in their schools' instructional leadership, they become less isolated. They gain satisfaction from knowing that they are making their schools more satisfying places for them to work and for children to learn. All of these constructive experiences infuse new energy and ideas into their classroom teaching, helping teachers invest in their school rather than merely work there.

What Strong Instructional Leadership Looks Like in Schools

How do teachers know when their principal is acting as an instructional leader? They know when they see their principals and other school leaders enacting these behaviors:[57]

- The principal and other school leaders set and communicate high, easily understood, and public standards and appropriate challenging performance expectations for every student and teacher.
- The principal and other school leaders model and verbally express the school's values and practices at every opportunity.
- The principal and other school leaders create a learning-centered school culture that focuses clearly and repeatedly on improving teaching and learning.
- The principal and other school leaders develop a climate of caring, consideration, and trust among teachers, students, and parents.
- The principal and other school leaders frequently and informally observe classroom instruction, conduct targeted learning walks, and provide substantive and timely feedback to teachers for their instructional improvement.
- The principal and other school leaders systematically engage staff in discussions about current research, theory, and practice that help advance teacher learning and student achievement.
- The principal and other school leaders participate with teachers in professional development activities during faculty meetings, grade-level, and content area meetings.
- The principal and other school leaders develop teacher leadership, encouraging faculty members to collaborate and learn from each other using individual and team strengths.
- The principal and other school leaders involve teachers in the design and implementation of important decisions and policies affecting them and their students.
- The principal and other school leaders actively seek input from teachers, students, parents, and the community to develop the school's improvement plan.

- The principal and other school leaders provide sufficient resources for effective instruction, including professional development and time and opportunity for collaborative planning and learning.
- The principal and other school leaders ensure an effective, ongoing system for monitoring and evaluating student learning and the school's progress toward its goals and communicating this with faculty, students, parents, and the community.
- The principal and other school leaders structure the school organization, including teachers' classroom locations and schedules, to facilitate collaboration.
- The principal and other school leaders buffer staff from distractions to their instructional work.
- The principal and other school leaders publicly celebrate student achievement in academics.
- The principal and other school leaders promptly and effectively address student concerns and troubles, proactively if possible, to keep students engaged, in school, and learning.

14.2b Correlate: Clear and Focused Mission

Today's school mission emphasizes teaching and learning an appropriate balance between learning how to comprehend and apply complex conceptual knowledge and mastering basic academic skills. It holds true for low-income and underserved children and also for affluent and middle-class children. The mission advocates *learning for all*, focusing on both the "learning" (what the student is doing and mastering) and the teachers' continuous professional growth. Outcomes—not merely inputs—matter.

Research and Discussion

School leaders begin to make their schools into positive learning environments for students and teachers by defining a compelling vision and a focused mission. A **vision** is an intelligent sense of what a better future can be; a **mission** is the purpose or direction pursued to reach that end.[58] "A vision is a target that beckons,"[59] claim business leadership experts. For instance, in 1961 when President John Kennedy set the then-almost-unimaginable goal of placing a man on the moon by 1970, and in 1975 when Bill Gates aimed to put a computer on every desk and in every home, these leaders concentrated attention on worthwhile, highly challenging, and attainable achievements. A vision provides a bridge from the present to the future. Only when one knows where one wants to go can one plan how to get there.

Vision and *mission* are not always thought of as two separate things. Instead, they may both be aspects of the same whole. Stephen R. Covey, author of *The Seven Habits of Highly Effective People*, sees a vision as telling where one wants to go and a mission as telling how one will get there.[60] Effective schools assume vision is part of a clear and focused mission. Both deal with values and purpose as different locations on the same continuum. One step is a prerequisite for the next.

Effective leaders bring vision into action by sharing it with others. An essential leadership skill is the capacity to influence and organize meaning for the organization's members. Leaders define and articulate what has previously remained unsaid. They invent images, metaphors, and mental models that help direct attention and energies. They depict a desirable future state of their organization for us to embrace and act upon.

In an effective school, first the principal and then other school leaders champion a persuasive, shared vision and a clear, focused mission that defines what is important and directs the organization on how to reach it. Rather than only a part of an annual "back-to-school" speech, "vision and mission talk" continues throughout the school day and year as school leaders make every event an opportunity to reinforce what the school community values and highlight how what they are doing now is helping them "get there." Vision and mission create meaning for everyone in the organization and make the world understandable. They help explain why things are being done the way they are and why certain things are considered good and rewarded but others are not.

Research shows that by fostering group goals, modeling the desired behaviors for others, and providing intellectual stimulation and individual support (through personal interactions and professional development), principals directly affect a school's culture and climate and indirectly influence student achievement.[61] Nevertheless, teachers are the essential agents who turn the mission into daily actions. Once the teachers and staff see the "big picture"—such as teachers working collaboratively to increase each student's learning opportunities and reducing the achievement gap between low-income and affluent students—the team members can understand how their own jobs relate to it. They can fit their skills and interests into the school's master plan to help it get where it intends to go as well as use this goal to realize their own deepest desires for meaning, accomplishment, and self-fulfillment. Having an easily understood and focused mission makes teaching more than a job. It becomes a way for teachers to live out their deepest values and fully engage their energies and talents as they educate children for lifelong learning, mature awareness and behavior, and economic opportunities.

Involving teachers in the change process increases their investment in the school's success. Teachers as well as principals should be able to speak enthusiastically about the school's vision and mission. Having a key role in bringing a desired future into the present keeps effective and influential teachers in the school despite the traditionally high turnover rate among teachers early in their careers. Creating a supportive atmosphere in which teachers are considered members of a professional community with opportunities to continue their own development both inside and outside the school leads teachers—and all their students—toward excellence.

Involving teachers in the change process increases their investment in the school's success.
iStock/Wavebreakmedia

What a Clear and Focused Mission Looks Like in Schools

In an effective school with a clear and focused mission, these characteristics are present:[62]

- Everyone (teachers, students, staff, parents, community) can tell you that teaching effectively so every student learns to state standards (or above) is one of the school's top goals.
- The school expresses a clear vision about what effective instruction should look like and accomplish in the school.
- The school implements its vision by setting (and meeting) goals and performance expectations for teachers and students.
- Principals, teachers, and staff model aspirational and ethical practices.

- The school provides professional development for new teachers about the school's instructional model and for every teacher's continual growth in pedagogy.
- Teachers receive clear, ongoing, and substantive feedback about their pedagogical strengths and weaknesses based on multiple data sources, including student achievement data.
- The school gives continual informed attention to every student's successful achievement.
- Student learning goals are high and measurable and aligned with state and national standards.
- Leaders use multiple forms of student data to inform improvement efforts.
- Students tell you that they are learning a lot in most of their classes.
- All students' learning includes both basic-level academic skills and higher-level cognitive abilities with sufficient time and help to master them.
- Teachers present academic work in ways that students find interesting, personally relevant, varied, intellectually engaging, and actively involving.
- Teachers use frequent formative assessments to identify students' current gaps in understanding and then provide the specific assistance needed.
- The school engages the school community in a collaborative process for developing the school's vision, mission, and goals that include in-depth study and assessment of identified shared values and information sources.
- The school establishes regular two-way communication with stakeholders about how well the vision is being implemented and met.
- The achievement gap between middle-class and low-income and racial and ethnic minority students is markedly decreasing or eliminated altogether as every student's achievement rises.

14.2c Correlate: Safe and Orderly Environment

Today's effective schools emphasize the presence of certain desirable behaviors. A **safe and orderly environment** is an organized, purposeful, cooperative, and nurturing atmosphere free from threat of harm in a school culture and climate that supports teaching and learning. In addition, all parties show respect for and appreciation of human diversity and democratic values.[63]

Research and Discussion

A safe and orderly environment as previously defined is foundational to any effective schooling. It is essential that teachers and students feel physically and emotionally safe and comfortable if they are to have the psychological energy needed for teaching and learning. Without a minimum level of security, organization, and calm, a school has little chance of positively affecting student achievement.

Many studies have singled out a safe and orderly environment as essential to academic achievement.[64] It is significantly correlated with less student fear, lower dropout rates, and higher student commitment to their learning.[65] Anxiety about safety shifts the brain's attention. When students and teachers worry about their personal safety, their focus insistently turns to protecting themselves. They become cautious and watchful as they stay hyperalert to potential dangers. At such times, the emotional parts of their brain are more fully aroused, and their cognitive areas become less active. In such environments, they cannot find extra energy to pay attention to teaching and learning. Achievement suffers. Conversely, in a school with a safe and orderly environment, teachers and students feel no personal danger. Thus, their cognitive capacities can become more fully engaged.

In this climate, the learning environment is well structured and businesslike. Teachers are committed to creating a strong, encouraging academic focus with high but achievable goals for students, and they work together collaboratively to make student success happen. Likewise, students work hard on academic matters, are highly motivated, and respect peers who achieve academically. And when they aren't achieving, caring adults listen to them to help them identify and resolve obstacles to their learning.

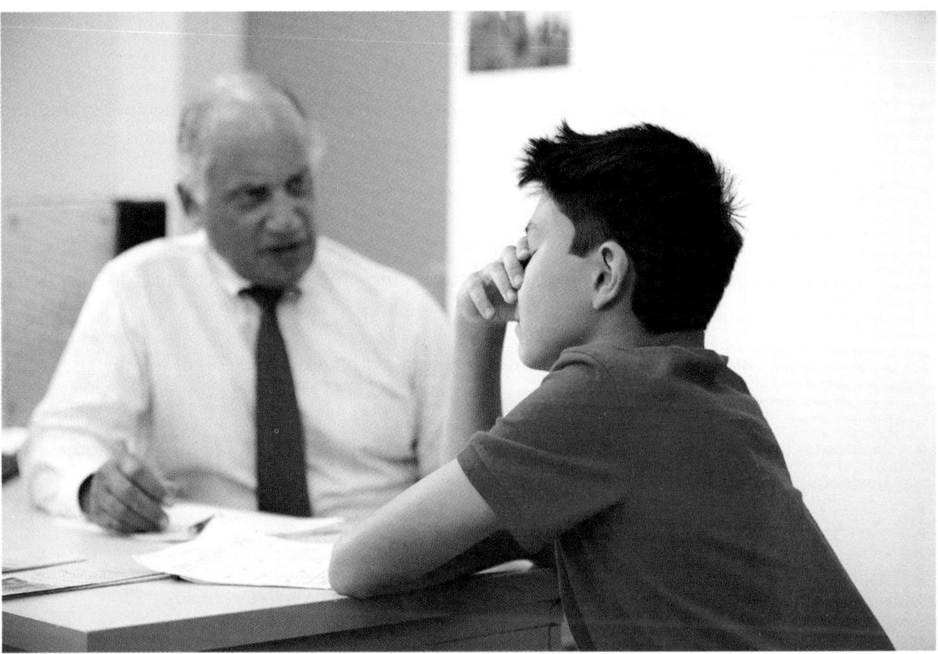

Students meet regularly with in-school mentors to discuss concerns and solve problems.
iStock/monkeybusinessimages

What a Safe and Orderly Environment Looks Like in Schools

A school has a safe and orderly environment when it meets the following criteria:[66]

- The school is clean, inviting, and comfortable. Throughout the day, custodians clean the halls and common areas after students use them, promptly noticing and removing graffiti or disorder.
- The school maintains ambitious and high expectations and standards for student and educator behaviors.
- Students and teachers report that the curriculum includes and reflects students' backgrounds.
- School leaders and teachers identify the diverse types of social and intellectual capital students bring with them to school and leverage these in their interactions with students to motivate learning.
- Students, faculty, staff, and parents at the school say that they feel safe, cared for, and trusted.
- Students at the school tell visitors that they and their friends want to learn (and are doing so).
- Students sit in mixed-race and gender groups in the cafeteria and classrooms.
- People in the building smile at one another freely and frequently.
- Rules and expectations are openly and visibly communicated (and frequently reviewed and enforced) to students (and parents), stressing mutual respect and responsibility.
- Teachers, administrators, and other adults are visible in the halls and common areas whenever students are using them, from morning entry through afternoon dismissal.
- Teachers, staff, parents, and the community have formal and informal ways to give ideas about improving the school's functioning.
- The principal and administrators are aware of the details and undercurrents in running the school, have early recognition systems to identify potentially disruptive students, and use this information to prevent and solve problems.

- All adults (principal, teachers, administrative personnel, custodians, cafeteria workers) help students learn self-discipline and responsibility.
- Students breaking rules receive fair and consistently administered consequences, including problem-solving to help prevent repeat errors in judgment.
- The school has low discipline referral rates and few (and declining) suspensions for disciplinary infractions.
- The school recognizes student, faculty, and staff achievements and celebrates these in a variety of ways.
- Challenging students have in-school adult mentors with whom they regularly discuss concerns and solve problems.
- Students stay after school to work one-on-one with teachers to make up or gain more understanding about their schoolwork.
- Teachers and students participate actively in developing the school's rules.
- The learning environment is cognitively challenging for all students.
- The curriculum includes multicultural education.

14.2d Correlate: Climate of High Expectations

To maintain a climate of high expectations for students, teachers must first hold high expectations for themselves. In effective schools, teachers believe in both their students' ability to master the curriculum and in their own collective efficacy in making it happen. Additionally, schools as cultural organizations transform from institutions designed for "instruction" to institutions designed to ensure "learning."

Research and Discussion

Students' and teachers' perceptions and expectations determine the goals they set for achievement; the strategies they use to meet these goals; the skills, energy, and other resources they use to apply these strategies; and the rewards they anticipate from making this effort.[67] The research on effective schools reinforces the importance of teacher expectations in determining student performance. Many other studies concur.[68]

Researchers clarify several relationships between teachers' expectations and student achievement:

- Teachers form expectations for student performance.[69]
- Teachers tend to treat students differently depending on these expectations.[70]
- Teachers' perceptions of current students' performance as well as their judgments for students' future performance are generally accurate.[71]
- Once set, teachers' expectations change little.[72] In school, first impressions matter.
- Student characteristics such as physical attractiveness, socioeconomic status, race, use of standard English, and history of grade retention are related to teacher expectations for academic achievement.[73]
- Teachers who expect students to be low achievers attribute their improved achievement to luck, whereas teachers attribute the perceived high achievers' success to their ability.[74]
- Teachers overestimate the achievement of high achievers, underestimate the achievement of low achievers, and predict least accurately low achievers' responses.[75]
- The better the teachers know their students, the more accurate their expectations for student academic success, especially in the early elementary grades (Grades 1 and 2).[76]

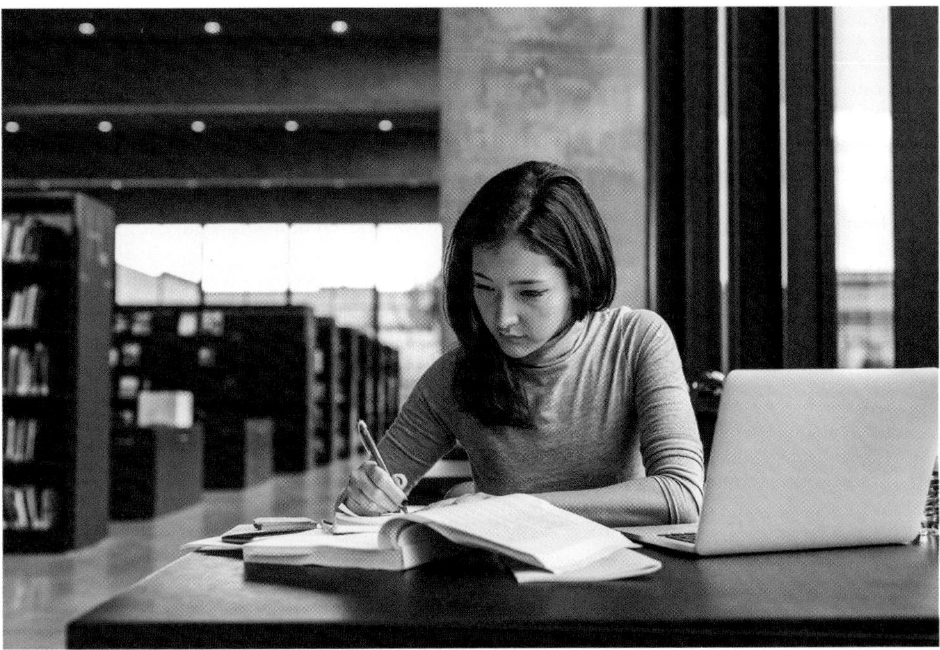

High expectations for student learning lead to high student achievement.
iStock/Jacob Ammentorp Lund

In a self-fulfilling prophesy, the more effective the teaching, the more effective the learning. Notably, studies find that as teachers improve their instructional practices, the more students learn, and the more optimistic teachers become about their students' success. In turn, their students became more successful and more confident in their ability to learn.[77] Each player's positive expectations influence the other in a mutually reinforcing manner. It is possible that when teachers become more effective in their classrooms and more children achieve well, teachers may treat all students as high achievers—providing them with similar praise and feedback and making similar demands for work and effort.

Researchers have also found that higher teachers' beliefs in their own and their colleagues' abilities to help all students make the academic advances that their school is asking of them, the higher the correlation with achievement levels and gains.[78] In short, teachers' initial expectations about students' being high or low achievers weaken as teachers commit to a learning-for-all mission and develop the expertise and confidence in their own and their colleagues' effectiveness to have all their students successfully learn the curriculum.

To understand more completely how strong instructional leadership, a clear and focused mission, a safe and orderly environment, and a climate of high expectations interact to create a positive, motivating learning environment in which teachers and students can do their best work, complete the activity in the **Reflect & Engage** box, Relating Four Correlates to Student and Teacher Success.

What a Climate of High Expectations Looks Like in Schools

What do schools with high expectations for student achievement look like?[79]

- The school has developed a shared vision of a school with all students regardless of family background achieving high levels of success in a rigorous curriculum.
- Every student has access to the high-status curriculum.
- Teachers, administrators, and parents expect all students to learn a full range of skills—from basic mastery of needed skills to higher-level, complex problem-solving—and they act on this belief.
- The school has expectations and practices in place to avoid both grade retention and social promotion by keeping all students learning apace throughout the year.

- Teachers have confidence in their skills to help all their students master the basic and higher-level skills, regardless of their family background. They not only act on this belief but continually upgrade their pedagogical skills.
- Teachers clearly inform students and parents of what students are expected to know and be able to do by the end of the unit or semester.
- Teachers help students use what they already know to learn new knowledge, develop new skills, and expand their understanding.
- Teachers use a variety of effective instructional approaches to enable every student to master a challenging curriculum.
- Students and teachers work together during class time (and before/after school if needed) to master the expected content and skills.
- The school has ongoing, collegial professional development tied to the classroom curriculum to help every teacher improve his or her instructional effectiveness.
- Students are encouraged to set and monitor high learning goals for themselves.
- Students and teachers believe that their effort is just as—if not more—important as their ability in producing their final achievement, and they invest effort in learning.
- Students with disabilities receive instruction in the regular classrooms from the regular teacher with assistance from a collaborating teacher.
- English language learners receive support to learn academics in the regular classroom.
- The school has very low suspension and dropout rates and very high promotion or graduation rates.
- Students and parents believe that their teachers have confidence in students' ability to learn the curriculum and expect them to do well.
- Students and parents say their schoolwork is challenging but doable.

REFLECT & ENGAGE: RELATING FOUR CORRELATES TO STUDENT AND TEACHER SUCCESS

The correlates of strong instructional leadership, a clear and focused mission, a safe and orderly environment, and a climate of high expectations interact to create a positive, motivating learning environment in which teachers and students can do their best work.

The following activity involves creating a mind map.

A. Working in pairs, use these four effective schools correlates to create a mind map that shows how they interact in ways to create a positive, supportive learning climate for students and teachers.

B. When your mind maps are complete, present them to the class and explain your ideas.

C. Selecting the ideas that make the most sense and meaning to the class, create a collaborative mind map on a large piece of newsprint, whiteboard, or other media to illustrate how these four correlates interact to support effective schools.

14.2e Correlate: Frequent Monitoring of Student Progress

School leaders regard assessment as pivotal to measuring student progress as well as developing the data from which to make decisions about program adjustments. These data efforts inform individual students' progress, teacher and department effectiveness (and identify needs for professional development), and overall school performance.

Accordingly, in today's effective schools, measurement of student progress has shifted away from overwhelming reliance on summative, standardized, norm-referenced tests to daily and weekly formative measurements of student learning using an array of assessments, including students' projects, performances, and portfolios.[80] Teachers pay attention to aligning the intended, taught, learned, and tested curricula.

Research and Discussion

Educational accountability has become the primary public space in which we focus on racial, ethnic, class, and educational inequities (as discussed in detail in Chapters 7, 11, and 13). Although standardized tests—typically summative assessments used at the end of the learning process—provide valuable information about student attainment, they cannot measure many of learning's important aspects. In fact, standardized tests sometimes narrow the range of cognitive skills used and remove knowledge from real-world uses.

Likewise, standardized tests cannot identify individual students' specific learning weakness in ways and at times when teachers can quickly diagnose them and intervene to remediate and advance student learning. To increase each student's learning, teachers in effective schools use assessments in a wider variety of ways.

Rather, effective schools frequently use formative assessment as a continuing and integral part of the teaching and learning process. Typically, checking student progress is a daily and weekly occurrence embedded within the learning activity. It takes a few minutes to provide finely grained information, focusing on what the students are learning this day or during this particular instructional unit. Teachers use it to modify teaching and learning activities to meet student needs. Students use it to clearly understand the teachers' learning goals, help them assess their current position in relation to these goals, and give them the cognitive tools to span the gap between the two. Likewise, using a broad array of assessments throughout the school year—including daily observations, classwork, and interviews and frequent projects, portfolios, and presentations—teachers can give students specific and timely feedback on their learning progress in ways that support student achievement and increase the types and qualities of student learning.

Research supports the idea that these recurrent and varied performance assessments offer a way to increase every student's achievement. Studies indicate that students who receive formative assessments perform better on a variety of achievement indicators than their peers without formative assessments as part of their learning activities.[81] Importantly, while formative assessment helps all students, it has an outsized beneficial impact on low-achieving students,[82] in part because it reinforces the students' mindset that learning takes effort (not only innate ability), and they can improve their understanding and mastery by making targeted changes. Additionally, regular engagement with performance tasks as part of assessment also increases students' ability to use—that is, transfer—this knowledge for real-world problem-solving. Despite the methodological limitations, experts agree that the practice of assessment for learning shows promise in its ability to improve student performance.[83]

What Frequent Monitoring of Student Progress Looks Like in Schools

What do schools that use frequent monitoring of student progress look like?

- Teachers clarify their intentions for student learning and their criteria for success.
- Teachers analyze and interpret a variety of formative student assessment data to monitor and advance student learning, not merely to measure it.
- Teachers use feedback from multiple formal and informal student assessments to update (and adapt) their daily instruction to meet individual and groups' learning needs.
- Teachers provide feedback to individual students that advance their learning.
- Indicators of students' and the school's achievement are visibly posted and celebrated within the school.
- Teachers promptly grade and return student work with useful feedback.

- Teachers diagnose student learning difficulties early and act to fix them.
- Students believe that their academic goals are challenging and that they can meet them.
- Students talk with each other about their shared understanding about intended learning and the criteria for success.
- Students have an increasingly active role in assessing and evaluating their own progress.
- Students use prompt feedback to extend and deepen their learning.
- Students and parents can describe students' achievement status and growth.
- Individual student reports on achievement are regularly updated to track growth.
- Students and parents understand how students' work is assessed and graded.
- The principal and leadership team use a variety of achievement data to monitor the effectiveness of curriculum, instruction, and assessment and their impact on student learning in an ongoing manner.
- The principal and leadership team use a variety of student achievement data to monitor the effectiveness of individual teachers and academic departments to identity needs for professional development to advance teacher learning.
- The principal recognizes and celebrates teachers' and students' accomplishments and acknowledges (and learns from) failures.

14.2f Correlate: Positive Home–School Relations

Almost 60 years of research finds the most accurate predictor of a student's academic achievement is the extent to which families encourage learning at home and involve themselves in their child's education. And teachers who encourage parent engagement often see a substantial change in their classrooms: more highly motivated students, improved student behavior, and higher grades. **Parental involvement**—those parental or familial actions expected to improve student performance or behavior[84]—can be the driver (or at least a catalyst or reinforcer) of their children's school achievement.

In contemporary effective schools, the parent–school relationship becomes a genuine partnership. Teachers learn about their students' cultures and the local community and use these insights to inform their relationships and instruction. At the same time, the professional staff engage with parents and the community in ways that strengthen student learning. Both parents and teachers have much to learn from one another about how to best inspire their students to learn what the school teaches. To help all parties realize their mutual goal—an effective home and school for every child—educators and parents need to build actual trust and engage in clear, two-way communication.

Research and Discussion

Joyce Epstein, Johns Hopkins professor and an expert in school–family relationships, notices, "The way schools care about children is reflected in the way schools care about the children's families. If educators view children simply as *students*, they are likely to see the family as separate from the school. If educators view students as *children*, they are likely to see both the family and the community as partners with the school in children's education and development."[85]

The importance of including parents or guardians in their children's educational process becomes self-evident when we think about how much home and family shape student learning and achievement. Effective leaders see their outside partners as untapped resources and make connections with the community to promote the broad participation from parents, families, and other community members who can add to students' positive learning experiences.

Much research supports the assertion that parent involvement leads to improved academic achievement.[86] Studies also indicate that family involvement enhances children's academic, social, and emotional development.[87]

Recent studies find a significant but moderate association between parent participation and children's academic outcomes,[88] and this outcome is generally true for children of all races and at all academic levels.[89] Meta-analyses on studies conducted between 2000 and 2013 find that the strongest associations between parents and their children's academic achievement come when families have high academic expectations for their children,[90] develop and maintain communication with them about school activities,[91] and help them to develop good reading habits.[92] The Chicago Consortium of School Research shows that parent and community ties can have a systemic and sustained effect on children's learning outcomes as well as whole-school improvement when linked with other vital supports such as strong school leadership, a high-quality faculty, community engagement and partnership, a student-centered learning climate, and effective instructional guidance for teachers.[93] Surprisingly, the relationship between parental help with their children's homework and academic achievement is either very small,[94] mixed,[95] or negative.[96] Parent involvement has the largest effect for secondary education, followed by primary education. The least parental effects occur in kindergarten.[97]

More specifically, research documents that when schools work together with families to promote student learning, children tend to succeed not just in school but in life as well. These students attain the following results:[98]

- Earn higher grades and test scores and enroll in higher-level programs
- Attend school regularly and do more homework
- Gain promotions, pass their classes, and earn more course credits
- Show higher math and reading proficiency
- Receive fewer placements in special education
- Use better social skills, show improved behavior, and adapt well to school
- Receive fewer disciplinary actions
- Display higher graduation rates
- Secure greater enrollment in postsecondary education

Just as importantly, research shows that what a family *does* is more important to student success than what a family *is* or *earns.* Parental involvement is the most reliable predictor of academic achievement whether the child is in preschool or upper grades, whether the family is financially struggling or affluent, and whether the parents finished high school or earned graduate degrees.[99] Regardless of family income, children succeed in school when their families are able to accomplish the following:

- Create a home environment that encourages learning
- Express high (but not unrealistic) expectations for their children's achievement and future careers
- Become involved in their children's education in school and in the community

Family involvement can reduce the obstacles that low-income and racially/ethnically diverse students typically encounter in school. Research shows that when schools support families to develop these three conditions, children from low-income families and diverse cultural backgrounds earn the school grades and test scores that approach those attained by students from middle-class families. They are more likely to take advantage of a full range of educational opportunities after graduating from high school. Even when only one or two of these conditions are in place, children do measurably better in school.[100]

Families clearly benefit from forging close ties to schools. When they do, the teachers they work with have higher confidence in the parents and higher expectations for the children. In turn, parents develop more confidence about helping their children learn at home, about the school, and about themselves as parents. In addition, when parents become involved in their children's education, they often enroll in continuing education courses to advance their own learning.[101]

Schools and communities benefit from stronger family–school ties as well. Schools that work well with families realize the following advantages:[102]

- Improved teacher morale
- Higher ratings of teachers by parents
- More support from families
- Higher student achievement
- Better reputations in the community

The bottom line: When parents are genuinely involved in their children's education, their children do better in school and in life.

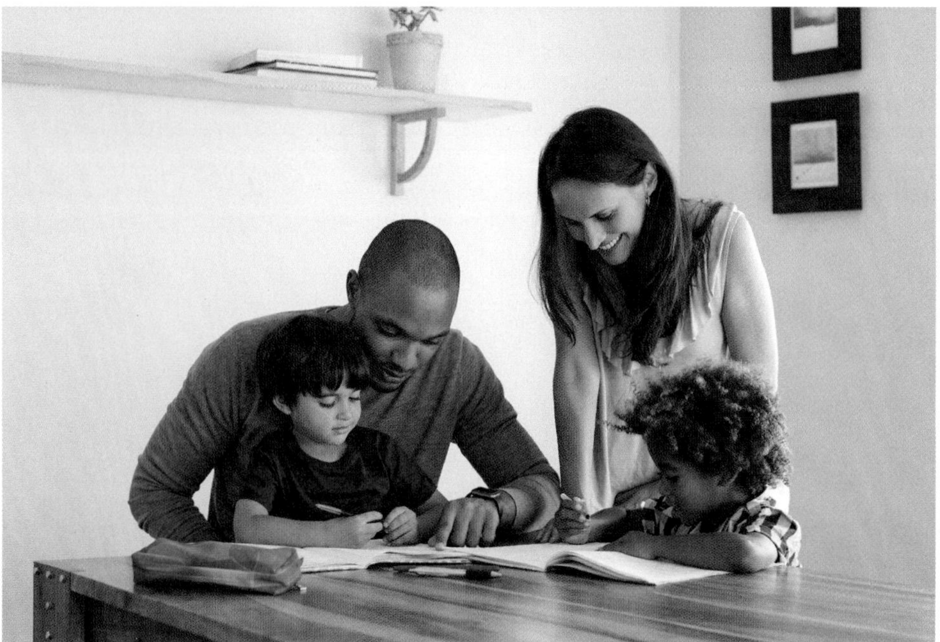

Research finds that family involvement has a powerful influence on student learning and achievement.
iStock/Ridofranz

What Positive Home–School Relations Look Like in Schools

When parents and educators work together successfully, the following behaviors are apparent in schools (as appropriate to the students' ages and maturity):

- Teachers understand and relate positively to students of diverse backgrounds.
- Parents and teachers meet together in formal conferences at least once a year.
- Teachers call on parents to use their talents and interests in school to help children learn.
- The school encourages parents to use various avenues for involvement.
- Teachers regularly call or email parents to discuss their child's progress and problems, and parents respond constructively to teachers' concerns.
- Teachers schedule regular interactive homework that requires students to demonstrate and discuss what they are learning with a family member.

- Teachers feel comfortable understanding and discussing parents' concerns about their child's academic, social, and behavioral progress.
- Parents feel increasingly comfortable in the school and supporting their children's learning at home.
- Teachers and administrators continually look for ways to involve parents and seek their input when making decisions and policies that affect their children's education.
- Schools provide clear information in the parents' preferred language about ways parents can help students learn at home by providing time, quiet, and space for homework and conduct other curricular-related activities.
- The school provides easily understood information to parents about the curriculum, assessments, and achievement levels; and parents and students make informed decisions annually about courses and programs of study.
- Teachers and parents are aware of and use community resources to enhance teaching and learning.
- Bilingual or multilingual employees work in school locations and are ready to welcome, meet, and greet parents and assist with parent–teacher conferences.
- Parent volunteers from various student demographics work visibly in the school.
- Students are aware of the school's importance to their family and better understand and follow school rules and policies because they have discussed these issues with their parents.
- The school schedules its events at different times during the day and evening so that all families can attend some throughout the year.

14.2g Correlate: Opportunity to Learn/Student Time on Task

Opportunity to learn (OTL) refers to equitable conditions or circumstances within the school or classroom that promote learning for all students. It means that *all* students—low-income, middle class, and affluent—have equal opportunities to receive high-quality teachers, rigorous curricula, relevant learning materials, well-presented and engaging instructional experiences, and well-maintained facilities that enable them to achieve high standards and avoid barriers that prevent learning. Of all school-level factors that affect student achievement, research finds that opportunity to learn has the strongest impact.[103]

Providing the access and finding enough time and high-quality resources to ensure every child's learning is a challenge for teachers. **Students' time on task** refers to the reality that learning is based on *time* to learn, not on the *rate* of learning. Some students master complex content quickly and often independently; others master it more slowly and with more assistance. Since effective schools intend that every child, not only those from affluent backgrounds, reaches the same high-quality educational outcomes, additional time and effort invested to advance certain students' learning gets better results. This is a matter of equity: Those who need more time and resources get them.

Much of the OTL research has focused on three types of indicators: curricula, pedagogy, and instructional resources. The *curricula* (instructional content) includes the degree and depth in which teachers cover academic material for different student groups. *Pedagogical processes* focus on how teachers organize classroom work and reflect teachers' varying instructional skill levels. *Instructional resources* comprise the supplies used in delivering instruction, including curricular materials, technology, safe and secure school facilities, and time availability and use. To some degree, these categories overlap.[104]

Curriculum and Opportunity to Learn

Having a **guaranteed and viable curriculum**—a combination of a rigorous curriculum to which every student has access with sufficient time and materials for teachers to successfully teach it—is strongly correlated with academic achievement. These factors are so interdependent that they may be considered as one feature.[105] Students have their opportunity to learn when they have a sufficient, up-to-date, and aligned curriculum taught by experienced, effective teachers who have enough uninterrupted time to present it and engage students with it. When teachers and students lack these essential resources, opportunity to learn suffers.

Schools actually have four curricula. The **intended curriculum** is the content specified by the state, district, or school to be addressed in a particular course at a particular grade level. The **taught curriculum** is the content the teacher delivers in the classroom. The **attained curriculum** is the one the students actually learn, and the **tested curriculum** is the one about which students must answer questions on classroom and standardized tests. Any mismatches detract from students' learning and reduce their OTL.

It may seem surprising that the intended curriculum and the taught curriculum are not always the same. Although public education provides teachers with much guidance on content standards for specific courses and grade levels, and school districts often develop curricula tied to these standards for teachers to use, teachers commonly make independent decisions about what they will cover and how deeply. Different teachers omit or include different topics, or they may spend 2 days or 2 weeks on the same topic. This practice frequently creates sizable holes in the *taught* curriculum—and in students' opportunity to learn the *intended* curriculum.

In a high-stakes testing environment such as we are now in, it is very important that every student has opportunities to learn the same information and skills to the same levels of depth and complexity that the standards specify, that they will see on assessments, and that they will need for more advanced courses and life outside school. Unless all students have the chance to learn the expected content to the same level of complexity that the assessment will measure it—or that the next course's teacher and real-world problem-solving require—they will be missing the opportunity to learn.

Effective Teaching and Opportunity to Learn

Improving students' opportunity to learn requires high levels of professional teaching competence. Teachers must know their subject and the standards to which they and their students will be held accountable. They must develop effective diagnostic skills to identify each student's learning obstacles in every required topic or skill. Teachers must deliver instruction in a variety of ways, adjusting their strategies to best suit the material and their students. They must design lessons that connect students to the content in ways that learners find personally meaningful and relevant. In turn, students must have occasions for demonstration, practice, and prompt feedback that they can immediately use to increase their learning. Further, these teachers and resources must be available to every student in every classroom. To teach in these ways requires teachers to become lifelong learners themselves as they keep enhancing their professional expertise and expanding their repertoire of teaching skills.

OTL teaching also means that teachers form partnerships with parents and guardians, encouraging them to support students' good learning and study habits at home. Ideally, teachers and parents will frequently communicate about students' progress and academic programs and support the others' efforts in their own ways.

Time and Opportunity to Learn

Time is a critical OTL variable. Before the Common Core State Standards, classroom teachers estimated that it would take 15,465 hours to adequately address the 200 standards and 3,039 benchmarks in national- and state-level documents covering 14 different subject areas.[106] Clearly, 15,465 hours of standards do not fit into 13,104 hours of K–12 instructional time. In part, the Common Core State Standards attempt to remedy the "mile wide and inch deep" curricula to better focus and pare it so students will have a realistic opportunity to learn them.

The school learning climate also impacts OTL. A school that values OTL deliberately organizes the school day (and time) in ways that best support instructional planning, teacher collaboration, and teaching itself. School leaders protect teachers from interruptions and unrealistic demands.[107] For example, administrators design a master schedule that coordinates teachers' preparation periods and designs common planning time for those teaching the same grade level, cluster or subject; ensure that all teachers have the curriculum and material they need for the subjects they teach; and reduce administrative tasks that have little or nothing to do with teaching or supporting students. And teachers may need additional time to analyze students' learning needs and respond with additional supports.[108]

What Opportunity to Learn/Time on Task Looks Like in Schools

What does opportunity to learn/time on task look like in schools?

- Schools establish curricular priorities, ensure appropriate teacher assignments, and provide students with needed supports.
- All students are enrolled in high-challenge, high-status courses with high-quality curriculum and effective teachers.
- Schools keep the expectations for student achievement high but vary the time and other resources needed to help every student reach the standards.
- Teachers involve all students in analyzing, synthesizing, generalizing, explaining, hypothesizing, and drawing conclusions to increase meaning and understanding.
- Teachers identify students' individual learning problems or misunderstandings early in the learning process and provide them with additional supports (time, individual assistance) as necessary.
- Teachers use a variety of instructional strategies to meet students' learning needs.
- Teachers receive the relevant materials, equipment, and ongoing professional development necessary for their successful job performance.
- Teachers use effective classroom management and organizational strategies to maximize learning time.
- Teachers design challenging (but not unduly frustrating) learning tasks for students that are adjusted to accommodate students' unique learning needs while ensuring they achieve high levels of mastery to meaningful standards.
- Classroom instructional resources for learning are equally accessible to all students.
- No public address announcements or other classroom interruptions occur during instructional time.
- Transitions between instructional activities and classroom routines occur smoothly with little time loss.
- Students with disabilities are included in all academic classes and receive collaborative teaching support.
- Students have opportunities to receive additional individualized assistance that addresses their specific learning challenges (e.g., teacher or classroom aide, peer tutor, interactive technology-based instructional resources aligned with the curriculum).
- Students who fail tests receive meaningful opportunities for remediation that focus on the test's knowledge and skills and give enough time to correct any weakness in that area before retaking the test.

14.3 EFFECTIVE SCHOOLS REPRISE

The effective schools correlates appear repeatedly in achieving schools at all grade levels, in separate regions, and among independent researchers. This consistency assures us that these correlates exist and have merit. That critics question the research methodology or claim that these schools' increased achievement scores may be random fluctuations simply means that the effective schools correlates are not a panacea for all ills affecting the U.S. educational system, nor are they easily infused into schools.[109] Other critics challenge the definitions used, the student demographics of these schools, and the stability of schools initially labeled as "effective" but then after a few years, fall back into low test scores.[110] But the critics of the effective schools correlates have never tried to discount their usefulness in promoting student learning.

Nonetheless, educators cannot completely close the achievement gap by intensively implementing the reforms advocated by proponents of the Effective Schools Movement without also tackling the underlying social problems that affect the children who attend our schools.[111] According to William J. Mathis, managing director of the National Education Policy Center in Boulder, Colorado, "To pretend that schools can single-handedly overcome a lifetime of deprivation through a 'whole-school action plan' or through rigorous and intensive adherence to a particular reading program is more an exercise in ritualistic magic than a realistic solution to social, economic, and personal problems."[112] Many children come to school with issues affecting their health, mobility, housing, nutrition, parents' unemployment, family structure, and medical and dental care—all of which have profound implications for how well they learn.

By themselves, these educational approaches cannot be completely successful. Six hours of daily instruction delivered over 180 days per year cannot overcome the effects of an impoverished or stressful home environment for 18 hours a day, 365 days a year. The data show, however, that when educators, parents, and communities integrate the effective schools correlates into their schools' daily life, they create important opportunities for more students to learn the high-level knowledge, skills, and habits of mind necessary for 21st century citizenship and self-sufficiency. Whatever the name, effective schools correlates have become "best practices." If a democracy thrives only with an educated populace, making every school effective is the best hope for our nation's future.

Despite their widespread success over the years—with or without the "effective schools" label—the Effective Schools Movement has identified certain realities that shape what the correlates can and cannot do to improve schools. Table 14.1 identifies many of these.

For a more complete understanding of how frequent monitoring of student progress, positive home–school relations, and opportunity to learn/student time on task contribute to every student's school success—regardless of personal background—complete the activity in the **Reflect & Engage** box, More Correlates Support Student Learning.

TABLE 14.1 ■ Effective Schools Realities

Effective School Factor	Explanation
No one model of effective schools exists.	No single set of variables can produce an effective school. Each school has its unique student and community factors that will influence how the correlates will work.
The correlates are prerequisites—not guarantees.	The correlates are proxies showing that the school is moving toward more successfully generating student achievement for every student demographic. They are necessary but not sufficient conditions for attaining high achievement for all and equitable achievement levels for low-income and students of color.
The correlates interact synergistically.	The correlates work together and influence one another in unique ways in different school environments. The practices may not look exactly the same in each school.
The correlates are challenges for schools to meet—not "recipes" to create high-achieving schools.	Each correlate has many steps that must be implemented correctly for each school's individual situation and in recognition of its interplay with the other correlates. Making a successful learning experience for every student is a very complex endeavor.
Schools must monitor and attend to all the correlates.	Schools are interacting systems. Changes in one place create ripples elsewhere. Schools must continually look for and account for (and if needed, remedy) the possible obstacles and repercussions their implementation may produce.

Effective School Factor	Explanation
Schools cannot undertake all of the correlates at one time.	Nor can they overlook implementing any one of them. All the correlates must eventually be present if student achievement for every student is to increase.
Each school's community socioeconomic context influences student achievement.	Both families and schools contribute to student learning. The best outcomes for students occur when both work together.
Underserved and low-income students' skills in effective schools are at least as well developed as those of middle-class children.	In effective schools, a child's SES cannot be determined by looking at test scores because all children are achieving well.

FLIPSIDES

Which Matters Most in Student Achievement: Families or Schools?

Too often, schools serving low-income and children of color have educators who believe that families—not schools—hold the overwhelming influence in student achievement. In contrast, educators in effective schools believe that high expectations for teachers and students with certain replicable practices—*along with family involvement*—can boost student learning and achievement regardless of their background. After comparing the two sets of beliefs and practices, which approach do you think does the most to increase student achievement?

Families—not schools—make the most difference in student achievement. Schools cannot overcome students' background limitations.	Schools—with families' support—can make the most difference in increasing student learning and achievement.
• Family background—socioeconomic status (SES), parenting practices, health issues, and housing stability, among other aspects—determines how well children learn in school. Schools cannot overcome these factors.	• Family background strongly influences children's learning, but high-quality instructional leadership, effective teachers, high-quality curricula, frequent assessments, and OTL can overcome many background factors.
• Teacher expectations for students' academic achievement are influenced by students' SES, race, ethnicity, use of standard English, and history of grade retention.	• Teachers with high expectations for each child's achievement, regardless of SES, are committed to delivering the instruction needed to help every child achieve at (or above) grade level.
• Teachers focus on helping students learn basic-level academic skills, often by providing remedial work, before they teach for "big ideas" and higher-level thinking.	• Teachers focus on helping every student learn basic-level academic skills, "big ideas," and high-level cognitive abilities within the same units by making the lessons meaningful to all students.
• Teachers give students opportunities to learn the standard school curriculum using regular instruction during the regular school day.	• Teachers give students opportunities to learn a high-quality curriculum with high levels of teaching competence and sufficient time and support (during and outside class) to learn it.
• Teachers use formative assessments to give students daily grades and rely on summative assessments to measure students' final achievement.	• Teachers use frequent formative assessments to monitor student learning progress, give students prompt feedback, and revise instructional plans; summative assessments are part of measuring students' final achievement.

Families—not schools—make the most difference in student achievement. Schools cannot overcome students' background limitations.	Schools—with families' support—can make the most difference in increasing student learning and achievement.
• Teachers believe that many of their low-income students and students of color will likely not complete high school or attend college.	• Teachers believe that their low-income students and students of color will complete high school and perhaps college.
• Teachers have an instructional role in the school and can be found in their classroom or in the teachers' workroom.	• Teachers have instructional and leadership roles in the school and can be found in the classroom and anywhere in the building.
• Teachers are assumed competent, and they continue their professional learning at their own discretion.	• Teachers are assumed competent, and schools give them opportunities to continue to extend and refine their abilities throughout their careers.
• Principals emphasize collegial and informal relationships with teachers and staff and stress general public relations. They are relatively easygoing with students and have good relationships with them.	• Principals as instructional leaders express (and enforce) high expectations for student behavior and teacher performance and regularly evaluate how well the students and teachers are achieving academic objectives.
• The achievement gap between middle-class and low-income and underserved students is large. One can guess students' SES by knowing their achievement test scores.	• The achievement gap between middle-class and low-income and underserved students is decreased or closed. One cannot accurately guess students' SES by knowing their achievement test scores.
• The school has very high suspension and dropout rates and a very low promotion and graduation rate.	• The school has very low suspension and dropout rates and a very high promotion and graduation rate.
• Teachers and administrators are fatalistic about current student achievement levels and have no plans to improve them.	• Teachers and administrators are dissatisfied about current student achievement levels and develop interventions to improve them.
• Teachers complain about lack of parent or family support for student achievement.	• Teachers find innovative ways to constructively involve parents and families in their students' learning.

Evidence supports the view that schools—with family support—can make a significant difference in low-income and underserved students' achievement. Schools that develop the culture and implement the practices of high expectations for all students (and teachers), regardless of family background, can raise student achievement to high levels.

REFLECT & ENGAGE: MORE CORRELATES SUPPORT STUDENT LEARNING

This activity involves creating a wordle (word cloud). Frequent monitoring of student progress, positive home-school relations, and opportunity to learn/student time on task are additional effective schools correlates that support student learning and teaching efficacy. Consider how these correlates interact with the four correlates discussed earlier.

A. Working alone, create a wordle using a digital tool such as Vizzlo using the seven correlates and related details to illustrate their relationships to each other and the ways they support successful teaching and learning.

B. Share your wordles in groups of four, each explaining his or her product and its meaning.

C. As a group, construct a wordle that reflects what you collaboratively see as the best ideas from the group members.

D. Present the group's wordle to the class. Identify which correlates you believe have the most personal meaning and relevance to you and explain why.

E. Discuss the correlate whose influence on teaching and learning surprises you the most and explain how that reshapes your ideas about how to generate the highest student outcomes.

F. Discuss how you as future teachers can use your knowledge of effective schools to focus your attention and gain valuable learning experiences during your teacher preparation program.

14.4 EDUCATING EVERYONE'S CHILDREN

Effective schools differ from other schools because they integrate the elements that make school success achievable for *every* student—instructional leadership, a clear and focused mission, a safe and orderly environment, a climate of high expectations, frequent monitoring of student progress, positive home–school relations, and opportunity to learn/time on task. Every child deserves to attend an effective school, and every teacher deserves to work in one.

14.4a Public Schools and the Public Good in a Pluralistic Society

Wanting to prove that well-run public schools with a vision for improving student outcomes could help children overcome limitations that their circumstances place on them, Ron Edmonds focused on what public schools could do. Today, public schools educate 90% of American children.[113] Most future teachers will work in public schools. After a chapter describing how effective schools can change a child's life trajectory for the better, it is reasonable to ask, *Do public schools serve a public good?*

A **public good** is a service provided without profit that benefits all members of the community, whether or not they contribute to its upkeep or use it themselves. Viewing public schools as providing a common civic advantage is anchored in humanistic and democratic values. When children receive a strong education and grow up to be gainfully employed, law-abiding citizens, that is a public good. By comparison, a **private good** benefits the individual, serving mainly those people who use them.[114] Of course, the community and nation benefits generally from having educated citizens, regardless of where their schooling occurred.

A brief history refresher helps explain why U.S. public schools are a public good. From its inception, the United States was viewed as a safety-valve—a way to relieve population, economic, and religious pressures in Europe. Immigration of varied people from assorted cultures, socioeconomic backgrounds, and belief systems was a fact of colonial life. English, Dutch, Germans, Scotch-Irish, Spanish, French, Swedes, and others migrated to North America, and they and their offspring adapted to their new surroundings. Even those living in the 13 English colonies were a mixture of races, cultures, religions, and languages.[115]

Not all the new settlers arrived in first-class cabins. Estimates suggest that Great Britain sent as many as 50,000 criminals to the 13 colonies. Perhaps as many as one half of all white immigrants during most of the colonial period were "indentured," unable to pay their travel or living expenses. Ship captains auctioned them off for a period of service to pay for their trans-Atlantic trip. About one fifth of the 18th century immigrants were Africans brought by force. In 1760, 15 years before the American Revolutionary War, about one third of colonists were born outside of America. Starting in 1820, immigration to the United States grew quickly each decade, exceeding 500,000 during the 1830s and rising above 2.5 million in the 1850s.[116]

Taxpayer-funded public schools would become the means to make all these diverse peoples Americans. Public schools provided a way to educate the community's children into the shared language, values, culture, and mutual respect needed to live safely and cooperatively together in communities within a shared nation. Both the individual and the larger society benefit from sharing general knowledge, critical thinking abilities for making decisions about societal problems, and the norms of civility and community engagement. Public schools continue to do this to this day.

"Our rights to privacy, free assembly, or the vote are protected only when citizens recognize their shared interests in these rights and work to safeguard the political process."[117] Accordingly, the public school curricula in history, civics, literature, language, and more enable students to appreciate these shared liberties and gain the knowledge to defend them. Public schools make these advantages widely available to children from all social classes, races, and ethnicities through a universal, tuition-free educational system.

By comparison, private schools do not serve these same ends. They may be founded on religious or sectarian values that may not always align to these civic ideas. Rather than be accessible to everyone, they tend to be tuition-based, excluding children from families who cannot afford (or who choose not) to pay these school costs out of pocket. Arguably, the intended or unintended separation or exclusion of students based on social class, intellectual ability, religious affiliation, sexuality, race, ethnicity, or other attribute weakens the larger community's power to champion the safeguarding of shared rights expected in a pluralist society.

Investigators who study the differences between U.S. public and private schools find substantial contrasts between the two types of educational institutions.[118] These differences include large variances in student demographics that affect their school achievement;[119] large disparities in the degree of government regulation and public accountability;[120] wide variances in openness to curricular and instructional innovation and effective professional practices;[121] and the presence of teachers with state-validated teaching certification (licenses).[122] Their conclusion: On average, public schools offer students a high-quality (or even superior) education at public expense.

14.4b Teaching as a Public Service

If public schools serve the public good, teaching in public school can be considered an essential public service, offering a keen sense of purpose and meaningful work that helps people in tangible and intangible ways. Today, we know the combination of school, home, and community factors that enable teachers to work successfully with children from every background. Developing the necessary pedagogical skills and excellence-plus-equity orientation can help teachers and school leaders give everyone's children, even those from low-income families, more opportunities to learn and achieve at high levels.

Many future teachers are highly idealistic, selecting a teaching career to help people and the larger society. Valuing the job's intrinsic rewards (such as interest and challenge) rather than its extrinsic rewards (such as income and prestige) is a highly commendable motive. But research finds that idealism may not be enough to keep new teachers in the profession.[123] Once inside their own classrooms, idealistic novice teachers with a generic sense of "wanting to make the world a better place" tend to become very frustrated and uncertain about the value of their work. As a result, they often quit the profession. By comparison, new teachers with eyes wide-open about public school realities (as this text has presented), a healthy dose of optimism and sense of humor linked with dogged persistence, and a love of children and lifelong learning may be better positioned to successfully meet the realities ahead.

Like John Dewey (1932) and scholars who followed,[124] educators with a bent for social justice see teaching as centered amid the cultural, racial, economic, and political tensions of their era. They want to ensure that every student has access to the high-quality curricula and the essential academic and moral supports to help them succeed in these classrooms and in adult life. They want to provide each of their students with opportunities to learn how to think and analyze critically, to be able to assess and evaluate the conditions in their world, and develop the academic skills needed to navigate these and take appropriate social action to improve it.[125] These teachers view public schools' frustrations as worthy challenges to overcome, and they have the vision, skill sets, energies, and (hopefully) the collegial supports to bend them toward fairness. With this social justice orientation, new teachers feel empowered rather than defeated.[126] Moreover, studies affirm that new teachers with this involvement positions them as valued leaders at their school sites and keeps them in the profession longer than average.[127]

Of course, public schools are imperfect. Every institution or organization has its weaknesses. But public schools welcome all eligible enrollees. And now we know how to create the learning conditions that enable children from various communities or origins to succeed and share in our common

American future. With an excellence-and-equity orientation, best practices in hand, and knowing what to look for—and work toward—in an educational setting, new teachers can transition into teaching more sure-footedly than with a naïve idealism. In short, the value of public schools and public school teachers extends well beyond individual benefits to include important civic priorities: They both prepare American students to live successfully in a pluralistic society in a democratic republic.

For a more complete understanding of how teachers and public schools contribute to our communities' and our national economic and political well-being, complete the activity in the **Reflect & Engage** box, U.S. Public Schools Are a Public Good, and Teaching Is a Public Service.

REFLECT & ENGAGE: U.S. PUBLIC SCHOOLS ARE A PUBLIC GOOD, AND TEACHING IS A PUBLIC SERVICE

This activity involves a role play. As a public good, taxpayer-funded public schools provide a way to educate the community's children in the shared values and culture needed to live safely and cooperatively together in communities. Teachers conduct a public service by facilitating the process.

You have all been named "Teachers of the Year" in school districts across your state because of the high esteem in which your colleagues, students, and parents hold you. Here is your situation:

About 90% of the students in your state attend public schools. Despite your highly diverse student population, student achievement is slightly above the national average. Teachers and administrators hold high expectations for students' achievement and behavior. Low-income children's achievement is improving but still lags behind that of their more affluent classmates. Teachers have confidence in their own and their colleagues' capacities to teach every child to high academic levels. Professional development for instructional improvement is ongoing and collaborative. Mostly, your school climates are calm and safe, the curricula are rigorous, and the students who need extra time and supports to master it receive them. Although your public schools are working respectably well, you are not satisfied. Room for improvement exists.

At the same time, private schools across the state are actively lobbying the state legislature to redirect public education funds into vouchers for parents to have their children attend private schools.

Your superintendents have asked you to work together to present a strong case to your local taxpayers' associations about why they should urge your state legislators to pass bills for the governor's signature to maintain or increase (not reduce or redirect) public schools' funding by persuading them that public schools are a public good and teachers perform a vital public service that both benefit the community, state, and nation.

A. Working in small groups of four, use this chapter to prepare a 5-minute persuasive talk to your local taxpayers' association on behalf of your goal. You can use graphic aids.

B. After about 20 minutes, each group presents its case to the rest of the class (i.e., the taxpayers' association).

C. As a class, discuss your views on whether or not you believe that public schools are a public good.

D. As a class, discuss whether or not they think teaching is a public service.

E. As a class, consider how new teachers who have a positive vision for what they realistically can do in schools to help every student overcome the "opportunity gap" (and who have in-school or professional network support for this role) tend to experience more success as a teacher (and remain in the profession) than being purely idealistic about "helping people."

KEY TAKE-AWAYS

Learning Objective 14.1 Examine the Effective Schools Movement's beginnings and its findings about schools' capacity to provide high-quality education for low-income students and students of color.

- Ron Edmonds: "No notion about schooling is more widely held than the belief that the family is somehow the principal determinant of whether or not a child will do well in school.... Such a belief has the effect of absolving educators of their professional responsibility to be instructionally effective."

- In the late 1970s and early 1980s, independent investigators across the country developed a body of research affirming that schools control the factors needed to ensure student mastery and high academic achievement among low-income and underserved students of the core curriculum, and the family plays a crucial role in promoting student learning.
- An **effective school** is one in which school practices enable low-income and underserved students' basic skills to be at least as well developed as the middle-class children's skills, closing the achievement gap between low- and high-SES students.
- Early investigators found that schools where low-income and racial and ethnic minority children achieved highly consistently shared certain beliefs and practices ("correlates") as prerequisites: strong principal or staff leadership, high expectations for student achievement, a clear set of instructional goals, an effective schoolwide staff professional development program, an emphasis on order and discipline, and a system for monitoring students' progress.
- No single combination of variables will produce an effective school; a pupil's family background neither causes nor prevents elementary school instructional effectiveness; the relationship between effective schools correlates and increased student achievement is correlational rather than cause-and-effect; and principals and teachers are responsible for instructional effectiveness.
- Effective school research has been subject to criticism of its principle, its theory, its methodology, its objectivity, and its practice. In answering its critics, much school effectiveness research recognizes the actual complexity of education goes well beyond test scores and is difficult (if not impossible) to separate schools' functioning from its larger social, economic, cultural, and political context.
- Today, effective schools practices have become best practices (with or without the *effective schools* label).

Learning Objective 14.2 Assess how each of the seven effective schools correlates contributes to student achievement and influences teachers' roles, as well as what each correlate looks like in schools.

STRONG INSTRUCTIONAL LEADERSHIP

- A large body of high-quality evidence demonstrates the modest but consistently significant contributions that school leadership makes indirectly to student learning, as well as the catalytic effects this leadership has on other essential aspects of the school and its community.
- As the school's "official" leader, the principal sets the climate, creates the expectations, clarifies the school's direction, and delivers the resources needed to make teaching and learning satisfying and successful endeavors. School leaders build their organizational cultures through participatory decision-making and collaborative planning, working closely with teacher leaders to define and express a clear and focused school vision and mission, setting goals, solving problems, and socializing their faculty to continue improving their pedagogy.
- When the current school's practices and structures do not allow principals to reach these goals, strong instructional leaders change the school organization to permit the vision and mission to flourish.
- The principal and other school leaders model and verbally express the school's values and practices at every opportunity, develop teacher leadership, and encourage faculty members to collaborate and learn from each other using individual and team strengths.

CLEAR AND FOCUSED MISSION

- A **vision** is an intelligent sense of what a better future can be; a **mission** is the purpose or direction pursued to reach that end. Vision tells where one wants to go, and a mission tells how one will get there. But vision and mission are not always thought of as two separate things. Effective leaders bring vision into action by sharing it with others.

- In an effective school, the principal and other school leaders continually champion a persuasive, shared vision and a clear, focused mission that defines what is important and directs the organization on how to reach it. The mission advocates *learning for all*, focusing on both the "learning" (what the student is doing and gaining) and the teachers' continuous professional growth (what the teachers are learning, doing, and gaining). Outcomes—not merely inputs—matter.
- The school implements its vision by setting (and meeting) goals and performance expectations for teachers and students. Teachers are the essential agents who turn the mission into daily actions. Seeing one's role in the "big picture" helps teachers see how their own jobs relate to it, and they can fit their skills and interests into the school's plan to help it get where it intends to go. Understanding the vision/mission helps the teachers' work life make sense and have meaning.
- Teachers as well as principals should be able to articulate enthusiastically the school's vision and mission. In enacting it, teachers present rigorous academic work in ways that students find interesting, personally relevant, varied, intellectually engaging, and actively involving.
- The school establishes regular two-way communication with stakeholders about how well the vision is being implemented and met.

Safe and Orderly Environment

- A safe and orderly environment is an organized, purposeful, cooperative, and nurturing atmosphere free from threat of harm in a school culture and climate that supports teaching and learning. All parties show respect for and appreciation of human diversity and democratic values.
- Many studies have singled out a safe and orderly environment as foundational to academic achievement. Teachers and students must feel physically and emotionally safe and comfortable if they are to have the psychological energy needed for teaching and learning. A secure and organized environment is significantly correlated with less student fear, lower dropout rates, and higher student commitment to their learning.
- Concern about one's physical or emotional safety shifts the brain's attention. At such times, the emotional parts of the brain are more fully aroused, and cognitive areas become less active. In such environments, individuals cannot find extra energy to pay attention to teaching and learning. Achievement suffers.
- School leaders and teachers help make the school psychologically safe when they work to ensure that every child succeeds academically, identify the diverse types of social and intellectual capital students bring with them to school, and leverage these in their interactions with students to motivate learning.

Climate of High Expectations

- To maintain a climate of high expectations for students, teachers must first hold high expectations for themselves.
- Researchers have also found that higher teachers' beliefs in their own and their colleagues' abilities to help all students make the academic advances that their school is asking of them, the higher the correlation with achievement levels and gains.
- Research finds that student characteristics such as physical attractiveness, socioeconomic status, race, use of standard English, and history of grade retention are related to teacher expectations for academic achievement. Teachers tend to treat students differently depending on these expectations.
- In a self-fulfilling prophesy, the more effective the teaching, the more effective the learning. As teachers improve their instructional practices, the more students learn, and teachers become

increasingly optimistic about their students' success. In turn, their students become more successful.

Frequent monitoring of student progress

- Effective schools include ongoing daily and weekly formative measurements of student mastery to guide their instruction and give students prompt corrective feedback to help them improve their learning. Although standardized tests and other summative assessments used at the end of the learning process provide valuable information about student attainment, they cannot measure many of learning's important aspects.
- Embedding the monitoring of student progress within the learning activity provides a steady stream of information to be used as feedback that teachers use to modify teaching and learning activities to meet student needs.
- Students use frequent feedback from formative assessments to clearly understand the teachers' learning goals, help them assess their current position in relation to these goals, and give them the cognitive tools to span the gap between the two.
- Research supports the idea that these recurrent and varied performance assessments offer a way to increase every student's achievement. Students who receive formative assessment perform better on a variety of achievement indicators than their peers without formative assessment as part of their learning activities. This is especially true for low-achieving students because it reinforces their mindset that learning takes effort, and they can improve by making specific changes.

Positive home–school relations

- Almost 60 years of research finds the most accurate predictor of a student's academic achievement is the extent to which families encourage learning at home and involve themselves in their child's education. This outcome is generally true for children of all races, SES, and at all academic levels. Studies also indicate that family involvement enhances children's academic, social, and emotional development.
- Research shows that regardless of family income, children succeed in school when their families are able to create a home environment that encourages learning; express high (but not unrealistic) expectations for their children's achievement and future careers; and become involved in their children's education in school and in the community.
- Joyce Epstein: "The way schools care about children is reflected in the way schools care about the children's families. If educators view children simply as *students*, they are likely to see the family as separate from the school. If educators view students as *children*, they are likely to see both the family and the community as partners with the school in children's education and development."
- Teachers who encourage parent engagement often see a substantial change in their classrooms: more highly motivated students, improved student behavior, and higher grades.
- Parent–school partnerships are collaborative relationships and activities involving school staff, parents and other family members, and communities to actively support children's learning and development. These partnerships recognize that all parties share responsibility and overlapping spheres of influence and vary in formats and complexity.

Opportunity to learn/Student time on task

- **Opportunity to learn (OTL)** refers to equitable conditions or circumstances within the school or classroom—such as high-quality teachers, rigorous curricula, relevant learning materials, well-presented and engaging instructional experiences, and well-maintained facilities—that promote learning for all students. Of all school-level factors that affect student achievement, opportunity to learn has the strongest impact.
- Students' time on task refers to the reality that learning is based on time to learn, not on the rate of learning. Some students master complex content quickly and often independently; others master

it more slowly and with more assistance. This is a matter of equity: Those who need more time and resources get them.

- Much of the OTL research has focused on three types of indicators: curriculum, pedagogy, and instructional resources. Having a guaranteed and viable curriculum—a combination of a rigorous curriculum to which every student has access with sufficient time and materials for teachers to successfully teach it—is strongly correlated with academic achievement. Unless all students have the chance to learn the expected content to the same level of complexity that the assessment will measure it—or that the next course's teacher and real-world problem-solving require—they miss OTL.
- Improving students' opportunity to learn requires high levels of professional teaching competence and sufficient time for each teacher to teach it and each student to learn it.

Learning Objective 14.3 Critique the rationale that the effective schools correlates by themselves cannot be completely successful in raising every student's achievement.

- No one model of effective schools exists. Each school has its unique student and community factors that will influence how the correlates will work. The correlates, interacting synergistically, are *prerequisites*—not a guarantee or recipe—for attaining high and equitable achievement levels for low-income and underserved students.
- Educators cannot completely close the achievement gap without also tackling the underlying social problems that affect the children who attend our schools.

Learning Objective 14.4 Defend the views of public schools as a public good and teaching as a public service.

- Public schools educate everyone's children, including those who most need caring and competent educators' interventions. Today, public schools educate 90% of American children.
- A public good is a service provided without profit that benefits all members of the community, whether or not they contribute to its upkeep or use it themselves. When children receive a strong education and grow up to be gainfully employed, law-abiding citizens, that is a public good. By comparison, a private good benefits the individual, serving mainly those people who use them.
- Immigration of varied people from assorted cultures, socioeconomic backgrounds, and belief systems was a fact of colonial life, and taxpayer-funded public schools became the means to make all these diverse peoples Americans, with a shared language, values, and culture needed to live together safely and cooperatively in society.
- Investigators who study the differences between U.S. public and private schools find substantial contrasts between the two types of educational institutions in areas of student demographics that affect student achievement, degree of government regulation and accountability, openness to curricular and instructional innovation, and presence of state-certified teachers. On average, public schools offer students a high-quality (or even superior) education at public expense.
- Teaching in public school can be considered an essential public service, offering a sharp sense of purpose and meaningful work that helps people in tangible and intangible ways. Developing the necessary pedagogical skills and excellence-plus-equity orientation can help teachers and school leaders give every child, even those from low-income and underserved families, more opportunities to learn and achieve at high levels.
- Research suggests that future teachers with eyes wide-open about public school realities, a healthy dose of optimism and humor linked with dogged persistence, a bent for social justice, and a love of children and lifelong learning may be better positioned to successfully meet the challenges ahead than a future teacher who is naively "idealistic" and prone to discouragement and burnout.

TEACHER SCENARIO: IT'S YOUR TURN

You have been invited to interview for your first teaching position. The interview begins with a writing sample. You are to respond to the following question:

Discuss what you see as the five most important aspects ("correlates"), in order of importance, that you would see in an effective school. Explain why you ranked them in the order you did, relate what you would see and what the school climate would be like if they were actively working in the school, and describe your own role in making these correlates a reality for all students.

NOTES

1. Edmonds, R. (1979, October). Effective schools for the urban poor. *Educational Leadership, 37*(1), 23.
2. Lezotte, L. (2001). *Revolutionary and evolutionary: The effective schools movement.* Effective Schools Products Ltd., p. 2; Lezotte, L. W., & Snyder, K. M. (2011). *What effective schools do: Re-envisioning the correlates.* Solution Tree Press.
3. Edmonds, 1979, p. 21.
4. Coleman, J., et al. (1966). *Equality of educational opportunity.* U.S. Government Printing Office.
5. Jencks surmised that students' achievement was primarily a function of the students' background. See Jencks, C., et al. (1972). *Inequality: A reassessment of the effect of family and schooling in America.* Basic Books, pp. 255–256.
6. Socioeconomic status is usually determined by considering parents' education and income.
7. Orlich, D. C. (1989, March). Education reforms: Mistakes, misconceptions, miscues. *Phi Delta Kappan, 70*(7), 516.
8. Scheerens, J., & Bosker, R. J. (1997). *The foundations of educational effectiveness.* Elsevier.
9. Scheerens & Bosker, 1997.
10. Good, T. L., & Brophy, J. E. (1986). School effects. In M. C. Wittrock (Ed.), *Handbook of research on teaching* (3rd ed.; pp. 570–602, 582). Macmillan.
11. Edmonds, R. R. (1982, December). Programs of school improvement: An overview. *Educational Leadership, 40*(3), 4–11.
12. Edmonds, 1982, p. 4.
13. Fredericksen, J. (1975). *School effectiveness and equality of educational opportunity.* Harvard University, Center for Urban Studies.
14. Lezotte, L., Edmonds, R., & Ratner, G. (1974). *Remedy for school failure to equitably deliver basic school skills.* Harvard University, Center for Urban Studies; Association for Effective Schools.
15. Edmonds's studies looked at relatively few and largely homogenous schools using norm-referenced tests, which made it difficult to see actual student learning gains or schools' effectiveness. For more on the critical reviews, see Purkey, S. C., & Smith, M. S. (1983, March). Effective schools: A review. *Journal of Elementary Education, 83*(4), 426–452.
16. Studies on teacher effectiveness have found that teacher effects explain more than the students' family backgrounds in producing student achievement. See: Chetty, R., Friedman, J. N., & Rockoff, J. E. (2014, May). Measuring the impacts of teachers II: Teacher value-added and student outcomes in adulthood. *American Economic Review, 104*(9), 2633–2679; Mendro, R. A., Jordan, H. R., Gomez, E., Anderson, M. C., & Bembry, K. L. (1998). *An application of multiple linear regression in determining longitudinal teacher effectiveness.* Dallas Independent School District; Sanders, W. L., & Horn, S. P. (1995). Educational assessment reassessed: The usefulness of standardized and alternative measures of student achievement as indicates for the assessment of educational outcomes. *Education Policy Analysis Archives, 3*(6), 1–15.
17. Marzano, R. (2000). *A new era for school reform: Going where the research takes us.* Mid-continent Research for Education and Learning, p. 13.
18. Brookover, W. B., & Lezotte, L. W. (1977). *Changes in school characteristics coincident with changes in student achievement.* Michigan State University, College of Urban Development.
19. Wimpelberg, R. K., Teddlie, C., & Stringfield, S. (1989). Sensitivity to context: The past and future of effective schools research. *Educational Administration Quarterly, 25*(1), 82–107.

20. Purkey, S. C., & Smith, M. S. (1983). Effective schools: A review. *The Elementary School Journal, 83*(4), 327–452.

21. Levine, D. U. (1990, Autumn). Update on effective schools: Findings and implications from research and practice. *The Journal of Negro Education, 59*(4), 577–584 (p. 582).

22. Teddlie, C., & Reynolds, D. (Eds.). (2000). *The international handbook on school effectiveness research.* Falmer.

23. Scheerens & Bosker, 1997; Scheerens, J. (1992). *Effective schooling: Research, theory, and practice.* Cassell; Bosker, R. J. (1992). *The stability and consistency of school effects in primary education.* University of Twente; Bosker, R. J., & Witziers, B. (1995, January). *School effects, problems, solutions, and a meta-analysis.* Paper presented at the International Congress for School Effectiveness and School Improvement, Leeuwarden, The Netherlands; Bosker, R. J., & Witziers, B. (1996). *The magnitude of school effects: Or, does it really matter which school a student attends?* Paper presented at the annual meeting of the American Educational Research Association, New York.

24. Heck, R. H. (2000). Examining the impact of school quality on school outcomes and improvement: A value-added approach. *Educational Administration Quarterly, 36*(4), 513–552; Heck, R. H. (2005). Examining school achievement over time: A multilevel, multi-group approach. In W. K. Hoy & C. G. Miskal (Eds.), *Contemporary issues in educational policy and school outcomes* (pp. 1–28). Information Age.

25. Heck, 2000.

26. Miller, R. J., & Rowan, B. (2006). Effects of organic management on student achievement. *American Educational Research Journal, 43*(2), 219–253.

27. Goddard, R. D., Sweetland, S. R., & Hoy, W. K. (2000) Academic emphasis and student achievement: A multi-level analysis. *Educational Administration Quarterly, 5*, 683–702; Goddard, R. D., Tschannen-Moran, M., & Hoy, W. K. (2001). Teacher trust in students and parents: A multilevel examination of the distribution and effects of teacher trust in urban elementary schools. *Elementary School Journal, 102*, 3–17; Goddard, R. D., LoGerfo, L., & Hoy, W. K. (2003, April). *Collective efficacy and student achievement in public high school: A path analysis.* Paper presented at the annual meeting of the American Educational Research Association, Chicago, IL.

28. Leithwood, K., Louis, K. S., Anderson, K. S., & Wahlstrom, K. (2004). *How leadership influences student learning. Review of research.* Wallace Foundation. https://conservancy.umn.edu/bitstream/handle/11299/2035/?sequence=1; Wallace Foundation. (2013, January). The school principal as leader: Guiding schools to better teaching and learning. Expanded edition. https://www.wallacefoundation.org/knowledge-center/Documents/The-School-Principal-as-Leader-Guiding-Schools-to-Better-Teaching-and-Learning-2nd-Ed.pdf

29. In 2020, Leithwood and colleagues revisited—and modified—their view of the principal as the school's number-two factor in advancing student achievement. Rather, they determined that because so many school factors affected student achievement, many of which the principal significantly influences, and although the principal is vital to school success, researchers cannot accurately assert that principals are number two. There is no number-two school influencer, but if there were, the principal would be it. See: Leithwood, K., Harris, A., & Hopkins, D. (2020). Seven strong claims about successful school leaders revisited. *School Leadership & Management, 40* (1), 5–22.

30. Fidler, B. (2004). A structural critique of school effectiveness and school improvement. In A. Harris & N. Bennett (Eds.), *School effectiveness and school improvement. Alternative perspectives* (pp. 47–74). Continuum; Luyten, H., Visscher, A., & Witziers, B. (2005). School effectiveness research: From a review of the criticism to recommendations for further development. *School Effectiveness and School Improvement, 16*(3), 249–279; Sandoval-Hernandez, A. (2008, March). School effectiveness research: A review of criticism and some proposals to address them. *Educate. Special Issue*, 31–44. http://www.educatejournal.org/index.php/educate/article/viewFile/141/152

31. Hargreaves, D. (1994). *Changing teachers, changing times.* Cassell.

32. Goldstein, H., & Woodhouse, G. (2000). School effectiveness research and educational policy. *Oxford Review of Education, 26*(3/4), 353–363. http://www.bristol.ac.uk/media-library/sites/cmm/migrated/documents/school-effectiveness-research-and-educational-policy.pdf

33. Goldstein, H., & Myers, K. (1996). Freedom of information: Towards a code of ethics for performance indicators. *Research Intelligence, 57*(1), 12–16; Pring, R. (1995). Educating persons: Putting education back into educational research (The 1995 SERA lecture). *Scottish Educational Review, 27*(2), 101–112.

34. Luyten, H., Visscher, A., & Witziers, B. (2005). School effectiveness research: From a review of the criticism to recommendations for further development. *School Effectiveness and School Improvement, 16* (3), 249–279.

35. Lauder, H., Jamieson, I., & Wikeley, F. (1998). Models of effective schools: Limits and capabilities. In R. Slee, G. Weiner, & S. Tomlinson (Eds.), *School effectiveness for whom?* Falmer.

36. McLaughlin, M. W. (1998) Listening and learning from the field: Tales of policy implementation and situated practice. In A. Hargreaves, A. Lieberman, M. Fullan, & D. Hopkins (Eds.), *International handbook of educational change: Kluwer international handbooks of education* (Vol. 5). Springer. https://doi.org/10.1007/978-94-011-4944-0; Miles, M. B. (1998) Finding keys to school change: A 40-year odyssey. In A. Hargreaves, A. Liberman, M. Fullan, & D. Hopkins (Eds.), *International handbook of school change* (Vol. 5, pp. 37–39). Kluwer Academic.

37. Cuban, L. (2018, June 3). *Whatever happened to effective schools? Classroom Practice.* https://larrycuban.wordpress.com/2018/06/03/whatever-happened-to-effective-schools/

38. Finn, C. (1986). *What works: Research about teaching and learning.* U.S. Department of Education.

39. U.S. Department of Education. (2004). *Teachers improve student performance. Comprehensive school reform program.* Archived Information. https://www2.ed.gov/programs/compreform/2pager.html

40. Smith, M. S., & O'Day, J. (1990, April). Systemic school reform. *Journal of Education Policy, 5*(5), 233–267.

41. These schools had at least 60% of students eligible for free or reduced-price lunch and they scored at least 5 points above the state average in mathematics or English language arts. Eighteen of the 30 schools outperformed school district peers by 20 points or more in math or ELAS. See: Kaplan, C. (2011). *Time well spent: Eight powerful practices of successful expanded-time schools.* National Center on Time & Learning. https://files.eric.ed.gov/fulltext/ED534903.pdf

42. Tuttle, C. C., Gill, B., Gleason, P., Knechtel, V., Nichols-Barrer, I., & Resch, A. (2013, February 27). KIPP middle schools: Impacts on achievement and other outcomes. *Mathematica Policy Research.* https://files.eric.ed.gov/fulltext/ED540912.pdf

43. The Education Trust. (2005, November). *Gaining traction gaining ground. How some high schools accelerate learning for struggling students.* https://edtrust.org/wp-content/uploads/2013/10/GainingTractionGainingGround.pdf

44. Charter Schools Institute. (2013). Harlem Village Academy leadership charter school. School evaluation report 2012-13. *School evaluation visit. Benchmark conclusions and evidence* (pp. 10–14). https://www.newyorkcharters.org/wp-content/uploads/Harlem-Village-Academy-Leadership-School-Evaluation-2012-13.pdf

45. Lezotte, L. (1991). *Correlates of effective schools: The first and second generation.* Okemos, MI: Effective Schools; Lezotte and Snyder, 2011.

46. Hallinger, P. (2008, March). *A review of PIMRS studies of principal instructional leadership: Assessment of progress over 25 years.* Paper presented at the annual meeting of the American Educational Research Association (AERA), New York; Hallinger, P., & Murphy, J. (1985). Assessing the instructional leadership behavior of principals. *Elementary School Journal, 86*(2), 217–248.

47. Hallinger, P. (2010). Developing instructional leadership. In B. Davies & M. Brundrett (Eds.), *Developing successful leadership* (Chap. 5; pp. 61–76). Springer.

48. Leithwood et al., 2004, p. 7.; Leithwood, K., Harris, A., & Hopkins, D. (2020). Seven strong claims about successful school leadership revisited. *School Leadership & Management, 40*(1), 5–22.

49. Grissom, J. A., Loeb, S., & Master, B. (2013). Effective instructional time use for school leaders. *Educational Researcher, 42*(8), 433–444.

50. Marzano, R. J., Waters, T., & McNulty, B. A. (2005). *School leadership that works: From research to results.* Association for Supervision and Curriculum Development.

51. Branch, G., Hanushek, E. A., & Rivkin, S. G. (2013. Winter). School leaders matter. *EducationNext, 13*(1), http://hanushek.stanford.edu/sites/default/files/publications/Branch%2BHanushek%2BRivkin%20 2013%20EdNext%2013%281%29_0.pdf

52. Leithwood et al., 2020.

53. Hoy, W., Tarter, J., & Wolfolk-Hoy, A. (2006). Academic optimism of schools: A force for student achievement. *American Educational Research Journal, 43*(3), 425–446.

54. Leithwood, K., &. Sun, J. (2018). Academic culture: A promising mediator of school leaders' influence on student learning. *Journal of Educational Administration, 56*(3), 350–363.

55. Berebitsky, D., & Salloum, S. J. (2017). The relationship between collective efficacy and teachers' social networks in urban middle schools. *AERA Open, 3*(4). doi:10.1177/2332858417743927

56. Leithwood, K., Harris, A., & Hopkins, D. (2008). Seven strong claims about successful school leadership. *School Leadership and Management, 28*(1), 27–42 (p. 2).

57. Heck, R. (2000, October). Examining the impact of school quality on school outcomes and improvement: A value-added approach. *Educational Administration Quarterly, 36*(4), 541; Hitt, D. H., & Tucker, P. D. (2016). Systematic review of key leader practices found to influence student achievement: A unified framework. *Review of Educational Research, 86*(2), 531–569; Leithwood et al., 2020; Waters, T., Marzano, R. J., & McNulty, B. (2003). *Balanced leadership. What 30 years of research tells us about the effect of leadership on student achievement. A working paper.* Mid-continent Research for Education and Learning.

58. The Effective Schools Movement did not use the term "vision." Its *mission* assumed *vision* as an integral part. To the members of this movement, a "clear and focused mission" meant challenging the conventional wisdom that students' achievement depended almost totally on their family backgrounds, which schools could not overcome.

59. Bennis, W., & Nanus, B. (1997). *Leaders: Strategies for taking charge.* HarperCollins, p. 82.

60. Covey, S. R. (1989). *The seven habits of highly effective people.* Simon and Schuster, p. 106.

61. Leithwood, K. (1994). Leadership for school restructuring. *Educational Administration Quarterly, 30*(4), 498–518.

62. Heck, 2000, p. 542; Fitzpatrick, K. A. (1998, July). *Indicators of schools of quality. Volume 1: Schoolwide indicators of quality.* National Study of School Evaluation, p. 149; Hitt & Tucker, 2016; Leithwood et al., 2020.

63. Lezotte, 1991, pp. 1–2; Lezotte & Snyder, 2011, pp. 101–113.

64. Mayer, D. P., Hoy, W. K., & Hannun, J. (1997). Middle school climate: An empirical assessment of organizational health and student achievement. *Educational Administration Quarterly, 33*(3), 290–311; Mullens, J. E., Moore, M. T., & Ralph, J. (2000). *Monitoring school quality: An indicators report.* U.S. Department of Education, National Center for Education Statistics; Grogger, J. (1997). Local violence and educational attainment. *Journal of Human Resources, 32*(4), 659–692.

65. Hoy & Hannun, 1997; Hoy, W. K., Hannum, J., & Tschannen-Moran, M. (1998, July). Organizational climate and student achievement: A parsimonious and longitudinal view. *Journal of School Leadership, 8*(4), 1–22; Hoy, W. K., & Sabo, D. (1998). *Quality middle schools: Open and healthy.* Corwin; Goddard, R. D., Sweetland, S. R., & Hoy, W. K. (2000). Academic emphasis of urban elementary schools and student achievement: A multi-level analysis. *Educational Administration Quarterly, 36*(5), 683–702.

66. Heck, 2000; Hitt & Tucker, 2016; Marzano, 2003, pp. 55–59.

67. Ferguson, R. R. (2003). Teachers' perceptions and expectations in the black-white test score gap. *Urban Education 38*(4), 460–507.

68. Brookover, W. B., & Lezotte, L. W. (1979). *Changes in school characteristics coincident with changes in student achievement.* Michigan State University, Institute for Research on Teaching; Edmonds, R. R., & Fredericksen, J. R. (1978). *Search for effective schools: The identification and analysis of city schools that are instructionally effective for poor children.* Harvard University, Center for Urban Studies; Brophy, J. E., & Evertson, C. (1976). *Learning from teaching: A developmental perspective.* Allyn & Bacon; McDonald, R., & Elias, P. (1976). The effects of teaching performance on pupil learning: Vol. I, final report. *Beginning teacher evaluation study, phase 2, 1974–1976.* Educational Testing Service; Rotter, M., Maughan, B., Mortimore, P., Ouston, J., & Smith, A. (1979). *Fifteen thousand hours: Secondary schools and their effects of children.* Harvard University Press.

69. Brophy, J., & Good, T. (1970). Teachers' communication of differential expectations for children's classroom performance: Some behavioral data. *Journal of Educational Psychology, 61*, 365–374; Dusek, J. B., & O'Connell, E. J. (1973). Teacher expectancy effects on the achievement test performance of elementary school children. *Journal of Educational Psychology, 65*, 371–377; O'Connell, E., Dusek, J., & Wheeler, R. (1974). A follow-up study of teacher expectancy effects. *Journal of Educational Psychology, 66*, 325–328; Rist, R. (1970). Students' social class and teacher expectations: The self-fulfilling prophesy in ghetto education. *Harvard Educational Review, 40*, 411–451.

70. Brophy & Good, 1970; Dusek, J. B. (1975). Do teachers bias children's learning? *Review of Educational Research, 45*, 661–684; Rosenthal, R. (1973). *On the social psychology of the self-fulfilling prophesy: Further evidence for Pygmalion effects and their mediating mechanisms.* Module 53. MSS Modular Publications; Rosenthal, R. (1976). *Experimenter effects in behavioral research* (2nd ed.). Irvington.

71. Egan, O., & Archer, P. (1985). The accuracy of teachers' rating of ability: A regression model. *American Educational Research Journal, 22*, 25–34; Hoge, R., & Butcher, R. (1984). Analysis of teacher judgments of pupil achievement level. *Journal of Educational Psychology, 76*, 777–781; Mittman, A. (1985). Teachers' differential behavior toward higher and lower achieving students and its relation to selected teacher characteristics. *Journal of Educational Psychology, 77*, 149–161; Monk, M. (1983). Teacher expectations? Pupil responses to teacher mediated classroom climate. *British Educational Research Journal, 9*, 153–166; Pedulla, J., Airasian, P., & Madaus, G. (1980). Do teacher ratings and standardized test results of students yield the same information? *American Educational Research Journal, 17*, 303–307; Good, T.

L. (1987). Two decades of research on teacher expectations: Findings and future direction. *Journal of Teacher Education, 4*, 32–47.

72. Ferguson, 2003.

73. Cecil, N. L. (1988). Black dialect and academic success: A study of teacher expectations. *Reading Improvement, 25*(1), 34–38; Dusek, J. B., & Joseph, G. (1983). The bases of teacher expectancies: A meta-analysis. *Journal of Educational Psychology, 75*(3), 327–346; Gaines, M. L., & Davis, M. (1990, April). *Accuracy of teacher prediction of elementary student achievement.* Paper presented at the annual meeting of the American Educational Research Association, Boston, MA (ERIC Document Reproduction Service No. ED 320 942); Kenealy, P., Neil, F., & Shaw, W. (1988). Influences of children's physical attractiveness on teacher expectations. *Journal of Social Psychology, 128*(3), 373–383: Williams, J. H., & Muehl, S. (1978). Relations among student and teacher perceptions of behavior. *Journal of Negro Education, 47*, 328–336.

74. Peterson, P. L., & Barger, S. A. (1984). Attribution theory and teacher expectancy. In J. B. Dusek (Ed.), *Teacher expectancies* (pp. 159–184). Lawrence Erlbaum.

75. Coladarci, T. (1986). Accuracy of teacher judgments of student response to standardized test items. *Journal of Educational Psychology, 78*(2), 141–146; Hoge, R. D., & Butcher, R. (1984). Analysis of teacher judgments of pupil achievement level. *Journal of Educational Psychology, 76* (5), 777–781; Patriarca, L. A., & Kragt, D. M. (1986, May/June). Teacher expectations and student achievement: The ghost of Christmas future. *American Review*, 48–50.

76. Raudenbush, S. W. (1984). Magnitude of teacher expectancy effects on pupil IQ as a function of the credibility of expectancy induction: A synthesis of findings from eighteen experiments. *Journal of Educational Psychology, 76*(1), 85–97.

77. Ferguson, 2003, p. 483; Guskey, T. (1982, July–August). The effects of change in instructional effectiveness on the relationship of teacher expectations and student achievement. *Journal of Educational Research, 75*(6), 345–349.

78. Waters et al., 2003; Heck, 2000.

79. Waters et al., 2003; Heck, 2000.

80. Lezotte, 1991; Lezotte & Snyder, 2011, pp. 91–100.

81. Black, P., & Wiliam, D. (1998). Assessment and classroom learning. *Assessment in Education: Principles, Policy & Practice, 5*(1), 7–74; Black, P., & Wiliam, D. (2009, February). Developing the theory of formative assessment. *Educational Assessment, Evaluation and Accountability, 21*(1), 8; Hanover Research. (2014, August). *The impact of formative assessment and learning intentions on student achievement.* https://www.hanoverresearch.com/media/The-Impact-of-Formative-Assessment-and-Learning-Intentions-on-Student-Achievement.pdf; Madison-Harris, R., & Muoneke, A. (2012, January). *Using formative assessment to improve student achievement in the core content areas.* Briefing papers. American Institutes for Research. http://www.sedl.org/secc/resources/briefs/formative_assessment_core_content/

82. Black & Wiliam, 2009, 5–31.

83. Black & Wiliam, 2009, 8; Hanover Research. (2014, August). *The impact of formative assessment and learning intentions on student achievement.* https://www.hanoverresearch.com/media/The-Impact-of-Formative-Assessment-and-Learning-Intentions-on-Student-Achievement.pdf

84. McNeal, R. B., Jr. (2014). Parent involvement and academic achievement, and the role of student attitudes and behaviors as mediators. *Universal Journal of Educational Research, 2*(8), 564–576.

85. Epstein, J. L. (1995, May). School/family/community partnerships: Caring for the children we share. *Phi Delta Kappan, 76*(9), 701–712.

86. Casreo, M., Exposito-Casas, E., Lopez-Martin, E., Lizasoain, L., Navarro-Ascensio, E., & Gaviria, J. L. (2015, February). Parental involvement on student academic achievement: A meta-analysis. *Educational Research Review, 14*(1), 33–46; Epstein, J. (1991). Effects on student achievement of teachers' practices of parent involvement. *Advances in Reading/Language Research, 5*, 261–276; Hill, N. E., & Tyson, D. F. (2009). Parental involvement in middle school: A meta-analytic assessment of the strategies that promote achievement. *Developmental Psychology, 45*(3), 740–763.

87. Banerjee, M., Harrell, Z. A. T., & Johnson, D. J. (2011). Racial/ethnic socialization and parental involvement in education as predictors of cognitive ability and achievement in African American children. *Journal of Youth and Adolescence, 40*, 595–605; Farkas, M. S., & Grolnick, W. S. (2010). Examining the components and concomitants of parental structure in the academic domain. *Motivation and Emotion, 34*, 266–279; Jeynes, W. (2012). A meta-analysis of the efficacy of different types of parental involvement programs for urban students. *Urban Education, 47*(4), 706–742; Mapp, K. L., & Kuttner, P. J. (2013). *Partners in education: A dual capacity-building framework for family-school partnerships.* SEDL & U.S. Department of Education. http://www2.ed.gov/documents/family-community/partners-education.pdf

88. Casreo et al., 2015.

89. Jeynes W. H. (2003). A meta-analysis: The effects of parental involvement on minority children's academic achievement. *Education and Urban Society, 35*(2), 202–218; Jeynes, W. H. (2005). The effects of parental involvement on the academic achievement of African American youth. *Journal of Negro Education, 74*(3), 260–274; Jeynes, W. H. (2012). A meta-analysis of the efficacy of different types of parental involvement programs for urban students. *Urban Education, 47*(4), 706–742; Wilder, S. (2014). Effects of parental involvement on academic achievement: A meta-synthesis. *Educational Review, 66*(3), 377–397.

90. Casreo et al., 2015; Wilder, 2014; Jeynes, 2007.

91. Casreo et al., 2015; Jeynes, 2003, 2005.

92. Casreo et al., 2015.

93. Bryk, A. S., Sebring, P. B., & Allensworth, E. (2009). *Organizing schools for improvement: Lessons from Chicago.* University of Chicago Press.

94. Casreo et al., 2015; Patall, E., Cooper, H., & Robinson, J.D. (2008). Parent involvement in homework: A research synthesis: *Review of Educational Research, 78*(4), 1039–1101; Wilder, 2014.

95. Patall et al., 2008.

96. Barger, M. M., Kim, E. M., Kuncel, N. R., & Pomerantz, E. M. (2019, July). The relation between parents' involvement in children's schooling and children's adjustment: A meta-analysis. *Psychological Bulletin, 145*(9), 855–890; Casreo et al., 2015; Hill & Tyson, 2009.

97. Casreo et al., 2015; Jeynes, 2012.

98. Henderson, A. T., & Berla, N. (Eds.). (1994*). A new generation of evidence: The family is critical in student achievement.* National Committee for Citizens in Education, p. 1. https://files.eric.ed.gov/fulltext/ED375968.pdf; Epstein, J. L. (1991). Effects of students' achievement of teacher practices of parent involvement. In S. B. Silvern (Ed.), *Advances in teaching/language research: Vol. 5. Literacy through family, community, and school interaction* (pp. 261–276). JAI Press; Henderson, A. T., &. Mapp, K. L. (2002). *A new wave of evidence: The impact of school, family and community connections on student achievement. Annual synthesis 2002.* National Center for Family and Community Connections With Schools. https://www.sedl.org/connections/resources/evidence.pdf; Jeynes, W. H. (2007). The relationship between parental involvement and urban secondary school student academic achievement. *Urban Education, 42*(1), 82–110.

99. Henderson & Berla, 1994; Henderson & Mapp. 2002.

100. See: Catsambis, S. (2001). Expanding knowledge of parental involvement in children's secondary education: Connections with high school seniors' academic success. *Social Psychology of Education 5*, 149–177; Sheldon, S. B., & Epstein, J. L. (2004). Getting students to school: Using family and community involvement to reduce chronic absenteeism. *School Community Journal, 4*(2), 39–56; Sheldon, S. B., & Epstein, J. L. (2005a). Involvement counts: Family and community partnership and math achievement. *Journal of Educational Research, 98*, 196–206; Sheldon, S. B., & Epstein, J. L. (2005b). School programs of family and community involvement to support children's reading and literacy development across the grades. In J. Flood & P. Anders (Eds.), *Literacy development of students in urban schools: Research and policy* (pp. 107–138). International Reading Association; Simon, B. S. (2004). High school outreach and family involvement. *Social Psychology of Education, 7*, 185–209.

101. Henderson & Berla, 1994.

102. Henderson & Berla, 1994.

103. Marzano, R. J. (2003). *What works in schools: Translating research into action.* Association for Supervision and Curriculum Development, pp. 22–25.

104. Venezia, A., & Maxwell-Jolly, J. (2007). *The unequal opportunity to learn in California schools: Crafting standards to track quality.* University of California, Policy Analysis for California Education.

105. Marzano, 2003, p. 22.

106. Kendall, J. S., & Marzano, R. J. (2000). *Content knowledge: A compendium of standards and benchmarks for K-12 students* (3rd ed.). Association for Supervision and Curriculum Development; Marzano, R. J., Kendall, J. S., & Gaddy, B. B. (1999). *Essential knowledge: The debate over what American students should know.* Mid-continent Regional Educational Laboratory, pp. 24–25.

107. Johnson, S. M. (2019, June). *Where teachers thrive: Organizing schools for success.* Harvard Education Press.

108. Anderson, J. (2019, September 17). *The fit of teacher time. Making teachers' time a valued resource in our school.* Harvard Graduate School of Education. https://www.gse.harvard.edu/news/uk/19/09/gift-teacher-time

109. Mathis, W. J. (2005, April). Bridging the achievement gap. A bridge too far? *Phi Delta Kappan, 86*(8), 591.

110. Fullan, M. (2008, January). From school effectiveness to system improvement: An inevitable conceptual evolution. Paper prepared for *Journal für Schulentwicklung.* OISE/ University of Toronto. https://michaelfullan.ca/wp-content/uploads/2016/06/Untitled_Document_25.pdf; Teddlie, C., & Stringfield, S. (2007, January). A history of school effectiveness and improvement research in the USA focusing on the past quarter century. In T. Townsend (Ed.*), International handbook of school effectiveness and improvement* (pp. 131–166). Springer; Silver, H. (1995, June). *Good schools, effective schools: Judgments and their histories.* School Development Series. Books International.

111. Borman, G. D., & Hewes, G. M. (2002, Winter). The long-term effects and cost-effectiveness of success for all. *Educational Evaluation and Policy Analysis, 24*(4), 243–266; Rothstein, R. (2004). *Class and schools: Using social, economic, and educational reform to close the black-white achievement gap.* Teachers College Press.

112. Mathis, 2005, p. 591.

113. Fuerstein, A. (2017, February 28). America's kids: Let's not make our educational system more unequal than it already is. *The Hechinger Report.* https://hechingerreport.org/traditional-public-schools-educate-90-percent-americas-kids-lets-not-make-educational-system-unequal-already/

114. Labaree, D. F. (2018, November). Public schools for private gain: The declining American commitment to serving the public good. *Phi Delta Kappan, 100*(3), 8–13.

115. Schlesinger, A. M. (1921, July). The significance of immigration in American history. *American Journal of Sociology, 27*(1), 71–85.

116. As discussed in Schlesinger, 1921.

117. Abowitz, K. K., & Stitzlein, S. M. (2018, November). Public schools, public goods, and public work. *Phi Delta Kappan, 100*(3), 33–37 (p. 35).

118. Braun, H. (2007, March–April). Are private schools better than public schools? *Principal, 86*(4), 22–25. https://www.naesp.org/sites/default/files/resources/2/Principal/2007/M-Ap22.pdf; Lubienski, C. A., & Lubienski, S. T. (2014). *The public school advantage: Why public schools outperform private schools.* The University of Chicago Press; Weglinsky, H. (2007). *Are private high schools better academically than public high schools*? Center on Education Policy.

119. These student demographic differences include socioeconomic backgrounds, parents' education and occupations (and the social capital that comes with these), prior school achievement, and other factors. When researchers statistically control student achievement data by student demographics, they find that public schools tend to perform no worse academically than—and often perform far superior to—private schools in student achievement. See: Lubienski & Lubienski, 2014.

120. High governmental regulations and public accountability for student achievement and financial stewardship in public schools but not in private schools.

121. Investigators found public schools more welcoming to curricular and instructional innovation and effective teaching practices than they found in private schools.

122. Some research shows the positive effects of teacher certification and a college major in the subject one will teach on student achievement. See: Darling-Hammond, L. (2000). Teacher quality and student achievement. *Education Policy Analysis Archives, 8*(1), 1–44. https://epaa.asu.edu/ojs/article/view/392/515; Darling-Hammond, L., Berry, B., & Thoreson, A. (2001). Does teacher certification matter? Evaluating the evidence. *Educational Evaluation and Policy Analysis, 23*(1), 57–77; Goldhaber, D., & Brewer, D.J. (2000). Does teacher certification matter? High school teacher certification status and student achievement. *Educational Evaluation and Policy Analysis, 22*(2), 129–145; Greenwald, R., Hedges, L., & Laine, R. (1996). The effect of school resources on school achievement. *Review of Educational Research, 66*(3), 361–396.

123. Hong, J. Y. (2010). Preservice and beginning teachers' professional identity and its relation to dropping out of the profession. *Teaching and Teacher Education, 26*(8), 1530–1543; Miech, R. A., & Elder, G. H., Jr. (1996, July). The service ethic and teaching. *Sociology of Education, 69*(3), 237–253.

124. Dewey, J. (1932). *The school and society.* University of Chicago Press; Counts, G. (1932). *Dare the school build a new social order?* Derek Day; Anyon, J. (1981). Social class and school knowledge. *Curriculum Inquiry, 11*(1), 3–10; Banks, J. (2006). Democracy, diversity, and social justice: Educating citizens for the public interest in a global age. In G. Ladson-Billings & W. F. Tate (Eds.), *Education research in the*

public interest. Teachers College Press; Giroux, H. J. A., & McLaren, P. (1986). Teacher education and the politics of engagement: The case for democratic schooling. *Harvard Educational Review, 56*(3), 213–238.

125. Cochran-Smith, M. (2004). *Walking the road: Race, diversity, and social justice in teacher education*. Teachers College Press; Giroux, H. (1995). Teachers, public life, and curriculum reform. In A. C. Ornstein & L. S. Behar-Hornstein (Eds.), *Contemporary issues in curriculum* (2nd ed.). Allyn & Bacon; Oakes, J., & Lipton, M. (2006). *Teaching to change the world* (3rd ed.). McGraw-Hill Higher Education; Picower, B. (2011, Fall). Learning to teach and teaching to learn: Supporting the development of new social justice educators. *Teacher Education Quarterly*, 38(4), 7–24; Westheimer, J., & Kahne, J. Introduction. *Equity & Excellence in Education, 40*(2), 97–100.

126. Duncan-Andrade, J. M. R. (2004). Toward teacher development for the urban in urban teaching. *Teaching Education, 15*(4), 339–350; Picower, B. (2007). Teacher education does not end at graduation: Supporting new teachers to teach for social justice. *Penn GSE Perspectives on Urban Education, 5*(1), 1–22. https://files.eric.ed.gov/fulltext/EJ852632.pdf; Quartz, K. (2003). "Too angry to leave": Supporting new teachers' commitment to transform urban schools. *Journal of Teacher Education, 54*(2), 99–111.

127. Quartz, 2003.

GLOSSARY

529 Plans. Formerly called tax-advantaged college investment (savings) accounts, they allow parents and grandparents to contribute to their child's college savings and deduct their annual contributions for "qualifying expenses" (including tuition, books, fees, supplies, and some room and board) from their income taxes. Since December 2017, the Tax Cuts and Jobs Act expands 529 accounts to include private and religious K–12 schooling.

Ability. Having the capacity or skill to do something.

Ability grouping. The school practice that flexibly separates students into homogeneous groups according to perceived abilities, past academic achievements, and presumed educational needs according to the purpose of study. Students can change groups for different subjects or learning purposes by the day, week, or project.

Academic freedom. The concept that teachers have some choices in the teaching methods they use as long as the teaching methods meet professional standards. Teachers have the professional freedom to monitor and adjust their teaching strategies if their students are not mastering the content. Academic freedom does not mean that teachers can say whatever they would like—or teach whatever they want—in the classroom.

Academy. An institution in the early New England colonies that provided schooling beyond town schools to fill commercial and early industrial economies, which demanded a modest number of people to fill those professions—later called "white-collar" positions—that required higher schooling.

Accountable. To hold answerable for, to act in a creditable manner; and capable of being explained.

Accreditation. In teacher education programs, a means of self-policing and quality control, usually voluntary.

Achievement gap ("opportunity gap"). The unequal achievement systematically shown by different student populations.

"Acting white". A cultural meme describing a set of social interactions in which racial and ethnic minority adolescents who earn good grades in school enjoy less social popularity than white students who do well academically.

Adequacy. Providing sufficient fiscal, personnel, and material resources to accomplish the job of educating our all our children, including those from low-income families, children with disabilities, and English language learners; a money-related issue affecting fairness in school funding.

Affect. The personal response to events, including expression of emotion or feelings, values, and beliefs. Current neuroscience research suggests that learning occurs, in part, through a person's affective development.

Affectionate discipline. A form of classroom management that depends on teachers and students forging deeply personal, warm, individualized relationships, like an ideal family. In theory, these positive emotional ties would trigger students' conscience, self-surveillance, and obedience and induce them to work conscientiously to learn in school.

Alternate teacher routes. Career preparation pathways that typically allow candidates to begin teaching while working on teacher program coursework and requirements at the same time to speed entry into the teaching occupation. Teach for America (TFA) and The New Teacher Project (TNTP) Teaching Fellows are two examples.

"Apprenticeship of observation". The phrase that Daniel C. Lortie coined in a sociological study, *School Teacher* (1975), to describe the phenomenon where laypersons who have spent thousands of hours as schoolchildren watching and judging teachers in practice develop many false ideas about teaching and mistakenly consider themselves to be "experts."

Assault. A mental violation or the threat that someone will receive a physical injury.

Asset thinking. The mindset or orientation that identifies and uses the student's personal strengths and interests to facilitate learning; also identifies and remedies the limiting social, environmental, and attitudinal barriers to that child's learning; the opposite of *deficit thinking*.

Attained curriculum. The content and skills that students actually learn.

Authentic (or performance) assessment. A type of appraisal that requires students to enact, demonstrate, construct, or develop a product or solution under defined conditions or standards—including presentations, portfolios, dramatic enactments, concerts, projects, exhibits, fairs, and debates—that capture aspects of students' learning that standardized tests cannot.

Battery. What happens when an assault becomes physical.

Bell curve (normal distribution). A statistical concept in which random scores spread out around a range from high to low with half the scores above and half below the mean.

Benchmarks. Academic criteria that identify specific content and performance expectations for certain grade levels or groups of grade levels.

Bureaucratic discipline. A form of classroom management that uses impersonal institutional authority other than the teacher—often advanced students acting as monitors, a status earned by merit—to enforce the school's rules.

Career academies. High school programs of study designed to equip each student for both college and career by combining core academic subjects with career-technical classes related to an occupational theme, such as health and bioscience, business and finance, arts and communications, education and child development, or engineering and information technology.

Career pathways. Sometimes called *career ladders* or *career lattice*, these offer teachers multiple routes to new roles and responsibilities that best fit their career interests and goals. Teachers can earn additional pay as they increase their capacities and take on new roles that contribute to improved student outcomes.

Case law. The legal precedents that judges create in their written opinions when they decide legal cases—by interpreting statutory law or prior judicial decisions—that influence virtually every aspect of education.

Case studies. Research in which investigators examine a small set of items (i.e., people, schools) in depth.

Certification (or licensure). The state's formal approval of teaching candidates for professional practice. This term is used interchangeably with *licensure*.

Charter schools. Public or private schools that claim to offer students more innovation and higher performance than available in traditional public schools (TPS) in exchange for taxpayer dollars, greater flexibility, and less oversight.

Child study movement. An educational innovation pioneered by American psychologist G. Stanley Hall that investigated how children's minds and personalities developed at the age when they entered school.

Children with disabilities. Identified by PL 94-142 (1975) as those who are intellectually challenged, hard of hearing, deaf, speech and language impaired, visually impaired (including blindness), seriously emotionally disturbed, orthopedically impaired, or otherwise health impaired, as well as children with specific learning disabilities as entitled to certain educational rights and services.

Chronic absentees. Missing 10% or more of the school year. Absenteeism becomes problematic as early as preschool because missing classroom instruction jeopardizes children's learning.

Classroom climate (instructional climate). The teaching, behavioral, and personal aspects of the classroom experience that can propel or hinder student learning.

Cocurricula. The activities, programs, and learning experiences that complement what students are learning in their academic classrooms, such as student newspapers and yearbooks, musical performances, art exhibits, debate competitions, and engineering teams that may occur outside the classroom or after regular school hours.

Cognition. The act of acquiring knowledge, including remembering, understanding, applying, analyzing, evaluating, and creating.

Cognitive capacity. The ability to identify and create relationships among pieces of information and develop increasingly complex structures for using and categorizing what the individual has learned is an essential foundation for building knowledge and developing reasoning ability.

Cognitive dissonance theory. The construct that an individual can experience an unpleasant psychological tension when new knowledge or information does not fit with what he or she already knows or believes; this anxiety motivates the individuals to reduce the discomfort by revising original beliefs or denying new information. This theory has implications for teaching and learning.

Collective bargaining. A formal process that gives union members a voice in management decisions that affect their compensation and work lives.

College and career readiness curricula. High school programs of study that prepare students for college, careers, and life. Courses objectives include mastery of rigorous knowledge and skills in core academic discipline of language, math, and sciences; the ability to communicate effectively orally and in writing; to think critically and develop informed arguments; to solve problems; to analyze information and data; and collaborate with others.

Common Core State Standards. A contemporary approach to improving K–12 public schools' curricula by focusing on rigorous academic content and the application of knowledge using higher-order thinking skills. Informed by curricula in top-performing countries, the standards incorporate the knowledge and skills that high school graduates need to master to succeed in college and careers in a global environment.

Compatible learning goals. The extent that teachers' and students' interests, values, perceptions, and learning objectives are "on the same page"; they work together toward the same ends in mutually satisfying ways.

Concurrent validity. An indication of the consistency or correlation between two independent measures of the same characteristic taken near the same time.

Content. The subject matter or topic that students learn in school. Since skills complement content, they are usually taught together.

Content validity. Whether the assessment provides an adequate sample or representation of the information that is supposed to be assessed to make the assessment results meaningful.

Continuing contract status (tenure). The legal status that restricts a school's ability to fire teachers without "just cause" and provides a degree of job security and a right of continued employment for teachers. Once on continuing contract or tenured, a teacher cannot be dismissed without legal due process. Continuing contract status or tenure does not guarantee lifelong employment.

Corporal punishment in schools. Any punishment in which physical force is used and intended to cause the student a degree of pain or discomfort, however mild (i.e., pinching, smacking, slapping, or spanking). This practice in schools has declined substantially in recent decades.

Critical dispositions. An Interstate New Teacher Assessment Support Consortium (InTASC) dimension that indicates the cognitive habits of professional action and moral commitments that anchor teacher actions.

Critical pedagogy. An instructional perspective whose purpose is to transform teachers, schools, and society into agents for social justice.

Critical theorists. Scholars who advance the critical theory philosophy of education and would have teachers help students critique the status quo and work for social justice in their society.

Critical theory. An educational philosophy that rejects schools' transmission of traditional mainstream culture and values as indoctrination to society's privileged interests that shape our schools by making their curriculum our "official knowledge."

Cultural capital. The language, values, and meanings used by a society's dominant social classes.

Cultural/family influences. The traditional values and behaviors that reflect the student's background as they play out in the family and community.

Cultural hegemony. The critical theory belief that public schools are controlled by the dominant class's worldview that imposes the colonial Western European settlers' traditions on today's ethnically and culturally diverse students.

Cultural literacy. The belief that reading comprehension depends on formal decoding skills, a wide vocabulary, and on far-ranging background knowledge based in European-American thought that literate writers and speakers assume their audiences already share.

Cultural pluralism. The concept that individual ethnic groups can keep their cultural heritages and their ancestral pride within the larger society even as they become full-hearted and patriotic Americans.

Culturally diverse learners. Students who may differ from their peers and teachers by ethnicity, race, socioeconomic status, language, gender, sexual identity, learning preferences, and/or cognitive and social development.

Culturally responsive pedagogy. The idea that students' backgrounds are assets that students can and should use in the service of their learning and that teachers of all backgrounds should develop the skills to teach all students effectively; another way of saying *culturally responsive teaching*.

Culturally responsive teaching (CRT). A research-based approach in which teachers make meaningful connections between what students learn in school and their cultures, languages, and life experiences by viewing these as assets that can aid students' learning.

Culture. A systems of values, concepts, assumptions, sensibilities, or ways of thinking that create a perceptual lens through which people interpret life events and guide communities of people in their daily lives.

Curriculum. The plan that guides the work of schools.

Cut score. A point on the continuum from the lowest possible score to the highest. Those students who fall below the cut score have not been able to demonstrate that they have met the educational standard. Deciding where to place the cut score is both an objective (psychometric) problem and a subjective (professional judgment and values) issue.

Cyberbullying. The deliberate and repeated harm inflicted through the use of computers, cell phones, and other electronic devices.

Deep learning. The conceptual skills that prepare students to master core academic content, think critically and solve complex problems, work collaboratively, communicate effectively, and learn how to learn.

Deficit thinking. The mindset or orientation of looking at students' socially defined weaknesses (as compared with able, middle-class white children with stable families and communities) rather than their strengths; the opposite of *asset thinking*.

Defined benefit (DB) plans. A pension arrangement in which the employer guarantees the employee a contracted retirement income based on years of experience and salary level.

Diagnostic assessments. Highly specialized interventions into student learning involving detailed and professionally prepared tests administered by a special education teacher, school psychologist, speech/language pathologist, occupational therapist, or regular teacher trained for this task.

Differentiated salary schedules. The practice of paying effective teachers more than their colleagues with similar years of experience if they agree to teach hard-to-staff subjects or work in hard-to-staff schools.

Digital citizenship. The ability to participate safely, intelligently, productively, and responsibly in the computerized world.

Disaggregate. Separating student achievement data by race, ethnicity, grade, and student subgroups in all grades tested to show academic progress and hold schools accountable for successfully educating every student.

Disidentification (withdrawal of psychic investment). A strategy that some students use to remove themselves from perceived threat of failing in school. For example, to save face they rationalize their poor performance as a lack of interest in the subject rather than as an inability to master it.

Diverse learners. Children who differ racially, ethnically, culturally, and linguistically or in other visible or invisible ways that differ from the stereotypical "white Anglo-Saxon" student of America's colonial past.

Due process. The legal protections for tenured teachers that include a formal hearing and presentation of proof of sufficient cause to meet the statutory requirements for removal from the position.

Early childhood. The years from birth to age 8 that educators and psychologists widely accept as a distinct phase of human development in which children mature key physical, emotional, and cognitive skills.

Early childhood education (ECE). Preschool (birth to age 3) learning programs.

Economic goals. Schools' purposes that intend to prepare students for their later occupational roles and to select, train, and distribute individuals into the society's division of labor.

Education privatization movement. Sometimes called *school choice*, it advocates giving parents more options about how and where to educate their children using taxpayer dollars by creating charter schools, using vouchers, and engaging in public–private partnerships where schools contract out education services.

Education savings accounts (ESA). Taxpayer dollars set aside, usually based on per-pupil funding formulas, in individual savings accounts for participating students. Parents can withdraw these dollars to spend on approved educational expenses, including private and parochial school tuition, homeschooling, curriculum materials, standardized test fees, or transportation. Parents can roll over unused ESA funds for future K–12 and higher-education costs.

Educational accountability. The process[es] by which school districts and states attempt to ensure that schools systems meet their goals. Although accountability includes academic assessment, accountability is much broader in scope.

Educational assessment. A comprehensive process of describing, judging, and communicating the quality of students' learning and performances.

Educational inflation. The situation in which the supply of well-educated individuals increases, yet employee wages and advanced degrees' value decline because so many qualified and available persons exist to fill the positions.

Educational philosophies. Viewpoints that help educators interpret, find meaning, and guide their work.

Educational standards. Criteria that clearly identify what students should know and be able to do after completing courses of study at a particular grade level.

Effective accountability systems. Comprehensive methods of monitoring and assessing students' academic progress, containing multiple measures of student achievement. Students' poor or excellent school achievement never has only one single cause.

Effective school. Defined by Ron Edmonds, educator and leader of the Effective Schools Movement, as one in which low-income and underserved students' basic skills are at least as well developed as the middle-class children's skills.

Efficacy. The belief in one's own ability to make a difference.

Effort. The amount of time and energy that students spend in meeting teachers' or schools' formal academic requirements (such as completing homework, attending school, coming to class prepared).

"Egg crate" structure. The traditional school format in which teachers work alone rather than as members of an integrated and tiered organization because the teaching profession lacked career stages.

English language learners. Students who come from a range of home/native languages, cultural backgrounds, and levels of English proficiency. They may be U.S. born or refugees with extensive or no prior school experiences.

Environmental limitations. The specific conditions under which a standardized test must be administered. All students must take it under identical conditions if their scores are to mean what they are intended to mean.

Equality. Providing the same services for all students regardless of the students' or locality's needs.

Equality of opportunity. The condition in which all members of a society have the same chances to enter any occupation or social class and to compete for any place in society. It does not mean that everyone will have the same income and status or that everyone will achieve the same outcome.

Equity. Providing the services students actually need; a fairness issue, equity is a basic tenet of our school finance system.

Essential knowledge. In Interstate New Teacher Assessment Support Consortium (InTASC), the importance of declarative and procedural knowledge as the bedrock of effective practice.

Essentialist. A traditional educational philosophy that selects curricula from the Western canon that adherents believe would be most relevant to the current student generation.

Ethical caring. A more highly abstract caring emotion that teachers feel toward their students; less intense or intimate than mother-child caring; also known as *natural caring*.

Ethics. The rules or widely accepted standards of practice—the voluntary norms, values, beliefs, habits, and attitudes—that govern members' professional conduct.

Every Student Succeeds Act (ESSA). The 2015 reauthorization of the Elementary and Secondary Education Act (ESEA) that replaced No Child Left Behind (NCLB); the U.S. Congress's efforts to improve upon NCLB's strengths while ending its weaknesses.

Existential philosophy of education. A viewpoint in which curriculum and instruction encourage deep personal reflection on one's identity, commitments, and choices. Its approach is cognitive, affective, and highly individual.

Existentialism. A philosophy that focuses on the existence of the individual and individual responsibility. Existentialists believe that people must create themselves by shaping their own meaning and choices.

Expertise. Possessing a high level of knowledge or skill in an area; comes with repeated involvement with a particular content or situation.

Explicit or conscious bias. Discrimination against people of certain races, ethnicities, religions, abilities, or other characteristics that exists within conscious awareness and allows the individual to act intentionally to express these prejudices, such as with verbal harassment or by not calling on a student with a disability to participate in class.

Expulsion. A long-term or permanent separation from the school program.

Face validity. Usually used in relation to a test; the appearance of legitimacy; not a technical aspect, but rather a marketing one.

Faculty psychology. The late 19th century viewpoint that intellect, will, and emotions all had their own "place" or compartments in the mind, and the mind could be trained by a uniform procedure of mental discipline and drill.

Formative assessments. Assessment for learning. "Formative" does not refer to the content, but rather to the manner in which the assessments are used.

Free speech. The Constitutional right that says the government must tolerate and cannot restrain the exercise of people's right to express information, ideas, and opinions in open public debate regardless of whether that speech is offensive, tumultuous, or discordant (subject to reasonable limitations).

Gifted students. Students who have been formally or informally identified as having superior abilities in areas or academic achievement, cognition, creative thinking, and or visual/performing arts. Gifted children from marginalized groups may be underidentified as gifted students.

Growth mindset. The belief that intelligence is not fixed and one's brain is capable of change—with dedicated effort, trying new strategies, asking for help when needed, and persistence—when faced with challenges.

Guaranteed and viable curriculum. A combination of a rigorous curriculum to which every student has access with sufficient time and materials for teachers to successfully teach it; strongly correlated with academic achievement.

Head Start. Federal programs for preschool education classes intended to give children ages 3 to 5 from economically disadvantaged homes the cognitive and social development or readiness for school success.

Hidden curricula. The unwritten, unofficial, and often unintended lessons, values, and viewpoints that students learn in school. Part of the school's culture and climate, it consists of the unspoken or implicit intellectual, social, and environmental messages—the social norms and expectations—that the school communicates to students.

Holistic (student-centered) accountability. Balances both quantitative and qualitative indicators of student performance. It presents the story behind the numbers, including teaching practices, curriculum practices, leadership practices, parent involvement, faculty communication, professional development, and funding adequacy.

Hornbook. An early reading primer in the New England colonies consisting of a single page protected by a transparent sheet of flattened cattle horn.

Human capital. Includes the skills, knowledge, talents, and social and personal attributes and experiences that an individual or a population possesses that creates value to their organization or country. Its cumulative total represents a form of wealth that organizations and nations can use to accomplish their goals. Education is foundational to its development.

Hybrid roles. Providing "release time" or a part-time classroom schedule that supports teacher instructional leadership activities during (and after) the school day.

Identity. Who you are, the way you think about yourself, and the way the world views you.

In loco parentis (in the place of the parent). The legal role of schools in overseeing and managing students' well-being while enrolled in their institution.

Inclusion model. The practice of having students with disabilities receive most, if not all, of their instruction in a general education classroom. Typically, a special education teacher or assistant will also participate in the class, often coteaching with the regular classroom teacher.

Induction. A comprehensive, coherent, and sustained professional development process that the school district organizes to train, support, and retain new teachers.

Infant schools. An educational innovation (that Robert Owen originated in Scotland, 1816) that prepared very young children (ages 3–5) to attend the common school, partly to let youngsters have some fun before they entered factory life and partly to provide them with moral and intellectual training.

Instruction. The methods and techniques by which teachers bring curriculum to life in the classroom to help children learn the information and skills.

Instructional (or classroom) climate. The teaching, behavioral, and personal aspects of the classroom experience that can propel or hinder student learning.

Instructional leadership. Leadership for learning, for enforcing the school's roles that define the school's mission, for managing the instructional program, and for promoting a positive learning climate. Typically includes the principal, assistant principals, and teachers, among others.

InTASC. The Interstate Teacher Assessment and Support Consortium, a program of the Council of Chief State School Officers; a Model Core Teaching Standards for licensing teachers that outlines what new teachers should know and be able to do to ensure that every K–12 student reaches the goal of being college and career ready.

Integrated curriculum. A way of organizing learning content that cuts across different areas of study by stressing the concepts that unify them, making connections for students, and engaging them in relevant, meaningful activities that can be linked to real life.

Intellectual goals. School purposes intended to teach essential cognitive skills such as reading for comprehension, writing for clarity of expression, mathematics for numerical reasoning in life and sciences, and higher-level critical thinking and reasoning.

Intended curriculum. The content specified by the state, district, or school to be addressed in a particular course at a particular grade level.

Interpersonal relationships. Primarily, in the context of this book, the quality of the teacher–student bond.

Intersectionality. A relatively recent theory; stresses that individuals develop their social identities in a holistic, integrated manner and considers their meaning and consequences for the person or group in the larger society.

Intrinsic motivation. The experience of wanting to engage in an activity because it is interesting, enjoyable, or helps achieve one's chosen goals.

Knowledge- and skills-based pay. Salary incentive programs that give teachers extra compensation for acquiring new knowledge and practices the school and district believe are critical to their goals, such as improved student outcomes.

Knowledge demands. In the Common Core Standards, the continuum between easier-reading texts, which make few assumptions about the readers' life experiences and depth of their cultural and content knowledge, and more demanding writings, which make many assumptions about one or more of these areas.

Language conventionality and clarity. In the Common Core Standards, the continuum of English from easily understood, clear, typical, conversational language to more challenging word use that is figurative, ironic, ambiguous, or purposefully misleading.

Learner-centered curriculum. A learning plan focused on including student needs, interests, and goals in what is taught rather than strictly transmitting a prescribed set of facts and skills, allowing learners to have input into their own education though their choices.

Learning. What happens when the learner actively constructs knowledge (produces new understanding by reconciling prior knowledge with new information) that results in meaningful changes in the way they know, think, and act. It is a complex cognitive and affective process.

LGBTQ+. An acronym for lesbian, gay, bisexual, transgender, transvestite, and queer or questioning a sexual orientation or gender identity; persons who challenge our societal assumptions about gender and sexuality and the ways many people actually lead their lives.

Liberal arts. The vision of education believes that mastering the academic disciplines—mathematics, logic, philosophy, sciences, history, literature, and the arts—characterizes the educated person.

Low birth weight. An infant's weight (less than 5 lbs. 8 oz.). Low birth weight babies tend to come from mothers in poor health or from lower socioeconomic status women (who may have poor pregnancy nutrition, inadequate prenatal care, and pregnancy complications).

Massive resistance. The practice of closing public schools to keep African American students from enrolling with white students that characterized several southern states' efforts to block racially desegregated education after *Brown v. Board of Education* (1954).

Mastery goals. Learning purposes that focus on gaining skills, comprehension, or competence based on student effort and personal improvement (which students believe are within their control).

Mental discipline theory. The pedagogy of American schooling that suggested studying certain rigorous academic subjects strengthens the student's mind and character. This theory is related to faculty psychology.

Mentoring. A specific type of induction program consisting of a collegial, supportive relationship developed between a veteran and a new teacher to ease the transition into the realities of daily classroom teaching.

Microaggression theory. The idea that underserved persons in this culture experience small daily hostilities, intended or unintended, from white persons.

Microaggressions. Short, everyday, indirect, subtle, intentional or unintentional statements, actions, environmental slights, put-downs, or insults that communicate hostile, derogatory, or negative messages to persons based solely on their marginalized group membership.

Middle class. The socioeconomic group that includes professionals, managers, and small-business owners (upper-middle class) as well as technical workers, technicians, sales personnel, and clerical workers (lower-middle class).

Mindset. The set of assumptions, values, and beliefs about one's self and one's world that include how a person perceives, interprets, and acts upon their environment.

Mission. The school's purpose or direction, often used interchangeably with *vision*.

Motivation. The condition that activates and sustains behavior toward a goal, that develops and changes over time with adjustments in the individual's interests and goals, developmental skills, environment, and sociocultural influences.

Multicultural education. The content of education or teaching that incorporates histories, texts, values, beliefs, and perspectives of people from varied cultural backgrounds into the curriculum. It is a response to the U.S. cultural pluralism and the relative absence of minority viewpoints in the public school curriculum and society.

National Assessment of Educational Progress (NAEP). A federally funded assessment used as a common metric for all states, sometimes called *The Nation's Report Card*.

Negligence. Conduct that is blameworthy because it falls short of what a reasonable person would do to protect another individual from a foreseeable risk of harm. A teacher is negligent when, without intending any wrong, he or she either acts or fails to take a precaution that, under the circumstances, an ordinary prudent and reasonably intelligent teacher ought to foresee would expose another person to unnecessary risk of harm.

No Child Left Behind Act (NCLB). A 2002 reauthorization of Elementary and Secondary Education Act funds, the federal government's first serious attempt to hold states, districts, and schools accountable for remedying the unequal achievement among different student populations, especially low-income students, racial/ethnic minority students, English language learners, and students with disabilities. Every Student Succeeds Act (2015) is its current successor.

Normal schools. In the early national period, 1- or 2-year training institutions (actually secondary schools) that prepared teachers for elementary schools. Normal schools were not college-level institutions.

Objectives. Specific school learning outcomes as compared to the terms "goals" or "purposes" to refer to broad directions.

Opportunity gap ("achievement gap"). The systematic unequal achievement shown by different student populations caused, many believe, because marginalized children typically do not receive the same access or resources as do middle-class and affluent children.

Opportunity to learn (OTL). Refers to equitable conditions or circumstances within the school or classroom that enable *all* students—low income, middle class, and affluent—to have equal opportunities to receive high-quality teachers, rigorous curricula, relevant learning materials, well-presented and engaging instructional experiences, and well-maintained facilities—that help them achieve high standards and avoid barriers that prevent learning.

Opportunity-to-learn standards. A set of conditions that schools, districts, and states must meet to ensure that students have enough occasions to meet expectations for their performance. Student achievement depends not only on students' abilities but also on whether they actually attended the class and whether the teacher has taught the subject in class with enough explanation, time, practice, feedback, and support in an appropriate learning environment necessary for students to absorb and master it.

Oppositional culture theory. Sometimes called *academic disengagement theory*, it is a belief that students from some racial and ethnic groups underachieve academically because they view schooling and the education system as extensions of the dominant culture that threatens their group's cultural identity and reproduces societal inequities.

Outlier studies. In statistical terminology, something that is relatively unusual and lies at the far end of the distribution.

Parental involvement. Those maternal, paternal, guardian, or familial actions expected to improve student performance or behavior.

Pedagogy. The art and science of teaching as a profession with certain methods, techniques, and materials to promote student learning.

Perennialists. Adherents of the traditional educational philosophy that focuses on teaching what adherents view as universal truths through Western civilization's classics.

Performance. In InTASC, the teaching behaviors that can be observed and assessed in teaching practice.

Performance (or authentic) assessment. A type of appraisal that requires students to enact, demonstrate, construct, or develop a product or solution under defined conditions or standards (such as presentations, portfolios, dramatic enactments, concerts, projects, exhibits, fairs, and debates) that capture aspects of students' learning that standardized tests cannot.

Performance goals. The learning purposes that stress being best as compared with others that tend to rely on students' ability (which students tend to believe is inherited and beyond their control).

Performance pay. Sometimes called *merit pay* or *performance awards*, it usually means a system of employee compensation that links salary to measures of work quality or goals such as increasing student achievement.

Personalized learning (or personalization). A student-centered approach to tailoring education to meet different students' needs. The term is ambiguous and can mean any number of educational arrangements.

Philosophy. The investigation of causes and laws underlying reality or a system of motivating concepts of principles or values by which one lives.

Political goals. School purposes that intend aim to instill loyalty to the country and to its existing political order. Schools are supposed to encourage patriotism and responsible public behaviors.

Prekindergarten. Schooling for children age 4.

Preschool. Schooling for children birth to age 3 that provides early, organized social and academic learning opportunities aligned with the district's K–3 curriculum.

Prestige. The level of social respect or standing, the good reputation, and high esteem accorded to an individual or a group because of their position's status in that society.

Private good. A service that benefits the individual, serving mainly those people who use them.

Private (nonpublic) schools. Educational institutions usually controlled by a private corporation, religious or nonaffiliated (not a government agency or board), and that are mainly supported by private funds and tuition.

Probable cause. Legally, a reasonable belief that a person has committed a crime; needed in order for police to conduct a search.

Probationary period. Usually 3 years working under an annual contract (sometimes called *untenured*).

Problem-based curriculum. An active, integrated, and constructive process that uses real-life issues to teach students how to identify a problem, search for solutions by gathering and evaluating relevant information from varied disciplines and sources, and devise a solution. Assigned problems are often complex, ill-structured, open-ended, and captivating enough to lead students toward investigation. Students must communicate, collaborate, and cooperate with classmates to solve the problems.

Procedural due process. The legal requirement when faced with disciplinary action that involves separation from school. Students must be given oral or written notice of the charges, an explanation of the evidence against them, and an opportunity to present their side of the story.

Profession. An exclusive occupational group that applies abstract knowledge and specialized skills to particular cases and has expertise and influence to practice in a given domain or field. A profession can keep its authority if the public accepts its claims of expertise and if the profession's internal structure of well-defined and agreed-upon knowledge and skills support it.

Professional boundaries. The legal, ethical, and organizational frameworks of care, expectations, and limits within which the worker–client relationship occurs.

Professional codes of ethics. The rules that guide professional decisions and actions, ensuring high standards of practice, protecting the public, and guiding practitioners in their decision-making.

Professional culture. The set of beliefs, values, assumptions, and relationships that educators and staff share about teaching and learning that influence every aspect of how a school functions, including the practices that support new teachers.

Professionalism. Accepting responsibility for developing and growing one's expertise in the skills and attitudes of those who think they are (or aspire to be) professionals.

Professionalization. An occupation's qualities, usually enhanced by increasing training or raising required qualifications.

Progressive. A relatively contemporary philosophical and educational perspective, defined as moving forward, ongoing, advancing; a person who favors or strives for reform in politics, education, or other fields.

Progressive education. An educational reform movement that focused on educating the "whole child"—intellectually, physically, and emotionally—begun as a reaction to the alleged narrowness and formalism of traditional education.

Progressive philosophy of education. The philosophical orientation that views students, rather than content, as education's focus. In this perspective, education's purpose is to prepare students to be lifelong learners in an ever-changing society.

Psychology. The scientific study of human behavior in general and the mind in particular arising in the late 19th century that placed students and how they learned—not subjects—at teaching's center.

Public good. A service provided without profit that benefits all members of the community, whether or not they contribute to its upkeep or use it themselves.

Race. A social construction; a cultural invention based on human physical appearance (such as skin or hair color and texture, facial features), ancestry, nationality, and culture. People invented the idea of race to make sense of their experiences in a world filled with people who lived elsewhere and looked and acted unlike themselves.

Racial, ethnic, and cultural identities. A sense of collective self based on a person's perception that he or she shares a common heritage with a particular racial, ethnic, or cultural group.

Reasonable suspicion. The legal standard that schools need credible information from a reliable source before they can justify searching a student on school property; a less demanding standard than probable cause.

Reciprocity. An agreement between states to accept each other's teaching credentials.

Resilience. The process or capacity to have successful outcomes despite challenging or threatening circumstances, influenced by the interplay between an individual's characteristics as well as social and environmental factors.

Resource rooms. Classrooms where teachers provide specialized instruction to students with disabilities who come in for part of the school day, either individually or in small groups.

Rubrics. Scoring guides that provide the most specific expectations for students' performance by identifying what they are supposed to accomplish on individual assignments and assessments.

Safe and orderly environment. One of the effective schools correlates; an organized, purposeful, cooperative, and nurturing atmosphere free from threat of harm in a school culture and climate that supports teaching and learning in which all parties show respect for and appreciation of human diversity and democratic values.

Scaffolding. A general term that describes the extra time and academic and moral supports put in place by schools to help economically and culturally diverse students and students with disabilities overcome their education gaps and learn to the highest levels.

School climate. The physical, intellectual, psychological, and social environment in which teachers' and students' behaviors occur within schools. School climate is the school's "feel" at the building and classroom levels.

School readiness. Children's physical, cognitive, social, and emotional development that enables them to benefit from early formal schooling and succeed academically, largely (but not completely) shaped at home before they ever reach the classroom.

School vouchers. State fiscal programs that give certificates for a fixed amount of public funding that parents can use to enroll their child in any school the parent chooses that accepts vouchers, including private, religious, and home schools.

Scientific management. A process developed by Frederick Taylor, the world's first efficiency expert, for businesses and factories to increase institutional competence by standardization to ensure quality with lower costs and applied to schools.

Selective tradition. The choices that those of social, economic, and political influence make in deciding the curricular knowledge and values that needs to be taught to everyone. Curriculum is not neutral.

Self-contained classrooms. Classroom specifically set aside for teachers and other support personnel to work with children with disabilities the majority of their school day.

Self-efficacy. Teachers' and learners' expectations about their ability to accomplish a given task.

Skills. The abilities to use one's knowledge (the content) competently in performance. Since skills completement content, they are usually taught together.

Social capital. The individual's capacity to access scarce resources because of their membership in networks or broader social structures.

Social class. A term used to distinguish a person's position relative to others within that society. Parental occupation, educational level, income, housing value, and political influence are the basis for determining a student's social class.

Social efficiency. A classroom model that emphasizes classroom control, management, obedience to authority, and a structured curriculum that focuses on memorization and rote skills.

Social–emotional learning (SEL). A form of emotional intelligence; the process by which children and adults gain and effectively apply the knowledge, attitudes, and skills needed to manage their emotions, set and realize worthwhile goals, feel and show empathy for others, keep positive relationships, and make responsible decisions.

Social goals. Schools' purposes that include helping prevent or solve societal problems, and along with family and religious organizations (among others), help to socialize children into society's various roles, behaviors, and values.

Social mobility. The movement of individuals, families, or groups though a system of their society's hierarchy.

Social promotion. The practice by which struggling students are advanced to the next grade with their same-age peers despite their lack of satisfactory academic progress.

Social reconstruction. The progressive education movement's more radical offshoot in the 1930s that advocated for serious societal reform and eventually led to the development of critical theory.

Socialization process. The means of educating children to develop a shared culture, behaviors, values, and loyalty essential to any society's long-term stability.

Socioeconomic status (SES). A term used to distinguish a person's position relative to others within that society. Parental occupation, educational level, income, housing value, and political influence are the basis for determining a student's social class or SES.

Sorting and selecting machine. The public school process that separates "human capital" (students) by their observed or presumed abilities and interests into certain curricular programs matched to appropriate future jobs.

Statistical norm. On the bell curve, the mean (average) place around the 50th percentile.

Status. The position or standing in society that confers certain benefits and privileges. Factors such as remuneration, knowledge, responsibility, social utility, and prestige contribute to social status.

Stereotype threat theory. The idea that people tend to underperform when confronted with situations that might confirm negative stereotypes about their social, racial, ethnic, or cultural group.

Stewardship. The practice of looking out for and managing an estate's or organization's affairs, tracking and accounting for resources given, and consciously, purposefully, and intentionally aligning our goals and actions with our values.

Strikes. Employee work stoppages in support of demands made on their employer, such as higher pay or improved conditions.

Structure. On the Common Core Standards for reading, the continuum between simple, well-marked, traditional organization to more complicated, implicit, and unconventional language construction.

Students' time on task. One of the effective schools correlates; the reality that learning is based on *time* to learn, not on the *rate* of learning. Some students master complex content quickly and often independently; others master it more slowly and with more assistance.

Students with disabilities. Students identified with one of 13 different disability conditions that adversely affect their educational performance.

Subject-centered curriculum. A learning plan organized around academic fields such as biology, mathematics, or literature as a way for students to acquire knowledge. For the most part, each teacher keeps instructional content to his or her own separate discipline.

Subjective status. The self-perception of rank or prestige that emphasizes personal achievement.

Summative assessments. The assessment of learning. Summative assessments are the final task at a unit's end used to make a concluding judgment about whether the student has met a certain required level of accomplishment.

Supplementary schools. Educational units that emerged during the early national era to fill in the learning gaps for individuals whose school attendance had ended prematurely or for students having unique educational needs that the community thought best met in separate facilities. Children attending supplemental schools included those with disabilities, youths alleged to be delinquent, and African American and Native American children judged to be unacceptable in regular classrooms.

Suspicionless searches. The legal category of reasonable encroachments on privacy in school that permit testing for drugs and alcohol without showing individualized suspicion.

Taught curriculum. The content the teacher delivers in the classroom.

Tax-credit scholarships (TCS). State-offered tax credits to encourage businesses or individuals to donate to a scholarship-granting organization, which then gives the money to eligible students to use toward tuition expenses at a private school.

Teacher preparation. The series of courses and field experiences that educate individuals to become teachers.

Teachers' professional boundaries. The verbal, physical, emotional, and social distances that an educator must maintain in order to ensure structure, security, and predictability in an educational environment.

Teaching (instruction). The work or method that carries out the school's educational plan.

Tenure (continuing contract status). The legal protection that restricts a school's ability to fire teachers without "just cause" and so provides a degree of job security and a right of continued employment for teachers. Tenure does not guarantee lifelong employment.

Test bias. When assessment results show provable and systematic differences in people's outcomes based on group membership. Test bias incorporates both psychometric and sociocultural factors, and both perspectives are necessary to draw a complete picture of test bias.

Test reliability. The extent to which an assessment is repeatable and yields consistent scores obtained by the same persons when retested with the identical test or with an equivalent form.

Tested curriculum. The content and skills about which students must answer questions on classroom and standardized assessments.

Title I. A federal program intended to supplement academic resources for low-income children who needed extra reading and math help in the early grades.

Tort. A civil wrong or some type of harm that one person causes another person, outside of a contract, for which the courts may award damages.

Toxic stress. The hormonal changes that happen in response to severely or repeated frightening or threatening events or conditions (e.g., growing up in unsafe and unstable environments); can disrupt children's behavior, cognitive capacity, and emotional and physical health.

Tracked curriculum. A sequence of academic classes that range from slow-paced remedial courses to demanding academic ones along with an array of electives, exploratory, vocational, and physical education classes into which school officials place students to pursue a particular program of study.

Tracking (curriculum tracking). A school practice of rigidly sorting students into homogeneous courses according to their perceived abilities, past academic achievements, and presumed and expected vocational directions and keeping students in this placement throughout their schooling.

Traditional assessments. Measures of student performance that commonly include paper-and-pencil or online tests with multiple-choice questions designed to compare students across the school district, state, or nation. Their scores on these tests identify whether students have developed the core knowledge and skills the standards expected.

Transmission of meaning. The traditional educational view that teachers hold knowledge in their heads, and their job is to transmit it in the most efficient way into students' heads.

Unconscious, implicit bias. Negative stereotypes or beliefs that operate outside a person's mindful awareness, appearing in the person's attitudes, understandings, and behaviors and directly contradicting what a person says he or she values. Implicit bias can interfere with relationship building and decision-making, tainting the learning climate and harming both teacher and student.

Underclass. The socioeconomic group within the working or lower class with many members as the third or fourth generation who live in poverty, depend on public assistance to maintain a relatively spare existence, and tend to live clustered in inner-city slums or in rundown rural areas. After several generations without visible social or economic progress, members of the underclass usually lose hope of improving their economic and social situation.

Union. A group of employees who come together voluntarily with the shared goal of improving their working conditions and having a voice at their place of employment.

"Unstaged" career. An occupation lacking a progression of steps through which one could advance, such as teaching has traditionally been.

Upper class. Usually defined as wealthy persons with considerable money, property, and investments.

Validity. The extent to which a test measures what it is supposed to measure.

Virtual (online) charter schools. Scholastic programs that attempt to educate full-time students primarily through the computer via the internet with synchronous or asynchronous lessons.

Vision. An intelligent sense of what a better future can be; a *mission* is the purpose or direction pursued to reach that end. The terms are often used interchangeably.

"White," "whiteness". A set of social processes and practices; a way Caucasian people see themselves and others; and a set of cultural behaviors usually "unmarked and unnamed." Being white is so interwoven into everyday living that whites, at times, cannot step outside and see their beliefs, values, and behaviors as creating a distinct cultural group.

White fragility theory. A concept that proposes a state of reduced psychological stamina in which even a minimal amount of racial stress for white persons becomes seemingly unbearable, "triggering" a range of defensive behaviors and racial stress that comes from recognizing that a dissenting view is challenging one's own perceptions of self in the world as a moral, unbiased person.

White privilege theory. A concept that proposes the unseen, unconscious, built-in advantage that white people gain (i.e., having more access to power and resources than people of color in the same situation) from being Caucasian in our Western culture.

Working class. The socioeconomic group that includes skilled craftsworkers (upper-working class) and unskilled manual and service workers (lower-working class). Skilled workers may either be middle or working class, depending on their education, income, and home neighborhood.

Workplace. Defined by the U.S. Supreme Court (1987) as "those areas and items that are related to work and are generally within the employer's control," including offices, hallways, cafeterias, desks, file cabinets, lockers, and other areas. In these locations, an employee does not have an expectation of privacy, and the school may search them.

INDEX